**Association for
Computing Machinery**

Advancing Computing as a Science & Profession

June 30-July 3, 2019
Boston, MA, USA

I0027515

WebSci'19

Proceedings of the 11th ACM Conference on
Web Science

Sponsored by:
ACM SIGWEB

Supported by:
**WebScience Trust, Gesis - Leibniz Institute for the Social Sciences
& Rensselaer**

Association for Computing Machinery

Advancing Computing as a Science & Profession

The Association for Computing Machinery
2 Penn Plaza, Suite 701
New York, New York 10121-0701

ISBN: 978-1-4503-6202-3 (Digital)

ISBN: 978-1-4503-7070-7 (Print)

Additional copies may be ordered prepaid from:

ACM Order Department
PO Box 30777
New York, NY 10087-0777, USA

Phone: 1-800-342-6626 (USA and Canada)
+1-212-626-0500 (Global)
Fax: +1-212-944-1318
E-mail: acmhelp@acm.org
Hours of Operation: 8:30 am – 4:30 pm ET

Web Science 2019 – General and Program Chairs' Welcome Message

It is our great pleasure to welcome you to the 11th ACM Conference on Web Science (Websci'19), June 30 – July 3, 2019, Boston, MA, USA.

This year, the conference theme is "Synergies for the Good: The Web and Society". We welcomed interdisciplinary contributions, especially those that had a broad perspective on the web, including those that combined analyses of web data with other types of data (e.g., from surveys or interviews) to better understand user behavior (online and offline); carried out longitudinal studies; presented successful cases of interdisciplinary and cross-disciplinary web research; used mixed-method approaches; critically reflected on the methods used; discussed responsible forms of Web Science (e.g. regarding standards, methods, generalizability of results); and/or those that reflected on the societal impact of web research, how the web is perceived in the media and in society, and whether this clashes with our self-image of Web Science. Thus, research on the interaction of society and the web was invited, and we received submissions highlighting web implications, synergies derived, and how the web as a socio-technical system will evolve in future.

WebSci'19 was a unique conference where a multitude of disciplines converged in a creative and critical dialogue with the aim of understanding the web and its impacts. WebSci'19 welcomed participation from diverse fields including (but not limited to) art, anthropology, computer and information sciences, communication, economics, humanities, informatics, law, linguistics, philosophy, political science, psychology, and sociology. Following the tradition of earlier conferences, contributions to WebSci'19 aimed to cross traditional disciplinary boundaries. The community engaged with novel and thought-provoking ideas and discussed original research, work in progress, analysis, and practice in the field of Web Science, its current theoretical, methodological, and epistemological challenges as well as Web practices of individuals, collectives, institutions, and platforms.

This year we were very pleased to accept 41 submissions for the regular research track chosen out of 130 submissions. We are grateful for the support of the Program Committee which consisted of 16 senior members and 66 regular members who selected an interesting, varied, exciting program comprising 31 long and 10 short papers. In addition to the posters selected from the Call for Posters, eight contributions were invited to be presented as a poster because they sparked fruitful discussions among the reviewers and were deemed to be of great interest and relevance to the WebSci'19 community.

This year WebSci'19 encouraged authors to particularly prepare and publish reproducibility information of conducted research and resources, such as source code and datasets. Authors were asked to add (if possible) a link (e.g. DOI or URL) to data or any other information relevant to their submission. With this measure WebSci'19 aimed at raising awareness of the reproducibility issue and demonstrated that, as a community-driven conference, it subscribes to and actively promotes Open Science principles in research.

General Chairs:
Paolo Boldi, Università degli Studi, *Milano, Italy*
Brooke Foucault Welles, Northeastern University, *Boston, USA*
Katharina Kinder-Kurlanda, GESIS - Leibniz Institute for the Social Sciences, *Cologne, Germany*
Christo Wilson, Northeastern University, *Boston, USA*

Program Chairs:
Isabella Peters, ZBW Leibniz Information Center for Economics & Kiel University, *Kiel, Germany*
Wagner Meira Jr., Universidade Federal de Minas Gerais, *Belo Horizonte, Brazil*

Table of Contents

Presentations

WebSci 2019 Conference Organization

General Chairs: Paolo Boldi *(Università degli Studi, Milan, Italy)*
Brooke Foucault Welles *(Northeastern University, Boston, US)*
Katharina Kinder-Kurlanda *(GESIS, Cologne, Germany)*
Christo Wilson *(Northeastern University, Boston, US)*

Program Chair: Isabella Peters *(Leibniz Information Center for Economics & Kiel University)*
Wagner Meira Jr. *(Federal University of Minas, Gerais, Brazil)*

Workshop & Tutorial Chairs: Stefan Dietze *(GESIS, Cologne, Germany)*
Katya Ognyanova *(Rutgers University, Camden, US)*

Poster Chairs: Momin Malik *(Harvard University, Boston, US)*

Ingmar Weber *(Qatar Computing Research Institute, Doha, Qatar)*

PhD Symposium Chairs: Sibel Adali *(Rensselaer Polytechnic Institute, Troy, US)*
Mark Weal *(University of Southampton, UK)*
Ilaria Liccardi *(MIT, Cambridge, US)*

Publication Chair: Massimo Santini *(Università degli Studi, Milan, Italy)*

Sponsorship Chair: Julia Neidhardt *(TU WIEN, Vienna, Austria)*

Web Chair: Nicole Samay *(Northeastern university, Boston, US)*

Program Committee: Tobias Ley (Tallinn University)
Yelena Mejova (ISI Foundation)
Katharina Kinder-Kurlanda (GESIS Leibniz Institute for the Social Sciences)
Eni Mustafaraj (Wellesley College)
Cristina Sarasua (University of Zurich)
Fariba Karimi (GESIS)
Elena Kochkina (The University of Warwick)
Seth Frey (Dartmouth College)
Katrin Weller (GESIS - Leibniz Institute for the Social Sciences)
Jussara Almeida (UFMG)
OshaniSeneviratne (Rensselaer Polytechnic Institute)
Peter Dolog (Aalborg University)
Eva Zangerle (Databases and Information Systems, Department of Computer Science, University of Innsbruck)
David Millard (University of Southampton)
Ujwal Gadiraju (L3S Research Center)
Wilhelm Hasselbring (Kiel University)
Tommi Mikkonen (University of Helsinki)
Geert-Jan Houben (Delft University of Technology)
Stasa Milojevic (Indiana University Bloomington)
Chris Snijders (Eindhoven University of Technology)
Mark Weal (University of Southampton)
Alessandro Piscopo (University of Southampton)
Bruno Gonçalves (New York University)
Harith Alani (The Open University)
Michael Granitzer (University of Passau)
Diogo Pacheco (Indiana University Bloomington)
Athanasios Mazarakis (Kiel University / ZBW)
Fabien Gandon (INRIA)
Robert Ackland (Australian National University)
Clare J.Hooper (University of Southampton)
Carlos Canal (University of Málaga)
Keith Burghardt (University of Southern California)
Onur Varol (Northeastern University)
Pinelopi Troullinou (The Open University)
Michael Cochez
Matthew Weber (Rutgers University)
Andres Abeliuk (University of Southern California)
Cornelius Puschmann (Alexander von Humboldt Institute for Internet and Society)
Nishanth Sastry (King's College London)
René Arnold (WIK-Consult GmbH)

WebSci 2019 Sponsors & Supporters

Sponsors:

Supporters:

Differences in Emotional Reactions to Social Media Content: The Role of Location and Content Type

Farhad Mohammad Afzali
University of Nebraska at Omaha
Omaha, NE, USA
farhadafzali@fulbrightmail.org

Christian Haas
University of Nebraska at Omaha
Omaha, NE, USA
christianhaas@unomaha.edu

Margeret Hall
University of Nebraska at Omaha
Omaha, NE, USA
mahall@unomaha.edu

ABSTRACT

Individuals in diaspora tend to engage and interact with the people of their origin. Afghans in the 1980s and 90s, still one of the largest diaspora communities, used traditional channels such as Radio and Television to communicate with their loved ones inside Afghanistan. The Internet facilitated changing their mode of communication to near real-time updates. Diaspora and local communities engage in the same Social Awareness Streams (SAS), but there is a lack of research focusing on difference and similarities of these communities. This paper investigates the differences in emotional disclosure and expression between diaspora and local communities in Afghanistan using data from 'Afghanistan My Passion', the largest public Afghan Facebook community page. We investigate a corpus of 2,165 Persian language words considering the location and gender of the social media user. This work provides the first analysis towards understanding differences in diaspora and local communities' emotional reactions to social media content and extends the body of literature on Persian language sentiment analysis.

CCS CONCEPTS

• **Human-centered computing → Social media; Social networking sites**.

KEYWORDS

social networks, social awareness streams, sentiment analysis

ACM Reference Format:
Farhad Mohammad Afzali, Christian Haas, and Margeret Hall. 2019. Differences in Emotional Reactions to Social Media Content: The Role of Location and Content Type. In *11th ACM Conference on Web Science (WebSci '19), June 30–July 3, 2019, Boston, MA, USA.* ACM, New York, NY, USA, 5 pages. https://doi.org/10.1145/3292522.3326035

1 INTRODUCTION

Diaspora communities are necessarily linked with displacement, dispersal, and migration [21], yet researchers have different opinions regarding its characteristics. Conner considers individuals living outside their homeland as diaspora communities [8], while another study describes diaspora as migrants who are immigrants,

guest workers, asylum seekers, ethnic minorities, and displaced populations as [21]. Hiller, adding to the definition of diaspora, states that there are three phases of migration cycle: pre-migrants, post-migrants, and settled migrants [11]. Afghan refugees make a large portion of the world's total diaspora community. We could not find Afghan Diaspora statistics around the world, but following refugee statistics provide a sense of the size of the Afghan diaspora. Afghan refugees had the largest worldwide refugee community for 32 years [19] before being surpassed by Syrian refugees in 2014 [1]. Afghans started fleeing the country in 1978 – after the Saur revolution – and outward migration has continued since then. In 2014, there were over 3.7 million Afghan refugees, with most of them living in Iran and Pakistan [19]. In comparison, Afghanistan has a population of over 34 million people as of 2017.

Afghans in diaspora have had an active role in the country's politics, reconstruction, and capacity building. Since 2001, Afghan presidents – Hamid Karzai and Ashraf Ghani – have been diasporic individuals [23]. Furthermore, three of four political groups attending the 2001 Bonn talks – gathered to decide the transitional government of Afghanistan after 9/11 – came from the diaspora [22]. Besides the country's leadership, diaspora members were given key positions such as ministries in the interim governments [23]. Nassery's report on the role of the Afghan-American diaspora in peacebuilding and reconstruction states: "Individual and group behaviors are an important element as of peacebuilding as are education or skill level, and by behaving professionally and collectively, the Afghan-American diaspora can best influence policy planning and implementation of reconstruction in Afghanistan" [[18], p. 1].

Diaspora communities – Afghans in the above mentioned cases – play a significant role their origin homeland. However, there is limited research on how Afghan diasporic identities are shaped and reshaped as they interact with their homeland. [9] discusses that 21st century is quite different from prior diasopras as new technologies pave the way for a faster and real-time communication to virtually engage in the events happening in their homeland. Social media's broad and deep discourses allow researchers to observe these interactions unobtrusively [14]. Social media has affected the integration and presence of diaspora communities as they virtually engage with their homeland at the expense of physical engagement with their adopted communities [13], which helps with studying the mutual impact of locals and diaspora alike. Afghans inside and outside of their country discuss issues and share opinions on current affairs using Social Awareness Streams (SAS) – a kind of semi-public communication used in social media. However, thoughts and emotions regarding events could differ between people based on their location and gender. An Afghan living in diaspora might

Table 1: Afghanistan My Passion fans by country

#	Country of Residence	#Fans
1	Afghanistan	1,592,397
2	Pakistan	475,146
3	Germany	142,278
4	Saudi Arabia	128,189
5	Iran	98,723
6	India	89,529
7	United Arab Emirates	88,806
8	Turkey	70,319
9	United States of America	50,074
10	Bangladesh	43,922

see corruption in the public sector differently compared to an individual residing inside the country and being part of the system. Similarly, a woman might view a new law introduced by the government differently compared to how a man sees it. For analyses of discourse in countries with high external populations, correct pre-classification is a necessary step. However diasporic communication and its differences compared to local populations is a mostly unaddressed subject in social media analysis. Also, it is unknown if different content types – posted by moderators – activate higher or lower emotional responses. This leads to our research questions:

RQ1: How do location and gender impact the sentiment of users' emotional expression?

RQ2: Which types of posts generate high emotional responses?

We chose Facebook as our data source to investigate these research questions as it is the most used social network in Afghanistan [1] and is the most accessible communication service in the country. As of 2015, mobile service providers, covering 89% of the population [2], offered Facebook packages where the subscriber did not need to have an active mobile data or Internet subscription to use Facebook [2]. It cost around one U.S. dollar to activate this service for one month. The coverage has increased and rates has gone down since then. 'Afghanistan My Passion' is the Facebook page with the largest audience among Afghans inside the country and in diaspora. The page – launched in 2011 – had 3.9 million fans in 2018, 42.9% of whom live inside the country [3] (see Table 1 for the top ten countries with the highest number of fans). The page admin posts various types of events happening across the country.

2 RELATED WORK

2.1 Diasporic Communication

Tsagarousianou states that connectivity defines diaspora better than displacement [21]. Diaspora communities have been communicating with their loved ones in their first home over generations. The type of communication has changed over time though. If we think about two centuries ago, it would take months for someone to communicate a single message with people in their homeland, probably by sending a letter and receiving a response. The emergence of

technology and the facility to communicate with others without a binding to distance or time has changed the shape of diasporic communications. The Internet brings members of a community closer to a global village where all the members have real-time connectivity to any other member of the community [16]. Media technology like social media, voice over internet protocols (VoIP) and diasporic media have a crucial role in forming diasporic identities and diaspora in general [21]. With media technology facilitating interactions among the diaspora communities, the concept of e-diaspora is getting popular [16]. Research in the role of ICT (Information and Communication Technology) in the lives of diasporic peoples contributes to a definition of the concept of e-diaspora, understood here as the result of the unwilling dispersal of members of a nation across several countries [16].

2.2 Social Network Sites (SNS)

Social network sites or social networking sites are web-based services used by individuals for constructing a public or semi-public profile within a bounded system, forming a list of users with whom they may connect, and exploring the list of connections [4]. Users interact online by creating profiles and providing (semi)personal information in the form of text, photos and other media [10]. As social networking and media platforms are generally based on true identities or variants thereof [10, 15], they are well suited for digital community analyses [10]. Social media and social networking sites have quickly ascended from a novelty of the early 2000's to a fact of life, and daily necessity. SNS like Facebook, LinkedIn, Twitter, Google Plus have become extremely popular in the recent years [5]. With the help of SNS, users – diasporic individuals – create social identities by creating social profiles and building social networks, which creates a sense of belonging to the network. Users consider themselves as part of the community psychologically if they: see themselves emotionally involved with the online community; evaluate self-worth based on the membership to a particular social group; or sense self-awareness of being part of the group [6].

2.3 Social Awareness Streams (SAS)

Social Network Sites have changed the shape of communications and interactions among people. SAS is one of the types of communication services that leverage the SNS. A kind of semi-public communication, i.e., Facebook and Twitter, which are very popular [12]. In this communication style, a user posts messages, photos or videos. What a user posts will appear to his/her contacts' news feed. The users can react synchronously or asynchronously with, for example, a like, comment or share, to what they see in their news feed posted by other people in his/her network [17]. Naaman et al. argue that the public nature of communication, the brevity of published content, and a highly connected social space are the three main factors that distinguish SAS from other types of communication services [17]. Therefore, we chose a Facebook page, Afghanistan My Passion, for this study.

3 RESEARCH DESIGN

In order to answer our research questions, we leveraged Python scripts to extract the data from Facebook. Between 2011-2017, there were 8,404 status updates by page admins. The total number of

---

[1]https://www.internews.org/news/social-media-afghanistan-users -and-engagement
[2]https://www.independent.co.uk/life-style/gadgets-and-tech/features/how-social-media-is-empowering-young-afghan-women-the-facebook-effect-10375022.html
[3]https://www.socialbakers.com/statistics/facebook/ pages/total/afghanistan

comments on these mentioned statuses is 646,399. We focused on data between July 13, 2017, and August 07, 2017, specifically on comments with 150+ words (n=480) because all types of topics found across all the page's posts were covered in that three week interval. We included only text written in Persian (Dari dialect) using Persian characters. English, transliterated texts, and other languages are excluded from this initial study as current language processing packages are unable to simultaneously analyze multiple languages or indeed even interpret the same language written in differing scripts. 91 of the total comments in our data set were English, Pashto, or transliterated. We removed those comments to keep our analysis based on Persian (Dari). After cleaning the comments, we had 389 of them to extract our sample from. Due to lack of availability of automatic processing tools for Persian data classification and manual identification of comment author's gender and location, we took a sample of 100 comments as to manually identify the gender and location of comment authors [4]. We used Quintly [5] to get the demographics of the fans based on the country they reside in. Quintly is a web-based social analytics tool that helps with scraping of information from social media sites.

3.1 Data Classification

To classify the data in common themes of content types, four Persian native speakers analyzed and coded the data individually. The coders used a jury format to reach a consensus regarding the common themes. The common themes (post types) identified were Cultural, Religious, Historical, Education, Racial Discrimination, Security Situation, and Healthcare. We then identified the comment author location and their gender by viewing their Facebook profiles. We dropped three profiles for which locations were not identifiable and two profiles for whose gender could not be identified.

3.2 Sentiment Analysis Tools

Following the data collection and classification, the biggest challenge was the lack of available tools that can analyze Persian/Dari sentiment. SentiStrength [20] was one of the tools that support Persian sentiment analysis. However, we found out that their Persian dictionary is still not mature as it leaves most of the words uncategorized. We used Polyglot [3] as the tool for sentiment analysis as it categorized most of the words, as it proved to be the most efficient sentiment analysis tool for the Persian Language. Polyglot is a python package that has robust features such as tokenization, language detection, Named Entity Recognition, Parts of Speech Tagging, Sentiment Analysis, Word Embedding, Morphological Analysis, and Transliteration of 100+ languages. It determines the polarity of words based on their negativity and positivity by assigning scores of -1 (negative words), 0 (neutral words), and +1 (positive words) to the words respectively. The analysis found 2,165 emotionally intoned terms in the posts and comments.

4 ANALYSIS AND RESULTS

In this section, we describe the analyses we performed on the data and the corresponding results. First, a word frequency-based analysis was conducted to determine commonalities between admins and

Figure 1: Frequency of words in posts by admin.

Figure 2: Frequency of words used in comments by fans.

fans, as well as to identify popular topics. Second, a sentiment analysis was performed to evaluate potential differences in sentiment across different topics, groups, and genders.

4.1 Word Frequencies and Topics

As a first analysis, we counted the frequency of the words used in all posts and comments since the start of Afghanistan My Passion, 2011. It helped us understand what the most common topics were and how the fans reacted to the posts. We generated two word clouds using wordclouds.com (see Figure 1 and 2). The figures demonstrate that there was a similarity in the topics discussed in posts by the admin and comments shared by the users. Additionally, the major issues addressed were positive, which indicates that the fans regardless of their location have similar sentiment about the topics discussed.

The word cloud in Figure 1 demonstrates the words used in the posts made by the admin of the page. The five most frequent words used by admins in the posts (Figure 1), from highest to lowest, were وطن، سال، زن، جان، افغانستان. English translations of these words are Afghanistan, life (or dear), woman, year, and homeland. Besides the five terms mentioned, most of the high frequency used words had positive messages in them. The words used in comments by fans (Figure 2) had positive tones in them as well. The most frequently used word used in comments was identical to the one used in posts, افغانستان. The remaining four highest frequency

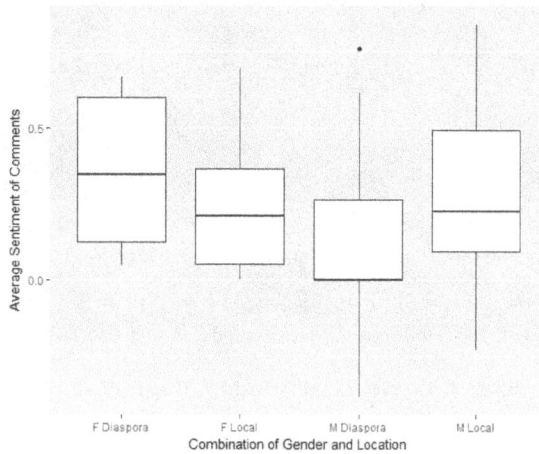

Figure 3: Comment sentiment based on gender and location

used words were زنده ، وطن ، جان ، خداوند. English translation of these words are (highest to lowest): Afghanistan, God, life (it means dear, too), homeland, and alive. Looking at the most frequent words, frequently discussed topics tend to be related to religion, life, and security. Combining the top ten words used in the statuses and comments we found that they all had positive valence. While more than a half of the fans reside outside the country, the most frequent words were about 'Afghanistan' and 'homeland'. This indicates that Afghans in diaspora discuss the country and the situations in the country as often as the local Afghans do, revealing an active interest that the diaspora has for its home country.

4.2 Sentiment Analysis

For the subsequent analysis, we concentrated on the comment-level sentiment. Comment sentiment was defined as the average percentage of positive and negative words in a comment; thus ranging from -1 to 1. For example, if a comment had two positive and one negative word, the average sentiment score was $(2 - 1)/3 = 0.33$. Figure 3 shows the distribution of comment sentiment based on location and gender. The average comment sentiment is 0.309 for Local and Male, 0.248 for Local and Female, 0.162 for Diaspora and Male, and 0.339 for Diaspora and Female. We had a total of 14.5% comments from women, and 43.5% of the comments were from Diaspora. An analysis of the total number of positive and negative words per comment revealed no statistically significant difference based on Location or Gender. To address the RQs, we conducted several statistical analyses based on the previously described data. Analysis of Variance (ANOVA) was used for the subsequent analyses, as the assumption of Gaussian distributions of the sentiment scores cannot be rejected at the 0.05 level. First, we considered the effect of gender (M/F) and location (Local/Diaspora) on the average comment sentiment. A two-way ANOVA with interaction effect found that neither main or interaction effects were significant at the 0.05 level, however the p-value of the location impacting the average comment sentiment was close to significance with 0.055 (see Table 2). Subsequent t-tests for the subgroups revealed the difference between Local and Diaspora was significant for Male

comments based on a p-value of 0.02. Neither gender nor the interaction of gender and location was significant. Next, we included

Table 2: Effects of gender and location on sentiment score

	Df	Sum Sq	Mean Sq	F	p-value
Gender	1	0.076	0.07629	1.042	0.311
Location	1	0.279	0.27941	3.817	0.055
Gender:Location	1	0.145	0.14488	1.979	0.164
Residuals	65	4.758	0.07320		

the type of post in the analyses. Post types were either cultural, religious, educational, historical, healthcare, racial discrimination, and security. Including the post type in the ANOVA did not change the resulting outcome, i.e., neither the post type nor its interactions with gender/location were found to be significant (see Table 3). This can, however, be a result of the currently used number of comments and could change by including a larger number of comments in subsequent studies. Third, when using an ANOVA with only the post

Table 3: Effects of gender, location, and post type on sentiment score

	Df	Sum Sq	Mean Sq	F	p-value
Gender	1	0.076	0.07629	1.002	0.322
Location	1	0.279	0.27941	3.670	0.061
Post_Type	6	0.282	0.04696	0.617	0.716
Gender:Location	1	0.193	0.19297	2.534	0.118
Gender:Post_Type	4	0.441	0.11023	1.448	0.232
Location:Post_Type	4	0.104	0.02606	0.342	0.848
Residuals	51	3.883	0.07614		

type groups, we found that the post type significantly influences the number of positive/negative words in the comments at the 0.05 level (see Table 4). Specifically, Fisher's Least Significant Difference test showed that posts concerning Racial Discrimination lead to a higher number of positive/negative sentiment words than posts about culture, religion, security, or education. Also, history related posts lead to a higher number of words than posts about religious topics. This indicates that Racial Discrimination in particular seems to lead to more discussions on Facebook.

Table 4: Effects of post type on positive/negative words

	Df	Sum Sq	Mean Sq	F	p-value
Post_Type	6	2937	489.6	2.651	0.0236
Residuals	62	11451	184.7		

Similarly, Table 5 shows an overview of average sentiment scores based on the Location (Diaspora vs Local) and Post Type. The NA values indicate that no posts were observed in this category. Based on the table, Cultural topics seem to correspond to more positive sentiment as compared to other topics. In addition, differences between the Local and Diaspora sentiment are observable in posts about Racial Discrimination, Religion, and Education. However, another two-way ANOVA with Post Type and Location as well as their interaction reveals no significance at the 0.05 level, with Location having the smallest p-value of 0.056. Finally, investigated whether there is a correlation between the sentiment of the original post (i.e., post by the site admin) and the sentiment of the comments. With a correlation coefficient of 0.08, the analysis revealed that there is little correlation between these two aspects.

Table 5: Location and post type sentiment differences

Post_Type	Diaspora	Local
Cultural	0.38396624	0.2763158
Educational	0.16666667	0.3150685
Healthcare	0.33333333	NA
Historical	0.12068966	0.2222222
Racial Discrimination	0.01075269	0.5121951
Religious	0.05405405	0.2719101
Security	0.06666667	NA

5 DISCUSSION & CONCLUSION

This study explored the sentiment of diasporic individuals in comparison to locals. It also examined the interactions of communities on social media and analyzed emotional characteristics based on their location and gender. Regarding RQ1, we find no statistical differences between the populations based on their declared gender. Differences in location between locals and diasporic individuals tends towards significance, which is the basis of any future work in this direction. Our analysis demonstrated that Afghans are more sensitive to racial discrimination and engage in talking about history more than any other category. These types of posts generate the highest emotional responses (RQ2). Finally, this paper contributes to the community of practice. The social media community activists, specifically Afghan communities, can predict the sensitivity and commonality of a post before publishing it. By doing so, they can post the right content at the right time. Social media can also be leveraged for various purposes to address local and diaspora communities. Cogburn & Espinoza-Vasquez, for instance, found that leveraging Web 2.0 helped Obama 08 campaign "translate online activity to on-the-ground activity" [[7], p. 200]. Hence, we believe that activists can take advantage of the existence of social media to develop a unified virtual local and diaspora community to promote causes and/or spread awareness.

6 LIMITATIONS & FUTURE WORK

This study has several limitations. We tried to identify the sentiment of fans based on their gender and location generally. This is manually intensive and results in a small-n phenomenon. In the next phase we will examine the more extensive dataset – collecting data from several pages – with more categories of admin posts to ensure maximum coverage of the page content in our analysis. We also plan to analyze the sentiment on the user level. The current research is hampered by the lack of robust Persian language tools. We argue that introducing or identifying a sentiment analysis tool with a more complete dictionary and the sentence-level sentiment

analysis functionality will be a significant contribution to the computational analysis of the Persian language. The small range of Polyglot may contribute to the lack of significance in the results, where a more fine-tuned tool like LIWC [6] may display differences across characteristics in language use.

REFERENCES

[1] 2014. Syria tops the world as source of refugees | News | Al Jazeera. https://bit.ly/1dxhXKR
[2] 2015. Ministry of Communication and IT (MCIT). https://mcit.gov.af/en
[3] Rami Al-Rfou, Bryan Perozzi, and Steven Skiena. 2013. Polyglot: Distributed Word Representations for Multilingual NLP. (2013). https://doi.org/10.1007/s10479-011-0841-3
[4] Danah Boyd and Nicole Ellison. 2010. Social network sites: definition, history, and scholarship. *IEEE Engineering Management Review* 3, 38 (2010), 16–31.
[5] Mustapha Cheikh-Ammar and Henri Barki. 2016. The Influence of Social Presence, Social Exchange and Feedback Features on SNS Continuous Use:. *Journal of Organizational and End User Computing* 28, 2 (2016), 33–52. https://doi.org/10.4018/JOEUC.2016040103
[6] Christy M K Cheung, Pui Yee Chiu, and Matthew K O Lee. 2011. Online social networks: Why do students use facebook? *Computers in Human Behavior* 27, 4 (2011), 1337–1343. https://doi.org/10.1016/j.chb.2010.07.028
[7] Derrick L. Cogburn and Fatima K. Espinoza-Vasquez. 2011. From networked nominee to networked nation: Examining the impact of web 2.0 and social media on political participation and civic engagement in the 2008 obama campaign. *Journal of Political Marketing* 10, 1-2 (2011), 189–213. https://doi.org/10.1080/15377857.2011.540224
[8] Walker Conner. 1986. The impact of homelands upon diasporas.
[9] Shehina Fazal and Roza Tsagarousianou. 2002. Diasporic communication: Transnational cultural practices and communicative spaces. *Javnost* 9, 1 (2002), 5–18. https://doi.org/10.1080/13183222.2002.11008790
[10] Margeret Hall and Simon Caton. 2017. Am I Who I Say I am ? Unobtrusive Self-Representation and Personality Recognition on Facebook. *PLOS One* 12, 9 (2017), e0184417. https://doi.org/10.1371/journal.pone.0184417
[11] Harry H. Hiller and Tara M. Franz. 2004. New ties, old ties and lost ties: the use of the internet in diaspora. *New Media & Society* 6, 6 (12 2004), 731–752. https://doi.org/10.1177/146144804044327
[12] Funda Kivran-swaine and Mor Naaman. 2009. Network Properties and Social Sharing of Emotions in Social Awareness Streams. *Media* July (2009), 379–382. https://doi.org/10.1145/1958824.1958882
[13] Lee Komito and Jessica Bates. 2009. Virtually local: social media and community among Polish nationals in Dublin. *Aslib Proceedings* 61, 3 (2009), 232–244. https://doi.org/10.1108/00012530910959790
[14] Andreas Lindner, Margeret Hall, Claudia Niemeyer, and Simon Caton. 2015. BeWell: A Sentiment Aggregator for Proactive Community Management. In *CHI'15 Extended Abstracts*, Vol. 18. ACM Press, Seoul, 1055–1060. https://doi.org/10.1145/2702613.2732787
[15] Jessa Lingel, Mor Naaman, and danah boyd. 2014. City, self, network: transnational migrants and online identity work. In *CSCW'14*. 1502–1510. https://doi.org/10.1145/2531602.25311693
[16] Marta Marcheva. 2011. The Networked Diaspora : Bulgarian Migrants on Facebook Facebook. 14, 2 (2011), 17–19.
[17] M. Naaman, J. Boase, and C.H. Lai. 2010. Is it Really About Me? Message Content in Social Awareness Streams. *Dot-Me.of-Cour.Se* (2010), 0–3. https://doi.org/10.1145/1718918.1718953
[18] Homira G. Nassery. 2003. *The Reverse Brain Drain: Afghan-American Diaspora in Post-Conflict Peacebuilding and Reconstruction.* Technical Report.
[19] Catherine Putz. 2015. Afghanistan's 32-Year Refugee Crisis. http://thediplomat.com/2015/09/afghanistans-32-year-refugee-crisis/
[20] Mike Thelwall, Kevan Buckley, and Georgios Paltoglou. 2012. Sentiment strength detection for the social web. *Journal of the American Society for Information Science and Technology* 63, 1 (1 2012), 163–173. https://doi.org/10.1002/asi.21662
[21] R Tsagarousianou. 2004. Rethinking the concept of diaspora: mobility, connectivity, and communication in a globalised world. *Communication and Media Research Institute University of Westminster* 1, 1 (2004), 52–65. https://doi.org/10.1017/CBO9781107415324.004
[22] Nicholas Van Hear. 2014. From" Durable Solutions" to" Transnational Relations": Home and Exile Among Refugee Diasporas. *Occasional Paper* 23 (2014), 232–251.
[23] Wolfram Zunzer. 2004. Diaspora Communities and Civil Conflict Transformation. *Berghof Occasional Paper* 26 (2004), 1–56. http://hdl.handle.net/10454/4186

---

[6]https://liwc.wpengine.com/

New Tab Page Recommendations Strongly Concentrate Web Browsing to Familiar Sources

Homanga Bharadhwaj
Computer Science, IIT Kanpur
homangab@cse.iitk.ac.in

Nisheeth Srivastava
Computer Science, IIT Kanpur
nsrivast@cse.iitk.ac.in

ABSTRACT

To what extent do contemporary web technologies that seek to personalize users' browsing experience trap them in filter bubbles? Existing research has yielded mixed results on the possibility of such influence, but empirical research in this area has been entirely cross-sectional. In this paper, we report results from a longitudinal controlled web experiment conducted to determine whether passive recommendations embedded in common computer user-interfaces (UIs) reinforce users' habitual browsing behaviors, to the detriment of the diversity of the set of pages they tend to visit online. Inspired by classical demonstrations of a part-set cueing effect in memory, our experimental design manipulates the behaviour of the 'New Tab' page for consenting volunteers over a two month-long period in randomized time blocks of equal length. Analysis of their browsing behavior shows that users visit on average 15% fewer unique web pages while their browser's 'New Tab' page displays recommendations based on conventional frequency and recency-based algorithms, than if the display is left blank. This effect is seen systematically for all participants in our study. Further analysis of browsing behavior in this experiment clearly identifies the source of the difference between these modes of browsing: users consistently visit a greater diversity of web pages while typing in URLs in the URL/search bar when there are no recommendations on the 'New Tab' page. Finally, using a simulation study, modelling user behavior as a random walk on a graph, we extracted quantitative predictions about the extent to which discovery of new sources of information may be hindered by the concentration of browsing driven by such personalized 'New Tab' recommendations in classical browser UIs.

CCS CONCEPTS

• **Human-centered computing → Empirical studies in HCI**; *User studies*; *Web-based interaction*;

KEYWORDS

filter bubble, personalization, habitual web browsing, information diet, cognitive science

WebSci '19, June 30-July 3, 2019, Boston, MA, USA
© 2019 Association for Computing Machinery.
ACM ISBN 978-1-4503-6202-3/19/06...$15.00
https://doi.org/10.1145/3292522.3326011

ACM Reference Format:
Homanga Bharadhwaj and Nisheeth Srivastava. 2019. New Tab Page Recommendations Strongly Concentrate Web Browsing to Familiar Sources. In *11th ACM Conference on Web Science (WebSci '19), June 30–July 3, 2019, Boston, MA, USA*. ACM, New York, NY, USA, 10 pages. https://doi.org/10.1145/3292522.3326011

1 INTRODUCTION

The medium is the message [19]. McLuhan's gnomic aphorism has, in the half-century since its utterance, launched countless humanistic appraisals of the manner in which the form of modern communication technologies have shaped, and continue to shape the way people think. Given the extent to which web-based technologies now saturate our lived environment, substantiating these critiques quantitatively is very important.

For instance, it seems intuitively plausible, even likely, that the hyper-linked nature of web interfaces, in contrast with the linear nature of books, leads to greater distraction and shallower processing of information [5]. A survey of recent empirical research addressing this question, however, notes that even though the basic hypothesis is borne out - students reading material on screens do worse on tests than students reading material on paper, this performance differential appears to reduce quite rapidly with practice [20]. While it is still too early to conclude definitively either way about the validity of this particular critique, a general point remains: access to empirical data permits broad critiques of technology's influence on cognition to themselves be substantiated.

A similar story can be told about yet another intuitively appealing hypothesis - the filter bubble [24]. Here, the claim is that web-based recommendation services, by virtue of their algorithmic logic, recommend digital objects to people that they are already known to prefer, thus reducing the possibility for them to experience new content that they may or may not like. Again, the claim is easily believable, but has proved difficult to substantiate empirically. An analysis of the effect of accepting movie recommendations from the Movielens system showed that while the set of movies recommended became gradually less diverse with time, users who chose to follow the system's recommendations received more diverse recommendations than users who ignored them [22]. Recent research seeking to evaluate the existence of filter bubbles in Google News' personalization algorithm reported extremely minor differences in news articles presented to different user accounts explicitly set up to provoke differentiation [13]. Mixed evidence for filter bubbles was obtained from an analysis conducted by Microsoft on the news reading habits of 50000 Internet Explorer users, which found that while political articles accessed via social media or search engines are more politically extreme than those accessed directly from websites, the use of these channels is also more associated with exposure to opposite political views than direct access [10].

There is an interesting dichotomy between theoretical and empirical evaluations of the filter bubble. Whereas theoretical critiques focus heavily on how recommendations could potentially narrow the diversity of users' demand patterns for digital media [24], empirical research focuses on identifying whether recommendation systems are narrowing the diversity of content providers' *supply* of digital objects [13, 22]. Work that explicitly tracks users' *consumption* patterns does appear to detect a small bubble effect [10], but the restriction of this study to studying only political diversity reduces the generalizability of its results.

In this paper, we report results from an experimental study of an extremely general version of the filter bubble hypothesis, evaluated strictly on consumption patterns rather than supply, and without restricting the nature of content consumed. Specifically, we investigate whether the presence of frequently visited tabs on 'new tab' pages in modern browsers leads to a concentration of browsing behavior into a more restricted set of websites than when such recommendation-based displays are absent. We conducted a controlled, longitudinal, within-subject experiment wherein we manipulated the behavior of consenting volunteers' new tab page displays without their knowledge and analyzed their browsing history at the end of the observation period to measure the degree to which our covert manipulations influenced users' web browsing behavior. We found strong statistical support for our hypothesis. Usage of new tab pages with personalized recommendations considerably reduced the number of unique websites visited by users, suggesting concentration of website browsing repertoires. Additional analyses revealed that this concentration was not uniform, and was seen most clearly precisely during browsing events most strongly associated with free memory recall - users typing URLs into address bars in the new tab page display, with recommendations visible underneath.

To assess the extent to which this measured concentration in web information sources could affect the diversity of users' experience on the web, we also ran a simulation study, using our data to set parameters for a random walk model of a web surfer seeking information from diverse sources. We found that, for empirically grounded values of non-habitual browsing, the size of suppression effects seen in our empirical sample would correspond to reductions in the frequency with which diverse information sources are accessed, of nearly 50% for the median user.

Thus, in this paper, we present empirical and simulation evidence to show that the presence of a set of web page icon recommendations on browser new tab pages reduces users' propensity to access infrequently visited web pages by nearly half. We also discuss the implications of this striking finding on the filter bubble literature, the principles of designing communication interfaces, and ethical considerations of web-mediated communication.

2 A CONTROLLED FILTER BUBBLE EXPERIMENT

We anticipated large individual differences in browsing behavior across subjects, suggesting that cohort-level differences may or may not be representative of the median user's experience. Therefore, we focused on designing a within-subject experiment, with experimental manipulations that each participant in the experiment would experience in different time blocks.

2.1 Experiment design

We designed a Firefox web extension using JavaScript, HTML and CSS. It broadly consists of three parts, a webpage to replace the default new tab display, a browser action page to log the browsing data into a local file and a remote script located in the experimenter's server that is used to tweak the type of websites displayed in the new tab page, as shown in Figure 1. In this design, the experimenter does not have access to the participant's data during the course of the experiment. At the end of the experiment, the experimenter explicitly asks for the logs, and participants are advised to curate their history to remove personal and private content before handing them over, if they choose to do so.

We programmed four different behavior modes in the replacement new tab page generated when people install our extension, controlled by a parameter in the extension script that we could change remotely without the user's knowledge. Each participant's replacement new tab page shows the web page icons as per exactly one of the following four modes at a given time.

(1) Display the **most** visited sites in browsing history
(2) Display the **least** visited sites in browsing history (at least one visit, naturally)
(3) **Default** behavior, following Mozilla's frecency algorithm - a combination of frequency and recency [11]
(4) Display a **blank** page

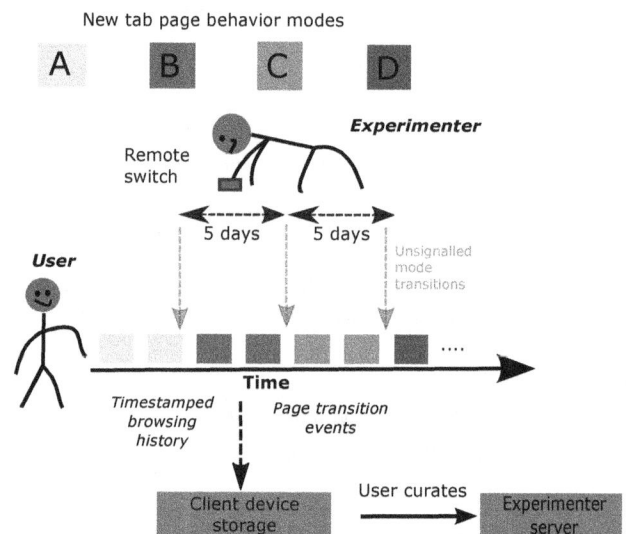

Figure 1: The experiment design

Our web-extension logs the webpages the user visits, the time of visits and the transition type from one webpage to the next - **typed** in the address or search bar, **linked** to from the content of a different site, or **clicked** through the browser UI. It also automatically logs all the websites currently displayed in the new tab page whenever it is opened. The replacement new tab page is designed to visually resemble the default Firefox new tab page so that after a certain period of time, the user is not very conscious of the extension running in background. Once the extension is installed on a participant's computer, the experimenter can change the behavior of the replacement new tab page by simply changing a parameter in a participant-specific file hosted on the experimenter's server. We used a fixed switching interval of 5 days, with all participants beginning with the default mode of new tab behavior, and with further switches assigned pseudo-randomly, ensuring that all participants received at least one block of 5 days' worth exposure to each of the three new behavior modes. Since we used a rolling recruitment process the 5-day blocks don't systematically interact with weekends for all participants, an important consideration in a behavior measurement experiment. This interaction is approximately random across subjects in our experiment.

2.2 Sample

Eighty volunteers from the general population (32 female, age 28.2 ± 6.1 years), recruited on a rolling basis, consented to participate in our experiment. 30% of them were university students, 40% were employed in the industry (excluding software industry), 20% were employed in the software industry and 10% were employed in the academia (lecturer/post-doc/professor). There were no web-developers in the sample, who used the browser for development. Participants were recruited through advertisements in newspapers, on social media websites and emails. Participants were not incentivized and were naive to the purpose of the study. We explained to them that we were interested in analyzing their web browsing history for a research experiment using a software extension they would install into their browser, that our extension would only store their data locally, and that they would have complete control over the curation process that would determine what part of their history they would share with the experimenters. The participants used various devices including laptops, desktops, tablet computers and mobile phones and no restriction on the type of device for a participant was imposed. A total of 10 participants reported to have used mobile phones / tablet computers while the remaining participants used either a laptop / desktop computer for installing the extension. At the end of two months of browsing for each participant, we asked them to curate the log files and share them with us, retaining the option to refuse. The two-month long browsing logs volunteered by these eighty participants formed our primary dataset.

At the time of submission of the logs, we asked the participants what fraction of the website logs had been curated by them. None of the eighty participants had curated more than 5% of the total content, with most participants not curating at all, which is reasonable and does not negatively affect our study. We had not disclosed to these participants that we intended to manipulate their new tab page's behavior remotely. To assess the extent to which they may have become aware of this possibility, at the time of collecting the logs we also asked them whether anything about the websites displayed in the new tab page 'bothered' them over the past two months. They were asked to express their opinion on a 0-10 scale with 0 being the 'not aware' state and 10 the 'very aware' state. They were not specifically asked if they thought the type of websites shown were being altered remotely to avoid experimenter demand effects [6]. Subjects' responses are shown in Table 1.

Table 1: Participants' level of awareness of our experimental manipulation.

Opinion	0-4	5-7	8-10
Number of subjects	70	7	3

These survey results suggest that the majority of our participants remained naive to the purpose of the experiment, and continued to behave naturally in the face of our remote manipulations.

2.3 Data processing

The self-curated browsing logs obtained from all 80 participants in the experiment constituted our primary analysis material. These logs contained time-stamped instances of different website URLs visited by the participants. From these logs, we filtered out pop-ups and ads using a white-list, and used a 30-minute gap between page views to delimit browsing sessions. We collapsed web-pages visited on the same primary web domain into multiple visits to the same website, and likewise collapsed page refreshes (immediate repetitions of the same page in the log) as a single visit to the page. The few occurrences of dynamic web-pages in the browsing log were collapsed to that of the parent domain. We explicitly handled pages visited from search engines in the browser. For all occurrences of Google, Yahoo, Bing, Ask.com, Baidu, Wolframalpha and DuckDuckGo in the browsing log, we considered the page clicked immediately afterwards in the search results. If the search engine address was typed out in the new tab page, we treated the page clicked from the search results as if it was typed out in the address bar. Table 2 lists out a few anecdotal examples of the most visited and least visited websites across participants.

3 RESULTS

Since our hypothesis generally concerns the potential reduction of the diversity of websites that users visit as a consequence of the format of the new tab page display, our first coarse measurement of this property was the number of unique websites (defined via the primary web-domain in each URL) visited by our experiment participants during each mode of the new tab page's display properties.

Combining the default and most visited modes' data into one sample and for the blank and least visited modes' data into another, a two-sample T-test yields strong statistical significance $p < 10^{-3}$ and a very large effect size (Cohen's d = 1.81) as shown in Figure 2. Thus, there is clearly a large difference in user behavior across these experimental cohorts, in the predicted direction. Users visit a lot more unique websites on average when the new tab page is blank or shows infrequently visited websites, suggesting that the presence of recommendations by default is suppressing the repertoire of webpages they might naturally visit. For completeness, we show the results of bonferroni corrected pair-wise T-test among

Table 2: Representative examples of most visited (1st Quartile) and least visited (4th Quartile) websites of participants

Most Visited	Least Visited
Google	weebly
Facebook	Joomla
Youtube	icrc
Twitter	Netscape
Amazon	Scribd
Quora	Godaddy
Netflix	Nasa
Instagram	Yahoo
CNN	hotmail
Overleaf	Orkut

all the pairs of conditions in our study (Table 3). However, the

Table 3: Results of bonferroni corrected pairwise T-test for all the pairs of conditions (as shown in Fig. 3). Number of unique website counts for each of the four modes are averaged over 80 individuals.

Condition 1	Condition 2	p-value
Most visited	Least visited	0.000011
Most visited	Default UI	0.620102
Most visited	Blank UI	0.000008
Least visited	Default UI	0.000024
Least visited	Blank UI	0.522001
Default UI	Blank UI	0.000018

heterogeneity of web browsing behavior across individuals could conceivably inflate these statistics, in the sense that a few highly prolific web users in our participant pool could skew the cohort-level differences should they happen to conform to our hypothesis. Thus, it is important to also analyze the data at the individual-level. We plot the difference between behavior during blank UI mode and default mode for all participants in Figure 3. Note that not a single of the eighty participants visited more unique websites while the new tab page behaved under its default settings, vis-a-vis when the default recommendation display was switched off (Blank UI mode). A one-sample T test of these absolute differences with respect to zero sample mean was statistically significant at $p < 10^{-6}$. The average participant's unique site visit count increased by 15% (median improvement 12%) when the new tab page was set to display a blank page over their corresponding counts when the new tab page worked by default.

It is reasonable to conclude from this observation that changing the behavior of the new tab page does in fact alter the diversity of websites browsed. In particular, enabling recommendations in the new tab page, as per the default frecency scheme causes a reduction in the diversity of information sources (websites) accessed by the users. But this analysis does not substantiate our hypothesis

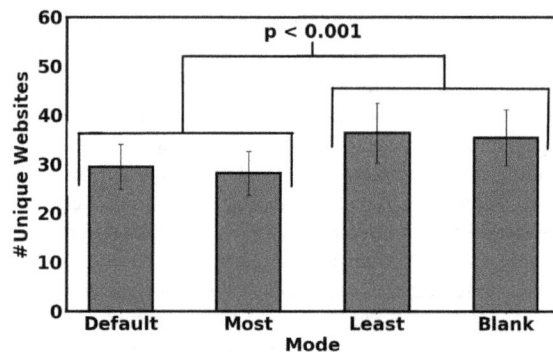

Figure 2: Number of unique website count for each of the four modes averaged over all 80 individuals. Error bars represent ± 1 Standard Deviation (S.D.).

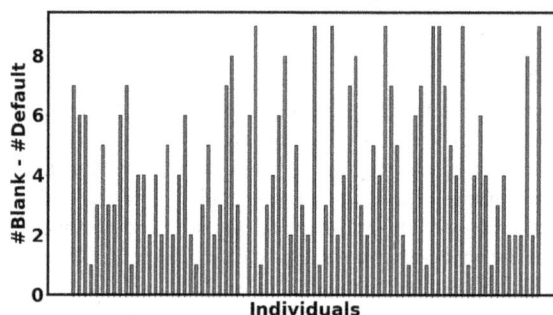

Figure 3: Absolute difference between the number of unique websites visited under the blank new tab page mode and under the default mode for all experiment participants.

about the mechanism responsible for this reduction in diversity - an increase in users' proclivity to concentrate web browsing to familiar sources , caused by interaction with the new tab page interface.

We needed a more granular view of the data to see if this might actually be true. Recall that we store both the timestamped page visit, and the web event that brings the user to that page. We categorized the pages according to visit frequency and transition type to focus especially on page visits wherewith we can analyze the nuances of users' visits to commonly visited and uncommonly visited websites and understand the implications of altering the new tab page display on the same.

This categorization is illustrated with a pseudo-flowchart in Figure 4, showing visually how we use the two decision points (frequency and transition type) to categorize web page visits into non-exclusive categories. To interpret the set-theoretic implications of the flowchart correctly, both *UI* and *pure* uncommon are subsets of uncommon, but *uncommon* and *common* are mutually exclusive. A brief description of these terms and their rationale follows.

- **Common.** Websites with high visit counts (removing the influence of interstitial URLs) are expected to correspond to content that users are in the habit of accessing and which correspond to commonly visited information sources. Since the number of webpages an individual visits will inform what constitutes high for them, we categorize as *common* visits all page visits to webpages whose visit frequency occurs in the fourth quartile (Q_4) of visit frequencies sorted in ascending order per browsing history log. In a measure of the heavy skew in the distribution of webpage counts, this quartile accounts for about 70% of all site visits across all participants' data. A distinct sub-category "pure common" takes into account frequently visited webpages visited by typed transitions from the address bar (or search the web box) of an existing tab.

- **Uncommon.** As above, it is intuitive that when people are browsing websites that are not commonly visited by them, such browsing will be marked by visiting new sources of content, hence new webpages. We mark as *uncommon* visits all visits to pages that fall in the first quartile (Q_1) of visit frequencies sorted in ascending order per browsing history log[1]. This quartile accounts for about 9% of all site visits across all participants' data.

- **Content / Event-driven.** Since we are interested in the interaction between the user's propensity to visit diverse information sources and the browser interface, we want to remove from our analysis all webpage visits that originate from an information source outside of these two. To this end, we mark all hyperlink based visits (marked in our logs as having the transition type 'link') irrespective of their frequency rank as content-driven, and exclude them from our analysis.

- **UI common.** The presence of clickable page icons obviously makes those webpages more accessible to users, over and above their mental propensity to visit these sites. Websites that users visit frequently, but use the UI to access, constitute an interesting sub-category of the *common* category. For these webpages, it is not as clear as for others that repeated visitation is indicative of conditioning due to passive recommendations that appear in the new tab page . The increased accessibility of the pages is clearly, but unquantifiably, also a factor. We refer to this category of pages, selecting all common pages arrived at either via UI clicks or by typing in the URL bar while the specific page icon was visible in the new tab page, as *UI common* pages.

- **UI uncommon.** When users visit rarely visited webpages via interaction with UI elements, we can infer that the UI interaction is driving them away from their typical sources of information. This makes the subset of *uncommon* pages that users arrive at from the new tab page (whether with transition 'link 'or 'typed '), especially interesting. We call this sub-category *UI uncommon*.

- **Pure uncommon.** The final category we define is, expectedly, sparsely populated, representing about 3% of all web page visits in our dataset. We define this as the subset of

uncommon pages whose icons are not displayed on the new tab page, have a transition type of 'typed' and have been transitioned to directly from the new tab page. To be a member of this set, the user has to have entered the webpage URL (at least its first few letters, keeping in mind auto-complete capabilities of browsers) with no input from the browser UI. Visiting rarely visited sites without the (measured) influence of either other websites' content or the content of UI elements means that this subset of webpage visits reflect visits to uncommon sources of information driven purely by the interaction of users' internal preferences for URLs with the browser's new tab page. Privileging users' internal URL preferences in a semantic sense, we label this category *pure* uncommon. Within this category, we make two further distinctions: *manipulated* pure uncommon takes into account only typed transitions to rarely visited pages from the new tab page. *Un-manipulated* pure uncommon takes into account typed transitions to rarely visited pages from the address bar (or web search box) from an existing tab.

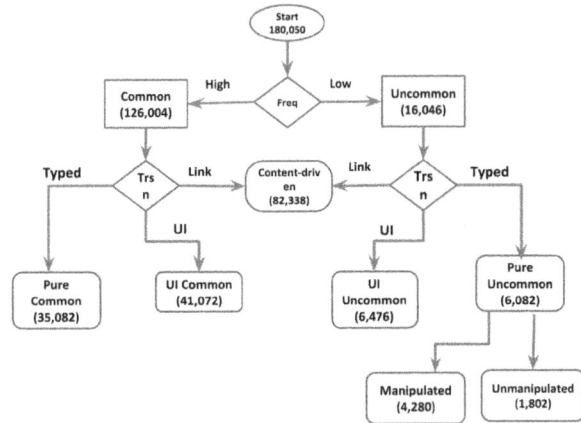

Figure 4: The analysis flowchart. The two decision points (diamond boxes) represent decisions by frequency (high = 4th quartile, low = 1st quartile) and transition type (link, typed, UI). Numbers inside boxes represent the number of webpage visits categorized under each category.

Using this categorization of browsing events, we sought to quantify the category-wise change in users' web browsing behavior across the three different UI manipulations. Because the different categories defined above have vastly different base rates, it is most sensible to measure the change across UI modes in terms of the category-wise percentage change,

$$100 \times \left(\frac{\text{New- category- occurrence- frequency}}{\text{Default- category- occurrence -frequency}} - 1 \right),$$

where the category occurrence frequency is mode-sensitive and is simply the number of page visits marked in a particular category for a user divided by their total page visits while their browser's new tab page's behavior was *in a particular mode.*

---

[1] Not all visits to infrequently visited webpages imply a correlation with the passive recommendations in the new tab display. Sometimes users may have only need to go to a website, like a bank website very infrequently, on purpose. Thus, our definition overestimates the amount of 'diversity' as measured by this metric. Since we are ultimately interested, as we will see below, in the change in the amount of diversity of browsed web sources under controlled manipulation, this overestimation of the absolute quantity ends up not being crucial.

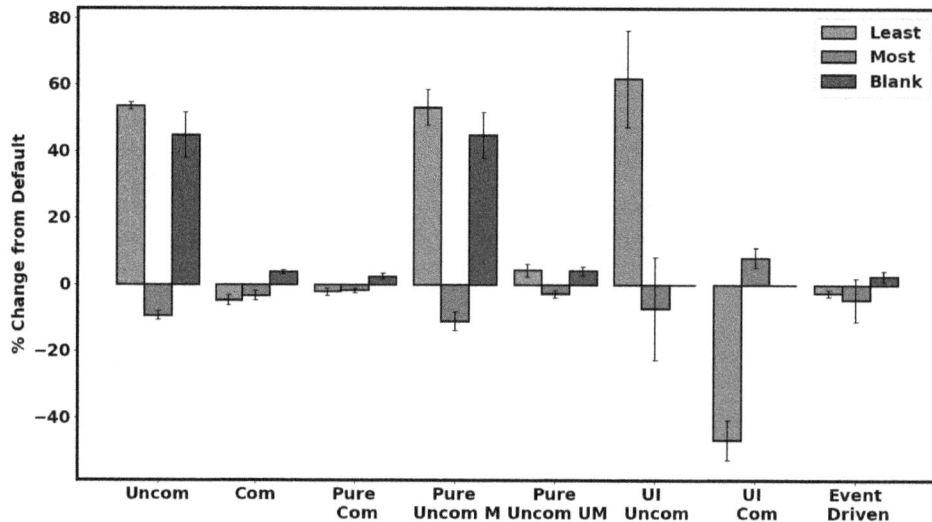

Figure 5: The change in each category's occurrence fraction with respect to the same fraction seen in the default mode per subject, averaged across all subjects. Error bars represent ±1 S.D. Com and uncom respectively denote the *common* and *uncommon* categories.

If the presence of web page recommendations on the new tab page affects browsing behavior by strongly concentrating visits to familiar information sources, we expected to see that our uncommon-linked categories would show positive percentage changes with respect to the default condition when we remove all page icons from the new tab display (the 'empty UI' condition) and when we present users with their least visited webpages as icons in the new tab display (the 'least visited' condition). As Figure 5 shows, this prediction is borne out clearly by our data. For both these conditions (least visited and empty UI), uncommon and pure uncommon categories showed large positive changes (∼ 50%) with respect to the baseline condition (the default frecency-based UI web page icons display). These conclusions are statistically significant in Bonferroni-corrected pairwise T-tests ($p < 0.001$), with effect sizes {0.83,0.89} for uncommon and {0.87, 0.85} for pure uncommon, for the least visited and blank UI display with respect to the default condition respectively.

Further, note also in Figure 5 that pages in the *manipulated* pure uncommon category accounted for almost all the change in the pure uncommon category as a whole; there are only marginal increases in the *non-manipulated* pure uncommon category. The difference between these two categories was only that the manipulated category page visits started with typing in URLs while the new tab page recommendations were visible, whereas the non-manipulated category page visits started from other pages, with new tab recommendations not visible. Since all other aspects of the users' experience were constant across these two sub-categories, the stark difference in browsing behavior emerges only by virtue of the new tab page recommendations being visible or invisible. This performance dissociation allows us to confidently pinpoint the source of the difference in browsing behavior - the recommendations on the new tab page - with precision, and to infer its psychological

provenance also - interference in memory while retrieving website URLs to type in the URL bar by alternative displayed page icons.

Thus, we conclude that (a) the presence of new tab page recommendations causes people to visit fewer unique web pages than they do in the absence of new tab page recommendations, (b) the reduction in unique web page visits is most evident for websites users visit infrequently, and (c) a very large fraction of the reduction is caused by memory interference when people try to type in URLs on the new tab page.

4 QUANTIFYING THE CONSEQUENCES OF SOURCE CONCENTRATION

Our experiment shows that users' web browsing behavior adapts to manipulations of the browser new tab display along lines predicted by theories of filter bubble and shallower processing of information on the web, and that this adaptation is *statistically* significant both across and within individuals. We have not, however, established that this adaptation is also *practically* significant. *Prima facie*, the changes in behavior are only apparent at the margins, not in the large aggregate of browsing patterns in our subjects, which comprises overwhelmingly of habitual access to highly visited websites. Viewed from this aggregate perspective, the deviations we have managed to introduce are of the order of about 0.5% of all page visits. Why should this miniscule change in behavior be consequential? This is the question we have sought to answer using the *in silico* experiments we report below.

Our primary hypothesis in this phase of the project was that minor changes in propensity to visit diverse information sources would affect the facility with which users can access crucial transition nodes in their information network that connect them to fresh sources of information that they do not commonly encounter during routine browsing. This hypothesis was inspired by related observations about the role of social preference feedback in the polarization of internet communities - a phenomenon recently popularized by the term 'filter bubble' [24].

In classic filter bubble settings, the source of feedback and recommendations is external, but tuned to personal preferences. It is this personalization that, perversely, reduces the diversity of information sources that the user acquires their social media-mediated knowledge from [24]. In our case, unlike in conventional filter bubble settings, there are no external sources of information and/or feedback. The browser UI is simply passively reflecting the habitual behavior of the user, modulo some modelling of the inter-temporal preferences for various forms of content of users.

Nonetheless, we think the filtering effect of reinforcement of existing preferences works by the exact same mechanism in our case, suppressing the user's propensity to sample content from diverse sources. Since the user's response to their own previous history is much more observable than social influences seen in social media recommender systems, we can try to quantify the extent to which suppression effects of the size seen in our empirical data might influence the diversity of information sourcing for model agents.

To do this, we have modelled website browsing behavior for an individual agent as a random walk on a graph. Within the graph for each subject, each node represents a distinct website. With this abstract representation in place, the next step is to realize that the structure of the graph itself must reflect the Zipfian nature of webpage-website counts - users visits a small number of sites a large number of times, and a large number of sites a small number of times [14].

To capture these particular dynamics while maintaining analytic simplicity, we specialized the network stucture we consider to be the family of all graphs with two pseudo-cliques wherein the cross-links between these pseudo-cliques are controlled by an ϵ parameter such that with a probability of ϵ, a link gets set up between two cross-pseudoclique nodes[2]. When we simulate a random walk on any one such graph, the reasons for this construction become clear. Nodes within pseudo-cliques have several short paths connecting them, and so are likelier to be visited by a random walker known to be situated at another node within the clique. Nodes in different pseudo-cliques will have longer shortest paths on average, so depending on the distribution of length of random walks for the agent, visits across pseudo-cliques will be rarer. Thus, we induce differences in accessibility of different nodes in the graph by assuming its structure to take this particular shape.

Unlike more intricate agent-based models of browsing behavior, such as in [14], which try to capture both within and across website browsing behavior, the model we use above makes predictions only for the quantity we are interested in - the across website browsing behavior of the user. Dwell times and page depths within websites are not modelled in our approach. We offload as much of the preference information about browsing behavior as possible onto the graph structure, resulting in the simplest possible observer model for the user - a random walk on the graph - that retrieves the Zipfian cross-site browsing behavior we are interested in simulating. The key difference between our simplistic model and the actual model of the web in terms of structure is that there are multiple pseudo-cliques in the web corresponding to different localizations of information [8]. The results we demonstrate for two pseudo-cliques can be shown for any pairs of pseudo-cliques without loss of generality, thus generalizing to more complicated web models as in [14].

The core of our succeeding analysis is identifying the slope of the relationship between the ϵ parameter, which controls the number of cross-links between the two pseudo-cliques, and the average first hitting time between nodes in different pseudo-cliques. Such an analysis does not require that the graphs contain pseudo-cliques of only equal size, or that they contain only two pseudo-cliques. We consider the simplest subset that instantiates the distance asymmetry we require. As a consequence of this distance asymmetry, we are able to map user behavior to network structure. Movements within a clique correspond to visitation of commonly accessed information sources while a leap from one clique to another corresponds to uncommon visits. Embedding the usually common, occasionally uncommon visitation behavior of users in this way in our graph model, we can say formally that there is on average uncommon visitation behavior ϵ of the time and visit to commonly accessed sources $1 - \epsilon$ of the time, assuming random initial node initialization in our specific graph structure. The same general principle is expected to hold for a much more general family of graphs - graphs with k pseudo-cliques, interconnected by cross-links generated via a stochastic process mediated by the parameter matrix $\epsilon_{ij}, i, j \in \{1, \cdots k\}$.

In this setup we are interested, fundamentally, in quantitatively characterizing the relationship between changes in ϵ and changes in the average first hitting time between cross-pseudoclique nodes. The first hitting time between two nodes is simply the expected number of moves a random walker originating at node i will take to first reach node j across multiple random walks originating at i. Since the UI manipulation affects ϵ by a large relative amount but a small absolute amount, we are interested in measuring the extent to which this small parametric change affects the visibility of cross-pseudoclique nodes in the graph, which corresponds in our browsing user model to the average first hitting time. Users will access websites that lie within their radius of experience, as measured by hitting time. First hitting times larger than the typical radius of experience - measured in terms of walk length - will correspond to websites typically inaccessible to the user.

Although theoretical properties of first hitting times on graphs have been investigated for random graphs [15, 31, 35], no direct results are specifically relevant for our analysis. Known theory suggests, on average, that adding extra nodes or edge to a graph increases the first hitting time of any two nodes in the graph but such analyses are true only on average across random graphs [2]. We, on the other hand, are interested in graphs with a very specific direction of variation in structure, changing from barbell style graphs for low values of ϵ into well-connected graphs as ϵ rises. A figure showing various graphs generated corresponding to different ϵ values is present in the supplementary material. The important

---

[2]A pseudo-clique is defined as the graph structure obtained by removing some edges from a clique. We generate pseudo-cliques by first assuming an exponential degree distribution within a pseudo-clique of nodes, then assigning edges to nodes randomly in decreasing order of degree, permitting ±1 changes in the original degree assigned to each node to handle conflicts in edge assignment. In our experiments, we used pseudo-cliques of size N=10 with highest degree 4.

thing to note is the rapidity with which adding cross-links changes sample graphs drawn generatively using different values of ϵ from barbell style graphs (known to have worst case shortest path distances) to well-connected graphs, with much smaller shortest path distances. Even though the graphs with higher ϵ have more edges, we intuitively expect that the non-random manner in which the new edges are introduced by our graph generative model counteracts the mere fact that they are being added, and reduces the first hitting time.

The generative model for our graph has two free parameters, the size of the graph N and the cross-linking parameter ϵ. We fit this generative model to our data by fixing the size of the graph and the value of the ϵ parameter using the typical size of our users' unique website repertoire and their measured non-habitual behavior/habitual behavior ratios in our dataset respectively. The modal value of N (the number of unique sites visited by a user in a month) is 25. To approximate this, each of our simulated graphs used 20 nodes divided into two pseudo-cliques of equal sizes. We generated graphs using ϵ values varied between 0 and 0.2 in steps of 0.005.

Once an (N, ϵ) graph for a particular value of epsilon is ready, we empirically measured the hitting time of every cross-pseudoclique node pair by simulating random walks between all cross-pseudoclique node pairs. We calculated the average first hitting time for 100 such random walks across all cross-pseudoclique node pairs for each of 100 (N, ϵ) generated graphs for each ϵ value. Figure 6a shows the result of this simulation, plotting average first hitting times obtained from this experiment for different values of ϵ.

We found empirically that the range of ϵ, measured as the ratio of uncommonly visited to commonly visited pages for each subject, is $0.005 - 0.07$ across our subjects. In this range, as illustrated in Figure 6a we observe an approximately exponential decline in hitting time with increase in ϵ. This is because, as anticipated, the effect of the 'cliqueish' structure of the graph dominates over increase in number of edges with ϵ. Gradually, as ϵ increases, the effect of increase in number of edges between pseudo-cliques starts dominating and hence the average hitting time asymptotes beyond $\epsilon \approx 0.1$, and will likely increase for still higher values. The key finding, also as anticipated, is that within the range of parametric values seen in our experiment, even small changes in ϵ cause large changes in the first hitting time. As we describe above, first hitting times represent website accessibility in our model, so the result obtained here implies that small changes in ϵ cause exponential declines in the accessibility of infrequently visited (cross-pseudoclique) websites for users.

Finally, the relationship between a finite random walk and the probability that it will pass through any given node is straighforward to estimate. It is simply the probability that a random walk as long as N might occur in the empirical distribution of first hitting times for that specific node. Hence, the p-value of a one-sided probability hypothesis test will give us exactly the probabilistic quantity of most interest to us - the probability with which a user with non-habitual browsing propensity ϵ will access a diverse information source in any given browsing session of any particular estimated length.

We identified individual sessions in our participants' browsing logs using a 30 minute interval to determine the boundaries of individual sessions (as mentioned in Section 2.3), and counting total

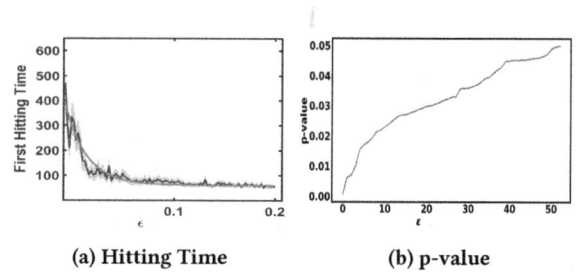

| (a) Hitting Time | (b) p-value |

Figure 6: (a) Plot of average and 95% confidence bound of first hitting time for all cross-pseudoclique nodes empirically measured across 100 simulated random walks in each of 100 graphs generated for each value of ϵ. The best fit exponential for the data is also shown.(b) Variation of p-value of the average session length with ϵ. p-value is averaged across multiple cross-pseudoclique node-pairs and graphs.

page visits as one step in the random walk. Across all participants, the average session length came out to be around 20 for our dataset. Next, we measured the kurtosis of the histogram of hitting times for each node pair in multiple random walks on a particular graph. We found that the kurtosis values themselves were well-represented by a normal distribution with mean 3.1 and SD 0.2. Hence, the first hitting time distribution for each node pair could be considered approximately Gaussian.

So, we ran one-sided z-tests testing whether a session length of $k = 20$ or lower might occur naturally in the hitting time distribution of cross-clique node pairs. We ran this calculation for 100 randomly sampled cross-pseudoclique node pairs across 100 graphs generated for each value of ϵ and plotted the p-values obtained against ϵ. This relationship is visualized in Figure 6b, and is approximately linear. This observation quantifies concretely the importance of large relative changes in the propensity to visit diverse information sources, even if this propensity constitutes a small relative share of overall browsing behavior. While the change in behavior is on the margin in terms of aggregate browsing behavior, it has non-marginal consequences on which information sources users will be able to access.

5 DISCUSSION

Since the beginning of internet browsing, designers have always tried to design browsers in ways that reduce the user's typing effort. In early browsers, this was done using history auto-complete suggestions. More recently, both OS and browser designers have sought to reduce typing effort still further by adding apps to home screens and frequent (and recent) web pages to 'new tab' pages. The inarguable logic of such design is that, because website visit counts are approximately power law distributed, being able to simply click on the most visited pages optimizes the number of typing responses needed over the course of users' use of the browser.

But website visits are a means to an end, not an end in themselves. Ultimately, they are expressions of our information preferences [25]. This paper makes the case that, by showing people the sites they visit most frequently over and over again in new tab displays, current practice in browser and OS UI design traps people into a solipsistic feedback loop, reinforcing their strongest preferences to the detriment of weaker ones that potentially offer more scope for diversity of experience and learning [29, 33]. We quantified the size of this feedback effect at its source - natural browsing behavior - by collecting browsing history from subjects who consented to having the behavior of their new tab page manipulated remotely via a plug-in they installed in their browsers. With *in silico* experiments, we further demonstrated the impact of the change in browsing behavior on peoples' proclivity for acquiring information from diverse sources.

5.1 Related work

Our work follows a rich vein of empirical research in human-computer interaction that is increasingly discovering subtle but powerful ways in which website interaction, access and even simple UI decisions can influence human decisions. For example, posting to Facebook has been shown to increase users' activity on the website immediately before and immediately after the posting, on the timescale of days [12]. More substantively, time of day of Twitter activity has been shown, strikingly, to correlate strongly with the probability of users being clinically depressed [7]. Even more strikingly, Epstein and colleagues have shown that presenting potential voters with search results for potential candidates in an actual national election in a UI with artificially manipulated search result rankings can shift the voting pool's vote fraction by up to 2% in the experimenter's chosen direction, a shift large enough to sway a reasonably close election [9]. There have also been recent works studying memory recall in simple tasks like clicking of pictures through different capture modalities [23]. We identify a large and consequential psychological effect: conventional UI design choices suppress peoples' propensity to access diverse information sources while accessing the web. This finding is not as specific as the ones documented previously in the literature, but also as a consequence, is likely affecting a lot more people at any given point in time by virtue of its generality.

Our results also relate to research efforts ongoing to characterize and surmount the recommender systems (RS) *filter bubble* [4, 18, 28]. There is mixed evidence regarding the effects of recommender systems on users' consumption patterns. Whereas work focused on identifying changes in content *supply* as a function of personalization tools has found no effects [13], other work studying *consumption* patterns have reported both negative [4, 10] and positive effects on consumption diversity [22]. Our work finds unambiguous and large negative effects on information diversity driven by the use of recommendations. By our simplest measure of diversity - count of unique websites visited - users operating browsers with blank new tab pages visited on an average 15% more unique websites over a two month period.

One possible reason for previously reported null or positive results in the literature might be that the *active* use of recommender systems like Movielens involves users actively looking for information they don't already possess, an explicit cognitive task where they are aware that they must evaluate the incoming information quasi-critically [30]. In contrast, constantly stopping by the new tab page during transitions between websites is a much subtler phenomenon; the recommendations here are *passive*, in the sense that the ostensible function of these bookmarks is to facilitate access to frequently visited pages, not to shift preferences. People can reason through, or actively ignore, redundant information while they are actively deciding what to do. It is harder for them to guard against the subtle impact of memory inhibition through visual presentation of web page icons time after time in the normal flow of their interaction with the browser [21].

While it might seem superficially strange that such a small UI design component could potentially have such a large impact on browsing behavior, behavioral economics offers striking examples of similar subconscious nudges significantly affecting behavior for better and for worse [16]. Similarly, Thaler and Sunstein offer striking examples of how small and often insignificant things can influence (nudge) behavior [17]. As McLuhan foresaw, but many modern empirical analyses ignore, the peril in informative computer interfaces is not that they may feed us bad information against our will, it is that the *form* in which they present information to use will subtly change our expectations of what we want to look for.

The classic ideal observer in web browsing - Pirolli & Card's *information forager* - models humans as observers optimizing information acquisition under information-theoretic constraints [25–27]. Our demonstration of large priming effects caused by as innocuous a source as the new tab page interface could help further nuance such models by incorporating the effect of psychological biases in the same way the influential cognitive biases literature has influenced the design of microeconomic models [34].

Our description of the delicate interaction between mind and machine in this most humdrum of tasks - web browsing - should also stimulate further exploration of the negative externalities of personalization, recommender systems and other methods of preference influence common in HCI applications. At present, such influence is sometimes justified by discriminating between malevolent and benevolent deception in UI design, with the basic difference being that a benevolent deception is meant to benefit the user [1]. Our study presents a clear example of the inadequacy of such ethical definitions - in our case, the developer, in principle, gains nothing by presenting frequently viewed web pages as clickable icons; the UI is designed the way it is to minimize the user's need to type. Nonetheless, this benevolent deception, conflating accessibility with preference via the subconscious impact of presentation on memory, ends up affecting user behavior substantially, as our results show.

5.2 Limitations

A natural limitation of this work is the size and representativeness of the population sample we used to establish the basic fact that presentation of commonly used websites' page icons on the new tab display interferes with users' proclivity to visit diverse information locales and concentrates web browsing to familiar sources . Nonetheless, the empirical results we describe in this paper are statistically significant by all conventional standards of measurements, and our sample is quite diverse with respect to gender, education, and occupational status. While one can never have too many participants in a study making claims about internet browsing behavior, the large effect sizes we find, consistently seen both across and within participants, suggest that our study was adequately powered to discern the specific hypothesis it investigated.

It is also possible to question how well conclusions from this study, with a mean sample age of 28, may generalize to the experience of older adults. At the same time, it must be remembered that while our sample is not representative of the general population, it is certainly more representative of *heavy* internet users [3, 32], who are the population most likely to be affected by the UI design decisions critiqued in this paper. We also note that the average age of our population is very close to the median age of the country this study was conducted in, suggesting that there is no significant age-bias in our recruitment.

5.3 Conclusion

In this paper, we contribute two basic results. One, we show empirically that subtle UI manipulations of the new tab page in common browsers can create large relative reductions in users' propensity to explore sites outside the repertoire of sites they commonly visit. Two, we show using a simulation study informed by empirically measured parameters that large relative changes in web source concentration manifest linearly in large absolute changes in the visibility of diverse information sources in a user's browsing experience. Together, these results present striking evidence that the current design practice of showing frequently visited webpages on new tab pages is suppressing the expression of web surfers' tendencies to visit diverse information sources on the web.

Considering how ubiquitous computers and the internet have become, this effect would span even mobile devices. In fact, since small screen sizes in hand held mobile phones or tablets are likely to bias users towards clicking the new tab page icons over typing in the address bar, the concentration of web browsing to familiar sources is likely to be exacerbated, as an admittedly small *post hoc* cohort analysis of our data shows. Further research is needed to quantify the extent of this difference.

Finally, we note that all common browsers offer users the ability to use a blank page as their new tab page, making our conclusions immediately actionable. Based on our results, people should decide for themselves whether the convenience of clicking through to commonly visited web pages is worth the potential curtailment of their curiosity.

ACKNOWLEDGEMENT

We thank DST, Government of India for their funding in support of the project through grant DST/CSRI/2017/334 (G). We also thank all the anonymous reviewers for their valuable feedback.

REFERENCES

[1] Eytan Adar, Desney S Tan, and Jaime Teevan. 2013. Benevolent deception in human computer interaction. In *Proceedings of the SIGCHI conference on human factors in computing systems*. ACM, 1863–1872.

[2] David Aldous. 1989. An introduction to covering problems for random walks on graphs. *Journal of Theoretical Probability* 2, 1 (1989), 87–89.

[3] Henry Assael. 2005. A demographic and psychographic profile of heavy internet users and users by type of internet usage. *Journal of advertising research* 45, 1 (2005), 93–123.

[4] Eytan Bakshy, Solomon Messing, and Lada A Adamic. 2015. Exposure to ideologically diverse news and opinion on Facebook. *Science* 348, 6239 (2015), 1130–1132.

[5] Nicholas Carr. 2010. *The shallows: How the internet is changing the way we think, read and remember.* Atlantic Books Ltd.

[6] Gary Charness, Uri Gneezy, and Michael A Kuhn. 2012. Experimental methods: Between-subject and within-subject design. *Journal of Economic Behavior & Organization* 81, 1 (2012), 1–8.

[7] Munmun De Choudhury, Michael Gamon, Scott Counts, and Eric Horvitz. 2013. Predicting Depression via Social Media. *ICWSM* 13 (2013), 1–10.

[8] Zoltan Dezsö, Eivind Almaas, András Lukács, Balázs Rácz, István Szakadát, and A-L Barabási. 2006. Dynamics of information access on the web. *Physical Review E* 73, 6 (2006), 066132.

[9] Robert Epstein and Ronald E Robertson. 2015. The search engine manipulation effect (SEME) and its possible impact on the outcomes of elections. *Proceedings of the National Academy of Sciences* 112, 33 (2015), E4512–E4521.

[10] Seth Flaxman, Sharad Goel, and Justin M Rao. 2016. Filter bubbles, echo chambers, and online news consumption. *Public opinion quarterly* 80, S1 (2016), 298–320.

[11] Mozilla Foundation. 2014. Frecency algorithm. Blog. Retrieved September 19, 2017 from https://developer.mozilla.org/en-US/docs/Mozilla/Tech/Places/Frecency_algorithm.

[12] Nir Grinberg, P Alex Dow, Lada A Adamic, and Mor Naaman. 2016. Changes in engagement before and after posting to facebook. In *Proceedings of the 2016 CHI Conference on Human Factors in Computing Systems*. ACM, 564–574.

[13] Mario Haim, Andreas Graefe, and Hans-Bernd Brosius. 2018. Burst of the filter bubble? Effects of personalization on the diversity of Google News. *Digital Journalism* 6, 3 (2018), 330–343.

[14] Bernardo A Huberman, Peter LT Pirolli, James E Pitkow, and Rajan M Lukose. 1998. Strong regularities in world wide web surfing. *Science* 280, 5360 (1998), 95–97.

[15] Satoshi Ikeda, Izumi Kubo, and Masafumi Yamashita. 2009. The hitting and cover times of random walks on finite graphs using local degree information. *Theoretical Computer Science* 410, 1 (2009), 94–100.

[16] Thomas C Leonard. 2008. Richard H. Thaler, Cass R. Sunstein, Nudge: Improving decisions about health, wealth, and happiness.

[17] Thomas C Leonard. 2008. Richard H. Thaler, Cass R. Sunstein, Nudge: Improving decisions about health, wealth, and happiness.

[18] Q Vera Liao and Wai-Tat Fu. 2013. Beyond the filter bubble: interactive effects of perceived threat and topic involvement on selective exposure to information. In *Proceedings of the SIGCHI conference on human factors in computing systems*. ACM, 2359–2368.

[19] Marshall McLuhan, MARSHALL AUTOR MCLUHAN, and Lewis H Lapham. 1994. *Understanding media: The extensions of man.* MIT press.

[20] Caroline Myrberg and Ninna Wiberg. 2015. Screen vs. paper: what is the difference for reading and learning? *Insights* 28, 2 (2015).

[21] Ben R Newell and David R Shanks. 2014. Unconscious influences on decision making: A critical review. *Behavioral and Brain Sciences* 37, 1 (2014), 1–19.

[22] Tien T Nguyen, Pik-Mai Hui, F Maxwell Harper, Loren Terveen, and Joseph A Konstan. 2014. Exploring the filter bubble: the effect of using recommender systems on content diversity. In *Proceedings of the 23rd international conference on World wide web*. ACM, 677–686.

[23] Evangelos Niforatos, Caterina Cinel, Cathleen Cortis Mack, Marc Langheinrich, and Geoff Ward. 2017. Can Less be More?: Contrasting Limited, Unlimited, and Automatic Picture Capture for Augmenting Memory Recall. *Proceedings of the ACM on Interactive, Mobile, Wearable and Ubiquitous Technologies* 1, 2 (2017), 21.

[24] Eli Pariser. 2011. *The filter bubble: What the Internet is hiding from you.* Penguin UK.

[25] Peter Pirolli and Stuart Card. 1995. Information foraging in information access environments. In *Proceedings of the SIGCHI conference on Human factors in computing systems*. ACM Press/Addison-Wesley Publishing Co., 51–58.

[26] Peter Pirolli and Stuart Card. 1999. Information foraging. *Psychological review* 106, 4 (1999), 643.

[27] Peter Pirolli and Wai-Tat Fu. 2003. SNIF-ACT: A model of information foraging on the World Wide Web. *User modeling 2003* (2003), 146–146.

[28] Paul Resnick, R Kelly Garrett, Travis Kriplean, Sean A Munson, and Natalie Jomini Stroud. 2013. Bursting your (filter) bubble: strategies for promoting diverse exposure. In *Proceedings of the 2013 conference on Computer supported cooperative work companion*. ACM, 95–100.

[29] Jürgen Schmidhuber. 2010. Formal theory of creativity, fun, and intrinsic motivation (1990–2010). *IEEE Transactions on Autonomous Mental Development* 2, 3 (2010), 230–247.

[30] Rashmi Sinha and Kirsten Swearingen. 2002. The role of transparency in recommender systems. In *CHI'02 extended abstracts on Human factors in computing systems*. ACM, 830–831.

[31] Vishal Sood, Sidney Redner, and Dani Ben-Avraham. 2004. First-passage properties of the Erdős–Renyi random graph. *Journal of Physics A: Mathematical and General* 38, 1 (2004), 109.

[32] Lori C Soule, L Wayne Shell, and Betty A Kleen. 2003. Exploring Internet addiction: Demographic characteristics and stereotypes of heavy Internet users. *Journal of Computer Information Systems* 44, 1 (2003), 64–73.

[33] Nisheeth Srivastava, Komal Kapoor, and Paul R Schrater. 2011. A cognitive basis for theories of intrinsic motivation. In *Development and Learning (ICDL), 2011 IEEE International Conference on*, Vol. 2. IEEE, 1–6.

[34] Amos Tversky and Daniel Kahneman. 1974. Judgment under uncertainty: Heuristics and biases. *science* 185, 4157 (1974), 1124–1131.

[35] Kôhei Uchiyama et al. 2011. The first hitting time of a single point for random walks. *Electronic Journal of Probability* 16 (2011), 1960–2000.

Explainable Machine Learning for Fake News Detection

Julio C. S. Reis, André Correia, Fabrício Murai, Adriano Veloso, Fabrício Benevenuto
Universidade Federal de Minas Gerais, Computer Science Department
Belo Horizonte, Minas Gerais, Brazil
{julio.reis,andre.correia,murai,adrianov,fabricio}@dcc.ufmg.br

ABSTRACT

Recently, there have been many research efforts aiming to understand fake news phenomena and to identify typical patterns and features of fake news. Yet, the real discriminating power of these features is still unknown: some are more general, but others perform well only with specific data. In this work, we conduct a highly exploratory investigation that produced hundreds of thousands of models from a large and diverse set of features. These models are unbiased in the sense that their features are randomly chosen from the pool of available features. While the vast majority of models are ineffective, we were able to produce a number of models that yield highly accurate decisions, thus effectively separating fake news from actual stories. Specifically, we focused our analysis on models that rank a randomly chosen fake news story higher than a randomly chosen fact with more than 0.85 probability. For these models we found a strong link between features and model predictions, showing that some features are clearly tailored for detecting certain types of fake news, thus evidencing that different combinations of features cover a specific region of the fake news space. Finally, we present an explanation of factors contributing to model decisions, thus promoting civic reasoning by complementing our ability to evaluate digital content and reach warranted conclusions.

CCS CONCEPTS

• **Human-centered computing** → **Social media**; • **Applied computing** → *Sociology*.

KEYWORDS

Fake News; Civic Reasoning; Features; Social Media

ACM Reference Format:
Julio C. S. Reis, André Correia, Fabrício Murai, Adriano Veloso, Fabrício Benevenuto. 2019. Explainable Machine Learning for Fake News Detection. In *11th ACM Conference on Web Science (WebSci '19), June 30–July 3, 2019, Boston, MA, USA*. ACM, New York, NY, USA, 10 pages. https://doi.org/10.1145/3292522.3326027

1 INTRODUCTION

More than a decade after their emergence, social media systems are used by over a third of the world's population [13]. These

systems have significantly changed the way users interact and communicate online, spawning a whole new wave of applications and reshaping existing information ecosystems. In particular, social media systems have been dramatically changing the way news is produced, disseminated, and consumed in our society.

These changes, however, started an actual information war in the few last years, favoring misinformation campaigns, reducing the credibility of news outlets in these environments [35], and potentially affecting news readers opinions on critical matters for our society. Misinformation, spin, lies and deceit have of course been around forever, but the emergence of fake news has quickly evolved into a worldwide phenomenon, and while there are efforts attempting to better comprehend this phenomenon [14, 20], it is not surprising that most existing efforts are devoted to detecting fake news [9, 37, 39, 41]. Typically, most of these efforts reduce the problem to a classification task, in which news stories are labeled as fact/fake and supervised learning is then used to separate fact from fake with a model learned from the data. Fake news detection gained traction and attention, especially in assisting fact checkers to identify stories that are worth investigating [17, 28].

Despite the undeniable importance of the existing efforts in this direction, they are mostly concurrent work, which propose complementary solutions and features to train a classifier, providing hints and insights that are rarely or never tested together. Little is known about the discriminating power of features proposed in the literature, either individually or when combined with others. Some may be adequate for pinpointing specific types of fake news, while others are more general but not sufficiently discriminating. Moreover, while explaining the decisions made by the proposed models is central to understand the structure of fake content, this discussion is often left aside. In this work, we address all of these issues.

In particular, we want to provide answers to the following questions. *How hard is the detection task? Do we really need all these features, or should we focus on a smaller set of more representative features? Is there a trade-off between feature discriminating power and robustness to pattern variations? Is there a clear link between features and the type of fake news they can detect?*

To answer these questions, we first conduct a systematic survey, identifying existing features for fake news detection and proposing new ones. This results in almost 200 features to consider. To implement and evaluate these features, we used a public dataset recently released by BuzzFeed that was enhanced with Facebook commentaries on labeled news stories [32]. Since the considered features may have a variety of complex nonlinear interactions, we employ a classification algorithm with significant flexibility. Specifically, we chose a fast and effective learning algorithm called extreme gradient boosting machines, or simply XGB [7]. Finally, we performed an unbiased search for XGB models, so that each model is composed of a set of randomly chosen features. We enumerated roughly 300K models, enabling us to perform a unique macro-to-micro investigation of the considered features.

Findings: Our analysis unveil the real impact of a sleigh of features for fake news detection. Particularly, our results show that:

- Our unbiased model exploration reveals how hard is fake news detection, as only 2.2% of the models achieve a detection performance higher than 0.85 in terms of the area under the ROC curve (or simply, AUC);
- We found that among the best models, some features appear up to five times more often than others;
- We distinguish a small set of features that are not only highly effective but also contribute the most to increasing the robustness of the models;
- We place models in a high dimensional space, so that models that output similar decisions are placed close to each other. We then cluster the model space, and a centroid analysis reveals that prototype models are very distinct from each other. Our cluster analysis by AUC reinforce these results. For centroid prototypes, we present an explanation of factors contributing to their decisions. Our findings suggest that models within different groups separate fake from real content based on very different underlying reasons.

Additionally, our effort provides other valuable contributions as we survey a large number of recent and related works and we attempt to implement all previously explored features to detect fake news. We also proposed novel features which showed to be useful for the best models we generated. On the other hand, we emphasize that this paper is not about proposing the best combination of features or the best XGB model, but about investigating features' informativeness and simple models that can be generated from them, as well as using these models to explain predictions made for news stories.

The rest of the paper is organized as follows. Section 2 presents the background, including important definitions, related works and an overview of the main features for fake news detection proposed in the literature. In Section 3, we describe our experimental methodology proposed for this work. We then present and discuss our results and their implications in Section 4. Finally, we present in Section 5 concluding remarks and directions for future work.

2 BACKGROUND AND RELATED WORK

We begin by providing important definitions used in our work, then we describe our effort to survey existing works that propose features for detecting fake news.

2.1 Definitions

Fake news is a topic that still lacks a clear or universally accepted definition. In this work we adopt the definition of fake news and fake news detection used in previous works [2, 35].

Definition 2.1. **(Fake News)** *"is a news article that is intentionally and verifiable false".*

Definition 2.2. **(Fake News Detection.)** Given an unlabeled piece of news $a \in \mathcal{A}$, a model for fake news detection assigns a score $S(a) \in [0, 1]$ indicating the extent to which a is believed to be fake. For instance, if $S(a') > S(a)$, a' is more likely to be fake than a according to the model. A threshold τ can be defined such that the prediction function $F : \mathcal{A} \rightarrow \{\text{fake, not fake}\}$ is

$$F(a) = \begin{cases} \text{fake} & \text{if } S(a) > \tau, \\ \text{not fake} & \text{otherwise.} \end{cases}$$

2.2 Features for Fake News Detection

Broadly speaking there are two kinds of efforts to tackle the fake news problem. The first kind aims at better comprehending the phenomenon [20, 40]. Particularly, Vosoughi *et al.* [40] shows that fake news tends to spread faster than the real news. Lazer *et al.* [20] call for an interdisciplinary task force to approach this complex problem. The second kind of existing efforts comprises those that propose solutions to the problem or provide insights on how to detect fake news, i.e. discussing typical patterns that can be used as features. For instance, Pérez-Rosas *et al.* [25] conduct a set of learning experiments to build accurate fake news detectors using linguistic features. Similarly, Volkova *et al.* [39] build linguistic models to classify suspicious and trusted news. Overall, most of the existing efforts in this space are concurrent work which use specific data and feature sets to train classifiers without providing clear guidelines on which features are useful to detect and explain fake news.

The literature is quite broad if we consider efforts related to information credibility, rumor detection, and news spread. Next, we conduct a systematic survey on these efforts aiming to identify the features proposed by them. Table 1 presents a summary of this survey along with some of techniques used to extract those features. At a high-level, we can categorize features explored in previous works as follows: (i) features extracted from news content (e.g. language processing techniques) [15, 39, 42, 43]; (ii) features from source (e.g. reliability and trustworthiness) [21]; and finally (iii) features extracted from the environment, which usually involves signals extracted from the social network repercussion and spread [8].

Overall, our work provides contributions that encompass the two kinds of efforts previously described, since (i) we provide a better understanding of the fake news phenomena by explaining how these features are used in the decisions taken by computation models designed to detect fake news, and (ii) we evaluate the use of machine learning with different combinations of features. Our survey on existing features is also an important contribution on its own.

3 METHODOLOGY

In this section, we describe the dataset used in this work as well as implementation details for a large set of features for fake news detection. In addition to features from previous works, we propose a novel set of features for fake news detection that includes features that measure text quality. Finally, we describe our experimental setup and present our framework for quantifying the informativeness of features for fake news detection.

Extracted from...	Feature Set	Techniques mostly used	References
News Content	Language Structures (Syntax)	Sentence-level features, such bag-of-words approaches, "n-grams", part-of-speech (POS tagging)	[9, 19, 27, 31, 35, 42]
	Lexical Features	Character level and word-level features, such as number of words, characters per word, hashtags, similarity between words, etc	[1, 5, 6, 15, 18, 27, 29, 35, 42, 43]
	Moral Foundation Cues	Moral foundation features	[39]
	Images and Videos	Indicators of manipulation and image distributions	[16]
	Psycholinguistic Cues	Additional signals of persuasive language such as anger, sadness, etc and indicators of biased language	[15, 19, 31, 39, 40]
	Semantic Structure	Word embeddings, "n-grams" extensions, topic models (e.g. latent Dirichlet allocation (LDA)), contextual informations	[5, 8, 9, 12, 31, 41–43]
	Subjectivity Cues	Subjectivity score, sentiment analysis, opinion lexicons	[27, 31, 39]
News Source	Bias Cues	Indicators of bias (e.g. politics), polarization	[29]
	Credibility and Trustworthiness	Estimation of user' perception of source credibility	[6, 34, 35]
Environment (Social Media)	Engagement	Number of page views, likes (on Facebook), retweets (on Twitter), etc	[6, 11, 12, 15, 18, 33, 35, 37, 40]
	Network Structure	Friendship network, complex network metrics	[6, 9, 12, 15, 18, 27, 33–35, 38–40]
	Temporal Patterns and Novelty	Time-series, propagation, novelty metrics	[6, 11, 12, 19, 33–35, 38, 40]
	User' Information	Users' profiles and characteristics across individual level and group level (e.g. their friends and followers)	[6, 15, 19, 27, 29, 33–35, 37, 38, 40]

Table 1: Overview of features for fake news detection presented in previous work.

3.1 Dataset

Most of the existing efforts to detect fake news are limited by the data they use. Ideally, to implement all features from previous efforts we would need a dataset that contains for each news story labeled by specialists, their textual content, information about their sources, and about the dissemination of these news, particularly in social media systems. We use a recently created dataset, named BuzzFace [32], with almost all of these characteristics. It consists of 2,282 news articles related to the 2016 U.S. election labeled by BuzzFeed journalists [36]. The BuzzFace dataset consists of an enriched version of the one created by BuzzFeed, with over 1.6 million comments associated to the news stories as well shares and reactions from Facebook users.

The news stories in the dataset are labeled into four categories: mostly true, accounting to 73% of all news articles, mostly false (4%), mixture of true and false (11%) and non-factual (12%). For simplicity, we discarded the non-factual content and merged the mostly false with the mixture of true and false into one single class, referred as "fake news" (349 out of 2,018 stories). The rationale is that stories that mix true and false facts may represent attempts to mislead readers. Thus, we focus our analysis into understanding how features are able to distinguish two classes, true and fake news.

Note: A typical pre-processing step is to separate factual from non-factual content. This task is easier than classifying factual data as fake or true since it is not necessary to check the veracity of the information using external sources. For illustration purposes, we conduct a small experiment to evaluate the accuracy of XGB [7] when discriminating factual and non-factual news using the features that will be described in Section 3.2. Our simple classifier performed very well, yielding 0.882 ± 0.024 of AUC. It is possible to achieve even higher performance levels by choosing features better tailored for this task. For this reason, this work assumes that non-factual data was already removed and only factual data is used as input. The alternative approach is to consider a multi-label classification problem, but this has the potential to increase the number of instances that need to be verified by an expert.

3.2 Our Implementation of Features for Fake News Detection

Next, we briefly describe how we implemented or adapted the features summarized in Table 1. In total we considered 172 features for fake news detection.

3.2.1 News Content. We consider as news content not only the news story but also its headline and any message that was posted by a news source when releasing it in online social networks. For news articles embedded in images and videos, we applied image processing techniques for extracting text shown on them. In total, we evaluated 141 textual features. The main feature sets are described next.

Language Structures (SYNT, for syntax). We implemented 31 sentence-level features, including number of words and syllables per sentence. Features also include indicators of the word categories (such as noun, verb, adjective). In addition, to evaluate writers' style as potential indicators of text quality, we also implemented features based on text readability [10].

Lexical Features (LEXI). We implemented 59 linguistic features, including number of words, first-person pronouns, demonstrative pronouns, verbs, hashtags, all punctuations counts, etc.

Psycholinguistic Cues (PSYC). Linguistic Inquiry and Word Count (LIWC) [24] is a dictionary-based text mining software. We use its latest version (2015) to extract 44 features that capture additional signals of persuasive and biased language.

Semantic Structure (SEMA). We implemented semantic features, including the toxicity score obtained from Google's API[1]. The API uses machine learning models to quantify the extent to which a text (or comment, for instance) can be perceived as "toxic". We did not consider strategies for topic extraction since the dataset used in this work was built based on news articles about the same topic or category (i.e. politics).

Subjectivity Cues (SUBJ). Using TextBlob's API[2], we compute subjectivity and sentiment scores of a text.

---

[1] https://www.perspectiveapi.com/#/
[2] http://textblob.readthedocs.io/en/dev/

3.2.2 News Source. To extract features from news source, we first parsed all news URLs and extracted the domain information. When the URL was unavailable, we associated the official URL of news outlet to news article. Therefore, we extract 8 (eight) indicators of political bias, credibility and source trustworthiness, and use them as detailed next. Moreover, in this category, we introduce a new set composed by 5 (five) features, called domain localization (see below).

Bias Cues (BIAS). We use the political biases of news outlets from BuzzFeed dataset as a feature.

Credibility and Trustworthiness (CRED). In this feature set, we introduce 7 (seven) new features to capture aspects of credibility (or popularity) and trustworthiness of domains. We collect, using Facebook's API[3], user engagement metrics of Facebook pages that published news articles (i.e. page talking about count and page fan count). Then, we use the Alexa API to get the relative position of news domain on the Alexa Ranking [4]. Furthermore, using this same API, we collect Alexa's top 500 newspapers. Based on the hypothesis that some unreliable domains may try to disguise themselves using domains similar to those of well-known newspapers, we define the dissimilarity between domains from the Alexa ranking and news domains in our dataset (measured by the minimum non-zero edit distance) as features. Last, we use indicators of low credibility of domains compiled in [34] as features.

Domain Location (DOML). Ever since creating fake news became a profitable job, some cities have become famous because of residents who create and disseminate fake news [5]. In order to exploit the information that Domain localization could carry, a pipeline was built to take each news website URL and extract new features, such as IP, latitude, longitude, city, and country. First, for each domain, the corresponding IP was extracted using the traceroute Linux command. Then the ipstack API is used to retrieve the location features. Although localization information (i.e. IP) has previously been used in works that exploit bots or spam detection [26], to the best of our knowledge there are no works that explore this data in fake news detection context.

3.2.3 Environment (Social Media). As indicators of user engagement and temporal patterns, we use information from Facebook. Next, we detail the 21 features from this category.

Engagement (ENGA). We use number of likes, shares and comments from Facebook users. Moreover, we compute the number of comments within intervals from publication time (900, 1800, 2700, 3600, 7200, 14400, 28800, 57600 and 86400 seconds), summing up to 12 features.

Temporal Patterns (TEMP). To capture temporal patterns from user commenting activities, we compute the rate at which comments are posted for the same time windows defined before.

3.2.4 Novel and Disregarded Features. Despite our efforts to include all the features described before, a few of them could not be included for various reasons. First, BuzzFace does not contain information related to network structure (i.e. Facebook connections).

[3]https://developers.facebook.com
[4]https://www.alexa.com
[5]https://www.bbc.com/news/magazine-38168281

Additionally, some features, such as those extracted from images and videos were used in related problems [39], but are out of the scope of this work as our dataset contains mostly textual data.

More importantly, 19 of the previously described features are novel. In particular, we proposed all features related to domain, including IP, latitude, longitude, city, county, and domain credibility. We also proposed other features such as toxicity and readability to assess the writing style of news stories. Later on we show that some of these features were proven valuable for fake news detection.

3.3 Unbiased Model Generation

The exact approach to assess the real impact of features for fake news detection would require the exhaustive enumeration of all possible combinations of features, so that one model is obtained for each combination in the power set. Obviously, inspecting all possible subsets of features is computationally prohibitive. Instead, we sample the model space by randomly selecting the features that compose a model. More precisely, we begin by enumerating all possible 1-feature and 2-feature models (172 and 14,706 models, respectively). Next, we take each of the 2-feature models and include one new feature chosen uniformly at random, so as to build 3-feature models. This step is repeated until we reach models composed of 20 features (a total of 294,292 models). In each step we ensure that each feature is included the same number of times and that no feature appears twice within the same model. This compensates for the smaller number of few-feature models by keeping the number of models constant regardless of the number of features.

3.3.1 Classification Algorithm. The features we consider may have a variety of complex nonlinear interactions. Capturing these interactions requires a classification algorithm with significant flexibility. For this reason, we chose a learning algorithm called gradient boosting machines. The main idea of gradient boosting machines is to combine multiple models into a stronger one. More specifically, models are iteratively trained so that each model is trained on the errors of the previous models, thus giving more importance to the difficult cases. At each iteration, the errors are computed and a model is fitted to these errors. Finally, the contribution of each base model to the final one is found by minimizing the overall error of the final model. Fitting the base models is computationally challenging so we used a recent, high performance implementation of gradient boosting machines, called XGBoost (or simply, XGB) [7].

3.3.2 Evaluation. In order to evaluate how accurate the learned models are, we employ the standard area under the ROC curve (AUC [4]), which takes into account the sensitivity-specificity trade-off. Basically, the AUC is an estimate of the probability that a model will rank a randomly chosen fake news case higher than a randomly chosen fact case. The AUC is robust to class imbalance and considers all possible classification thresholds.

For each model, we performed a 5-fold cross-validation. The dataset is partitioned into five partitions, out of which four are used as training data, and the remaining one is used as the validation-set. The process is then repeated five times with each of the sets used exactly once as the validation-set, thus producing five results. Hence, the reported AUC values are averaged over the five runs. Further, we employ the mean absolute deviation (or simply, MAD) in order to get a sense of how spread out the AUC values are through the five validation sets. Therefore, for each model we have an estimate of its predictive accuracy and variability.

3.4 Feature Importance and Shapley Additive Explanations

Effective models perform decisions that are usually hard to explain. However, understanding why a model has made a specific decision is paramount in any fake news detection application scenario, as it provides insight into the reasons why the content was considered to be fake, tooling fact-checkers with the facts that contributed most to the decision.

The typical approach for explaining the decisions of a model is based on calculating the impact (or importance) each feature has on the decision. Feature importance can be defined as the increase in the model prediction error after feature values are permuted, since this operation breaks the relationship between the feature and the outcome. Therefore, a feature is important if permuting its values increases the model error, because the model relied on the feature for the correct decision. On the other hand, a feature is not important if permuting its values keeps the model error unchanged, because the model ignored the feature for the decision.

Often, however, features interact with each other in many different and complex ways in order to perform accurate decisions. Thus, the feature importance is also given as a function of the interplay between the features. In this case, Shapley values [22] can be used to find a fair division scheme that defines how the total importance should be distributed among the features. In fact, Shapley values are theoretically optimal and are the unique consistent and locally accurate attribution values. Unfortunately, Shapley values can be challenging to compute, and thus we focus on explaining only the top-most effective models.

4 RESULTS

In this section we describe the results of the experiments designed to answer our research questions. In Section 4.1, we investigate the predictive accuracy and variability of the features. In Section 4.2, we focus only on the best performing models in order to evaluate models in terms of effectiveness and variability. Then, in Section 4.3, we cluster the model space according to the features present in each model, and we construct an investigation to understand the role of features in the model decisions. Finally, we attempt to explain the decisions made by some prototype models in Section 4.4.

4.1 Features: Accuracy and Variability

We quantify the predictive accuracy of a feature by considering all models in which the feature was included. More specifically, the predictive accuracy of a feature is given as the average AUC value of all models in which the feature was included. Similarly, the variability of a feature is given as the average MAD value of all models in which the feature was included. Figure 1 shows how features are distributed in terms of predictive accuracy and variability. Clearly, there is a small number of features for which the predictive accuracy is significantly higher. Specifically, around 5% of the considered features are included into models in which the average AUC values are higher than 0.85. The majority of the

features are associated with significantly lower average AUC values. The same trend is observed when we investigate the distribution of features in terms of variability. Around 3% of the considered features are associated with relatively low variability.

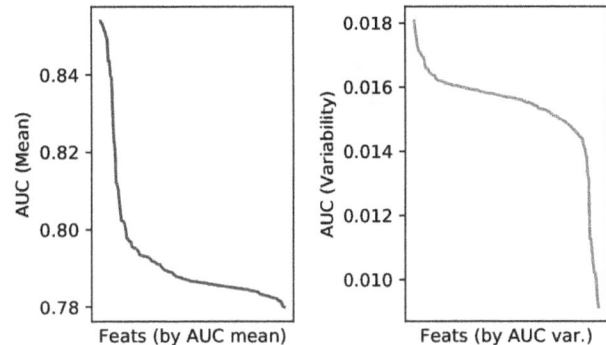

Figure 1: Distribution of features. Left – Predictive accuracy. Right – Variability.

4.2 Top 10 % Models: Accuracy and Variability

Now we investigate whether relatively simple models (composed by up to 20 features) can perform consistently well across the dataset. In order to do so, we take the top 10% models w.r.t. AUC. Among the best performing models, we are interested in those that exhibit low variability.

Figure 2 shows a scatter plot of the top 10% models w.r.t AUC, each represented by a dot. Each dot diameter is proportional to the ratio between the respective model's AUC mean and variability. Cartesian coordinates of each dot center are obtained from the vector of the probabilities assigned by the model to each fake news case in the validation set.

First, we note that the mean AUC is in the range $[0.855, 0.885]$ and, therefore, the different diameters are mostly due to AUC's variability. We observe the presence of very few models with excellent performance on average (yellow dots, AUC > 0.88), but with high variability. On the other hand, there are many models with lower variability, but with lower average AUC values (medium-sized purple and blue models, AUC < 0.865). Finally, there are two models with the good trade-off between performance and variability (pinkish dots, AUC ≈ 0.87). These cases will be discussed in the next sections.

To better understand the relationship between features and model performance, we take the best performing models and compute the prevalence of features. Also, to understand the relationship between them and AUC variability, we take, from the top performing models, the 10% with the highest and 10% with the lowest variability and compute the prevalence of features in these sets.

4.2.1 Accuracy. Considering models with the highest AUC values, features extracted from the environment (i.e. from social media), are more frequent (e.g. the number of shares (40%) and reactions count (29%)). Moreover, features that capture information regarding the location and credibility of domains (e.g. ranking position of domain

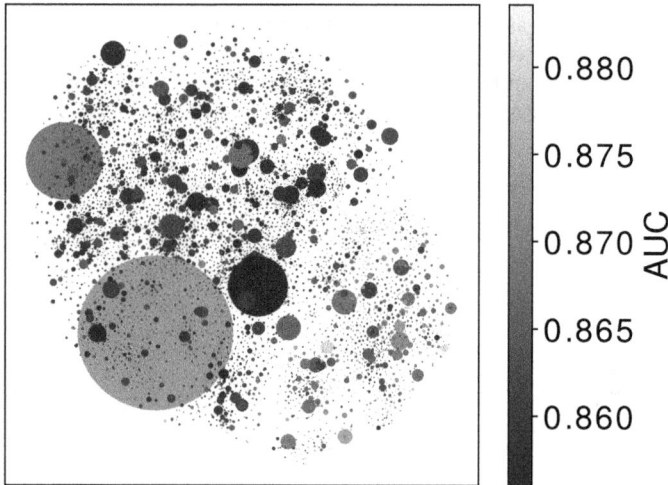

Figure 2: Each point represents a model. Color indicates AUC value. Diameter indicates accuracy consistency across folds (i.e., larger diameter implies lower variability). Probabilities associated to fake news stories by each model are taken as a vector to compute its 2D t-SNE [23] representation (i.e., for defining the model's position in the plot).

from Social Alexa (39%), page reactions from users on social media (29%), IP of domain (28%), etc., are very frequent in this group of models. Finally, features that capture political bias of news outlet (i.e. mainstream, left-leaning, and right-leaning (37%)) are quite prevalent in the best models. On the other hand, character level, word-level and sentence-level features (e.g. count) are less frequent in best models (7% of models on average).

4.2.2 Variability. While features from the social media (e.g. share count (13%)), IP of domain (14%) and semantic structure (e.g. toxicity (13%)) are very frequent in models with low variability, features from user engagement (from social media) (e.g. number of comments on first 7200 seconds (12%), political bias (12%) and Facebook page (12%)), occurred more often in models with high variability. Sentence level-features and Psycholinguistic features are very frequent both in models with high and low variability.

In sum, we conclude that there are many combinations of features that yield models with high performance and low variability. In the next section, we investigate whether these models are redundant (i.e. identify similar sets of fake news) or complementary.

4.3 Clustering the Model Space

In order to understand whether the top 10% models cover different regions of the space of fake news, we cluster them from binary vector representations that indicate which features are present in each model. To cluster these models, we use the standard K-Means algorithm based on Euclidean distances [3]. To find the optimum value of K, we use the Silhouette Score [30], which measures, on average, how tightly grouped all the members in different clusters are, and select the value of K, for which the Silhouette Score is the highest. In this work, we use $K = 6$. The sizes of the resulting clusters vary from 3,769 to 5,921 (mean 4,908 and std. dev. 703).

Once again, we embed the models in a 2D space based on the probabilities assigned to fake news cases and color code the models according to the cluster they belong to. Hence cohesive clusters indicate that models within the same cluster are better at identifying specific types of fake news. If this is the case, models that belong to the same cluster (i.e. share similar features) are expected to be close to each other in the embedding, indicating that they assign similar scores to the fake news in the test set. In fact, this is what we observe in Figure 3. Next, we analyze which types of features best describe each cluster.

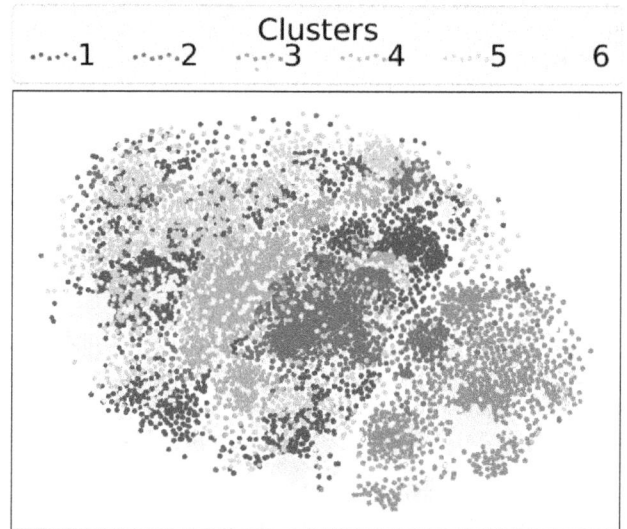

Figure 3: t-SNE representations [23] of models based on the scores associated to each fake news in the validation set. Colors indicate clusters found from binary vectors indicating which features were used in each model. Proximity between models from the same cluster suggest correlation between features used and fake news correctly detected.

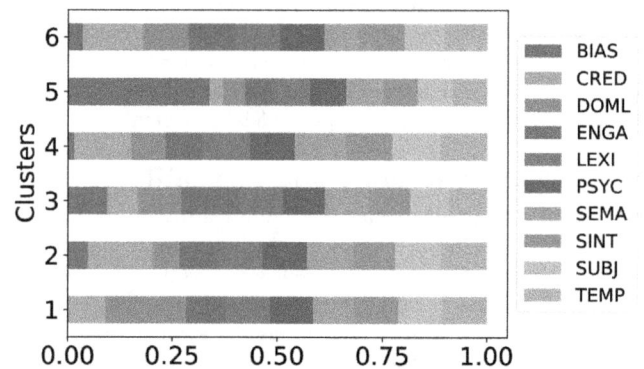

Figure 4: Descriptions of clusters in terms of feature sets, represented as segments. Segment lengths are normalized $R_{i,t}$ ratios and indicate how much more/less often features of type t appear in cluster i than in a random null model.

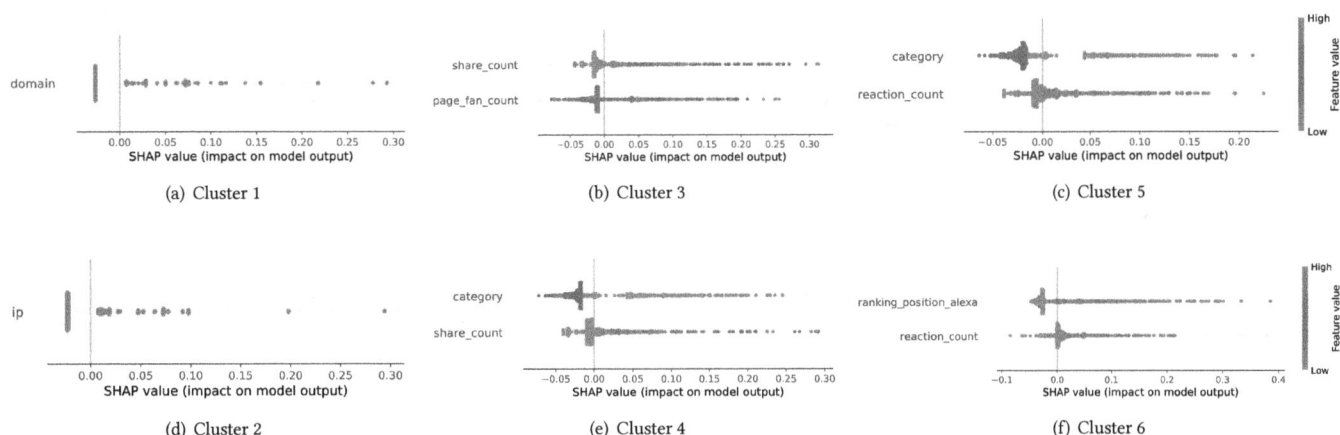

(a) Cluster 1

(b) Cluster 3

(c) Cluster 5

(d) Cluster 2

(e) Cluster 4

(f) Cluster 6

Figure 5: SHAP summaries for the closest models to each cluster centroid. These violin plots show the impact of each feature on model output (positive values on x-axis mean increased chance of being fake). Features are color-coded according to its values (highest: red, lowest: blue), except for Domain and IP, which do not have a meaningful scale. For instance, for Cluster 5's centroid, high values of `reaction_count` are associated to positive SHAP values.

4.3.1 Describing clusters in terms of types of features. When we focus on the analysis of the top 10% performing models, features no longer appear with the same frequency. In addition, clusters include different numbers of models, each of which can include any number of features. In order to compare the frequency of specific types of features across clusters, we define a (random) null model. This allows us to determine how much more (less) often than expected a given feature type appears in a cluster.

Let $C_{i,t}$ be the number of times features of type t appear in models from cluster i for $t \in$ BIAS, CRED, ..., TEMP and $i = 1, \ldots, 6$. Multiple features of the same type are counted multiple times. Also, let $C_i = \sum_t C_{i,t}$ be the total number of features in cluster i. Denote by $N_t = \sum_i C_{i,t}$ the number of times features of type t appear among the top 10% performing models. The expectation of $C_{i,t}$ if features were assigned to clusters completely at random is $C_i N_t / \sum_t N_t$. Therefore, the ratio $R_{i,t} = C_{i,t}/(C_i N_t / \sum_t N_t)$ measures how much more (less) often features of type t appear in cluster i than in a random null model.

Figure 4 shows ratios $R_{i,t}$ normalized for each cluster i (i.e. divided by $\sum_t R_{i,t}$). Normalized ratios allow us to identify which types of features better describe each cluster. We note that clusters comprise combinations of features types in different proportions. All clusters use features from all features types, except for cluster 1, which does not include BIAS features. These features are more frequent in cluster 5 and less so in cluster 4. CRED features are very prevalent in clusters 2, 4 and 6, but less used by models in cluster 5. Finally, DOML features are very prevalent in cluster 1. Therefore, these observations combined with Figure 3 corroborate the hypothesis that models generated from different combinations of features are able to correctly identify different fake news groups.

4.4 Explaining Model Decisions

In this section, we use SHAP [22] to explain why news are classified as fake or not by representative models of each cluster. SHAP is short for SHapley Additive exPlanations. It is a unified approach to interpreting model predictions. As such, SHAP assigns a "force" or importance value – positive or negative – to each feature in a particular prediction [22]. The output value (prediction) consists of the sum of the base value (average prediction over the validation set) and these forces (closer to 1.0 means more likely to be fake). In addition, SHAP allows us (i) to summarize the importance of a feature, and (ii) to associate low/high feature values to an increase/decrease in output values, through color-coded violin plots built from all predictions.

Representative models of each cluster were selected according to the following criteria: (1) by centroid proximity, where we select the closest model to the cluster centroid (Figure 5); and (2) by AUC, where we select in each cluster the model with the best performance w.r.t AUC (Figure 6).

Figure 5 shows violin plots of SHAP values for features used by each of the selected centroid models. Interestingly, we note that the closest models to the centroids have either one or two features, all of which come from feature sets DOML, BIAS, ENGA and CRED.

The representative models of clusters 1 and 2 have a single feature, domain and ip, respectively. In either case, we remove the feature value color-coding since low/high feature values are not meaningful in these cases. These plots are very similar, as there is a close mapping from ips to domains. We found that the three domains that have a large negative impact (i.e. less likely fake) on the output value are politico.com, abcnews.go.com and cnn.com. For models within cluster 3, high page fan counts have large impact – positive or negative – over predictions. Extremely high values though, are almost always associated with negative impact, since popular pages are less likely to share fake news. Large numbers of shares, however, tend to increase output values. This is consistent

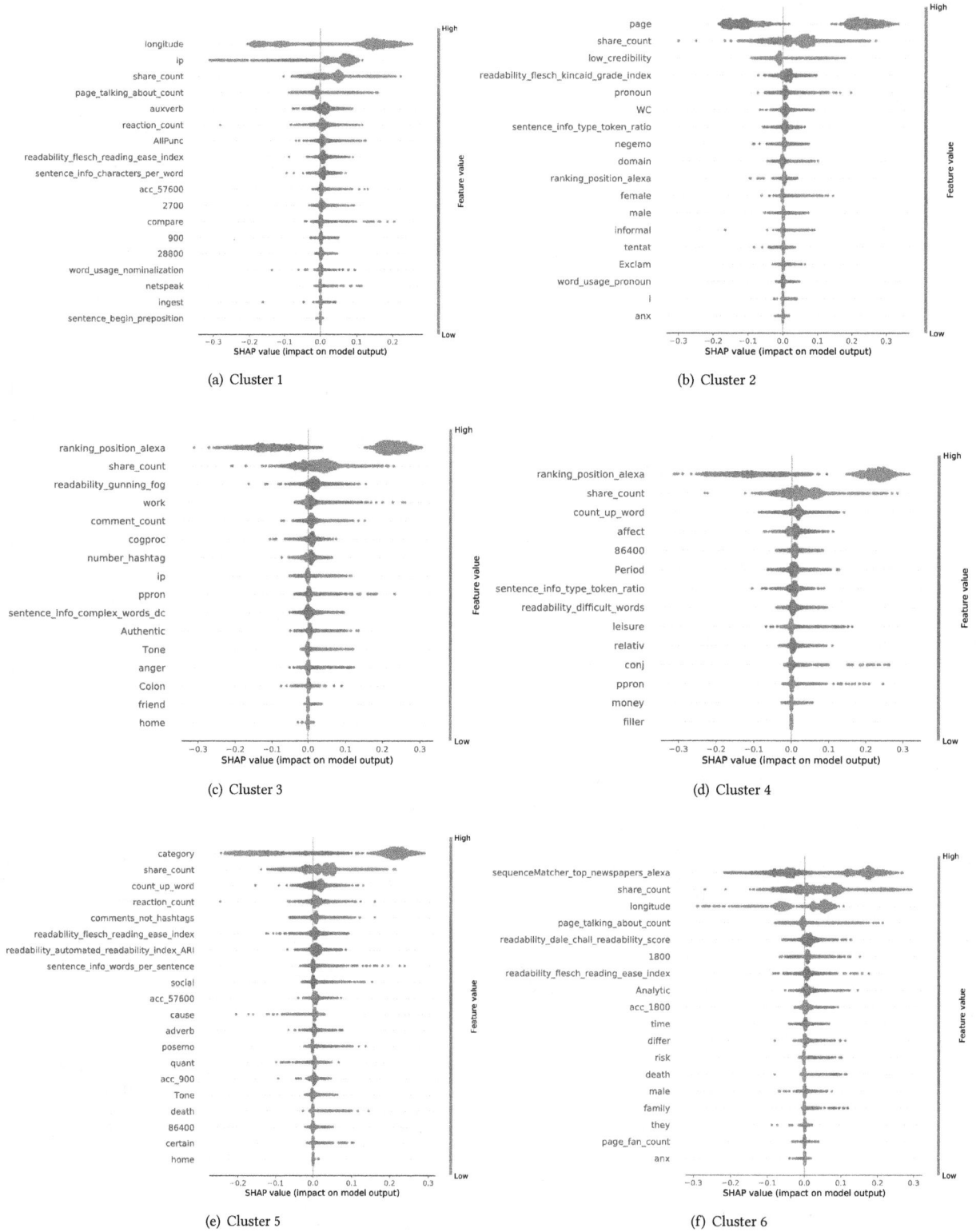

(a) Cluster 1

(b) Cluster 2

(c) Cluster 3

(d) Cluster 4

(e) Cluster 5

(f) Cluster 6

Figure 6: SHAP summaries for the highest AUC model in each cluster.

(a) Cluster 3, predicted: fake

(b) Cluster 3, predicted: not fake

(c) Cluster 4, predicted: fake

(d) Cluster 4, predicted: not fake

(e) Cluster 5, predicted: fake

(f) Cluster 5, predicted: not fake

(g) Cluster 6, predicted: fake

(h) Cluster 6, predicted: not fake

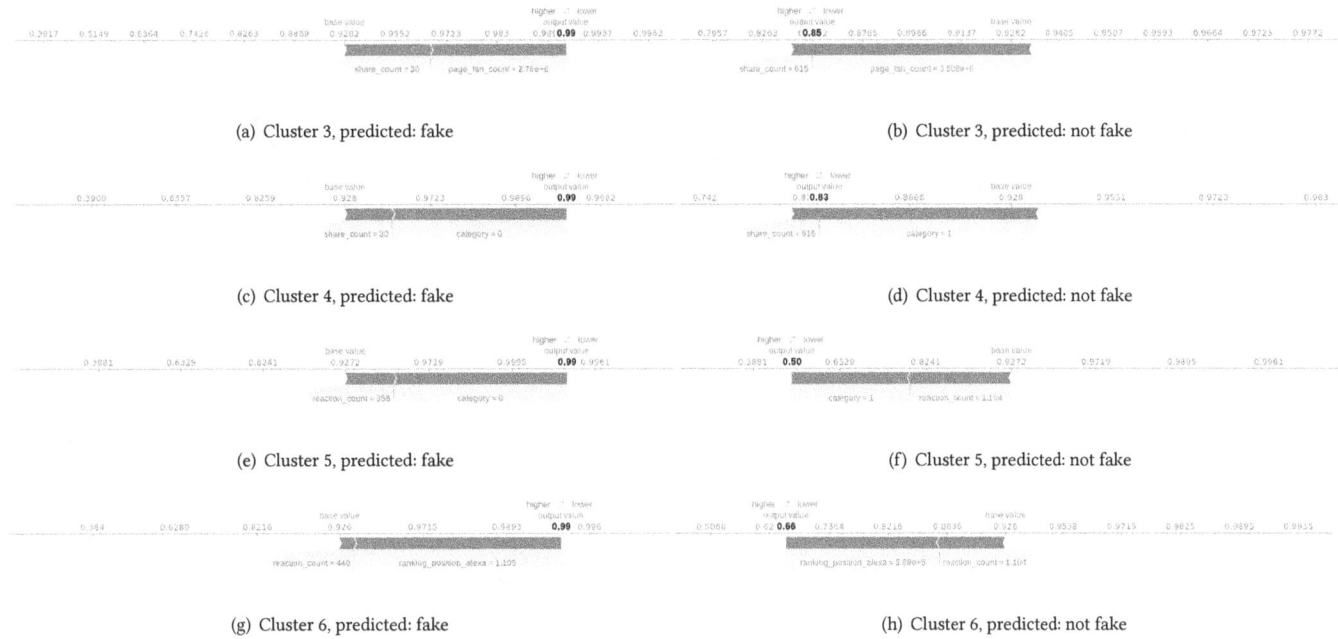

Figure 7: SHAP results on test cases for representative centroid models of each cluster. Base value (0.926) is the score of an instance with average feature values. Feature values that increase (decrease) prediction score are shown below red (blue) bars whose lengths depict the corresponding amount. Output value = base value + length of red bars – length of blue bars.

with recent research that shows that fake news are more likely to be shared [20, 40]. Models within cluster 4 also include number of shares as a feature and can be interpreted in the same way. Representative models of cluster 4 and 5 include categories of political bias as a feature, which takes on three values: -1 for left-leaning, 0 for mainstream and 1 for right-leaning. As expected, category has a negative impact on output for mainstream news (purple dots), but increases the prediction value if the source exhibits political bias. Models representing cluster 5 and 6 share number of reactions as a feature. In the same way as number of shares, higher values of this feature increase the chances that a piece of news is classified as fake. Last, the model representing cluster 6 also includes the ranking position retrieved from Alexa as a feature. As expected, very low values (top of the ranking) tend to have a large negative impact on the output.

In Figure 6 we present the SHAP results for the top performing models w.r.t AUC. Differently from the models closest to the centroids that have one or two features, the clusters in Figure 6 have much more features. Cluster 1 uses localization and Domain features, longitude and ip, which are features proposed in the present work. Clusters 2 and 3 rank engagement features nearly as the most influential features. For Clusters 3 and 4 Alexa's ranking position appears as one of the most important features, similar to the Centroid clusters. Cluster 5 and Cluster 6 are a mix of localization, Domain and Engagement features, which are top-of-the-rank features on the others clusters. Psycholinguistic cues are shown to be relevant in all clusters, once they appear in every model. Similar findings were obtained when analyzing the lowest variability models in each

cluster, where most of them contain Psycholinguistic cues, Domain and Engagement Features.

Last, focusing on centroid models, we include, for each of the representative models, examples of news stories that are scored higher (lower) than average, indicating it is more (less) likely to be fake. Figure 7 shows SHAP results on different news stories, which explain the role that each feature had on the decision. For ethical reasons, we omit the results corresponding to Clusters 1 and 2, which respectively indicate domains and IPs less/more likely to publish fake news. Figures 7 (a,b) shows that very high page fan counts decrease the output value, while the effect of share counts may depend on the former feature. In Figures 7 (c,d) we observe that news from mainstream media (category 0) tend to have lower output values, whereas news from politically biased sources (categories -1 and 1) often receive a positive bump in their outputs. In Figures 7 (e,f) we observe other examples of category's impact and that the number of reactions has a similar behavior as the number of shares. Finally, in Figures 7 (g,h) we note that being at the bottom (top) of the Alexa's ranking has a negative (positive) impact on the output value.

5 CONCLUDING DISCUSSION

In this work we provide many contributions that are relevant to the field. First, we survey a large number of recent and related works as an attempt to implement all potential features to detect fake news. We proposed novel features, such as those related to the source domain, which appear within the best models up to five times more often than other features. Second, our framework reveals how hard is to detect fake news, as only a small fraction of the models (only

2.2%) achieve a detection performance higher than 0.85 in terms of AUC. We hope our effort can become a baseline for other solutions to the same problem.

Finally, our findings suggest that certain types of fake news tend to be identified by models with specific combinations of features. As a consequence, different models separate fake stories from real ones based on very different reasoning. This shows the complexity of the problem and allow us to understand how hard it is for a single solution to tackle all forms of fake news stories. As future work we plan to categorize the fake news stories as a strategy to construct effective and robust ensembles of classifiers. For instance, in this work we showed the different models of clusters that are made of random combinations of features. This indicates that ensemble techniques that combine models from different clusters are a promising avenue for investigation.

ACKNOWLEDGMENTS

This work was partially supported by the project FAPEMIG-PRONEX-MASWeb, Models, Algorithms and Systems for the Web, process number APQ-01400-1, as well as grants from Google, CNPq, CAPES, and Fapemig.

REFERENCES

[1] Hadeer Ahmed, Issa Traore, and Sherif Saad. 2017. Detection of online fake news using N-gram analysis and machine learning techniques. In *Int'l Conference on Intelligent, Secure, and Dependable Systems in Distributed and Cloud Environments (ISDDC)*.
[2] Hunt Allcott and Matthew Gentzkow. 2017. Social media and fake news in the 2016 election. *Journal of Economic Perspectives* 31, 2 (2017), 211–36.
[3] David Arthur and Sergei Vassilvitskii. 2007. k-means++: The advantages of careful seeding. In *Proc. of the Annual ACM-SIAM symposium on Discrete Algorithms (SODA)*. Society for Industrial and Applied Mathematics.
[4] Ricardo Baeza-Yates and Berthier Ribeiro-Neto. 1999. *Modern information retrieval*. Vol. 463. ACM press New York.
[5] Sreyasee Das Bhattacharjee, Ashit Talukder, and Bala Venkatram Balantrapu. 2017. Active learning based news veracity detection with feature weighting and deep-shallow fusion. In *Proc. of the Int'l Conference on Big Data (Big Data)*. IEEE.
[6] Carlos Castillo, Marcelo Mendoza, and Barbara Poblete. 2011. Information credibility on twitter. In *Proc. of the Int'l Conference on World Wide Web (WWW)*.
[7] Tianqi Chen and Carlos Guestrin. 2016. Xgboost: A scalable tree boosting system. In *Proc. of the Int'l Conference on Knowledge Discovery and Data Mining (KDD)*.
[8] Giovanni Luca Ciampaglia, Prashant Shiralkar, Luis M Rocha, Johan Bollen, Filippo Menczer, and Alessandro Flammini. 2015. Computational fact checking from knowledge networks. *PLOS ONE* 10, 6 (2015).
[9] Niall J Conroy, Victoria L Rubin, and Yimin Chen. 2015. Automatic deception detection: Methods for finding fake news. In *Proc. of the Annual Meeting of the (ASIS&T)*.
[10] Daniel H Dalip, Marcos André Gonçalves, Marco Cristo, and Pável Calado. 2017. A general multiview framework for assessing the quality of collaboratively created content on web 2.0. *Journal of the Association for Information Science and Technology* 68, 2 (2017), 286–308.
[11] Samantha Finn, Panagiotis Takis Metaxas, Eni Mustafaraj, Megan OâĂŹKeefe, Lindsay Tang, Susan Tang, and Laura Zeng. 2014. TRAILS: A system for monitoring the propagation of rumors on twitter. In *Proc. of the Computation + Journalism Conference (C+J)*.
[12] Adrien Friggeri, Lada A Adamic, Dean Eckles, and Justin Cheng. 2014. Rumor Cascades. In *Proc. of the Int'l AAAI Conference on Weblogs and Social (ICWSM)*.
[13] Kevin Gallagher. 2017. The Social Media Demographics Report: Differences in age, gender, and income at the top platforms. *http://www.businessinsider.com/the-social-media-demographics-report-2017-8*, Business Insider (2017).
[14] Jennifer Golbeck, Matthew Mauriello, Brooke Auxier, Keval H Bhanushali, Christopher Bonk, Mohamed Amine Bouzaghrane, Cody Buntain, Riya Chanduka, Paul Cheakalos, Jennine B Everett, and others. 2018. Fake News vs Satire: A Dataset and Analysis. In *Proc. of the Int'l Conference on Web Science (WebScience)*.
[15] Aditi Gupta, Ponnurangam Kumaraguru, Carlos Castillo, and Patrick Meier. 2014. Tweetcred: Real-time credibility assessment of content on twitter. In *Proc. of the Int'l Conference on Social Informatics (SocInfo)*.
[16] Zhiwei Jin, Juan Cao, Yongdong Zhang, Jianshe Zhou, and Qi Tian. 2017. Novel visual and statistical image features for microblogs news verification. *IEEE Transactions on Multimedia* 19, 3 (2017), 598–608.
[17] Jooyeon Kim, Behzad Tabibian, Alice Oh, Bernhard Schölkopf, and Manuel Gomez-Rodriguez. 2018. Leveraging the crowd to detect and reduce the spread of fake news and misinformation. In *Proc. of the Int'l Conference on Web Search and Data Mining (WSDM)*.
[18] Srijan Kumar, Robert West, and Jure Leskovec. 2016. Disinformation on the web: Impact, characteristics, and detection of wikipedia hoaxes. In *Proc. of the WWW Companion*.
[19] Sejeong Kwon, Meeyoung Cha, and Kyomin Jung. 2017. Rumor detection over varying time windows. *PLOS ONE* 12, 1 (2017).
[20] David MJ Lazer, Matthew A Baum, Yochai Benkler, Adam J Berinsky, Kelly M Greenhill, Filippo Menczer, Miriam J Metzger, Brendan Nyhan, Gordon Pennycook, David Rothschild, and others. 2018. The science of fake news. *Science* 359, 6380 (2018), 1094–1096.
[21] Yaliang Li, Qi Li, Jing Gao, Lu Su, Bo Zhao, Wei Fan, and Jiawei Han. 2015. On the discovery of evolving truth. In *Proc. of the Int'l Conference on Knowledge Discovery and Data Mining (KDD)*.
[22] Scott M Lundberg and Su-In Lee. 2017. A Unified Approach to Interpreting Model Predictions. In *Proc. of the Neural Information Processing Systems (NIPS)*, I. Guyon, U. V. Luxburg, S. Bengio, H. Wallach, R. Fergus, S. Vishwanathan, and R. Garnett (Eds.). Curran Associates, Inc.
[23] Laurens van der Maaten and Geoffrey Hinton. 2008. Visualizing Data Using t-SNE. *Journal of machine learning research* 9, Nov (2008), 2579–2605.
[24] J. W. Pennebaker, M. E. Francis, and R. J. Booth. 2001. Linguistic inquiry and word count: LIWC 2001. *Mahway: Lawrence Erlbaum Associates* (2001).
[25] Verónica Pérez-Rosas, Bennett Kleinberg, Alexandra Lefevre, and Rada Mihalcea. 2017. Automatic detection of fake news. *Proc. of the Int'l Conference on Computational Linguistics* (2017).
[26] Anirudh Ramachandran and Nick Feamster. 2006. Understanding the network-level behavior of spammers. In *Proc. of the Conference on Applications, Technologies, Architectures, and Protocols for Computer Communications (SIGCOMM)*.
[27] Jacob Ratkiewicz, Michael Conover, Mark R Meiss, Bruno Gonçalves, Alessandro Flammini, and Filippo Menczer. 2011. Detecting and tracking political abuse in social media. In *Proc. of the Int'l AAAI Conference on Weblogs and Social (ICWSM)*.
[28] Julio C. S. Reis, André Correia, Fabrício Murai, Adriano Veloso, and Fabrício Benevenuto. 2019. Supervised Learning for Fake News Detection. *IEEE Intelligent Systems* 34, 2 (2019).
[29] Manoel H. Ribeiro, Pedro H. C. Guerra, Wagner Meira Jr., and VirgÃnlio Almeida. 2017. "Everything I Disagree With is# FakeNews": Correlating Political Polarization and Spread of Misinformation. In *Proc. of Data Science + Journalism Workshop*.
[30] Peter J Rousseeuw. 1987. Silhouettes: a graphical aid to the interpretation and validation of cluster analysis. *Journal of computational and applied mathematics* 20 (1987), 53–65.
[31] Victoria Rubin, Niall Conroy, Yimin Chen, and Sarah Cornwell. 2016. Fake news or truth? using satirical cues to detect potentially misleading news. In *Proc. of the Workshop on Computational Approaches to Deception Detection (NAACL-HLT)*.
[32] Giovanni Santia and Jake Williams. 2018. BuzzFace: A News Veracity Dataset with Facebook User Commentary and Egos. In *Proc. of the Int'l AAAI Conference on Weblogs and Social (ICWSM)*.
[33] Chengcheng Shao, Giovanni Luca Ciampaglia, Alessandro Flammini, and Filippo Menczer. 2016. Hoaxy: A platform for tracking online misinformation. In *Proc. of the WWW Companion*.
[34] Chengcheng Shao, Giovanni Luca Ciampaglia, Onur Varol, Kai-Cheng Yang, Alessandro Flammini, and Filippo Menczer. 2018. The spread of low-credibility content by social bots. *Nature communications* 9, 1 (2018), 4787.
[35] Kai Shu, Amy Sliva, Suhang Wang, Jiliang Tang, and Huan Liu. 2017. Fake news detection on social media: A data mining perspective. *ACM SIGKDD Explorations Newsletter* 19, 1 (2017), 22–36.
[36] C. Silverman, L. Strapagiel, H. Shaban, E. Hall, , and J. Singer-Vine. 2016. Hyperpartisan facebook pages are publishing false and misleading information at an alarming rate. *https://www.buzzfeed.com/craigsilverman/partisan-fb-pages-analysis*, Buzzfeed (2016).
[37] Eugenio Tacchini, Gabriele Ballarin, Marco L Della Vedova, Stefano Moret, and Luca de Alfaro. 2017. Some like it hoax: Automated fake news detection in social networks. In *Proc. of the Workshop on Data Science for Social Good (SoGood)*.
[38] Sebastian Tschiatschek, Adish Singla, Manuel Gomez Rodriguez, Arpit Merchant, and Andreas Krause. 2018. Fake News Detection in Social Networks via Crowd Signals. In *Proc. of the WWW Companion*.
[39] Svitlana Volkova, Kyle Shaffer, Jin Yea Jang, and Nathan Hodas. 2017. Separating facts from fiction: Linguistic models to classify suspicious and trusted news posts on twitter. In *Proc. of the Annual Meeting of the ACL*.
[40] Soroush Vosoughi, Deb Roy, and Sinan Aral. 2018. The spread of true and false news online. *Science* 359, 6380 (2018), 1146–1151.
[41] William Yang Wang. 2017. "Liar, Liar Pants on Fire": A New Benchmark Dataset for Fake News Detection. In *Proc. of the Annual Meeting of the ACL*.
[42] Wei Wei and Xiaojun Wan. 2017. Learning to identify ambiguous and misleading news headlines. In *Proc. of the Int'l Joint Conference on AI (IJCAI)*.
[43] Zhe Zhao, Paul Resnick, and Qiaozhu Mei. 2015. Enquiring minds: Early detection of rumors in social media from enquiry posts. In *Proc. of the WWW Companion*.

Characterizing Attention Cascades in WhatsApp Groups

Josemar Alves Caetano
josemarcaetano@dcc.ufmg.br
Dept. of Computer Science,
Universidade Federal de Minas Gerais
(UFMG), Brazil

Gabriel Magno
magno@dcc.ufmg.br
Dept. of Computer Science,
Universidade Federal de Minas Gerais
(UFMG), Brazil

Marcos Gonçalves
mgoncalv@dcc.ufmg.br
Dept. of Computer Science,
Universidade Federal de Minas Gerais
(UFMG), Brazil

Jussara Almeida
jussara@dcc.ufmg.br
Dept. of Computer Science,
Universidade Federal de Minas Gerais
(UFMG), Brazil

Humberto T. Marques-Neto
humberto@pucminas.br
Dept. of Computer Science, Pontifícia
Universidade Católica de Minas
Gerais (PUC Minas), Brazil

Virgílio Almeida*
virgilio@dcc.ufmg.br
Dept. of Computer Science,
Universidade Federal de Minas Gerais
(UFMG), Brazil

ABSTRACT

An important political and social phenomena discussed in several
countries, like India and Brazil, is the use of WhatsApp to spread
false or misleading content. However, little is known about the
information dissemination process in WhatsApp groups. Attention
affects the dissemination of information in WhatsApp groups, determining what topics or subjects are more attractive to participants
of a group. In this paper, we characterize and analyze how attention
propagates among the participants of a WhatsApp group. An attention cascade begins when a user asserts a topic in a message to the
group, which could include written text, photos, or links to articles
online. Others then propagate the information by responding to it.
We analyzed attention cascades in more than 1.7 million messages
posted in 120 groups over one year. Our analysis focused on the
structural and temporal evolution of attention cascades as well as
on the behavior of users that participate in them. We found specific
characteristics in cascades associated with groups that discuss political subjects and false information. For instance, we observe that
cascades with false information tend to be deeper, reach more users,
and last longer in political groups than in non-political groups.

CCS CONCEPTS

• **Networks** → **Online social networks**; • **Information systems** → *Chat*.

KEYWORDS

WhatsApp; Cascades; Information Diffusion; Misinformation; Social Computing

---

*Also with Berkman Klein Center for Internet & Society, Harvard University, USA.

ACM Reference Format:
Josemar Alves Caetano, Gabriel Magno, Marcos Gonçalves, Jussara Almeida,
Humberto T. Marques-Neto, and Virgílio Almeida. 2019. Characterizing
Attention Cascades in WhatsApp Groups. In *11th ACM Conference on Web
Science (WebSci '19), June 30–July 3, 2019, Boston, MA, USA*. ACM, New York,
NY, USA, 10 pages. https://doi.org/10.1145/3292522.3326018

1 INTRODUCTION

Global mobile messenger apps, such as WhatsApp, WeChat, Signal,
Telegram, and Facebook-Messenger, are popular all over the world.
WhatsApp, in particular, with more than 1.5 billion users [11], has
an expressive penetration in many countries like South Africa, India, Brazil, and Great Britain. Messenger apps are an important
medium by which individuals communicate, share news and information, access services and do business and politics. With end-
to-end encryption added to every conversation, WhatsApp sets
the bar for the privacy of digital communications worldwide. As
a consequence, in many countries, WhatsApp has been used by
political parties and religious activists to send messages and distribute news. The combination of encrypted messages and group
messaging has proved to be a valuable tool for mobilizing political
support and disseminating political ideas [21]. There is growing evidence of unprecedented disinformation and fake news campaigns
in WhatsApp. In India, false rumors and fake news intended to
inflame sectarian tensions have gone viral on WhatsApp, leading
to lynching mobs and death of dozens of people [16]. Misleading
messages with fake news and photos containing disinformation
have been used to influence real-world behavior in the Brazilian
elections in 2018 [3].

A key component of the WhatsApp architecture is group chats,
which allow group messaging. Groups are unstructured spaces
where participants can share messages, photos, and videos with up
to 256 people at once. Much of the political action in WhatsApp
takes place in private groups and through direct messaging, which
are impossible to analyze due to the encryption protocol. However,
there is a large number of groups that are often publicized in well-
known websites. These groups are open to new participants. After
joining a group, a participant can post messages and receive the
messages that circulate in the group. Unstructured conversations
are the most usual form of conversation in a group chat.

Differently, from Facebook and Twitter, WhatsApp groups do
not have many features that have been pointed out as responsible

for the dissemination of false information [19]. WhatsApp does not have ads, promoted tweets, News Feed or timeline, which are controlled by algorithms. In a group chat, anybody can propose a discussion or start a new discussion in response to a piece of content or join an existing discussion at any time and any depth. There is no algorithm or human curator moderating discussions in a WhatsApp group. In such a domain, a natural question that arises is: What are the ingredients of the WhatsApp architecture that makes it a weaponizable social media platform to distribute misinformation? The goal of this paper is to take a first step towards understanding information diffusion in WhatsApp groups. Our work is an essential step in order to increase knowledge about misinformation dissemination in messenger apps.

The approach we use to understand information spreading in a WhatsApp group is a combination of two concepts: information cascade and attention. WhatsApp allows a participant to explicitly mention a message she intends to reply or refer to, by using the reply function. The reply function in WhatsApp creates a sequence of interrelated messages, which can be tracked and viewed as a cascade of interrelated messages. Every time a participant "replies" to a message, all other participants are notified by the message that appears on the screen. A *reply* has the effect of re-gaining the attention for a specific piece of information.

In a chaotic environment of a WhatsApp group chat, participants are sometimes swamped by messages, which characterizes a typical information overload situation, that competes for the cognitive resources of the participants. Herbert Simon [10] was the one who first theorized about information overload, proposing the concept of economy of attention. "A wealth of information creates a poverty of attention" said Simon [26]. *Attention cascades* can be viewed as a structure that represents the process of information creation and consumption, which models new patterns of collective attention. They capture the connections fostered among group participants, their comments and their reactions in the group discussion setting. We want to increase our understanding of information dissemination processes that underlie the dynamics of a group discussion. Our initial research questions are the following:

- *How different are attention cascades in political and non-political groups on WhatsApp?*
- *What is the impact of false information on the characteristics of attention cascades?*

To illuminate the behavior of attention cascades, we study the dissemination processes of cascades in political and non-political groups as well as cascades with previously reported false information and with unclassified information. We show that the attention cascades are markedly different in their time evolution and structure. More broadly, by characterizing the attention cascades of different types of groups, we can better understand the information spreading process in group discussions and explore the contextual factors driving their differences.

In this paper, we present a large-scale study of attention cascades in WhatsApp groups. Attention cascades can help to understand the process of information dissemination in WhatsApp groups. With an in-depth analysis of a large number of messages of two groups, political and non-political, each containing verified false information and unclassified information, we demonstrate that the

structural and temporal characteristics of the two classes of cascades are different. We show that attention cascades in WhatsApp groups reflect real-world events that capture public attention. We also demonstrate that political cascades last longer than non-political ones. We show that cascades with false information in political groups are deeper, broader and reach more users than the same type of cascades in non-political groups.

The remainder of this paper is organized as follows. We first review related work. Next, we discuss the concept of attention cascade that drives our study and describes each step of our methodology. We present our results for each research question posed, and then discuss our main conclusions and directions for future work.

2 RELATED WORK

Characterizing cascades structure and growth on online social networks is a key task to understand their dynamics. Many studies have analyzed cascades formed on networks like Facebook and Twitter. In [13], authors analyzed large cascades of reshared photos on Facebook, more specifically one cascade of a reshared American President Barack Obama's photo posted on his page following his reelection victory, which in 2013 it had had over 4.4M likes, and another photo posted by a common Norwegian Facebook user (Petter Kverneng), which got one million likes on his humorous post. This paper shows that these two large cascades spread around the world in 24 hours and it points out that studying information cascades is important to understand how information is disseminated on today's very well-connected online environment. On the other hand, analyzing Twitter's cascades, the authors of [25] analyzed the cascades from the point of view of users. This paper measures how Twitter users observe the retweets on their own timelines and how is their engagement with retweet cascades in counterpoint with non-retweeted content. Nevertheless, we need to understand cascades' properties on emerging online communication platforms like WhatsApp (which has millions of users organized in groups) to better understand the phenomenon of the quick information spread and its impact on users decisions and actions.

Recently, the paper [8] shows how some diffusion protocols affect 98 large information cascades of photo, video, or link reshares on Facebook. Authors identify four classes of protocols characterized by the individual effort for user participates in a cascade and by the social cost of user stays out. The proposed classes, *transient copy protocol*, *persistent copy protocol*, *nomination protocol*, and *volunteer protocol*, may used to understand the cascade growth and structure. This paper indicates that as individual effort increase the information dissemination decreases and as higher the social costs users wait and observe more the group before making a decision or do any action.

The cascades can be viewed as complex dynamic objects. Thus, identifying their recurrence and predicting their growth are not trivial tasks. In [6], authors present a framework to address cascade prediction problems, which observe the nature of initial reshares as well as some characteristics of the post, such as caption, language, and content. Moreover, authors of [7] analyze cascades bursts and show how their recurrence would occur over time. Predicting cascades growth, evolution, and recurrence could be useful to mitigate the spread of rumors [14] and of misinformation in general, especially in the political context, which has received much attention lately.

Some studies analyzed attention on online platforms. Ciampaglia et al. [10] analyze Wikipedia network traffic to measure the attention span and their spikes through time. They found that collective attention is associated with the law of supply and demand for goods, in this case, information. Moreover, the authors show that the creation of new Wikipedia articles is associated with shifts of collective attention. Wu et al. [28] studies the collective attention towards news story from the political news webiste *digg.com*. The authors analyze how the group attention shifts considering the novelty of the news and the process of fade with time as they spread among people.

Regarding WhatsApp, there are few studies analyzing data extracted from groups. The majority of works explore the WhatsApp effects on education activities. For instance, Cetinkaya [5] inspect the impact of WhatsApp usage on school performance and Bouhnik et al. [4] analyze how students and teachers interact using WhatsApp. Other works compare WhatsApp with other applications. Church et al. [9] analyzes the difference of between WhatsApp and SMS messaging and in Rosler et al. [24], authors present a systematical analysis of security characteristics of WhatsApp and of two other messaging applications. These studies use qualitative methodologies and data related to (but not directly from) WhatsApp to perform the study. However, few works actually characterize WhatsApp usage using its data. Recently, Garimella et al. [15] proposes a data collection methodology and perform a statistical exploration to allow researchers to understand how public WhatsApp groups data can be collected and analyzed. Rosenfeld et al. [23] analyze 6 million encrypted messages from over 100 users to build demographic prediction models that use activity data but not the content of these messages. In [22], authors collected WhatsApp messages to monitor critical events during the Ghana 2016 presidential elections.

This paper greatly builds on top of prior study [27], where the authors analyzed the diffusion of verified true and false news stories distributed on Twitter. They classified news as true or false using information from six independent fact-checking organizations. They found that falsehood diffused farther, deeper, and more broadly than the truth in all categories of information, especially for false political news. They also found that false news was more novel than true news and false stories inspired fear, disgust, and surprise in replies, whereas true stories inspired anticipation, sadness, joy, and trust.

In our work, we also adjust the methodology proposed in [27] on WhatsApp to analyze cascades properties and user relationships of political and non-political groups. We also analyze and compare cascades with and without identifiable falsehood using the information on Brazilian fact-checking websites. Nevertheless, we extend the work [27] by applying the methodology on WhatsApp groups that are entirely different online environments when we compare to Twitter or Facebook. Finally, we exploit an *attention perspective* in our analyses, which brings a somewhat different view of the problem of misinformation dissemination.

3 ATTENTION CASCADES IN WHATSAPP

WhatsApp enables one-to-one communication through private chats as well as one-to-many and many-to-many communication through groups, allowing users to send textual and media (image, video, audio) messages. Compared to other online social networking applications (e.g., Facebook, Twitter), WhatsApp may be considered an unsophisticated platform as information is shared through a very loosely structured interface. Shared content is shown in temporal order, with each message accompanied by the posting time and, in case of groups, its origin (identification or telephone of the user who posted it). Yet, WhatsApp is a major communication platform in various countries of the world, offering an increasingly popular vehicle for information dissemination and social mobilization during important events [21].

One important feature of WhatsApp is *reply*, which allows a user to explicitly mention a message she intends to reply or refer to, bringing it forward in a conversation thread. This kind of interaction among users mentioning, replying or sharing each other's messages is common in other online social networks (e.g., reply and retweet in Twitter, share and post on Facebook). However, in WhatsApp this feature plays a key role in facilitating navigation through the sequence of messages, allowing one to keep track of different ongoing conversation threads. This is particularly important in the case of WhatsApp groups, where different subsets of the participating users may engage in different, possibly weakly related (or even unrelated) conversations simultaneously. Thus it becomes hard to keep track of each conversation thread, losing attention and ultimately diverting.

Our goal in this paper is to study the information dissemination process in WhatsApp groups, focusing mainly on how user attention, a key channel for such process, is characterized in such unstructured, yet increasingly popular environment. To that end, we use the concept of *cascades* [27] as a structural representation of how users' attention is dedicated to different conversation threads within a WhatsApp group. We emphasize that conversations in WhatsApp have the distinguishing characteristic of *not* being influenced or driven by any algorithm as in other social networks (e.g., newsfeed in the Facebook, content recommendation, etc.). They depend solely on the active participation of users of the group, as messages posted by others catch their attention.

More specifically, an *attention cascade* begins when a user makes an assertion about a topic in a message to the group. This message is the root of the cascade. Other users join and establish a conversation thread by explicitly replying to the root message or to other messages that replied to it. We say that the root or subsequent messages in the cascade *caught the attention* of a group member, motivating her to interact. Thus, we focus on messages that were explicitly linked by the *reply* feature[1]. We consider the specific use of the reply feature as a signal that the user's attention was caught by the message she is replying to and that the cascade is a (semi-)structured representation modeling emergent patterns of *collective* attention. As in any real conversation of a group of people, attention may drift to other (possibly weakly related) topics as the

---

[1]Users may not necessarily use the reply feature to respond to a previous message. However identifying such implicit links would require processing the content of the messages, which is outside the present scope.

conversation goes on. Note however that in an explicit reply, the message that is being replied to is shown to everyone, just before the reply itself, serving as a means to "re-gain" or keep (part of) the original attention that motivated the user to participate in the cascade. Thus, the root message triggers the initial attention of some users, and the conversation is kept alive among a subset of participating users (which may change over time) as they continue replying to successive messages.

We also note that, unlike prior uses of the cascade model to understand the propagation of a particular piece of content [13, 25], we here use it to represent the participation (thus attention) of multiple users in an explicitly defined conversation thread, despite other messages and conversations that might be simultaneously happening in the same group. Thus, we refer to such structural representation of how collective attention is dedicated to a particular conversation thread within a WhatsApp group as *attention cascade*.

4 METHODOLOGY

In this section, we describe our methodology to gather data and characterize attention cascades in WhatsApp groups. We analyze cascades concerning three dimensions, namely, structural and temporal properties as well as user participation. The first two capture the main patterns describing how collective attention is dedicated to a conversation thread and how it evolves. The latter captures how individuals participate in such process, interacting with each other via replies. Given the extensive use of WhatsApp for discussions related to politics and other social movements [21], we collected data from groups oriented towards political and non-political topics. We define the topic of a cascade as the topic of the group it belongs to, and we analyze political and non-political cascades separately. Similarly, we also analyze cascades with identified false information separately from the rest.

In the following, we start by describing our methodology to collect WhatsApp data (Section 4.1), and present how we identify and build cascades from such data (Section 4.2). We discuss our group and cascade labelling method (Section 4.3) and present the attributes used in our characterization (Section 4.4).

4.1 Data Collection

We collected a WhatsApp dataset consisting of all messages posted in 120 Brazilian WhatsApp groups from October 16th 2017 to November 6th 2018. Despite offering private chats by default, WhatsApp allows group administrators to share invites to join such groups on blogs, web pages, and other online platforms. Such feature effectively turns the access to the group and the content shared in it public since anyone who has the invite can choose to join the group, receiving all the messages posted after that.

We focus on groups whose access is publicly available. To find invites to such groups online, we leveraged the fact that all links shared by group administrators have the term chat.whatsapp.com as part of their URLs. Thus, we used Selenium scripts on Google Search website to search for web pages containing this term and located in Brazil (according to Google). We parsed all pages returned as a result of the search, extracting the URLs to WhatsApp groups.

The monitoring and data collection process of each group requires an actual device and valid SIM card to join the group. Thus

we were restricted to join a limited number of WhatsApp groups by the available memory in our devices. We randomly selected and joined 120 groups to monitor. These groups cover different topics which can be further categorized into political oriented subjects or not, as will be discussed in Section 4.3. We then used the same process described in [15] to collect data from those groups, preserving user anonymity and complying with WhatsApp privacy policies. Specifically, we extracted the WhatsApp messages from our monitoring devices (smartphones) using scripts provided by the authors[2], replacing each unique telephone number by a random unique ID. Throughout the paper, we refer to such a unique ID by the term *user*[3].

In total, our dataset consists of 1,751,054 messages posted by 30,760 users engaged in the 120 WhatsApp as mentioned earlier groups [4].

4.2 Attention Cascade Identification

Recall that an attention cascade is composed by a tree of messages, which are pairwise connected by the reply feature, posted by one or more users. We identify cascades on WhatsApp by taking the following approach. We model each group as a directed acyclic graph where each node is a message (text or media content) posted in the group and there is a direct edge from message A to message B if message B is a reply to message A[5]. Each connected component of such a graph, which by definition is a tree, is identified as a cascade. Note that we chose not to impose any time constraint on the cascade identification because we consider the use of a reply as strong evidence of the connection between messages. Thus, all cascade leaves are messages that did *not* receive any reply (in our dataset).

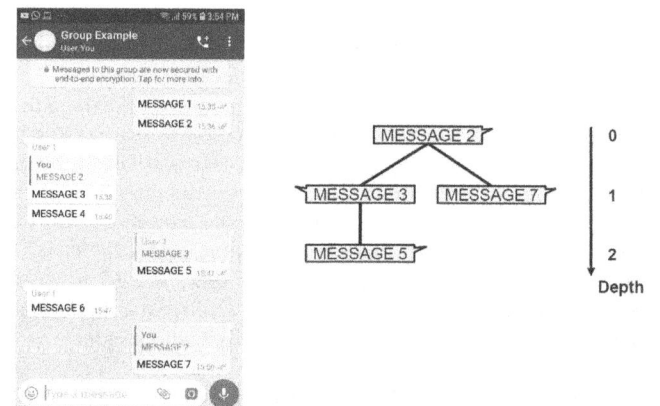

Figure 1: Example of a cascade on WhatsApp.

Figure 1 illustrates how we identify cascades from messages posted in a WhatsApp group. Figure 1 (left) shows a sequence of 7 messages. The cascade starts with "MESSAGE 2", the root, which was posted at time 15:35. At time 15:38, another user replied to that

---

[2]https://github.com/gvrkiran/whatsapp-public-groups
[3]We are not able to identify multiple telephone numbers belonging to the same person.
[4]Readers can contact the first author to request the anonymized dataset used in this work. We would be pleased to provide it.
[5]Thus, message B was necessarily posted after message A.

message by posting "MESSAGE 3", which was then followed by another reply, "MESSAGE 5". At time 15:50, user "You" replied the root message by posting "MESSAGE 7". Note that "MESSAGE 4" and "MESSAGE 6" posted during this time interval do not belong to the cascade as they are not explicit replies to any previous message in the cascade. Moreover, "MESSAGE 1" does not belong to the cascade either, since the message was posted before the root message. Moreover, since it did not receive any reply, it does not belong to *any* cascade. Finally, note that "MESSAGE 7" is a reply made by the same user who posted "MESSAGE 2", thus it is a self-reply. By such an example, it becomes clear that there might be multiple on-going cascades simultaneously in the same group.

4.3 Classifying Groups and Cascades

As mentioned, we analyze cascades of different topics, notably political and non-political topics, as well as cascades containing false information separately, aiming at identifying attributes that distinguish them. In this section, we discuss how we label each cascade according to such categorization.

WhatsApp groups are identified by names that reflect the general topic that the discussions in the group should cover. Examples of group names in our dataset (translated to English) are *Brazilian news*, *Friendship without borders* and *Right wing vs. Left wing*. Our data collection span several periods of significant social mobilization in Brazil. For instance, the 2018 Brazilian general election, during which WhatsApp was reportedly a significant vehicle of political debates[6]. Thus, we chose to classify groups into two categories: political oriented and non-political. To that end, we manually labeled the groups according to their names. For instance, group names that refer to specific candidates or political debates were labeled as political groups, whereas all others were labeled as non-political. Out of the three examples above, the first two illustrate non-political groups, whereas the last one (*Right wing vs. Left wing*) is clearly politically oriented. Our labeling effort identified 78 political and 42 non-political groups in our dataset.

We refer to an attention cascade in a political group as a *political cascade*. Similarly, cascades in non-political groups are labeled as *non-political*. Such definition is a simple cascade categorization since the specific topic(s) discussed in a cascade may diverge from the group's meant subject. Nevertheless, we argue that, in general, inheriting the group label is a reasonable approximation, and we leave for the future a more specific content-based cascade categorization.

Orthogonally, we also distinguish cascades containing reportedly false information (e.g., rumor) or, more generally speaking, *falsehood*, from the others. To that end, we relied on previously identified fake news reported by six Brazilian fact-checking websites (*Aos Fatos, Agência Lupa, Comprova, Boatos.org, Checagem Truco,* and *Fato ou Fake*) [7]. We first collected all news identified as fake by those six Brazilian fact-checking websites, totalling 3,072 fake news fact-checks. Next, we filtered fake news in text, that is,

we removed fact-checks that analyzed fake content only in media formats (audio, video or image). In total, we selected 862 fake news texts.

We then turned to the messages in our identified cascades, focusing on textual content and URLs shared. The latter often refers to news webpages. Thus, we extracted the texts from those URLs using the newspaper[8] Python library, which is specialized to retrieve the textual content of news portals and websites. We discarded all URLs for which the library was not able to recover the text (returned NULL).

In total, we identified 337,861 pieces of text on the cascades (327,530 textual messages and 10,331 texts from URLs). For the sake of readability, we refer to all of them as merely text messages.

In order to identify text messages with falsehood, we first processed all fake news and text messages by removing stopwords and performing lemmatization using the Natural Language Toolkit [2]. We then modeled each piece of content (fake news and text message) as a vector of size n, where n is the number of distinct lemmas identified in all text messages and fake news. Each position in the vector contains the weight of the corresponding lemma, defined as the term frequency (i.e., the number of times that the term appeared in the corresponding text).

We compared each text message against each fake news by computing the cosine similarity [18] between their vector representations. Specifically, given a text message (vector) m and fake news (vector) f, we computed their textual similarity as:

$$similarity(m, f) = \frac{m \cdot f}{\|m\| \, \|f\|} = \frac{\sum_{i=1}^{n} m_i f_i}{\sqrt{\sum_{i=1}^{n} m_i^2} \sqrt{\sum_{i=1}^{n} f_i^2}} \quad (1)$$

where m_i and f_i are the weights in text vectors m and f. The cosine similarity returns a value between 0 and 1. The closer the value to 1, the stronger the similarity between the vectors.

In order to reduce noise, we focused on text pairs with similarity above 0.5. We manually inspected each such text pair and identified a total of 677 out of 2271 messages whose textual content referred to fake news reported by Brazilian fact-checking websites. We label any cascade containing at least one of such messages as *cascade with falsehood*[9]. We refer to all other cascades as *unclassified*. Note that we cannot guarantee the absence of falsehood in the unclassified cascades as we only analyzed fake news in text format, and we are restricted by the available fake news in such format reported by fact-checking websites. Nevertheless, we assume that the most popular fake fake news disseminated as textual content were identified and listed by Brazilian fact-checking services.

In total, we identified 666 cascades with falsehood (49 non-political and 617 political cascades) and 149,528 unclassified ones (52,689 non-political and 96,839 political cascades).

---

[6]Another example was a national truck drivers strike which greatly affected the country with the shutdown of highways in most states which caused unavailability of food and medicine for two weeks in late May 2018.
[7]https://aosfatos.org/, https://piaui.folha.uol.com.br/lupa/, https://projetocomprova.com.br/,https://www.boatos.org/,https://apublica.org/checagem/,https://g1.globo.com/fato-ou-fake/

[8]https://pypi.org/project/newspaper/
[9]Although we do not impose restrictions on the depth of such message, we note that in the vast majority of the cases (93%), the root message of such cascades carried false information.

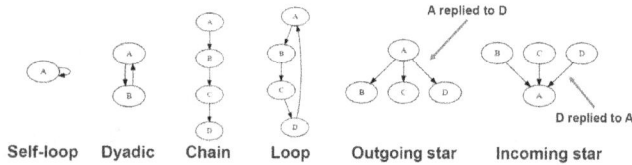

Figure 2: Six motifs considered for analysis. Each node is a user and an edge (i, j) represents that a user i replied a user j in a given cascade.

4.4 Cascade Attributes

We characterize attention cascades concerning several attributes which can be grouped into three main dimensions: structural properties, temporal properties, and user participation. The structural properties consist of the number of nodes, depth, maximum breadth, and structural virality. The number of nodes corresponds to the total number of messages in the cascade. The depth of a particular message m in a cascade is the number of edges from the root message to m (i.e., number of replies from m back to the root). The depth of a cascade is then defined as the maximum depth reached by a message in the cascade. The breadth of a cascade is defined according to a certain depth and corresponds to the number of messages in that particular depth of the cascade. Thus, the maximum breadth of a cascade is defined based on the breadth at all depth levels in the cascade. The structural virality of a cascade is defined as the average distance between all pairs of nodes [17]. The higher the structural virality value, the stronger the indication that, on average, the messages are distant of each other, thus suggesting viral diffusion of content in that cascade [17].

The main temporal attribute analyzed is the cascade duration, defined as the time interval between the last message belonging to the cascade and its root. We also characterize the temporal evolution of each cascade by analyzing its structural properties over time. When analyzing structural and temporal attributes that are in function of another attribute, we normalize their values in order to compare cascades with different values ranges. For example, when we analyze depth over time, we averaged (and measured standard error) at every depth considering the maximum depth of the cascade. Thus 50% depth means the depth at the middle of any cascade. Therefore, we can analyze the average number of minutes it took to reach a certain percentage depth in a cascade and compare with others.

Regarding the third dimension, user participation, we characterize each cascade in terms of the number of unique users participating in the cascade as well as the patterns of social communication established by them. For the latter, we first build a user-level representation of each cascade, that is, we build a directed graph whose vertices are users and an edge between vertice X and vertice Y is added if user X replied to user Y in the given cascade. We identify patterns of social communication occurring between users in such representation using motifs. To that end, we borrow from [29], where the authors proposed network motifs as a tool to analyze patterns of information propagation in social networks. The authors proposed four types of motifs (i.e., long chain, ping pong, loop, and star), we here extend the definition by analyzing six motifs, which

are shown in Figure 2. Specifically, we propose the self-loop motif and divide the star motif into two other motifs by differentiating it according to its edge orientation (incoming star and outgoing star). Moreover, we choose to rename long chain to chain and ping pong to dyadic.

We identify motifs in cascades testing if a cascade graph is isomorphic to a motif template. We define templates for the motifs in Figure 2 as follows. Self-loop and dyadic motifs are considered templates, as the total number of nodes is fixed (one and two, respectively). For the remaining motifs, we generate templates with the number of nodes ranging from 2 (chain) or 3 (loop, outgoing star, incoming star) up to n, where n is the maximum number of unique users in any cascade analyzed. To detect graph isomorphism, we used the implementation of the VF2 algorithm proposed by Cordella *et al.* [12] available in the *networkx* Python library. The VF2 algorithm identifies both graph and subgraph isomorphism. Our analysis considers the presence of a motif in a given cascade if the cascade is a graph (or subgraph) isomorphic to the corresponding template.

5 CASCADE CHARACTERIZATION

In order to understand the characteristics of the attention cascades as well as the hidden structures existing in the interaction between participants of a group, we adopt a three-dimension approach to characterize attention cascades. To that end, we look at the structural and temporal characteristics of the cascades and the different communication forms that participants of a cascade interact with each other. In the following, we present the analysis and discussion of the findings in each dimension.

5.1 Overall cascade analysis

In this section, we look at the number of cascades identified in our dataset of messages. To do so, and rather than viewing the set of all cascades, we segment the cascades into two classes, namely: political and non-political. For each class, we separate the cascades into two sub-classes: cascades with verified false information and unclassified cascades, that may have both true and false information, but it was not verified.

Figure 3 shows the total number of cascades in the dataset collected from WhatsApp groups during the period from October 2017 to November 2018. As it is evident from Figure 3, there are two peaks of cascades in political groups. These peaks shown in the leftmost graph are associated with key events of the electoral campaign in Brazil. One peak occurred when the presidential candidate, Jair Bolsonaro, was stabbed in the stomach during a campaign rally at the beginning of September. The other event was the day of the first round of voting, at the beginning of October. It is worth noting that the peak of the number of political cascades with false information is also associated with the date of the first round of voting, that was widely publicized by the media [3]. The non-political cascades with falsehood remained stable during the election period, as exhibited in the rightmost graph of Figure 3. In the leftmost graph, the peak for non-political cascades occurred by the end of May, coinciding with the truckers' strike that halted Brazil, with protesters blocking traffic on hundreds of highways [20]. These two

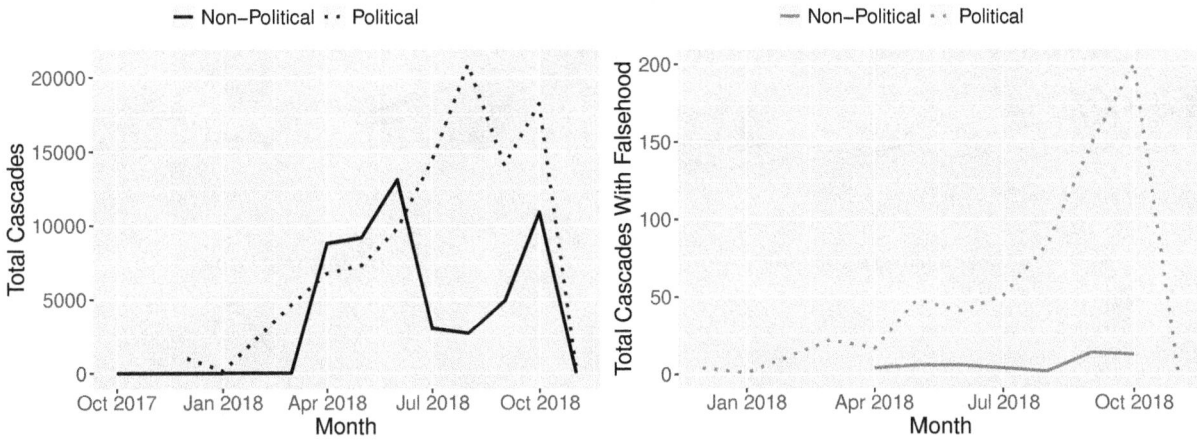

Figure 3: Total cascades over time.

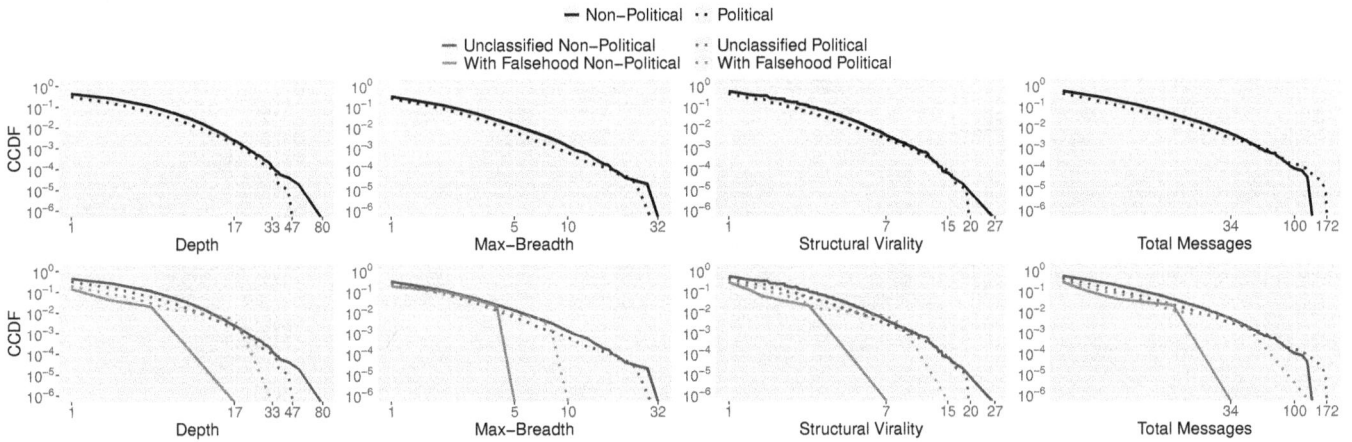

Figure 4: Depth, maximum breadth, structural virality, and total messages.

graphs clearly show that attention cascades in WhatsApp groups reflect real-world events that capture the public attention.

We also analyzed temporal relationships among different cascades of each group [1]. We found that in 99.2% of the cases there is no temporal overlap (i.e., one cascade finishes before others start). Therefore, our dataset shows that most of the time only one thread of discussion dominates the attention of the group.

5.2 Structural Characteristics

In this section, we focus on the structural characteristics of the cascades, that are defined in section 4.4. Figure 4 shows the CCDF of the empirical distribution of the main structural characteristics of the two classes of cascades, political and non-political and the sub-classes, represented by cascades with false information and unclassified cascades. The upper row shows the comparison between political (dotted) and non-political (regular) groups. The lower row shows the comparison between 'unclassified' (blue) and 'with false-hood' (red), besides the previous segmentation between political and non-political, totaling four lines of distribution.

A natural question concerning the structure of attention cascades in different WhatsApp groups is whether they exhibit a similar structural profile. When analyzing the cascades on political and non-political groups (upper row) in Figure 4, we observe that the graphs show similar curves for both classes, with small differences in the probability of the maximum values for the two classes. We observe that non-political cascades are deeper and broader than political cascades. Moreover, despite the structural virality of political and non-political cascades are very similar, when we look at the graph that shows the structural virality of the sub-classes of cascades (lower row), we note that the virality of cascades with false information in political groups is more significant than the virality in a non-political group. Recall that higher virality suggests viral diffusion, which maybe interpreted as a sign that false information in political groups spread farther than in non-political groups. Finally, the total number of messages attribute calls our attention since the number of messages in political discussions exceeds the number in non-political discussions, indicating that political subjects stimulate more interaction among participants.

— Non–Political ·· Political

■ Unclassified Non–Political ■ Unclassified Political ▨ With Falsehood Non–Political ▨ With Falsehood Political

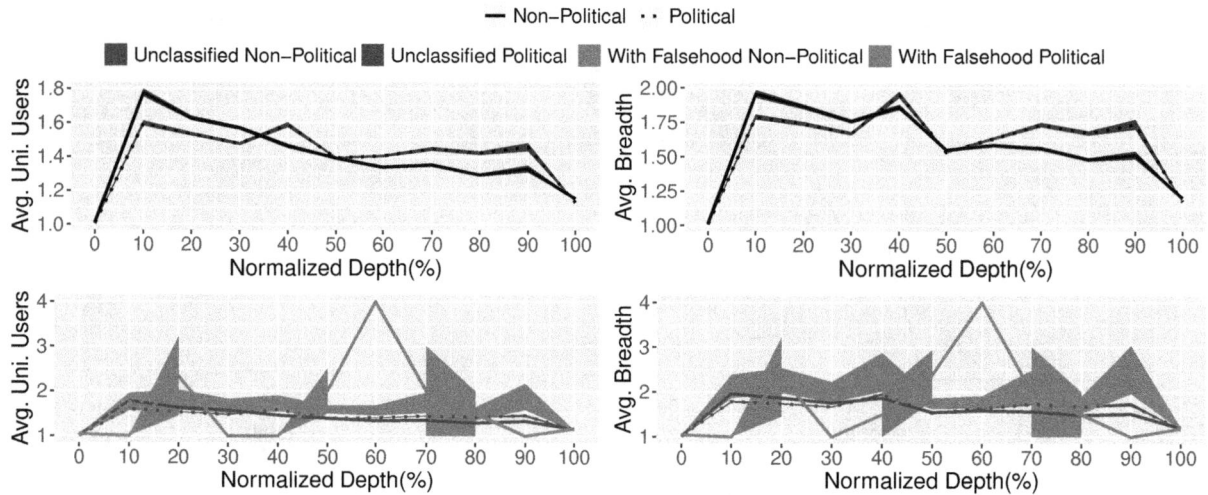

Figure 5: Breadth vs. depth and unique users vs. depth of cascades from political and non-political WhatsApp groups.

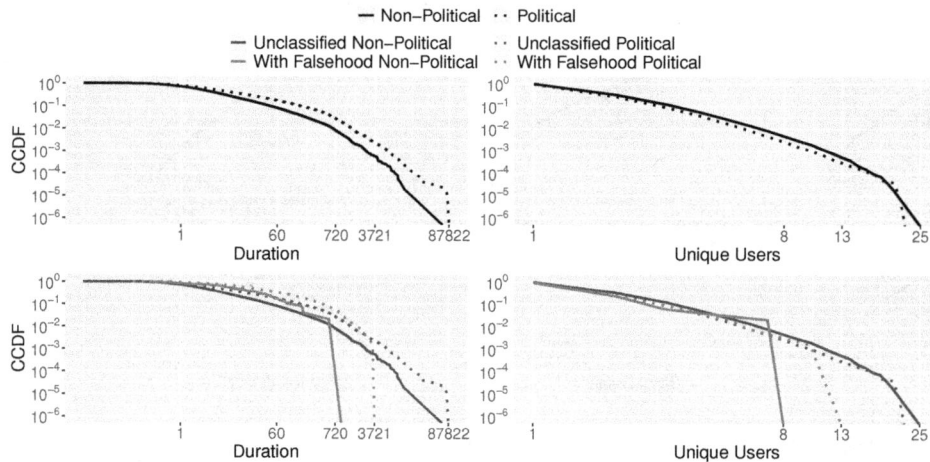

Figure 6: Cascade duration and unique users.

Now we analyze the cascade attributes as a function of depth. We observe in Figure 5 that cascades of political groups have on average more users than cascades of non-political groups after 35% of the maximum depth. The cascades in political groups are on average wider than non-political ones after the half of the maximum depth, indicating that cascades of political groups finish with more parallel interactions (branches) than the non-political ones. Regarding misinformation comparison, we note that cascades with falsehood in political groups reach on average more users than the other types of cascades for higher depth. Note that cascades with falsehood of non-political groups have an unstable behavior. The cascades with falsehood of political groups reach on average more people at every depth as the cascades were deepened.

5.3 Temporal Characteristics

We now turn our focus to the length of time of the attention cascades. The first column of Figure 6 displays the CCDF of the cascade duration. The top graph of the this column shows that political cascades last longer than non-political ones. A possible explanation is that political cascades stir more debate among the participants of the group. The graph at the bottom of the first column of Figure 6 shows the CCDF of the duration of unclassified cascades and cascades with false information. As we can see from the graph, in both types of groups, political and non-political, the presence of false information reduces the duration of the cascades. We conjecture that when false information or fake news is identified in the cascade, the participants of the group start losing interest in the discussion and terminate the cascade.

Regarding temporal cascade attributes as a function of depth and unique users, we observe on the topmost left graph of Figure 7 that

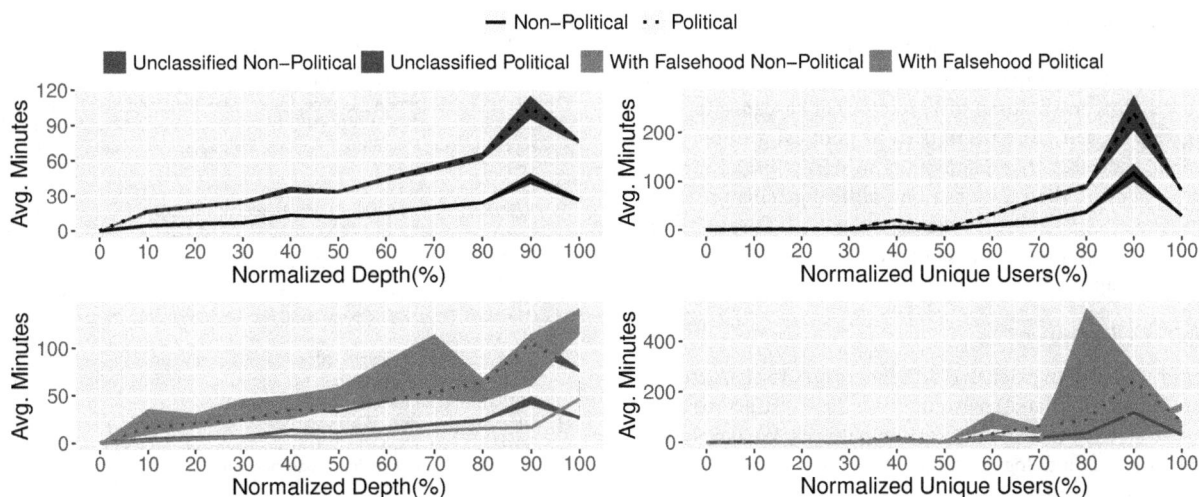

Figure 7: Depth over time and unique users over time of cascades from political and non-political WhatsApp groups.

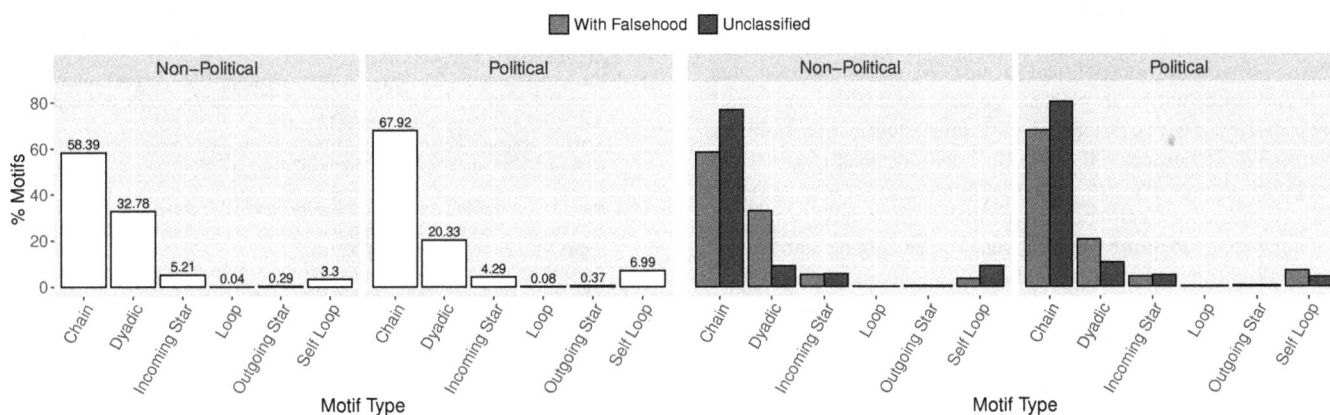

Figure 8: User motifs.

cascades in political groups take two times longer than cascades in non-political groups to reach their maximum depth. The topmost right graph indicates that cascades in political groups take considerable more time to reach 90% of unique users than non-political groups. Moreover, both graphs are that attention allocation in a WhatsApp group clearly depends on the nature of the content that starts the cascade. One possible explanation is that political discussions spur hot debates that last longer. In the lower part of Figure 7, we also note that political cascades with falsehood take longer to reach the maximum depth. However, non-political cascades with falsehood take less time to reach the maximum depth. Although we have not explored the content in messages, we conjecture that political fake news has a significant impact on group discussion and generate more debate than non-political fake news, as shown in the leftmost graph of Figure 7.

5.4 User Participation in Cascades

In this section, we focus on the following question: how participants of a cascade interact with the other participants? We analyze the relative frequency of the six motifs that represent the most common patterns of social communication among participants of the cascades. Figure 8 shows that the most common pattern of communication among participants of a cascade is *chain*, for both political and non-political groups. *Chain* is the most popular motif in the two classes of groups. The percentage of *chain* is more than half of the total motifs identified in the cascades. It is interesting to observe that the fraction of *self-loops* in political groups is two times greater than the percentage of *self-loops* in non-political groups. Regarding misinformation analysis, the rightmost graph of Figure 8 displays that cascades with falsehood of political groups have a higher percentage of chain and self-loops than corresponding non-political cascades. One possible explanation for the higher percentage of self-loops is that in political discussions a participant might want to emphasize or defend her position or idea and makes explicit reference to her previous message in the cascade.

Regarding the total number of users participating in cascades, we note on the second column of Figure 6 that cascades in non-political groups reach more users than in political groups. This characteristic indicates that discussions in non-political groups draw more attention than the ones on political groups probably because of their content. Moreover, cascades with falsehood on political groups reach more users than cascades with falsehood on non-political groups.

6 CONCLUSION

In this paper we used an extensive set of messages to characterize attention cascades in WhatsApp groups from three distinct perspectives: structural, temporal and interaction patterns. We developed a data collection methodology and model each group as a directed acyclic graph, where each connected component is identified as a cascade. In addition to providing a new way of looking at information dissemination in small groups through the concept of attention, our study has unveiled several interesting findings, regarding political groups and misinformation. These findings include differences in the structural and temporal characteristics of political groups when compared to non-political groups. We show that cascades with false information in political groups are deeper, wider and reach more users than cascades with falsehood in non-political groups. We demonstrate that political cascades last longer than non-political ones. We also show that attention cascades in WhatsApp groups reflect real-world events that capture public attention.

Our current and future work is focused on leveraging many of the findings and conclusions presented in this paper along with several dimensions. First, we are looking into using information about content to understand their impact on the structure and temporal characteristics of attention cascades. Questions we want to answer in the future include the following: What kind of content would extend the duration of attention cascades? What is an adequate metric for quantifying attention in a group chat? What is the impact of hate content on the characteristics of attention cascades? Finally, we want to construct tools to generate synthetic attention cascades to model different types of group chats.

7 ACKNOWLEDGEMENTS

This work was partially supported by CNPq, CAPES, FAPEMIG and the projects InWeb, MASWEB and INCT-Cyber.

REFERENCES

[1] James F. Allen. 1983. Maintaining Knowledge About Temporal Intervals. *Commun. ACM* 26, 11 (Nov. 1983), 832–843. https://doi.org/10.1145/182.358434
[2] Steven Bird, Edward Loper, and Ewan Klein. 2009. *Natural language processing with Python.* O'Reilly Media Inc., New York, US.
[3] Anthony Boadle. 2018. Facebook's WhatsApp flooded with fake news in Brazil election. https://reut.rs/2OLpbZu Accessed on February 18, 2019.
[4] Dan Bouhnik and Mor Deshen. 2014. WhatsApp Goes to School: Mobile Instant Messaging between Teachers and Students. *Journal of Information Technology Education: Research* 13 (2014), 217–231.
[5] Levent Cetinkaya. 2017. The Impact of Whatsapp Use on Success in Education Process. *The International Review of Research in Open and Distributed Learning* 18, 7 (November 2017), 8.
[6] Justin Cheng, Lada Adamic, P. Alex Dow, Jon Michael Kleinberg, and Jure Leskovec. 2014. Can Cascades Be Predicted?. In *Proceedings of the 23rd International Conference on World Wide Web (WWW '14)*. ACM, New York, NY, USA, 925–936. https://doi.org/10.1145/2566486.2567997
[7] Justin Cheng, Lada A. Adamic, Jon M. Kleinberg, and Jure Leskovec. 2016. Do Cascades Recur?. In *WWW (WWW '16)*. International World Wide Web Conferences Steering Committee, Geneva, Switzerland, 671–681. https://doi.org/10.1145/2872427.2882993
[8] Justin Cheng, Jon M. Kleinberg, Jure Leskovec, David Liben-Nowell, Bogdan State, Karthik Subbian, and Lada A. Adamic. 2018. Do Diffusion Protocols Govern Cascade Growth?. In *ICWSM 2018, Stanford, California, USA, June 25-28, 2018.* AAAI, Palo Alto, California, U.S., 32–41.
[9] Karen Church and Rodrigo de Oliveira. 2013. What's Up with Whatsapp?: Comparing Mobile Instant Messaging Behaviors with Traditional SMS. In *MobileHCI (MobileHCI '13)*. ACM, New York, NY, USA, 352–361. https://doi.org/10.1145/2493190.2493225
[10] Giovanni Luca Ciampaglia, Alessandro Flammini, and Filippo Menczer. 2015. The production of information in the attention economy. *Scientific Reports* 5, 9452 (2015), 1. https://doi.org/10.1038/srep09452
[11] John Constine. 2018. WhatsApp hits 1.5 billion monthly users. $19B? Not so bad. Retrieved from https://tcrn.ch/2LdlavD. Accessed on February 18, 2019.
[12] L. P. Cordella, P. Foggia, C. Sansone, and M. Vento. 2004. A (sub)graph isomorphism algorithm for matching large graphs. *IEEE Transactions on Pattern Analysis and Machine Intelligence* 26, 10 (Oct 2004), 1367–1372. https://doi.org/10.1109/TPAMI.2004.75
[13] P. Alex Dow, Lada A. Adamic, and Adrien Friggeri. 2013. The Anatomy of Large Facebook Cascades. In *ICWSM*. AAAI, Palo Alto, California, U.S., 8.
[14] Adrien Friggeri, Lada A. Adamic, Dean Eckles, and Justin Cheng. 2014. Rumor Cascades. In *Proceedings of the Eighth International Conference on Weblogs and Social Media, ICWSM 2014, Ann Arbor, Michigan, USA, June 1-4, 2014.* AAAI, Palo Alto, California, U.S., 8.
[15] Kiran Garimella and Gareth Tyson. 2018. WhatApp Doc? A First Look at WhatsApp Public Group Data. In *International AAAI Conference on Web and Social Media.* AAAI, Palo Alto, California, U.S., 1–8.
[16] Jeffrey Gettleman and Hari Kumar. 2018. A Minister Fetes a Convicted Lynch Mob, and Many Indians Recoil. https://nyti.ms/2Obz66O Accessed on February 18, 2019.
[17] Sharad Goel, Ashton Anderson, Jake Hofman, and Duncan J. Watts. 2016. The Structural Virality of Online Diffusion. *Management Science* 62, 1 (2016), 180–196. https://doi.org/10.1287/mnsc.2015.2158
[18] Anna Huang. 2008. Similarity Measures for Text Document Clustering.
[19] Mike Isaac. 2018. Facebook Overhauls News Feed to Focus on What Friends and Family Share. https://nyti.ms/2qXYhSv Accessed on February 18, 2019.
[20] Marina Lopes. 2018. In Brazil, a truckers' strike brings Latin America's largest economy to a halt. https://goo.gl/obWnNK Accessed on February 18, 2019.
[21] Marina Lopes. 2018. WhatsApp is upending the role of unions in Brazil. Next, it may transform politics. Retrieved from The Washington Post (https://goo.gl/WY6nxZ). Accessed on February 18, 2019.
[22] Andrés Moreno, Philip Garrison, and Karthik Bhat. 2017. WhatsApp for Monitoring and Response during Critical Events: Aggie in the Ghana 2016 Election. In *14th Int'l Conf. on Information Systems for Crisis Response and Management.* Collections at UNU, Albi, Ghana.
[23] Avi Rosenfeld, Sigal Sina, David Sarne, Or Avidov, and Sarit Kraus. 2018. WhatsApp usage patterns and prediction of demographic characteristics without access to message content. *Demographic Research* 39, 22 (2018), 647–670. https://doi.org/10.4054/DemRes.2018.39.22
[24] Paul Rösler, Christian Mainka, and Jörg Schwenk. 2017. More is Less: How Group Chats Weaken the Security of Instant Messengers Signal, WhatsApp, and Threema. *Cryptology ePrint Archive* 1, 1 (2017), 1–8.
[25] Rahmtin Rotabi, Krishna Kamath, Jon Kleinberg, and Aneesh Sharma. 2017. Cascades: A View from Audience. In *WWW (WWW '17)*. International World Wide Web Conferences Steering Committee, Republic and Canton of Geneva, Switzerland, 587–596. https://doi.org/10.1145/3038912.3052647
[26] Herbert A. Simon. 1971. Designing organizations for an information rich world. In *Computers, communications, and the public interest*, Martin Greenberger (Ed.). The Johns Hopkins University Press, Baltimore, 37–72.
[27] Soroush Vosoughi, Deb Roy, and Sinan Aral. 2018. The spread of true and false news online. *Science* 359, 6380 (2018), 1146–1151. https://doi.org/10.1126/science.aap9559
[28] Fang Wu and Bernardo A. Huberman. 2007. Novelty and collective attention. *Proceedings of the National Academy of Sciences* 104, 45 (2007), 17599–17601. https://doi.org/10.1073/pnas.0704916104
[29] Qiankun Zhao, Yuan Tian, Qi He, Nuria Oliver, Ruoming Jin, and Wang-Chien Lee. 2010. Communication Motifs: A Tool to Characterize Social Communications. In *Proceedings of the 19th ACM International Conference on Information and Knowledge Management (CIKM '10)*. ACM, New York, NY, USA, 1645–1648. https://doi.org/10.1145/1871437.1871694

Minority Report: Cyberbullying Prediction on Instagram

Charalampos Chelmis
cchelmis@albany.edu
Department of Computer Science
University at Albany, State University of New York
Albany, New York, United States

Mengfan Yao
myao@albany.edu
Department of Computer Science
University at Albany, State University of New York
Albany, New York, United States

ABSTRACT

Introduction. Cyberbullying, as a form of abusive online behavior, although not well–defined, is a repetitive process, i.e., a sequence of harassing messages sent from a bully to a victim over a period of time with the intent to harm the victim. Numerous automated, data–driven approaches have been developed for the automatic classification of cyberbullying instances, with emphasis on classification accuracy. While the importance of highly accurate classifiers is undoubted, a key pitfall of existing cyberbullying detection methods is that (i) they disregard the repetitive nature of the harassing process, and (ii) they work retrospectively (i.e., after a cyberbullying incident has occurred), making it difficult to intervene before an interaction escalates. Motivated by the scarcity of methods to anticipate cyberbullying, we focus on cyberbullying prediction with the goal of reducing the time from detection to intervention.

Methods. We formulate the prediction of the number of harassing comments a media session will receive over a period of time as a regularized multi–task regression problem. In our formulation, we consider two settings where (i) the progression of cyberbullying behavior from some time point in the near future to subsequent time points further into the future is modeled given limited knowledge of the recent past, and (ii) increasingly more historical data is accumulated to improve prediction accuracy. To validate our approach, we conduct an extensive experimental evaluation on a real–world dataset from Instagram, the online social media platform with the highest percentage of users reporting experiencing cyberbullying.

Results. Intuitively, the larger the number of observed comments in the recent past of a media session, the better the predictive power of our approach. The downside to using more historical data is that decisions must be postponed until more comments are collected. Therefore, the trade–off between accuracy and decision speed is examined. In general, our approach outperforms competing approaches by up to 31.4% and 46.2% in Recall and Mathew correlation coefficient respectively.

Discussion. Our approach can be used to effectively prioritize media sessions for increased monitoring as time goes by or for immediate intervention before a conversation escalates. In future work, we plan to incorporate additional features and investigate the generalizability of our approach on other key social networking

venues where users frequently become victims of cyberbullying. Beyond cyberbullying prediction, our work is, to the best of our knowledge, the first to provide insights on the forecasting performance of multi–task regression as a function of the prediction horizon and the length of available historical data. We thus believe that our work can serve as a reference point on the forecasting performance of multi–task regression both for researchers and practitioners.

CCS CONCEPTS

• **Information systems** → *World Wide Web*; *Social networks*; • **Computing methodologies** → *Machine learning*.

KEYWORDS

Web and society; cyberharassment; cybersafety; online well–being

ACM Reference Format:
Charalampos Chelmis and Mengfan Yao. 2019. Minority Report: Cyberbullying Prediction on Instagram. In *11th ACM Conference on Web Science (WebSci '19), June 30–July 3, 2019, Boston, MA, USA*. ACM, New York, NY, USA, 9 pages. https://doi.org/10.1145/3292522.3326024

1 INTRODUCTION

A growing number of online users abuse the Internet to harass other users, leading to a tide of cyberbullying incidents [12, 18]. Bullying, once limited to physical spaces (e.g., schools, workplaces or sports fields) and particular times of the day (e.g., school hours), can now occur anytime, anywhere [24, 37]. Cyberbullying, a type of cyberharassment, can take many forms, typically however, refers to repetitive hostile behavior using digital media (e.g., hurtful comments, videos and images) in an effort to intentionally and repeatedly harass or harm individuals [24]. Cyberbullying is permanent (i.e., content remains accessible online unless removed) and potentially widespread (i.e., online social media provide a wide audience, and quick spread of online posts).

The potentially devastating real–world consequences to victims, which include but are not limited to psychological suffering and isolation, escalated physical confrontations, and suicide [18, 20], have led to the development of numerous methods for the automatic classification of cyberbullying instances [1, 35, 36] in a variety of online social networks and with a plethora of constraints [5, 8, 32, 33, 43, 44]. While highly accurate classifiers are of paramount importance to greatly reduce the burden on human moderators employed by online social media platforms, a key pitfall of existing cyberbullying detection methods is that they work retrospectively (i.e., after a cyberbullying incident has occurred), making it difficult to intervene before an interaction escalates. In contrast, approaches for cyberbullying prediction would be advantageous in

(i) identifying in advance vulnerable users that may fall victims of cyberbullying (i.e., before toxic comments, from which text–based features can be extracted, appear), using only limited data such as the image and caption provided by the creator of the media, and (ii) scaling detection methods to the staggering rates at which content is generated (e.g., 95 million photos and videos are shared on Instagram per day[1]) in online social media by targeting available computational resources on the subset of media sessions projected to experience cyberbullying, rather than blindly classifying all media sessions indiscriminately.

Present Work. Motivated by the scarcity of methods to anticipate cyberbullying [22, 26], and the fact that most existing approaches disregard the repetitive nature of the harassing process [44], we focus on cyberbullying prediction on Instagram, the online social media platform with the highest percentage of users reporting experiencing cyberbullying [18]. Instagram has more than 800 million registered users as of Sep. 2017, and over 40 billion uploaded photos as of Oct. 2015.

Instead of trying to detect all possible harassment, aggressive, antisocial, inflammatory, or toxic content in online social media, we focus on *harassing comments*, that are common to a number of types of unwanted behavior, including cyberharassment and cyberbullying. More importantly, we are interested in exploiting the *temporal dynamics* of the *repetitive* bullying behavior over time directly in our modeling. To this end, we formulate cyberbullying prediction as regularized multi–task regression [2, 4, 13], where the progression of the number of hateful comments Instagram content will receive over time is estimated from limited historical data. Our experimental results show that our proposed approach consistently outperforms competing methods. We also perform sensitivity analysis to examine the impact of the parameters on the performance of the proposed approach.

Our main contributions can be summarized as follows:

- **Novel Formulation:** We propose a novel formulation of cyberbullying prediction on Instagram as a regularized multi–task regression problem. In order to support different intervention strategies, as well as to assess the difficulty of variants of this problem, we consider two settings as follows. In our first formulation, we estimate the progression of harassment from some time point in the near future to subsequent time points further into the future based on limited knowledge of the recent past. In our second formulation, increasingly more historical data is accumulated to improve prediction accuracy. A model learned from the first formulation would result in projections at multiple times in the future, therefore providing a potential timeline for escalating discourses, whereas, the second formulation attempts to improve overall prediction accuracy by leveraging common knowledge shared across the forecasting tasks.
- **Experimental Evaluation:** We evaluate the forecasting accuracy of our approach as a function of the prediction horizon and the length of historical data on a real–world dataset of 10K Instagram comments. To ensure the **reproducibility**

of our work, we make the source code of our approach available at https://github.com/IDIASLab/CyberBullyingPrediction.
- **Broader Applicability:** Intuitively, the predictive power of forecasting models improves with the accumulation of historical data and deteriorates further into the future predictions. To the best of our knowledge, this is the first work to examine the forecasting performance of multi–task regression as a function of the prediction horizon and the length of available historical data.

Outline. The rest of this paper is organized as follows. We first review prior and related work in Section 2. We formulate the problem of cyberbullying prediction in online social networks in Section 3. We describe our evaluation methodology and results on a real–world dataset in Section 4. We conclude with a discussion of our results, limitations, and possible future directions in Section 5.

2   RELATED WORK

Cyberbullying Detection. We argue that it is imperative to predict the potential of a media session to receive harassing comments in the future so as to facilitate timely interventions. However, with the exception of few recent attempts at cyberbullying prediction [22, 26], the majority of prior work, an overview of which can be found at [1, 35, 36], focuses on cyberbullying detection. Nevertheless, with the exception of [44], no prior work has studied cyberbullying as a repetitive process. Out of the two recent methods for cyberbullying prediction, [22] examined prediction feasibility given only the initial image–content and text caption of an Instagram post, whereas [26] focused on predicting harassment escalation in comments following the first hostile comment in a discussion. In contrast to these methods, the approach presented in this work can make predictions at any given time.

Cyberbullying Indicators. Despite the scarce research work on cyberbullying prediction, features that may be useful for predicting cyberbullying instances have been explored in the context of cyberbullying detection. Specifically, text has been a major factor in detecting cyberbullying in online social media. However, features ranging from gender information, user context, linguistic and non–verbal features, and graph properties have also been used [5, 6, 9, 46]. The use of profanity and hate speech has been well correlated with toxic comments on the Web [10, 11, 16, 17]. However, what may constitute hate speech and profanity is context dependent (i.e., relative to time and location) [3]. The sociological literature review in [26] motivated some of the features used in this work.

Hostility & Harassment Detection. The related problem of detecting harassing and hostile behavior on the Web has been very well studied [5, 7, 10, 16, 21, 23, 25, 28, 29, 34, 38, 42], with the majority of this body of work having primarily focused on text–based features, excluding critical information in the various modalities (e.g., image, video, user profile, time, and location) typically associated with content shared on online social media [8]. Similarly to state–of–the–art for cyberbulying detection, to the best of our knowledge, all existing approaches for detecting hostile content on the Web ignore the fact that as a process that unfolds with time, cyberbullying is repetitive in nature [44].

---

[1]33 Mind–Boggling Instagram Stats & Facts for 2018: https://www.wordstream.com/blog/ws/2017/04/20/instagram-statistics

Multi–Task Learning. Multi–task learning utilizes commonalities among multiple related prediction problems to improve performance [2, 4, 13]. The key challenges in multi–task learning are to define and exploit such relatedness [13], while maintaining a small number of predictive features shared across all learned models [2]. Multi–task learning approaches have been applied in many domains, however, to the best of our knowledge, ours is the first work that applies multi–task learning for harassment intensity prediction. More importantly, no prior work has examined the forecasting power of the multi–task learning framework as a function of the prediction horizon and the length of historical data.

3 PROBLEM FORMULATION

Consider a large set $\mathcal{M}$ of N media sessions, where each media session $s \in \mathcal{M}$ belongs to user $u \in \mathcal{U}$, has an associated media object (i.e., image or video) along with its corresponding caption and hashtags, and a set of comments $\{(c_1, t_1), \ldots, (c_{N_s}, t_{N_s})\}$ from users in $\mathcal{U}$, where $c_i, i \leq N_s$ indicates the i–th comment with corresponding timestamp t_i, and N_s denotes the number of comments in s. For training and testing purposes, we additionally consider $\forall s \in \mathcal{M}$ set $\{y_1, \ldots, y_{N_s}\}$, where y_i denotes the cumulative number of harassing comments session s has received up to time t_i.

Our goal is to predict **harassment intensity** (i.e., the future number of harassing comments) at t time points in the future, for any given media session. Specifically, given time point γ, we wish to estimate harassment intensity up to timestamp $\gamma + h$, where h is the prediction horizon. In this context, *short–* and *long–term* prediction refer to the scenarios where $h = 1$ (e.g., the next time point) and $h > 1$, respectively.

From an intervention perspective, a greater prediction horizon provides more flexibility in taking preventative measures as the time between the final comment observed by the system and the time of escalation increases. However, the ability to accurately forecast the number of harassing comments up to some time in the future may depend on (i) the number of past comments on a media session (i.e., *length of historical data*), and (ii) how far ahead in the future a prediction is to be made (i.e., *prediction horizon*). Intuitively, long–term prediction is harder than short–term prediction, as many factors can potentially affect human behavior online [30].

Figure 1 shows the evolution of harassment intensity over time for a random sample of media sessions in our dataset (Section 4.3). As expected, not all media sessions experience the same level of harassment. More importantly, harassing behavior tends not to be evenly spread out in time. Both (i) bursts of harassing comments, which may be indicative of abusive behavior in which several people gang up on a victim [39], and (ii) incremental changes, which may reflect repetitive harassing comments from a single individual, can be observed.

To capture such dynamics, we formulate the problem of harassment intensity prediction as a **regression problem**. Specifically, in order to predict at time γ the harassment intensity, $y_s^{\gamma+h}$, of media session s at future time $\gamma + h$, we extract training features x_s^{γ} from the past *lag* comments (i.e., at times $\gamma - 1, \gamma - 2, \ldots, \gamma - lag$). For each media session, we construct a training input x_s^{γ} and output $y_s^{\gamma+h}$, and we wish to learn a function $y_s^{\gamma+h} = f(x_s^{\gamma}, h)$ for multiple

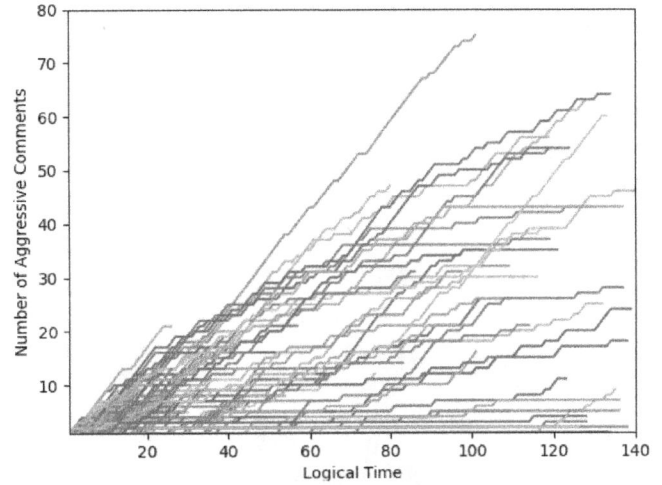

Figure 1: Temporal dynamics of harassment intensity in a random sample of Instagram media sessions in our dataset. Each curve corresponds to a media session, and shows the cumulative number of harassing comments the session attracts over time. The x–axis represents logical time, which increases for each media session when a new harassing comment arrives.

combinations of γ and h. By considering the prediction of harassment intensity at a single time point as a regression task, a simple approach to learn $f(x_s^{\gamma}, h)$ is to train one model for each combination of γ and h independently. However, different time points in the future may be represented as distinct tasks, or alternatively, tasks can be defined by the length of historical data used for prediction. Additionally, jointly training multiple regression problems for different combinations of γ and h may be advantageous due to the intrinsic temporal smoothness relationship among the regression problems (e.g., the difference in the number of harassing comments between two consecutive time points should in general be small).

The above reasoning motivates us to formulate harassment intensity prediction as a multi–task regression problem [2, 4, 13]. Specifically, we consider two formulations, namely:

- Fixed–Lag Varying–Horizon Prediction Model (*FLVH*), and
- Varying–Lag Fixed–Horizon Prediction Model (*VLFH*),

which are detailed in Sections 3.1 and 3.2 respectively. *FLVH* attempts to model the progression of cyberbullying behavior from some time point in the near future to subsequent time points further into the future, given a limited knowledge of the recent past (this knowledge of the recent past is common among tasks). Conversely, *VLFH* focuses on improving the prediction of harassment intensity at a given point in time (common to all tasks) by accumulating increasingly more historical data. Figure 2 provides a visual illustration of our proposed formulations.

3.1 Fixed–Lag Varying–Horizon Prediction Model

Consider a multi–task regression problem of t time points with n training samples of d features each. Let $X_i = \{X_{i,1}, ..., X_{i,n}\}, 1 \leq$

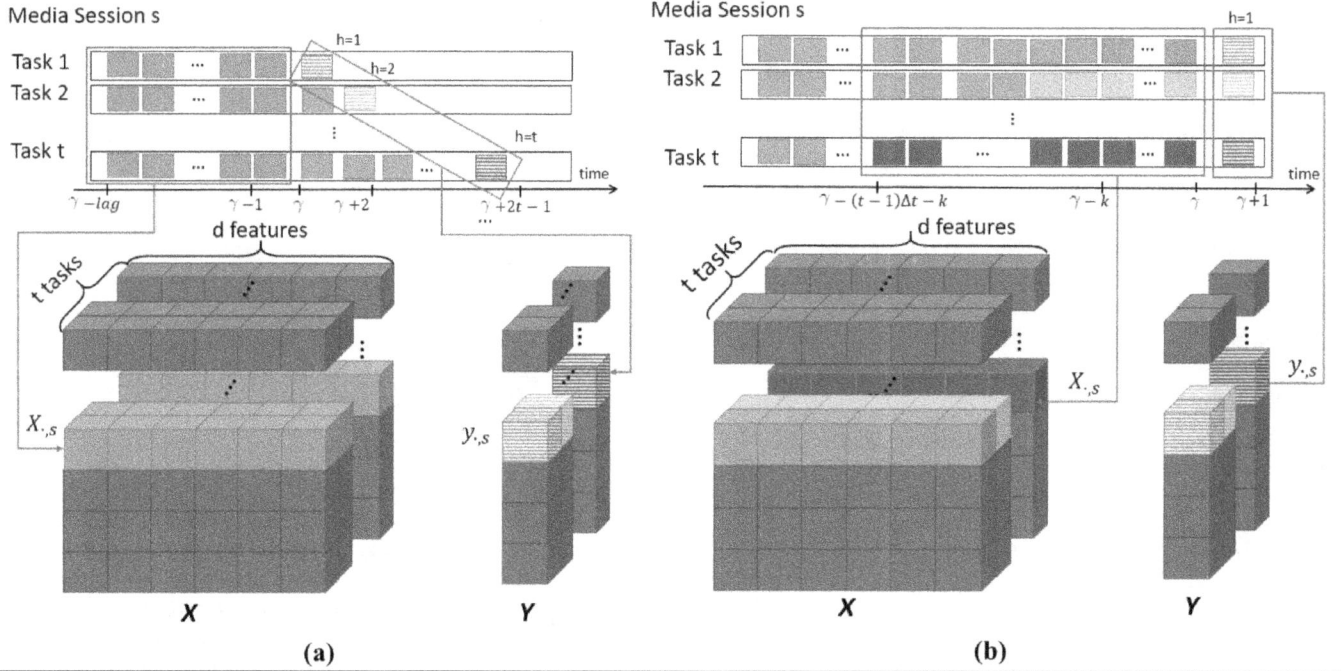

Figure 2: Illustration (better seen in color) of the proposed formulations for cyberbullying prediction on Instagram. (a) Fixed–Lag Varying–Horizon prediction model (Section 3.1). (b) Varying–Lag Fixed–Horizon prediction model (Section 3.2)

$i \leq t$ be the input data, and $Y_i = \{y_{i,1}, .., y_{i,n}\}$ be the targets, where $X_{i,s}$ is a vector of length d, each element of which is a feature extracted from the set of observed comments for task i, and $y_{i,s}$ is the predicted number of aggressive comments that media session s will receive up to future time $h_i = i\tau$. Parameter $\tau \in \mathbb{Z}^+$ is used to introduce prediction gaps (i.e., make the time points for which prediction is to be made non consecutive). The goal is to learn t models $f^i(X_i) = X_i^T W_i$, with weight matrix $\mathbf{W} = \{W_i | i = 1, ..., t\}$, where a linear model W_i is to be estimated for $\forall i$ so as to predict a harassment intensity score Y_i for each media session up to future time h_i, given X_i. Therefore, our objective is to estimate matrix $\mathbf{W}$. Figure 2(a) illustrates this formulation.

The rationale behind this formulation is that in practical applications, it can be used to predict the progression of harassment in a media session over time, from the near future (e.g., $h = 1$), to a time $h = t\tau$ further into the future, where t or τ can be arbitrarily large, given only limited knowledge (i.e., k comments) from the recent past. Note that long–term prediction is generally harder than short–term prediction considering the many factors that can potentially affect the discourse of social interactions in online social networks [30]. Typically two broad categories of methods exist for long–term prediction [41]: (i) training a model for each prediction horizon, and (ii) iteratively use previously predicted values as input to the next prediction task. We chose the first category when formulating *FLVH* to avoid the error accumulation problem of iterative methods [41].

3.2 Varying–Lag Fixed–Horizon Prediction Model

Similarly to our *FLVH* model, our goal in this formulation is to learn t models $\mathbf{W} = \{W_i | i = 1, ..., t\}$ to predict the number of aggressive comments a media session will receive by a future time h. However, unlike *FLVH* in which the number of observed comments across the t tasks is fixed, here, we vary the length of the historical data used in each task by considering varying lags, $lag_i = (i - 1) \cdot \Delta t + k$, so as to incorporate progressively more historical data into the predictive model. Variable $k \geq 1$ controls the minimum number of comments considered. In other words, *VLFH* is designed to predict harassment intensity for each media session at a future time point h (which is common across tasks) by learning a model based on past comments, starting from the k most recent comments, and incorporating Δt more comments at a time. Input data X and targets Y are constructed in the same manner as in *FLVH*. Figure 2(b) illustrates this formulation.

The benefit of this formulation is that the impact (if any) of additional past information on the performance of harassment intensity prediction can be quantitatively evaluated.

3.3 Loss Function

Each of the t tasks in our two formulations above can be learned independently using conventional single–task learning. However, independently learning models to predict far into the future could result in inferior predictive power; intuitively the further the prediction into the future, the less indicative historical data becomes. Moreover, the majority of media sessions on Instagram has been shown to receive ≤ 15 comments on average [22], leading to a sparsity problem (i.e., not enough training data).

To address these challenges, both of our proposed formulations learn all prediction tasks simultaneously, leveraging in this way commonalities among tasks (e.g., shared features extracted from the same historical data) to effectively address the training data sparsity problem, as well as the intrinsic temporal smoothness among different tasks (i.e., the number of harassing comments cannot vary significantly from one timestamp to another) to potentially improve overall prediction performance. The additional advantage of our proposed formulations is that they can both be used in an online setting; a prediction can be made at any point in the lifetime of a session once training has been performed.

Formally, each of our proposed formulations solves the following general optimization problem: $\min_{\mathbf{W}} \mathcal{L}(\mathbf{W}) + \lambda\Omega(\mathbf{W})$, where $\mathcal{L}(\mathbf{W})$ denotes the empirical loss function, $\Omega(\mathbf{W})$ encompasses regularization terms that encode task relatedness, and λ is a vector of tuning parameters used to balance the trade–off between the loss and regularization terms. Specifically, the goal for each task i is to learn matrix $\mathbf{W}$, such that the penalized empirical loss

$$\mathcal{L}(\mathbf{W}, \mathbf{X}, \mathbf{Y}) = \sum_{i=1}^{t} \|X_{i,s}W_i - Y_i\|_F^2 + \lambda_1 \|\mathbf{W}\|_F^2 +$$
$$\lambda_2 \sum_{i=1}^{t-1} \|W_i - W_{i+1}\|_F^2 + \lambda_3 \|\mathbf{W}\|_{2,1} \qquad (1)$$

is minimized. In Eq. 1, the first term corresponds to the least–squares loss function. The first regularization term, $\lambda_1 \|\mathbf{W}\|_F^2$, controls the generalization error, λ_1 controls the sparsity of $\mathbf{W}$ (equivalently the complexity of the trained models), and $\|.\|_F^2$ is the square of Frobenius norm of a matrix. The second regularization term, $\lambda_2 \sum_{i=1}^{t-1} \|W_i - W_{i+1}\|_F^2$, controls the similarity between two neighboring tasks. When λ_2 is large, the difference between any two neighboring tasks is forced to be small (i.e., large prediction deviations at neighboring time points are penalized). The group Lasso regularization term, $\lambda_3 \|W\|_{2,1}$, based on the $\ell_{2,1}$–norm penalty for feature selection [45], ensures that all models at different time points share a common set of features. This is achieved by introducing row sparsity in $\mathbf{W}$ across all tasks using the $\ell_{2,1}$–norm.

Learning all models requires obtaining the optimal weight matrix $\mathbf{W}$ by computing: $\mathbf{W}^* = \arg\min_{\mathbf{W}} \mathcal{L}(\mathbf{W}, \mathbf{X}, \mathbf{Y})$. As the objective function consists of smooth and non–smooth terms, methods such as subgradient descent can be used to tackle convex and non–differentiable functions, but have high complexity $O(\frac{1}{\sqrt{K}})$, where K denotes the number of iterations. For faster convergence rate, we use the accelerated gradient descent method, an iterative algorithm with $O(\frac{1}{K^2})$ complexity [27]. In accelerated gradient descent, the solution $W_i + 1$ on each step is computed as a gradient of the current search point W_i. The key operation in this iterative process is the computation of the proximal operator $\mathbf{W}^* = \arg\min_{\mathbf{W}} \frac{\eta}{2} \left\| \mathbf{W} - (W_i - \frac{1}{\eta}\nabla\mathcal{L}(W_i)) \right\|^2 + \Omega(\mathbf{W})$, where η is the step size, to find the next search point W^* based on the current search point W_i. Accelerated gradient descent differs from the subgradient method in the sense that the current search point W_i is the affine combination of the previous two points with parameter

α, instead of only using the latest one. Specifically, W_i is updated as $W_{i+1} = W_i - \alpha(W_i - W_{i-1})$, where W_i is initialized by $X_i \times Y_i$, and the stopping criterion is set to 10^{-5}. Parameters α and η are initialized to -1 and 1, respectively.

4 EXPERIMENTAL EVALUATION

In this section, we provide a thorough experimental evaluation of our proposed formulations. Specifically, we begin by evaluating the effectiveness and efficiency of our approach on real data in comparison to baselines. We continue by studying the parameter sensitivity of our formulations. In our experiments, we considered $t = 10$ tasks, and set $k = 10$ and $\tau = 1$ for both FLVH and VLFH, and $\Delta t = 2$ for VLFH. All experiments were conducted on a 64–bit machine with a dual–core Intel processor @2.7GHz and 16GB memory.

4.1 Baselines

To the best of our knowledge, only two methods have thus far been proposed for cyberbullying prediction, both on Instagram [22, 26]. We included both of these methods in our experimental evaluation for performance comparison.

- **LRFS [22]:** Logistic Regression classifier with forward Feature Selection for cyberbullying prediction on Instagram media sessions based on a cohort of features extracted from the first 15 comments and caption, post time, user properties, and image content. Our performance comparison in Section 4.5 demonstrates the superiority of our approach over LRFS, while using only a fraction of the features used by LRFS.
- **LRLR [26]:** Logistic Regression classifier with L2 Regularization that, given all comments up to and including the first hostile comment, predicts whether the total number of hostile comments on a media session will be greater than or equal to a predetermined threshold N after some future time h. LRLR has been shown to achieve its best performance for a threshold of 10 (i.e., $N = 10$) and a lead time of 3 hours (i.e., $h = 3$) [26]. We reached the same conclusion in our experiments, and thus set parameters $N = 10$ and $h = 3$ (this corresponds to ~ 1 timestep, on average, in our formulation) for a fair comparison in Section 4.5.

In addition to state–of–the–art for cyberbullying prediction, we are also interested in evaluating the benefit of learning multiple tasks simultaneously as opposed to learning t tasks independently. Therefore, we consider a final baseline, termed **STL** for Single Task Learning, in which the penalized empirical loss function in Eq. 1 is used, but contrary to our methods, all models are trained independently by setting the term $\lambda_2 \sum_{i=1}^{t-1} \|W_i - W_{i+1}\|_F^2 = 0$ in Eq. 1.

4.2 Evaluation Metrics

We use coefficient of determination (i.e., R^2 score) as our main evaluation criterion to measure how well observed outcomes are replicated, based on the proportion of total variation of outcomes explained by the model [40]. A negative R^2 score indicates bad fit, whereas $R^2 = 1$ indicates perfect fit. The regularization terms in our loss function used to learn a more generalizable model (i.e., reduce overfitting) are expected to result in a relatively low R^2 score due to larger mean squared error. Additionally, the frequency of harassing comments could be arbitrarily large, leading to unbounded errors.

We further consider the most prevalent performance metrics in empirically evaluating the classification performance of cyberbullying detection methods. These include accuracy, precision, recall, and F–measure. As such metrics however can result in misleading conclusions in highly imbalanced datasets [19], we additionally consider the Matthews correlation coefficient (MCC), which is less sensitive to data skewness as it considers mutual accuracies of both classes and all four values of the confusion matrix [31]. We compute these metrics for the cyberbullying class by treating the harassment intensity prediction problem as a binary classification task. Specifically, we consider a naive classification rule motivated by the definition in [22], where a media session is classified as an instance of cybebullying if the predicted frequency of aggressive comments is ≥ 2. This simplified classification problem additionally enables a direct and fair comparison with the baselines.

4.3 Dataset

We use comments spanning 22.1% of all media sessions containing $\geq 40\%$ profanities from the Instagram dataset available by [22]. Comments have been manually annotated by 10 experts. The original dataset has been collected using snowball sampling starting from a random seed node. For each user, all media the user shared, users who commented on the media, and the comments posted on the media had been collected. Of all media sessions containing at least 40% profanities 47.5% had been manually labeled as positive if *"there are negative words and/or comments with intent to harm someone or other, and the posts include two or more repeated negativity against a victim"* [22]. We performed 3–fold cross validation for model selection, where within each fold, 2/3 of the data was used for training, and the rest for testing.

4.4 Feature Engineering

Although feature engineering may be as important as modeling in a prediction problem, our main objective in this work is to improve upon existing cyberbullying prediction methods. For a fair comparison, we consider the following features: #. of mentions, #. of words, density of uppercase, density of punctuation, #. of hashtags, #. of urls, density of bad words from a dictionary [14], compound Vader sentiment [15], and ten unigrams selected by [22] and [26]. Although [26] uses additional features (i.e., unigrams, word2vec, and lexicons), incorporating all such features into our multi–task regression formulation could be problematic in terms of efficiently solving the optimization problem to find **W**. The use of a much smaller subset of features as compared to [26] could put our approach at a major disadvantage in terms of data representation. Nevertheless, our results show improvements over *LRLR* even with such a significantly smaller feature set.

Table 1 shows the specific features, ranked from highest to lowest, selected by our proposed formulations across different tasks. The features selected are very relevant to cyberbullying detection, as well as consistent across tasks.

Approach	Features
FLVH	"fuck", "bitch", #. of mentions, "hate", #. of uppercase letters, "beauty", text length
VLFH	"fuck", "bitch", #. of mentions, "hate", #. of uppercase letters, "ugly", # of hashtags, "shut", "gay"

Table 1: Top features (ranked by coefficients) selected by *FLVH* (top) and *VLFH* (bottom).

	Accuracy	Recall	Precision	F-measure	MCC
FLVH (h = 1)	0.7087	0.8807	0.6085	0.7173	0.4743
FLVH (h = 2)	0.7152	0.8841	0.6290	0.7330	0.4807
FLVH (h = 3)	0.7138	0.8984	0.6365	0.7431	0.4792
FLVH (h = 4)	0.7198	0.9079	0.6497	0.7558	0.4868
FLVH (h = 5)	0.7237	0.9164	0.6592	0.7653	0.4914
FLVH (h = 6)	0.7261	0.9305	0.6656	0.7747	0.4945
FLVH (h = 7)	0.7317	0.9350	0.6758	0.7834	0.4992
FLVH (h = 8)	0.7345	0.9390	0.6829	0.7897	0.4990
FLVH (h = 9)	0.7412	0.9405	0.6939	0.7975	0.5049
FLVH (h = 10)	0.7431	0.9471	0.6982	0.8026	0.5055
LRFS	0.7489	0.7206	0.7217	0.7211	0.4768

Table 2: *FLVH* performance comparison with *LRFS* [22].

4.5 Performance Comparisons

1) Fixed–Lag Varying–Horizon Prediction: LRFS [22] resembles our *FLVH* model in that a fixed number of comments is used to classify media sessions. However, unlike *FLVH*, in which predictions are made in predetermined points h in the future from any given time γ, a "prediction" by *LRFS* is made only after the last comment for a given media session becomes available. We also report the aggregate performance of *FLVH* across all tasks for comparison with *LRFS*. Note that this comparison is unfair to our model since the problem we are trying to solve does not concern the "eventual" status of media sessions (i.e., binary classification after the last comment for a given media session becomes available). Instead, *FLVH* focuses on predicting the number of harassment comments a session is expected to receive in the near future (i.e., regression problem).

Table 2 summarizes this performance comparison. The results indicate that our approach significantly outperforms *LRFS* with respect to recall, F-measure and MCC both for individual tasks (i.e., different prediction horizons) and on average.

2) Varying–Lag Fixed–Horizon Prediction: LRLR [26] uses all available comments in a media session to predict the presence of cyberbullying 3 hours after the most recent hostile comment. We found the average number of comments received within 3 consecutive hours in our dataset to be 0.042. Since *LRLR* uses a fixed prediction horizon for all media sessions, it is more similar to our proposed *VLFH* method when the prediction horizon is set to 1. Unlike *VLFH* where in task i, only $k + \Delta i$ lag comments are used, *LRLR* uses all past comments up to the first hostile comment to predict harassment intensity for all media sessions. Nevertheless, to verify the extent to which the amount of past knowledge affects (if at all) prediction performance, we compare all *VLFH* tasks to *LRLR*.

Table 3 shows the results. Notably, the performance of *VLFH* across all metrics improves as more past comments are considered.

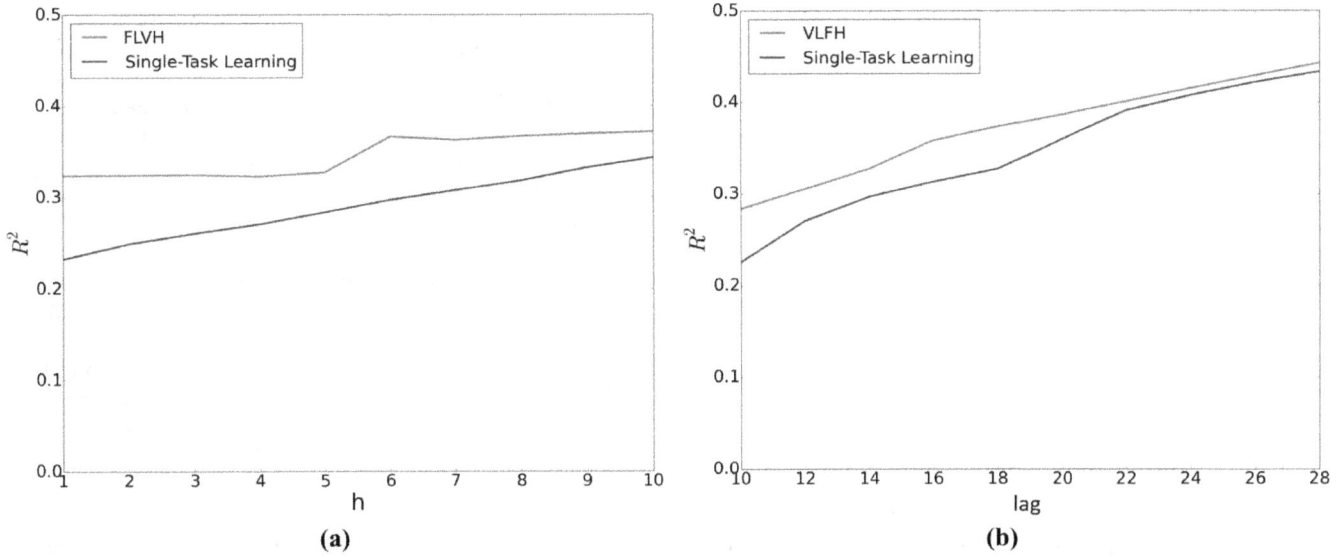

Figure 3: Comparison between (a) *FLVH* and (b) *VLFH* with single–task learning in terms of R^2 score.

	Accuracy	Recall	Precision	F–measure	MCC
VLFH (lag = 10)	0.7131	0.8759	0.6237	0.7286	0.4712
VLFH (lag = 12)	0.7272	0.9179	0.6504	0.7613	0.5020
VLFH (lag = 14)	0.7395	0.9370	0.6728	0.7832	0.5204
VLFH (lag = 16)	0.7560	0.9517	0.6970	0.8047	0.5441
VLFH (lag = 18)	0.7740	0.9651	0.7196	0.8244	0.5719
VLFH (lag = 20)	0.7883	0.9698	0.7392	0.8389	0.5902
VLFH (lag = 22)	0.8002	0.9731	0.7557	0.8508	0.6052
VLFH (lag = 24)	0.8087	0.9761	0.7677	0.8594	0.6149
VLFH (lag = 26)	0.8151	0.9784	0.7772	0.8662	0.6198
VLFH (lag = 28)	0.8157	0.9803	0.7800	0.8688	0.6161
LRLR	0.5918	0.4759	0.3193	0.3704	0.1017

Table 3: *VLFH* performance comparison with *LRLR* [26].

The results also show that *VLFH* consistently outperforms *LRLR* in terms of accuracy, recall, precision, F–measure and MCC.

3) Advantage of Multi–Task Regression: Figure 3 reveals the advantage of *FLVH* and *VLFH* in predicting the future by training tasks jointly given the same amount of access to past information. Both of our models take advantage of the commonality between tasks to address the sparsity of training samples and improve the forecasting performance for all future time points, as opposed to *STL* (i.e., single–task learning model) in terms of R^2 score. Specifically, the results demonstrate that learning all tasks jointly is advantageous to single–task learning under the assumption that the further in the future a prediction is to be made, the less indicative the present (similarly, the recent past) becomes.

4.6 Parameter Sensitivity Analysis

An important issue in the practical application of *FLVH* and *VLFH* is the selection of regularization parameters λ_1, λ_2, and λ_3. Ideally, λ_1 and λ_3 should each be set to a large value so that only the most powerful features will be selected, and the time complexity of the learned model becomes small. Similarly, a large value for λ_2 should

be used to penalize large prediction deviations at neighboring time points. Setting $\lambda_2 = 1000$, while varying parameter λ_1 and λ_3 accordingly from 0 to 1000 with a step size of 200, we found the maximum difference between accuracy scores across all tasks to be less than 0.9%. We obtained similar results for λ_2 when keeping λ_1 fixed. We obtained these results for both *FLVH* and *VLFH*. The "insensitivity" to parameter λ_3 can be potentially explained by the large variance in the discriminating capability of features for the particular problem of harassment intensity prediction. In other words, it is possible that even without regularization (i.e. $\lambda_3 = 0$), the coefficients of "less important" features are already set close to zero.

Next, we focus on the sensitivity (if any) of *FLVH* and *VLFH* on the number of observed comments used for prediction (i.e., *lag*), and prediction horizon h. Figure 4 shows the sensitivity results of varying the value of h from 5 to 20 for *FLVH* (i.e., a task refers to a time point progressively further away in the future). In general, for all tasks, accuracy increases as h increases. Intuitively, the larger the number of observed comments in the recent past of a media session, the better the predictive power of the model, even for 10 comments into the future. Thus, setting h to larger values can yield better accuracy. The downside to setting h to larger values is that decisions must be postponed until more comments are collected. Therefore, the trade–off between accuracy and speed of decision must be considered when deciding which value of h to use.

Figure 5 shows the sensitivity results of *VLFH* (i.e., the number of observed comments varies across tasks) on the prediction horizon, in the range {3, 5, 10, 15, 20}. Note that in our dataset, the maximum number of comments in a media session is 147. Thus, for *lag* > 28, no media sessions exist with enough comments to train a model with > 6 tasks. Accuracy is relatively stable for all tasks, with a slight increase as h increases for $10 \leq lag \leq 16$ (i.e., for up to 16 past comments). Accuracy is quite stable even when h is large,

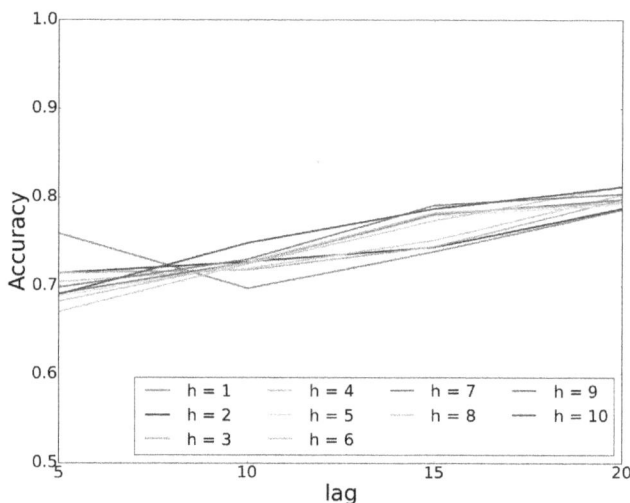

Figure 4: Sensitivity analysis of the proposed *FLVH* model on the number of observed comments (i.e., *lag*).

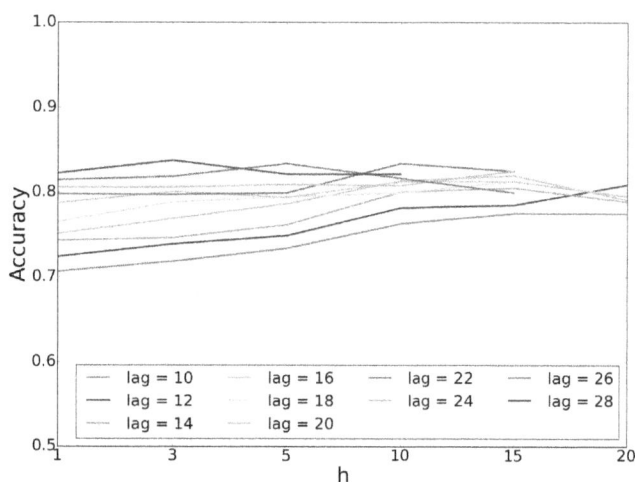

Figure 5: Sensitivity analysis of the proposed *VLFH* model on prediction horizon.

demonstrating that a good prediction can be made even with a small number of observed comments.

5 CONCLUSION

Contributions. In this paper, we presented two novel multi–task regression formulations to the problem of harassment intensity prediction on Instagram given a limited amount of historical data. By distinguishing between media sessions that are more likely to receive many harassing comments in the future, and those that are expected to receive few or none, our proposed approach can be used to effectively prioritize media sessions either for increased monitoring as time goes by or for immediate intervention before a conversation escalates, rather than investigating an event after its occurrence.

Our work considered the estimation of predictive models at different time points in the future with both fixed and varying lengths of historical data as a multi–task regression problem. Our extensive experimental evaluation results demonstrate the benefit of leveraging shared information between prediction tasks, which effectively increases the sample size, and incorporating into the training process the intrinsic temporal smoothness relationship between tasks to improve forecasting accuracy. Our results additionally showed that our approach can effectively predict harassment intensity on Instagram media sessions, outperforming competing methods by up to 31.4% and 46.2% in recall and Mathew correlation coefficient respectively.

Future Directions. In our ongoing work, we focus on features that have been shown to be informative for cyberbullying classification and more recently for harassment prediction. Given that Instagram is primarily a photo-sharing site, in future work, we plan to investigate the predictive power of non–text features extracted from image classification algorithms. Attributes engineered from user profiles and activity history as well as network structure information may provide additional context for forecasting. Finally, it may be possible to extract from these data insights into human behavior. For example, it may be possible to identify responses (if any) that may diffuse, as opposed to escalate, harassment in online social media. We are also planning to evaluate the performance of our approach on additional datasets from diverse platforms including Ask.fm and Twitter, which are reported to be key social networking venues where users frequently become victims of cyberbullying.

Broader Applicability. Beyond cyberbullying, our work is, to the best of our knowledge, the first to examine the forecasting power of the multi–task regression framework as a function of the prediction horizon and the length of historical data. Our findings based on our experimental results reveal the advantage of multi–task regression over traditional single–task learning methods for forecasting, particularly so as the prediction horizon increases. We thus believe that our work can serve as a reference point on the forecasting performance of multi–task learning both for researchers and practitioners.

REFERENCES

[1] Mohammed Ali Al-garadi, Kasturi Dewi Varathan, and Sri Devi Ravana. 2016. Cybercrime detection in online communications: The experimental case of cyberbullying detection in the Twitter network. *Computers in Human Behavior* 63 (2016), 433–443.

[2] Andreas Argyriou, Theodoros Evgeniou, and Massimiliano Pontil. 2006. Multi-task feature learning. In *Proceedings of the 19th International Conference on Neural Information Processing Systems (NIPS'06)*. MIT Press, Cambridge, MA, USA, 41–48.

[3] Amy Bellmore, Angela J Calvin, Jun-Ming Xu, and Xiaojin Zhu. 2015. The Five w's of "Bullying" on Twitter: Who, What, Why, Where, and When. *Computers in Human Behavior* 44 (2015), 305–314.

[4] Rich Caruana. 1997. Multitask learning. *Machine learning* 28, 1 (1997), 41–75.

[5] Despoina Chatzakou, Nicolas Kourtellis, Jeremy Blackburn, Emiliano De Cristofaro, Gianluca Stringhini, and Athena Vakali. 2017. Mean birds: Detecting aggression and bullying on twitter. In *Proceedings of the 2017 ACM on Web Science Conference*. ACM, 13–22.

[6] Charalampos Chelmis, Daphney-Stavroula Zois, and Mengfan Yao. 2017. Mining patterns of cyberbullying on twitter. In *Data Mining Workshops (ICDMW), 2017 IEEE International Conference on*. IEEE, 126–133.

[7] Ying Chen, Yilu Zhou, Sencun Zhu, and Heng Xu. 2012. Detecting offensive language in social media to protect adolescent online safety. In *Privacy, Security, Risk and Trust (PASSAT), 2012 International Conference on and 2012 International Confernece on Social Computing (SocialCom)*. IEEE, 71–80.

[8] Lu Cheng, Jundong Li, Yasin N Silva, Deborah L Hall, and Huan Liu. 2019. XBully: Cyberbullying Detection within a Multi-Modal Context. In *Proceedings of the Twelfth ACM International Conference on Web Search and Data Mining*. ACM, 339–347.

[9] Maral Dadvar, Dolf Trieschnigg, Roeland Ordelman, and Franciska de Jong. 2013. Improving cyberbullying detection with user context. In *European Conference on Information Retrieval*. Springer, 693–696.

[10] Thomas Davidson, Dana Warmsley, Michael Macy, and Ingmar Weber. 2017. Automated hate speech detection and the problem of offensive language. In *International AAAI Conference on Web and Social Media*.

[11] Karthik Dinakar, Roi Reichart, and Henry Lieberman. 2011. Modeling the detection of textual cyberbullying. *The Social Mobile Web* 11, 02 (2011), 11–17.

[12] Maeve Duggan. 2017. Online harassment 2017. http://www.pewinternet.org/2014/10/22/online-harassment/.

[13] Theodoros Evgeniou and Massimiliano Pontil. 2004. Regularized multi-task learning. In *Proceedings of the Tenth ACM SIGKDD International Conference on Knowledge Discovery and Data Mining (KDD '04)*. ACM, New York, NY, USA, 109–117.

[14] FrontGate Media. 2014. A list of 723 bad words to blacklist & how to use Facebook's moderation tool. https://www.frontgatemedia.com/a-list-of-723-bad-words-to-blacklist-and-how-to-use-facebooks-moderation-tool/.

[15] CJ Hutto Eric Gilbert. 2014. Vader: A parsimonious rule-based model for sentiment analysis of social media text. In *Eighth International Conference on Weblogs and Social Media*.

[16] Njagi Dennis Gitari, Zhang Zuping, Hanyurwimfura Damien, and Jun Long. 2015. A lexicon-based approach for hate speech detection. *International Journal of Multimedia and Ubiquitous Engineering* 10, 4 (2015), 215–230.

[17] Jennifer Golbeck, Zahra Ashktorab, Rashad O Banjo, Alexandra Berlinger, Siddharth Bhagwan, Cody Buntain, Paul Cheakalos, Alicia A Geller, Quint Gergory, Rajesh Kumar Gnanasekaran, et al. 2017. A large labeled corpus for online harassment research. In *Proceedings of the 2017 ACM on Web Science Conference*. ACM, 229–233.

[18] Leam Hackett. 2017. The Annual Bullying Survey 2017. https://www.ditchthelabel.org/wp-content/uploads/2017/07/The-Annual-Bullying-Survey-2017-1.pdf.

[19] Haibo He and Edwardo A. Garcia. 2009. Learning from imbalanced data. *IEEE Trans. on Knowl. and Data Eng.* 21, 9 (Sept. 2009), 1263–1284.

[20] Sameer Hinduja and Justin W Patchin. 2010. Bullying, cyberbullying, and suicide. *Archives of suicide research* 14, 3 (2010), 206–221.

[21] Homa Hosseinmardi, Amir Ghasemianlangroodi, Richard Han, Qin Lv, and Shivakant Mishra. 2014. Towards understanding cyberbullying behavior in a semi-anonymous social network. In *2014 IEEE/ACM International Conference on Advances in Social Networks Analysis and Mining (ASONAM)*. IEEE, 244–252.

[22] Homa Hosseinmardi, Rahat Ibn Rafiq, Richard Han, Qin Lv, and Shivakant Mishra. 2016. Prediction of cyberbullying incidents in a media-based social network. In *Proceedings of the 2016 IEEE/ACM International Conference on Advances in Social Networks Analysis and Mining*. IEEE Press, 186–192.

[23] April Kontostathis, Kelly Reynolds, Andy Garron, and Lynne Edwards. 2013. Detecting cyberbullying: Query terms and techniques. In *Proceedings of the 5th Annual ACM Web Science Conference (WebSci '13)*. ACM, New York, NY, USA, 195–204.

[24] Robin M Kowalski, Susan P Limber, Sue Limber, and Patricia W Agatston. 2012. *Cyberbullying: Bullying in the digital age*. John Wiley & Sons.

[25] Srijan Kumar, Justin Cheng, and Jure Leskovec. 2017. Antisocial behavior on the Web: Characterization and detection. In *Proceedings of the 26th International Conference on World Wide Web Companion*. International World Wide Web Conferences Steering Committee, 947–950.

[26] Ping Liu, Joshua Guberman, Libby Hemphill, and Aron Culotta. 2018. Forecasting the presence and intensity of hostility on Instagram using linguistic and social features. In *Twelfth International AAAI Conference on Web and Social Media*.

[27] Yurii Nesterov. 2013. *Introductory lectures on convex optimization: A basic course*. Vol. 87. Springer Science & Business Media.

[28] Chikashi Nobata, Joel Tetreault, Achint Thomas, Yashar Mehdad, and Yi Chang. 2016. Abusive language detection in online user content. In *Proceedings of the 25th International Conference on World Wide Web*. International World Wide Web Conferences Steering Committee, 145–153.

[29] Alexandra Olteanu, Kartik Talamadupula, and Kush R Varshney. 2017. The limits of abstract evaluation metrics: The case of hate speech detection. In *Proceedings of the 2017 ACM on Web Science Conference*. ACM, 405–406.

[30] Zizi Papacharissi. 2009. The virtual geographies of social networks: a comparative analysis of Facebook, LinkedIn and A SmallWorld. *New media & society* 11, 1-2 (2009), 199–220.

[31] David Martin Powers. 2011. Evaluation: from precision, recall and F-measure to ROC, informedness, markedness and correlation. (2011).

[32] Rahat Ibn Rafiq, Homa Hosseinmardi, Richard Han, Qin Lv, and Shivakant Mishra. 2018. Scalable and Timely Detection of Cyberbullying in Online Social Networks. In *Proceedings of the 33rd Annual ACM Symposium on Applied Computing (SAC '18)*. ACM, New York, NY, USA, 1738–1747.

[33] Elaheh Raisi and Bert Huang. 2018. Weakly supervised cyberbullying detection with participant-vocabulary consistency. *Social Network Analysis and Mining* 8, 1 (2018), 38.

[34] Mohammadreza Rezvan, Saeedeh Shekarpour, Lakshika Balasuriya, Krishnaprasad Thirunarayan, Valerie L Shalin, and Amit Sheth. 2018. A quality type-aware annotated corpus and lexicon for harassment research. In *Proceedings of the 10th ACM Conference on Web Science*. ACM, 33–36.

[35] H Rosa, N Pereira, R Ribeiro, PC Ferreira, JP Carvalho, S Oliveira, L Coheur, P Paulino, AM Veiga Simão, and I Trancoso. 2019. Automatic cyberbullying detection: A systematic review. *Computers in Human Behavior* 93 (2019), 333–345.

[36] Semiu Salawu, Yulan He, and Joanna Lumsden. 2017. Approaches to automated detection of cyberbullying: A survey. *IEEE Transactions on Affective Computing* 1 (2017), 1–1.

[37] Robert Slonje and Peter K Smith. 2008. Cyberbullying: Another main type of bullying? *Scandinavian journal of psychology* 49, 2 (2008), 147–154.

[38] Sara Owsley Sood, Elizabeth F Churchill, and Judd Antin. 2012. Automatic identification of personal insults on social news sites. *Journal of the American Society for Information Science and Technology* 63, 2 (2012), 270–285.

[39] A. Squicciarini, S. Rajtmajer, Y. Liu, and C. Griffin. 2015. Identification and Characterization of Cyberbullying Dynamics in an Online Social Network. In *Proceedings of the 2015 IEEE/ACM International Conference on Advances in Social Networks Analysis and Mining 2015 (ASONAM '15)*. ACM, New York, NY, USA, 280–285.

[40] Robert George Douglas Steel and James Hiram Torrie. 1960. *Principles and procedures of statistics: with special reference to the biological sciences*. McGraw-Hill.

[41] Andreas S Weigend. 2018. *Time series prediction: forecasting the future and understanding the past*. Routledge.

[42] Jun-Ming Xu, Kwang-Sung Jun, Xiaojin Zhu, and Amy Bellmore. 2012. Learning from bullying traces in social media. In *Proceedings of the 2012 Conference of the North American Chapter of the Association for Computational Linguistics: Human Language Technologies (NAACL HLT '12)*. Association for Computational Linguistics, Stroudsburg, PA, USA, 656–666.

[43] Mengfan Yao, Charalampos Chelmis, and Daphney-Stavroula Zois. 2018. Cyberbullying detection on Instagram with optimal online feature selection. In *2018 IEEE/ACM International Conference on Advances in Social Networks Analysis and Mining (ASONAM)*. IEEE, 401–408.

[44] Mengfan Yao, Charalampos Chelmis, and Daphney-Stavroula Zois. 2019. Cyberbullying ends here: Towards robust detection of cyberbullying in social media. In *Proceedings of the International Conference on World Wide Web*. International World Wide Web Conferences Steering Committee.

[45] Ming Yuan and Yi Lin. 2006. Model selection and estimation in regression with grouped variables. *Journal of the Royal Statistical Society: Series B (Statistical Methodology)* 68, 1 (2006), 49–67.

[46] Haoti Zhong, Hao Li, Anna Squicciarini, Sarah Rajtmajer, Christopher Griffin, David Miller, and Cornelia Caragea. 2016. Content-driven detection of cyberbullying on the Instagram social network. In *Proceedings of the Twenty-Fifth International Joint Conference on Artificial Intelligence (IJCAI'16)*. AAAI Press, 3952–3958.

Better Safe Than Sorry:
an Adversarial Approach to improve Social Bot Detection

Stefano Cresci, Marinella Petrocchi
IIT-CNR, Pisa, Italy
[name.surname]@iit.cnr.it

Angelo Spognardi
Dept. of Computer Science,
Sapienza University of Rome, Italy
spognardi@di.uniroma1.it

Stefano Tognazzi
IMT School for Advanced Studies
Lucca, Italy
stefano.tognazzi@imtlucca.it

ABSTRACT

The arm race between spambots and spambot-detectors is made of several cycles (or generations): a new wave of spambots is created (and new spam is spread), new spambot filters are derived and old spambots mutate (or *evolve*) to new species. Recently, with the diffusion of the adversarial learning approach, a new practice is emerging: to manipulate on purpose target samples in order to make stronger detection models. Here, we manipulate generations of Twitter social bots, to obtain - and study - their possible future evolutions, with the aim of eventually deriving more effective detection techniques. In detail, we propose and experiment with a novel genetic algorithm for the synthesis of online accounts. The algorithm allows to create synthetic *evolved* versions of current state-of-the-art social bots. Results demonstrate that synthetic bots really escape current detection techniques. However, they give all the needed elements to improve such techniques, making possible a proactive approach for the design of social bot detection systems.

KEYWORDS

Social bots; online social networks security; adversarial classifier evasion; genetic algorithms; Twitter

ACM Reference Format:
Stefano Cresci, Marinella Petrocchi, Angelo Spognardi, and Stefano Tognazzi. 2019. Better Safe Than Sorry: an Adversarial Approach to improve Social Bot Detection. In *11th ACM Conference on Web Science (WebSci '19), June 30-July 3, 2019, Boston, MA, USA*. ACM, New York, NY, USA, 10 pages. https://doi.org/10.1145/3292522.3326030

1 INTRODUCTION

A worrying peculiarity of spammers and bots (or spambots) is that they *evolve* over time, adopting sophisticated techniques to evade well-established detection systems [12, 49]. In the context of Online Social Networks (ONSs), newer social spambots often feature advanced characteristics that make them way harder to detect with respect to older ones, since capable of mimicking human behaviors and interaction patterns better than ever before [12, 20]. These automated accounts represent – to the best of the literature knowledge – the third and most novel generation of social bots,

following the original wave dated back in the 00s, and passing through a second generation dated around 2011 [49]. The latest social bots are capable of sharing (credible) fake news, inflating the popularity of OSN users, and reshaping political debates [40, 41]. Given this picture, it is not surprising that evolution mechanisms (together with coordination and synchronization ones) represent one of the key factors that currently allow malicious accounts to massively tamper with our social ecosystems [14].

Despite malicious accounts evolution representing a sort of Pandora's box, little to no attention has been posed towards studying – and possibly anticipating – such evolution. In fact, in past years, as social bots gradually became clever in escaping detection, scholars and OSNs administrators tried to keep pace (i.e., *reacted*), by proposing ever more complex detection techniques, as described in the Related Work section. The natural consequence of this *reactive* approach – according to which a new technique is designed only after having collected evidence of new mischiefs of evolved bots – is that researchers and OSN admins are constantly one step behind the bot developers [43].

The classification task of recognising if an online account is genuine or not is *adversarial* in nature, being focused on distinguishing *bad* samples from *good* ones. Nonetheless, a new approach is gaining momentum in the wide field of artificial intelligence, leveraging the concept of *adversarial learning*: the automatic learning within a hostile environment [28]. This allows to both discover vulnerabilities in learning algorithms and to test algorithmic techniques which yield more robust learning [44]. Intuitively, the evolution of new waves of social bots can be seen as a problem of *adversarial classifier evasion*, where the attacker changes the generated samples to evade detection. Thus, the core idea of this paper is to manipulate *on purpose* target samples in order to produce stronger detection models. Inspired by the adversarial learning approach, for the first time to the best of our knowledge, we carry out an exploratory investigation to define and implement a *proactive* technique to study and detect evolving social bots.

Specifically, we aim at answering the following critical, yet unexplored, research questions:

RQ1 – *Can we develop an analytical framework for simulating spambot evolutions?*

RQ2 – *Can we use such framework for synthesizing new generations of spambots? And, most importantly, are these evolved spambots capable of going undetected by state-of-the-art techniques?*

RQ3 – *Can we leverage this proactive and adversarial study of spambot evolutions to improve current detection techniques?*

Approach. Our methodological approach to answer the three questions stems from the so-called *digital DNA* technique [11], where the behavioral lifetime of an account is encoded as a sequence of characters, built according to the chronological sequence of actions performed by the account. The adoption of this behavioral modeling technique offers a DNA-like representation for the lifetime of each account, including new social spambots. We feed the DNA sequences to a custom-designed genetic algorithm, so as to study possible evolutions of the accounts [36]. The customized genetic algorithm iteratively selects the *best* evolutions, so as to converge towards synthetic bots capable of resembling behavioral characteristics of legitimate accounts. Furthermore, by constraining possible evolutions within the algorithm, the approach allows to obtain synthetic accounts capable of performing specific tasks (e.g., viral marketing, message spamming, mass retweeting, etc.). Notably, the digital DNA behavioral modeling technique has been exploited in the past as the building block of a state-of-the-art detection system [13]. Thus, we can also apply such detection technique on the synthetically evolved accounts, to evaluate whether they are capable of evading detection.

Contributions. This work contributes along several dimensions. Firstly, (i) we propose GenBot, a novel genetic algorithm specifically designed for social spambot evolutions. By employing a cost function that quantifies the difference between a new generation of spambots and a group of legitimate accounts, GenBot is capable of generating spambots whose behavior is similar to that of the legitimate ones. Notably, our results outperform previous attempts to simulate the behavior of human accounts [16]. Then, (ii) we discuss the design of an analytical framework for simulating possible social spambot evolutions that leverages both the digital DNA behavioral modeling technique and the genetic algorithm previously defined. We experiment with this framework to synthesize a novel generation of evolved spambots, with the aim of producing adversarial samples. Furthermore, (iii) we assess the extent to which the newly synthesized social bots are detected by 3 state-of-the-art techniques. Results show that, with the proposed framework, it is possible to create an adversarial behavioral fingerprint that allow bots to escape detection. Finally, (iv) by studying the characteristics of the synthetic evolved spambots, we draw useful insights into which account features could be considered in order to improve the detection of real evolving spambots.

Broadening the approach. We ground our study on a recently-proposed proactive approach to spambot detection [43]. In order to carry out extensive experimentation on real-world data, without loss of generality, here we implement it by focusing on the behavior (i.e., the sequences of actions that accounts perform) of spambots and legitimate accounts. This choice opens up the possibility to leverage, for our experiments, the *digital DNA* behavioral modeling technique [11] as well as the *social fingerprinting* spambot detection technique [13]. However, despite this particular implementation of the proactive approach, similar analyses could be carried out, by relying on different modeling and spambot detection techniques, such as those based on network/graph analysis and those based on content analysis.

Reproducibility. Both the data[1] and the code[2] used in this study are publicly available for scientific purposes.

---
[1]http://mib.projects.iit.cnr.it/dataset.html
[2]http://sysma.imtlucca.it/tools/digdna-genetic-algorithm/

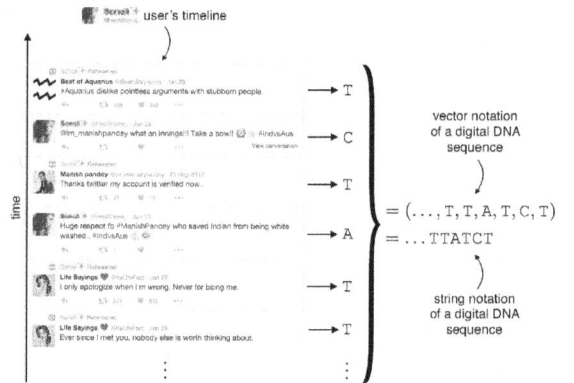

Figure 1: Excerpt of a digital DNA extraction process for a Twitter user with the alphabet $\mathbb{B} = \{A,C,T\}$, where T is assigned to every tweet, C to every reply, and A to every retweet.

2 BACKGROUND AND NOTATION

Here, we provide a succinct description of the main concepts related to digital DNA sequences and genetic algorithms, as well as notations and metrics adopted in the remainder of this study.

2.1 Digital DNA

Digital DNA sequences. We define a digital DNA sequence s as a row-vector of characters (i.e., a string),

$$\mathbf{s} = (b_1, b_2, \ldots, b_n) \quad b_i \in \mathbb{B} \ \forall \ i = 1, \ldots, n$$

Characters b_i in s are also called the (DNA) *bases* and are drawn from a finite set $\mathbb{B}$, called *alphabet*,

$$\mathbb{B} = \{B_1, B_2, \ldots, B_N\} \quad \forall \ i \neq j : B_i \neq B_j$$

Online users' behaviors can be represented by encoding each user action, in chronological order, with an appropriate base. In this way, we obtain the sequence of characters that makes up the digital DNA sequence of the user. For example, Figure 1 shows the process of extracting the digital DNA sequence of a Twitter user, by scanning its timeline according to the alphabet $\mathbb{B} = \{A,C,T\}$, where T is assigned to every tweet, C to every reply, and A to every retweet. A digital DNA sequence can be represented, then, with a compact string like $\mathbf{s} = \ldots$ TTATCT. Additional details about the theoretical foundations of digital DNA can be found in [11, 13].

Similarity between digital DNA sequences. In order to analyze groups of users rather than single users, we need to study multiple digital DNA sequences as a whole. A group A of $M = |A|$ users can be described by the strings representing the digital DNA sequences of the M users.

To perform our analyses on digital DNA sequences, we can rely on recent advances in the fields of bio-informatics and string mining [23]. One of the possible means to quantify similarities between sequential data representations is the *longest common substring* [3]. Given two strings, $\mathbf{s}_i$ of length n and $\mathbf{s}_j$ of length m, their longest common substring (henceforth LCS) is the longest string that is a substring of both $\mathbf{s}_i$ and $\mathbf{s}_j$. For example, given

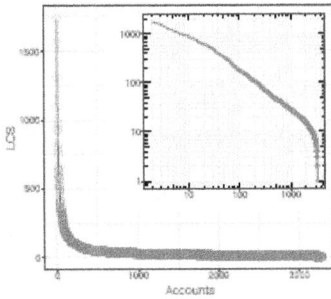

Figure 2: LCS curve of a group of legitimate (human-operated) accounts.

s_i = MASSACHUSETTS and s_j = PARACHUTE, their LCS is the string ACHU and the LCS length is 4. The extended version of this problem, which considers an arbitrary finite number of strings, is called the *k-common substring* problem [9]. In this case, given a vector $A = (s_1, \ldots, s_M)$ of M strings, the problem is that of finding the LCS that is common to at least k of these strings, for each $2 \leq k \leq M$. Notably, both the *longest common substring* and the *k-common substring* problems can be solved in linear time and space, by resorting to the generalized suffix tree and by implementing state-of-the-art algorithms, such as those proposed in [3]. Given that, in the *k-common substring* problem, the LCS is computed for each $2 \leq k \leq M$, it is possible to plot a *LCS curve*, showing the relationship between the length of the LCS and the number k of strings [13].

Figure 2 depicts the LCS curve computed for a group of legitimate (human-operated) Twitter accounts, via the alphabet $\mathbb{B} = \{A, C, T\}$. On the x axis is reported the number k of accounts (corresponding to the k digital DNA sequences used to compute LCS values) and on the y axis the length of the LCS common to at least k accounts. Therefore, each point in a LCS curve corresponds to a subset of k accounts that share the longest substring (of length y) among all those shared between all the other possible subsets of k accounts.

A LCS curve is a representation of the behavioral similarities among a group of users, since it is an ordered sequence of substring lengths. To obtain a single value as *measure* of similarity for the whole group, we can compute the area under the LCS curve (AUC) [19, 21]. Since LCS curves are discrete functions defined over the $[2, M]$ range, their AUC can be computed straightaway, without approximations, with the following trapezoid rule,

$$\text{AUC} = \sum_{k=3}^{M} \frac{(\text{LCS}[k-1] + \text{LCS}[k])\Delta_k}{2} \tag{1}$$

Compared to LCS, the definition of AUC, given in Equation (1), allows to quantitatively and directly compare the overall behavioral similarity among different groups. This notion of AUC is exploited in Section 5 to evaluate the results of this study.

2.2 Genetic algorithms

Genetic algorithms [36] represent a popular meta-heuristic technique to solve optimization problems. It is inspired by the natural evolution, in which only the best candidates of some species survive across several subsequent generations. Starting from a random sample of candidate solutions (a so-called *population* of *individuals*), only the best ones are elected to evolve. Similarly to what happens in nature, through a mechanism of recombination and mutation of those individuals, a new *generation* is obtained. This evolved generation is expected to have a better quality with respect to the previous one. The quality of individuals is evaluated by associating a *fitness score* to all of them. The score is computed by a given *fitness function* that is designed according to the task at hand. During each generation, the current population is modified via either a single input function called *mutation* or a two input function called *crossover*. The outputs of these functions are called *offsprings* and a new generation is formed by merging some of the individuals from the previous generation with some of the offsprings. In our experimental scenario, when we refer to an individual, we refer to a group of users. Thus, our population is composed of different groups of users that evolve passing from a generation to the next one.

Notations. We call P_0 the initial population and P_i the population at the i-th generation. Given a population P_i, $G_j = \{u_1, u_2, \ldots, u_M\}$ is the j-th individual (i.e., a group of users) of P_i. Then, $G_j[k] = u_k$ is the k-th user of the group G_j, characterized by its digital DNA sequence. In other words, u_k is a digital DNA sequence encoding the behavior of the k-th Twitter user. We define v_j as the fitness score of the j-th individual. The population $P_i = \{(G_1, v_1), (G_2, v_2), \ldots, (G_J, v_J)\}$ is a set of pairs containing the individuals and their associated fitness scores.

3 AN ALGORITHM FOR SIMULATING BOT EVOLUTIONS

The design of a custom genetic algorithm for solving a given task involves the definition of the parameters and functions used by the algorithm in its iterative execution. In this section, we first describe the design choices and building blocks of the GENBOT algorithm and we conclude by defining the algorithm itself.

3.1 Building blocks: fitness, mutation and crossover

Fitness. In our scenario, individuals of best quality are groups of bots that best emulate the behavior of a group of legitimate (human-operated) accounts. To formalize this intuition, we rely on the notion of behavioral similarity expressed by digital DNA and LCS curves. More specifically, our goal for this task is to *minimize* the distance between the LCS curve (i.e., the behavioral representation) of a group of legitimate accounts and the LCS curve of a population of synthetic evolved bots.

We rely on the Kullback-Liebler distance (D_{KL}) to compute the distance between two LCS curves, since it has already been fruitfully employed in recent similar work [16, 46]. D_{KL} is an information theoretic metric that measures how much information is lost when a target probability distribution $P_X(x)$ is approximated by $\hat{P}_X(x)$. In detail, D_{KL} is the symmetric version of the Kullback-Liebler divergence d_{KL} (defined as, $d_{KL}(\hat{P}_X, P_X) = \sum_x \ln\left(\frac{\hat{P}_X(x)}{P_X(x)}\right) \hat{P}_X(x)$), where,

$$D_{KL}(\hat{P}_X, P_X) = \frac{d_{KL}(P_X, \hat{P}_X) + d_{KL}(\hat{P}_X, P_X)}{2} \tag{2}$$

Fit(G_j, b)	GCO(G_x, G_y, r)
1 $g \leftarrow LCS(G_j)$	1 for $i \in \{1, \ldots, r\}$ do
2 $v_j \leftarrow D_{KL}(g, b)$	2 $G_{xy}[i] \leftarrow G_x[i]$
3 return v_j	3 $G_{yx}[i] \leftarrow G_y[i]$
	4 for $i \in \{r+1, \ldots, |G_x|\}$ do
	5 $G_{xy}[i] \leftarrow G_y[i]$
	6 $G_{yx}[i] \leftarrow G_x[i]$
	7 return G_{xy}, G_{yx}

In the GenBot algorithm, the target distribution $P_X(x)$ is obtained from the LCS curve of legitimate accounts, while the approximating distribution $\hat{P}_X(x)$ is obtained from the LCS curve of a group of bots. The D_{KL} distance is computed by the fitness function Fit($\cdot$) that accepts as input an individual G_j and the target LCS curve b of legitimate accounts. The output is a scalar v_j that represents the fitness score of the individual G_j.

Mutation. The mutation is an operator commonly used in many genetic algorithms [36]. It typically consists in making some bases of the DNA sequences of an individual to mutate into a different base (e.g., A $\xrightarrow{\text{mutation}}$ C).

Previous studies showed that the distribution of bases within the digital DNA sequences of legitimate users is not uniform [13, 16]. Quite intuitively, some actions tend to occur more often than others, such as the tweeting action. For this reason, in GenBot we design a mutation operator that favors mutations from the C (replies) and T (retweets) bases to the A (tweets) base. Nonetheless, also mutations from A to C and T are possible, although with a lower probability. Our Mutation($\cdot$) function accepts two parameters: P_i, which is the full population at the i-th generation of the genetic algorithm; and L, which is the length of the digital DNA sequences. The output returned by the function is the mutated P_i population.

Mutation(P_i, L)
1   for $(G_j, v_j) \in P_i$ do
2   for $u_k \in G_j$ do
3   for $l \in \{1, \ldots, L\}$ do
4      $r \leftarrow$ rand()
5   if $r <$ MUT-PROB then
6   if $u_k[l] = $ C or $u_k[l] = $ T then
7        $u_k[l] = $ A
8   else
9   if $r < 0.5$ then
10        $u_k[l] = $ C
11   else
12        $u_k[l] = $ T
13   return P_i

Crossover. Traditionally, a crossover operator has two parent individuals as input, and generates two offsprings as the output [36]. The offsprings are obtained via a recombination of the DNA sequences of the two parents. Remarkably, in this study an individual G_j is a group of users $G_j = \{u_1, u_2, \ldots, u_M\}$ rather than a single user with its DNA sequence. Thus, by following the traditional crossover approach, we have two groups of users as input (the parents) and we obtain two groups of users as output (the offsprings). Recombinations at this level (i.e., at the group-level) can occur by mixing users between the two parent groups, rather than by mixing

DNA sequences. Within GenBot, this crossover strategy is implemented with the function GCO($\cdot$) (*Group CrossOver*). GCO($\cdot$) uses a one-point crossover technique. In detail, it randomly selects two groups $G_x, G_y \in P_i$ as the parents and a random crossover point r. Then, it generates the offspring G_{xy} as the combination of the first parent up to point r with the second parent from point r onwards, and the offspring G_{yx} viceversa. Figure 3 gives an intuitive idea of how our group-level crossover operator works.

Since our individuals are composed of many users, we can complement the previous crossover strategy with additional fine-grained crossovers working at the user-level. Specifically, we define two user-level crossover operators, referred to as the *User CrossOver* operator, defined in function UCO($\cdot$), and the *User Reverse CrossOver* operator, defined in function URCO($\cdot$). Function UCO($\cdot$) is a one-point crossover operator that acts at user-level. Similarly to the GCO($\cdot$) operator, two parents $u_x, u_y \in G_j$ and one crossover point r are randomly picked. Next, two offsprings – respectively u_{xy} and u_{yx} – are generated as the combination of the first parent up to point r with the second parent from point r onwards, and viceversa. Figure 4 gives an intuitive idea of how our UCO($\cdot$) user-level crossover operator works, in comparison with the group-level crossover.

Function URCO($\cdot$) differs from UCO($\cdot$) in the way the second parent u_y is exploited. In fact, in URCO($\cdot$), the digital DNA sequence of u_y is reversed before being recombined with that of the first parent u_x. This simple operation allows to create much more variability in the DNA sequences of the offsprings and it demonstrates very effective in practice.

Contrarily to traditional genetic algorithms, we exploit the richness of the DNA-based behavioral representations, by designing a multi-level crossover strategy. At the user-level, the fine-grained UCO($\cdot$) and URCO($\cdot$) operators apply recombinations to the DNA sequences of single users. Furthermore, at the group-level, the coarse-grained GCO($\cdot$) operator shuffles users between different groups.

UCO(u_x, u_y, r)	URCO(u_x, u_y, r)
1 for $i \in \{1, \ldots, r\}$ do	1 for $i \in \{1, \ldots, r\}$ do
2 $u_{xy}[i] \leftarrow u_x[i]$	2 $u_{xy}[i] \leftarrow u_x[i]$
3 $u_{yx}[i] \leftarrow u_y[i]$	3 $u_{yx}[i] \leftarrow u_y[|u_y| - i]$
4 for $i \in \{r+1, \ldots, |u_x|\}$ do	4 for $i \in \{r+1, \ldots, |u_x|\}$ do
5 $u_{xy}[i] \leftarrow u_y[i]$	5 $u_{xy}[i] \leftarrow u_y[|u_y| - i]$
6 $u_{yx}[i] \leftarrow u_x[i]$	6 $u_{yx}[i] \leftarrow u_x[i]$
7 return u_{xy}, u_{yx}	7 return u_{xy}, u_{yx}

3.2 The GenBot algorithm

We implemented GenBot by following the steps of the (1+1)-evolutionary algorithm scheme [18]. In its simplest definition, a (1+1)-EA is a *randomized hill climbing technique* [26] that relies on mutations only. In the GenBot algorithm, the simple (1+1)-EA scheme is extended by the adoption of a multi-level crossover strategy (i.e., 1 group-level and 2 user-level crossovers), as previously defined.

The core of the GenBot algorithm is represented in Algorithm 1 by the *for loop* at lines 7–37. Each iteration of the loop applies the mutation and crossover operators to obtain a new generation of spambots. In detail, the evolutionary steps in GenBot begin by mutating the current population and continue by substituting

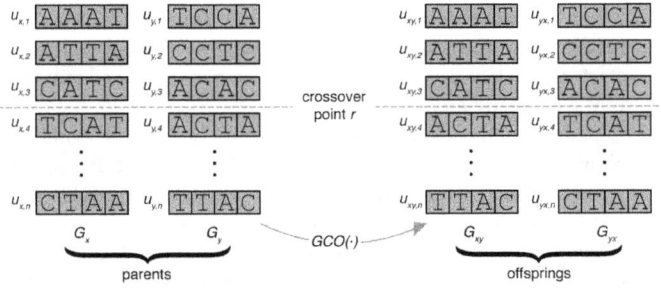

Figure 3: Group-level crossover: GCO(·) operator.

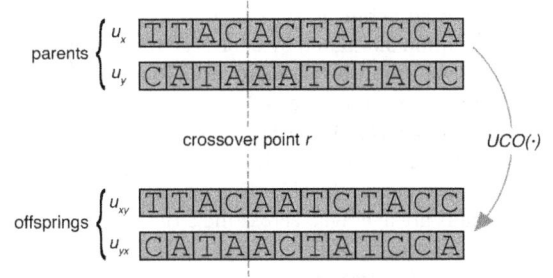

Figure 4: User-level crossover: UCO(·) operator.

Algorithm 1 GenBot

input : target legitimate group $G_{\text{legitimate}}$, initial population P_0
output : last generation of evolved spambots P_{best}

1   $b \leftarrow \text{LCS}(G_{\text{legitimate}})$
2   $U \leftarrow \text{numOfUsers}(G_{\text{legitimate}})$
3   $T \leftarrow \text{numOfTweets}(G_{\text{legitimate}})$
4   $P_{\text{best}} \leftarrow \text{null}$
5   **for** $G_i \in P_0$ **do**
6     $v_i \leftarrow \text{Fit}(G_i, b)$ // initial fitness score
7   **for** $i \in \{1, \ldots, \text{MAX-GEN}\}$ **do**
8     $mut = \text{Mutation}(P_{i-1}, T)$ // apply mutations
9   **for** $m_j \in mut$ **do**
10       $mv_j \leftarrow \text{Fit}(m_j, b)$
11   **if** $mv_j < v_j$ **then**
12         $(G_j, v_j) \leftarrow (m_j, mv_j)$
13   **for** $(G_k, v_k) \in P_i$ **do**
14       $x \leftarrow \text{rand}(1, \text{POP-SIZE})$
15       $y \leftarrow \text{rand}(1, \text{POP-SIZE})$
16       $G_{xy} \leftarrow \text{GCO}(G_x, G_y, U)$ // apply group crossovers
17   **for** $j \in \{1, \ldots, \text{NUM-URCO}\}$ **do**   // apply user reverse crossovers
18         $u_x \leftarrow \text{rand}(1, U)$
19         $u_y \leftarrow \text{rand}(1, U)$
20         $(u_{xy}, u_{yx}) \leftarrow \text{URCO}(G_j[u_x], G_j[u_y], T)$
21         $G_{xy}[u_x] \leftarrow u_{xy}$
22         $G_{xy}[u_y] \leftarrow u_{yx}$
23       $mv_k \leftarrow \text{Fit}(G_{xy}, b)$
24   **if** $mv_k < v_k$ **then**
25         $(G_k, v_k) \leftarrow (G_{xy}, mv_k)$
26   **for** $(G_k, v_k) \in P_i$ **do**
27   **for** $j \in \{1, \ldots, \text{NUM-UCO}\}$ **do**   // apply user crossovers
28         $u_x \leftarrow \text{rand}(1, U)$
29         $u_y \leftarrow \text{rand}(1, U)$
30         $(u_{xy}, u_{yx}) \leftarrow \text{UCO}(G_j[u_x], G_j[u_y], T)$
31         $G_{xy}[u_x] \leftarrow u_{xy}$
32         $G_{xy}[u_y] \leftarrow u_{yx}$
33       $mv_k \leftarrow \text{Fit}(G_{xy}, b)$
34   **if** $mv_k < v_k$ **then**
35         $(G_k, v_k) \leftarrow (G_{xy}, mv_k)$
36     $P_{i+1} \leftarrow P_i$
37     $P_{\text{best}} \leftarrow P_i$ // update evolved spambots
38 **return** P_{best}

---

the individuals that improve as a consequence of the mutations. Then, the group-level (coarse-grained) crossover GCO(·) is applied. Finally, also the 2 user-level (fine-grained) crossovers are applied. Specifically, at first URCO(·) is applied and the obtained offsprings are evaluated. Only those offsprings that improved the fitness score are retained. Subsequently, UCO(·) is applied and the offsprings are evaluated one last time, thus obtaining a new population that becomes the starting point of the next iteration of the algorithm.

Notably, traditional evolutionary heuristics based on genetic algorithms perform only one update of the population at each iteration of the algorithm. In GenBot however, each generation is the combination of three intermediate generations, respectively obtained via (i) mutations, (ii) a combination of group-level and reverse user-level crossovers, and (iii) user-level crossovers.

4 EXPERIMENTS, SETUP AND EVALUATION

4.1 Dataset

The dataset for this study is composed of the timelines of 3,474 legitimate Twitter accounts.

In order to build this dataset of certified human-operated accounts, random Twitter users were contacted by mentioning them in tweets. Then, contacted users were asked simple questions in natural language. Possible answers to such questions were collected by means of a Twitter crawler[3]. Upon manually verifying the answers, all 3,474 accounts that answered were certified as legitimate ones. Notably, this dataset has already been used in recent works [11–13, 16] and it is considered an important resource in the field of spambot and automation detection.

4.2 Experimental setup

The GenBot algorithm is implemented in C++ and the code is publicly available for scientific purposes (link in the introduction). For an efficient, linear-time computation of the LCS curves, we rely on an adapted version of the GLCR toolkit[4] implementing the algorithms in [3]. All the experiments ran on a machine with an Intel Xeon E7-4830v4, with a 64-bits architecture at 2 GHz, 112 cores and 500 GB of RAM. As the reference with which to compare our results, we consider the last (most recent) 2,000 actions performed by the legitimate accounts in our dataset.

We run GenBot with a population of 30 individuals per run (POP-SIZE) and a generation limit of 20,000 epochs as a stopping criterion (MAX-GEN). The initial population P_0 is composed of 30 identical individuals. Each individual represents a group of accounts and the starting point for all the individuals is a DNA sequence of length 2,000 (same DNA length of the legitimate accounts), whose first 1,000 positions are filled with the DNA base A, followed by 500 positions filled with the base C and the last 500 positions filled with the base T. Regarding the mutation operator, the probability

---

[3] https://developer.twitter.com/en/docs
[4] https://www.uni-ulm.de/in/theo/research/seqana.html

to mutate each action is set equal to 0.0002 (MUT-PROB). For each generation simulated by GenBot, a total of 30 offsprings are generated via group-level crossovers. Concerning the user-level crossovers, for each individual 2 offsprings are generated via the URCO(·) operator (NUM-URCO), while 12 offsprings are generated via the UCO(·) operator (NUM-UCO). Each experiment is repeated 5 times and each run of the algorithm starts with a different random seed. Results are averaged across the 5 runs.

4.3   Experimental evaluation

In the next section, we provide results for our experiments. In each experiment, the quality of the solutions generated by the the GenBot algorithm is evaluated by comparing the LCS curve of the last generation of spambots with that of the reference group. The LCS curve of the last generation of spambots is computed by applying the point-to-point average of all the LCS curves of the spambots groups constituting the last generation. We give both a qualitative and a quantitative evaluation of the results, as follows: (i) we provide a graphical comparison of LCS curves, giving a direct and intuitive insight into the quality of our results; (ii) we compute and compare the AUC of the LCS curves with Equation (1); (iii) we measure the distance between the LCS curves by means of the D_{KL} defined in Equation (2).

5   RESULTS

The last generation of spambots generated by GenBot (i.e., the one under evaluation) is referred to as *evolved spambots*.

5.1   Behavioral analysis of evolved spambots

Here, we evaluate the extent to which the evolved spambots generated by GenBot are capable of emulating the behavior of legitimate users. The first – and to the best of our knowledge, unique – scientific attempt to solve this task was documented in [16], where the authors employed a set of resampling techniques to generate new behavioral fingerprints, as similar as possible to those of legitimate users. In order to provide a comparison between GenBot and [16], we applied the best performing techniques described in [16] to our dataset. Specifically, 3 types of DNA resampling techniques were used: (i) a statistical resampling of the digital DNA sequences of legitimate users based on the average characteristics of those users (labeled *average*); (ii) a block permutation with block size = 5 (labeled *5-permutation*); and (iii) a block bootstrap with block size = 5 (labeled *5-bootstrap*). For the sake of clarity, Figure 8 pictorially shows the way to perform a block resampling on a digital DNA sequence [16].

Qualitative results of this experiment are shown in Figure 5. The LCS curve of the group of legitimate accounts is labeled *benchmark*. As shown, the LCS curve of the spambots generated with GenBot is almost completely overlapping the benchmark. The only exception is in the tail of the LCS curve and it is visible in the log-log inset of Figure 5. The comparison between previous techniques and GenBot is clearly in favor of the latter. In fact, all previous techniques greatly struggle to fit the head of the LCS curve, while instead they perform better in the tail. To this regard, our approach and those described in [16] seem to be complementary, with our GenBot algorithm capable of fitting all the LCS curve except for the tail,

which instead is well fit by the resampling approaches of [16]. One further improvement could be the adoption of block resampling strategies in GenBot, adding them to the mutations and crossovers that we already employ.

A quantitative evaluation of the quality of evolved spambots is obtained by comparing the AUC of the LCS curves of the spambots with that of the legitimate accounts. As shown in Table 1, the spambots obtained with GenBot were able to reproduce the LCS of legitimate users with a percentage error of only 2.98% in excess. Instead, all other techniques managed to reproduce only about half of the behavioral similarities expected within a group of legitimate accounts.

5.2   Detection of evolved spambots

Going further, we are now interested in evaluating whether the evolved spambots are able to avoid detection by state-of-the-art techniques [13]. We design this experiment by replicating the working conditions of most spambot detection systems – that is, we focus on the analysis of an unknown group of users that contains both spambots and legitimate users.

In detail, we start by mixing together part of our evolved spambots with part of the legitimate users. Then, we compare the LCS curve of the mixed group with that of the legitimate users only. Figure 6 shows a qualitative result of this comparison. As shown, the LCS curve of the mixed group lays very close to that of the legitimate users. In turn, this means that also the mixed group of evolved spambots and legitimate users still behaves like a group solely composed of legitimate users. Table 2 presents the comparison in terms of AUC values, which quantitatively confirm the result, although showing a larger error than that reported in the previous experiment of Table 1.

Finally, we apply 2 state-of-the-art spam and bot detection techniques [13, 35] to the mixed group, and we assess their performance in detecting the evolved spambots. We compare these results with those measured while applying the techniques in [13, 35] to a group of non-evolved spambots. Results are reported in Table 4 and show that the evolved spambots generated by GenBot largely evade detection (mean $F1 \simeq 0.260$). In addition to the techniques tested in Table 4, we also applied the system in [1] to our evolved spambots. Similarly to [13, 35], also [1] proves incapable of accurately detecting the evolved bots with $Accuracy = 0.495$ and $MCC = -0.071$. This result is in contrast with previous work [11, 13] where the detection rate for non-evolved spambots was $F1 = 0.923$.

5.3   Generalizability

In this section, we evaluate the generalizability of the GenBot algorithm and of the previously shown results. We change the group of legitimate accounts and we assess whether the evolved spambots generated by GenBot are still similar to the legitimate accounts. We first randomly split the original group of legitimate accounts into 2 disjunct subgroups (labeled *Group A* and *Group B*), each subgroup counting about 50% of the accounts of the original group. These subgroups are the 2 new references for GenBot to generate evolved spambots. Then, we compare the behavioral similarity between the evolved spambots and the subgroup (either *Group A* or *Group B*) used to generate them. Figure 7 shows the results of

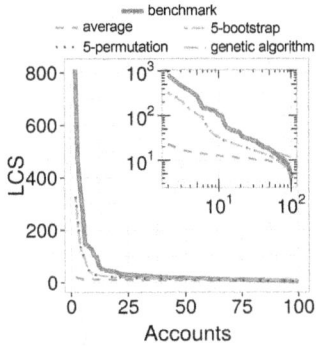

Figure 5: Qualitative analysis of evolved spambots and comparison with previous techniques.

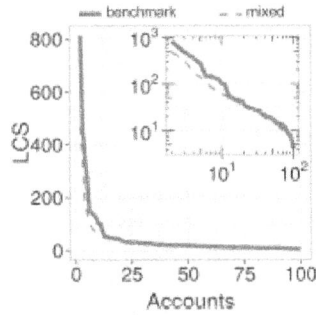

Figure 6: Comparison of the LCS curve of legitimate users with that of a mixed group composed of evolved spambots and legitimate users.

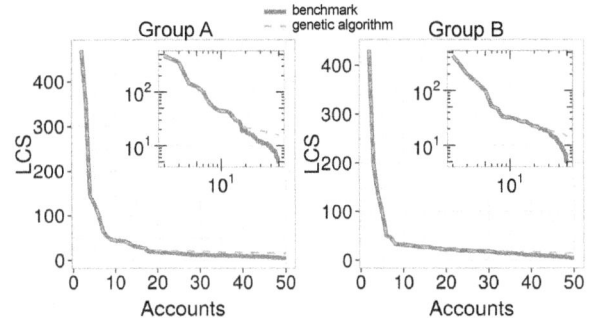

Figure 7: Qualitative comparison of evolved spambots against 2 different groups of legitimate accounts. Despite the different shape of the LCS curves of *Group A* and *Group B*, the corresponding evolved spambots closely match their behavior.

technique	AUC	% error
benchmark	3961.0	–
average	971.9	−75.46%
5-bootstrap	2001.7	−49.46%
5-permutation	2019.8	−49.01%
genetic algorithm	4079.0	+2.98%

Table 1: Quantitative analysis: comparison with previous techniques.

group	AUC	% error
benchmark (legitimate)	3961.0	–
mixed (bot + legitimate)	3090.2	−21.98%

Table 2: AUC comparison (group of legitimate users vs mixed groups: evolved spambots and legitimate users).

technique	Group A		Group B	
	AUC	% error	AUC	% error
benchmark	1797.0	–	1521.50	–
genetic algorithm	2025.6	+12.72%	1632.20	+07.28%

Table 3: Quantitative comparison of evolved spambots against 2 different groups of legitimate accounts.

technique	accounts	evaluation metrics					
		Precision	Recall	Specificity	Accuracy	F1	MCC
Cresci *et al.* [13]	non-evolved spambots	1.000	0.858	1.000	0.929	0.923	0.867
Miller *et al.* [35]	non-evolved spambots	0.555	0.358	0.698	0.526	0.435	0.059
Cresci *et al.* [13]	evolved spambots (GENBOT)	0.512	0.210	0.800	0.505	0.298	0.012
Miller *et al.* [35]	evolved spambots (GENBOT)	0.720	0.360	0.860	0.610	0.480	0.254

Table 4: Performances of 2 state-of-the-art spam and bot detection techniques towards the detection of non-evolved spambots and evolved spambots generated with GENBOT. The evolved spambots largely go undetected.

target group	D_{KL}	
	mean	std
legitimate full	32.64	2.97
legitimate *Group A*	73.83	11.44
legitimate *Group B*	34.16	2.33

Table 5: Variability of our results across 5 runs of our algorithm for different experiments.

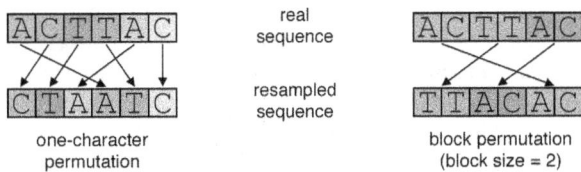

Figure 8: Application of block resampling to a digital DNA sequence, and comparison with one-character resampling.

a qualitative comparison. Despite the different shape of the LCS curves of *Group A* and *Group B* of legitimate accounts (solid red line), the corresponding evolved spambots closely match their behavior. This testifies that even by changing the characteristics of the accounts to mimic, GENBOT is capable of generating spambots that behave in a similar way with respect to the legitimate ones.

Moreover, this also implies that GENBOT is capable of generating spambots featuring different characteristics. Interestingly, Figure 7 also shows a rather poor performance in fitting the tail of the LCS curve, similarly to what we already saw in Figure 5. Finally, Table 3 reports quantitative results for the 2 subgroups of legitimate accounts, showing a low percentage error for both groups.

The experiments were executed 5 times, with random seeds to assess variability. In particular, we measure the mean and the standard deviation (std) of the distance between the LCS curve of the evolved spambots generated by GENBOT and that of legitimate accounts, across 5 runs of the algorithm. The distance between LCS curves is measured by means of the D_{KL} distance defined in Equation (2). As shown in Table 5, the standard deviation of D_{KL} is rather low in every experiment, and significantly lower than the mean, which suggests low variability in the results.

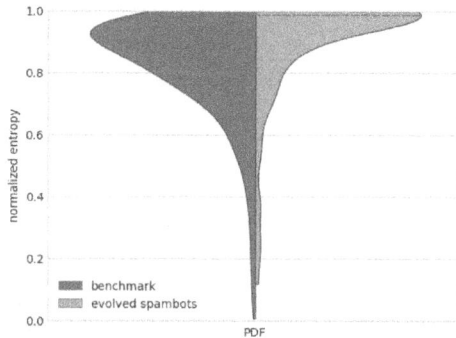

Figure 9: Beanplot showing the PDF of the normalized Shannon entropy of DNA sequences related to evolved spambots and legitimate accounts. DNA sequences of the evolved spambots feature a suspiciously high entropy.

5.4 Improving current detection techniques

As demonstrated above, the GenBot-generated spambots are able to avoid actual detection techniques. We can see that collectively, the evolved spambots do not leave traces of their automated nature, since they accurately reproduce the LCS curve of legitimate accounts. However, interesting insights can be gained by studying the single digital DNA sequences of every spambot. Indeed, a close inspection reveals that the digital DNA sequences of the spambots generated by GenBot have very few repetitions and almost no regularities at all[5]. In turn, such DNA sequences represent very erratic and heterogeneous behaviors. This finding is in contrast with the known characteristics of legitimate accounts [13, 16] that tend to favor certain actions in their behaviors. As a consequence, digital DNA sequences of legitimate accounts have a prevalence for certain DNA bases (e.g., the A base for tweets). We formalize this intuition by relying on the notion of normalized Shannon entropy (H_{norm}). In particular, we compute the entropy of each digital DNA sequence, for all the evolved spambots and all the legitimate accounts. Figure 9 shows a beanplot of the empirical probability density function (PDF) of the normalized entropy, comparing measurements for evolved spambots with those of legitimate accounts. As expected, the spambots generated by GenBot have mean $H_{norm} \simeq 1$, whereas for legitimate accounts mean $H_{norm} = 0.8$ (dashed red lines in Figure 9). A straightforward consequence of this observation is the possibility to extend current detection techniques based on the accounts' behavior, such as [11, 13], by also considering information related to the repetitions and regularities within sequences, thus making current systems more robust against possible future spambot evolutions. Although limited in scope, this experiment nonetheless testifies the usefulness – and one among many possible applications – of the proposed analytical framework for simulating spambot evolutions.

6 DISCUSSION

Our results demonstrated the possibility to combine the behavioral representation of digital DNA with the computational framework

---

[5]Here we are interested in repetitions *within* sequences rather than *across* sequences, as it was for the case of studying the LCS.

of genetic algorithms, in order to create evolved spambots capable of escaping current state-of-the-art detection techniques, based on the accounts' behavior [13] and on the content of posts [1, 35].

In particular, we designed an analytical framework for simulating spambot evolutions, thus answering to the first of our research questions (**RQ1**). In such framework, social spambots behavior is modeled via digital DNA. Then, DNA sequences are fed to the novel genetic algorithm (GenBot), designed to simulate spambot evolutions. After thousands of subsequent iterations, the output of GenBot is a novel generation of *evolved spambots*, described by their digital DNA. Notably, in this work we grounded the framework for simulating possible spambot evolutions on (i) genetic algorithms and (ii) the recent advances in digital DNA behavioral modeling, since they currently represent its key enabling factors. However, it is likely that in the near future the same methodological approach for studying spambot evolution could leverage different techniques and methodologies, thus widening its applicability.

Aiming to answer **RQ2**, we then evaluated the extent to which the evolved spambots are capable of going undetected by state-of-the-art techniques. Since our experiments grounded on modeling the actions in the timelines of the accounts under investigation, it was natural to consider detection techniques based on accounts behavior and posted contents. Thus, with regards to the technique in [13], we showed that (i) the behavioral fingerprint of the spambots generated by GenBot is similar to that of legitimate users, (ii) a group containing both our evolved spambots and legitimate users is almost indistinguishable from a group solely composed of legitimate users, and (iii) the *social fingerprinting* detection technique largely fails in detecting the evolved spambots. Moreover, 2 other recent detection techniques, based on the content of posts [1, 35], also fail in detecting the spambots generated by GenBot. These results raise concerns towards the vulnerabilities of current state-of-the-art techniques.

Finally, we studied the characteristics of the evolved spambots, with the goal of answering to **RQ3** – that is, looking for ways to improve (at least a subset of) current detection techniques. Specifically, we investigated whether the evolved spambots still had some peculiar characteristics that would make them detectable. We noticed that, although the group of evolved spambots behaves like a group of legitimate users, the digital DNA of the spambots is more *entropic* than that of legitimate users. Thus, we argue that it would be possible and fruitful to extend current detection techniques by also considering the amount of entropy within digital DNA sequences. This last finding thus represents a useful suggestion for improving current spambot detection techniques.

This study – the very first of its kind – moves in the direction of a *proactive* spambot detection. For the first time since the advent of OSNs, we have the chance to proactively study spambot evolutions and to design more robust detection techniques, possibly capable of withstanding the next evolutions of social spambots. Although unlikely to completely defeat spambots and other malicious accounts, the application of the proposed proactive approach would nonetheless bring groundbreaking benefits. The capability to foresee possible spambot evolutions would not only allow to test the detection rate of state-of-the-art techniques (including techniques based, e.g., on the exploration of the social graph of the accounts, or on their profiles and posting aptitudes), but also and above all, to *a priori* adapt them and even to design new detection techniques. As a consequence of the additional design and experimentation allowed by the proactive approach, many spambot evolutions will be detected from *day 0*. Spambots will see their chances to harm severely restricted, with clear and immediate benefits for our online environments, and ultimately, for our societies (e.g., less fake news and biased propaganda). Notably, for those few spambot evolutions still not foreseen by this proactive approach, we will still be able to fall back to the traditional reactive approach, at no additional cost.

7 ETHICAL CONSIDERATIONS

With the rise of AI, our daily lives are increasingly influenced by decisions taken on our behalf by automated systems. Algorithmic filtering (which leads to filter bubbles, echo chambers, and eventually polarization), algorithmic bias and current limits in explainability of predictive models already raise serious ethical concerns on the development and adoption of AI solutions. Within this context, algorithmic approaches to the characterization, development, and detection of social bots make no exception [17, 42]. For instance, one might naively think that all endeavors devoted to the development of social bots are to be blamed. However, not all social bots are nefarious by nature [20]. Indeed, bots can be programmed to automatically post information about news and academic papers [24, 32], and even to provide help during emergencies [4, 39]. Undeniably, the provision of useful services by benign bots will make them become an established presence on social platforms [37]. Meanwhile, other researchers investigated malicious bots [2, 15, 29, 33], in an effort to better understand their evolution, impact and interactions with benign users. The so-recognized existence of benign versus malicious bots sparked heated debates about the rights of automated accounts. For instance, both researchers and everyday social media users wondered the extent to which social bots should be considered equal to humans, as far as censorship[6,7] and suppression of free speech [34] are concerned.

While advancing the state of the art in the fascinating field of AI, we are aware that the successful implementation of new technologies will pose greater challenges to discriminate between human and automated behaviors. Now more than ever, spambot evolution and their subsequent detection meet ethical considerations. The framework proposed in this paper should not be seen merely as a technical exercise. In fact, our evolved spambots have not been conceived to support botnet developers (a criticism that could be very well posed to all the above-cited research). Instead, we remark that one of the main goals of this paper is to proactively sharpen detection techniques to cope with future evolutions of spambots, as typically done in the well-recognized field of adversarial learning.

Lastly, [50] clearly explains that "a supervised machine learning tool is only as good as the data used for its training". Since spambot detection is a rapidly-evolving field, we are all involved in the quest for up-to-date datasets. By playing with the parameters of the evolutionary algorithm here proposed, we advocate the capability to create a huge variety of fresh data, to re-train and fine-tune existing detection mechanisms.

8 RELATED WORK

Although representing an effective heuristic to solve complex optimization problems [36], genetic algorithms usually require a string-based genetic encoding of information to be applied. This requirement severely limited their applicability. Remarkably, in recent years, we assisted to the proliferation of many studies on modeling and analyzing online behaviors. A stream of research focused on specific behavioral analytics tasks, such as detecting specific behavioral patterns [6, 27, 38], predicting future behaviors [30, 55], and detecting anomalous ones [7, 11, 13, 45, 53, 54]. Others instead achieved more general results. In [25] authors showed that individuals have persistent and distinct online inter-event time distributions, while [16] focused on modeling human tweeting behaviors, showing that such behaviors are very diverse and heterogeneous, although far from being random. One result achieved in behavioral analytics is the possibility to encode the behavioral information of an account in a DNA-like string of characters [11, 16]. The characterization of the account behavior through this *digital DNA* modeling technique, coupled with the capability to carry out evolutionary simulations by means of genetic algorithms, opens up the unprecedented opportunity to quantitatively experiment with spambot evolutions and motivates our research.

Meanwhile, progress has been made towards the detection of malicious accounts (e.g., fakes, bots, spammers). As such accounts put in place complex mechanisms to evade existing detection systems, scholars tried to keep pace by proposing powerful techniques based on profile- [5, 10, 54], posting- [5, 8, 11, 13, 22, 48], and network-characteristics [5, 31, 47, 48, 51–53] of the accounts. However, until now, new detection systems have been developed only as a consequence of spambot evolutions [12]. In fact, no work has ever been done towards studying, and possibly anticipating, such evolutions. In other words, malicious accounts detection has always been tackled with a *reactive* approach, which is in contrast with the novel *proactive* approach envisaged in this research.

9 CONCLUSIONS

We presented the first exploratory study to carry out a quantitative analysis of spambot evolutions. Specifically, riding the wave of the adversarial learning line of research, we first designed a novel genetic algorithm for simulating spambot behavioral evolutions. Then, we evaluated the extent to which the evolved spambots are capable of evading 3 state-of-the-art detection systems, based on evaluating the accounts' behavior and the content of posts. Testing the first system, results showed that as much as 79% of the evolved spambots evade detection. Additionally, we also investigated the characteristics of the evolved spambots, highlighting distinctive features (e.g., entropy within digital DNA sequences) that would allow to distinguish them from legitimate accounts. Considering these features in current detection systems based on behavioral characteristics of the accounts would make them more robust against possible future spambot evolutions.

Further experimentation could lead to new results not only in bot design (e.g., chatbots), but also and foremost in the development of spambot detection systems. Indeed, until now, researchers had to *react* to bot evolutions. However, for the first time since the advent of OSNs, there is the concrete chance to *proactively* tackle the

---

[6]https://www.nytimes.com/2018/09/05/technology/lawmakers-facebook-twitter-for eign-influence-hearing.html

[7]https://www.theguardian.com/technology/2018/oct/16/facebook-political-activis m-pages-inauthentic-behavior-censorship

challenging task of spambot detection. Although here instantiated for a specific modeling and detection technique, we thus argue that the proactive approach will provide the scientific community with the possibility to experiment with and simulate future spambot evolutions, substantially raising the bar for spambot developers.

ACKNOWLEDGEMENTS

Research supported in part by TOFFEe (TOol for Fighting FakEs), a PAI ('Progetto di Attività Integrate') project of IMT School For Advanced Studies Lucca and by MIUR under grant 'Dipartimenti di eccellenza 2018-2022', Computer Science Dept., Sapienza University.

REFERENCES

[1] Faraz Ahmed and Muhammad Abulaish. 2013. A generic statistical approach for spam detection in Online Social Networks. *Computer Communications* 36, 10 (2013), 1120–1129.
[2] Luca Maria Aiello, Martina Deplano, Rossano Schifanella, and Giancarlo Ruffo. 2012. People are Strange when you're a Stranger: Impact and Influence of Bots on Social Networks. In *ICWSM*. AAAI.
[3] Michael Arnold and Enno Ohlebusch. 2011. Linear time algorithms for generalizations of the longest common substring problem. *Algorithmica* 60, 4 (2011).
[4] Marco Avvenuti, Salvatore Bellomo, Stefano Cresci, Mariantonietta Noemi La Polla, and Maurizio Tesconi. 2017. Hybrid crowdsensing: A novel paradigm to combine the strengths of opportunistic and participatory crowdsensing. In *WWW Companion*. ACM.
[5] Prudhvi Ratna Badri Satya, Kyumin Lee, Dongwon Lee, Thanh Tran, and Jason Jiasheng Zhang. 2016. Uncovering fake likers in online social networks. In *CIKM*. ACM.
[6] Hakan Bagci and Pinar Karagoz. 2015. Random walk based context-aware activity recommendation for location based social networks. In *DSAA*. IEEE.
[7] Chiyu Cai, Linjing Li, and Daniel Zeng. 2017. Detecting Social Bots by Jointly Modeling Deep Behavior and Content Information. In *CIKM*. ACM.
[8] Nikan Chavoshi, Hossein Hamooni, and Abdullah Mueen. 2016. DeBot: Twitter Bot Detection via Warped Correlation.. In *ICDM*. IEEE.
[9] Lucas Chi and Kwong Hui. 1992. Color set size problem with applications to string matching. In *Combinatorial Pattern Matching*. Springer.
[10] Stefano Cresci, Roberto Di Pietro, Marinella Petrocchi, Angelo Spognardi, and Maurizio Tesconi. 2015. Fame for sale: Efficient detection of fake Twitter followers. *Decision Support Systems* 80 (2015).
[11] Stefano Cresci, Roberto Di Pietro, Marinella Petrocchi, Angelo Spognardi, and Maurizio Tesconi. 2016. DNA-inspired online behavioral modeling and its application to spambot detection. *IEEE Intelligent Systems* 31, 5 (2016).
[12] Stefano Cresci, Roberto Di Pietro, Marinella Petrocchi, Angelo Spognardi, and Maurizio Tesconi. 2017. The Paradigm-Shift of Social Spambots: Evidence, Theories, and Tools for the Arms Race. In *WWW Companion*. ACM.
[13] Stefano Cresci, Roberto Di Pietro, Marinella Petrocchi, Angelo Spognardi, and Maurizio Tesconi. 2017. Social fingerprinting: detection of spambot groups through DNA-inspired behavioral modeling. *IEEE TDSC* (2017).
[14] Stefano Cresci, Fabrizio Lillo, Daniele Regoli, Serena Tardelli, and Maurizio Tesconi. 2018. $FAKE: Evidence of spam and bot activity in stock microblogs on Twitter. In *ICWSM*. AAAI.
[15] Stefano Cresci, Marinella Petrocchi, Angelo Spognardi, and Stefano Tognazzi. 2019. On the capability of evolved spambots to evade detection via genetic engineering. *Online Social Networks and Media* 9 (2019).
[16] Stefano Cresci, Roberto Di Pietro, Marinella Petrocchi, Angelo Spognardi, and Maurizio Tesconi. 2017. Exploiting digital DNA for the analysis of similarities in Twitter behaviours. In *DSAA*. IEEE.
[17] Carolina Alves de Lima Salge and Nicholas Berente. 2017. Is that social bot behaving unethically? *Commun. ACM* 60, 9 (2017).
[18] Stefan Droste, Thomas Jansen, and Ingo Wegener. 2002. On the Analysis of the (1+1) Evolutionary Algorithm. *Theoretical Computer Science* 276 (2002).
[19] Tom Fawcett. 2006. An introduction to ROC analysis. *Pattern recognition letters* 27, 8 (2006).
[20] Emilio Ferrara, Onur Varol, Clayton Davis, Filippo Menczer, and Alessandro Flammini. 2016. The rise of social bots. *Commun. ACM* 59, 7 (2016).
[21] Jerome Friedman, Trevor Hastie, and Robert Tibshirani. 2001. *The elements of statistical learning*. Vol. 1. Springer Series in Statistics.
[22] Maria Giatsoglou, Despoina Chatzakou, Neil Shah, Alex Beutel, Christos Faloutsos, and Athena Vakali. 2015. ND-Sync: Detecting Synchronized Fraud Activities. In *PAKDD*.
[23] Dan Gusfield. 1997. *Algorithms on strings, trees and sequences: computer science and computational biology*. Cambridge University Press.
[24] Stefanie Haustein, Timothy D. Bowman, Kim Holmberg, Andrew Tsou, Cassidy R. Sugimoto, and Vincent Larivière. 2016. Tweets As Impact Indicators: Examining the Implications of Automated "Bot" Accounts on Twitter. *J. Assoc. Inf. Sci. Technol.* 67, 1 (2016).
[25] Jiwan Jeong and Sue Moon. 2017. Interval Signature: Persistence and Distinctiveness of Inter-event Time Distributions in Online Human Behavior. In *WWW Companion*. ACM.
[26] Ari Juels and Martin Wattenberg. 1996. Stochastic hillclimbing as a baseline method for evaluating genetic algorithms. In *NIPS*.
[27] Srijan Kumar, Justin Cheng, and Jure Leskovec. 2017. Antisocial Behavior on the Web: Characterization and Detection. In *WWW Companion*. ACM.
[28] Alexey Kurakin, Ian Goodfellow, and Samy Bengio. 2017. Adversarial machine learning at scale. In *ICLR*.
[29] Kyumin Lee, Brian Eoff, and James Caverlee. 2011. Seven Months with the Devils: A Long-Term Study of Content Polluters on Twitter. In *ICWSM*. AAAI.
[30] Kang Li and Yun Fu. 2014. Prediction of human activity by discovering temporal sequence patterns. *IEEE TPAMI* 36, 8 (2014).
[31] Shenghua Liu, Bryan Hooi, and Christos Faloutsos. 2017. HoloScope: Topology-and-Spike Aware Fraud Detection. In *CIKM*. ACM.
[32] Tetyana Lokot and Nicholas Diakopoulos. 2016. News Bots: Automating news and information dissemination on Twitter. *Digital Journalism* 4, 6 (2016).
[33] Gregory Maus. 2017. A Typology of Socialbots (Abbrev.). In *WebSci*. ACM.
[34] Jeffrey Mervis. 2014. An Internet research project draws conservative ire. *Science* 346, 6210 (2014).
[35] Zachary Miller, Brian Dickinson, William Deitrick, Wei Hu, and Alex Hai Wang. 2014. Twitter spammer detection using data stream clustering. *Information Sciences* 260 (2014).
[36] Melanie Mitchell. 1998. *An Introduction to Genetic Algorithms*. MIT Press.
[37] Bjarke Monsted, Piotr Sapiezynski, Emilio Ferrara, and Sune Lehmann. 2017. Evidence of complex contagion of information in social media: An experiment using Twitter bots. *PloS one* 12, 9 (2017).
[38] Marcel Salathé, Duy Q Vu, Shashank Khandelwal, and David R Hunter. 2013. The dynamics of health behavior sentiments on a large online social network. *EPJ Data Science* 2, 1 (2013).
[39] Saiph Savage, Andres Monroy-Hernandez, and Tobias Höllerer. 2016. Botivist: Calling volunteers to action using online bots. In *CSCW*. ACM.
[40] Indira Sen, Anupama Aggarwal, Shiven Mian, Siddharth Singh, Ponnurangam Kumaraguru, and Anwitaman Datta. 2018. Worth its Weight in Likes: Towards Detecting Fake Likes on Instagram. In *WebSci*. ACM.
[41] L Steward, Ahmer Arif, and Kate Starbird. 2018. Examining Trolls and Polarization with a Retweet Network. In *WSDM Workshops*. ACM.
[42] Andree Thieltges, Florian Schmidt, and Simon Hegelich. 2016. The devil's triangle: Ethical considerations on developing bot detection methods. In *Spring Symposium Series*. AAAI.
[43] Stefano Tognazzi, Stefano Cresci, Marinella Petrocchi, and Angelo Spognardi. 2018. From Reaction to Proaction: Unexplored Ways to the Detection of Evolving Spambots. In *WWW Companion*. ACM.
[44] Liang Tong, Bo Li, Chen Hajaj, and Yevgeniy Vorobeychik. 2017. Hardening Classifiers against Evasion: the Good, the Bad, and the Ugly. *CoRR* abs/1708.08327 (2017). arXiv:1708.08327 http://arxiv.org/abs/1708.08327
[45] Onur Varol, Emilio Ferrara, Clayton Davis, Filippo Menczer, and Alessandro Flammini. 2017. Online Human-Bot Interactions: Detection, Estimation, and Characterization. In *ICWSM*. AAAI.
[46] Bimal Viswanath, Muhammad Ahmad Bashir, Muhammad Bilal Zafar, Simon Bouget, Saikat Guha, Krishna P Gummadi, Aniket Kate, and Alan Mislove. 2015. Strength in Numbers: Robust Tamper Detection in Crowd Computations. In *COSN*. ACM.
[47] Binghui Wang, Neil Zhenqiang Gong, and Hao Fu. 2017. GANG: Detecting Fraudulent Users in Online Social Networks via Guilt-by-Association on Directed Graphs. In *ICDM*. IEEE.
[48] Fangzhao Wu, Jinyun Shu, Yongfeng Huang, and Zhigang Yuan. 2015. Social spammer and spam message co-detection in microblogging with social context regularization. In *CIKM*. ACM.
[49] Chao Yang, Robert Harkreader, and Guofei Gu. 2013. Empirical evaluation and new design for fighting evolving Twitter spammers. *IEEE TIFS* 8, 8 (2013).
[50] K. C Yang, O. Varol, C. A. Davis, E. Ferrara, A. Flammini, and F. Menczer. 2019. Arming the public with AI to counter social bots. *Human Behavior and Emerging Technologies* (2019).
[51] Zhi Yang, Christo Wilson, Xiao Wang, Tingting Gao, Ben Y Zhao, and Yafei Dai. 2014. Uncovering social network sybils in the wild. *ACM TKDD* 8, 1 (2014).
[52] Rose Yu, Xinran He, and Yan Liu. 2014. GLAD: group anomaly detection in social media analysis. In *KDD*. ACM.
[53] Shuhan Yuan, Xintao Wu, Jun Li, and Aidong Lu. 2017. Spectrum-based deep neural networks for fraud detection. In *CIKM*. ACM.
[54] Reza Zafarani and Huan Liu. 2015. 10 Bits of Surprise: Detecting malicious users with minimum information. In *CIKM*. ACM.
[55] Aoying Zhou, Weining Qian, and Haixin Ma. 2012. Social media data analysis for revealing collective behaviors. In *KDD*. ACM.

Harnessing Collective Intelligence in P2P Lending

Henry K. Dambanemuya
Northwestern University
Evanston, Illinois
hdambane@u.northwestern.edu

Emőke-Ágnes Horvát[*]
Northwestern University
Evanston, Illinois
a-horvat@northwestern.edu

Abstract

Crowd financing is a burgeoning phenomenon that promises to improve access to capital by enabling borrowers with limited financial opportunities to receive small contributions from individual lenders towards unsecured loan requests. Faced with information asymmetry about borrowers' credibility, individual lenders bear the entire loss in case of loan default. Predicting loan payment is therefore crucial for lenders and for the sustainability of these platforms. To this end, we examine whether the "wisdom" of the lending crowd can provide reliable decision support with respect to projects' long-term success. Using data from Prosper.com, we investigate the association between the dynamics of lending behaviour and successful loan payment through interpretable classification models. We find evidence for collective intelligence signals in lending behaviour and observe variability in crowd wisdom across loan categories. We find that the wisdom of the lending crowd is most prominent in the auto loan category, but it is statistically significant for all other categories except student debt. Our study contributes new insights on how signals deduced from lending behaviour can improve the efficiency of crowd financing thereby contributing to economic growth and societal development.

Keywords

Crowdsourcing, Crowdfunding, Herding, Signalling, Wisdom of Crowds, Decision-Making, Dynamics

ACM Reference Format:
Henry K. Dambanemuya and Emőke-Ágnes Horvát. 2019. Harnessing Collective Intelligence in P2P Lending. In 11th ACM Conference on Web Science (WebSci '19), June 30–July 3, 2019, Boston, MA, USA. ACM, New York, NY, USA, 8 pages. https://doi.org/10.1145/3292522.3326040

1 Introduction

Peer-to-Peer (P2P) lending services are social platforms that connect individual borrowers to lenders who compete through a bidding process to invest outside of traditional financial institutions [1, 5, 26]. Although such online financing is a relatively new phenomenon, several studies have already investigated determinants of successful fundraising [2–4, 11, 12, 15, 16, 19–21, 24–26, 31–34]. Understanding who will receive funding is a crucial component

[*]Corresponding author

of the crowd financing model. However, crowd financing platforms also need to recognise how to attract and keep lenders. From the lenders' perspective, the key outcome is whether a borrower pays the loan on time [14, 21, 30]. Making this determination is extremely hard, even for experienced institutional lenders, let alone for untrained individuals who face additional information asymmetry compared to offline lenders, because they have less access to factual information about borrowers' credibility such as credit history, income, or employment. Lenders bear the entire loss in case of loan default and might quit using crowd financing, which could impact the viability of several online platforms. Typically, lenders consider loan characteristics such as amount, interest rate, and credit score when making lending decisions. However, lenders may also have additional criteria and since information about bids is made public on the platform, their behaviour can influence others. Such social learning is prevalent when individuals find it difficult to evaluate an object's true quality [28, 29] and can lead to information cascades and herding [6, 13], which might result in sub-optimal outcomes. Research on P2P lending suggests, however, that herding can help novice lenders identify which borrowers are the best risk [35]. Motivated by this work, we propose to scrutinise the collective intelligence of the lending crowd and identify a set of indicators that are associated with accurate predictions of loan success. We argue that lenders can capitalise on each other's evaluation of the borrowers' creditworthiness to improve their decision-making as a collective.

Specifically, *we investigate whether the wisdom of the lending crowd can help estimate the likelihood that a borrower will pay the loan years down the line*, i.e., the long-term success of borrowers' projects. To this end, we develop a set of features that characterise lending behaviour and account for potential learning effects and changes in the lender population. We then aggregate these features to describe the lender crowd contributing to individual projects. Finally, we train classification models with loan, borrower, and lending dynamics features to investigate which factors are associated with loan payment. By improving on a random-estimator baseline, we establish a basis for non-trivial prediction of loan payment from features which summarise lenders' actions and are determinants of long-term project success. We conclude by investigating the lending dynamics features that make prediction possible and further investigate whether the lending crowd is wiser in predicting the long-term success of certain project categories than others. The premise of our work is not to debate whether lender dynamics are more important than borrower or loan features in evaluating loan payment. Rather, *we argue that dynamics in lending behaviour add significant value to the estimation accuracy of machine learning models for predicting loan payment*. Since it is not known how these dynamics manifest themselves, we are compelled to investigate a range of potential collective intelligence indicators and test which signals contribute to the reliable inference of projects' long-term success.

First and foremost, our findings provide new insights on how lender behaviour can improve crowd financing efficiency and thereby contribute to economic growth and societal development. Specifically, we complement existing research on who receives funding [2–4, 11, 12, 15, 16, 19–21, 24–26, 31–34] with an investigation of the lesser understood determinants of loan payment or default. Additionally, our approach also informs the study of broadly relevant problems of collective decision-making under high uncertainty. Crowd financing is essentially a prototypical case of decision-making with substantial associated ambiguity: It is mediated by an online marketplace and presents challenges in determining, for instance, the veracity of identities, reliability of claims, merit of ideas, and their expected appeal to an indefinite crowd. The tasks tackled by lenders are therefore representative of the problems that arise in a suite of other P2P platforms such as consumer-to-consumer e-commerce websites (eBay), as well as task-service (TaskRabbit) and hospitality (AirBnB) platforms. By creating a framework that separates domain-specific predictors of long-term success from generalisable indicators of collective intelligence, the latter are expected to find use also beyond the context of crowd financing.

The rest of the paper is organised as follows: Section 2 summarises related research on crowd financing. Section 3 introduces data from Prosper.com. Section 4 describes measures and models used for predicting long-term success, while Section 5 provides our results. We conclude the paper in Section 6.

2   Related Work

Crowdfunding is an emerging topic of research in fields ranging from social computing [11, 15, 23, 24, 34] to economics [1, 5, 26]. A key strand of literature examines which projects receive funding. Factors such as description quality [25], specific language use [4], project updates [34], the ability to attract funders early in the campaign [12, 15], promotional activities on social media [24], and the project creator's reputation [11] as well as their social capital [3, 16, 20, 31] have been found to be associated with higher rates of fundraising. Some of this research highlights the role of herding and information cascades among investors in successfully raising capital [2, 32], leaving the question open whether the crowd's herding was rational or not. In the low-information P2P lending context, Zhang and Liu argued that herding can be beneficial for novice lenders [35]. They found that, in general, lenders are savvy enough to know when to follow the herd, but that they are also more inclined to herd on well-funded listings.

Due to these potentially adverse herding effects, when determining whether the crowd produced actual collective intelligence, one needs to look beyond who received funding and tackle questions like who payed the loan back, set up a business successfully, or produced the promised project deliverables? Collecting data on such long-term outcomes is difficult and hence literature examining determinants of long-term project success is scarce. Few exceptions have studied default in P2P lending marketplaces: Serrano-Cinca et al. demonstrated via a logistic regression model that borrowers' credit information is the most predictive factor of loan default [30]. The authors also found evidence for the relevance of borrowers'

annual income, homeownership status, credit history, and indebtedness to loan payment. Emekter et al. found similar loan and borrower features to be important predictors of default [14]. To extend the problem's relevance beyond lenders' profitability, Klafft advocated for a thorough analysis from a lender's perspective as a path to increase the future business potential of P2P lending platforms. Acknowledging the severity of the information asymmetry problem, the author suggested that lenders following simple, portfolio-based investment rules can attain acceptable returns for all credit rating categories, with the exception of high-risk loans. Finally, in another study examining the performance of P2P lending platforms, Iyer et al. found that non-expert lenders predict the likelihood of loan default with 45% greater accuracy than the borrowers' exact credit score and achieve 87% of the predictive power of the best possible default predictor that an econometrician could have constructed using all available standard financial information about borrowers.

In a different spirit, centred on the temporal progression of lenders' bidding behaviour, the study by Ceyhan et al. used Prosper.com data to predict both short- and long-term project success [10]. Instead of making inferences based on a large number of traditional creditworthiness indicators, the authors modelled the temporal dynamics of bidding to grasp "how the market feels" and to gain information that was not present in borrower characteristics like credit grade and debt-to-income-ratio. Due to similarities in terms of data and focus, this study is most closely related to our research. Ceyhan et al. fit the progression of bids with a sigmoid function and leave it unclear how their model relates to collective intelligence theories at large.

In sum, our literature review indicates that while much is understood about short-term funding success (i.e., who receives funding), little is known about long-term payment success (i.e., who delivers). Moreover, aside from the Ceyhan et al. study, previous work on long-term success has concentrated on loan and borrower determinants of default. We see this as a knowledge gap in understanding the wisdom of lending crowds in P2P marketplaces. To fill this gap, our work concentrates on determinants of long-term project success deduced from lending dynamics that could improve crowd financing efficiency.

3   Data: Prosper Marketplace

Prosper.com is a peer-to-peer lending platform that allows borrowers to receive funding from members of a large online marketplace. Borrowers request loans by creating *listings* for a specific amount between $1,000 and $25,000 and specifying the maximum interest rate they are willing to pay if the listing turns into a loan. Lenders then *bid* to fund a fraction of the amount at a chosen interest rate. When a listing reaches at least 100% of its requested amount, bids with the lowest interest rates are pooled into a single *loan* awarded to the borrower at a final *interest rate* determined by Prosper.

Lenders make their decisions based on information displayed on the platform. Included on the listings are borrowers' financial information such as *debt-to-income ratio*, *credit grade*, and *Prosper score*, as well as the loan *amount*, project *description* and *category*. These details are available for all the 415,157 listings created between November 2005 and October 2008, belonging to six loan categories ranging from student loans to auto loans (see Section 4.2 for definitions). In 2009, Prosper changed its privacy policy and stopped showing borrowers' credit score information. To account for this change in platform features, we restrict our study to data prior to this event.

To predict loan payment, we further limit our data to listings that were successfully completed by November 2008 and were either fully paid or defaulted due to, e.g., delinquency, bankruptcy, or a borrower being deceased. This sample excludes loan payments that were still ongoing, late, cancelled, repurchased, or charged off. By design, this sample only considers the activity of borrowers who requested at least one successful loan and lenders with at least one participating bid in a funded listing. The final data contains 3,948,777 bids on 28,935 successfully funded listings. These listings belong to 26,404 borrowers whose projects were funded by 50,264 lenders. Of the 28,935 loans, 18,279 were successfully repaid, while 10,656 defaulted. The average requested loan size for all completed listings was $6,171 (standard deviation = $5,585) with a mean of 21.2% in maximum borrower rate. The total amount lent to borrowers through Prosper in this three year period was $178,556,824.

4 Predicting Long-Term Success

In this section, we describe the experimental setup of our study. We begin by defining the problem of predicting long-term success as a binary classification task, then list the learning methods used for prediction as well as the performance metrics used to evaluate the classifiers. Finally, we discuss our feature selection methodology, providing detailed explanations about how we computed new features from Prosper.com data.

4.1 Experimental Setup

For prediction, we represent listings by a set of features that describe attributes of the borrower, terms of the loan, and features that summarise the behaviour of the lenders who contributed to the loan. We use standard scaling to normalise the feature set by subtracting the mean and scaling to unit variance. Each listing's long-term success is indicated by whether the borrower successfully paid the loan (1) or not (0). We tackle this binary classification problem with a variety of learning methods: Random Forests (RF) [7], Classification and Regression Trees (CART), Adaptive Boosting (ADB) [17], Logistic Regression (LR), Gaussian Naive Bayes (GNB), and Quadratic Discriminant Analysis (QDA). We rely on Scikit-Learn's Python API for method implementation [27].

To perform out of sample tests, in all learning setups, we do 5-fold cross validation and report the classification accuracy, precision, recall, F1 score, and area under the receiver operating characteristic curve (AUC). We also use 5-fold cross validation for parameterisation. To compare the predictive performance of each feature, we use the Random Forest Variable Importance (viRF) computed via Gini Importance [8]. Furthermore, to understand the factors associated with payment success for different loan categories, we run separate classification models and feature importance evaluations within each individual category represented in the data.

4.2 Determinants of Long-Term Success

We proceed by describing factors that contribute to loan payment. We divide these factors into three groups: loan, borrower, and lending dynamics determinants. When designing composite

features within each group, we weigh components of the composite feature using their viRF scores as described below.

4.2.1 Loan Determinants We examine each project's loan features provided by Prosper.com. These features describe standard characteristics of the loan such as the *amount requested, monthly loan payment, loan term*, estimated annualised loss rate on the loan (*estimated loss*), and the rate the borrower pays on the loan (*interest rate*). We also include the *length of the project description* measured by the number of words in the project description as a proxy of the effort borrowers invested in their listings [10]. For each listing, Prosper also provides a *credit grade* that indicates the loan's estimated average annualised loss rate range. This is calculated based on Prosper's proprietary system and allows the platform to maintain consistency when evaluating individual loan requests.

4.2.2 Borrower Determinants We also make use of standard borrower features. Consistent with existing literature, we consider borrowers' *homeownership* status. Furthermore, on Prosper.com, a member can be simultaneously a borrower, lender, and group leader, which leads to a simple feature that summarises their engagement with the platform by counting their roles (*role count*). For each listing, we additionally measure *borrower age* as the number of days between a borrower became a Prosper member and posted their listing. To evaluate *borrower experience* during this time, we sum up the ratio of the borrower's funded listings to their total listings and the ratio of their paid loans to their total loans. The two components are weighted by their viRF scores obtained from a random forest model that contains both ratios. Borrower experience therefore measures borrowers' *past* success on the platform, prior to their current listing and is zero for each borrower's first project.

To investigate the effect of credit information on the predictive performance of borrower features and to emulate realistic decision-making scenarios where credit information might not be available, we group borrower features into sensitive and non-sensitive features. The borrower features introduced so far were non-sensitive. Sensitive borrower features include: *i.) credit volatility* defined as the difference between a borrower's highest and lowest credit score rating as obtained from reporting agencies; *ii.) Prosper score*, which is a custom risk score built using historical Prosper.com data; and *iii.) debt-to-income ratio*.

4.2.3 Determinants of Lending Dynamics Intuitively, the more people a listing attracts, the more likely it is that a project meets its funding goals and the more compelled the borrower will be to pay back the lenders. As the most straightforward lender feature, we thus count the total *number of bids* for each listing and expect this to correlate with success (c.f. Ceyhan et al. [10]).

Since we also anticipate that lenders' investment outcomes will improve with the amount of time they spend on the platform and the number of funding attempts they make, we compute lender features that correspond to borrower age and experience. In this case, however, we aggregate age and experience over every lender who contributed to a specific loan. The age of individual lenders is defined as the number of days between they became Prosper members and made a bid on the current listing. Lenders' age for a given listing is therefore characterised by the *median lender age*. Lenders' experience is defined as the sum of the fraction of lenders' winning bids (i.e., the ones that have not been outbid by others), their contributions to funded as opposed to not funded listings, and participation in successfully paid loans as opposed to defaulted ones. Components of the sum are weighted according to viRF scores obtained from a random forest model that contains the three fractions individually. *Average lender experience* is computed from the *past* successes of the entire group of lenders, prior to the current listing.

The temporal aspects of the crowd's bidding dynamics might also indicate confidence in a listing's merit, hence we develop a set of features that describe the speed at which funds are accumulating, i.e., how fast lenders make their determination of the projects' potential. For each listing, we compute the *time to first bid* as the difference between the first bid and the time the listing was posted, as well as the *time between the first and last bid* when the listing completed. Additionally, we measure the *coefficient of variation* in inter-bid event times as the ratio between the mean and standard deviation of the time intervals between consecutive bids. This measure quantifies the difference in bidding times between subsequent lenders and indicates potential plateaus and surges in the accumulation of bids.

Finally, we include a set of features that are tied to the accumulated bid amounts. First, based on Vulkan et al.'s observation that the largest amount in a successfully funded project accounted for about 30% of the total capital sought, as opposed to 5.4% of the not funded project's target [33], we measure the *maximum lender bid amount* for each listing. This amount might not only be important for its contribution towards a project's fundraising success, but it can also indirectly signal loan quality. Second, we calculate the *mean bid amount per second*, i.e., dollars per unit time. This feature essentially indicates a contribution frequency that captures both the bid amount and the timing of lender activity, and has been shown to correlate with fundraising success [9]. Third, we explicitly quantify herding based on correlations between the contributed amounts. We use a measure that is similar to Goh and Barabási's memory coefficient [18]. Given the consecutive bid amounts $\{B_1, B_2, ..., B_N\}$, the *coefficient of herding* is defined as the ratio between the co-variation of the sequences $S1 = \{B_1, B_2, ..., B_{N-1}\}$ and $S2 = \{B_2, B_3, ..., B_N\}$ and the product of the standard deviation of these sequences:

$$\frac{1}{N} \sum_{i=1}^{N} \frac{(B_i - \mu_{S1})(B_{i+1} - \mu_{S2})}{\sigma_{S1}\sigma_{S2}},$$

where N is the number of bids in the loan, μ_{S1}, μ_{S2} and σ_{S1}, σ_{S2} are the mean and standard deviation of the first ($S1$) and second ($S2$) sequence, respectively. While we also considered longer range correlations, pair-wise correlations were the most predictive of long-term success.

The proposed *lending features evolve with respect to each bid* that a lender makes and with each listing that a lender contributes to. This is important, because through the repeated re-computation of lending dynamics features, we account for potential learning effects and changes in lender population without making any assumptions about how learning and attrition affect our diverse lender population. Our features are thus general and may describe collective intelligence in a variety of settings that involve decision-making online. If shown that minimally constraining features deduced from lenders' actions are predictive of loan payments, one can argue that the lending crowd's behaviour can help improve crowd financing efficiency through better predicting which loans might be successful.

5 Results

Using all the 23 features introduced above, we were able to predict project long-term success with a random forest accuracy of 0.7147, 95% confidence interval: (0.7144, 0.7149), and AUC score of 0.707 (a random estimator would achieve an AUC of 0.5). Table 1 shows the evaluation results for all six machine learning models. Our results, obtained with different sets of features, are comparable to the currently state-of-the-art model by Ceyhan et al. [10].

Table 1: Long-term success prediction results. Random Forest classifier yielded best estimation results with an AUC score of 0.707.

Model	Accuracy	Precision	Recall	F-Score	AUC
QDA	0.704	0.766	0.765	0.766	0.682
CART	0.645	0.721	0.714	0.718	0.620
GNB	0.694	0.749	0.775	0.762	0.665
RF	**0.715**	0.797	0.736	0.765	**0.707**
LR	0.626	0.865	0.483	0.620	0.677
ADB	0.725	0.754	0.837	0.793	0.685

Correlations between features. Before comparing the predictive power of loan, borrower, and lending features, we investigate the correlations between features belonging to individual groups (see Table 2). Among loan features, there are unsurprising positive correlations between *i.)* the amount requested and the monthly loan payment, *ii.)* the amount requested and the credit grade, *iii.)* the estimated loss and interest rate, as well as *iv.)* credit grade and monthly loan payment. Equally expected is the negative correlation between credit grade and estimated loss. The highest correlation among borrower features is between borrower age and experience. This is to be expected given that we built both of these features to describe borrowers' familiarity with the platform. We also find that the Prosper score correlates somewhat with borrower age and credit volatility, giving us an intuition for the criteria Prosper's algorithm uses when assigning this score. We learn more about the components of Prosper score by inspecting its correlations with borrower features. Accordingly, Prosper score has a negative correlation with interest rate, estimated loss, and loan age, as well a positive correlation with credit grade.

The correlations among lending dynamics features are more interesting. There is a strong positive correlation between the maximum amount bid by a single lender and the coefficient of variation for inter-bid times, meaning that in the presence of a high maximal bid, inter-bid times are spread more widely. We find further, albeit smaller positive correlations between the coefficient of herding and average lender experience, the coefficient of herding and time between first and last bid, as well as bid count and time between first and last bid. The remaining correlations are rather small, indicating that the developed lending features are different across the considered sample of projects. Furthermore, most of the correlations between lending dynamics features and loan or borrower features are weak, demonstrating that lending decisions are based

Table 2: Correlations between loan, borrower, and lending features. Several weak correlations between lending dynamics features and loan or borrower features indicate that lending decisions are based on additional subtle information that is directly observed from the platform. * p < 0.05; ** p < 0.01; *** p < 0.001.

	Loan Features							Lender Features									Borrower Features						
	1	2	3	4	5	6	7	8	9	10	11	12	13	14	15	16	17	18	19	20	21	22	23
1. Interest Rate	-																						
2. Monthly Loan Payment	-0.074***	-																					
3. Estimated Loss	0.480***	0.105***	-																				
4. Description Length	0.160***	0.073***	0.185***	-																			
5. Credit Grade	-0.700***	0.369***	-0.409***	-0.228***	-																		
6. Loan Age	-0.013*	-0.039***	-0.045***	0.081***	-0.206***	-																	
7. Amount Requested	-0.155***	0.985***	0.061***	0.059***	0.424***	-0.043***	-																
8. Average Lender Experience	-0.0794***	-0.048***	-0.128***	-0.003	0.097***	-0.046***	-0.043***	-															
9. Bid Amount Per Second	-0.159***	0.058***	-0.113***	-0.105***	0.186***	-0.090***	0.070***	0.040***	-														
10. Time Between First and Last Bid	-0.274***	0.173***	-0.119***	0.054***	0.256***	-0.157***	0.196***	0.085***	-0.128***	-													
11. Median Lender Age	-0.027***	-0.004	0.008	-0.098***	0.207***	-0.688***	-0.003	0.091***	0.082***	0.053***	-												
12. Time to First Bid	0.129***	-0.114***	0.096***	0.114***	-0.198***	-0.047***	-0.119***	-0.051***	-0.102***	-0.186***	0.021***	-											
13. Coefficient of Herding	-0.004	0.083***	-0.068***	0.030***	0.139***	-0.033***	0.081***	0.269***	-0.028***	0.246***	-0.026***	-0.097***	-										
14. Bid Count	-0.312***	0.728***	-0.067***	0.068***	0.450***	-0.174***	0.768***	-0.003	0.037***	0.417***	0.055***	-0.102***	0.153***	-									
15. Coefficient of Variation	0.106***	0.312***	0.101***	0.110***	0.054***	0.034***	0.298***	0.020***	-0.048***	0.072***	0.011	0.022***	0.133***	0.118***	-								
16. Max Lender Bid Amount	-0.003	0.386***	0.089***	0.064***	0.068***	0.016**	0.382***	-0.123***	0.039***	-0.019***	0.047***	0.028***	-0.206***	0.132***	0.709***	-							
17. Prosper Score	-0.345***	-0.070***	-0.418***	-0.133***	0.396***	-0.678***	-0.041***	0.121***	0.153***	0.217***	0.480***	-0.009	0.080***	0.147***	-0.093***	-0.089***	-						
18. Debt to Income Ratio	0.026***	0.079***	0.058***	0.066***	0.015*	0.027***	0.072***	0.004	-0.027***	0.005	-0.038***	0.013*	0.009	0.028***	0.058***	0.056***	-0.018**	-					
19. Borrower Age	-0.008	-0.024***	-0.019***	0.029***	0.060***	-0.291***	-0.022***	0.021***	0.007	0.053***	0.263***	0.037***	-0.000	0.031***	0.018**	0.018**	0.214***	-0.010	-				
20. Credit Volatility	0.069***	0.063***	0.004	-0.012*	0.057***	-0.470***	0.061***	0.020***	0.020***	0.066***	0.306***	-0.200***	-0.005	0.096***	0.008	0.031***	0.271***	-0.011	0.123***	-			
21. Role Count	-0.216***	-0.009	-0.141***	0.027***	0.191***	0.038***	0.003	0.032***	-0.008	0.092***	0.016**	-0.002	0.035***	0.062***	-0.001	-0.011	0.088***	-0.005	0.190***	-0.134***	-		
22. Borrower Experience	-0.045***	0.008	-0.020***	-0.005	0.062***	-0.177***	0.012*	0.021***	0.031***	0.034***	0.183***	-0.006	0.010	0.041***	0.026***	0.028***	0.139***	-0.009	0.575***	0.070***	0.120***	-	
23. Homeownership	-0.166***	0.231***	-0.021***	-0.054***	0.325***	-0.186***	0.243***	0.096***	0.058	0.114***	0.171***	-0.056***	0.056***	0.252***	0.058***	0.051***	0.133***	0.029***	0.051***	0.106***	0.070***	0.049***	-

also on more subtle information than what is directly provided by the platform. The only high positive correlations we find between lending and loan features are with bid count. As expected, more lenders contributing to a listing is associated with a higher requested amount, higher credit grade, and more monthly loan payment. Finally, the correlations between median lender age and borrower features, indicate that experienced lenders tend to prefer borrowers who have used the platform for longer, have a high Prosper score, and even have more volatile credit. The latter could be attractive to lenders, because it gives them the opportunity to charge higher interest rates.

We also inspect correlations between characteristics of borrowers and loan payment outcome. For example, people with low credit grade are considered risky borrowers and likely to have a higher estimated loss on return (Pearson coefficient: $r = -0.409, p < 0.001$) and therefore high interest rate ($r = -0.700, p < 0.001$, c.f. Klafft [22]). Consequently, as shown in Figure 1, having a high interest rate significantly decreases the odds of successful loan payment (Odds ratio: $OR = 0.460, p < 0.001$). While people with high Prosper scores and credit grades may be good borrowers, they are also likely

to enjoy favourable loan terms such as low interest rates, which increases the odds of successful payment. While we found no significant differences in borrowers' odds of successful payment based on their homeownership status, a further investigation based on borrowers' level of indebtedness (i.e., debt-to-income ratio) yields interesting results. After grouping borrowers into three levels of indebtedness based on the lower, inter, and upper-quartile ranges in debt-to-income ratio, respectively, we observe that whether or not a borrower is a homeowner significantly increases the odds of successful payment if the borrower has low debt-to-income ratio ($OR = 1.172, p < 0.001$), but it decreases the odds of successful payment otherwise ($OR = 0.869, p < 0.001$). Our data shows that 72.8% of homeowners with low indebtedness successfully pay their loans compared to 63.8% of their non-homeowner peers (see Table 3). On the contrary, only 53% of homeowners with high indebtedness successfully pay their loans compare to 60.7% of non-homeowners with similar levels of debt. These findings suggest that loan payment is affected by a combination of features. Hence, in this study we employ a set of multivariate models that are capable of investigating the effects of higher-order dependencies between borrower, loan, and lender features on long-term project success.

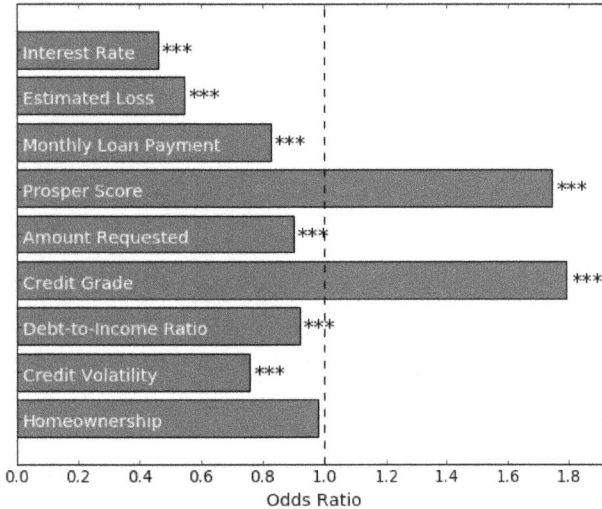

Figure 1: Odds of successful loan payment for observable platform features characteristic of loans and borrowers. High credit grade and Prosper score increase teh odds of successful loan payment.

Table 3: Percentage of successfully paid loans by homeownership and level of indebtedness.

		Debt-to-Income Ratio		
		Low	Medium	High
Homeowner	True	72.8%	63.8%	53.8%
	False	63.0%	64.4%	60.7%

Lending dynamics features summarise other features. We further examine how different feature categories perform with respect to predicting long-term success. Using the best performing model from the previous experiment, random forest, we compare the predictive performance of lending dynamics, sensitive and non-sensitive borrower, as well as loan determinants. Unsurprisingly, the model with all feature categories performs best with an accuracy of 0.715. As expected, loan features have higher estimation accuracy (0.658) compared to lending dynamics (0.600) and borrower (0.627) features. We find this observation in agreement with previous studies that demonstrate the relevance of loan characteristics to borrowers' likelihood of fully paying their loans [14, 30]. To investigate the impact of borrowers' credit information, we use borrower features with and without sensitive information. When we train and evaluate the random forest classifier on the two sets of borrower features, we observe that excluding sensitive credit information from the model considerably lowers the estimation accuracy of borrower features by a margin of 0.214. In other words, non-sensitive borrower features attain a significantly lower accuracy than lending dynamics features. However, when we combine sensitive and non-sensitive borrower features with loan and lending dynamics features (i.e., use

all features), we observe that eliminating sensitive credit information has little effect on the model's accuracy (-0.293). This indicates that lending dynamics features must have picked up nearly all of the valuable signal from sensitive borrower information. Our finding suggests thus that despite the differences in lenders' experience and investment expertise, *as a collective, lenders successfully recovered and used credit information available in loan specifications and borrower profiles.* Moreover, the gleaned information is successfully captured in the proposed simple lending dynamics features.

Table 4: Feature importance ranking of predictive features for long-term success categorised into groups and ranked by feature importance score. Lender features have relatively higher viRF scores compared to most loan and borrower features, accounting for 38.6% of the predictive performance. * denotes sensitive credit information.

Group	Feature	Rank	viRF
Loan	Interest Rate	1	0.124
	Monthly Loan Payment	2	0.069
	Estimated Loss	3	0.055
	Description Length	8	0.045
	Credit Grade	15	0.039
	Loan Age	17	0.035
	Amount Requested	18	0.034
Lender	Average Lender Experience	5	0.052
	Bid Amount Per Second	6	0.045
	Time between First and Last Bid	7	0.045
	Median Lender Age	9	0.045
	Time to First Bid	10	0.044
	Coefficient of Herding	11	0.043
	Bid Count	12	0.043
	Coefficient of Variation	13	0.042
	Max Lender Bid Amount	20	0.027
Borrower	Prosper Score*	4	0.053
	Debt-to-Income Ratio*	14	0.041
	Borrower Age	16	0.038
	Credit Volatility*	19	0.028
	Role Count	21	0.025
	Borrower Experience	22	0.019
	Homeownership	23	0.010

Lending dynamics features rank higher than most features. Next, we investigate the relative importance of individual features for prediction. Table 4 shows all features ranked using random forest variable importance (viRF) scores. Loan features are most predictive of long-term success: loan interest rate, estimated loss, and monthly payment consistently rank highest in viRF scores, while loan term and credit grade have poor viRF scores.

Although the top-3 features with the highest viRF scores are loan features, we observe that lending dynamics features have relatively higher viRF scores compared to most borrower features as well as other loan features such as credit grade, requested loan amount, and loan age. Of the three feature groups, lending dynamics features account for 38.6% of the predictive performance and therefore add significant value to the prediction of loan payment. This indicates that lenders do not only evaluate borrowers' *displayed* information when making lending decisions, but also rely on, e.g., potential informal information about borrowers. Furthermore, average lender age and experience are among the most important lending dynamics features, which means that the more time lenders spend participating on the platform and the more successful they are, the more they contribute to the group's collective intelligence. Lenders' bid amount per second and the time between first and last bid are also indicative of successful loan payment. Indirectly linked to this speed of action is herding, which alongside the number of bids and the coefficient of variation, has medium importance among our set of features.

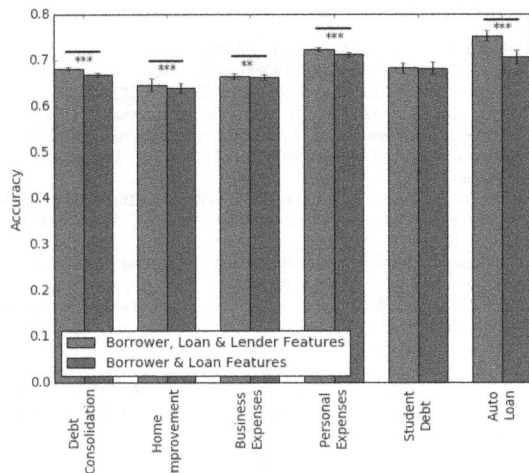

Figure 2: Model accuracy by feature group and project category. Lender features contribute significant marginal gains in estimation accuracy indicative of collective intelligence beyond summarising loan and borrower information.

Lenders demonstrate collective intelligence and their accuracy varies by loan category. We find that lenders demonstrate collective intelligence as lending dynamics features achieve 83.7% of the predictive power of all the indicators of long-term project success combined, which is consistent with the results of Iyer et al. [21]. While a random forest estimator trained only on loan and borrower features yielded an estimation accuracy of 0.7026, 95% confidence interval: (0.7024, 0.7029), adding lending dynamics features to the model slightly improved the prediction accuracy to 0.7147, 95% confidence interval: (0.7144, 0.7149). This marginal gain in estimation accuracy suggests that *lending decisions provide more than a simple summation of loan and borrower information* furnished through the platform. As a point of further inquiry, we investigate how lender wisdom varies by loan category and how the features describing lending dynamics change in importance ranking across those categories.

Adding lending dynamics features to loan and borrower features consistently improves estimation accuracy across loan categories. The wisdom of the lending crowd is most prominent in the auto loan category, but it is also statistically significant for all other categories except student debt (see Figure 2). This means that lenders are going beyond just summarising loan and borrower features. Instead, they augment available direct information with their own perceptions and interpretations of indirect signals, which leads to them being able to select creditworthy borrowers. Lenders are most accurate

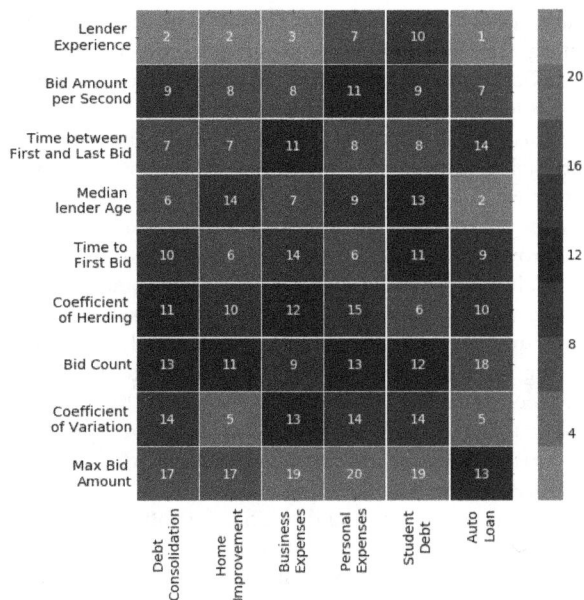

Figure 3: Analysis of feature ranking by project category. Displayed are only the ranks for lending dynamics features. We observe no systematic ranking patterns among lending features.

in the case of auto loans most probably because of their own experiences with this category of personal investment. They are least reliable in assessing the likelihood of successful payment for student loans. Although our data set does not enable more detailed investigations in this direction, we assume that predicting student debt payment is compounded by uncertainties in post-education outcomes that may affect borrowers' opportunities to pay.

Finally, an analysis of the importance of lender features by loan categories shows that average lender experience is overall the most important, while maximum bid amount is the least important predictor for most loan categories. Note that the analysis underlying Figure 3 contained all three groups of features, but we display only the ranks of lending dynamics features relative to loan and borrower features. Aside of the consistent trends for average lender experience and maximum bid amount, there are no systematic ranking patterns among the other lending features, which suggests that one can hardly reduce lender characteristics to a single aspect of lender behaviour that is consistent across all loan categories.

6 Discussion & Conclusions

The wisdom of crowds idea suggests that untrained lenders working in low-information environments could possess a collective intelligence that allows superior decision-making comparable to or even exceeding that of expert institutional lenders. In P2P lending, a par excellence low-information decision-making context, determining whether borrowers will fully pay their loans is especially hard due to significant information asymmetry about their credibility. Notwithstanding this challenge, we found that lenders demonstrate collective intelligence that can be harnessed to predict future loan payment and help improve efficiencies in P2P markets' capital allocation.

Our contributions are threefold. First, we provide new knowledge about signals deduced from lending behaviour that can contribute to the efficiency of crowd financing. Characteristics of lending dynamics such as lenders' previous successes, the bid amount per second, as well as the coefficients of variation and herding provide reliable estimates of long-term project success. These findings suggest that lenders' collective intelligence can be harnessed to increase the effectiveness of crowd financing. Second, we contribute to the growing literature on the wisdom of crowds by providing new insights about novel expressions of collective intelligence and potential ways to harvest it. We expect that our results will inform further research into crowd-aware system design on crowd financing platforms and beyond. Third, the proposed collective intelligence signals are general and easily transfer to various other crowd-sourcing settings. They are thus valuable in exploring contexts, where it is less straightforward to establish whether and how individuals delivered on their tasks.

There are several exciting directions for future research. For instance, further investigation into collective intelligence signals that enhance crowd financing outcomes could rely on more detailed observations of social signalling to understand its subtle effects on lenders' collective decision-making. Our results indicate that learning effects in crowds can help reveal innovative strategies to improve lending outcomes, especially for novice lenders. Identifying the conditions that optimise individual learning in this context is another fruitful avenue for future research. Finally, empirically testing the forecasting power of lending dynamics while the fundraising activity is still in progress has considerable practical appeal.

We believe that a better understanding of lender determinants of long-term project success promoted in this paper will help improve the efficiency of capital allocation in P2P markets, ultimately helping individuals get out of debt, improving household economic welfare, and enhancing entrepreneurship.

Acknowledgments

The authors would like to thank Brian Uzzi and Jayaram Uparna for providing the data. The authors would also like to thank the anonymous referees for their valuable comments and helpful suggestions. The work is supported by the U.S. National Science Foundation under Grant No. IIS-1755873.

References

[1] Ajay Agrawal, Christian Catalini, and Avi Goldfarb. 2014. Some simple economics of crowdfunding. *Innovation Policy and the Economy* 14, 1 (2014), 63–97.
[2] Ajay Agrawal, Christian Catalini, and Avi Goldfarb. 2015. Crowdfunding: Geography, social networks, and the timing of investment decisions. *Journal of Economics & Management Strategy* 24, 2 (2015), 253–274.
[3] Gerrit KC Ahlers, Douglas Cumming, Christina Günther, and Denis Schweizer. 2015. Signaling in equity crowdfunding. *Entrepreneurship Theory and Practice* 39, 4 (2015), 955–980.
[4] Tim Althoff, Cristian Danescu-Niculescu-Mizil, and Dan Jurafsky. 2014. How to ask for a favor: A case study on the success of altruistic requests. In *ICWSM*.
[5] Paul Belleflamme, Thomas Lambert, and Armin Schwienbacher. 2014. Crowdfunding: Tapping the right crowd. *Journal of Business Venturing* 29, 5 (2014), 585–609.
[6] Sushil Bikhchandani, David Hirshleifer, and Ivo Welch. 1998. Learning from the behavior of others: Conformity, fads, and informational cascades. *Journal of Economic Perspectives* 12, 3 (1998), 151–170.
[7] Leo Breiman. 2001. Random forests. *Machine learning* 45, 1 (2001), 5–32.
[8] Leo Breiman. 2017. *Classification and regression trees.* Routledge.
[9] Gordon Burtch, Anindya Ghose, and Sunil Wattal. 2013. An empirical examination of the antecedents and consequences of contribution patterns in crowd-funded

[10] Simla Ceyhan, Xiaolin Shi, and Jure Leskovec. 2011. Dynamics of bidding in a P2P lending service: Effects of herding and predicting loan success. In *Proceedings of the 20th International Conference on World Wide Web.* ACM, 547–556.
[11] Benjamin C Collier and Robert Hampshire. 2010. Sending mixed signals: Multilevel reputation effects in peer-to-peer lending markets. In *Proceedings of the 2010 ACM Conference on Computer Supported Cooperative Work.* ACM, 197–206.
[12] Massimo G Colombo, Chiara Franzoni, and Cristina Rossi-Lamastra. 2015. Internal social capital and the attraction of early contributions in crowdfunding. *Entrepreneurship Theory and Practice* 39, 1 (2015), 75–100.
[13] David Easley and Jon Kleinberg. 2010. *Networks, crowds, and markets: Reasoning about a highly connected world.* Cambridge University Press.
[14] Riza Emekter, Yanbin Tu, Benjamas Jirasakuldech, and Min Lu. 2015. Evaluating credit risk and loan performance in online Peer-to-Peer (P2P) lending. *Applied Economics* 47, 1 (2015), 54–70.
[15] Vincent Etter, Matthias Grossglauser, and Patrick Thiran. 2013. Launch hard or go home!: Predicting the success of Kickstarter campaigns. In *Proceedings of the first ACM Conference on Online Social Networks.* ACM, 177–182.
[16] Seth Freedman and Ginger Zhe Jin. 2008. *Do social networks solve information problems for peer-to-peer lending? Evidence from Prosper.com.* Technical Report 08-43. Indiana University, Bloomington: School of Public & Environmental Affairs, Bloomington, IN.
[17] Yoav Freund and Robert E Schapire. 1997. A decision-theoretic generalization of on-line learning and an application to boosting. *J. Comput. System Sci.* 55, 1 (1997), 119–139.
[18] K-I Goh and A-L Barabási. 2008. Burstiness and memory in complex systems. *EPL (Europhysics Letters)* 81, 4 (2008), 48002.
[19] Michael D Greenberg, Bryan Pardo, Karthic Hariharan, and Elizabeth Gerber. 2013. Crowdfunding support tools: Predicting success & failure. In *CHI'13 Extended Abstracts on Human Factors in Computing Systems.* ACM, 1815–1820.
[20] Emőke-Ágnes Horvát, Jayaram Uparna, and Brian Uzzi. 2015. Network vs market relations: The effect of friends in crowdfunding. In *Proceedings of the 2015 IEEE/ACM International Conference on Advances in Social Networks Analysis and Mining 2015.* ACM, 226–233.
[21] Rajkamal Iyer, Asim Ijaz Khwaja, Erzo FP Luttmer, and Kelly Shue. 2015. Screening peers softly: Inferring the quality of small borrowers. *Management Science* 62, 6 (2015), 1554–1577.
[22] Michael Klafft. 2008. Online peer-to-peer lending: A lenders' perspective. In *Proceedings of the International Conference on E-Learning, E-Business, Enterprise Information Systems, and E-Government, EEE.*
[23] Yang Liu, Roy Chen, Yan Chen, Qiaozhu Mei, and Suzy Salib. 2012. I loan because...: Understanding motivations for pro-social lending. In *Proceedings of the fifth ACM International Conference on Web Search and Data Mining.* ACM, 503–512.
[24] Chun-Ta Lu, Sihong Xie, Xiangnan Kong, and Philip S Yu. 2014. Inferring the impacts of social media on crowdfunding. In *Proceedings of the 7th ACM International Conference on Web Search and Data Mining.* ACM, 573–582.
[25] Dan Marom and Orly Sade. 2013. Are the life and death of an early stage venture indeed in the power of the tongue? Lessons from online crowdfunding pitches. *Unpublished. Working Paper Hebrew University* (2013).
[26] Ethan Mollick. 2014. The dynamics of crowdfunding: An exploratory study. *Journal of Business Venturing* 29, 1 (2014), 1–16.
[27] F. Pedregosa, G. Varoquaux, A. Gramfort, V. Michel, B. Thirion, O. Grisel, M. Blondel, P. Prettenhofer, R. Weiss, V. Dubourg, J. Vanderplas, A. Passos, D. Cournapeau, M. Brucher, M. Perrot, and E. Duchesnay. 2011. Scikit-learn: Machine Learning in Python. *Journal of Machine Learning Research* 12 (2011), 2825–2830.
[28] Matthew J Salganik, Peter Sheridan Dodds, and Duncan J Watts. 2006. Experimental study of inequality and unpredictability in an artificial cultural market. *Science* 311, 5762 (2006), 854–856.
[29] Matthew J Salganik and Duncan J Watts. 2008. Leading the herd astray: An experimental study of self-fulfilling prophecies in an artificial cultural market. *Social Psychology Quarterly* 71, 4 (2008), 338–355.
[30] Carlos Serrano-Cinca, Begona Gutierrez-Nieto, and Luz López-Palacios. 2015. Determinants of default in P2P lending. *PloS One* 10, 10 (2015), e0139427.
[31] Silvio Vismara. 2016. Equity retention and social network theory in equity crowdfunding. *Small Business Economics* 46, 4 (2016), 579–590.
[32] Silvio Vismara. 2016. Information cascades among investors in equity crowdfunding. *Entrepreneurship Theory and Practice* (2016).
[33] Nir Vulkan, Thomas Åstebro, and Manuel Fernandez Sierra. 2016. Equity crowdfunding: A new phenomenon. *Journal of Business Venturing Insights* 5 (2016), 37–49.
[34] Anbang Xu, Xiao Yang, Huaming Rao, Wai-Tat Fu, Shih-Wen Huang, and Brian P Bailey. 2014. Show me the money!: An analysis of project updates during crowdfunding campaigns. In *Proceedings of the SIGCHI Conference on Human Factors in Computing Systems.* ACM, 591–600.
[35] Juanjuan Zhang and Peng Liu. 2012. Rational herding in microloan markets. *Management Science* 58, 5 (2012), 892–912.

markets. *Information Systems Research* 24, 3 (2013), 499–519.

Towards a Cyberphysical Web Science:
A Social Machines Perspective on Pokémon GO!

David De Roure
Oxford e-Research Centre,
University of Oxford
Oxford, United Kingdom
david.deroure@oerc.ox.ac.uk

James A. Hendler
Institute for Data Exploration
and Applications
Rensselaer Polytechnic Institute (RPI)
Troy, NY
hendler@cs.rpi.edu

Diccon James
Independent Researcher
Oxford, United Kingdom
ddm03021@gmail.com

Terhi Nurmikko-Fuller
Centre for Digital Humanities
Research,
Australian National University
Canberra, Australia
Terhi.Nurmikko-Fuller@anu.edu.au

Max Van Kleek
Dept of Computer Science,
University of Oxford
Oxford, United Kingdom
emax@cs.ox.ac.uk

Pip Willcox
Oxford e-Research Centre,
University of Oxford
Oxford, United Kingdom
pip.willcox@bodleian.ox.ac.uk

ABSTRACT

The concept of Social Machines has become an established lens to describe the sociotechnical systems of Web Science, and has been applied to some archetypical cyberphysical systems. In this paper we apply this lens to a larger system, the location based online augmented reality game *Pokémon Go!*. The contributions are an illustrative application of the descriptive Social Machines lens to a system of this scale and type, and the use of simulation as a method for an executable description, which includes use of an ontology to represent partially the universe of the game.

CCS CONCEPTS

• **Information systems** → **Web applications**; *Collaborative and social computing systems and tools*; • **Human-centered computing** → **Collaborative and social computing theory, concepts and paradigms**; *Ubiquitous and mobile computing*;

KEYWORDS

Social Machines, Internet of Things, Cyberphysical systems, game design, Pokémon Go!

ACM Reference Format:
David De Roure, James A. Hendler, Diccon James, Terhi Nurmikko-Fuller, Max Van Kleek, and Pip Willcox. 2019. Towards a Cyberphysical Web Science: A Social Machines Perspective on Pokémon GO!. In *11th ACM Conference on Web Science (WebSci '19), June 30–July 3, 2019, Boston, MA, USA.* ACM, New York, NY, USA, 5 pages. https://doi.org/10.1145/3292522.3326043

1 INTRODUCTION

The Web Science community has studied the Web as a co-constituted 'digital world' through which humans interact. Mobile devices bring into play geographical location and movement, attaching the Web to our physical world. For example, health and fitness apps rely on movement and data gathered from health devices in order to facilitate behavioural interventions. With growing deployment of the Internet of Things we anticipate increasing numbers of connected 'smart' devices deployed around our person, home, transport and environment. Hence increasingly Web Science is becoming 'cyberphysical', with a deepening intertwining of the digital and physical worlds and the algorithms that connect them. How then shall we describe, analyse and design these systems in order to conduct Web Science?

The concept of Social Machines has become an established lens to describe the sociotechnical systems of Web Science, [8] and has already been applied to some archetypical cyberphysical systems [5]. In this paper we apply this lens to a larger system, the location based online augmented reality game *Pokémon Go!*. We see this as a poignant exemplar in our rehearsal for future systems, due to its scale, the evolving ecosystem in which it is situated, the application in massively multiplayer online gaming, the early use of augmented reality, and the rich commentary it has attracted.

The main contribution of this paper is the illustrative application of the Social Machines lens to a cyberphysical Web Science system, to inform future studies. In addition we report on a further method of description which uses a simulator, and we hope this will attract further work; this includes a preliminary Pokémon ontology.

Section 2 introduces the game of *Pokémon Go!* from the point of view of a single player. In Section 3 we extend the description to social effects, illustrating a social machine within the game. Our ecosystem approach in Section 4 shows *Pokémon Go!* in the context of interrelated social machines. We introduce a new descriptive approach through simulation in Section 5, and close with a discussion in section 6.

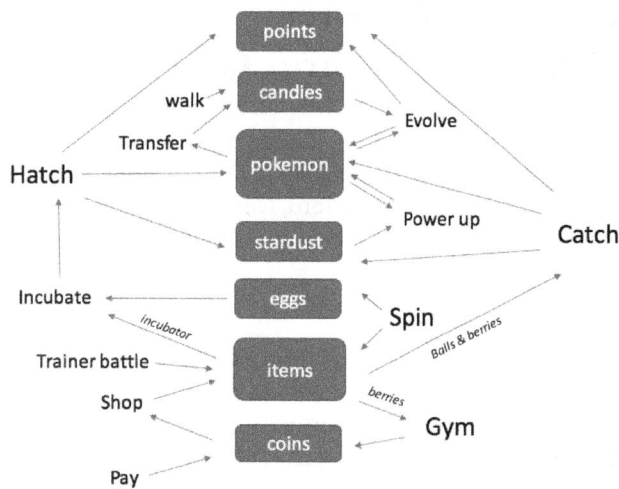

Figure 1: Diagrammatic representation of the game from the point of view of a single player and what they carry.

2 THE GAME OF *POKÉMON GO!*

Pokémon Go! is a location-based augmented reality game. Available for iOS and Android devices since 2016, the app enables the player to collect virtual creatures called Pokémon (from 'pocket monsters') by finding and capturing them as they are automatically spawned and appear virtually in real-world locations. The clear objective of the game is in its slogan: "gotta catch 'em all". To date there are around 460 different types of Pokémon which can be caught, of over 800 in the Pokémon franchise [1].

Players progress up levels (from 1–40), with successively harder goals and larger number of points needed between levels, and higher value Pokémon available to catch. Levelling up, catching Pokémon including rare and powerful types, and completing *badges*, are thus the gamification elements of the *Pokémon Go!* app.

The diagram in figure 1 provides a description of the game from the point of view of a single player whose character is carrying various game objects, and the actions that cause changes to the objects carried. Those playing the game will typically have a conceptual model equivalent to this, though they may choose to express it in different ways. Part of our methodology over several years has been to invite people to provide diagrams of social machines, and the particular diagrams in this paper come from the authors [2, 3].

Here we describe the game loop and structure, with social aspects discussed in Section 3, and then in Section 4 we consider the co-evolution of social machines in the broader ecosystem in which this is situated. This sequence of sections, with textual and diagrammatic descriptions, illustrates what we are describing methodologically as a social machines lens, as we zoom out from individual to crowd.

In game, players are known as *trainers* and carry Pokémon *storage* and a *backpack* of game items. Caught Pokémon are kept in the storage, and every time a new type is captured this is recorded in the player's *Pokédex*, a form of catalogue which enables the trainer to see the completeness of their collection. The backpack contains

---

[1]https://en.wikipedia.org/wiki/List_of_Pokemon

Poké Balls, Incubators, Berries, Revives, Potions and other game items. The player also carries a number of *Pokécoins, Stardust* and numbers of *Candies* associated with particular Pokémon types, and none of these variables occupies storage. Trainers accumulate experience points (XP), which dictate their level between 1 and 40. Other variables associated with individual trainers include distance walked and badges awarded.

In the spirit of "gotta catch 'em all", trainers walk around and encounter geolocated Pokémon which are spawned automatically for a period of time (minutes). The frequency of particular Pokémon spawning is influenced by geographical features, a link between the physical and digital. Trainers can catch a Pokémon by throwing Poké Balls at it repeatedly until the capture succeeds (effectively virtual dice are rolled each time). Different types of Poké Ball have different levels of effectiveness, and capture is made easier by feeding the Pokémon different types of *Berry*. Poké Balls and Berries are obtained when the trainer encounters and spins a PokéStop or Gym. Multiple players will see the same Pokémon in the same location and can all capture it, obtaining independent instances which are only associated by their provenance. Although creation of copies is a familiar affordance of the digital, this cloning is perhaps dissonant from the physical world that is overlaid; however, this cloning encourages cooperation, rather than competition, in social engagement between players.

Trainers can *evolve* Pokémon according to a scheme of evolutionary relationships which is defined in the *Pokémon Go!* universe. This uses up *Candies* for that Pokémon type and generates XP. They can also power them up by using *Stardust*, bringing the Pokémon up through levels as per the player. Collecting Pokémon and hatching eggs generate Candies, XP and Stardust, so the whole game is fuelled by the 'grind' of walking, catching and hatching. Evolving and powering up enables trainers to improve their collections.

Pokémon Go! can be seen as an 'exergame' with walking incentivised by the need to capture Pokémon and also to visit and spin PokéStops, which replenish game items in the backpack again randomly. Spinning may also provide an egg if the trainer has space: up to nine eggs can be carried in Pokémon storage, and can hatch Pokémon by placing them in up to nine *Incubators* and walking 2, 5, 7 or 10km. Additionally covering a distance with a 'buddy' Pokémon generates candies, and there are rewards for the player walking distances (e.g. 50km) in a week.

3 SOCIAL EFFECTS

The second major game incentive is to train Pokémon in Gyms. A Gym belongs to whichever of the three teams has captured it, and a player can choose a team to join on reaching Level 5. Multiple trainers can come together to capture a Gym, and a Gym belonging to one team might be attacked simultaneously by trainers from other teams. An incentive for battles is that the longer the Pokémon stay in the captured Gym, the more Pokécoins the trainer gets when the Pokémon leaves the Gym, up to a maximum of 50 coins per day. The other way to gain coins is by buying them with real-world money. Hence Gyms are where players come together, and illustrate how Pokémon has real-world social effects. Gyms may be attacked in an *ad hoc* manner by nearby solo players, or else players may form small groups of the same Pokémon team, and proactively take over a Gym or a series of Gyms.

Real-world social effects also occur when players gather to win a Gym *raid*, sometimes in large numbers. A raid is where a Pokémon spontaneously becomes the *Gym boss* for a limited time period; defeating the Gym boss gives each trainer involved in the *battle* a bonus opportunity to capture another instance of that type of Pokémon. Raids are beneficial for both combat and capture: they are the mechanism for capturing 'legendary' Pokémon, which do not appear through hatching or in the wild, and which can subsequently be used to attack (though not defend) Gyms.

There are other social features. Each trainer can have friends of various degrees of closeness, and can send them gifts (which contain randomly selected game items). They can also trade Pokémon when physically colocated, subject to various constraints, and hold 'person versus person' battles with friends and with other players encountered in real life.

How do we describe these social features and effects? This is where we call on the notion of *Social Machines*, a term introduced by Tim Berners-Lee in 1999 [1]. Today we see them as networks of people and devices at scale, their behaviour co-created by human participants and technological components. They harness the power of the crowd, with everyone able to contribute—to document situations, cooperate on tasks, exchange information, or to play. Through social machines, existing social processes may be scaled up, and new processes enabled, to solve problems, augment reality, create new sources of value, and disrupt existing practice. [8]

Raids are a classic social machine: they cause humans to come together to solve a problem. While the numbers involved in an individual raid may be 10s, *Pokémon Go!* operates at massive scale. There have been "Global Catch Challenges" where the global extent of activity (e.g. 3 billion Pokémon captured globally in 7 days) triggers predetermined rewards to players, such as increased points and stardust.

We have made use of a notation called a *sociogram*, which was developed as a successful workshopping tool, has also been used in teaching, and was developed further as a specification language [7]. A full sociogram schematic for *Pokémon Go!* would be extensive and complex, but we illustrate it in figure 2 which describes a Raid.

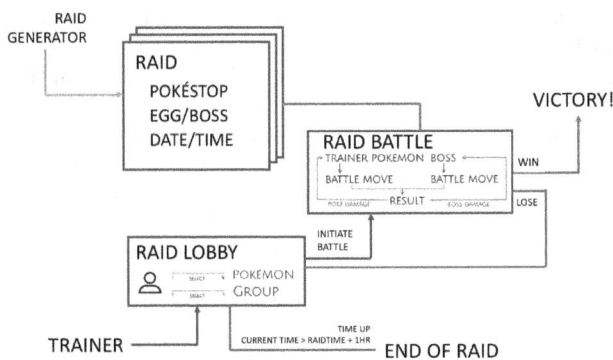

Figure 2: A Raid, described in a notation inspired by sociograms.

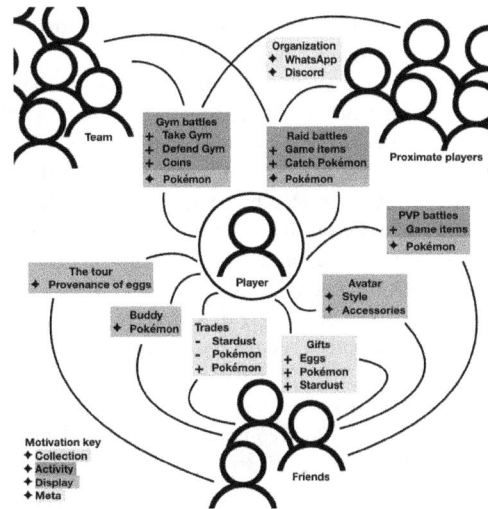

Figure 3: A description which includes other players.

4 THE POKÉMON GO! SOCIAL MACHINES ECOSYSTEM

The diagrams in figure 1 and 2 are from the perspective of a single player who is experiencing the game with increasing social features. Figure 3 focuses on the social, with teams, friends, and proximate players. Importantly, as indicated at the top of the diagram, *Pokémon Go!* does not operate in isolation of established social machines and in turn it has given rise to new ones. It is coupled by its human players into the social machines ecosystem, with players interacting with multiple social machines during play. For example, without in-game communication mechanisms between players, the use of other social platforms to support *Pokémon Go!* is an important aspect of the social characteristic of the game: very often the need for people to act simultaneously in Gym and raid battles requires coordination out of game through social media apps such as Facebook, the gamer network 'Discord', WhatsApp and Reddit channels.

Pokémon Go! is in fact based on an earlier social machine. *Ingress* is the forerunner of *Pokémon Go!* and feeds directly into it by providing the locations of PokéStops and Gyms. Also a location-based, augmented-reality exergame, *Ingress* was released by Niantic in 2012 for Android and 2014 for iOS. In *Ingress* there are two teams, as opposed to the three of *Pokémon Go!*, and they aim to capture geolocated portals and link them to control geographical regions. In the backstory, the earth has been seeded with 'exotic matter' (XM) by an alien race regarded by the 'Enlightened' faction as benevolent, while the 'Resistance' faction fight to protect humanity. Players gain XM by walking. Emergent social behaviours during gameplay include establishing neutral zones, as well as training and creating rules of engagement.

The portals of *Ingress* are located at landmarks which have historical or cultural significance. These include public and historical buildings, tourist and recreational spaces, and public art. These locations are crowdsourced, with millions of submissions received by Niantic, and the portals subsequently provided the locations of PokéStops. Hence the social machine of *Ingress* portals has fed directly into the social machine of *Pokémon Go!*

The *Silph Road*[2] is a research-focused grassroots network of *Pokémon Go!* players on Reddit, conducting research projects to help understand game mechanics and features, as well as providing community support for *Pokémon Go!* enthusiasts. With emergent rules for conducting the research projects, and proactive moderation to ensure constructive discussion in line with the objectives, the Silph Road can be seen as a social machine which in turn is constructed within the Reddit social machine.

As an example, some of the research projects have explored the distribution of apparently random outcomes to see what factors may actually influence them. The moveset (attacks) that a Pokémon has after evolution appears random, as if by dice roll. In a study of moveset factors the Silph Road community gathered data from over 10,000 evolutions and tested against 11 factors, with a null hypothesis that a Pokémon's moves are selected in a uniformly random fashion from the moves available. No evidence of correlation was found, and the distribution was found to be uniform.

IV calculators also result from reverse-engineering the programming of the game. Internally to an instance of a Pokémon are three variables known as the *Individual Values* (IVs), representing Attack, Defence, and Stamina with an integer between 0 and 15. The IVs determine how powerful a Pokémon will be when it is fully powered up, in addition to the species-specific *base stats*. The user interface keeps these variables hidden, but provides derived *Combat Power* and *Hit Points* values as well as the amount of stardust needed to power up the Pokémon. Additionally an *appraise* mechanism provides an automated textual appraisal of the Pokémon, which further constrains the possible IVs. This is sufficient information to be able to infer the IVs, or at the least sets of possible values. The result is that the equations used to derive the visible values have been reverse engineered by the community, and many online IV calculators have been provided.

Other social machines have come about to assist *Pokémon Go!* players. There are crowdsourced maps showing locations of PokéStops and Gyms, and multiple efforts to crowdsource the location of Pokémon. Established social machines have also modified their behaviour to couple with the *Pokémon Go!* social machine, for example Yelp included a feature to enable users to report the proximity of PokéStops to listed businesses [4].

5 THE SIMULATOR AND ONTOLOGY

In order to explore our understanding of the game, and investigate the prospect of simulation as part of social machine design methodology, we have built a simulator for a subset of the *Pokémon Go!* game structure and metagame. A secondary goal was to experiment in describing player behaviour in pseudocode—by asking players to write down the rules they are using in play, and implementing these in the simulator, we begin to establish a domain specific language to represent behaviour. The simulator enables us to explore the relationship between the 'micro' and the 'macro' effects. [6]

The simulation is built using NetLogo, which is an open source programmable modelling environment designed for modelling a complex system consisting of hundreds of independent "agents",

[2]https://thesilphroad.com

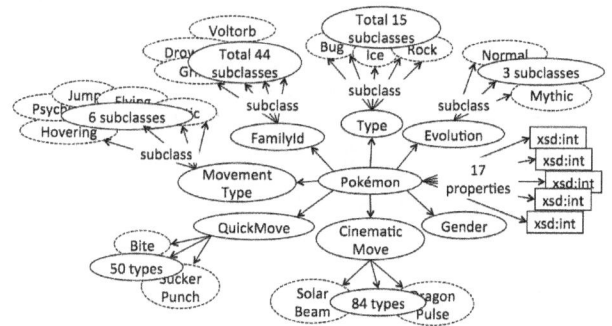

Figure 4: Visualization of the Pokéontology

as it develops over time. The programmer defines the micro-level behaviour of agents, using an extension of the Logo programming language, and runs the simulation in order to investigate the macro-level behaviours that emerge. Typical examples of NetLogo simulations are drawn from biology, medicine, physics, chemistry, mathematics, computer science, economics and social psychology.

The *Pokémon Go!* simulator has agents which represent the geolocated Pokémon, PokéStops and Gyms. These do not move, and the Pokémon are spawned only for a period of time. Other agents represent the trainers belonging to one of the three teams, and move around to visit the PokéStops and Gyms and to capture Pokémon. Simulation parameters include numbers of Pokémon, PokéStops, Gyms, players, and the maximum number of Pokémon a player can keep. A plot keeps track of the number of uncaptured and captured Pokémon, and the number of Poké Balls.

The simulator makes it possible to encode different player behaviours and see the consequences over time. In particular, making small changes to individual player behaviour may have consequences in terms of mobility and also interactions with other players. Apart from this ability to conduct 'what-if' experiments, the principal benefit of these exercises is in finding ways to describe the individual behaviours. For the initial simulator, we wrote pseudocode which attempts to describe the decision-making by one player in the field. As experience grows in this process, we are essentially creating a domain-specific language in which players can describe their behaviour. We suggest that this exercise could be replicated for other social machines, and tells us something about the primitives of human behaviour in the machine.

Coding the simulation also necessitated some clarity about the Pokémon ontology. The term 'Pokémon' is used ambiguously: it can refer to a specific instance, to a multitude, to a type, to a series of types. Pokémon can change type, while retaining some characteristics, on 'evolution' (which might better be thought of as metamorphosis, given that it occurs at speed and to an individual Pokémon).

The *Pokéontology* was designed to capture several different aspects of the Pokémon, both at a generic (overview) level of types and the separate stages of the biography of a specific individual. It was complicated by the lack of narrative continuity between different instances of the Pokémon universe across the franchise. For example, Pokémon can be traded in earlier games, whereas this feature was only recently introduced in *Pokémon Go!* in June 2018. The process of ontology development was complicated by the changes the Pokémon universe had undergone in different stages of the franchise's growth. Individual Pokémon level up, acquire new skills, and evolve or metamorphosize. The number of species has also dramatically increased from 151 in the first generation, resulting in more complex arrangements of phenotypes, morphologies and categories. Later generations introduced new species which are polymorphic, and can break the category boundaries of earlier species (such as the third generation Pokémon Wurmple, which can evolve into a Silcoon and then a Beautifly, or into a Cascoon and then a Dustox), so the ontology was designed to represent the entirety of the biodiversity of the Pokémon universe, rather than be built up sequentially representing the development of that universe.

As Pokémon evolve or metamorphosize from one subspecies to another, they improve in skill and increase in power. Representing this progression in an ontological structure necessitates the capture of diachronic change (occurring to one specific individual). These features were added to the ontological structure which also included characteristics such as details of the non-playable attributes of the phenotype (colour and size).

Underlying the ontological structure is the hypothesis that each instance of a Pokémon is an abstract concept prior to capture. Once captured, it becomes a unique specimen of a specific (sub)species (an instance of a type) and it is awarded a unique ID.

6 DISCUSSION AND FUTURE WORK

Our methodology for this work has been for the authors to describe social machines through different diagrams, text, and through pseudocode. We hope the examples here help convey the social machines 'lens'. A broader range of descriptive approaches, including a wider range of diagrams, can be found in the social machines literature [8].

Reflecting on the work, we see a clear resonance between social machines and games, and this suggests that practice in games design could be usefully applicable to social machines. Ethical issues in games design also translate to social machines, and hence to Web Science. For example, *Pokémon Go!* can be seen as an 'open ethical game' in which the players' values are used in developing a relation with the game world, and the game world accepts and encourages this player-driven ethical affordance [9].

One apparent difference might be the 'fantasy' backstory in games, but our social machines are not without associated narratives and universes too. Looking through the lens the other way, it seems entirely possible to view social machines as games. We have virtual persona on social platforms and it is not a great stretch to see Facebook and Twitter as about role-playing. Consider a comparison of Linked-In and *Pokémon Go!*–both involve collecting, competing, improving.

We have also found the notion of the *metagame* useful. In the ecosystem perspective on social machines, we do not so much design and deploy a machine as make an intervention in the ecosystem. The clear attention to metagame design as 'engaging with life', versus the in-game structure, is something we believe should be just as explicit in social machine design. Gamers frequently speak of 'the meta' and we feel there is still much understanding to be gained in 'the meta' of social machines.

Finally, the simulator has proved to be a useful tool, as much in programming it as in using it. We are not aware of previous work on agent-based models of social machines *per se*, and in we fact might be cautious about a methodology that risks being deterministic—more machine than social. However the simulator enabled us to capture behaviours, to test our understanding, and to try 'what-if' scenarios that could not be achieved 'in the wild'. There is further work to be done on describing player behaviour and the 'primitives' of the social machine. We recommend the use of simulation as part of social machines design in the future.

We expect Web Science to be increasingly situated in the physical world, thanks to smart devices and the broadening deployment of the Internet of Things. The fact that *Pokémon Go!* is location-based makes it an exemplar in this respect also. There is still much to be explored about situated social machines going forward, including the dimensions of ethics and responsible innovation, and the incorporation of the emerging techniques of artificial intelligence.

Our presentation of *Pokémon Go!* has been from a social machines perspective, presenting the game design, social effects and context in the social machines ecosystem. We hope that this serves to illustrate social machines thinking, and that this paper has set the scene for future work at the intersection of games and social machines, particularly with respect to design.

7 ACKNOWLEDGMENTS

The work of the University of Oxford has previously been supported by *SOCIAM: The Theory and Practice of Social Machines*, funded by the UK Engineering and Physical Sciences Research Council (EPSRC), under PETRAS, grant number EP/J017728/2; De Roure and Van Kleek are also supported by grant number EP/N02298X/1. We wish to thank our SOCIAM colleagues, past and present.

REFERENCES

[1] Tim Berners-Lee. 1999. *Weaving the Web: The Original Design and Ultimate Destiny of the World Wide Web by Its Inventor.* Harper San Francisco.
[2] David De Roure, Clare Hooper, Megan Meredith-Lobay, Kevin Page, Ségolène Tarte, Don Cruickshank, and Catherine De Roure. 2013. Observing Social Machines Part 1: What to Observe?. In *Proceedings of the 22Nd International Conference on World Wide Web (WWW '13 Companion).* ACM, New York, NY, USA, 901–904. https://doi.org/10.1145/2487788.2488077
[3] David De Roure, Clare Hooper, Kevin Page, Ségolène Tarte, and Pip Willcox. 2015. Observing Social Machines Part 2: How to Observe?. In *Proceedings of the ACM Web Science Conference (WebSci '15).* ACM, New York, NY, USA, Article 13, 5 pages. https://doi.org/10.1145/2786451.2786475
[4] Pavan Ravikanth Kondamudi, Bradley Protano, and Hamed Alhoori. 2017. Poké-Mon Go: Impact on Yelp Restaurant Reviews. In *Proceedings of the 2017 ACM on Web Science Conference (WebSci '17).* ACM, New York, NY, USA, 393–394. https://doi.org/10.1145/3091478.3098861
[5] Aastha Madaan, Jason R. C. Nurse, David De Roure, Kieron O'Hara, Wendy Hall, and Sadie Creese. 2018. A Storm in an IoT Cup: The Emergence of Cyber-Physical Social Machines. *CoRR* abs/1809.05904 (2018). arXiv:1809.05904 http://arxiv.org/abs/1809.05904
[6] Kieron O'Hara, Noshir S Contractor, Wendy Hall, James A Hendler, Nigel Shadbolt, et al. 2013. Web Science: Understanding the emergence of macro-level features on the world wide web. *Foundations and Trends® in Web Science* 4, 2–3 (2013), 103–267.
[7] P. Papapanagiotou, D. Murray-Rust, M. Van Kleek, A. Davoust, A. Manataki, and D. Robertson. 2017. Rapid Assembly of Social Machines with the Lightweight Social Calculus. In *2017 Workshop on Hybrid Human-Machine Computing (HHMC 2017).*
[8] Nigel Shadbolt, Kieron O'Hara, David De Roure, and Wendy Hall. 2019. *The Theory and Practice of Social Machines.* Springer, Springer Nature Switzerland AG 2019.
[9] Miguel Sicart. 2009. *The Ethics of Computer Games.* MIT Press.

Using the Web for Science in the Classroom:
Online Citizen Science Participation in Teaching and Learning

Cathal Doyle
School of Information
Management
Victoria University of Wellington
Wellington, New Zealand
cathal.doyle@vuw.ac.nz

Rodreck David
School of Information
Management
Victoria University of Wellington
Wellington, New Zealand
rodreck.david@vuw.ac.nz

Yevgeniya Li
School of Information
Management
Victoria University of Wellington
Wellington, New Zealand
jane.li@vuw.ac.nz

Markus Luczak-Roesch
School of Information
Management
Victoria University of Wellington
Wellington, New Zealand
markus.luczak-roesch@vuw.ac.nz

Dayle Anderson
School of Education
Victoria University of Wellington
Wellington, New Zealand
dayle.anderson@vuw.ac.nz

Cameron M. Pierson
School of Information
Management
Victoria University of Wellington
Wellington, New Zealand
cameron.pierson@vuw.ac.nz

ABSTRACT

Introduction: Citizen involvement in scientific projects has become a way of encouraging curiosity and greater understanding of science whilst providing an unprecedented engagement between professional scientists and the general public. In this paper we specifically focus on the impact of online citizen science (OCS) participation in the science education of primary school age children in New Zealand.

Methods: We use four exploratory cases within a broader research project to examine the nature and impact of embedding OCS projects that use web based online crowdsourcing and collaboration tools within classroom environments of primary school science learners.

Results & Discussion: Our findings provide insights into primary school teachers' perception of OCS. They offer initial insights into how teachers embed OCS in a classroom environment, and why this improves science learning aptitudes, inquisitiveness and capabilities in primary school age children. We also notice that successfully embedding OCS projects in education is affected by the project context, how the results are disseminated, and inclusivity in socio-cultural aspects.

KEYWORDS

citizen science, online citizen science, education, learning

ACM Reference format:

Cathal Doyle, Rodreck David, Yevgeniya Li, Markus Luczak-Roesch, Dayle Anderson and Cameron M. Pierson. 2019. Using the Web for Science in the Classroom: Online Citizen Science Participation in Teaching and Learning. In *WebSci'19: 11th ACM Conference on Web Science, June 30-July 3, 2019, Boston, MA, USA.* ACM, New York, NY, USA, 10 pages. https://doi.org/10.1145/3292522.3326022

1 INTRODUCTION

Participatory science, crowd-sourced science, or citizen science (CS), are a few of the many terms that refer to the modern phenomenon of scientific endeavor which involves amateur volunteers as contributors to real-world science projects. CS projects involve citizens - who are called citizen scientists - to collect field data (e.g. take pictures of sightings of specific plants or animals), while others ask citizen scientists to classify pre-collected data or annotate whether some particular features can be observed (e.g. a particular pattern in a plotted graph). When these contributions are enabled by the Internet, researchers also use the term online citizen science (OCS), which is the focus for this paper.

Considerable research in this area investigates the design of successful OCS projects from the perspective of professional scientists tapping into citizen science as part of their projects, or from the perspective of facilitators of citizen science such as the providers of OCS digital platforms for crowdsourcing and collaboration [1-5]. For scientists, the questions addressed often relate to how one can ensure sustained motivation and engagement of citizens so that a project reaches its target [6]. However, this point of view is limited, only regarding OCS projects as a part of the research life-cycle of professional scientists' line of inquiry. For OCS platform providers, amassing a large number of participants and adoption is an obvious incentive to their platform business model [3]. This also means they have a vested interest that does not necessarily account for the interests of the participants themselves. This raises interesting questions such as: How do users (other than professional scientists and facilitators) who engage with OCS perceive its utility and usefulness? Do these groups have a different understanding of the purpose of OCS? Do professional scientists consider these groups when developing their OCS projects?

We consider these questions, from the perspective of primary school teachers, focusing on the impact of OCS participation on the science education of children. This is an important foundation that has a potential to provide professional scientists who design and implement OCS projects with an understanding of what is needed if they wish to embed their OCS projects in learning environments, whilst simultaneously benefitting teaching and learning for educators and learners. From this, we then introduce four case studies that consist of primary school teachers who embedded an OCS project into a teaching unit, where we gain a perspective of OCS from primary school teachers.

Our findings reveal that OCS is seen as an opportunity for students to engage with topics that otherwise are inaccessible in a classroom or lab setting (e.g. space), but also there is a mismatch between how OCS projects frame their suitability for in-class use (if they do that at all) and intended use as outlined by teachers. Further, teachers indicated the importance of seeing the results of contributions made and the final outcome of the project, while professional scientists are often more concerned with presenting their results to the scientific community through publication of academic papers. We also find that projects with a link to the local context are preferred by teachers and highlight an important but understudied aspect, namely the cultural responsiveness of online citizen science.

The remainder of this paper is structured as follows: We provide a brief background to the study and the broader project from which it is embedded. We review related work, discussing the conceptualisations of citizen science in offline and online environments as well as its fit in the education sector. We then explain the research methods, particularly the design of the cases used in our inquiry. Thereafter, we present our findings, with a discussion that synthesizes and links them to the current conversations about OCS in related literature. We conclude the paper by summarizing the contributions and some limitations.

1.1 Brief Background to the Study

Authors of this paper are involved in a larger project titled *"Citizen Scientists in the Classroom: Investigating the Role of Online Citizen Science in the Science Education of School Age Children"*,

funded by the Teaching and Learning Research Initiative (TLRI)[1] of New Zealand. This project is designed as a co-constructive partnership between researchers and four primary school teachers who are advocates of science education in New Zealand. Partnership agreements with the teachers' four schools, including necessary ethics procedures, have been obtained for this research. The four teachers have been purposefully invited to be part of this research project because of their sound understanding of the role of Science Capabilities for Citizenship[2] in the New Zealand curriculum for science, and knowledge of how to implement these capabilities in primary school science classrooms. All four teachers are from the Science Teaching Leadership Programme (STLP) in New Zealand[3]. Their participation in the STLP means they have experience in the science learning area and an interest in promoting science among other teachers and schools. Exploratory in-depth case studies were conducted with each of the four teachers.

2 REVIEW OF RELATED LITERATURE

2.1 Science Education

Science education is a crucial and strategic focus of education sectors in many countries. Increasing science literacy, aptitudes and capabilities is seen as a way of both enlightening the general citizenry and developing keen interests in professional and technical skills required to drive innovativeness, scientific discovery and national development [7]. In 2014, the New Zealand government launched a national strategic initiative to improve public engagement with science and technology, and build greater scientific literacy amongst its citizenry in a project titled: *A Nation of Curious Minds - He Whenua Hihiri i te Mahara* [7]. The New Zealand Curriculum (NZC) introduced in 2007, already had at the core of its science learning area an aim to build students' ability to engage with science and scientific issues of interest to them, through its *Participating and Contributing* sub-strand [8]. The stated purpose of the science learning area as a whole is that "students explore how both the natural physical world and science itself work so that they can participate as critical, informed, and responsible citizens in a society in which science plays a significant role" [8, p.17]. This explicit embedding of science and inquiry-based learning in the NZC is just one example of how science education in general has become an integral part of many primary and secondary school curricula around the world [9, 10].

Given this increased importance of science education in school curricula, it is noteworthy that student engagement with science is declining, reflecting international trends [11-14]. One way of improving scientific engagement, and at the same time developing capabilities with science useful as members of society, may be through the inclusion of citizen science in school programmes which provides new opportunities for the general public to participate in real scientific projects.

---

[1] http://www.tlri.org.nz/
[2] https://scienceonline.tki.org.nz/Science-capabilities-for-citizenship/
[3] https://royalsociety.org.nz/what-we-do/funds-and-opportunities/science-teaching-leadership-programme/

2.2 Citizen Science (CS)

Citizen science is a scientific practice [15, 16] originating in the 1700s [15], involving members of the public [17-20] actively engaging with professional scientists [16, 18, 20] in scientific work [18]. The members of the public participating can be referred to as citizen scientists [15, 16] or volunteers [15, 17, 18, 20]. Such engagement requires following an established protocol [18] that is created by the professional scientist [21] and can include one or more of the following tasks: data collection [15, 17, 20]; data processing [22, 23]; data analysis & interpretation [15, 17, 18]; and/or dissemination of results [17, 21]. Outcomes from citizen science projects include advancements in scientific research [16, 19], as well as increasing the public's understanding of science [15, 19, 20].

Based on the above understanding of citizen science, we adopt the following working definition: Citizen science is a process that involves professional scientists and citizen scientists engaging on a scientific project. This engagement follows an established protocol, created by the professional scientists, which can include one or more of the following tasks: data collection, data processing, data analysis & interpretation, and/or dissemination of results. Outcomes should be advancements in scientific research, as well as an increase in the public's understanding of science.

While this provides us with an understanding, and definition of CS, online citizen science (OCS) differs in various ways. We suggest that it is important to highlight these differences, in particular in light of increasingly digital learning environments. Emphasising that digital technologies are a utility for some scientific endeavours - but not all of them (or not all stages of all of them) - bares the potential to create awareness to be critical when utilising almost ubiquitous technologies and ask whether the technologies are utilised purposefully. Thus, an overview of OCS is presented next, along with a working definition.

2.3 Online Citizen Science (OCS)

Since the introduction of the Internet, and advancements in technology, citizen science has evolved to move the process online [15], allowing professional scientists to engage with citizen scientists in new ways [15, 16, 20]. This includes being able to provide easier access to large datasets [15, 19]; making tools available to support engagement from citizen scientists that are geographically distributed [18-20]; enabling communication between citizen scientists [15]; and providing a wider reach to a broader audience of citizen scientists [18, 20]. These citizen science projects can be aided by technology [18] or can be completely mediated online through technology [17, 18]. This extension of citizen science has been called online citizen science [15, 17, 24], and digital citizen science [20].

Expanding on our working definition of citizen science we adopt the following working definition of online citizen science: Online citizen science is an extension of citizen science, where the tasks to be completed are aided, or completely mediated, through the Internet. Engagement can occur in different ways such as submitting data collected by citizen scientists, providing large datasets to be analysed; making tools available to support engagement with citizen scientists that are geographically distributed; enabling communication between citizen scientists; and providing a wider reach to a broader audience of citizen scientists.

3 RESEARCH QUESTIONS

While it is evident from previous research that there is a good understanding of CS and OCS from an academic perspective, what is unclear is how teachers perceive it, the methods they use to embed it in learning, and the overall impact it has on science learning for primary school children. We thus develop our three guiding research questions as follows:

RQ1. How do primary school teachers perceive OCS projects?

RQ2. Why is embedding OCS projects in primary school science learning beneficial?

RQ3. How do primary school teachers embed OCS projects in learning environments?

4 RESEARCH METHODS

4.1 Multiple Case Study Design and Justification

Our inquiry sought to answer *how* teachers embed web-based OCS in a classroom environment and *why* this improves science learning aptitudes, inquisitiveness and capabilities in primary school age children, making it very relevant to use an exploratory case study design [25]. We needed to explore and understand primary school teachers' perspectives of OCS, how they use it in classroom environments, and the overall fit it has with promoting science education whilst meeting specific project goals. By exploring a unique set of cases of four different teachers' perceptions and contextual experiences in an unfolding project, and accumulating a promisingly rich dataset, we found these elements of our study corresponding to the norms of using case study inquiry [26-29].

4.2 Description of the Case Context, Data Sources and Methods

To develop the perspectives that primary school teachers have of OCS, an exploratory multiple-case study design was adopted for this study. These cases involved four primary school teachers in New Zealand, who each embedded an OCS project into their teaching units. The specific learning intended in each case was determined by the teacher's particular teaching unit, which was in turn determined by a wider school plan. Once each teacher knew what unit they would be teaching during the time set for the project, they reviewed and selected a relevant OCS project(s) that could be linked with the unit topic and goals. They implemented their units over the course of a term, introducing and embedding their selected OCS project(s). Below we provide a description of the four cases (see Table 1 for a summary), an overview of the data collection activities, and conclude by explaining our data analysis methods.

Table 1: Summary of Case Studies

Case	Teacher	Topic Focus	OCS Used	# of Students
Case 1	A	Animal identification	Identify New Zealand Animals[4]	25
Case 2	B	Pollution in streams	The Plastic Tide[5]	62
Case 3	C	Light & sound	Agent Exoplanet[6] & Planet Hunters[7]	44
Case 4	D	Power of light	Globe at Night[8]	21

4.2.1 Case 1 – Teacher A. The first case consisted of 25 students between the ages of 9-11, where the focus of the unit was around local animal identification, and their behavior, which ran for more than 3 weeks. Within this unit, Teacher A identified a number of learning outcomes, including: how to make observations and collect data about pests; understand how scientists collect data and make observations from it; appreciate how technology can assist in making these observations; and develop an understanding of *Kaitiakitanga* [9] (the Māori concept of guardianship, for the sky, the sea, the land and living things.). To help achieve these outcomes, Teacher A selected an OCS project called *Identify New Zealand Animals*. The project aims to understand the impact that introduced mammalian predators, such as rats and stoats, have on urban environments. Citizen scientists were required to detect and classify animals on photos taken by motion-activated cameras around different New Zealand cities. The students had the added benefit of the professional scientist who setup this project coming into the classroom to discuss it with them before they started. Students initially used the project tutorial to understand what they were required to do, and then used the OCS website to classify the animals in the photos provided there. They also trapped predators at their school, an activity that Teacher A was linking with the OCS project.

4.2.2 Case 2 – Teacher B. The second case consisted of 62 students between the ages of 6-10, where the focus of the unit was on the impact of plastic in waterways (this was part of a larger project focusing on pollution in streams) and ran over twenty weeks. With this unit, Teacher B identified a number of learning outcomes, including understanding how scientists use observations to help answer questions about our world; identify and understand how humans have changed the stream habitat and water quality; identify and reflect on actions to help protect waterways. To help achieve these outcomes, Teacher B chose an OCS project called *The Plastic Tide*. The project aim is to build an open source machine learning algorithm that can detect plastic washed up on beaches using images captured by drones. Citizen scientists are involved in training this algorithm by classifying the plastic and litter they see in the photos provided. Teacher B initially discussed with the students where plastic comes from and the impact plastic litter has on the environment. The teacher then introduced sand samples she had collected from a local beach containing a range of plastic items. Students identified and sorted these plastics into groups of different types. Following this activity, students were introduced to the OCS project, where they were asked to tag and classify the types of litter in the photos of beaches around the world.

4.2.3 Case 3 – Teacher C. The third case consisted of 44 students between the ages of 11-13, where the focus of the unit was light and sound, which ran for 10 weeks. With this unit, Teacher C identified a number of learning outcomes, including: how exploration and investigation allows us to study the behaviour of light and sound; understanding of these behaviours and features; and a variety of applications of light and sound. In order to achieve these learning outcomes, the students undertook a number of activities aimed at developing their understanding of the properties of light and sound. Teacher C then chose two OCS projects - *Agent Exoplanet* and *Planet Hunters* as an application of light properties. The aim of both projects is to identify exoplanets. Agent Exoplanet provides citizen scientists with images taken by telescopes to classify, while Planet Hunters provides graphs of stars' light curves to classify. Teacher C initially introduced students to exoplanet types, and used models to show how the brightness of stars can be measured by gaging the dip in light intensity that occurs when a planet passes between the star and the receiving telescope. Following these activities, students used support material provided by the teacher, *Agent Exoplanet* and *Planet Hunters* to understand the task they had to complete for each. When familiar with each, they participated in interpreting the graphs and images.

4.2.4 Case 4 – Teacher D. The fourth case consisted of 21 students between the ages of 8-10, where the focus of the unit was the power of light, and ran for 9 weeks. With this unit, Teacher D identified a number of learning outcomes, including: understanding the physics of light; how light pollution impacts the living and physical world; to get an appreciation of how science is a way of explaining the world, that science knowledge changes over time; and how to critically evaluate the reliability of data. In order to achieve these understandings, Teacher D selected an OCS project called *Globe at Night*. The project aims to raise public awareness of the impact of light pollution. Citizen scientists were required to collect and submit data by observing their night skies, providing information about date, time, location, and how it compared to one of 7 magnitude charts. Teacher D spent the initial 4 weeks building students' understanding of light, covering topics such as properties of light, methods for measuring light,

---

[4] https://www.zooniverse.org/projects/vykanton/identify-new-zealand-animals
[5] https://www.theplastictide.com/
[6] https://lco.global/agentexoplanet/

[7] https://www.planethunters.org/
[8] https://www.globeatnight.org/
[9] https://teara.govt.nz/en/kaitiakitanga-guardianship-and-conservation/page-4

sources of light, and light pollution. Following this, the OCS project was introduced, where Teacher D created a "treasure hunt" of the OCS website to familiarize students with the site. They then used some of the support material provided by Globe at Night, including video and documentation. While the initial plan was for students to contribute to the OCS project by taking pictures of their night skies, this was not possible due to weather conditions. However, Teacher D was able to take some pictures that they could use with the magnitude charts to categorise the degree of light pollution. Students were also asked to examine data collected over a period of years from the *Globe at Night* website to identify and suggest explanations for any patterns and trends, and then compare the data with images available from satellite maps, considering the reliability of each data set.

4.3 Overview of Data Collection

Data was collected using guided interviews with teachers, their planning documentation, and collaborative workshops attended by the teachers, providing us with multiple sources of evidence from which to triangulate and validate our findings. In order to capture the teachers' experiences when embedding the OCS projects, three questionnaires were administered at three different stages: a pre-intervention stage; a mid-intervention stage; and a post-intervention stage (see Appendix B). Lastly, after completing each stage, we ran a full-day workshop with the teachers, to discuss their progress and experiences. The pre-intervention stage consisted of the teachers creating their teaching units to embed OCS, and occurred in April 2018. When this stage was completed, each of the teachers completed a questionnaire. The questions were structured to understand the teachers' view of how the OCS project they chose linked with the learning outcomes of their unit; what challenges they expect to face; and how it fits with the science capabilities of the NZ curriculum.

Teachers then implemented their teaching units, with the OCS project embedded. A mid-intervention stage in May 2018 captured the progress of embedding, with the teachers again completing an additional questionnaire. These questions were structured to understand what was working well, what difficulties they encountered, and what actions they took to support student learning with respect to the OCS project. This was followed by another workshop. Lastly, a post-intervention stage in July 2018 captured the teachers' experiences having completed the implementation of their unit, where each of the teachers completed a final questionnaire. These questions asked teachers to explain how they helped students to engage with the OCS project, what successes and challenges they experienced in using the OCS, and what information they think teachers require when considering an OCS project as part of a science unit. A final workshop was run to again discuss their experiences in greater detail. Additionally, documentation also consisted of the unit plans that each of the teachers created when planning their units, identifying how they were going to embed an OCS project in their units.

4.4 Data Analysis

In terms of analysis of the cases, a multi-case study approach allows for cross-case analysis and comparison, and for the phenomenon to be investigated across multiple settings [26, 29]. As the research method used was multiple-case study, cross-case synthesis is the most appropriate analytic technique that can be used for analysing the data [28]. This consisted of a thematic analysis, where an inductive coding approach was adopted, allowing themes to emerge from the data. One of the investigators coded the unit plans and questionnaires, which was then reviewed independently by two other investigators for confirmation of the emerging themes. All three agreed on the themes that had emerged from the collected data. Presented in the next section is an overview of the four cases, which is then followed by the findings and a discussion about each of them.

5 RESULTS AND DISCUSSION

The findings are structured according to the research questions. First we present and discuss teachers' perspectives regarding OCS projects. Here we also discuss teachers' perspectives on why embedding OCS is helpful in primary school science teaching and learning. Second, we discuss how teachers embed OCS projects and their suggestions on how embedding may be optimised. Additionally, we discuss an emergent theme of cultural inclusivity in OCS projects.

5.1 Teachers' Perspectives on OCS Projects – Importance, Engagement & Feedback

Teachers expressed both interest and excitement that OCS can be a new, engaging tool and method for teaching that attracts young learners into science. Our cases revealed *why* embedding OCS was helpful in primary school science learning. It supported the very notion of having OCS – it attracted students towards science learning, encouraged them to approach scientific tasks and data with curiosity and supported critical thinking, inference, and learning. We had several instances during the field study when both teachers and students expressed excitement, a sense of discovery, and practical experiences that reinforced and supplemented previously learnt content.

For example, to support critical thinking and critiquing evidence capabilities, Teacher D used satellite maps along with Globe at Night to show the difference between reported light pollution from OCS and the image taken from space. This led to an important discussion on students' understanding about missing data, reliability of OCS, and reasons why light pollution for certain areas might not be reported and present on the OCS map, yet exist in real life. During the project, teachers reported that students felt drawn to being or feeling like actual "scientists".

> *"...they are scientists and they are doing science"*
> (Case 2, Teacher B)

"They can go right on to interpreting the graphs, and be fully engaged and excited by the fact that they are using REAL data and that their interpretations are used by REAL scientists for a REAL purpose."
(Case 3, Teacher C)

This participation can encourage the attitude of "I can do science" which is one of the pivotal points for OCS [15, p.6]. In addition, evidence from the cases showed that dissemination of results of the OCS project itself was an important feedback element. It was a critical aspect of promoting participation. While developing science capabilities and a better understanding of the scientific process are primary reasons for OCS involvement, teachers further indicated that seeing results of contributions made was also very important. They indicated the importance of being able to see the output(s) and the progress of the OCS project that the students participated in, to see how their efforts contributed to a real world scientific project, and that their active involvement had some tangible outcomes. As such, feedback regarding the output of OCS projects was expected to provide satisfaction for the work done, and stimulate a willingness to engage in OCS projects in the future.

"Our data will contribute to a global data set that we can then discuss and use for our own investigations. As well as being part of our Science unit, this data could be linked in with maths, literacy, social sciences, art etc." (Case 4, Teacher D)

However, this may be different from the typical goal of professional scientists. Often, professional scientists are more concerned with the positive findings in relation to their research question(s), and the publication(s) that will result from those findings. This view is especially prevalent in academic research projects in which end results are primarily in the form of scholarly publications as these are tied to rewards such as promotion and scholarly recognition. Such a view prevents some of the goals that OCS is supposed to help achieve, and possibly hinders the growth of science that can be achieved through such projects. Another issue is that the results of the project may not be easily accessible by the general public if they are presented in specialized conferences and academic journals. Scientific papers written by and for academics might also be difficult to understand for general public audiences, as the results are presented using specialist language and formatting. The reading age requirements to understand these papers is often beyond the scope of primary students.

Therefore, it is important that if professional scientists are engaging with students in their OCS projects, they need to be prepared to look beyond the academic paper. They need to engage with the students who are assisting them, disseminating the results in ways students and other non-scientists can interpret and understand. This can be achieved in numerous forms, such as presentations, student and non-scientist friendly blog posts, wikis, Q&A sessions, and forums. Doing so can help students and others see the "bigger" picture in terms of their contributions, and helps form their opinion on science, and professional scientists themselves. For example, in the first case, Teacher A had the

scientist who was running the OCS project come into the classroom and introduce it to the students, which greatly increased the interest, and engagement, in the project.

"Having the 'author' introduce the project was a real win in engagement. [He] talked about why he was doing what he was doing, the process, and how. He showed the class a motion-detecting camera as well. The class was hooked right from the start!"
(Case 1, Teacher A)

Further, by having such engagement, the citizen scientists may be more careful in terms of how they complete the task required of them, increasing accuracy of results:

"This was hugely supported I believe by having [him] come and talk about the importance of his work. The students were so excited to help him and make sure they made cautious observations - nothing rushed."
(Case 1, Teacher A)

Such engagement can also come from professional scientists who might not be part of the OCS project. For example, Teacher D had a professional scientist, who is an expert on the topic they were studying, to talk about it.

"Inviting [professional scientist] in to talk about light pollution and share his experience was really successful in engaging students. [He] talked about the difficulties in measuring light pollution around the globe and introduced students to the idea of using scientific measurement tools to accurately gauge light pollution levels."
(Case 4, Teacher D)

This again encourages the attitude of "I can do science" [15, p.6]. Further, it ties in with Raddick, Bracey [15] argument, which draws on Chambers [30], that students and the public become more aware of scientists, how they work, and gives them confidence that they can take on such roles in the future.

"Reminding them about the Scientist who visited and why they were doing this spurred them along. A real insight into how science can be tedious at times but persistence is important."
(Case 1, Teacher A)

"Sharing their work with scientists will add value to the work in the eyes of the children"
(Case 2, Teacher B)

Finally, students themselves can become disseminators of knowledge, where they bring their new knowledge back to the home, and community in which they are part. This is in line with the goal of curious minds [7]. It is not just about trying to create a nation of scientists, but encouraging citizens to be able to use their science knowledge to participate as critical, informed, and responsible citizens. Such endeavours can help disseminate scientific knowledge in a local context.

"We shared what we were doing with parents via class blog and class newsletter. Lots of interest!"
(Case 1, Teacher A)

"It gave the children a global appreciation of a local problem and has encouraged them to pursue their local study and present their findings to our local community."
(Case 2, Teacher B)

5.2 Embedding OCS in Learning Environments & Suggestions for Improvement

When setting up an OCS project, there are many aspects that need to be considered such as: choosing the research question(s) to be addressed; forming a project team (if necessary); and developing, testing, and refining protocols to be followed by the citizen scientists [21]. While OCS projects outside school environments have found that these aspects may also involve participating citizen scientists, we found that in a primary school environment, teachers and their classes are not necessarily interested in these 'project' aspects. Instead, it was much easier for the professional scientist(s) to set up these aspects, such as creating relevant research questions based on their experience and knowledge of what they want to study. In addition to their normal duties, attempting to include teachers in OCS project planning appeared to stretch their already limited time. We found that teachers are interested in the material that helps them and their classes to understand (i) the requirements of a project, (ii) if it is suitable for their students, and (iii) how it can fit in their classrooms. This was evidenced by the teachers already considering this in the pre-implementation stage, when they were looking at OCS projects that would be a good fit for their scenarios. For example, in the first case, Teacher A was considering the tutorials that their potential OCS project provided for new participants when reviewing suitable projects. More so, all the four teachers in our cases indicated that they found explanatory material provided to be very helpful in their strategies for embedding the projects into student learning activities.

"The tutorial provided by the OCS project was also very helpful."
(Case 1, Teacher A)

"Introduce The Plastic tide: Share how to use the website."
(Case 2, Teacher B)

However, an issue that arose in the fourth case, was that while the OCS project provided support in the form of videos and documentation, Teacher D's class found the material to be difficult to understand. Although the documentation was provided for students to help understand the work that was required of them, issues arose with students not being able to read or understand it, particularly with regards to the technology being used. This may be not only because they had limited understanding of science in general, but also that the supporting material may have been pitched higher than primary school student level.

Therefore, it is important for professional scientists to carefully and properly prepare supporting material. Such material should be simple enough to convey the intended message that the targeted recipients can understand. Training materials that are richer in content, including images, videos, and other interactive content, that complement each other were reported to provide a better explanation than plain text only. Additionally, teachers indicated that interactive user interfaces (UI) and engaging user experiences (UX) provided by the design of the web-based platforms through which students access and use material in an OCS project can have a positive effect on students' initial impression, willingness to actively participate, and overall engagement throughout a project. For instance, Teacher A reported that,

"I was thrilled with how everyone was engaged right from the start! Able students and those less able. This was a wonderful UDL [10] tool - the online hook -in and clear instructions with check boxes that meant everyone could understand what to do."
(Case 1, Teacher A)

Therefore, in creating supporting material, professional scientists should consider their audience, richness of the material, UI & UX design, and the appropriate level of detail required. By making such information explicit, and providing engaging tools, teachers would better understand the project as a whole, and successfully embed it in teaching and learning activities in their classroom environments. Such practice may also encourage greater participation from general citizens.

We further asked teachers to consider what information they looked for from an OCS project in order for them to select an appropriate one for use in their classroom. Suggestions that were provided can be seen in Table 2. The most common suggestions included the timeframe of when students could contribute to the project, the age range of a project, technology requirements of a project, and the science skills that are supported in participating in the project. These were the critical elements that teachers needed to successfully embed OCS in primary school learning environments.

Table 2: Suggestions from teachers about information required about OCS projects

Case	Suggestions from Teachers
Case 1, Teacher A	• Length of time for project
	• Age range
	• Curriculum links
	• Ways to integrate with other learning areas
	• Technology requirements
Case 2, Teacher B	• Contexts that the project could be meaningfully linked to
	• Estimated age ranges the project is appropriate for

---

[10] Universal Design for Learning - designing learning experiences inclusive of students with special learning needs

	• Science skills or capabilities that are supported by the use of the project • What links can be made to local / hands on activities • The science strands that are covered by the project
Case 3, Teacher C	• Curriculum strand • Nature of Science strands • Science Capabilities developed • Broad age range / curriculum level • Ideas / stories / resources from teacher who have used it • Technology requirements
Case 4, Teacher D	• A general idea of the age and curriculum range the project is most appropriate for • An approximate reading age for the material supplied with the project • The type of engagement supported (data gathering, interpretation etc.) and the timeframe and level of commitment required • Can individuals access their own data? Are contributions or progress tracked? Can the data be taken from the project to be used in different contexts?

Considering the feedback from our four primary school teachers, we developed a set of criteria that professional scientists should consider if they want to attract teachers to use their OCS projects in their classrooms. We then had cycles of iterative feedback meetings with the teachers, discussing the criteria, to confirm and refine them. This was intended to ensure that each criterion represents the teachers' needs and expectations from OCS projects. These criteria are presented and explained in Table 3. Having explicit information about each criterion allows teachers to better understand the OCS project, its potential relevance to their students, and how to successfully embed it in teaching and learning. As OCS proliferates in primary level learning environments, the criteria are an important finding for productive engagement between professional scientist(s) (who are clients) and the school teachers and their classes (who are the hosts).

Of course, a question that might be posed is why scientists should care about their OCS projects being used by primary school children? We argue that school children are the future, and embedding OCS projects in their learning process, inculcates aptitudes for science learning that may encourage them to get involved with science and even pursuing science careers in the future. Additionally, the more participants for a project, the more beneficial it is for the scientists, and the OCS platform. Using OCS in a school is one way of encouraging this participation with a simultaneous benefit to the learners and higher participation and contributions for OCS projects.

Table 3: Important contextual descriptions required for an OCS project to be used in the classroom

Context	Explanation
Purpose of the project	Provide a general overview of the project, explaining the purpose, and what it wants to achieve, including the area of focus
Project timeframe	State when the project will start, how long it will run for, what stages participants will be required to complete their tasks (including when they will be expected to do so), and when and how results will be disseminated
Requirements	Technical requirements such as: • Devices that can be used • App(s) and software needed • Accessibility (is an individual account required, or will a group one do?) Skill requirements such as: • Numeracy skills • Literacy skills • Technical/Computer skills
Support provided	Specify what support will be provided for the participants for the different stages of the project. This includes materials that are available to gain an understanding of the project, what's expected of the participants, such as videos and/or documentation
Age level	Indicate what the minimum suitable age level for participation is
Relevance to students' learning	Explain the area of focus for the project, what aspects of this area will be touched on during the project, and how students will be exposed to it by their participation
Geographic scope	Indicate if the OCS project is of local, national, or international interest
Data availability	Indicate if the data that is gathered, or used, in the project is available for access outside of the project itself for further manipulation, such as being able to collaboratively compare it with other classes/schools locally, nationally, and/or internationally

5.3 Cultural Inclusivity in OCS

Our study was carried out in New Zealand. While there is a significant overlap between the New Zealand curriculum to the curricula of other countries, New Zealand features a unique bi-cultural context that recognizes the special place of indigenous Māori culture. Hence, cultural responsiveness of the online citizen science projects that are to be selected for learning activities is a major concern to teachers and students alike. At the time of this study, we were not aware of OCS projects that incorporate any form of cultural responsiveness. We thus found this to be revelatory. This could start from being available in other languages than just English (which does already exist in some projects), but could go as far as a careful consideration of what may be regarded as sacred topics in indigenous cultures, or even to questioning the nature of the scientific inquiry and the adequacy of the underlying knowledge system [31]. For example, all the teachers described culturally responsive practices in embedding OCS:

> "We talked about our school RIMU[11] values - especially Integrity and how as citizen scientists we had to show integrity with our observations."
> (Case 1, Teacher A)

> "Whole-school focus on Matariki[12] - connect by talking about how light travels through space. Polynesian peoples navigated by the light of the stars and used the light of stars as their calendar. Today we know about the universe through observing and measuring light from stars."
> (Case 3, Teacher C)

> "Link with Matariki - students will identify and observe the Matariki constellation and explore how astronomical observations were used to measure time."
> (Case 4, Teacher D)

This is further explained by Teacher B, who introduced a type of learning that encourages a traditional Māori model of learning:

> "Use a tuakana / teina[13] model of learning so older children are supporting the younger children"
> (Case 2, Teacher B)

While this seems to be a major cultural shortcoming of existing OCS projects, it can equally be a great opportunity for a large-scale participatory exercise. Teachers can pick up the topics represented by the different OCS projects and ask their students to talk to senior citizens of their indigenous communities to provide their stories about these topics, e.g. in New Zealand the Matariki and navigation stories about the stars at night.

> "I used the context of constellations as an opportunity to explore traditional stories. Before we began to explore the OCS students were asked to find traditional stories from their own cultures relating to the stars or constellations for homework. Despite a very culturally diverse class, many students struggled to find stories from their own cultures and instead chose stories relating to the Greek and Zodiac constellations familiar in Western culture. However, one student shared a Māori story (a legend of Matariki) and other shared Sri Lankan, Samoan and Chinese legends"
> (Case 4, Teacher D)

This would not only be a genuine enrichment of the citizen science landscape but would contribute to the importance of acknowledging this knowledge as being owned by the indigenous people of an area. This further contributes to valuing citizens for their many knowledge systems and validating their place in citizen science.

5 CONCLUSION

As the trend towards the use of OCS projects in education is increasing, with a promising potential to provide rich experiences in science teaching and enhancing science learning aptitudes and capabilities in particular, it is important to have a closer look at how the participants of such projects view and are affected by them. Our exploratory study is the 'first of its kind' in doing so. It provides early insights that provoke reflection about the perspectives of primary school teachers regarding OCS. We find that at primary school level, OCS provides unique opportunities for teachers and their students to engage with professional scientists in learning environments, to stimulate interest and curiosities about science in young learners, and to support the learning and acquiring of critical skills and capabilities. It provides the criteria that are important for productive and successful engagement between professional scientist(s), school teachers and their classes. The study further provides some initial insights into the importance of rich content as well as the use of engaging UI and interactive UX designs in web-based OCS platforms intended for a primary school classroom environment. Additionally, OCS projects in educational environments should have feedback cycles in which learners are updated about the impact of their previous engagements. This provides young learners with a sense of real scientific contribution which goes beyond the immediate learning activities and reinforces aptitudes towards science learning. Therefore, our findings and associated recommendations provide professional scientists with insights about how to engage school teachers and the meaningful ways in which such engagements can be productive and successful to both science learning in schools and OCS-enabled scientific research projects. These findings are a significant step towards an understanding of OCS in teaching and learning at the primary school level.

There are some limitations to the study. First is that the focus is on the NZ curriculum, which has its own peculiarities that may not be applicable to other countries. We also acknowledge the limitation of the scope with the four cases in this exploratory study, considering that the findings are based on the teachers' perspectives only. However, as this is part of a bigger research project, we have ongoing endeavours to expand this scope. In particular, we will include the student's perspectives and intend to expand our assessment and evaluation of the benefits of OCS in teaching and learning. Overall, the provoking insights emerging from this exploratory study are difficult to ignore and can be a start in building blocks towards successful OCS projects from both the perspectives of professional scientists and teachers and learners in educational environments.

---

[11] Related to Māori values and native forest
[12] Māori name for the cluster of stars also known as the Pleiades

[13] http://tereomaori.tki.org.nz/Curriculum-guidelines/Teaching-and-learning-te-reo-Maori/Aspects-of-planning/The-concept-of-a-tuakana-teina-relationship

ACKNOWLEDGEMENTS

This work is funded by Teaching and Learning Research Initiative (TLRI) of New Zealand under Project No. 9182.[14] TLRI supports and enhances links between educational research and teaching practices to improve outcomes for learners.

The authors would also like to thank the anonymous reviewers for their valuable comments and helpful suggestions.

REFERENCES

[1] Tinati, R., M. Van Kleek, E. Simperl, M. Luczak-Rösch, R. Simpson, and N. Shadbolt. 2015. Designing for citizen data analysis: A cross-sectional case study of a multi-domain citizen science platform. In Proceedings of the 33rd Annual ACM Conference on Human Factors in Computing Systems (CHI '15). ACM Press, 4069-4078.

[2] Tinati, R., M. Luczak-Roesch, E. Simperl, and W. Hall. 2017. An investigation of player motivations in Eyewire, a gamified citizen science project. Computers in Human Behavior, 73, 527-540.

[3] Jay, C., R. Dunne, D. Gelsthorpe, and M. Vigo. 2016. To sign up, or not to sign up?: maximizing citizen science contribution rates through optional registration. In Proceedings of the 2016 CHI Conference on Human Factors in Computing Systems. ACM, 1827-1832.

[4] Tinati, R., M. Luczak-Roesch, E. Simperl, and W. Hall. 2016. Because science is awesome: studying participation in a citizen science game. In Proceedings of the 8th ACM Conference on Web Science. ACM, 45-54.

[5] Oliveira, N., E. Jun, and K. Reinecke. 2017. Citizen Science Opportunities in Volunteer-Based Online Experiments. In Proceedings of the 2017 CHI Conference on Human Factors in Computing Systems. ACM, 6800-6812.

[6] Law, E., K.Z. Gajos, A. Wiggins, M.L. Gray, and A.C. Williams. 2017. Crowdsourcing as a Tool for Research: Implications of Uncertainty. In CSCW. 1544-1561.

[7] What is Curious Minds? Available at: https://www.curiousminds.nz/about/. Last access: 15th February 2019.

[8] 2007. Ministry of Education. The New Zealand curriculum. Wellington: Learning Media.

[9] Hofstein, A. and V.N. Lunetta. 1982. The role of the laboratory in science teaching: Neglected aspects of research. Review of educational research, 52(2), 201-217.

[10] Hofstein, A. and V.N. Lunetta. 2004. The laboratory in science education: Foundations for the twenty-first century. Science education, 88(1), 28-54.

[11] Bolstad, R. and R. Hipkins. 2008. Seeing yourself in science. Wellington, New Zealand: New Zealand Council For Educational Research.

[12] Tytler, R., D. Symington, V. Kirkwood, and C. Malcolm. 2008. Engaging students in authentic science through school--community links: learning from the rural experience. Teaching Science: The Journal of the Australian Science Teachers Association, 54(3).

[13] Caygill, R., V. Hanlar, and C. Harris-Miller. 2016. Student attitudes to maths and science: what we know from New Zealand's TIMSS 2014/15 results for Year 5 and Year 9. Retrieved 15th February, 2019 from: http://www.education-counts.govt.nz/publications/series/2571/timss-201415/student-attitudes-to-maths-and-science-what-we-know-from-new-zealands-timss-201415-results-for-year-5-and-year-9.

[14] Educational Assessment Research Unit and New Zealand Council for Educational Research. Wānangatia te Putanga Tauira National Monitoring Study of Student Achievement Science. 2012. Available at: http://nmssa.otago.ac.nz/-reports/2012_Science_ONLINE.pdf. Last access: 15th February 2019.

[15] Raddick, M.J., G. Bracey, K. Carney, G. Gyuk, K. Borne, J. Wallin, S. Jacoby, and A. Planetarium. 2009. Citizen science: status and research directions for the coming decade. AGB Stars and Related Phenomenastro 2010: The Astronomy and Astrophysics Decadal Survey, 2010, 46P.

[16] Raddick, M.J., G. Bracey, P.L. Gay, C.J. Lintott, C. Cardamone, P. Murray, K. Schawinski, A.S. Szalay, and J. Vandenberg. 2013. Galaxy Zoo: Motivations of citizen scientists. arXiv preprint arXiv:1303.6886.

[17] Crowston, K., E. Mitchell, and C. Østerlund. 2018. Coordinating Advanced Crowd Work: Extending Citizen Science. In Proceedings of the 51st Hawaii International Conference on System Sciences.

[18] Wiggins, A. and K. Crowston. 2011. From conservation to crowdsourcing: A typology of citizen science. In Proceedings of the 44th Hawaii International Conference on System Sciences. IEEE, 1-10.

[19] Hassman, K., G. Mugar, C. Østerlund, and C. Jackson. 2013. Learning at the seafloor, looking at the sky: The relationship between individual tasks and collaborative engagement in two citizen science projects. In proceedings for 10th International Conference on Computer Supported Collaborative Learning.

[20] Nov, O., O. Arazy, and D. Anderson. 2011. Dusting for science: motivation and participation of digital citizen science volunteers. In Proceedings of the 2011 iConference. ACM, 68-74.

[21] Lewenstein, B.V. 2004. What does citizen science accomplish.

[22] Yadav, P. and J. Darlington. 2017. Conceptual Frameworks for Building Online Citizen Science Projects. arXiv preprint arXiv:1704.05084.

[23] Curtis, V. 2014. Online citizen science games: opportunities for the biological sciences. Applied & translational genomics, 3(4), 90-94.

[24] Raddick, M., G. Bracey, P. Gay, C. Lintott, P. Murray, K. Schawinski, A. Szalay, and J. Vandenberg. 2010. Galaxy zoo: Exploring the motivations of citizen science volunteers. Sept. Astronomy Education Review, 9(1).

[25] Yin, R.K. 2009. Case study research: Design and methods (applied social research methods). London and Singapore: Sage.

[26] Benbasat, I., D.K. Goldstein, and M. Mead. 1987. The case research strategy in studies of information systems. MIS quarterly, 11(3), 369-386.

[27] Eisenhardt, K.M. 1989. Building theories from case study research. Academy of management review, 14(4), 532-550.

[28] Yin, R.K. 1994. Case study research: design and methods. 1994. Thousand Oaks, CA.

[29] Darke, P., G. Shanks, and M. Broadbent. 1998. Successfully completing case study research: combining rigour, relevance and pragmatism. Information systems journal, 8(4), 273-289.

[30] Chambers, D.W. 1983. Stereotypic images of the scientist: The Draw-a-Scientist Test. Science education, 67(2), 255-265.

[31] Smith, L.T., Decolonizing methodologies: Research and indigenous peoples. 2013: Zed Books Ltd.

---

[14] http://www.tlri.org.nz/tlri-research/research-progress/school-sector/citizen-scientists-classroom-investigating-role-online

Concept of Keystone Species in Web Systems: Identifying Small Yet Influential Online Bulletin Board Threads

Shota Ejima
Graduate School of Systems and Information Engineering, University of Tsukuba, Japan
eji@websci.cs.tsukuba.ac.jp

Mizuki Oka
Graduate School of Systems and Information Engineering, University of Tsukuba, Japan
ALTERNATIVE MACHINE Inc., Japan
mizuki@cs.tsukuba.ac.jp

Takashi Ikegami
Graduate School of Arts and Sciences, The University of Tokyo, Japan
ikeg@sacral.c.u-tokyo.ac.jp

ABSTRACT

Research is being conducted to understand social and innovative behavior in human interactions on the Web as a biological ecosystem. Keystone species in a biological ecosystem are defined as a set of species that significantly impacts the ecosystem if they are removed from the system, irrespective of its small biomass. Identifying keystone species is an important problem as they play an important role in maintaining diversity and stability in ecosystems. A human community in the web system also possesses keystone species. They can be influential users or contents on the web systems, even though their commitments to the web are relatively small. We use data from an online bulletin board, and identify keystone threads (= "species") that have a large impact if they are removed or become unpopular, despite their small population size. Here, the removal of threads can be regarded as a state in which there is no attention or actions by users on the thread. The multivariate Hawkes process is used to measure the degree of influence among all threads and calculate the overall activity level on the online bulletin board. Our analysis confirms that keystone threads do exist in the system. Apparently, the number of keystone species increases along with the service maturation. The keystone concept in online services proposed in this study gives a new viewpoint for their stable operation.

CCS CONCEPTS

• **Human-centered computing** → **Web-based interaction**; *Social network analysis*; • **Information systems** → *Web log analysis*.

KEYWORDS

online discussion threads, Hawkes process, keystone species

ACM Reference Format:
Shota Ejima, Mizuki Oka, and Takashi Ikegami. 2019. Concept of Keystone Species in Web Systems: Identifying Small Yet Influential Online Bulletin Board Threads. In *11th ACM Conference on Web Science (WebSci '19), June 30–July 3, 2019, Boston, MA, USA*. ACM, New York, NY, USA, 5 pages. https://doi.org/10.1145/3292522.3326023

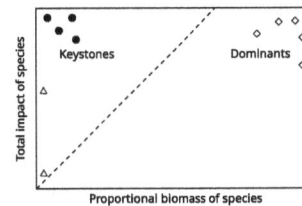

Figure 1: View of keystone species drawn with inference to [19]. Plots on the upper left are keystone species whose proportional biomass (population) is small but their impact is large, and plots in the upper right are dominant species whose proportional biomass (population) and impact are both large. The dashed line represents $y = x$, indicating a proportional relationship between population and impact.

1 INTRODUCTION

In recent years, various online communities, such as online bulletin boards, chat tools, and social network services, have been widely used. People's communication in an online community creates enormous log data on a daily basis and their interactions create new ideas that spread through social networks. Richard Dawkins called the spread of influence and information as memes analogous to genes [2]. This "meme evolution theory" has recently regained attention as large amounts of traces of individual actions and remarks are constantly recorded and accumulated on the Web, and they can be analyzed quantitatively [12, 20]. Furthermore, such an evolutionary biological perspective and its mathematical framework have been proposed for social media analysis [1, 13]. These studies suggest that an analogy can be borrowed from biological systems, and if correctly applied to social systems, it can open new perspectives on analyzing social systems.

In biological ecosystems, the concept of *dominant* and *keystone* species exists to define influential species [19]. The dominant species are defined as species having both high biomass and large impact on the ecosystem. On the other hand, keystone species are the ones having large impact on the ecosystem despite their low biomass proportional to the ecosystem. Figure 1 depicts the relationship of dominant and keystone species with the abundance of species and their impacts on ecosystems. It has been reported that, if keystone species are removed from the ecosystem, the balance of the ecosystem collapses, causing extinction of many other species [17]. Many experiments on biological ecosystems have demonstrated that less abundant species also have strong effects on communities and ecosystems [3, 18], and finding and protecting those species is important from the perspective of the system's stability. In contrast to dominant species, keystone species are considered difficult to identify, as their population is small.

In online social-communication systems, identifying keystone species in ecosystems can be regarded as identifying influential users or contents, which have been extensively studies in the literature. These studies include identifying influential users based on follow-follower networks [10] or diffusion models of the spread of influence and information through social networks [9, 21]. The influential users or contents obtained from these studies can be regarded as identified *dominants* species in the biological ecosystem, and to the best of our knowledge, few studies have discussed keystone species in the context of online communities. Therefore, in this study, we introduce the concept of keystone species in an online communication system and propose a method to identify them. In contrast to the standard biological definition of keystone species, we extend it to more dynamic and network-based ones [8]. That is, we treat the keystone species as time-varying and context-dependent (i.e., the combinations of other species) processes.

Specifically, we apply the concept of keystone species to online bulletin boards by considering a thread as a species. On the online bulletin board, users create threads related to specific topics and themes to communicate. Threads can be said to influence each other because users move back and forth among threads. In other words, threads are in a competitive relationship to get a limited number of user resources. Such an environment can be considered similar to the competitive relationship between species in biological ecosystems. If keystone threads are identified, online bulletin board service providers can perform necessary interventions, such as protection of keystone threads, for stable operation.

We model each thread as an event sequence of all the actions performed by users (i.e., views, comments, replies, and claps) and estimate the influence among threads by using the multivariate Hawkes process [7], a self-exciting stochastic point process. The Hawkes process was originally used to analyze earthquakes [15] and applied to many other fields such as financial market modeling [5]. In recent years, it has been used for influential user identification [23] and recommendations [22], user interest modeling [11], and steering user activity by controlling dynamics [4] on social media.

For identifying keystone species, it is necessary to measure the degree of impact when the species is removed from the system. Gupta et al. proposed a method for characterizing the effect of removing selected events in the history of the Hawkes process [6]. We also employ a similar method in this study to simulate the degree of impact caused by thread deletion. Specifically, we use the fitted parameters of the multivariate Hawkes process and simulate the model to compute the degree of impact caused by deleting each thread from the system. This is done by computing the *activity level* of the entire bulletin board [16] and comparing the activity levels from before and after the removal and regard that as an *impact* of the removal of each thread. If a thread has a high degree of impact despite a small density (i.e., the number of users participating in the thread), then we identify the thread as a keystone thread.

The contributions of this study are summarized below.

- We introduce the concept of keystone species of the biological ecosystems in a web system to identify influential contents.
- We propose a method to identify keystone species in a web system via the multivariate Hawkes process and measure the difference of impact before and after the removal of a species (i.e., content).
- We apply our method to online bulletin board data and show the existence of keystone species on the Web, as well as the results of our analysis on the found keystone species.

2 DEFINITION OF KEYSTONE SPECIES AND HAWKES PROCESS

2.1 Keystone species in biological ecosystems

The keystone species has a large impact on the ecosystem despite its proportionally small biomass in the ecosystem. Starfish have been reported as a keystone species. When starfish, which is the apex of a food chain in a intertidal zone, was removed, the mussel population, on which starfish was feeding, increased abnormally and the balance of the ecosystem was destroyed [17]. Consequently, many other species living in the intertidal zone have become extinct. That is, keystone species play an important role in maintaining stability in ecosystems.

For the definition of keystone species, we use the population density p_i occupied by species i in the ecosystem and the *impact* I_i when i is removed from the ecosystem. The *impact* is defined as how a quantitative value representing the nature of the ecosystem, such as the population of all species in the ecosystem, will change before and after removing the species i. Let t_N be the quantitative value representing the nature of the ecosystem before removing species i, and t_D be the value after removal. The *impact* I_i of removal of the species i is shown below[19].

$$I_i = \frac{t_N - t_D}{t_N} \tag{1}$$

Intuitively, if you draw a scatter plot with population density p_i plotted on the horizontal axis and the impact I_i plotted on the vertical axis, the points on the upper left of the figure are keystone species (see Figure 1). Further, plots in the upper right in the graph, that is, the species whose impact and proportional population density are both large, are called dominant species.

In this study, let p_{max} and I_{max} be the maximum population density and maximum impact of all the target species, respectively. The species i that satisfies the following two conditions is defined as a keystone species [8]:

$$p_i \leq c_p \times p_{max} \tag{2}$$
$$c_I \times I_{max} \leq I_i \tag{3}$$

where c_p and c_I are the threshold coefficients, which are used to compute thresholds for population density and impact, respectively. Note that the threshold values $c_p \times p_{max}$ and $c_I \times I_{max}$ become different depending on the values of p_{max} and I_{max}, respectively. When the computed p_i is smaller than the threshold of population density and I_i is higher than the threshold of impact, the species i

is identified as a keystone species. We also define CI_i as the community importance of the species i, which indicates the keystonness of the species [14] . The higher this value, the higher is the keystonness of the species.

$$CI_i = \frac{I_i}{p_i} = \frac{t_N - t_D}{t_N} \frac{1}{p_i} \qquad (4)$$

2.2 Multivariate Hawkes Process

Hawkes process[7] is a self-exciting stochastic point process, and is a probabilistic model that takes into account the influence of past event occurrences on future event occurrences. We consider *threads* in an online bulletin board as species and estimate the degree of influences between threads by modeling event sequences via the multivariate Hawkes process. Then, we calculate the *impact* on the online bulletin board when each thread is deleted by using the estimated degree of influence. By using this impact value and the density defined for each thread, a thread that has a high overall impact when deleted, despite its small density, is identified as a keystone. Event sequences of a thread are composed of user actions such as accesses, comments, and claps.

The intensity function $\lambda_i(t)$ of the event sequences at time t of thread i is represented as follows:

$$\lambda_i(t) = \mu_i + \sum_{j=1}^{D} \sum_{t_k^j < t} \phi(t - t_k^j) \qquad (5)$$

where D is the number of threads, μ_i is the base intensity of thread i, and t_k^j represents the k-th event sequence of thread j. ϕ is called the kernel function, and we use the exponential kernel function $\phi(t) = \alpha_{ij}e^{-\beta_{ij}t}$. α_{ij} represents the degree of the influence of thread j on thread i, and β_{ij} represents the decay rate of the intensity of thread i raised by the event sequences in thread j. These parameters can be obtained analytically by the maximum likelihood method, given an event sequence [15].

We define threads as nodes, set the estimated parameter α_{ij} as the edge representing the degree of influence from thread i to j, and construct a network. We consider this thread network as an ecosystem and identify the keystone thread that plays an important role in maintaining the stability of the network, that is, for stable communication within the online bulletin board.

2.3 Impact of removal of a thread

To calculate keystone threads, we need to calculate the impact I_i on the ecosystem, viz., the thread network, when thread i is removed. Here, we use cascading condition C, which represents the activity level of network [16]. Let $\boldsymbol{\alpha} = \{\alpha_{ij}\}_{i,j=1,\cdots,D}, \boldsymbol{\mu} = \{\mu_i\}_{i=1,\cdots,D}$ be the parameters estimated via the multivariate Hawkes process. Then C is defined as follows:

$$C \equiv \frac{\sum_{i,j}(L\Lambda L^T)_{ij}}{\sum_i \langle \lambda_i \rangle}, \qquad (6)$$

where $L = \sum_{n=0}^{\infty} \boldsymbol{\alpha} = (I - \boldsymbol{\alpha})^{-1}, \Lambda = \text{diag}(\langle \boldsymbol{\lambda} \rangle) = \text{diag}(\{\langle \lambda_i \rangle\}_{i=1,\cdots,D})$
$= \text{diag}(L\boldsymbol{\mu})$. The value of C becomes higher as the event sequence of each node (threads) of the network becomes more bursty. We define this burstiness to represent the activity level of the network.

Table 1: Descriptive statistics of online bulletin board

	pregnant women	mothers
periods	03/2017 ~ 09/2018	
# of unique users	10,687	10,945
# of unique threads	425	399
# of accesses	112,868	105,821
# of comments	22,777	23,978
# claps	136,211	97,820
average # of actions per thread	640	570

The change in activity level of the network ΔC_i when deleting a certain thread i in the network is defined as follows:

$$\Delta C_i = \sum_{j \neq i}(C - C_j'), \qquad (7)$$

where C_j' is the cascading condition calculated by setting the influence between threads i and $j(\neq i)$ (i.e., α_{ij}, α_{ji}) to 0. Performing the same calculation for all $j \neq i$, and calculating the differences with the original C and all the C_j', we obtain ΔC_i by adding the differences. This ΔC_i is equivalent to $t_N - t_D$ in the equation (1). We can thus define the impact I_i by removing the thread i from the network as follows:

$$I_i = \frac{t_N - t_D}{t_N} = \frac{\Delta C_i}{C} \qquad (8)$$

3 EXPERIMENTS

3.1 Data

The data used by us was provided by QON Inc., which is an online community service in Japan [1]. More than 100 companies use this service as an online bulletin board for communication between a client company and consumers, and the total number of users exceeds 1 million. Each company is provided a community in which the company can run its own bulletin board. We analyzed two communities among them[2]. One targeted women before or during pregnancy, and the other targeted mothers who were raising children. Table 1 shows the statistics of the data of the two communities of the online bulletin board. On the online bulletin board, users can communicate with other users by posting threads and replying to the threads by commenting and clicking claps (corresponds to likes) for threads and/or comments.

We analyzed the event sequences composed of user actions, such as views, comments, and claps, on threads. The event sequences are divided into two-week windows (30 windows were obtained for the period between March 2017 and September 2018), and the parameters are fitted using the multivariate Hawkes process for each window. We disregard threads having less than 50 actions in the event sequences, as fitting cannot be performed if the number of actions is too small. Accordingly, 218 unique threads out of 435 threads are targeted for our analysis (51.3 % of the total number of unique threads). The number of overlapping target threads for analysis in all windows is 449. For the other community, the number of unique target threads is 213 out of 399 threads (53.3%). The number of overlapping target threads in all windows is 427.

---

[1]https://www.q-o-n.com
[2]The data we used in this study is publicly available at
https://github.com/AlternativeMachine/keystone

There are two types of threads, viz., threads created by community service administrators (called thread by administrators) and by general users (called thread by users). In the thread by administrators, because questionnaires and gift campaigns for users are often conducted, many users gather, and therefore the number of actions is larger compared to thread by users. On the other hand, thread by users is mainly used for chatting and consultation about daily life. The number of users who participated per thread as well as the number of actions are smaller compared to thread by administrators.

For the population density, which we need to identify for calculating keystone threads, we use the number of users participating in the thread. Let N be the number of target threads and u_i be the number of unique users who have taken action at least once in thread i in a window. Then the population density p_i of thread i can be calculated as follows:

$$p_i = \frac{u_i}{\sum_{j=1}^{N} u_j}. \qquad (9)$$

The threshold coefficients c_p and c_I are set to 0.25 and 0.5, respectively, with reference to [8]. That is, the thread i whose p_i is less than one-fourth of the maximum population thread c_{max} and I_i is more than half of the maximum impact thread I_{max} in a window, is identified as a keystone thread. It is noteworthy that thresholds are computed in relation to the maximum values for population and impacts, respectively; the threshold values become different for each window. Figure 2-left shows the temporal development of keystone thresholds for p_i and I_i computed for each window and the number of threads for each window in the bar graph. We can see that the number of threads maximizes at window ID = 15 and the threshold values correlate roughly with the number of threads for each window. Figure 2-right shows the number of windows selected as keystones for each thread sorted in descending order. One of the threads is selected the maximum number of times, viz., six times, over the period.

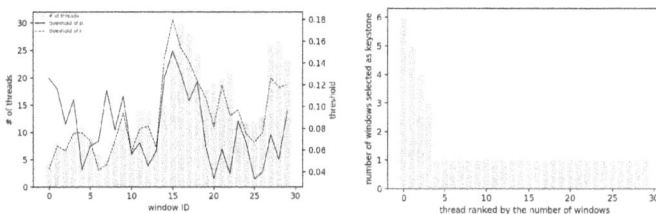

Figure 2: (left) Temporal development of keystone thresholds for p_i and I_i computed for each window and the total number of threads in each window denoted by the bar graph. (right) The number of windows selected as keystones for identified keystone threads.

4 RESULTS

Because of the limitation of space in the paper, we mainly show the results of one community (pregnant women). First we show the time development of population density p_i of all the threads in all the windows during the whole period in Figure 3. If a thread in a window is selected as a keystone thread, it is colored red. We can see that keystone threads tend to appear more as the time elapses or the community matures.

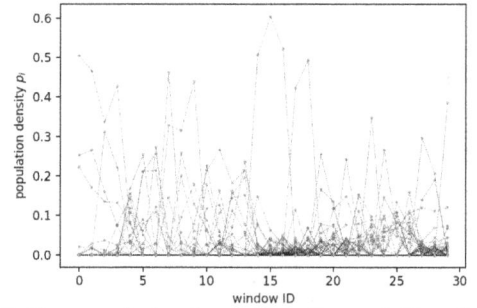

Figure 3: Temporal development of population density p_i over windows for all the threads. Each line indicates the development of each thread and it is colored red when selected as a keystone thread.

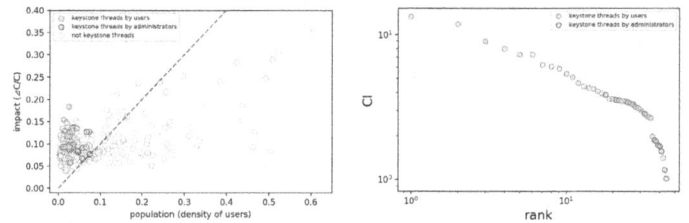

Figure 4: (left) Scatter plot with p_i on the horizontal axis and I_i on the vertical axis of all windows. The dashed line represents $y = x$ indicating a proportional relationship between population and impact. Keystone threads by users (red=32), administrators (blue=12), and other non-keystone threads (white=405). (right) CI values of keystone threads are arranged in rank order. Red: keystone threads by users, blue: keystone threads by administrators.

Figure 4-left shows a scatter plot with population density p_i and impact I_i on the horizontal and vertical axes, respectively. The results of all threads are plotted here. This figure shows the results of all windows. Because the thresholds for keystones are computed considering the maximum values for population and impacts in each window, the threshold values become different for each window. The dashed line in the figure indicates $y = x$, and threads being on this line indicates that their impacts on removal are proportional to the population density. The colored (red and blue) circles are threads identified as keystones. If a thread is by users, it is colored red and is blue if it is by administrators. Other non-keystone threads are in white. The number of threads identified as keystones is 44 among 449 threads. Of the 44 threads identified as keystone threads, 32 (72.7%) are threads by users. This indicates a possibility that the thread by users is more likely to be selected as a keystone thread.

Figure 4-right shows the keystone threads sorted by community importance CI_i. Reds are keystone threads by users and blues are keystone threads by administrators. The top 16 ranked CI_i are of threads by users. Among keystone threads, the average CI_i of keystone threads by users is 4.88, and the average CI_i of keystone threads by administrators is 2.33. The analysis using CI_i also confirms that keystoneness tends to be higher for threads created by users than by administrators.

Figure 5: Example of the thread network (window ID = 19) in which a keystone thread is colored red.

To investigate what types of threads by users are identified as keystones, we also categorized each thread according to its content and found five major categories such as chatting (12 threads), word-chain-game (9), consultation (7), picture sharing (2), and reports on winning the lottery (1). One interesting category is keystone threads with word-chain-games. The most keystone-selected thread (six times) as well as the top CI_i ranked thread is also a word-chain-game thread. Although the number of participating users is small, a thread with active interaction between users is more likely to be identified as a keystone thread.

Figure 5 shows a thread- network (α_{ij}) of in a window (window ID = 19) in which the word-chain-game thread exists[3]. Each node corresponds to a thread and the edge width corresponds to the influential strength among nodes. The red-colored node is the keystone thread that is the only one selected as the keystone thread. Moreover, the nodes connected with strong influences are those of dominant threads. Network analysis on centralities (degree, betweenness, and pagerank) show that the discovered keystone node has neither high nor low values, but rather, median values. Nevertheless, their impacts are large enough to collapse the entire system.

From this result, it became clear that thread by users is important for the stable operation and autonomy of an online bulletin board. The results on the other community (mother community) showed very similar results, that is, the keystoneness is higher in threads by users than threads by administrators. Among 427 threads, 64 threads are identified as keystone threads, and 38 threads (59.4%) are threads by users, more than the majority. The average values of CI_i of keystone threads are 10.4 and 4.82 for threads by users and administrators, respectively.

5 CONCLUSION

In this study, we introduced the concept of keystone species, which is important for keeping the biological ecosystem stable, on the online bulletin board, and proposed a new influential-content identification method in the online community. We considered threads in online bulletin boards as species in a biological ecosystem and modeled influences among threads by using the multivariate Hawkes process. We constructed a thread network with threads as nodes, estimated the influence as edges, and calculated the degree of impact on the activity level of the entire network when a thread is removed. Accordingly, we showed that there are threads that play keystone roles. An analysis of threads from the viewpoint of thread

by users and thread by administrators shows that all dominant threads are occupied by thread by administrators, and in contrast, thread by users is more likely to be identified as a keystone thread.

Keystone species plays an important role in preserving the stability of biological ecosystems. When considering an online community as an ecosystem, its stability is realized by its high level of activity and engagement by the user. Identifying content that may work to increase the activity of the community despite its small population or event occurrence is difficult in the existing method, so the proposed method gives a new perspective for stable operation of the service.

In this study, we only analyzed two communities, both of which showed similar tendencies, but in the future, we would like to analyze all communities (more than 100) in the bulletin board service and verify the overall tendency. Moreover, we would like to analyze how the types of keystone threads or their numbers differ when grouping threads with semantics. Finally, our method is general and can be applied for identifying, for example, keystone users in other online communities such as social network services.

ACKNOWLEDGMENTS

This work was supported by JSPS KAKENHI Grant Numbers JP17H01821 and JP19H04214.

REFERENCES

[1] Lada A Adamic, Thomas M Lento, Eytan Adar, and Pauline C Ng. 2016. Information evolution in social networks. In *Proc. of the 9th ACM International Conference on Web Search and Data Mining*. 473–482.
[2] Richard Dawkins. 1976. *The selfish gene*. Oxford University Press New York. 224 pages.
[3] James A. Estes, Alexander Burdin, and Daniel F. Doak. 2016. Sea otters, kelp forest, and the extinction of Steller's sea cow. *Proc. of the National Academy of Sciences of the United States of America* 113, 4 (2016), 880–885.
[4] Mehrdad Farajtabar, Xiaojing Ye, Sahar Harati, Le Song, and Hongyuan Zha. 2016. Multistage Campaigning in Social Networks. In *Proc. of the 29th International Conference on Neural Information Processing Systems (NIPS 2016)*. 4725–4733.
[5] Vladimir Filimonov and Didier Sornette. 2012. Quantifying reflexivity in financial markets: Toward a prediction of flash crashes. *Physical Review E* 85, 5 (2012), 056108.
[6] Amrita Gupta, Mehrdad Farajtabar, Bistra Dilkina, and Hongyuan Zha. 2018. Discrete Interventions in Hawkes Processes with Applications in Invasive Species Management. In *Proc. of the 27th International Joint Conference on Artificial Intelligence*. 3385–3392.
[7] Alan G Hawkes. 1971. Point spectra of some mutually exciting point processes. *Journal of the Royal Statistical Society. Series B (Methodological)* (1971), 438–443.
[8] Takashi Ikegami. 2005. Neutral phenotypes as network keystone species. *Population Ecology* 47, 1 (2005), 21–29.
[9] Tomoharu Iwata, Amar Shah, and Zoubin Ghahramani. 2013. Discovering latent influence in online social activities via shared cascade poisson processes. In *Proc. of the 19th ACM SIGKDD International Conference on Knowledge Discovery and Data Mining*. 266–274.
[10] Haewoon Kwak, Changhyun Lee, Hosung Park, and Sue Moon. 2010. What is Twitter, a social network or a news media?. In *Proc. of the 19th International Conference on World Wide Web*. 591–600.
[11] Andrew S Lan, Jonathan C Spencer, Ziqi Chen, Christopher G Brinton, and Mung Chiang. 2018. Personalized Thread Recommendation for MOOC Discussion Forums. In *Proc. of the Joint European Conference on Machine Learning and Knowledge Discovery in Databases*. 725–740.
[12] Jure Leskovec, Lars Backstrom, and Jon Kleinberg. 2009. Meme-tracking and the Dynamics of the News Cycle. In *Proc. of the 15th ACM SIGKDD International Conference on Knowledge Discovery and Data Mining*. 497–506.
[13] Yasuko Matsubara, Yasushi Sakurai, and Christos Faloutsos. 2015. The web as a jungle: Non-linear dynamical systems for co-evolving online activities. In *Proc. of the 24th International Conference on World Wide Web*. 721–731.
[14] L Scott Mills, Michael E Soulé, and Daniel F Doak. 1993. The keystone-species concept in ecology and conservation. *BioScience* 43, 4 (1993), 219–224.
[15] Yoshihiko Ogata. 1988. Statistical models for earthquake occurrences and residual analysis for point processes. *Journal of the American Statistical association* 83, 401 (1988), 9–27.
[16] Tomokatsu Onaga and Shigeru Shinomoto. 2016. Emergence of event cascades in inhomogeneous networks. *Scientific reports* 6 (2016), 33321.
[17] Robert T Paine. 1966. Food web complexity and species diversity. *The American Naturalist* 100, 910 (1966), 65–75.
[18] Robert T. Paine. 1969. A note on trophic complexity and community stability. *American Naturalist* 103 (1969), 91–93.
[19] Mary E Power, David Tilman, James A Estes, Bruce A Menge, William J Bond, L Scott Mills, Gretchen Daily, Juan Carlos Castilla, Jane Lubchenco, and Robert T Paine. 1996. Challenges in the Quest for Keystones: Identifying keystone species is difficult—but essential to understanding how loss of species will affect ecosystems. *BioScience* 46, 8 (1996), 609–620.
[20] Elad Segev, Asaf Nissenbaum, Nathan Stolero, and Limor Shifman. 2015. Families and networks of internet memes: the relationship between cohesiveness, uniqueness, and quiddity concreteness. *Journal of Computer-Mediated Communication* 20, 4 (2015), 417–433.
[21] Greg Ver Steeg and Aram Galstyan. 2012. Information transfer in social media. In *Proc. of the 21st International Conference on World Wide Web*. 509–518.
[22] Ali Zarezade, Utkarsh Upadhyay, Hamid R Rabiee, and Manuel Gomez-Rodriguez. 2017. Redqueen: An online algorithm for smart broadcasting in social networks. In *Proc. of the 10th ACM International Conference on Web Search and Data Mining*. 51–60.
[23] Ke Zhou, Hongyuan Zha, and Le Song. 2013. Learning social infectivity in sparse low-rank networks using multidimensional hawkes processes. In *Proc. of the 16th International Conference on Artificial Intelligence and Statistics*. 641–649.

---

[3]A threshold is set to draw the edges of the network. The threshold value is set using an average value of α_{ij} excluding the diagonal components, and the edges are drawn if the values are larger greater than the this threshold.

Exploring Misogyny across the Manosphere in Reddit

Tracie Farrell
tracie.farrel@open.ac.uk
Open University

Miriam Fernandez
miriam.fernandez@open.ac.uk
Open University

Jakub Novotny
novotny.jakub@gmail.com
No affiliation

Harith Alani
h.alani@open.ac.uk
Open University

ABSTRACT

The 'manosphere' has been a recent subject of feminist scholarship on the web. Serious accusations have been levied against it for its role in encouraging misogyny and violent threats towards women online, as well as for potentially radicalising lonely or disenfranchised men. Feminist scholars evidence this through a shift in the language and interests of some men's rights activists on the manosphere, away from traditional subjects of family law or mental health and towards more sexually explicit, violent, racist and homophobic language. In this paper, we study this phenomenon by investigating the flow of extreme language across seven online communities on Reddit, with openly misogynistic members (e.g., Men Going Their Own Way, Involuntarily Celibates), and investigate if and how misogynistic ideas spread within and across these communities. Grounded on feminist critiques of language, we created nine lexicons capturing specific misogynistic rhetoric (Physical Violence, Sexual Violence, Hostility, Patriarchy, Stoicism, Racism, Homophobia, Belittling, and Flipped Narrative) and used these lexicons to explore how language evolves within and across misogynistic groups. This analysis was conducted on 6 million posts, from 300K conversations created between 2011 and December 2018. Our results shows increasing patterns on misogynistic content and users as well as violent attitudes, corroborating existing theories of feminist studies that the amount of misogyny, hostility and violence is steadily increasing in the manosphere.

CCS CONCEPTS

• **Information systems** → **Social networking sites**; *Data mining*; *Web mining*.

KEYWORDS

Hate, misogyny, Reddit, feminist studies

ACM Reference Format:
Tracie Farrell, Miriam Fernandez, Jakub Novotny, and Harith Alani. 2019. Exploring Misogyny across the Manosphere in Reddit. In *11th ACM Conference on Web Science (WebSci '19), June 30–July 3, 2019, Boston, MA, USA*. ACM, New York, NY, USA, 10 pages. https://doi.org/10.1145/3292522.3326045

1 INTRODUCTION

The 'manosphere' is a group of loosely incorporated websites and social media communities where men's perspectives, needs, gripes, frustrations and desires are explicitly explored. Women and feminism are typically targets of hostility [14, 32]. In these spaces, discourse tends to revolve around a concept of "men's rights activism", which highlights experiences of discrimination against men, including issues from child custody, to homelessness and forced conscription [14].

The manosphere phenomena has been linked to several prominent, violent crimes perpetrated in the real world by individuals belonging to online communities of self-proclaimed misogynists [1, 2]. These acts were justified, *in the words of the perpetrators*, by a deep hatred for women, whom they perceived as having rejected and betrayed them [32]. These high-profile cases have renewed discussions that surfaced previously during the GamerGate and TheFappening controversies [31], more specifically, about how exposure to misogynistic ideas online may lead to increased violence and threats against women.

Feminist analysis of the manosphere concludes that there is an *ideological shift* away from the men's rights topics that used to unite members toward more misogynistic and violent ideas. Recent discourse analyses of the popular men's rights websites, A Voice for Men[1] and Men Going Their Own Way (MGTOW)[2] point to a backlash toward feminism [31, 32, 38], where even positive sentiments toward rape in some circumstances may be utilised to attract men who feel concerned or excluded by the direction of sexual politics [19].

While these discourse analysis studies provide in-depth observations of misogynistic rhetoric, they are usually conducted over a small subset of conversations, and over a very limited period of time. Full manual analysis is impractical and thus, automatic techniques need to be used.

Existing automatic methods to analyse online misogyny are, however, scarce and mainly focused on the analysis of Twitter (a platform where communities are not well-defined) and conducted by using a snapshot of tweets (generally in the thousands) collected over a few months. In addition, except for the work of Hardaker and

---

[1]https://www.avoiceformen.com/
[2]https://www.mgtow.com/

McClashan [20], existing computational studies do not usually build over the extensive knowledge and years of research from discourse studies and feminist linguistic models of online misogyny.

In this paper, we triangulate our investigation of misogyny online between feminist theories, social theories, and computational methodologies to gain a better understanding of misogyny online. In particular, we explore how extreme and violent language, specifically relative to women, is expressed and how it evolves across seven different communities from Reddit[3], where users group around shared interests, ideologies, and subcultural language. Our study is conducted over 7 online communities including 6M posts grouped around 300K conversations, which, to the best of our knowledge, forms the largest study of this topic so far. Our research is guided by the following research questions:

- *What is the strength and evolution of misogynistic ideas within and across different online communities?* To tackle this question we propose an approach based on Natural Language Processing that captures 9 prevalent misogynistic ideas (or categories of misogyny) from feminist studies and translates these categories into lexicons to automatically track their emergence and evolution within and across communities.
- *Which groups express the most violent attitudes and what are the most popular forms of online misogynistic violence?* To conduct this study we assess communities considering the amount of content and users expressing violent attitudes, the type of violent attitudes expressed, and the key terminology used for this purpose.

By investigating these research questions, we provide the following contributions:

- A summary of a wide range of theories and models of online misogyny from the feminist literature, as well as an analysis of the works that have targeted the problem of online misogyny from a computational perspective.
- The translation of different categories of misogyny, identified in feminist theory, into lexicons of hate terms to study the evolution of language within the manosphere.
- An in-depth analysis of different manifestations and evolution of misogyny across the Reddit manosphere.
- We corroborated existing feminist theories and models around the phenomenon of the manosphere by conducting a large-scale observational analysis.

The rest of the paper is structured as follows: Section 2 describes related work, including feminist models of online misogyny, linguistic models of online misogyny and computational approaches. Section 3 shows our proposed approach to operationalise well known manifestations of misogyny from social science and feminist studies to lexicons of terms and expressions that we can track computationally. Sections 4 and 5 describe our analysis of the manosphere on Reddit.Section 6 discusses our results and implications, and Section 7 concludes the work.

2 RELATED WORK

Misogyny is hatred or contempt for women [8]. Yoon described misogyny as "the police force of sexism"[37], linguistically and

---
[3]reddit.com

behaviourally subjugating or excluding women within what appears to be a patriarchal society [8]. Misogyny is often positioned in opposition to feminism, and as evidence for the ongoing need for feminism to continue [5, 14]. From a feminist perspective, misogyny is *visibly carried out online*, evidenced by the documented hate that has been targeted specifically at women celebrities, politicians, and other professionals for no apparent reason other than their gender. To provide two high-profile examples, nude photos of celebrities leaked during what was called "The Fappening" affected almost exclusively women. It was also largely women in the gaming industry, who were targeted with violent messages and threats during the #GamerGate controversy, in response to what was perceived by some men as undue progressiveness in gaming [31].

Using violent and misogynistic language online is not trivial, even if some individuals do not intend to act on any of their statements. Online men's groups have given space to members' glorification of tragedies like the Isla Vista Killings, in which Elliot Roger killed 6 people and wounded 14 others, after communicating extensively online about his contempt for women (and people of colour) [1]. That rhetoric is believed to have attracted others, including Alek Minassian, the alleged perpetrator of the Toronto van attack that killed 10 and wounded 16 people [2]. Along with the #GamerGate and #TheFappening controversies, which impacted hundreds of women [31], there are growing concerns that misogyny *online* has some worrying qualities in scope and scale that women are unable to avoid [25].

In this section, we discuss some of the ways in which feminist scholars have attempted to shed light on the issue of misogyny online and the limitations of these approaches with regard to scope and scale. We also explore existing computational approaches and present some of the challenges that those approaches have not yet addressed.

2.1 Feminist Models of Online Misogyny

Feminist scholarship explores misogyny online through research questions that acknowledge culturally and socially embedded experience [7, 8, 23], including:

- the nature of misogyny and attempts to characterise it
- exacerbating factors, both social and technological
- impacts on society and culture

Feminist theory explores misogyny historically [8], as well as in contemporary contexts, to demonstrate how misogyny evolves alongside culture [14]. Misogyny is presented not only as behaviour that objectifies, reduces, or degrades women, but also as the exclusion of women, manifesting itself in discrimination, physical and sexual violence, as well as hostile attitudes toward women [8]. Feminist scholarship argues that framing misogyny in this way is important for examining the overarching structures and conditions that allow misogyny to persist [29, 37]. Defensive hashtags, such as notallmen or FemalePrivilege, imply that because not all men are misogynist and some women are more powerful than some men, misogyny does not really exist as part of cultural or political hegemony [18].

However, feminist studies on the nature of misogyny online are typically conducted by a small number of authors looking at a small amount of data intensively. For example, both Kendall [26] and Lin

[28] joined online groups to observe and interview group members about misogynistic views (Kendall joined what she called the BlueSky community, Lin joined MGTOW). Lin builds her argument through comparing and contrasting community members' statements with one another, and contextualising them within a timeline of current events [28]. Kendall spent 3 years as a member of the group, having informal contact as well as conducting interviews with other members [26]. The data from such studies is very rich, but it is insufficient to *structure* deeply entrenched or networked misogyny, as we see online [5].

Zuckerberg investigated networked misogyny through her analysis of rhetoric on the 'manosphere' and the ways in which misogyny is justified within it. She found that these groups often shared an exploitation of "deeply misogynistic" ancient, Hellenistic philosophy that allow them to reframe history and promote violence against women. According to Zuckerberg, the manosphere flips the narrative of oppression and positions men both as victims of exclusion under the authority of feminism [38]. However, Zuckerberg's analysis is based on an inductive logic of community discourse, making it difficult to understand how deeply she examined communities and for how long.

Misogyny is exacerbated by both social and technological factors, according to feminist scholars [30]. Feminists connect the disenfranchisement of women with many other categories of exclusion, such as race, ethnicity and sexual orientation [8, 10]. Anonymity and technology affordances are believed to play an further aggravating role in this phenomenon, by giving perpetrators a way of voicing extreme sentiments without taking responsibility for their words or their consequences [5]. Stoeffel, for example, analysed case studies involving women's experience of violent threats online. She argued that anonymity not only disproportionately impacts women, it puts professional women in particular danger, as they engage as their real selves against anonymous abusers [35]. From a cyberfeminist perspective, these events signify that "toxic technocultures" have developed online and their power is being used to exclude, humiliate, extort and injure women [31].

Feminist studies about misogyny online measure impact by looking at the types and volume of hate abuse received [35], spikes in abuse accompanying perceived "gains" in feminism [5], but also the impact on men, who also experience hostility in the form of feminisation of their own character or insults to female members of their family [24]. Methods of feminist research in this area are typically observational or case studies, tracing women's behaviours and sentiments across various online platforms, and capturing the violent responses to this from men [24]. These studies are discursive and illuminate important relationships and dependencies. However, for a high level picture of the evolution of such relationships over time, computational approaches could provide valuable evidence.

Massanari, for example, studied the infrastructure of the platform Reddit, the same platform we studied in our research. She found that Reddit's karma point and subreddit systems, ease of account creation and loose governance structure/policies were creating an environment for "toxic technocultures" to proliferate [31]. While this study included a manual historical analysis of activity across the subreddits she was observing, Massanari's research is limited without a way of systematically observing the evolution of communities over a clear period of time, which could help interrogate her theories of how toxic masculinity spreads online.

2.2 Linguistic Models of Online Misogyny

Feminist theorists of language and gender address many themes, from different uses of language by men and women, socialisation through language, the power of definition of terms, as well as language and identity construction [11]. The assumption at the heart of each of these themes, is that power determines who sets the rules for language and that language can therefore be used to control or subjugate. Feminist studies on the use of language on the internet should be viewed through this lens - that language is political as it is personal and cultural.

Sundén and Paasonen, for example, examined different pejorative terms for women of a certain age and ideology, which women have now attempted to "reclaim" in the Swedish and Finnish context through discourse analysis [36]. Marwick and Caplan performed a critical discourse analysis on the word "misandry" (hatred or contempt for men) as it evolved through different online communication platforms from the 1990s to 2010s. They searched archives within Google Groups to search for misandry by year within different communities, as well as Google Trends, the Internet Archives' WayBack Machine, and MediaCloud, looking for spikes in usage, which they then examined in more granularity. They applied feminist discourse theory and grounded theory in the analysis of their data, to see how the concept has infiltrated the mainstream and the impact on perceptions of feminism as "a manhating movement which victimises men and boys" [30].

These two linguistic examples demonstrate a fruitful area where computational techniques can improve upon and enhance existing approaches, providing more efficient ways of identifying some types of anomalies and providing a historical picture of the evolution of language and activity over time.

2.3 Computational Approaches

While the problem of online hate speech has been the focus of a wide body of research during the last few years [15], computational approaches targeting the problem of misogyny in particular are scarce and very recent. Computational methods have been either used to **observe** and study the phenomenon of online misogyny [6, 20–22], to generate automatic misogynistic **content detection** methods [4, 12, 13], or to use the appearance of misogyny related words in online content as a **predictor** of criminal behaviour [16].

Regarding the **observational studies**, Jamie Bartlett and colleagues [6] analysed misogyny on Twitter by collecting English tweets containing the word 'rape' during a three month period between December 2013 and February 2014. Based on a sample of 138,662 tweets they studied the over time evolution of this word, and differentiated between casual and offensive misogyny.

Hardaker and McClashan [20] studied the case of online misogyny against the feminist campaigner Caroline Criado-Perez. 76,275 tweets were collected during a three month period (25/06/13 - 25/09/13) and quantitative and qualitative approaches were used to detect emergent discourse communities. As the authors pointed out, this notion of community is based on users who have no connection to each other rather than either supporting or abusing Caroline.

Hewitt and colleagues [21] gathered 5,500 tweets over the course of a week based on a set of 20 terms and annotated those tweets manually (each tweets was coded by one researcher as misogynistic or not). They used this exercise to discuss the problems of identifying misogynistic language on Twitter and other online social spaces, since it is not always trivial to determine what is misogynistic language. They propose the use of clustering analysis as a way to automatically mine the language that emerges from the data.

Jaki and colleagues [22] conducted a study of the online discussion forum Incels.me and its users. They analysed 65,000 messages posted during a 6-month period between November 2017 and May 2018. They identified the terms more frequently used by the community and did a qualitative analysis to identify key topics of discussion. Their analysis highlights that about 30% of the content is misogynistic, 15% homophobic and 3% racist.

One step further from observational studies, Maria Anzovino and colleagues [4] focus on the **automatic detection and categorisation** of misogynous language in social media. They design a taxonomy of manifestations of misogyny that includes five different categories: discredit, stereotype and objectification, sexual harassment and threats of violence, dominance, and derailing. They collected tweets based on the set of words proposed by Hewitt and colleagues [21] from July till November 2017. 2,227 tweets were annotated as (misogynistic or not) and (as belonging to one particular category). This dataset was further used to generate automatic identification methods. Extensions of this dataset, including English, Spanish and Italian tweets have been built by the authors and used within two competitions where the challenge is to create classifiers to automatically identify misogyny online; IberEval-2018 and EvalIta-2018.[4] This has lead to a series of papers investigating various classification methods to categorise misogyny including: Support Vector Machines (SVM), Logistic Regression, Ensemble Models, or Deep Learning [12, 13].

In addition to these studies Fulper and colleagues [16] investigated the potential of social media in **predicting** criminal behaviour, in particular rape and sexual abuse. For this purpose they compared the volume of misogynistic tweets and the rape crime statistics in the United States, finding a significant association. To identify misogynistic tweets they compiled a list of 90 terms (not described in the paper and, to the best of our knowledge, not publicly available). These terms were used to categorise 1.2Million tweets as containing misogynistic language.

As we can observe, our proposed study differentiates from previous works in several important directions. First of all, while our approach is also observational, our aim is not to study a particular use case [20], or a small sub sample of tweets collected during few months [6, 21, 22], but concrete communities, where users share in-group characteristics, like common ideology or subcultural language. Moreover, we do not aim to observe a time snapshot, but the full evolution of these communities from their inception. Our study is conducted over 7 online communities including 6M posts grouped around 300K conversations, which, to the best of our knowledge, is a significantly larger study than previous ones. The platform used

for our study is also different than the one used by previous works (Twitter). Not only Reddit enables the creation of communities around shared interested, it also allows for longer posts (not just the 280 characters of Twitter), providing a richer ground to analyse and explore linguistic phenomena. It is also important to highlight that, except the work of Hardaker and McClashan [20], existing computational works do not take advantage of the knowledge and years of experience from discourse studies and feminist linguistic models of online misogyny when conducting their analyses or proposing detection and prediction methods.

3 REPRESENTING MISOGYNY

Feminist theory describes misogyny as a range of activities from hostility toward women, to physical, psychological and systemic violence against them. The Encyclopedia of Feminist Theories [8] identifies six key activities that are connected with misogyny: (i) Physical violence towards women, (ii) Sexual violence towards women, (iii) Hostility towards women, (iv) Belittling of women (v) Exclusion of women and (vi) Promotion of Patriarchy or Male Privilege. Adding to these basic characteristics, we add those that arise in connection with misogyny online: (vii) Stoicism (from Zuckerberg) and, (viii) Flipping the Narrative (from Ging [18] and Flood [14]).

In this work, we aimed at linguistically characterising these manifestations of misogyny by building lexicons of hate with the terms and expressions that describe these particular ideas or categories of misogyny. We built a total of 9 lexicons including the above mentioned categories and two additional ones that encapsulate other hateful terms and expressions not necessarily targeted towards women, but that aim to capture the distinct levels of hateful speech within the manosphere. These categories are Homophobia and Racism. To build such lexicons we used seven existing lexicons of hate speech and studies of the specific rhetoric used within the manosphere. These list of lexicons include:

- *Harassment Corpus.* Built by Rezvan and colleagues[33],[5] this lexicon includes an annotated corpus of 713 harassment words and expressions including: sexual harassment (452 terms), racial harassment (153 terms), appearance-related harassment (14 terms), intellectual harassment (31 terms), political harassment (21 terms) and general (42 terms)
- *Violence verbs*: Built by Geen and Sonner [17], this lexicon encapsulates 322 verbs identified with several categories of violence including: torture, stabbing, murder, massacre and choke.
- *Hatebase (female)*: Hatebase is the world's largest structured repository of regionalised, multilingual hatespeech.[6] It contains 2,432 terms in 94 languages associated with hate. From this list, using Hatebase search capabilities, we filtered 36 hate terms commonly used towards females.

[4]https://amiibereval2018.wordpress.com/, https://amievalita2018.wordpress.com/

[5]https://github.com/Mrezvan94/Harassment-Corpus/blob/master/Harassment%20Lexicon.csv
[6]https://hatebase.org/

Table 1: Lexicons of Misogyny

Category of Misogyny	Num terms	Examples
Belittling	58	femoid, titties, stupid cow
Flipping the narrative	7	beta, normie, men's rights
Homophobia	126	dyke, fistfucker, faggot
Hostility	303	bitch, cunt, whore
Patriarchy	8	alpha male, subjugate, suppress
Physical Violence	73	hit, punch, choke
Racism	670	nigger, raghead, pikey
Sexual Violence	22	rape, sodomise, gangbang
Stoicism	33	blackpill, cuck, hypergamy

- *Hatebase (original)*: Davidson and colleagues [9] published with their work 1,034 terms from the original Hatebase dictionary.[7] To the best of our knowledge the current full Hatebase dictionary is not publicly available.
- *Profanity words*: Published by Robert J. Gabriel, this lexicon contains a list of 450 bad words and swear words banned by Google.[8]
- *Incel specific*: This dictionary, created by Tim Squirrel, contains an analysis of 57 specific neologisms from the Incel (Involuntary Celibates) community.

The collected 2,454 unique terms and expressions have been manually coded by the first author of this paper (native English speaker with a background in social science and cultural anthropology). Out of this annotation 1,300 terms have been selected, since they belong to one the above mentioned categories of misogyny. The created lexicons are available here.[9] The number of terms per category is listed in Table 1. To annotate these terms the following considerations were taken into account:

- The concept of stoicism is based on Zuckerberg's analysis of the manosphere [38]. It encapsulates terms and expressions of endurance of pain or hardship because of the lack of intimacy or beauty. Terms like 'kiss-less', 'hug-less' or 'involuntarily celibate' are part of this category.
- Patriarchy encapsulates that which has to do with women being considered less than men, or some men being better than others by virtue of having traditionally masculine qualities.
- Flipping the Narrative encapsulate terms and expressions that refer to men being oppressed by women or (indirectly or directly) by other men.
- Sexual Violence encapsulates any word explicitly connected with sexual violence (and nothing else).
- Physical Violence encapsulates any word explicitly connected with physical violence that is not explicitly sexual.
- Hostility includes violent verbs, and slurs that are not immediately racist or homophobic. However, if a verb is ambiguous (such as fucking), but it is made into a slur (such as fucker) it is coded it as hostility.
- Belittling encapsulates any word that is disrespectful or degrading women's experiences.

---
[7] https://github.com/t-davidson/hate-speech-and-offensive-language/tree/master/lexicons
[8] https://github.com/RobertJGabriel/google-profanity-words-node-module/blob/master/lib/profanity.js
[9] https://github.com/miriamfs/WebSci2019

- Homophobia encapsulates any word related to being homosexual or that mocks being homosexual. This category does not distinguish between terms that have to do explicitly with women and those that have to do with men, for reasons that this was a modifying category to assess general violent attitudes.
- Racism referred to any word that was supposed to represent a specific group of people based on where they are from or their perceived race or ethnicity. Xenophobia and racism are not separated in this category. We included terms like 'fresh off the boat', 'paddy' (pejorative for Irish person) and 'kraut' (pejorative for a German person), as well as terms referring specifically to race. The reason for this division is, similarly to the above, to simplify modifying categories about violent attitudes.

4 ANALYSIS SET-UP

In this section we describe the different online communities selected for this study as well as the analysis conducted to answer our research questions.

4.1 Selection of Online Communities

To choose our communities, we began with one community that had been in the media following the Toronto van attack, Incels [3]. Critical discourse analyses of these groups' communications online had uncovered predator-prey or master-servant dichotomies in their discussions about male-female relationships, and a reinforced sense of entitlement [3, 27]. For Incels, misogyny appeared to be coupled with racism as well, in particular for women of colour who are perceived as racially betraying darker skinned men in favour of white men [3, 34].

From this node, we intended to find a selection of related communities that have some shared ideologies. In April 2018, we identified 10 groups with the word "incel" in their community name or in their discussion threads, which were still active and online on Reddit. Of those 10 groups, we saw that 1 group was private, 4 groups were monitoring groups and 5 groups were active, self-identified groups of incels or men's rights activists. To help understand how such groups might differ from one another, we collected data from many different types of communities discussing some of the same information and ideas. In particular, to conduct our analysis we collected information from six popular communities on Reddit, which revolve around topics expressed in the manosphere, such as men's rights and difficulty with relationships:

- *r/MGTOW*: this is a subreddit of 'men going their own way', in which men claim that they wish to simply live a life without the interference from women.
- *r/badwomensanatomy*: this is a subreddit focusing on women's bodies in a misogynistic way.
- *r/Braincels*: this is the main incel subreddit since *r/incels* was removed from Reddit in November 2017 for violating site-wide rules. It is widely believed that this happened because of a post from an *r/incels* user about legal advice in which he pretended to be asking a "general question about how rapists get caught". Some members of Braincels were also

self-reported members of the website incels.me (now defunct), and the more current incels.is[10] or similar non-Reddit websites, where more violent content is posted.

- *r/IncelsWithoutHate*: this is a subreddit of individuals who are self-described as both incel but non-violent. This group supplies? somewhat of a control group, in that they will share some of the same vocabulary with other groups, but should express less misogyny and violence as other groups.
- *r/Inceltears*: this is a subreddit dedicated to calling out Incels. They screenshot and post particularly egregious content from r/braincels, incels.me, incels.is and other incel communities. They are partly responsible for a large number of incel communities being closed down.
- *r/IncelsInAction*: this is a subreddit that monitors activity from other incel communities, similarly to *r/Inceltears*.
- *r/Trufemcels*: this is a subreddit of women who are self-described incels. Male incels occasionally remark that it is not possible for a female incel to exist, given the advantages of women over men in finding a sexual partner.

4.1.1 Data Collection. We gathered all data from the above seven communities, from their inception until January 2019. This has led to the collection of 301,078 conversations and a total of 5,674,303 comments in those conversations (see Table 2). We collected this data via the pushshift API[11], a big-data storage project that maintains an archive of Reddit data. Table 2 shows a summary of the collected data, including the online community, its number of posts, and the dates of the first and last post. We collected a data snapshot from the beginning of each community until 11/01/2019. Note that for Braincels we have data until 01/10/2018, since this community has been put in quarantine by Reddit. We can observe that MGTOW is the largest community, in terms of contributions (nearly 200K posts) and also the one that has been active for longer (since June 2011). The most active community is however Braincels, which contains nearly 100K contributions done in one year from October 2017 till October 2018. The less active community is IncelsInAction, with only 330 posts, and the newest one is Trumfemcels, which originated in April 2018.

4.2 Conducted Analyses

We used the constructed lexicons to identify the amount and type of misogynistic content posted in each community. Let's C be the set of communities, P be the set of posts, and P_{c_i} the set of post

[10]https://incels.is/
[11]https://pushshift.io/

Community	numPosts	minDate	MaxDate
MGTOW	168124	2011-06-04	2019-01-11
badwomensanatomy	13010	2014-01-02	2019-01-11
IncelsWithoutHate	2309	2017-04-09	2019-01-11
IncelTears	15679	2017-05-19	2019-01-11
IncelsInAction	330	2017-06-24	2019-01-10
Braincels	96545	2017-10-21	2018-10-01
Trufemcels	5081	2018-04-04	2019-01-11

Table 2: Table captions should be placed below the table.

of a particular community c_i. Let's M be the set of misogynistic categories considered in this study, L the set of lexicons and l_j the lexicon that represents the category of misogyny m_j. We consider that a post $p \in P_{c_i}$ can be labelled as displaying the category of misogyny m_j if it exists a term t in the post p that belongs to l_j, i.e., $t \in p$ and $t \in l_j$. It is also important to notice that for the purpose of this study we do not differentiate between initial posts (i.e., those that start a new thread) and comments (i.e., contributions to an existing thread). Based on this proposed mapping of content to categories of misogyny we have conducted several analyses to answer our research questions:

- Table 3 shows the amount of misogynistic posts for each community and the distribution of these posts across categories. Percentages are provided as well as totals to assess the relative strength of each misogynistic category within each community.
- Table 4 shows the amount of users posting misogynistic content for each community and for each category within each community. Percentages are provided as well as totals to assess the relative size of the members of the community engaged in misogynistic behaviour.
- Table 5 shows the top terms used across all communities to describe the different categories of misogyny.
- Figure 1 displays the over time evolution of the different categories of misogyny for every community.
- Figure 2 displays the over time evolution of the number of active users for every community.

5 ANALYSIS RESULTS

In this section we display the results of our analyses and discuss key insights.

5.1 Strength and Evolution of Misogyny

Following RQ1 (see 1) this analysis investigates the strength and evolution of misogynistic ideas within communities. Table 3 shows a static snapshot of the number of posts for each community, the number of posts displaying misogyny (based on our lexicon-based approach), and the number of posts displaying each specific category of misogyny. Totals and percentages are provided in this table. In addition, Figure 1 displays the evolution of each category of misogyny within each of the online communities analysed.

As we can see from Table 3, while MGTOW and Braincels display the higher number of posts categorised as misogyny (726K and 451K respectively, since they are the biggest communities, in terms of percentages of misogynistic conversations, Braincels, IncelsInAction, IncelTears and IncelsWithoutHate all display more than 27%. In terms of specific categories of misogyny TruFemcels shows the highest percentage for belittling and racism, MGTOW shows the highest percentage for flipping the narrative, hostility and physical violence, Braincels shows the highest percentage for homophobia and patriarchy, IncelTears for sexual violence and IncelsWithoutHate for stoicism. We can also observe that Hostility, Stoicism and Physical violence, seem to be the most popular categories across communities.

These results can be triangulated with how these communities self-identify to further examine what we have observed. For example, members of IncelTears and IncelsInAction are reporting on extreme posts that they see on other subreddits where incels are active (such as Braincels). We would expect to see a higher concentration of misogynistic language on that subreddit, which we do. Similarly, however, we would expect IncelsWithoutHate, with the community's aim to spread *less* violent speech than other groups of incels, to have a lower percentage of some forms of misogyny than other groups. However, IncelsWithoutHate had the greatest percentage of posts including misogynistic language. Returning to the actual content on the subreddit, we observed that IncelsWithoutHate reference content they have seen posted by other more violent groups (similarly to IncelTears and IncelsInAction). There also appears to have been some infiltration of the group and harassment[12].

TruFemcels, as a community for women incels, is also difficult to interpret. Misogyny is not exclusive to men. Feminist scholars view internalised misogyny as evidence of patriarchy [6]. However, the explanation for this may also have to do with interference on the subreddit from agitators. Moderators of the subreddit have warned that TruFemcels are regularly harassed by what is believed to be male incels. This harassment include doxxing[13] and trolling threads.[14]

It is important to note that this is a static view of the communities (considering their full duration). We also analysed their evolution over time to observe the dynamics of these misogynistic ideas. The over-time (weekly) distributions are displayed in Figure 1. The first interesting element we observed is a significant difference in the time/posts distributions among the different communities. For MGTOW, categories of misogyny seem to have a similar evolution pattern, being very mild or nearly nonexistent during the first two years of the community, but displaying a constant increase since 2015 till the end of 2018 were we observe a slight decrease. This growth is parallel to the growth on the number of active members posting in the community (see Figure 2). Within this community hostility is the most prominent category, followed by physical violence and belittling. This is a similar pattern to that displayed by the subreddit badwomensanatomy with several exceptions. Categories are more interconnected (i.e., they are less prominent with respect to one another) and activity in the community (number of posts) is smaller. However, hostility, physical violence and belittling are also the most prominent categories.

For Braincels, we can observe a steady increase for all categories of misogyny, and a sharp increase around April 2018. One possible explanation for this may have to do with the Toronto van attack, allegedly perpetrated by self-proclaimed incel Alek Minassian during this same period [2]. We see peaks in other communities as well at this time. From our investigations, this could be extended media attention on the subject of incels, following the Toronto attack. Searches for the term incel on google trends shows spikes from April and November 2018 as well. After that, the weekly amount of misogynistic content produced on the subreddits we examined

stabilises. The top categories of misogyny that particularly stand out in this community are hostility and stoicism.

IncelsInAction, IncelsWithoutHate, IncelTears and TruFemcels display more constant patterns of growth with hostility and stoicism being prominent categories in all of them. For the first three groups, this is expected, as they are involved in re-posting content they view as particularly hateful or demeaning. For TruFemCels, this is once again difficult to interpret, considering the harassment that the group has received. However, after returning to the community to examine some usage of words in more detail, the high levels of stoicism appear to accurately characterise this group.

MGTOW, Braincels, IncelsWithoutHate and TruFemCelsFrom are the communities we studied that are actually for the incel or men's rights communities. In our analysis, we see stoicism in the four groups we examined increasing over the course of 2017 and 2018, with a slight downturn in late 2018. This supports Zuckerberg's proposition that stoicism is an important, over-arching narrative in these communities [38]. Interestingly, we also identified this characteristic in TruFemCels, where misogynistic attitudes are more related to belittling and self-deprecation.

It is also interesting to observe the steady and sometimes sharp growth of active members in these communities (see Figure 2). The activity within MGTOW and Braincels have been steadily growing, reaching picks of nearly 5,000 active users a week. For Braincels we can perceive a major and rapid increase of active members at the end of April 2018 followed by a sharp decrease around the end of the year, when the community was quarantined by Reddit. Badwomensanatomy and inceltears also display a steady increase, with an actual activity status of 3,000 active users every week. IncelsWithoutHate, Trufemcels and IncelsInAction display more moderated patterns of growth.

These findings, and our observations of the constant increase in the different categories of misogyny across all communities, support existing discourse analysis studies that violence and hostility are increasing toward women online [5, 30, 31].

5.2 Violent attitudes

Tables 3 and 4 display the amount of misogynistic content and the number of users spreading misogynistic content for every community. As we can see in this analysis, MGTOW, Braincels and badwomensanatomy (all groups that are actual incel or men's rights communities), are the communities with higher amounts of misogynistic content and users. Massanari's idea of "toxic technocultures" [31] can possibly be seen in this data, as the number of users posting misogynistic content and the amount of misogynistic content are both increasing across our groups of male incels and men's rights activists.

In terms of violent attitudes, (which we identify with the categories of sexual violence, physical violence, racism and homophobia) we can observe that for sexual violence, MGTOW and Braincels display the largest amount of posts, but IncelTears and IncelsInAction display the highest percentages. Again, as monitoring groups, we would expect to see a high level of misogynistic content in these subreddits, which has possibly come from MGTOW or Braincels. In terms of physical violence, MGTOW displays both the largest amount and the highest percentage of posts, followed by IncelTears

---

[12]https://tinyurl.com/y2cgbfav
[13]finding another users private information and making it public online
[14]https://tinyurl.com/y6z234r5

Community	N.Posts	Misogyny		Belittling		FlippingNarr		Homophobia		Hostility		Patriarchy		P. Violence		Racism		S. Violence		Stoicism	
		N	P	N	P	N	P	N	P	N	P	N	P	N	P	N	P	N	P	N	P
MGTOW	3136231	726621	23.17%	97039	3.09%	52755	1.68%	3399	0.11%	323867	10.33%	1799	0.06%	125916	4.01%	38444	1.23%	38408	1.22%	44994	1.43%
badwomensanatomy	496665	72046	14.51%	18278	3.68%	367	0.07%	237	0.05%	28003	5.64%	132	0.03%	12495	2.52%	7215	1.45%	3101	0.62%	2218	0.45%
IncelsWithoutHate	54789	16307	29.76%	2082	3.80%	626	1.14%	85	0.16%	4718	8.61%	51	0.09%	2114	3.86%	847	1.55%	455	0.83%	5329	9.73%
IncelTears	578659	161732	27.95%	17003	2.94%	3505	0.61%	903	0.16%	54404	9.40%	355	0.06%	22293	3.85%	9415	1.63%	12263	2.12%	41591	7.19%
IncelsInAction	3903	1055	27.03%	102	2.61%	8	0.20%	7	0.18%	340	8.71%	1	0.03%	121	3.10%	51	1.31%	75	1.92%	350	8.97%
Braincels	1629277	451754	27.73%	47489	2.91%	21384	1.31%	9218	0.57%	149179	9.16%	1279	0.08%	37766	2.32%	31944	1.96%	10048	0.62%	143447	8.80%
TruFemcels	75553	18045	23.88%	2940	3.89%	588	0.78%	72	0.10%	5608	7.42%	60	0.08%	2326	3.08%	1892	2.50%	326	0.43%	4233	5.60%

Table 3: Misogynistic content across categories and communities. N=Number of posts. P=Percentage of posts

Community	N.Users	Misogyny		Belittling		FlippingNarr		Homophobia		Hostility		Patriarchy		P. Violence		Racism		S. Violence		Stoicism	
		N	P	N	P	N	P	N	P	N	P	N	P	N	P	N	P	N	P	N	P
MGTOW	93596	33879	36.2%	14339	15.32%	9627	10.29%	1606	1.72%	25541	27.29%	1112	1.19%	16522	17.65%	9243	9.88%	8273	8.84%	9507	10.16%
badwomensanatomy	69076	19798	28.66%	8702	12.6%	310	0.45%	208	0.3%	11616	16.82%	115	0.17%	6433	9.31%	4379	6.34%	1982	2.87%	1536	2.22%
IncelsWithoutHate	5198	2205	42.42%	786	15.12%	330	6.35%	71	1.37%	1334	25.66%	40	0.77%	829	15.95%	439	8.45%	248	4.77%	1316	25.32%
IncelTears	56273	22867	40.64%	6725	11.95%	2058	3.66%	674	1.2%	13952	24.79%	284	0.5%	7861	13.97%	4340	7.71%	4821	8.57%	11615	20.64%
IncelsInAction	1642	496	30.21%	94	5.72%	9	0.55%	7	0.43%	236	14.37%	1	0.06%	98	5.97%	46	2.8%	57	3.47%	237	14.43%
Braincels	55516	22968	41.37%	8658	15.6%	5042	9.08%	2620	4.72%	16089	28.98%	681	1.23%	8599	15.49%	6652	11.98%	3554	6.4%	13899	25.04%
TruFemcels	7727	2680	34.68%	1017	13.16%	294	3.8%	59	0.76%	1506	19.49%	48	0.62%	879	11.38%	688	8.9%	174	2.25%	1305	16.89%

Table 4: Misogynistic users across categories and communities. N=Number of users. P=Percentage of users

Belittling		FlippingNarr		Homophobia		Hostility		Patriarchy		P. Violence		Racism		S. Violence		Stoicism	
word	freq	word	freq	word	freq	word	freq	word	freq	word	freq	word	freq	word	freq	word	freq
female	121549	mgtow	38862	faggot	7453	hate	89389	suppress	1188	hit	37142	black	49552	rape	58396	incel	111373
dumb	31312	beta	33450	fag	1856	bitch	54609	betabuxx	1023	kill	29006	bigger	15545	cock carousel	3750	chad	36081
roastie	9143	normie	16975	fags	1407	pussy	47869	omega	786	cut	21888	nigga	3575	pound	2703	cuck	31482
boobs	8354	mra	424	homo	1278	hurt	26440	subjugate	300	force	17740	nigger	1030	conquer	1543	cope	26169
failure	7952	overthrow	368	dyke	879	cunt	24150	oblige	255	attack	12061	niggas	1006	incest	1378	blackpill	13621

Table 5: Most used misogynistic terms across communities

(a monitoring group). Braincels is largely the most homophobic community and TruFemcels the one that displays a higher percentage of racist content. In terms of users, MGTOW shows the highest number of users talking about sexual and physical violence, while Braincels shows the highest percentage of users displaying homophobic and racial language.

Among the most used violent terms across communities 5 we can observe hit, kill, cut, and rape occurring with a high level of frequency in comparison to other words. One exception to this are neologisms that developed in the communities. The words incel, chad (normatively attractive white male) and blackpill (deterministic point of view on human relationships) are examples. Another exception is the collection of words that the communities have appropriated. Beta, for example, is a term for a man who is not an alpha male (white, attractive and successful). The word cuck has many different meanings from our examination of the subreddits, but broadly refers to anyone who does not accept what is perceived to be biologically determined hypergamy among women. The development of new language is another signal of the existence of a "culture" of misogyny that may exist within these online communities in the manosphere [5, 31].

6 DISCUSSION

With this observational analysis our goal has been to test existing feminist theories and models at scale. Our results do indeed corroborate some of these theories, particularly, the idea that violence and hostility are increasing towards women online [30], that violent rhetoric and misogyny are co-occurring [8, 10], and that stoicism and flipping the narrative are two contemporary responses to feminism [38]. Our research supports these positions by exploring the evolution of content and users over time in seven different communities. While we cannot indicate a clear motive for violence and hostility, we can say that it is increasing, that fluctuations exist in the misogynistic language used by these groups, and that stoicism and hostility are increasing and prominent across communities.

One limitation of using lexicons in this study is that they are unable to capture all of the words that might be relevant (lack of completeness). They also do not capture important details about the context of language [6, 21]. Despite these limitations, these lexicons helped in exposing the trends over time in the use of language. Indeed, we were able to support and extend the hypothesis of feminist studies that the amount of misogyny, hostility and violence is steadily increasing in the manosphere.

We utilised the efforts of only one coder to annotate the words in the lexicons. This could lead to potential bias or human error in annotating the data, and is subject to further work. Nevertheless, we

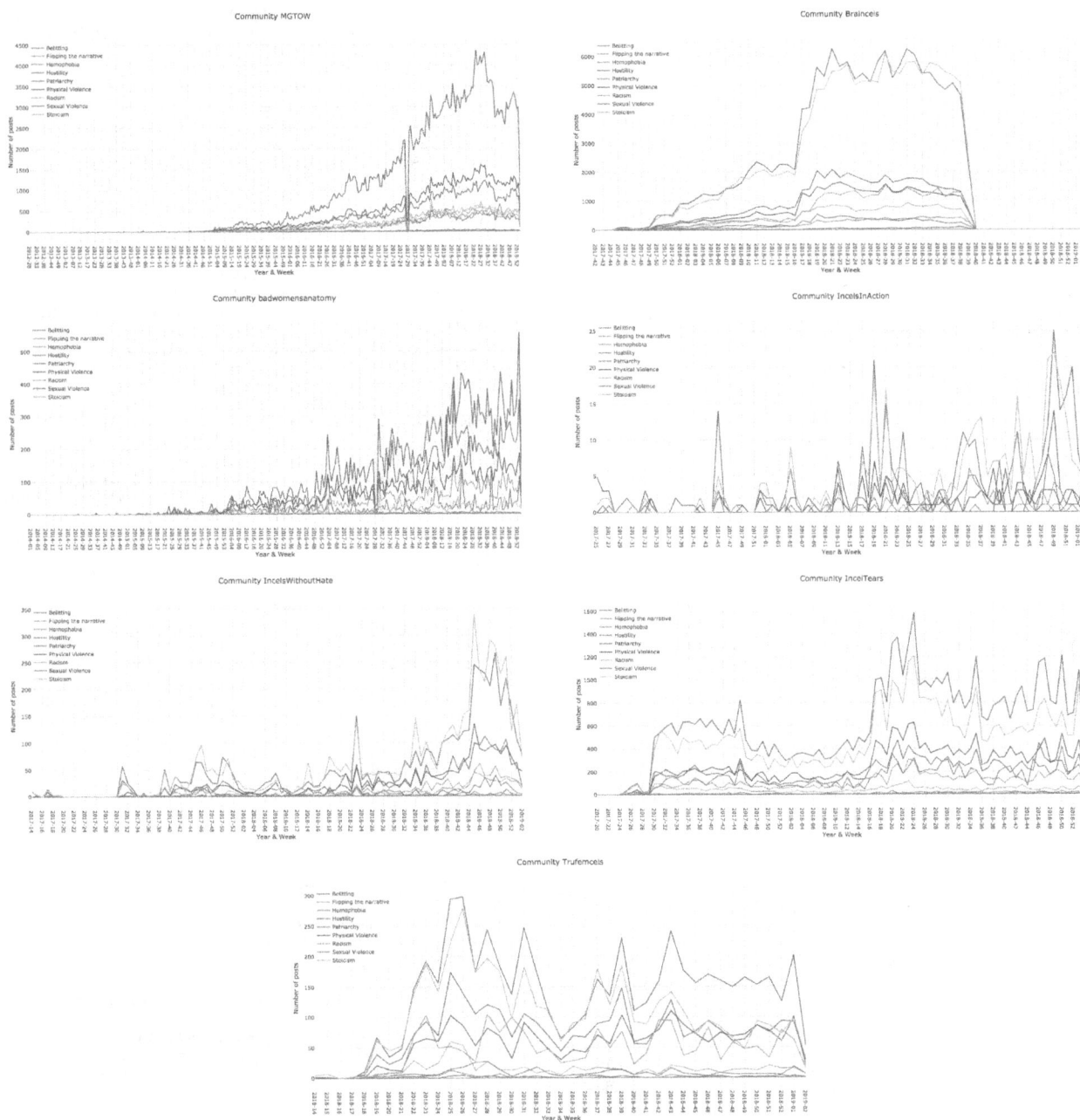

Figure 1: Distribution of misogynistic content posted per week for every category and community

believed it was more critical to have a person familiar with contemporary feminist theory working with the data and discussing codes with the rest of the research team. In the process of our analysis, we identified ways of optimising our lexicons by combining or adjusting categories, some of which we have already implemented and will continue to improve to make these lexicons an open resource for the research community.

In some categories, such as patriarchy or flipping the narrative, there were very few words available in the lexicons. It is possible

that some categories may be disadvantaged towards others, but we can see trends over time despite this limitation. Patriarchy, in particular, was also a difficult category to identify. It does not, therefore, feature prominently in our analysis at this time.

Neologisms may also play an important role, as we found a lexicon of many new terms originating in the incel and men's rights communities. Although 57 studied neologisms were incorporated in these lexicons, through the study of these communities we have detected newly emerged neologisms that we plan to study in the

Figure 2: Weekly active users across communities

future. In particular, we are interested in where these new terms emerge, how they are used by different communities and where divergence and similarities can be observed. This forms part of our future work.

Finally, we recognise that this is an observational study based on lexicons. An appropriate next step would be to explore the use of word embeddings or semantic concepts to better capture the context in which these terms are used. Data mining techniques, such as clustering, could also be used to identify linguistic patterns that may emerge from the data. A study of influence in terms of users and messages for those communities, is also planned to explore the influence of language, how it spreads and from whom.

Despite these limitations, we have achieved our aim to combine feminist studies and social science models to make interdisciplinary observations about misogyny in the manosphere, over time and at scale. While we still have many different challenges to resolve, this work is one of the very first attempts to understand the manosphere both socially and computationally.

7 CONCLUSIONS

In this paper, we test existing feminist theories and models around the phenomenon of the manosphere by conducting a large-scale observational analysis of seven different online communities on Reddit, with openly misogynistic members. Grounded on feminist critiques of language, we created nine lexicons capturing specific misogynistic rhetoric and used these lexicons to explore how language evolves within misogynistic groups. Our results corroborate existing theories of feminist studies, particularly the idea that violence and hostility are increasing toward women online [30], that violent rhetoric and misogyny are co-occurring [8, 10], and and that stoicism and flipping the narrative are two contemporary responses to feminism [38].

Acknowledgments. Trivalent, H2020, grant agreement 740934.

REFERENCES

[1] [n. d.]. 2014 Isla Vista Killings. https://www.bbc.co.uk/news/world-us-canada-43892189. Accessed: 2019-01-27.
[2] [n. d.]. Alek Minassian. https://www.telegraph.co.uk/news/2018/04/24/do-know-alek-minassian-arrested-toronto-van-attack/. Accessed: 2019-01-27.
[3] [n. d.]. INCELS. http://haenfler.sites.grinnell.edu/subcultures-and-scenes/incels/#ffs-tabbed-311. Accessed: 2019-01-27.
[4] Maria Anzovino, Elisabetta Fersini, and Paolo Rosso. 2018. Automatic identification and classification of misogynistic language on twitter. In *Int. Conf. Applications of Natural Language to Information Systems*. Springer.
[5] Sarah Banet-Weiser and Kate M Miltner. 2016. # MasculinitySoFragile: culture, structure, and networked misogyny. *Feminist Media Studies* 16, 1 (2016), 171–174.
[6] Jamie Bartlett, Richard Norrie, Sofia Patel, Rebekka Rumpel, and Simon Wibberley. 2014. Misogyny on twitter. *Demos* (2014), 1–18.
[7] Lorraine Code. 1991. *What can she know?: feminist theory and the construction of knowledge.* Cornell University Press.
[8] Lorraine Code. 2002. *Encyclopedia of feminist theories.* Routledge.
[9] Thomas Davidson, Dana Warmsley, Michael Macy, and Ingmar Weber. 2017. Automated hate speech detection and the problem of offensive language. *arXiv preprint arXiv:1703.04009* (2017).
[10] Lynn Davies. 2008. Gender, education, extremism and security. *Compare* 38, 5 (2008), 611–625.
[11] Penelope Eckert and Sally McConnell-Ginet. 2013. *Language and gender.* Cambridge University Press.
[12] Elisabetta Fersini, Debora Nozza, and Paolo Rosso. 2018. Overview of the evalita 2018 task on automatic misogyny identification (ami). *Proc. 6th evaluation campaign of Natural Language Processing and Speech tools for Italian (EVALITA), Turin, Italy* (2018).
[13] Elisabetta Fersini, Paolo Rosso, and Maria Anzovino. 2018. Overview of the task on automatic misogyny identification at ibereval 2018. (2018).
[14] Michael Flood. 2004. Backlash: Angry men's movements. In *The battle and backlash rage on: Why feminism cannot be obsolete.* Xlibris Press, 261–278.
[15] Paula Fortuna and Sérgio Nunes. 2018. A survey on automatic detection of hate speech in text. *ACM Computing Surveys (CSUR)* 51, 4 (2018), 85.
[16] Rachael Fulper, Giovanni Luca Ciampaglia, Emilio Ferrara, Y Ahn, Alessandro Flammini, Filippo Menczer, Bryce Lewis, and Kehontas Rowe. 2014. Misogynistic language on Twitter and sexual violence. In *Proc. ACM Web Science Workshop on Computational Approaches to Social Modeling (ChASM).*
[17] Russell G Geen and David Stonner. 1975. Primary associates to 20 verbs connoting violence. *Behavior Research Methods* 7, 4 (1975), 391–392.
[18] Debbie Ging. 2017. Alphas, betas, and incels: Theorizing the masculinities of the manosphere. *Men and Masculinities* (2017), 1097184X17706401.
[19] Lise Gotell and Emily Dutton. 2016. Sexual violence in the 'manosphere': Antifeminist men's rights discourses on rape. *Int. J. Crime, Justice and Social Democracy* 5, 2 (2016), 65–80.
[20] Claire Hardaker and Mark McGlashan. 2016. "Real men don't hate women": Twitter rape threats and group identity. *Journal of Pragmatics* 91 (2016).
[21] Sarah Hewitt, Thanassis Tiropanis, and Christian Bokhove. 2016. The problem of identifying misogynist language on Twitter (and other online social spaces). In *Proc. 8th ACM Conference on Web Science*. ACM, 333–335.
[22] Sylvia Jaki, Tom De Smedt, Maja Gwóźdź, Rudresh Panchal, Alexander Rossa, and Guy De Pauw. 2018. Online hatred of women in the Incels. me forum: Linguistic analysis and automatic detection. *Manuscript submitted* (2018).
[23] Marianne Janack. 2004. Feminist epistemology. Internet encyclopedia of philosophy.
[24] Emma Alice Jane. 2014. 'Back to the kitchen, cunt': speaking the unspeakable about online misogyny. *Continuum* 28, 4 (2014), 558–570.
[25] Emma A Jane. 2016. *Misogyny online: A short (and brutish) history.* Sage.
[26] Lori Kendall. 2002. *Hanging out in the virtual pub: Masculinities and relationships online.* Univ of California Press.
[27] Mary Lilly. 2016. *'The World is Not a Safe Place for Men': The Representational Politics of the Manosphere.* Ph.D. Dissertation. Université d'Ottawa/University of Ottawa.
[28] Jie Liang Lin. 2017. Antifeminism Online. MGTOW (Men Going Their Own Way). (2017).
[29] Kate Manne. 2017. *Down Girl: The Logic of Misogyny.* Oxford University Press.
[30] Alice E Marwick and Robyn Caplan. 2018. Drinking male tears: language, the manosphere, and networked harassment. *Feminist Media Studies* 18, 4 (2018).
[31] Adrienne Massanari. 2017. # Gamergate and The Fappening: How Reddit's algorithm, governance, and culture support toxic technocultures. *New Media & Society* 19, 3 (2017), 329–346.
[32] Angela Nagle. 2017. *Kill all normies: Online culture wars from 4chan and Tumblr to Trump and the alt-right.* John Hunt Publishing.
[33] Mohammadreza Rezvan, Saeedeh Shekarpour, Lakshika Balasuriya, Krishnaprasad Thirunarayan, Valerie Shalin, and Amit Sheth. 2018. Publishing a Quality Context-aware Annotated Corpus and Lexicon for Harassment Research. *arXiv preprint arXiv:1802.09416* (2018).
[34] Katy Sian. 2018. Stupid Paki Loving Bitch: The Politics of Online Islamophobia and Misogyny. In *Media, Crime and Racism*. Springer, 117–138.
[35] Kat Stoeffel. 2014. Women pay the price for the Internet's culture of anonymity. *The Cut* 12 (2014).
[36] Jenny Sundén and Susanna Paasonen. 2018. Shameless hags and tolerance whores: feminist resistance and the affective circuits of online hate. *Feminist Media Studies* 18, 4 (2018), 643–656.
[37] Joewon Yoon. 2018. Down Girl: The Logic of Misogyny. *Asian Women* 34, 1 (2018), 109–112.
[38] Donna Zuckerberg. 2018. *Not All Dead White Men: Classics and Misogyny in the Digital Age.* Harvard University Press.

The Potential for Serious Spaceships to Make a Serious Difference

Robert Fleet
Australian National University
robert.fleet@anu.edu.au

Terhi Nurmikko-Fuller
Australian National University
terhi.nurmikko-fuller@anu.edu.au

ABSTRACT

Identifying, investigating, and potentially disrupting organised criminal networks is difficult. Data gathered by law enforcement and regulatory authorities are often inconsistent, incomplete, and inaccurate. Computational criminology attempts to address these limitations by modelling the behaviour of virtual "humans" in virtual places. However, virtual humans are rule-based and can never fully replicate actual human behaviour. This study takes a new approach by utilising the benefits of the observable and controllable environment of virtual worlds but examining real people and real behaviour. To do this, it explores real people's behaviour in a virtual environment similar to the circumstances found in organised criminal networks. Massively Multiplayer Online (MMO) video games with player-driven markets present real humans with similar circumstances in controlled and observable virtual environments.

Market conditions within MMO games and illicit markets are both characterised by trust, reputation and, when all else fails, violence. Overall, MMO games are a novel data source to identify, investigate, and provide prevention strategies to the problem of organised criminal networks. Using social network analysis of real-world players from data broadcast by EVE Online (an MMO); spatial, temporal, and behavioural patterns of both offenders and victims are examined. The data broadcast from the game is consistent, complete, and accurate and provides a much larger sample size than obtainable in real-world environments.

The data set consists of a seven-year period containing approximately 7M-9M events. It captures the activities of 600,000 individuals and 2,500 groups. This paper proposes that video games can approximate the circumstances found in the real world and human agents can and do act in the most rational way to maximise success in those circumstances. Overall, MMO games offer a powerful social science data generator that offers insights into real-world social problems (such as organised criminal networks) that are typically difficult to examine.

CCS CONCEPTS

• **Networks → Online social networks;** • **Applied computing → Law; Sociology;**

KEYWORDS

Online Behaviour, Massively Multiplayer Online Games, Social Network Analysis, Surveillance, Victimisation, Computational Criminology

ACM Reference Format:
Robert Fleet and Terhi Nurmikko-Fuller. 2019. The Potential for Serious Spaceships to Make a Serious Difference. In *11th ACM Conference on Web Science (WebSci '19), June 30-July 3, 2019, Boston, MA, USA.* ACM, New York, NY, USA, 8 pages. https://doi.org/10.1145/3292522.3326017

1 INTRODUCTION

Information about the actions of illicit market groups can be difficult to accurately observe and record [9, 10, 42, 45, 46]. Yet these activities are of interest to law enforcement agencies (who seek prohibition), regulatory agencies (who seek both tax revenue, and links between legitimate and illicit market activities) and criminal justice systems (who are required to make/enforce policy to deal with illicit markets) [3, 4, 20]. By necessity, illicit market groups are covert in their operations and resistant to infiltration [35]. Even when individuals and groups allow researchers to observe and record their actions and decisions, the data must be approached with some caution as to its accuracy and reliability [43].

The lack of accurate observation leaves a gap in the knowledge about the activities and social structures of covert illicit market groups. This paper argues that interested researchers must look for novel ways of improving the observation of individual and group behaviour in conditions that allow markets to form that are characterised by reputation, trust, and violence. In order to address this lack of "observability", this paper argues that novel data sources should be investigated. A novel extant data source that addresses the present limitations are player-driven markets found in Massively Multiplayer Online games (MMOs). These are virtual markets that can be observed that hold similarities to physical world illicit markets in that groups operate to control a market position and make profit while utilising violence as a tool to resolve disputes, protect market positions and enforce financial obligations.

More recent attempts to define organised crime beyond an ethnic commonality or a particular criminal activity have highlighted a common profit-motivated thread amongst what are identified as organised criminal groups. There has been some consensus that organised crime is often based on profit-motivated criminal enterprise [1, 39, 44]. The process of committing ongoing crime is itself identified as the inherent danger of criminal organisations and while loosely associated turf-focused groups do exist, there has been a distinct shift in group activities towards being involved in illicit markets [16, 18]. Therefore there is some ongoing interest amongst interested regulatory and criminal justice organisations in monitoring and disrupting ongoing criminal enterprise. Especially in light of the suspected links of organised crime to terrorist activities through financial support [32, 34].

Critics argue that the analogy between legitimate and illicit enterprises can only be extended so far and that comparisons tend to overlook some key differences [16, 17, 35, 37, 38]. However there are still some significant characteristics that allow legitimate and illicit enterprises to be compared and contrasted [16, 17]. Each characteristic is centred on a key business need or decision that legitimate and illicit enterprises face in conducting business. The objective of each decision is similar for each enterprise group but the factors that weigh into the decision making process are specific to the enterprise's chosen market [40, 41]. The understanding that the process of organised crime is based on on-going yet fluid collaborative relationships between individuals and groups suggests that an appropriate approach to investigating organised criminal groups is to adopt a network model [17]. Further given the consensus that there is an aspect of criminal enterprise to the majority of the activities of criminal groups, an economic model is also applicable to any investigation [17]. The use of these two models will allow the paper to focus predominantly on self-organising networks of collaborating individuals whom are interested in operating and protecting a for-profit enterprise across the three distinct market types (legitimate, illicit, and virtual).

2 RELATED WORK

Virtual worlds can provide insight into physical world phenomena [5]. Previous research has established the benefits and usefulness of using Massively Multiplayer Online Role-Playing Games (MMORPGs) as a reliable and valid source to study physical world social phenomena, including criminal activities. Whilst epidemiology (the study and analysis of the distribution and determinants of conditions within a population) has been used as a basis for crime research, especially repeat victimisation and hotspot analysis [7], social network analysis has been applied to co-offending and repeat victimisation studies [10]. Economic theory has, in turn, been used to understand and reinforce rational choice and decision-making in property crimes [38].

2.1 Epidemiology

Epidemiologists have utilised MMORPG to study the outbreak of diseases. For example, in 2005 an unforeseen error in the computer code controlling the game world of a popular MMO, World of Warcraft, introduced an outbreak of a disease-like bug into the game [31]. The outbreak was the unintended consequence of a new type of computer-controlled behaviour escaping the strict confines of the area in which it was supposed to operate. The disease (known as a *debuff* in-game) was intended to be limited to a particular area (it was attached to a certain computer controlled enemy); within that area it would be annoying but not fatal to those infected (a moderate continuous drain on player health) and able to spread between other players in the same immediate area. By use of a certain action in the game (a teleport spell) the disease was ported to populous areas outside of the containment area. Due to the disease being intended to infect more powerful higher level players (more powerful translates to higher health numbers,

greater resistances to debuffs and higher health recovery rates) once released into the common areas, where players of all levels congregated, it proved to be fatal to players of lower levels. Also due to this contagious nature it spread rapidly in areas of high population concentrations. It took a number of concentrated efforts by the company that runs the game to eliminate this problem. This outbreak provided epidemiologists and social scientists a wealth of information on both disease behaviour and public behaviour in response to wide-scale infectious outbreaks [31]. They found that virtual disease displayed similar traits to physical world disease. This example illustrates the experimental value of virtual worlds.

2.2 Complex networks

Virtual worlds have been useful in studying the ways in which networks form between individuals and entities. Complex networks have been observed in a number of different scientific fields including computing, biology, economics and social networks [6]. In a cross-comparison between the different field type networks there have been a number of features that have been found to be similar between them. Similar features include average shortest-path length; high clustering coefficients and scale-free connectivity are almost universal in complex networks across the differing fields. The features have also been observed in social networks formed in virtual game worlds [21].

The difficulties of studying covert behaviour have been made easier with the use of virtual game worlds. Virtual game worlds have been used to study dark networks (clandestine networks of criminal individuals or entities that are used to channel information, funds and goods between each other). Due to their clandestine nature the networks that exist in the physical world are hard to locate and characterise in full. Law enforcement and intelligence agencies are interested in characterising these networks as a number of criminal and terrorist organisations rely on these dark networks for the gathering of funds and the distribution of information and material. Similar networks exist in virtual game worlds that seek to exploit the virtual game worlds for physical world profits [26].

Gold farming, power levelling, and account/equipment sales for real money are all activities that are prohibited in almost all virtual game worlds, as they have a detrimental effect on the economy and fairness of the game worlds that they exploit for profit [14]. As such, the people who engage in these activities form dark networks, which are similar to physical world dark networks. The motivation to form dark networks in order to conceal the activity from game administrators (and at the same time maximise effectiveness) mirror the same reasons dark networks form in the physical world [33]. The ability to identify and visualise the network topology of in-game dark networks allows for researchers to better characterise the hidden networks in the physical world which would otherwise be problematic.

The usefulness of using virtual worlds has also been demonstrated in studying dynamics of a network. Complex networks are not fixed, with relationships forming and breaking over time. The change in relationships between network entities changes the shape and flow of information and resources across the network [22]. These changes can be hard to capture in the physical world, especially for highly mobile social networks. The virtual world's ability to record and playback activities allows for these hard-to-visualise changes to be tracked and observed. This ability also allows for the investigation of network attack tolerance and network adaption [2]. Attack tolerance and network adaption are related concepts about the changes networks undergo when network entities are deliberately removed. This has applications in the studies of drug trafficking organisations and other organised crime groups [46].

2.3 Economics

Another area where virtual game world have shown extensive promise is economics studies. Virtual economies have been observed to emulate physical world and theoretical economies accurately [11]. The economies observed in virtual game worlds are often player-driven, free market economies where players directly influence the supply and demand of goods within them. Due to the similarities between the game economies and physical world economies the rational decision making processes and economic strategies found in the game world are useful in characterising and predicting physical world economic behaviour [30].

Economics plays a significant part in the way players approach MMORPGs [47]. Game economies provide suitable ways of measuring player success and self-efficacy in the absence of more traditional physical world measures [27]. Surplus in-game currency is used to obtain goods that will visually display the player's status and power to other individuals. The need to acquire certain goods that indicate elite status or special powers over other players can be a driving factor in gaming addiction and other problematic game related behaviours [24].

Game economies are also linked to cybercrime activity with virtual game worlds. The ability to illegally convert or sell in-game currency for physical world currency has spawned a number of behaviours that while officially banned by the game developers still continues. Syndicates of individuals will play the game in a deliberate fashion to exploit the game design to extract the largest amount of in-game currency for the least effort in a timely fashion (gold farming) [28]. The in-game currency that is farmed is later sold outside of the game for physical world money. Other illegal player syndicates will exploit the game design to obtain rare or unique in-game items that can be later traded outside of the game (for example, via eBay) for physical world currency [23]. These real money trading activities provides motivation for criminal exploitation of the game and an alternative, though strictly illegal, pathway for legal players to exploit for their own in game benefit [29].

In summary, virtual worlds have provided researchers with a reliable and valid source. Virtual worlds have been utilised in a broad range of research areas including criminal activities. Virtual worlds display similar features to physical world activities, providing accurate representations of the physical world to allow players to make similar decisions in the game as they would in the physical world. The benefits of virtual worlds (especially MMORPG) include capturing a large data samples, in a timely fashion, and are even able to identify covert behaviour.

3 METHODOLOGY

Our analysis focuses on data collected from EVE Online, a MMORPG set in a persistent futuristic science fiction setting. The game is a

subscription-based service meaning that the players must pay a monthly fee to access the game [12]. The aim of the game is to accumulate in-game wealth and power. Player also gains reputation that extends from within the game to the physical world through meta-gaming channels. While the game itself has objectives for the player to accomplish there is little in the way of narrative engagement thus allowing players enough freedom to insert their own narrative and play objectives. In this case the most effective way of achieving high levels of wealth, power and reputation is to group up with other players [12, 13].

The computer system controlling EVE Online generates a report in real time every time a player-controlled ship is destroyed. The report (referred to as *killmails*) is sent to the victim and the aggressor who laid the final blow. Killmails can be thought of as being analogous to the homicide/crime reports gathered in the physical world by law enforcement agencies. The computer system controlling EVE online also broadcasts them to third parties with an API.

The broadcast data contain a range of information relating to the circumstances of the ship loss, including the involved parties, their group affiliations, time and location as well as financial losses. These reports form the basis for the analyses used in this research, as they contain information that is not always apparent from physical world homicide reports (for example, a definitive list of all parties involved in the event). This data can be analysed in ways similar to the ways information from the physical world can be. Furthermore, reports generated in close temporal and spatial proximity to each other might be considered part of a larger conflict event.

Killmails were gathered from a third party which records all killmails broadcast by the game via the API. It is proposed that the data set being used includes the activities of all players engaged in violence over a period of 7 years (2007-2014). The data set contains the records of approximately 500,000 individual players and encompasses approximately 9,800,000 individual events.

The data gathered was examined using Social Network Analysis (SNA). SNA allows the generation of descriptive statistics in regards to the size and characteristics of in-game co-operating groups, whilst at the same time allowing for the investigation of conflict between individuals and groups and provide descriptive statistics on the amount of victimisation and violence occurring. The temporal and spatial distributions of the events will be examined in future using a Geographic Information System (GIS).

The data subset used in the preliminary investigation outlined in this paper was drawn from the entire data set between the time stamps 2007/12/05T23:26:00 and 2007/12/06T09:01:00 and contains 920 nodes and 3457 edges. The network graphs and visualisations (Figures 1 – 4) were produced in Gephi (0.9.2).

4 EVE ONLINE

EVE is notable for a number of features that differentiate it from other games in the genre [25]. These features make it more suitable for research than some other games within the genre. These features more accurately mirror the physical world in the degrees of freedom given to the player to act as they might in the physical world. Firstly, all of the players are hosted on a single server cluster meaning that any player accessing the game occupies the same virtual space as every other player. As this is feature is computationally difficult to achieve for very large numbers of players many other games split the players up into separate yet identical virtual worlds hosted on separate servers [12]. EVE Online has approximately 350,000 subscribers with an average concurrent user figure of approximately 21,000 players. The record for peak concurrent users is 65,303 players online at one time [12].

Secondly, the game employs a laisse-faire free market economy that is solely driven by the players. This means that the in game economy is reliant on player intervention and actions to operate. Players must obtain raw materials, manufacture goods and sell these goods on the open market to make money [13]. This means that the players must be engaged with the virtual world to progress in the game, as the one of the purposes of the game is to accumulate wealth in order to more effectively accumulate wealth. In the absence of a formal score keeping mechanism, wealth is a useful measure of overall power in the game [25].

Finally of note is the way in which the game deals with player development. Within EVE players have the capacity to train any skill that they feel best suits the requirements of the way they approach playing the game. The learning of skills provides a number of benefits to the player by being able to utilise more advanced ships, modules and weapons as well as making the use of these items and other facilities more effective [25]. EVE uses a time-based model of skill development rather than skill acquisition being based on repeated in-game actions as in many other games. Skills are learnt over time on a passive basis as players receive a set number of skill points per hour in real time. Skills continue to develop in real time even if the player is not actively playing the game. Simple skills may take minutes to learn while skills that are more complex can take months to learn [13]. To illustrate, in order to fly one of the most powerful military vessels in the game it requires knowledge of over 20 different skills and a total training time of 194d 6h 24m 16s. This is the minimum amount of time required to simply pilot the vessel, as further skills would be required to most effectively use the ship in battle [13].

4.1 Environmental Characteristics

The EVE environment is composed of a contiguous interconnected network of systems that are grouped into loose constellations [12]. Systems can be thought of as being analogous to street corners, city blocks or census mesh blocks and therefore form one of the basic geographic units of analysis in the research. Constellations can be thought to be analogous to neighbourhoods, jurisdictions or other geographic divisions within urban areas and therefore form another basic geographic unit of analysis in the research. A constellation is a close grouping of systems that contain more links to one another than to other systems. Constellations are typically separated from each other by a small number of systems that serve as bridges between the adjacent constellations. These bridging systems provide natural bottlenecks and barriers to travel, as the space between systems and constellations is impassable [13].

Systems and constellations form the main activity sites for players to access resources and to interact with other players. The systems provide valuable resources to players similar to locations for the provision of illicit services and goods in the physical world.

Players need to act collectively in self-organising groups to effectively claim and defend areas from other groups [13]. Systems that can be claimed by player-controlled groups are the likely sites of conflict between competing player-controlled groups. Player groups identify with the occupied space as their home areas and will invest time and effort improving and solidifying their territories. All these are activities that can be observed in the physical world [25].

The virtual game space is divided into two distinct areas; Computer Controlled Space and Player Controlled Space. Computer controlled space because of its rigidly controlled nature, high traffic volumes and central location can be thought of as being analogous to the CBD of a large city [12]. Within computer-controlled space, formal behavioural control of violent activity is provided by a computer generated police response in the form of an in-game police force (CONCORD) [25]. CONCORD will respond to inter-player violence within computer controlled spaced based on a rating given to each system. As the systems in computer-controlled space get farther away from the central systems the rating given to each system decreases from 1.0 to 0.1. CONCORD response times become increasingly longer as the rating falls [13]. This reflects a measure of policing effectiveness in the physical world with inner suburbs being better patrolled and more likely to draw a timely response while outer suburbs and rural locations are less likely to have immediate responses.

Player controlled space consists of the systems and constellations surrounding computer controlled space. These systems can be thought of as being analogous to drug street corners, territories and organised criminal groups set spaces. The systems in this space are not controlled by the computer and are therefore free to be claimed and defended by player formed groups [12]. Player groups can further improve controlled systems to make them more profitable to occupy which means that there is also an incentive to continue to hold and defend these systems [13].

It takes time to travel within and between systems; while travelling the player is also exposed to risks from other players and computer controlled enemies [13]. This introduces a type of friction similar in the physical world to the distances willing to be travelled by players. Meaning that players are more likely to travel shorter distances than longer distances due to the time and effort it takes to travel longer distances as well as the increased risk. Without this friction, a player could quickly and with little effort jump across the long distances between the systems that would not be possible in the physical world.

4.2 Individual Player Characteristics

Individual players are one of the primary units of analysis in this research. In the game world player characteristics are derived from the skills those players choose to train. As noted before skills take physical world time to develop; with higher level and advanced skills taking much longer to train than lower level basic skills. Skills and skill training can therefore be thought of as representing experiential knowledge in the physical world [25]. In the physical world individuals receive training and gain experience in their chosen activities that make them more effective at doing that activity in the future. In the game the skill system achieves the same effect.

The player's combined skill set reflects the type of game play style that the player chooses. Aggressive players will train skills that will aid in combat whereas acquisitive players will train skills that aid in manufacture and sales. Skills also determine the types of space vessels that a player is able to operate and the equipment that can be fitted to the vessel. Higher skill levels allow for better vessels to be used, better equipment to be fitted and more effective operations of both [25].

Vessels form the primary tool for interfacing between the game world and other players in the game. Vessels are the player's physical presence in the game that when combined with a skill set represent the player's capacity to effectively perform an activity in the game [12]. This is similar to the physical world where experiential knowledge and physical ability add together to make performing activities more effective.

For other players the vessel that is being flown by an individual represents that individual's strength and level of threat posed by that player. The vessel also represents the potential reward that might come from victimising the player [13]. This parallels the types of information used by offenders in the physical world to make assessments of the risks and rewards associated with offending.

Players also have security ratings that reflect their activities in the game. Negative ratings indicate aggressive and violent acts while positive ratings indicate friendly acts towards computer-controlled players and groups [12]. This is another source of information that players can use to assess the threat posed by other players in the game. Strong negative ratings indicate that a player may have participated in violence before and is therefore more adept at using violence [13]. Security ratings are similar to physical world criminal records held by law enforcement agencies.

4.3 Player Group Characteristics

Players are able to organise themselves into groups known as corporations (sub-groups). Each corporation has a unique name and identifier in game. Corporations have a hierarchy of membership roles that can be assigned to individual players or groups of players. Corporations have the capacity to pool resources and funds in common locations for all members to access [12]. Players will group together to more effectively achieve in-game activities (Maniac, 2004). These types of characteristics are commonly found in similar types of groups in the physical world. However given the virtual world's lack of legal recourse to resolve disputes between corporations often corporations will be involved in violence as a means of dispute resolution. This makes corporations more like physical world criminal organisations.

Corporations by themselves are unable to claim territory in player-controlled space. Corporations must team-up with other corporations to form alliances (groups). Alliances are able to claim sovereignty over systems in player-controlled space [12]. Claiming sovereignty means that claimed system belongs to the alliance and allows the owner to exploit the resources present. The alliance may also invest in the system to improve the resources present [13]. Claimed systems must be defended, as they are open to attack by other groups who wish to claim sovereignty [25]. This is parallel to the physical world where smaller groups of offenders group

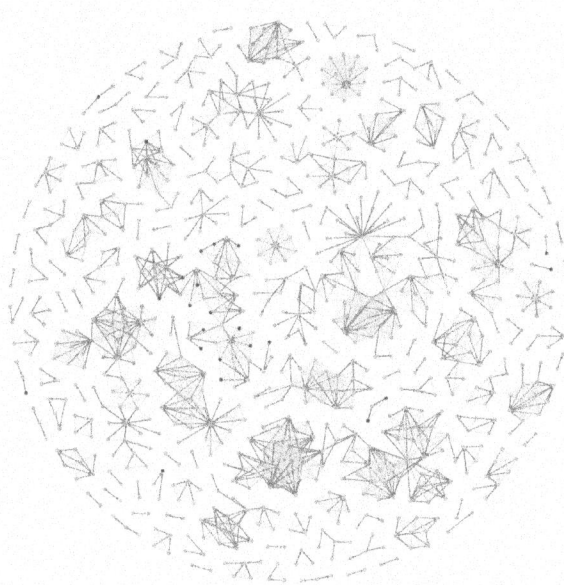

Figure 1: Complete Network Diagram for EVE Online 2007/12/05T23:26-2007/12/06T09:01 (Fruchterman Reingold)

together to form coalitions to more effectively occupy and defend valuable territory and resources from outside interference.

5 ANALYSIS

The initial exploratory analysis of the data set focuses on producing network descriptive statistics and visualisation for the observation of patterns. Figure 1, complete network, displays the social network graph for all nodes within the sample data set. In this instance, the nodes are coloured by the top 7 player groups (alliance) by node count. Edges are displayed in green for co-offending (non-directed edges) and red for victimisation (directed edges) with arrows indicating the relationship from offender to victim. Figure 2, large connected component, shows the largest connected component from within the the network graph shown in Figure 1. The connected component shows the structure, relationships and violent victimisations of a group with the in game Alliance name of "Triumvirate". The nodes which are associated with the group are shown in green.

Simple metrics such as degree distribution (a measure of the distribution of edges per node) demonstrate the overall shape and nature of the network. Figure 3, co-offending, shows that the distribution of co-offending links in the network graph. It can be seen that while there is variability in the distribution of these links it does conform to a scale-free distribution that we would expect to see in a non-random collaboration network [8]. There are a number of things that can be inferred from this distribution. There is a large number of unconnected nodes which indicates that the majority of offending that takes place is simple one-on-one opportunistic assaults rather than coordinated attacks. While much lower in number multiple offender attacks with less than 15 co-offenders still make up the remaining majority of attacks. This may demonstrate

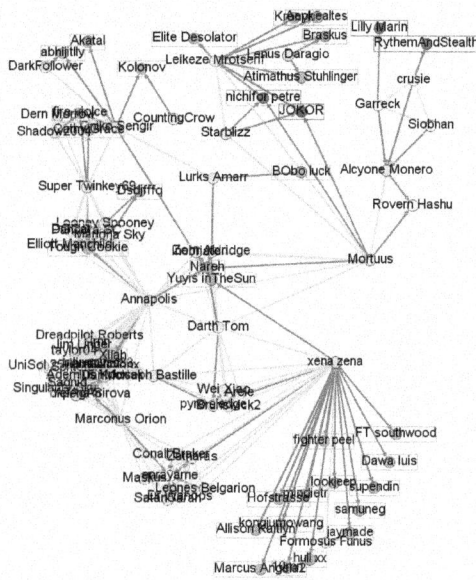

Figure 2: Large Connected Component - Triumvirate (in green)

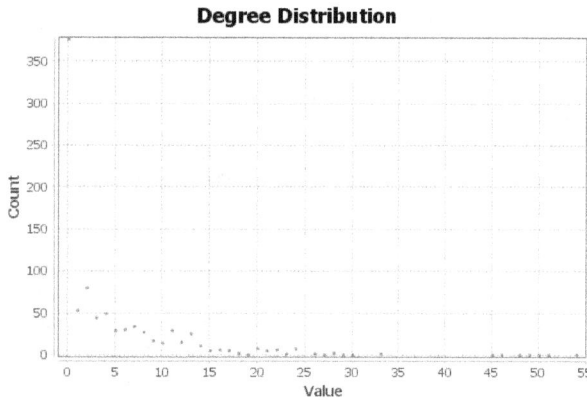

Figure 3: Co-offending Degree Distribution - all nodes

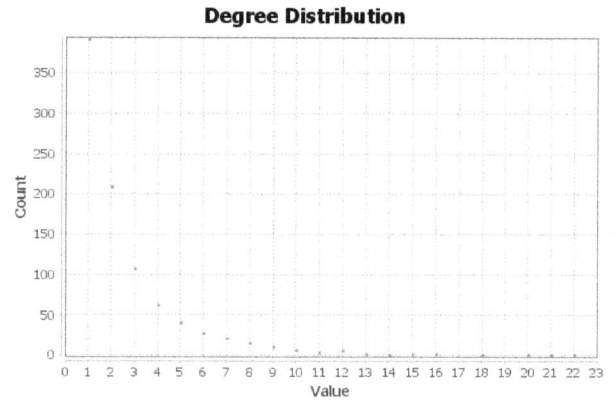

Figure 4: Victimisation Degree Distribution - all nodes

a level of organisation to the offending but further analysis is likely to uncover that these groups are ad-hoc in nature and only come together to achieve a specific goal or take advantage of a transient opportunity before disbanding. It is also observed that there are a small number of highly connected nodes. These nodes act to connect groups across space and time. These nodes are referred to as Brokers and are of significant interest to law enforcement and regulatory agencies due to their position in criminal networks. Removal of individuals in brokerage positions is likely to cause widespread disruption to the network [36].

Figure 4, Victimisation, also shows a scale-free distribution. In this case the distribution is closer to a power law distribution. This is close to the ideal distribution that would be observed in the physical world for vistimisation rates. There are a large number of individuals who are victimised once and not again while there is only a small number of individuals who experience multi-victimisation [19]. Further observations can be made about the network structure if a single large connected component is isolated from the larger network graph. Figure 2 provides a number of examples in regards to how social network graphs can be used to uncover important information about the activities of a group over time and space. Within the graph an individual (label: Xena Zena) has a high number of out-degree edges. It is likely that this individual is taking advantage of a criminal opportunity where there are a number of vulnerable targets and a lack of disincentives to commit the violence. While this highly violent behaviour would likely cause this individual to be brought to the notice of law enforcement quickly it can be observed that this individual is not highly connected to the core group. The arrest of this individual while important will have little affect on disrupting the overall network. It can also be observed that the highly violent individual is not heavily involved in the conflict that can be observed between the main group (green nodes) and the rival group (yellow nodes).

As mentioned previously it can be observed that there are a small number of highly connected individuals that serve as brokers between clusters of the main group. It can be observed that the individual (label: Annapolis) is connected to the main group and as well as being placed between three larger sub-groupings as well as other brokers. Further investigation shows that this particular individual connects the main group and sub-groups across multiple locations and times. The removal of this individual from the network would cause significant disruption to the main group's activity and would therefore be of most interest to law enforcement and regulatory agencies. In contrast to the highly violent individual the broker does not participate in many violent encounters so may not be readily identifiable depending on how the violent incidents are investigated and/or observed by law enforcement. Further there is no direct link between this individual and the highly violent individual meaning that while the highly visible and dangerous individual will likely come to the attention of law enforcement they are unlikely to be able to expose the key brokering individual.

The final feature of note is revenge. Towards the top right of the graph a pair of green nodes (label: Mortuus and Alcyone Monero) have attacked a rival yellow node (label: Rovern Hashu). Subsequently, one of the green nodes (label: Alcyone Monero) is attacked by three rival yellow nodes (label: Siobhan, Garreck, cruise). This demonstrates that there is a current conflict occurring between these two groups. Further investigation in the future would be needed to uncover the dynamics and scale of this conflict which is not contained within the current sample. It is also noticeable that the person victimised does not retaliate directly but is avenged by other members of the group. Additionally, the victim of the revenge is isolated from the group and therefore more vulnerable. While proximity to the original event is likely to play a part in why the revenge act was targeted at the player it also highlights the vulnerability of members of the group who are not tightly bound to the core active members of the group. This is similar to the physical world where the rivalry and retaliatory violence is more likely to be waged between rank-and-file members than higher ranking members of a group [15].

6 CONCLUSIONS

Existing research has proved the applicability and suitability of data collected from virtual worlds to shed light on research questions and to provide insights into physical world phenomena in the context of epidemiology, complex networks, and economics. In this paper we have argued that data collected from virtual environments, specifically MMORPGs such as EVE Online and World of Warcraft, can be effectively used to model and thus increase our understanding of criminal behaviour and dark networks.

Our case study example, which applied SNA techniques to a sample data set capturing almost 400 individual events engaged in by some 920 individuals over an nine and a half hour period illustrate that the patterns which are emerging tend to match those patterns that can be observed in general crime statistics and from within the descriptive literature surrounding crime science and computational criminology.

Thus, virtual environments can be seen to have a proven legitimacy as an information source regarding human behaviour, and ought to play an increasingly significant role in future research and modelling endeavours, providing rich and diverse data to researchers across several disciplinary boundaries.

7 ACKNOWLEDGEMENTS

This research has been carried out as part of a PhD thesis supported by an Australian Government Research Training Program (RTP) Scholarship.

REFERENCES

[1] Sabrina Adamoli, Andrea Di Nicola, Ernesto U Savona, and Paola Zoffi. 1998. *Organised crime around the world.* Heuni Helsinki.
[2] Reka Albert, Hawoong Jeong, and Albert-Laszlo Barabasi. 2000. Error and attack tolerance of complex networks. *Nature* 406, 6794 (2000), 378–382. http://dx.doi.org/10.1038/35019019
[3] Peter Andreas. 2004. Illicit international political economy: the clandestine side of globalization. *Review of International Political Economy* 11, 3 (2004), 641–652.
[4] Pino Arlacchi. 1998. Some observations on illegal markets. *The new European criminology: Crime and social order in Europe* (1998), 203–215.
[5] William Sims Bainbridge. 2007. The scientific research potential of virtual worlds. *science* 317, 5837 (2007), 472–476.
[6] Stephen P. Borgatti, Ajay Mehra, Daniel J. Brass, and Giuseppe Labianca. 2009. Network Analysis in the Social Sciences. *Science* 323, 5916 (2009), 892–895. https://doi.org/10.1126/science.1165821
[7] Paul J Brantingham and Patricia L Brantingham. 1993. Environment, routine and situation: Toward a pattern theory of crime. *Advances in criminological theory* 5 (1993), 259–294.
[8] DA Bright, C Greenhill, and N Levenkova. 2010. Attack of the nodes: Scale-free criminal networks and vulnerability to targeted law enforcement interventions. In *2nd Illicit Networks Workshop, Wollongong, Australia*.
[9] David A Bright and Jordan J Delaney. 2013. Evolution of a drug trafficking network: Mapping changes in network structure and function across time. *Global Crime* 14, 2-3 (2013), 238–260.
[10] David A Bright, Caitlin E Hughes, and Jenny Chalmers. 2012. Illuminating dark networks: a social network analysis of an Australian drug trafficking syndicate. *Crime, Law and Social Change* 57, 2 (2012), 151–176.
[11] Edward Castronova, Dmitri Williams, Cuihua Shen, Rabindra Ratan, Li Xiong, Yun Huang, and Brian Keegan. 2009. As real as real? Macroeconomic behavior in a large-scale virtual world. *New Media & Society* 11, 5 (2009), 685–707.
[12] CCP. 2019. EVE Online. (2019). https://www.eveonline.com/
[13] CCP. 2019. EVElopedia. (2019). https://www.evelopedia.org/Main_Page
[14] Kim-Kwang Raymond Choo and Russell G Smith. 2008. Criminal exploitation of online systems by organised crime groups. *Asian journal of criminology* 3, 1 (2008), 37–59.
[15] Scott H Decker. 1996. Collective and normative features of gang violence. *Justice Quarterly* 13, 2 (1996), 243–264.
[16] Frederick Desroches. 2007. Research on upper level drug trafficking: a review. *Journal of Drug Issues* 37, 4 (2007), 827–844.
[17] Frederick John Desroches. 2005. *The crime that pays: Drug trafficking and organized crime in Canada.* Canadian Scholars' Press.
[18] Adam Edwards and Pete Gill. 2002. Crime as enterprise?–The case of"transnational organised crime". *Crime, Law and Social Change* 37, 3 (2002), 203–223.
[19] Graham Farrell. 1992. Multiple victimisation: its extent and significance. *International Review of Victimology* 2, 2 (1992), 85–102.
[20] H Richard Friman and Peter Andreas. 1999. *The illicit global economy and state power.* Rowman & Littlefield.
[21] Andrzej Grabowski and Natalia Kruszewska. 2007. Experimental study of the structure of a social network and human dynamics in a virtual society. *International Journal of Modern Physics C* 18, 10 (2007), 1527–1535.
[22] A Grabowski, N Kruszewska, and RA Kosiński. 2008. Dynamic phenomena and human activity in an artificial society. *Physical Review E* 78, 6 (2008), 066110.
[23] Yue Guo and Stuart Barnes. 2007. Why people buy virtual items in virtual worlds with real money. *ACM SIGMIS Database* 38, 4 (2007), 69–76.
[24] Maria C Haagsma, Marcel E Pieterse, Oscar Peters, and Daniel L King. 2013. How Gaming May Become a Problem: A Qualitative Analysis of the Role of Gaming Related Experiences and Cognitions in the Development of Problematic Game Behavior. *International Journal of Mental Health and Addiction* (2013), 1–12.
[25] hideodate. 2019. EVE University. (2019). https://www.eveuniversity.org/
[26] Brian Keegan, Muhammad Aurangzeb Ahmed, Dmitri Williams, Jaideep Srivastava, and Noshir Contractor. 2010. Dark gold: Statistical properties of clandestine networks in massively multiplayer online games. In *Social Computing (SocialCom), 2010 IEEE Second International Conference on.* IEEE, 201–208.
[27] Julia Kneer, Sabine Glock, Sara Beskes, and Gary Bente. 2012. Are digital games perceived as fun or danger? Supporting and suppressing different game-related concepts. *Cyberpsychology, Behavior, and Social Networking* 15, 11 (2012), 604–609.
[28] Yungchang Ku, Ying-Chieh Chen, Kuo-Ching Wu, and Chaochang Chiu. 2007. *An empirical analysis of online gaming crime characteristics from 2002 to 2004.* Springer, 34–45.
[29] Vili Lehdonvirta. 2005. Real-money trade of virtual assets: ten different user perceptions. *Proceedings of Digital Arts and Culture (DAC 2005), IT University of Copenhagen, Denmark* (2005), 52–58.
[30] Vili Lehdonvirta. 2009. Virtual item sales as a revenue model: identifying attributes that drive purchase decisions. *Electronic Commerce Research* 9, 1-2 (2009), 97–113.
[31] Eric T Lofgren and Nina H Fefferman. 2007. The untapped potential of virtual game worlds to shed light on real world epidemics. *The Lancet infectious diseases* 7, 9 (2007), 625–629.
[32] Tamara Makarenko. 2004. The crime-terror continuum: tracing the interplay between transnational organised crime and terrorism. *Global crime* 6, 1 (2004), 129–145.
[33] A. Malm and G. Bichler. 2011. Networks of Collaborating Criminals: Assessing the Structural Vulnerability of Drug Markets. *Journal of Research in Crime and Delinquency* 48, 2 (2011), 271–297. https://doi.org/Doi10.1177/0022427810391535
[34] Donato Masciandaro. 2017. *Global financial crime: terrorism, money laundering and offshore centres.* Taylor & Francis.
[35] Carlo Morselli, Cynthia Giguère, and Katia Petit. 2007. The efficiency/security trade-off in criminal networks. *Social Networks* 29, 1 (2007), 143–153.

[36] C. Morselli and J. Roy. 2008. Brokerage qualifications in ringing operations. *Criminology* 46, 1 (2008), 71–98. <GotoISI>://000254485300003

[37] Howard Rachlin. 2004. The behavioral economics of violence. *Annals of the New York Academy of Sciences* 1036, 1 (2004), 325–335.

[38] Peter Reuter. 1983. *Disorganized crime: The economics of the visible hand.* MIT press Cambridge, MA.

[39] Mark Shaw. 2014. Typologies of Transnational Organized Crime Groups. *Centre for International Crime Prevention, UNODC, accessed February* 12 (2014).

[40] Herbert A Simon. 1979. Rational decision making in business organizations. *The American economic review* 69, 4 (1979), 493–513.

[41] Herbert A Simon. 1982. Models of bounded rationality: Behavioral economics and business organizations. *Jg., Cambridge (MA)* (1982).

[42] Malcolm K Sparrow. 1991. The application of network analysis to criminal intelligence: An assessment of the prospects. *Social networks* 13, 3 (1991), 251–274.

[43] Petrus C Van Duyne and Maarten Van Dijck. 2007. *Assessing organised crime: the sad state of an impossible art.* Springer, 101–124.

[44] Alan Wright. 2013. *Organised crime.* Routledge.

[45] Jennifer Xu and Hsinchun Chen. 2005. Criminal network analysis and visualization. *Commun. ACM* 48, 6 (2005), 100–107.

[46] Jennifer Xu and Hsinchun Chen. 2008. The topology of dark networks. *Commun. ACM* 51, 10 (2008), 58–65. https://doi.org/10.1145/1400181.1400198

[47] Nick Yee. 2006. Motivations for play in online games. *CyberPsychology & Behavior* 9, 6 (2006), 772–775.

A Unified Deep Learning Architecture for Abuse Detection

Antigoni-Maria Founta
Aristotle University
Thessaloniki, Greece
founanti@csd.auth.gr

Despoina Chatzakou
Aristotle University
Thessaloniki, Greece
deppych@csd.auth.gr

Nicolas Kourtellis
Telefonica Research
Barcelona, Spain
nicolas.kourtellis@telefonica.com

Jeremy Blackburn
University of Alabama
Alabama, USA
blackburn@uab.edu

Athena Vakali
Aristotle University
Thessaloniki, Greece
avakali@csd.auth.gr

Ilias Leontiadis
Telefonica Research
Barcelona, Spain
ilias.leontiadis@telefonica.com

ABSTRACT

Hate speech, offensive language, sexism, racism, and other types of abusive behavior have become a common phenomenon in many online social media platforms. In recent years, such diverse abusive behaviors have been manifesting with increased frequency and levels of intensity, e.g., [9]. Despite social media's efforts to combat online abusive behaviors [23, 33] this problem is still apparent. In fact, up to now, they have entered an arms race with the perpetrators, who constantly change tactics to evade the detection algorithms deployed by these platforms. Such algorithms, not disclosed to the public for obvious reasons, are typically custom-designed and tuned to detect only one specific type of abusive behavior, but usually miss other related behaviors. In the present paper, we study this complex problem by following a more holistic approach, which considers the various aspects of abusive behavior. We focus on Twitter, due to its popularity, and analyze user and textual properties from different angles of abusive posting behavior. We propose a deep learning architecture, which utilizes a wide variety of available metadata, and combines it with automatically-extracted hidden patterns within the text of the tweets, to detect multiple abusive behavioral norms which are highly inter-related. The proposed unified architecture is applied in a seamless and transparent fashion without the need for any change of the architecture but only training a model for each task (i.e., different types of abusive behavior). We test the proposed approach with multiple datasets addressing different abusive behaviors on Twitter. Our results demonstrate high performance across all datasets, with the AUC value to range from 92% to 98%.

KEYWORDS

Abusive Behavior, Hate Speech, Twitter, Deep Learning

ACM Reference Format:
Antigoni-Maria Founta, Despoina Chatzakou, Nicolas Kourtellis, Jeremy Blackburn, Athena Vakali, and Ilias Leontiadis. 2019. A Unified Deep Learning Architecture for Abuse Detection. In *11th ACM Conference on Web Science (WebSci '19), June 30–July 3, 2019, Boston, MA, USA*. ACM, New York, NY, USA, 10 pages. https://doi.org/10.1145/3292522.3326028

1 INTRODUCTION

Social media ubiquity has raised concerns about emerging problematic phenomena such as the intensity of abusive behavior. Unfortunately, this problem is difficult to deal with since it has many "faces" and exhibits complex interactions among social media users. Such multifaceted abusive behavior involves instances of hate speech, offensive, sexist and racist language, aggression, cyberbullying, harassment, and trolling [34, 41]. Each form of abusive behavior has its own characteristics, and manifests differently, depending on the social media objectives, the users participating in it, and the topic's sensitivity. Indeed, popular social media platforms like Twitter and Facebook are not immune to abusive behavior, even though they have devoted substantial resources to deal with it [32].

This type of behavior is harmful both socially, reducing the proclivity and trust of users to the particular online social media platform, as well as from a business perspective. For instance, concerns about racist and sexist attacks on Twitter seem to have impacted a potential sale of the company [18]. Even though social media platforms have increased their measures against abusive behaviors online [37], there is always the need to develop advanced mechanism to be one step ahead of the abusers.

Apart from the social media platforms themselves, the research community has also made attempts at detecting abusive behavior. For example, there have been various works attempting to detect hate speech [2, 12, 40, 42], cyberbullying [6, 11, 16], and abusive behavior in general [7, 10, 27]. Furthermore, various techniques have been applied to detect offensive language [26, 43], and even racism and sexism [20, 22, 24]. However, these solutions are typically custom built and tuned for a specific platform and *type* of abusive behavior, and not generalizable.

Additionally, abusive behavior cannot be assumed just by a "monolithic" consideration of the content (e.g., text of an individual post). Instead, in this work, we follow a more "holistic" approach to consider other facts that may carry important signals and predictors for this type of behavior. Such features can include users' prior posts, social network, popularity, account settings, and even the metadata of posts, to reveal a more global abusive behavior tendency. We study all such user activities as they can help capture different facets of the abusive behavior. We tackle the problem by designing a novel, *unified* deep learning architecture, able to digest and combine any available attributes, to detect abusive behavior. The deep learning approach allows us to capture subtle, hidden commonalities and differences among the various abusive behaviors within the same model, while being careful not to overfit on the available data.

Our method is a global and lightweight solution with respect to computational resources needed, with the capacity to consider the plethora of available (meta)data, to recognize various types of abusive behavior, and without too much feature engineering and model tuning. Even though the feature engineering for every behavior to be analyzed and detected can offer a better understanding about the data and domain at hand, it can be a very laborious process which has no guarantees that it will provide a significantly improved performance, if any. We show that the combination of all available metadata with the proposed training methodology can substantially outperform the state of the art over various datasets, each of which captures a different facet of abusive behavior: i) cyberbullying, ii) hateful, iii) offensive, and iv) sarcasm.

More concretely, we make the following contributions:

- We demonstrate the importance of combining all available (meta)data for detecting abusive behavior. We measure its importance by experimenting and producing superior results, with a deep-learning-based architecture able to combine the available input. To the best of our knowledge, we are the *first to demonstrate the power of such a unified architecture in detecting various facets of abuse* in online social networks.
- We show how naive training methodology fails to make optimal use of heterogeneous inputs. To address this, we implement a training technique that focuses separately on each input by alternating training between them. *This optimization substantially boosts detection capabilities*, as it allows the model to avoid considering only the most dominant features for each task.
- We show that our architecture is *portable* across different forms of abusive behavior, as opposed to previous works which use customized detectors for each type of abuse. We experiment on five datasets covering several forms of abuse, and find that our unified architecture works across all *without the need for any tuning or reconfiguring*. Our architecture can handle the imbalance of the various classes without special tuning, and especially for the minority classes. Our results shed light on how different feature types contribute to abuse detection, and provide evidence that text-only features alone are insufficient to reliably detect generic abusive behavior.
- We demonstrate that our methodology can be easily adapted for the detection of toxic behavior in domains such as online gaming, *without further tuning*.
- We provide our implementation to the community, which will be made available on github.com.

2 BACKGROUND AND RELATED WORK

Abuse detection is an increasingly trending topic over the past few years. Numerous studies have been published, trying to address this problem especially in social networks, and in various forms. Hate speech detection [2, 12, 25, 40, 42], cyberbullying identification [6, 11, 16], and the detection of abusive [7, 10, 27] or offensive language [8, 26, 43], are some of the facets of this problem. Some works try to detect more specific types of hateful behavior, such as racism [22, 24] or sexism [20]. However, as [41] points out, there are many similarities between these subtasks, and scholars tend to group them under "umbrella terms" - like [36] do for hate speech - or use them interchangeably. Yet, major advancements on these tasks are quite new and many of the related studies are preliminary.

Table 1: Comparison of our method with past works. TF: text, UF: user, CF: content, NF: network features.

Related Work	Features				ML method used		Platform	
	TF	UF	CF	NF	Neural Nets	Classic	Twitter	Other
[2],[21], [15],[28], [13],[44]	x				x		x	
[35]	x		x		x		x	
[30]	x	x			x		x	
[38]	x		x		x	x	x	x
[1]	x				x	x		x
[6]	x	x		x		x	x	
[42]	x	x				x	x	
[10], [31]	x		x			x	x	
[25]	x					x	x	
This work	x	x	x	x	x	x	x	x

Most of previous works use traditional machine learning classifiers, such as logistic regression [10, 42, 43] and support vector machines [40], or ensemble classifiers of such traditional methods [5]. Some studies experiment with deep learning on this task, especially after the major advancements of the last years. Due to the large amount of related research concerning these tasks, we only analyze works that are most relevant with ours in terms of domain and methodology, like in [2, 15, 28]. Table 1 compares our method to those that are most relevant to our problem setting. Under the features category four main types of features are listed, i.e., text-, user-, content-, and network-based. N-grams, term frequency, or word embeddings are commonly used text-based features. The user-based features contain information extracted from a user's profile (e.g., number of posts, accounts age, etc.), while the network-based are related to a user's friendship network (e.g., number of followers and friends). Finally, the content-based features are highly related to a user's behavioral patterns, as for instance the average number of the used hashtags and/or urls in his posts, the average words' and posts' length, or the expressed sentiments/emotions.

Twitter Data Sources. Authors in [2] focus on hate speech detection, and specifically attempt to detect racism and sexism based on various deep learning architectures. These architectures include Convolutional Neural Networks (CNNs), Long Short-Term Memory Networks (LSTMs), and FastText [21], combined with numerous features like TF-IDF and Bag of Words (BoW) vectors. Their LSTM classifier with random embeddings results to significantly improved performance compared to baseline methods. In [44] a CNN with GRU network is used, combined with word embeddings, to detect hate speech on Twitter. The proposed method is tested on various datasets, in order to either discriminate among racism, sexism, and neither (or both), or between hate and non-hate tweets. Compared to existing methods, the authors achieved the highest F1-score.

In [15] authors also use deep learning models to address hate speech on Twitter. Specifically, they proceed with CNNs and feature embeddings, such as one-hot encoded character n-gram vectors and word embeddings. They outperform the baseline in terms of precision and F1 score, but not on recall. Similarly, [28] also uses CNNs with character- and word-level inputs for the same task. However, it investigates two different cases; performing the classification for all three labels (i.e., none, sexist, and racist) at once, or beginning with the detection of 'abusive language' and then further distinguishing between sexist or racist. The results show that, in general, the two cases can have equally good performance. The deep learning model, though, does not seem to perform as well as traditional machine learning algorithms when it comes to the two-step approach. All previously mentioned works experiment with the dataset that was published in [42] and we also use it to compare the results.

Authors in [13] proceed with Italian text sources extracted from both Twitter and Facebook to detect hate speech. A neural network setup combined with word embeddings is used to show the effect of merging data from different sources. The results show small improvement compared to classifying texts separately. In [35] the focus is on identifying offensive language in German tweets. Two neural network setups are used, where text data (i.e., word embeddings) alone or combined with linguistic features (e.g., # of punctuation, sentiment, etc.) are used on top of an LSTM network. Overall, the combination of different features leads to a higher F1-score. Finally, authors in [30], based on an ensemble LSTM setup and a word-based frequency vectorization, focus on detecting racism, sexism, and neutral Twitter data. Best results are achieved when both text and behavioral (e.g., gender) features are used.

Other Social Media Platforms. Literature on the topic of hate detection on Twitter using deep learning has been sparse. However, there are some works addressing this problem in different online platforms. E.g., the study in [27] deals with Yahoo news comments which have been annotated as abusive or not, by trained Yahoo employees. More specifically, they employ several datasets from comments found on Yahoo! Finance and News. Most of them were annotated by employees of the company, one was crowdsourced using Amazon's Mechanical Turk, and one was provided from [12]. In [12], the authors also classify hate speech on Yahoo comments, using the continuous BOW neural language model to train word and comment representations into 'paragraph embeddings' (named *paragraph2vec*). They use logistic regression for classification.

Nobata et al. [27] compare directly their research with [12], due to their similarities. Except from working on the same task and domain, they also employ similar features, i.e., comment embeddings (named *comment2vec*). However, they treat these embeddings differently, without using deep learning based models. In addition to the embeddings, they construct a number of other features, all derived from the comment's text. For the classification task they use the Vowpal Wabbit's regression model,[1] and they outperform [12] by 0.10 in AUC with 82.6% F1-score. In [38] both traditional and deep neural networks (i.e., CNN, LSTM) are used to detect aggressive behavior on Facebook and Twitter posts, as well as on Hindi-English Code-Mixed texts. The best results are obtained with the CCN setup when combined with both text and content based features. Finally, authors in [1] succeed to detect aggression on Facebook posts with an LSTM classifier combined with word embeddings.

Contributions. This work studies in depth the application of deep learning on the detection of abuse in all its forms with a unified architecture. Departing from the previous works that use mostly textual or custom, task-specific, features, we design a neural network architecture that is able to digest all available input (both text and numerical metadata). Furthermore, training the proposed multi-input network is not straightforward. We introduce an interleaved approach that has only been adapted from image recommendation

---

[1] https://github.com/JohnLangford/vowpal_wabbit

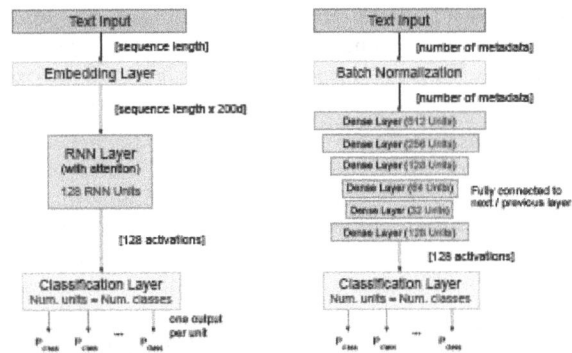

Figure 1: The individual classifiers that are the basis of the combined model. Left: the text-only classifier, Right: the metadata-only classifier.

systems [19], and explain all technical details needed for its repeatability. As far as we know, we are the first to experiment with this architecture on classification of text. To sum up, our work is the first proposed unified technological solution to detect a diverse set of abusive behaviors on platforms like Twitter, while the results show significant improvement over various state-of-the-art methods.

3 DEEP LEARNING ARCHITECTURES

Our overarching goal is to introduce a novel classifier built on cutting-edge technology such as deep learning, that can detect nuanced forms of abusive behavior. There is a host of literature that tackles this problem and uses a variety of approaches to do so. A key takeaway from the majority of this work is that building a model based on text is outperformed by those that additionally take domain specific features into account. Unfortunately, this is a cumbersome process, with slightly different problems and data sources requiring specially constructed models using different architectures. Ideally, we would prefer to have a *single* model/architecture that incorporates *domain specific* metadata, as well as text content and is performant on a large number of abusive content detection tasks.

To that end, we present a unified classification model for abusive behavior. Our approach is treating i) raw text, and ii) domain specific metadata, separately at first, and later combining them into a single model. Domain-specific data here means features that can be computed on the platform under study, such as popularity of users in the network, reposting counts, etc., depending on what functionalities are available.

In the remainder of this section, we provide details on how our final network is built from its component parts, paying particular attention to the specifics of how to train such a multi-input model. First, we present the two individual classifiers that we later fuse: the text and the metadata classifier. Next, we discuss technical details related to the classifier building, lessons learned and tradeoffs in the design and implementation of the classifier. In particular, we discuss how we can combine the various classifiers, either as an ensemble or a single network. Finally, we present the different ways of effectively training such a multi-path network.

3.1 Text Classification Network

This classifier only considers the raw text as input. There are several choices for the class of neural network to base our classifier on.

We use Recurrent Neural Networks (RNN) since they have proven successful at understanding sequences of words and interpreting their meaning. We experimented with both character- and word-level RNNs. The latter is the most performant across all our datasets.

Text preprocessing: Before feeding any text to the network, we need to transform each sample to a sequence of words. As neural networks are trained in mini-batches, every sample in a batch must have the same sequence length (number of words). Tweets containing more words than the sequence length are trimmed, whereas tweets with fewer words are left-padded with zeros (the model learns they carry no information). Ideally, we want to setup a sequence length that is large enough to contain most text from the samples, but avoids outliers as they waste resources (feeding zeros in the network), making the training of the network slower. Therefore, we take the 95th percentile of length of tweets (with respect to the number of words) in the input corpus as the optimal sequence length. For tweets, this results in sequences of 30 words (in effect, 5% of tweets that contain more than 30 words are truncated). We additionally remove any words that appear only once in the corpus, as they are most likely typos and can result in over-fitting. Once preprocessed, the input text is fed to the network for learning.

Word embedding layer: The first layer of the network performs a word embedding, which maps each word to a high-dimensional vector (typically 25-300 dimensions). Word embedding has proved to be a highly effective technique for text classification tasks, while also reduces the number of training samples required to reach good performance. We settled on using pre-trained word embeddings from GloVe [29], which is constructed on more than 2 billion tweets. We choose the highest dimension embeddings (200) available, as these produce the best results across all abusive behaviors investigated. If a word is not found in the GloVe dataset, we initialize it as random vector. The following layers will just treat it as an individual word and potentially learn its significance in this context.

Recurrent layer: The next layer is an RNN with 128 units (neurons): we tried different sizes, and this gave best results for all datasets. As mentioned previously, RNNs learn sequences of words by updating an internal state. After experimenting with several choices for the RNN architecture (Gated Recurrent Unit or GRUs, Long Short-Term Memory or LSTMs, and Bidirectional RNNs), we find that due to the rather small sequences of length in social media (typically less than 100 words per post, just 30 for Twitter), simple GRUs are performing as well as more complex units. To avoid over-fitting we use a recurrent dropout with $p = 0.5$ (i.e., individual neurons were available for activation with probability 0.5), as it empirically provided the best results across all studied behaviors. Finally, an attention layer [3] can be added as it provides a mechanism for the RNN to "focus" on individual parts of the text that contain information related to the task. Attention is particularly useful to tackle texts that contain longer sequences of words (e.g., forum posts). Empirically, we find this only helps for texts that exceed 100 words and, thus, disable it for any classification task that involves tweets.

Classification layer: Finally, we use a fully connected output layer (a.k.a. Dense layer) with one neuron per class we want to predict, and a softmax activation function to normalize output values between 0 and 1. The output of each neuron at this stage represents the probability of the sample belonging to each respective class.

Note that this is the layer that is sliced off when we fuse the text and metadata models into the final combined classifier.

3.2 Metadata Network

The metadata network considers non-sequential data. For example, on Twitter, it might evaluate the number of followers, the location, account age, total number of (posted/favorited/liked) tweets, etc., of a user (see Section 4 for a detailed list).

Metadata preprocessing: Before feeding the data into the neural network, we need to transform any categorical data into numerical, either via enumeration or one-hot encoding, depending on the particulars of the input. Then, each sample is thus represented as a vector of numerical features.

Batch normalization layer: Neural network layers work best when the input data have zero mean and unit variance, as it enables faster learning and higher overall accuracy. Thus, we pass the data through a Batch Normalization layer that takes care of this transformation at each batch.

Dense layers: We use a simple network of several fully connected (dense) layers to learn the metadata. We design our network so that a bottleneck is formed. Such a bottleneck has been shown to result in automatic construction of high-level features [17, 39]. In our implementation, we experimented with multiple architectures and we ended up using 5 layers of size 512, 245, 128, 64, 32, which provide good results across all studied behaviors. On top of this layer, we add an additional (6th) layer which ensures that this network has the same dimensionality as the text-only network; this ends up enhancing performance when we fuse the two networks. Finally, we use *tanh* as activation function, since it works better with standardized numerical data.

Classification layer: As with the test only network, we use one neuron per class with softmax activation.

3.3 Combining the Two Classification Paths

The two classifiers presented above can handle individually either the raw text or the metadata. To build a multi-input classifier we need to combine these two paths. There are two possible ways to perform such a task: i) just use the output of the two classifiers (probabilities of belonging to a given class) as input of a new classifier, or ii) combine the two classifiers on the previous layer that represents the automatically constructed features (Figure 2).

Instead of combining an ensemble of pre-trained classifiers, neural networks allow us to create arbitrary combinations of layers and construct complex architectures that resemble graphs. So, instead of training and then combining two separate classifiers, we can design from the beginning a single architecture that combines both paths before their inputs are squashed into classification probabilities (Figure 2). Therefore, we concatenate the text and metadata networks at their penultimate layer: i) the text path where sequences of raw text are input and 128 activations are produced (one for each RNN unit) and ii) the metadata path where each input produces 128 activations. We can think of this architecture as merging together 128 automatically constructed features from each input and then attempting the final classification task based on this vector.

Contrary to traditional machine learning, this architecture allows us to mix a diverse set of data (sequences of text and discrete metadata) without having to explicitly construct the text features

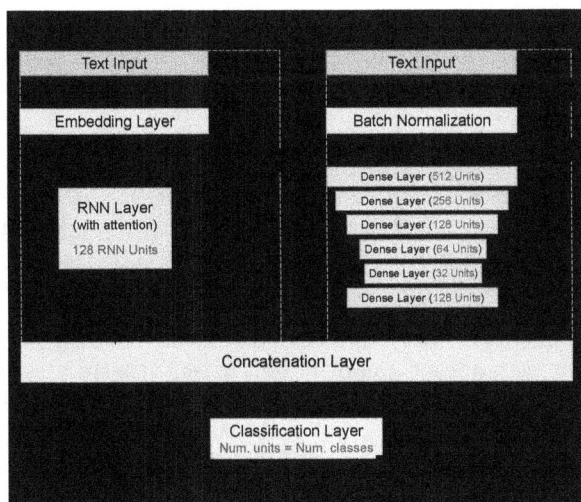

Figure 2: The combined classifier. The output of the two individual paths are concatenated and a classification layer is added over the merged data.

(e.g., TF-IDF vectors). Furthermore, we utilize the power of word embedding that have been pre-trained on much larger datasets.

3.4 Training the Combined Network

While the combined architecture is straightforward, just training the whole network at once is not the most optimal way. In fact, there are several ways to train the combined network: below, we list some of the possible ways and on the Evaluation Section we compare their performance.

Training the entire network at once (Naive Training): The simplest approach is to train the entire network at once; i.e., to treat it as a single classification network with two inputs. However, the performance we achieve from this training technique is suboptimal: the two paths have different convergence rates (i.e., one of the paths might converge faster, and thus dominate any subsequent training epochs). Furthermore, standard backpropagation across the whole network can also induce unpredictable interactions as we allow the weights to be modified at both paths simultaneously.

Transfer learning: We can avoid this problem by *pre-training* the two paths separately and only afterwards join them together to build the architecture of Figure 2. This involves a number of steps:

(1) We pre-train separately the text and the metadata classifiers.
(2) We *remove* the classification layer of each classifier, effectively exposing the activations of their penultimate layer. We treat these as the features that the two pre-trained networks have constructed based on their training.
(3) We freeze the weights of both networks, so no further retraining of their weights is possible.
(4) We add a concatenation layer and a classification layer, effectively transforming the separate models of Figure 1 into the architecture of the combined model (Figure 2).
(5) We train again the combined model. Only the final layer's weights are trainable.

Note: this model resembles an ensemble but with a key difference: the input is not the final class probabilities (num_{class}+num_{class}

features) but features learned by the previous layer of the pre-trained models (128+128 features).

Transfer learning with fine tuning (FT): This approach is the same as above, except we do not freeze the weights on the original networks. The practical result of this is that our pre-training serves only to initialize the weights, which the fused network can later adapt when we merge the two paths.

Combined learning with interleaving (Interleaved): As discussed, standard training of the whole network at once may lead to poor performance due to the interaction of updating both data paths at once. The training approaches presented in the previous sections try to mitigate this problem by training the two paths separately and then concatenating the two pre-trained models together. Instead, here we introduce a way that allows us to *train the full network simultaneously while mitigating the aforementioned drawbacks* achieving increased performance.

To do this, we can design our training in a way that, at each mini-batch, data flow through the whole network, but only one of the paths is updated, i.e., we train the two paths in an alternating fashion. E.g., on even-numbered mini-batches the gradient descent only updates the text path whereas on odd-numbered batches the metadata ones. Finally, between epochs we also alternate the paths so both paths get a chance to observe the whole dataset.

To implement this interleaved approach (e.g., in Keras), we initialize two identical models A and B with the architecture shown in Figure 2. However, before compiling the models, we introduce a single difference: the text-path of A is defined as non-trainable ('frozen') and, similarly, the metadata-path on B is also 'frozen.' During training, at each mini-batch we alternate these models:

- If (*batch_number* + *epoch_number*) is even, then use model A (else, use B). Notice, the input will pass through both paths, however, the gradient will only update the weights of a single path.
- Copy the newly updated weights to the unused model. Now both models have equal weights.
- Repeat for next mini-batch.

At the end of this process, we have two identical models, each trained one-path-at-a-time. Our empirical results shown that mini-batches of 64 to 512 samples perform similar on all datasets and we chose 512 as it speeds up training.

This results in a more optimal, balanced network as the gradient is only able to change one path at a time, thus avoiding unwanted interactions. At the same time, the loss function is calculated over the whole, combined, network (notice that the input does pass through the whole network).

The interleaving architecture, originally introduced in [19], used parallel training on two RNNs for multimedia and textual features, and applied for video and product recommendations. However, our work is the first one to introduce it on text classification.

4 DATASET

Here, we first describe the features we extract. Then, we analyze the datasets used in the experiments and how they fit the scope of our analysis. Table 2 summarizes the basic properties (e.g., number of tweets, involved users) and the available metadata per dataset.

Dataset	Tweets	Classes	Users	WV	CF	UF	NF
Cyberbullying	6,091	8.5% Bully 5.5% Aggressive 86% Normal	891	✓	✓	✓	✓
Hateful	16,059	12% Racism 20% Sexism 68% None	1,236	✓	✓	✓	
Offensive	24,783	6% Hate 77% Offensive 17% Neither		✓	✓		
Sarcasm]	61,075	10.5% Sarcastic 89.5% Normal	60,255	✓	✓	✓	
Abusive	85,984	31.7% Abusive 5.7% Hate 62.6% Normal	81,448	✓	✓	✓	✓

Table 2: A descriptive analysis of the datasets with information about: the # of tweets/users, the distribution of the classes, and if we have the correspondent word vector (WV), content- (CF), user- (UF) and network-based (NF) metadata.

4.1 Feature Extraction

Text-based features: Word Vectors (WV). Are representations of words into a vector space (word2vec). As explained earlier, and using the GloVe method [29], the words from tweets are mapped, or embedded, into a high-dimensional vector of 200 dimensions.

Metadata Features. Similar to the work presented in [6] a set of metadata is considered, either content-, user-, or network-based, since they have been proven effective for a similar task. More specifically, these metadata are of three general categories:

Content-based (CF): some common and basic textual data are considered, frequently used on Twitter; namely the amount of hashtags and mentions of other users; how many emoticons exist in the tweet; how many words there are with uppercase letters only; the amount of URLs included. Moreover, tweets' sentiment (i.e., positive/negative score), specific emotions (i.e., anger, disgust, fear, joy, sadness, and surprise), and offensiveness scores are considered.

User-based (UF): for the author level, we extract a few basic metadata regarding his popularity (i.e., number of followers/friends). Also, we consider his activity based on the number of posted and favorited tweets, the subscribed lists, and the age of his account.

Network-based (NF): we analyze a user's network by considering his followers (i.e., someone who follows a user) and friends (i.e., someone who is followed by a user). Based on [6], the considered metadata indicate a user' popularity (i.e., the number of followers and friends, and the ratio of them), the extent to which a user tends to reciprocate the follower connections he receives, the power difference between a user and his mentions, the user's position in his network (i.e., hub, authority, eigenvector and closeness centrality), and his tendency to cluster with others (i.e., clustering coefficient).

4.2 Cyberbullying Dataset

The dataset provided by [6] was collected for the purpose of detecting two instances of abusive behavior on Twitter: cyberbullying and cyberaggression. In addition to a baseline, the authors collected a set of tweets between June and August 2016, using snowball sampling around the GamerGate controversy, which is known to

have produced many instances of cyberbullying and cyberaggression. The 9,484 tweets were grouped into 1,303 per user "batches" and labeled via crowdsourced workers into one of four categories: 1) bullying, 2) aggressive, 3) spam, or 4) normal. The authors are careful to differentiate between aggressive and bullying behavior. An aggressor was defined as "someone who posts at least one tweet or retweet with negative meaning, with the intent to harm or insult other users" and a bully was defined as "someone who posts multiple tweets or retweets with negative meaning for the same topic and in a repeated fashion, with the intent to harm or insult other users." The aggressive and bullying labels make up about 8% of the dataset, spam makes up about 1/3, with the remainder normal. For our purposes, we remove the batches labeled as spam, as they can be handled with more specialized techniques [6]. We note that the authors were focused on identifying bullying and aggressive users, but we are interested in classifying individual tweets and thus, we break up each batch into individual tweets, each labeled with whatever label their batch was given. In addition to word vectors (WV), this dataset includes all types of metadata, i.e., CF, UF, NF.

4.3 Hateful Dataset

The dataset provided by [42], is focused on racism and sexism. Collected over a two-month period, the authors manually searched for common hateful terms targeting groups, e.g., ethnicity, sexual orientation, gender, religion, etc. The search results were narrowed down to a set of users that seemed to espouse a lot of racist and sexist views. After collection, the data were preprocessed to remove Twitter specific content (e.g., retweets and mentions), punctuation, and all stop words except "not." The tweets were labeled as racist or sexist according to a set of criteria, e.g., if the tweet attacks, criticizes, or seeks to silence a minority, if it promotes hate speech or violence, or if there is use of sexist or racial slurs.

Data were manually annotated (not via crowdsourcing) and resulted in 2k racist and 3k sexist tweets, out of 16k total. This dataset is a good benchmark for the present work as it has been used by several similar studies, e.g., [2, 15, 28]. When working with this dataset, except from the word vectors (WV), we also employ both CF and UF metadata. We do not use network-related metadata (NF), due to time limitations (it takes a significant amount of computation and network effort to crawl users' profiles with Twitter API rate limits).

4.4 Offensive Dataset

Tweets characterized as hateful, offensive, or neither are provided by [10]. Here, hate speech is defined as language that is used to express hatred, insult, or to humiliate a targeted group or its members. Offensive language is less clearly defined as speech that uses offensive words, but does not necessarily have offensive meaning. Thus, this dataset makes the distinction that offensive language can be used in context that is not necessarily hateful. Of 80 million tweets they collected, a 25k were labeled by crowdsourced workers, with a resulting intercoder-agreement score of 92%. 77% of the tweets were labeled as offensive, with only 6% labeled as hateful. The authors only made the text of the tweets available, and so we have no metadata to use, other than WV.

4.5 Sarcasm Dataset

In the dataset by [31], tweets are characterized as sarcastic or non-sarcastic. Sarcasm, in this work, is defined as 'a way of using words that are the opposite of what you mean in order to be unpleasant to somebody or to make fun of them.' In some online settings such as Twitter or Facebook, with not enough context on the topic of discussion or interest to be civil, sarcasm can be considered impolite and even aggressive behavior. Though this dataset is slightly different from the rest, considering the task at hand, we believe it can bring a useful dimension to the plurality and complexity of abusive behavior, and can inform our method to detect such language.

The data collection was conducted based on self-described users' annotations. Specifically, the authors collected only tweets that contained the hashtags #sarcasm and #not and filtered out tweets that did not contain these hashtags at the end of them, to eliminate tweets that referred to sarcasm but were not sarcastic. They also removed non-english tweets, retweets, tweets with less than three words, and tweets that contained mentions or URLs.

The final dataset consists of almost $91k$ tweets, where 10% are sarcastic. Since not all data were still publicly available through Twitter API, we ended up with $60k$ - preserving the portion of sarcastic tweets. Finally, during the classification, we removed the #sarcasm and #not hashtags. Similar to the Hateful dataset, we employ WV, CF and UF, but no NF. We use the original highly imbalanced dataset since it adapts better to real cases. Hence, we compare our classification performance with the imbalanced results of the baseline.

4.6 Abusive Dataset

In the abusive dataset provided by [14] tweets are characterized as abusive, hateful, spam, and normal. To conclude to the aforementioned inappropriate speech categories, the authors initially proceeded with a series of annotation rounds where different types of abusive behaviors were considered, i.e., offensive, abusive, hateful speech, aggressive, bullying, spam, and normal. Then, an exploratory study took place, to identify the most representative labels related to the types of abusive content. Based on statistical analysis the authors either merged or removed a set of labels to conclude to the most representative set.

Overall, $100k$ tweets were characterized using the Figure Eight platform. Similar to the Cyberbullying dataset, the spam-related tweets were removed to proceed with the following analysis. For this dataset, apart from the WV, we also used all types of metadata, i.e., CF, UF, and NF. For the NF only the number of followers, friends, and the ratio of them was used, since the users' two hop friendship network was not available.

5 EVALUATION

Here, we describe in detail our experimental setup and results while testing the performance of our method on the different datasets used. All results shown here are based on 10-fold cross validation.

5.1 Experimental Setup

For our implementation we use Keras[2] with Theano[3] as back-end for the deep learning models implementation. We use the functional

[2]https://keras.io/
[3]http://deeplearning.net/software/theano/

API to implement our multi-input single-output model and run the experiments on a server equipped with three Tesla K40c GPUs.

In terms of training, we use *categorical cross-entropy* as loss function and *Adam* as the optimization function. A maximum of 100 epochs is allowed, but we also employ a separate validation set to perform *early stopping*: training is interrupted if the validation loss did not drop in 10 consecutive epochs and the weights of the best epoch are restored.

It is important to notice that the same model (with the same architecture, number of layers, number of units and parameters) is used for all datasets, as we want to demonstrate the performance of this architecture across different tasks. The performance of the algorithm might increase even further if the parameters are tuned specifically for each task (e.g., using a larger network when there are more training samples). Overall, the model, excluding the pre-trained word embeddings, contains approximately $250k$ trainable parameters (i.e., weights).

Finally, except from each dataset's state-of-the-art, we also compare our results with a basic Naive Bayes model, using the TF-IDF weights for each tweet. For this baseline, we only use the raw text. First, we perform some basic preprocessing of the data; we convert all characters to lowercase and remove all stop words for 14 frequently spoken languages, as well as some twitter-specific stop words. Finally, we tokenize the tweet based on some Twitter-specific markers (hashtags, URLs, and mentions) and punctuation. Afterwards, we experiment with both Porter and Snowball stemmers, lemmatization, keeping the most frequent words and the combinations of all the previously mentioned. We find that the most efficient step is keeping only the most frequent words. We also experiment on the amount of frequent words we need to keep and find that the best results are yielded using the top $10k$ words.

5.2 Experimental Results

In this section we present the classification performance of the proposed methodology on the five datasets. Next, we examine which are the inputs that contribute the most. Finally, we discuss how the different training strategies affect the classification performance.

Training methodology: We apply the same model over all five datasets and the results of AUC, Accuracy, Precision, Recall, and F1-score are summarized in Table 3. Here, we test the training methods discussed earlier to choose the best method to compare with the state-of-art. Firstly, we observe that training with the whole network at once (naive training) results to suboptimal performance (e.g., AUC of 0.94 in the cyberbullying dataset). The reason is that allowing the gradient descent to update both paths simultaneously might result in unwanted interactions between the two. For example, one path might converge faster than the other, dominating in the decisions. In fact, when we examine the standalone classifiers, we observe that the text classifier requires 25-40 epochs to converge whereas the metadata classifier only requires 7-12. By training the whole network together, the metadata side can start overfitting.

A step towards the right direction is to train each path separately, as individual classifiers, and then transfer the constructed features to a new classifier (transfer learning). This method slightly improves the results as it reduces the interactions between the two paths. Notice that, due to the fact that most of the network has been already trained, the additional layer converges after just 3-5 epochs.

	AUC	Acc.	Prec.	Rec.	F1
Cyberbullying Dataset (3 classes)					
DL-Baseline Naive Bayes	0.73	0.88	0.88	0.88	0.88
Chatzakou et al. 2017	0.91	0.91	0.90	0.92	0.91
DL-Metadata only	0.93	0.88	0.91	0.88	0.89
DL-Text only	0.92	0.89	0.91	0.89	0.89
DL-Text & Metadata (Naive Train.)	0.94	0.89	0.90	0.90	0.90
DL-Text & Metadata (Tran. Lear.)	0.95	0.90	0.92	0.90	0.90
DL-Text & Metadata (Tran. Lear. FT)	0.95	0.90	0.91	0.90	0.91
DL-Text & Metadata (Interleaved)	0.96	0.92	0.93	0.92	0.93
Hateful Dataset					
Baseline Naive Bayes	0.79	0.81	0.81	0.81	0.81
Waseem and Hovy 2016	-	-	0.74	0.73	0.78
Badjatiya et al. 2017	-	-	0.93	0.93	0.93
Pitsilis et al. 2018	-	-	0.93	0.93	0.93
DL-Metadata only	0.91	0.74	0.81	0.74	0.76
DL-Text only	0.93	0.83	0.84	0.83	0.83
DL-Text & Metadata (Naive Train.)	0.93	0.85	0.86	0.86	0.86
DL-Text & Metadata (Tran. Lear.)	0.95	0.85	0.86	0.85	0.85
DL-Text & Metadata (Tran. Lear. FT)	0.95	0.86	0.87	0.86	0.86
DL-Text & Metadata (Interleaved)	0.96	0.87	0.88	0.87	0.87
Offensive Dataset					
Baseline Naive Bayes	0.71	0.87	0.84	0.87	0.85
Davidson et al. 2017	0.87	0.89	0.91	0.9	0.9
DL-Metadata only	0.75	0.61	0.80	0.61	0.66
DL-Text only	0.91	0.87	0.89	0.87	0.88
DL-Text & Metadata (Naive Train.)	0.90	0.87	0.89	0.87	0.88
DL-Text & Metadata (Tran. Lear.)	0.91	0.87	0.89	0.87	0.88
DL-Text & Metadata (Tran. Lear. FT)	0.90	0.87	0.89	0.87	0.88
DL-Text & Metadata (Interleaved)	0.92	0.90	0.89	0.89	0.89
Sarcasm Dataset					
Baseline Naive Bayes	0.66	0.90	0.89	0.9	0.89
Rajadesingan, Zafarani, and Liu 2015	0.7	0.93	-	-	-
DL-Metadata only	0.96	0.92	0.94	0.92	0.92
DL-Text only	0.81	0.89	0.89	0.89	0.89
DL-Text & Metadata (Naive Train.)	0.97	0.96	0.96	0.96	0.96
DL-Text & Metadata (Tran. Lear.)	0.97	0.95	0.95	0.95	0.95
DL-Text & Metadata (Tran. Lear. FT)	0.97	0.95	0.95	0.95	0.95
DL-Text & Metadata (Interleaved)	0.98	0.97	0.96	0.97	0.97
Abusive Dataset					
Baseline Naive Bayes	0.80	0.39	0.66	0.39	0.31
DL-Text & Metadata (Interleaved)	0.93	0.84	0.85	0.85	0.85

Table 3: Final results of the baselines and our experiments, for each one of the datasets.

Finally, by employing alternate training (interleaved), we further improve the predictive power of the resulting model reaching 0.96 AUC in the cyberbullying. This shows that multi-input models such as this can benefit from alternate training. The reason is that this methodology avoids any interactions that might result when weights are updated simultaneously in both paths.

Classification performance: Across all datasets and abusive behaviors, the proposed classifier (Interleaved) outperforms in almost all of the cases both the baseline and the state-of-art, as reported in recent publications, for two reasons. First, the proposed approach that combines the raw text and the metadata achieves notably higher performance when compared to the ones using a single set of attributes, as it takes advantage of the additional information from the users' profile and network. This is consistent across all five datasets. Second, the word embeddings allow us to transfer features that were constructed over a billion of tweets, and it enables us to model complex tasks with fewer samples (such as this one).

Looking at the five datasets, on the cyberbullying dataset we observe that using a single set of attributes (text or metadata) we achieve better AUC (0.92 or 0.93, respectively) but worse accuracy (0.89 or 0.88, respectively) than the method proposed in the state-of-the-art (AUC 0.91, accuracy 0.91) [6]. However, the interleaved training of our model substantially outperforms the baseline (AUC 0.96, accuracy 0.92). Having said that, we need to mention here that the comparison with this dataset is not direct. The results reported on [6] are on user-level, while ours are on tweet-level. Therefore, while we can get an understanding on how well their data can be classified with our algorithm, we cannot parallelize the two cases. Nevertheless, the results we achieve on tweet-level are very high, which shows that our model distinguishes very well between the classes, regardless of the comparison.

On the sarcasm dataset, we largely outperform the previous results, as the existing work did not consider metadata. Specifically, we reach an AUC of 0.98 compared to 0.7 of the existing methodology, as in this case the text is not carrying significant information to detect if a tweet is sarcastic. However, the remaining metadata (user, network, content-level metadata) do reveal such information. In case of the hateful dataset, there was no AUC reported in the already existing works, but concerning the precision and recall values we are falling behind for 5% and 6%, respectively. When both text and metadata are combined we reach a precision and recall of 0.88 and 0.87, respectively, when compared to 0.81 of the baseline.

In the offensive dataset the interleaved model is able to reach an AUC of 0.92. Here, even though the precision and recall are similar to those presented in [10], our AUC and accuracy scores still outperform. This is due to the fact that we could not find any user or network metadata related to this dataset and, therefore, our classifier is only using the raw text and the content-based metadata.

Large-scale performance: We run the proposed method on the large-scale abusive dataset to evaluate its performance when executed on larger samples of tweets. Since we are the first that build upon such a dataset, we only compare the interleaved approach with a baseline algorithm, i.e., Naive Bayes. The overall AUC achieved is 0.93, which is significantly higher than the 0.80 achieved with the simple baseline, while also the precision and recall values of 0.85 highlight the efficiency of the proposed approach when executed on larger datasets, and in comparison to the baseline values of 0.31-0.66 for the same performance metrics.

Metadata importance: As described earlier, we use a number of metadata features extracted from the tweets and their authors, namely content-based, user-based, and network-based. These metadata play an important role on the improvement of the performance. When combined with the raw text, they substantially increase all the metrics. However, not all of them have the same impact on the performance (some are more essential than others). In order to determine how each one of these metadata affects our model, we experiment with the cyberbullying dataset and calculate their importance. The results on the AUC are presented in Table 4. We chose this dataset as we have all groups of metadata available (user, content, network, text) and, therefore, it is possible to examine how each of them contributes to the model. The results for other datasets are following similar trends and are omitted due to limited space.

Firstly, by examining individual metadata, we observe that models which are built with individual metadata result in the poorest performance. For example, network-level metadata are the least

Metadata Features	Acronym	AUC
Network Only	NF	0.641
Content Only	CF	0.799
User Only	UF	0.806
User & Content	UF+CF	0.887
Network & Content	NF+CF	0.908
Text Only	WV	0.915
User & Network	UF+NF	0.915
All-metadata Only	CF+UF+NF	0.923
Text & Content	WV+CF	0.930
Text & Network	WV+NF	0.931
Text & User & Content	WV+UF+CF	0.933
Text & Network & Content	WV+NF+CF	0.936
Text & User	WV+UF	0.938
Text & User & Network	WV+UF+NF	0.955
All	WV+CF+UF+NF	0.961

Table 4: Metadata Importance. The values are obtained using the Cyberbullying dataset.

descriptive (AUC of just 0.64) whereas content- and user-based are slightly better (AUC 0.8). By far, raw text is the best feature for this task, as it can lead to a model with particularly higher AUC of 0.91.

Furthermore, combining two or more metadata classes together (user, network, content) does increase performance. This indicates that the information provided is not overlapping and it all adds to better performance. When all the metadata are combined, we reach an AUC of 0.923 which is higher than any other metadata combination. Moreover, using all metadata does result in better classification when compared to just using the text, showing that these metadata carry at least as much predictive power as text does.

Nevertheless, the strongest models were built when text is combined with metadata showing how much the raw text contributes in this classification task. For example, just combining text with user-level metadata is enough to reach an impressive performance (0.94 AUC). Adding network data bumps the performance to 0.955.

Finally, the best performance is reached when all attributes are used. This also demonstrates the fact that the metadata information does not overlap the information that can be extracted from raw text, and this is why the proposed model can be quite powerful and outperforms the state-of-art models for these tasks.

Regarding the network performance, text was by far the most important factor decelerating the training of the whole model. Due to the content path being an RNN, training was eminently more slow than the case of experiments where this path was not used. All other metadata have been two orders of magnitude faster than text, without any significant differences between them. Therefore, there is no tradeoff decisions to be made on whether or not some of the metadata should be excluded for slowing down training.

6 GENERALIZING TO OTHER PLATFORMS: TOXIC BEHAVIOR IN ONLINE GAMING

Though in this work we primarily focus on Twitter to demonstrate how our unified approach works with the same set of features, the same methodology can be applied to other domains *with no modifications*. To demonstrate this, we run the same architecture over a dataset from a completely different domain. We acquired the dataset from the authors of [4] who built a classifier to detect toxic behavior in an online video game. Their dataset is collected from a crowdsourced system that presents reviewers with instances of

millions of matches, where toxic behavior is potentially exhibited. The match data include a variety of details such as the full in-game chat logs, players' in-game performance, the most common reason the match was reported for, the outcome of the match, etc. Matches are labeled for either *pardon* or *punish* by a jury of other players who cast votes in either direction.

From the 1 million individual matches provided to us, we extracted a set of features. Like the datasets used earlier in this work, we extract the chat logs of each potentially offending player. We also extract a set of domain specific metadata features (e.g., features that describe the offenders' performance, as well as the performance of other players, the outcome of the game, how many reports the match received, the most common report type, etc.). Each match is also labeled with the final decision of the crowdsourced worker (either, pardon or punish).

Even though, at a high level, this dataset is structured similarly to the five datasets presented earlier (i.e., it is divided into text based and domain specific categories), there are important differences. First, the text is *much* larger (on average, offenders use 2,500 words per match compared to just 30 words per tweet). Next, the domain specific nature of the metadata does not really have an analogue in the Twitter datasets we used. Finally, the language used in the chat logs themselves, while English, is littered with domain specific jargon. Thus, applying our architecture to this dataset makes a strong case for its portability to different domains.

In [4], the authors evaluated several sub-tasks, with varying degrees of difficulty. The first was the general problem of predicting whether a player will be pardoned or punished, where their best model had an AUC of 0.80. They also experimented with trying to predict only overwhelming decisions, an easier problem, and achieve AUCs of 0.88 and 0.75 for overwhelming pardon and punish decisions, respectively.

We tackled the more general problem by running the dataset through the model presented in our Architecture Section. We enabled an attention layer to deal with the length of the text, however, no other changes were made to the architecture. While we expected *reasonable* performance, we achieved an accuracy of 0.93 and an AUC of 0.89, beating the performance of even the easiest task presented in [4]. These results provide a strong indication that our architecture is suitable for finding abusive behavior in a wide variety of domains.

7 SUMMARY

Unified deep learning classifier is possible: In this work, we built and applied the exact same deep learning model architecture in all five datasets and demonstrated that it can efficiently handle each type of abusive behavior. While fine-tuning the classifier parameters for each dataset can squeeze some more performance, the proposed methodology does beat the current state of the art (in almost all cases) in each behavior detection. Importantly, our architecture can handle the imbalance of the various classes without special tuning, and especially for the minority classes.

All inputs help: We demonstrated how each of the attributes (text, user, network, content) contribute in each task, i.e., identification of specific type of abusive behavior. Our proposed architecture can seamlessly combine this input into a single classification model, without particular tuning.

Training methodology: Training a multi-input network is not straightforward. We introduced a methodology that alternates training between the two input paths to further increase performance in all datasets tested. We compared the proposed training paradigm with various other possible training methodologies (ensemble, feature transfer, concurrent training) and show that it can substantially outperform them.

Flexible to other data: In this paper, we show the ability of our approach to combine two different paths: text and metadata. However, one can simply concatenate more input paths to the architecture. For example, in an image classification problem, a CNN-based network can be used to extract image features and it could be joined with text information (tags and user comments) and image metadata (time and location taken, how many pictures the user has taken, the uploader's social network, etc.). Similarly, in an audio classification task, an audio path can be merged with text and metadata. We leave this exploration as future work.

Generalizing to other platforms: Finally, we showed that our proposed architecture can be easily applied, in a plug-and-play fashion, to detect abusive behavior in other online domains beyond Twitter. As an example, we presented results on detecting toxic behavior in an online gaming network, with superior performance over the state of art. We leave further explorations as future work.

REFERENCES

[1] Segun Taofeek Aroyehun and Alexander Gelbukh. 2018. Aggression detection in social media: Using deep neural networks, data augmentation, and pseudo labeling. In *Proceedings of TRAC-2018*.
[2] Pinkesh Badjatiya, Shashank Gupta, Manish Gupta, and Vasudeva Varma. 2017. Deep learning for hate speech detection in tweets. In *26th ACM WWW Companion*.
[3] Dzmitry Bahdanau, Kyunghyun Cho, and Yoshua Bengio. 2014. Neural machine translation by jointly learning to align and translate. *arXiv preprint arXiv:1409.0473* (2014).
[4] Jeremy Blackburn and Haewoon Kwak. 2014. STFU NOOB!: Predicting Crowdsourced Decisions on Toxic Behavior in Online Games. In *23rd ACM WWW*.
[5] Pete Burnap and Matthew L Williams. 2015. Cyber hate speech on twitter: An application of machine classification and statistical modeling for policy and decision making. *Policy & Internet* 7, 2 (2015), 223–242.
[6] Despoina Chatzakou, Nicolas Kourtellis, Jeremy Blackburn, Emiliano De Cristofaro, Gianluca Stringhini, and Athena Vakali. 2017. Mean Birds: Detecting Aggression and Bullying on Twitter. In *9th ACM WebScience*.
[7] Ying Chen, Yilu Zhou, Sencun Zhu, and Heng Xu. 2012. Detecting offensive language in social media to protect adolescent online safety. In *IEEE PASSAT & SocialCom*.
[8] Isobelle Clarke and Jack Grieve. 2017. Dimensions of Abusive Language on Twitter. In *Proceedings of the First Workshop on Abusive Language Online*.
[9] Sam Cook. 2018. Cyberbullying facts and statistics for 2016-2018. https://www.comparitech.com/internet-providers/cyberbullying-statistics/.
[10] Thomas Davidson, Dana Warmsley, Michael Macy, and Ingmar Weber. 2017. Automated Hate Speech Detection and the Problem of Offensive Language. In *ICWSM*.
[11] Karthik Dinakar, Roi Reichart, and Henry Lieberman. 2011. Modeling the detection of Textual Cyberbullying. *The Social Mobile Web* 11, 02 (2011).
[12] Nemanja Djuric, Jing Zhou, Robin Morris, Mihajlo Grbovic, Vladan Radosavljevic, and Narayan Bhamidipati. 2015. Hate speech detection with comment embeddings. In *24th ACM WWW*.
[13] Paula Fortuna, Ilaria Bonavita, and Sérgio Nunes. [n. d.]. Merging datasets for hate speech classification in Italian. ([n. d.]).
[14] Antigoni-Maria Founta, Constantinos Djouvas, Despoina Chatzakou, Ilias Leontiadis, Jeremy Blackburn, Gianluca Stringhini, Athena Vakali, Michael Sirivianos, and Nicolas Kourtellis. 2018. Large Scale Crowdsourcing and Characterization of Twitter Abusive Behavior. In *12th AAAI ICWSM*.
[15] Björn Gambäck and Utpal Kumar Sikdar. 2017. Using Convolutional Neural Networks to Classify Hate-Speech. In *1st Workshop on Abusive Language Online*.
[16] Hariani and Imam Riadi. 2017. Detection Of Cyberbullying On Social Media Using Data Mining Techniques. *International Journal of Computer Science and Information Security* 15, 3 (2017), 244.

[17] Kaiming He, Xiangyu Zhang, Shaoqing Ren, and Jian Sun. 2016. Deep residual learning for image recognition. In *Proceedings of the IEEE conference on computer vision and pattern recognition*.
[18] Alex Hern. 2016. Did trolls cost Twitter $3.5bn and its sale? https://www.theguardian.com/technology/2016/oct/18/did-trolls-cost-twitter-35bn.
[19] Balázs Hidasi, Massimo Quadrana, Alexandros Karatzoglou, and Domonkos Tikk. 2016. Parallel recurrent neural network architectures for feature-rich session-based recommendations. In *10th ACM RecSys*.
[20] Akshita Jha and Radhika Mamidi. 2017. When does a compliment become sexist? Analysis and classification of ambivalent sexism using twitter data. In *2nd Workshop on NLP and Computational Social Science*.
[21] Armand Joulin, Edouard Grave, Piotr Bojanowski, and Tomas Mikolov. 2016. Bag of tricks for efficient text classification. *arXiv preprint arXiv:1607.01759* (2016).
[22] Irene Kwok and Yuzhou Wang. 2013. Locate the Hate: Detecting Tweets against Blacks.
[23] Daniel Lowd. 2017. Can Facebook use AI to fight online abuse? http://theconversation.com/can-facebook-use-ai-to-fight-online-abuse-95203.
[24] Estefanía Lozano, Jorge Cedeño, Galo Castillo, Fabricio Layedra, Henry Lasso, and Carmen Vaca. 2017. Requiem for online harassers: Identifying racism from political tweets. In *4th IEEE Conference on eDemocracy & eGovernment (ICEDEG)*.
[25] Shervin Malmasi and Marcos Zampieri. 2018. Challenges in discriminating profanity from hate speech. *Journal of Experimental & Theoretical Artificial Intelligence* 30, 2 (2018), 187–202.
[26] Yashar Mehdad and Joel R Tetreault. 2016. Do Characters Abuse More Than Words?. In *SIGDIAL*.
[27] Chikashi Nobata, Joel Tetreault, Achint Thomas, Yashar Mehdad, and Yi Chang. 2016. Abusive language detection in online user content. In *25th ACM WWW Companion*.
[28] Ji Ho Park and Pascale Fung. 2017. One-step and Two-step Classification for Abusive Language Detection on Twitter. *arXiv preprint arXiv:1706.01206* (2017).
[29] Jeffrey Pennington, Richard Socher, and Christopher D. Manning. 2014. GloVe: Global Vectors for Word Representation. In *EMNLP*.
[30] Georgios K Pitsilis, Heri Ramampiaro, and Helge Langseth. 2018. Effective hate-speech detection in Twitter data using recurrent neural networks. *Applied Intelligence* 48, 12 (2018), 4730–4742.
[31] Ashwin Rajadesingan, Reza Zafarani, and Huan Liu. 2015. Sarcasm detection on twitter: A behavioral modeling approach. In *8th ACM WSDM*.
[32] Matthew Rozsa. 2016. Twitter trolls are now abusing the company?s bottom line. https://www.salon.com/2016/10/19/twitter-trolls-are-now-abusing-the-companys-bottom-line/.
[33] Twitter Safety. 2017. Enforcing new rules to reduce hateful conduct and abusive behavior. https://blog.twitter.com/official/en_us/topics/company/2017/safetypoliciesdec2017.html.
[34] Huascar Sanchez and Shreyas Kumar. 2011. Twitter bullying detection. *NSDI*.
[35] Johannes Schäfer. 2018. HIIwiStJS at GermEval-2018: Integrating Linguistic Features in a Neural Network for the Identification of Offensive Language in Microposts. *Austrian Academy of Sciences, Vienna September 21, 2018* (2018).
[36] Anna Schmidt and Michael Wiegand. 2017. A survey on hate speech detection using natural language processing. In *5th SocialNLP*.
[37] Elizabeth Schulze. 2019. EU says Facebook, Google and Twitter are getting faster at removing hate speech online. goo.gl/XPQzGC.
[38] Vinay Singh, Aman Varshney, Syed Sarfaraz Akhtar, Deepanshu Vijay, and Manish Shrivastava. 2018. Aggression Detection on Social Media Text Using Deep Neural Networks. In *Proceedings of ALW2*.
[39] Naftali Tishby and Noga Zaslavsky. 2015. Deep learning and the information bottleneck principle. In *IEEE Information Theory Workshop*.
[40] William Warner and Julia Hirschberg. 2012. Detecting hate speech on the world wide web. In *2nd Workshop on Language in Social Media*.
[41] Zeerak Waseem, Thomas Davidson, Dana Warmsley, and Ingmar Weber. 2017. Understanding Abuse: A Typology of Abusive Language Detection Subtasks. *arXiv preprint arXiv:1705.09899* (2017).
[42] Zeerak Waseem and Dirk Hovy. 2016. Hateful Symbols or Hateful People? Predictive Features for Hate Speech Detection on Twitter.. In *SRW@ HLT-NAACL*.
[43] Guang Xiang, Bin Fan, Ling Wang, Jason Hong, and Carolyn Rose. 2012. Detecting offensive tweets via topical feature discovery over a large scale twitter corpus. In *21st ACM CIKM*.
[44] Ziqi Zhang, David Robinson, and Jonathan Tepper. 2018. Detecting Hate Speech on Twitter Using a Convolution-GRU Based Deep Neural Network. In *European Semantic Web Conference*. Springer.

8 ACKNOWLEDGMENTS

The authors acknowledge research funding from the European Union's Horizon 2020 research and innovation programme under the Marie Skłodowska-Curie ENCASE project, Grant Agreement No. 691025.

The Web We Mix: Benevolent AIs for a Resilient Web

Fabien Gandon
Fabien.Gandon@inria.fr
Inria, Université Côte d'Azur, CNRS, I3S, France
Sophia Antipolis, France

ABSTRACT

The Web was initially perceived and used as a globally distributed hypertext space for humans. But from its inception, the Web has always been more: its hypermedia architecture is in fact linking programs world-wide through remote procedure calls [12]. In parallel to the social expansion of the Web we witnessed in the 90s, a more hidden but as important extension started very early to make it more and more machine friendly [4] supporting the publication and consumption by software agents of worldwide linked data published on a semantic Web [13]. The Web managed to become at the same time the largest social application on earth and the default and most adopted architecture and framework for internet applications. It is now a space where more than three billion users interact with billions of pages and numerous software. These evolution trends of the Web were joined by many others (mobile Web, Web of things, etc.)[1] and as a result the Web became a collaborative space for natural and artificial intelligence distributed and situated everywhere. Nowadays when a link is followed – when a call is made on the Web – the answer can come from an arbitrary source of knowledge or form of intelligence, be it natural or artificial. The Web we weaved effectively is a universal social and programming space linking data, programs, users,... everything in a unified and standardized architecture, for better and for worse, so Web science needs to speak now.

This Web we mix should pursue a synergistic connection of intelligent forms for the good of the Web and society. If "The Web We Want [is] a public good[,] a basic right, and (...) a catalyst for social justice and human rights."[2] ensuring, freedom of expression, access, neutrality and privacy to everyone, diversity, decentralization and openness, then we need AI on the Web to be aiming for that by design.

In this keynote I will mention a number of works from the research team Wimmics[3] (pronounced "we mix") that has been studying the challenges in bridging social semantics and formal semantics on the Web [15]. These contributions address some of the challenges in connecting AIs to the Web.

The Web is already populated by many bots and a number of classical tasks we perform on the Web can benefit from AI e.g. to ease search [7], support exploration [21, 24] and browsing, optimize

[1] see W3C Rec. https://www.w3.org/TR/

[2] https://webwewant.org/about/

[3] https://team.inria.fr/wimmics/

WebSci '19, June 30–July3, 2019, Boston, MA, USA
© 2019 Copyright held by the owner/author(s).
ACM ISBN 978-1-4503-6202-3/19/06.
https://doi.org/10.1145/3292522.3329406

crawling [19], integrate data sources [23], etc. There is also a special mutual benefit in the relation between AI and the data(sets) found on the Web. AI can of course help us extract, curate, enrich, share and maintain knowledge graphs [26]. Inversely AI can be fed by data from the Web to learn and reason e.g. to provide external knowledge to improve robots interactions [6] and behaviors [27] or to improve data analysis and predictions in very different domains such as smart cities [20] or health-care [18].

With the advent of the Web, we individually have to face humanity in all its scale and diversity and AI can help us, users, scale to the Web scale. Goal-driven Web bots can actively participate to the online activity and, for instance, prevent bullying and harassment [1]. The coupling of AI and the Web has the potential to take our interactions to the next level of intelligence [16] and to take into account complex aspects of them such as the role of emotions in online debates [3]. An important goal for Web Science therefore is the production of AIs benevolent-by-design for the good of the Web and society. For instance, educational AI could help educate Web users in many domains [25] including the many dimensions of Web itself (technical, social, economical, etc.).

The more we study intelligence, the more diversified it becomes: we identify ever more forms of intelligence and smart behaviours. The Web can both benefit and contribute to this. First the Web is a great tool to study this diversity of intelligence and the multidisciplinary nature of Web Science [11] puts it in an ideal position to explore and expand the forms of intelligence. Inversely, the Web requires a diversity of forms of intelligence to address the many types of diversity we find online (content, users, contexts, tasks, usages, resources, etc.). By nature and to address its expansion and evolution, the Web needs advances in distributed intelligence and situated intelligence. This study must include different forms of natural intelligence (e.g. people, connected animals, connected plants) and different forms of artificial intelligence (reasoning, learning, inducing, etc.) [14]. The challenge will also be to study their interactions with the resources of the Web (linked pages, linked data, connected objects, etc.) [8]. Distributed AI and the multi-agent systems have a rendezvous with the Web and its sciences [10] to study and design hybrid societies of natural intelligence and artificial intelligence on the Web and their normative rules [17].

This research program can also be seen as making Web Science a meeting point between two research fields born in the 50s: "AI" for Artificial Intelligence [22] and "IA" for Intelligence Amplification [2] and Intelligence Augmentation [9]. The long term potential of the Web is to augment and link all forms of intelligence and we need to prepare for a time when we will be "All Watched Over by a Web of Loving Grace" [5]

CCS CONCEPTS

• **Information systems** → **World Wide Web**; • **Computing methodologies** → **Artificial intelligence**.

KEYWORDS

web, web science, artificial intelligence, AI

BIOGRAPHY

Fabien's PhD in 2002 [10] at Inria pioneered the joint use of distributed artificial intelligence (AI) and semantic Web to manage a variety of data sources and users above a Web architecture. Then, at Carnegie Mellon University, he proposed an AI method to enforce privacy preferences in querying and reasoning about personal data. In

Figure 1: Fabien Gandon

2004, as a researcher at Inria, he started to study models and algorithms to integrate social media and knowledge based AI systems on the Web. In 2012 he became the representative of Inria at W3C and founded Wimmics, a joint research team between Univesité Côte d'Azur, Inria, CNRS and I3S, on bridging social and formal semantics on the Web. In 2014, Fabien became a research director (DR). He supervised 10 PhD, chaired major international conferences (e.g. WWW 2012 and 2018, ESWC 2015, ISWC 2019) and authored 23 journal papers, 136 conference and workshop papers, 2 books and 11 book chapters. In 2015 he initiated a series of bilingual MOOCs on the national FUN platform on semantic Web and linked data. In 2017 he established and became the director of the joint research laboratory between Inria and the QWANT search engine and he also became responsible for the research convention between the Ministry of Culture and Inria. In 2018 Fabien became Vice Head of Science of Inria Sophia Antipolis – Méditerranée. http://fabien.info

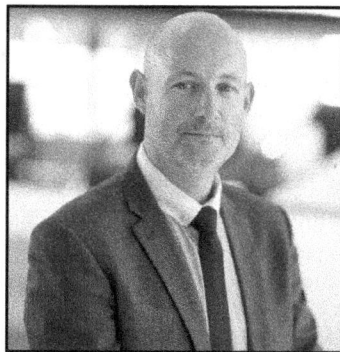

REFERENCES

[1] Pinar Arslan, Michele Corazza, Elena Cabrio, and Serena Villata. 2019. Overwhelmed by Negative Emotions? Maybe You Are Being Cyber-bullied!. In *SAC 2019 - The 34th ACM/SIGAPP Symposium On Applied Computing*. Cyprus.
[2] Ross Ashby. 1956. Design for an intelligence-amplifier. *Automata studies* 400 (1956), 215–233.
[3] Sahbi Benlamine, Maher Chaouachi, Serena Villata, Elena Cabrio, Claude Frasson, and Fabien Gandon. 2015. Emotions in Argumentation: an Empirical Evaluation. In *International Joint Conference on Artificial Intelligence, IJCAI 2015 (Proceedings of the Twenty-Fourth International Joint Conference on Artificial Intelligence, IJCAI 2015)*. Buenos Aires, Argentina, 156–163. https://hal.inria.fr/hal-01152966
[4] Tim Berners-Lee, Robert Cailliau, Ari Luotonen, Henrik Frystyk Nielsen, and Arthur Secret. 1994. The World-Wide Web. *Commun. ACM* 37, 8 (Aug. 1994), 76–82. https://doi.org/10.1145/179606.179671
[5] Richard Brautigan. 1968. All watched over by machines of loving grace. *TriQuarterly* 11 (1968), 194.
[6] Michel Buffa, Catherine Faron Zucker, Thierry Bergeron, and Hatim Aouzal. 2016. Semantic Web Technologies for improving remote visits of museums, using a mobile robot. Proceedings of the ISWC 2016 Posters & Demonstrations Track co-located with 15th International Semantic Web Conference (ISWC2016). https://hal.inria.fr/hal-01400924 Poster.
[7] Elena Cabrio, Julien Cojan, Alessio Palmero Aprosio, Bernardo Magnini, Alberto Lavelli, and Fabien Gandon. 2012. QAKiS: an Open Domain QA System based

on Relational Patterns. International Semantic Web Conference, ISWC 2012. https://hal.inria.fr/hal-01171115 Poster.
[8] Andrei Ciortea, Simon Mayer, Fabien Gandon, Olivier Boissier, Alessandro Ricci, and Antoine Zimmermann. 2019. A Decade in Hindsight: The Missing Bridge Between Multi-Agent Systems and the World Wide Web. In *AAMAS 2019 - 18th International Conference on Autonomous Agents and Multiagent Systems*. Montréal, Canada, 5p. https://hal-emse.ccsd.cnrs.fr/emse-02070625
[9] Douglas C Engelbart. 1962. *Augmenting human intellect: A Conceptual Framework*. SRI Summary Report AFOSR-3223. Stanford Research Institute.
[10] Fabien Gandon. 2002. *Distributed Artificial Intelligence And Knowledge Management: Ontologies And Multi-Agent Systems For A Corporate Semantic Web*. Theses. Université Nice Sophia Antipolis. https://tel.archives-ouvertes.fr/tel-00378201
[11] Fabien Gandon. 2014. The three 'W' of the World Wide Web call for the three 'M' of a Massively Multidisciplinary Methodology. In *WEBIST 2014 - 10th International Conference (Web Information Systems and Technologies)*, Valérie Monfort and Karl-Heinz Krempels (Eds.), Vol. 226. Springer International Publishing, Barcelona, Spain. https://doi.org/10.1007/978-3-319-27030-2
[12] Fabien Gandon. 2017. For everything: Tim Berners-Lee, winner of the 2016 Turing award for having invented… the Web. *1024 : Bulletin de la Société Informatique de France* 11 (Sept. 2017), 21. https://hal.inria.fr/hal-01843967
[13] Fabien Gandon. 2018. A Survey of the First 20 Years of Research on Semantic Web and Linked Data. *Revue des Sciences et Technologies de l'Information - Série ISI : Ingénierie des Systèmes d'Information* (Dec. 2018). https://doi.org/10.3166/ISI.23.3-4.11-56
[14] Fabien Gandon. 2019. *Web Science, Artificial Intelligence and Intelligence Augmentation (in Dagstuhl Perspectives Workshop 18262 - 10 Years of Web Science: Closing The Loop)*. Other. Dagstuhl. https://hal.inria.fr/hal-01976768
[15] Fabien Gandon, Michel Buffa, Elena Cabrio, Olivier Corby, Catherine Faron Zucker, Alain Giboin, Nhan Le Thanh, Isabelle Mirbel, Peter Sander, Andrea G. B. Tettamanzi, and Serena Villata. 2013. Challenges in Bridging Social Semantics and Formal Semantics on the Web. In *5h International Conference, ICEIS 2013 (Lecture Notes in Business Information Processing)*, Hammoudi, S., Cordeiro, J., Maciaszek, L.A., Filipe, and J. (Eds.), Vol. 190. Springer, Angers, France, 3–15.
[16] Fabien Gandon and Alain Giboin. 2017. Paving the WAI: Defining Web-Augmented Interactions.. In *Web Science 2017 (WebSci17)*. Troy, NY, United States, 381 – 382. https://doi.org/10.1038/nbt0609-508
[17] Fabien Gandon, Guido Governatori, and Serena Villata. 2017. Normative Requirements as Linked Data. In *JURIX 2017 - The 30th international conference on Legal Knowledge and Information Systems* . Luxembourg, Luxembourg, 1–10. https://hal.archives-ouvertes.fr/hal-01643769
[18] Raphaël Gazzotti, Catherine Faron Zucker, Fabien Gandon, Virginie Lacroix-Hugues, and David Darmon. 2019. Injecting Domain Knowledge in Electronic Medical Records to Improve Hospitalization Prediction. In *ESWC 2019 - The 16th European Semantic Web Conference*. Portorož, Slovenia. https://hal.archives-ouvertes.fr/hal-02064421
[19] Hai Huang and Fabien Gandon. 2019. Learning URI Selection Criteria to Improve the Crawling of Linked Open Data. In *ESWC2019 - The 16th Extended Semantic Web Conference*. Portoroz, Slovenia. https://hal.inria.fr/hal-02073854
[20] Freddy Lécué, Simone Tallevi-Diotallevi, Jer Hayes, Robert Tucker, Veli Bicer, Marco Luca Sbodio, and Pierpaolo Tommasi. 2014. Smart traffic analytics in the semantic web with STAR-CITY: Scenarios, system and lessons learned in Dublin City. *Journal of Web Semantics* 27-28 (2014), 26–33.
[21] Nicolas Marie. 2012. *Rough Paths, Gaussian Processes and Applications*. Theses. Université Paul Sabatier - Toulouse III. https://tel.archives-ouvertes.fr/tel-00783931
[22] John McCarthy, Marvin Minsky, Nathaniel Rochester, and Claude Shannon. 1955. A proposal for the Dartmouth summer research project on artificial intelligence. http://raysolomonoff.com/dartmouth/boxa/dart564props.pdf
[23] Franck Michel, Catherine Faron Zucker, Olivier Corby, and Fabien Gandon. 2019. Enabling Automatic Discovery and Querying of Web APIs at Web Scale using Linked Data Standards. In *WWW 2019 - LDOW/LDDL Workshop of the World Wide Web Conference*. San Francisco, United States. https://doi.org/10.1145/3308560.3317073
[24] Emilie Palagi. 2018. *Evaluating exploratory search engines : designing a set of user-centered methods based on a modeling of the exploratory search process*. Theses. Université Côte d'Azur. https://tel.archives-ouvertes.fr/tel-01976017
[25] Oscar Rodríguez Rocha, Catherine Faron Zucker, and Alain Giboin. 2018. Extraction of Relevant Resources and Questions from DBpedia to Automatically Generate Quizzes on Specific Domains. In *International Conference on Intelligent Tutoring Systems 2018*. Montreal, Canada. https://hal.inria.fr/hal-01811490
[26] Andrea G. B. Tettamanzi, Catherine Faron Zucker, and Fabien Gandon. 2015. Dynamically Time-Capped Possibilistic Testing of SubClassOf Axioms Against RDF Data to Enrich Schemas. In *The 8th International Conference on Knowledge Capture, K-CAP 2015*. Palisades, NY, United States.
[27] Jay Young, Valerio Basile, Lars Kunze, Elena Cabrio, and Nick Hawes. 2016. Towards Lifelong Object Learning by Integrating Situated Robot Perception and Semantic Web Mining. In *Proceedings of the European Conference on Artificial Intelligence (ECAI) 2016 conference*. The Hague, Netherlands.

Empowering Borrowers in their Choice of Lenders: Decoding Service Quality from Customer Complaints

Aniruddha M. Godbole
agodbole@indiana.edu
School of Informatics, Computing, and Engineering
Indiana University
Bloomington, Indiana

David J. Crandall
djcran@indiana.edu
School of Informatics, Computing, and Engineering
Indiana University
Bloomington, Indiana

ABSTRACT

When shopping for lenders, most consumers choose a financial institution based on just a few key factors: the interest rate, the distance to the lender's nearest branch, an existing relationship with the lender, and the reputation of that lender. But most consumers fail to consider an important element that will be key to their long-term satisfaction: whether the customer service provided by the lender is commensurate with the price. Our underlying assumption in this paper is that a consumer's personality traits are associated with the issues they will face. We use state-of-the-art cross-domain word vector space mapping and representative trait vectors in this space to estimate ten personality traits corresponding to each text and use topic modeling for finding the topics in a complaint. We then use two modified collaborative topic regression methods to create two complaint topic trait spaces for each lender, and test our underlying assumption by using statistical tests for this unsupervised learning problem in three cases: mortgage loans, student loans, and payday loans. We propose that lenders could be recommended for a specific user by analyzing this space, recommending a lender with the fewest number of complaints per retail customer of that lender in the complaint space neighborhood of the customer. We suggest future work that may be undertaken for the three types of loans, including the possibility that lenders evaluate their service from a customer's perspective to track customer satisfaction over time, and extensions to other parts of the service economy.

CCS CONCEPTS

• **Information systems** → **Recommender systems**; *Data analytics*; • **Social and professional topics** → User characteristics; • **Human-centered computing** → Collaborative and social computing.

KEYWORDS

Complaint, finance, customer service, personality traits, cross-domain word vector mapping, recommender system, collaborative topic regression, unsupervised learning

ACM Reference Format:
Aniruddha M. Godbole and David J. Crandall. 2019. Empowering Borrowers in their Choice of Lenders: Decoding Service Quality from Customer Complaints. In *11th ACM Conference on Web Science (WebSci '19), June 30–July 3, 2019, Boston, MA, USA*. ACM, New York, NY, USA, 8 pages. https://doi.org/10.1145/3292522.3326021

1 INTRODUCTION

Historically, lenders have either not been evaluated by their customers for quality of service, or they have been assessed using aggregate-level reports based on subjective ratings in surveys. The U.S. Consumer Financial Protection Bureau [12] reports that almost half of all borrowers do not shop around when arranging a mortgage loan. In the absence of an easy way to compare lenders based on their customer service, consumers tend to compare based just on price (interest rate), the existence of a relationship with the lender, the distance to the nearest branch, and the reputation of the lender [12]. In general, whether for mortgages or other types of loans, there is almost no emphasis on customer service [6, 14, 53].

There is thus a need to create tools and information for consumers to make better-informed decisions based on the quality of service provided by a lender, and how it will conform with their own expectations. While machine learning has been applied extensively to the financial sector, we are not aware of any work that analyzes complaints from a customer's perspective. Even the customer-centric use cases of credit scoring, client-facing chatbots, and selling of insurance to customers [10] are actually formulated from a lender's perspective.

Our goal in this paper is to take a first step towards testing whether it is possible to automatically recommend lenders to a particular consumer based on which lenders are least likely to lead to consumer complaints. To do this, we apply machine learning and data mining techniques to a large-scale dataset of consumer complaints, looking for patterns (topics) in them. We also analyze a large-scale dataset of Twitter text, trying to infer personalities traits of individual users from it. We then look for connections between these personality profiles and the complaints for different lenders. We are not trying to resolve the complaints [24] better or faster. Rather, our goal is to try to identify lenders that are likely to give fewer reasons for making complaints.

1.1 Research Questions and Scope

In particular, we investigate two specific research questions:

(1) Is the association among the set of personality traits and complaint topics different for each lender?

(2) Is it feasible to make personalized recommendations to customers about suitable lenders based on customer service?

To study these questions, we use three specific datasets: (1) the Consumer Financial Protection Bureau (CFPB) Complaints Dataset (as of 31 July 2018) [2], (2) the TREC 2011 Microblog Dataset [41], and (3) the World Well-Being Project's [52] correlations between personality traits and words. We restrict our attention to three specific types of loans: mortgage loans, student loans, and payday loans. We do not consider temporal modeling aspects, nor do we benchmark the proxy personality trait scores. The impact of lenders selling their loans and borrowers refinancing their loan is considered to neutralize each other — for groups of customers and groups of lenders — as a simplifying assumption.

1.2 Contributions

Our main contributions are:

(1) We show it is feasible to use machine learning on a publicly available complaints dataset to empower retail customers with personalized recommendations about service providers based on their customer service;

(2) We find a general association between the set of personality traits and complaint topics in the case of payday loans, and show how lenders differ through visualizations of the latent space;

(3) We undertake domain adaptation within the English language using Cross-Domain Word Vector Space Mapping;

(4) We propose to recommend lenders based on analyzing the neighborhood around the customer in latent topic space;

(5) We propose to use a large number of topics that include a few that are semantically interpretable by the consumer;

(6) We compare different techniques for building a joint space between the topics and and personality traits; and

(7) We make our code publicly available at https://github.com/godboleam/service-quality.

2 RELATED WORK

So far, the focus in work related to complaint data has generally been on the lender's usage of the data [47, 50]. Financial firms have reportedly lobbied against a publicly available complaints dataset [19]. The focus has been to look at the dataset from the lenders' perspective [34] even though the intent of the CFPB has clearly been in favor of giving primacy to the interests of the borrower. An unspoken adversarial relationship between lenders and customers is unnecessary and perhaps short-sighted [9]. Given that the CFPB oversight seems to have not affected the overall volume of mortgage lending [23] there may not be a trade-off between lenders' interest and customers' interests even in the short-term.

Customers often regret — when they even exercise a choice — an interest rate-based selection of a lender [29]. J.D. Power Ratings says top-performing banks have fewer reported complaints and problems [30]. Their 2017 study was based on more than 5,784 responses. Deloitte suggests modification to products and processes based on complaint analysis [20], and this development is encouraging even though it is from a lender's perspective.

Despite our best efforts we could not find prior literature that explores the CFPB complaints dataset for either exploring the association between personality traits and complaint topics, or for making personalized recommendations to customers based on a lender's customer service.

3 METHODS

Our goal is to analyze a large-scale, publicly-available dataset of complaints against lenders, and to develop a word embedding space to connect the complaints to personality traits inferred through analyzing consumers' Twitter feeds. A major challenge in making this connection is that the style and vocabulary of complaints is typically very different from those of informal tweets. Moreover, we need complaints topics that are interpretable by humans, and we need to evaluate the proposed methodology without labeled ground truth data.

Our overall approach is as follows. We created word embeddings separately for the complaints text and the tweets text. Only the English tweets were considered. We then used a cross-domain word vector space mapping so that domain adaptation helps in two cases: for finding word vectors of words that are correlated with the five personality traits (on bipolar scales), and for finding the proxy traits for a Twitter users. We separately use topic modeling for the complaints dataset (without using the word vectors as [21] was not conclusive about using word vectors for topic modeling). We use the probability of that topic as a score for that topic in the complaint. We then use modified Collaborative Topic Regression (CTR) by two methods to build a joint space between complaint topics and personality traits.

We now describe the approach in more detail.

3.1 Definitions

We define a *complaint user* to be a retail customer who has made a complaint in our dataset. A *Twitter user* is a prospective borrower or someone who has sought a personalized recommendation in the past. We assume that the text of the tweets of a user reflect something about the person's personality. The *proxy trait scores* are the ten scores associated with the five personality traits, on bipolar scales. The *complaint language* is based on the complaint narrative texts in the CFPB complaints dataset. This includes all complaints irrespective of the type of the loan. The *Tweet language* is based on the tweet text (detected as English) in the TREC 2011 Microblog Dataset. Although complaints and tweets are written in the same language (English), the styles and vocabularies are quite different, as if they were different dialects. We build a *Complaint Topic Trait Space* to connect complaints and personality traits.

3.2 Data

We use three main datasets, collected as of July 31, 2018.

3.2.1 Complaints data. Around 1.5 million complaints [15] have been sent to the CFPB, and the publicly available dataset has 1,087,269 (1.08 million). This is probably the largest dataset of its kind. About 30% (0.307 million) have accompanying narratives or unstructured complaint text. We believe this complaints dataset can be considered a reasonable proxy for measuring customer service. It is believed that the pain for a loss is felt much more than the joy felt for a similar magnitude of gain [31]. This asymmetrical relationship implies that complaints are very valuable for evaluating customer service, and a recent JD Power survey reached this conclusion for the financial sector in particular [30]. A variety of negative emotions are seen in almost half of the complaint narratives about lenders [22].

We use the complaints data independently to generate word embeddings and for topic modeling. In the case of the word embeddings, we apply the following pre-processing steps: (1) convert to lower case, (2) drop most punctuation and symbols (but retain ', $, and %), (3) replace all numbers with ∗, (4) replace all tokens such as XXXXX (which indicate private information that was scrubbed by the CFPB before releasing the data) with &, (5) remove extra spaces, and (6) use utf-8 encoding. We then apply the fastText [11] Python wrapper to create the word embeddings.

The complaints dataset does not include unique identifiers for each customer, so we cannot detect if a single customer makes multiple complaints. We thus make the (naive) assumption that each customer in the dataset has made exactly one complaint.

3.2.2 World Well-Being Project data. We use the gender and age-controlled list of 1-gram word correlations for the five personality traits (on bipolar scales) from the World Well-Being Project [52]. Most of these are words used in informal English, like the language often used on Twitter.

3.2.3 Tweets data. We use the TREC 2011 Microblog dataset [41], which had 10,617,146 (10.6mn) tweets as of mid-2018. The tweets corpus was downloaded using Twitter Tools [39] and the TREC 2011 Twitter Collection Downloader [5]. Language detection done using a port of Google's language detection library to Python [3] indicated that around two-thirds of the tweets are not in English. Only the English tweets were considered for creating the tweet language word embeddings, and we used the following preprocessing before applying fastText [11]: (1) drop most symbols and punctuation (but retain ', !, and @), (2) replace all URLs by ˆ, (3) replace all numbers by ∗, (4) replace all Twitter handles with @, (5) remove extra spaces, and (6) use utf-8 encoding. We believe that our collection of over one million tweets will probably suffice for building word embeddings, as more will likely not give significantly superior results [38].

3.3 Word Vector Space and Cross-Domain Word Vector Space

We address the challenge of inferring personality traits from complaint and Twitter text using cross-domain word vector space mapping, and by using personality trait proxies (see Section 3.5) in this same space. The fastText Python wrapper was used to create a complaint language word vector space and a tweet language word vector space, both of 200 dimensions. Earlier uses of cross-domain vector spaces has focused on unsupervised translation between two languages [8, 37]. We used the state-of-the-art Vecmap opensource project code [1] to create a mapping from the complaint language space to the tweet language space. This algorithm includes Cross-domain Similarity Local Scaling (CSLS) proposed by Lample et al. [37] We used the 'identical' parameter to specify that words in the tweet text that are common to the complaint text ought to have

	CFPB Classification as available in the dataset	
Our Classification	Product	Sub-product
Mortgage loan	Mortgage	Conventional home mortgage Conventional fixed mortgage Conventional adjustable mortgage (ARM)
	Debt collection	Mortgage Mortgage debt
Student loan	Student loan	Federal student loan servicing Private student loan Non-federal student loan
	Debt collection	Federal student loan Federal student loan debt Non-federal student loan Private student loan debt
Payday loan	Payday loan	—
	Debt collection	Payday loan Payday loan debt

Table 1: Mapping from CFPB loan type classifications to our three classifications (mortgage, payday, student loan).

the same meaning. The Vecmap output word2vec [42] embeddings were consumed using the gensim [46] library.

3.4 Topic Modeling of Complaints

Out of the 1.08 million complaints in the dataset, the total number of complaints with a narrative is 307,120. Of these, 128,314 are such that the lender's response is not disputed by the customer. We used only the undisputed complaints for topic modeling, since these are more likely to be genuine complaints and thus higher-quality data. We considered three types of loans, mortgage loans, student loans, and payday loans.

The CFPB's classification and nomenclature of products and issue options underwent a change in April 2017 [13]. Also, the product and debt collection are identified separately by the CFPB. The map of our classification of the loans to the CFPB classification is given in Table 1. The nomenclature, both prior to and after April 2017, is aligned with how banks are organizationally structured, which means they are designed from the perspective of efficient issue resolution by a lender and not from a customer's perspective.

Of the over 100,000 undisputed complaints, we have 12,772 for mortgage loans, 8,687 for student loans, and 2,698 for payday loans. For student loans, we considered only lenders who are involved in both product and debt collection of both Federal and private student loans, to be able to analyze the complaints throughout the life of the product. We assume that a company is involved with a product or with debt collection if there is at least one complaint against it.

About 58% (76) of the mortgage debt collection companies are involved in both mortgage product and mortgage debt collection. There are 92 companies associated with Federal student loan debt collection, 154 with Private student loan debt collections, and 54 who do both. Thirty-six companies are associated with both Federal and private student loans and have at least one undisputed complaint with a narrative. About 60% (243) of the payday product companies are involved in both payday loans and payday loan debt collection.

```
bank payment loan go i from my saying download being info XXXX pay student
company account paying loans payments I mortgage the home house property We
The XX because Bank America Wells Fargo They ,u''n t'' $ time told \n\n As
money debt he day work said called calls phone number He payday Mae Sallie
month debt receive pay go send ask sell borrower facility time year month
robo middle check debt daughter week year session pg xxxxpage mis friend
credit yard human citi acre someone i. chairman name manner refer corporation
grandmother cc cycle people girlfriend onset resource preciousdriver gal man
daughter georgia agi boundrie set thank ed bill significance bless what i k
fedloan hotel crew head performer c. bofa. hail agent me.all that:1.1 crystal
statusdespite layer hr midst absence situation error modification loss!?!?!?!.
doing grandmother retirement st husband sir girl what i lady claiming senior
colleague birth use drafting sake red path navient yrs xxxxgreatlake ring
thousand dog d definite minus bofa. co. speaker head difference box sewer
spart loan/ init service director boss site means est brother hundred kin noon
yesterday essential avenue tomorrow sent whom slrp female since brotherinlaws
page usefuleness trid purple tid elbow lilac circuit sending abbreviation
woman door name because weekend wk basic thing rank navient someone 48hrs
dinner it me progress member dismiss
```

Figure 1: List of 222 custom stop words.

3.4.1 Preprocessing. For topic modeling, we used spaCy [26] to tokenize complaints. Only the lemmatized version of tokens tagged as nouns by spaCy were used, as these tokens generally seemed to offer better interpretability [21]. We then applied Hierarchical Dirichlet Process (HDP) topic modeling using the gensim library to identify 150 topics for each of the three types of loans. We found in initial work that the topics were often dominated by frequent but not distinctive words, making it difficult to interpret the topics. To refine our topic models, we used a heuristic procedure that iteratively identified these words and added them to a list of stop words:

(1) An HDP model's $150 \times k$ inference matrix, where k is the number of complaints (sampled from the complaints for that type of loan, sampling was required as spaCy—used for tokenization and Parts of Speech tagging—by default works with up to a million words) was fetched using the gensim library. We used the spaCy default stop word list in the first iteration.
(2) The probabilities in this matrix were set to zero if they were in the bottom or top quartiles (otherwise the interpretability of topics became difficult when attempted at the end of an iteration).
(3) For each topic the median probability (from among the k complaints) was considered to be representative for that topic.
(4) We then found the top 10 topics.
(5) Based on the keywords in the 10 topics (across mortgage loans, payday loans, student loans), appropriate additional stop words were added to the stop words list.
(6) Repeat above steps five times.

In all, 222 additional custom stop words were added to the default spaCy list in the four iterations. The topic modeling was undertaken five times for each of the three types of loans. The list of the custom stop words are shown in Figure 1.

3.4.2 Scoring. A complaint topic score is the probability of a specific topic being associated with a specific complaint. We did not rescale these scores as this would force all topics to have similar scores, which would implicitly make the unnecessary and unreasonable assumption that all topics are equally important.

Chang et al [18] found a trade-off between predictive perplexity and interpretability of latent topics. In our work, partial interpretability — i.e. having only a few of the 150 topics as interpretable — is acceptable because we only need a small set of topic importance scores from a Twitter user. The higher the relative importance score, the more important the issue/topic to that customer.

3.4.3 Sample topics. To give an idea of the topics found by our analysis, we give two examples. The top seven words in Topic #13 in our analysis included the words disbursement, afternon, violationno, confirmation, correspondence, bankrupty, and postcard, all with probabilities of about 0.003. This topic seems to correspond with complaints about rights under bankruptcy not being respected. Topic #141 seems to correspond with fraudulent advertisement, with words heat, fault, 839,i, work, checking, advertisement, and clerk, again with probabilities about 0.003.

3.5 Personality Trait Proxies

Big5 is a popular and standard personality test [17] that uses bipolar scales for extraversion, neuroticism, agreeableness, conscientiousness, and openness. Correlations between bipolar scales of the five personality traits and associated words are available [52]. Our intuition behind developing personality trait proxies is to infer personality trait-like information for word embeddings in the cross-domain vector space by considering the similarity of these word embeddings with the proxy representative trait vectors. For each of the ten (two polarities for each of five scales) traits, we compute a weighted average word vector in the vector space, yielding the ten proxy representative trait vectors. The weights are the correlations between the personality trait and the words associated with that personality trait. For each word for which there exists a word vector in the cross-domain word vector space, we find that word's similarity with a proxy representative trait vector. The same is done for other words in the given text (which could be a complaint narrative or a tweet). Then we take the average of the similarities to get a single proxy trait score for that text, and repeat for the other nine traits.

3.6 Modified Collaborative Topic Regression

Human interpretability of topics is useful in practice so that a prospective borrower could give her input on specific topics that are of interest to her, although it is sufficient for only a subset of the 150 topics to be interpretable. We address the challenge of human interpretability with a modification to Collaborative Topic Regression [56]. In the case of each complaint, we compute 160 scores: 150 scores corresponding to each of the 150 topics and 10 scores for each of the proxy personality traits. We use root mean squared error (RMSE) as the loss function given that we are doing a regression [57]. The complaints are mapped to a Complaint Topic Trait Space using the predicted values for the 160 scores. We use the Funk SVD implementation of the Surprise [27] library. Additionally, we use a hybrid (neural network) implementation of the Spotlight [7] library which uses a bilinear neural network — which in turn uses the Pytorch library [45] — for another such Complaint Topic Trait Space. In all we have two Complaint Topic Trait Spaces for each of the three types of loans: mortgage loans, student loans and payday loans.

For Funk SVD, we considered 4 latent factors, one epoch, and default values for all other hyperparameters. The hybrid method consists of a set of independent fully-connected layers for the user, and a set of independent fully-connected layers for the scores (complaint topics, personality trait proxies), and the outputs of these two sets are combined by a dot product [35]. We increased the regularization parameter (as compared to the default values of the Spotlight library) in order reduce the instability in the prediction space [16]. Key hyperparameter values for the hybrid method are given in Table 2. Table 3 reports the RMSEs for different approaches.

Table 4 presents sample Complaint Topic Trait Space visualizations, each corresponding to the first two principal components. Each gray dot corresponds to a complaint. Each red dot corresponds to a complaint about the concerned lender. The blue dot corresponds to a prospective borrower and is discussed in detail later in this paper.

3.7 Challenges in evaluation

The RMSE gives some indication of whether the predicted Complaint Topic Trait Space is an acceptable generalization of the data, but is otherwise of limited utility [36]. It is not a reliable metric in the case of predicting scores for a customer who interacts for another loan or with another lender in the future, or in the case of a new customer [32]. Nevertheless, our RMSE scores seem to suggest a generalization in the data compared with the maximum scores.

A major challenge in evaluating our work is that it is a case of unsupervised learning, and we do not have even a small labeled subset of the dataset. Given the large number of lenders, a controlled experiment would not be practical, so the best lender for a specific borrower — from a customer perspective — cannot be known with certainty or with a high confidence. While finding a true best lender is impractical, given that an alternative baseline is a random selection from a service quality perspective, we believe that recommendations to the customer (discussed in the next section) could be empowering even if the improvement (given that service quality is not the only factor) were incremental.

3.8 Making personalized recommendations

Table 4 shows samples visualizations of the topic trait embedding spaces. For each of the two techniques (Funk SVD and hybrid), and for each type of loan, the figure shows the spaces created from the complaint data of two (anonymized) banks or lenders. The blue dots correspond to a hypothetical prospective mortgage loan borrower (one of the authors!) using tweets from the hypothetical prospective borrower's Twitter handle. The Python-Twitter library [4] was used to fetch tweets (retweets are excluded) and infer the proxy personality traits. The hypothetical proxy borrower is asked to give relative importance scores for two randomly selected topics from the set of interpretable topics. Modified Collaborative Topic Regression is used to find the predicted 160 scores (predicted scores for the 10 proxy personality traits and two complaint topics are also included). The first two principal components are used to visualize the hypothetical proxy borrower as the blue dot.

We hypothesize that personalized recommendations can be made by finding a lender with the least number of complaints in the neighborhood of the prospective borrower, normalized by number of customers for that lender. The U.S. Federal Reserve publishes the number of branches of various lenders, and we use the number of branches as a proxy for the number of retail customers. One significant limitation of this proxy is that it ignores other (non-branch) channels of lending, and moreover assumes that all the considered lenders make loans of different types in a similar proportion, which is a significant approximation [54]. Unfortunately, the names of the lenders in the CFPB dataset and in the Federal Reserve Statistical Release [48] are often not identical, so we used the Levenshtein distance [43] to map between lender names. In the case where a lender is missing, we conservatively consider that lender to have only one branch.

These assumptions and approximations are significant limitations to the preliminary work we present here and which could be addressed with adequate time and effort. Because of this and because our intent is to present a methodology rather than a production ready system, we present anonymized lender names in Table 4.

4 RESULTS

We use the Freeman and Halton Exact Test [51] to very conservatively evaluate our proposed methodology. Halkidi et al [25] say that for an external criteria test the null hypothesis is that the dataset is randomly structured. We apply external criteria to the Complaint Topic Trait Space at the lender level. It is feasible that the sub-space of interest has distinctive frequency distributions across lenders. Besides, groups of lenders may be similar at the aggregate level. We consider only the first principal component of the Complaint Topic Trait Space. We discretized the first principal component into twenty discrete levels. Then we find the frequency distribution based on the discrete level corresponding to each complaint. We did not consider other principal components, so our application of external validation is a very conservative test. In the case of the Freeman and Halton Exact Test, the alternative hypothesis is about general (and not linear) association. Table 5 presents p-values of the Freeman and Halton Exact Test for Complaint Topic Trait Spaces specified by the Funk SVD modified Collaborative Topic Regression and the Hybrid modified Collaborative Topic Regression in the case of the three types of loans.

According to the results, at an aggregate level and at a 0.20 level of significance, the Complaint Topic Trait Space is distinctive for the lenders in the case of payday loans. However, we cannot make such an inference in the case of mortgage loans and student loans. It is interesting that the p-values for the Complaint Topic Trait Space built using the Hybrid method are lower in the case of mortgage loans and student loans, which suggests that perhaps additional experimentation of the neural network topology and hyperparameters could lead to more distinctive spaces for the lenders (at an aggregate level). As discussed above, this test is very conservative.

Sample recommendations using this space are shown in Table 6.

5 DISCUSSION

New datasets and open-source algorithms have made it possible to study complaints against financial institutions at a large scale. In particular, the availability of a cross-domain word embedding implementation like Vecmap as an open source project has been an

Type of loan	User layers	Item layers	Regularization	Learning rate	Iterations	Batch size
Mortgage	(12773,64), (64,16), (16,4), (4,4)	(160,4), (4,4)	0.01	0.01	1	12773
Student	(2699,16), (16,4), (4,4)	(160,4), (4,4)	0.01	0.01	1	2699
Payday	(2699,16), (16,4), (4,4)	(160,4), (4,4)	0.01	0.01	1	2699

Table 2: Parameter values used for topic regression.

Type of loan	Sample Size	Complaint Topic Space	RMSE
Mortgage	12,772	Funk SVD	0.053
		Hybrid	0.054
Student	8,687	Funk SVD	0.055
		Hybrid	0.055
Payday	2,698	Funk SVD	0.059
		Hybrid	0.059

Table 3: Results of collaborative topic space regression, for different types of loans and different approaches.

essential tool that has made it — in conjunction with TREC 2011 Microblog Dataset and the WWBP — much easier to explore the utility of machine learning on a large complaints dataset from a customer's perspective. Interpretability of topics is a very significant problem and the use of modified Collaborative Topic Regression to meaningfully use a mix of interpretable and non-interpretable topic scores makes it possible to go beyond merely predicting based on personality traits alone. An alternative approach would have been to ignore an explicit consideration of complaint topics and instead use only personality trait embeddings [44]. This would require labeled data and would be an oversimplification, ignoring variations among people with similar personality traits but different appreciation of pain points. Domain adaptation in the case of such an alternative method would have to be implemented in a different way, perhaps as suggested in Rieman [49].

The hybrid method for building a Complaint Topic Trait Space seems promising given the substantially lower Freeman and Halton test p-values than with the Funk SVD for mortgage and student loans. While the use of complaints as a proxy for customer service is reasonable it has a limitation: it implicitly ignores positive actions by the lenders which may have a lesser but nevertheless important role in customer service. In case of a passive Twitter user, non-text inputs would be useful for inferring personality traits [55], however the inference of the personality proxy traits in such a case would be very different. Our method assumes that complaint users are representative of all retail customers.

Our work underscores that publicly available complaints datasets can be a gold mine for customers and service providers alike. Unfortunately, it has been reported that the CFPB complaints dataset may be withdrawn from the public [33]. In our view, in order to further empower the customer, more anonymized data (and not less) could be made available, including data about the originator of the loan, servicer of the loan, and each lender's number of retail customers for each type of loan by geography on a quarterly basis.

6 CONCLUSION AND FUTURE WORK

We proposed to analyze a public complaints dataset from the retail customer's perspective. We showed that the Complaint Topic Trait Space is distinct for each lender in the case of payday loans but not distinct for mortgage and student loans. Some possible causes for this include a smaller intersection of lenders originating loans and debt collectors, more frequent transfer of loans (among lenders), more heterogeneity among sub-products, and heterogeneity in service quality in different geographies. We proposed a method to make personalized recommendations based on the customer service provided by lenders. The visualizations of the Complaint Topic Trait Spaces suggest that the same method could be suitable for mortgage loans and student loans depending on the location of the Twitter user in the Complaint Topic Trait Space. To confirm the same frequency distributions of the complaints in the Complaint Topic Trait Sub-spaces in the neighborhood of Twitter users and the distributions of the Complaint Topic Trait Sub-spaces for groups of lenders in the neighborhood of Twitter users, we test using external criteria like the Freeman and Halton Exact tests.

In line with *primum non nocere*, given that the Freeman and Halton Exact test only tells us whether the structure of the dataset is not random, it would be prudent to use our proposed method only on the subset of payday loan lenders (and to mortgage loan lenders and student loans lenders based on future work) which in a specific customer's eyes are similar. In other words, at least initially, the Twitter user ought to be asked for her shortlist of potential lenders from whom she is inclined to borrow and our proposed methodology ought to recommend from that shortlist. In the future, lenders may analyze complaints against them across time to evaluate variation in quality of service. This may be especially useful for analyzing complaints before and after the launch of new products, and refinement of products based on such analyses. Use of anomaly detection (e.g. [40]) for finding both nominal and abnormal points in the Complaint Topic Trait Space could potentially give interesting insights.

Competitive pressures that could result from a customer focus on quality are desirable, and could help lenders move away from "a race to the bottom" based primarily on pricing (which also contributes— along with other factors— to unviable low interest rates which may be accompanied by asset price bubbles and hence a less stable economy). Future work could include use of the proposed method in the case of other publicly available complaints datasets, better interpretability of topics by multiple experts, use of bigrams and trigrams, experimentation with the hyperparameters and additional topologies for the hybrid method for building the Complaint Topic Trait Spaces, benchmarking of proxy personality trait scores, and use of Facebook text [28] or an ensemble of tweets and Facebook posts. Mortgage loan sub-products could be analyzed separately.

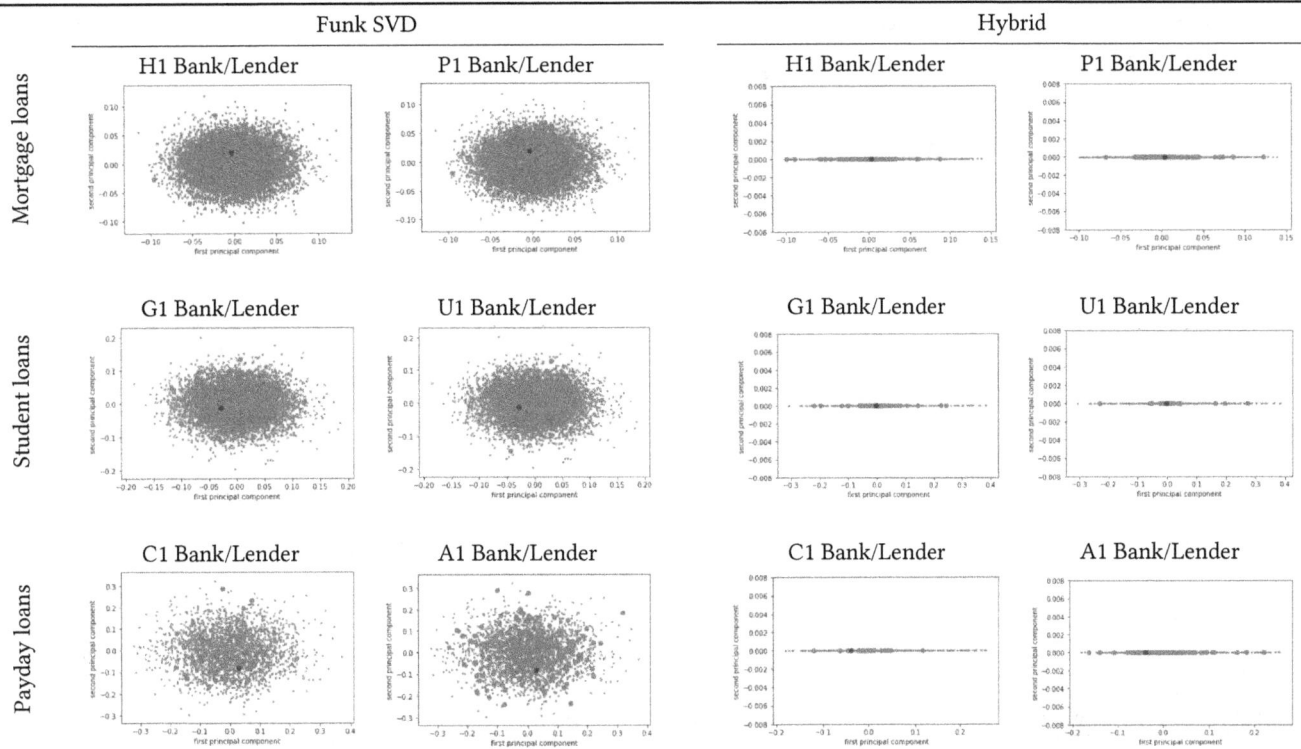

Table 4: Visualizations of complaint topic trait spaces. For each technique (Funk SVD and hybrid) and for each type of loan (mortgage, student loan, payday loan), we show a 2d projection of the embedding space for two sample (anonymized) lenders.

Loan type	Sample size	# samples	Space	p-value
Mortgage	12,772	1,000,000	Funk SVD	0.8029 ± 0.0010
			Hybrid	0.4962 ± 0.0013
Student	8,687	200,000	Funk SVD	0.6177 ± 0.0028
			Hybrid	0.5380 ± 0.0029
Payday	2,698	200,000	Funk SVD	0.0985 ± 0.0017
			Hybrid	0.1593 ± 0.0021

Table 5: Results of topic trait space analysis.

Federal student loans and private student loans could also be analyzed separately. Analysis may also be undertaken by geography. Under the assumption that it is the meanings of words that is relevant for association with a personality trait, an extension to other languages will also be feasible using Cross-Lingual word embeddings. Finally, our techniques could be extended and applied to other parts of the service economy.

7 ACKNOWLEDGMENTS

We first heard about the asymmetrical effect of loss/gain associated with pain/joy from A. V. Rajwade (1936-2018). We thank Maciej Kula for help with modifying the Spotlight library. This research was supported in part by Lilly Endowment, Inc., through its support for the Indiana University Pervasive Technology Institute, and in part by the Indiana METACyt Initiative.

REFERENCES

[1] [n. d.]. https://github.com/artetxem/vecmap.
[2] [n. d.]. https://www.consumerfinance.gov/data-research/consumer-complaints/.
[3] [n. d.]. Port of Google's Language Detection library to Python. https://pypi.org/project/langdetect/.
[4] [n. d.]. python-twitter: A Python wrapper around the Twitter API. https://python-twitter.readthedocs.io/en/latest/.
[5] [n. d.]. TREC 2011 Twitter Collection Downloader. https://github.com/cmlonder/trec-collection-downloader.
[6] 2017. How To Choose the Right Bank for You. *ABC News* (2017).
[7] 2017. Spotlight. https://github.com/maciejkula/spotlight.
[8] Mikel Artetxe, Gorka Labaka, and Eneko Agirre. 2018. A robust self-learning method for fully unsupervised cross-lingual mappings of word embeddings. In *Annual Meeting of the Association for Computational Linguistics*.
[9] Ian Ayres, Jeff Lingwall, and Sonia Steinway. 2013. Skeletons In The Database: An Early Analysis Of The CFPB's Consumer Complaints. *Fordham Journal of Corporate & Financial Law* XIX (2013).
[10] Financial Stability Board. 2017. Artificial intelligence and machine learning in financial services: Market developments and financial stability implications. , 11-15 pages.
[11] Piotr Bojanowski, Edouard Grave, Armand Joulin, and Tomas Mikolov. 2016. Enriching Word Vectors with Subword Information. *arXiv:1607.04606* (2016).
[12] Consumer Financial Protection Bureau. 2015. Consumers' mortgage shopping experience: A first look at results from the National Survey of Mortgage Borrowers.
[13] Consumer Financial Protection Bureau. 2017. CFPB Summary of product and sub-product changes.
[14] Consumer Financial Protection Bureau. 2018. Buying a house: Tools and resources for homebuyers. https://www.consumerfinance.gov/owning-a-home/process/compare.
[15] Bureau Of Consumer Financial Protection. 2018. Complaint snapshot: Debt collection.
[16] Antal Buza and Piroska B. Kis. 2014. Instability Of Matrix Factorization Used In Recommender Systems. *Annales Univ. Sci. Budapest., Sect. Comp.* 42 (2014).

(a) Funk SVD

(b) Hybrid

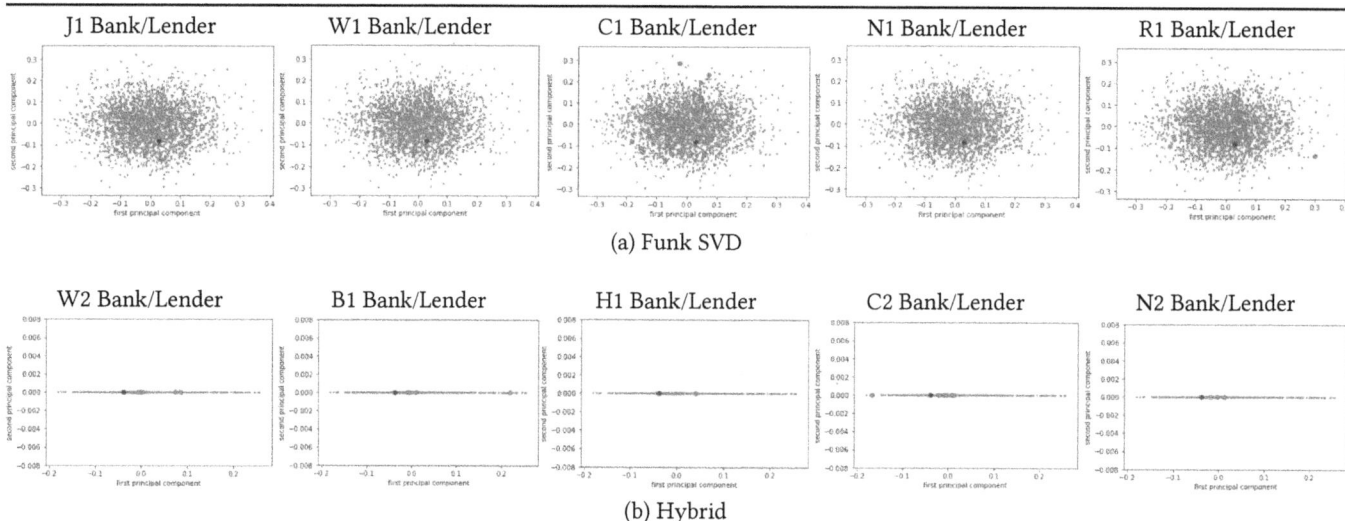

Table 6: Sample recommendations using the complaint topic space with Funk SVD (top) and the Hybrid method (bottom).

[17] Fabio Celli, Fabio Pianesi, David Stillwell, and Michal Kosinski. 2013. Workshop on Computational Personality Recognition: Shared Task. In *ICWSM Workshops*.
[18] Jonathan Chang, Jordan Boyd-Graber, Sean Gerrish, Chong Wang, and David Blei. 2009. Reading Tea Leaves: How Humans Interpret Topic Models. In *Neural Information Processing Systems*.
[19] Stacy Cowley. 2018. Consumer Bureau Looks to End Public View of Complaints Database. *New York Times* (2018).
[20] Deloitte. 2015. The power of complaints: Unlocking the value of customer dissatisfaction.
[21] Fabrizio Esposito, Anna Corazza, and Francessco Cutugno. 2016. Topic Modeling with Word Embeddings. In *Third Italian Conference on Computational Linguistics*.
[22] Pamela Foohey. 2017. Calling On The CPFB For Help: Telling Stories And Consumer Protection. In *80 Law & Contemporary Problems (Forthcoming) Indiana Legal Studies Research Paper No. 356*.
[23] Andreas Fuster, Matthew Plosser, and James Vickery. 2018. Does CFPB Oversight Crimp Credit? . *Federal Reserve Bank of New York Staff Reports* 857 (2018).
[24] Boris A. Galitsky and Josep Lluis de la Rosa. 2011. Learning Adversarial Reasoning Patterns in Customer Complaints. In *AAAI Workshop on Applied Adversarial Reasoning and Risk Modeling*.
[25] Maria Halkidi, Yannis Batistakis, and Michalis Vazirgiannis. 2001. On Clustering Validation Techniques. *Journal of Intelligent Information Systems* 17, 2/3 (2001).
[26] Matthew Honnibal and Mark Johnson. 2015. An Improved Non-monotonic Transition System for Dependency Parsing. In *EMNLP*. 1373–1378.
[27] Nicolas Hug. 2017. Surprise, a Python library for recommender systems. http://surpriselib.com.
[28] Kokil Jaidka, Sharath Chandra Guntuku, Anneke Buffone, H. Schwartz, and Lyle Ungar. 2018. Facebook vs. Twitter: Differences in Self-disclosure and Trait Prediction. In *ICWSM*.
[29] J.D. Power Ratings. 2016. Buyer's Remorse Is Relatively High despite Rising Satisfaction.
[30] J.D. Power Ratings. 2017. Secret to Nationwide, Multiproduct Success in Retail Banking: Not Making Mistakes.
[31] D. Kahneman and A. Tversky. 1979. Prospect Theory: An Analysis of Decision under Risk. *Econometrica* 47, 4 (1979), 263âĂŞ291.
[32] Frank Kane. [n. d.]. Building Recommender Systems with Machine Learning and AI. https://www.udemy.com/building-recommender-systems-with-machine-learning-and-ai/.
[33] Ted Knutson. 2018. CFPB Chief: I could make consumer complaints secret. *Forbes* (2018).
[34] KPMG. 2017. KPMG Client Alert, America's FS Regulatory Center of Excellence: Complaints Monitoring and Risk Management.
[35] Maciej Kula. 2016. Hybrid Recommender Systems at Py-Data Amsterdam 2016. https://speakerdeck.com/maciejkula/hybrid-recommender-systems-at-pydata-amsterdam-2016?slide=21.
[36] Maciej Kula. 2018. Implicit and explicit feedback recommenders: And the curse of RMSE. https://resources.bibblio.org/hubfs/share/2018-01-24-RecSysLDN-Ravelin.pdf.

[37] Guillaume Lample, Alexis Conneau, Ludovic Denoyer, and Marc'Aurelio Ranzato. 2018. Unsupervised Machine Translation Using Monolingual Corpora Only. In *ICLR*.
[38] Quanzhi Li, Sameena Shah, Xiaomo Liu, and Armineh Nourbakhsh. 2017. Word Embeddings Learned from Tweets and General Data. In *ICWSM*.
[39] Jimmy Lin. [n. d.]. Twitter tools. https://github.com/lintool/twitter-tools.
[40] Fei Tony Liu, Kai Ming Ting, and Zhi-Hua Zhou. 2012. Isolation-based Anomaly Detection. *ACM Transactions on Knowledge Discovery from Data* 6, 1 (March 2012).
[41] Richard McCreadie, Ian Soboroff, Jimmy Lin, Craig Macdonald, Iadh Ounis, and Dean McCullough. 2012. On building a reliable Twitter corpus. In *SIGIR*.
[42] Tomas Mikolov, Kai Chen, Greg Corrado, and Jeffrey Dean. 2013. Efficient Estimation of Word Representations in Vector Space. *arXiv* (2013).
[43] David Necas. [n. d.]. python-Levenshtein:Python extension for computing string edit distances and similarities. https://pypi.org/project/python-Levenshtein/.
[44] Yair Neuman and Yochai Cohen. 2014. A Vectorial Semantics Approach to Personality Assessment. *Scientific Reports* 4 (2014).
[45] Adam Paszke, Sam Gross, Soumith Chintala, Gregory Chanan, Edward Yang, Zachary DeVito, Zeming Lin, Alban Desmaison, Luca Antiga, and Adam Lerer. 2017. Automatic differentiation in PyTorch. In *NeurIPS*.
[46] Rehurek Radim and Petr Sojka. 2010. Software Framework for Topic Modelling with Large Corpora. In *Workshop on New Challenges for NLP Frameworks*.
[47] Lucia Rahilly. 2018. *McKinsey on Risk*.
[48] Federal Reserve Statistical Release. 2018. Large Commercial Banks: Insured U.S.-Chartered Commercial Banks that have Consolidated Assets of $300 million or more, ranked by Consolidated Assets.
[49] Daniel Rieman, Kokil Jaidka, H. Schwartz, and Lyle Ungar. 2017. Domain Adaptation from User-level Facebook Models to County-level Twitter Predictions. In *International Joint Conference on Natural Language Processing*.
[50] Tom Sabo. 2017. *Applying Text Analytics and Machine Learning to Assess Consumer Financial Complaints*. Technical Report. SAS Institute.
[51] SAS. [n. d.]. Chapter 28 FREQ Procedure. SAS OnlineDoc Version 8. https://support.sas.com/documentation/onlinedoc/stat/131/freq.pdf.
[52] H. Schwartz, Johannes Eichstaedt, Margaret Kern, Lukasz Dziurzynski, Stephanie Ramones, Megha Agrawal, Achal Shah, Michal Kosinski, David Stillwell, Martin Seligman, and Lyle H. Ungar. 2013. Personality, Gender, and Age in the Language of Social Media: The Open-Vocabulary Approach. *PLOS ONE* 8, 9 (Sept 2013).
[53] Laura Shin. 2014. How To Choose A Bank Account: 10 Things To Look For. *Forbes* (2014).
[54] Trefis Group. 2017. A breakdown of the loan portfolios of the largest U.S. banks.
[55] Svitlana Volkova, Yoram Bachrach, and Benjamin Van Durme. 2016. Mining User Interests to Predict Perceived Psycho-Demographic Traits on Twitter. In *Second International Conference on Big Data Computing Service and Applications*.
[56] Chong Wang and David Blei. 2011. Collaborative Topic Modeling for Recommending Scientific Articles. In *KDD*.
[57] Yandex. [n. d.]. Big Data Applications: Machine Learning at Scale, Coursera. https://www.coursera.org/lecture/machine-learning-applications-big-data/recsys-mf-ii-Bq6m2.

Dogs Good, Trump Bad:
The Impact of Social Media Content on Sense of Well-Being

Jennifer Golbeck
University of Maryland
College Park, MD

ABSTRACT

Social media can impact how people feel both in the short and long term. Most studies in this area have focused on longer-term feelings of happiness and life satisfaction, but the immediate impact on users' sense of well-being and anxiety levels are not well studied. In this work, we had 1,880 subjects complete surveys about their immediate sense of well-being and contentment and then view one of three possible social media pages: a collection of happy dog pictures and videos; a collection of non-dog related images and videos that generally were funny, non-political, and popular; and Donald Trump's Twitter account. After viewing this content, they were re-surveyed on their sense of well-being. We found viewing dogs led to a large and significant increase in the sense of well-being, viewing popular content led to a smaller but still significant improvement, and viewing Donald Trump's Twitter account led to a very large decrease in sense of well-being. This work has implications for recommender systems, which may consider these results as a step toward optimizing user well-being rather than simply engagement, and for users who may want to manage their own happiness through social media channels and following patterns.

KEYWORDS

social media; well being; recommender systems

ACM Reference Format:
Jennifer Golbeck. 2019. Dogs Good, Trump Bad: The Impact of Social Media Content on Sense of Well-Being. In 11th ACM Conference on Web Science (WebSci '19), June 30-July 3, 2019, Boston, MA, USA. ACM, New York, NY, USA, 5 pages. https://doi.org/10.1145/3292522.3326009

1 INTRODUCTION

Social media platforms are good at measuring engagement with content; time viewed, likes, shares, and comments are all easy and straightforward to track. Content recommender

Figure 1: Does this picture spark joy? For our subjects, it did.

systems generally rely on these engagement metrics to recommend content, based on the general idea that the things we spend more time interacting with are the things we want to see. However, studies into the overall impacts of social media on users repeatedly show mixed effects. There are plenty of positive impacts but also plenty of negative ones. This suggests the question: what social media is good for people to view?

With this in mind, we set out to understand the impact that different types of content have on users' immediate sense of well-being. With 1,880 subjects, we created an experiment where subjects would complete a short survey to measure well-being before and after viewing selected social media content. Subjects were randomly assigned to one of three experimental content conditions: posts featuring pictures and videos of dogs, popular posts that tended to be funny and were non-political, and Donald Trump's Twitter feed. These were selected to cover a range of topics from the cute and non-controversial to the politically-charged.

We found that dog posts created a large and highly significant increase in immediate sense of well-being, as did popular posts to a lesser extent. Viewing Donald Trump's

Twitter feed led to a large and significant decrease in immediate sense of well-being.

These results are not designed to suggest that one type of content is objectively good or bad, but rather to establish that there are marked differences in how content impacts users and to drive future research toward measuring and using well-being as a factor in content recommendation.

In this paper, we frame this work in existing studies of the impacts of social media. We present our experiment and results and discuss future directions for building systems that not only engage people but that help them feel better.

2 RELATED WORK

2.1 Social Media and Well-Being

Social media's impact on well-being has been studied from a variety of perspectives. Much of this work focuses on the impact of interactions on social media or the general experience of consuming content, rather than our approach which looks at the impacts of different types of content.

On Facebook, researchers found that one-to-one interactions made people feel more bonded and less lonely, but as they consumed more content, these feelings were reduced [6]. A 2015 experimental study found that immediately after consuming social media content, subjects had increased stress and lower happiness [5]. This is echoed in a clinical study that found problematic social media use connected with depressive states [16].

A meta-review that focused on adolescents found that the impacts were mixed in most of the 43 studies they analyzed. Some studies found benefits like increased self-esteem and social capital along with negatives like depression and social isolation [4]. While focused on adolescents, this meta review presents the main result: results are mixed. Social media is linked to improvements and detriments, often for the same person. Thus, trying to understand "is social media good or bad" is an oversimplified question.

There are few studies on the impact of content on well-being from the same perspective. There are plenty of studies that look at a particular type of content that a person may seek out - e.g. healthcare [15], mental health[8], eating disorders [7]. However, our studies differ in that we want to measure the impact of content users may naturally come across (or be recommended) in their feeds.

2.2 The Benefits of Dogs

There has been extensive research into the health and mental health benefits of dogs. People who own pets tend to be healthier overall [11], have lower blood pressure reactions to stressful situations [2], and even have better longevity after cardiac events [9].

The physical presence of a dog can reduce stress and anxiety [3, 12]. A meta-review found that children who read to dogs experience reduced stress and better performance [10].

These benefits extend to viewing images of dogs. Researchers in Japan found viewing pictures of cute animals reduced

stress and improved performance [14]. Viewing other pleasant images did not have the same beneficial effect. This suggests that our study on well-being may see similar results, where images of dogs improve well-being in a way that other popular, funny content or political content does not.

3 METHODOLOGY

3.1 Surveys

Subjects began by completing the Anxiety and Depression Association of America's Depression screener and Anxiety screener. They also answered basic questions about their social media use.

Next, we measured their baseline sense of well-being using the Patient Evaluation of Emotional Comfort Experienced (PEECE) survey [17]. This survey has 12 statements that begin with "I feel " and are followed by aspects of well-being: relaxed, valued, safe, calm, cared for, at ease, like smiling, energized, content, in control, informed, and thankful. Subjects rate each feeling on a 5 point scale from 1 (not at all) to 5 (extremely). The test is scored by averaging their answers.

After establishing that baseline, subjects were randomly assigned to view one of three possible conditions: a Twitter page with pictures and videos of dogs, a Twitter page with non-dog-related and non-political popular posts that tended to be funny, or Donald Trump's Twitter feed. We curated the pages for the first two conditions. Subjects were required to spend at least 5 minutes browsing the content on each page and were prevented from continuing in the study by a timer.

Once they had spent time in the condition, they re-completed the PEECE survey so we could measure changes in their immediate sense of well-being.

Finally, subjects provided information about their demographic traits. Because we included Donald Trump's Twitter feed as one of the conditions, we also asked about their approval of his performance as President using the language from the Washington Post -ABC News Approval Poll: "Do you approve or disapprove of the way Donald Trump is handling his job as President?". Subjects could answer "Approve", "Disapprove", or "Neutral/No Opinion".

3.2 Subjects

Subjects were recruited via social media postings on Twitter, Instagram, Facebook, and Snapchat asking them to participate in a survey about how social media content affected their well-being. Subjects were not compensated.

We had 1,880 subjects complete the experiment. The average age was 29 years old (SD = 11.0). Gender distribution was 82.1% female, 15.9% male, and 2% other or fluid. The majority of our subjects were from the United States (73.0%) with another 9.4% from the UK and 6.0% from Canada.

On the depression screener, subjects rated how much they were bothered by various aspects of depression, like having a poor appetite or low energy, on a scale from 1 (not bothered at all) to 5 (bothered every day). The average score was 1.9 (SD=1.0). On the anxiety screener, subjects answered Yes

Table 1: Sample posts from the three social media feed conditions in our experiment

| (Dogs) | (Popular Posts) | (Donald Trump) |

or No to questions about symptoms of anxiety like "Do you experience excessive worry?" and "Is your worry excessive in intensity, frequency, or amount of distress it causes?". Subjects answered yes to 61.3% of the questions.

With respect to the background questions that relate to the content subjects viewed, our sample had some clear biases.

The subjects overwhelmingly disapproved of Donald Trump as President with 91.2% disapproving, 2.7% approving, and 6.1% Neural or with no opinion. This survey was administered while the US Government was shutdown from December 2018 to January 2019 which may be responsible for the higher-than-normal disapproval rates. For reference, the Washington Post - ABC Poll data from the same time period showed a disapproval rating of 58% with 37% approval [1].

We also asked subjects to rate how much the statement "I love dogs" applied to them. The vast majority, 93.7% said it applied strongly or somewhat while 2.0% were neutral and 4.3% said not much or not at all.

While this indicates a biased subject sample, we are able to control for this to some extent, as discussed in the results below. Furthermore, our goal is not to offer an objective assessment of what content is good for people's well-being, but rather to illustrate the viewing different types of content does have a significant impact on individuals.

4 RESULTS

Overall, subjects' initial scores on the PEECE survey averaged 3.28 on a 1 to 5 scale, where 5 represents the highest well-being. There was no significant difference in average initial score among the three experimental conditions (dog-viewers, popular post-viewers, and Trump-viewers). When dividing subjects by anxiety level, into those who answered Yes to 3 to 4 of the 4 anxiety questions from those who answered Yes to 2 or fewer, there were significant differences in initial sense of well-being. The less anxious people had an initial well-being score of 3.54 vs 3.08 for more anxious subjects.

Group	Before	After
Trump	3.27	2.08
Dogs	3.27	3.81
Popular	3.29	3.43

Table 2: Average PEECE scores before and after viewing the experimental content for each group. All results are significant for $p < 0.001$.

After viewing the content, there were significant changes among all three experimental groups, shown in table ??. Viewing Donald Trump's tweets led to a large and significant decline in sense of well-being, while the other two conditions led to significant increases. Dogs generated the highest increase. All results are highly significant, with $p < 0.001$.

Given that Donald Trump was so' unpopular among our subjects, we analyzed the impact of viewing his content on the people who did not disapprove of him. Only 16 of our 1,808 subjects approved of the job he was doing and were placed in the condition where they viewed his tweets. Their sense of well-being appeared to decline from 3.64 to 3.58, but the change was not statistically significant, as would be expected with such a small sample. If we included both people who approved and who were neutral or had no opinion about Trump, we found the decrease in well-being was significant, from 3.39 to 3.30 ($p < 0.05$).

Among people who were neutral or negative on dogs, only 19 saw the dog condition. Even with this small sample, the increase in well-being ratings increased significantly from 3.09 to 3.59 ($p < 0.001$)[1]

Both the more and less anxious sub-groups saw changes in well-being that mimicked the overall population. All had large, significant decreases in well-being after viewing Trump's account while they saw increases in the other two conditions, and the largest increase with the dog condition.

5 DISCUSSION

As mentioned above, the point of this research was not to establish that dogs (or any other content type) were universally and objectively good for well-being or that Trump was universally bad viewing. Instead, we have established that, for a large sample, the content someone sees does have a significant, immediate impact on their sense of well-being.

While our results here may not be surprising to some people, it lays the foundation for discussions about how content recommendation systems should work. Currently, most are engineered to increase engagement. However, accounts that have high engagement can still damage well-being in the short term. Donald Trump's account is often recommended as a follow for new Twitter users, but our results show that for at least some - and potentially a substantial number - of users, seeing his content can make them feel worse.

We are also not arguing that we should all only look at things that make us happy. However, if we circle back to work that looks at the impact of social media on users, it is important to consider how content in general, and recommended content in particular, is impacting them. Obviously, social media platforms want to increase engagement and time users spend with them, since this increases the potential for profit. However, that does not mean that engagement is a good measure of people's enjoyment on their platform. Indeed, highly engaging posts can often be quite toxic [13].

We suggest that an important area for future research is into recommending well-being-enhancing content on social media. This will require new methods for measuring well-being, as users obviously cannot be completing questionnaires after each browsing session. Once such metrics are developed, creating mechanisms for including this as a feature in recommender systems will be important. Users may want to manually balance well-being vs. engagement in their timelines (e.g. I may want to see almost exclusively things that make me happier vs. someone who wants a mix of well-being-enhancement and news, even if the news makes them feel worse) or algorithms may seek to strike this balance automatically. The correct approach remains to be seen, but we believe this is a promising and important area of future work.

For individual users, this research suggests that they may want to more carefully curate their social media feeds. Whether through lists or multiple accounts, it could be beneficial to have a curated set of content that will improve well-being separate from content that may be useful but detrimental to well-being.

6 CONCLUSION

In this paper, we studied the impact that different types of social media posts had on subjects' immediate sense of well-being. We had 1,880 subjects complete a short survey about their present well-being, and then had them spend time looking at one of three experimental conditions: pictures and videos of dogs; popular, generally funny social media posts; and Donald Trump's Twitter account. After browsing, subjects re-took the well-being survey. We found significant increases in well-being after viewing the dog and popular post conditions, with dog posts driving the biggest increase. Viewing Donald Trump's Twitter account led to a significant decrease in subjects' sense of well-being.

We believe this work lays the foundation for a larger body of future research focused on measuring how different types of content impact an individual's sense of well being which, in turn, can be incorporated into content recommender systems. With all the concern about the impact social media has on its users, algorithms that bring people content that makes them feel better has a clear place in the research discussion. We have shown that such effects do exist, and call for new work to make these initial insights operationalizable.

---

[1] We note this group is markedly less happy initially than the average. We hypothesize, with some bias, that if they liked dogs, they might be happier.

REFERENCES

[1] 2019. Washington Post-ABC News poll Jan. 21-24, 2019. Washington Post (Feb 2019). https://www.washingtonpost.com/politics/polling/donald-trump-approvedisapprove-president/2019/02/07/3bba9b70-20cf-11e9-a759-2b8541bbbe20_page.html

[2] Karen Allen, Barbara E Shykoff, and Joseph L Izzo Jr. 2001. Pet ownership, but not ACE inhibitor therapy, blunts home blood pressure responses to mental stress. Hypertension 38, 4 (2001), 815–820.

[3] Karen M Allen, Jim Blascovich, Joe Tomaka, and Robert M Kelsey. 1991. Presence of human friends and pet dogs as moderators of autonomic responses to stress in women. Journal of personality and social psychology 61, 4 (1991), 582.

[4] Paul Best, Roger Manktelow, and Brian Taylor. 2014. Online communication, social media and adolescent wellbeing: A systematic narrative review. Children and Youth Services Review 41 (2014), 27–36.

[5] Stoney Brooks. 2015. Does personal social media usage affect efficiency and well-being? Computers in Human Behavior 46 (2015), 26–37.

[6] Moira Burke, Cameron Marlow, and Thomas Lento. 2010. Social network activity and social well-being. In Proceedings of the SIGCHI conference on human factors in computing systems. ACM, 1909–1912.

[7] Stevie Chancellor, Zhiyuan Jerry Lin, and Munmun De Choudhury. 2016. This Post Will Just Get Taken Down: Characterizing Removed Pro-Eating Disorder Social Media Content. In Proceedings of the 2016 CHI Conference on Human Factors in Computing Systems. ACM, 1157–1162.

[8] Munmun De Choudhury, Emre Kiciman, Mark Dredze, Glen Coppersmith, and Mrinal Kumar. 2016. Discovering shifts to suicidal ideation from mental health content in social media. In Proceedings of the 2016 CHI conference on human factors in computing systems. ACM, 2098–2110.

[9] Erika Friedmann, Aaron H Katcher, James J Lynch, and Sue Ann Thomas. 1980. Animal companions and one-year survival of patients after discharge from a coronary care unit. Public health reports 95, 4 (1980), 307.

[10] Sophie Susannah Hall, Nancy R Gee, and Daniel Simon Mills. 2016. Children reading to dogs: A systematic review of the literature. PloS one 11, 2 (2016), e0149759.

[11] Bruce Headey, Fu Na, and Richard Zheng. 2008. Pet dogs benefit owners health: A natural experiment in China. Social Indicators Research 87, 3 (2008), 481–493.

[12] Bronwyn A Kingwell, Andrea Lomdahl, and Warwick P Anderson. 2001. Presence of a pet dog and human cardiovascular responses to mild mental stress. Clinical Autonomic Research 11, 5 (2001), 313–317.

[13] Delia Mocanu, Luca Rossi, Qian Zhang, Marton Karsai, and Walter Quattrociocchi. 2015. Collective attention in the age of (mis)information. Computers in Human Behavior 51 (2015), 1198–1204.

[14] Hiroshi Nittono, Michiko Fukushima, Akihiro Yano, and Hiroki Moriya. 2012. The power of kawaii: Viewing cute images promotes a careful behavior and narrows attentional focus. PloS one 7, 9 (2012), e46362.

[15] Edin Smailhodzic, Wyanda Hooijsma, Albert Boonstra, and David J Langley. 2016. Social media use in healthcare: a systematic review of effects on patients and on their relationship with healthcare professionals. BMC health services research 16, 1 (2016), 442.

[16] Antonius J Van Rooij, Christopher J Ferguson, Dike Van de Mheen, and Tim M Schoenmakers. 2017. Time to abandon Internet Addiction? Predicting problematic Internet, game, and social media use from psychosocial well-being and application use. Clinical Neuropsychiatry 14, 1 (2017), 113–121.

[17] AM Williams, Leanne Lester, Caroline Bulsara, Anna Petterson, Kellie Bennett, E Allen, and David Joske. 2017. Patient Evaluation of Emotional Comfort Experienced (PEECE): developing and testing a measurement instrument. BMJ open 7, 1 (2017), e012999.

Decoding the Social World

Sandra González-Bailón
Annenberg School for Communication
University of Pennsylvania
sgonzalezbailon@asc.upenn.edu

ABSTRACT

Social life is full of paradoxes. Our intentional actions often trigger outcomes that we did not intend or even envision. How do we explain those unintended effects and what can we do to regulate them? In this talk, I will discuss research that illustrates how data science and digital traces help us solve the puzzle of unintended consequences—offering the solution to a social paradox that has intrigued thinkers for centuries. Communication has always been the force that makes a collection of people more than the sum of individuals, but only now can we explain why: digital technologies have made it possible to parse the information we generate by being social in new, imaginative ways. Yet we must look at that data, I will argue, through the lens of theories that capture the nature of social life. The technologies we use, in the end, are also a manifestation of the social world we inhabit.

In this talk I will discuss how the unpredictability of social life relates to communication networks, social influence, and the unintended effects that derive from individual decisions. I will focus on empirical research in the field of political communication, with special emphasis on the analysis of social media, mobilization dynamics, exposure to information, and news consumption. I will describe how communication generates social dynamics in aggregate (leading to episodes of "collective effervescence") and I will discuss the mechanisms that underlie large-scale diffusion, when information and behavior spread "like wildfire." I will use the theory of networks to illuminate why collective outcomes can differ drastically even when they arise from the same individual actions. By opening the black box of unintended effects, and how they relate to communication dynamics, I hope to identify strategies for social intervention and illuminate policy implications—and how data science and the analysis of digital traces embolden critical thinking in a world that is constantly changing.

CCS Concepts/ACM Classifiers
Collaborative and social computing; social networks; social media; social network analysis; behavioral sciences; sociology.

Author Keywords
Computational social science; networks; political communication.

BIOGRAPHY

Sandra González-Bailón is an Associate Professor at the Annenberg School for Communication, University of Pennsylvania, and affiliated faculty at the Warren Center for Network and Data Sciences. Prior to joining Penn, she was a Research Fellow at the Oxford Internet Institute, where she is now a Research Associate. Her research lies at the intersection of network science, data mining, computational tools, and political communication. She is the author of the book Decoding the Social World (MIT Press) and co-editor of The Oxford Handbook of Networked Communication (OUP). She is an associate editor of the journals *Social Networks, EPJ Data Science*, and the *International Journal of Press/Politics*.

REFERENCES

[1] González-Bailón, S. (2017). Decoding the Social World. Data Science and the Unintended Consequences of Communication, Boston, MA: MIT Press.

[2] Foucault-Welles, B. and González-Bailón, S. (eds.) (2018). The Oxford Handbook of Networked Communication, Oxford: Oxford University Press.

How Representative is an Abortion Debate on Twitter?

Eduardo Graells-Garrido
Universidad del Desarrollo
Santiago, Chile
egraells@udd.cl

Ricardo Baeza-Yates
NTENT & Northeastern University
California, USA
rbaeza@acm.org

Mounia Lalmas
Spotify
London, UK
mounia@acm.org

ABSTRACT

Today, more than ever, social networks and micro-blogging platforms are used as tools for political exchange. However, these platforms are biased in several aspects, from their algorithms to the population participating in them. With respect to the latter, we analyze the discussion on Twitter about an abortion bill in Chile, proposed in January 2015, and approved as law in September 2017. We find that Twitter has strong biases in population representation. Still, when carefully paired with demographic attributes, Twitter-based insights on the characteristics of political discussion match those from national-level surveys.

CCS CONCEPTS

• **Human-centered computing** → **Social network analysis**;

1 INTRODUCTION

A prominent usage of the social platforms on the Web is the exchange of points of view. These platforms are biased in several aspects, from their algorithms to the population that participates in them [1]. Experiments have shown that, when controlling for demographic factors, social media users do not show different political behavior than non-social media ones [6]. However, it remains unclear to which extent insights from social-media discussion reflect those from the general population. In this work, we address the longitudinal discussion on a specific controversial issue, *abortion*. Its discussion on micro-blogging platforms has been studied before, delivering insights on how the different stances on the issue relate [3, 7]. In this context, we analyze a discussion about abortion in Chile, where we measure the *representativeness* of insights derived from the discussion. We processed more than one million tweets published during the entire life cycle of an abortion bill (2015—2017). The analysis included inference of political stance of users, estimation of population bias, and comparison between platform-insights with those from nationally representative opinion surveys.

As result, we confirm that Twitter is demographically biased; however, when incorporating demographic factors in the analysis, it provides insights comparable to traditional sources.

2 DATA SETS

We used three data sources, a data set of Twitter Discussion during 2015–2017, a census from 2017, and a survey of political opinions:

WebSci '19, June 30–July 3, 2019, Boston, MA, USA
© 2019 Copyright held by the owner/author(s).
ACM ISBN 978-1-4503-6202-3/19/06.
https://doi.org/10.1145/3292522.3326057

- A Twitter dataset, collected between Jan. 1, 2015, and Dec. 31, 2017, using the Streaming API. Query keywords included abortion vocabulary, mentions, hashtags, and contextual keywords (*e.g.*, #marchaabortolegal –protest for legal abortion–). This resulted in 1,443,865 tweets from 104,938 users.
- The Chilean government held a population census on April 2017 [4]. Chile has 17.5M inhabitants, with 14.5M aged 13 years old or greater (13 years old is the minimum Twitter user age according to the Terms of Service). The census is available as open-data.
- The Centro de Estudios Públicos (CEP) think-tank holds public opinion surveys every three months. In April 2017, they held one survey about abortion [2], in the context of the last year of the life cycle of the abortion bill.

With these three data sets we aim to measure the representativeness of insights obtained from the Twitter discussion.

3 ATTRIBUTE INFERENCE AND WEIGHTING

For each user in the data set we inferred demographic attributes, an stance with respect to abortion, and a weight with respect to the general population.

Demographic Attributes of Users. We are interested in age and gender. Since both attributes are not usually reported, we inferred them. First, we used heuristics to find users with self-reported attributes. For age, we matched common phrases in biographies that disclosed age or date of birth. For gender, in addition to such types of phrases, we analyzed the self-reported first name of the account. As result, we had a labeled set of users with gender (binary male/female) and age (in cohorts, *e.g.*, 18–24, 25–34, *etc.*). We built a feature matrix for all users with a biography (TF-IDF weighted document-term matrix of biography content), and objective arrays with the preliminary labels. We propagated the labels to the unlabeled users using LinearSVC for age (0.94 mean accuracy, 10-fold c.v.), and SGD with log-loss for gender (0.83 mean accuracy, 10-fold c.v.). In total, 89.21% of users were labelled with both age and gender (males 56.28%, females 43.72%).

Stance with respect to Abortion. We treated stance inference as a binary classification problem. Given a user profile (*e.g.*, the concatenation of her/his tweets), the task is to infer the corresponding stance: in *opposition*, or in *defense*. To do so, we built a list of seed keywords associated with each stance, based on previous work analyzing abortion in Chile [3]. Seed keywords for the *defense* stance include #abortolibre (unrestricted abortion), the NGO @miles_chile, and the hashtag #obligadasaparir (forced to give birth). Seed keywords for the *opposition* stance include #sialavida (yes to life), #salvemoslas2vidas (let's save the two lives), and the conservative site hazteoir.org. The seed keywords were used to fit a

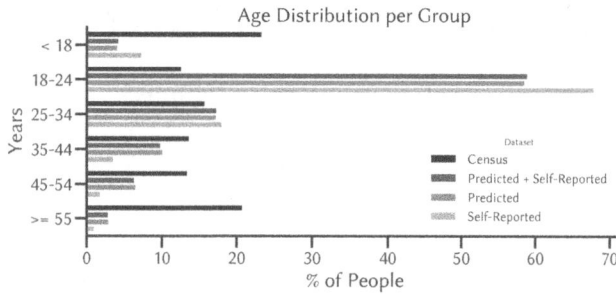

Figure 1: Distribution of age cohorts in the Census [4], and in our data set, including self-reported and inferred ages.

Table 1: Gender distribution in the data sets under study.

	Self-Reported	Inferred	S.R. + Inferred	Census
Males	57.42%	50.91%	55.70%	48.59%
Females	42.58%	45.22%	43.28%	51.41%
F/M Ratio	0.7414	0.8882	0.7769	1.0580

topic model, SeededLDA [5]. Seeded LDA is a semi-supervised variation of Latent Dirichlet Allocation, where the *a priori* information of words guide the topic inference. As input, we used a user-term matrix built using the tweets in the discussion. After fitting, the model provides $P(s \mid u)$, the probability of user u being associated with stance s. To label a user u with a stance s, we calibrated the threshold for $P(s \mid u)$ using profiles with self-reported abortion stances in their biographies. The accuracy of the model was 0.84.

Profile Weighting. For each user in the Twitter data set, we established a profile weight based on the representativeness of her/his demographic attributes according to the census.

4 REPRESENTATIVENESS AND CONCLUSION

To understand representativeness, we first analyzed how the Twitter demographic distributions differ from those in the census. Figure 1 shows the age cohort distribution. For each cohort, the figure contains bar charts of population distributions: census, all inferred Twitter profiles, and profiles with self-reported ages. We observe that younger people are more likely to report their age in their profile, and that the 25–34 range is the most similar in terms of census representation. Note that after predicting age for the rest of the data set, this bias is less pronounced. However, Chilean Twitter users still have an over-representation of 18–24 year old people.

Regarding gender, Table 1 shows the gender distribution in the data set, considering self-reported and inferred users. As result, females are severely under-represented in Twitter, as the female/male ratio is 0.78, in contrast with the census ratio of 1.06.

Representativeness of Insights. Next, we analyzed whether the insights that could be inferred from Twitter could be compared with those from a national level survey. A common way of analyzing survey data is through regression. We therefore decided to perform the same type of analysis in our data sets. In our case, the analysis would be representative (or not) according to the similarities in the coefficients of each model. If all Twitter coefficients have the same magnitude and sign than the survey coefficients,

Table 2: Regression results (N = 93,614 in Twitter models, N = 1,481 in CEP Survey). Positive coefficients show association to the *defense* stance; negative ones, to *opposition*. Significance: *** : $p < 0.001$ (Bonferroni corrected).

Coefficient	Twitter	Weighted	CEP Survey
Intercept (female, 18–24)	1.33***	1.33***	1.30***
male	-0.28***	-0.29***	-0.22
< 18	-0.24***	-0.24***	—
25–34	-0.18***	-0.18***	-0.06
35–44	-0.27***	-0.27***	-0.31
45–54	-0.37***	-0.37***	-0.50
≥ 55	-0.48***	-0.47***	-0.58

then the inference is representative of the general public opinion. We constructed three logistic regression models of the form: $P_{pop}(Y = \text{stance} \mid X = \text{gender, age cohort})$, where *pop* was one of: the Twitter population, the weighted Twitter population, and the population from the CEP opinion survey. All models considered being female with age 18–24 as reference, thus, each β coefficient represents the influence of a change in the respective attribute, all else being equal. A positive value is associated with *defense* (a negative with *opposition*)

Table 2 shows the model results. All models have coefficients with the same signs and similar magnitudes. Here, insights of interest for social scientists would include, for instance, that males are more likely to be in *opposition* ($\beta_{male} < 0$), which is arguably expected, due to males not risking their lives through abortion. Other insight is that older adults are also more likely to be in *opposition*, in comparison with the 18–24 age cohort ($\beta_{\geq 55} < \beta_{45-54} < \beta_{35-44} < \beta_{25-34}$) — as people grow, they could be more likely to have a family, which could be a relevant factor in catholic countries like Chile. Thus, our procedure matched the tools (regression) and insights (interpretation of coefficients) that would be made by domain experts when analyzing social issues, implying that the analysis is equivalent to those from representative sources.

Conclusion. Regarding abortion in Chile, Twitter models augmented with demographic information have equivalent outcomes from those of surveys. Biased sources can deliver valuable insights, if taking proper care of who and what is being analyzed.

REFERENCES
[1] Ricardo Baeza-Yates. 2018. Bias on the Web. *Commun. ACM* 61, 6 (May 2018), 54–61.
[2] CEP. 2017. National Survey of Public Opinion, April–May 2017. https://www.cepchile.cl/cep/site/artic/20170601/asocfile/20170601155007/encuestacep_abr_may2017.pdf. [Online; accessed November 2th, 2018].
[3] Eduardo Graells-Garrido, Mounia Lalmas, and Ricardo Baeza-Yates. 2015. Finding intermediary topics between people of opposing views: a case study. In *Social Personalisation & Search*, Christoph Trattner, Denis Parra, Peter Brusilovsky, and Leandro Balby Marinho (Eds.). CEUR, Santiago, Chile.
[4] Instituto Nacional de Estadísticas. 2018. Censo 2017. http://www.censo2017.cl/microdatos/. [Online; accessed February 18th, 2019].
[5] Jagadeesh Jagarlamudi, Hal Daumé III, and Raghavendra Udupa. 2012. Incorporating lexical priors into topic models. In *Proceedings of the 13th Conference of the European Chapter of the Association for Computational Linguistics*. Association for Computational Linguistics, Avignon, France, 204–213.
[6] Jonathan Mellon and Christopher Prosser. 2017. Twitter and Facebook are not representative of the general population: Political attitudes and demographics of British social media users. *Research & Politics* 4, 3 (2017), 2053168017720008.
[7] Amy X Zhang and Scott Counts. 2016. Gender and Ideology in the Spread of Anti-Abortion Policy. In *Proceedings of the 2016 CHI Conference on Human Factors in Computing Systems*. ACM, San Jose, CA, USA, 3378–3389.

Efficient Tracking of Breaking News in Twitter

Tuan-Anh Hoang

GESIS Leibniz Institute for the Social Sciences, Germany

tuan-anh.hoang@gesis.org

Thi-Huyen Nguyen, Wolfgang Nejdl

L3S Research Center, Germany

{nguyen,nejdl}@l3s.de

ABSTRACT

We present an efficient graph-based method for filtering tweets relevant to a given breaking news from large tweet streams. Unlike existing models that either require manual effort, strong supervision, and/or not scalable, our method can automatically and effectively filter incoming relevant tweets starting from just a small number of past relevant tweets. Extensive experiments on both synthetic and real datasets show that our proposed method significantly outperforms other methods in filtering the relevant tweets while being as fast as the most efficient state-of-the-art method.

ACM Reference Format:

Tuan-Anh Hoang and Thi-Huyen Nguyen, Wolfgang Nejdl. 2019. Efficient Tracking of Breaking News in Twitter. In *11th ACM Conference on Web Science (WebSci '19), June 30-July 3, 2019, Boston, MA, USA*. ACM, New York, NY, USA, 2 pages. https://doi.org/10.1145/3292522.3326058

1 INTRODUCTION

Real-time acquisition of tweets related to breaking news in real-time is vital for many important applications, such as social sensing and public opinion monitoring. This task is challenging due to the large scale of the Twitter data stream and the prevalence of noise and the wide range of covered topics in Twitter. These challenges require efficient methods for filtering relevant tweets from large streams. Existing works on real-time tweet filtering however require much manual effort and/or strong supervision which are often not available for the breaking news. Moreover, most of these methods are not scalable as they rely on supervised learning models whose training process is computationally expensive. We address these shortcomings by developing a lightweight method that requires minimal supervision yet obtains high performance. Precisely, we consider the filtering task in the following context:

Given a small set of tweets relevant to breaking news, we have to automatically decide, in real-time, if subsequent tweets in the tweet stream are relevant to the news.

In the following sections, we present a brief overview of our proposed method and some major experiment results. Readers are encouraged to refer to the full version of this paper [2] for the detailed description of the proposed method and the experiments.

2 METHODOLOGIES

The main idea of our proposed method is to employ a graph based approach for measuring tweets' relevance to the breaking news and

to the *background*. With background we refer to a representation of all topics in the tweet stream S that occur at around the same time with the news. As the stream consists of tweets in a vast variety of topics, we assume that incoming tweets are mostly relevant to the background and irrelevant to the news we want to track, and that news-relevant tweets are outliers. We therefore adopt a simple outlier detection approach to distinguish the news-relevant tweets based on the ratio of their relevance scores to the news and background. Our method consists of the following phases.

Initialization phase. We build the term graphs G_N and G_B from the set of initial relevant tweets T_N - which is given as input - and a set of tweets T_B that is randomly selected from all ones published within a short time window before the start filtering time. To do that, we preprocess each tweet by removing stopwords, punctuation marks, and special symbols (e.g., braces and quotations). The remaining tokens, which we call *terms*, are converted to lower-case, except the URLs embedded in tweets which are case sensitive. The node set then consists of all terms appearing in some preprocessed tweet(s). For a preprocessed tweet m and a pair of terms u and v, if both two terms appear in some window size L of m, then a undirected edge is drawn between u and v in the graph. A window size L of m is a sequence of at most L consecutive terms in m. The weight of edge (u, v) is the number of tweets in T that contain the edge. We then compute the importance of terms in G_N and G_B using Pagerank method. Finally, we compute the mean μ_N and variance σ_N of relevance scores of tweets in T_N - i.e., the relevant tweets - to the news, and compute mean μ_R and variance σ_R of *relevance ratio* of tweets in $T_N \cup T_B$. Here, a tweet's relevance ratio is the ratio between its relevance scores to the news and background. We will describe in detail the computation of tweets' relevance score in subsection below.

Filtering phase. For each incoming tweet m, its relevance scores to news r_N and background r_B are measured using the term graph G_N and G_B respectively. If $r_B > 0$, the ratio r_N/r_B is used to update μ_R and σ_R. Next, m's relevance label is determined as described below. If m is relevant then it is emitted as output and also added in T_N. The graph G_N is also updated using terms and edges induced by m. If m is irrelevant, with some probability $p < 1$, it is chosen for updating the background graph G_B and added into T_B. Regardless of m's relevance to the news, it is also used for checking whether updating of terms' importance is needed. The condition for this can be either time difference or number of (relevant) tweets found since the last update. If an update is needed, the oldest tweets in T_N and T_B are removed, and term graphs G_N and G_B are updated accordingly to the removed tweets. Also, term importance in the graphs is re-computed, and values of μ_N, σ_N, μ_R, and σ_R are reassigned accordingly.

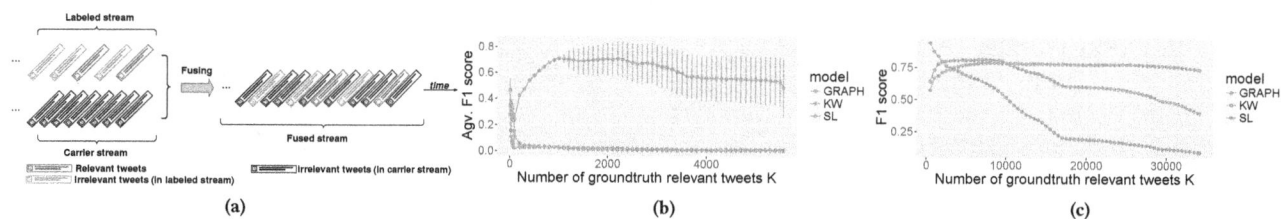

Figure 1: (a) Procedure for generating synthetic datasets, and experimental result on synthetic (b) and real datasets (c)

2.1 Computing Tweet Relevance Score

Given a term graph $G = (V, E)$ and a tweet m, our approach for measuring m's relevance to the news represented by G leverages both importance of terms and of edges in G. Precisely, the relevance score r of m is computed as follows.

$$r = \sum_{(u,v) \in E_m \cap E} \left[\pi(u) \frac{w(u,v)}{w(u,\cdot)} + \pi(v) \frac{w(u,v)}{w(\cdot,v)} \right] \quad (1)$$

In Equation 1, E_m is the set of edges induced by tweet m. $\pi(u)$ and $\pi(v)$ are importance of terms u and v in G respectively, $w(u,v)$ is the weight of edge (u,v), $w(u,\cdot)$ and $w(\cdot,v)$ are the summations of weights of all u's edges and v's edges respectively, i.e., $w(u,\cdot) = \sum_{(u,v') \in E} w(u,v')$ and $w(\cdot,v) = \sum_{(u',v) \in E} w(u',v)$.

2.2 Determining Tweets' Relevance Label

For a tweet m, if its relevance score to background $r_B = 0$, we decide that m is irrelevant. Otherwise, we determine relevance label of m based on its relevance scores to the news r_N and the ratio r_N/r_B. We assume that r_N follows a Gaussian distribution with mean μ_N and variance σ_N, while the ratio r_N/r_B follows a Gaussian distribution with mean μ_R and variance σ_R. We therefore measure the deviation d_N of respectively r_N and deviation d_R of r_N/r_B from their means as follows.

$$d_N = \frac{r_N - \mu_N}{\sigma_N} \quad \text{and} \quad d_R = \frac{(r_N/r_B) - \mu_R}{\sigma_R} \quad (2)$$

Then, m is assigned *relevance* label if $d_N \geq -1.3$ and $d_R \geq 1.05$. That means, only tweets whose relevance score is out of the bottom 10% and whose relevance ratio is among the top 15% are considered relevant to the news.

3 EXPERIMENTS

3.1 Datasets

Synthetic datasets with groundtruth. These datasets are synthesized following the procedure shown in Figure 1 (a). We re-used the set of tweets about the *Sandy Hurricane*[1] that were collected by [4] to simulate labeled stream. To simulate the carrier streams, we crawled tweets in 2017 using Twitter's realtime sample API. For each event, the labeled stream is fused into 15 different time durations of the carrier stream to create different datasets.

Real datasets with proxy groundtruth. Our real datasets consist of *2017 Westminster Attack*[2] and the tweet stream that are formed

[1]https://en.wikipedia.org/wiki/Hurricane_Sandy
[2]https://en.wikipedia.org/wiki/2017_Westminster_attack

by crawling Twitter using its sample API as above. We used a Twitter-LDA topic model [5] to mine topics of tweets returned by the filtering methods.The obtained topics are then manually judged for relevance based on their top terms and top tweets. A tweet m is considered relevant if $p(z|m) \geq \theta = 0.6$ for some annotated-relevant topic z. Relevant tweets of all filtering methods are pooled to form the proxy groundtruth for evaluating their performance.

3.2 Results

Figure 1 (b) shows the F_1 scores over time of the filtering methods on 15 *Sandy Hurricane* datasets. Since all the datasets have the same groundtruth, we average their scores. Here we compare our proposed method -denoted by **GRAPH** with two baselines: **KW** proposed by Cotelo et al. [1] - which is the state-of-the-art keyword based methods, and **SL** proposed by Magdy et al. [3] - which is the state-of-the-art supervised learning based methods. Similarly, Figure 1 (c) shows the scores of the three methods on *2017 Westminster Attack* dataset. The figures show that both the two baseline methods have better performance than ours in a short time duration after the news happens when there are not many relevant tweets. However, their performance decreases rapidly later when there are many more relevant tweets. This is due to the fact that, at first, the baseline methods' filters are unigram-based and weakly trained by datasets with only a small number of truly relevant tweets (i.e., the set of input relevant tweets). The figures also show that our method is much more robust against the news' evolution as it obtains lower performance at earlier stages but significantly outperforms the baseline methods to obtain much higher performance consistently across subsequent states.

ACKNOWLEDGEMENT

This research is supported by the ERC Grant (339233) ALEXAN-DRIA and the DFG Grant (NI-1760/1-1) Managed Forgetting.

REFERENCES

[1] Juan M Cotelo, Fermin L Cruz, and Jose A Troyano. Dynamic topic-related tweet retrieval. *JAIST*, 65(3):513–523, 2014.
[2] Tuan-Anh Hoang, Thi-Huyen Nguyen, and Wolfgang Nejdl. Efficient tracking of breaking news in twitter. https://www.dropbox.com/s/uz54vtp8z3ort68/attt.pdf.
[3] Walid Magdy and Tamer Elsayed. Unsupervised adaptive microblog filtering for broad dynamic topics. *IPM*, 52(4):513–528, 2016.
[4] Alexandra Olteanu, Carlos Castillo, Fernando Diaz, and Sarah Vieweg. Crisislex: A lexicon for collecting and filtering microblogged communications in crises. In *ICWSM*, 2014.
[5] Wayne Xin Zhao, Jing Jiang, Jianshu Weng, Jing He, Ee-Peng Lim, Hongfei Yan, and Xiaoming Li. Comparing twitter and traditional media using topic models. In *ECIR*, 2011.

Characterising Third Party Cookie Usage in the EU after GDPR

Xuehui Hu
King's Collage London
London, UK
xuehui.hu@kcl.ac.uk

Nishanth Sastry
King's Collage London
London, UK
nishanth.sastry@kcl.ac.uk

ABSTRACT

The recently introduced General Data Protection Regulation (GDPR) requires that when obtaining information online that could be used to identify individuals, their consents must be obtained. Among other things, this affects many common forms of cookies, and users in the EU have been presented with notices asking their approvals for data collection. This paper examines the prevalence of third party cookies before and after GDPR by using two datasets: accesses to top 500 websites according to `Alexa.com`, and weekly data of cookies placed in users' browsers by websites accessed by 16 UK and China users across one year.

We find that on average the number of third parties dropped by more than 10% after GDPR, but when we examine real users' browsing histories over a year, we find that there is no material reduction in long-term numbers of third party cookies, suggesting that users are not making use of the choices offered by GDPR for increased privacy. Also, among websites which offer users a choice in whether and how they are tracked, accepting the default choices typically ends up storing more cookies on average than on websites which provide a notice of cookies stored but without giving users a choice of which cookies, or those that do not provide a cookie notice at all. We also find that top non-EU websites have fewer cookie notices, suggesting higher levels of tracking when visiting international sites. Our findings have deep implications both for understanding compliance with GDPR as well as understanding the evolution of tracking on the web.

CCS CONCEPTS

• **Security and privacy → Privacy protections;** • **Social and professional topics → Governmental regulations;**

KEYWORDS

GDPR; Privacy; Cookie notice

ACM Reference Format:
Xuehui Hu and Nishanth Sastry. 2019. Characterising Third Party Cookie Usage in the EU after GDPR. In *11th ACM Conference on Web Science (WebSci '19), June 30-July 3, 2019, Boston, MA, USA.* ACM, New York, NY, USA, 5 pages. https://doi.org/10.1145/3292522.3326039

1 INTRODUCTION

The General Data Protection Regulation (GDPR) is a sweeping regulation that came into effect on May 25, 2018 in the European Union (EU), to protect the online privacy of its residents [13]. GDPR affects many aspects of personal data collection [15], although some argue that it does not go nearly far enough [19]. A central tenet of GDPR is that whenever personal data is collected about a user, it has to be done with the consent of the user.

This notion of user consents has affected a large number of sites that have used various mechanisms including analytics, tracking, and targeted advertising to track users. Such websites are now required to inform users. Consent for cookies which can be used to identify a user uniquely is explicitly mentioned in Recital 30 [1].

The need to inform users has led to a large number of cookie notices to users. Different websites have adopted different practices as shown in Fig. 1. Some, such as Forbes and LinkedIn (Fig. 1 (a) & (b)) have provided users with several choices, allowing them to select or unselect different options. Others, such as Office.com (Fig. 1 (c)) simply inform (without giving the user any choice) that user-specific cookies are being used, and this notice needs to be accepted if the website is accessed. The last option is not to issue any notice at all, because either no user-specific cookie has been used, or non-compliance of GDPR. Many websites appear to have chosen one of the first two options (cookie notice with or without choice) because GDPR non-compliance can attract fines of up to the higher of 20 Million Euros or 4% of the turnover of a company[1].

In this paper, we investigate GDPR cookie notices on two sets of websites. The first is the set of top sites according to Alexa Web Traffic Analysis. The second set comprises websites visited by real users in an ongoing study[2]. In both cases, we focus on so-called *third party cookies*, i.e., cookies set not by the "first party" sites visited by the users, but by other third parties used by the first party sites. For example, if a user visits a site that uses Google Analytics, a Google (Analytics) cookie is placed in the user's browser. Third party sites hold enormous power since they obtain a panoramic view of a user's browsing history across different sites using the same third party.

We access these sets of websites from a vantage point in the EU, and obtain the following results:

(1) Generally, websites which offer users a choice store *more* third-party cookies (when users accept default options offered), than sites which do not give users a choice. Some websites appear to continue placing cookies that are used to track users even after they explicitly decline consent[3].

---

[1]Art. 83(4) and 84(5) of the GDPR. https://gdpr-info.eu/art-83-gdpr/
[2]All collected data have been obtained with agreement from participants and under Research Ethics Minimal Risk Registration process at our university to ensure the permissions of approvals relevant to this research (Ethics approval no. MRS-1718-6539)
[3]Example screencast videos for such websites in Top500: https://bit.ly/2GnWrim

(a) **Levelled cookies setting in Forbes.com**   (b) **Detailed Cookie Table provided by LinkedIn.com**

(c) **Office.com provides a cookie notice but no choice**

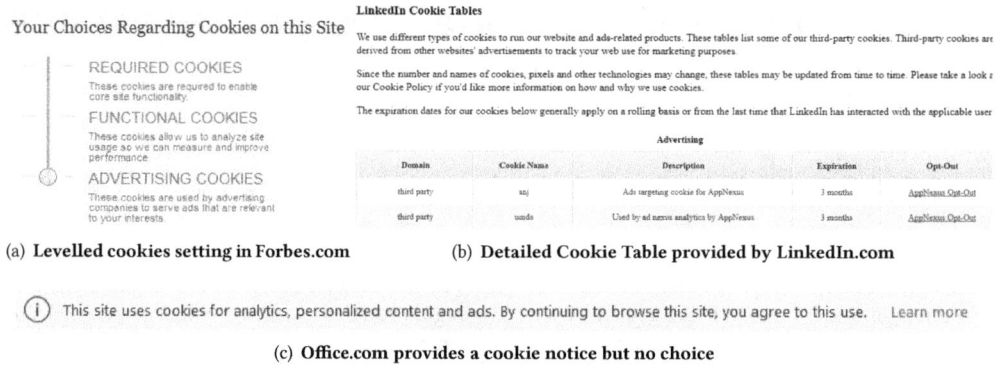

Figure 1: Examples of cookie notices provided by website owners to EU users after GDPR came into effect (May 25, 2018)

(2) The number of third party cookies, as well as the manner of GDPR consent notices, vary across different categories of websites. Adult websites are the least likely to offer GDPR consent and choices, but also appear to contain fewer third party cookies, likely because several common third parties such as Facebook and DoubleClick do not work with adult sites. In contrast, news websites have the highest number of third parties, and also provide more cookie consent notices.

(3) The prevalence of third-party cookies appears to differ across countries: Nearly 90% (66%) websites in the Alexa.com Top 100 in China (USA) do not issue any third party cookie notices, or provide no choice to users on the manner of tracking.

(4) On average, the number of third-party cookies from UK websites drops by 10% after May 25, 2018, suggesting that GDPR has been successful and sites are complying with the regulation. However, this reduction appears to not be reflected in real users' browsing histories, and third party cookie numbers in 2019 show little change since before GDPR.

2 DATASETS

Our results are based on two datasets. The first dataset focuses on the top websites, i.e., those which obtain the maximum amount of traffic according to Alexa.com [2]. We first analysed the top 100 sites in the UK one week before and one week after the introduction of GDPR (May 25 2018), focusing on differences in cookie numbers. In addition, we manually examine the types of cookie notices served by the top 500 websites in the UK after GDPR has been introduced.

The second dataset is obtained from a study in which anonymised browser histories are being collected weekly from 15 users (9 in the UK; 6 in China). We have instrumented the browsers of these users using a modified version of a browser plugin, Lightbeam [10] which runs also on Google Chrome. Our plugins collect information about both the first party websites they visit, as well as the third party cookies placed as a result of visiting those first party sites. Altogether these users have visited around 15k first-party websites across the year, which have led to over 187k third-party domains from which cookies are placed on their computers (Table 1). We focus on the UK users who have visited around 8416 websites and have cookies from nearly 113K third-party domains.

3 GDPR NOTICES IN ALEXA TOP WEBSITES

We first study GDPR cookie notices in popular websites. Our study comprises three steps. First we capture cookies one week before

User Group	No. 1st party sites	No. 3rd party cookies
UK Users	8416	113,003
CN Users	6144	74,313
Total	14827	187,316

Table 1: Data collected from Jan. 2018 to Jan. 2019

and one week after GDPR comes into effect, among the Alexa.com Top 100 sites in the UK, which, as a current member of the EU, is subject to GDPR. Next we compare UK cookie notices after GDPR was introduced, with those from outside the EU, taking USA and China as examplar non-EU countries, and also using Alexa.com's global lists of top sites in various important categories of the web, such as shopping and technology. We then manually examine the different kinds of cookie notices among the top 500 websites in the UK, and discuss the impact on tracking and GDPR compliance.

3.1 Cookie notices among Alexa Top 100 sites

After 25th May in 2018, websites started to pop up cookie notices to users before data from them is collected. Generally, there are three types of cookie notices: The first one is that the website owner provides users with a privacy choice of opting out from the data sharing, e.g., Forbes and LinkedIn (Fig. 1 (a) & (b)). Other examples include Reddit, Twitter and Amazon. The second kind of websites includes vendors that provide a notice of cookie collection but they do not offer a way to change the setting, e.g., Office.com (Fig. 1 (c)). Essentially, the user has to choose between using the website with cookies being used, and not using the website at all. The final kind of websites provide no cookie collection notice. A handful of websites also stop their business and support for European users. This includes several prominent non-EU sites such as LAtimes.com, ChicagoTribune.com, QQ.com, Unroll.me, etc.

Fig. 2 studies GDPR cookie notices of the Alexa.com Top 100 websites in the UK. Nearly 80% of these sites display some form of cookie notice (Fig. 2 (a) & (b)), and half of all collected websites provide an option on whether to receive personalised ads or not (Fig. 2 (a)). When the websites provide a choice, we accept the default settings and observe the number of cookies stored[4]. 22 websites in the top 100 do not serve any cookie notice.

As expected, GDPR appears to have had an effect on the *number* of third party cookies immediately after the law came into effect. Amongst websites which allow users to set their choices (Fig. 2 (a)),

---

[4]Note that some of the cookies stored are simply to note the fact that the cookie notice has been served and accepted. We discard these cookies from our counts.

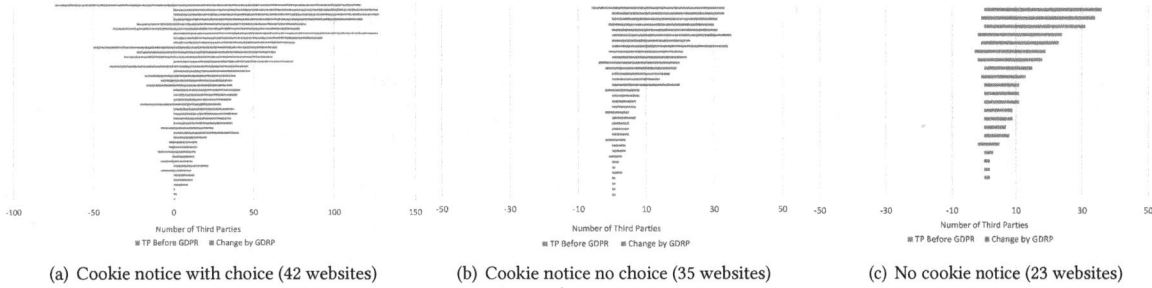

(a) Cookie notice with choice (42 websites)   (b) Cookie notice no choice (35 websites)   (c) No cookie notice (23 websites)

Figure 2: The changes on the number of third-party cookies of Alexa Top100 Websites (one week before and after GDPR), if the default choice is accepted. Each horizontal line denotes a site, totally 100 lines across three subgraphs. For each site, blue shows the number of third-party cookies served before GDPR, and red the *change* in the number of cookies after GDPR. Three categories are observed: (a) Sites which serve users with cookie notices. (Green indicate sites which store cookies even if users explicitly opt out) (b) Sites which serve cookie notices but offer no choice to users. (c) Sites which serve no notices after GDPR.

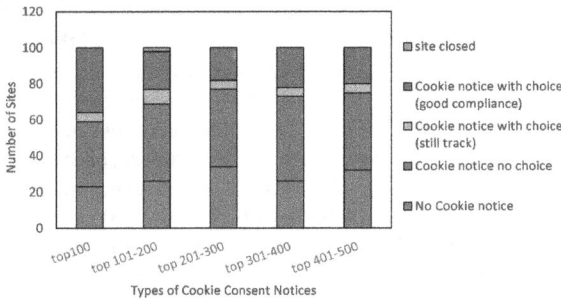

Figure 3: Detailed study of UK top500 sites' Cookie Types.

the average number of third party cookies dropped from 34 to 28; websites which show a cookie notice but provide no choice in the matter (Fig. 2 (b)) show a minor reduction from 16 cookies on average before GDPR to 15 after; those which do not issue cookie notices (Fig. 2 (c)) show no change, with an average of 13 third party cookies before and after GDPR.

Degree of GDPR compliance: It is interesting and notable that websites which appear to be transparent and offer users a choice (Fig. 2 (a)) store *more* cookies (avg. 28) when the default option is accepted, than those which provide no choice (avg. 15). Similarly, several websites which offer an option seem to have used the opportunity to *increase* the number of third-party cookies (Red lines on the positive side of Fig. 2 (a)). Examining manually, we see that websites which do not serve cookie notices *use some of the same third party trackers (e.g., Google Analytics or Facebook cookies) which are found among websites that do serve notices*, which suggests that perhaps such websites *should* be serving cookie notices and asking for user consent, or could be not compliant with GDPR.

Furthermore, in our manual examination of websites that do provide users with a choice, we see cases where tracking cookies are being placed even after opting out of tracking and personalisation (i.e., even when we choose non-default choices that maximise privacy), highly indicative of GDPR non-compliance (See footnote 3, Pg. 1). Fig. 2 (a) shows these websites with green, and it is interesting to note that these websites have higher than average number of cookies among those that provide cookie notices with choice.

Finally, Fig.3 expands our study from the top 100 sites we have been looking at so far to the Alexa.com top 500 sites. As expected,

the fraction of sites offering users a choice drops drastically after the top 100. Many sites also close and stop serving EU users.

3.2 Cookie notices of top non-EU websites

GDPR compliance is a requirement for all websites that wish to operate within or can be accessed from EU locations. Therefore, we are interested in understanding how non-EU websites have dealt with the introduction of GDPR as they will also be subject to the regulation if serving EU citizens in the EU. As mentioned previously, several prominent websites such as LATimes.com (Alexa.com rank 163 in the USA), Chicagotribune.com (Alexa.com USA rank 342) and QQ.com (Alexa.com rank 2 in China), have once stopped serving users in the EU, serving up a banner that says they do not operate within EU boundaries because of GDPR.

Therefore, as a baseline, we manually examine how Alexa.com top 100 sites in China and the USA serve cookie notices when accessed from the UK. Table 2 shows the comparison of top 100 sites in the UK (also studied in Fig. 2) and those in China (CN) and USA (US). In contrast with the UK, only 10% (respectively 34%) of sites in China (USA) offer users a choice of which cookies to store, and only a further 6% (14%) serve a cookie notice with no choice. Thus the vast majority (84% in CN, 52% in the US) of top sites are currently operating without a cookie notice. A large proportion also serve a notice that tracking cookies are being used, but users are not able to opt out of such cookies and continue to use the websites. Indeed, only a small fraction 10% (34%) of top sites in CN (US) offer users a cookie notice with choice. Therefore, it appears that *users of international non-EU websites in the UK obtain little protection, and little choice about their privacy and tracking.*

	UK	US	CN
Choice (UK)	42%	34%	10%
Notice no Choice (UK)	35%	14%	6%
No Cookie Choice (UK)	23%	52%	84%

Table 2: Percentage distribution of different kinds of cookie notices in Alexa.com Top 100 websites from US, CN and UK.

We next turn to global top sites across categories in Alexa.com, to understand GDPR compliance among different kinds of websites. Fig. 4 shows the categories ranked by the number of third parties

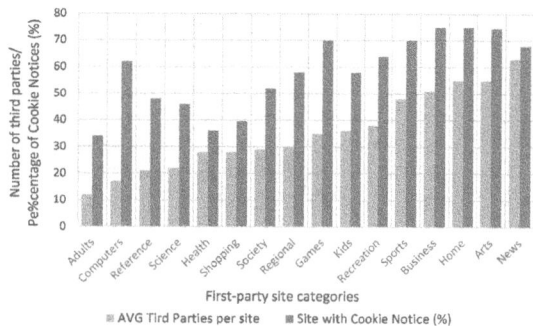

Figure 4: The average number of third parties per site and percent of cookie notices in each category.

per site for each category on average. The count in Adult websites is the least, likely because they typically are not able to access the most common third-party cookie providers such as Facebook or Google Analytics. However, Adult websites also have the lowest fraction of websites serving cookie notices. News and home related websites have the largest number of third parties, but also show the highest levels of compliance (i.e., serve cookie notices). In general however, no individual category of global websites achieves the same level of compliance as the top 100 UK websites.

4 COOKIE NOTICES TO REAL USERS

Until now, we have been studying how top sites around the web serve third-party cookie notices. However, any given user may have niche interests, and will likely access sites outside the list of Alexa.com top sites. To understand how compliant those less popular sites are, we turn to an ongoing user study we are conducting on third-party trackers collected by browser plugins, using a live user group. We also wish to understand whether real users see a decrease in number of tracking third party cookies after GDPR.

Cookie notices in real users' browsing histories We use 1528 websites collected by UK users in the weeks from Jan - Mar 2018 and evaluate the popularity of those sites by their visiting frequency to group them into 5 quintiles. Quintile 1 comprises 133 sites visited by over 80% participants, quintile 2 has 150 sites visited by around 60% - 80% users, quintile 3 is 148 sites visited by 40% - 60% users, quintile 4 168 sites by 20% - 40% users and quintile 5 has by far the most number of sites (929), but each site is visited by less than 20% participants. Even the Alexa.com top 100 sites are evenly distributed across the five quintiles – 15 of the Alexa.com UK top 100 sites fall in quintile 5, i.e., are visited by fewer than 20% of users. 19 Alexa.com top100 sites are not accessed by *any* user.

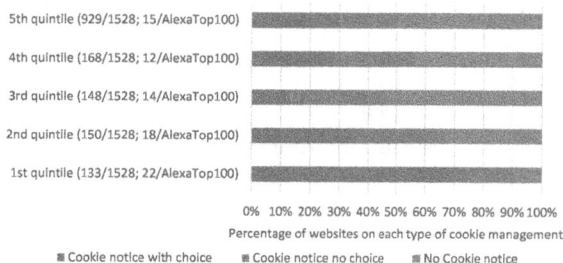

Figure 5: Cookie notices among the five quintiles of websites accessed by a real user base.

Fig. 5 shows the distribution of different kinds of cookie notices among the websites in different quintiles. Reassuringly, websites which are visited by most of the users in the study (quintile 1) has the highest fraction of websites which serve some form of cookie notice. However, as we go towards more niche interest websites, those visited by smaller numbers in our user study, the fraction that serve GDPR cookie notices drops drastically (there is a steady decline up to quintile 3, and although there is a brief uptick in quintiles 4 and 5, the fraction serving cookie notices are still below the top 2 quintiles). This suggests that users may need to be careful about niche websites.

Did GDPR affect third party cookie numbers for real users? Whereas previous sections have looked at synthetic or programmatically generated browser visits to websites, we can also ask the *extent to which users explicitly make use of the choice provided by GDPR cookie notices* and choose to block third-party tracking. We examine this using the anonymised cookie data from one year of browser histories of the UK users in our study. Fig. 6 shows that although there was a brief reduction in the number of third-party cookies when GDPR was introduced in May 2018, the overall number of cookies among the 9 UK users has stayed relatively the same between Jan 2018 and Jan 2019. The reductions between Mar 2018 and Jun 2018 appear to coincide with the beginning of the preparations for GDPR cookie compliance and the cookie consent manager rollouts of the widely used OneTrust [11] (Mar 2018) and TrustArc [16] (Apr 2018) for GDPR compliance, and similar reductions also reported by others[8]. However, Do Not Track cookies and GDPR consent cookies expire; cookie caches get cleaned etc, and *it appears that users in our study have subsequently mostly chosen default settings or have made choices that do not increase their privacy – there is little change in the numbers of third-party cookies per website visited between early 2018 and early 2019.* Table 3 shows how the numbers of cookies varied for selected sites of different Alexa.com ranks between Feb 2018 and Feb 2019, with a minimum being seen around the time GDPR introduced in May 2018. Interestingly, users in China experience *fewer* third party cookies throughout the duration.

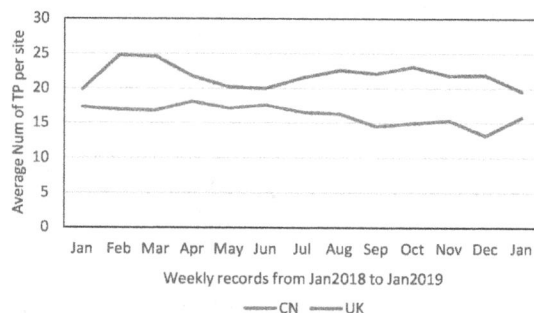

Figure 6: Average number of third parties per site, based on weekly browsing records of UK and China participants.

	Site A (top100)	Site B (top200)	Site C (top300)	Site D (top400)	Site E (top500)
Feb., 2018	13	14	20	21	37
May, 2018	8	8	16	17	29
Feb 2019	12	8	22	18	32

Table 3: Number of cookies on websites visited by real users.

5 RELATED WORK

GDPR is newly introduced, and so there have only been a handful of measurements and analyses: [6] concluded that tracking flows mostly stay within the EU. In a periodic survey of top 500 sites, [3] found that around one-sixth of websites (15.7%) had reorganised privacy policies by May 25, 2018. [17] investigated cookie synchronisation and show that GDPR cookie consents are insufficient to prevent leakages. Our work differs from these studies as we examine GDPR over a long duration, using real users' browsing histories and focusing on third-party cookies.

Senzing Inc. [14] suggests that around 60% of European companies are not yet prepared for GDPR and 44% of the EU's larges companies are worried about compliance with GDPR. [18] studies kids and teenagers' privacy and finds the EU children may be subject to more third party tracking compared to the US. [8] examines news websites and finds that UK in particular has a high level of tracking. Results such as these corroborate our findings that sites may not be offering a choice, or offering a choice and then not respecting users' choice (see examples from footnote 3).

Different from studying the behaviour of actual websites is to take an economic, policy or legal perspective. However, even in these fields, it is now being recognised that choice may be difficult for users to deal with, given the complexity of these sites and the technology used [5, 12]. [7] develops a tool to examine privacy policies of websites to see if all third parties are being disclosed, and finds that privacy policies are extremely complicated, and several third parties are not being disclosed. Our results (Fig. 6) also suggest that in practice users may not make choices that maximise privacy.

Our work focuses on GDPR consent cookies, but fits within the overall area of studying third-party tracking. Gomer *et al.* [4] posited three key questions to explore: the relationship between search context and tracking services, the extent of tracking and the characteristics of tracking services. We focus on the extent of tracking, and on the characteristics. [9] checked the coverage of top 10 trackers and showed that Doubleclick might cover over 80%. Such works highlight the importance of third-party websites in leaking personal information and motivate our study of third-party cookies and consent notices about their use.

6 DISCUSSION AND CONCLUSIONS

In this paper, we took an in-depth look at the effect of GDPR, which requires cookie notices when sites are using third-party cookies that collect personal data. We find that although UK-based websites comply in general (i.e., serve some form of cookie notice), non-EU sites are less likely to offer fine-grained choices for users to decide their privacy preferences. Availability of choice also varies across different categories of websites, with adult websites being the least likely to offer a cookie notice, but also with many fewer third-party cookies than other categories such as news websites.

Fine grained choices are not necessarily what is "best" for the users: First, though UK websites are meeting the cookie consent requirement by presenting users with a choice, this choice can be a false one – if default choices are accepted, it could sometimes lead to higher numbers of third-party cookies than before. Second, by studying the numbers of third party cookies in real users' browsing histories, we find that GDPR has had little long term effect on the numbers of cookies. In practice, the choices, when offered, can be very fine grained (e.g., Fig. 1 (b)), allowing users to opt out of cookies from specific third parties that are being used by the website while still allowing them to opt in for cookies from other third parties. We speculate that users may be fatigued by the effort of having to choose their privacy preferences on every website they visit, and end up accepting the default choices offered by the websites (which in a majority of sites, is to have tracking turned on). Interestingly, users in the UK appear to have *larger* numbers of third party cookies than countries like China. Unfortunately, tracking is the default on many sites where users are not given a choice at all, and the only real choice for users appears to be a forced one of either accepting tracking and third party cookies, or not using the website at all.

In summary, we find that by and large, the relationship between website operators and users remains unbalanced, and GDPR may in practice be falling short of the level of protection that it aims to deliver.

REFERENCES

[1] GDPR Recital 30. 2018. Online identifiers for profiling and identification. https://gdpr-info.eu/recitals/no-30/. Accessed on 2018-07-25.
[2] Alexa. 2018. Global Top Websites. https://www.alexa.com/topsites. Accessed on 2018-05-20.
[3] Martin Degeling, Christine Utz, Christopher Lentzsch, Henry Hosseini, Florian Schaub, and Thorsten Holz. 2018. We Value Your Privacy... Now Take Some Cookies: Measuring the GDPR's Impact on Web Privacy. *The Network and Distributed System Security Symposium* (2018).
[4] Richard Gomer, Eduarda Mendes Rodrigues, Natasa Milic-Frayling, and mc schraefel. 2013. Network analysis of third party tracking: User exposure to tracking cookies through search. In *Proc. WI - IAT-Volume 01*. IEEE Computer Society.
[5] KL Hui and I Png. 2006. Economics of privacy. T. Hendershott, ed., Handbooks in Information Systems, Vol. 1.
[6] Costas Iordanou, Georgios Smaragdakis, Ingmar Poese, and Nikolaos Laoutaris. 2018. Tracing Cross Border Web Tracking. In *Proceedings of the Internet Measurement Conference 2018 (IMC '18)*. ACM, New York, NY, USA, 329–342. https://doi.org/10.1145/3278532.3278561
[7] Timothy Libert. 2018. An automated approach to auditing disclosure of third-party data collection in website privacy policies. In *2018 Proc. WWW*. International World Wide Web Conferences Steering Committee, 207–216.
[8] Timothy Libert, Lucas Graves, and Rasmus Kleis Nielsen. 2018. Changes in third-party content on European News Websites after GDPR. (2018).
[9] Hassan Metwalley, Stefano Traverso, Marco Mellia, Stanislav Miskovic, and Mario Baldi. 2015. The online tracking horde: a view from passive measurements. In *International Workshop on Traffic Monitoring and Analysis*. Springer, 111–125.
[10] Mozilla. 2012. *Firefox Lightbeam*.
[11] OneTrust. 2018. OneTrust launches Universal Consent Management and Preference Management. https://bit.ly/2V674Qq. Accessed on 2019-02-10.
[12] Marc Pelteret and Jacques Ophoff. 2016. A review of information privacy and its importance to consumers and organizations. *Informing Science: The International Journal of an Emerging Transdiscipline* 19 (2016), 277–301.
[13] GDPR Portal. 2018. EU GDPR Information Portal. https://www.eugdpr.org/. Accessed on 2018-06-11.
[14] Senzing. 2019. Finding the missing link in GDPR compliance. https://bit.ly/2IGzUjA. Accessed on 2019-02-08.
[15] Christina Tikkinen-Piri, Anna Rohunen, and Jouni Markkula. 2018. EU General Data Protection Regulation: Changes and implications for personal data collecting companies. *Computer Law & Security Review* 34, 1 (2018), 134–153.
[16] TrustArc. 2018. TrustArc Launches GDPR Validation, Empowering Companies to Demonstrate GDPR Compliance Status. https://bit.ly/2PgBaet. Accessed on 2019-02-10.
[17] Tobias Urban, Dennis Tatang, Martin Degeling, Thorsten Holz, and Norbert Pohlmann. 2018. The Unwanted Sharing Economy: An Analysis of Cookie Syncing and User Transparency under GDPR.
[18] Natalija Vlajic, Marmara El Masri, Gianluigi M Riva, Marguerite Barry, and Derek Doran. 2018. Online Tracking of Kids and Teens by Means of Invisible Images: COPPA vs. GDPR. In *2th Proc. MPS*. ACM, 96–103.
[19] Tal Z Zarsky. 2016. Incompatible: The GDPR in the Age of Big Data. *Seton Hall L. Rev.* 47 (2016), 995.

Temporal Analysis of Supply and Demand of Topics on The Web*

Masahiro Inoue
Kyoto University
inoue@dl.soc.i.kyoto-u.ac.jp

Keishi Tajima
Kyoto University
tajima@i.kyoto-u.ac.jp

ABSTRACT

Timing of supply and demand for information on a topic does not always coincide. Sometimes one of them rises first, then the other follows. We show a classification of hot topics on the Web in the past based on the temporal relationship between their supply and demand, and also show that our classification is useful for predicting the timing of supply peaks in some cases.

1 INTRODUCTION

Supply and demand for some information on the Web have correlation, but their timing does not always coincide. Sometimes one of them appears first, and the other follows. The timing they reach their peaks may also be different. In this paper, we show a classification of hot topics on the Web based on the temporal relationship between their supply and demand to investigate their properties.

There have been some research on supply and demand for information. McNie [3] discussed discrepancy between supply and demand of scientific information. McVicar et al. [4] analyzed the geographic discrepancy between supply and demand for musics by independent artists. The keynote talk by Fedyk [1] discussed the behavior of the consumers of the news from major news media. However, this is the first research on temporal relationship between supply and demand for information on the Web.

2 DETECTING SUPPLY AND DEMAND

For our purpose, we need to know when the information on each topic was demanded and when it was supplied.

A good indicator of the demand is the frequency of queries related to the topic submitted to Web search engines. Although query logs of major search engines are not available to the public, we can indirectly know when the demand for a topic rose through Google Trends[1]. We use the date when the topic appeared on Google Trends, denoted by T, to approximate when the demand rose.

On the other hand, there is no easy way to know when the information on a topic was supplied. In this research, we approximate it by retrieving web pages related to the topic through a search engine, producing a timeline showing how many pages newly appeared on each day, and detecting the peak and upsurge on the timeline.

In order to produce such a timeline, we need to know the creation date of each web page. Although creation dates of pages are not

---

*This work was supported by JSPS KAKENHI JP18H03245.
[1] http://www.google.com/trends/

Table 1: Six Categories and their Ratio

Condition on Relative Position of T	Abbreviation	Ratio
$U \leq T = P$	$T = P$	19%
$U \leq T < P, T = P - 1$	$T = P - 1$	11%
$U \leq T < P, T = P - 2$ or $P - 3$	$T = P - 2, 3$	1.6%
$P - 3 \leq T < U \leq P$	$T < U$	1.3%
$U \leq P < T \leq P + 3$	$P < T$	1.3%
$T < P - 3$ or $P + 3 < T$	$\|T - P\| > 3$	66%

always explicit under the present Web, many web pages, e.g., most news articles and blogs, are created with some content management systems (CMSs), and CMSs usually embed creation dates on pages. We developed a system that detects such timestamps on pages [2]. The program is available as an open source library[2].

Our system retrieves top 200 web pages through a search engine, and detects the peak and upsurge on the timeline produced from them. If the ranking by a search engines is influenced by the creation dates of pages, estimating the timelines only by using top 200 web pages given by a search engine would be biased. In order to avoid that, we select topics that are old enough, for which we expect that the temporal factor in the top ranking has become ignorable.

We define the peak day, P, on a timeline as the day when the most web pages appeared. Starting from P, we trace back successive previous days with new page appearances until we reach a day without a page appearance. We define the upsurge date, U, as the last day with page appearances we could trace back. Notice that $U \leq P$. If the peak day has less than three pages, we determine the topic has no supply peak, and exclude the topic from our experiments.

Because we only use the top 200 pages, we rarely have pages irrelevant to the given topic, but we miss many relevant pages. Our purpose is, however, to find P and U. Our experiment shows that 200 pages are enough to find the correct P. For about half of queries in our experiment, even top 20 pages are enough to detect the same peak as with 200 pages, and for three fourth of our queries, top 100 pages are enough. On the other hand, if we include more pages, we will obtain earlier days for U. However, it can affect our classification only when the upsurge of supply is later than the date from Google Trends, which is very rare as we explain later.

Our system does not always detect correct timestamps on pages, and it can also affect our classification, but our system had the precision higher than 90% in our experiment, and errors in timestamp detection rarely affected the estimation of P and U.

3 CLASSIFICATION

We collected 4,000 queries from Google Trends, top 20 queries for each of 200 days starting from January 1st, 2011. Eliminating queries for which the peak has less than three pages as mentioned before,

---

[2] https://github.com/kkjk21/Timestamp-Extractor

Table 2: Query Examples

#	Category	Queries	U	P	T
1	$T = P$	inside job documentary	02/27	02/27	02/27
2	$T = P - 1$	critics choice awards 2011	01/12	01/15	01/14
3	$T = P - 2$	nfl draft	04/25	04/30	04/28
4	$T = P - 2$	arizona shooting	01/10	01/12	01/10
5	$T < U$	billy walters	01/17	01/17	01/16
6	$T < U$	prader willi syndrome	01/27	01/27	01/26
7	$P < T$	qwiki	01/20	01/20	01/22
8	$P < T$	super bowl food	01/31	02/04	02/05

we classified the remaining 2,695 queries. We classify them into six categories based on the temporal position of T relative to U and P. Table 1 lists the conditions defining the six categories, their abbreviated names, and the ratio of the queries classified into each category. Table 2 shows some examples of the queries. The dates are in 2011 and their format is "mm/dd". In the following, we explain the details of these six categories.

(1) $T = P$

This is the second largest group of queries in our experiment. Typical topics in this group are news or events occurred on the day P. The query #1 in Table 2 is a typical example. For most queries in this group, $U = P$ also holds. Therefore, we can expect that T and P for this type of topic will be the day of the news or event in most cases. The supply will not increase and have a higher peak later.

(2) $T = P - 1$

This is the third largest group. $T = P - 1$ means the peak of the supply appears on the next day of the rise of the demand. Typically, several web pages appeared on T as prompt reports, after which most web pages with full contents, typically articles on news sites, appeared on $T + 1$. In the case of the query #2 in Table 2, T is the day of the announcement of the award winners, P was the next day, and U, the upsurge of the supply, started several days before T.

In this group, $U = T$ holds only for 7% of queries, while it holds for most queries in $T = P$ group as explained before. It means most queries that satisfy $U = T$ also satisfy $U = T = P$. Therefore, we can predict whether a new topic is in the group $T = P$ or not on the day T in the following way. Suppose a new topic appeared in Google Trends on the day T. We then detect U by tracing back the appearance of related pages starting from T, and if $U = T$, we can expect that $T = P$, i.e., the peak of the supply is also on T, and the supply will decrease next day. On the contrary, if $U < T$, we can expect that $T < P$, i.e., the supply will increase next day.

(3) $T = P - 2$, $T = P - 3$

Although this group is the forth largest, it includes far fewer queries than the previous two groups. For about 70% of queries in this group, $U \leq T$ holds, i.e., the supply started before the query became a trend. For these queries, the supply started early but it continued for long time and reached its peak after the demand rose.

Typical queries in this group are those about long term events or discussions which ended up with some interesting results. The query #3 in Table 2 is an example of such a type. In this group, $P - T$ is larger than in the group $T = P - 1$ by definition, and our experiment shows that $T - U$ is also larger than in the group

$T = P - 1$ on average. Therefore, if we find $T - U$ is large on the day T, we can expect that $P - T$ will be also large.

This group also includes topics for which more reports appeared as time went by after the event on T. The query #4 in Table 2 is an example. This happens only for a small number of very big news.

(4) $T < U$

Among queries satisfying $T = P - 1$, $T = P - 2$, or $T = P - 3$, there are a small number of queries where $T < U$ holds. The condition $T < U$ means even the upsurge, usually the earliest reports on the topic, appeared later than the demand for the information.

Most of such queries are related to some real-world events not of type that are reported by news media. Most of them are related to TV programs. The query #5 and #6 in Table 2 are examples of this type. These queries were not triggered by news events but by the information appeared on TV. Because of that, the information was not reported much on the day T, but more web pages appeared later due to the appearance of the query in Google Trends. Such queries are typical examples where demand triggered supply.

(5) $P < T$

There also exist a few queries where $P < T$ holds. We can imagine why $P \geq T$ holds for most queries: it usually takes longer to make a report on an event and publish it than just to submit a query. Therefore, $P < T$ queries are rare, and this group is worth focusing on. We found there are mainly two types of queries in this group.

In one type, there was quick reports on it on the Web, but the search by people rose later because it took time for the people to get to know about it. The query #7 is an example of this type. A new web service "qwiki" was announced and it was reported by many blogs, but it took some time for people to know about the service. This is an example where supply triggered demand.

The query #8 is an example of the second type. In this case, much information on "super bowl food" was published in advance of the date in the near future when the information is expected to be demanded. For this type of queries, supply "foresaw" demand.

(6) $|T - P| > 3$

Many queries in this group are common nouns or popular proper nouns, e.g., names of celebrities or popular places. Such topics are continually demanded and supplied. For many of them, our system failed to find the peak corresponding to the demand, and as a result, $|T - P|$ was large. In our experiment, many queries were classified in this group, but if we can detect the peak more accurately, we can classify more queries in this group into the other groups.

4 CONCLUSION

We classified topics on the web based on the temporal relationship between their supply and demand. Our classification is useful for predicting supply peak in some cases, as explained in Section 3.

REFERENCES

[1] Anastassia Fedyk. 2015. Supply and Demand: Propagation and Absorption of News. In *NewsWWW (WWW 2015 Companion)*. 883–883.
[2] Masahiro Inoue and Keishi Tajima. 2012. Noise robust detection of the emergence and spread of topics on the Web. In *TempWeb (WWW 2012 Companion)*. 9–16.
[3] Elizabeth C. McNie. 2007. Reconciling the supply of scientific information with user demands: an analysis of the problem and review of the literature. *Environmental Science & Policy* 10, 1 (2007), 17 – 38.
[4] Matt McVicar, Cédric Mesnage, Jeffrey Lijffijt, Eirini Spyropoulou, and Tijl De Bie. 2015. Supply and Demand of Independent UK Music Artists on the Web. In *WebSci*. 48:1–48:2.

Incentivized Blockchain-based Social Media Platforms: A Case Study of *Steemit*

Chao Li
School of Computing and Information
University of Pittsburgh
Pittsburgh, USA
chl205@pitt.edu

Balaji Palanisamy
School of Computing and Information
University of Pittsburgh
Pittsburgh, USA
bpalan@pitt.edu

ABSTRACT

Advances in Blockchain and distributed ledger technologies are driving the rise of incentivized social media platforms over Blockchains, where no single entity can take control of the information and users can receive cryptocurrency as rewards for creating or curating high-quality contents. This paper presents an empirical analysis of *Steemit*, a key representative of these emerging platforms, to understand and evaluate the actual level of decentralization and the practical effects of cryptocurrency-driven reward system in these modern social media platforms. Similar to Bitcoin, *Steemit* is operated by a decentralized community, where 21 members are periodically elected to cooperatively operate the platform through the Delegated Proof-of-Stake (DPoS) consensus protocol. Our study performed on 539 million operations performed by 1.12 million *Steemit* users during the period 2016/03 to 2018/08 reveals that the actual level of decentralization in *Steemit* is far lower than the ideal level, indicating that the DPoS consensus protocol may not be a desirable approach for establishing a highly decentralized social media platform. In *Steemit*, users create contents as posts which get curated based on votes from other users. The platform periodically issues cryptocurrency as rewards to creators and curators of popular posts. Although such a reward system is originally driven by the desire to incentivize users to contribute to high-quality contents, our analysis of the underlying cryptocurrency transfer network on the blockchain reveals that more than 16% transfers of cryptocurrency in *Steemit* are sent to curators suspected to be bots and also finds the existence of an underlying supply network for the bots, both suggesting a significant misuse of the current reward system in *Steemit*. Our study is designed to provide insights on the current state of this emerging blockchain-based social media platform including the effectiveness of its design and the operation of the consensus protocols and the reward system.

CCS CONCEPTS

• **Security and privacy** → **Social network security and privacy**; • **Networks** → **Social media networks**.

KEYWORDS

blockchain, social media, decentralization, reward system, bot

ACM Reference Format:
Chao Li and Balaji Palanisamy. 2019. Incentivized Blockchain-based Social Media Platforms: A Case Study of Steemit. In *11th ACM Conference on Web Science (WebSci '19), June 30-July 3, 2019, Boston, MA, USA.* ACM, New York, NY, USA, 10 pages. https://doi.org/10.1145/3292522.3326041

1 INTRODUCTION

Recent advances in Blockchain and distributed ledger technologies [26] are driving the rise of incentivized social media platforms over Blockchains. Examples of such platforms include *Steemit*[1], *Indorse*[2], *Sapien*[3] and *SocialX*[4]. Unique features of these blockchain-powered social media platforms include decentralization of data generated in the platforms and deep integration of social platforms with the underlying cryptocurrency transfer networks on the blockchain. *Steemit* is the first blockchain-powered social media platform that incentivizes both creator of user-generated content and content curators. It has kept its leading position during the last two and a half years and its native cryptocurrency, *STEEM*, has the highest market capitalization among all cryptocurrencies issued by blockchain-based social networking projects. Its market capital is estimated over 266 million USD in 09/30/2018 [24].

In *Steemit*, users can create and share contents as blog posts. Once posted, a blog can get replied, reposted or voted by other users. Depending on the weight of received votes, posts get ranked and the top ranked posts make them to the front page. All data generated by *Steemit* users are stored in the Steem-blockchain [3]. Similar to other blockchains like Bitcoin [26] and Ethereum [4], data stored in the Steem-blockchain is publicly accessible and it is hard to be manipulated. At the core of *Steemit* are its decentralization and its cryptocurrency-driven reward system used for rewarding the content creators and curators. Instead of operating as a single entity like *Reddit* and *Quora*, the *Steemit* platform is operated by a group of 21 witnesses elected by its shareholders (uses owning *Steemit* shares) through the Delegated Proof of Stake (DPoS) consensus protocol [23]. Unlike traditional social media platforms that typically do not reward their users, *Steemit* issues three types of rewards to its users: (1) producer reward; (2) author reward; (3) curation reward. The producer rewards are issued to the elected witnesses producing blocks. It incentivizes users of *Steemit*

[1]https://steemit.com/
[2]https://indorse.io/
[3]https://beta.sapien.network/
[4]https://socialx.network/

to compete for the top-21 witnesses. The author rewards and curation rewards are issued to users creating posts (authors) and users voting for posts (curators) respectively. These incentivize authors to produce posts that attract more votes and curators to vote for posts that have higher potential to be voted by other users. By the end of 2018/08, *Steemit* has issued over 40 million USD worth of rewards to its users [14].

This paper presents an empirical analysis of *Steemit*, a key representative of emerging blockchain-based incentivized social media platforms. Our study targets two core features of *Steemit*, namely its decentralized operation and its cryptocurrency-driven reward system. By analyzing over 539 million operations performed by 1.12 million users during the period 2016/03 to 2018/08, we aim at obtaining several key insights including the answers for the following set of key questions:

- Do the members of the witness group in the platform have a high update rate or do the same set of users serve in the group? What is the power of big shareholders on the decentralization properties of the platform? Is it possible that a single big shareholder can determine who to join the witness group?
- What are the factors correlated with rewards issued to authors and curators? How does the reward system influence users' behavior? Can incentives be misused by users such as buying votes from bots to promote their posts?

Our analysis reveals interesting details on the decentralized operation in *Steemit* and its reward system. Our study on decentralization in *Steemit* shows that the witness group tends to show a relatively low update rate and its seats may actually be controlled by a few large shareholders. Our analysis also indicates that the majority of top witnesses and top electors form a value-transfer network. These findings together reveals that the actual level of decentralization in *Steemit* is far lower than the ideal level, indicating that DPoS consensus protocol may not be a desirable approach for establishing a highly decentralized social media platform. Our analysis of the reward system in *Steemit* shows that author rewards earned by an author are correlated with a number of factors, including the number of followers, number of created posts and owned *Steemit* shares. However, our analysis of the *transfer* and *vote* operations show that more than 16% transfers in the dataset are sent to curators suspected to be bots. A deeper analysis also reveals the existence of an underlying supply network for the bots, where big shareholders delegate their *Steemit* shares to bots to earn profit. These results together suggests that the current cryptocurrency-driven reward system in *Steemit* is under substantial misuse that deviates from the original intended goal of rewarding high-quality contents. We point out that the current consensus protocols and reward systems can hardly achieve their design targets and identify the key reasons and suggest potential solutions. We believe that the findings in this paper can facilitate the improvement of existing blockchain-based social media platforms and the design of future blockchain-powered websites.

2 BACKGROUND

In this section, we introduce the *Steemit* social media platform that runs over the Steem-blockchain[3]. We present the key use cases of *Steemit* and discuss how *Steemit* leverages the underlying

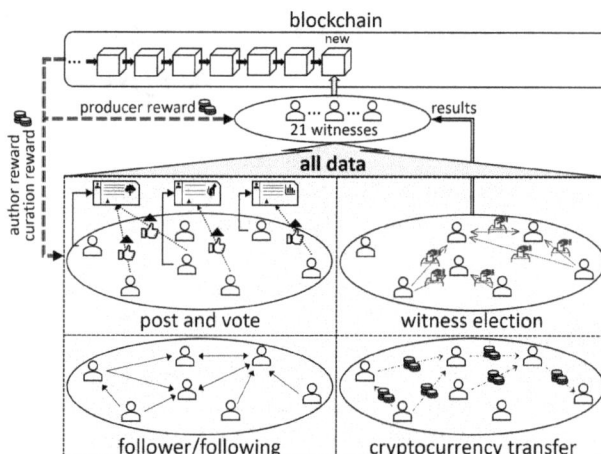

Figure 1: Steem blockchain overview

blockchain to function as a decentralized social site that incentivizes users with cryptocurrency-based rewards.

Steemit. Users of *Steemit* can create and share contents as blog posts. A blog post can get replied, reposted or voted by other users. Based on the weights of received votes, posts get ranked and the top ranked posts make them to the front page.

Steem-blockchain. *Steemit* uses the Steem-blockchain[3] to store the underlying data of the platform as a chain of blocks. Every three seconds, a new block is produced, which includes all confirmed operations performed by users during the last three seconds. *Steemit* allows its users to perform more than thirty different type of operations. In Figure 1, we display four categories of operations that are most relevant to the analysis presented in this paper. While post/vote and follower/following are common features offered by social sites (e.g., Reddit [30] and Quora [34]), operations such as witness election and cryptocurrency transfer are features specific to blockchains.

Witness election and DPoS. Witnesses in *Steemit* are producers of blocks, who continuously collect data from the entire network, bundle data into blocks and append the blocks to the Steem-blockchain. The role of witnesses in *Steemit* is similar to that of miners in Bitcoin [26]. In Bitcoin, miners keep solving Proof-of-Work (PoW) problems and winners have the right to produce blocks. With PoW, Bitcoin achieves a maximum throughput of 7 transactions/sec [7]. However, transaction rates of typical mainstream social sites are substantially higher. For example, Twitter has an average throughput of more than 5000 tweets/sec [16]. Hence, *Steemit* adopts the Delegated Proof of Stake (DPoS) [23] consensus protocol to increase the speed and scalability of the platform without compromising the decentralized reward system of the blockchain. In DPoS systems, users vote to elect a number of witnesses as their delegates. In *Steemit*, each user can vote for at most 30 witnesses. The top-20 elected witnesses and a seat randomly assigned out of the top-20 witnesses produce the blocks. With DPoS, consensus only needs to be reached among the 21-member witness group, rather than the entire blockchain network like Bitcoin. This significantly improves the system throughput.

Cryptocurrency - shares and rewards. In *Steemit*, each vote casting a post or electing a witness is associated with a weight that is proportional to the shares of *Steemit* held by the voter. Like most blockchains, the Steem-blockchain issues its native cryptocurrencies called *STEEM* and Steem Dollars (*SBD*). To receive shares of *Steemit*, a user needs to 'lock' *STEEM/SBD* in *Steemit* to receive Steem Power (*SP*) at the rate of 1 *STEEM* = 1 *SP* and each *SP* is assigned about 2000 vested shares (*VESTS*) of *Steemit*. A user may withdraw invested *STEEM/SBD* at any time, but the claimed fund will be automatically split into thirteen equal portions to be withdrawn in the next thirteen subsequent weeks. For example, in day 1, Alice may invest 13 *STEEM* to *Steemit* that makes her vote obtain a weight of 13 *SP* (about 26000 *VESTS*). Later, in day 8, Alice may decide to withdraw her 13 invested *STEEM*. Here, instead of seeing her 13 *STEEM* in wallet immediately, her *STEEM* balance will increase by 1 *STEEM* each week from day 8 and during that period, her *SP* will decrease by 1 *SP* every week.

Through Steem-blockchain, *Steemit* issues three types of rewards to its users: (1) producer reward; (2) author reward and (3) curation reward. The amount of producer reward is about 0.2 *STEEM* per block in 2018/08, meaning that a witness producing blocks for a whole day can earn about 14,400 *STEEM*. Each day, the Steem-blockchain issues a number of *STEEM* (about 53,800 *STEEM* per day in 2018/08) to form the post reward pool and posts compete against each other to divide up the reward pool based on the total weight of votes received within seven days from the post creation time. Here, 75% of reward received by a post goes to the post author and the rest is shared by the post curators based on their vote weight.

In the rest of this paper, for ease of exposition and comparison, we transfer all values of *STEEM/SBD/SP/VESTS* to US dollars (*USD* denoted by $), based on their median transfer rate from 2018/01 to 2018/08, which is $1 = 1 *SBD* ≈ 0.4 *STEEM* = 0.4 *SP* ≈ 800 *VESTS* [13].

3 DATASET AND PRELIMINARY RESULTS

In this section, we describe our data collection methodology and present some preliminary results including the growth of *Steemit* over time and the usage of operations in the platform.

3.1 Data collection

The Steem-blockchain offers an Interactive Application Programming Interface (API) for developers and researchers to collect and parse the blockchain data [12]. From block 1 (created at 2016/03/24 16:05:00) to block 25,563,499 (created at 2018/09/01 00:00:00), we collected 539,817,204 operations performed by 1,120,166 users of *Steemit* during the period 2016/03 to 2018/08. The collected data also includes 121,619,828 virtual operations performed in the *Steemit* platform, such as issuing rewards to witnesses, authors and curators, during the same time period. In the data collected, we recognized 36 types of operations performed by users and 11 types of virtual operations. In table 1, we summarize the key operations (OP) and virtual operations (VO) focused in this paper.

3.2 Preliminary results

Growth of *Steemit*. We first investigate the growth of *Steemit* over time and find that the platform growth is highly impacted by the cryptocurrency market. In Figure 2, we plot the numbers of newly registered users and newly performed operations per month

OP (social)	Description
comment	users create posts, reply to posts or replies
vote	users vote for posts
custom_json	users follow other users, repost a blog

OP (witness-election)	Description
witness_update	users join the witness pool to be elected, witnesses in pool update their information
witness_vote	users vote for witnesses by themselves
witness_proxy	users cast votes to the same witnesses voted by another user by setting that user as their election proxy

OP (value-transfer)	Description
transfer	users transfer *STEEM/SBD* to other users
transfer_to_vesting	users transfer *STEEM/SBD* to *VESTS*
delegate_vesting_shares	users delegate *VESTS* to other users
withdraw_vesting	users transfer *VESTS* to *STEEM*

VO (reward)	Description
producer_reward	platform issues rewards to producers
author_reward	platform issues rewards to authors
curation_reward	platform issues rewards to curators

Table 1: Summary of operations and virtual operations

and the changes of *Bitcoin* and *STEEM* price during the period 2016/03 to 2018/08. Apart from the initial boost in the first month, the platform witnessed three times of robust growth, which happened during 2016/05 to 2016/07, 2017/04 to 2017/06 and 2017/11 to 2018/01, respectively. We can observe a strong correlation between the monthly increment of users and the changes in the *STEEM* price. This is due to the fact that more *Steemit* users investing in trading may drive up the *STEEM* price while higher *STEEM* price may in turn attract more people joining *Steemit*. Next, in cryptocurrency market, the changes of *Bitcoin* price are usually seen as the most important market signals. During all the three rising periods, we see the surge in *Bitcoin* price, which illustrates the high influence of the cryptocurrency market on the growth of *Steemit* and also suggests that most *Steemit* users may have a background understanding of cryptocurrency and blockchain. Finally, by comparing the user curve and the operation curve, we find that even though the user growth rate drops after all the three rising periods, the operation growth rate keeps maintaining stability after boosting, which may reflect that most users who joined *Steemit* during the rising periods remain active after the end of the rising periods.

Usage of operations. As discussed in section 3.1, users in *Steemit* may perform a variety of operations and these operations are recorded by the Steem-blockchain. By investigating the usage of these operations, we aim to answer the following questions: (1) which categories of operations are more frequently performed by users?, (2) do users use *Steemit* more like a social media platform or like a cryptocurrency wallet? In Figure 3 and Figure 4, we plot the numbers of social/witness-election operations and value-transfer operations performed in different months, respectively. The functionality of these operations is described in Table 1. Among the three categories of operations, the social operations show the highest utilization rate, which indicates that users are using more social functions offered by *Steemit* than transfer functions. Among the three social operations, the *vote* operation is the most frequently

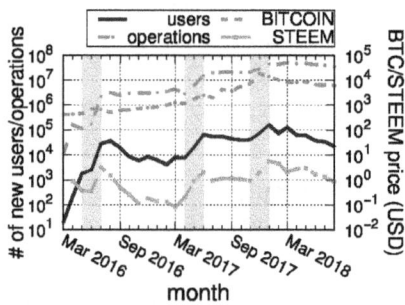

Figure 2: New users/operations per month (2016/03 to 2018/08)

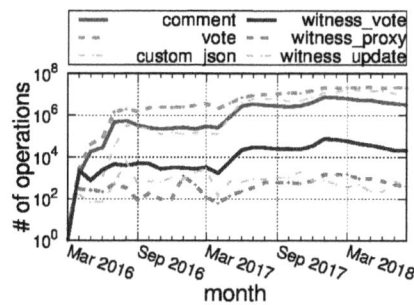

Figure 3: New social/witness-election operations per month (2016/03 to 2018/08)

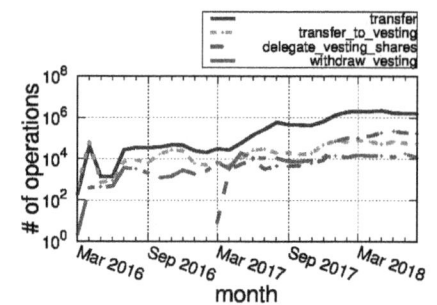

Figure 4: New value-transfer operations per month (2016/03 to 2018/08)

used one. In 2018/08, more than 21 million votes were cast to posts. Unlike other voting-based social media platforms such as *Reddit*, in *Steemit*, votes cast by users owning *Steemit* shares have real monetary value, which may incentivize *Steemit* users to keep voting for posts with some frequency to avoid wasting their voting power. We will discuss more about voting and rewarding mechanisms in section 5. Among the four value-transfer operations, users perform the *transfer* operation more frequently. Since the *transfer* operation is the only operation among the four that is not associated with *VESTS*, namely shares of *Steemit*, the fact may reflect that more trading behaviors are happening in *Steemit* than investing behaviors. Finally, the number of performed witness-election operations are relatively small, compared with the other two categories. Each month, we see only thousands of users setting or updating their witness votes through the *witness_vote* and *witness_proxy* operations and only hundreds of users joining the witness pool or updating their witness information through the *witness_update* operation. This reflects a relatively low participation rate in witness election regarding both elector and electee and could impact the level of decentralization in the platform. We discuss witness election in more detail in section 4.

4 DECENTRALIZATION IN *STEEMIT*

As a blockchain-based social media platform, *Steemit* distinguishes itself from traditional social sites through the decentralization brought by the blockchain. In this section, we investigate the actual level of decentralization in *Steemit* by analyzing the witness election process of DPoS in detail.

4.1 Decentralized platform operation

Centralization and decentralization. In traditional social media platforms, such as *Reddit* and *Quora*, a single entity (i.e., Reddit, Inc. and Quora, Inc.) owns the complete data generated by users and operates the websites. In contrast, *Steemit* not only open sources its front-end, *Condenser* and the back-end Steem-blockchain [29], but also makes all its data in the blockchain available for public access [3]. Rather than functioning as a single entity, the *Steemit* platform is operated by a group of 21 witnesses elected by its users. Any user in *Steemit* can run a server, install the Steem-blockchain and synchronize the blockchain data to the latest block. Then, by sending a *witness_update* operation to the network, the user can become a witness and have a chance to operate the website and

earn producer rewards if he or she can gather enough support from the electors to join the 21-member witness group.

Steemit-2 and STEEM-2. As anyone can copy the code and data of *Steemit*, one may naturally doubt that an adversary, say Bob, may build a 'fake' *Steemit* platform, *Steemit-2* that has exactly same the functionality and historical data as *Steemit*. To distinguish *Steemit-2* from *Steemit*, we name the cryptocurrency issued by *Steemit-2* as *STEEM-2* (and also *SBD-2*). Here, a natural question that arises is what makes people believe that *Steemit*, rather than *Steemit-2*, is the 'real' one? In the decentralized network, the opinion of 'which one is real' is determined by the consensus of *Steemit* users or, to be more precise, the shareholders. With the DPoS consensus protocol, each block storing data of *Steemit* is signed by a top witness elected by the shareholders, which may represent the consensus among the shareholders. Therefore, unless most of shareholders switch to *Steemit-2*, the new blocks generated in *Steemit-2* will be signed by witnesses elected by a few shareholders and will not be recognized by the entire community.

Factors affecting decentralization of *Steemit*. In our work, we study the characteristics of decentralization in *Steemit* by analyzing the witness election process. In general, we consider *Steemit* to have an ideal level of decentralization if members of the 21-member witness group are frequently updated and if these members all have different interests. We also consider *Steemit* to have a relatively high decentralization closer to the ideal level if it allows more people to join the 21-member witness group, if the power of big shareholders is not decisive and if the election is not heavily correlated with value-transfer operations. We investigate these aspects in the following subsection.

4.2 Analyzing witness election

Update of the 21-member witness group. To investigate the update of the 21-member witness group, we extract the producer of each block from block 1 to block 25,563,499 and plot the results as a heatmap in Figure 5. We first compute the number of blocks produced by each witness and sort the witnesses based on their produced blocks in total. For the top-30 witnesses that have the highest number of produced blocks, we plot their attendance rate in the 21-member witness group during the thirty months. During a month that has thirty days, there should be $30 * 24 * 60 * 60/3 = 864,000$ blocks generated because blocks are generated every three seconds. For every 21 blocks (63 seconds), the 21 elected witnesses

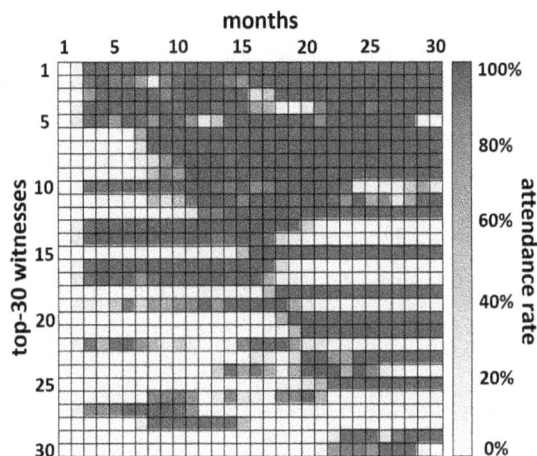

Figure 5: Heatmap of top-30 witnesses' attendance rate in the 21-member witness group during 30 months from 2016/03 to 2018/08

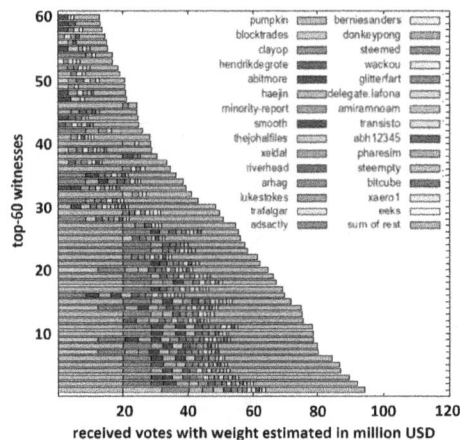

Figure 6: A snapshot of weighted votes received by top-60 witnesses at block 25,563,499. The votes are weighted by shares (estimated in *USD*) owned by the electors. We show the votes cast by the top-29 electors owning the highest weight and use 'sum of rest' to represent the sum of weighted votes cast by all other electors.

are shuffled to determine their order for generating the next 21 blocks. Therefore, if a witness has a 100% attendance rate in the elected group, it can at most produce $864000/21 \approx 41,142$ blocks in a thirty-day month. In Figure 5, we find that most of the top-30 witnesses, once entering the 21-member witness group, maintained a high attendance rate closer to 100% for a long time. From month 12 to month 30, namely one and a half year, the top-12 witnesses firmly held at least 10 seats, nearly half of positions in the 21-member witness group. From month 23 to month 30, 17 seats were held by 18 witnesses. From witness 13 to witness 30, we can observe a transition period, namely month 15 to month 20, during which the places of nine old witnesses were gradually taken by nine new witnesses. Overall, the 21-member witness group tends to show a relatively low update rate. The majority of seats were firmly controlled by a small group of witnesses. We do observe some switch of seats but that happened only in a low frequency.

Power of big shareholders. Next, we investigate the influence of big shareholders in the witness election. As described in Table 1, a user has two ways to vote for witnesses. The first option is to perform *witness_vote* operations to directly vote for at most 30 witnesses. The second option is to perform a *witness_proxy* operation to set another user as an election proxy. For example, Alice may set Bob to be her proxy. Then, if both Alice and Bob own $100 worth of shares, any vote cast by Bob will be associated with a weight of $200 worth of shares. Once Alice deletes the proxy, the weight of Bob's votes will reduce to $100 worth of shares immediately. In Figure 6, we plot the stacked bar chart representing a snapshot of weighted votes received by the top-60 witnesses, who have produced the highest amounts of blocks, at block 25,563,499. The figure shows the distribution of votes cast by the top-29 electors whose votes have the highest weight, either brought by their own shares or shares belonging to users setting these electors as proxy. The sum of weighted votes cast by all other electors outside the top-29 is represented as 'sum of rest'. From Figure 6, we see a few top electors have their votes weighted by striking amounts of shares. The top-1 elector has his or her votes weighted by $19,800,000 worth of shares. A deeper investigation regarding the top-1 elector shows that all

the shares affecting his or her weight are not directly owned by this user, but owned by another user, who set the top-1 elector as proxy. The runner-up elector, which is the account belonging to the main exchange used by *Steemit* users, has its votes associated with a weight of $12,100,000 worth of shares. From the figure, we see all the 27 witnesses voted by the top-1 elector enter the top-50, all the 18 witnesses receiving votes from both the top-2 electors enter the top-30 and the only witness receiving votes from all the top-3 electors becomes the top-1 witness. We can also observe that 19 out of the top-20 witnesses receive at least two votes from the top-3 electors and 29 out of the top-30 witnesses receive at least one vote from the top-3 electors. As illustrated by the results, the distribution of weight of votes in witness election is heavily skewed, which suggests that the election of 21 witnesses may be significantly impacted by a few big shareholders, This phenomenon may not be a good indication for a decentralized social media platform. In the worst case, if the 21-member witness group is controlled by a single shareholder, the platform will simply function as a centralized model.

Value-transfer operations among election stakeholders. Finally, we investigate the value-transfer operations performed among the top-30 witnesses, top-29 electors and the accounts selecting top-29 electors as proxy. The data is plotted as a directed graph in Figure 7, where edges are colored by their source node color. The edge thickness represents the amount of transferred value from source to target, which is the sum of value transferred through *transfer* and *transfer_to_vesting* operations. Since most *Steemit* users use runner-up elector to trade cryptocurrency, the graph does not show edges connected with that account. Our first observation about this graph is that only two out of top-30 witnesses and three out of top-29 electors never perform value-transfer operations while all other investigated users form a value-transfer network, which has 3.34 average degree, 0.21 average clustering coefficient and 3.96 average path length. In the network, we find a cluster of users who select top-29 electors as proxy. After manually checking the profiles

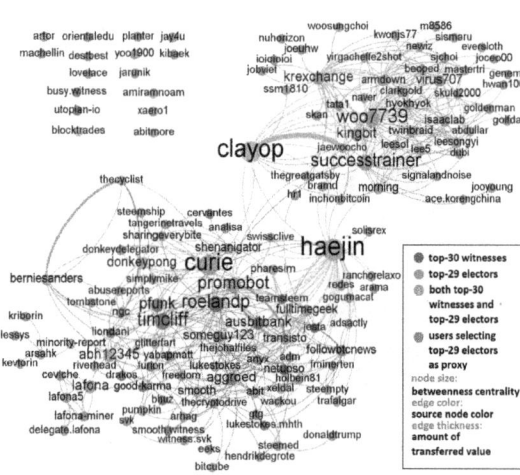

Figure 7: Graph of value-transfer operations performed among the top-30 witnesses, the top-29 electors and the accounts selecting these electors as proxy. The graph was plotted using Gephi [2].

of these users, we find that this cluster represents a community of Korean users, which is connected to the rest of the network mainly through several leaders of the Korean community. Overall, what we observed from the value-transfer operations suggests that the majority of the investigated election stakeholders have economic interactions, which may not be a good indication of a perfectly decentralized witness group where the members are expected to have different interests.

4.3 Discussion

Our study in this section demonstrates that the 21-member witness group tends to show a relatively low update rate and these seats may actually be controlled by a few big shareholders. Our study also indicates that the majority of top witnesses and top electors form a value-transfer network and have economic interactions. Together, these results suggest that the actual level of decentralization in *Steemit* is far lower than the ideal level. One key reason for the low decentralization is the use of DPoS consensus protocol. The DPoS consensus protocol has been widely adopted by mainstream blockchain-based platforms such as BTS and EOS and has been proved to be an effective approach of enhancing transaction rates of blockchains. However, there has been a long debate surrounding decentralization of DPoS. The opponents of DPoS censure that DPoS-powered platforms trade decentralization for scalability as the consensus in these platforms is only reached among a small committee (e.g., the 21-member witness group in *Steemit*), instead of among all interested members (e.g., all miners in Bitcoin and Ethereum powered by Proof-of-Work (PoW) consensus). The supporters of DPoS argue that those PoW-powered platforms has been controlled by a few mining pools, showing even lower decentralization than the DPoS-powered platforms. The data-driven analysis in this section deeply investigates the underlying behaviors of participants interested in the core component of DPoS, namely the witness election. The results reveal that the current electoral system is making the decentralization quite fragile, as the committee intended to be decentralized is actually quite centralized in practice. A quick solution to address the symptoms is to restrict the power of

big stakeholders, such as cutting the number of times that big stakeholders can vote in the election. A better way of solving the problem is to replace DPoS with more advanced consensus protocols, that can form the committee without an election involving interactions among users. For example, Algorand [9], a recent cryptocurrency, proposed a new Byzantine Agreement (BA) protocol that makes the election be fairly performed by the Verifiable Random Functions in cryptography, rather than by users.

5 REWARD SYSTEM IN *STEEMIT*

A core feature of *Steemit* is its reward system. As a blockchain-based social media network that issues its own cryptocurrencies, *Steemit* leverages its native cryptocurrencies to incentivize authors and curators of posts for rewarding contributors to the platform, who either create good contents or screen out good contents. In this subsection, we theoretically analyze the reward system in *Steemit* and study the factors correlated with rewards earned by authors and curators. We also jointly investigate the value-transfer operations and *vote* operations to understand if the reward system is being misused by *Steemit* users, such as buying votes from bots to promote their posts for the purpose of earning higher profit. Such misuse may deviate from the original intended goal of the *Steemit* reward system.

5.1 Reward system

To the best of our knowledge, *Steemit* [15] never formally published the details of its reward system, so we investigated its source code to understand its reward system [29] in detail. Each time a user votes for a post, the vote contributes a certain amount of reward shares (*rshares*, denoted as *rs*) to that post. It is computed as

$$rs = e\_VESTS * \frac{vp * vw - 0.0049}{50}$$

where e_VESTS refers to effective vesting shares (*VESTS*), vp stands for voting power and vw denotes voting weight. In *Steemit*, users can deposit or withdraw *VESTS* through *transfer_to_vesting* operation and *withdraw_vesting* operation, respectively. However, as described in Table 1, a user may also delegate *VESTS* to other users through *delegate_vesting_shares* operation. For example, if Alice owns 100 *VESTS* and if she delegates 50 *VESTS* to Bob and if she also receives 30 *VESTS* delegated to her by Carol, then her $e\_VESTS = 100 - 50 + 30 = 80$ *VESTS*. A user may set voting weight vw to any value between 0% and 100%. *Steemit* leverages voting power vp to restrict the number of weighted votes cast by users per day. Initially, each user has $vp = 100\%$. Then, if a user casts a vote to a post, this user's vp will drop to $(1 - \frac{1-0.0049}{50}) * 100\%$, which is roughly 98% if he/she sets $vw = 100\%$. That is, if a user keeps voting, his/her vp will also keep dropping. Once vp drops to 0%, his/her vote will contribute no *rshares* to posts and the user and post authors will not earn rewards from this vote. Each day, vp recovers 20% before it is back to 100%.

A post, after being created, can accumulate *rshares* from received votes during a 7-day time window. At the end of the time window, the post will use the accumulated *rshares* to compete with accumulated *rshares* of other posts to divide up the post reward pool (about 53,800 *STEEM* per day in 2018/08). After that, 75% of the post reward (denoted as *pr*) is directly issued to the post author as

(a) Followers

(b) Post numbers

(c) Vesting shares

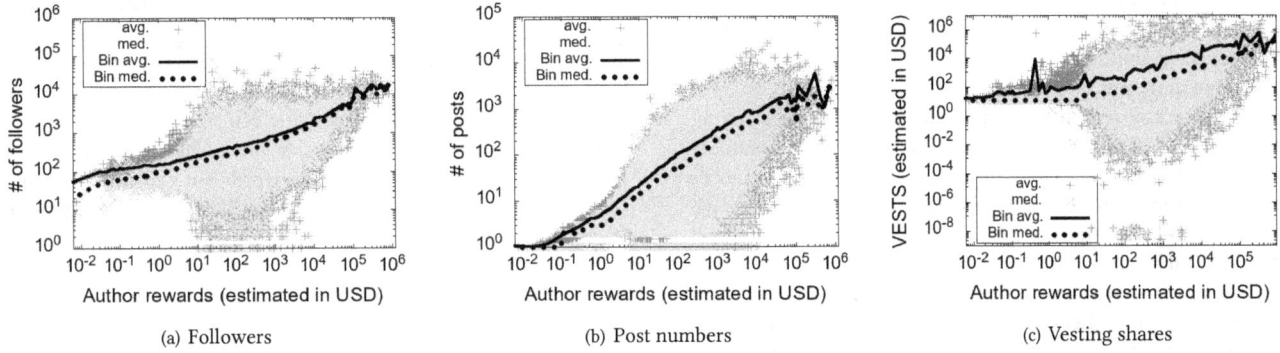

Figure 8: Scatter plot investigating correlation between followers (post numbers, vesting shares) and author rewards

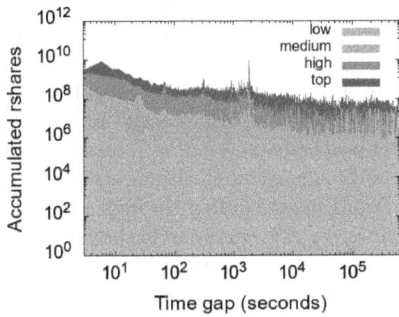

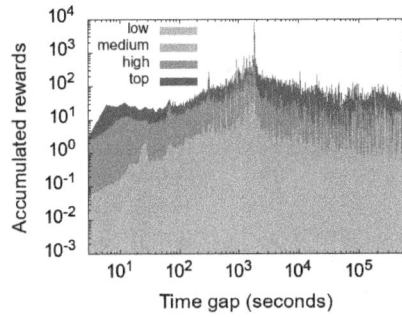

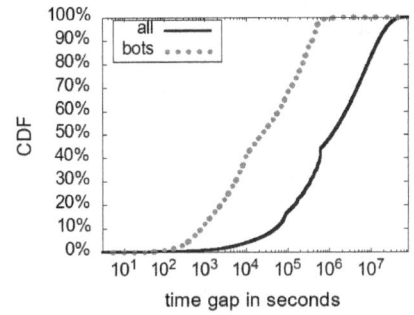

Figure 9: Distribution of accumulated *rshares* over time after post creation time

Figure 10: Distribution of accumulated curation rewards over time

Figure 11: CDF investigating the time gap between post creation time and bot voting time

author reward (denoted as *ar*) and the rest 25% is finally shared by all curators who voted for the post during the 7-day time window, namely their curation rewards (denoted as *cr*). The curation reward received by a single curator can be computed as:

$$cr = 0.25 * pr * \frac{\sqrt{rs_b + rs} - \sqrt{rs_b}}{\sqrt{rs_T}} * min(\frac{td}{30}, 1)$$

As can be seen, *cr* is computed from 25% of *pr*, but is affected by two factors. The first factor is the ratio between $\sqrt{rs_b + rs} - \sqrt{rs_b}$ and $\sqrt{rs_T}$, where rs_b denotes the *rshares* accumulated by the post before this user's vote and rs_T refers to the total accumulated *rshares* by the post during the 7-day time window. This is a very interesting factor as it suggests that curators who want to earn higher *cr* should vote for posts as early as possible to make rs_b smaller. It also suggests that such curators vote for posts that have higher probability to accumulate higher rs_T by the end of 7-day time window. However, the second factor forces curators to reconsider the early vote strategy. It is the minimum of $\frac{td}{30}$ and 1, where *td* denotes the time difference in minutes between the post creation time and voting time. For example, if Alice votes for a post one minute after the post creation time, she will only receive $\frac{1}{30}$ of the curation rewards assigned to her while the rest $\frac{29}{30}$ is again issued to the post author. Instead, if Alice casts her vote 30 minutes after the post creation time, she can completely earn the assigned curation rewards. Because of the second factor, a post author usually receives more than 75% of the post reward. In summary, the two factors in

the curation reward equation make it hard to determine the best strategy of the voting time in the reward earning game. However, it is clear that voting for posts that are likely to be voted by more users in the future is certainly helpful.

5.2 Factors correlated with rewards

After theoretically analyzing the reward system, we now investigate the blockchain data to learn the factors correlated with author rewards and curation rewards.

Author rewards. Regarding author rewards, we investigate three factors: (1) number of followers owned by an author; (2) number of posts created by an author; (3) amount of vesting shares (*VESTS*) owned by an author. In order to gauge the correlation between these factors and author rewards, for each factor, we plot in Figure 8 the average and median of values of the factor (*y*) against author rewards estimated in USD (*x*). Following the methodology used by Kwak *et al.* [22], we also bin the value of author rewards in log scale and plot the average and median per bin in lines. In Figure 8(a), we see the line of average is always above the line of median, indicating that some users with followers more than average do not receive expected degree of support from their followers regarding their posts. The gap between the two line is larger for users receiving lower author rewards, but becomes relatively small for the top authors earning rewards more than $1000. The median number of followers grows steadily without showing a flat period or a surge. Next, in Figure 8(b), we investigate correlation between number of posts created by an author and rewards received by an author. Again, we find that the line of average keeps itself above the line of median, indicating that some users post more blogs than average but do not receive more rewards as they may expect. This may suggest that some authors slow down their posting speed while improving the quality of their posts. Until $30,000 rewards, the median number of posts shows a relatively stable growth. After that, it experiences a fluctuation among the top authors. Finally, in Figure 8(c), we investigate correlation between VESTS owned by an author and rewards received by an author. From the observation that the line of median lies nearly always below the line of average, we may infer that some users own higher shares of *Steemit* than average but fail to increase their author rewards to the same scale. By observing the line of median, we find that the median number of VESTS stays relatively flat at $12.5 before author rewards reach $10. The $12.5 worth of VESTS is equal to 5 *STEEM*, which is the minimum line that *Steemit* suggests that its user transfer to *VESTS* for the purpose of maintaining the user's account in a normal state. From $10 worth of author rewards, the median points start to disperse. It is interesting to find that many authors earning rewards more than $10 maintain very low *VESTS*, even lower than the suggested minimum line. However, beyond $10 worth of author rewards, the line of median still shows a positive trend.

Overall, our results illustrate a positive correlation between all the three factors and author rewards. Our results do not imply causation, but they suggest that users, both authors and curators, consider the three factors as indicators of the potential popularity of posts.

Curation rewards. As we have analyzed in section 5.1, the curation reward assigned to a single curator is affected by two factors. The first factor suggests that reward-driven curators cast their votes early and vote for posts with high potential for popularity. However, the second factor penalizes the early votes. Regarding the potential popularity of posts, a reward-driven curator may leverage the number of followers/posts/VESTS of post authors as indicators. However, due to the conflict suggestions from the two factors in the curation reward computation equation, it is hard to determine the best voting time for maximizing curation rewards. Therefore, we decide to investigate what are the choices made by users in the data set. To observe decisions made by different levels of shareholders, we divide users into four groups based on their owned *VESTS*, namely low ($< 10^4$), medium ($10^4 - 10^6$), high ($10^6 - 10^8$) and top ($> 10^8$). In Figure 9, we plot the distribution of the accumulated *rshares* that have been contributed by all votes to all posts every second after the post creation time. Since *rshares* is the most important factor of post rewards and also the key value of votes, this figure helps revealing users' strategies on selecting voting time. As can be seen from results, there are two peaks that happened. The first peak is at the sixth second, which indicates that many curators choose to vote for a post after six seconds (two blocks) of the post creation time. This may reflect that many users are still using the early vote strategy. The second peak is more interesting. It happens at the 1803 second, namely the first block after the 30-minute time period penalized by the second factor of the curation reward computation equation. This reflects that some users do understand the punishment mechanism and are deliberately avoiding from being penalized. We can also observe that the low-level shareholders tend

to not pay special attention to the voting strategies while all the other three groups of shareholders tend to contribute more to the two peaks and are more likely to vote earlier besides the two peaks. The results of the distribution of accumulated curation rewards along time are shown in Figure 10, which show a clear effect of the punishment mechanism on the early votes. The results suggest that curators who want to earn more rewards vote around the time of the second peak, namely the end of the 30-minute penalty period.

5.3 Misuse of reward system

The reward system in *Steemit* may be a good way to reward contributors to the platform, but it may also be misused by some users in ways that deviate from the original intended goal in *Steemit*, such as buying votes from bots to promote some meaningless posts for the purpose of earning profit. In this subsection, we aim at understanding to what extent such behaviors are performed in *Steemit*.

Temporal correlation. We study this topic by investigating the temporal correlation between *transfer* operations and *vote* operations. Concretely, if there is a suspicious vote cast by a curator to an author through a *vote* operation, there should also be a suspicious fund transferred to the curator from the author through a *transfer* operation that happens before the *vote* operation is performed by the curator. Specifically, we consider a *transfer* operation is suspicious if the 'memo' area (allowing sender to leave a message) of the *transfer* operation only contains a link pointing to a recent post created by the sender. If in addition, the recipient of the *transfer* operation, after receiving the fund from the sender, votes for the post matching that link within the 7-days time window after the post creation time, we consider it as a suspicious trade between a post author and a voting bot.

After parsing the 18,172,530 *transfer* operations in blockchain, we find that 5,031,737 (27.69%) of them only contain a single post link in the 'memo' area. By further investigating the *vote* operation, we find that 2,939,051 (16.17%) of the total *transfer* operations are followed by a suspicious *vote* operation voting for the post link within the 7-days time window, which are performed by the recipients of the funds. Among all the fund recipients, the top one has performed such trade for 113,068 times and earned nearly 1 million USD.

Voting time of suspicious curators. To further investigate the features of the curators suspected to be bots, in Figure 11, we plot the cumulative distribution function (CDF) of the time gap between the post creation time and voting time. The solid line refers to the CDF of votes cast by all curators who ever received any amount of fund from the authors of voted posts at any time point in the past. The dotted line describes the CDF of votes cast by curators suspected to be bots. As can be seen, the curators suspected to be bots cast their votes much earlier than the average. The dotted line reaches 98.9% at the 604,800 second, which refers that nearly all their votes are sent within the 7-day time window and they are internationally contributing *rshares* of their votes to the posts.

An example bot network. In Figure 12, we plot an example bot network, which describes the *transfer* operations sent to the curators suspected to be bots from the top-30 post authors, who most frequently had contacted with these suspected curators. The node sizes are weighted by weighted in-degree. As can be seen,

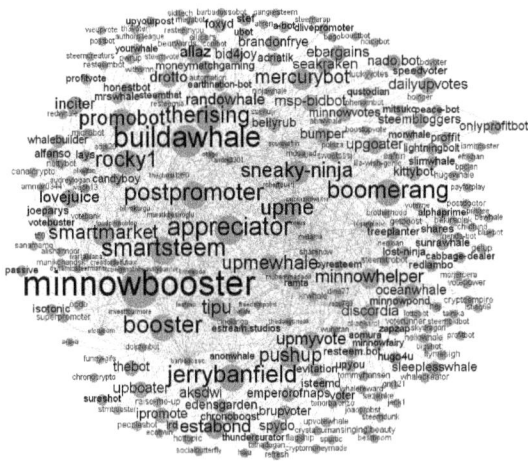

Figure 12: Graph of *transfer* operations sent from selected post authors (red) to the curators suspected to be bots (blue). The graph was plotted using Gephi [2].

Figure 13: Graph of *delegate_vesting_shares* operations and *transfer* operations among the top-30 curators suspected to be bots (red) and their suspected suppliers (blue). The graph was plotted using Gephi [2].

the thirty authors contacted a large number of suspected curators because they may need *rshares* from more than one suspected curator to promote their posts. We can also observe that most suspected curators have their account name containing suspected keywords, such as *boost, promote, whale* and *upvote*.

An example supply network for bots. Finally, we analyze where do these suspected curators get large amounts of *VESTS* to make their votes weighted by higher *rshares*. After a deep analysis, we find that there is an underlying supply network, where some big shareholders delegate their *VESTS* to the suspected curators through *delegate_vesting_shares* operations and the suspected curators periodically pay 'rent' to these *VESTS* suppliers through *transfer* operations. In Figure 13, we plot an example supply network for bots, which describes the *delegate_vesting_shares* operations sent to the

top-30 suspected curators with highest earnings and the *transfer* operations sent from the top-30 suspected curators with amount higher than $100. The node size reflects weighted degree and the edge thickness is weighted by the amount of transferred value. From the graph, we find that most of the top-30 suspected curators own a number of suppliers and a few of them have many. It is interesting to find that the top-1 supplier is the same user who also stands behind the top-1 witness presented in section 4.2. We find that this user has earned more than 1.5 million USD by delegating his or her *VESTS* to the curators suspected to be bots.

5.4 Discussion

In summary, we have discussed the design principle, current use status and underlying misuse of the cryptocurrency-driven reward system of *Steemit* in this section. The rise of social bots and the harm caused by them to the online ecosystems has been widely recognized [8]. Our results in this section reveal that bots have broadly appeared in the emerging incentivized blockchain-based social media networks. In *Steemit*, the monetary value of cryptocurrencies and the deep integration of social operations and value-transfer operations have jointly led to the special supply chain, where bots buy voting powers from big stakeholders and sell the voting powers to users who want to promote posts. Clearly, such behaviours violate the original intention of the reward system and may eventually result in a front page occupied by valueless posts or spams promoted by bots. Moreover, due to the decentralized operation, it is difficult to delete these problem posts appeared at the front page because no single entity has this power. Our discussion in this section also suggests a way of detecting bots through investigating the temporal correlation between *transfer* operations and *vote* operations. We believe this detection approach is effective at the current stage when bots prefer to trade with the native cryptocurrency *STEEM*, which is detectable through the Steem-blockchain. However, smarter bots may hide the temporal correlation between *transfer* operations and *vote* operations by asking their clients to pay them through other cryptocurrencies such as Bitcoin or even privacy-preserving cryptocurrencies such as Zerocash [27]. Then we need to rely on other approaches, such as Deep Neural Networks [21], to detect bots.

6 RELATED WORK

In recent years, due to the rapid growth and consistent popularity, social media platforms have received significant attention from researchers. A large number of research papers have analyzed several popular social media platforms from various perspectives [1, 10, 11, 28, 30, 31, 34]. Tan *et al.* [31] investigated users' behavior in *Reddit* and found that users continually post in new communities. Singer *et al.* [28] observed a general quality drop of comments made by users during activity sessions. Hessel *et al.* [11] investigated the interactions between highly related communities and found that users engaged in a newer community tend to be more active in their original community. In [10], the authors studied the browsing and voting behavior of *Reddit* users and found that most users do not read the article that they vote on. An extensive survey of recent research on *Reddit* is provided in [25]. Besides *Reddit*, several other social media platforms have also been analyzed by researchers. Wang *et al.* [34] analyzed the *Quora* platform and found that the quality of Quora's knowledge base is mainly contributed by its user heterogeneity and question graphs. Anderson *et al.* [1] investigated the *Stack Overflow* platform and observed significant assortativity in the reputations of co-answerers, relationships between reputation and answer speed.

Recent advances in blockchain and distributed ledger technologies in terms of scalability [17, 19], efficiency [6, 33] and privacy [5, 20, 27] have empowered blockchains to support various services beyond money transfer, including incentivized blockchain-based social media platforms such as *Steemit*. Recently, this new type of social media platform has drawn some attention from researchers. Thelwall *et al.* [32] analyzed the first posts made by 925,092 *Steemit* users to understand the factors that may drive the post authors higher rewards. Their results suggest that new users of *Steemit* start from a friendly introduction about themselves rather than immediately providing useful content. In a very recent work, Kiayias *et al.* [18] studied the decentralized content curation mechanism from a computational perspective. They defined an abstract model of a post-voting system, along with a particularization inspired by *Steemit*. Through simulation of voting procedure under various conditions, their work identified the conditions under which *Steemit* can successfully curate arbitrary lists of posts and also revealed the fact that selfish participant behavior may hurt curation quality. To the best of our knowledge, the work presented in this paper is the first research that investigates the reward system and decentralization features of incentivized blockchain-based social media platforms through a rigorous empirical analysis of the operations reflected in the underlying blockchain data.

7 CONCLUSION

In this paper, we presented an empirical analysis of *Steemit*, a blockchain-based incentivized social media platform where no single entity can take control of the information and users are rewarded for the contributions they make. We analyzed over 539 million operations performed by 1.12 million users during the period 2016/03 to 2018/08. Our results show interesting details about two core features of *Steemit*, namely its decentralized management and its reward system. Our study on decentralization in *Steemit* shows the actual level of decentralization in *Steemit* is far lower than the ideal level, indicating that DPoS consensus protocol may not be a desirable approach for establishing a highly decentralized social media platform. Our analysis of the reward system reveals the fact that more than 16% transfers of cryptocurrency in *Steemit* are sent to curators suspected to be bots and also finds the existence of an underlying supply network for the bots, both suggesting that the current cryptocurrency-driven reward system in *Steemit* is under severe misuse that deviates from the original intended goal of rewarding high-quality contents.. Overall, we believe that the results in this paper provide insights on the current state of the emerging blockchain-based social media platforms including the effectiveness of the design and the operation of the consensus protocols and the reward system.

REFERENCE

[1] Ashton Anderson et al. Discovering value from community activity on focused question answering sites: a case study of stack overflow. In *Proceedings of the 18th ACM SIGKDD*, pages 850–858. ACM, 2012.

[2] Mathieu Bastian et al. Gephi: an open source software for exploring and manipulating networks. *Icwsm*, 8(2009):361–362, 2009.

[3] Steem blockchain [Internet]. Available from. https://developers.steem.io/. Accessed Oct. 2018.

[4] Vitalik Buterin et al. A next-generation smart contract and decentralized application platform. *white paper*, 2014.

[5] Jan Camenisch, Manu Drijvers, and Maria Dubovitskaya. Practical uc-secure delegatable credentials with attributes and their application to blockchain. In *Proceedings of the 2017 CCS*, pages 683–699. ACM, 2017.

[6] Melissa Chase and Sarah Meiklejohn. Transparency overlays and applications. In *Proceedings of the 2016 ACM SIGSAC Conference on Computer and Communications Security*, pages 168–179. ACM, 2016.

[7] Kyle Croman et al. On scaling decentralized blockchains. In *International Conference on Financial Cryptography and Data Security*, pages 106–125, 2016.

[8] Emilio Ferrara et al. The rise of social bots. *Communications of the ACM*, 59(7):96–104, 2016.

[9] Yossi Gilad, Rotem Hemo, Silvio Micali, Georgios Vlachos, and Nickolai Zeldovich. Algorand: Scaling byzantine agreements for cryptocurrencies. In *Proceedings of the 26th Symposium on Operating Systems Principles*, pages 51–68. ACM, 2017.

[10] Maria Glenski, Corey Pennycuff, and Tim Weninger. Consumers and curators: Browsing and voting patterns on reddit. *IEEE Transactions on Computational Social Systems*, 4(4):196–206, 2017.

[11] Jack Hessel et al. Science, askscience, and badscience: On the coexistence of highly related communities. In *ICWSM*, pages 171–180, 2016.

[12] Interactive Steem API [Internet]. Available from. https://steem.esteem.ws/. Accessed Oct. 2018.

[13] STEEM Price [Internet]. Available from. https://coinmarketcap.com/currencies/steem/. Accessed Oct. 2018.

[14] Steem Total Rewards [Internet]. Available from. https://steem.io/. Accessed Oct. 2018.

[15] Steem Whitepaper [Internet]. Available from. https://steem.io/steem-whitepaper.pdf. Accessed Oct. 2018.

[16] Twitter Usage Statistics [Internet]. Available from. http://www.internetlivestats.com/twitter-statistics/. Accessed Oct. 2018.

[17] Harry Kalodner et al. Arbitrum: Scalable, private smart contracts. In *Proceedings of the 27th USENIX Conference on Security Symposium*, pages 1353–1370. USENIX Association, 2018.

[18] Aggelos andothers Kiayias. A puff of steem: Security analysis of decentralized content curation. *arXiv preprint arXiv:1810.01719*, 2018.

[19] Eleftherios Kokoris-Kogias et al. Omniledger: A secure, scale-out, decentralized ledger via sharding. In *2018 IEEE Symposium on Security and Privacy (SP)*, pages 583–598. IEEE, 2018.

[20] Ahmed Kosba et al. Hawk: The blockchain model of cryptography and privacy-preserving smart contracts. In *2016 IEEE symposium on security and privacy (SP)*, pages 839–858. IEEE, 2016.

[21] Sneha Kudugunta and Emilio Ferrara. Deep neural networks for bot detection. *Information Sciences*, 467:312–322, 2018.

[22] Haewoon Kwak, Changhyun Lee, Hosung Park, and Sue Moon. What is twitter, a social network or a news media? In *Proceedings of the 19th international conference on World wide web*, pages 591–600. ACM, 2010.

[23] Daniel Larimer. Delegated proof-of-stake (dpos). *Bitshare whitepaper*, 2014.

[24] Steem market cap [Internet]. Available from. https://coinmarketcap.com/currencies/steem/. Accessed Oct. 2018.

[25] Alexey N Medvedev et al. The anatomy of reddit: An overview of academic research. *arXiv preprint arXiv:1810.10881*, 2018.

[26] Satoshi Nakamoto. Bitcoin: A peer-to-peer electronic cash system. 2008.

[27] Eli Ben Sasson et al. Zerocash: Decentralized anonymous payments from bitcoin. In *2014 IEEE Symposium on Security and Privacy (SP)*, pages 459–474. IEEE, 2014.

[28] Philipp Singer, Emilio Ferrara, Farshad Kooti, Markus Strohmaier, and Kristina Lerman. Evidence of online performance deterioration in user sessions on reddit. *PloS one*, 11(8):e0161636, 2016.

[29] Steemit souce code [Internet]. Available from. https://github.com/steemit. Accessed Oct. 2018.

[30] Greg Stoddard. Popularity and quality in social news aggregators: A study of reddit and hacker news. In *Proceedings of the 24th WWW*, pages 815–818. ACM, 2015.

[31] Chenhao Tan and Lillian Lee. All who wander: On the prevalence and characteristics of multi-community engagement. In *Proceedings of the 24th WWW*, pages 1056–1066, 2015.

[32] Mike Thelwall. Can social news websites pay for content and curation? the steemit cryptocurrency model. *Journal of Information Science*, page 0165551517748290, 2017.

[33] Alin Tomescu and Srinivas Devadas. Catena: Efficient non-equivocation via bitcoin. In *2017 38th IEEE Symposium on Security and Privacy (SP)*, pages 393–409. IEEE, 2017.

[34] Gang Wang, Konark Gill, Manish Mohanlal, Haitao Zheng, and Ben Y Zhao. Wisdom in the social crowd: an analysis of quora. In *Proceedings of the 22nd international conference on World Wide Web*, pages 1341–1352. ACM, 2013.

Good News for People Who Love Bad News: Centralization, Privacy, and Transparency on US News Sites

Timothy Libert
Carnegie Mellon University
timlibert@cmu.edu

Reuben Binns
University of Oxford
reuben.binns@cs.ox.ac.uk

Figure 1: The New York Times homepage exposes visitors to 61 third-party domains.

ABSTRACT

The democratic role of the press relies on maintaining independence, ensuring citizens can access controversial materials without fear of persecution, and promoting transparency. However, as news has moved to the web, reliance on third-parties has centralized revenue and hosting infrastructure, fostered an environment of pervasive surveillance, and lead to widespread adoption of opaque and poorly-disclosed tracking practices.

In this study, 4,000 US-based news sites, 4,000 non-news sites, and privacy policies for 1,892 news sites and 2,194 non-news sites are examined. We find news sites are more reliant on third-parties than non-news sites, user privacy is compromised to a greater degree on news sites, and privacy policies lack transparency in regards to observed tracking behaviors. Overall, findings indicate the democratic role of the press is being undermined by reliance on the "surveillance capitalism" funding model.

CCS CONCEPTS

• **Security and privacy → Human and societal aspects of security and privacy**; **Usability in security and privacy**;

KEYWORDS

Web; Privacy; Security; Tracking; News Media

ACM Reference format:
Timothy Libert and Reuben Binns. 2019. Good News for People Who Love Bad News: Centralization, Privacy, and Transparency on US News Sites. In *Proceedings of 11th ACM Conference on Web Science, Boston, MA, USA, June 30–July 3, 2019 (WebSci '19)*, 10 pages.
https://doi.org/10.1145/3292522.3326019

1 INTRODUCTION

News media in the United States has historically been decentralized and reliant upon a mixture of subscription and advertising revenue [31].[1][2] In legacy media such as print, radio, and television, advertisements are targeted at specific audiences only to the degree that given publications or programs are known to be popular with certain groups, such as young women, sports fans, or retirees. The

---

[1] Publicly-funded news media have a larger role in other Western democracies and the findings of this study are limited to the US market.
[2] The degree of centralization has increased over time due to mergers.

best means of determining the impact of advertisements are indirect measures of sales volume and brand awareness.

As news consumption has shifted to the web, subscription revenue has declined and advertisements are now primarily brokered by specialized advertising technology ("adtech") companies [26]. In contrast to legacy media, the web facilitates monitoring the actions of specific users, allowing advertisers to target messages based on inferences gleaned from "tracking" users as they browse the web, a process known as "online behavioral advertising" (OBA). The technological systems facilitating OBA are highly centralized, allowing a handful of companies to monitor the web browsing behaviors of billions of people and broker the flow of advertising revenue to millions of sites.

The most common way user behavior is monitored is via the inclusion of third-party services on web pages which initiate network connections between a user and a given third-party. Such connections often occur without user interaction and may expose users to persistent tracking carried out by cookies, browser fingerprints, and other identifiers. Prior research has determined that news websites contain significantly more behavioral tracking mechanisms than other types of sites [4, 7] and the news industry is reliant on a handful of adtech firms for revenue [26].

Beyond advertising, news sites may expose users to a range of third-parties that provide services for measuring the number of visitors to a page, recommending related articles, facilitating the sharing of articles on social media, and hosting content. From the perspective of the publisher, being able to target advertisements and offload the development of core site functions to outside parties makes economic sense: limited space on a given page may be used to display the most relevant advertisements, developer time may be spent on adding custom features rather than duplicating third-party services, and the complexities of hosting web pages may be delegated to cloud hosting companies.

While the centralization of advertising and hosting has a well-documented impact across the web [7, 19], the news sector represents a specific case for concern because the press serves an important democratic role in holding powerful actors to public account. There are three primary aspects of this role pertinent to today's adtech-driven web. First, as an independent social institution, the press should be free from outside influence and control [3, 5, 16]. Second, the press functions best when citizens are free to access information without fear of persecution: freedom to listen and read is as important as freedom to speak [33]. Third, the press must be transparent and honest so that citizens can have well-placed trust in the information they receive [16].

Reliance on third-parties compromises the above functions in several ways. First, while press outlets require independence to operate without influence, today's web fosters a centralization of both revenue and content-delivery infrastructure, which gives a handful of advertising and hosting firms massive unseen leverage over the press. This leverage has manifested itself in at least one known effort by Google to coerce a news outlet to include additional tracking code on their pages by asserting that not using the code would cause "search results [to] suffer" [13]. Second, citizens rely on *privacy* to enable them to safely seek out potentially controversial content [33] and web tracking directly undermines the privacy and security of readers. Research demonstrates that

awareness of surveillance reduces citizens' comfort in seeking out information [22] and commenting on controversial topics [39]. Last, the essential nature of online advertising is premised on extracting user data in covert ways which run directly counter to the goal of transparency, potentially eroding the most essential resource of any news organization: trust.

To examine the impacts of third-parties on news sites, 4,000 US-based news sites are analyzed to determine how often users are exposed to third-party services, the privacy impacts of such exposure, and the nature of third-party services. To understand how news sites differ from other popular sites, an additional 4,000 popular non-news sites in the US are analyzed to provide a comparative benchmark. 12.5 million requests for third-party content and 3.4 million third-party cookies are examined to measure privacy impacts of several types of third-party services. Finally, 1,892 news and 2,194 non-news privacy policies are examined to determine if policies are clearly written and if third-parties are transparently disclosed.

We find news sites are highly dependent on third-parties for advertising revenue, core page functionality, and web hosting. 97% of news pages include content from Google, with 84% using the DoubleClick advertising service. A range of services from audience measurement to social media are hosted by third-parties, and just three web hosting companies are responsible for 43% of all news pages examined. The privacy impacts of centralization are profound: 99% of news pages examined load third-party content from an average of 41 distinct domains. 91% of sites include a third-party cookies, of those that have such cookies, we find 63 on average. This tracking is designed to be invisible to users and privacy policies are difficult to understand, time consuming to read, and only disclose 10% of observed third-party tracking. The majority of these measures are significantly worse for news than non-news pages.

2 BACKGROUND & RESEARCH QUESTIONS

While there are general risks associated with tracking on any category of site, there are particular concerns associated with tracking on news sites which may be organized by three themes: independence, privacy, and transparency. The following sections outline each of these concerns and their attendant research questions.

2.1 Independence

The Internet has been characterized as a decentralized network which distributes media power away from legacy intermediaries and into the hands of the public writ large [23]. However, the rise of a corporate giants in search (Google) and social media (Facebook, Twitter), shows that instead of removing intermediaries, the web has centralized even more power into fewer hands [40]. Pew's 2015 State of News Report revealed that Google, Facebook, Microsoft, Yahoo and Aol were responsible for "61% of total domestic digital ad revenue in 2014", with Google accounting for 38% of digital revenue [26]. Thus, a move to the web does not necessarily equate with increased independence, rather the dominance of behavioral advertising and centralized hosting services may reduce the underlying independence publishers have enjoyed for centuries.

The concept of press independence is well-defined and scholars have noted that press independence "has come to mean working with freedom: from state control or interference, from monopoly, from market forces, as well as freedom to report, comment, create and document without fear of persecution" [3]. Likewise, independence is a value held closely by "reporters across the globe [who] feel that their work can only thrive and flourish in a society that protects its media from censorship; in a company that saves its journalists from the marketers" [5]. Freedom from commercial influence is additionally put at risk by "native advertising and other practices online that blur the line between journalism and sponsored content" thereby threatening "the fundamentals of journalistic independence" [15].

Press independence may be undermined if a small group of organizations controls the underlying revenue generation function of the press or if a small group controls the publishing infrastructure which is now composed of servers and data centers rather than printing presses. If such centralization exists, the press may find themselves less able to challenge powerful entities, resist privacy-invasive business practices, and may be exposed to censorship if intermediaries are coerced into removing content. We pursue the following questions related to independence:

- How centralized, or distributed, are revenue generating mechanisms on news websites?
- How centralized, or distributed, is the use of third-party content on news websites?
- How centralized, or distributed, is the hosting of news websites?

2.2 Privacy

In the same way the free press depends on free speech to be able to write controversial content without interference, citizens rely on *privacy* to enable them to seek out content without being watched. Richards notes that there is little value in being free to write what you want if surveillance makes citizens too afraid to read it [33]. A 2015 study of search trends before and after revelations of NSA surveillance revealed that "there is a chilling effect on search behavior from government surveillance on the Internet" [22]. Likewise, users primed to be cognizant of government surveillance were significantly less likely to comment on a fictional news story describing US military action [39]. If news consumers feel they are being monitored they may be less likely to visit news websites which offer an adversarial take on the actions of the government, or discuss controversial matters with other citizens.

Web tracking techniques are designed to centralize the collection of reader habits into corporate-controlled databases as part of a economic model referred to as "panoptic" [11], "platform"[30, 38], "cognitive"[27], or "surveillance"[10, 44] capitalism. Regardless of the name, the underlying concept is that data gleaned from monitoring users may be used to generate profit, leading to an unending search for new sources of data.

These trends also make it easier for governments to leverage commercial surveillance for political and security needs as corporations may be exploited or coerced into giving access to data to government intelligence agencies such as the NSA [2]. Even without coercion, so-called "data brokers" may sell personal information to military and law enforcement organizations. A 2009 report revealed that the FBI's National Security Branch Analysis

Center (NSAC) possessed "nearly 200 million records transferred from private data brokers such Accurint, Acxiom and Choicepoint" [36]. Likewise, according to an internal email regarding the now-defunct US Department of Defense "Total Information Awareness" project, a military official discussed obtaining Acxiom's data with the company's Chief Privacy Officer in 2002 [14].

Prior research has noted that news websites tend to have more tracking mechanisms than other websites [4, 7], but to date there have been few large-scale studies of tracking on news sites specifically (the Trackography project is one notable exception[3]). To add to existing knowledge on the topic, we pursue the following research questions:

- How is user privacy impacted by different types of third-party content?
- Does third-party content expose users to state surveillance?

2.3 Transparency

More than ink, paper, or advertising revenue, the press has always relied on the trust of readers to thrive. Reader trust is first and foremost grounded in the degree to which news organizations provide transparent accounting of relevant events. However, the technical underpinnings of web tracking rely on covert surveillance of users' web browsing habits, which is fundamentally antithetical to principals of transparency. One way this situation could be partially remedied is if privacy policies on news websites disclose the tracking taking place. Thus, a final question is asked:

- Do the privacy policies of news websites transparently disclose data flows to third-parties?

Pursuing the above questions provides insights into how third-party services could negatively impact the democratic role of the press, and require a multifaceted methodological approach.

3 METHODOLOGY

To answer our research questions, we collect and analyze a set of news and non-news web pages across several dimensions. Considerations regarding the design of the set of pages examined, methods for capturing and categorizing third-party content, and locating privacy policies are described below.

3.1 Data sampling and page collection

To determine if the risks associated with news sites are comparable to other types of popular sites we assemble lists of popular news and non-news websites. News sites are drawn from the US Newspaper List (USNPL.com), a well-organized and up-to-date list of newspapers, news-related magazines, television, and radio stations. From this list we scan over 7,000 pages to identify those that do not redirect to another domain and have at least 50 internal links, indicating the site has a variety of content and is not a placeholder.[4] We find 4,000 pages that meet our criteria. To build the non-news set of pages we draw 4,000 pages from the Alexa top 7,000 US sites which also do not redirect and have at least 50 internal links. The Alexa list is commonly used in web measurement research [7, 19, 34].

---

[3]https://myshadow.org/trackography
[4]We judged redirection based on the pubsuffix, thus "example.com" and "www.example.com" are not counted as a redirect whereas "example.com" and "example.net" are. We use the same criteria to define "internal link".

Given the dynamic nature of modern websites, we load the homepages from each set ten times to capture requests which may not have been found on a single page load. This yields a total of 80,000 page loads, 12.5 million third-party HTTP requests, and 3.4 million third-party cookies inclusive of news and non-news data sets. The computer used for this study is located at an academic institution in the United States, and data collection is performed in April, 2019.

3.2 Detecting third-party services

Once the sets of pages are established the open-source software tool webXray is used to detect third-party HTTP requests and cookies. webXray is given a list of URLs and loads each page in the Chrome web browser, closely reflecting real user behavior. During page loading the browser waits 45 seconds to give an opportunity for page scripts to download and execute. For each page load, webXray creates a fresh Chrome user profile which is free of prior browsing history and cookie data. During page loading no interaction takes place, meaning that notifications to accept cookies are not acted on, and all cookies are set without express user consent. webXray is an established tool used in prior web privacy measurement studies [12, 19–21].

The main benefit of webXray for this study is it provides fine-grained attribution library of the entities which operate third-party web services. While requests to third-party services are made to a specified domain, it is not always clear who owns a domain. For example, third-party content hosted on the the domain "1e100.net" comes from Google and content from "fbcdn.net" is hosted by Facebook. The webXray domain owner library is organized in a hierarchical fashion so that a single domain may be traced to its parent companies. For example, the domain "doubleclick.net" is owned by the DoubleClick service, which is a subsidiary of Google, which is a subsidiary of Alphabet. The webXray domain ownership library has been used to augment findings using the OpenWPM platform as well as studies of Android applications [7, 32].

3.3 Categorization of third-party content

There are a variety of reasons why a first-party site may include third-party services, and the webXray domain ownership library is extended with a service categorization. For over 200 services and companies, the homepage is visited to manually evaluate why a first-party would include content for the given service. It is important to note that our categorization is from the perspective of the *first*-party as the *third*-party may have different objectives. For example, while a site may utilize Google Analytics to gain insights into site traffic, Google may use that data for marketing purposes. This process yields several types of content, details of which are as follows:

- **Advertising** services are used to identify consumers, track their browsing behavior, predict their purchasing interests, and show them advertisements reflective of such predictions.
- **Audience measurement** systems allow site operators to learn about the people who visit a site and the actions they perform.
- **Compliance** tools allow sites to manage their privacy policies and consent notifications in order to comply with data protection laws.

- **Content recommendation** systems are often found at the bottom of articles and provide links to related articles on the same site and partner sites, as well as sponsored advertising content.
- **Design optimization** tools allow site designers to experiment with different designs (a process often called "A/B Testing").
- **Hosting services** run the physical infrastructure which delivers site content. Specialized types of content such as code libraries, fonts, and videos may be hosted from third-party domains. Likewise, generic hosting domains may serve first-party content under a third-party address.
- **Security** services exist to help site operators cope with threats such as distributed denial of service (DDoS) attacks and to prevent criminals using automated means to commit ad fraud and scrape content.
- **Social media** services have two main purposes: embedding user-generated content in a given page and facilitating users sharing a given URL on their social network of choice.
- **Tag managers** are a type of hosted code library with a specific function: helping sites to cope with large volumes of third-party tracking scripts ("tags"). Instead of reducing the number of tags, these services assist web developers with adding even more.

3.4 Identifying web hosting providers

To investigate the hosting of websites, we determine the parties which own a site's IP address using *whois* data. Such owners could be the entity which owns the site, as well as cloud-hosting providers such as Amazon Web Services. We calculate the average number of unique sites hosted by a given provider, revealing how centralized hosting is across the pages examined.

3.5 Collecting and analyzing privacy policies

In addition to monitoring content and cookies, webXray searches for and extracts links to privacy policies on a given page. The text of all links is evaluated to find matches in a list of terms associated with privacy policies. Once policy links are discovered, a second tool, policyXray, is used to harvest and analyze privacy policies.

policyXray has been used in prior research for auditing privacy policies [21]. policyXray uses the open-source Javascript library "Readability.js" to isolate and extract policy text [28]. The use of Readability.js is an essential step as it removes sections of the page which are not part of the policy. For sites with sidebar or footer links to Facebook or Twitter, removing non-policy content ensures that such text is not interpreted as part of the policy.

Once policy text is extracted, mentions of third-party services identified by webXray are searched for. If the names of companies are found, they are interpreted as disclosed in the policy. To give the most opportunities for disclosure, both the owner of the domain, variations on its spelling, and its parent companies are searched for. For example, if the domain "doubleclick.net" is found, the policy is searched to find matches for the strings "DoubleClick", "Double Click" (with a space), "Google", and "Alphabet". Additionally, policyXray analyzes the difficulty of reading a given policy using the English-language Flesch Reading Ease and Flesch-Kinkaid

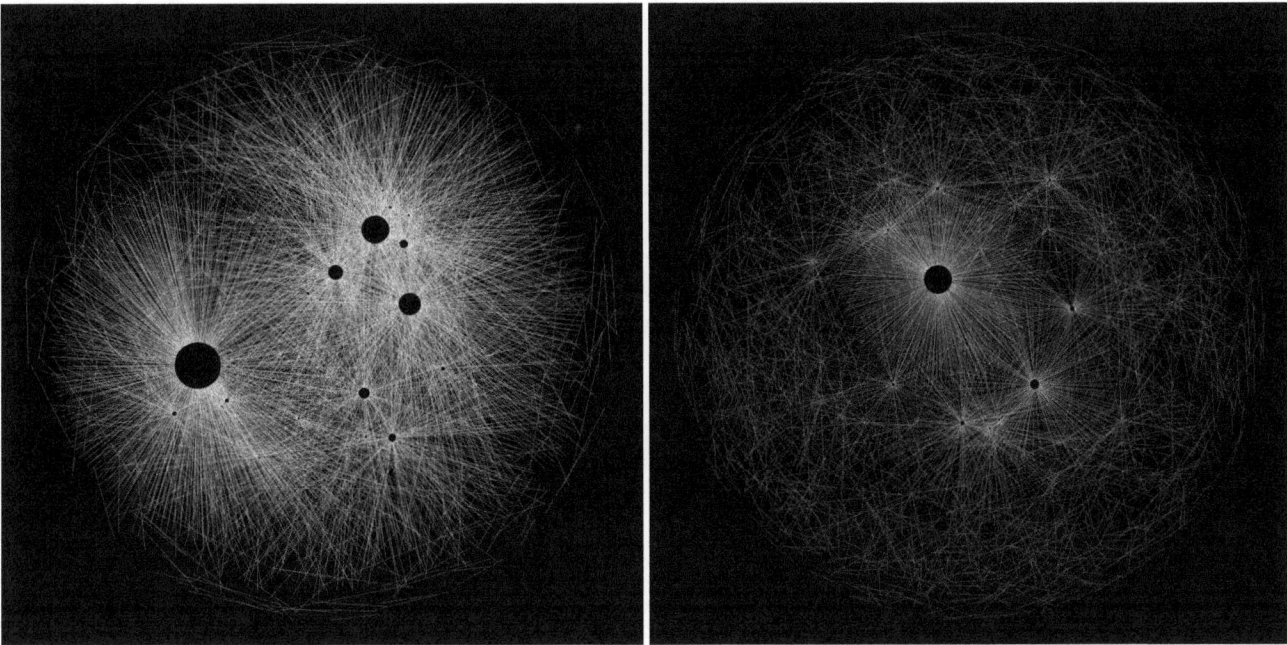

Figure 2: News sites (left) exhibit greater hosting centralization than non-news (right).

Grade Level metrics. We follow MacDonald and Cranor's prior work in this regard [24].

3.6 Limitations

There are several potential limitations to the approaches detailed above. First, the set of pages may not be fully comprehensive and thus not representative of larger trends. Second, webXray may potentially miss some tracking mechanisms, or be flagged as a "bot", resulting in an under-count of exposure. Third, webXray may miss some links to privacy policies if they do not match expected policy text. Finally, policyXray is not always able to parse the text found in a policy and sections of a policy may be erroneously discarded, thereby impacting the accuracy of disclosure measurements.

4 FINDINGS

Across all dimensions examined, use of third-party content by news websites has a negative impact on the democratic utility of the press. News websites rely on highly centralized revenue and hosting infrastructure, placing user privacy at risk, and such risks are not revealed in privacy policies. Furthermore, when compared to non-news sites, news website exhibit more centralization, worse privacy, and less transparency.

4.1 Centralization of revenue, third-party services, and hosting

To explore the independence of news sites we examine revenue generation, reliance on third-party services, and site hosting. We position the possibilities between two extremes: on the first, sites may broker their own advertisements, develop their own code, and host their own sites. Traditionally, news publishers have done many

equivalent tasks in-house. For example, one of the authors delivered newspapers in his youth. On the other extreme, a small number of companies could control the purse strings for an entire industry, unilaterally make essential decisions on digital infrastructure, and own the physical apparatus which delivers the news. We find news on the web tracks closer to the second extreme.

Figure 3 shows the top ten third-party service providers found on news pages along with their equivalent reach on non-news pages. Of the top ten companies, only Amazon is not primarily an advertiser (though that is quickly changing as Amazon's ad services expand). The most remarkable finding is one company, Google, is found on 98% of news and 97% of non-news sites. Likewise, Facebook is able to track users on 53% of news and 51% of non-news sites. While these companies are dominant on both sets of sites, an additional nine companies are found on over 40% of news sites. In contrast, on non-news sites, only Google and Facebook cross the 40% threshold. Thus, while there is a diversity of third-parties, each party has a significantly more central role in the news ecosystem and the overwhelming majority of the most prevalent parties broker advertising.

These findings suggest two main threats to revenue independence. First, the scale of major advertising networks obviates the need for advertisers to engage with publishers directly, making it harder for news outlets to operate independently. Second, Pew found that digital advertising on news websites is dominated by "display ads such as banners or video" as opposed to "search ads" [26]. These types of ads rely on behavioral data for targeting, which is only possible when data is collected from a large range of sites and users. Although a news outlet may want to take control of their advertising, the inventory they offer advertisers will be more cumbersome to buy and less targeted to specific users.

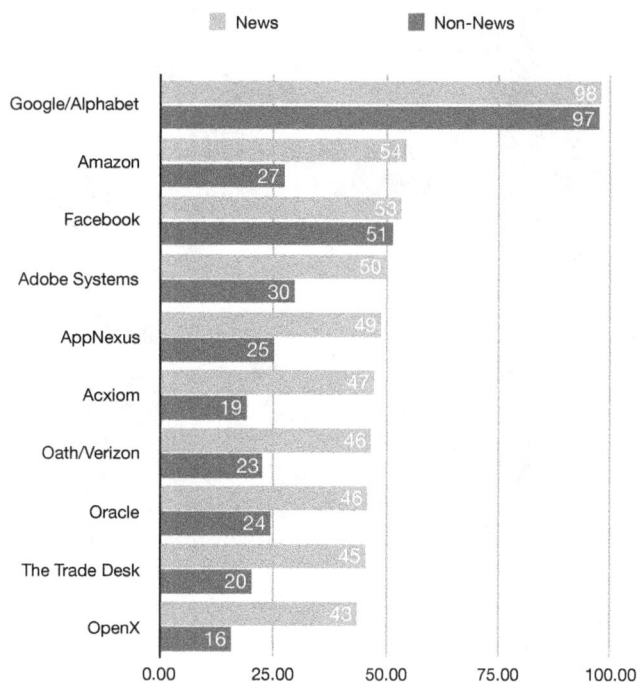

Figure 3: A large percentage of pages include content from a relatively small number of third-parties, a trend more pronounced in news.

Beyond third-party advertising revenue, websites may enhance the bottom line by utilizing third-party services for essential page functions, in turn reducing personnel expenses related to hiring software engineers and maintaining code. This is a less direct form of centralization than revenue, yet in some ways is more powerful. While a given company may part ways with an advertising network, replacing core page functionality can be enormously expensive, thereby establishing a hidden dependence.

Third-parties provide a number of services, and Table 1 shows the prevalence across sites examined. 85% of news sites contain third-party advertising content whereas only 76% of non-news sites do. Likewise, we find much higher reliance on marketing-driven content recommendation systems in news (19%) than non-news (10%). Due to the nature of news funding in the United States this is not a surprising finding. However, what is more surprising is that among sites which do have advertising, news sites use 21 distinct third-parties on average, whereas non-news use half as many (9).

Table 1 details the utilization of third-party services across several categories. In only two categories, design optimization and fonts, do non-news sites exhibit higher dependence on third-parties. For two categories, audience measurement and hosting, there is general parity between news and non-news. For the remaining eight categories, advertising, code, compliance, content recommendation, security, social media, tag management, and video, news sites exhibit higher dependence on third-parties. News shows much higher use of social media (72% vs 64%) - an issue we revisit in the privacy analysis.

The above measures only account for the number of network connections made, rather than the volume of data transferred. We find a high level of centralization when looking at data transfer: 64% of all data on news websites comes from a third-party domain, compared to 41% for non-news. Google is responsible for delivering the most third-party data (15% for news, 8% for non-news). The cost of hosting a website is often directly related to the volume of data transferred and using third-party services may keep costs down while simultaneously fostering dependence.

News websites also rely on third-parties to deliver *first-party* website content. Transferring this data takes physical material resources (e.g. electricity, computer hardware, air conditioning) which are comparable to what was formerly needed to deliver newspapers (e.g. paper, printing presses, delivery persons). We find most publishers outsource the hosting of their sites. Centralization of first-party hosting is in some ways the most troublesome issue related to press freedoms as it opens the door for authorities to conduct censorship for a large number of news outlets by putting pressure on a much smaller number of hosting providers.

We find a total of 268 unique web hosts for news sites compared to 1,084 for non-news, a nearly four-fold difference. Not only are the number of hosts for news sites far smaller, but only three companies (Lee Enterprises, Incapsula, and Amazon) host 44% of all US news sites examined. In contrast, for non-news, only one company hosts more than 7% of sites. Figure 2 illustrates site hosting networks, with several prominent nodes shown hosting news sites.

A final risk to publisher independence is large volumes of third-party advertising and tracking content may make news pages more expensive to view and slower to load than non-news websites. News websites take an average of 28 seconds to complete downloading compared to 17 seconds for non-news.[5] This may lead users to get their news from social media or aggregator websites which control which articles get presented to users, sidestepping news editors, and reducing the likelihood users will develop long-term relationships with a news outlet. The two most frequently detected third-parties on news sites, Google and Facebook, aggregate, select, and optimize delivery of news articles in centralized systems (*AMP* and *Instant Articles* respectively), making them direct competitors to news outlets. As with advertising, giving these companies access to user browsing histories allows them to provide targeting and selection of news content which may be superior to that provided by decentralized news outlets. For many users, download time will be the least of their worries when it comes to visiting news websites.

4.2 Privacy

While users may turn to the news to learn of the ways in which corporations compromise their privacy, it is news sites where we find the greatest risks to privacy. While nearly all sites expose user browsing behavior to third-parties (99% for news, 98% for non-news), on a per-page basis, news sites expose users to an average of 41 third-parties simultaneously compared to 21 for non-news. News sites expose users to third-party cookies on 91% of pages, compared to 84% for non-news. On a per-page basis, the number

---

[5]Measures of time are useful as relative rather than absolute measures given variations in network latency across locations and times. However, in this case pages are loaded from two computers sitting next to each other.

of third-party cookies is nearly three times greater: 63 on averag for news compared to 23 for non-news. News sites also exhib poorer security: only 70% of news pages use transport encryptio compared to 85% of non-news pages. While top-level analysis i dicates that news sites fare more poorly in their stewardship user security and privacy, further examination reveals differe third-party services impact user privacy and security in distin ways.

While all third-party requests expose users to potential trac ing via analysis of HTTP log data [43], the presence of third-par cookies is a strong indicator that a given third-party is making *purposeful attempt* to compromise users' privacy by tracking the as they navigate between sites.[6] As Table 1 details, different typ of services set cookies at considerably different rates, and for nev sites, cookies are often set at greater rates. Advertising content se cookies at high rates: 76% of news and non-news pages with a vertising contain an advertising cookie. Content recommendatio which is arguably a sub-type of advertising, sets cookies at eve greater rates (82% for news, 81% for non-news).

Service Type	% of Pages		% w Cookie	
	News	Non-News	News	Non-News
Advertising	85	76	76	76
- Content Rec	19	10	82	81
Audience Measure	93	93	45	23
Compliance	14	4	0	2
Design Optimize	14	28	45	44
Hosting	95	94	7	5
- Code	88	74	0	0
- Font	3	16	0	0
- Video	23	22	22	29
Security	28	16	4	6
Social Media	72	64	40	47
Tag Manager	77	61	0	0

Table 1: Most types of content are more prevalent on new sites, with the presence of cookies varying considerably.

Furthermore, each page with advertising content has an average of 21 distinct third-party domains compared with nine for non-news. There is a finite amount of room for advertising on a given page and even the most insufferable designs cannot accommodate 21 banner advertisements. Thus, the presence of seemingly redundant advertising content is best explained by the fact that even in cases where ads are not shown, an advertising network may track user behavior to display targeted advertisements on *other* pages.

Other types of services which utilize cookies at fairly high rates are audience measurement (44% news, 23% non-news), design optimization (45% news, 44% non-news), and social media (40% news, 47% non-news). In the case of audience measurement, privacy concerns are high as these systems are specifically used to record browsing behaviors. Cookies utilized by design optimization tools

---

[6]Although this analysis focuses on third-party cookies, it is also possible to track users with first-party cookies.

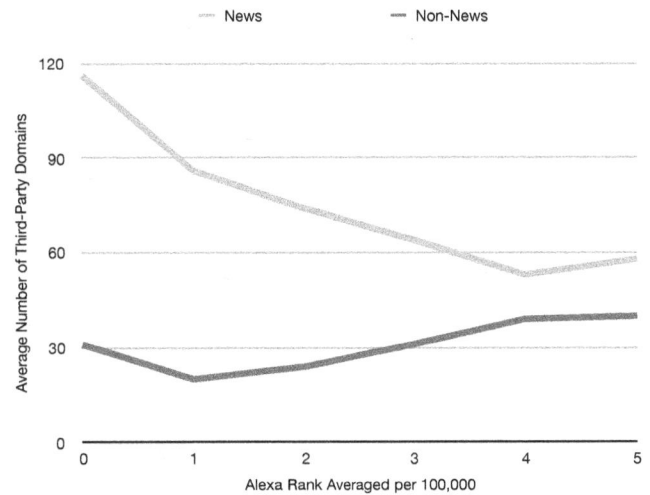

Figure 4: Of sites ranked in the top 500,000 in the United States, higher-ranked news sites have the most third-parties and news sites have more third-parties than non-news sites.

may not be designed for tracking users across sites, but may nevertheless represent a privacy risk. Social media content comes with the added privacy concern that cookies may be linked with specific off-line identities (Facebook for example requires the use of "real" names). Cookies are rarely, if ever, set for services related to compliance, fonts, code libraries, and tag managers, suggesting that these types of services may not be intentionally tracking users.

As noted above, under "surveillance capitalism" we might hypothesise that non-profit news outlets would likely have fewer privacy-compromising features than commercial news outlets. Although an imperfect proxy, the use of the "org" and "com" top-level domains are reliable indicators if a given site is a non-profit or commercial organization and thus provide a rough means to test this hypothesis. Of news sites examined, 3% are "org" and 92% are "com", a breakdown which may reflect the commercial nature of US news media. As expected, we find non-profit sites exhibit a much lower percentage of sites with third-party cookies (78% for "org" vs 92% for "com"), and among sites with third-party cookies, commercial sites have over four times more (15 for "org" vs 66 for "com"). While the percentage of "org" and "com' sites with any third-party content is similar (98% for "org", 99% for "com"), the average number of third-party domains is nearly three times greater (15 for "org" vs 43 for "com"). Furthermore, sites which are ranked higher by Alexa, and which are likely more profitable, also have the greatest number of third-parties, as illustrated in Figure 4. The highest-ranked news site, The New York Times, leaks user data to 61 third-party domains (see Figure 1).

4.3 State surveillance

Some of the biggest risks deriving from poor privacy are related to state surveillance. Third-parties potentially expose users to two forms of state surveillance. In the first, third-parties may either be compromised or forced to disclose users' web browsing information to authorities. In the second, companies which sell or share

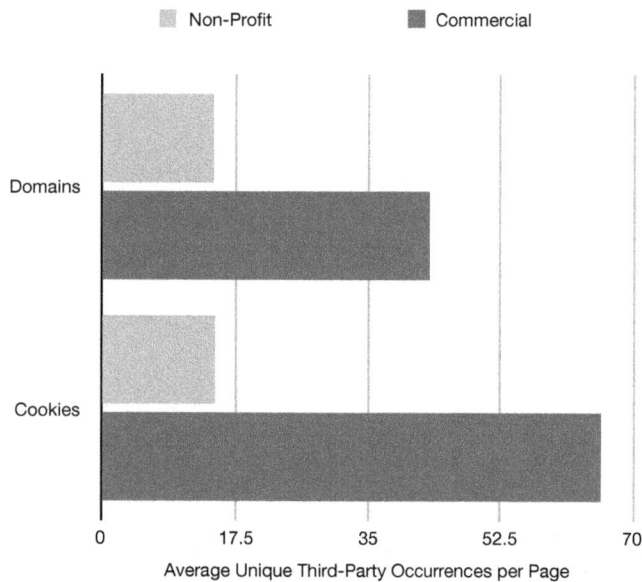

Figure 5: Non-profit news sites have fewer third-party domains and cookies than commercial sites.

personal data directly to the government may include web browsing information. Given the role of news media in exposing state surveillance, it is particularly relevant if news websites facilitate such outcomes themselves.

In 2013, former US National Security Agency (NSA) contractor Edward Snowden leaked details on how the NSA has used web browsing data for spying purposes. According to former Deputy US Chief Technology Officer Ed Felten, Snowden's disclosures revealed "a link between the sort of tracking that's done by Web sites for analytics and advertising and NSA exploitation activities" [37]. Likewise, *The Guardian* revealed a specific Google cookie, "Doubleclick ID", was used in efforts to spy on users of the Tor anonymity service [29]. Englehardt et al studied third-party cookies in 2015 and found users are "vulnerable to the NSA's dragnet surveillance".[8] This problem has not gone away: 74% of news and 50% of non-news pages include DoubleClick cookies.[7]

As noted above, the data broker Acxiom has discussed or sold user data to both the US Department of Defense and the FBI. We find Acxiom on 47% of news and 19% of non-news pages. Another company receiving large volumes of user data from news websites is Oracle, which has content on 46% of news and 24% of non-news pages. Of particular importance to the subject of state surveillance, Oracle has deep ties to US military and law enforcement: among Oracle's divisions are "Immigration and Border Control" which assist with "managing the tracking of individuals within national boundaries".[8]

It is not possible to determine if data Acxiom or Oracle collects from visitors to news websites is made available to government clients, but as noted above, the possibility *alone* is enough to dissuade users from accessing politically sensitive material [22, 39]. The blurring of boundaries between commercial and state surveillance is well-documented, but it is especially concerning given the special role of news media in the democratic process.

One reason to discount the chilling effects of surveillance is users who do not know about surveillance may not be dissuaded from seeking out politically controversial news. However, lack of awareness is another way in which reliance on third-parties may undermine the press.

4.4 Transparency: policy readability and third-party disclosure

To determine if a given web page's privacy policies are both clear and transparent, we harvest the privacy policies of 1,892 news sites (47% of the total), and 2,194 privacy policies of non-news sites (55% of the total). Next, three sets of measures are taken. First, we evaluate how difficult it is to read privacy policies. Second, we estimate how long it would take to read an average policy. Third, each page with a privacy policy is evaluated with policyxray to determine if the entities receiving data on the page are disclosed.

A given privacy policy may contain information which is valuable to users and informs them of privacy risks, yet for such information to be useful, it would need to be stated in terms a user could comprehend. The Flesch-Reading Ease (FRE) score is a 0-100 scale of reading difficulty, with 100 being easiest to read. The Flesch-Kinkaid Grade-Level score pegs a text against the US K-12 education system. Scores significantly above grade 12 become increasingly meaningless as the Flesch-Kinkaid formula may generate an infinitely high score. A grade-level score above 20 does not mean a PhD is needed to read the text, it means the text exceeds the utility of the grade-level scale.

Both news and non-news policies have poor FRE scores, 21 and 28 respectively. Likewise, their grade-level scores, 28 and 34 respectively, demonstrate a breakdown of the very applicability of grade-level metrics. While no enforceable standards exist for the readability of online privacy policies, insurance policies written below an FRE level of 45 are not enforceable in Florida [21]. Thus, if these were insurance, rather than privacy, polices they would not meet minimum legal requirements for clarity. Standards of transparency expected of the press should exceed what the state of Florida expects from insurers, yet the failure here is clear.

Privacy polices are also time consuming to read, raising an additional burden to users. On average, privacy policies for news sites are 2,263 words in length and require 9 minutes to read. In comparison, privacy policies for non-news sites average 2,033 words and require slightly over 8 minutes to read. While this amount of time may not initially appear onerous, MacDonald and Cranor have previously calculated the cost in time to read all such policies for an average user is considerable, and Libert has determined the time to read *both* first- and third-party policies exceeds 80 minutes for an average site [21, 24]. It is possible that disclosing a larger number of third-parties makes news policies lengthier, yet this explanation may be ruled out.

Although vague statements about sharing user data with "affiliates" or "partners" may be viewed as a *type* of disclosure, this

---

[7]Note the "ID" cookie appears to have been deprecated and "DSID" and "IDE" are now used.

[8]See http://www.oracle.com/us/industries/public-sector/046927.html.

Company	% of Pages Tracked	% Disclosed in Policies
Alphabet (Google)	95	38
Facebook	52	16
Amazon	46	2
Oracle	45	<1
Acxiom	41	0
Verizon (Oath)	40	<1
comScore	38	0
Twitter	34	4
AppNexus	32	1
OpenX	30	<1

Table 2: News privacy policies lack transparency, especially in regards to companies with no consumer-facing products such as Axiom and AppNexus.

study takes the approach that disclosure entails mentioning the *specific* third-parties present on a site. [9] Policies for both news and non-news sites fail to disclose the vast majority of third-parties. Only 10% of third-parties are disclosed in news privacy policies and only 14% in non-news policies. Both news sites and non-news sites share problematic features, with news sites once again faring worse.

Low rates of disclosure are not uniform and there is significant variability in the degree to which different third-parties are disclosed (see Table 2). Companies with services users may already be aware of such as search (Google) and social media (Facebook and Twitter) are more likely to be disclosed than those which users may not directly interact with such as AppNexus and Acxiom. Many parties are not mentioned in any privacy policies despite appearing on large numbers of pages. On news pages, 241 third-parties are found, of these, 169 (70%) are never mentioned in a privacy policy. On non-news pages, 266 third-parties are found, of these 202 (76%) are never mentioned. Thus, even users who make an effort to read privacy policies will likely never learn of many third-party services which may observe their browsing behavior. Given the very essence of journalism is transparency and disclosure, the state of privacy policies on news sites makes a poor case for citizens to place trust in these institutions.

5 RELATED WORK

Work related to the value of the press is detailed in the background section, and it is helpful to provide more context on related technical work here. There is a large literature devoted to the privacy and security impacts of web tracking. One early study correctly predicted that privacy would be at risk if an "advertising agency could add measurement code to the banner ads it distributes" [9]. A number of studies have investigated the presence of browser "fingerprinting" techniques which are used to track users without cookies [1, 6, 43]. Web measurement literature has been documenting the spread of tracking mechanisms at large scale since at least

2006 [17]. Recent studies have expanded the scale and scope of such investigations to document tracking across millions, or even billions, of sites [7, 19, 35] and examined how practices have changed over time [18, 41].

Researchers have also investigated the "notice and choice" privacy regulation framework while relies on users being notified of tracking by reading privacy policies. A large body of research has demonstrated this approach is ineffective as privacy policies are difficult to understand for most users [21, 24, 25], and they rarely disclose the third-party services [21]. Approaches such as crowdsourcing the interpretation of privacy policies may help alleviate this [42], but it remains difficult for users to learn of web tracking practices in general.

6 CONCLUSION

It is important to acknowledge that the ability of news outlets to stay in business is currently tied to a highly-centralized revenue model which is largely out of their control and fundamentally hostile to user privacy. However, difficult financial considerations do not absolve news media of responsibility for minimizing the amount of third-party content or increasing transparency of practices which impact user privacy. Likewise, news outlets have performed admirably when reporting on state surveillance and corporate privacy scandals, but rarely disclose how they also benefit from tracking users, raising the troubling question of what institutions users may rely upon to inform them of web tracking. Nevertheless, many would agree an imperfect press is better than no press at all.

Despite its democratic role, respect for the press is not universal. US President Donald Trump has stated that the news media "is the enemy of the American People". [10] While many around the world have grown weary of, and even inured to, this rhetoric, it is unwise to assume the significant powers of the US government could not be turned against the news media, especially if justified under the pretence of national emergency.

The ability of the press to withstand attempts at censorship and discovery of citizens' reading habits are deeply undermined by centralization of revenue and hosting. The fact that only three companies host 43% of news pages (Lee Enterprises, Incapsula, and Amazon) combined with duopolies in search (Google, Microsoft) and social media (Facebook, Twitter), means pressure on only seven companies could result in rapid and widespread information suppression and identification of political dissidents. While these scenarios may seem far-fetched, sober evaluation of the findings presented herein demands we consider the current state of centralization, privacy, and transparency on the web as a threat to democracy.

7 ACKNOWLEDGEMENTS

The authors thank reviewers for their insightful comments and Prof. Jonathan Smith for use of computing resources.

REFERENCES

[1] Gunes Acar, Marc Juarez, Nick Nikiforakis, Claudia Diaz, Seda Gürses, Frank Piessens, and Bart Preneel. 2013. FPDetective: dusting the web for fingerprinters. In *Proceedings of the 2013 ACM SIGSAC Conference on Computer & Communications Security*. ACM, 1129–1140.

---

⁹While this study is based on a sample of US sites, it is instructive to note that EU data protection guidelines recommend that data controllers should typically disclose specific recipients rather than broad categories; see Article 29 Working Party Guidelines on Transparency WP260 rev.01, p37.

¹⁰https://twitter.com/realDonaldTrump/status/832708293516632065

[2] James Ball. 2013. NSA's PRISM surveillance program: how it works and what it can do. *The Guardian* 8 (2013).

[3] James Bennett, James Bennett, and Niki Strange. 2015. Introduction: the utopia of independent media: independence, working with freedom and working for free. *Media Independence: Working with Freedom or Working for Free* (2015), 1–28.

[4] Ceren Budak, Sharad Goel, Justin Rao, and Georgios Zervas. 2016. Understanding emerging threats to online advertising. In *Proceedings of the 2016 ACM Conference on Economics and Computation*. ACM, 561–578.

[5] Mark Deuze. 2005. What is journalism? Professional identity and ideology of journalists reconsidered. *Journalism* 6, 4 (2005), 442–464.

[6] Peter Eckersley. 2010. How unique is your web browser?. In *Privacy Enhancing Technologies Symposium*. Springer, 1–18.

[7] Steven Englehardt and Arvind Narayanan. 2016. Online tracking: A 1-million-site measurement and analysis. In *Proceedings of the 2016 ACM SIGSAC Conference on Computer and Communications Security*. ACM, 1388–1401.

[8] Steven Englehardt, Dillon Reisman, Christian Eubank, Peter Zimmerman, Jonathan Mayer, Arvind Narayanan, and Edward W Felten. 2015. Cookies that give you away: The surveillance implications of web tracking. In *Proceedings of the 24th International Conference on World Wide Web*. International World Wide Web Conferences Steering Committee, 289–299.

[9] Edward W Felten and Michael A Schneider. 2000. Timing attacks on web privacy. In *Proceedings of the 7th ACM Conference on Computer and Communications Security*. ACM, 25–32.

[10] John Bellamy Foster and Robert W McChesney. 2014. Surveillance capitalism: Monopoly-finance capital, the military-industrial complex, and the digital age. *Monthly Review* 66, 3 (2014), 1.

[11] Oscar Gandy. 2005. If it weren't for bad luck. *14th Annual Walter and Lee Annenberg Distinguished Lecture* (2005).

[12] Christian Hauschke. 2016. Third-Party-Elemente in deutschen Bibliothekswebseiten. *Informationspraxis* 2, 2 (2016).

[13] Kashmir Hill. 2017. Yes, Google Uses Its Power to Quash Ideas It Doesn't Like—I Know Because It Happened to Me. *Gizmodo* (2017).

[14] Chris Jay Hoofnagle. 2003. Big Brother's Little Helpers: How ChoicePoint and Other Commercial Data Brokers Collect and Package Your Data for Law Enforcement. *North Carolina Journal of International Law and Commercial Regulation* 29 (2003), 595.

[15] Kari Karppinen and Hallvard Moe. 2016. What We Talk About When Talk About "Media Independence". *Javnost-The Public* 23, 2 (2016), 105–119.

[16] Bill Kovach and Tom Rosenstiel. 2007. *The elements of journalism: What newspeople should know and the public should expect*. Three Rivers Press (CA).

[17] Balachander Krishnamurthy and Craig E Wills. 2006. Generating a privacy footprint on the internet. In *Proceedings of the 6th ACM SIGCOMM Conference on Internet Measurement*. ACM, 65–70.

[18] Adam Lerner, Anna Kornfeld Simpson, Tadayoshi Kohno, and Franziska Roesner. 2016. Internet Jones and the Raiders of the Lost Trackers: An Archaeological Study of Web Tracking from 1996 to 2016. In *25th USENIX Security Symposium (USENIX Security 16)*. USENIX Association, Austin, TX. https://www.usenix.org/conference/usenixsecurity16/technical-sessions/presentation/lerner

[19] Timothy Libert. 2015. Exposing the Hidden Web: Third-Party HTTP Requests On One Million Websites. *International Journal of Communication* (2015).

[20] Timothy Libert. 2015. Privacy Implications of Health Information Seeking on the Web. *Commun. ACM* (2015).

[21] Timothy Libert. 2018. An Automated Approach to Auditing Disclosure of Third-Party Data Collection in site Privacy Policies. *Proceedings of the 2018 World Wide Web Conference* (2018), 207–216.

[22] Alex Marthews and Catherine E Tucker. 2015. Government surveillance and internet search behavior. *SSRN* (2015).

[23] Robert W McChesney. 2013. *Digital disconnect: How capitalism is turning the Internet against democracy*. New Press, The.

[24] Aleecia M McDonald and Lorrie Faith Cranor. 2008. The Cost of reading privacy policies. *I/S: A Journal Of Law And Policy For The Information Society* 4 (2008), 543.

[25] Aleecia M McDonald, Robert W Reeder, Patrick Gage Kelley, and Lorrie Faith Cranor. 2009. A comparative study of online privacy policies and formats. In *Privacy Enhancing Technologies*. Springer, 37–55.

[26] Amy Mitchell and Tom Rosenstiel. 2015. State of the news media 2015. *Pew Research Center. Journalism & Media* (2015).

[27] Yann Moulier-Boutang. 2011. *Cognitive capitalism*. Polity.

[28] Mozilla. 2017. Readability.js. https://github.com/mozilla/readability. (07 2017).

[29] National Security Agency. 2013. Tor Stinks Presentation. *The Guardian* http://www.theguardian.com/world/interactive/2013/oct/04/tor-stinks-nsa-presentation-document (2013).

[30] Frank Pasquale. 2016. Two narratives of platform capitalism. *Yale L. & Pol'y Rev.* 35 (2016), 309.

[31] Victor Pickard. 2014. *America's Battle for Media Democracy*. Cambridge University Press.

[32] Max Van Kleek Jun Zhao Timothy Libert Nigel Shadbolt. Reuben Binns, Ulrik Lyngs. 2018. Third Party Tracking in the Mobile Ecosystem. *WebSci âĂŹ18: 10th ACM Conference on Web Science* (2018).

[33] Neil M Richards. 2008. Intellectual privacy. *Texas Law Review* 87 (2008), 387.

[34] Franziska Roesner, Tadayoshi Kohno, and David Wetherall. 2012. Detecting and defending against third-party tracking on the web. In *Proceedings of the 9th USENIX conference on Networked Systems Design and Implementation*. USENIX Association, 12–12.

[35] Sebastian Schelter and Jérôme Kunegis. 2016. On the Ubiquity of Web Tracking: Insights from a Billion-Page Web Crawl. *arXiv preprint arXiv:1607.07403* (2016).

[36] Ryan Singel. 2008. Newly declassified files detail massive FBI data-mining project. (2008).

[37] Ashkan Soltani, Andrea Peterson, and Barton Gellman. 2013. NSA uses Google cookies to pinpoint targets for hacking. *The Washington Post* https://www.washingtonpost.com/blogs/the-switch/wp/2013/12/10/nsa-uses-google-cookies-to-pinpoint-targets-for-hacking (2013).

[38] Nick Srnicek. 2017. *Platform capitalism*. John Wiley & Sons.

[39] Elizabeth Stoycheff. 2016. Under surveillance examining Facebook's spiral of silence effects in the wake of NSA internet monitoring. *Journalism & Mass Communication Quarterly* (2016), 1077699016630255.

[40] Siva Vaidhyanathan. 2012. *The Googlization of everything:(and why we should worry)*. University of California Press.

[41] Tim Wambach and Katharina Bräunlich. 2016. Retrospective Study of Third-party Web Tracking. In *Proceedings of the 2nd International Conference on Information Systems Security and Privacy*. 138–145. https://doi.org/10.5220/0005741301380145

[42] Shomir Wilson, Florian Schaub, Rohan Ramanath, Norman Sadeh, Fei Liu, Noah A Smith, and Frederick Liu. 2016. Crowdsourcing Annotations for Websites' Privacy Policies: Can It Really Work?. In *Proceedings of the 25th International Conference on World Wide Web*. International World Wide Web Conferences Steering Committee, 133–143.

[43] Ting-Fang Yen, Yinglian Xie, Fang Yu, Roger Peng Yu, and Martın Abadi. 2012. Host fingerprinting and tracking on the web: Privacy and security implications. In *Proceedings of the Network and Distributed System Security Symposium*.

[44] Shoshana Zuboff. 2015. Big other: surveillance capitalism and the prospects of an information civilization. *Journal of Information Technology* 30, 1 (2015), 75–89.

A Data-Driven Examination of Hotelling's Linear City Model

Xin Liu
University of Pittsburgh
Pittsburgh, Pennsylvania
xil178@pitt.edu

Konstantinos Pelechrinis
University of Pittsburgh
Pittsburgh, Pennsylvania
kpele@pitt.edu

ABSTRACT

In his seminal work *stability in competition*, Hotelling developed a model for identifying the spatial equilibrium for two competing firms such that they maximize their market-share. He considered a linear area of fixed length and he showed that in this setting the two competing firms should be located side-by-side in the middle of the line. Hotelling's study has been then adopted and used to analyze and explain other phenomena in a variety of fields. However, the linear city model is purely theoretical, without any empirical validation. The goal of this study is to explore Hotelling's Law in its original space - i.e., that of firm competition - and identify possible adjustments needed to describe its application/validity in a non-linear city. In particular, we collect data from location-based social networks that include information for the number of customers in a venue and we compare them with the expectations from Hotelling's original law. Overall, we identify that at a large geographic scale there is correlation between the market-share and the inter-venue distance, which is consistent with the Hotelling's Law. However, as we zoom into smaller scales there are deviations from the expectations from Hotelling's law, possibly due to higher sensitivity to the necessary assumptions. Our findings enhance the literature on optimal location placement for a venue and can provide additional insights for owners in regards to the linear city model.

ACM Reference Format:
Xin Liu and Konstantinos Pelechrinis. 2019. A Data-Driven Examination of Hotelling's Linear City Model. In *11th ACM Conference on Web Science (WebSci '19), June 30-July 3, 2019, Boston, MA, USA.* ACM, New York, NY, USA, 5 pages. https://doi.org/10.1145/3292522.3326020

1 INTRODUCTION

"Location, location, location". This has been the mantra of real-estate agents when it comes to valuing a property. This is true for local businesses as well. Location is an important driver for the success of a business, that being a restaurant, a cafe, a retail store etc. [27]. Location can impact the success of a business both through convenient access to it, but also through agglomeration of other businesses (even if they are competing in nature). For example, it may be reasonable for a venue v to operate in an area with limited options for the service provided by v in order to achieve oligopoly/monopoly. However, competition can be beneficial in a multitude of ways. For

one, it motivates the improvement of the services provided by v [5]. More importantly though, an area with multiple venue options will overall attract more people that are interested in exploring the area and hence, all the venues will potentially enjoy the benefits from the associated network effects [21].

There has been a significant volume of research on the impact of location on the revenue of a local business and the of *optimal* sites for a business. One of the first pieces that dealt with the problem of business location is what is known today as Hotelling's Law or Hotelling's Linear City (HLC) Model [13]. What Hotelling theorized, is that if there are two competing stores v_1 and v_2 on a street and their goal is to maximize their market share, ceteris paribus, their optimal location is right in the middle of the street, next to each other.

More specifically, Hotelling developed a linear city model to identify a spatial equilibrium point for two competing venues that offer identical products aiming at maximizing their market-share. Hence, as shown in Figure 1, for location z on the street segment (i.e., $z \in [0,1]$) and M total customers uniformly distributed over the linear street segment, there will be $M \cdot z$ customers on the segment $[0, z]$ and $M \cdot (1 - z)$ customers on the segment $(z, 1]$. The utility a customer will get by visiting venue j (i.e., v_j) depends on (i) the unit transportation cost t, (ii) the prices at venue j, p_j and (iii) the gross customer surplus from visiting venue j, s_j. Overall, the utility is expressed by:

$$u_j = s_j - p_j - t \cdot d_j. \tag{1}$$

where d_j is the distance between the customer and v_j. Under the assumption that the market is *covered* (i.e., the excess surplus for every customer is large enough for them to be willing to buy), and that v_1 is at point $z = 0$ and v_2 is at point $z = 1$, the equilibrium point $\hat{z}$ at which a customer is indifferent to the two venues is [18]:

$$\hat{z} = (t + p_2 - p_1 + s_1 - s_2)/(2t). \tag{2}$$

This is also the location where the two venues need to locate their stores. For the case of venues that offer identical services, customers will get the same gross surplus from the two venues (i.e., $s_1 = s_2$), while the prices will be equal (i.e., $p_1 = p_2$), leading to $\hat{z} = 1 - \hat{z} = \frac{1}{2}$. Therefore, HLC states that the Nash equilibrium in this case is for the two venues to be located one by the other on the middle of the line. Despite the rather unrealistic assumptions of HLC (e.g., uniform distribution of customers, linear geography etc.), the model provides very important insights that can impact the site location of businesses. HLC is generalized as Salop's circular city model [18], where N venues (instead of 2 venues) are distributed uniformly over a circle. More generally, HLC implies that businesses will benefit if they are located near their competitors. In particular, given that the businesses offer similar quality product and at similar prices, each should get their fair share of the market.

WebSci '19, June 30-July 3, 2019, Boston, MA, USA
© 2019 Association for Computing Machinery.
ACM ISBN 978-1-4503-6202-3/19/06...$15.00
https://doi.org/10.1145/3292522.3326020

This is counter-intuitive at a first glance, since this co-location will significantly increase competition and there can be customer spill-over from v_1 to v_2 and vice-versa. Of course, Hotelling's Linear City model is a purely theoretical law that is based on a set of (idealized) assumptions, such as a uniform mobility model. Under the latter, customers will arrive uniformly on the length of the street and therefore, v_1 will be the closest venue to approximately half of them and v_2 the closest for the rest half. Starbucks have been reported to make site choices based on the mobility patterns and even have stores very close to each other (as HLC would suggest) [1], while clustering observed in gas stations [26], fast food restaurants [25], pharmacies [11] and other retail stores [24] is also an artifact of ideas in Hotelling's Law. Despite these anecdotal stories, to the best of our knowledge, the *validity* of HLC has not been examined through real-world dataset, and especially, in the digital marketing and social media era, where *hyper-locality*, i.e., the ability to obtain information for areas not in our immediate vicinity, can alleviate some of the disadvantages experienced by a remote, potentially isolated, venue.

In this study, we use data from Foursquare, the largest location-based social network to date, and iExit, a service that provides information about Points-of-Interest at highway exits, to explore whether the outcomes expected by HLC hold in the real-world. We focus on a specific setting in order to minimize influence from other factors to the extent possible. In particular, we examine the distribution of customer visits to fast food restaurants that are clustered in highway exists. This mimics the original setting of HLC to a large extent - that is, venues that offer the same service and in similar prices, while also being very close to each other. We analyze the number of customers as a function of the distance between the venues in different scales. Our results indicate that, as we zoom-in to smaller (geographic) scales, the *validity* of HLC is reduced. This can possibly be attributed to many of the Hotelling's Law assumptions that might be harder to hold in the real-world in small scales. The contribution of our work is twofold: we provide evidence for the validity of HLC in a real-world setting and that in small geographic scales some of Hotelling's Laws assumption might not hold.

Related Literature: A large number of studies have analyzed the spatial influences on store competitions and customers' characteristics (e.g., [10, 12, 23]). Furthermore, there is a large volume of studies that aim into identifying optimal locations for business stores and Daskin *et al.* [9] present a detailed taxonomy of the various sub-problems in optimal site identification. In general, a retail store is expected to be more successful if located within a shopping center or a central business district, which provides convenient transportation access and attractiveness [17]. Given also the correlation between retail store density and street network centrality [19, 20], a central location will be preferable. Jensen [14, 15] also considers network effects in interactions between different types of venues, while Aboolian *et al.* [2] develop a spatial interaction model that seeks to simultaneously optimize location and design decisions for a set of new venues. However, the proposed model assumes a purely homogeneous customers base, that is, all customers are identical with respect to their venue preferences and expenditure decisions. Furthermore, the lack of detailed customer volume for the venues, creates issues for estimating the potential total market share for a venue in an area. In a subsequent series of studies [3, 4] the authors assume that customers' demand for a venue v (i.e., the probability

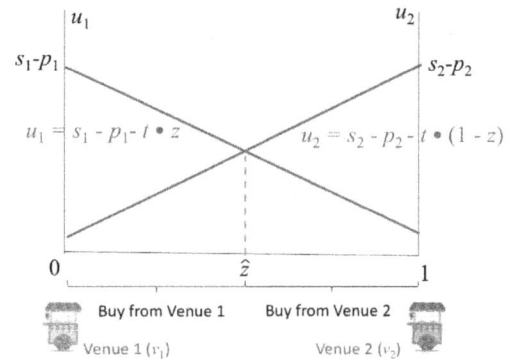

Figure 1: Based on the HLC model, a user that is on the middle of the street ($\hat{z} = 0.5$) is indifferent to the two venues. This is also the location where the two venues need to locate their stores to maximize their customer share.

of visiting the venue) decreases with the distance from v and increases with the *attractiveness* of it. Based on this assumption, the authors provide a spatial interaction model for locating a set of new facilities that compete for market share. Their models are applied and evaluated on synthetic data, showing the efficiency of the proposed algorithmic solution to the discrete multi-venue competitive interaction optimization problem. However, it is not clear how they will perform in the real-world. Other approaches [6] identify the optimal location for a store by maximizing the number of customers expected to be covered taking mobility patterns into consideration . Bozkaya *et al.* [7] use a genetic algorithm to select a single site among several candidate locations to maximize the market share under budget constraints. The results are verified by a real-world dataset of a supermarket chain in City of Istanbul. However, the methods of selecting candidate locations are not explained. Furhtermore, Karamshuk *et al.* [16] study the predictive power of various geographic and mobility-related features on the popularity of retail stores in New York City using Foursquare data. Even though the authors do not focus particularly on the HLC model, some of the features chosen are relevant to Hotelling's Law (at least at an intuitive level). In particular, the number of competing venues in an area, the density of venues in an area as well as the diversity of venues within an area are features that are examined among others.

2 DATASET AND EXPERIMENTAL SETUP

In order to complete our study we need data for customer visitation in local businesses. Furthermore, as aforementioned, we want to focus on cases that *match* - to the extend possible - the assumptions made by the HLC model. For that we focus on a specific type of venues, namely fast food restaurants, and on a particular environment, that is, highway exits. With this setting, our analysis will include venues that offer the same service, at very similar quality and price points.

For our study we focus on the state of Pennsylvania (PA), and we use the iExit API[1] that provides information about points-of-interest at highway exists. Every point of interest is a tuple of the following form: <id, phone, latitude, longitude, address, name, category, rating, price tier, brand name, exit ID>. We collect a total of 1,537 tuples that

---

[1] https://iexit.readme.io/

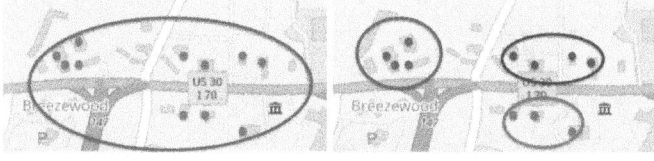

Figure 2: The different scales for our analysis. At a large scale (left) we consider a set of individual venues that are accessible from the same highway exits. At a small scale analysis we consider clusters of venues (right).

correspond to fast foods over the highway network in Pennsylvania over 482 exits. 95.1% of them belong to the lowest price tier, which means that venues in our dataset have very similar prices. We then query Foursquare's public venue API[2] to obtain information about the number of check-ins in each of these venues.

We begin by calculating the average daily check-ins for every venue in our dataset. For this we use the number of days that each venue has been on Foursquare up to the day of data collection (i.e., 19/06/2018). By using the average daily number of check-ins we essentially alleviate problems associated with the fact that older venues might have higher number of total check-ins simply by virtue of being on the system for longer. We also want to filter out venues that did not have a check-in for an extended period of time, which can be a sign of a venue that has been closed, and hence, we remove all venues with average daily check-ins less than 0.1.

According to our earlier discussion when venues - offering similar service quality at similar prices - are co-located, they expect to obtain their fair share of the market. That is, if there is a total of N check-ins in an *area* and k *closely* located venues, each will get approximately (N/k) check-ins. Based on this observation, the objective of our study is to examine whether there are any deviations from this expectation.

Geographic Scale: Intuitively, referring to the original setting for HLC, the geographic scale is related to the length of the linear street and the part of the street covered by businesses and customers. In our case the geographic scale will be initially defined through the area covered from the venues in the vicinity of each highway exit. Based on the data from the iExit API, a venue can be accessed from multiple exits[3]. Venues sharing the same group of highway exits through which they are accessible are all geographically close to each other and they can be considered as co-located at a large-scale. There is a total of 150 such clusters that will form our initial analysis unit and we will refer to them as *large* clusters. In this setting, every venue (i.e., fast food restaurant) within the cluster will be one of the competing venues in the Hotelling's Law. This setting is presented on the left part of Figure 2, where the blue circles correspond to a large cluster of fast food restaurants around a set of highway exits.

In order to examine how the expectations from HLC are met as we *zoom in* to smaller scales, we further divide the large clusters to smaller sub-clusters and explore the market share in these smaller scales. We identify sub-clusters based on their density using HDBSCAN with haversine distance [8]. We identify a total of 256 sub-clusters, which we will refer to them as *small* clusters. Focusing on these smaller clusters we are going calculate the market share of

each venue within this smaller scale and compare it with the expectations from HLC. We will refer to this case as the small scale setting (right part of Figure 2). To obtain an idea of the actual length scales the different settings refer to we calculate the maximum pairwise distance in each case for all the clusters. The average of these maximum pairwise distances are 2.44 miles and 0.51 miles for large and small scale respectively.

Recall that the HLC model suggests that it is at the best interest of competing venues to locate as close to each other as possible. In order to capture the degree to which this is satisfied in each setting, we calculate the average pairwise haversine distance of venues within the area of interest. In particular, in the case of the large scale this corresponds to the average pairwise distance of all the venues in a large cluster. Formally, with $d(i, j)$ being the distance between venues i and j, that belong to cluster A, the average pairwise distance of venues d_A, in cluster A, is given by:

$$d_A = [\sum_{i,j=1, i \neq j}^{N} d(i,j)]/N_d \qquad (3)$$

where N is the number of venues in cluster A and $N_d = N(N-1)/2$ is the number of venue pairs within A. For the case of the small scale setting the average pairwise distance is calculated in the same way, using only the venues within the corresponding small cluster.

Market Share Fairness: Every set of venues A (let us assume a large-scale cluster WLOG) can be described through a vector $C_A = [c_1, c_2, \ldots, c_N]$, where c_i is the average daily check-ins in venue i of cluster A. According to the HLC model, vector C_A should exhibit *fairness*, that is, every venue in A obtains their fair share of the market. To quantify the market share fairness f_A in the set of venues A we are going to use the coefficient of variation of C_A [22]:

$$f_A = \text{std}(C_A)/\text{mean}(C_A) \qquad (4)$$

When the total market within cluster A is allocated fairly across the venues in A, f_A will be 0. Hence, a smaller value of f_A corresponds to more fair allocation of the market share within the cluster venues.

3 RESULTS

In order for our analysis to provide evidence supporting (or not) the HLC model, we should examine the correlation between d_A and f_A. Based on HLC, this correlation needs to be positive, i.e., smaller average pairwise distance for the venues in A should lead to more fairness in the market share, which corresponds to smaller f_A. Of course, simply examining the correlation between these two variables (e.g., through the Pearson correlation coefficient) is not appropriate since there are other factors that can affect the market share fairness for a set of venues even if our dataset consists of venues with similar quality of service (all are fast foods venues) and similar pricing. Hence, in order to control for these factors we will start by building a regression model where our dependent variable will be the market share fairness f_A and our independent variables will include various covariates - additional to d_A - that can have an impact on f_A. In particular, we include the following three variables in our model:

Venue reputation: Even though one expects that fast food restaurants offer a similar quality of service, the *reputation* of specific brands might impact the market share they get. To get an estimate for the reputation of a venue we use the average Foursquare rating of all the brand's venues in the 10 largest cities in PA. We then use the

---

[2]https://developer.foursquare.com/
[3]These exits typically correspond to different directions on the same highway, or exits that are located close enough to provide accessibility to the same venues.

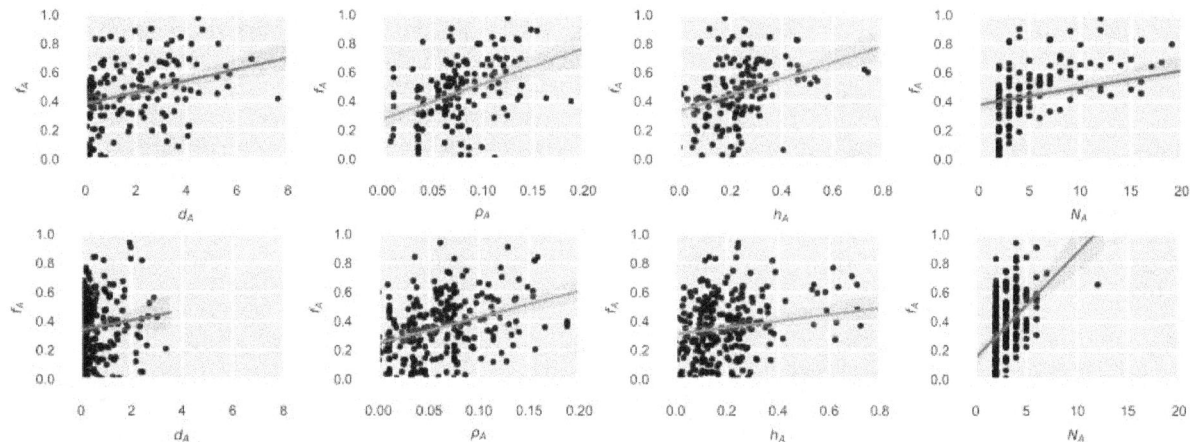

Figure 3: The relationship between pairwise venue distance d_A and market share fairness is strong in the large scale environment (top row) as compared to the small scale environment (bottom row).

coefficient of variation for the reputation ρ_A of the venues within a cluster A as an independent variable in our regression.

Hours of operations: If a venue within a cluster has significantly different hours of operations (e.g., shorter hours of operations), then this will potentially affect the market share it obtains. Hence, we collected hours of operation for every venue in our dataset and calculated the coefficient of variation for the weekly hours of operations h_A for the venues in each cluster A.

Number of venues: Figure 3 presents the correlations between the independent variables and the market share fairness for both scales examined, while Table 1 presents the results from our regression models. As we can see, even after controlling for other covariates, the distance between the venues is still significantly and positively correlated with the market share fairness in the large scale setting. However, in the small scale the relationship is less strong and not significant. Consequently, it has very limited explanatory power. While in the large scale setting the average venue pairwise distance explains about 11% of the total variance in the market share fairness, in small scale it merely explains 1% of it.

Part for this difference could be attributed to the much smaller variability of the pairwise distance in the small scale setting (as it is evident from the x-axis range in Figure 3). In particular, the variance of d_L for the large scale clusters L is $\sigma^2_{d_L} = 3$, while for the small scale clusters S is $\sigma^2_{d_S} = 0.45$. With a small variability in the regressor it is extremely difficult to identify any meaningful relationship even if one exists. However, apart from that one of the key ideas behind the HLC model is that the distance to the venue is an important factor in the decision making process. For the small scale setting, since all venues are extremely close to each others the market share fairness can be very sensitive to other parameters that we have assumed are similar among venues in our setting (e.g., pricing and service quality), while factors such as the venue reputation are more important for the customer's decision (thus, if there is a larger skew in the reputation of the cluster's venues this translates to a skew at the market share). In contrast, at the large scale, while venues are relatively close to each other as well, they are also reachable from many different highway exits. This means that specific venues might be preferable to others purely based on the *direction* of arrival in the large cluster, leading to

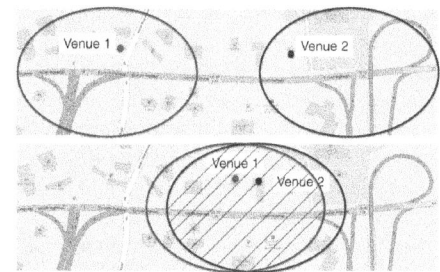

Figure 4: In a large scale cluster (top), two venues will be accessible from different exits leading to a more fair allocation of the customers, while in a small scale cluster (bottom) there will be significant overlap in the *service areas* of the venues and hence, the market share can be extremely sensitive to other factors.

a more fair share of the market. I.e., the relative co-location of venues attracts drivers from many different exits but then their relatively *larger* pairwise distance - as compared to that between venues in the small clusters - can be the deciding factor for the customer's choice. We visualize this idea in Figure 4, where on the top we have two venues belonging to the same large cluster, while on the bottom we have two venues belonging to the same small cluster. In the former case, the venues are accessible from different exits and the circled areas include the ingress points from the highway. Customers within these areas will prefer the corresponding venue (similar to the HLC model on a line). However, in the small scale cluster, these areas have significant overlap, which means that now customers from this area might use other criteria to choose between these venues.

Overall, we can say our results support the HLC model at a high level. In particular, at a large scale, the co-location of venues provides agglomeration effects, while at the same time the slight distance between the venues allows them to attract customers arriving from different directions and hence, obtain a market share closer to the fair allocation. As we move to smaller geographic scales, the strength of HLC model reduces, and this might be due to the fact that in very small scales, given the negligible distance between venues (especially compared to the overall distance traveled on the highway), the market

	large scale		small scale	
variable	d_A only	all features	d_A only	all features
intercept	0.381***	0.166***	0.340***	0.111***
	(0.025)	(0.043)	(0.017)	(0.030)
d_A	0.0402***	0.0170*	0.0337*	0.0092
	(0.010)	(0.010)	(0.019)	(0.017)
ρ_A		1.7273***		1.0881***
		(0.432)		(0.299)
h_A		0.3870***		0.0524
		(0.115)		(0.067)
N_A		0.0060***		0.0565***
		(0.002)		(0.010)
N	150	150	256	256
R^2	0.108	0.345	0.012	0.250

$^{***}p < 0.01$, $^{**}p < 0.05$, $^{*}p < 0.1$

Table 1: Our regression model results.

share can be very sensitive to HLC assumptions (e.g., quality of service and pricing). Thus, our results do not necessarily say that Hotelling's Law does not hold in small scales, but (possibly) that the model is more sensitive to its assumptions in this scale.

4 DISCUSSIONS AND CONCLUSIONS

In this paper our objective has been to explore the *validity* of Hotelling's Law in the real-world. We identified a specific setting that satisfies the main assumptions of HLC, namely, similar service quality and pricing. Under HLC venues will maximize their market share (and in fact they will get their fair share of the market) when they are located close to each other. Our results indicate that for large scale clusters, when the average pairwise distance between the venues is smaller, the market share for each venue is closer to its fair share, supporting the idea that clustering of competing venues can have significant agglomeration effects for a business. When focusing on smaller scale clusters, this relationship is not significant anymore, potentially due to the higher sensitivity of the model to its assumptions.

Of course, our study exhibits limitations. Firstly, even though mobile and web-platforms like Foursquare offer a convenient way to obtain data that can verify theoretical constructs (like the HLC model), we are aware of possible biases that exist in the use of platforms such as Foursquare and the underlying assumption is that check-in volume is representative of actual *popularity*/customers of a venue, which might not be true. Furthermore, despite the evidence provided here in support of HLC, the setting analyzed is not very representative of a dense urban environment. For example, in the highway setting we focused on in this study, the transportation cost can be neglected given the type of trips that pass through these highways/exits. In an urban environment, especially a dense one, this can be crucial. Moreover, we focused specifically on fast food restaurants that tend to exhibit similar characteristics in terms of quality, pricing and outlook to customers. However, in an urban environment venues that seemingly offer the same service (e.g., restaurants) can exhibit significantly diverse characteristics, and clustering might have small impact on the market share a business obtains. In addition, the sensitivity to the HLC's model assumptions can be higher in a dense urban setting, similar to the small scale setting in this study.

REFERENCES

[1] 2012. Starbucks' Store Location Approach Examined. https://www.10news.com/news/starbucks-store-location-approach-examined.
[2] Robert Aboolian, Oded Berman, and Dmitry Krass. 2007. Competitive facility location and design problem. *European Journal of Operational Research* 182, 1 (2007), 40–62.
[3] Robert Aboolian, Oded Berman, and Dmitry Krass. 2007. Competitive facility location model with concave demand. *European Journal of Operational Research* 181, 2 (2007), 598–619.
[4] Robert Aboolian, Oded Berman, and Dmitry Krass. 2009. Efficient solution approaches for a discrete multi-facility competitive interaction model. *Annals of Operations Research* 167, 1 (2009), 297–306.
[5] Rajiv D. Banker, Inder Khosla, and Kingshuk K. Sinha. 1998. Quality and Competition. *Management Science* 44, 9 (1998), 1179–1192. http://www.jstor.org/stable/2634708
[6] Oded Berman and Dmitry Krass. 2002. The generalized maximal covering location problem. *Computers & Operations Research* 29, 6 (2002), 563–581.
[7] Burcin Bozkaya, Seda Yanik, and Selim Balcisoy. 2010. A GIS-based optimization framework for competitive multi-facility location-routing problem. *Networks and Spatial Economics* 10, 3 (2010), 297–320.
[8] Ricardo J. G. B. Campello, Davoud Moulavi, and Joerg Sander. 2013. Density-Based Clustering Based on Hierarchical Density Estimates. In *Advances in Knowledge Discovery and Data Mining*, Jian Pei, Vincent S. Tseng, Longbing Cao, Hiroshi Motoda, and Guandong Xu (Eds.). 160–172.
[9] Mark S Daskin. 2008. What you should know about location modeling. *Naval Research Logistics (NRL)* 55, 4 (2008), 283–294.
[10] Alon Eizenberg, Saul Lach, and Merav Yiftach. 2015. Retail prices in a city: an empirical analysis. *Maurice Falk Institute for Economic Research in Israel. Discussion paper series.* 7 (2015), 0_1.
[11] Susan Feyder. [n. d.]. Nation's biggest pharmacies sidle right up to each other. Retrieved November 1, 2018 from http://www.startribune.com/nation-s-biggest-pharmacies-sidle-right-up-to-each-other/176188911/
[12] Rachel Griffith, Ephraim Leibtag, Andrew Leicester, and Aviv Nevo. 2009. Consumer shopping behavior: how much do consumers save? *Journal of Economic Perspectives* 23, 2 (2009), 99–120.
[13] Harold Hotelling. 1990. Stability in competition. In *The Collected Economics Articles of Harold Hotelling*. Springer, 50–63.
[14] Pablo Jensen. 2006. Network-based predictions of retail store commercial categories and optimal locations. *Physical Review E* 74, 3 (2006), 035101.
[15] Pablo Jensen. 2009. Analyzing the localization of retail stores with complex systems tools. In *International Symposium on Intelligent Data Analysis*. Springer, 10–20.
[16] Dmytro Karamshuk, Anastasios Noulas, Salvatore Scellato, Vincenzo Nicosia, and Cecilia Mascolo. 2013. Geo-spotting: mining online location-based services for optimal retail store placement. In *Proceedings of the 19th ACM SIGKDD international conference on Knowledge discovery and data mining*. ACM, 793–801.
[17] Alexander Kubis and Maria Hartmann. 2007. Analysis of location of large-area shopping centres. A probabilistic Gravity Model for the Halle–Leipzig area. *Jahrbuch für Regionalwissenschaft* 27, 1 (2007), 43–57.
[18] Andreu Mas-Colell, Michael Dennis Whinston, Jerry R Green, et al. 1995. *Microeconomic theory.* Vol. 1. Oxford university press New York.
[19] Sergio Porta, Vito Latora, Fahui Wang, Salvador Rueda, Emanuele Strano, Salvatore Scellato, Alessio Cardillo, Eugenio Belli, Francisco Cardenas, Berta Cormenzana, et al. 2012. Street centrality and the location of economic activities in Barcelona. *Urban Studies* 49, 7 (2012), 1471–1488.
[20] Sergio Porta, Emanuele Strano, Valentino Iacoviello, Roberto Messora, Vito Latora, Alessio Cardillo, Fahui Wang, and Salvatore Scellato. 2009. Street centrality and densities of retail and services in Bologna, Italy. *Environment and Planning B: Planning and design* 36, 3 (2009), 450–465.
[21] Stuart S Rosenthal and William C Strange. 2004. Evidence on the nature and sources of agglomeration economies. In *Handbook of regional and urban economics.* Vol. 4. Elsevier, 2119–2171.
[22] Michael Sheret. 1984. Note on Methodology: The Coefficient of Variation. *Comparative Education Review* 28, 3 (1984), 467–476. http://www.jstor.org/stable/1187327
[23] Howard Smith and Donald Hay. 2005. Streets, malls, and supermarkets. *Journal of Economics & Management Strategy* 14, 1 (2005), 29–59.
[24] Ken Steif. [n. d.]. Why Do Certain Retail Stores Cluster Together? Retrieved November 1, 2018 from https://www.planetizen.com/node/65765
[25] Presh Talwalkar. [n. d.]. Why are McDonalds and Burger King usually located near each other? Fast food location game theory. Retrieved November 1, 2018 from https://mindyourdecisions.com/blog/2012/10/23/why-are-mcdonalds-and-burger-king-usually-located-near-each-other-fast-food-location-game-theory/
[26] Presh Talwalkar. 2014. *The joy of game theory: An introduction to strategic thinking.* CreateSpace Independent Publishing Platform.
[27] Kerry D. Vendell and Charles C. Carter. 1993. Retail Store Location and Market Analysis: A Review of the Research. *Journal of Real Estate Literature* 1, 1 (1993), 13–45. http://www.jstor.org/stable/44103233

Link Prediction via Second Order Cone Programming

Shreya Malani
BingAds Applied Research
Microsoft, India
shreyam@microsoft.com

Dinesh Dileep Gaurav
BingAds Applied Research
Microsoft, India
digaurav@microsoft.com

Rahul Agrawal
BingAds Applied Research
Microsoft, India
rahulagr@microsoft.com

ACM Reference Format:
Shreya Malani, Dinesh Dileep Gaurav, and Rahul Agrawal. 2019. Link Prediction via Second Order Cone Programming. In *11th ACM Conference on Web Science (WebSci '19), June 30–July 3, 2019, Boston, MA, USA.* ACM, New York, NY, USA, 2 pages. https://doi.org/10.1145/3292522.3326053

1 INTRODUCTION

Link Prediction in social Networks (e.g. Facebook, Twitter) is a widely studied research area in the quest to understand user relationships. Most networks rarely seek explicit positive/neutral feedback from a user on their relations and even more rarely do they ask for stating a negative vote/sentiment. However, predicting this relation is interesting from the network's perspective, as it is useful in various social network analysis tasks of commercial interest like Community Detection, Node Ranking, Node classification, Recommendation and many more [5, 7]. Positive links are far more easier to obtain compared to negative links (e.g. friends in Facebook). In most of these social graphs, we also have access to user interaction data which is very rich in information on links, for e.g., the posts and comments from Facebook, or tweets in Twitter. In [5] and other contemporary works, these additional information is leveraged for link prediction. For more recent results in link prediction, we refer the interested reader to [6, 8].

In this paper, we formulate the link prediction as a learning problem based on the features of links closely following the lines of [5] and reference therein. Though the proposed approaches in [5] and related papers show promise, they inherently suffer from the computational complexity of the learning frameworks they use. We follow a classification-after-clustering approach wherein we cluster the classes individually before applying a learning framework. We design maximum margin classifiers on this clustered data which can be then converted into standard Second Order Cone programs.

2 PROPOSED LEARNING APPROACH

Our proposed approach is combination of clustering and a learning framework. Initially, we will cluster each link type into different clusters (feature vector generation is explained later) using an off-the-shelf clustering approach. For each cluster, we will estimate the cluster center and the covariance matrix given as $(\bar{x}_i, \Sigma_i)$. For our classification, we will use a two-class classification model. Thus, clusters belonging to class 1 will have label 1 and -1 for the other. Let $y_i \in \{1, -1\}$ denote the label of cluster i.

In first formulation, we propose to fit an ellipse to each cluster i whose center and covariance matrix are given as $(\bar{x}_i, \Sigma_i)$. In first formulation, we propose to fit an ellipse to each mixture i whose center, variance are given as $(\bar{x}_i, \Sigma_i)$. In addition, we define a user-defined parameter γ_i which controls the radius of ellipse fitting cluster i. This allows us to consider an optimization problem where we try to find a hyperplane which accurately separates the ellipses corresponding to clusters of both the classes. Let $\mathcal{E}(\bar{x}_i, \Sigma_i, \gamma_i)$ denote the ellipse corresponding to cluster i. Our approach is similar to standard soft-margin SVM formulation, where individual points in each class are supposed to be separated by the optimal hyperplane. Similarly, we require the ellipses in same class to lie on the same side of the maximum margin hyperplane and also the points in them. This can be formulated as

$$\min_{\mathbf{w}, b, \epsilon} ||\mathbf{w}||_2^2 + \sum_{i=1}^{K} \epsilon_i$$
$$\text{s.t. } y_i(\mathbf{w}^T \mathbf{x}_i + b) \geq 1 - \epsilon_i, \forall \mathbf{x}_i \in \mathcal{E}(\bar{x}_i, \Sigma_i, \gamma_i)$$
$$\epsilon_i \geq 0 \; i \in \{1, \ldots, K\} \tag{1}$$

Consider each ellipse constraint in (1) which should be satisfied for every point $\mathbf{x}_i$ in the ellipse. It is not hard to prove that each elliptical constraint of (1) is equivalent to the Second Order Cone constraint [4]

$$y_i(\mathbf{w}^T \bar{x}_i + b) \geq 1 - \epsilon_i + \gamma_i ||\Sigma_i^{\frac{1}{2}} \mathbf{w}||_2 \tag{2}$$

Substituting (2) into (1), we have the following Second-Order Cone Program (SOCP)

$$\min_{\mathbf{w}, b, \epsilon} ||\mathbf{w}||_2^2 + \sum_{i=1}^{K} \epsilon_i$$
$$\text{s.t. } y_i(\mathbf{w}^T \bar{x}_i + b) \geq 1 - \epsilon_i + \gamma_i ||\Sigma_i^{\frac{1}{2}} \mathbf{w}||_2, \forall i$$
$$\epsilon_i \geq 0 \; i \in \{1, \ldots, K\} \tag{3}$$

We note that the complexity of above formulation is in the order of $O(K^6)$, which is the number of clusters (typically within hundreds). Though, this is high, the reduction in computation compared to using the entire set of data points can be useful in most situations. It is noteworthy that in earlier works [3, 5], the sample size is a determining factor in the complexity of the proposed approach. However, as the size of the social graph increases, this can be a limiting factor. However, clustering prior to the classification, significantly reduces the computational complexity while still retaining a comparable performance. Any standard convex package for Cone Programs can be used for solving the optimization problem in (3). We forsake the algebraic conversion of (3) into standard SOCP format as this is widely known[4]. In our second formulation, we set $\gamma_i = 0$ which is equivalent to reducing the elliptical radius to zero. It is straightforward to see that (3) now reduces to a standard SVM with centroids as the data points. This also further reduces the complexity to $O(K^2)$, possibly at cost of accuracy in classification. We also note that determining the clusters for a given dataset is a well studied problem. For instance, a straight forward approach would be to do a nearest neighbor clustering [4] which will give a rough estimate for K. For more accuracy, we can also use more sophisticated approaches as in [2].

3 EXPERIMENTS

3.1 Methodology

We experimented our proposed framework on the publicly available Epinions graph which is well studied in previous literature as well[3, 5]. Epinions network allows users to explicitly state their trust (positive links) or distrust (negative links) on other users. We refer the interested reader to [3, 5] for a brief overview and a detailed study of the statistical nature of Epinions graph. Missing links correspond to the nonexisting edges. However, negative links are extremely scarce compared to positive and missing links. To alleviate this, we follow algorithm 1 in [5] to construct the negative links based on additional content centric information (available as comments and ratings in Epinions). Positive links are directly taken from the Epinions graph. We follow the lines of [5] and references therein for feature extraction from links. As explained earlier, we constructed two class experiments held across different combinations of missing links, negative links and positive links. For instance, in one of the experiments, negative links will be considered as the first class whereas positive links were considered the second, and vice-versa. Once such a class separation is decided, we constructed clusters on each class (using their feature vectors) using a standard implementation of Gaussian Mixture Models. We note that one can use more advanced clustering mechanisms like BIRCH which scale really well to massive data sets. Once the centroids and the covariances are estimated, we use it as input to our proposed models in (3). We used the convex package CVX [1] to solve the cone programs. We rerun our experiments for different combinations of clusters on each classes as well as different class separations. We choose to report only relevant results due to brevity of space.

3.2 Results and Discussions

In Table 1, we present the performances of our proposed models for each class separation. *Neg, Pos, Miss* denotes negative, positive and missing links respectively. First column contains the class type in the named order. Second column states the respective number of clusters in colon separated form. We experimented with multiple combinations of number of clusters on each class type and report the precision and recall for predicting class 1. We choose to report only selected combinations of clusters with acceptable performances. We observe that the proposed model has varied performance across different classification scenarios. Further it seems that the performance is superior when class 1 is the larger class (negative links are scarce). However, performance achieved when predicting negative links against positive links is acceptable in comparison to models proposed in [3, 5]. However, the performance was not satisfactory when the comparison was between negative link and missing links. Intuitively, this can be ascribed to the scarcity

Table 1: Performance of Proposed Model

Type	Clusters	Precision	Recall
Neg vs *Pos*	10:3	0.304	0.478
Pos vs *Neg*	50:60	0.873	0.91
Neg vs *Pos* within 4 Hops	5:70	0.202	0.5731
Pos vs *Neg* within 4 Hops	10:3	0.950	0.8123
Neg vs *Miss*	30:30	0.107	0.258
Neg vs *Miss* within 4 Hops	50:60	0.112	0.235
Miss vs *Neg* within 4 Hops	10:2	0.909	0.899

of negative links. We note that missing links can exist between any two chosen nodes in the graph, however negative links and positive links exist only in a neighborhood depending on the relationship/interactions between nodes[1] in social graphs. This rather makes missing links arbitrary and difficult to model via clusters. Thus, further experiments were conducted restricting the neighborhood of a link to within 4 hops. This numbers are also reported in Table 1 which seems to improve the precision and recall. We observe that the performance reported here is comparable to earlier works [3, 5] (skipped due to brevity of space). We remark that this performance comes at a significant reduction of complexity due to the clustering-before-classification approach.

3.3 Future Work

An interesting direction is to pursue and evaluate more advanced clustering techniques as this does seem to affect the performance. Further, though the proposed model scales really well, it is impacted by the large number of missing links which is on the order of billions. Thus, it will be interesting to limit all missing links within a neighborhood of the given node whose relationships with others has to be studied.

REFERENCES

[1] M Andersen, Joachim Dahl, and Lieven Vandenberghe. 2013. CVXOPT: A Python package for convex optimization. *abel. ee. ucla. edu/cvxopt* (2013).
[2] Mario A. T. Figueiredo and Anil K. Jain. 2002. Unsupervised learning of finite mixture models. *IEEE Transactions on Pattern Analysis & Machine Intelligence* 3 (2002), 381–396.
[3] Jure Leskovec, Daniel Huttenlocher, and Jon Kleinberg. 2010. Predicting positive and negative links in online social networks. In *Proceedings of the 19th international conference on World wide web*. ACM, 641–650.
[4] Pannagadatta K Shivaswamy, Chiranjib Bhattacharyya, and Alexander J Smola. 2006. Second order cone programming approaches for handling missing and uncertain data. *Journal of Machine Learning Research* 7, Jul (2006), 1283–1314.
[5] Jiliang Tang, Shiyu Chang, Charu Aggarwal, and Huan Liu. 2015. Negative link prediction in social media. In *Proceedings of the eighth ACM international conference on web search and data mining*. ACM, 87–96.
[6] Jiliang Tang, Yi Chang, Charu Aggarwal, and Huan Liu. 2015. A survey of signed network mining in social media. *arXiv preprint arXiv:1511.07569* (2015).
[7] Jiliang Tang, Yi Chang, Charu Aggarwal, and Huan Liu. 2016. A survey of signed network mining in social media. *ACM Computing Surveys (CSUR)* 49, 3 (2016), 42.
[8] Peng Wang, BaoWen Xu, YuRong Wu, and XiaoYu Zhou. 2015. Link prediction in social networks: the state-of-the-art. *Science China Information Sciences* 58, 1 (2015), 1–38.

Spread of Hate Speech in Online Social Media

Binny Mathew
Indian Institute of Technology Kharagpur
Kharagpur, India
binnymathew@iitkgp.ac.in

Ritam Dutt
Indian Institute of Technology Kharagpur
Kharagpur, India
ritam.dutt@gmail.com

Pawan Goyal
Indian Institute of Technology Kharagpur
Kharagpur, India
pawang.iitk@gmail.com

Animesh Mukherjee
Indian Institute of Technology Kharagpur
Kharagpur, India
animeshm@gmail.com

ABSTRACT

Hate speech is considered to be one of the major issues currently plaguing the online social media. With online hate speech culminating in gruesome scenarios like the Rohingya genocide in Myanmar, anti-Muslim mob violence in Sri Lanka, and the Pittsburgh synagogue shooting, there is a dire need to understand the dynamics of user interaction that facilitate the spread of such hateful content. In this paper, we perform the first study that looks into the diffusion dynamics of the posts made by hateful and non-hateful users on Gab[1]. We collect a massive dataset of 341K users with 21M posts and investigate the diffusion of the posts generated by hateful and non-hateful users. We observe that the content generated by the hateful users tend to spread faster, farther and reach a much wider audience as compared to the content generated by normal users. We further analyze the hateful and non-hateful users on the basis of their account and network characteristics. An important finding is that the hateful users are far more densely connected among themselves. Overall, our study provides the first cross-sectional view of how hateful users diffuse hate content in online social media.

CCS CONCEPTS

• **Networks** → **Online social networks**; • **Human-centered computing** → *Social content sharing*; *Social media*; *Empirical studies in collaborative and social computing*; **Social network analysis**.

KEYWORDS

Hate Speech, Gab, Online Social Media, Information Diffusion, De-Groot Model

ACM Reference Format:
Binny Mathew, Ritam Dutt, Pawan Goyal, and Animesh Mukherjee. 2019. Spread of Hate Speech in Online Social Media. In *11th ACM Conference on Web Science (WebSci '19), June 30–July 3, 2019, Boston, MA, USA*. ACM, New York, NY, USA, 10 pages. https://doi.org/10.1145/3292522.3326034

---

[1]gab.com

1 INTRODUCTION

The Internet is one of the greatest innovations of mankind which has brought together people from every race, religion, and nationality. Social media sites such as Twitter and Facebook have connected billions of people[2] and allowed them to share their ideas and opinions instantly. That being said, there are several ill consequences as well such as online harassment, trolling, cyber-bullying, and *hate speech*.

The rise of hate speech: Hate speech has recently received a lot of research attention with several works that focus on detecting hate speech in online social media [4, 10, 12, 21, 35]. Even though several government and social media sites are trying to curb all forms of hate speech, it is still plaguing our society. With hate crimes increasing in several states[3], there is an urgent need to have a better understanding of how the users spread hateful posts in online social media. Companies like Facebook have been accused for instigating anti-Muslim mob violence in Sri Lanka that left three people dead[4] and a United Nations report blamed them for playing a leading role in the possible genocide of the Rohingya community in Myanmar by spreading hate speech[5]. In response to the UN report, Facebook later banned several accounts belonging to Myanmar military officials[6] for spreading hate speech. In the recent Pittsburgh synagogue shooting[7], the sole suspect, *Robert Gregory Bowers*, maintained an account (@onedingo) on Gab[1] and posted his final message before the shooting[8]. Inspection of his Gab account shows months of antisemitc and racist posts that were endorsed by a lot of users on Gab.

The present work: In this paper, we perform the first study which looks into the diffusion dynamics of the posts by hateful users in Gab. We choose Gab for all our analysis. This choice is primarily motivated by the nature of Gab. Unlike other social media sites such as Twitter and Facebook, Gab promotes "free speech" and allows users to post content that may be hateful in nature without any fear of repercussion. This has led to the migration of several

---

[2]https://techcrunch.com/2018/07/25/facebook-2-5-billion-people
[3]http://www.aaiusa.org/unprecedented_increase_expected_in_upcoming_fbi_hate_crime_report
[4]https://www.theguardian.com/world/2018/mar/14/facebook-accused-by-sri-lanka-of-failing-to-control-hate-speech
[5]https://www.reuters.com/investigates/special-report/myanmar-facebook-hate
[6]https://www.reuters.com/article/us-myanmar-facebook/facebook-bans-myanmar-army-chief-others-in-unprecedented-move-idUSKCN1LC0R7
[7] https://en.wikipedia.org/wiki/Pittsburgh_synagogue_shooting
[8]https://www.independent.co.uk/news/world/americas/pittsburgh-synagogue-shooter-gab-robert-bowers-final-posts-online-comments-a8605721.html

Twitter users who were banned/suspended for violating its terms of service, namely for abusive and/or hateful behavior [45]. This provides a unique opportunity to study how the hateful content would spread in the online medium, if there were no restrictions.

To this end, we crawl the Gab platform and acquire 21M posts by 341K users over a period of 20 Months (October, 2016 to June, 2018). Our analysis reveals that the posts by hateful users tend to spread faster, farther, and wider as compared to normal users.

Our **main contributions** are as follows.

- We perform the first study which looks into the diffusion dynamics of posts by hateful user accounts.
- We find that the hate users in our dataset (which constitute 0.67% of the total number of users) are very densely connected and are responsible for 26.80% of posts generated in Gab.
- We find that the posts of hate users tend to spread fast, farther, and reach a much wider audience as compared to the non-hateful users.

In summary, our analysis reveals that the posts by hateful users have a much higher spreading velocity. These posts receive a much larger audience and as well at a faster rate. As a case study, we also investigate the detailed account characteristics of *Robert Gregory Bowers*, the sole suspect of the Pittsburgh synagogue shooting[7].

2 DATASET

2.1 The Gab social network

Gab[1] is a social media platform launched in August 2016 known for promoting itself as the "Champion of free speech", but has been critised for being a shield for alt-right users [45]. The site is very similar to Twitter, but has very loose moderation policy. According to the Gab guidelines, the site does not allow illegal pornography and promotion of violence and terrorism[9]. All other forms of speech are allowed on Gab. The site allows users to read and write posts of upto 3,000 characters, called "gabs". The site employs an upvoting and downvoting mechanism for posts and allows categorization of posts into topics such as News, Sports, Politics etc.

2.2 Dataset collection

In order to understand the diffusion dynamics in Gab, we collect a massive dataset of posts and users by following the crawling methodology described in Zannettou et al. [45]. We use Gab's API to crawl the site using the well-known snowball strategy. We first obtain the data for the most popular user as returned by Gab's API and then collect the data for all their followers and followings. We collect different types of information as follows: 1) basic details about each user like username, score, account creation date; 2) all the posts of each user; 3) all the followers and followings for each users. This resulted in a massive dataset whose details are presented in Table 1. We have only collected the publicly available data posted in Gab and make no attempt to de-anonymize the users. We outline the procedure to distinguish between hateful and non-hateful users in the following section.

Property	Value
Number of posts	21,207,961
Number of reply posts	6,601,521
Number of quote posts	2,085,828
Number of reposts	5,850,331
Number of posts with attachments	9,669,374
Number of user accounts	341,332
Average follower per account	62.56
Average following per account	60.93

Table 1: Description of the dataset.

2.3 Identifying hateful users

Gab has been at the center of several hate activity. With the recent Pittsburg shooting, and removal of the app from play store, it has become quite infamous. The volume of hateful content in Gab is 2.4 times higher than that of Twitter [45] which justifies our choice of Gab. We adopted a multi step approach to curate our dateset.

2.3.1 Lexicon based filtering. We created a lexicon[10] of 45 high-precision unigrams and bigrams that are often associated with hate like 'kike' (slur against Jews), 'paki' (slur against Muslims), 'beached whale' (slur against fat people). These hate words were initially selected from the Hatebase[11] and Urban dictionary[12]. Words such as 'banana', 'bubble' are present in Hatebase which could easily appear in benign context. In order to avoid ambiguity, we ran multiple iterations and carefully chose those keywords which were not ambiguous in Gab.

We leverage these high precision keywords to identify explicit hate posts based on their textual content. The total number of unique posts which have been identified explicitly as 'Hate' were 280,468 or 1.32% of the entire dataset. However, since posts need not necessarily contain solely textual information (45.59% of all posts include an attachment in the form of images, videos, and URLs), we resort to a diffusion based model of identifying hate users in the social network.

2.3.2 Extraction of hateful users. Using the high precision lexicon would miss out on several users who might be hateful in nature but are not selected as they did not post any content with words from our lexicon (like using images and videos). In order to capture such obscure hate users, we leverage the methodology used by Ribeiro et al. [33]. We enumerate the steps of our methodology below.

- We identify the initial set of hateful users as those who have written at least 10 posts, with at least one hateful keyword in each of them. This results in a set of 2,769 hateful users.
- We create a repost network where nodes represent the users and edge-weights denote posting and reposting frequency. We convert the repost network into a belief network by reversing the edges in the original network and normalizing the edge weights between 0 and 1. We explain this further in the subsequent section.

---

[9]https://gab.com/about/guidelines

[10]The lexicons: www.github.com/binny-mathew/Spread_Hate_Speech_WebSci19
[11]https://www.hatebase.org
[12]https://www.urbandictionary.com

- We then run a diffusion process based on the DeGroot's learning model [19] on the belief network. We assign an initial belief value of 1 to the 2,769 users identified earlier and 0 to all the other users. The diffusion model aims to identify users who did not explicitly use any of the hateful keywords, yet have a high potential of being a hateful user due to homophily.
- We observe the belief values of all the users in the network after *five* iterations of the diffusion process and divide the users into four strata, $[0, .25)$, $[.25, .50)$, $[.50, .75)$ and $[.75, 1]$ according to their associated belief.

We define users whose belief values lie within $[.75, 1]$ as hateful and those whose belief values lie within $[0, .25]$ as non-hateful with the additional constraint that each of these users should have at least *five* posts. We do so since it is difficult to judge a person on the basis of a single post. We thus obtain a set of 2,290 hateful users and 58,803 non-hateful users, which comprises $\sim 0.67\%$ and $\sim 17.23\%$ of the entire dataset. We refer to the set of hateful and non-hateful users as KH (read 'Known hateful user') and NH (read 'Not hateful user') respectively henceforth.

2.3.3 DeGroot's model of information diffusion. : We illustrate a repost network with three users (A, B, C) in Figure 1a. An edge-weight of 9 from B to A denotes that user B has reposted 9 posts of A while a self loop of A of weight 17 denotes that A has posted 17 times. We convert the repost network into a diffusion network as shown in 1b by reversing the edges, with the edge-weights normalized. The edge weights are normalized by dividing the edge weight from C to A in the original network by the sum of the edge weights originating from C (including self loops). For example, user C in Figure 1a has reposted A 5 times and has posted 10 times. Thus the value of edge weights from A to C is $\frac{5}{15}$ or 0.33 and the weight of the self-loop at C is $\frac{10}{15}$ or 0.67 as shown in Figure 1b. The normalized edge-weight is a measure of the user's belief being influenced by her neighbors. Let us denote the belief of A, B and C at the time instant i as b_A^i, b_B^i, b_C^i respectively. The belief of user C at time instant $i + 1$ can be written as

$$b_C^{i+1} = 0.33 \times b_A^i + 0.67 \times b_C^i \tag{1}$$

Thus belief propagation takes place in an iterative fashion using the DeGroot's model. If we consider the initial beliefs of A, B and C to be 1, 0 and 0 respectively, their corresponding beliefs at time instant 1 would be 1, 0.75 and 0.33 as demonstrated in Figure 1c.

2.4 Quality of the labels

We evaluate the quality of the final dataset of hateful and non-hateful accounts through human judgment. We ask four annotators to determine if a given account is hateful or non-hateful as per their perception. The annotators consisted of three undergraduate students with major in Computer Science and one PhD student in Social Computing. Since Gab does not have any policy for hate speech, we use the guidelines defined by Twitter[13] for this task. We provide the annotators with a class balanced random sample of 200 user accounts[14]. Each account was evaluated by two independent

[13]https://help.twitter.com/en/rules-and-policies/hateful-conduct-policy
[14]We have used a random sample of 200 accounts per class to keep the monetary cost manageable

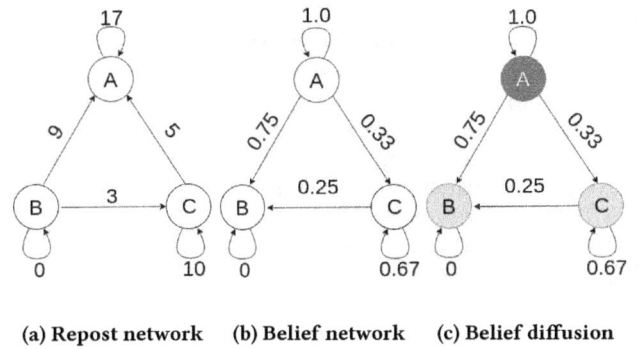

(a) Repost network   (b) Belief network   (c) Belief diffusion

Figure 1: Description of the DeGroot's model for information diffusion in a toy network.

annotators. We follow the definition used by ElSherief et al. [14] to identify a post as hateful. The authors define hate speech as a "*direct and serious attack on any protected category of people based on their race, ethnicity, national origin, religion, sex, gender, sexual orientation, disability or disease*".

We observe that the two annotators found 86.9% and 93.2% of the hate accounts from our sample as hateful, yielding a substantial high Cohen's κ score of 0.69. Likewise 92.2% and 99.4% of the non-hateful accounts from our sample were adjudged to be non-hateful yielding a very high κ score of 0.87. These results show that the dataset generated by our method is of high quality with minimal noise.

3 USER CHARACTERISTICS

We first try to understand the characteristic differences between the KH and NH users identified by our method.

3.1 Account characteristics

Here we analyze the differences in the account characteristics of hateful and non-hateful users. The different account characteristics include the number of posts, followers and followings (normalized over time) and the number of likes, dislikes, replies, reposts (normalized over the number of posts) of the KH and NH users. The normalization over time is done by dividing the account characteristic (say number of posts) of a user by the number of days elapsed from the first post of the user to the date the last post was crawled. We report the mean and median details of these characteristics in Table 2. We measure the statistical significance between the two distributions using the two sample K-S test and observe that each of the account characteristics are significantly different (p-value<0.001). The inordinate difference in the mean and median values between NH and KH can be attributed to the prolific activity of hateful users. The raw quantity of posts generated by the KH and NH amount to 26.80% (5.68M) and 45.53% (9.65M) of all posts, respectively. This implies that as small as *0.67% of the users generated 26.80% of all the content in Gab*. Some of the striking observations from the table are that the normalized number of followers of the KH users is more than double the number for the NH users. Although the normalized number of likes for the KH users is larger than that of the NH users, what is more notable is that the normalized number of dislikes for the KH users is more than double compared to the NH users. This indicates that there is a (possibly growing) mass in Gab (albeit small) who have built an overall opposition against hate speech and we believe that this could be attributed to the rising influence of counter speech and the corresponding counter speakers. Typically, the posts from the KH users receive double the number of replies and reposts compared to the NH users.

Feature	Mean KH	Mean NH	Median KH	Median NH
post	6.899	0.633	1.813	0.075
follower	1.651	0.639	0.629	0.138
following	1.658	0.881	0.299	0.052
like	2.628	1.533	1.490	0.678
dislike	0.124	0.051	0.038	0.000
score	2.576	1.733	1.453	0.875
reply	0.222	0.116	0.162	0.000
repost	0.401	0.224	0.146	0.000
F:F	4.732	5.219	1.545	1.611

Table 2: Account characteristics of the hateful and the non-hateful users. Hateful users generate more popular content and also posts frequently. All the differences in account characteristics are significant (*p*-value<0.001 and marked in different color), except F:F(Follower/Following).

3.2 Network characteristics

In this section, we investigate the network characteristics of the KH and the NH users on the basis of their follower-following relationship. We construct a subgraph over the entire network with nodes being the set of KH and NH users and edges representing the follower-following relationship between these users only. This subgraph so formed has 61.1K nodes and 7.56 M edges. We observe that the network of KH users (2.29K nodes, 156.1K edges) is ≈ 16.74 times more dense than the NH users (58.8K nodes, 6.15M edges). The KH users also demonstrate higher reciprocity values (35.00%) as opposed to the NH users (32.75%) with (*p*-value~0.0). Moreover, an NH user is 5.4 times more likely to follow a KH user than a KH user following a NH user, inkling at the higher popularity of KH users. It is also 20.675 times more likely that a KH user will follow another KH user than a NH one. This indicates strong cohesiveness among the KH users. Typically, the KH users seem to operate in closed groups or clans which is a well-known property of extremist networks [31].

4 DIFFUSION DYNAMICS OF POSTS

In this section, we observe the diffusion of information throughout the network and analyze the differences in diffusion of posts generated by the KH users and those generated by the NH users.

4.1 Model description

We refer to the path traced by a post as it is reposted by other users as a cascade and the original user as the root user. Since it is not possible to trace the exact influence path, i.e., the user who influenced the reposting, we leverage the social network connections (followers and friends) as means of information diffusion and influence

similar to Taxidou and Fischer [38]. In all the models, an edge is formed between two users if there exists a follower-following relationship between the users. We deploy the Least Recent Influencer Model (LRIF) [5] to observe the information diffusion. Previous research [2, 38] have also used such models to study the diffusion of information in online social media. In the LRIF model, users are influenced by the first exposure to a message even if they do not act immediately. Essentially, the model seeks to avoid exhaustive search by converting the network into a directed acyclic graph, thereby, reducing the time complexity. We illustrate the DAG generated by the LRIF models in Figure 2. The sample network is shown in Figure 2a comprising five users. A directed edge between any two users (say from B to A) specifies the follower-following relationship (B follows A). The number beside each user specifies the time of reposting, with A being the root user. The DAG generated by the LRIF model is shown in Figure 2b.

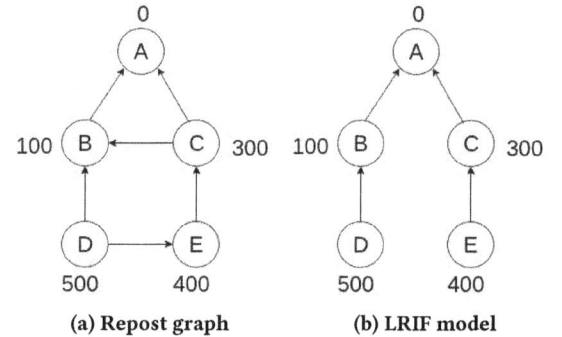

(a) Repost graph   (b) LRIF model

Figure 2: DAG generated by the LRIF model on a sample repost network. The numbers indicate the time in seconds of reposting. The links are formed between User C and A since A posted earlier than B.

4.2 Characteristic cascade parameters

In order to characterize the cascades generated by KH and NH users, we employ the following features as used in Vosoughi et al. [39].

- **Size** represents the number of nodes in the DAG which are reachable from the root user. It corresponds to the total number of unique users involved in the cascade of the post.
- **Depth** is the length of the largest path from the root node of the cascade. The depth of a cascade, D, with n nodes is defined as

$$D = \max(d_i), 0 \leq i \leq n \qquad (2)$$

where d_i is the depth of node i.

- **Average depth** is the average path length of all nodes reachable from the root user. For a cascade with n nodes, we define its average depth (AD) as

$$AD = \frac{1}{n-1} \sum_{i=1}^{n} d_i \qquad (3)$$

where d_i is the depth of the node i.

	Posts				Attachments				Topics			
	KH		NH		KH		NH		KT		NT	
	Mean	Max	Mean	Max	Mean	Max	Mean	Max	Mean	Max	Mean	Max
Size	1.28	447	1.21	602	1.34	447	1.23	455	1.68	237	1.51	252
Depth	0.13	7	0.09	7	0.16	7	0.11	7	0.30	11	0.24	6
Breadth	1.13	275	1.10	533	1.15	275	1.11	391	1.30	162	1.24	189
Average depth	0.11	4.82	0.08	4.53	0.14	4.82	0.10	4.53	0.26	4.52	0.22	3.74
Structural virality	0.13	5.46	0.09	5.07	0.16	5.46	0.11	5.07	0.31	6.10	0.25	4.89

Table 3: Diffusion characteristics of posts of the KH and the NH users. The minimum value for all the characteristics were same: a post with no repost.

- **Breadth** is the maximum no. of nodes present at any particular depth in the DAG.

$$B = \max(b_i), 0 \le i \le d \tag{4}$$

where b_i denotes the breadth of the cascade at depth i and d denotes the maximum depth of the cascade.

- **Structural virality** as defined by Goel et al. [18], is the average distance between all pairs of nodes in the DAG, assuming the DAG to be a tree. It is simply the Weiner index.

$$SV = \frac{1}{n(n-1)} \sum_{i=1}^{n} \sum_{j=1}^{n} d_{ij} \tag{5}$$

where d_{ij} represents the length of the shortest path between nodes i and j.

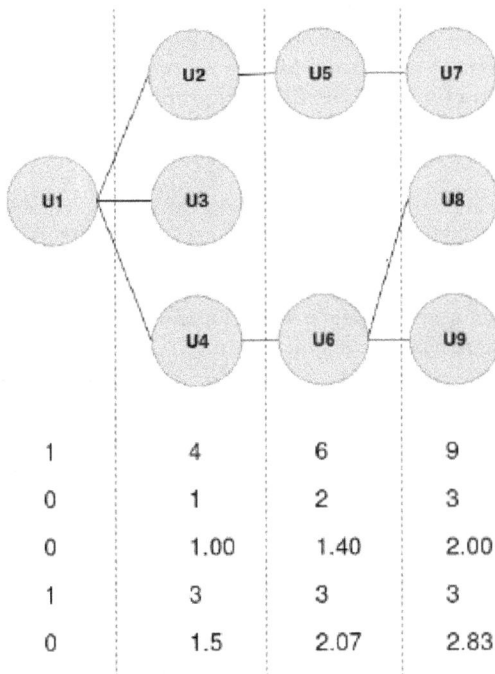

Figure 3: Repost path between a set of Gab users. At each level we show the various cascade properties.

In Figure 3, we show an example cascade in which we show the different values of the above measures at each level of the cascade.

4.3 Experiments on varied nature of posts

All subsequent evaluation is carried out on the DAG generated by the LRIF model. KH users had 2.73M posts and NH users had 6.87M posts which we considered as the root posts for our cascade. We do not include the posts of KH and NH users which are 'quotes' or 'replies', since such posts might not represent the user's actual opinion. We also observe the diffusion characteristics for posts having attachments (images or media content) separately since such posts are hypothesized to be more viral. The supposed virality is attributed to the appeal of an image/ meme over plain textual information. Finally, in order to observe the topic perspective, we look into posts which have been posted in topics. We report the mean and max score of the cascade features for the different experiments in Table 3. Note that we did not report min values since they were the same for the KH and NH users for all the cascade features.

4.4 Characteristic differences in cascades of the KH and NH users

4.4.1 General cascade parameters. The mean size (number of unique users) of a cascade is larger for posts of KH users than NH users as observed from Table 3. Figure 4a shows the Complementary Cumulative Distribution Function (CCDF) of a cascade's size for both KH and NH users. We observe that almost 90% of the posts do not get reposted for both KH and NH users. Although the maximum size of the NH's cascade is larger, the cascade's size is significantly larger for KH users especially for the initial stages. Thus, the posts of KH users have a larger audience.

The mean breadth of a cascade is also larger for posts generated by KH users implying that such posts spread wider (farther amongst a user's followers) than those generated by NH users. The CCDF of a cascade's breadth 4b exhibits similar characteristics as a cascade's size. Only the top 0.1% of the NH user's cascade had more breadth as compared to the KH user's cascade.

The mean depth, mean average depth and mean structural virality of a cascade are also significantly larger for posts generated by KH users. Not only does it imply that such posts diffuse deeper into the network but they are also more viral [18]. Moreover, as the CCDF for depth, avg-depth and virality (Figures 4c, 4d and 4e

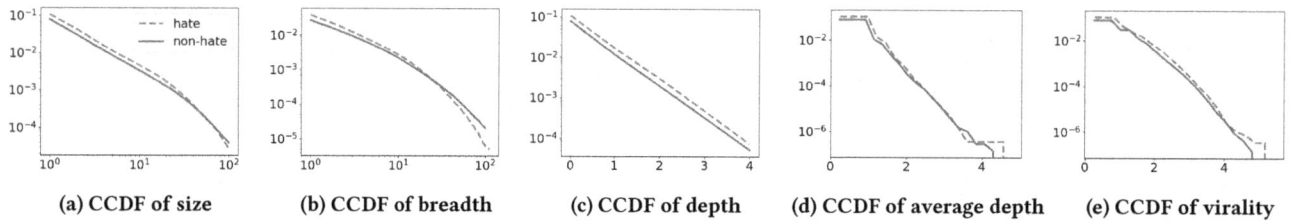

| (a) CCDF of size | (b) CCDF of breadth | (c) CCDF of depth | (d) CCDF of average depth | (e) CCDF of virality |

Figure 4: Different diffusion dynamics of the posts by hate and non-hate users using LRIF model. The cascade properties namely size, breadth, depth, average depth and virality are larger for the posts of hateful users.

respectively) depicts, these properties remain consistently larger for the KH users throughout their entire distribution.

4.4.2 Posts with attachment. In order to understand the diffusion dynamics of posts with attachment, we consider only those posts which have an attachment. The attachment can be images, videos or urls. From Table 3, it is observed that posts with attachments have a larger mean size, breadth, depth, average depth and structural virality implying that such posts have a greater outreach, diffuse wider, deeper and are more viral. This agrees with our hypothesis that attachments with memes and images are more instrumental in information diffusion than textual content. The different characteristics manifest as significant (p-value < 0.01) according to the KS-test for posts and attachments.

4.4.3 Posts in topics. Topics represent sub-communities in Gab catered to a certain cause or serving a niche interest. We attempt to compare topics having a higher proportion of hateful content with those having a lower proportion of hateful content. We consider topics which have at least 100 users and at least 500 posts to ensure that our cascades formed are well represented. We then rank the topics in decreasing fraction of hateful content and take the top 250 topics as hateful topics (HT) and the bottom 250 topics as non-hateful topics (NT). We show some of the top 10 instances of hateful and non-hateful topics in Table 4. We observe that HT consists of topics which aim to promote hate speech in the community.

The cascade properties of the posts in the HT and NT topics are summarized in Table 3. It is evident that community involvement has increased the cascade properties significantly.

HT	Jews Are The Synagogue Of Satan, The Black Race SUCKS, Street Shitter, Israel Holocaust Remembrance Day
NT	Xenoblade Chronicles 2(Spoilers), 2018 memes to amuse you, What's Going On?, Landscape, Classic Cars and Trucks,

Table 4: Prominent hateful and non-hateful topics of Gab.

4.4.4 Early adopters in a cascade. Figures 5a and 5b illustrate the proportion of hateful and non-hateful propagators at each depth. It is evident that the hateful users are early adopters in the cascades of KH users, exhibiting strong degree of homophily. The reverse also holds true for non-hateful users who are the early adopters in the cascades of NH users. The change in monotonicity of the curves in both the diagrams after depth 4 can be attributed to the small

number of cascades whose depth exceeded 4 levels (0.0065% and 0.0057% of KH and NH users respectively). These are fast cascades where the information was propagated by a larger fraction of hateful users in KH posts and larger fraction of non-hateful users in NH posts.

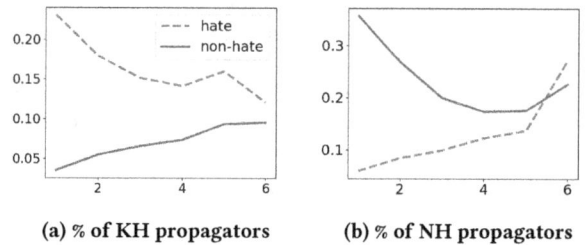

| (a) % of KH propagators | (b) % of NH propagators |

Figure 5: The proportion of hateful and non-hateful users who have reposted the root user across different depths. Here, the X-axis represents the depth of the cascade while the Y-axis represent the proportion of users. Hate users are early propagators for the posts of hateful users while non-hateful users are the early propagators for the posts of non-hateful users.

4.4.5 Dynamics of the cascade properties. We also explore the different dynamic properties of the cascade parameters. In particular, we investigated the temporal aspects as well as the relationship between the parameters of the cascade.

Temporal aspects: The temporal aspects of information diffusion, namely the evolution of different cascade parameters over time are illustrated for both KH and NH cascades in terms of size, breadth, depth, average depth and structural virality via the Figures 6a, 6b, 6c, 6d and 6e respectively. For all such diagrams, the x-axis represents the specific characteristic (like size or depth) and the y-axis represent the time taken in thousand seconds. It is quite evident that the time taken for the KH cascades to reach a particular value is lower in the initial stages implying that KH cascades are significantly faster initially. This can be attributed to the high proportion of KH users as early propagators.

Dynamic relationship between diffusion parameters: Next, we observe the dynamic relationship between the cascade parameters. In Figure 7a, we observe that the cascade of KH users reach a higher depth for almost all the values of breadth. We note similar results for other relations such as size vs avg. depth (Figure 7b), size vs vepth (Figure 7d), and size vs virality (Figure 7e). In case of size vs breadth (Figure 7c), we observe that this does not hold. The posts of KH users seem to have smaller breath for almost every size of the cascade as compared to the posts of NH users.

4.4.6 Summary.

- The posts of KH users diffuse significantly farther, wider, deeper and faster than the NH ones.
- Posts having attachments tend to be more viral.
- KH users are more proactive and cohesive. This observation is based on their fast repost rate and the high proportion of them being early propagators.

5 CASE STUDY: THE PITTSBURG SHOOTING

In the aftermath of the Pittsburg synagogue shooting[7], the Gab website owners were forced to shutdown the site temporarily for a week[15]. The reason behind the decision to ban the website arose from Robert Bowers' history of posting antisemitic messages on Gab (under the username @onedingo). Bowers allegedly killed eleven people at a Pittsburgh synagogue with a gun on October 27, 2018.

We illustrate the account characteristics of @onedingo that were present in our dataset in Table 5. We observe that all the characteristics of @onedingo are close to the characteristics of the KH users shown in Table 2. We also manually inspected into the user's posts and found several hateful instances such as the following.

> Kikes are enemy number one. Dealing with anything after will be a relative piece of cake. I will not fire on someone who is shooting my enemy.

Moreover, 40.9% of onedingo's followings were KH users, also 25.4% of his followers were KH users.

We observed the cascade properties of onedingo and found that it aligns more with the non-hateful users. Thus, if one only looks at the cascade properties it would be very difficult to ascertain the vindictive nature of this user. The user successfully managed to camouflage himself and portray a non-hateful behavior in its message cascading patterns. However, at a micro level, a closer observation of the posts made by the user, reveals that several of the posts of onedingo talk about killing and genocide of Jews. We would need models that can differentiate between different intensities of hate speech for obtaining clearer insights in such nuanced cases. We plan to take this work up as an immediate future work.

6 ADDITIONAL OBSERVATIONS

In this section we put forward certain additional observations that we believe are necessary to render completion to this research.

6.1 Influential users

As posts of KH users have higher virality as compared to the NH users, we wanted to know how much of it was due to user popularity. To get a better understanding of the popularity, we analyze the users based on two different criteria: 1) the number of followers; 2) the user PageRank.

Account characteristics			Cascade characteristics	
Property	Value	Normalized value	Property	Mean value
post	206	1.355	size	1.158
follower	212	1.395	depth	0.105
following	232	1.526	breadth	1.052
like	568	2.757	average depth	0.087
dislike	2	0.01	virality	0.078
score	566	2.748		
reply	113	0.549		
repost	114	0.553		
F:F	0.91379	- -		

Table 5: Description of onedingo's characteristics.

We compute the PageRank on the follower/following network of the Gab users and rank them according to their scores. We take the top k users in the PageRank score and compute the percentage of users that are tagged as KH and NH. We try different values of k ranging from 50 to 10000. We can observe from Figure 8 that there are much more (around 6 times) NH users in the top k position as compared to the KH users. We got similar results using the number of followers (data not shown).

These results indicate that the NH user group consisted of much more popular users as compared the KH users. Thus the overall popularity of users does not seem to bear any correlation with the spread dynamics of posts on Gab.

6.2 Domains used

Next, we identify what kind of links were being shared by the posts of the KH and NH users. To this end, we inspect the urls mentioned by the KH and NH users in their posts. We first extract the domains of all the links that are present in the root posts of the cascades for both the KH and NH users. Then, we filter out all the domains which are not present in at least 200 unique posts. Next, we find the fraction of times a domain was used in the post of a KH user to the post of NH user. We report the top domains used by the KH and NH users in Table 6 according to the fraction of usage. We observe that the KH user posts contained domains such as *dailystormer* which is an American neo-Nazi site, white supremacist, and Holocaust denial commentary board. The website advocates for the genocide of Jews and considers itself a part of the alt-right movement. These websites are also responsible for the spread of conspiracy theories. Since we know that fake news tend to spread faster [40], we posit that fake news and hate speech tend to go hand in hand. We would be interested to investigate this relationship between hate speech and fake news in more details in a future work.

6.3 Top 1% viral hateful and non-hateful posts

Next, We study the difference of the top 1% of the hate and non-hate posts according to structural virality. We first check the presence of profane words using a lexicon[16]. We found that among the top viral hate posts, 32.91% contained one or more profane words. Only

---

[15]https://www.technadu.com/godaddy-forces-gab-shut-down-temporarily/46040

[16]https://github.com/RobertJGabriel/Google-profanity-words/blob/master/list.txt

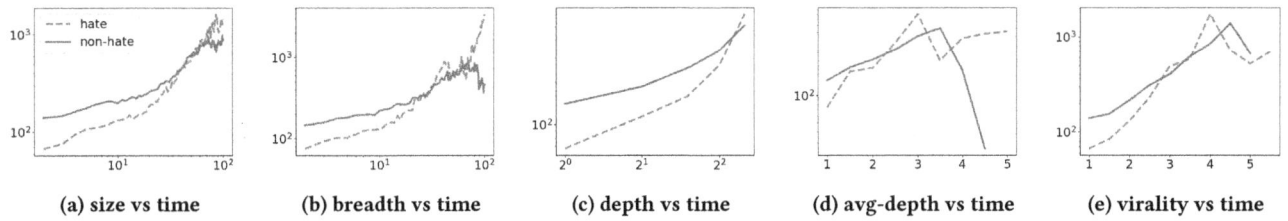

(a) size vs time   (b) breadth vs time   (c) depth vs time   (d) avg-depth vs time   (e) virality vs time

Figure 6: Temporal profiles of diffusion properties of the cascades generated by the posts of the KH and the NH users. Here, the Y-axis represents time (taken in 10^3 seconds) and X-axis represents the cascade characteristics. The posts of KH users spread farther, wider and deeper more quickly in the initial stages.

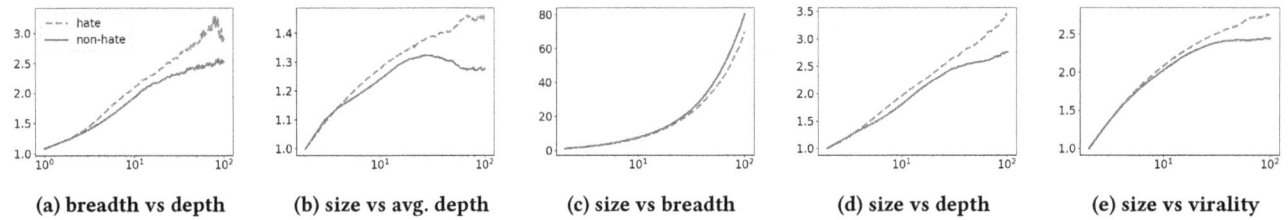

(a) breadth vs depth   (b) size vs avg. depth   (c) size vs breadth   (d) size vs depth   (e) size vs virality

Figure 7: Diffusion dynamics of different properties of the cascades. For each figure, the first property represents the X-axis and the second property represents the Y-axis.

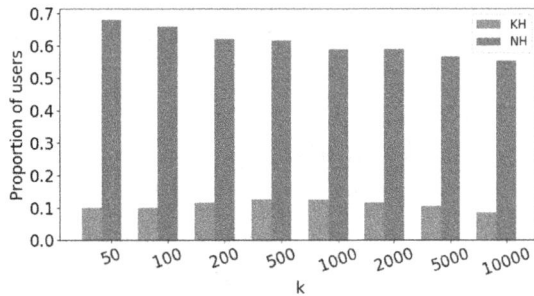

Figure 8: Proportion of KH and NH in the top k PageRank score.

User	Domains
KH	*dailystormer*, imageshack, *radioaryan*, endculturalmarxism, *christophercantwell*, *infostormer*, rationalwiki, skepdic
NH	xxxbios, bring-back-america, yourlawyer, Energy-Ingenuity, petreporters, internetmarketingexperience, strippersforyou

Table 6: Top domain that are used by KH and NH users.

26.23% of the top non-hate posts contained one or more profane words.

We also observed the type of content that is shared by the top 1% of the posts. We found that 16.47% of KH user posts did not contain any form of attachment. The same for NH users was 13.04%. On the other hand, NH users seem to be using urls in their posts a lot; 34.1% of the top NH user posts had at least one url, whereas only 21.24% of the KH user posts had at least one url. We also found that KH users use image and gif in 58.54% of their posts whereas NH users use it in 48.73% of their posts.

7 DISCUSSION

In this section we discuss the implications of this work and note the limitations of the study.

7.1 Real world impact of online hate

The spread of hate speech in the online medium in a grave concern to the society. This is particularly problematic for several unsuspecting victims who might form an unnecessary outgroup prejudice against a particular community [36]. The frequent and repetitive exposure to hate speech leads to desensitization to this form of verbal violence and subsequently to lower evaluations of the victims and greater distancing, thus increasing the outgroup prejudice.

One of the prime examples of this was the Rohingya crisis in Myanmar. Many of the people who helped in disseminating hate on Facebook had not even met a single Rohingya in their life. Their view of the target community was completely manipulated by the rampant spread of hate speech on Facebook. Our results show that the "hate-workers" form cohesive groups is a testimony to why campaigns like the above usually succeed; the spread of the hate content is a well-orchestrated collective effort that helps the content to spread like wildfire as opposed to individual efforts which could never have been so successful.

7.2 Design of online platforms

The online social media platforms facilitates the fast spread of any kind of information. The users with malicious intents normally make use of such features to disseminate their messages. As we have seen from our analysis, the KH users are most active in the early stages of content spread, our recommendation would be that these social media platforms should curtail the spread of harmful content by *suppressing its initial spread*. This way the harmful posts would appear on the home feed of fewer people and thus cause less damage. The posts that people receive in their home feed reinforces generally their world views. The platforms could thus monitor the spread of hate speech and reduce its effect by showing it in less people's home feed.

Another suitable alternative to fight hate speech without harming freedom of speech would be using counter speech. This strategy is even endorsed by companies like Facebook that has stated in public that it believes counter speech is not only potentially more effective, but also more likely to succeed in the long run [6]. By understanding the spread of hate speech in online social media, the sites could employ appropriate counter speech strategies that could mitigate/neutralize the effects of hate speech.

7.3 Limitations of the current study

In our analysis we have relied on the user account to study the cascade. We assume that the hateful posts of these hateful accounts would generate majority of the reposts. This means that few of the reposts of these hateful accounts might not be hateful in nature. However, while we cannot claim to have captured the full picture, our analysis provided a peek into the cascade dynamics of the hateful posts in Gab.

8 RELATED WORK

Diffusion in online media: To the best of our knowledge there has not been any work that tries to study the diffusion of hate in online social media. However, there are several works that looks into diffusion of fake news [27, 39, 43], Linkedin [3], retweet cascade [8, 9, 18, 39], rumours [11, 17, 20, 22, 47] and Tumblr [1, 2, 7, 44]. Cheng et al. [9] perform a large scale analysis of recurring cascades in Facebook. They observe that content virality is the main driver for recurrence. In Del Vicario et al. [11], the authors perform a large scale analysis of Facebook and observe that selective exposure to content is the primary driver of content diffusion and generates the formation echo chambers. Stuart [37] systematically profiled all Islamist-related terror offenses in the United Kingdom between 1998 to 2015 and found that over a quarter (28%) of Islamist related terror offenses were demonstrably inspired by the rhetoric or propaganda of a proscribed terrorist organisation.

Research on Gab: There is little research done on Gab. Zannettou et al. [45] performed the first study in which the author collected and analyzed a large dataset of Gab and found that the site is predominantly used for discussion of news, world events, and politics. They also found that Gab contains 2.4 times more hate speech as compared to Twitter. Lima et al. [23] also found that Gab is very politically oriented and users who abuse the lack of moderation disseminate hate. Zannettou et al. [46] perform a large scale measurement study of the meme ecosystem by introducing a novel image processing pipeline. Gab has substantially higher number of posts with racist memes. Gab shares hateful and racist memes at a higher rate than mainstream communities. In similar lines, Finkelstein et al. [16] study millions of comments and images from alt-right web communities like 4chan's Politically Incorrect board (/pol/) and the Twitter clone, Gab and quantify the escalation and spread of antisemitism.

Research on hate speech: The majority of the research in hate speech has been done in automatic detection in various social media platforms like Twitter [4, 10, 32, 42], Facebook [12], Yahoo! Finance and News [13, 28, 41] and Whisper [26]. In another online effort, a Canadian NGO, the Sentinel Project[17], launched a site in 2013 called HateBase[18], which invites Internet users to add to a list of slurs and insulting words in many languages. There are some works which have tried to characterize the hateful users [24, 34]. In Ribeiro et al. [34], the authors study the user characteristics of hateful accounts on Twitter and found that the hateful user accounts differ significantly from normal user accounts on the basis of activity, network centrality, and the type of content they produce. In ElSherief et al. [15], the authors perform a comparative study of the hate speech instigators and target users on Twitter. They found that the hate instigators target more popular and high profile Twitter users, which leads to greater online visibility. Mathew et al. [25] studies the effect of counterspeech in hateful YouTube videos and develops machine learning models to automatically detect counterspeech in YouTube comments. In ElSherief et al. [14], the authors focus on studying the target of the hate speech - directed and generalized. They observe that while directed hate speech is more personal, informal and express anger, the generalized hate is more of religious type and uses lethal words such as 'murder', 'exterminate', and 'kill'. Ottoni et al. [30] analyze the hate, violence, and discriminatory bias in a selection of right-wing YouTube channels. The authors found that these channels are more specific in their content, discussing topics such as war and terrorism, and have a higher percentage of negative category words such as aggression and violence. In Olteanu et al. [29], the authors study the effect of external events on hate speech in two social media: Twitter and Reddit. They observe that extremist violence tends to increase hate speech in online medium, especially messages which advocate violence.

9 CONCLUSION AND FUTURE WORK

In this paper, we perform the first study which observes the nuances of the diffusion characteristics of the posts made by hateful and non-hateful users. We used high precision keywords to select hateful users and provide them as input to DeGroot's model to identify the hateful and non-hateful set of users. We then analyse the diffusion characteristics of the posts of these users. We found that the posts made by hateful users tend to spread farther, faster, and wider. These hateful users are densely connected with each other and generate almost 1/4th of the content in Gab despite comprising 0.67% of the users.

Our work also points to several open research avenues. A large fraction of the posts were in the form of images in case of hate users. For future work, we would like to take up the task of building a classification system that can distinguish between images/videos that are hateful in nature. Another interesting direction would be

---

[17]https://thesentinelproject.org/
[18]https://www.hatebase.org/

to look into the diffusion characteristics of the individual hateful posts instead of the accounts.

REFERENCES

[1] Nora Alrajebah. 2015. Investigating the structural characteristics of cascades on Tumblr. In *Advances in Social Networks Analysis and Mining (ASONAM), 2015 IEEE/ACM International Conference on*. IEEE, 910–917.

[2] Nora Alrajebah, Leslie Carr, Markus Luczak-Roesch, and Thanassis Tiropanis. 2017. Deconstructing diffusion on Tumblr: structural and temporal aspects. In *Proceedings of the 2017 ACM on Web Science Conference*. ACM, 319–328.

[3] Ashton Anderson, Daniel Huttenlocher, Jon Kleinberg, Jure Leskovec, and Mitul Tiwari. 2015. Global diffusion via cascading invitations: Structure, growth, and homophily. In *Proceedings of the 24th International Conference on World Wide Web*. International World Wide Web Conferences Steering Committee, 66–76.

[4] Pinkesh Badjatiya, Shashank Gupta, Manish Gupta, and Vasudeva Varma. 2017. Deep Learning for Hate Speech Detection in Tweets *(WWW)*. 759–760.

[5] Eytan Bakshy, Jake M Hofman, Winter A Mason, and Duncan J Watts. 2011. Everyone's an influencer: quantifying influence on twitter. In *Proceedings of the fourth ACM international conference on Web search and data mining*. ACM, 65–74.

[6] Jamie Bartlett and Alex Krasodomski-Jones. 2015. Counter-speech examining content that challenges extremism online. *Demos. Available at: http://www.demos.co.uk/wp-content/uploads/2015/10/Counter-speech.pdf* (2015).

[7] Yi Chang, Lei Tang, Yoshiyuki Inagaki, and Yan Liu. 2014. What is tumblr: A statistical overview and comparison. *ACM SIGKDD explorations newsletter* 16, 1 (2014), 21–29.

[8] Justin Cheng, Lada Adamic, P. Alex Dow, Jon Michael Kleinberg, and Jure Leskovec. 2014. Can Cascades Be Predicted?. In *Proceedings of the 23rd International Conference on World Wide Web (WWW '14)*. ACM, New York, NY, USA, 925–936. https://doi.org/10.1145/2566486.2567997

[9] Justin Cheng, Lada A Adamic, Jon M Kleinberg, and Jure Leskovec. 2016. Do cascades recur?. In *Proceedings of the 25th International Conference on World Wide Web*. International World Wide Web Conferences Steering Committee, 671–681.

[10] Thomas Davidson, Dana Warmsley, Michael Macy, and Ingmar Weber. 2017. Automated Hate Speech Detection and the Problem of Offensive Language. (2017).

[11] Michela Del Vicario, Alessandro Bessi, Fabiana Zollo, Fabio Petroni, Antonio Scala, Guido Caldarelli, H Eugene Stanley, and Walter Quattrociocchi. 2016. The spreading of misinformation online. *Proceedings of the National Academy of Sciences* 113, 3 (2016), 554–559.

[12] Fabio Del Vigna, Andrea Cimino, Felice DellâÄŹOrletta, Marinella Petrocchi, and Maurizio Tesconi. 2017. Hate me, hate me not: Hate speech detection on Facebook. (2017).

[13] Nemanja Djuric, Jing Zhou, Robin Morris, Mihajlo Grbovic, Vladan Radosavljevic, and Narayan Bhamidipati. 2015. Hate Speech Detection with Comment Embeddings. In *WWW '15 Companion*. 29–30.

[14] Mai ElSherief, Vivek Kulkarni, Dana Nguyen, William Y. Wang, and Elizabeth Belding. 2018. Hate Lingo: A Target-based Linguistic Analysis of Hate Speech in Social Media *(ICWSM '18)*.

[15] Mai ElSherief, Shirin Nilizadeh, Dana Nguyen, Giovanni Vigna, and Elizabeth Belding. 2018. Peer to Peer Hate: Hate Speech Instigators and Their Targets. (2018).

[16] Joel Finkelstein, Savvas Zannettou, Barry Bradlyn, and Jeremy Blackburn. 2018. A Quantitative Approach to Understanding Online Antisemitism. *arXiv preprint arXiv:1809.01644* (2018).

[17] Adrien Friggeri, Lada A Adamic, Dean Eckles, and Justin Cheng. 2014. Rumor Cascades.. In *ICWSM*.

[18] Sharad Goel, Ashton Anderson, Jake Hofman, and Duncan J Watts. 2015. The structural virality of online diffusion. *Management Science* 62, 1 (2015), 180–196.

[19] Benjamin Golub and Matthew O Jackson. 2010. Naive learning in social networks and the wisdom of crowds. *American Economic Journal: Microeconomics* 2, 1 (2010), 112–49.

[20] Fang Jin, Edward Dougherty, Parang Saraf, Yang Cao, and Naren Ramakrishnan. 2013. Epidemiological modeling of news and rumors on twitter. In *Proceedings of the 7th Workshop on Social Network Mining and Analysis*. ACM, 8.

[21] Rohan Kshirsagar, Tyrus Cukuvac, Kathy McKeown, and Susan McGregor. 2018. Predictive Embeddings for Hate Speech Detection on Twitter. In *Proceedings of the 2nd Workshop on Abusive Language Online (ALW2)*. 26–32.

[22] Jure Leskovec, Mary McGlohon, Christos Faloutsos, Natalie Glance, and Matthew Hurst. 2007. Patterns of cascading behavior in large blog graphs. In *Proceedings of the 2007 SIAM international conference on data mining*. SIAM, 551–556.

[23] Lucas Riguete Pereira De Lima, Julio C. S. Reis, Philipe F. Melo, Fabricio Murai, Leandro Araújo Silva, Pantelis Vikatos, and Fabrício Benevenuto. 2018. Inside the Right-Leaning Echo Chambers: Characterizing Gab, an Unmoderated Social System. *ASONAM* (2018).

[24] Binny Mathew, Navish Kumar, Pawan Goyal, Animesh Mukherjee, et al. 2018. Analyzing the hate and counter speech accounts on Twitter. *arXiv preprint arXiv:1812.02712* (2018).

[25] Binny Mathew, Hardik Tharad, Subham Rajgaria, Prajwal Singhania, Suman Kalyan Maity, Pawan Goyal, and Animesh Mukherje. 2018. Thou shalt not hate: Countering Online Hate Speech. *arXiv preprint arXiv:1808.04409* (2018).

[26] Mainack Mondal, Leandro Araujo Silva, and Fabricio Benevenuto. 2017. A Measurement Study of Hate Speech in Social Media. In *HT*.

[27] Eni Mustafaraj and Panagiotis Takis Metaxas. 2017. The fake news spreading plague: was it preventable?. In *Proceedings of the 2017 ACM on Web Science Conference*. ACM, 235–239.

[28] Chikashi Nobata, Joel Tetreault, Achint Thomas, Yashar Mehdad, and Yi Chang. 2016. Abusive Language Detection in Online User Content. In *WWW '16*. 145–153.

[29] Alexandra Olteanu, Carlos Castillo, Jeremy Boy, and Kush R Varshney. 2018. The Effect of Extremist Violence on Hateful Speech Online. (2018).

[30] Raphael Ottoni, Evandro Cunha, Gabriel Magno, Pedro Bernardina, Wagner Meira Jr, and Virgílio Almeida. 2018. Analyzing Right-wing YouTube Channels: Hate, Violence and Discrimination. In *Proceedings of the 10th ACM Conference on Web Science*. ACM, 323–332.

[31] Arie Perliger and Ami Pedahzur. 2011. Social Network Analysis in the Study of Terrorism and Political Violence. *Political Science and Politics* 44, 2 (2011).

[32] Jing Qian, Mai ElSherief, Elizabeth M. Belding-Royer, and William Yang Wang. 2018. Hierarchical CVAE for Fine-Grained Hate Speech Classification. *EMNLP* abs/1809.00088 (2018).

[33] Manoel Ribeiro, Pedro Calais, Yuri Santos, VirgÃŋlio Almeida, and Wagner Meira Jr. 2018. Characterizing and Detecting Hateful Users on Twitter *(ICWSM '18)*.

[34] Manoel Horta Ribeiro, Pedro H Calais, Yuri A Santos, Virgílio AF Almeida, and Wagner Meira Jr. 2017. " Like Sheep Among Wolves": Characterizing Hateful Users on Twitter. In *WSDM workshop on Misinformation and Misbehavior Mining on the Web (MIS2)*. 8.

[35] Punyajoy Saha, Binny Mathew, Pawan Goyal, and Animesh Mukherjee. 2018. Hateminers: Detecting Hate speech against Women. *arXiv preprint arXiv:1812.06700* (2018).

[36] Wiktor Soral, Michał Bilewicz, and Mikołaj Winiewski. 2018. Exposure to hate speech increases prejudice through desensitization. *Aggressive behavior* 44, 2 (2018), 136–146.

[37] Hannah Stuart. 2017. *Islamist Terrorism: Analysis of Offence and Attacks in the UK (1998-2015)*. Henry Jackson Society.

[38] Io Taxidou and Peter M. Fischer. 2014. Online Analysis of Information Diffusion in Twitter. In *Proceedings of the 23rd International Conference on World Wide Web (WWW '14 Companion)*. ACM, 1313–1318.

[39] Soroush Vosoughi, Deb Roy, and Sinan Aral. 2018. The spread of true and false news online. *Science* 359, 6380 (2018), 1146–1151. https://doi.org/10.1126/science. aap9559

[40] Soroush Vosoughi, Deb Roy, and Sinan Aral. 2018. The spread of true and false news online. *Science* 359, 6380 (2018), 1146–1151.

[41] William Warner and Julia Hirschberg. 2012. Detecting Hate Speech on the World Wide Web. In *Proceedings of the Second Workshop on Language in Social Media (LSM '12)*. 19–26.

[42] Zeerak Waseem and Dirk Hovy. 2016. Hateful symbols or hateful people? predictive features for hate speech detection on twitter. In *Proceedings of the NAACL student research workshop*. 88–93.

[43] Liang Wu and Huan Liu. 2018. Tracing fake-news footprints: Characterizing social media messages by how they propagate. In *Proceedings of the Eleventh ACM International Conference on Web Search and Data Mining*. ACM, 637–645.

[44] Jiejun Xu, Ryan Compton, Tsai-Ching Lu, and David Allen. 2014. Rolling through tumblr: characterizing behavioral patterns of the microblogging platform. In *Proceedings of the 2014 ACM conference on Web science*. ACM, 13–22.

[45] Savvas Zannettou, Barry Bradlyn, Emiliano De Cristofaro, Haewoon Kwak, Michael Sirivianos, Gianluca Stringini, and Jeremy Blackburn. 2018. What is Gab: A Bastion of Free Speech or an Alt-Right Echo Chamber. In *Companion of the The Web Conference 2018 on The Web Conference 2018*. 1007–1014.

[46] Savvas Zannettou, Tristan Caulfield, Jeremy Blackburn, Emiliano De Cristofaro, Michael Sirivianos, Gianluca Stringhini, and Guillermo Suarez-Tangil. 2018. On the Origins of Memes by Means of Fringe Web Communities. *arXiv preprint arXiv:1805.12512* (2018).

[47] Zhe Zhao, Paul Resnick, and Qiaozhu Mei. 2015. Enquiring minds: Early detection of rumors in social media from enquiry posts. In *Proceedings of the 24th International Conference on World Wide Web*. International World Wide Web Conferences Steering Committee, 1395–1405.

RTBUST: Exploiting Temporal Patterns
for Botnet Detection on Twitter

Michele Mazza
IIT-CNR, Italy
michele.mazza@iit.cnr.it

Stefano Cresci*
IIT-CNR, Italy
stefano.cresci@iit.cnr.it

Marco Avvenuti
University of Pisa, Italy
marco.avvenuti@unipi.it

Walter Quattrociocchi
Ca' Foscari University of Venice, Italy
w.quattrociocchi@unive.it

Maurizio Tesconi
IIT-CNR, Italy
maurizio.tesconi@iit.cnr.it

ABSTRACT

Within OSNs, many of our supposedly online friends may instead be fake accounts called *social bots*, part of large groups that purposely re-share targeted content. Here, we study retweeting behaviors on Twitter, with the ultimate goal of detecting retweeting social bots. We collect a dataset of 10M retweets. We design a novel visualization that we leverage to highlight benign and malicious patterns of retweeting activity. In this way, we uncover a "normal" retweeting pattern that is peculiar of human-operated accounts, and 3 suspicious patterns related to bot activities. Then, we propose a bot detection technique that stems from the previous exploration of retweeting behaviors. Our technique, called RETWEET-BUSTER (RTBUST), leverages unsupervised feature extraction and clustering. An LSTM autoencoder converts the retweet time series into compact and informative latent feature vectors, which are then clustered with a hierarchical density-based algorithm. Accounts belonging to large clusters characterized by malicious retweeting patterns are labeled as bots. RTBUST obtains excellent detection results, with $F1 = 0.87$, whereas competitors achieve $F1 \leq 0.76$. Finally, we apply RTBUST to a large dataset of retweets, uncovering 2 previously unknown active botnets with hundreds of accounts.

CCS CONCEPTS

• **Information systems** → *Social networking sites.*

KEYWORDS

Social bots, retweet patterns, OSN security, Twitter

ACM Reference Format:

Michele Mazza, Stefano Cresci, Marco Avvenuti, Walter Quattrociocchi, and Maurizio Tesconi. 2019. RTBUST: Exploiting Temporal Patterns for Botnet Detection on Twitter. In *11th ACM Conference on Web Science (WebSci '19), June 30–July 3, 2019, Boston, MA, USA*. ACM, New York, NY, USA, 10 pages. https://doi.org/10.1145/3292522.3326015

*This is the corresponding author.

1 INTRODUCTION

In 2016 the Oxford dictionary elected "Post-Truth" as the word of the year and in 2017 Collins dictionary did the same for "Fake News". In 2017 the World Economic Forum raised a warning on the potential distortion effect of social media on user perceptions of reality[1]. Recent studies, targeting Facebook, showed the tendency of the users to interact with information adhering to their preferred narrative [3, 13] and to ignore dissenting information [45]. Confirmation bias seems to account for user decisions about consuming and spreading content and at the same time, aggregation of favored information within those communities reinforces selective exposure and group polarization [38]. As we interact with our peers, we are exposed to the effects of echo chambers, which may result in polarization and hate speech [14]. In this scenario the role of bots is not clear, both for the difficulties in quantifying their impact as well as for the accuracy of detection algorithms. However, any of our supposedly online friends may instead be fake, automated accounts (*social bots*), and a part of large coordinated groups that purposely (re-)share targeted content [16]. Along this challenge, in this work we propose a new method for the detection of groups of bots, accounting for their statistical traces induced by their coordinated behavior on Twitter.

Specifically, we focus on re-sharing (i.e., retweeting) patterns with the ultimate goal of detecting retweeting social bots. Indeed, by artificially boosting retweet counts, these bots may affect users' popularity or influence, thus "reshaping political debates [40]. They can defraud businesses and ruin reputations"[2]. Moreover, large retweet counts indicate influential users, and can be monetized. Thus, there are strong economic and sociopolitical incentives for malicious bots to tamper with retweets [18, 41]. Hence, fast and accurate removal of these bots might be crucial for ensuring the healthiness of our online social ecosystems.

Both researchers and OSN administrators have recently been very active towards the detection of social bots, and many different techniques have been proposed to this end. Unfortunately, the same also applies to malicious bot developers. In fact, as soon as new detection techniques are deployed, bot developers tweak the characteristics of their accounts, thus allowing them to evade detection [8]. This "never-ending clash" led to the current situation where social bots are so sophisticatedly engineered as to mimic legitimate accounts, becoming almost indistinguishable from them [42]. A

---

[1] http://reports.weforum.org/global-risks-2017/acknowledgements/
[2] https://www.nytimes.com/interactive/2018/01/27/technology/social-media-bots.html

straightforward consequence of this situation is that standard machine learning classification approaches, where each account is analyzed individually, are no longer profitable. Instead, the scientific frontier of bot detection now focuses on groups of suspicious accounts as a whole. Analyzing groups has the advantage that, no matter how sophisticated a single bot can be, a large enough group of them will still leave traces of automation, since they do share a common goal (e.g., increasing someone's popularity) [8]. For the same reasons, unsupervised approaches are preferred over supervised ones [44].

The possibility to exploit more data for the analysis, opened up by the approaches that target groups rather than individual accounts, is however counterbalanced by the difficulties in collecting and processing that much data. For instance, the behavior-based technique described in [7, 9] requires collecting and comparing data of the Twitter timelines of all analyzed accounts. Similarly, graph-based techniques such as [26] require building and analyzing the social graph of a large group of accounts. The amount of data and computational power needed to complete these analyses, inevitably limits the large-scale applicability of these techniques. In short, the next generation of bot detection techniques should strike the balance between accuracy and data/algorithmic efficiency.

Contributions. We propose a novel technique for the detection of retweeting social bots, called RETWEET-BUSTER (RTBUST), having all the desirable features previously discussed. Our technique only requires the timestamps of retweets (and of the retweeted tweets) for each analyzed account, thus avoiding the need for full user timelines or social graphs. Then, it compares the temporal patterns of retweeting activity of large groups of users. Leveraging previous findings in the field, RTBUST looks for groups of accounts with distinctive and synchronized patterns. Evaluation results on a large dataset of retweets demonstrate excellent bot detection performances, with $F1 = 0.87$, whereas competitors achieve $F1 \leq 0.76$. Summarizing, our detailed contributions are as follows.

- We analyze retweeting behaviors of a large set of users by introducing a simple – yet effective – visualization, which we then leverage to highlight benign and malicious patterns of retweeting activity.
- We design a group-analysis technique that is capable of detecting accounts having the same retweeting patterns. Accounts belonging to a large group characterized by the same malicious patterns are labeled as bots.
- We compare detection results of our technique with those obtained by baselines and other state-of-the-art techniques, demonstrating the effectiveness of our approach.
- By applying our technique to a large dataset of retweets, we uncover 2 previously unknown active botnets.

2 RELATED WORK IN BOT DETECTION

The vast majority of previous attempts at bot detection are based on supervised machine learning [8]. The first challenge in developing a supervised detector is related to the availability of a ground truth (i.e., labeled) dataset, to be used in the learning phase of the classifier. In most cases, a real ground truth is lacking and the labels are simply given by human operators that manually analyze the data. Critical issues arise since there is no "standard" definition of what a social

bot is [34, 44]. Moreover, humans have been proven to largely fail at spotting sophisticated bots, with only $\simeq 24\%$ bots correctly labeled as such [8]. As anticipated, these criticalities support the development of unsupervised techniques.

Regarding features to exploit for the detection, 3 classes have been mainly considered: (i) profile features [12, 28]; (ii) features extracted from the posts, such as posting behavior and content of posted messages [5, 30, 36]; and (iii) features derived from the social or interaction graph of the accounts [26, 27, 31]. The classes of features exploited by the detection technique have a strong impact on both the performances of the detector as well as its efficiency [6]. For instance, in Twitter it has been demonstrated that those features that mostly contribute towards the predictive power of bot detectors (e.g., measures of centrality in the social graph), are also the most costly ones.

The difficulties in detecting sophisticated bots with supervised approaches that are based on the analysis of individual accounts, recently gave rise to a new research trend that aims to analyze groups of accounts as a whole [8]. This new approach to bot detection is proving particularly effective at detecting coordinated and synchronized bots, such as those targeted in our work. For instance, the technique discussed in [7, 9] associates each account to a sequence of characters that encodes its behavioral information. Such sequences are then compared between one another to find anomalous similarities among sequences of a subgroup of accounts. The similarity is computed by measuring the longest common subsequence shared by all the accounts of the group. Accounts that share a suspiciously long subsequence are then labeled as bots. Instead, the family of systems described in [26, 31, 32] build a bipartite graph of accounts and their interactions with content (e.g., retweets to some other tweets) or with other accounts (e.g., becoming followers of other accounts). Then, they aim to detect anomalously dense blocks in the graph, which might be representative of coordinated and synchronized attacks. A possible drawback of group approaches is that they exacerbate challenges related to data and algorithmic costs, since they typically involve a large number of comparisons between all accounts in a given group [9, 43].

Lastly, a trailblazing direction of research involves the application of adversarial machine learning to bot detection. Until now, bot detection has mostly followed a *reactive* schema, where countermeasures are taken only after having witnessed evidence of bot mischiefs [42]. Instead, in [42] is proposed an adversarial framework enabling *proactive* analyses. The framework has been later instantiated in [10] by using evolutionary algorithms to test current detection techniques against a wider range of unseen, sophisticated bots. Another preliminary work in adversarial bot detection is described in [21]. Among the positive outcomes of adversarial approaches to bot detection, is a more rapid understanding of the drawbacks of current detectors and the opportunity to gain insights into new features for achieving more robust and more reliable detectors.

3 DATA COLLECTION AND ANNOTATION

Our dataset for this study is composed of *all* Italian retweets shared in a 2 weeks time span – specifically, between 18 June 2018 and 1 July 2018 (inclusive). Overall, our dataset comprises 9,989,819 retweets, shared by 1,446,250 distinct users. Thus, on average, each

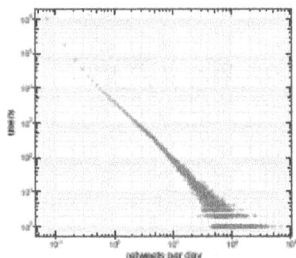

Figure 1: Daily retweets per user.

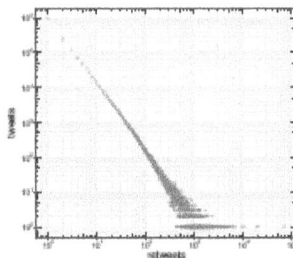

Figure 2: Total retweets per tweet.

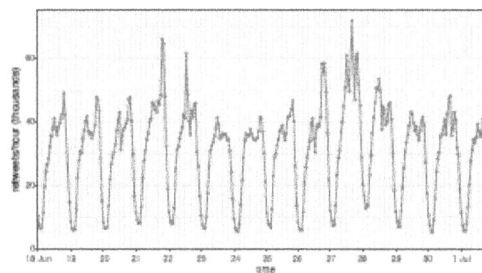

Figure 3: Hourly volume of retweets across the 2 considered weeks.

user in our dataset retweeted 7 times per day, in line with recent statistics reporting between 2 and 50 daily retweets for legitimate users [17]. However, our dataset also includes many "extreme" users, as visible in Figure 1 showing the distribution of retweets per day per user, which features a typical heavy-tailed shape. The 9,989,819 retweets are related to 1,691,865 distinct original tweets, which are also included in the dataset. Figure 2 shows the distribution of retweets per original tweet, while Figure 3 shows the hourly volume of retweets across the 2 considered weeks.

For each tweet, retweet, and user in our dataset we have access to all Twitter metadata fields, as provided by Twitter APIs. To collect this dataset, we resorted to Twitter Premium Search API[3] with the following query parameters: lang:IT and is:retweet. Here, the exploitation of the Premium Search API is important since it allowed us to build a *complete* dataset of retweets. In fact, the Standard Search API[4] used in the majority of previous works, does not guarantee completeness, meaning that not all tweets matching the query criteria are returned. Notably, although our dataset for this study is limited to tweets in the Italian language, both the data collection approach and the analytical process described in the remainder of the paper, are totally language independent. The language of collected tweets can be easily changed with the lang: parameter, and our analyses only exploit timestamps.

After data collection, we performed data filtering and annotation. A manual inspection of those users exhibiting the largest number of retweets per day quickly revealed their automated nature. However, it turned out that all such accounts, despite being bots, were not malicious ones. Their automated nature was manifest, they did not try to disguise as human-operated accounts, and they were not acting coordinatedly nor trying to inflate the popularity of some specific content. The presence of this kind of bots is well known [19]. They do not pose a threat to OSNs and, in fact, some of them are even benign [2, 39]. Thus, we excluded such accounts from future analyses, since they are not the target of our work. Similarly, we also excluded accounts featuring a very small number of retweets. Operationally, we set our filtering thresholds by leveraging statistics in [17] – that is, we retained only those users with a mean number of retweets per day ≥ 2 and ≤ 50. In this way, we ended up with 63,762 distinct users exhibiting human-like retweeting behaviors. The goal

of our next analyses is to tell apart the sophisticated human-like bots from the real human-operated accounts.

Although our detection technique is unsupervised and hence it does not require a labeled ground truth, we nonetheless carried out manual annotation of a small subset of our dataset. This is useful in order to evaluate the extent to which our technique is capable of correctly spotting the bots. We thus annotated $\simeq 1,000$ accounts from our dataset, following the latest annotation guidelines for datasets containing social bots [8]. We ended up with an almost balanced annotated dataset[5], comprising 51% bots and 49% legitimate (i.e., human-operated) accounts.

4 PATTERNS OF RETWEETING ACTIVITY

Here, we investigate the temporal dynamics of retweeting activity of all the 47,947 accounts in our dataset. By also leveraging class labels of the annotated accounts, we aim at highlighting retweeting behaviors that are indicative of normal versus suspicious activity.

To ease the exploration of a user's retweeting activity, we propose a compact – yet informative – scatterplot visualization called RETWEET-TWEET (RTT). Given a user and the list of all his retweets, RTT plots the timestamp of each retweet (x axis) against the timestamp of the corresponding original tweet (y axis). By the definition of RTT, points laying in different areas of the plot imply different retweeting behaviors. Figure 4a shows the semantics of this visualization, by means of a visual explanation of the most common behaviors caught by the RTT plot. In detail, no point can ever appear above the main diagonal of the plot, since that would break causality (i.e., it would correspond to a retweet that anticipates the original tweet, which is clearly impossible). Points laying near to the main diagonal represent retweets occurring rapidly after the publication time of the original tweet. Conversely, points that lay far from the diagonal imply a large temporal distance between a tweet and its retweet (i.e., retweets of very old tweets), which is an uncommon behavior.

Normal behaviors – droplet pattern. Figure 4b shows the typical RTT plot of a "normal", legitimate user. As shown, the vast majority of points concentrates slightly below the main diagonal. This is the expected behavior on the past-paced Twitter OSN, since retweets typically occur with short delay (e.g., between 1 and 10 minutes) from the original tweets [20]. Occasionally, legitimate users retweet a sequence of tweets with increasing delays. In RTT

[3]https://developer.twitter.com/en/docs/tweets/search/api-reference/premium-search.html
[4]https://developer.twitter.com/en/docs/tweets/search/api-reference/get-search-tweets.html

[5]The dataset is avaible at https://doi.org/10.5281/zenodo.2653137

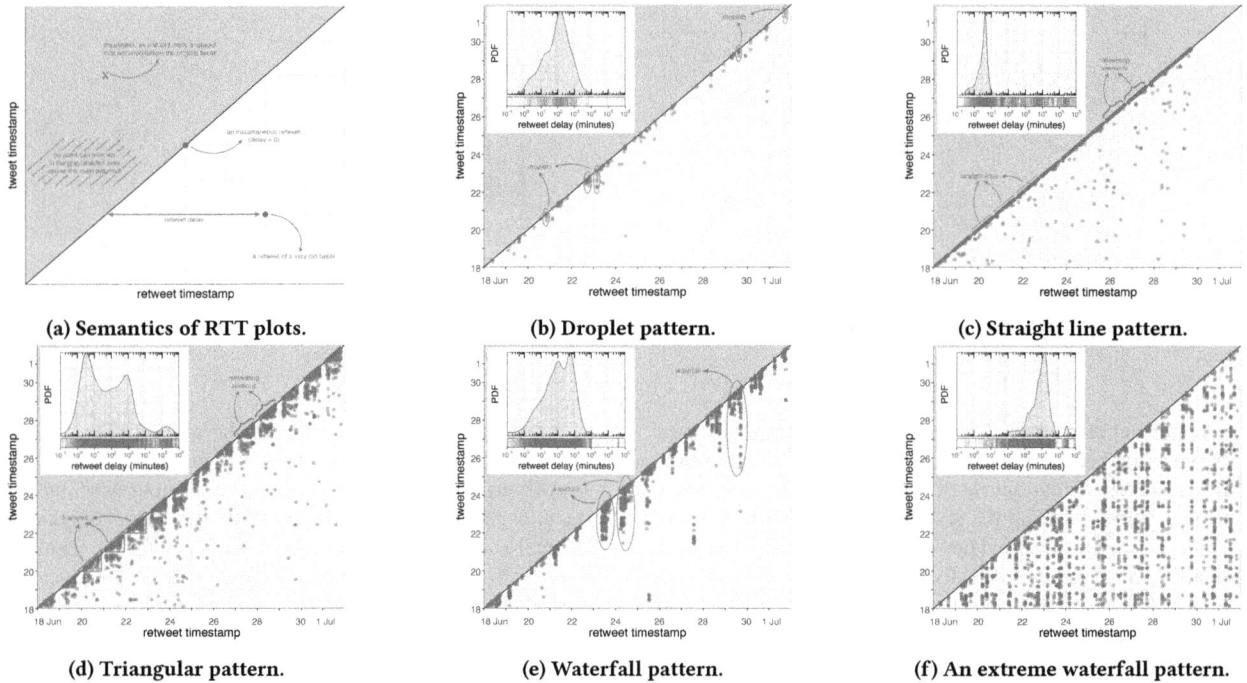

(a) Semantics of RTT plots.

(b) Droplet pattern.

(c) Straight line pattern.

(d) Triangular pattern.

(e) Waterfall pattern.

(f) An extreme waterfall pattern.

Figure 4: RTT **plots depicting a normal tweeting behavior (blue colored) and many suspicious ones (red colored). The insets of** RTT **plots show the empirical probability density function (PDF) and a rug plot of retweet delays.**

plots, this retweeting behavior creates a few vertically-stacked points that we refer to as *droplets*. We found this pattern to be frequent among legitimate users. In fact, the droplet pattern occurs each time a user retweets a Twitter feed (e.g., search results) or a user timeline. Since feeds and timelines are rendered – both in the Web application and via APIs – in reverse chronological order, retweeting a sequence of such tweets results in increasing retweet delays, just because tweets retweeted last are actually the oldest ones. Apart from these observations, no other clear pattern emerges in the RTT plot of Figure 4b. The possible presence of distinctive patterns in RTT plots is particularly relevant since it implies some form of regularity in a user's retweeting activity. In turn, striking regularities are typically caused by automated actions – that is, they are representative of bot behaviors, as previous literature already highlighted [5, 9, 31].

Suspicious behaviors – straight line pattern. The RTT plot in Figure 4c shows different retweeting behaviors. Almost all points in the plot are laying precisely above the main diagonal, meaning that the user almost always retweets in a matter of a few seconds from the original tweets. The user's activity is also clearly split into different sessions, separated by small gaps denoting inactivity.

Suspicious behaviors – triangular pattern. Figure 4d shows yet another suspicious pattern. This time the activity sessions are very regular, with always roughly the same length and the same inactivity time that separates subsequent sessions. Moreover, sessions seem to create a peculiar *triangular* pattern below the diagonal of the RTT plot. This means that, within a given session, the user retweets past tweets only up to a fixed point in time that roughly corresponds to the starting time of the session.

Suspicious behaviors – waterfall pattern. Finally, Figure 4e shows the behavior of a user whose retweets go way back in time. In figure, this is represented by points forming solid vertical lines. These lines are significantly longer than those representing droplets in Figure 4b and are probably caused by systematic retweeting of a Twitter feed or timeline in reverse chronological order. Since many vertical lines are present in the RTT plots showing this retweeting behavior, we call this a *waterfall* pattern. Apart from the vertical lines, mild signs of retweeting sessions are also visible in the plot. Although the presence of the *waterfall* pattern shown in Figure 4e is already indicative of automated behaviors, for some users this behavior is truly extreme, as shown in Figure 4f.

As highlighted by the previous analyses, the RTT plot is useful for studying the retweeting behavior of a given user. It is a valuable tool *per se*, that can empower human analysts for getting insights into the behaviors of Twitter accounts. Moving forward, in the next section we build on the results of these analyses by designing a fully automatic technique for spotting malicious retweeting bots.

5 INTRODUCING RETWEET-BUSTER

As highlighted in the previous sections, unsupervised group-based approaches currently represent the most promising research direction for social bot detection [8, 44]. Thus, in this section we propose an unsupervised technique that leverages the temporal distribution of the retweets of large groups of users, in order to detect malicious retweeting bots. Since we aim to design an unsupervised technique, we can not simply learn a detector for spotting the suspicious patterns identified in Section 4. Instead, our goal

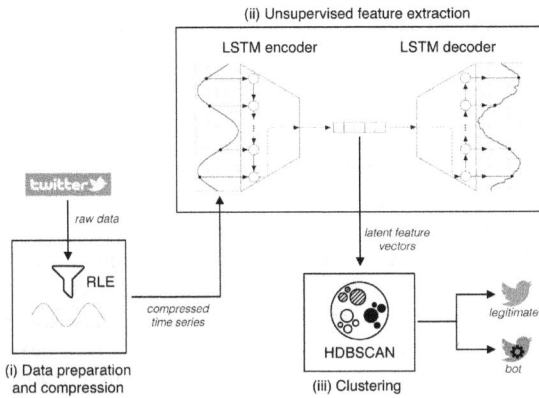

Figure 5: Main logical components of RTBUST.

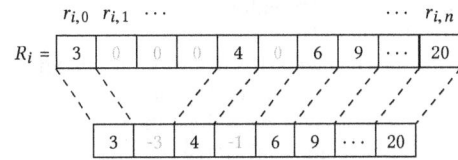

Figure 6: Excerpt of a retweet time series compressed with RLE. Observations affected by RLE are orange-colored.

is to develop a technique that is capable of spotting such suspicious patterns, *as well as possible other patterns* that might exist in a dataset describing temporal retweeting activities. In other words, the technique should be able to automatically identify meaningful patterns from the data, rather than be able to recognize only those patterns that we manually labeled as suspicious.

Thus, building on these considerations, we propose a retweeting bot detection technique, called RETWEET-BUSTER (RTBUST), based on automatic unsupervised feature extraction. Then, in order to implement a group-analysis technique, such automatically-learned features are passed to a density-based clustering algorithm. The rationale for clustering stems from previous research in human and bot behaviors, in that humans have been proven to exhibit much more behavioral heterogeneity than automated accounts [5, 11]. As a consequence, we expect that the heterogeneous humans will not be sufficiently "dense" to be clustered. In fact, they will act pretty much like a background noise in the features space. Conversely, groups of coordinated and synchronized bots will be organized in much denser groups in the features space, thus resulting in nice density-based clusters. In detail, our proposed RTBUST technique is organized in 3 main steps, as also shown in Figure 5: (i) time series data preparation and compression; (ii) unsupervised feature extraction; and (iii) user clustering.

Data preparation and compression. Let t_{REF} be a reference timestamp set at the start of the analysis time window. In our case t_{REF} corresponds to 17 June, 2018 at 00:00:00. Then, $t(x)$ denotes the publication timestamp of tweet ID = x. The raw data exploited to carry out bot detection with RTBUST is the same used in the RTT plots of Section 4, that is tweet and retweet timestamps. In RTBUST such timestamps are organized as a retweet time series $R_i = \{r_{i,0}, r_{i,1}, \ldots, r_{i,n}\}$ for each user u_i, where,

$$r_{i,j} = \begin{cases} |t(x) - t_{REF}| & \text{if } u_i \text{ retweeted tweet ID} = x \text{ at time } t_j \\ 0 & \text{if } u_i \text{ did not retweet at time } t_j \end{cases}$$

The temporal granularity of our time series is that of seconds, which is the same granularity as Twitter timestamps. That is, we have one $r_{i,j}$ observation per second per user. Hence, our time series have a very fine temporal grain. However, overall they are very sparse because users retweet, on average, only once in a few minutes.

At this step, we want to maximize the informativeness of our time series, while minimizing the amount of data to store and process. To beat this trade off, we employ a modified version of the run-length encoding (RLE) compression scheme. RLE is a simple and widely-used lossless sequence compression scheme that encodes consecutive equal data values with one single *<value, length>* tuple. In our case, we use RLE to reduce the sparsity in our time series by compressing the many consecutive zeros that represent no retweeting activity. Since we only need to compress zeros, we do not need to use the typical RLE *<value, length>* tuples. In fact, just the *length* will suffice. We have however to make a distinction between RLE lengths and the $|t(x) - t_{REF}|$ observations that represent retweets. Since by definition, $r_{i,j}$ observations that represent retweets are always positive, one straightforward way to make such distinction is to substitute consecutive zeros with the opposite of RLE lengths. Figure 6 graphically summarizes this data preparation and compression step. As a result of this step, we have one single compact time series for each user. Furthermore, such time series efficiently encodes multiple information, such as inactivity periods as well as tweets and retweets timestamps.

Unsupervised feature extraction. So far, we obtained a compact representation of the temporal retweeting behaviors of our users. Now, we need to turn this representation into a limited number of highly-informative features. Specifically, we have 3 goals for this step: (i) obtain features for a subsequent machine learning task (i.e., density-based clustering) in an unsupervised way; (ii) obtain fixed-length feature vectors, whereas user time series have variable length; (iii) maximize the amount of information in our features, while minimizing the number of features.

Basically, all our goals can be achieved with a well thought out application of dimensionality reduction techniques to our run-length-encoded time series. Specifically, we take a feature projection approach, where we aim to transform our compressed time series into lower-dimensional feature vectors. Feature projection can be achieved via a large number of different techniques. Here, we propose a solution based on *variational autoencoders*, a particular type of deep neural networks, because of their favorable characteristics [29]. In Section 6 we also show comparisons with other dimensionality reduction and feature projection techniques (e.g., PCA, TICA).

Variational autoencoders (VAEs) are an unsupervised learning technique that leverages neural networks for learning a probabilistic representation (i.e., learning features) of the input. As shown in Figure 5, a VAE is composed of 2 main modules: an encoder network and a decoder network. The encoder takes the original input and learns a compressed knowledge representation. Dually, the decoder takes the compressed representation and tries to reconstruct the original input at its best. During the (unsupervised) training phase of the network, the encoder learns to create a meaningful and informative compressed representation of the input, so that the decoder can accurately reconstruct it. Notably, if the input dimensions are largely independent of one another, the compression performed by the encoder results in a loss of valuable information and the subsequent reconstruction becomes a very difficult task. However, if some sort of structure (i.e., patterns) exists in the input data, such as the peculiar patterns that we uncovered in Section 4, that structure can be learned by the encoder and consequently leveraged when converting the input into its compressed representation. In other words, this encoding learns latent features of the input data, which is precisely what we require from this unsupervised feature extraction step. Because deep neural networks are capable of learning nonlinear relationships, this encoding can be thought of as a more powerful generalization of PCA [35]. In our work, the decoder is only used for training the VAE, since we are not really interested in reconstructing our time series. Instead, once trained, the encoder becomes our unsupervised feature extractor. The dimension of the latent feature vector generated by the encoder is a parameter of the VAE, with which we extensively experiment in the next section. The lower the dimension, the more compressed is the representation of the input. However, a low-dimensional representation mitigates possible issues during the subsequent clustering step, caused by the curse of dimensionality [15].

Regarding the deep learning architecture used for implementing the VAE, we relied on a long short-term memory (LSTM) network. LSTMs are well-known and widely used recurrent neural networks. Because of their memory states, they are well-suited for performing tasks on time series, which are often characterized by temporal correlations and by lags of unknown duration between relevant events [23]. Specifically, LSTMs have been proven very accurate at extracting patterns in input space, where input data spans over long sequences. Furthermore, they are also suitable for dealing with sequences of variable length, such as our time series, while still being able to produce fixed-lengths data representations.

User clustering. Now that our users are represented by their latent feature vectors computed by the LSTM encoder, we can apply density-based clustering in order to check for common retweeting behaviors. If large clusters of users are found, then we might have detected a coordinated and synchronized group of accounts, possibly constituting a retweeting botnet. We base our clustering step on a recent efficient algorithm that combines density- and hierarchical-based clustering: HDBSCAN [4]. Among the advantages of this algorithm is its effectiveness in finding clusters with variable degrees of density, a much desirable feature when dealing with noisy real-world data. In addition, HDBSCAN also proved about twice as fast as its predecessor DBSCAN. Regarding algorithm parameters, HDBSCAN removed the need to specify a global density threshold (the ϵ parameter in DBSCAN) by employing an optimization strategy for finding the best cluster stability [4]. The only mandatory parameter to set is the minimum cardinality of the clusters found by HDBSCAN. We experiment with this parameter in the next section. Concluding, after running our density-based

clusering step, we label as bots all those accounts that end up clustered. Conversely, we label as legitimate all those account that are treated as noise (i.e., that are not clustered) by HDBSCAN.

6 EXPERIMENTS AND RESULTS

Here we present results obtained while searching for the best set of parameters of RTBUST, as well as overall bot detection results.

Evaluation methodology. In all the experiments described in this section we analyze all 63,762 accounts of our dataset. Then, we evaluate the effectiveness of different techniques, possibly executed with different configurations of parameters, in correctly classifying the $\simeq 1,000$ annotated accounts. Thus, the bot detection task is framed as a binary classification task, with the 2 classes being: *bot* (positive class) and *human* (negative class). For presenting evaluation results we rely on 5 standard, well-known metrics used for evaluating binary machine learning classifiers, specifically: precision, recall, accuracy, F1-Score ($F1$), and Matthews correlation coefficient (MCC) [37].

Comparisons. While evaluating the bot detection results of RTBUST, we also perform extensive comparisons with other baselines and state-of-the-art techniques for social bot detection.

In Section 5 we grounded the unsupervised feature extraction step of RTBUST on a variational autoencoder. However, a number of other techniques could be used to achieve the same goal. Thus, for the sake of experimentation we implemented 2 more versions of RTBUST that are based respectively on principal component analysis (PCA) and time independent component analysis (TICA) for feature extraction [25]. PCA is a well-known linear statistical technique for dimensionality reduction. By choosing an appropriate number of principal components found by PCA, it is possible to greatly reduce the dimensionality of a problem, while minimizing the loss of information. Similarly, TICA is another dimensionality reduction technique that is particularly suitable for dealing with time series. While PCA finds high-variance linear combinations of the input dimensions, TICA aims to find high-autocorrelation linear combinations. Thus, when using PCA and TICA for feature extraction, the features resulting from PCA are likely to convey different information with respect to those obtained from TICA.

As typically done for many machine learning tasks, we also experiment with a small set of handcrafted features. These features take into account characteristics of the retweet time series of the users (e.g., inter-retweet times, retweeting delays and sessions), as well as other characteristics not available from retweet time series, but that might still contribute to bot detection (e.g., the distribution of retweeted accounts). Table 1 lists the 12 handcrafted features. Notably, some of them – such as inter-retweet times – have been largely used in previous retweeter bot detection systems [24, 43]. In our subsequent experiments, these handcrafted features are tested in RTBUST in place of those automatically extracted by PCA, TICA, and the VAE.

Regarding comparisons with other state-of-the-art bot detection techniques, we experiment with the supervised version of the *Social fingerprinting* technique proposed in [7, 9] and with the unsupervised *HoloScope* technique proposed in [31]. Both techniques are designed to detect synchronized and coordinated groups of bots, and have been briefly described in Section 2. In addition, we also

	feature	description
1	RT users entropy	Shannon entropy of the distribution of retweeted users
2	RT days entropy	Shannon entropy of the distribution of the publication days of retweeted tweets
3	RT rate	number of retweets per time unit
4	daily mean RTs	daily mean of the number of retweets
5	RT days	number of distinct days during which the user retweeted at least once
6	minimum IRT	minimum of the inter-retweet times
7	mean IRT	mean of the inter-retweet times
8	stdev IRT	standard deviation of the inter-retweet times
9	minimum RT delay	minimum of the retweet delays
10	mean RT delay	mean of the retweet delays
11	stdev RT delay	standard deviation of the retweet delays
12	RT sessions	number of detected retweeting sessions

Table 1: List of handcrafted features computed for each user.

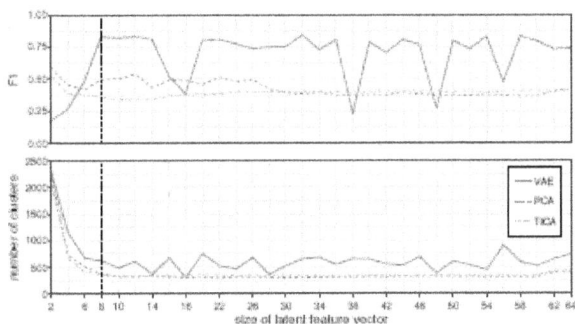

Figure 7: Dependence of clustering stability and bot detection performances on the number of features extracted by PCA, TICA and the VAE. Best results are obtained with the VAE, starting from 8 features (dashed vertical line).

experiment with the *Botometer* system [12]. *Botometer* is a publicly-available service[6] to evaluate the similarity of a Twitter account with the known characteristics of social bots. It leverages an off-the-shelf supervised machine learning classifier that exploits more than 1,000 features of the accounts under investigation. Similarly to the majority of existing systems, *Botometer* performs account-by-account analyses, rather than group analyses.

Finally, as a simple comparison baseline we also try classifying as bots all those accounts whose retweet rate (i.e., retweets per unit of time) is higher than a fixed threshold. We set this threshold as the third quartile of the distribution of retweet rates for our 63,762 accounts. This comparison helps understand if simply looking at the number of retweets is enough for gaining insights into the nature (bot/legitimate) of an account.

Parameters configuration. The most important parameter of RTBUST is the dimension of the latent feature vectors generated by the VAE. It affects both the quality of the subsequent clustering step, which in turn affects bot detection performances, as well as the time/computation needed to complete it. The same also applies

---

[6] https://botometer.iuni.iu.edu

to the number of projected dimensions obtained with PCA or TICA. Thus, we designed an experiment to evaluate the performances of RTBUST, implemented with VAE, PCA, and TICA for feature extraction, in relation to the number of considered latent features.

Figure 7 shows results for this experiment, in terms of the overall $F1$ obtained for the classification of bots and humans, and of the total number of clusters found by HDBSCAN. Regarding the number of clusters, all 3 implementations show the same qualitative behavior. When considering a very limited number of features, HDBSCAN finds a large number of clusters. Increasing the number of features results in fewer clusters, up to a point (size of latent feature vector = 10) where the number of clusters stops decreasing. Regarding bot detection performance, Figure 7 shows a very different behavior between the VAE implementation of RTBUST, with respect to the PCA and TICA ones. Features extracted by PCA and TICA seem to provide significantly less information for bot detection with respect to those extracted by the VAE, as demonstrated by a lower $F1$. Moreover, increasing the number of considered PCA and TICA features seems of no help, since the $F1$ remains almost the same for each latent feature vector size. Instead, the VAE implementation shows a behavior that is consistent with the results obtained for the number of clusters. The $F1$ rapidly increases when considering a larger number of features, up to a point (size of latent feature vector = 8) where it reaches and maintains its maximum (apart from a few fluctuations). Overall, these results demonstrate that the VAE is much more powerful than PCA and TICA for the unsupervised feature extraction from our retweet time series. Furthermore, as little as 8 VAE features seem to be enough for stabilizing the clustering and achieving good bot detection results.

We repeated this experiment by also varying the minimum cluster cardinality (i.e., the only HDBSCAN parameter). We omit detailed results due to space limitations, however we report finding the best results with clusters larger than 10 accounts, a threshold that is both intuitive (i.e., it is not very meaningful to look for minuscule botnets) and operationally effective.

Quantitative evaluation of bot detection. Next, we present detailed bot detection results for all the considered techniques. For the VAE, PCA and TICA implementations of RTBUST, we use only 8 features, leveraging results of our previous experiment.

Table 2 shows retweeter bot detection results. The best detection performances ($F1 = 0.87$) are achieved by the proposed RTBUST technique using the VAE for unsupervised feature extraction. In fact, it beats all other competitors in each evaluation metric, with the only exception of the *recall* metric. All other implementations of RTBUST achieve worse results, with $F1 \leq 0.67$. As anticipated, this is a strong point in favor of the VAE for extracting informative features from our retweet time series. The second best overall results are obtained by the *Social fingerprinting*, achieving an encouraging $F1 = 0.76$. Instead, the other state-of-the-art techniques obtain much worse results, with *Botometer*'s $F1 = 0.43$ and *Holo-Scope*'s $F1 = 0.01$. Interestingly, the majority of evaluated techniques achieve their worst results in the *precision* metric, meaning that many legitimate accounts are misclassified as bots. This results is in contrast with previous results in bot detection [8]. However, previous works mainly experimented with supervised techniques, while here we mainly explore unsupervised ones. Thus, combined

technique	type	features	evaluation metrics				
			precision	*recall*	*accuracy*	*F1*	*MCC*
baseline							
retweet rate	–	1	0.3534	0.3585	0.3440	0.3559	−0.3124
comparisons							
Botometer [12]	supervised	> 1, 000	0.6951	0.3098	0.5830	0.4286	0.2051
HoloScope [31]	unsupervised	–	0.2857	0.0049	0.4908	0.0096	−0.0410
Social fingerprinting [7, 9]	supervised	–	0.6562	0.8978	0.7114	0.7582	0.4536
our contributions							
RTBUST (handcrafted features)	unsupervised	12	0.5284	0.7707	0.5364	0.6270	0.0767
RTBUST (PCA)	unsupervised	8	0.5111	**0.9512**	0.5154	0.6649	0.0446
RTBUST (TICA)	unsupervised	8	0.5228	**0.9512**	0.5364	0.6747	0.1168
RTBUST (VAE)	unsupervised	8	**0.9304**	0.8146	**0.8755**	**0.8687**	**0.7572**

Table 2: Retweeter bot detection results of RTBUST and comparison with a baseline and other state-of-the-art techniques. Best results in each evaluation metric are shown in bold.

Figure 8: Visual exploration of RTBUST (VAE) bot detection results, and comparison with t-SNE.

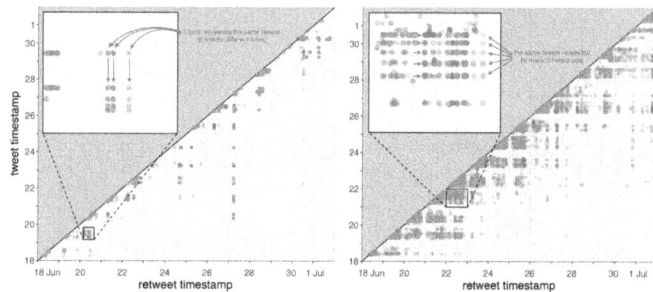

(a) *Cars* botnet.

(b) *Singer* botnet.

Figure 9: RTT plots of the 2 botnets discovered with RTBUST.

Figure 10: A subset of accounts from the *singer* botnet.

results of our study and previous ones might suggest that supervised approaches to social bot detection are more prone to type II errors (false negatives), while unsupervised approaches are more prone to type I errors (false positives).

In Figure 8, we use t-SNE [33] for plotting our annotated accounts in a bi-dimensional space, where each account is colored according to the RTBUST (VAE) cluster it belongs to, and 2 different symbols represent bots and legitimate accounts according to our ground truth. Since in RTBUST each clustered account is labeled as bot while unclustered ones are labeled as humans, by comparing colors and symbols of the accounts in figure, it is possible to visually assess the quality of bot classification. Furthermore, Figure 8 also allows a comparison between our clustering and that resulting from t-SNE. Regarding bot detection, we can see few clustered legitimate accounts. Similarly, only a minority of bots are grey-colored (i.e., unclustered). Concerning the comparison between t-SNE and RTBUST, the 2 algorithms produce rather different clusters. For instance, multiple RTBUST clusters collapse in a single t-SNE cluster and vice versa. However, the overall distinction between bots and humans seem to hold for both RTBUST and t-SNE. The majority of legitimate accounts are both grey-colored and spread across the central region of Figure 8. In other words, they do not belong to any cluster neither for t-SNE nor for RTBUST. Dually, the

majority of bots appear as colored and positioned near other bots. Thus, both t-SNE and RTBUST seem to recognize bot similarities although organizing the bots differently, despite the very different inner functioning of the 2 techniques. Given the usefulness and widespread application of t-SNE, these similarities support results of RTBUST (VAE).

Qualitative evaluation of bot detection. Given the good results achieved by RTBUST (VAE) at spotting the annotated bots in our dataset, we now analyze also those non-annotated accounts that have been labeled as bots by the same technique. This manual and qualitative validation might serve as an additional evaluation of the outcomes of RTBUST.

In particular, RTBUST found 2 notable clusters of non-annotated accounts. The smallest of such clusters counts 44 accounts. A manual inspection of these accounts revealed that they actually belong to a small botnet with some peculiar characteristics. First and foremost, they almost only retweet 3 accounts (@peugeotitalia, @citroenitalia and @motorionline). Thus, this botnet has a specific focus on cars. Moreover, they only post retweets or images, no account of the botnet has a real profile picture, and they are loosely synchronized, meaning that they tend to retweet the same tweets but at different moments in time. In order to get further insights into their behavior, we produced a combined RTT visualization of all the accounts of the botnet, as shown in Figure 9a. Each point in figure is a retweet made by one of the botnet's account and colors represent different bots. Interestingly, clear patterns emerge in some portions of the RTT plot, as seen in the inset of Figure 9a. Such patterns testify the synchronized retweeting activity of the botnet.

The other notable cluster of bot accounts found by RTBUST is composed of almost 300 accounts that almost exclusively retweet 2 accounts (@Valerio_Scanu and @ArmataScanu). Similarly to the previous smaller botnet, also this larger one seems to retweet with a specific focus – that is, publicizing tweets related to the Italian pop singer Valerio Scanu[7]. Figure 9b shows the RTT plot of this botnet, which exhibits a mixture of the triangular and waterfall patterns that we described in Section 4. Figure 10 also displays the appearance of the profiles of some of these accounts. As seen, some accounts of the botnet are tightly synchronized, while the botnet as a whole is loosely synchronized.

This qualitative evaluation revealed that, not only did RTBUST achieve good results on the annotated accounts, but it also allowed to discover 2 previously unknown active retweeting botnets.

7 DISCUSSION

Visualizing suspicious behaviors. In this work we provided several contributions. The first of such contributions is the development of the RTT visualization. In figures 4 and 9 we showed that RTT plots represent a useful tool for analyzing the retweeting behavior of an account, or of a group of accounts. Human analysts can gain valuable insights into the behaviors of suspicious accounts by leveraging RTT plots. The possibility to leverage RTT plots might be particularly valuable in future data annotation tasks, considering the current difficulties faced by human annotators in correctly labeling social bots [8]. Another favorable application scenario is related to the banning of bots from OSNs. Indeed, despite the recent advances in machine learning-based detectors, manual verification of accounts to assess their degree of automation is still carried out by OSN administrators [16]. To this end, RTT plots might contribute to speed-up the process and to reduce possible human mistakes.

Notably, a few previous works also proposed some simple visualizations with the goal of highlighting suspicious behaviors in OSNs [18, 26, 27]. However, previous visualizations for spotting suspicious behaviors require much more data than that needed by RTT

plots. For example, the visualizations used in [26] are based on the full social graph of considered accounts. Similarly, the visualizations proposed in [18] require building retweet threads/cascades, which in turn require friend/followers information of each retweeter. Conversely, with RTT plots we can spot suspicious retweeting behaviors with as little information as retweet-tweet timestamps.

Generalizability and robustness. Our second, and largest, contribution is the development of the RETWEET-BUSTER (RTBUST) bot detection technique. RTBUST is an unsupervised technique that is capable of automatically spotting meaningful patterns in retweet data. Because of this feature, RTBUST is potentially capable of detecting retweeting bots exhibiting a behavior that has not been witnessed before. We believe this to be an important feature, considering that we still lack a "standard" and "well-agreed" definition of what a social bot is [34, 44] – and consequently, of its expected behaviors [1]. Hence, the capability to spot a broad set of different behaviors, surely comes in handy. Moreover, it has been now largely demonstrated that social bots do *evolve* to escape detection techniques [8, 42]. Thus, the generalizability of RTBUST and its robustness to evasion is a much desirable feature because it allows us to better withstand the next evolution of social bots.

Explainability. Model and decision explainability has now become one of the major practical and ethical concerns around AI [22]. To this regard, one of the possible drawbacks of RTBUST lies in the difficulty to "explain" the reasons for labeling an account as bot or legitimate. This is largely due to the difficulty in interpreting the latent features used for clustering, which in turn depend on the adoption of the "black-box" variational autoencoder for unsupervised feature extraction. This issue is not peculiar of our technique, but it is rather a well-known limitation of all deep learning techniques [22]. Here, to mitigate this issue we again propose to resort to RTT plots. As demonstrated in Figure 9, our visualization can be profitably used also *after* the application of RTBUST, with the goal of understanding the characteristics of those accounts that have been labeled as bots.

8 CONCLUSIONS

In this work, we investigated patterns of retweeting activity on Twitter, with the specific goal of detecting malicious retweeting bots. To this end, our work provides several contributions.

Firstly, we proposed a novel visualization technique called RETWEET-TWEET (RTT). As thoroughly shown, RTT plots are an effective and efficient mean to gain valuable insights into the retweeting behaviors of Twitter accounts. By leveraging RTT plots we analyzed the "normal" retweeting behavior of legitimate users, and we uncovered 3 suspicious behaviors that are caused by automated retweeting – and thus, that are representative of bot activities. Furthermore, we discussed how RTT plots can empower human analysts when manually annotating a dataset comprising social bots, as well as OSN administrators looking for evidence of automation when deciding about banning accounts from social platforms. Finally, we highlighted that RTT plots can also be used to explain decisions of black-box bot detectors, thus contributing towards explainable and interpretable AI.

Next, we designed an unsupervised group-analysis technique, called RETWEET-BUSTER (RTBUST), for detecting retweeting social

---

[7] https://en.wikipedia.org/wiki/Valerio_Scanu

bots. The core of RTBUST is an LSTM variational autoencoder that we trained to extract a minimum number of highly informative latent features from the retweet time series of each account. The decision about an account (whether it is bot or legitimate) is based on the outcome of a hierarchical density-based clustering algorithm. In detail, accounts belonging to large clusters are labeled as bots, while unclustered accounts are labeled as legitimate. We compared different implementations of RTBUST with baselines and state-of-the-art social bot detection techniques. RTBUST outperformed all competitors achieving $F1 = 0.87$, in contrast with $F1 \leq 0.76$ of other techniques. By applying RTBUST to a large dataset of retweets, we also discovered 2 previously unknown active botnets comprising hundreds of accounts.

For future work we plan to improve the decisions taken by RTBUST. In fact, here we adopted a rather naive solution revolving around accounts being clustered or not. However, we can augment the final decision step of RTBUST by considering additional information, such as the hierarchy of clusters produced by the clustering algorithm and other internal and external clustering validation measures. In this way, we could prune some clusters or some accounts belonging to a cluster, thus improving *precision*. Similarly, we could expand some clusters by adding borderline accounts, thus possibly also improving *recall*, which currently is the bottleneck of RTBUST. Other than improving RTBUST, we also plan to apply it *in the wild* for discovering and analyzing active botnets.

REFERENCES

[1] Abdullah Almaatouq, Ahmad Alabdulkareem, Mariam Nouh, Erez Shmueli, Mansour Alsaleh, Vivek K Singh, Abdulrahman Alarifi, Anas Alfaris, and Alex Sandy Pentland. 2014. Twitter: who gets caught? observed trends in social microblogging spam. In *ACM WebSci*.
[2] Marco Avvenuti, Salvatore Bellomo, Stefano Cresci, Mariantonietta Noemi La Polla, and Maurizio Tesconi. 2017. Hybrid crowdsensing: A novel paradigm to combine the strengths of opportunistic and participatory crowdsensing. In *ACM WWW Companion*.
[3] Alessandro Bessi, Mauro Coletto, George Alexandru Davidescu, Antonio Scala, Guido Caldarelli, and Walter Quattrociocchi. 2015. Science vs conspiracy: Collective narratives in the age of misinformation. *PloS one* 10, 2 (2015).
[4] Ricardo JGB Campello, Davoud Moulavi, and Jörg Sander. 2013. Density-based clustering based on hierarchical density estimates. In *PAKDD*.
[5] Nikan Chavoshi, Hossein Hamooni, and Abdullah Mueen. 2016. DeBot: Twitter Bot Detection via Warped Correlation. In *IEEE ICDM*.
[6] Stefano Cresci, Roberto Di Pietro, Marinella Petrocchi, Angelo Spognardi, and Maurizio Tesconi. 2015. Fame for sale: Efficient detection of fake Twitter followers. *Decision Support Systems* 80 (2015).
[7] Stefano Cresci, Roberto Di Pietro, Marinella Petrocchi, Angelo Spognardi, and Maurizio Tesconi. 2016. DNA-inspired online behavioral modeling and its application to spambot detection. *IEEE Intelligent Systems* 31, 5 (2016).
[8] Stefano Cresci, Roberto Di Pietro, Marinella Petrocchi, Angelo Spognardi, and Maurizio Tesconi. 2017. The Paradigm-Shift of Social Spambots: Evidence, Theories, and Tools for the Arms Race. In *ACM WWW Companion*.
[9] Stefano Cresci, Roberto Di Pietro, Marinella Petrocchi, Angelo Spognardi, and Maurizio Tesconi. 2018. Social Fingerprinting: detection of spambot groups through DNA-inspired behavioral modeling. *IEEE TDSC* 15, 4 (2018).
[10] Stefano Cresci, Marinella Petrocchi, Angelo Spognardi, and Stefano Tognazzi. 2019. On the capability of evolved spambots to evade detection via genetic engineering. *Online Social Networks and Media* 9 (2019).
[11] Stefano Cresci, Roberto Di Pietro, Marinella Petrocchi, Angelo Spognardi, and Maurizio Tesconi. 2017. Exploiting digital DNA for the analysis of similarities in Twitter behaviours. In *IEEE DSAA*.
[12] Clayton Allen Davis, Onur Varol, Emilio Ferrara, Alessandro Flammini, and Filippo Menczer. 2016. BotOrNot: A System to Evaluate Social Bots. In *ACM WWW Companion*.
[13] Michela Del Vicario, Alessandro Bessi, Fabiana Zollo, Fabio Petroni, Antonio Scala, Guido Caldarelli, H Eugene Stanley, and Walter Quattrociocchi. 2016. The spreading of misinformation online. *PNAS* 113, 3 (2016).
[14] Michela Del Vicario, Gianna Vivaldo, Alessandro Bessi, Fabiana Zollo, Antonio Scala, Guido Caldarelli, and Walter Quattrociocchi. 2016. Echo chambers: Emotional contagion and group polarization on facebook. *Scientific reports* 6 (2016).
[15] Pedro Domingos. 2012. A few useful things to know about machine learning. *Commun. ACM* 55, 10 (2012).
[16] Emilio Ferrara, Onur Varol, Clayton Davis, Filippo Menczer, and Alessandro Flammini. 2016. The rise of social bots. *Commun. ACM* 59, 7 (2016).
[17] Syeda Nadia Firdaus, Chen Ding, and Alireza Sadeghian. 2018. Retweet: A popular information diffusion mechanism–A survey paper. *Online Social Networks and Media* 6 (2018).
[18] Maria Giatsoglou, Despoina Chatzakou, Neil Shah, Christos Faloutsos, and Athena Vakali. 2015. Retweeting activity on twitter: Signs of deception. In *PAKDD*.
[19] Zafar Gilani, Ekaterina Kochmar, and Jon Crowcroft. 2017. Classification of twitter accounts into automated agents and human users. In *IEEE/ACM ASONAM*.
[20] Manuel Gomez-Rodriguez, Krishna P Gummadi, and Bernhard Schoelkopf. 2014. Quantifying Information Overload in Social Media and Its Impact on Social Contagions. In *AAAI ICWSM*.
[21] Christian Grimme, Dennis Assenmacher, and Lena Adam. 2018. Changing Perspectives: Is It Sufficient to Detect Social Bots?. In *SCSM*.
[22] Riccardo Guidotti, Anna Monreale, Salvatore Ruggieri, Franco Turini, Fosca Giannotti, and Dino Pedreschi. 2018. A survey of methods for explaining black box models. *ACM CSUR* 51, 5 (2018).
[23] Tian Guo, Zhao Xu, Xin Yao, Haifeng Chen, Karl Aberer, and Koichi Funaya. 2016. Robust online time series prediction with recurrent neural networks. In *IEEE DSAA*.
[24] Sonu Gupta, Ponnurangam Kumaraguru, and Tanmoy Chakraborty. 2019. MalReG: Detecting and Analyzing Malicious Retweeter Groups. In *ACM CoDS-COMAD*.
[25] Carlos X Hernández, Hannah K Wayment-Steele, Mohammad M Sultan, Brooke E Husic, and Vijay S Pande. 2018. Variational encoding of complex dynamics. *Physical Review E* 97, 6 (2018).
[26] Meng Jiang, Peng Cui, Alex Beutel, Christos Faloutsos, and Shiqiang Yang. 2016. Catching Synchronized Behaviors in Large Networks: A Graph Mining Approach. *ACM TKDD* 10, 4 (2016).
[27] Meng Jiang, Peng Cui, Alex Beutel, Christos Faloutsos, and Shiqiang Yang. 2016. Inferring lockstep behavior from connectivity pattern in large graphs. *KAIS* 48, 2 (2016).
[28] Christian Kater and Robert Jäschke. 2016. You shall not pass: detecting malicious users at registration time. In *ACM WebSci Workshops*.
[29] Diederik P Kingma and Max Welling. 2013. Auto-encoding variational bayes. In *IEEE ICML*.
[30] Sangho Lee and Jong Kim. 2014. Early filtering of ephemeral malicious accounts on Twitter. *Computer Communications* 54 (2014).
[31] Shenghua Liu, Bryan Hooi, and Christos Faloutsos. 2017. HoloScope: Topology-and-Spike Aware Fraud Detection. In *ACM CIKM*.
[32] Shenghua Liu, Bryan Hooi, and Christos Faloutsos. 2018. A Contrast Metric for Fraud Detection in Rich Graphs. *IEEE TKDE* (2018).
[33] Laurens van der Maaten and Geoffrey Hinton. 2008. Visualizing data using t-SNE. *Journal of machine learning research* (2008).
[34] Gregory Maus. 2017. A Typology of Socialbots (Abbrev.). In *ACM WebSci*.
[35] Qinxue Meng, Daniel Catchpoole, David Skillicom, and Paul J Kennedy. 2017. Relational autoencoder for feature extraction. In *IEEE IJCNN*.
[36] Zachary Miller, Brian Dickinson, William Deitrick, Wei Hu, and Alex Hai Wang. 2014. Twitter spammer detection using data stream clustering. *Information Sciences* 260 (2014).
[37] David Martin Ward Powers. 2011. Evaluation: from Precision, Recall and F-Measure to ROC, informedness, markedness and correlation. *International Journal of Machine Learning Technologies* 2, 1 (2011).
[38] Walter Quattrociocchi. 2017. Inside the echo chamber. *Scientific American* 316, 4 (2017).
[39] Saiph Savage, Andres Monroy-Hernandez, and Tobias Höllerer. 2016. Botivist: Calling volunteers to action using online bots. In *ACM CSCW*.
[40] Massimo Stella, Emilio Ferrara, and Manlio De Domenico. 2018. Bots increase exposure to negative and inflammatory content in online social systems. *PNAS* 115, 49 (2018).
[41] L Steward, Ahmer Arif, and Kate Starbird. 2018. Examining Trolls and Polarization with a Retweet Network. In *ACM WSDM Workshops*.
[42] Stefano Tognazzi, Stefano Cresci, Marinella Petrocchi, and Angelo Spognardi. 2018. From Reaction to Proaction: Unexplored Ways to the Detection of Evolving Spambots. In *ACM WWW Companion*.
[43] Nguyen Vo, Kyumin Lee, Cheng Cao, Thanh Tran, and Hongkyu Choi. 2017. Revealing and detecting malicious retweeter groups. In *IEEE/ACM ASONAM*.
[44] Kai-Cheng Yang, Onur Varol, Clayton A Davis, Emilio Ferrara, Alessandro Flammini, and Filippo Menczer. 2019. Arming the public with AI to counter social bots. *Human Behavior and Emerging Technologies* (2019).
[45] Fabiana Zollo, Alessandro Bessi, Michela Del Vicario, Antonio Scala, Guido Caldarelli, Louis Shekhtman, Shlomo Havlin, and Walter Quattrociocchi. 2017. Debunking in a world of tribes. *PloS one* 12, 7 (2017).

As the Tweet, so the Reply? Gender Bias in Digital Communication with Politicians

Armin Mertens
Cologne Center for Comparative Politics
Cologne, Germany
mertens@wiso.uni-koeln.de

Franziska Pradel
Cologne Center for Comparative Politics
Cologne, Germany
pradel@wiso.uni-koeln.de

Ayjeren Rozyjumayeva
Faculty of Management, Economics and Social Sciences
Cologne, Germany
rozyjumayeva@wiso.uni-koeln.de

Jens Wäckerle
Cologne Center for Comparative Politics
Cologne, Germany
jens.waeckerle@uni-koeln.de

ABSTRACT

This study investigates gender bias in political interactions on digital platforms by considering how politicians present themselves on Twitter and how they are approached by others. Incorporating social identity theory, we use dictionary analyses to detect biases in individual tweets connected to the German federal elections in 2017. Besides sentiment analysis, we introduce a new measure of personal- vs. job-related content in text data, that is validated with structural topic models. Our results indicate that politicians' communication on Twitter is driven by party identity rather than gender. However, we find systematic gender differences in tweets directed at politicians: female politicians are significantly more likely to be reduced to their gender rather than to their profession compared to male politicians.

CCS CONCEPTS

• **General and reference** → **Empirical studies**; • **Information systems** → **Social networking sites**.

KEYWORDS

bias, dictionary analysis, gender, topic models, twitter

ACM Reference Format:
Armin Mertens, Franziska Pradel, Ayjeren Rozyjumayeva, and Jens Wäckerle. 2019. As the Tweet, so the Reply? Gender Bias in Digital Communication with Politicians. In *11th ACM Conference on Web Science (WebSci '19)*, June 30–July 3, 2019, Boston, MA, USA. ACM, New York, NY, USA, 9 pages. https://doi.org/10.1145/3292522.3326013

1 INTRODUCTION

> "Why do you even care for the #BER [Berlin airport] opening? Because you have to choose your clothes for the opening ceremony??"[1]

This tweet directed at a female German politician resembles an often observed and reported phenomenon in our digital society: digital communication is driven by gender stereotypes rather than job-related content. This, in turn, can lead to bias and discrimination towards female professionals. Building on insights from research on social identities [60, 61] as well as gender biases and gender roles in politics [1, 9, 52], we expect to find gender biased communication on Twitter coming from — but also directed at — politicians. One of the key elements of social identity theory is group membership and categorization: individuals have several identities (i.e. categorizations) assigned by themselves and by others. In politics, a female political candidate can have several identities such as a politician, party member, mother or wife. Based on our own identities and those we assign to others we have different expectations, behave, and engage accordingly with others. Linked to this cognitive process, stereotypes and prejudices can emerge that are related to group categorization [60, 61].

Uncovering gender biased communication on Twitter is especially important since gender stereotypes impact the assessment of politicians and their perceived eligibility for being in office [19, 20, 32, 41]. Little knowledge exists, however, on how gender roles and biases interact in social media communication and how they can be analyzed systematically. Hence, our research extends the current literature by uncovering whether and how politicians are treated differently based on their gender and how this aligns with the presentation of politicians themselves within social networks.

This paper takes up the challenge of identifying latent gender biases in digital communication by analyzing 22.12 million tweets that were collected during the German federal elections in 2017.[2] After pre-processing and subsetting the data into tweets *by* and tweets *at* politicians, we apply two different dictionaries to the

---

[1] The original tweet in German can be accessed via: https://twitter.com/KohlmeierSPD/status/772378753032937472?ref_src=twsrc.
[2] The dataset containing the relevant tweet IDs was collected by GESIS [58] and can be accessed via: doi:10.4232/1.12992. All replication materials are available here: https://github.com/arminmertens/ACM_digital_communication

data: (1) We assess the sentiment of each tweet by calculating the *log* ratio of positive to negative words. The dictionary is validated with human coding and has been shown to accurately capture dynamics in political science [47]. (2) We introduce a new measure quantifying gender bias in digital communication on Twitter: a ratio of personal- versus job-related words using LIWC-dictionaries [62]. For personal-related words, the "family", "friends" and "leisure" dictionaries are used while job-related words are captured with the "work" dictionary. The resulting measure can identify whether a tweet is covering more private and personal or professional and job-related communication. We validate the new dictionary using structural topic models [50]. To estimate the effects of gender and political party affiliations on the resulting dictionary measures, different mixed-effects models and predicted values are calculated (see Section 3).

Overall, we find evidence that politicians tend to behave more according to party ideology than their gender identity on Twitter. Additionally, government politicians are more positive than opposition politicians. We also do not find more personal- than job-related tweets by politicians of either sex, suggesting that politicians on Twitter behave more according to their professional identity as party or government members. However, digital communication directed *at* politicians is mainly a function of the politicians' gender, with tweets at female politicians being more personal than tweets at male politicians. Furthermore, tweets directed at politicians are more positive for right-leaning women and left-leaning men. One of the main contributions of this paper is the combination of sentiment analyses with a new personal- versus job-related communication measure uncovering gender bias in the content of tweets. Finally, our findings on substantial differences between tweets directed at politicians and communicated by them provides an empirical test of assumptions of social identity theory on online platforms.

2 RELATED WORK

Politicians and Twitter

Twitter arguably became one of the most important communication arenas in daily political life of many citizens. Initially conceived as a website to share personal status updates, it has now more than 335 million users globally sharing an average of 500 million tweets per day. One distinct characteristic of this social network platform is the presence of not only individuals but also private and public institutions and organizations. Virtually every legislator, political party and candidate in developed democracies has an active Twitter account. Irrespective of their offline identities, they all interact within the same linguistic and symbolic framework. This plethora of data allows social scientists to test a variety of questions.

Theoretical and empirical research. Social science research done on Twitter is diverse both methodologically as well as theoretically. Although reviewing all of Twitter research is beyond the scope of the current article, we review some of the major branches related to our paper. While the vast majority of research focusing on Twitter are purely empirical [35], some studies within political communication and behavior studies are providing a fertile ground for theory-driven research.

Changing the nature of media systems. Addressing the question from the media systems perspective, for instance, Chadwick [16] argues that new media actors, such as Twitter, Facebook and Google, are redefining the power relationships between more traditional institutions. Traditional media is considered to have an important role in keeping public and private institutions accountable to the masses [30]. But with ever more competitive markets, traditional media is becoming both more exclusive and less trusted by the general public. By studying how the gate-keeping role of traditional media outlets is challenged by the newly emerging actors, Chadwick [16] concludes that Western democracies have entered the age of hybrid media systems. Theoretical background to the hybrid media systems research is provided by established areas of communication research. Namely, communication theories on agenda setting [14, 45, 55], framing [27, 34] as well as selective exposure [4, 53].

Political mobilization and protest. Research on mobilization through social networks emerged in the early 2000s with studies focusing on how political actors in the United States mobilized voters through newly emerging personal websites [31, 48]. Due to its geographic focus on the US, the research primarily focused on how emerging technologies are changing the ad-driven nature of political campaigning. Specifically, studies investigate how political actors strategize (try to involve, connect and mobilize citizens) [31] through newly emerging platforms [5] and how campaign communication differs based on gender [18, 54].

Political polarization and opinion formation. Yet another variable through which the effect of Twitter-driven communication is being tested is connected to political polarization and attitude formation [63]. The findings, however, are still inconclusive as to what exactly this technology does to polarization. Liang and Nordin [39] find that high-speed internet access increases online news consumption but has little to no impact on political attitudes. Using quasi-random variation in broadband internet access due to state-level, right-of-way legislation, Lelkes [38] argues that social media platforms exacerbate already existing political tensions. Thus, many argue that the introduction of social networking sites as a prevalent communication tool is contributing to this trend [24]. Empirical evidence of echo-chambers in online communication networks suggests that Internet and social media may aggravate political polarization [2, 17, 59]. That is, research on homogeneous communication networks offline is simply replicated on Internet platforms [6, 25, 29].

On the other hand, Newman et al. [43] find that people who use social networks are exposed to diverse news at a greater rate than people who do not use social networks. This is not surprising if we consider that the majority of ties in any user's personal network are weak — acquaintances, co-workers and distant relatives. Weak ties play a key role in information diffusion on social media [7]. They are important because of their contribution to the spread of novel information which has a higher chance of being ideologically diverse. Barberá [8] provides rigorous empirical evidence of this statement by analyzing how a user following at least one political account becomes slightly more moderate. Finally, Boxell et al. [12] suggest that the relationship between internet and polarization is likely to be complicated and is a function of a particular citizen's level of engagement with news and politics. Lastly, most recent research on Twitter deals with questions of political misinformation and fake news [28, 33, 37]. Actors spreading false information are arguably enabled by the advertising-driven nature of social media networks [3, 37].

Politicians, gender and online platforms

Prior research on gender and politics, more generally, has shown that the activation of stereotypes impacts the evaluation of candidates and voting decisions [9, 52]. Similarly, a study by Aalberg [1] revealed that gender stereotypes lead to changes in the assessment of politicians, their communication and party support. This bias might treat women either as less capable for politics compared to men, or not fit for political office altogether [19, 20, 32, 41]. However, while candidate gender may be a convenient way to make a judgment in an experimental setting, this situation might not be transferable to real voting decisions [21]. Additionally, men and women are attributed with different strengths in politics: men are considered to be more competent in aspects of military and national security, while women ought to be more compassionate [20, 36]. Gender stereotypes might therefore hurt women in some situations, but give them an advantage in others [52].

In the digital age, online platforms such as Twitter, Wikipedia, Facebook and search engines give voters access to information and the possibility to engage with politicians. However, studies found structural gender biases inherent in these platforms. Women are structurally underrepresented on Wikipedia [26, 65] and there are differences in the presence and interaction on Twitter such as women being less retweeted and followed [40].

Twitter is a special case since it allows politicians to communicate with their voters, to campaign and to represent themselves. Likewise, voters have the chance to interact directly with them or to talk about them with a greater audience. Research has, however, repeatedly shown that the tweets with politicians resemble gender stereotypical communication [22, 23, 42, 65].

While politicians change their Twitter communication during campaigning not only their communication style, but also its impact on electoral success, vary with the gender of the politician [42]. For example, research showed that U.S. Senate candidates were more interactive on Twitter when they were women. Both women and men used a more personalized communication style (also termed "feminine communication style"), which can be viewed as a beneficial strategy for mimicking direct (face-to-face) communication [42].

Focusing on gender biased communication with related professionals, research [64] revealed that female political journalists for the U.S. Congress mainly interchange with other women, but men mainly with other men on Twitter. Similarly, Parmelee et al. [46] showed that the behavior of journalists and their interaction on twitter is varying with their gender and generation by using a content analysis of tweets from US political journalists. Their research examined the interactivity by manually categorizing the type of interactivity and the type of users by human coders. Their results suggest that while men were significantly more active in mutual discourse than women, women engaged significantly more in responsive dialogue. Furthermore, their study provided insights

into the interaction with politicians. Male journalists engaged more than twice as much as politicians compared to female journalists.

3 METHODS

In order to detect gender differences in the communication with politicians on Twitter, we construct two measures with automated text analyses: first, we shed light on the sentiment of tweets. The sentiment measure creates a log ratio of positive to negative words that have been identified with cross-country validated dictionaries. Second, we introduce a new measure quantifying whether a tweet is covering more personal or professional communication.

Sentiment

We use a sentiment dictionary as proposed by Proksch et al. [47]. It creates a log ratio of positive to negative words and has been shown to accurately capture dynamics in political science, with positive numbers indicating positive sentiment. The dictionary is validated with human coding (for details see [47]). It is based on the Lexicoder Sentiment Dictionary (LSD), which was then translated to German [66].

$$sentiment = log\left(\frac{positive\ words + 0.5}{negative\ words + 0.5}\right) \tag{1}$$

The LSD tries to achieve both high recall (detecting a wide range of sentiment words), but also high precision (not detecting many false positives). In practice, this is not easy: some words might be associated with positive speech (e.g. military power during wartime) at one point in time and for a certain part of the public, while they are not used positively in other times or by other people. Therefore, the LSD mainly consists of words that are clearly dealing with issues of affection and emotion while avoiding policy-related terms. This approach has been used to study newspaper coverage [56, 57] and legislative debates [47] and we propose to extend this to political use of social media.[3]

Personal- versus job-related communication

Research on gender roles and stereotypes argues and provides evidence that women are generally taken less serious and perceived as less competent compared to men [1, 13]. Therefore, it is reasonable to expect that female politicians receive more personal rather than professional tweets. Following the procedure of Proksch et al. [47] for constructing a sentiment measure, we understand the personal-versus job-related communication measure as a "one-dimensional quantity expressed using a relatively language-specific and possibly institutionally fixed set of lexical resources". A log ratio of personal- versus job-related words is therefore constructed (see table 1)[4] by using a combination of LIWC-dictionaries [62] that relate either to personal and private words ("family", "friends" and "leisure" dictionary) or job-related words ("work" dictionary). LIWC dictionaries have initially been constructed in order to have a new

---

[3]We expect the dictionary to work adequately at high levels of aggregation. This means that at the level of the individual tweet, a dictionary approach will often have difficulty classifying the tweet as positive or negative, while human coding will typically manage to do so.
[4]The words in table 1 have been translated, original words of the dictionary are in German.

efficient analysis procedure covering psychological processes in the content of writings or talking and it has repeatedly been validated [62].

$$personal \ vs. \ job = log \left(\frac{personal + 0.5}{job + 0.5} \right) \qquad (2)$$

The resulting measure uncovers personal- relative to role-related information. Thus, a more positive score indicates more personal- compared to job-related tweets, while a more negative one suggests more job- compared to personal-related tweets.

Personal	Job
family (e.g. "children", "husband")	work (e.g. "meeting", "office", "project", "colleague", "negotiate", "contract")
friends (e.g. "boyfriend", "friend") leisure (e.g. 'beach", "cinema")	

Table 1: Constructing dictionaries for "personal" and "job"-related communication

Structural Topic Models

As a complementing measure to dictionary-based analysis, we also look at the results of a more automated text analysis. Namely, we applied topic modelling to our dataset to find if there are additional or contradictory insights to be gained. Topic modelling is one branch of text mining which allows for automatic pattern detection in a large body of unstructured text. The basic goal of topic modelling is to identify topics across documents. Topics consist of specific words and any single document can contain several topics. While there is a variety of different implementations of topic modelling, one of the most frequently used models is the Latent Dirichlet Allocation (LDA) and its various extensions. LDA models define topics as clusters of words that tend to co-occur. Clusters are then compared by a variety of semantic similarity measures. To find these co-occurring clusters, software combs through a textual corpus and compares the occurrence of topics within individual documents to the assignment of clusters in other documents to find the best matches[10, 11].

We chose to use one of the recent LDA-based topic modelling methods called structural topic modelling (STM). The STM's major advantage is that it allows to vary the distribution of topics as a function of document-level covariates [49, 51]. The inclusion of covariates in the model makes it possible to build and test hypotheses in a regression-like setting. That is, one can to look at covariation between topic prevalence and variables of interest. In this paper, the STM's ability to incorporate covariates means that we can examine directly our main questions concerning gendered communication. Specifically, we can test if the topics within our corpus are linked to the gender of the political actor who received the tweets. Moreover, the STM allows us to control for other factors that may be related with topic prevalence, such as time, party affiliation and others.

We estimate topic models using the STM package in R [51]. The models are computed with a spectral initialization algorithm which

is robust to changes in parameter specification. In practice, this means that irrespective of the seeds set while running the models, one obtains the best results in a consistent manner [44, 49]. Varying the number of topics, we evaluated 61 topics that produced enough information for labelling. After a qualitative labelling of the most-probable words and documents of the models' topics in the range of 61 topics, we selected 40 topics from the model as the most useful for understanding the degree of gendered communication.

Statistical models

To estimate the effects of gender and political party affiliation on the sentiment of tweets by politicians and the measure for personal- vs. job-related content, respectively, we calculated several mixed-effects regression models. Since tweets sent by the same politician cannot be assumed to be independent of each other, hierarchical models with random effects at the politician level were estimated. We used multiple linear regressions for analyzing the sentiment and personal vs. job-related content of tweets at politicians. The coefficient plots displayed in Section 5 contain predicted values for sentiment and the job-vs.-personal measure with 95% confidence intervals for gender and party.

4 DATA

The twitter data we used in our analysis consists of ~22.12 million tweets that were collected by Stier et al. [58] in the period from July 5, 2017 until September 30, 2017 — the period around the German federal elections in the same year. Since the provided data only contains the tweet-IDs, we scraped the text of each tweet and relevant adjacent data (screen name, tweet creation date, number of words, number of retweets, favourite count, etc.) by ourselves. After collecting the data, we filtered it according to certain criteria:

(1) Selecting only those tweets where the text column does not have missing values.
(2) Selecting only tweets that were written in German.
(3) Subsetting for tweets that were sent by politicians.
(4) Subsetting another dataset for tweets that were directly sent *to* politicians.

To identify German politicians, we merged the Twitter data with a dataset provided by Castanho Silva and Proksch [15], containing the name, party affiliation and social media handles by most German politicians. After subsetting the data, we received 561,770 tweets which were sent directly to politicians by 86,098 different users and 37,463 tweets which were tweeted by a total of 231 politicians.

Hence, the number of tweets was reduced quite substantially during the process of filtering and subsetting the data. A large number of tweets were simply not directly related to communication with or by politicians, another large chunk of tweets were deleted (by Twitter or the respective users themselves), and some tweets were not related to the German elections but were still acquired during the gathering process.

5 RESULTS

Descriptive statistics

Figure 1 and Figure 2 show the descriptive statistics — i.e. the total number of tweets by party and gender — for all tweets used in the analysis. Several aspects are worth discussing in greater detail. First, looking at Figure 1, it can be observed that politicians from parties in government (CDU/CSU and SPD, indicated by parties displayed above the dashed vertical line) tweet most frequently compared to all opposition parties. This fact, however, might simply be explained by the size of those parties as they are the largest parties in the German political system. More specifically, in conservative parties on the right of the political spectrum (CDU and FDP) tweets by female politicians are extremely rare compared to tweets by male politicians. Second, while in the SPD female politicians also tweet less often than male politicians, the distribution is the opposite for parties more to the left of the political left-right scale: for the Greens and the Left party, female politicians do, in fact, tweet more often the male politicians. One clear particularity is the tweeting behavior of AfD (Alternative for Germany) politicians, the newly introduced far-right party in Germany: there was not a single tweet by a male AfD politician during the German federal elections in 2017 in our sample. Hence, while the ratio of women in the AfD, in general, is very low (less than 11% in the German Bundestag), the debate on social media platforms like Twitter is entirely dominated by female politicians.

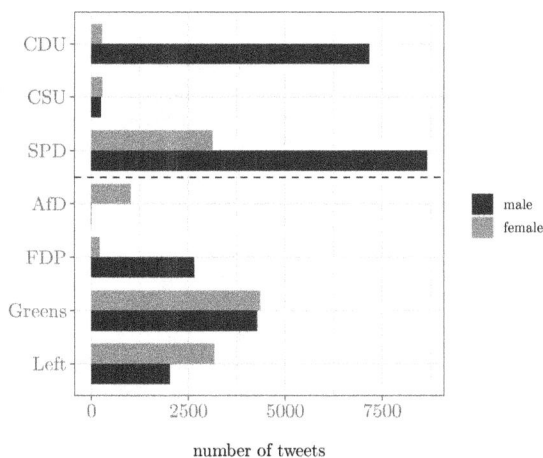

Figure 1: Number of tweets by politicians by party and gender (dashed vertical line indicates government-opposition divide)

When looking at Figure 2, in comparison, most patterns described for tweets *by* politicians can also be found for tweets sent *to* politicians: government parties receive the most tweets compared to opposition parties, although Christian Democrats (CDU) received far less tweets compared to the Social Democratic Party (SPD). Looking at gender differences, for CDU, CSU, SPD and FDP male politicians received almost the entire attention. Only a marginal amount of tweets was sent to female politicians of the respective parties. For the Greens, male politicians also received the majority of tweets. This is especially interesting for the Green Party, as female politicians themselves tweeted slightly more often compared

to male politicians (see Figure 1). For the Left Party, female politicians did not only sent out the most tweets, they also received the majority of replies and attention. Lastly, the most striking feature of Figure 2 is the number of tweets sent to AfD politicians. With a comparatively low amount of tweets sent by female AfD politicians (1,016 tweets), the attention those politicians receive is superior to almost all other parties (~120,000 tweets). Only rivalled by the SPD (receiving ~ 152,000 tweets), AfD politicians seem to be very effective in gathering social media attention, which is even more significant, since the attention is focused solely on female politicians.

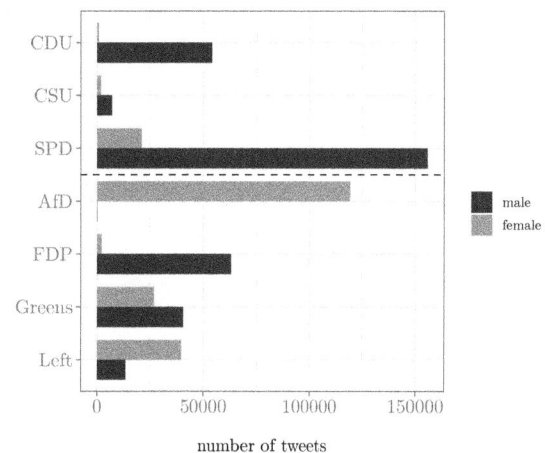

Figure 2: Number of tweets at politicians by party and gender (dashed vertical line indicates government-opposition divide)

Sentiment

Twitter communication by politicians. Figure 3 shows the sentiment of tweets sent out by politicians. Politicians from parties in government (CDU, CSU and SPD) tweet the most positive, irrespective of their gender. Meanwhile, politicians from opposition parties, specifically from the right-wing AfD and the Left, are the most negative. This clearly shows a government-opposition divide of politicians on Twitter, similar to findings of sentiment analysis in parliaments [47]. Gender, on the other hand, does not seem to play a large role for politicians on Twitter. This suggests that politicians act **according to their party identity** on Twitter.

Twitter communication at politicians. In tweets directed at politicians, we can see clear gender differences that seem to be dependent on party. Figure 4 shows that tweets directed at conservative politicians (CDU, CSU) are more positive when the recipient is female and more negative towards male politicians. Meanwhile, male politicians in the SPD and the Left receive more positive tweets than women for these parties. This suggests that politicians are approached **according to their gender identity** by other users on Twitter.

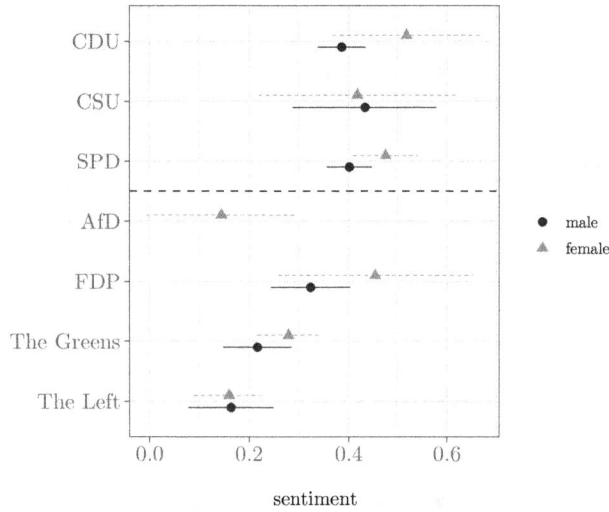

Figure 3: Sentiment in tweets by politicians (dashed vertical line indicates government-opposition divide)

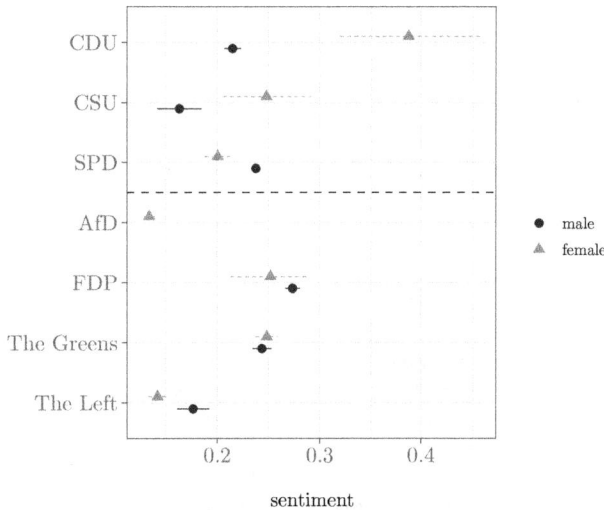

Figure 4: Sentiment in tweets at politicians (dashed vertical line indicates government-opposition divide)

Personal- versus job-related communication

Twitter communication by politicians. The predicted effects of personal- versus job-related communication by politicians (see Figure 5) indicate that their tweets are mainly **a function of their party membership** rather than their gender. One exception, female CDU politicians share the highest amount of personal tweets compared to professional tweets. When comparing politicians being in the

government with those being in the opposition, the predicted effects reveal a slightly higher share of personal tweets compared to professional ones for governmental parties. The party AfD has the least personal tweets.

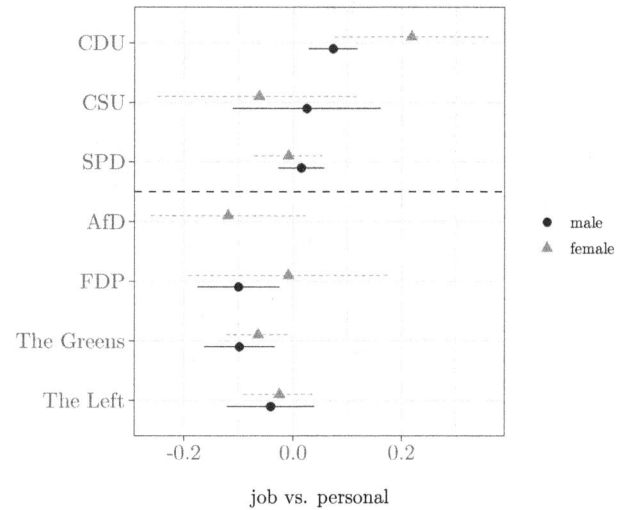

Figure 5: Job vs. personal ratio in tweets by politicians (dashed vertical line indicates government-opposition divide)

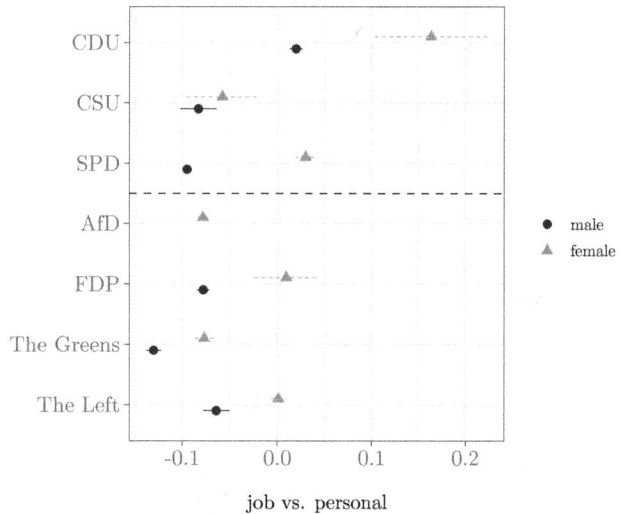

Figure 6: Job vs. personal ratio in tweets at politicians (dashed vertical line indicates government-opposition divide)

Twitter communication at politicians. In contrast, when looking at tweets at politicians the findings look very different. While the personalization of tweets by politicians does not seem to be driven by gender, the predicted effects of personal- versus job-related tweets sent at politicians are mainly **driven by the politicians' gender** (see Figure 6). Specifically, female politicians get more personal than professional tweets. Moreover, the greatest divide between tweets at male and female politicians is observable for politicians belonging to the party CDU, followed by SPD and FDP. Politicians from the Green party receive the lowest amount of personal tweets.

Structural Topic Models

Models derived by using the STM package confirm our findings in the previous section. Namely, we find a significant difference between the type of communication female and male politicians receive on Twitter. Out of 60 topics identified in our Twitter data, only 40 topics were amenable to labelling. That is, we could define — based on the high probability of exclusive words for a given topic — that the topic was dealing with a specific topic (such as democracy, for example). In 65 per cent of cases, there was a significant ($\alpha \leq 0.05$) difference when controlling for gender as a covariate. While covariate effects within the STM models are difficult to interpret substantially, one can study the specific words that are more likely to occur within one topic as opposed to the other.

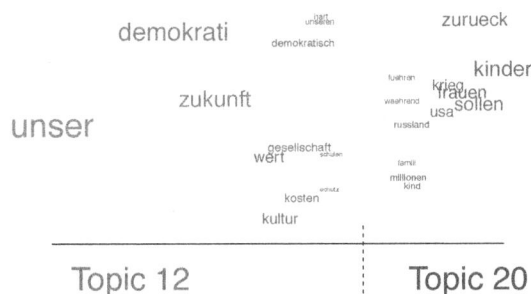

Figure 7: Topic differences based on politicians' gender (from Structural Topic Models)

In Figure 7, we compare two such topics. As can be seen, there are substantial differences within the Tweets received by women (Topic 20) and that by men (Topic 12). Words most frequently occurring within the topic more likely to be received by men (topic 12) are: "our", "democra", "future", "society", "schools", "democratic", schools", "costs, "culture". Women, on the other hand, are more likely - as opposed to men - to receive Topic 20 containing words such as: "children","child", "women", "family", "war" and "should".

Some of the other labelled topics within which we found significant gender differences are presented in Table 2. For topics related to labour markets, labour equality, taxes and pensions, open borders and refugees, there were no gender differences. But for certain areas - especially involving democracy, children and women, foreign affairs, jobs and parenting - women politicians are more likely to be the recipients (as opposed to their male counterparts). In conclusion, substantial review of the vocabulary within topics supports our findings above that there is gendered communication on Twitter, especially when one looks at the types of messages received by political actors.

6 CONCLUSION

Overall, we find evidence that the Twitter communication by politicians can mainly be explained by their party membership rather than their gender. Additionally, the analyses revealed that government politicians tweet more positive than opposition politicians. We find no evidence for gender differences in the amount of personal- compared to job-related tweets by politicians. This suggests that politicians using Twitter behave more according to their professional identity as party or government members and less to their gender identity with the aligned stereotypes. However, we find systematic gender differences in digital communication directed *at* politicians, with tweets at female politicians being more personal than tweets at male politicians. Moreover, tweets at politicians are more positive for right-leaning women and left-leaning men.

The main contribution of this work is the combination of sentiment analysis with a new personal- versus job-related communication measure uncovering gender bias in the content of tweets. This research may also provide valuable insights for adjacent scientific fields such as gender biases on online platforms in general, measurement of social group discrimination and communication biases towards female professionals.

A somewhat related question that could be raised with this study concerns the existence of various combinations of sentiment and personalization in tweets and the effects on individuals: Under which circumstances are personalized or professional tweets negatively, positively or neutrally formulated — and does this vary significantly with the gender and party of the politician? How do the different combinations of sentiment and personalization affect voters? When dissecting tweets sent to politicians, the gender and ideology of the sender should be taken into account: Are negative tweets towards female left-leaning politicians sent by their own party supporters or are supporters of right-leaning parties targeting left-leaning women and vice versa?

No Gender Differences	Significant Gender Differences
Endangered labour markets; Elections; Taxes and pensions; Labour equality; Merkel, open borders and refugees	Children and women; Jobs and parenting, working parents; Anti-fascist movement; Greens and Environmental policy; Rights; Democracy and future; Germany, Turkey and the EU; Foreign affairs; Religion and politics.

Table 2: Gender differences in Structural Topic Models

In addition, other factors such as seniority or ministry position may also be crucial for explaining the tweeting behavior of politicians. Future research is needed to investigate their effects and their moderating role. Moreover, this line of research could benefit from including previously unavailable measures of the political orientation and gender of twitter users into the analysis. Finally, using a similar approach, research should explore whether other societal biases are also reflected on online platforms, such as Twitter, and how these biases influence political behavior.

REFERENCES

[1] Toril Aalberg and Anders T. Jennsen. 2007. Gender stereotyping of political candidates. *Nordicom Review* 28, 1 (2007), 17–32.
[2] Lada A. Adamic and Natalie Glance. 2005. The political blogosphere and the 2004 US election: divided they blog. In *Proceedings of the 3rd international workshop on Link discovery*. ACM, 36–43.
[3] Hunt Allcott and Matthew Gentzkow. 2017. Social Media and Fake News in the 2016 Election. *Journal of Economic Perspectives* 31, 2 (2017), 211–236. https://doi.org/10.1257/jep.31.2.211 arXiv:1704.07506
[4] Scott L. Althaus and David Tewksbury. 2002. Agenda setting and the âĂŸnewâĂİ news: Patterns of issue importance among readers of the paper and online versions of the New York Times. *Communication Research* 29, 2 (2002), 180–207.
[5] Nick Anstead and Andrew Chadwick. 2009. *Parties, election campaigning, and the Internet: Toward a comparative institutional approach*. Routledge, London and New YorN.
[6] Eytan Bakshy, Solomon Messing, and Lada A. Adamic. 2015. Exposure to ideologically diverse news and opinion on Facebook. *Science* 348, 6239 (2015), 1130–1132.
[7] Eytan Bakshy, Itamar Rosenn, Cameron Marlow, and Lada A. Adamic. 2012. The role of social networks in information diffusion. In *Proceedings of the 21st international conference on World Wide Web*. ACM, 519–528.
[8] Pablo Barberá, Ning Wang, Richard Bonneau, John T. Jost, Jonathan Nagler, Joshua Tucker, and Sandra González-Bailón. 2015. The critical periphery in the growth of social protests. *PLoS ONE* 10, 11 (2015), 1–15. https://doi.org/10.1371/journal.pone.0143611 arXiv:e0143611
[9] Nicole M. Bauer. 2015. Emotional, Sensitive, and Unfit for Office? Gender Stereotype Activation and Support Female Candidates: Emotional, Sensitive, and Unfit for Office? *Political Psychology* 36, 6 (2015), 691–708.
[10] David Blei, Lawrence Carin, and David Dunson. 2010. Probabilistic Topic Models: A focus on graphical model design and applications to document and image analysis. *IEEE signal processing magazine* 27, 6 (2010), 55.
[11] David M. Blei, Andrew Y. Ng, and Michael I. Jordan. 2003. Latent dirichlet allocation. *Journal of machine Learning research* 3, Jan (2003), 993–1022.
[12] Levi Boxell, Matthew Gentzkow, and Jesse Shapiro. 2017. Is the Internet Causing Political Polarization? Evidence from Demographics. (2017). https://doi.org/10.3386/w23258
[13] Regina Branton, Ashley English, Samantha Pettey, and Tiffany D. Barnes. 2018. The impact of gender and quality opposition on the relative assessment of candidate competency. *Electoral Studies* 54 (2018), 35–43.
[14] Marcel Broersma and Todd Graham. 2012. Social media as beat: Tweets as a news source during the 2010 British and Dutch elections. *Journalism Practice* 6, 3 (2012), 403–419.
[15] Bruno Castanho Silva and Sven-Oliver Proksch. 2018. Talking Europe: Politicians' Discourse about the EU on Twitter and in Parliament. Paper presented at the 114 APSA Annual Meeting, Aug 29–Sep 01. Boston, MA.
[16] Andrew Chadwick. 2017. *The hybrid media system: Politics and power*. Oxford University Press.
[17] Elanor Colleoni, Alessandro Rozza, and Adam Arvidsson. 2014. Echo chamber or public sphere? Predicting political orientation and measuring political homophily in Twitter using big data. *Journal of Communication* 64, 2 (2014), 317–332.
[18] Evandro Cunha, Gabriel Magno, Marcos André Gonçalves, César Cambraia, and Virgílio Almeida. 2014. He votes or she votes? Female and male discursive strategies in twitter political hashtags. *PLoS ONE* 9, 1 (2014). https://doi.org/10.1371/journal.pone.0087041
[19] Tessa M. Ditonto, Allison J. Hamilton, and David P. Redlawsk. 2014. Gender Stereo-types, Information Search, and Voting Behavior in Political Campaigns. *Political Behaviour* 36 (2014), 335–358.
[20] Kathleen Dolan. 2010. The Impact of Gender Stereotyped Evaluations on Support for Women Candidates. *Political Behaviour* 32, 1 (2010), 69–88.
[21] Kathleen Dolan and Timothy Lynch. 2014. It Takes a Survey: Understanding Gender Stereotypes, Abstract Attitudes, and Voting for Women Candidates. *American Politics Research* 42, 4 (2014), 656–676.
[22] Heather Evans. 2016. Do women only talk about "female issues"? Gender and issue discussion on Twitter. *Online Information Review* 40, 5 (2016), 660–672.
[23] Heather K. Evans and Jennifer Hayes Clark. 2016. "You Tweet Like a Girl!" How Female Candidates Campaign on Twitter. *American Politics Research* 44, 2 (2016), 326–352.
[24] Henry Farrell. 2012. The consequences of the internet for politics. *Annual review of political science* 15 (2012).
[25] Matthew Gentzkow and Jesse M Shapiro. 2011. Ideological segregation online and offline. *The Quarterly Journal of Economics* 126, 4 (2011), 1799–1839.
[26] Peter A. Gloor, Joao Marcos, Patrick M. de Boer, Hauke Fuehres, Wei Lo, and Keiichi Nemoto. 2015. Cultural anthropology through the lens of Wikipedia: Historical leader networks, gender bias, and news-based sentiment. *arXiv preprint arXiv:1508.00055* (2015).
[27] Jacob Groshek and Ahmed Al-Rawi. 2013. Public sentiment and critical framing in social media content during the 2012 US presidential campaign. *Social Science Computer Review* 31, 5 (2013), 563–576.
[28] Andrew Guess, Brendan Nyhan, and Jason Reifler. 2018. Selective exposure to misinformation: Evidence from the consumption of fake news during the 2016 US presidential campaign. *European Research Council* 9 (2018).
[29] Yosh Halberstam and Brian Knight. 2016. Homophily, group size, and the diffusion of political information in social networks: Evidence from Twitter. *Journal of Public Economics* 143 (2016), 73–88.
[30] R. Lance Holbert, R. Kelly Garrett, and Laurel S. Gleason. 2010. A new era of minimal effects? A response to Bennett and Iyengar. *Journal of Communication* 60, 1 (2010), 15–34. https://doi.org/10.1111/j.1460-2466.2009.01470.x
[31] Philip N. Howard. 2006. *New media campaigns and the managed citizen*. Cambridge University Press.
[32] Leonie Huddy and Nayda Tekildsen. 1993. Gender Stereotypes and the Perception of Male and Female Candidates. *American Journal of Political Science* 37, 1 (1993), 119–147.
[33] John T. Jost, Pablo Barberá, Richard Bonneau, Melanie Langer, Megan Metzger, Jonathan Nagler, Joanna Sterling, and Joshua A. Tucker. 2018. How Social Media Facilitates Political Protest: Information, Motivation, and Social Networks. *Political Psychology* 39, 3 (2018), 85–118. https://doi.org/10.1111/pops.12478
[34] Hyun Jung Oh, Thomas Hove, Hye-Jin Paek, Byoungkwan Lee, Hyegyu Lee, and Sun Kyu Song. 2012. Attention cycles and the H1N1 pandemic: A cross-national study of US and Korean newspaper coverage. *Asian Journal of Communication* 22, 2 (2012), 214–232.
[35] Andreas Jungherr. 2013. Tweets and votes, a special relationship. *Proceedings of the 2nd workshop on Politics, elections and data - PLEAD '13* (2013), 5–14. https://doi.org/10.1145/2508436.2508437
[36] Jeffry W. Koch. 1999. Candidate Gender and Assessments of Senate Candidates. *Social Science Quarterly* 80, 1 (1999), 84–96.
[37] David M. J. Lazer, Matthew A. Baum, Yochai Benkler, Adam J. Berinsky, Kelly M. Greenhill, Filippo Menczer, Miriam J. Metzger, Brendan Nyhan, Gordon Pennycook, David Rothschild, Michael Schudson, Steven A. Sloman, Cass R. Sunstein, Emily A. Thorson, Duncan J. Watts, and Jonathan L. Zittrain. 2018. The science of fake news. *Science* 359, 6380 (2018), 1094–1096. https://doi.org/10.1126/science.aao2998
[38] Yphtach Lelkes. 2016. Mass polarization: Manifestations and measurements. *Public Opinion Quarterly* 80, S1 (2016), 392–410.
[39] Che-Yuan Liang and Mattias Nordin. 2013. The Internet, News Consumption, and Political Attitudes–Evidence for Sweden. *The BE Journal of Economic Analysis & Policy* 13, 2 (2013), 1071–1093.
[40] J. Nathan Matias, Sarah Szalavitz, and Ethan Zuckerman. 2017. FollowBias: Supporting Behavior Change toward Gender Equality by Networked Gatekeepers on Social Media. In *Proceedings of the 2017 ACM Conference on Computer Supported Cooperative Work and Social Computing*. ACM, 1082–1095.
[41] Monika L. McDermott. 1998. Race and Gender Cues in Low-Information Elections. *Political Research Quarterly* 51, 4 (1998), 895–918.
[42] Lindsey Meeks. 2016. Gendered styles, gendered differences: Candidates' use of personalization and interactivity on Twitter. *Journal of Information Technology & Politics* 13, 4 (2016), 295–310.
[43] Nic Newman, Richard Fletcher, Antonis Kalogeropoulos, David AL Levy, and Rasmus Kleis Nielsen. 2017. Reuters Institute digital news report 2017. (2017).
[44] Derek O'Callaghan, Derek Greene, Joe Carthy, and Pádraig Cunningham. 2015. An analysis of the coherence of descriptors in topic modeling. *Expert Systems with Applications* 42, 13 (2015), 5645–5657.
[45] John H Parmelee. 2013. Political journalists and Twitter: Influences on norms and practices. *Journal of Media Practice* 14, 4 (2013), 291–305.
[46] John H. Parmelee, Nataliya Roman, Berrin Beasley, and Stephynie C Perkins. 2017. Gender and generational differences in political reporters' interactivity on Twitter. *Journalism Studies* (2017), 1–16.
[47] Sven-Oliver Proksch, Will Lowe, Jens Wäckerle, and Stuart Soroka. 2019. Multilingual Sentiment Analysis: A New Approach to Measuring Conflict in Legislative Speeches. *Legislative Studies Quarterly* 44, 1 (2019), 97–131.
[48] Lee Rainie, Aaron Smith, Kay Lehman Schlozman, Henry Brady, and Sidney Verba. 2012. Social media and political engagement. *Pew Internet & American Life Project* 19 (2012), 2–13.

[49] Margaret E. Roberts, Brandon M. Stewart, and Edoardo M. Airoldi. 2016. A model of text for experimentation in the social sciences. *J. Amer. Statist. Assoc.* 111, 515 (2016), 988–1003.

[50] Margaret E. Roberts, Brandon M. Stewart, and Dustin Tingley. 2018. *stm: R Package for Structural Topic Models.* http://www.structuraltopicmodel.com R package version 1.3.3.

[51] Margaret E. Roberts, Brandon M. Stewart, Dustin Tingley, Christopher Lucas, Jetson Leder-Luis, Shana Kushner Gadarian, Bethany Albertson, and David G. Rand. 2014. Structural topic models for open-ended survey responses. *American Journal of Political Science* 58, 4 (2014), 1064–1082.

[52] Kira Sanbonmatsu. 2002. Gender Stereotypes and Vote Choice. *American Journal of Political Science* 46, 1 (2002), 20–34.

[53] Dietram A. Scheufele and Matthew C. Nisbet. 2013. Commentary: Online news and the demise of political disagreement. *Annals of the International Communication Association* 36, 1 (2013), 45–53.

[54] Lei Shi, Neeraj Agarwal, Ankur Agrawal, Rahul Garg, and Jacob Spoelstra. 2012. Predicting US Primary Elections with Twitter. (2012), 1–8. https://doi.org/10.1.1.252.8161

[55] Eli Skogerbø, Axel Bruns, Andrew Quodling, and Thomas Ingebretsen. 2016. Agenda-setting revisited: Social media and sourcing in mainstream journalism. *The Routledge companion to social media and politics* (2016), 104–120.

[56] Stuart N. Soroka. 2006. Good News and Bad News: Asymmetric Responses to Economic Information. *Journal of Politics* 68, 2 (2006), 372–385. https://doi.org/10.1111/j.1468-2508.2006.00413.x arXiv:https://onlinelibrary.wiley.com/doi/pdf/10.1111/j.1468-2508.2006.00413.x

[57] Stuart N. Soroka. 2014. *Negativity in Democratic Politics: Causes and Consequences.* Cambridge University Press. https://doi.org/10.1017/CBO9781107477971

[58] Sebastian Stier, Arnim Bleier, Malte Bonart, Fabian Mörsheim, Mahdi Bohlouli, Margarita Nizhegorodov, Lisa Posch, Jürgen Maier, Tobias Rothmund, and Steffen Staab. 2018. Systematically Monitoring Social Media: The case of the German federal election 2017. *GESIS papers* 04 (2018).

[59] Cass R Sunstein. 2001. *One case at a time: Judicial minimalism on the Supreme Court.* Harvard University Press.

[60] Henry Tajfel. 1970. Experiments in intergroup discrimination. *Scientific American* 223, 5 (1970), 96–103.

[61] Henri Tajfel and John C. Turner. 1979. *The social psychology of intergroup relations.* Number 4. Brooks/Cole, Monterey, CA, Chapter An integrative theory of intergroup conflict. The Social Psychology of Intergroup Relations, 33–37.

[62] Yla R. Tausczik and James W. Pennebaker. 2010. The psychological meaning of words: LIWC and computerized text analysis methods. *Journal of Language and Social Psychology* 29, 1 (2010), 24–54.

[63] Joshua A. Tucker, Andrew Guess, Pablo Barberá, Cristian Vaccari, Alexandra Siegel, Sergey Sanovich, Denis Stukal, and Brendan Nyhan. 2018. Social Media, Political Polarization, and Political Disinformation: A Review of the Scientific Literature. March (2018), 1–95.

[64] Nikki Usher, Jesse Holcomb, and Justin Littman. 2018. Twitter makes it worse: Political journalists, gendered echo chambers, and the amplification of gender bias. *The International Journal of Press/Politics* 23, 3 (2018), 324–344.

[65] Kevin M. Wagner, Jason Gainous, and Mirya R. Holman. 2017. I am woman, hear me tweet! Gender differences in twitter use among congressional candidates. *Journal of Women, Politics & Policy* 38, 4 (2017), 430–455.

[66] Lori Young and Stuart Soroka. 2012. Affective News: The Automated Coding of Sentiment in Political Texts. *Political Communication* 29, 2 (2012), 205–231. https://doi.org/10.1080/10584609.2012.671234 arXiv:https://doi.org/10.1080/10584609.2012.671234

ACKNOWLEDGMENTS

We would like to thank the jury members at the Euro CSS 2018 Symposium for useful comments on an earlier version of this article as well as Sven-Oliver Proksch and Ingo Rohlfing for their support throughout the project. We also thank three anonymous reviewers for their comments in finalizing the manuscript. In addition, Franziska Pradel is grateful for support by the Digital Society research program funded by the Ministry of Culture and Science of the German State of North Rhine-Westphalia.

Extremist Propaganda Tweet Classification with Deep Learning in Realistic Scenarios

Leonardo Nizzoli
University of Pisa and IIT-CNR, Italy
leonardo.nizzoli@iit.cnr.it

Marco Avvenuti
Dept. of Information Engineering,
University of Pisa, Italy
marco.avvenuti@unipi.it

Stefano Cresci, Maurizio
Tesconi
IIT-CNR, Italy
[name.surname]@iit.cnr.it

ABSTRACT

In this work, we tackled the problem of the automatic classification of the extremist propaganda on Twitter, focusing on the Islamic State of Iraq and al-Sham (ISIS). We built and published several datasets, obtained by mixing 15,684 ISIS propaganda tweets with a variable number of neutral tweets, related to ISIS, and random ones, accounting for imbalances up to 1%. We considered three state-of-the-art, deep learning techniques, representative of the main current approaches to text classification, and two strong linear machine learning baselines. We compared their performance when varying the composition of the training and test sets, in order to explore different training strategies, and to evaluate the results when approaching realistic conditions. We demonstrated that a Recurrent-Convolutional Neural Network, based on pre-trained word embeddings, can reach an excellent F1 score of 0.9 on the most challenging test condition (1%-imbalance).

CCS CONCEPTS

• **Computing methodologies** → **Natural language processing**; **Neural networks**.

KEYWORDS

Extremist propaganda; artificial neural networks; cyber intelligence; Twitter

ACM Reference Format:
Leonardo Nizzoli, Marco Avvenuti, and Stefano Cresci, Maurizio Tesconi. 2019. Extremist Propaganda Tweet Classification with Deep Learning in Realistic Scenarios. In *11th ACM Conference on Web Science (WebSci '19), June 30-July 3, 2019, Boston, MA, USA*. ACM, New York, NY, USA, 2 pages. https://doi.org/10.1145/3292522.3326050

1 INTRODUCTION

The volume and variety of the Twitter stream ensure a comfortable hideout to malicious propaganda activities. Hence, the Social Media Intelligence (SOCMINT) research community has devoted increasing efforts in developing automatic methods to filter malicious tweets [10]. If literature provides several contributions on this topic [6], the proposed techniques are generally tested and evaluated in laboratory conditions [1, 2, 7]. Therefore, stakeholders cannot estimate how those models would perform in the wild.

Motivation. In this work, we focused on the Islamic State of Iraq and al-Sham (ISIS). We addressed the needs of a potential stakeholder who leverages the Twitter Streaming API [4] to obtain a mixture of ISIS propaganda tweets (pro-ISIS), tweets reporting ISIS related content but not supporting the organization (about-ISIS), and completely random ones, with unknown relative proportion. The stakeholder is interested in choosing the suitable state-of-the-art text classification technique, together with the optimal training strategy, to separate pro-ISIS tweets from the others, and in having an estimation of the expected performance.

Contribution. We selected three state-of-the-art, deep learning techniques, representative of the main current approaches to text classification, covering both character- and word-level text representations, and convolutional and recurrent architectures. For comparison purposes, we also included two strong linear baselines. Starting from 15,684 pro-ISIS tweets, we built several datasets accounting for a wide range of positive class imbalances (up to 1%). The results of this extensive investigation addressed the objectives of identifying a good candidate technique, together with a proper training strategy, and of estimating the performance in realistic conditions. In particular, we obtained an excellent F1 score of 0.9 under the most challenging condition of 1%-imbalanced test set. As a key contribution, we published the experimental datasets.

2 MATERIALS AND METHODS

Datasets. In order to reproduce the features of a realistic scenario, we built several datasets by combining pro-ISIS, about-ISIS and random tweets, with different proportions. The 15,684 pro-ISIS English tweets were sampled from a large, reliable, publicly available dataset[1], published by *Fifth Tribe*, a digital agency providing services to US government. We sampled the about-ISIS tweets from a dataset[2] including tweets containing at least one ISIS related keyword. We collected random tweets via the Twitter Streaming API, by means of the *GET statuses/sample* method, which returns a small random sample of all public statuses. The largest and most imbalanced (1%) dataset included, for each pro-ISIS tweet, 6 about-ISIS and 93 random tweets. Less imbalanced datasets (from 2% to 10%, and balanced) were derived from more imbalanced ones, by removing negative instances. Each dataset underwent stratified splitting to create training (64%), validation (16%) and test sets (20%). We published the datasets[3] for reproducibility and further research.

---

[1] https://www.kaggle.com/fifthtribe/how-isis-uses-twitter
[2] https://www.kaggle.com/activegalaxy/isis-related-tweets
[3] http://ci.iit.cnr.it/ept. For the login credentials, please e-mail leonardo.nizzoli@iit.cnr.it.

Learning techniques. Deep learning, based on Artificial Neural Networks (ANNs), represents the current state-of-the-art for text classification. The main advantages are higher performance, automatic feature extraction and higher generalizability [5]. Limiting ourselves to the state-of-the-art, we identified a possible taxonomy as follows: (i) Convolutional (CNN) vs. Recurrent-Convolutional (RCNN) Neural Network architectures and (ii) character- vs. word-based text representations. CNNs result very effective in capturing the text semantic, whereas RCNNs, due to their sequential architecture, excel in capturing contextual information and long-term semantic features. Characters-based representations enable to learn multi-language models and abnormal character combinations (very common in tweets [3]). Instead, word-based representations commonly leverage word embeddings to incorporate distributional information about words, learned in large text corpora. Due to the different pros and cons of each approach, we decided to compare: (i) a character-based CNN model (ChCNN), proposed in [12]; (ii) a RCNN (WeRCNN), combined with max pooling [8] and based on pre-trained FastText word embeddings [9]; (iii) an evolution of the previous one (We2DRCNN), in which convolution and max pooling were carried out in a two-dimensional arrangement [13], and (iv) two linear baselines (SVM), trained on bag-of-character (ChSVM) and bag-of-word (WoSVM) n-grams [11].

3 RESULTS AND DISCUSSION

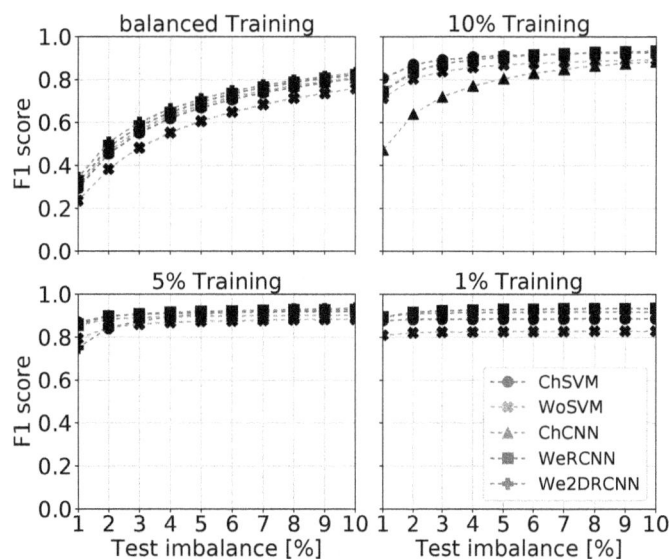

Figure 1: F1 score trends, for different training strategies, when varying the test set imbalance. On 1% training, ChCNN performed like a majority classifier (undefined F1 score).

We trained models on balanced, 10%, 5%, 1% training sets, and we evaluated their performance when varying the imbalance of the test sets in the range [1%, 10%]. Figure 1 shows the obtained F1 score trends. Models trained on the balanced training set suffered a serious performance worsening when decreasing the percentage of positive instances in the test set. Instead, the performance showed

a more stable trend when we increased the number of negative examples in the training set. The linear baseline ChSVM obtained the highest F1 score when using the 10% training set, but it was outperformed on the 1%. ChCNN was competitive with the 5% training set, but resulted in a majority classifier, with an undefined F1 score, on the 1% one. Word-based RCNNs clearly outperformed the other candidates on the most imbalanced 1% dataset, keeping very stable on the whole investigated range. In particular, WeRCNN obtained the highest F1 score (0.895) on 1% test set.

Fig. 1 trends address the needs of the potential stakeholders, as summarized in Section 1. In fact, they outline RCNNs, based on pre-trained word embeddings, as suitable techniques. Moreover, they support the choice of highly imbalanced training set if an unknown, high imbalance is expected in the real tweet stream. Finally, they allow a performance estimation over a wide range of conditions.

4 CONCLUSIONS

We outlined a framework for solving the task of extremist propaganda tweet classification in realistic scenarios. We provided the performance trends of several text classification techniques, when varying the training strategies and the test conditions. Those trends address the needs of possible stakeholders seeking for a suitable text classification technique, an efficient training strategy and an estimation of the performance expected in the wild. Focusing on the most challenging test condition (1% imbalance), we demonstrated that Recurrent Convolutional Neural Network, based on pre-trained word embeddings, reached a F1 score as high as 0.9 when trained with the same imbalance. Moreover, the measured trends provide a performance estimation on a wide range of conditions. Finally, the dataset were published for reproducibility and further research.

REFERENCES

[1] Swati Agarwal and Ashish Sureka. 2015. Using KNN and SVM based one-class classifier for detecting online radicalization on Twitter. In *ICDCIT'15*. Springer, 431–442.
[2] Michael Ashcroft, Ali Fisher, Lisa Kaati, Enghin Omer, and Nico Prucha. 2015. Detecting jihadist messages on twitter. In *EISIC'15*. IEEE, 161–164.
[3] Marco Avvenuti, Stefano Cresci, Leonardo Nizzoli, and Maurizio Tesconi. 2018. GSP (Geo-Semantic-Parsing): Geoparsing and Geotagging with machine learning on top of linked data. In *ESWC'18*. Springer, 17–32.
[4] Stefano Cresci, Salvatore Minutoli, Leonardo Nizzoli, Serena Tardelli, and Maurizio Tesconi. 2019. Enriching Digital Libraries with Crowdsensed Data. In *IRCDL'19*. Springer, 144–158.
[5] Tiziano Fagni, Leonardo Nizzoli, Marinella Petrocchi, and Maurizio Tesconi. 2019. Six Things I Hate About You (in Italian) and Six Classification Strategies to More and More Effectively Find Them. In *ITASEC'19*.
[6] Emilio Ferrara, Wen-Qiang Wang, Onur Varol, Alessandro Flammini, and Aram Galstyan. 2016. Predicting online extremism, content adopters, and interaction reciprocity. In *SOCINFO'16*. Springer, 22–39.
[7] Andrew H Johnston and Gary M Weiss. 2017. Identifying Sunni extremist propaganda with deep learning. In *SSCI'2017*. IEEE, 1–6.
[8] Siwei Lai, Liheng Xu, Kang Liu, and Jun Zhao. 2015. Recurrent convolutional neural networks for text classification. In *AAAI'15*, Vol. 333. 2267–2273.
[9] Tomas Mikolov, Edouard Grave, Piotr Bojanowski, Christian Puhrsch, and Armand Joulin. 2018. Advances in pre-training distributed word representations. In *LREC'18*. ELRA.
[10] David Omand, Jamie Bartlett, and Carl Miller. 2012. Introducing social media intelligence (SOCMINT). *Intelligence and National Security* 27, 6 (2012), 801–823.
[11] Sida Wang and Christopher D Manning. 2012. Baselines and bigrams: Simple, good sentiment and topic classification. In *ACL'12*. 90–94.
[12] Xiang Zhang, Junbo Zhao, and Yann LeCun. 2015. Character-level convolutional networks for text classification. In *NIPS'15*. 649–657.
[13] Peng Zhou, Zhenyu Qi, Suncong Zheng, Jiaming Xu, Hongyun Bao, and Bo Xu. 2016. Text classification improved by integrating bidirectional LSTM with two-dimensional max pooling. In *COLING'16*. 3485–3495.

An Automated Cyclic Planning Framework Based on Plan-Do-Check-Act for Web of Things Composition

Mahda Noura
Martin Gaedke
mahda.noura@informatik.tu-chemnitz.de
martin.gaedke@informatik.tu-chemnitz.de
Technische Universität Chemnitz
Chemnitz, Germany

ABSTRACT

Empowering end users to be directly involved in the development and composition of their smart devices surrounding them that achieves their goals is a major challenge for End User Development (EUD) in the context of Web of Things (WoT). This can be achieved through Artificial Intelligence (AI) planning. Planning is intended as the ability of a WoT system to construct a sequence of actions, that when executed by the smart devices, achieves an effect on the environment in response to an end user issued goal. The problem of planning specifically for the WoT domain has not been sufficiently dealt with in the existing literature. The existing planning approaches do not deal with one or more of the following important factors in the context of WoT: (1) random unexpected events (2) unpredictable device effects leading to side effects at runtime, and (3) durative effects. In this work, we propose a cyclic planning system which adopted a PDCA (Plan-Do-Check-Act) process solution to deal with the existing shortcomings for continuous improvement. The planner employs domain knowledge based on the WoTDL (Web of Things Description Language) ontology.The cyclic planner enables continuous plan monitoring to cope with inconsistencies with user issued goals. We demonstrate the feasibility of the proposed approach on our smart home testbed. The proposed planner further enhances the ease of use for end users in the context of our goal-oriented approach GrOWTH.

CCS CONCEPTS

• **Human-centered computing** → *Ubiquitous and mobile computing*; • **Computing methodologies** → **Planning and scheduling**; Knowledge representation and reasoning; Intelligent agents.

KEYWORDS

Internet of Things; Web of Things; Plan-Do-Check-Act; Artificial Intelligence; Planning; Semantic Web

ACM Reference Format:
Mahda Noura and Martin Gaedke. 2019. An Automated Cyclic Planning Framework Based on Plan-Do-Check-Act for Web of Things Composition. In *11th ACM Conference on Web Science (WebSci '19), June 30-July 3, 2019, Boston, MA, USA*. ACM, New York, NY, USA, 10 pages. https://doi.org/10.1145/3292522.3326044

1 INTRODUCTION

The term Internet of Things (IoT), coined by Kevin Ashton [1], has been an emerging technological trend in recent years in a broad range of domains. The idea of IoT is to enrich physical things ("objects") and places with wireless accessible sensing, computing, and actuating capabilities [4]. The increase in use of smart devices have already changed the way people live, ranging from interactive smart homes to smart parking systems in cities.

One of the main research challenges is how to enable end users to exploit the diverse behaviors of these smart devices and be able to control/monitor and compose them to create new, added-value services [5]. To reach this objective, it is vital that users can easily control how to use their smart objects (i.e., sense data from sensors and affect the physical environment) and how to combine the behavior of different objects to reach some desired goal. The integration of existing Web standards with IoT devices, called the Web of Things (WoT) [8] has simplified access to these smart devices for web developers by allowing the functionality of physical devices to be abstracted and exposed as services on the Web either using RESTful Web Services or WS-* protocol stack.

Automated planning approaches in the Artificial Intelligence (AI) domain would further contribute towards empowering end user's without technical expertise to automatically interact with different WoT devices to reach their goal of interest. They enable the user to specify a coarse-grained goal (What) without providing a concrete way (How). For example, in the smart home domain there are many devices that can change the current situation of the home (like smart lamps, shades, etc.), and can be exploited to provide contextual (i.e., luminosity, humidity, etc.,) information and act automatically in response to a user goal. Some goals in a smart home setting include "increase the temperature", "I want to read a book".

From academia, some approaches [12, 13, 15, 16, 20, 22] have adopted AI planning techniques with the aim to facilitate users achieve their goal in the context of smart environments. However, the existing planning solutions do not consider one or more of the following problems in the context of WoT:

(1) **Unpredictable device effects**: The majority of the solutions assume that each device actuation is defined in terms of preconditions and effects. This means that at design time, the device provider must predict all the possible effects of each WoT device actuation in different scenarios. However, in most cases the device providers only considers the direct effects while either ignoring or simply not being able to predict indirect effects in different situations. Even the predicted effects are not quantifiable since it is impossible to model any kind of complex interaction between arbitrary combinations of devices and the physical environment. For example, how well a heating device can warm the house depends on many criteria's such as where the heater is located, type of heater, whether a window is open, etc. Therefore, it cannot be assumed that the device provider will offer a quantifiable and precise description of all the possible effects.

(2) **Random unexpected events**: In the context of real-world WoT applications such as smart home, smart city, etc. they are characterized by dynamic internal and external factors that can influence reaching the goal of a user. For example, the weather conditions or the unpredictable human behavior can affect the correctness of the produced plan (external event). Moreover, the different WoT devices may join or leave the network at arbitrary times during execution, making device availability unpredictable at runtime (internal event). Therefore, a plan can fail because of an event like malfunctioning device.

(3) **Durative effects**: For some smart devices the effects of an actuation are not instantaneous. This means that the controller must wait for the effects of an actuation to take place. Unlike Web Service composition, in WoT environments the link to the physical world adds a duration dimension to the planning problems because physical actuations require a duration to show the effects and cannot be accelerated on a software level (e.g., by using faster CPU, faster algorithms, etc.,).

Clearly, the above-mentioned factors will have a high impact on the actual execution of device operations which may lead to unexpected behaviour and undesirable user experience and should therefore not be disregarded.

To address the shortcomings of the existing approaches, the contribution of this work is to propose and develop a cyclic planner inspired by the Plan-Do-Check-Act (PDCA) [2] paradigm in business management to deal with unpredictable device effects, random unexpected effects and durative effects. To achieve a level of automation, the planner uses domain knowledge based on the WoTDL[1] (Web of Things Description Language) ontology and WoTDL2API [19] for it's automatic conversion to the OpenAPI specification.The WoTDL ontology has been designed based on our analysis in [17]. The domain knowledge in this work describes the capability of each WoT device in terms of the possible device actuations (preconditions and effects) without restricting the device provider to predict all the possible effects in different environmental contexts. The solution to the plan is realized by employing state of the art AI planners. A fully-working prototype has been implemented which

---

[1] https://vsr.informatik.tu-chemnitz.de/projects/2019/growth/wotdl/

provides the backend to facilitating end users achieve their goals automatically at runtime and on-demand, depending merely on the knowledge of WoT device capabilities, and the user's personal goals. The feasibility of the proposed solution is demonstrated on our smart home testbed consisting of various physical devices by examining a set of realistic case studies. The current contributions are developed in the context of GrOWTH [18], which aims to support EUD for WoT using a goal-oriented technique.

The rest of the paper is structured as follows. Section 2 discusses the related work for planning in smart environments. Then, in Section 3 we show the motivation of the work through a scenario in the smart home domain. In Section 4, the definition of planning for WoT composition regarding the proposed approach is provided. The WoT composition domain is formulated to planning domain definition language in Section 5, and the proposed PDCA-based cyclic planning solution is introduced in Section 6. Section 7 provides the evaluation and results. Finally, Section 8 concludes the paper and provides future insights.

2 RELATED WORK

There is a great deal of research related to planning for web service composition and ubiquitous computing separately. Planning in the context of WoT environments is a relatively new topic and there are few solutions that address this issue directly. This section studies the related work concerning some of the specific AI planning techniques employed from representative studies in different domains, providing a base for extracting the advantages and limitations.

2.1 AI planning in Ubiquitous Computing

The benefits of integrating AI planning techniques with ubiquitous and pervasive computing have long been recognized. Some of the related examples are [3, 10, 14]. In 2003, Heider [10] proposed a solution to simplify complex infrastructures such as multimedia systems. He describes a method to employ AI-based planning techniques to end user applications using a goal-based approach. In this solution, the intelligent components provide a semantic description, so that the planner can independently choose the right devices to reach the user's goal. Although a detailed information about error handling is not presented, the system can respond to the dynamic situation in the application environment. Krüger et al. [14] provides a user interface for controlling intelligent environments to proactively support end users. However, the planning step is performed at design time. In contrast, solutions targeted for end users without the required expertise should be capable of adapt themselves automatically at run-time without the intervention of a domain expert. Chen et al.[3] provides a goal-based solution for service robots using a automatic Hierarchical Task Network Planner (HTN) to achieve the goal. The system also uses a semantic description supported by ontology to make decisions in a context-sensitive context and also takes into account the preferences learned from the user. All of these solutions suffer from the same limitation as they do not consider any kind of uncertainty which makes them unsuitable for highly dynamic environments. However, in smart environments this must be considered as the default and not an option.

2.2 AI planning for Web Service Composition

AI planning techniques have also been used in many approaches to automate (Web) service composition. In this category, the composition process is regarded as the planning problem and services are considered as actions. For example, the SWORD [21] project is an automated web service composition solution based on planning algorithms aimed at minimizing development time and effort. The services are considered as rules and then an expert system decides whether the desired service composition can be realized using the available resources. Based on the planning problem, a service is formulated as an action, with the inputs representing the precondition and the outputs the effects. However, they assumed that the services have a description of the respective inputs and outputs which is a time consuming task to model. In contrast, the project is not aimed for end user's but rather for developers. If there is no plan due to any circumstances, the developer must intervene manually. The PORSCE II framework [9] uses semantic web technologies for service composition. Similar to our approach, they transform the service composition problem into a planning problem and describe it according to the standard PDDL. The problem is then solved by an AI planner and they transfer the solution back to the terminology of the service compositions. It is also capable of identifying service failures by using equivalent services. In contrast, the WoT devices in this work are described using WoTDL (Web of Things Description Language) which is an extension to OWL-S ontology supporting WoT devices. On the other hand, a more elaborate solution for service composition is provided in [12] which also takes the problem of uncertainty into account. In this work planning is performed continuously using Constraint Satisfaction Problem (CSP), such that the steps are predicted offline and revised at execution time. By comparison in our approach we do not perform offline planning and the plans are generated dynamically at runtime per user goal. Wang et al [23] proposed a Graphplan algorithm which considers the problem of uncertainty of execution effect for web service composition.

2.3 AI Planning for Web of Things

The problem of Web service composition is similar to planning for WoT devices based on the REST architectural style, because the main objective of both problems is to combine actions (represented as web services) in a dynamic manner. However, due to the lack of physical devices in this domain executing requests to Web services is almost instantaneous and unlike physical devices do not require processing time and a duration for the actual effect to take place. Furthermore, WoT environments are non-deterministic due to it's connection to the physical world. Towards the approaches developed for WoT composition we can highlight the works of [7, 16, 22, 24]. Mayer et al. [16] proposed a goal-based solution for automatic configuration of intelligent environments. Users use a visual programming tool to indicate which properties their environment should have according to their goals and the system checks whether the target can be reached with the available resources. Since the composition is generated at runtime, the proposed system can also operate in highly dynamic environments which are common in the IoT field. In contrast, they only consider device failures by informing the user with a status code and assume complete

knowledge about device effects. Yau et al. [24] attempts to meet the user-expected requirements for a mobile cloud IoT system through markov decision planning. The user communicates the functional and quality requirements to the scheduling system, which would then identify all the smart and non-smart devices in the application environment and after analyzing the device status, would enable the designer to calculate the actions to be taken. More recently, [7] aims to find an automatic solution for detecting and resolving conflicts between the actions of different IoT devices using an AI planner. A recent approach, [22] extends the CSP planner in [12] to a weighted CSP in order to attain partial goal fulfillment for resolving conflicts in a multi-user smart home setting.

To the best of our knowledge, none of the currently proposed approaches consider random unexpected events, unpredictable device effects and durative effects at the same time. The aspect of device failure has been partially addressed in some of the existing literature but the other two aspects are ignored and not dealt with.

3 MOTIVATING SCENARIOS

To show the problems considered in this work, a scenario from the smart home domain is described. Lets suppose Mary is in her smart home and would like to issue the goal: "I want to read a book". For reading a book, she has preferences for light and noise condition. The smart home first measures the ambient luminosity in the room, and finds out that it is too dark, then reacts by switching the lamp on. It also senses the amount of noise in the room and finds out that the noise is above a certain threshold, then turns the TV off. After some time, Mary wants to chill on the couch and issues this goal to the smart home. Based on Mary's preferences the system knows she likes dimmed lights, soft jazz music and the temperature set to 22 degrees. The current temperature in the room is 18 degrees. The fulfillment of this goal cannot be predicted in advance and requires the smart home to be able to produce an initial plan for the increase of temperature and then to repeat the cycle of monitoring the temperature over a span of time until the desired effect (temperature) is reached. Depending on the time of the day, type of heater, location of the heater, an open window, etc., the plan and the time to reach the desired effect differs and obviously cannot be anticipated. Some time passes, and Mary utters to the smart home ("increase the brightness in the room"). The system finds out that it is daylight and decides to open the shutters. However, it is a very sunny hot day outside, and eventually the sun heats up the room and the temperature increases. Here the side effect of opening the shades is increase in the room temperature. The system monitors the environment finding an alternative plan depending on the available devices and acts by closing the shutter, switching the lamp on and turning the fan on. To further complicate things, when trying to close the shades, it does not work, and the service request fails. In this situation, the system should, if possible, be able to choose another device which produces a similar effect on the environment.

4 PLANNING FOR WEB OF THINGS COMPOSITION CONCEPTUAL MODEL

The WoT composition is considered as a planning domain, where actions link to the different operations of physical devices and the goal is derived from a user request that calls for a state change in the physical environment. All WoT devices are described according to the WoTDL ontology which is an extension to OWL-S [2] ontology for supporting the WoT domain. In this work, we assume that the descriptions of the WoT device operations is provided by a knowledge expert, who is responsible for formalizing the different operations of devices using RDF syntax in OWL ontology. Semantic Web ontologies have been previously used in the domain of planning, interested readers may refer to [9], however it is not the focus of this work.

Definition 1 (WoT composition): The WoT domain is defined as 5-tuple WoTD$=< S, s^o, A, s^*, \gamma >$, where:

$S = s_1, s_2, \ldots, s_n$ is a finite set of states including the initial state s^o and the goal state s^*. Each state is represented by a finite non-empty set of parameters $Par_s = p_1, p_2, \ldots, p_k$ expressing the facts known about this state. Each parameter $p_i \in Par_s$ has a finite domain of V^{p_i}.

A is the set of actions. An action $a \in A$ defines its functionality as 4-tuples: $a=(name(a), preconditions(a), effects(a), actuations(a))$, where: $name(a)$ is a unique name of the device action, e.g., ("TurnLampOn"), $preconditions(a)$ is a set of propositional formula over Par_s, which follows: $\phi: := prop|\phi \wedge \phi|\phi \vee \phi|\neg\phi$ and $prop \subset N \times O \times V$ represents an atomic fact, combining the name of the parameter $n(p_i) \in N$, operator $o(p_i) \in O = \{=, <, >, \#, \leq, \geq\}$ and the value $v(p_i) \in V^{p_i}$, $effects(a)$ is a combination of $(E(a), t_E)$, where effect $E(a)$ of action a on parameter $p_i \in Par_s$ can be of the following types:

- $increase(p_i)$ or $decrease(p_i)$ for increasing or decreasing p_i (e.g., increase VOLUME)
- $toggle(p_i)$ for switching between the possible values of p_i (e.g., from ON to OFF)
- $assign(p_i, v)$, for assigning constant value v to p_i (e.g., set TEMP to 22°C)

t_E (time to effect) is the duration stating the amount of time for an effect to occur cf. (Figure 1) (e.g., the time required for the actual increase in temperature in a room after the thermostat has completed its operation)

$actuations(a)$ are a set of HTTP requests that can be sent to the physical devices that invokes the operations on the devices. It is a tuple $(method, url, body, headers, t_0)$, where $method$ indicates the desired action to be performed on a Web device $GET|POST|PUT$, url the mechanism for retrieving the resource, $body$ the body of the HTTP message, $headers$ and t_0 is the time required for the physical operation triggered by this actuation cf. (Figure 1) (e.g., the time required to close a rolling shutter after the request is sent to the shutter).

$\gamma : S \times A \rightarrow S$ is the transition function between the states associated with actions from A performed by devices.

The solution to the planning problem described by the WoT composition is a finite sequence $\pi \in A^*$ of actions. This plan $\pi = a_1 \ldots a_n$ is executable from state s_0, if there exists a sequence of states $\sigma = s_0 \ldots s_n$ so that, for $i = 0, \ldots, n-1, s(i+1) = \gamma(s_i, a(i+1))$ the states form a consistent sequence of transitions and $s_n = s^*$ this sequence ends in the target state.

[2] https://www.w3.org/Submission/OWL-S/

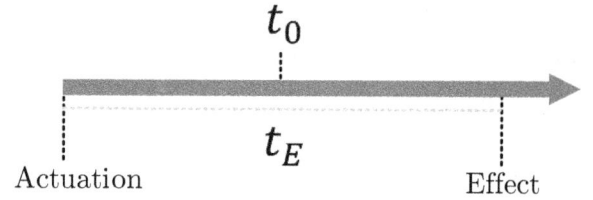

Figure 1: Timeline from the actuation to the actual effect

5 ENCODING THE WOT COMPOSITION IN PLANNING DOMAIN DEFINITION LANGUAGE

While most planning systems in different domains assume that the planning domain is defined by a domain expert at design time in the Planning Domain Description Language (PDDL) or similar, that is not possible for dynamic smart environments. In this work our method is driven by the requirement that the planning domain is constructed at run-time automatically in response to a user goal. Therefore, in this section we show how, given a user goal, the planning domain and the problem domain is automatically constructed from the WoTDL ontology in RDF to PDDL. The planning domain and the problem domain can then be used as input to any state-of-the-art planning technology to find a plan. In particular, we represent them making use of PDDL2.1 [6], which provides numeric features that are relevant for this work, e.g. to represent the value of temperature.

5.1 Planning Domain

In order to generate the planning domain file automatically, a parser is developed to transform the WoTDL ontology instances expressed in RDF to PDDL. A minimal example of TTL representation to PDDL planning file generation is presented in the top right of Figure 2, where the mappings are marked in different colours. It is worth noting that the ontology instance is not complete and only the relevant instances are shown for the sake of clarity.

The domain file, in it's minimal state, consists of a description of all *types, predicates,* and the *actions* in the environment. The *types* describe the different types of WoT devices that exists in the smart environment (red) like a thermostat, lamp, shutter, etc as well as the environmental characteristics such as the room temperature, ambient brightness. *Predicates* are the properties of objects and help to describe the state of the domain, for example, the *LampPowerState* can be used to check whether the Lamp is switched on or off (light green). The actions express the operations provided by the available devices and influence the state of the world. They are described in PDDL by a name (yellow), a list of parameters, preconditions, and effects. The example illustrates an action to turn off the lamp (*SwitchOffLamp*) and expects an argument for the variable $a1$ of type *lamp* as a parameter. The preconditions and effects are represented by logically linked predicates and refer to the variables passed to the action by the variable name. In the example, the action assumes as a precondition (aqua blue) that the *lamp* object passed to it must be in the "on" state. If the condition is met, the planner can select this action to produce the described effect (light blue). In this case,

```
<#PhillipsHue>
   a wotdl:CompositeDevice ;
   wotdl:hasActuator <#LampActuator> ;
   wotdl:hasSensor <#LightSensor>;
   wotdl:name "philipshue"^^xsd:string ;
   wotdl:type "lamp"^^xsd:string .
<#LampActuator>
   a wotdl:Actuator;
   wotdl:hasTransition <#LampOffTr>.
<#LampOffTr>
   a wotdl:Transition;
   wotdl:hasPrecondition <#LampOffPr>;
   wotdl:hasActuation <#LampOff>;
   wotdl:hasEffect <#DecreaseBrightness>, <#Off>.
<#LampOff>
   a wotdl:HttpRequest ;
   wotdl:httpMethod "POST"^^xsd:string ;
   wotdl:name "SwitchOffLamp"^^xsd:string ;
   wotdl:url "http://192.168.10.111/lights/off";
   wotdl:waitAfterActuation "1".
<#DecreaseBrightness>
   a wotdl:DecreaseEffect ;
   wotdl:affects <#AmbientLuminosity>;
   wotdl:decrement "680".
<#AmbientLuminosity>
   a wotdl:Parameter ;
   wotdl:name "AmbientLuminosity"^^xsd:string.
<#Off>
   a wotdl:FixedValueEffect ;
   wotdl:affects <#LampPowerState> ;
<#LampOffPr>
   a wotd :PreCondition ;
   wotdl:on <#LampPowerState> ;
   wotdl:value "on"^^xsd:string .
<#LampPowerState>
   a wotdl:Parameter;
   wotdl:name "LampPowerState".
```

```
(:types
lamp - device)

(:predicates
(LampPowerState ?dev - device))

(:functions
(AmbientLuminosity ?dev - device))

(:action SwitchOffLamp
:parameters (?a1 - lamp)
:precondition (and
(LampPowerState ?a1))

:effect (and (decrease
(AmbientLuminosity
?a1)680)(LampPowerState ?a1))
)
```

```
(:objects
phillipshue – lamp
GroveLightSensor – lightSensor)

(:init
(LampPowerState phillipshue)
(=(AmbientLuminosity phillipshue)19)
)

(:goal
(and (=(AmbientLuminosity
phillipshue)680))))
```

```
User Goal

{AmbientLuminosity}{IncreaseEffect}
```

Figure 2: WoTDL instance to PDDL transformation

the (*PowerLampState*) of the *lamp* object would be "true" after the operation is performed.

5.2 Problem Domain

The generation of the TTL to PDDL problem file is presented in the bottom right of Figure 2, The problem definition specifies the problem to be solved in PDDL syntax. This consists of the objects that are currently in the domain, the initial state and the desired target state. Initially, all object instances are listed with their assigned type a *philipshue* of the type *lamp* (dark orange). Following is the description of the initial state, which is displayed using the predicates from the domain definition, for example the Phillips Hue lamp is currently switched on and the ambient luminosity is equal to 19. The initial state of the environment is identified by sending an HTTP GET request to the different sensors. Finally, the description of the desired target state follows (pink), which is also displayed using the predicates. The planner should find a way to increase the brightness to 680. The goal state is expressed by the end user and converted into an appropriate format. All this information is then enough for a PDDL-capable AI planner to generate a plan as output.

6 PLAN-DO-CHECK-ACT BASED AUTOMATED PLANNING

In this section we present the methodology that is employed for planning for WoT composition. We propose a cyclic planner inspired by the Plan-Do-Control-Act (PDCA) [2] paradigm in the context of continuous improvement process in business management. This concept can be depicted as an analogy to the problem presented in this work where the achievement of the goal desired

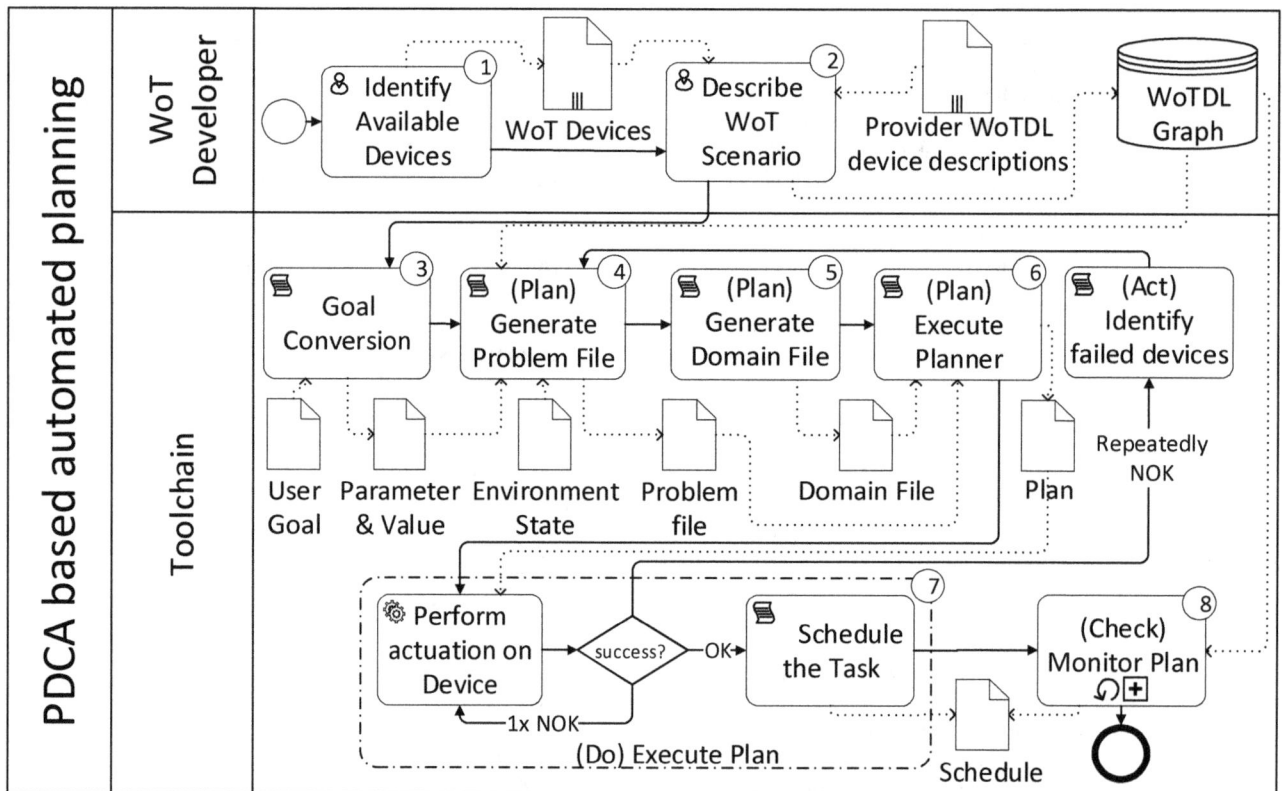

Figure 3: PDCA-based automated planning methodology for WoT composition

by the user can be regarded as a process which requires continuous observation and one or more possible re-planning iterations. The main idea behind our cyclic planner is to sense the environment continuously after an initial plan is executed in order to find and resolve inconsistencies with user issued goals. Figure 3 illustrates an overview of the workflow using BPMN. The PDCA-based automated planning for WoT composition architecture involves three main roles:

- *IoT Device Provider* is the role in charge of manufacturing and describing IoT devices and sensors according to the WoTDL ontology. The WoTDL ontology describes the key concepts of AI planning-based applications in the context of WoT.
- *End User* is the actor who will ultimately use the system and interacts with it by issuing goals (e.g., "It's too warm") using voice interactions.
- *Automated Planner Toolchain* is a system role representing our toolchain for supporting user issued goals through automatic generation and execution of a plan.

The planner involves four major steps:

- **Plan**: The planner generates an initial plan depending on the user goals, context, and available WoT devices (cf. steps 4-6)
- **Do**: The list of actions in the generated plan is executed by physical WoT devices through HTTP requests to produce the desired effect (cf. step 7)

- **Check**: The current environment state is compared to the goal state (cf. step 8)
- **Act**: If the current state and the goal state matches the cycle ends, otherwise the required procedure is taken to deal with unexpected events, unpredictable device effects and durative effects.

In the following we describe the steps of this process in sequential order.

Step 1- Identify Available Devices: Before the planning process starts the WoT developer needs to identify the set of IoT devices which will be utilized for the users scenario.

Step 2- Describe WoT Scenario : The WoT developer creates the WoTDL description by aggregating the device descriptions provided by the device providers for each device involved in the user scenario. Then, the resulting WoTDL description is stored as RDF graph according to the WoTDL ontology.

Step 3- Goal Conversion : The end users can then interact with the system for issuing goals to the WoT environment using voice interactions. The goal from the user is passed to this component and this phase is responsible for performing natural language processing to convert it in a form that can be processed by the machine. The output of this step is a JSON object representing a set of parameter and values. For example, the goal "it's too warm" is converted into {"temperature","24"}.

Step 4- Generate PDDL Problem File : Once the users desired goal is processed it should be transformed into a form that can be processed by an AI planner. In this step, the PDDL problem file is automatically generated from the WoTDL graph using a parser. To formulate the PDDL problem domain, the environment state (initial state) and the goal of the user are used as input. The initial state is identified by sensing the available sensors and actuators. More details about this step is discussed in Section 5.2.

Step 5- Generate PDDL Domain File : In this phase, the PDDL domain file is automatically generated using a parser. To create the domain file, the WoTDL graph is initially queried to retrieve all device instances that exists in the scenario as well as the environmental properties.More details about this step is discussed in Section 5.1.

Step 6- Execute Planner : Given the PDDL domain and problem files as input the planner produces an initial plan to the given planning problem to achieve the desired goal. In particular, the planner creates a planning graph with all existing states as vertices and the actions as edges. Then the Planner searches through all device actions that affect one of the goal variables to reach the goal state. After that, a sequence of steps (WoT devices actuations) to reach the goal is generated as output. It is worth noting that in this work, a state-of-the-art planner, Metric-FF [11], is used to produce the plan.

Step 7- Execute Plan : The plan generated by the Planner and the available actions from the previous step are passed as input to this phase. It then maps the steps of the plan to the actions and actuates each action by executing the associated HTTP request. These requests are defined in the device description in terms of HTTP method, URL, and body. The HTTP requests cause the physical WoT devices to produce the desired effects. This step also includes failure detection mechanism by sending a request to the unresponsive device for a maximum of three times. If the device does not respond after three times, the device is considered as fail and a re-plan is performed without the corresponding device. On the other hand, if it responds the task is scheduled for further monitoring.

Step 8- Monitor Plan : This phase constantly monitors the state of the environment to check whether the expected effect has occurred. All the available sensors from the WoTDL graph are queried at regular intervals to check whether an action for monitoring is listed. If so, the current sensor value is compared to the target state value. If these values match, the action was successful and can be excluded from further monitoring. However, if the values do not match the respective action is either executed again or the time for the next check is recalculated. If the effect of the respective action could not once again be evaluated as successful, it is marked as "failed" and a new planning process for the associated target is initiated. If there is no associated action for the respective sensor measurement parameter, the sensor value is only compared with the initial state of the measurement parameter. If these values are different from one another, there is a side effect and the user is informed accordingly. Inside this component there is a *TaskMonitor* which runs continuously as a service to monitor all sensors and the actions. Successful actions are removed because the goal has been reached, whereas failed actions inform the user or automated countermeasures are taken.

7 EVALUATION

In this section, we demonstrate the feasibility of the proposed cyclic planning approach using multiple smart home cases derived from Section 3 and explore the scalability over different number of devices. For each unique case the toolchain announced in Section 3 is tested in our smart home testbed located in the VSR laboratory to analyze the behavior of the approach based on the completion of the user issued goal.

In particular the testbed includes three sensors including temperature, humidity, light, and four actuators including lamp, fan cooler, shade and thermostat as listed in Table 1. Each of these IoT devices are accessed through different non-web interfaces. The Phillips Hue lamp is the exception, since it directly targets end users and therefore provides a web-based API. Given these devices and by following our methodology, we modeled the existing testbed using the WoTDL ontology in turtle format. Furthermore, the ontology instances of the smart home scenario are extracted to compose and deploy the standard OpenAPI specification based on the WoTDL2API [3] toolchain [19]. In this way, the IoT devices supporting different communication protocols are transformed into WoT devices. In order to offer the user an easy way to enter their goals into the system the Amazon Echo Dot is used. The Amazon Alexa Skill Kit [4] language service is utilized to create different intentions, so-called intents, which can be triggered with different utterances.

7.1 Study Cases

The evaluation cases applied to the testbed are extracted from the scenario mentioned previously in Section 3. For each case, we need to simulate the situation so that the PDCA planner can respond to the real situation. In the following, the cases are discussed:

Case A (device failure): This case represents random internal effects showing a malfunctioning device during runtime and if possible finding an alternative plan. At the beginning of the experiment both light sources are extinguished, i. the Philips lamp is off and the roller shutter lowered. Then the user expresses the goal "increase brightness". The system first tries to open the roller shutters to fulfill the goal. However, in order to simulate the problem situation, the power supply of the servomotor is disconnected to make the roller shutter fail. Figure 4a shows the results of using the cyclic planner to solve device failure. The X-axis shows the evaluation time since the users goal is issued at 0, and the Y-axis stands for the current value of brightness ranging from 0 to 600. The black lines with diamonds on top demonstrates important events occurred in the experiment during the user issued goal, each block of measurement shows a different period in the PDCA cycle. The main events in this figure are as follows: (a)The goal is extracted from the user and the planner delivers the plan, (b) the command to actuate the servomotor for the shutter is sent. Since the activation of the shutter requires 5 seconds (*waitForActuation*) the system waits in the meantime, (c) the execution is completed, (4) the *TaskMonitor* detects that the luminosity has not changed and therefore extends the waiting time by the value associated with the action (1 second), (d) the *TaskMonitor* again detects that the desired luminosity

---

[3]https://github.com/heseba/wotdl2api
[4]https://developer.amazon.com/alexa-skills-kit/

(a) Case A Failure Detection

(b) Case B Side Effect

(c) Case C Durative Effects

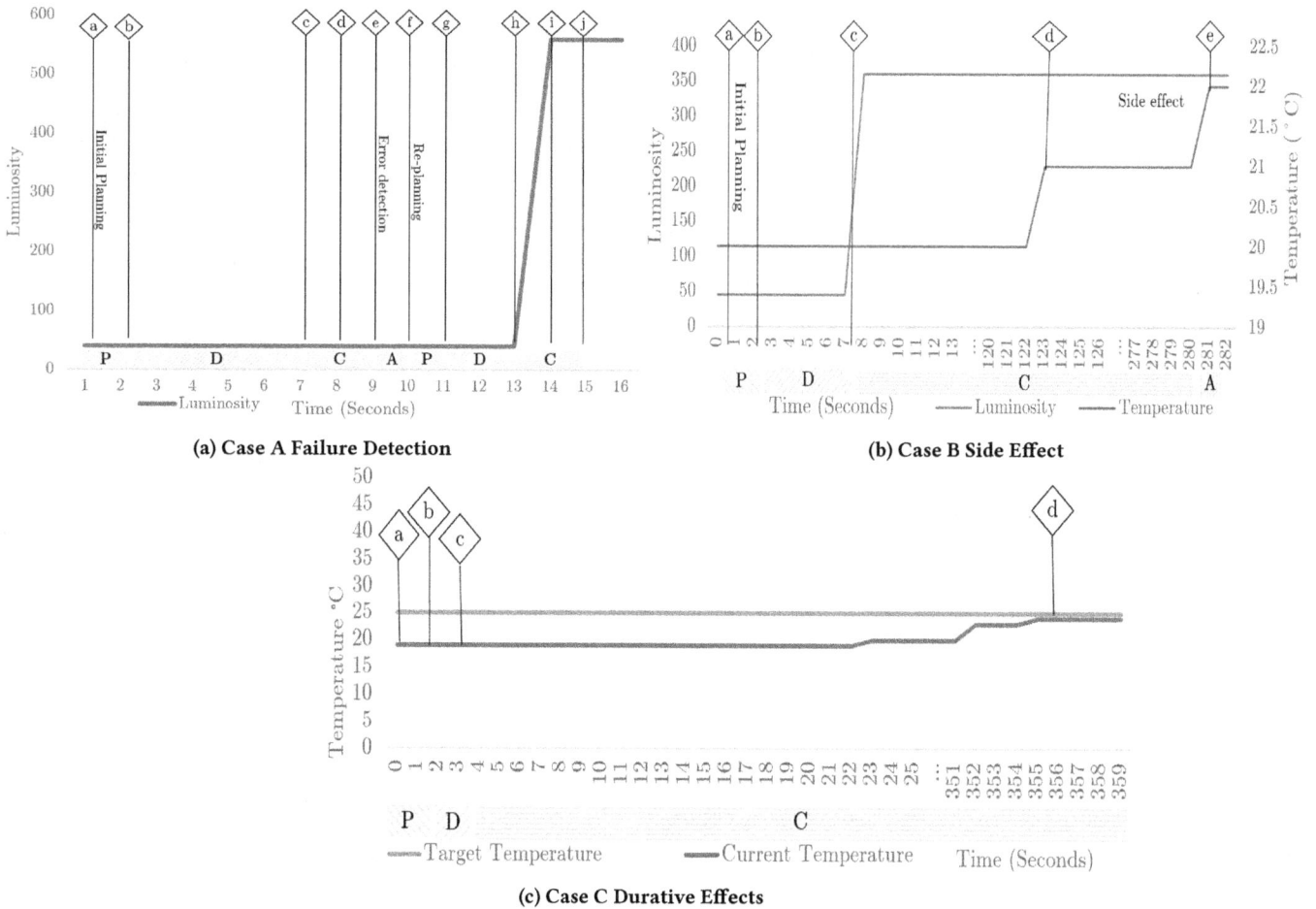

Figure 4: evaluation results on different study cases

Table 1: IoT devices in testbed for evaluation

Device Name	Protocol	Description
Phillips Hue Lamp	z-wave	Controls brightness and color of light
Shades Motor	Pulse Width Modulation	Motor for the curtains
Relay + Heating Panel	Custom Interval Control	Controls the heating
DHT11	Single-bus serial protocol	Temperature and Humidity Sensor
DC motor	Analog voltage-based	Mini Cooling Fan
Eqiva Thermostat	Bluetooth	Thermostat

has not been reached and again extends the monitoring period by one second. (e) On the third monitoring, the device is identified as faulty and is no longer considered during a new planning process, (f) the new PDDL files have been generated without considering the shutter and the planner provides a re-plan, (g) The actuation command to turn the Philips Hue lamp on is executed, (h) as a result of the actuation the luminosity increases, (i) finally the *TaskMonitor* recognizes the achievement of the desired light intensity and the goal is reached.

Case B (Side effects): The purpose of this case is to detect unwanted side effects due to incomplete knowledge about all the possible effects during the execution of the plan. In order to simulate an external event, the Bluetooth thermostat of a heating located outside the testbed is switched on to simulate the sunlight heating the room through the window. The initial situation in the house is that the Phillips Hue lamp is switched off and the roller shutter is closed. The user then specifies the goal "increase the brightness". The results of this case is shown in Figure 4b. This figure contains

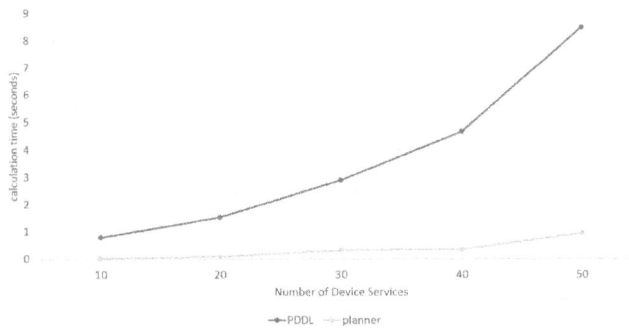

Figure 5: Planning time over many devices

two observations representing the change in temperature and luminosity. The blue line represents the temperature change and the orange line shows the luminosity. The meaning of the X-axis along with the events a and b are the same as case A. Some of the duration shown in blanks have been omitted due to brevity. The following events are worth highlighting: (c) The roller shutter is open in response to the plan executed in event b and therefore the ambient luminosity gradually increases in the room, (d) in the Control phase, the *TaskMonitor* recognizes the temperature rise from 20 to 21 degrees. In this phase, there is no detection yet, as the tolerance value is set to 1, (e) the temperature rises to 22 degrees and the *TaskMonitor* ultimately detects the unwanted side effect of opening the shutter.

Case C (Durative Effects): The purpose of this experiment is to show how the cyclic planner handles actuation's that require a longer period of time to produce the desired effect. The current temperature in the room is measured at 19 degrees and the user expresses the goal "increase the temperature to 25 degrees". By querying the WoTDL graph the *timeToEffect* of the heater is calculated as 6 minutes. The behaviour of the system is shown in Figure 4c. To explain this figure, the following events are considered: (a) the target temperature of 26 degrees is accepted by the system, the PDDL domain and problem files are generated and the planner creates a plan, (b) the thermostat is activated and set to the appropriate temperature, (c) the task is added to the *TaskList* for monitoring since the effect time is expected in 6 minutes. (d) the *TaskMonitor* realizes that the t*imeToEffect* span is expired and senses the current temperature. The temperature is sensed at 24.4 degrees which is in the tolerance range. Therefore the monitoring step is successfully completed.

To summarize, the results verify that the proposed cyclic planning approach works for the scenario we introduced before in Section 3 and can provide valid plans for user issued goals.

7.2 Scalability

One important concern with respect to all smart composition systems is how they scale with the growing number of physical devices. Therefore, We explored the scalability of our approach to demonstrate it's performance to control smart environments in realistic contexts. To demonstrate this, the WoTDL graph is supplied with

additional device instances and then the planning process is initiated. In this experiment, the time required for generating the PDDL files and running the AI planner we use in our system - Metric-FF [11]- were considered separately. The results (Figure 5) demonstrates the time it takes for the Metric-FF planner to find the solution is less than 1 second for 50 devices, but there is a sharp increase compared to the duration of only 40 devices. The time required for querying the WoTDL graph and generating the PDDL problem and domain files does significantly increase, but this can be easily resolved by caching the device capabilities locally and only generating the PDDL files whenever a change in the environment state occurs.

Although, the performance of the planning process is low, it is practical for up to a number of 20 devices. Up to this number of devices, the total time required to plan is about 2.2 seconds. Based on the current forecasts there will be about 15 smart appliances per household by 2020. We conclude that our approach is suitable to control smart environments like smart homes that do not contain a high number of devices. More optimization is necessary for larger scales and application scenarios with real-time constraint.

8 CONCLUSION AND FUTURE WORK

In this paper, we initially proposed a smart home scenario based on the unpredictable situations that can occur during planning for WoT composition. Then we proposed a fully automatic cyclic planning approach to facilitate the composition of WoT devices for end users. The solution considers three important situations in the context of WoT environments : device failure, unpredictable device effects causing side effects and durative effects. The device capabilities are described using the WoTDL ontology providing *interoperaility*, breaking down interoperability barriers through semantics and *flexibility* of supporting new device descriptions in an evolving way. Furthermore, the proposed solution is targeted for end users by only stating *what* has to be performed, without providing *how* it can be met. The results on our smart home testbed illustrated that the proposed approach can automatically solve the considered scenarios at runtime successfully without the involvement of a user. In the future, we will further optimize the solution for more realistic smart application domains. We also plan to extend the GrOWTH framework by extracting the device capabilities expressed in terms of actuations, preconditions and effects automatically, rather than adding these instances in the WoTDL ontology Graph by a domain expert. We expect that this would further improve the usability of the system for end users without domain expertise.

ACKNOWLEDGMENTS

We would like to thank Phil Dietrich for his contributions towards the implementation of this research.

REFERENCES

[1] Kevin Ashton and others. 2009. That 'internet of things' thing. *RFID journal* 22, 7 (2009), 97–114.
[2] Ron Basu. 2004. *Implementing quality: a practical guide to tools and techniques: enabling the power of operational excellence.* Cengage Learning EMEA.
[3] Chia Hung Chen, Alan Liu, and Pei Chuan Zhou. 2014. Controlling a service robot in a smart home with behavior planning and learning. *Conference Proceedings - IEEE International Conference on Systems, Man and Cybernetics* 2014-Janua, January (2014), 2821–2826. https://doi.org/10.1109/smc.2014.6974356

[4] Li Da Xu, Wu He, and Shancang Li. 2014. Internet of things in industries: A survey. *IEEE Transactions on industrial informatics* 10, 4 (2014), 2233–2243.

[5] Giuseppe Desolda, Carmelo Ardito, and Maristella Matera. 2017. Empowering End Users to Customize their Smart Environments. *ACM Transactions on Computer-Human Interaction* 24, 2 (2017), 1–52. https://doi.org/10.1145/3057859

[6] Maria Fox and Derek Long. 2003. PDDL2. 1: An extension to PDDL for expressing temporal planning domains. *Journal of artificial intelligence research* 20 (2003), 61–124.

[7] Emre Göynügür, Sara Bernardini, Geeth de Mel, Kartik Talamadupula, and Murat Sensoy. 2017. Policy conflict resolution in iot via planning. In *Canadian Conference on Artificial Intelligence*. Springer, 169–175.

[8] Dominique Guinard and Vlad Trifa. 2009. *Towards the web of things: Web mashups for embedded devices* (15 ed.). Madrid, Spain.

[9] Ourania Hatzi, Dimitris Vrakas, Nick Bassiliades, Dimosthenis Anagnostopoulos, and Ioannis Vlahavas. 2013. The PORSCE II framework: Using AI planning for automated semantic web service composition. *The Knowledge Engineering Review* 28, 2 (2013), 137–156.

[10] T Heider. 2003. Goal oriented assistance for extended multimedia systems and dynamic technical infrastructures. *Proceedings of the Seventh IASTED International Conference on Internet and Multimedia Systems and Applications* 7 (2003), 62–67.

[11] JÃŭrg Hoffmann. 2003. The Metric-FF Planning System: Translating "Ignoring Delete Lists" to Numeric State Variables. *Journal of artificial intelligence research* 20 (2003), 291–341.

[12] Eirini Kaldeli, Alexander Lazovik, and Marco Aiello. 2016. Domain-independent planning for services in uncertain and dynamic environments. *Artificial Intelligence* 236 (2016), 30–64. https://doi.org/10.1016/j.artint.2016.03.002

[13] Thomas Kirste, Thorsten Herfet, and Michael Schnaider. 2001. EMBASSI : Multimodal Assistance for Universal Access to Infotainment and Service Infrastructures. *Proceedings of the 2001 EC/NSF Workshop on Universal Accessibility of Ubiquitous Computing: Providing for the Elderly* (2001), 41–50. https://doi.org/10.1590/S0101-32622010000200006

[14] Frank Krüger, Gernot Ruscher, Sebastian Bader, and Thomas Kirste. 2011. A context-aware proactive controller for smart environments. *CEUR Workshop Proceedings* 747 (2011). https://doi.org/10.1524/icom.

[15] Simon Mayer, Dominic Plangger, Florian Michahelles, and Simon Rothfuss. 2016. UberManufacturing A Goal-Driven Collaborative Industrial Manufacturing Marketplace. *Proceedings of the 6th International Conference on the Internet of Things - IoT'16* (2016), 111–119. https://doi.org/10.1145/2991561.2991569

[16] Simon Mayer, Ruben Verborgh, Matthias Kovatsch, and Friedemann Mattern. 2016. Smart Configuration of Smart Environments. *IEEE Trans. Automation Science and Engineering* 13, 3 (2016), 1247–1255.

[17] Mahda Noura, Amelie Gyrard, Sebastian Heil, and Martin Gaedke. 2018. Concept extraction from the Web of Things knowledge bases. In *Proceedings of the International Conference WWW/Internet 2018*.

[18] Mahda Noura, Sebastian Heil, and Martin Gaedke. 2018. GrOWTH: Goal-Oriented End User Development for Web of Things Devices. In *International Conference on Web Engineering 2018*.

[19] Mahda Noura, Sebastian Heil, and Martin Gaedke. 2019. Webifying Heterogenous Internet of Things Devices. In *International Conference on Web Engineering 2019*.

[20] Javier Palanca, Elena del Val, Ana Garcia-Fornes, Holger Billhardt, Juan Manuel Corchado, and Vicente Julián. 2018. Designing a goal-oriented smart-home environment. *Information Systems Frontiers* 20, 1 (2018), 125–142. https://doi.org/10.1007/s10796-016-9670-x

[21] Shankar R Ponnekanti and Armando Fox. 2002. Sword: A developer toolkit for web service composition. In *Proc. of the Eleventh International World Wide Web Conference, Honolulu, HI*, Vol. 45.

[22] Noel Nuo Wi Tay, Janos Botzheim, and Naoyuki Kubota. 2018. Human-Centric Automation and Optimization for Smart Homes. *IEEE Transactions on Automation Science and Engineering* (2018), 1–13. https://doi.org/10.1109/TASE.2018.2789658

[23] Pengwei Wang, Zhijun Ding, Changjun Jiang, Mengchu Zhou, and Yuwei Zheng. 2016. Automatic web service composition based on uncertainty execution effects. *IEEE Transactions on Services Computing* 9, 4 (2016), 551–565. https://doi.org/10.1109/TSC.2015.2412943

[24] Stephen S. Yau and Arun Balaji Buduru. 2014. Intelligent Planning for Developing Mobile IoT Applications Using Cloud Systems. *2014 IEEE International Conference on Mobile Services* (2014), 55–62. https://doi.org/10.1109/MobServ.2014.17

What sets Verified Users apart?
Insights, Analysis and Prediction of Verified Users on Twitter

Indraneil Paul
IIIT Hyderabad
indraneil.paul@research.iiit.ac.in

Abhinav Khattar
IIIT Delhi
abhinav15120@iiitd.ac.in

Shaan Chopra
IIIT Delhi
shaan15090@iiitd.ac.in

Ponnurangam Kumaraguru*
IIIT Delhi
pk@iiitd.ac.in

Manish Gupta**
IIIT Hyderabad
manish.gupta@iiit.ac.in

ABSTRACT

Social network and publishing platforms, such as Twitter, support the concept of a secret proprietary *verification* process, for handles they deem worthy of platform-wide public interest. In line with significant prior work which suggests that possessing such a status symbolizes enhanced credibility in the eyes of the platform audience, a verified badge is clearly coveted among public figures and brands. What are less obvious are the inner workings of the verification process and what being verified represents. This lack of clarity, coupled with the flak that Twitter received by extending aforementioned status to political extremists in 2017, backed Twitter into publicly admitting that the process and what the status represented needed to be rethought.

With this in mind, we seek to unravel the aspects of a user's profile which likely engender or preclude verification. The aim of the paper is two-fold: First, we test if discerning the verification status of a handle from profile metadata and content features is feasible. Second, we unravel the features which have the greatest bearing on a handle's verification status. We collected a dataset consisting of profile metadata of all 231,235 verified English-speaking users (as of July 2018), a control sample of 175,930 non-verified English-speaking users and all their 494 million tweets over a one year collection period. Our proposed models are able to reliably identify verification status (Area under curve AUC > 99%). We show that number of public list memberships, presence of neutral sentiment in tweets and an authoritative language style are the most pertinent predictors of verification status.

To the best of our knowledge, this work represents the first attempt at discerning and classifying verification worthy users on Twitter.

---

* This work was partially done by the author while in sabbatical at IIIT Hyderabad (pk.guru@iiit.ac.in).
** The author is also a Principal Applied Researcher at Microsoft India (gmanish@microsoft.com).

CCS CONCEPTS

• **Information systems** → **Social networks**; *Relevance assessment*; Content analysis and feature selection; • **Networks** → **Social media networks**; **Online social networks**.

KEYWORDS

Twitter, Social Influence, Verified Users

ACM Reference Format:
Indraneil Paul, Abhinav Khattar, Shaan Chopra, Ponnurangam Kumaraguru, and Manish Gupta. 2019. What sets Verified Users apart? Insights, Analysis and Prediction of Verified Users on Twitter. In *11th ACM Conference on Web Science (WebSci '19), June 30–July 3, 2019, Boston, MA, USA.* ACM, New York, NY, USA, 10 pages. https://doi.org/10.1145/3292522.3326026

1 INTRODUCTION

The increased relevance of social media in our daily life has been accompanied by an exigent demand for a means to affirm the authenticity and authority of content sources. This challenge becomes even more apparent during the dissemination of real-time or breaking news, whose arrival on such platforms often precedes eventual traditional media reportage [19, 38]. In line with this need, major social networks such as Twitter, Facebook and Instagram have incorporated a verification process to authenticate handles they deem important enough to be worth impersonating. Usually conferred to accounts of well-known public personalities and businesses, *verified accounts*[1] are indicated with a badge next to the screen name (e.g., ☑ on Twitter and ☑ on Facebook). Twitter's verification policy [67] states that an account is verified if it belongs to a personality or business deemed to be of sufficient public interest in diverse fields, such as journalism, politics, sports, etc. However, the exact decision making process behind evaluating the strength of a user's case for verification remains a trade secret. This work attempts to unravel the likely factors that strengthen a user's case for verification by delving into the aspects of a user's Twitter presence, that most reliably predict platform verification.

1.1 Motivation

Our motivation behind this work was two-fold and is elaborated in the following text.

---

[1] The exact term varies by platform, with other social networks using the term "Verified Profiles". However in the interest of consistency, all owner-authenticated accounts are referred to as *verified accounts*, and their owners as *verified users*.

Lack of procedural clarity and imputation of bias: Despite repeated statements by Twitter about verification not being equivalent to endorsement, aspects of the process – the rarity of the status and its prominent visual signalling [68] – have led users to conflate authenticity and credibility. This perception was confirmed in full public view when Twitter was backed into suspending its requests for verification in response to being accused of granting verified status to political extremists [2], with the insinuation being that the verified badge lent their otherwise extremist opinions a facade of mainstream credibility.

This however, engendered accusations of Twitter's verification procedure harbouring a liberal bias. Multiple tweets imputing the same gave rise to the hashtag #VerifiedHate. Similar insinuations have been made by right-leaning Indian users of the platform in the lead up to the 2019 Indian General Elections under the hashtag #ProtestAgainstTwitter. These hitherto unfounded allegations of bias prompted us to delve deeper into understanding what may be driving the process and inferring whether these claims were justified or could the difference in status be explained away by less insidious factors relating to a user's profile and content.

Positive perception and coveted nature: Despite having its detractors, the fact remains that a verified badge is highly coveted amongst public figures and influencers. This is with good reason as in spite of being intended as a mark of authenticity, prior work in social sciences and psychology points to verified badges conferring additional credibility to a handle's posted tweets [11, 23, 51]. Psychological testing [24] has also revealed that the credibility of a message and its reception is influenced by its purported source and presentation rather than just its pertinence or credulity. Captology studies [21] indicate that widely endorsed information originating from a well-known source is easier to perceive as trustworthy and back up the former claim. This is pertinent as owners of verified accounts are usually well-known and their content is on an average more frequently liked and retweeted than that of the generic Twittersphere [58, 63].

Adding to the desirability of exclusive visual indicators is the demanding nature of credibility assessment on Twitter. The imposed character limit and a minimal scope of visually customizing content, coupled with the feverish rate at which content is consumed – with users on average devoting a mere three seconds of attention per tweet [17] – makes users resort to heuristics to judge online content. There is substantial work on heuristic based models for online credibility evaluation [14, 29, 61]. Particularly relevant to this inquiry is the *endorsement heuristic*, which is associated with credibility conferred to it (e.g. a verified badge) and the *consistency heuristic*, which stems from endorsements by several authorities (e.g. a user verified in one platform is likely to be verified on others).

Unsurprisingly, a verified status is highly sought after by preeminent entities, as evidenced by the prevalence of get-verified-quick schemes such as promoted tweets from the now suspended account '@verified845' [9, 65]. Our work attempts to obtain actionable insights into verification process, thus providing entities looking to get verified a means to strengthen their case.

1.2 Research Questions

The aforementioned motivating factors pose a few avenues of research inquiry that we attempt to answer, which are detailed below.

RQ1: Can the verification status of a user be predicted from profile metadata and tweet contents? If so what are the most reliably discriminative features?

RQ2: Do any inconsistencies exist between verified and non-verified users with respect to peripheral aspects like the choice and variety of topics they tweet about?

1.3 Contributions

Our contributions can be summarized as follows:

- We motivate and propose the problem of predicting verification status of a Twitter user.
- We detail a framework extracting a substantial set of features from data and meta-data about social media users, including friends, tweet content and sentiment, activity time series, and profile trajectories. We plan to make this dataset of 407,165 users and 494 million tweets, publicly available upon publication of the work.[3]
- Additionally, we factored in state-of-the-art bot detection analysis into our predictive model. We use these features to train highly-accurate models capable of discerning a user's verified status. For a general user, we are able to provide a zero to one score representing their likelihood of being verified in Twitter.
- We report the most informative features in discriminating verified users from non-verified ones and also shed light on the manner in which the span and gamut of topic coverage between their tweets differs.

The rest of the paper is organized as follows. Section 2 details relevant prior work, hence putting our work in perspective. Section 3 elaborates our data acquisition methodology. In Sections 4 and 5, we conduct a comparative analysis between verified and non-verified users, addressing RQ1 and RQ2 respectively, and attempt to uncover features that can reliably classify them. We conclude with a brief summary in Section 6.

2 RELATED WORK

Previous studies have focused on measuring user impact in social networks. As user impact might be a critical factor in deciding who gets verified on Twitter [67], it is important to study how certain users in particular networks have more impact/influence as compared to the others. Cha et al. [13] studied the dynamics of influence on Twitter based on three key measures: in-degree, retweeets, and user-mentions. They show that in-degree alone is not sufficient to measure the influence of a user on Twitter. Bakshy et al. [5] demonstrate that URLs from users who have been influential in the past tend to generate larger cascades on the Twitter follower graph. They also show that URLs considered more interesting and that kindle positive emotions, spread more. Canali et al. [10] identify key users on social networks who are important sources or targets for content disseminated online. They use a dimensionality-reduction based technique and conduct experiments with YouTube and Flickr

---

[2] https://www.bbc.com/news/technology-41934831

[3] http://precog.iiitd.edu.in/requester.php?dataset=twitterVerified19

datasets to obtain results which outperform the existing solutions by 15%. The novelty of their approach is that they use attribute rich user profiles and not just stay limited to their network information. On the other hand, Lampos et al. [40] predict user impact on Twitter using features, such as user statistics and tweet content, that are under the control of the user. They experiment with both linear and non-linear prediction techniques and find that Gaussian Processes based models perform the best for the prediction task. Klout [1] was a service that measured the influence of a person using information from multiple social networks. Their initial framework [56] used long lasting (e.g., in-degree, pagerank centrality, recommendations etc) and dynamic features (reactions to a post such as retweets, up-votes etc.) to estimate the influence of a person across nine different social networks.

Further studies have tried to classify users based on factors such as celebrity status, socioeconomic status etc. Lampos et al. [39] classify the socioeconomic status of users on Twitter as high, middle or lower socioeconomic, using features such as tweet content, topics of discussion, interaction behaviour, and user impact. They obtain an accuracy of 75% using a nonlinear, generative learning approach with a composite Gaussian Process kernel. Preoctiuc-Pietro et al. [54] present a Gaussian Process regression model, which predicts the income of the user on Twitter. They examined factors that help characterize user income on Twitter and analyze their relation with emotions, sentiments, perceived psycho-demographics, and language used in posts. Further, Marwick et al. [45] qualitatively study the behaviours of celebrities on Twitter and how it impacts creation and sharing of content online. They aim to conceptualize "celebrity as a practice" in terms of personal information revelation, language usage, interactions, and affiliation with followers, among other things. There are also other studies that try to characterize usage patterns [2] and personalities [62] of varied users on Twitter.

Multiple existing studies attempt to detect and analyze automated activity on Twitter [15, 16, 20, 25, 71, 78] and differentiate bot activity from human or partial-human activity. Conversely, Chu et al. [16] identify users on Twitter that generate automated content. The verification badge was a key feature used for the purpose. Holistically characterizing features that resemble automated activity, and the extent to which exhibiting the same can hurt a user's case for verification is further explored in Section 4.2.

Past studies on verified accounts have focused on elucidating their behaviors and properties on Twitter. Hentschel et al. [34] analyze verified users on Twitter and further use this information to identify trustworthy "regular" (not fake or spam) Twitter users. Castillo et al. [11] attempt to identify credible tweets based on a variety of profile features including whether the user was verified by the platform or not. Along similar lines, Morris et al. [51] examined factors that influence profile credibility perceptions on Twitter. They found that possessing an authenticated status is one of the most robust predictors of positive credibility. Paul et el. [52] performed multiple network analyses of the verified accounts present on Twitter and reveal how they diverge from earlier results on the network as a whole. Hence, to summarize, there exists a rich body of literature establishing the enhancement of credibility and perceived importance a verified badge endows a user with. However, no prior work, to the best of our knowledge, has attempted to characterize attributes that make the aforementioned status more attainable.

3 DATASET

In this section, we present details of our dataset and the data collection process along with a summary of the diverse features.

3.1 User Metadata

The '@verified' handle on Twitter follows all accounts on the platform that are currently verified. We queried this handle on the 18th of July 2018 and extracted the IDs of 297,776 users who were verified at the time. In the interest of verifying Twitter's assertion that likeliness of an handle's verification is commensurate with public interest in that handle and nothing else [66, 67], we sought to obtain a random controlled subset of non-verified users on the platform. Pursuant to this need, we leveraged Twitter's Firehose API – a near real-time stream of public tweets and accompanying author metadata – in order to acquire a random set of 284,312 non-verified users, controlling for a conventional measure of public interest, by ensuring that the number of followers of every non-verified user obtained was within 2% that of a unique verified user that we had previously acquired.

Twitter provides a REST Application Programming Interface (API) with various endpoints that make data retrieval from the site in an organized manner easier. We used the REST API to acquire profile metadata of the user handles obtained previously including account age, number of friends, followers and tweets. Additionally, we obtained the number of public Twitter lists a user was part of and the handle's profile description. Metadata features extracted from user profiles have previously been used for classifying users and inferring activity patterns on Twitter [48, 76]. We further focused our work to the subset of users who had English listed as their profile language thus enabling us to focus on the largest linguistic demographic on the platform [50] and leaving us with 231,235 English verified users and 175,930 non-verified users.

3.2 Content Features

Utilizing Twitter's Firehose API, we acquired all tweets authored by the aforementioned users over a one year collection period spanning from 1st June 2017 to 31st May 2018. In total, our collection process acquired roughly 494,452,786 tweets. The tweet texts were retained and any accompanying media such as GIFs were deemed surplus to requirements and discarded.

From the text we extracted linguistic and stylistic features such as the number and proportion of *Part-Of-Speech* (POS) tags, effectively obtaining a user's breakdown of natural language component usage. Work demonstrating the importance of content features in location inference [44], tweet classification [7], and network characterization [42] further led us to extract the frequency of hashtags, retweets, mentions and external links used by each user. Prompted by studies showing that the deceptiveness of tweets could be inferred from the length of sentences constituting them [4], we computed additional features including average words per sentence, average words per tweet, character level entropy and frequency and proportion of long words (word length greater than six letters) per user.

In the interest of better discerning the emotions conveyed by the tweets authored by a user and responses they may evoke in the

User Metadata		Temporal Features	
	Number of followers		Average number of followers last year
	Number of friends		Average number of friends last year
	Number of statuses		Average number of statuses last year
	Number of public list memberships		Proportion of followers gained in last 3 months
	Account age		Proportion of friends gained in last 3 months
			Proportion of statuses generated in last 3 months
			Proportion of followers gained in last 1 month
			Proportion of friends gained in last 1 month
			Proportion of statuses generated in last 1 month
			Average duration between statuses
Content Features	Number of POS tags[1]	**Miscellaneous Features**	LIWC analytic summary score
	Frequency of POS tags[1]		LIWC authentic summary score
	Average number of words per sentence		LIWC clout summary score
	Average number of words per tweet		LIWC tone summary score
	Character level entropy		Botometer complete automation probability
	Proportion of long words[2]		Botometer network score
	Positive sentiment score[3]		Botometer content score
	Negative sentiment score[3]		Botometer temporal score
	Neutral sentiment score[3]		Tweet topic distribution[4]
	Compound sentiment score[3]		
	Frequency of hashtags		
	Frequency of retweets		
	Frequency of mentions		
	Frequency of external links posted		

Table 1: List of features extracted per user by our framework.

[1] Part Of Speech (POS) tags include nouns, personal pronouns, impersonal pronouns, adjectives, adverbs, verbs, auxiliary verbs, prepositions and articles.
[2] Long words are defined as words longer than 6 letters.
[3] Sentiment scores are weighted over all tweets of a user by tweet length.
[4] Scores over 100 topics are extracted from the tweets.

potential audience, sentiment analysis presented itself as an effective tool. Sentiment gleaned from Twitter conversations has been used to predict financial outcomes [8], electoral outcomes [3] as well as the ease of content dissemination [22]. We used Vader [26], a popular social media sentiment analysis lexicon, which has previously been widely used in a plethora of applications ranging from predicting elections [3, 55] to forecasting cryptocurrency market fluctuations [59]. We extracted positive, negative and neutral sentiment scores and an additional fourth compound score, which is a nonlinear normalized sum of valence computed based on established heuristics [74] and a sentiment lexicon. All four scores are computed per user, weighted by tweet length.

3.3 Temporal Features

Existing research suggests that temporal features relating to content generation and activity levels on Twitter can be used to infer emergent trending topics [12] as well as influential users [41].

Leveraging the Twitter Firehose, we gathered fine-grained time series of user statistics including number of friends, followers and statuses, thus permitting us to compute their averages over our one year collection period. Furthermore, positing that a user's likelihood of verification may be predicated on how ascendant their reach in

the platform is, we compute the proportion of friends and followers gained over the last one month and the last three months of our collection period. Additionally, similar trajectory encoding features are computed for tweet activity levels over the aforementioned one and three month windows, and the average time between statuses is extracted using the status count time series on a per user basis.

3.4 Miscellaneous Features

Attempting to capture qualitative cognitive and emotional cues from a user's tweets, we acquired the four LIWC 2015 [53] summary statistics named Analytic, Clout, Authentic and Tone for each user in our dataset. The summary dimensions indicate the presence of logical and hierarchical thinking patterns, confidence and leadership, personal cues and emotional tone, respectively, in the tweets of a user. LIWC categories have been scientifically validated to perform well in determining affect on Twitter [18, 70] and have been previously used to detect sarcasm [27] and for mental health diagnoses from Twitter conversations [31].

Furthermore, positing that accounts perceived as being completely or partially automated may have a harder time getting verified, we leveraged Botometer – a flagship bot detection solution [69] that exposes a free public API. The system is trained on thousands of instances of social bots and the creators report AUC ROC scores between 0.89 and 0.95. Botometer utilizes features spanning the gamut from network attributes to temporal activity patterns. Additionally, it queries Twitter to extract 300 recent tweets and publicly available account metadata, and feeds these features to an ensemble of machine learning classifiers, which produce a Complete Automation Probability (CAP) score, which we acquire for every user in our dataset. We also augment our dataset with the temporal, network and content category automation scores for each user.

Finally, we also look to glean into the topics that users tweet about. Topic modelling has been effectively used in categorizing trending topics on Twitter [79] and inferring author attributes from tweet content [47]. To this end, we ran the Gibbs sampling based Mallet implementation of Latent Dirichlet Allocation (LDA) [46] setting the number of topics to 100 with 1000 iterations of sampling. Although, such a topic model could be applied on a per tweet basis and subsequently aggregated by user, we find this approach to not work very well as most tweets are simply a sentence long. To overcome this difficulty, we follow the workaround adopted by previous studies by aggregating all the tweets of a user into a single document [35, 75]. In effect, this treatment can be regarded as an application of the author-topic model [60] to tweets, where each document has a single author.

3.5 Rectifying Class Imbalance

Focusing our analysis on the Twitter Anglosphere left us with a substantially skewed class distribution of 231,235 verified users and 175,930 non-verified users in our dataset. In keeping with existing research on imbalanced learning on Twitter data [30, 49], we used a two-pronged approach to rectify this – a minority over-sampling technique named ADASYN [32] which generates samples based on the feature space of the minority examples and a hybrid over and under-sampling technique called SMOTETomek which additionally also eliminates samples of the over-represented class [36] and has been found to give exemplary results on imbalanced datasets[6]. Augmenting our classifier's training data in the aforementioned manner allowed us to attain near-perfect classification scores.

The data collected is classified and summarized in Table 1. We intend to anonymize and make this dataset accessible to the public in a manner compliant with Twitter terms, once this work is published.

4 INFERRING VERIFIED STATUS

We commence our analysis by eliminating all features that could be deemed surfeit to requirements. To this end, we employed an all-relevant feature selection model [37] which classifies features into three categories: confirmed, tentative and rejected. We only retain features that the model is able to confirm over 100 iterations.

To evaluate the effectiveness of our framework in discerning verification status of users, we examine five classification performance metrics – precision, recall, F1-score, accuracy and area under ROC curve – for five classifiers. The first two methods intended at establishing baselines were a Logistic Regressor and a Support Vector Classifier. Further, three methods were used to gauge how far the classification performance could be pushed using the features we collected. These were (1) a Generalized Additive Model

trained by nested iterations, setting all terms to smooth, (2) a Multi Layered Perceptron with 3 hidden layers of 100, 30 and 10 neurons respectively, using Adam as an optimiser and ReLU as activation and (3) state-of-the-art Gradient Boosting tool named XGBoost with a maximum tree depth of 6 and a learning rate of 0.2. The results obtained are detailed in Table 2. The first batch of results are obtained by training on the original unadulterated training split. Even without rectifying class distribution biases, we are able to attain a high classification accuracy of 98.9% on our most competitive classifier.

The second and third batches are trained on data rectified for class imbalance using the adaptive synthetic over-sampling method (ADASYN) and a hybrid over and under-sampling method (SMOTE-Tomek), respectively. The ADASYN algorithm generates samples based on the feature space of the minority class data points and is a powerful method that has seen success across many domains [33] in neutralizing the deleterious effects of class imbalance. The SMOTE-Tomek algorithm combines the above over-sampling strategy with an under-sampling method called Tomek link removal [64] to remove any bias introduced by over-sampling. This rectification did improve results, generally improving the performance of our two baseline choices and especially helping us inch closer to perfect performance with gradient boosting. However, particularly surprising was the detrimental effect of class re-balancing on the MLP classifier which in all likeliness also learned the non-salient patterns in the re-balanced data. Also unexpectedly, the ADASYN re-balancing outperformed the more sophisticated SMOTETomek re-balancing in pushing the performance limits of the support vector (89.1% accuracy) and gradient boosting (99.1% accuracy) approaches. This might be owing to the fact that the Tomek link removal method omits informative samples close to the classification boundary thus affecting the learned support vectors and decision tree splits.

Our results suggest that near perfect classification of the Twitter user verification status is possible without resorting to complex deep-learning pipelines that sacrifice interpretability.

4.1 Feature Importance Analysis

To compare the usefulness of various categories of features, we trained gradient boosting classifier, our most competitive model, using each category of features alone. While we achieved the best performance with user metadata features, content features were not far behind. Evaluated on multiple randomized train-test splits of our dataset, user metadata and content features were both able to consistently surpass 0.88 AUC. Additionally, temporal features alone are able to consistently attain an AUC of over 0.79.

The individual feature importances were determined using the Gini impurity reduction metric output by the gradient boosting model trained on the unmodified dataset. To rank the most important features reliably, the model was trained 100 times with varying combinations of hyperparameters (column sub-sampling, data sub-sampling and tree child weight) and the features determined to be the most important were noted. The most reliably discriminative features and their normalized density distributions over the values they attain are detailed in Figure 1. These features generally exhibit intuitive patterns of separation based on which an informed

Dataset	Classifier	Precision	Recall	F1-Score	Accuracy	ROC AUC Score
Original imbalanced data	Logistic Regression	0.86	0.86	0.86	0.859	0.854
	Support Vector Classifier	0.89	0.89	0.89	0.887	0.883
	Generalized Additive Model[1]	0.97	0.98	0.98	0.975	0.976
	3-Hidden layer NN (100,30,10) ReLU+Adam	0.98	0.98	0.98	0.983	0.977
	XGBoost Classifier	0.99	0.99	0.99	**0.989**	**0.990**
ADASYN class rebalancing	Logistic Regression	0.86	0.86	0.86	0.856	0.858
	Support Vector Classifier	0.89	0.89	0.89	0.891	0.891
	Generalized Additive Model[1]	0.97	0.97	0.97	0.974	0.973
	3-Hidden layer NN (100,30,10) ReLU+Adam	0.96	0.96	0.96	0.959	0.957
	XGBoost Classifier	0.99	0.99	0.99	**0.991**	**0.991**
SMOTETomek class rebalancing	Logistic Regression	0.86	0.86	0.86	0.860	0.856
	Support Vector Classifier	0.90	0.90	0.90	0.903	0.901
	Generalized Additive Model[1]	0.98	0.97	0.98	0.974	0.974
	3-Hidden layer NN (100,30,10) ReLU+Adam	0.97	0.97	0.97	0.966	0.968
	XGBoost Classifier	0.99	0.99	0.99	**0.990**	**0.991**

Table 2: Summary of classification performance of various approaches using metadata, temporal and contextual features on the original and balanced datasets.

[1] The generalized additive models were trained using all smooth terms.

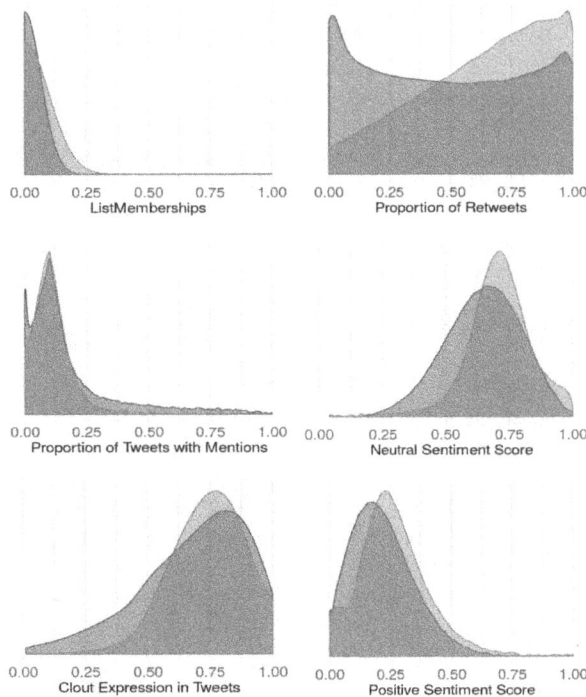

Figure 1: Normalized density estimations of the six most discriminative features for verified (blue) and non-verified users (red).

prediction can be attempted, e.g., the very highest echelons of public list membership counts are populated exclusively by verified users while the very low extremes of propensity for authoritative speech as indicated by LIWC Clout summary scores are exclusively displayed by non-verified users.

The top 6 features are sufficient to reach performance of 0.9 AUC on their own right and the top 10 features are sufficient to further push those numbers up to 0.93. This is largely owing to the fact that substantial redundancy was observed among sets of highly correlated features such as some linguistic (tendency to use long words and impersonal pronouns highly correlate with high analytic LIWC summary scores) and temporal trajectory (most ascendant users score highly in both the 1 month and 3 month features in terms of tweets authored and followers gained) features.

4.2 Clustering and characterization

In order to characterize accounts with a higher resolution than a binary verification status will permit, we apply K-Means++ on the normalized user vectors selecting the 30 most discriminative features indicated by the XGBoost model – our most competitive classifier. We settle on 8 different clusters based on evaluation including the inflection point of the clustering inertia curve and the proportion of variance explained. In the interest of an intuitive visualization, two dimensional embeddings obtained using t-SNE dimensionality reduction method [43] are presented. Tuning the perplexity metric appropriately, the method considers the similarity of data points in our feature space and embeds them in a manner that reflects their proximity in the feature space. The embeddings are plotted and our classifier responses for members of the different clusters are detailed in Figure 2.

Investigating these clusters allows us to further unravel combinations of attributes that strengthen a user's case for verification. Clusters C0 and C2 are composed nearly exclusively of non-verified

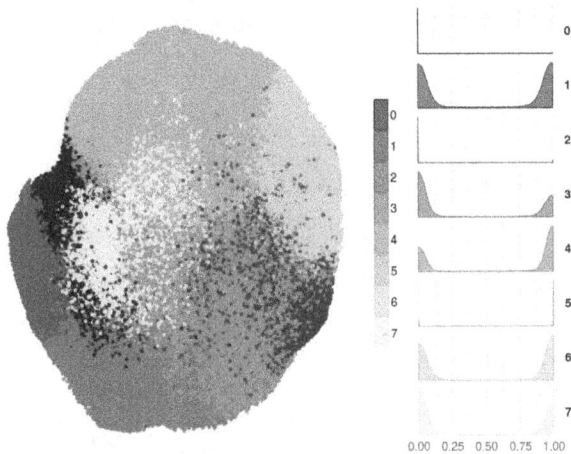

Figure 2: t-SNE embeddings of accounts coloured by cluster. The distribution of verification probabilities by cluster, as predicted by our classifier, are faceted on the right.

Cluster	Population	Accuracy	ROC AUC Score
C0	19462	0.996	0.989
C1	26259	0.986	0.986
C2	19356	0.994	0.984
C3	46178	0.988	0.987
C4	90843	0.989	0.987
C5	105701	0.993	0.986
C6	39248	0.990	0.989
C7	60118	0.987	0.986

Table 3: Classification performance of our most competitive model broken down by cluster.

users. Cluster C0 can largely be characterized as the Twitter layman with a high proportion of experiential tweets. This narrative further plays out in our collected features with members of this cluster on average having short tweets, high incidence of verb usage and scoring especially high in the LIWC Authenticity summary. Cluster C2 can be characterized as an amalgamation of accounts exhibiting bot-like behavior. Members of this cluster scored highly on the complete, network and content automation scores in our feature set. Furthermore, members in C2 possessed attributes previously linked to spammers such as copious usage of hashtags [77] and external links [72]. Manual inspection verified the substantial presence of automated content such as local weather updates in this cluster. Unsurprisingly, members of this cluster were predicted to possess the lowest verification probability by our classifier.

The composition of clusters C4 and C6 leans towards verified users, with members of C4 having a tendency to post longer tweets and retweet more frequently than author content, while members of C6 almost exclusively retweet on the platform with slightly over 93% of their content being such. Cluster C5 is nearly entirely comprised of verified users and includes elite Twitteratti that comprise the core of verified users on the platform. These users have by far the highest list memberships on average while also scoring very highly on the LIWC Clout summary. Predictably, members of this cluster were predicted to possess the highest verification probability by our classifier.

The remaining clusters C1, C3 and C7 are comprised of a mix of verified and non-verified users. However, further inspection revealed that they have very divergent trajectories. Members of cluster C1 are ascendant both in terms of reach and activity levels as evidenced by the proportion of their followers gained and statuses authored in the last one and three months of our collection period. These members can be said to constitute a nouveau-elite group of users. This is further backed up by the fact that these users are lacking in their presence in public lists as compared to the very established elite in cluster C5. Manual inspection also verifies that many of these users have attained verification during our collection

period. This is in stark contrast with members of C3 and C7 who are either stagnant or declining in their reach and activity levels and show very low engagement with the rest of the platform in terms of retweets and mentions. Remarkably, our classifier is able to make this distinction and rates members of C1 as slightly better candidates for verification on average than members of C3 or C7. The relative difficulty of classifying users in these mixed clusters is demonstrated in the performance breakdown detailed in Table 3.

5 COMPARATIVE TOPICAL USAGE ANALYSIS

Having deduced important predictive features present in a user's metadata, linguistic style and activity levels over time with respect to verification status, we next investigate the presence of similar predictive patterns in the choice and variety of tweet topic usage amongst users.

5.1 Content Topics

In order to obtain a topical breakdown of a user's tweets in an unsupervised manner, we ran the Gibbs sampling based Mallet implementation of Latent Dirichlet Allocation (LDA) [46] with 1000 iterations of sampling. Narrowing down on the correct number of topics T required us to execute multiple runs of the model while varying our choices for the number of topics. The model was executed for 30, 50, 100, 150 and 300 topics and the likelihood estimates were noted. It must be mentioned that in all cases the likelihood estimates stabilized well within the 1000 iteration limit we set. The likelihood keeps rising in value up to $T = 100$ topics, after which it sees a decline. This kind of profile is often seen when varying the hyperparameter of a statistical model, with the optimal model being rich enough to fit the information available in the data, yet not complex enough to begin fitting noise. This led us to conclude that the tweets we collected over a year are best accounted for by incorporating 100 separate topics. We set document-topic density $\alpha = T/50$ and topic-word density $\beta = 0.01$, which are the default settings recommended in prior studies [28] and maintain the sum of the Dirichlet hyperparameters, which can be interpreted as the number of virtual samples contributing to the smoothing of the topic distribution, as constant. The chosen value of β is small enough to permit a fine-grained breakdown of tweet topics covering various conversational areas.

Classifier	Precision	Recall	F1-Score	Accuracy	ROC AUC Score
Generalized Additive Model (GAM)[1]	0.83	0.83	0.83	0.832	0.831
3-Hidden layer NN (100,30,10) ReLU+Adam	0.88	0.88	0.88	**0.882**	**0.880**
XGBoost Classifier	0.82	0.82	0.82	0.824	0.823

Table 4: Summary of classification performance of various approaches on inferred topics.

[1] The generalized additive models were trained using all smooth terms.

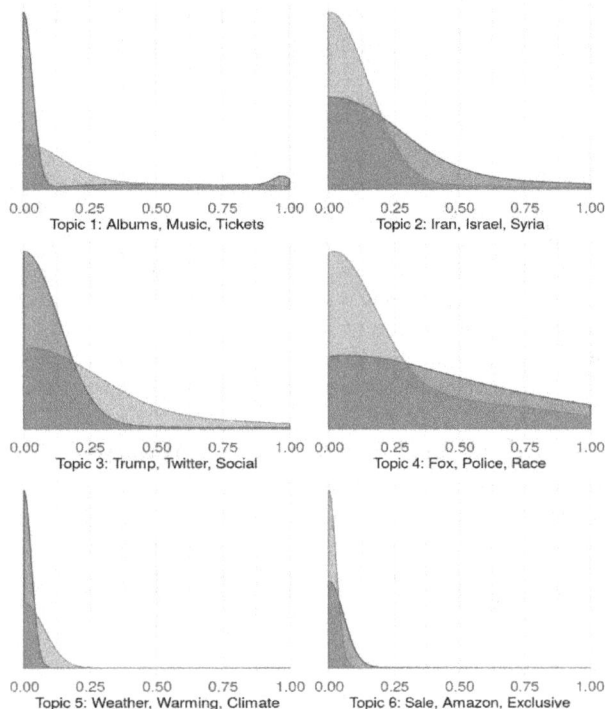

Figure 3: Normalized density estimations of usage for the six most discriminative topics for verified (blue) and non-verified users (red). Listed alongside are the top three most probable keywords for each topic.

We again commenced the prediction by pruning down our topical feature set using the all relevant feature selection method we used earlier [37] in Section 4. This allowed us to hone in on the 76 topics that were confirmed to be predictive of verification status. To evaluate the effectiveness of our framework in discerning verification status of users from topic cues, we examine five classification performance metrics – precision, recall, F1-score, accuracy and area under ROC curve – for the three classifiers that were most competitive in our previous classification task. These were (1) a Generalized Additive Model trained by nested iterations, setting all terms to smooth, (2) a Multi Layered Perceptron with 3 hidden layers of 100, 30 and 10 neurons respectively, using Adam as an optimiser and ReLU as activation and (3) Gradient Boosting tool named XGBoost with a maximum tree depth of 5 and a learning rate of 0.3. The results obtained are detailed in Table 4. The results demonstrate

that it is eminently possible to infer the verification status of a user purely using the distribution of topics they tweet about with a high accuracy. The MLP classifier was the most competitive in this task, reliably pushing past 88.2% accuracy.

In the interest of interpretability, we evaluate the predictive power of each topic with respect to the classification target. To this end, we obtain individual topic importances using the ANOVA F-Scores output by GAM – our second most competitive model on this task. In order to rank the features reliably, the procedure is run on 50 random train-test splits of the dataset and the topics with the lowest F-Scores noted. The most reliably discriminative topics and the normalized density distributions of their usage are detailed in Figure 3. Owing to multiple topics largely belonging to popular broad conversational categories such as sports and politics, some redundancy was observed in the way of multi-collinearity. This is further backed up by the fact that the top 15 most important topics alone can discern verification status with an AUC of 0.76 while the top 25 topics can push those numbers up to an AUC of 0.8 nearly approximating the GAM performance on the whole feature set (AUC 0.83). These topics generally exhibit intuitive patterns of separation based on which an informed prediction can be made, e.g., the users who tweet most frequently about climate change are all verified while controversial topics like middle-east geopolitics are something verified users prefer to devote limited attention to.

5.2 Topical Span

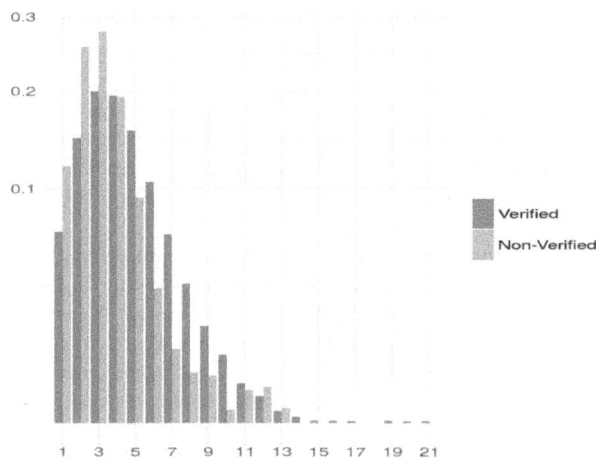

Figure 4: Square-root scaled proportion of users by optimal number of topics.

Peripheral aspects of topics such as their geographical distribution [57] and the viability of embeddings they induce for sentiment analysis [57] tasks have been explored before. This prompted us to extend our inquiry into peripheral measures such as inconsistencies in the variety and number of topics the two classes of users tweet about. In order to obtain an optimal mix of the number of topics per user in an unsupervised manner, we leveraged the use of an Hierarchical Dirichlet Process (HDP) model implementation [73] for topic inference. This method streams our corpus of tweets and performs an online Variational Bayes estimation to converge at an optimal number of topics T, for each user. Once again, we set $\alpha = T/50$ and $\beta = 0.01$, which are the default settings recommended in existing studies [28].

The distribution of cardinality for topic sets by verification status are detailed in Figure 4. Inspection of the distribution uncovers a clear trend with non-verified users clearly being over-represented in the lower reaches of the distribution (1–4 topics), while a comparatively substantial portion of verified users are situated in the middle of the distribution (5–10 topics). Also noteworthy is the fact that the very upper echelons of topical variety in tweets are occupied solely by verified users. We posit that this may be owing to the fact that news handles (e.g., '@BBC': 13 topics) and content aggregators (e.g., '@GIFs': 21 topics) are over represented in the set of verified users. The validation of this assertion is left for future work.

6 CONCLUSION

The coveted nature of platform verification on Twitter has led to the proliferation of verification scams and accusations of systemic bias against certain ideological demographics. Our work attempts to uncover actionable intelligence on the inner workings of the verification system, effectively formulating a checklist of profile attributes a user can work to improve upon to render verification more attainable.

This article presents a framework that computes the strength of a user's case for verification of Twitter. We introduce our machine learning system that extracts a multitude of features per user, belonging to different classes: user metadata, tweet content, temporal signatures, expressed sentiment, automation probabilities and preferred topics. We also categorize the users in our dataset into intuitive clusters and detail the reasons behind their likely divergent outcomes from the verification procedure. Additionally, we demonstrate role, that a user's choices and variety over conversational topics plays in precluding or effecting verification.

Our framework represents the first of its kind attempt at discerning and characterizing verification worthy users on Twitter and is able to attain a near perfect classification performance of 99.1% AUC. We believe this framework will empower the average Twitter user to significantly enhance the quality and reach of their online presence without resorting to prohibitively priced social media management solutions.

7 ACKNOWLEDGMENTS

We thank Language Technologies Research Centre (LTRC) lab at IIIT-Hyderabad and the Precog lab at IIIT-Delhi for their support.

Additionally, we would like to thank Microsoft India for granting access to their commercial Twitter solutions.

REFERENCES

[1] 2019. Klout. https://www.lithium.com/products/klout. Accessed: 2019-02-16.
[2] Hasan Al Maruf, Nagib Meshkat, Mohammed Eunus Ali, and Jalal Mahmud. 2015. Human behaviour in different social medias: A case study of Twitter and Disqus. In *2015 IEEE/ACM International Conference on Advances in Social Networks Analysis and Mining (ASONAM)*. IEEE, 270–273.
[3] David Anuta, Josh Churchin, and Jiebo Luo. 2017. Election bias: Comparing polls and twitter in the 2016 us election. *arXiv preprint arXiv:1701.06232* (2017).
[4] Darren Scott Appling, Erica J Briscoe, and Clayton J Hutto. 2015. Discriminative models for predicting deception strategies. In *Proceedings of the 24th International Conference on World Wide Web*. ACM, 947–952.
[5] Eytan Bakshy, Jake M Hofman, Winter A Mason, and Duncan J Watts. 2011. Everyone's an influencer: quantifying influence on twitter. In *Proceedings of the fourth ACM international conference on Web search and data mining*. ACM, 65–74.
[6] Gustavo EAPA Batista, Ronaldo C Prati, and Maria Carolina Monard. 2004. A study of the behavior of several methods for balancing machine learning training data. *ACM SIGKDD explorations newsletter* 6, 1 (2004), 20–29.
[7] Rabia Batool, Asad Masood Khattak, Jahanzeb Maqbool, and Sungyoung Lee. 2013. Precise tweet classification and sentiment analysis. In *Computer and Information Science (ICIS), 2013 IEEE/ACIS 12th International Conference on*. IEEE, 461–466.
[8] Johan Bollen, Huina Mao, and Xiaojun Zeng. 2011. Twitter mood predicts the stock market. *Journal of computational science* 2, 1 (2011), 1–8.
[9] Bustle. 2018. This Twitter Verification Scam Was Promoted By Twitter Itself, And The Consequences Are Terrifying. https://www.bustle.com/p/this-twitter-verification-scam-was-promoted-by-twitter-itself-the-consequences-are-terrifying-7833920. Accessed: 2018-12-27.
[10] Claudia Canali and Riccardo Lancellotti. 2012. A quantitative methodology based on component analysis to identify key users in social networks. *International Journal of Social Network Mining* 1, 1 (2012), 27–50.
[11] Carlos Castillo, Marcelo Mendoza, and Barbara Poblete. 2011. Information credibility on twitter. In *Proceedings of the 20th international conference on World wide web*. ACM, 675–684.
[12] Mario Cataldi, Luigi Di Caro, and Claudio Schifanella. 2010. Emerging topic detection on twitter based on temporal and social terms evaluation. In *Proceedings of the tenth international workshop on multimedia data mining*. ACM, 4.
[13] Meeyoung Cha, Hamed Haddadi, Fabricio Benevenuto, and Krishna P Gummadi. 2010. Measuring user influence in twitter: The million follower fallacy. In *fourth international AAAI conference on weblogs and social media*.
[14] Shelly Chaiken. 1980. Heuristic versus systematic information processing and the use of source versus message cues in persuasion. *Journal of personality and social psychology* 39, 5 (1980), 752.
[15] Nikan Chavoshi, Hossein Hamooni, and Abdullah Mueen. 2016. Identifying correlated bots in twitter. In *International Conference on Social Informatics*. Springer, 14–21.
[16] Zi Chu, Steven Gianvecchio, Haining Wang, and Sushil Jajodia. 2012. Detecting automation of twitter accounts: Are you a human, bot, or cyborg? *IEEE Transactions on Dependable and Secure Computing* 9, 6 (2012), 811–824.
[17] Scott Counts and Kristie Fisher. 2011. Taking It All In? Visual Attention in Microblog Consumption. *ICWSM* 11 (2011), 97–104.
[18] Munmun De Choudhury, Michael Gamon, Scott Counts, and Eric Horvitz. 2013. Predicting depression via social media. *ICWSM* 13 (2013), 1–10.
[19] Nicholas Diakopoulos and Arkaitz Zubiaga. 2014. Newsworthiness and Network Gatekeeping on Twitter: The Role of Social Deviance.. In *ICWSM*.
[20] John P Dickerson, Vadim Kagan, and VS Subrahmanian. 2014. Using sentiment to detect bots on twitter: Are humans more opinionated than bots?. In *Proceedings of the 2014 IEEE/ACM International Conference on Advances in Social Networks Analysis and Mining*. IEEE Press, 620–627.
[21] B Zafer Erdogan. 1999. Celebrity endorsement: A literature review. *Journal of marketing management* 15, 4 (1999), 291–314.
[22] Emilio Ferrara and Zeyao Yang. 2015. Measuring emotional contagion in social media. *PloS one* 10, 11 (2015), e0142390.
[23] Andrew J Flanagin and Miriam J Metzger. 2007. The role of site features, user attributes, and information verification behaviors on the perceived credibility of web-based information. *New media & society* 9, 2 (2007), 319–342.
[24] Brian J Fogg, Cathy Soohoo, David R Danielson, Leslie Marable, Julianne Stanford, and Ellen R Tauber. 2003. How do users evaluate the credibility of Web sites?: a study with over 2,500 participants. In *Proceedings of the 2003 conference on Designing for user experiences*. ACM, 1–15.
[25] Zafar Gilani, Reza Farahbakhsh, Gareth Tyson, Liang Wang, and Jon Crowcroft. 2017. An in-depth characterisation of Bots and Humans on Twitter. *arXiv preprint arXiv:1704.01508* (2017).
[26] CJ Hutto Eric Gilbert. 2014. Vader: A parsimonious rule-based model for sentiment analysis of social media text. In *Eighth International Conference on Weblogs and Social Media (ICWSM-14)*. Available at (20/04/16) http://comp. social. gatech. edu/papers/icwsm14. vader. hutto. pdf.

[27] Roberto González-Ibánez, Smaranda Muresan, and Nina Wacholder. 2011. Identifying sarcasm in Twitter: a closer look. In *Proceedings of the 49th Annual Meeting of the Association for Computational Linguistics: Human Language Technologies: Short Papers-Volume 2*. Association for Computational Linguistics, 581–586.

[28] Thomas L Griffiths and Mark Steyvers. 2004. Finding scientific topics. *Proceedings of the National academy of Sciences* 101, suppl 1 (2004), 5228–5235.

[29] Aditi Gupta, Ponnurangam Kumaraguru, Carlos Castillo, and Patrick Meier. 2014. Tweetcred: Real-time credibility assessment of content on twitter. In *International Conference on Social Informatics*. Springer, 228–243.

[30] Hussam Hamdan, Patrice Bellot, and Frederic Bechet. 2015. lsislif: Feature extraction and label weighting for sentiment analysis in twitter. In *Proceedings of the 9th International Workshop on Semantic Evaluation (SemEval 2015)*. 568–573.

[31] GACCT Harman and Mark H Dredze. 2014. Measuring post traumatic stress disorder in Twitter. In *ICWSM* (2014).

[32] Haibo He, Yang Bai, Edwardo A Garcia, and Shutao Li. 2008. ADASYN: Adaptive synthetic sampling approach for imbalanced learning. In *Neural Networks, 2008. IJCNN 2008.(IEEE World Congress on Computational Intelligence). IEEE International Joint Conference on*. IEEE, 1322–1328.

[33] Haibo He and Edwardo A Garcia. 2008. Learning from imbalanced data. *IEEE Transactions on Knowledge & Data Engineering* 9 (2008), 1263–1284.

[34] Martin Hentschel, Omar Alonso, Scott Counts, and Vasileios Kandylas. 2014. Finding users we trust: Scaling up verified Twitter users using their communication patterns. In *Eighth International AAAI Conference on Weblogs and Social Media*.

[35] Liangjie Hong and Brian D Davison. 2010. Empirical study of topic modeling in twitter. In *Proceedings of the first workshop on social media analytics*. ACM, 80–88.

[36] Miroslav Kubat, Stan Matwin, et al. 1997. Addressing the curse of imbalanced training sets: one-sided selection. In *Icml*, Vol. 97. Nashville, USA, 179–186.

[37] Miron B Kursa, Witold R Rudnicki, et al. 2010. Feature selection with the Boruta package. *J Stat Softw* 36, 11 (2010), 1–13.

[38] Haewoon Kwak, Changhyun Lee, Hosung Park, and Sue Moon. 2010. What is Twitter, a social network or a news media?. In *Proceedings of the 19th international conference on World wide web*. AcM, 591–600.

[39] Vasileios Lampos, Nikolaos Aletras, Jens K Geyti, Bin Zou, and Ingemar J Cox. 2016. Inferring the socioeconomic status of social media users based on behaviour and language. In *European Conference on Information Retrieval*. Springer, 689–695.

[40] Vasileios Lampos, Nikolaos Aletras, Daniel Preoţiuc-Pietro, and Trevor Cohn. 2014. Predicting and characterising user impact on Twitter. In *Proceedings of the 14th Conference of the European Chapter of the Association for Computational Linguistics*. 405–413.

[41] Changhyun Lee, Haewoon Kwak, Hosung Park, and Sue Moon. 2010. Finding influentials based on the temporal order of information adoption in twitter. In *Proceedings of the 19th international conference on World wide web*. ACM, 1137–1138.

[42] Jure Leskovec and Julian J Mcauley. 2012. Learning to discover social circles in ego networks. In *Advances in neural information processing systems*. 539–547.

[43] Laurens van der Maaten and Geoffrey Hinton. 2008. Visualizing data using t-SNE. *Journal of machine learning research* 9, Nov (2008), 2579–2605.

[44] Jalal Mahmud, Jeffrey Nichols, and Clemens Drews. 2012. Where Is This Tweet From? Inferring Home Locations of Twitter Users. *ICWSM* 12 (2012), 511–514.

[45] Alice Marwick and Danah Boyd. 2011. To see and be seen: Celebrity practice on Twitter. *Convergence* 17, 2 (2011), 139–158.

[46] Andrew Kachites McCallum. 2002. Mallet: A machine learning for language toolkit. (2002).

[47] Caitlin McCollister, Bo Luo, and Shu Huang. 2015. Building Topic Models to Predict Author Attributes from Twitter Messages.. In *CLEF*.

[48] Alan Mislove, Sune Lehmann, Yong-Yeol Ahn, Jukka-Pekka Onnela, and J Niels Rosenquist. 2011. Understanding the Demographics of Twitter Users. *ICWSM* 11, 5th (2011), 25.

[49] Yasuhide Miura, Shigeyuki Sakaki, Keigo Hattori, and Tomoko Ohkuma. 2014. TeamX: A sentiment analyzer with enhanced lexicon mapping and weighting scheme for unbalanced data. In *Proceedings of the 8th International Workshop on Semantic Evaluation (SemEval 2014)*. 628–632.

[50] Delia Mocanu, Andrea Baronchelli, Nicola Perra, Bruno Gonçalves, Qian Zhang, and Alessandro Vespignani. 2013. The twitter of babel: Mapping world languages through microblogging platforms. *PloS one* 8, 4 (2013), e61981.

[51] Meredith Ringel Morris, Scott Counts, Asta Roseway, Aaron Hoff, and Julia Schwarz. 2012. Tweeting is believing?: understanding microblog credibility perceptions. In *Proceedings of the ACM 2012 conference on computer supported cooperative work*. ACM, 441–450.

[52] Indraneil Paul, Abhinav Khattar, Ponnurangam Kumaraguru, Manish Gupta, and Shaan Chopra. 2018. Elites Tweet? Characterizing the Twitter Verified User Network. *arXiv preprint arXiv:1812.09710* (2018).

[53] James W Pennebaker, Ryan L Boyd, Kayla Jordan, and Kate Blackburn. 2015. *The development and psychometric properties of LIWC2015*. Technical Report.

[54] Daniel Preoţiuc-Pietro, Svitlana Volkova, Vasileios Lampos, Yoram Bachrach, and Nikolaos Aletras. 2015. Studying user income through language, behaviour and affect in social media. *PloS one* 10, 9 (2015), e0138717.

[55] Jyoti Ramteke, Samarth Shah, Darshan Godhia, and Aadil Shaikh. 2016. Election result prediction using Twitter sentiment analysis. In *Inventive Computation Technologies (ICICT), International Conference on*, Vol. 1. IEEE, 1–5.

[56] Adithya Rao, Nemanja Spasojevic, Zhisheng Li, and Trevor Dsouza. 2015. Klout score: Measuring influence across multiple social networks. In *2015 IEEE International Conference on Big Data (Big Data)*. IEEE, 2282–2289.

[57] Yafeng Ren, Yue Zhang, Meishan Zhang, and Donghong Ji. 2016. Improving twitter sentiment classification using topic-enriched multi-prototype word embeddings. In *Thirtieth AAAI conference on artificial intelligence*.

[58] Statista. 2018. Most popular tweets on Twitter as of November 2018, by number of retweets. https://www.statista.com/statistics/699462/twitter-most-retweeted-posts-all-time/. Accessed: 2018-12-22.

[59] Evita Stenqvist and Jacob Lönnö. 2017. Predicting Bitcoin price fluctuation with Twitter sentiment analysis.

[60] Mark Steyvers, Padhraic Smyth, Michal Rosen-Zvi, and Thomas Griffiths. 2004. Probabilistic author-topic models for information discovery. In *Proceedings of the tenth ACM SIGKDD international conference on Knowledge discovery and data mining*. ACM, 306–315.

[61] S Shyam Sundar. 2008. The MAIN model: A heuristic approach to understanding technology effects on credibility. *Digital media, youth, and credibility* 73100 (2008).

[62] Michael M Tadesse, Hongfei Lin, Bo Xu, and Liang Yang. 2018. Personality Predictions Based on User Behavior on the Facebook Social Media Platform. *IEEE Access* 6 (2018), 61959–61969.

[63] TechAcute. 2018. Top 40 List of the Most-Liked Tweets on Twitter. https://techacute.com/list-most-liked-tweets/. Accessed: 2018-12-22.

[64] Ivan Tomek. 1976. Two modifications of CNN. *IEEE Trans. Systems, Man and Cybernetics* 6 (1976), 769–772.

[65] TripWire. 2019. Get Verified Through a Promoted Tweet? Nope. ItâĂŹs a Scam! https://www.tripwire.com/state-of-security/latest-security-news/get-verified-promoted-tweet-nope-scam/. Accessed: 2019-1-29.

[66] Twitter. 2018. Verified account FAQs. https://help.twitter.com/en/managing-your-account/twitter-verified-accounts. Accessed: 2018-12-22.

[67] Twitter. 2019. About Verified Accounts: Twitter Help 2018. https://help.twitter.com/en/managing-your-account/about-twitter-verified-accounts. Accessed: 2018-12-22.

[68] Twitter. 2019. Twitter Support Statement. https://twitter.com/TwitterSupport/status/930926124892168192. Accessed: 2019-1-22.

[69] Onur Varol, Emilio Ferrara, Clayton Davis, Filippo Menczer, and Alessandro Flammini. 2017. Online Human-Bot Interactions: Detection, Estimation, and Characterization. https://aaai.org/ocs/index.php/ICWSM/ICWSM17/paper/view/15587/14817

[70] Svitlana Volkova, Kyle Shaffer, Jin Yea Jang, and Nathan Hodas. 2017. Separating facts from fiction: Linguistic models to classify suspicious and trusted news posts on twitter. In *Proceedings of the 55th Annual Meeting of the Association for Computational Linguistics (Volume 2: Short Papers)*, Vol. 2. 647–653.

[71] Alex Hai Wang. 2010. Detecting spam bots in online social networking sites: a machine learning approach. In *IFIP Annual Conference on Data and Applications Security and Privacy*. Springer, 335–342.

[72] Alex Hai Wang. 2010. Don't follow me: Spam detection in twitter. In *2010 international conference on security and cryptography (SECRYPT)*. IEEE, 1–10.

[73] Chong Wang, John Paisley, and David Blei. 2011. Online variational inference for the hierarchical Dirichlet process. In *Proceedings of the Fourteenth International Conference on Artificial Intelligence and Statistics*. 752–760.

[74] Amy Beth Warriner, Victor Kuperman, and Marc Brysbaert. 2013. Norms of valence, arousal, and dominance for 13,915 English lemmas. *Behavior research methods* 45, 4 (2013), 1191–1207.

[75] Jianshu Weng, Ee-Peng Lim, Jing Jiang, and Qi He. 2010. Twitterrank: finding topic-sensitive influential twitterers. In *Proceedings of the third ACM international conference on Web search and data mining*. ACM, 261–270.

[76] Shaomei Wu, Jake M Hofman, Winter A Mason, and Duncan J Watts. 2011. Who says what to whom on twitter. In *Proceedings of the 20th international conference on World wide web*. ACM, 705–714.

[77] Sarita Yardi, Daniel Romero, Grant Schoenebeck, et al. 2010. Detecting spam in a twitter network. *First Monday* 15, 1 (2010).

[78] Chao Michael Zhang and Vern Paxson. 2011. Detecting and analyzing automated activity on twitter. In *International Conference on Passive and Active Network Measurement*. Springer, 102–111.

[79] Arkaitz Zubiaga, Damiano Spina, Víctor Fresno, and Raquel Martínez. 2011. Classifying trending topics: a typology of conversation triggers on twitter. In *Proceedings of the 20th ACM international conference on Information and knowledge management*. ACM, 2461–2464.

Analyzing Textual (Mis)Information
Shared in WhatsApp Groups

Gustavo Resende
UFMG, Brazil
gustavo.jota@dcc.ufmg.br

Philipe Melo
UFMG, Brazil
philipe@dcc.ufmg.br

Julio C. S. Reis
UFMG, Brazil
julio.reis@dcc.ufmg.br

Marisa Vasconcelos
IBM Research
marisaav@br.ibm.com

Jussara M. Almeida
UFMG, Brazil
jussara@dcc.ufmg.br

Fabrício Benevenuto
UFMG, Brazil
fabricio@dcc.ufmg.br

ABSTRACT

Whatsapp is a messenger app that is currently very popular around the world. With a user-friendly interface, it allows people to instantaneously exchange messages in a very intuitive and fluid way. The app also allows people to interact using group chats, sharing messages, videos, audios, and images. These groups can also be a fertile ground to spread rumors and misinformation. In this work, we analyzed the messages shared on a number of political-oriented WhatsApp groups, focusing on *textual content*, as it is the most shared media type. Our study relied on a dataset containing all textual messages shared in those groups during the 2018 Brazilian presidential campaign. We identified the presence of misinformation in the contents of these messages using a dataset of priorly checked misinformation from six Brazilian fact-checking sites. Our study aims at identifying characteristics that distinguish such messages from the other textual messages (with unchecked content). To that end, we analyzed various properties of the textual content (e.g., language usage, main topics and sentiment of message's content) and propagation dynamics of both sets of messages. Our analyses revealed that textual messages with misinformation tend to be concentrated on fewer topics, often carrying words related to the cognitive process of *insight*, which characterizes chain messages. We also found that their propagation process is much more viral with a distinct behavior: they tend to propagate faster within particular groups but take longer to cross group boundaries.

CCS CONCEPTS

• **Human-centered computing** → **Social media**; • **Applied computing** → *Sociology*.

KEYWORDS

misinformation, content dissemination, WhatsApp, textual information

ACM Reference Format:
Gustavo Resende, Philipe Melo, Julio C. S. Reis, Marisa Vasconcelos, Jussara M. Almeida, and Fabrício Benevenuto. 2019. Analyzing Textual (Mis)Information Shared in WhatsApp Groups. In *11th ACM Conference on Web Science (WebSci '19), June 30-July 3, 2019, Boston, MA, USA*. ACM, New York, NY, USA, 10 pages. https://doi.org/10.1145/3292522.3326029

1 INTRODUCTION

Whatsapp is a messenger app that changed how people communicate when using smartphones. With a simple and easy-to-use interface, the app allows its users to exchange textual and multimedia messages in private and group conversations. Moreover, the possibility of sending messages via the Internet, instead of using a text messaging service (e.g., SMS), is a much cheaper choice. One could argue that such features highly contributed to turning WhatsApp into the most popular messaging app in the world, with 1.5 billion users in 180 countries and 1 billion daily active users[1].

The conversation in groups allows users to chat and interact instantly with all of those who joined the group. The visibility of such conversation is restricted to members of the group, being thus controlled by the group manager who decides who can join the group. However, access to a group can be made effectively public when the manager shares the link to join it in websites or social networks like Facebook and Twitter. In such a case, anyone with access to the link can join the group, which can be considered, from a practical perspective, public.

WhatsApp groups facilitate the dissemination of different types of content including chain messages, news, memes and rumors, including the so-called fake news. We here are particularly interested in the spread of *misinformation*, which refers to reportedly false (or inaccurate) information which is often intended to deceive people. In countries like India and Brazil where the app reportedly already reached 200 and 120 million users respectively[2], the spread of misinformation in WhatsApp has had consequences for society such as lynching episodes in India[3] and fake news flooding during Brazilian presidential elections[4]. Indeed, WhatsApp has acknowledged the importance of reducing the spread of misinformation by restricting the number of times a unique message can be forwarded

[1]http://www.businessofapps.com/data/whatsapp-statistics/
[2]https://www.financialexpress.com/industry/technology/whatsapp-now-has-1-5-billion-monthly-active-users-200-million-users-in-india/1044468/
[3]https://www.livemint.com/Technology/O6DLmIibCCV5luEG9XuJWL/How-widespread-is-WhatsApps-usage-in-India.html
[4]https://www.independent.co.uk/life-style/gadgets-and-tech/news/whatsapp-india-killings-latest-update-explained-app-fake-hoax-rumours-a8428746.html

by the same user in those two countries[5]. This is a first step to constrain the spread of fake news. Yet, given the great popularity of the application, its effectiveness is naturally limited. It is of utmost importance to identify characteristics of messages containing misinformation that distinguish them from regular content, as a step to build effective countermeasures against their dissemination.

Previous studies about WhatsApp focused on understanding the general patterns of how users interact with the application [5, 10] as well as its use on specific tasks (e.g., educational tasks, medical information exchange) [4, 31]. In a recent work [21], we have studied the dissemination of *images* in political public groups in WhatsApp, highlighting some differences in images containing previously identified misinformation from the rest. Yet, no prior study, not even ours, focused on exploring the presence of misinformation in *textual* messages, which is the most common type of content shared in the system, and whether there are particular features that distinguish them from the other textual messages.

Towards filling this gap, we here present an extensive investigation of the spread of textual messages within *WhatsApp public groups*. We focus on *political-oriented* public groups as we expect greater user engagement in topics of stronger social impact. We aim to compare the textual messages containing previously reported misinformation with other textual messages whose content was unchecked. We characterize these two sets of textual messages in terms of language usage, the main topics and sentiment of the message's content, as well as their propagation dynamics. More specifically, we tackle the following research questions.

RQ1: What are the differences in terms of textual features between messages containing misinformation and the rest?

RQ2: How are the propagation dynamics of the messages containing misinformation (i.e., how long they remain being spread, how many people and groups spread them) and how it differs from the propagation of other textual messages?

Towards tackling these questions, we used the dataset collected in [21]. However, unlike in that work, which focused on image content, we here analyze the textual messages. The dataset was collected from 364 politically oriented groups. We joined those groups and gathered the content shared within them for the time period of the Brazilian first round of general elections campaign (August 16th to October 7th, 2018). We also gathered fake news from six Brazilian fact-checking agencies and used it to identify misinformation in the textual messages of our collected dataset.

Our analyses unveiled a number of interesting findings regarding the dissemination of misinformation in textual messages in the WhatsApp groups monitored. We found that messages with misinformation tend to be slightly smaller (especially in number of words), partially due to the larger presence of URLs in their contents. Moreover they tend to be concentrated on fewer topics, often carrying words related to the cognitive process of *insight* (which characterizes chain messages). We also found that their propagation process is much more viral, reaching a larger number of users and groups, with a distinct behavior: they tend to propagate faster

within particular groups but take longer to cross group boundaries, which results in such message lasting longer on the system.

The remainder of this paper is organized as follows. Next section discusses related work, while Section 3 describes the WhatsApp dataset used in our analysis. Sections 4 and 5 present our analyses of textual features and propagation dynamics, thus addressing RQ1 and RQ2, respectively. Finally, Section 6 concludes the paper and gives directions for future work.

2 RELATED WORK

A number of recent studies have investigated how online social networks may impact many global political scenarios, such as the White Helmets in the Syria[25] and the 2016 US presidential campaign. The latter attracted the focus of various studies, from the role of *bots* and political advocates on Twitter [22] to the influence of *fake news* on the results of the election [1, 9].

Some authors focused on the propagation of misinformation on the Web. For example, Castillo *et al.* [6] analyzed the credibility of information shared on Twitter, discovering that there are measurable differences in the way credible and not credible messages propagate, whereas Vosoughi *et al.* [29] showed that fake news tend to spread faster than the real news. Others have proposed learning methods to automatically detect fake messages ranging from lexical to deep learning approaches exploring linguistic and network features [24, 30]. On this classification task, textual features are great semantic resources used very often on many approaches using the language structure [6], sentiment and other psycho-linguistic cues [29], topic models [11] and even political biases [2] of the messages. However, these prior efforts focused mostly on news articles and posts in online social networks such as Facebook [20], Twitter [6, 11] and Weibo [30]. None of them investigated the spread of misinformation on WhatsApp, which owns peculiarities that differ it from other platforms. For instance, WhatsApp groups are fundamentally chat rooms where any member can share a piece of content instantly reaching all other members. Unlike other social networks, WhatsApp groups form somewhat small communities[6] where content dissemination is driven solely by the members' intentions, with no influence of any recommendation or news feed algorithm. Thus, information spread is such environment may convey particular properties worth studying.

Yet, there have been reports that WhatsApp is being massively used not only as an important tool for marketing[7], but also as a vehicle for spreading fake news. For example, Cunha *et al.* [7] pointed WhatsApp as one of the leading sources of misinformation spreading, showing how users are easily manipulated through the spread of misleading information.

A few recent studies have investigated how users behave as they share messages in WhatsApp, particularly within chat groups. Garimella *et al.* [10] proposed a generalizable data collection methodology for WhatsApp public groups, whereas Seufert *et al.* [23] investigated the emerging group-based communication paradigm on WhatsApp and its implications on mobile network traffic. Caetano *et al.* [5] in turn analyzed user behavior in public groups using a three-layer hierarchical approach (e.g., message, user and

---

[5]https://www.theguardian.com/technology/2019/jan/21/whatsapp-limits-message-forwarding-fight-fake-news

[6]The number of members in a group is limited to 256.
[7]http://nyti.ms/2L3AV3M

groups). Finally, some studies [4, 31] focused on understanding how users interact using Whatsapp for performing different tasks such as educational tasks, medical information exchange, etc. To our knowledge, the only prior work to tackle the dissemination of misinformation in WhatsApp is our own recent study [21]. Yet, our focus in that work was on the dissemination of image content in the system, analyzing images containing misinformation and proposing some general countermeasures. We have not analyzed textual messages shared in the groups, as we do here. Also, we here do a more thorough comparison of the contents shared in the messages and their propagation dynamics, identifying features that clearly distinguish messages with misinformation from the rest.

In sum, while prior studies provide valuable knowledge about WhatsApp as an emerging social network and information dissemination vehicle, the analysis of misinformation in the system is still at a very early stage. This work greatly adds to the current literature by focusing on the textual properties and propagation dynamics of misinformation on WhatsApp.

3 WHATSAPP DATASET

As mentioned, this work relies on the same raw dataset of WhatsApp messages collected in our prior study [21]. Our present focus is on a large part of this dataset, covering the period of August 16th to October 7th, 2018 which precedes the first-round of the Brazilian general elections campaign when a new president, state governors, and House members were elected[8]. Moreover, unlike in [21], where our analyses were focused on image content, our present concern is on a different subset of the data, notably *textual* messages. In this section, we first present the filtered dataset used in this work (Section 3.1) and then describe our methodology to identify misinformation in the textual messages (Section 3.2).

As presented in [21], in order to gather a relevant WhatsApp dataset, we first identified a considerable number of public groups by searching for them using Google as well as Twitter and Facebook search engines. Specifically, we submitted the query "chat.whatsapp.com", a common piece of any URL containing an invite to join a WhatsApp group. We restricted our search space to groups related to Brazilian politics, by including in each search query a word from a dictionary related to the 2018 Brazilian elections[9]. This dictionary basically contains the name of all politicians, political parties, as well as words associated with political extremism. Finally, we performed a manual inspection of the collected group names to filter out those that are not related to politics. In total, we found 3,444 distinct links for public groups, out of which only 1,828 were valid. Due to memory restrictions, we were able to subscribe to 364 distinct groups, selected randomly out of the valid ones, using three cellphones we had available. After joining each group, the collection process was initiated.

Table 1: Overview of dataset.

Period	08/16 − 10/7/2018
#Public Groups	364
#Total Users	18,725
#Textual Messages	591,162
#Images	110,954
#Videos	73,310
#Audios	14,488
Filtering: textual messages with > 180 characters	
#Textual Messages	59,979
#Distinct Textual Messages	37,674
# URLs	19,502

WhatsApp uses end-to-end encryption, which makes access to the contents of the messages harder. Thus we used the *WebWhatsAppAPI*[10], which provides an interface in Python to send and receive messages by *WhatsApp Web* and uses *Sellenium* to automate the application through the browser. In total, we retrieved $591,162$ messages posted by $18,725$ unique users in the 364 groups. We emphasize that sensitive information such as user names and phone numbers were not stored in our dataset as we performed user anonymization before storing the data. Specifically, we mapped each telephone number to a unique user ID and we use these IDs to identify the source of each message[11]. For each message, we stored its content, the name of the group where the message was posted, group ID, user ID, date, and timestamp.

3.1 Our Filtered Dataset

Table 1 gives an overview of our collected dataset. Clearly, textual messages comprise the great majority on these groups, representing 75% of all messages shared. Since we aim at studying the presence of misinformation, we analyzed only messages with at least 180 characters to avoid small talks and greetings. This filtering left us with $59,979$ textual messages, many of which contain one or more URLs to websites and external news, summing up almost $19,502$ links in our analyzed messages.

We grouped similar content by computing the Jaccard similarity [8] between pairs of messages. The Jaccard similarity between messages m_i and m_j is computed as the ratio of the number of common words in both m_i and m_j to the number of words in the union of both messages. Messages with a similarity greater than 0.7 were considered the same and were grouped together and considered as (semi-)duplicates. The choice of threshold was made empirically. After manually inspected a sample of the messages, we note several messages that carried the same information despite differences in the use of words and emotions. In this process, a representative message for each content was selected, keeping information about the groups each content was sent to and their timestamps. In total, we identified $37,674$ distinct textual messages.

---

[8]The first round of elections occurred on October 7th. Most voted candidates who gathered more than 50% of the votes were automatically considered winners, which was the case of several candidates running for state governors. Otherwise, the two best-ranked candidates continued campaigning for a second round. This was the case of the presidential candidates.
[9]https://goo.gl/PdwAfV

---

[10]WhatsAppAPI available on http://github.com/mukulhase/WebWhatsapp-Wrapper
[11]Note that we are not able to identify individuals as the same person may have joined one or different groups using different telephone numbers.

3.2 Identifying Misinformation

To identify misinformation in our textual messages, we collected facts there were previously checked as *fake* by fact-checking websites and compared them the messages in (filtered) dataset. Specifically, we crawled checked information (news or claims) from six popular Brazilian fact-checking sites: "Aos fatos", "Me engana que eu posto", "e-farsas", "é ou não é (G1)", "Lupa" and "Boatos.org"[12]. We collected all posted facts published during the year of 2018, including title (or claim), URL, description, summary, associated images (links, if available), authors (if available), date, and label (i.e. fake or not). In total, 1,234 facts labeled as fake were collected.

We then computed the text similarity between each textual message(filtered) in our WhatsApp dataset and each collected fact labeled as fake by at least one of the fact-checking websites. For the latter, we experimented with using only the contents of the summary field and using the description, which contains a more detailed presentation of the fact. We found that using the summary leads to more accurate textual matching possibly because WhatsApp messages tend to be more direct to the point. We first pre-processed each piece of textual content (WhatsApp message and fact summary) using a version of the Spacy natural language processing toolkit specific to Portuguese[13] to remove stop words and accents as well as to stemming words. Each piece of content was then modeled as a bag of words, by means of a TF-IDF vectorial representation, widely used in information retrieval [16]. Given a WhatsApp message m and a fact summary s, represented by their TF-IDF vectors v_m and v_s, respectively, we computed their textual similarity by means of the cosine similarity, defined as $cos(v_m, v_s) = \frac{v_m \cdot v_s}{||v_m|| \cdot ||v_s||}$.[14]

We computed the similarity scores between all pairs of messages and fake fact summaries. Note that the two pieces of content may refer to the same fact and yet have (cosine) similarity below the maximum of 1. Thus, the identification of misinformation depends on some similarity threshold. To define such threshold, we first manually compared a sample of 100 WhatsApp messages with the fact summaries, determining whenever both referred to the same (fake) fact. We then compared this manual label with the similarity cosine scores. No match was found in our manual labeling between contents with cosine score below 0.4. Thus, any WhatsApp message whose cosine similarity with any of the fake fact summaries was above 0.4 was considered *suspicious of carrying misinformation*. All suspicious messages were then manually analyzed and compared against the fact summaries. We note that messages with high similarity score, but containing retractions (e.g., links to fact-checker websites refuting the original content) were manually excluded from misinformation dataset. This process led to the identification of 69 *distinct* textual messages containing previously checked misinformation. These messages were *shared* 578 times in our dataset[15].

In the following sections, we compare properties of the textual content and propagation dynamics of the messages containing misinformation with the other textual messages in our dataset. We refer to the latter as *unchecked*. We do not claim that there is no misinformation in the unchecked messages, given that such an assertion is restricted to the availability of checked facts. Yet, we expect that we were able to catch most textual messages containing misinformation in our dataset, especially those with greater impact on users, as they most probably were reported by the fact checkers.

4 TEXTUAL PROPERTIES OF MESSAGE CONTENT

In this section, we analyze textual properties of WhatsApp messages containing misinformation as well as unchecked content, highlighting differences between them. Our analyses cover message size, psychological linguistic features, sentiment analysis as well as main topics and frequent words present in each type of message. Note that, compared to [21], all these analyses, which are focused on textual content, are novel.

4.1 Message Sizes

We start by looking at the sizes of the messages shared on WhatsApp. Figures 1(a) and 1(b) show the cumulative distributions function (CDF) of the numbers of words and characters in the messages containing misinformation as well as in the messages whose content was unchecked. Recall that our filtered dataset contains only messages with more than 180 characters. According to Figure 1(a), 20% of the messages with misinformation have up to approximately 15 words. Those are often messages with links to websites or blogs publicizing fake news. In contrast, the same fraction of unchecked messages have up to 20 words. Indeed, considering only messages of intermediate size (up to 50 words), those carrying misinformation tends to be shorter. The two distributions continue very similar up to roughly 748 words, which is the maximum number of words in all messages with misinformation analyzed. Yet, there are a few longer messages (more than 5,000 words) with unchecked content in the dataset. In general, despite the variability in intermediate sizes, messages with misinformation tend to have fewer words[16].

Figure 1(b) shows that both distributions of numbers of characters are very similar up to around 4,000 characters. Roughly 60% of both types of messages have up to 280 characters, and the medium size is 459 and 472 characters for messages with misinformation and unchecked content, respectively. However, we do find some very long messages (up to 61,681 characters) among those with unchecked content.

4.2 Psychological Linguistic Features

Textual messages with misinformation may contain psychological and cognitive elements that can trigger specific reactions, possibly boosting the sharing of the message to others. In order to study the distribution of psycholinguistic elements in the textual messages, we extracted these types of features from the texts using the 2015 version of the Linguistic Inquiry and Word Count (LIWC) [26]. LIWC is a psycholinguistic lexicon system that categorizes words into psychologically meaningful groups. We used the dictionary

---

[12]aosfatos.org, veja.abril.com.br/blog/me-engana-que-eu-posto/, www.e-farsas.com, g1.globo.com/e-ou-nao-e/, piaui.folha.uol.com.br/lupa/, and www.boatos.org
[13]https://spacy.io/
[14]We did experiment with other similarity metrics, notably WMD (*Word Mover's Distance*)[13], which covers the semantics of sentences, and the results were similar, but with a higher cost of processing.
[15]Throughout this paper we use the term *sharing* a message as a synonym of posting a message in a WhatsApp group. In that sense, the same message (same content) may be shared/posted multiple times by one or more users.

[16] We note that the larger presence of links in messages with misinformation, as will be discussed in the next section, does not impact the difference in length as each link is counted as one word.

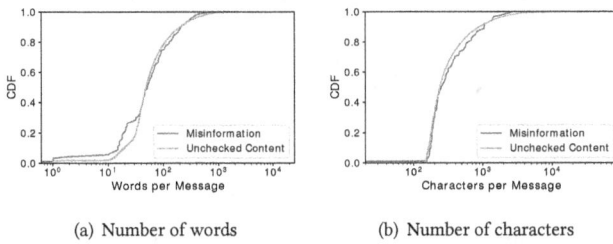

(a) Number of words (b) Number of characters

Figure 1: Distributions of message sizes

for the Portuguese language, which is organized as a hierarchy of categories and subcategories, all of which form the set of LIWC attributes. Examples include linguistic style attributes, affective attributes, and cognitive attributes. Positive emotions, negative emotions, anxiety, anger are examples of subcategories of the affective attributes, whereas insight, causation, discrepancy are examples of subcategories of the cognitive attributes. In total, there are 92 LIWC attributes. Each such (sub)category is characterized by a set of words from the dictionary. Examples of words representing the anger attribute in the LIWC Portuguese dictionary are *hate, kill, pissed* (translated to English). Given an input text, we compute the value of a LIWC attribute as the percentage of words in the text that represent the given attribute. Note that, as such, an attribute value is normalized to the size of each individual message.

We characterized both messages with misinformation and unchecked content with respect to the presence of psycholinguistic elements by computing the distributions of attribute values for each LIWC attribute for both sets of messages. As a first step to narrow our attention to the most distinguishing attributes, we compared both distributions using a Kolmogorov-Smirnov (KS) test [14], which is a non-parametric test of equality of continuous distributions, in which the null hypothesis states that the two input samples have the same distribution. We identified 7 (out of 92) attributes, for which the null hypothesis can be rejected with a confidence level of 0.95. We then computed the relative difference between the *average* values of each such attribute for messages with misinformation and messages with unchecked information.

Figure 2 shows the attributes with a greater presence in messages with misinformation. These are mainly subcategories of the linguistic attributes (*we, they, present, exclaim*) and psychological attributes (*insight, inhibition, sexual*).

Messages with misinformation have a larger presence of URLs: 50% of the messages with misinformation have at least one URL, whereas only 32% of the other messages contain such links. The presence of such URLs emphasizes the linguistic features related to punctuations that are frequent in links. Thus, in order to investigate the presence of other psycholinguistic features, we removed the links from all messages in this analysis. We identified some significant presence of the attributes *we* and *they*, representing words and verbs in the first and third-person plural respectively. The former was used in phrases aiming at aggregating the community towards the same goal, and the latter to refer to third parties. The attribute *present* indicate frequent use of verbs in the present tense and misinformation in current news and events. The exclamation mark was

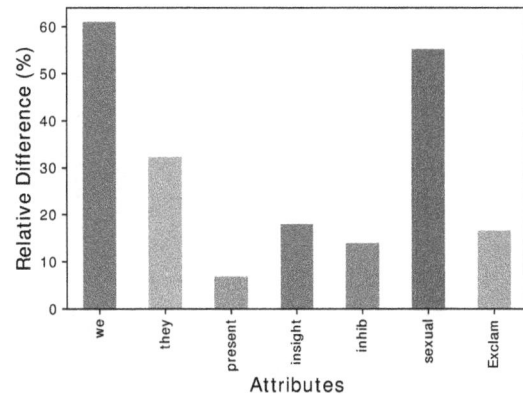

Figure 2: LIWC attributes that occur more frequently in messages with misinformation.

also observed with the attribute *Exclaim*, used in messages with misinformation content, to drive the attention and appeal to a more emotive speech.

The *insight* attribute is a cognitive process characterized by words like *attention, warning, look,* and *listen,* which occurred very often in messages with misinformation, especially those structured as chain messages, where warnings and verbs in the imperative are common. We also noticed that messages with those words tended to be shared 40% more times than the remaining, on average. Rumors about voter turnout and denial of previously reported facts were also observed in the messages with misinformation in our dataset, with a larger presence of words like *deny, null,* and *block* which characterize the *inhibition* attribute. The *sexual* attribute is represented by words such as *virgin, orgy* and *nudism*, often related to offensive content. We conjecture that the somewhat higher frequency of such attribute in messages with misinformation is due to the presence of false stories and hate speech content towards some political opposition groups. We also observed some sensationalist headlines that use sexual content to attract attention.

4.3 Sentiment Analysis

Sentiment analysis has become an extremely popular tool to capture text polarity, especially on social media data [15]. In order to investigate the overall subjective cues of sentiment in the WhatsApp textual messages, we used a Portuguese version[17] of SentiStrength method [28] to measure the polarity of each piece of content. SentiStrength is a well-established method that implements a combination of supervised learning techniques with a set of rules that impact the "strength" of the opinion contained in the message. This technique has already been applied in several domains (e.g., to capture the strength of sentiments expressed in headlines of online news [19]). We here employ it to investigate whether there are differences in the sentiment of messages carrying misinformation when compared to the rest.

Figure 3 shows the percentages of positive, neutral and negative messages with misinformation and carrying unchecked content. It

---

[17] Available in: sentistrength.wlv.ac.uk.

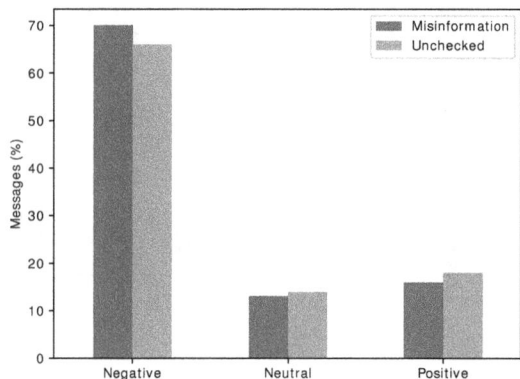

Figure 3: Sentiment polarity of messages.

Table 2: Topics inferred by LDA algorithm.

Topic	Most representative words (translated to English)
1	vote, president, Haddad, Lula, Ciro, apply, research, PT, elections, voter
2	no, ant, know, do, person, speak, find, thing, expensive, people
3	say, life, God, do, Lord, day, man, no, good, be
4	country, nation, Brazilian, Brazil, left-wing, political, power, party, govern, right-wing
5	be, laugh, city, governor, senator, yes, state federal, new, big
6	govern, money, do, work, company, millions, year, Brazilian real, pay, receive
7	Bolsonaro, Brazil, say, woman, support, Jair, defend, apply, see, favor
8	be, law, publish, form, education, leave, be, use, project, right, project
9	day, group, Facebook, video, today, folks, chat_whatsapp, friend, share, hour
10	year, cop, after, weapon, news, city, arrested, find, crime, where

is interesting to note the very large volume of negative messages in both groups. A large presence of negative content has also been previously reported for Twitter [27]. However, the results in Figure 3 suggest an even stronger bias towards a negative discourse on WhatsApp. Moreover, there are more positive messages than neutral ones (also in both groups), which evidences the polarized nature of the data, leaning more often towards more extreme feelings rather than neutral text.

Comparing messages with misinformation with those with unchecked content, we do observe some differences, but they are small. In particular, messages with misinformation are slightly more negative. Such difference is indeed statistically significant by a Kruskal-Wallis H-test [12], with p-value < 0.005. This finding is in agreement with previous observations that misinformation content tends to be more negative [33], especially within polarized communities. Moreover, inspired by previous results on online news [19], one could speculate that messages with misinformation tend to be more negative as a mechanism to attract readers. As we will see in Section 5.1, such messages are indeed shared a larger number of times.

4.4 Topic Analysis

Although we here focus on politically related groups, the contents of the messages vary greatly in terms of their topics. Political discussions, product/business marketing, and even humor are some examples. Thus, we further characterized the WhatsApp messages in terms of the topics they convey. To that end, we used Latent Dirichlet Allocation (LDA) [3], a generative statistical model to automatically infer the topics in a collection of documents. We applied LDA to all messages (with misinformation and with unchecked content) jointly, and then compare the distributions of the identified topics in each group of messages, aiming at identifying differences between them.

Specifically, we lowercased and tokenized all the words in the filtered dataset, and removed accents and stopwords using the Portuguese list provided by the Spacy toolkit. We then ran the LDA algorithm using *gensim* [18], a Python library for topic modeling. We chose the best number of topics k to be returned by the algorithm

based on the topic coherence metric [17], which captures whether different topics indeed have few words in common, as is commonly used. Specifically, we ran the LDA algorithm varying the number of topics k from 2 to 30 and chose the LDA model that produced the highest topic coherence score, which was for $k = 10$. These topics are presented in Table 2, which shows the most representative words (according to LDA) for each topic. Note that, although our collection methodology does favor political content, we do observe a great variety of topics, characterize by words such as *God, life, money, millions* and *Facebook*.

We then assigned one topic to each message by analyzing the probability of each word in the message belonging to each of the identified topics. We selected the topic with the highest aggregated probability considering all words in the message as its representative topic. Figures 4(a) and 4(b) show the histograms of topics for the messages with misinformation and for those with unchecked content, respectively.

Clearly, the distribution is much more biased towards fewer topics in the messages with misinformation. The most frequent topic in this group, *Topic 6*, was almost twice as much frequent in the messages with misinformation and is characterized by words such as *government, money, do,* and *work*. We found that many messages in this topic labeled as misinformation do indeed carry rumors about government's economic projects in the current or prior term of office. An extract of one such message is: *This is not fake news. It is on the website of the Chamber of Deputies - PT has a project for the confiscation of assets.* It refers to a false project of the political party that had been in Office previously (PT or Work Party), and probably was disseminated aiming at favoring candidates from opposing parties. As this topic is mainly characterized by subjects related to projects, economics and finance, it has no particular political side and their links point to economy news and even false propaganda.

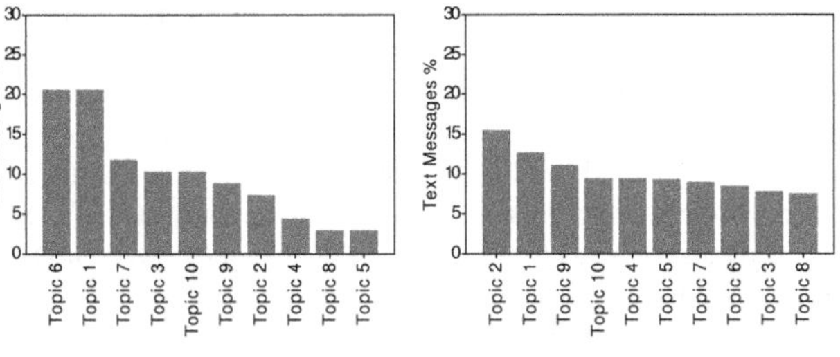

(a) Messages with misinformation (b) Messages with unchecked content

Figure 4: Distributions of topics inferred by LDA.

(a) Messages with misinformation

(b) Messages with unchecked content

Figure 5: Word clouds of the top 500 words (translated to English).

Topic 1 also has significant presence in the messages with misinformation and is characterized by words such as *Haddad, Lula,* and *Ciro* (names of candidates running for president) as well as *vote,* and *president.* Strongly related to the 2018 presidential election, this topic presents information about many candidates, it does not target any particular political side. The links present in the messages point to news about different candidates and polling surveys results. Similarly, *Topic 7*, containing mostly words related to Jair Bolsonaro, a candidate running for president, was also more frequent in messages with misinformation. This is consistent with reports of how the spread of misinformation in WhatsApp, targeting particular candidates, influenced the 2018 presidential election campaign in Brazil[18]. One example message related to *Topic 7* is (translated to English): *Bolsonaro proposes mass dismissal of teachers and distance education for all levels..* This fact was learned to be fake afterward, spread with the goal of harming the candidate's campaign. Another example is: *Please listen to what Father Marcelo Rossi talked about the current situation of the country and about Bolsonaro! He gave a class!.* This message refers to a very charismatic and beloved Brazilian priest who allegedly supported candidate Bolsonaro in a false audio that went viral. These two messages illustrate how misinformation propagation was used to harm but also to favor his campaign.

4.5 Frequent Terms

To further support our analyses of the contents of the WhatsApp messages, Figure 5 shows the word clouds of the top 500 most frequent words (translated to English) for both sets of messages (with misinformation and unchecked content). These word clouds were produced using the Wordle tool[19]. Note the frequent presence of many words related to the topics inferred using the LDA algorithm. Examples are *vote, Bolsonaro, Brazil, Lula* and, *PT*, which are related to the election. Words like *project, benefit,* and *income,* clearly related to *Topic 6* (see prior section) were also highlighted in the cloud for messages with misinformation.

We delved further into the contents of messages with misinformation by investigating whether there are particular patterns of word usage (e.g., prefixes or suffixes of sentences) that occur more frequently. Specifically, we used each of the top-50 most frequent words in Figure 5(a) as input to the Word tree visualization tool

[32], Given an entry word and a dataset of textual content, this tool generates a tree, with the given entry word as root, showing phrases that branch off from the root across all texts of the dataset.

Figure 6 shows one such word tree, rooted by the word *Please* (*Por favor,* in Portuguese). This was the root with the largest number of branches in the set of messages with misinformation. Indeed, as shown in Figure 6, we found 7 different phrases starting with the word *Please.* Those phrases were found in messages carrying misinformation, which were shared a total of 33 times in our dataset. We emphasize that, as shown in Figure 5(a), these phrases are related to different topics such as a particular candidate (Bolsonaro), health-related issues (e.g., hospital, life), and even a rumor about drugs. This variety of subjects indicate that the use of this particular word *Please* may indeed be a distinguishing feature of misinformation spread in WhatsApp textual messages in general, and not only during the period of elections. Words like *listen, publish, share,* and *spread* were also found in these phrases. These are words that characterize chain messages, being representative of the psychological process of *insight.* As found in Section 4.2, this psycholinguistic attribute does indeed occur more often in messages with misinformation.

5 PROPAGATION DYNAMICS

Besides characterizing the textual content of the messages, we also analyze their propagation dynamics within each group as well as across different groups. We analyze the message reach by quantifying the number of shares (Section 5.1) as well as temporal properties of the spread of a message in the system (Section 5.2). Compared

---
[18]https://www.nytimes.com/2018/10/17/opinion/brazil-election-fake-news-whatsapp.html?module=inline
[19]Available at: http://www.wordle.net/

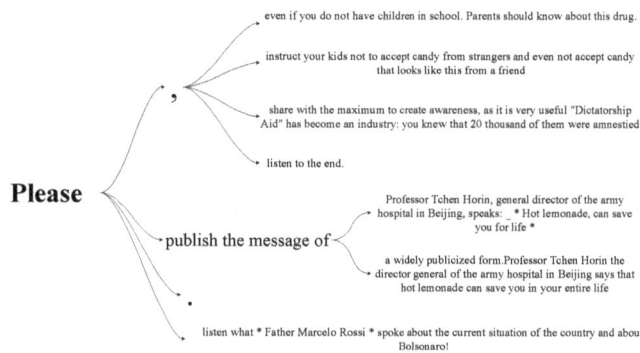

even if you do not have children in school. Parents should know about this drug.

instruct your kids not to accept candy from strangers and even not accept candy that looks like this from a friend

share with the maximum to create awareness, as it is very useful "Dictatorship Aid" has become an industry: you knew that 20 thousand of them were amnestied

listen to the end.

Please ,

Professor Tchen Horin, general director of the army hospital in Beijing, speaks: _ * Hot lemonade, can save you for life *

publish the message of

a widely publicized form.Professor Tchen Horin the director general of the army hospital in Beijing says that hot lemonade can save you in your entire life

.

listen what * Father Marcelo Rossi * spoke about the current situation of the country and about Bolsonaro!

Figure 6: Word tree for the word root *Please*.

to the results in [21], this provides a more detailed analysis of message propagation covering a larger number of metrics. Nevertheless, in the following, we explicitly compare our present findings with those in our prior work (despite the focus on different media types) for metrics analyzed in both studies.

5.1 Message Reach

Recall that, as presented in Section 3.1, we do group messages with very similar content together and consider them indistinctly duplicates of the same content. In this section, we analyze the reach of each such piece of content by quantifying the number of distinct users who posted the same message, the number of distinct groups in which the same message was posted as well as the total number of copies (shares) of the same message across all analyzed groups. Figures 7(a), 7(b) and 7(c) show the cumulative distributions of those measures for messages containing misinformation as well as messages with unchecked content.

As shown in Figure 7(a), roughly 60% of the unchecked messages were shared by up to 2 users, while the same fraction of messages with misinformation reached a much larger number of users (up to 7). Similarly, the messages with misinformation tend to reach a much larger number of distinct groups. Figure 7(b) indicates that roughly 80% of the messages were posted in up to 10 groups or, in other way, 20% of the messages reached more than 10 groups. In contrast, 80% of the messages with unchecked content was shared in only up to 2 distinct groups. According to Figure 7(c), the distinction between messages with misinformation and with unchecked content is similarly very drastic when it comes to the total number of shares. Roughly 80% of the latter were shared only once and practically all unchecked content was shared at most 10 times. In contrast, nearly half of the messages with misinformation were shared more than once, and 20% of them were shared more than 10 times. Clearly, textual messages with misinformation have a much greater reach in WhatsApp, suggesting a viral behavior within and across the WhatsApp groups.

5.2 Temporal Properties of Message Spread

In this section, we investigate the spread of a message over time, focusing on messages that were shared at least twice in our dataset 50% and 20% of the messages with misinformation and with unchecked content, respectively). We analyze temporal properties of this spread including message *lifetime* and the time between consecutive shares of the same message, here referred to as *burst time*. These two metrics were also analyzed in [21] for images, and we compare our results with those prior findings below. Since the computation of burst time disregards the particular group where each share happened, we further analyze the dissemination within and across different groups by analyzing the time interval of a share since the message was first shared in the group (*intra-group time*) and the time interval between the first shares of the same message in different groups (*inter-group time*).

5.2.1 Message Lifetimes.
The lifetime of a message is calculated as the time interval between the first and last occurrence of this message in our dataset, thus reflecting how long the message remained being replicated on WhatsApp, *as captured by our dataset*. Figure 8(a) shows the cumulative distributions of the lifetimes (in terms of days) for each set of messages. Clearly, the messages with misinformation tend to remain in the system for much longer: roughly half of the messages with misinformation in our dataset had a lifetime of at least 10 days. In contrast, most messages with unchecked content remained in the system for up to a single day, and less than 20% of them had lifetimes above 10 days. This result is in sharp contrast with our prior findings for images shared in WhatsApp groups[21], where we did *not* observe clear differences between the lifetimes of images with misinformation and unchecked content.

5.2.2 Burst Times.
The communication in messenger apps is often extremely fast. Thus, another metric to characterize the temporal dynamics of message propagation is the time interval between two consecutive shares of the same message (in the same group or in different groups), which we call burst time. Figure 8(b) shows the cumulative distributions of burst time for messages with misinformation and unchecked content. We note that the two distributions exhibit some distinction in their bodies (smaller values), though differences become unclear for burst times above 100 minutes. That is, for values up to 100 minutes, the burst times tend to be somewhat longer for messages with misinformation. That is, unchecked content is reshared faster. For example, around 20% of the messages with unchecked content is reshared within 3 minutes since the last post. In contrast, only 10% of the messages with misinformation are reshared within the same interval. We did observe the presence of messages from spammers with promotions and product offers among those with unchecked content. We speculate that those may explain the shorter burst times for such messages, as one may expect that spammers make an effort to publicize their content by resharing it often. Note that, for messages with misinformation, the longer time interval between successive shares of the same message may indeed contribute to the longer lifetimes observed in the previous section.

Once again, we observe differences with our previous findings for image content. In [21], we reported the opposite pattern, with shorter burst times for messages with misinformation. Recall that the two studies rely on data collected from the same WhatsApp groups during the same period, but focus on different types of messages. Thus, the misinformation propagation patterns does seem to vary depending on the media type. Extending this analysis to other media types, such as audio and video, is an interesting avenue for future work.

(a) Number of unique users per message   (b) Number of unique groups per message   (c) Total number of shares

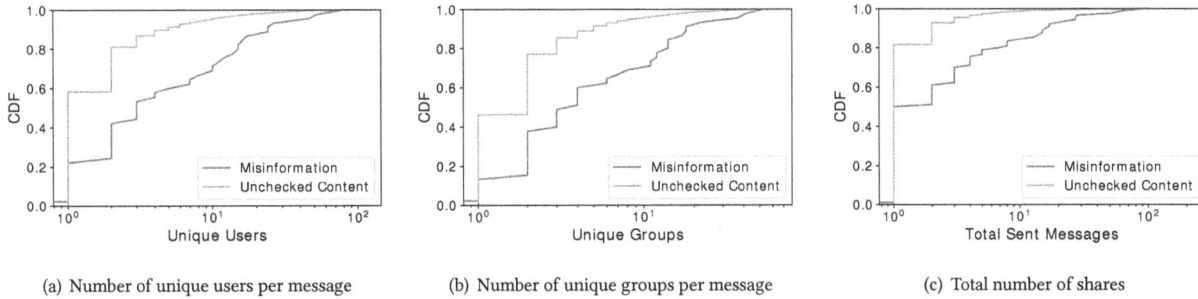

Figure 7: Cumulative distributions of the reach of each message in terms of distinct users, distinct groups and total shares.

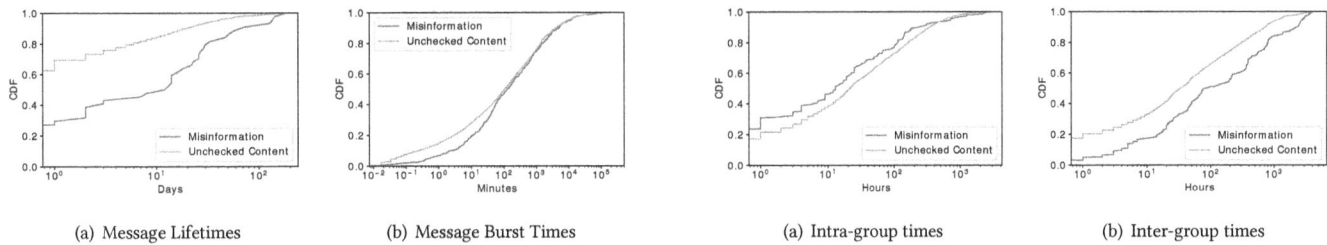

(a) Message Lifetimes   (b) Message Burst Times

Figure 8: Cumulative distributions of life and burst times.

(a) Intra-group times   (b) Inter-group times

Figure 9: Cumulative distributions of inter and intra-group times.

5.2.3 Intra and Inter Group Times. As our final analysis, we look into how the same message is disseminated within the same group and across different groups. Our goal is to understand how long it takes for a message to first appear in different groups as well as the time interval since this first appearance and the following shares within the same group. To that end, we define the intra and inter-group times. The *intra-group time* is defined as the time interval between the current share of a message and the *first time* the same message was shared in the group. Note that the same message may be shared multiple times in the same group by one or more users. This metric is computed for messages within each group separately, and is restricted to messages shared at least twice in the group 29% and 9% of messages with misinformation and unchecked content, respectively. The *inter-group time* is defined as the time interval between the first share of a message in a group and the first share of the message in any group. It captures the time interval between the first appearance of a content in different groups, and is measured only for messages that were shared in at least two groups 83% and 55% of messages with misinformation and unchecked content, respectively.

We note that the analysis of intra and inter times may help understanding the observed patterns in burst times, since, unlike the latter, the two metrics defined above explicitly capture the structure of groups and its role in the propagation of a message. The cumulative distributions of intra and inter-group times are shown in Figures 9(a) and 9(b), respectively. The distributions for messages with misinformation and with unchecked content are different. Within each group, the shares of messages with misinformation tend to be somewhat more concentrated in time, happening faster. As Figure 9(a) shows, in approximately 50% of the cases, a message with misinformation is reshared within 10 hours since the first time

it appeared in the group. For messages with unchecked content this fraction is smaller than 40%. In contrast, Figure 9(b) shows that crossing the group boundaries takes longer for messages with misinformation: in only 20% of the cases, they reappear in a different group within 10 hours. In contrast, for messages with unchecked content, 30% of the inter-group times are within the same limit.

By contrasting these results with those reported in the previous section, we conclude that although the overall spread of messages with misinformation is somewhat slower (greater burst times), these messages in general spread faster within particular groups, taking longer to propagate across different groups.

6 CONCLUDING REMARKS

We have analyzed textual properties and propagation dynamics of messages disseminated in a number of political-oriented WhatsApp groups. Our study was driven by the goal of identifying properties that distinguishing textual messages containing misinformation from other textual messages whose content is unchecked. To that end, we relied on a dataset of fake news reported by six Brazilian fact-checking websites, identifying their presence in the WhatsApp messages analyzed by means of textual similarity analysis.

Our results revealed a number of interesting findings. With respect to textual properties, we found only small differences in message sizes as messages with misinformation tend to be slightly smaller (especially in number of words). This may be partially due to the larger presence of URLs in their contents. By performing topic modeling, we also identified that textual messages with misinformation is more concentrated on fewer topics, related to presidential candidates and government projects. The prevalence of such topics was confirmed by a higher frequency of words related to them. Moreover, the analysis of the psychological elements indicated a frequent presence of the cognitive process of *insight* in the messages with misinformation. This attribute is characterized by words such as *attention, warning, look, listen* which are often used in chain messages. We also noted the frequent presence of phrases starting with the word *Please*, used in relation to various subjects, which may also be a feature of chain messages. Finally, despite the differences being small, we do find that the contents of messages with misinformation tend to be more negative, in agreement with previous analysis of misinformation [33].

Our analyses of propagation dynamics revealed a much more viral spread of misinformation content, as such messages are shared more times, by a larger number of users and in more groups. Moreover, messages with misinformation tend to spread faster within particular groups, but take longer to propagate across different groups, which results in such messages lasting longer on WhatsApp. Interestingly, these results are in contrast with our prior study of misinformation in *images* shared in WhatsApp [21], suggesting that the propagation dynamics of misinformation may indeed depend on the type of media used to convey the information.

We emphasize that although our findings were observed on a particular dataset and thus might be influenced by its collection methodology (e.g., focus on political groups, monitoring period), they might generalize, to some extent, to other WhatsApp groups and time period. For example, although the observed particular topics are biased by our collection methodology, the concentration of misinformation on fewer (more catchy and controversial) topics may be expected in general, and so are the longer lifetimes.

This study offers a first step towards understanding how misinformation disseminates in textual content on WhatsApp. We hope it motivates follow-up efforts covering other datasets, time periods, WhatsApp groups and media types. Exploring the analyzed features in the design of automatic mechanisms for detecting misinformation on WhatsApp is also a promising future work.

ACKNOWLEDGMENTS

This work was partially supported by the project FAPEMIG-PRONEX-MASWeb, Models, Algorithms and Systems for the Web, process number APQ-01400-1, as well as grants from Google, CNPq, CAPES, and Fapemig.

REFERENCES

[1] H. Allcott and M. Gentzkow. 2017. Social media and fake news in the 2016 election. *Journal of Economic Perspectives* 31, 2 (2017), 211–36.
[2] Mahmoudreza Babaei, Juhi Kulshrestha, Abhijnan Chakraborty, Fabricio Benevenuto, Krishna P. Gummadi, and Adrian Weller. 2018. Purple Feed: Identifying High Consensus News Posts on Social Media. In *Proc. of the Conf. on Artifical Intelligence, Ethics Society*.
[3] David M Blei, Andrew Y Ng, and Michael I Jordan. 2003. Latent dirichlet allocation. *Journal of machine Learning research* 3, Jan (2003), 993–1022.
[4] Dan Bouhnik and Mor Deshen. 2014. WhatsApp goes to school: Mobile instant messaging between teachers and students. *Journal of Information Technology Education: Research* 13, 1 (2014), 217–231.
[5] Josemar Alves Caetano, Jaqueline Faria de Oliveira, Hélder Seixas Lima, Humberto T Marques-Neto, Gabriel Magno, Wagner Meira Jr, and Virgílio AF Almeida. 2018. Analyzing and characterizing political discussions in WhatsApp public groups. *arXiv preprint arXiv:1804.00397* (2018).
[6] Carlos Castillo, Marcelo Mendoza, and Barbara Poblete. 2011. Information credibility on twitter. In *Proc. of the Int'l Conference on World Wide Web*.
[7] Evandro Cunha, Gabriel Magno, Josemar Caetano, Douglas Teixeira, and Virgilio Almeida. 2018. Fake news as we feel it: perception and conceptualization of the term 'fake news' in the media. In *Proc. of the Int'l Conference on Social Informatics*.
[8] Société Vaudoise des Sciences Naturelles. 1864. *Bulletin de la Société vaudoise des sciences naturelles*. Vol. 7. F. Rouge.

[9] A. Fourney, M. Racz, G. Ranade, M. Mobius, and E. Horvitz. 2017. Geographic and Temporal Trends in Fake News Consumption During the 2016 US Presidential Election. In *Proc. of the Int'l Conference on Information and Knowledge Management*.
[10] K. Garimella and G. Tyson. 2018. WhatsApp, Doc? A First Look at WhatsApp Public Group Data. In *Proc. of the Int'l Conference on Web and Social Media*.
[11] Jun Ito, Jing Song, Hiroyuki Toda, Yoshimasa Koike, and Satoshi Oyama. 2015. Assessment of tweet credibility with LDA features. In *Proc. of the Int'l Conference on World Wide Web*.
[12] H Kruskal and W Wallis. 1952. Use of ranks in one-criterion variance analysis. *Journal of the American statistical Association* 47, 260 (1952), 583–621.
[13] Matt Kusner, Yu Sun, Nicholas Kolkin, and Kilian Weinberger. 2015. From word embeddings to document distances. In *International Conference on Machine Learning*. 957–966.
[14] F. Massey Jr. 1951. The Kolmogorov-Smirnov test for goodness of fit. *Journal of the American statistical Association* 46, 253 (1951), 68–78.
[15] Philipe F Melo, Daniel H Dalip, Manoel M Junior, Marcos A Gonçalves, and Fabrício Benevenuto. 2019. 10SENT: A stable sentiment analysis method based on the combination of off-the-shelf approaches. *Journal of the Association for Information Science and Technology* (2019).
[16] Ashish Moon and T Raju. 2013. A survey on document clustering with similarity measures. *International Journal of Advanced Research in Computer Science and Software Engineering* 3, 11 (2013), 599–601.
[17] David Newman, Jey Han Lau, Karl Grieser, and Timothy Baldwin. 2010. Automatic evaluation of topic coherence. In *Proc. of the Annual Conference of the North American Chapter of the Association for Computational Linguistics*. ACL.
[18] Radim Rehurek and Petr Sojka. 2010. Software framework for topic modelling with large corpora. In *Proc. of the WS on New Challenges for NLP Frameworks*.
[19] Julio Reis, Fabricio Benevenuto, Pedro Vaz de Melo, Raquel Prates, Haewoon Kwak, and Jisun An. 2015. Breaking the News: First Impressions Matter on Online News. In *Proc. of the Int'l Conference on Web and Social Media*.
[20] Julio C. S. Reis, André Correia, Fabrício Murai, Adriano Veloso, and Fabrício Benevenuto. 2019. Supervised Learning for Fake News Detection. *IEEE Intelligent Systems* 34, 2 (2019).
[21] Gustavo Resende, Philipe Melo, Hugo Sousa, Johnnatan Messias, Marisa Vasconcelos, Jussara Almeida, and Fabrício Benevenuto. 2019. (Mis)Information Dissemination in WhatsApp: Gathering, Analyzing and Countermeasures. In *Proc. of the Web Conference*.
[22] Marian-Andrei Rizoiu, Timothy Graham, Rui Shang, Yifei Zhang, Robert Ackland, Lexing Xie, et al. 2018. # DebateNight: The Role and Influence of Socialbots on Twitter During the 1st 2016 US Presidential Debate. In *Proc. of the Int'l Conference on Web and Social Media*.
[23] Michael Seufert, Tobias Hoßfeld, Anika Schwind, Valentin Burger, and Phuoc Tran-Gia. 2016. Group-based communication in WhatsApp. In *Proc. of the IFIP Networking Conference and Workshops*. IEEE.
[24] Kai Shu, Amy Sliva, Suhang Wang, Jiliang Tang, and Huan Liu. 2017. Fake news detection on social media: A data mining perspective. *ACM SIGKDD Explorations Newsletter* 19, 1 (2017), 22–36.
[25] Kate Starbird, Ahmer Arif, Tom Wilson, Katherine Van Koevering, Katya Yefimova, and Daniel Scarnecchia. 2018. Ecosystem or Echo-System? Exploring Content Sharing across Alternative Media Domains. In *Proc. of the Int'l Conference on Web and Social Media*.
[26] Yla R Tausczik and James W Pennebaker. 2010. The psychological meaning of words: LIWC and computerized text analysis methods. *Journal of language and social psychology* 29, 1 (2010), 24–54.
[27] Mike Thelwall, Kevan Buckley, and Georgios Paltoglou. 2011. Sentiment in Twitter events. *Journal of the American Society for Information Science and Technology* 62, 2 (2011), 406–418.
[28] Mike Thelwall, Kevan Buckley, Georgios Paltoglou, Di Cai, and Arvid Kappas. 2010. Sentiment strength detection in short informal text. *Journal of the American Society for Information Science and Technology* 61, 12 (2010), 2544–2558.
[29] Soroush Vosoughi, Deb Roy, and Sinan Aral. 2018. The spread of true and false news online. *Science* 359, 6380 (2018), 1146–1151.
[30] Yaqing Wang, Fenglong Ma, Zhiwei Jin, Ye Yuan, Guangxu Xun, Kishlay Jha, Lu Su, and Jing Gao. 2018. EANN: Event Adversarial Neural Networks for Multi-Modal Fake News Detection. In *Proc. of the Int'l Conference on Knowledge Discovery & Data Mining*.
[31] Shabeer Ahmad Wani, Sari M Rabah, Sara AlFadil, Nancy Dewanjee, and Yahya Najmi. 2013. Efficacy of communication amongst staff members at plastic and reconstructive surgery section using smartphone and mobile WhatsApp. *Indian journal of plastic surgery: official publication of the Association of Plastic Surgeons of India* 46, 3 (2013), 502.
[32] Martin Wattenberg and Fernanda B Viégas. 2008. The word tree, an interactive visual concordance. *Transactions on visualization and computer graphics* 14, 6 (2008), 1221–1228.
[33] Fabiana Zollo, Petra Kralj Novak, Michela Del Vicario, Alessandro Bessi, Igor Mozetič, Antonio Scala, Guido Caldarelli, and Walter Quattrociocchi. 2015. Emotional dynamics in the age of misinformation. *PloS one* 10, 9 (2015), e0138740.

Auditing Autocomplete: Suggestion Networks and Recursive Algorithm Interrogation

Ronald E. Robertson
Northeastern University
rer@ccs.neu.edu

Shan Jiang
Northeastern University
sjiang@ccs.neu.edu

David Lazer
Northeastern University
d.lazer@neu.edu

Christo Wilson
Northeastern University
cbw@ccs.neu.edu

ABSTRACT

Autocomplete algorithms, by design, steer inquiry. When a user provides a root input, such as a search query, these algorithms dynamically retrieve, curate, and present a list of related inputs, such as search suggestions. Although ubiquitous in online platforms, a lack of research addressing the ephemerality of their outputs and the opacity of their functioning raises concerns of transparency and accountability on where inquiry is steered. Here, we introduce recursive algorithm interrogation (RAI), a breadth-first search method for auditing autocomplete by recursively submitting a root query and its child suggestions to create a network of algorithmic associations. We used RAI to conduct a longitudinal audit of autocomplete on Google and Bing using a focused set of root queries – the names of 38 US governors who were up for reelection – during the summer of 2018. Comparing across search engines, we found a higher turnover rate among longer and lower ranked suggestions on both search engines, a higher prevalence of social media websites in Google's suggestions, a higher prevalence of words classified as a swear or a negative emotion in Bing's suggestions, and periodic shocks that spanned across most of our root queries. We open source our code for conducting RAI and discuss how it could be applied to other platforms, topics, and settings.

CCS CONCEPTS

• Information systems → Content ranking;

KEYWORDS

search queries; autocomplete; suggestions; algorithm auditing

ACM Reference Format:
Ronald E. Robertson, Shan Jiang, David Lazer, and Christo Wilson. 2019. Auditing Autocomplete: Suggestion Networks and Recursive Algorithm Interrogation. In *11th ACM Conference on Web Science (WebSci '19), June 30-July 3, 2019, Boston, MA, USA.* ACM, New York, NY, USA, 10 pages. https://doi.org/10.1145/3292522.3326047

1 INTRODUCTION

When people seek out information beyond their social circles, they are generally limited to one of two options. They can either seek it out on their own, or seek out the assistance of a librarian – a specialist who manages bodies of information – and begin the complex, exploratory, and iterative process of formulating, communicating, and negotiating a *query* [3, 31, 48]. Historically, people would rely on libraries for this type of assistance [7], but today, libraries have been largely replaced by web indices, and librarians by algorithms. To illustrate, recent surveys have found that 82.3% of American adults use search engines one or more times a day [12], but only 48% of Americans over the age of 15 have visited a public library in the last year [25].

Among the most widely used and trusted information-seeking mediums of today are web search engines [4, 13, 15, 16, 19, 37, 49], and particularly analogous to the process of query negotiation with a librarian, is the interactive assistance that search engines offer users as they input their queries [23, 35]. On Google and Bing, which together account for 84.8% of all search engine traffic [36], this assistance comes in the form of algorithmically generated search suggestions. Much like how librarians save people time by guiding them to the right sections of a library, Google estimates that its suggestions reduce "typing by about 25 percent" and save "over 200 years of typing time per day" [18].

Given the immense amount of traffic that autocomplete algorithms receive [36], the influence that they have on the queries that people view and click (through filtering and ranking) [24, 34], and the inherent ephemerality of their output, it is crucial that we develop methods for mapping not only the explicit suggestions that they provide, but also the implicit associations underlying those suggestions [11, 27, 39, 52]. Such maps could potentially increase the interpretability of their outputs, help platform moderators proactively identify the inappropriate associations that autocomplete has a history of making, and enable researchers and the public to hold them accountable for those associations [39].

In this paper we present methods for preserving, mapping, and analyzing the autocomplete search suggestions that people are exposed to while conducting web searches. To construct these maps, we introduce *recursive algorithm interrogation* (RAI), a breadth first search method for auditing autocomplete by recursively submitting a root input and its child suggestions to recover their underlying associations. The data resulting from this process can be modeled as a weighted and directed tree-like network that we refer to as *suggestion networks*; where nodes are suggested items, links are algorithmic associations, and link weights are derived from each suggestion's ranking.

We conducted an exploratory experiment using RAI in which we held web identity constant by submitting root queries from a single server with a fixed location and user-agent. Using the names of 38 US Governors as root queries, we initiated RAI on Google and Bing's autocomplete algorithms in parallel twice a day, at 9am and 6pm, for approximately 10 weeks between June and August 2018. We then used a combination of descriptive statistics, NLP, and information theoretic measures to compare the suggestion networks produced by each search engine. We found similarities in the structural and linguistic bounds of their suggestion networks, but substantial differences in their content and temporal dynamics. For example, Google was twice as likely as Bing to suggest social media (especially YouTube), and Bing was more likely to make a suggestion that contained a word classified as a swear or a negative emotion. We also found a higher turnover rate among longer and lower ranked suggestions, and periodic shocks that spanned across most of our root queries and which could potentially indicate algorithm updates.

Overall, our work makes the following contributions:

- We introduced RAI, a generalizable method for mapping the associations generated by autocomplete algorithms.
- We used RAI to conduct the first parallel and longitudinal audit of Google and Bing's autocomplete algorithms.
- Our results suggest that RAI could be an effective and valid tool for expanding a set of root queries.
- We found patterns of periodic shocks that affected the suggestions produced for most root queries, potentially identifying algorithm updates.
- We open source our tools for conducting RAI and constructing association networks, with the hope that they will spur further research in other topic areas.

Outline. The rest of the study is organized as follows. First, we examine documentation on and prior audits of autocomplete (§ 2). Next, we introduce the components of RAI (§ 3), and describe the results of our exploratory audit using RAI and US Governors names as root inputs (§ 4). Finally, we discuss our limitations (§ 5) and findings (§ 6).

2 BACKGROUND

In this section, we review official documentation for Google and Bing's autocomplete algorithms and the limited number of audits conducted on them.

Autocomplete Documentation. While both Google and Bing offer some documentation for how their autocomplete algorithms work, the data and decisions governing these algorithms are largely opaque. The documentation for Google's autocomplete system states that their suggestions are based on factors including the terms you type, the popularity and freshness of those terms, your search and browsing histories, and trending topics in your area [17]. Documentation for Bing's autocomplete functionality is less explicit, though it also appears to be based on the characters entered and the popularity of terms [6]. Both search engines also provide

factors which might lead one to not see certain suggestions, including suggestions that (1) contain disparaging or sensitive terms, (2) violate a policy regarding sex, hate, violence, and/or dangerous speech, (3) are not novel enough, or (4) are not popular enough.

Given the ephemerality of their output and the opacity and lack of regulatory oversight on how autocomplete works [27], the influence that these systems have over user inquiry raises concerns of transparency and accountability. Among these are concerns about the data that is used to train them, the stereotypes and biases that they might implicitly or explicitly evoke, and the specific censorship rules that govern them. Within this line of concern, and motivating the root selection for our audit, Google has previously been criticized for it's suggestions related to political actors. For example, in mid-2016, people found that searches for "lying" returned "lying ted" as a suggestion, in reference to Republican candidate Ted Cruz, but "crooked" did not return "crooked hillary" as a suggestion, in reference to Democratic candidate Hillary Clinton [29]. Similarly, Google has come under international criticism and entered a wide array of legal disputes related to their autocomplete algorithm generating a "combination of words that [are] capable of conveying a deceitful or misleading message" [27].

Autocomplete Audits. One principled method for outlining patterns of algorithmic decision making is known as the *algorithm audit* [45]. This framework involves feeding an algorithm a set inputs while systematically varying who is asking, what they're asking, where they're asking from, and when they're asking. Examples of how this method has been applied include studies of political bias, personalization, and localization on Google [20, 26, 28, 42], racial and gender discrimination in the gig economy [14, 22], and dynamic pricing on Amazon [8, 21, 33]. Prior audits of autocomplete, however, are relatively scarce, and include informal Search Engine Optimization (SEO) blogs [46, 53], investigative computational journalism reports [10, 11], and a peer-reviewed article from critical discourse researchers [1].

The SEO industry posts were focused on how to manipulate Google's autocomplete to make positive suggestions for a client's name rise in the ranks, and how to make negative suggestions disappear [46, 53]. This research demonstrated that, in 2013, one could directly influence search suggestions by creating a crowdsourcing task where participants were instructed to enter a specific search query and click on the first result listed [46]. Furthermore, it demonstrated that it took approximately one week for the changes to take place, indicating significant lag in Google's autocomplete updates at the time.

The computational journalism reports provided a more rigorous examination, and focused on the topics of censorship and defamation. In the first study, Diakopoulos focused on the suggestions returned by Google and Bing for various sex and violence-related words [11] – topics that Google explicitly states it excludes from autocomplete [17]. He found that certain words were censored on Google – returning no suggestions – while others were not, and the differences were somewhat expected from Google's autocomplete FAQ, but were also somewhat arbitrary depending on how the query was formulated. In the defamation study, Diakopoulos looked at whether entering the names of public figures and corporations on Google's autocomplete produced suggestions that could be considered defamatory, finding that name disambiguation makes it hard to tease apart the associations between such queries and their suggestions [10].

In the critical discourse paper, Baker and Potts (2013) "interrogated" (inspiring the name of our method) Google in April 2011 by submitting a series of carefully crafted questions and documenting the outputs [1]. After selecting 12 identity groups (*e.g.,* Black, Muslim, Gay), the authors mapped these groups into 2,690 question fragments by adding a *wh-* starting string (*e.g.,* why do, what do, where do) or an auxiliary fronting (*e.g.,* should, are, do) to each group. Overall, Baker and Potts found that their method elicited questions that made relatively distinct associations about each group, including physical characteristics for Jewish and Black people, and negative stereotypes about Gay people. Although they did not consider how the presence of these stereotypes in autocomplete might affect users, they noted that, at the time, no method existed for users to flag inappropriate suggestions, a feature which Google has since added.

Although illuminating, most of these studies were never peer-reviewed or automated and scaled up, leaving open questions on how to audit autocomplete. While other studies have also been conducted on autocomplete, their primary focus was on user engagement and improving relevance, a different, more internally focused type of audit [2, 24, 34]. To the best of our knowledge, none of the studies conducted thus far on autocomplete have examined the structures and associations that emerge when collecting suggestions recursively.

3 METHOD

In this section we describe the three components of RAI: selecting root inputs, conducting a breadth first search, and trimming the resulting suggestion networks. In our application of RAI, we explicitly did *not* study personalization or user generated queries. Instead, we used a fixed set of *root queries* and held web identity constant by submitting queries from a single server with a fixed location in the Northeastern US. This approach enabled us to map the autocomplete search suggestions for a fixed set of queries – from the perspective of a fixed user with no history – and measure their change over time. That is, our audit is not focused on human behavior, but machine behavior: the algorithm is our subject [41].

Root Selection.   To seed RAI, we used the names of 38 US governors (26 Republican, 7 Democratic, 2 Independent, and 1 Democrat-Farmer-Labor) as our *root queries*. US Governors are popularly elected officials who serve four-year terms as "chief executive officers of the fifty states and five commonwealths and territories" [38]. We selected these roots for two primary reasons. First, because Google has previously been criticized for it's suggestions related to political actors [29]. Second, we used these root queries because 15 of the governors were up for reelection in 2018. These elections were spread across six days during our data collection window: 2018-06-05 (5), 2018-06-12 (3), 2018-06-26 (3), 2018-08-02 (1), 2018-08-04 (1), and 2018-08-07 (2). These events, tied directly to the root input, provided opportunities to measure the impact of external shocks on Google and Bing's autocomplete algorithms.

Breadth First Search.   To conduct a breadth first search on Google and Bing we first identified two URLs that we could leverage as APIs. We then designed a program to submit a single *root query* to each search engine in parallel, add each root's suggestions to its respective queue, and then recursively repeat this process until the queue was extinguished or until the process reached a maximum *depth* – the number of steps from the root – that we set at 8 for this study.[1] For example, using the name of the Massachusetts governor, "charlie baker," as our root, Google returned a set of suggestions, including "charlie baker email," "charlie baker height," "charlie baker twitter," "charlie baker salary," and "charlie baker approval rating." We then recorded the rank, depth, and time of collection for each of these, and then submitted each of them to Google, and so forth, generating a tree-like directed network structure that we refer to as *suggestion networks*, where the nodes are n-grams and the links indicate which node suggested which. While building these networks, we did not collect duplicate edges resulting from cycles. If we observed a suggestion that we had already seen, we drew the link but did not add the suggestion to the queue. If a given node was linked to twice or more, we kept its depth and rank from the first occurrence.

Suggestion Network Trimming.   Given that the goal of our audit was to examine the autocomplete associations relevant to the root queries we had selected, we explored our data for cases where the suggestions obviously deviated from the root input. We identified two cases that resulted in what we call *emergent roots*: a suggestion that (a) is not relevant but somehow related to the original root query (*e.g.,* "governor of california jerry brown biography" → "biography"), and (b) initiates a new and unrelated branching process (*e.g.,* Figure 1).

The first case of emergent roots involves a type of conceptual network teleportation. For example, in a network built for the root query "scott walker," we found an edge from "scott walker wisconsin recount" to "recount." The query "recount" then began spawning its own suggestion network, including morphological and informational suggestions – such as, "recounting," "recounted," and "recount definition" – that no longer had direct relevance to the original root query (Figure 1).

The second case involves root disambiguation, and occurs when there is a well-known person with the same name as, or a name similar to, the root query. For example, for the roots "matt mead" and "kate brown," the autocomplete algorithms began suggesting morphological variants, such as "matt meadows" or "matt meader" and "kate abramson" or "kate brannan." The breadth first search would then continue on with these new names, each functioning as its own emergent root, producing a large number of suggestions unrelated to our root query.

Both of these cases were more prevalent on Bing, where the output of RAI surged at depth 5 and onward due to emergent roots (Figure 2).[2] To trim our networks of these, and reduce the amount of noise in the suggestion networks we were building, we used a

---

[1] As a practical matter, we limited the depth because of the amount of time that it took to reach greater depths, and because submitting queries too quickly increased the risk of being rate limited.
[2] Note that the high variability at greater depths is due to a small number of networks that produced nodes at those depths.

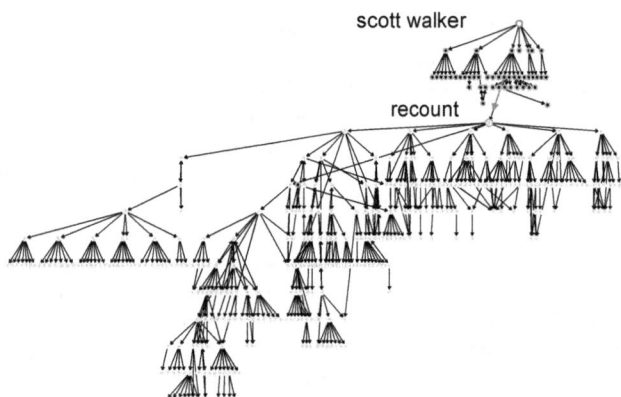

Figure 1: An example of our trimming on a suggestion network for the root "scott walker." The red edge leads from "scott walker wisconsin recount" to "recount," an emergent root that we trimmed from our suggestion networks in order to maintain their relevance to the root queries we selected.

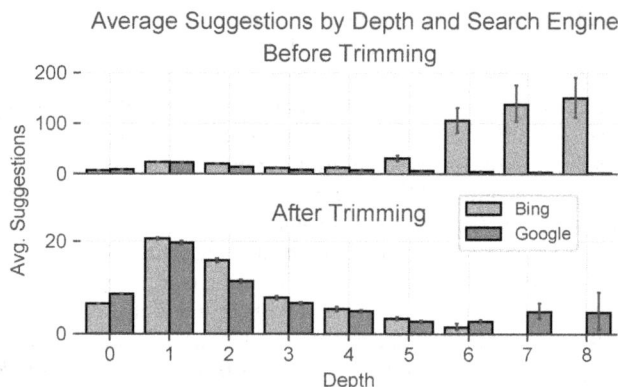

Figure 2: Before trimming, the suggestion networks produced by Bing were substantially larger at greater depths. However, after trimming the two cases of emergent roots we identified, the suggestion networks provided by Google and Bing were well aligned.

simple and conservative rule: trim any edges in which the target node did not contain both the first and last name of the root query. The result was largely a reduction in Bing's suggestions networks at depth 5 and onward, removing emergent roots, and leaving a distribution that more closely matched Google's (Figure 2).

4 RESULTS

Here we examine the suggestion networks that we collected using RAI and our root queries. More specifically, we describe and compare their structural and linguistic features, examine their change over time, and explore a method for reducing them down to a web of associated n-grams.

4.1 Structural Features

To characterize the structure of our suggestion networks, we calculated several canonical network science metrics. Out-degree (k_{out}), the number of out-bound links from a given node, has a clear interpretation (*i.e.,* the number of suggestions it produced). However, in-degree (k_{in}) has a less straightforward meaning. Excluding the roots, all nodes must have an in-degree of at least one (*i.e.,* they must have been suggested), so $k_{in} > 1$ is the result of converging suggestions, meaning that a node is relevant to multiple queries. These merge points could indicate a potentially important or ubiquitous association.

Most networks had right-skewed in- and out-degree distributions (Figure 3), indicating that most of the queries we submitted produced relatively few suggestions. This relationship varied by search engine, with Google never producing more than ten suggestions ($\mu = 1.2, SD = 2.1$), and Bing never producing more than eight ($\mu = 1.1, SD = 1.9$).[3] Using a Spearman's correlation, we found that as depth increased, the number of suggestions decreased for both search engines, but less so for Google than Bing (Google

$\rho = -0.11^{***}$; Bing $\rho = -0.34^{***}$).[4] Conversely, the number of merge points increased with depth for both search engines (Google $\rho = 0.52^{***}$; Bing $\rho = 0.43^{***}$).

4.2 Linguistic Features

We explored the linguistic features of suggestions networks in three respects: basic query characteristics, lexicon classifications, and the mentions of social media.

Query Characteristics. Considering all queries (*i.e.,* all roots and their child suggestions), the average query in our dataset consisted of 4.6 words ($SD = 1.2$), and this feature was not substantially different across Google and Bing (Figure 4). This finding aligns with prior work on real users in 2012, which found that the queries conducted on Google and Bing were on average 4.3 words [9], suggesting that RAI may sample queries from a similar distribution. However, our findings diverge from a 2010 report which indicated that 54.5% of queries conducted on Google were greater than three words [32]; 80.4% of the queries we conducted were greater than three words. This difference is likely a result of our root queries all being two words long, and the tendency for the autocomplete algorithms of both search engines to add rather than remove words when providing suggestions.

Indeed, in terms of the change from query (source node) to suggestion (target node), the difference in the number of words (target - source) was somewhat normally distributed around one (Figure 4). Overall, relative to their parent query, 87.7% of suggestions were longer by one or more words, while 11.8% of suggestions had the same number of words (*e.g.,* "asa hutchinson bio" → "asa hutchinson biography"), and the remaining 0.5% of suggestions decreased by one or two words (*e.g.,* "nathan deal new laws" → "nathan deal news").

---

[3]This maximum does not appear to be temporally stable – research conducted in 2017 found a maximum of only 4 suggestions for Google [43].

[4]Throughout the rest of the paper use the standard significance notation for P values, *** P < 0.001, ** P < 0.01, * P < 0.05

Suggestions (k_{out}) and Merge Points (k_{in})

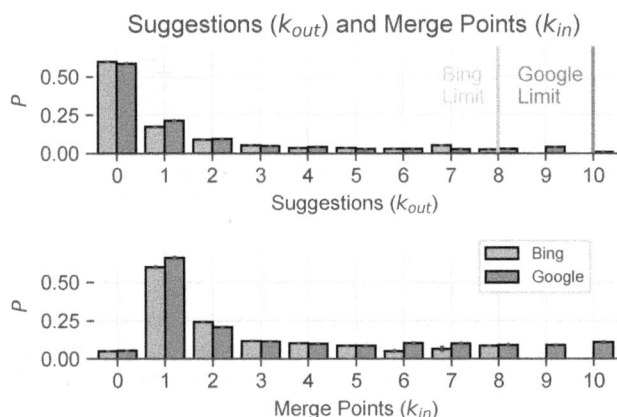

Figure 3: Mean probability of a query producing k_{out} suggestions (top) and being suggested k_{in} times (bottom). The blue and yellow vertical lines represent the maximum number of suggestions that Google and Bing provided, respectively.

N-gram Count and Change

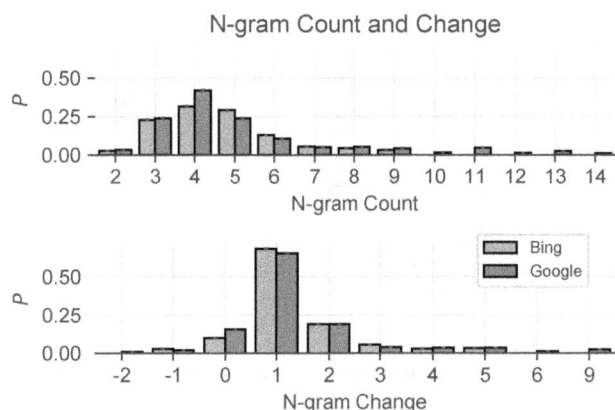

Figure 4: Most suggestions contained four or more words (top), and the majority of suggestions increased by one word or more relative to the query that produced them (bottom).

With respect to the interaction between the linguistic and structural features of suggestion networks, we found that longer queries are not only more likely to appear at greater depths, but they are also less likely to produce more suggestions. More specifically, query length (the number of words in a query) was positively correlated with depth (Google: $\rho = 0.61^{***}$; Bing: $\rho = 0.69^{***}$) and negatively correlated with k_{out} (Google $\rho = -0.33^{***}$; Bing $\rho = -0.50^{***}$).

Lexicon Classifications.   To attach qualitative context to the suggestions that we collected, while maintaining the automated nature of our method, we parsed our suggestions for n-grams that matched with words in the Linguistic Inquiry and Word Count lexicon (LIWC). LIWC is a widely used lexicon that was compiled by social scientists for classifying the psychological meaning of words [40, 47].

We observed several cases where suggestions were classified as containing "swear" words. For example, Bing returned the suggestion "gun control **idiot** jerry brown signs bill" at depth four and rank one for the root "jerry brown" (its immediate parent query was "jerry brown gun control"). This suggestion was short-lived, however, appearing at 9am and disappearing at 6pm on June 27, 2018. In contrast, the only Google suggestion that was classified as "swear" was "gina raimondo **freak**onomics" for the root "gina raimondo" at depth zero, rank nine. However, as people familiar with the popular economics book *Freakonomics* will recognize, this is clearly a misclassification by LIWC, and upon further investigation, we found that the suggestion likely resulted from Governor Raimondo appearing on a podcast of the same name. While the Jerry Brown examples demonstrate how suggestions can cast politicians in a negative light, the Gina Raimondo example stresses the importance of examining suggestions in the context of real world events.

While the cases for swear words are somewhat anecdotal, search engines frequently suggested words with negative emotions (i.e., "negemo" for LIWC) to their users. For example, Bing

produced the suggestions: "governor kate brown of oregon"→"kate brown governor of oregon **bad** law", "scott walker wisconsin economy"→"wisconsin economy **failing** under scott walker", and "andrew cuomo bar exam"→["andrew cuomo **failing** the bar exam 4 times", "andrew cuomo **failing** the bar exam"]. However, suggestions classified as containing negative emotions typically only survived for less than 10 days. In total, Google produced suggestions containing negative emotions for three (7.8%) root queries and Bing for six (15.8%) root queries.

Social Media Suggestions.   Given the growing concerns about how web search can funnel users towards social media (*e.g.,* Google's embedded Twitter and YouTube results [42]), we examined the rate at which major social media platforms – specifically, Facebook, Twitter, Instagram, LinkedIn, Reddit, and YouTube – were suggested in autocomplete. Overall, we found that Google's suggestions included references to social media twice as often (10.6%) as Bing's (4.6%). We also found differences by root, with Google including a suggestion to Twitter for all 38 roots, while Bing only did so for 32 roots. Suggestions mentioning Facebook were more equal (Google: 25, Bing: 23). Conversely, Bing mentioned Instagram for seven roots, while Google only did so for two. There were also substantial differences among suggestions that mentioned YouTube, where Google referenced it's sister platform for 14 roots, while Bing only mentioned YouTube for four roots.

There are several caveats here worth mentioning. Although we trimmed suggestions that did not explicitly mention the root, there are some disambiguation challenges that this did not resolve. For example, while both Google and Bing linked Dan Malloy, the governor of Connecticut, to Instagram, these suggestions typically also mentioned "surf" or "surfer." We looked into this and found that the 63 year old governor was not in fact an avid surfer, but there is another Dan Malloy who is. Similarly, Bing provided a suggestion for California governor Jerry Brown that mentioned Facebook, "jerry brown news3lv facebook," but this was in reference to the

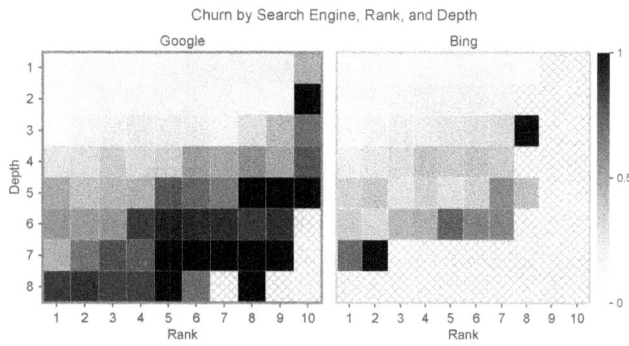

Figure 5: As rank and distance from the root increases, the suggestions of Google and Bing become less stable.

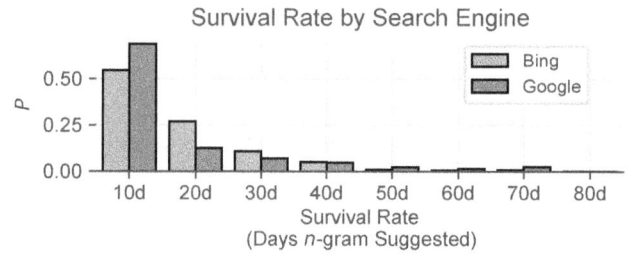

Figure 6: Most queries only appeared for a handful of days, indicating a generally high turnover rate among the suggestions made by search engines, as characterized by our method.

meteorologist Jerry Brown for News 3 Las Vegas. These findings highlight the challenges in automated methods for name disambiguation, especially in autocomplete [10], and again emphasize the need to consider context when evaluating suggestions.

4.3 Temporal Features

We explored the temporal change of suggestion networks in three ways, first by quantifying the *churn* of nodes, second by examining the *survival rate* of nodes, and third by calculating normalized mutual information over time. We found that the greatest variability among the suggestions produced by Google and Bing occurs among the lowest ranked nodes, that most nodes have a relatively short life lifespan, and some evidence that Google and Bing's autocomplete algorithms periodically shift in the suggestions they deliver. These shifts might occur due to real life events directly or peripherally involving the roots (*e.g.*, their primary elections), but also might occur when the algorithms are being updated.

Churn. Given the impact of depth on suggestion networks' structural and linguistic features, we calculated churn by examining each root query's suggestion network, and asking how often the n-grams at each rank and depth changed between that network and the one that we collected on the next crawl. More formally, let $S_{e,r,d}(t, q)$ represent the set of suggestions at time $t \in T$ for root query $q \in Q$ from search engine e at rank $r \in R$ and depth $d \in D$. Churn $c_{e,r,d}(t, q)$ is defined as the Jaccard Index between time t and $t + 1$, i.e.,

$$c_{e,r,d}(t, q) = 1 - \frac{|S_{e,r,d}(t+1, q) \cap S_{e,r,d}(t, q)|}{|S_{e,r,d}(t+1, q) \cup S_{e,r,d}(t, q)|}. \quad (1)$$

Then, we aggregate $c_{e,r,d}(t, q)$ over time t and root query q to get average churn $\bar{c}_{e,r,d}$ from search engine e at each rank r and depth d, i.e.,

$$\bar{c}_{e,r,d} = \frac{1}{|Q|} \frac{1}{|T|} \sum_{q \in Q} \sum_{t \in T} c_{e,r,d}(t, q). \quad (2)$$

We found that the churn for Google and Bing followed a similar pattern: turnover was higher for lower ranked suggestions and suggestions that appeared at greater depths (Figure 5). We also examined correlations between churn and depth (Google: $\rho = 0.43^{***}$; Bing: $\rho = 0.54^{***}$), churn and rank (Google: $\rho = 0.10^{***}$; Bing:

$\rho = 0.20^{***}$), and churn and query length (Google: $\rho = 0.29^{***}$; Bing: $\rho = 0.48^{***}$). While these correlations point towards the importance of depth and query length, it is also important to consider them in light of our findings from § 4.1, where we found that query length was positively correlated with depth (longer queries at greater depths) and out-degree was negatively correlated with depth (fewer suggestions at greater depths).

Taking the relationships between query length, depth, and churn into account, we examined the relationship between churn and rank at each depth and found the greatest correlation at depth zero (Google: $\rho = 0.39^{***}$; Bing: $\rho = 0.47^{***}$). Together, these findings indicate that (1) longer queries are more volatile over time, and (2) highly ranked suggestions tend to be more stable over time. The latter suggests a potential cumulative advantage for the associations that make it into highly ranked positions, in terms of user attention, because of the rank-biased way that users examine suggestions [24, 34]. This stability may also help to prevent attempts to game or manipulate the rankings, but our results are descriptive and we can only speculate on this matter.

Survival Rates. To examine the survival rate of suggestions, we tracked the number of days that each unique suggestion persisted across our data collection window. Using this count, we found that the majority (Google: 70%; Bing: 54.6%) of suggestions appeared for ten days or less (Figure 6), while less than 1% of suggestions (Google: 0.2%; Bing: 0.1%) appeared for the entire duration of our crawl. Given our previous findings related to query length, we also examined the relationship between query length and survival rate, but found no significant differences. We also examined the differences between the two search engines with respect to the LIWC classifications by ranking each LIWC category according to its mean survival rate. We found that these rankings were not correlated ($\rho = 0.17, P = 0.16$), indicating that the search engines' autocomplete algorithms deviate in the types of associations that they make for US politicians, according to LIWC classifications. These results indicate that for the suggestions that do churn, their life span is relatively short, potentially due to the presence of trending topics (or "freshness") as indicated in the autocomplete documentation.

External Shocks. To explore how suggestions might react to real world events, we examined the rate of change for each root's

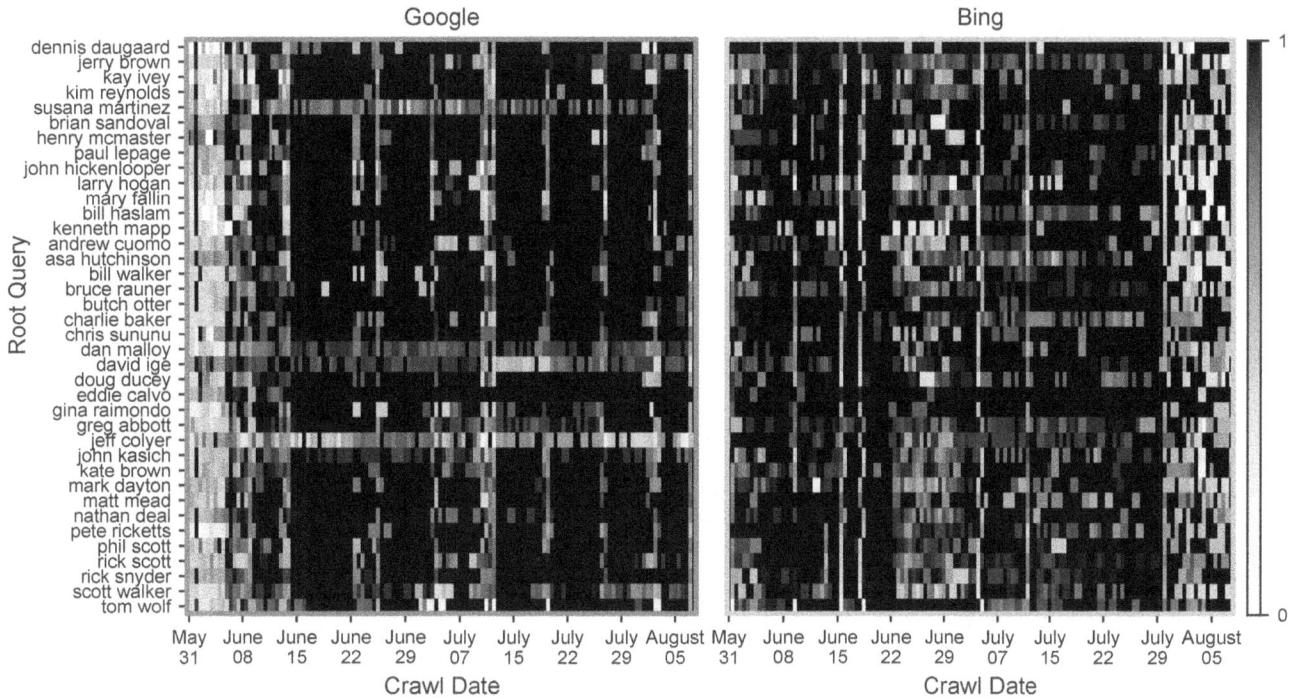

Figure 7: Normalized mutual information (NMI) over time and by search engine. A value of 1 indicates that there was no change in a root's information set since the previous time step, while a value of 0 indicates a complete change. Roots are clustered and arranged vertically by primary, and the red vertical lines represent the date of the primary for each clustering of governors.

suggestion network over time using normalized mutual information (NMI), a measure commonly used when comparing the overlap between two information sets [54]. At a high level, NMI measures the difference between two distributions and returns a value that scales from 0 to 1, where 0 means the distributions were completely different, and 1 means that they were the same. Here we explicitly ignore the ranking and depth of suggestions, as our primary interest is measuring any type of change in the information being retrieved for a given root query. While our analysis here was exploratory, our expectation was that external events would provide some sort of shock to the system, perhaps due to an increase in search volume.

We calculated NMI by first extracting all of the words present in each suggestion network at each time step. We excluded the root queries during this tokenization process to prevent them from inflating similarity. Then, for each root, we moved across each time step in our data collection window and measured the NMI for that root query between time t and time $t + 1$. More formally, following the notation we used for churn (Equation 1) and using $H(A)$ to denote the entropy of A, and $I(A; B)$ to denote the mutual information between A and B, we calculated NMI as:

$$NMI_{e,r,d}(t,q) = \frac{2 \times I(S_{e,r,d}(t,q); S_{e,r,d}(t+1,q))}{[H(S_{e,r,d}(t,q)) + H(S_{e,r,d}(t+1,q))]} \quad (3)$$

We then plotted this relationship over time, marking the gubernatorial primary dates of the 15 governors who had a primary during our data collection period (Figure 7). While we did not find a clear decrease in NMI among the roots during their respective elections

(which would have indicated a surge of novel suggestions) it did reveal relatively periodic shocks that appear to affect all roots, especially for Google. While both Google and Bing showed variations on these root-wide surges in NMI, the timings did not align well across the search engines, suggesting that some of these changes may be due to internal factors that affect each search engine differently; such as an algorithm update being pushed. These surges could also be tied to fluctuations in search activity more broadly, and different search engines have different users with different needs and habits.

4.4 Association Networks

To explore the underlying associations being made for politicians' names by Google and Bing, we first reduced each suggestion down to the new information that it contained relative to its root. That is, if the query "asa hutchinson" produced the suggestion "asa hutchinson biography," we reduced that suggestion to "biography." We executed this reduction with memory, so if at the next depth, "asa hutchinson biography" (now just "biography") linked to "asa hutchinson bio," the resulting edge was from "biography" to "bio." In effect, this procedure reduced the redundant information and enabled us to look at what we refer to as n-gram *association networks*.

After completing this process, we aggregated all of the resulting association networks into a single network for each search engine (Figure 8). The resulting networks reflect all of the associations made across our data collection window, giving us a new way of examining the associations that persist across all politicians, and

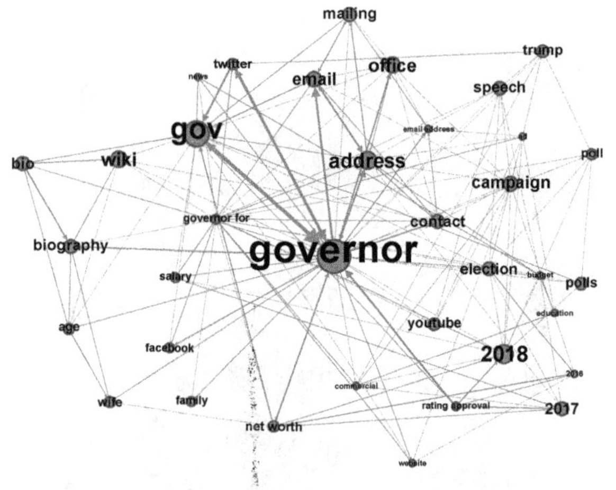

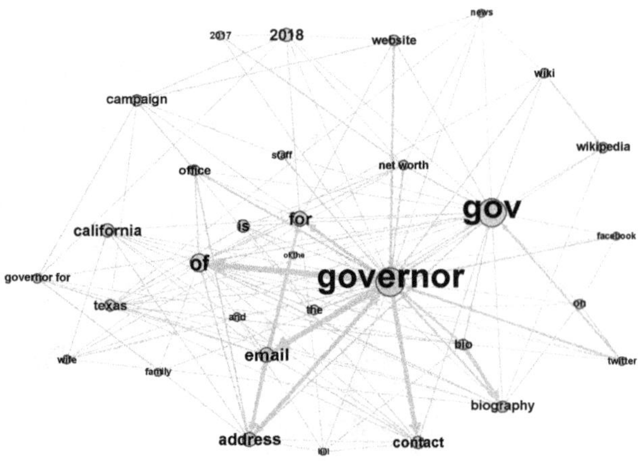

Figure 8: Association networks for Google (blue) and Bing (yellow) aggregated across root queries. The nodes represent n-grams, and the directed edges indicate a suggestion between two n-grams. The size of nodes and their labels are relative to their k_{in}, and edge size are representative of their weight – the total count for that suggestion across all crawls and roots. For visualization purposes we set a threshold of $k_{in} \geq 15$.

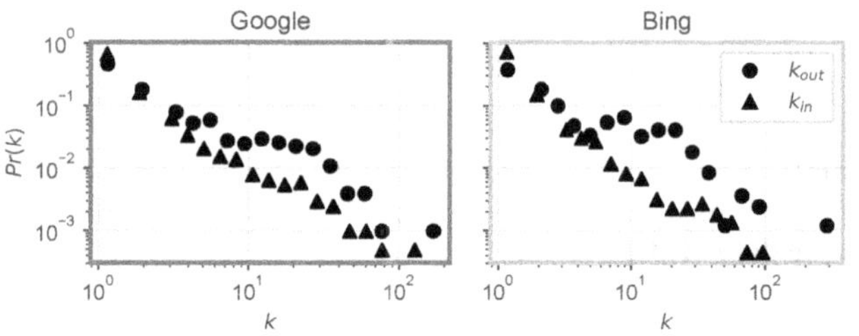

Figure 9: The in- and out-degree distributions for the aggregated association networks produced by both search engines were heavy tailed and fairly similar.

how these associations differ by search engine. Structurally, using the same standard network metrics as before (in- and out-degree), we found that Google and Bing both had similar heavy-tailed degree distributions (Figure 9). This structural similarity is related to the maximum number of suggestions that Bing and Google provided at the time of our audit, and is also likely limited by our trimming method.

Examining these associations networks more closely, we found moderate correlations between the n-gram associations produced by Google and Bing. More specifically, we used the in- and out-degree to rank all of the n-grams we observed, and found that both were moderately correlated (in-degree: $\rho = 0.49^{***}$; out-degree: $\rho = 0.38^{***}$). This means that there were significant differences in the associations being made for politicians by Google and Bing. The top-10 n-grams with the highest in-degree for Google were, rank-ordered: ['governor', 'email', 'twitter', 'gov', 'address', 'net worth', 'wife', 'rating approval', 'contact', 'facebook']. The same for Bing were: ['governor', 'gov', 'of', 'gov.', 'address', 'email', 'contact', 'twitter', 'for', 'bio'].

5 LIMITATIONS

Here we discuss the limitations of our approach, including disambiguation and context issues, the fixed and artificial nature of our queries, and the absence of user behavior and personalization.

Disambiguation. As noted in prior work, disambiguation is a problem inherent to audits of human names in autocomplete [10]. While our method for trimming suggestions (§ 3) proved to be a useful method for removing irrelevant queries generated by morphologically similar names, it did not solve the disambiguation problem, as we saw in our results on the presence of social media websites. However, the number of cases where this occurred was minimal, and it likely did not have an impact on our main findings. Although one could add an n-gram to their root queries to help disambiguate the search intent, this could further distance the root from a real user query, and further limit the number and breadth of suggestions returned. Future research should examine additional disambiguation techniques to trim suggestion networks.

Context. While we attempted to study autocomplete in isolation – by holding location, user, and queries constant – autocomplete is inherently tied to the social world. Suggestions occur, in part, because people are searching for them, and people search for things for myriad reasons. For example, suggestions might contain phrases that are ironic or satirical, but without context, could be classified and interpreted as negative. One potential way to capture this context is to expand our method to capture the search results returned for each suggestion, though without cooperation from a search engine, the amount of crawling required to collect this additional data is not feasible. On the other hand, it is likely that these mischaracterizations would wash out with a large enough sample.

Query Selection. Providing Google or Bing with a root input other than a name produces different types of suggestions, and adding characters to the end of the names we submitted (*e.g.*, name + "a") also produces a different set of suggestions than those generated by submitting the names alone, but there is typically overlap (*e.g.*, name + "age" often appears in both). However, as a practical matter, appending each letter of the English alphabet to the end of a set of root queries would expand the amount of data collected exponentially. More importantly, data collection on that scale would likely not be allowed by Google and Bing, as it would require a constant, high-speed stream in order to complete RAI for all root + alphabet combinations in a reasonable time window.

Similarly, we did not collect suggestions in the setting that they are typically encountered: as the user types. When typing a query into Google or Bing, each new character entered results in a flash of suggestions based on the characters entered up to that point. The structures that we collected are a coarse grain version of what information scientists refer to as *tries*; a tree of possible suggestions that is updated as each new character is inputted. Again, as a practical matter, collecting a trie for each root query is not feasible without unfettered access to a search engine's autocomplete. Despite this limitation, prior work has shown that 53% of user engagement with autocomplete occurs after the user has typed the last character of a word [34], which is essentially what we simulated with RAI.

Personalization. We reemphasize that our study was aimed at studying the behavior of Google and Bing's autocomplete algorithms under fixed conditions that eliminated user-based personalization and held localization constant. This approach made the suggestions we collected comparable across search engines, root queries, and time, but does not address the heterogeneity of real user behavior. That is, users have widely different search strategies [44], and in practice, these strategies would systematically affect the way that they formulate queries and therefore the suggestions that they are exposed to. One could incorporate real user queries – through a browser extension, for example – and measure differences across query categories, but then time and location would become confounding variables. Localization, on the other hand, could be incorporated into our study by submitting root queries from geographically dispersed servers. Prior work has shown that real user queries systematically vary by location, and this variance is correlated with demographic variables, suggesting that it could be used as a proxy to understand personalization [5, 51].

6 DISCUSSION

In this paper, we introduced RAI, a method for preserving and mapping an algorithm's associations around a given root input. Using the names of 38 US governors who were up for re-election in 2018 as root inputs, we applied RAI to conduct an exploratory and non-personalized audit of Google and Bing's autocomplete algorithm in parallel over the course of two months. Our results demonstrate consistency in the structural and linguistic bounds of the two search engines' autocomplete algorithms, and shed light on differences in their content and temporal dynamics.

We found that Google and Bing's suggestions generally have a high degree of churn that is mediated by (1) the rank of the suggestions, with highly ranked positions being more stable than lower ranked positions, and (2) the length of the query being submitted, with shorter queries producing suggestions that were more stable than suggestions produced by longer queries. (Figure 5 and Figure 6). Given the attention biases in how users interact with autocomplete (*e.g.*, order effects) [24, 34], this stability at high ranks may limit

exposure to volatile suggestions while not entirely excluding them. That is, highly ranked suggestions may be limited to stable trends around a given query, while lower ranked positions offer a more exploratory view of fleeting trends or breaking news. Limiting user exposure to volatile suggestions in this way may provide useful friction for combating inaccurate, offensive, or misleading information, and future research should explore this.

Our findings on the enhanced presence of social media in Google's suggestions, especially YouTube, has implications that could be seen as concerning. For example, YouTube is owned by the same parent company as Google, and regulators have previously levied record-breaking fines on Google for favoring its own products and services. Similarly, YouTube has recently come under heavy criticism for politically radicalizing its viewers [50], and in light of that, steering users who are searching politicians' names towards the video platform does not seem ideal. Future research should examine this link more in-depth, perhaps by examining the search results returned for queries that mention YouTube.

The periodic temporal dynamics that we picked up on may identify algorithm updates. These show up in Figure 7, where we observed approximately weekly shocks across roots, especially for Google. This finding ties in to prior work, which found that Google's suggestions took about a week to update [46]. These periods of accelerated turnover could be a particularly important time to conduct a more in-depth and qualitative analysis in future research.

The association networks that we derived from our data could potentially be used to assist human moderators by providing them with a macro view of the associations that an algorithm is making. Such a perspective could potentially reduce their viewing burden and enable them to more readily spot policy violations. Future research should examine methods for improving the filtering and visualization of these networks.

We hope our results and tools will provide a foundation for future research mapping information pathways on other platforms. For example, RAI could be applied to map YouTube recommendations, similar to the AlgoTransparency project [30]. Scholars who research fairness, accountability, transparency, and ethics in algorithms may wish to apply our method to study the associations that Google and Bing make with respect to gender, race, or other groups [39]. For example, do the suggestions for female or male names systematically differ? Although using more question-like root queries – as Baker and Potts did [1] – is an appealing idea, we explored a few such examples (*e.g.*, "why do <group>"), and found that they often returned zero suggestions on Google and Bing, suggesting that they are already being intentionally blocked. In hopes of spurring such research, we make our tools freely available at https://github.com/gitronald/suggests.

ACKNOWLEDGMENTS

We thank the anonymous reviewers for their helpful comments and Alexandra Olteanu, Piotr Sapieżyński, and others for invaluable discussions and comments on this work. This research was supported in part by NSF grant IIS-1553088. Any opinions, findings, and conclusions or recommendations expressed in this material are those of the authors and do not necessarily reflect the views of the NSF.

REFERENCES

[1] Paul Baker and Amanda Potts. 2013. 'Why Do White People Have Thin Lips?' Google and the Perpetuation of Stereotypes via Auto-Complete Search Forms. *Critical Discourse Studies* 10, 2 (May 2013), 187–204. https://doi.org/10.1080/17405904.2012.744320

[2] Ziv Bar-Yossef and Naama Kraus. 2011. Context-sensitive query auto-completion. In *Proceedings of the 20th international conference on World wide web*. ACM, 107–116.

[3] Nicholas J Belkin. 1980. Anomalous states of knowledge as a basis for information retrieval. *Canadian Journal of Information Science* 5, 1 (1980), 133–143.

[4] Edelman Berland. 2017. 2017 Edelman Trust Barometer. (2017). http://www.edelman.com/trust2017/ Accessed: 2017-03-07.

[5] Bin Bi, Milad Shokouhi, Michal Kosinski, and Thore Graepel. 2013. Inferring the Demographics of Search Users: Social Data Meets Search Queries. In *Proceedings of the 22nd International Conference on World Wide Web - WWW '13*. ACM Press, Rio de Janeiro, Brazil, 131–140. https://doi.org/10.1145/2488388.2488401

[6] Bing. 2018. A deeper look at autosuggest. https://blogs.bing.com/search/2013/03/25/a-deeper-look-at-autosuggest. (2018).

[7] Lionel Casson. [n. d.]. *Libraries in the Ancient World*. Yale University Press.

[8] Le Chen, Alan Mislove, and Christo Wilson. 2016. An Empirical Analysis of Algorithmic Pricing on Amazon Marketplace. In *Proceedings of the 25th International World Wide Web Conference*.

[9] Chitika. 2012. *Ask.com Has The Most Long-Winded Searchers, Report Says*. Technical Report. Chitika. http://searchengineland.com/ask-com-has-the-most-long-winded-searchers-report-says-109202

[10] Nick Diakopoulos. 2013. Algorithmic defamation: The case of the shameless autocomplete. http://www.nickdiakopoulos.com/2013/08/06/algorithmic-defamation-the-case-of-the-shameless-autocomplete/. (2013).

[11] Nick Diakopoulos. 2013. Sex, Violence, and Autocomplete Algorithms: Methods and Context. http://www.nickdiakopoulos.com/2013/08/01/sex-violence-and-autocomplete-algorithms-methods-and-context/. (2013).

[12] William H. Dutton, Bianca Christin Reisdorf, Elizabeth Dubois, and Grant Blank. [n. d.]. Search and Politics: The Uses and Impacts of Search in Britain, France, Germany, Italy, Poland, Spain, and the United States. ([n. d.]). https://doi.org/10.2139/ssrn.2960697

[13] William H. Dutton, Bianca Christin Reisdorf, Elizabeth Dubois, and Grant Blank. 2017. Search and Politics: The Uses and Impacts of Search in Britain, France, Germany, Italy, Poland, Spain, and the United States. (2017).

[14] Benjamin Edelman, Michael Luca, and Dan Svirsky. 2017. Racial discrimination in the sharing economy: Evidence from a field experiment. *American Economic Journal: Applied Economics* 9, 2 (2017), 1–22.

[15] Robert Epstein and Ronald E Robertson. 2015. The search engine manipulation effect (SEME) and its possible impact on the outcomes of elections. *Proceedings of the National Academy of Sciences* 112, 33 (2015), E4512–E4521.

[16] Robert Epstein, Ronald E. Robertson, David Lazer, and Christo Wilson. 2017. Suppressing the search engine manipulation effect (SEME). *Proceedings of the ACM: Human-Computer Interaction* 1, 42 (2017). Issue 2.

[17] Google. 2017. Search using autocomplete. https://support.google.com/websearch/answer/106230. (2017). Accessed: 2017-04-01.

[18] Google. 2018. How Google autocomplete works in Search. https://www.blog.google/products/search/how-google-autocomplete-works-search/. (2018).

[19] Jeffrey Gottfried and Elisa Shearer. 2016. News use across social media platforms. Pew Research Center. (2016). http://www.journalism.org/2016/05/26/news-use-across-social-media-platforms-2016/

[20] Aniko Hannak, Piotr Sapieżyński, Arash Molavi Kakhki, Balachander Krishnamurthy, David Lazer, Alan Mislove, and Christo Wilson. 2013. Measuring Personalization of Web Search. In *Proceedings of the 22nd International World Wide Web Conference*.

[21] Aniko Hannak, Gary Soeller, David Lazer, Alan Mislove, and Christo Wilson. 2014. Measuring Price Discrimination and Steering on E-commerce Web Sites. In *Proceedings of the 2014 ACM Conference on Internet Measurement*.

[22] Anikó Hannák, Claudia Wagner, David Garcia, Alan Mislove, Markus Strohmaier, and Christo Wilson. 2017. Bias in Online Freelance Marketplaces: Evidence from TaskRabbit and Fiverr.. In *CSCW*. 1914–1933.

[23] Donna Harman. 1988. Towards interactive query expansion. In *Proceedings of the 11th annual international ACM SIGIR conference on Research and development in information retrieval*. ACM, 321–331.

[24] Kajta Hofmann, Bhaskar Mitra, Filip Radlinski, and Milad Shokouhi. 2014. An eye-tracking study of user interactions with query auto completion. In *Proceedings of the 23rd ACM International Conference on Conference on Information and Knowledge Management*. ACM, 549–558.

[25] John B. Horrigan. [n. d.]. Library Usage and Engagement by Americans. ([n. d.]). http://www.pewinternet.org/2016/09/09/library-usage-and-engagement/

[26] Desheng Hu, Shan Jiang, Ronald E Robertson, and Christo Wilson. 2019. Auditing the Partisanship of Google Search Snippets. In *Proceedings of the 2019 World Wide Web Conference (WWW '19)*, Vol. 16. 58.

[27] Stavroula Karapapa and Maurizio Borghi. 2015. Search engine liability for autocomplete suggestions: Personality, privacy and the power of the algorithm. 23, 3

(2015), 261–289. https://doi.org/10.1093/ijlit/eav009

[28] Chloe Kliman-Silver, Aniko Hannak, David Lazer, Christo Wilson, and Alan Mislove. 2015. Location, Location, Location: The Impact of Geolocation on Web Search Personalization. In *Proceedings of the 2015 ACM Conference on Internet Measurement*.

[29] Search Engine Land. 2016. Google says it's not deliberately filtering "Crooked Hillary" suggested search to favor Clinton. https://searchengineland.com/google-crooked-hillary-251152. (2016). Accessed: 2017-04-01.

[30] Paul Lewis and Erin McCormick. 2018. How an Ex-YouTube Insider Investigated Its Secret Algorithm. *The Guardian* (Feb. 2018).

[31] Don McFadyen. 1975. The psychology of inquiry: reference service and the concept of information/experience. *Journal of Librarianship* 7, 1 (1975), 2–11.

[32] Matt McGee. 2010. Google weighs in on query length: Long tail alive and well. (2010). http://www.smallbusinessem.com/google-query-length/3273/.

[33] Jakub Mikians, László Gyarmati, Vijay Erramilli, and Nikolaos Laoutaris. 2012. Detecting price and search discrimination on the Internet. In *Proceedings of the 11th ACM Workshop on Hot Topics in Networks*.

[34] Bhaskar Mitra, Milad Shokouhi, Filip Radlinski, and Katja Hofmann. 2014. On user interactions with query auto-completion. In *Proceedings of the 37th international ACM SIGIR conference on Research & development in information retrieval*. ACM, 1055–1058.

[35] Yael Nemeth, Bracha Shapira, and Meirav Taeib-Maimon. 2004. Evaluation of the real and perceived value of automatic and interactive query expansion. In *Proceedings of the 27th annual international ACM SIGIR conference on Research and development in information retrieval*. ACM, 526–527.

[36] NetMarketShare. 2018. *Search engine market share*. Technical Report. NetMarketShare. https://www.netmarketshare.com/search-engine-market-share.aspx

[37] Nic Newman, David A. L. Levy, and Rasmus Kleis Nielsen. 2017. Reuters Institute Digital News Report 2017. *SSRN Electronic Journal* (2017). https://doi.org/10.2139/ssrn.2619576

[38] NGA. [n. d.]. Governors' Powers & Authority. ([n. d.]). https://www.nga.org/consulting/powers-and-authority/

[39] Safiya Umoja Noble. 2018. *Algorithms of oppression: How search engines reinforce racism*. New York University Press.

[40] James W Pennebaker, Martha E Francis, and Roger J Booth. 2001. Linguistic inquiry and word count: LIWC 2001. *Mahway: Lawrence Erlbaum Associates* 71 (2001).

[41] Iyad Rahwan, Manuel Cebrian, Nick Obradovich, Josh Bongard, Jean-François Bonnefon, Cynthia Breazeal, Jacob W Crandall, Nicholas A Christakis, Iain D Couzin, Matthew O Jackson, et al. 2019. Machine behaviour. *Nature* 568, 7753 (2019), 477.

[42] Ronald E Robertson, Shan Jiang, Kenneth Joseph, Lisa Friedland, David Lazer, and Christo Wilson. 2018. Auditing Partisan Audience Bias within Google Search. *Proceedings of the ACM: Human-Computer Interaction* 2 (2018).

[43] Ronald E Robertson, David Lazer, and Christo Wilson. 2018. Auditing the Personalization and Composition of Politically-Related Search Engine Results Pages. In *Proceedings of the 2018 World Wide Web Conference on World Wide Web*. International World Wide Web Conferences Steering Committee, 955–965.

[44] Daniel E. Rose and Danny Levinson. 2004. Understanding user goals in Web search. In *Proceedings of the 13th International Conference on World Wide Web (WWW '04)*. ACM, New York, NY, USA, 13–19.

[45] Christian Sandvig, Kevin Hamilton, Karrie Karahalios, and Cedric Langbort. 2014. Auditing algorithms: Research methods for detecting discrimination on internet platforms. In *Proceedings of "Data and Discrimination: Converting Critical Concerns into Productive Inquiry"*.

[46] Lauren Starling. 2013. How to remove a word from Google autocomplete. (2013). http://www.laurenstarling.org/how-to-remove-a-word-from-google-autocomplete/

[47] Yla R Tausczik and James W Pennebaker. 2010. The psychological meaning of words: LIWC and computerized text analysis methods. *Journal of language and social psychology* 29, 1 (2010), 24–54.

[48] Robert S. Taylor. 2015. Question-negotiation and information seeking in libraries. *College & Research Libraries* 76, 3 (March 2015), 251–267. https://doi.org/10.5860/crl.76.3.251

[49] Francesca Tripodi. 2018. Searching for Alternative Facts: Analyzing Scriptural Inference in Conservative News Practices. Data & Society. (May 2018).

[50] Zeynep Tufekci. 2018. Opinion | YouTube, the Great Radicalizer. *The New York Times* (June 2018).

[51] Ingmar Weber and Carlos Castillo. 2010. The demographics of web search. In *Proceedings of the 33rd international ACM SIGIR conference on Research and development in information retrieval*. ACM, 523–530.

[52] Wayne A. Wiegand. [n. d.]. The "Amherst Method": The Origins of the Dewey Decimal Classification Scheme. 33, 2 ([n. d.]), 175–194.

[53] Wiideman. 2010. Beat the autocomplete - A study of Google auto-suggest. (2010). https://www.wiideman.com/research/google-autocomplete/study-results

[54] Pan Zhang. 2015. Evaluating Accuracy of Community Detection Using the Relative Normalized Mutual Information. *Journal of Statistical Mechanics: Theory and Experiment* 2015, 11 (Nov. 2015), P11006.

Understanding Brand Consistency from Web Content

Soumyadeep Roy
IIT Kharagpur, India
soumyadeep.roy9@iitkgp.ac.in

Niloy Ganguly
IIT Kharagpur, India
niloy@cse.iitkgp.ac.in

Shamik Sural
IIT Kharagpur, India
shamik@cse.iitkgp.ac.in

Niyati Chhaya
Adobe Research, India
nchhaya@adobe.com

Anandhavelu Natarajan
Adobe Research, India
anandvn@adobe.com

ABSTRACT

Brands produce content to engage with the audience continually and tend to maintain a set of human characteristics in their marketing campaigns. In this era of digital marketing, they need to create a lot of content to keep up the engagement with their audiences. However, such kind of content authoring at scale introduces challenges in maintaining consistency in a brand's messaging tone, which is very important from a brand's perspective to ensure a persistent impression for its customers and audiences. In this work, we quantify brand personality and formulate its linguistic features. We score text articles extracted from brand communications on five personality dimensions: sincerity, excitement, competence, ruggedness and sophistication, and show that a linear SVM model achieves a decent F1 score of 0.822. The linear SVM allows us to annotate a large set of data points free of any annotation error. We utilize this huge annotated dataset to characterize the notion of brand consistency, which is maintaining a company's targeted brand personality across time and over different content categories; we make certain interesting observations. As per our knowledge, this is the first study which investigates brand personality from the company's official websites, and that formulates and analyzes the notion of brand consistency on such a large scale.

KEYWORDS

brand personality; reputation management; affective computing; text classification

ACM Reference Format:
Soumyadeep Roy, Niloy Ganguly, Shamik Sural, Niyati Chhaya, and Anandhavelu Natarajan. 2019. Understanding Brand Consistency from Web Content. In *11th ACM Conference on Web Science (WebSci '19), June 30–July 3, 2019, Boston, MA, USA.* ACM, New York, NY, USA, 9 pages. https://doi.org/10.1145/3292522.3326048

1 INTRODUCTION

Organizations tend to maintain a personality or a set of human characteristics in their marketing campaigns, which help them to uniquely position themselves in a market segment and differentiate from other products. For example, Red Bull positions itself as courageous and outgoing and Nike portrays itself as athletic. Aaker [1] formalizes the brand persona dimensions highlighted in Table 1. Maehle [15] attempts to understand how consumers form their perceptions of the brand persona dimensions and also what product or brand characteristics influence these perceptions. There exist very few studies [12, 27] that attempt to quantify this implicit notion of brand personality. Brand personality is one of the dimensions that forms the brand image of an organization and it also significantly contributes towards the understanding of consumer choice [19].

Trait	Explanation
Sincerity	A brand which portrays itself as honest, friendly, sincere, or down–to–earth.
Excitement	A brand portraying itself as spirited, imaginative, trendy, and contemporary.
Competence	If a brand describes its successes and achievements in its articles it comes out as being competent. Competence in general is evoked when the reader interprets a brand's success from its content.
Sophistication	A brand which portrays itself as glamorous, charming, or catering to the upper class.
Ruggedness	A brand which portrays itself as adventurous, outdoorsy, tough, or Western.

Table 1: Brand Dimensions

In the era of digital marketing, brands need to create a lot of online content to keep up the engagement with their audiences. Brands also tend to share a lot of posts not directly promoting the brand such as information about the product domain and utility related insights to engage with its audience. This kind of online content authoring at scale introduces challenges in maintaining consistency in a brand's messaging tone which is very important from a brand's perspective to ensure a persistent impression on its customers and audiences. Monitoring and maintaining such brand consistency on a large scale is difficult, and require costly human experts.

To this end, the paper exploits several classification algorithms to check the brand persona of a content. Delin [6] describes how brand personality and brand value are built based on brand content. This research on content articles published by brands follows four linguistic frameworks: chains of reference, participant roles, presupposition and assumption, and tenor. We leverage these linguistic features in our work to build a simple supervised classification model which needs annotated data. We scrapped the official websites of the Fortune 1000 companies of 2017 and accumulated around 30 gigabytes of textual data. We randomly select 600 articles and use Amazon Mechanical Turk for crowdsourcing the text annotation, thereby forming a human-annotated data set. With this gold standard dataset, a suite of standard classifiers are tested; out of which a linear SVM turns out to be the best achieving an F1-score of 0.822.

We classify the entire dataset (298112 web pages content covering 643 companies after several rounds of cleaning of the 30 GB data collected) using the selected linear SVM. Further, we consider a subset of the data which classify with a confidence value ≥ 0.095 and obtain a total of 93321 data points which covers web postings from 536 Fortune 1000 companies. The confidence threshold is considered to ensure the corresponding automatic annotations are not flawed. With the sanitized data MT_{large}, we now check the performance of companies with respect to their ability to maintain brand personae. As per our knowledge, this is the first study which attempts to quantify and investigate brand consistency in such a large scale. We conduct both temporal and non-temporal studies, find the type of brand personae displayed by different kinds of posts and identify the set of companies who are able to maintain their brand consistency over time.

The rest of the paper is structured as follows. In Section 2, we start with the prior art. Section 3 discusses the dataset collected and the process of cleaning the dataset as well as various observations regarding the dataset. Section 4 presents the proposed classification model followed by experimental results. In Section 5 we perform the large scale characterization study of brand consistency. The paper concludes with a summary of discussions and several directions for future work.

2 PRIOR RESEARCH

While sentiment and emotion analysis is extensively studied, unavailability of well-tagged datasets for other dimensions such as brand personality introduces a challenge in developing automated methods for detection and study of these dimensions.

Aaker [1] develops a theoretical framework for brand personality dimensions and lists five dimensions of brand personality. Xu et al. [27] present an approach for predicting perceived brand personality in social media, with the underlying hypothesis that brand perception depends on user imagery, employee imagery, and official announcements. Liu et al. [13, 14] further extend it to build a novel visual analysis tool, to help explain the association between brand personality and its above–mentioned driving factors on social media. Liu et al. [12] analyze how consumers and companies portray their brand perception in visual social media (images, instead of text) and attempt to capture the intangible differences between the two competing brands over the same product.

This issue of maintaining brand consistency and the cost associated with it is a well-established problem. This was a task in CLEF called RepLab [3], in which one focuses on monitoring the reputation of companies and individuals. However, the work is only on Twitter because it states that it is the critical media for early detection of potential reputational issues. The tweets are assigned

to one of the seven standard reputation dimensions (performance, products & services, leadership, citizenship, governance, workplace, innovation) of the RepTrak Framework [1], which reflect the affective and cognitive perceptions of a company by different stakeholder groups [4]. Spina et al. [20] addresses this reputation monitoring problem faced by experts by formulating it as a topic detection task. Their work focuses only on Twitter.

Various features including LIWC [23], Mairesse [16], character-level features, and responsive patterns [22] have been found to be useful in predicting human personality from text. [27] finds that the income and needs of the consumer affect consumption behavior as well as their personality traits.

Muller and Chandon [17] studied the effect of a forced visit to a company website on brand personality. Since, companies strategically place verbal or non-verbal cues in the websites to evoke specific emotions from their users, Douglas et. al. [7] proposed the Website Emotional Features Assessment Model (WEFAM) based on website features like site activation, site affection, site confidence, site serenity, site superiority and site surgency.

Su et al. [21] train an RNN with LIWC and other grammatical features as input to predict personality trait scores. Wei et al. [25] use CNN with 1,2,3-grams kernels to capture structures in text. Yang et al. [28] build a hierarchical representation of documents, constructed from words to sentences and then to the document level. Ling et al. [10] goes deeper than word-level towards character-level, while Liu et al. [11] extends their work for short texts. However, due to the limited amount of annotated data, deep learning framework cannot be used in this context.

3 DATASET

We collected text content of the Fortune 1000 companies for the year of 2017 from their official websites. We only consider the following pages - *about the company, media releases, blogs and communication* directed towards the customers. We perform an extensive crawl using the Scrapy[2] framework and filter the pages based on keyword-based inclusion and exclusion rules over the webpage URL. We consider the web page types that aim to engage with the customer directly, first in terms of portraying their brand characteristics like about, history, vision, commitment, who-we-are and secondly, in terms of informative content like blogs, media releases, investors, newsroom. We limit our crawling task by not considering product pages like showroom, products, store, and content not targeted explicitly for consumers like legal, policy, disclaimer. The inclusion keywords are - about, about-us, news, press, introduction, strength, investors, history, vision, benefits, commitment, people, why-choose-us, who-we-are, approach, media, blog, social, while the exclusion keywords are - job, jcr_content, events, legal, help, showroom, products, store, project, career, policy, disclaimer, report. For each company, we start from their home page and limit ourselves to pages within the same domain name. We filter the websites that contain non-English text content. Given a web page, we parse only the ASCII text content with the paragraph ($< p > ...ASCII text... < /p >$) HTML tags and concatenate

---

[1] $http$: $//www.reputationinstitute.com/about - reputation - institute/the - reptrak - framework$
[2] https://scrapy.org/

them together, separated by a paragraph separator marker. We are able to collect data from 299481 corporate web pages, covering 643 companies. We name this large dataset as MT_{large}.

3.1 Static and dynamic pages

Each of the company webpages consists of static and dynamic contents. Static pages are one which explicitly defines the brand which a company stands for like its mission, vision and core values. Generally, the frequency of such posts is quite less and mostly posted during the launch of the website. Dynamic web pages usually comprise of the content used for continually engaging with the audience. They are blogs, news, media or press releases, notes to investors posted at regular intervals. MT_{large} thus contains static pages and dynamic pages for 338 and 643 companies respectively. Static page content creates the brand impression while it is imperative that the dynamic content maintains that to ensure brand consistency. However, in this section, we perform some elementary data study to understand the nature of post of dynamic content.

Static keywords	introduction (34), about (573), commitment (45), people (252), vision (48), strength (429), history (1116), approach (571), benefits (930)
Dynamic keywords	media(19203), blog(36844), news(92448), press(52544), investors(5837)

Table 2: Keywords used to divide static and dynamic web content

3.2 Extracting temporal information from web content

We, therefore, need the timestamp information as to when a dynamic web page was posted by the company to understand the temporal behavior of the content. MT_{large} contain 298112 such dynamic posts covering 643 companies, from which we are able to timestamp information from only around 49.18%, accounting to 140,337 number of posts. We manually observe that the time-stamps usually have granularity in terms of days and weeks. 75.01% of these posts contain day-level information, while the remaining have a year as granularity. Here, we only consider company postings done between the period of January 2000 and September 2017.

3.3 Basic Observations

3.3.1 Volume of dynamic posts . We observe among the Fortune 1000 companies, the number of posts are roughly similar (Figure 1), although we find that there are occasional spikes representing companies who post way more than the average. These spikes are more prevalent among higher ranked companies.

3.3.2 Inter-arrival time between two postings. We analyze the inter-arrival time between two company postings and study the patterns that are prominent across different companies. By postings, we refer to only dynamic web content, and we consider the content where the date is present in the granularity of a day (52432 posts). We perform both sector-wise and industry-wide study. We

observe in Figure 1 that the inter-arrival time posting patterns is heavy-tailed and the pattern is similar across sectors. We select the top 5 sectors with the most number of posts– technology (48219), financials (11739), energy (4915), healthcare (4685) and business services (3747), for depicting their heavy-tailed behavior. Here, we consider the dynamic posts whose granularity is in days and whose inter−arrival time is non-zero, In Figure 1, we observe peaks appearing consistently after an interval of 30 to 33 days and further investigate this issue, by studying what type of dynamic posts are more prevalent during these peaks. We observe that a significant value of 77.96% of them are posted at the end of the month. We consider day 1, 2, 30, 31 of a month as month-end. We observe the following proportion of post types - media (9.63%), blog (13.98%), news (66.95%), press (25.67%) and investor (24.0%) and the highest being the dynamic post type 'news' .

4 CLASSIFICATION

In order to check the brand persona of a content, we build up a classifier. To have a supervised model, we require annotated data as well as feature extraction from the dataset. These steps are discussed next followed by the classification models and experimental results.

4.1 Annotation

Each article is annotated in two different ways (a). annotators follow a 5 point Likert scale to annotate the articles on each of the five dimensions of brand personality (similar to the one used by [9] and [18] for annotating formality), (b). they rank the five dimensions in the order in which they are evoked from a given article. Each article is annotated 3 times by different annotators. Consistency between the two methods of annotation is considered to judge the fidelity of the annotation.

Companies names are anonymized to reduce bias. Industry/domain information about the content is marked to provide context to the annotator. For example, Merrill Lynch is marked as a banking company. We randomly select 600 articles and use Amazon Mechanical Turk for crowdsourcing the text annotation. After filtering using consistency check mentioned above, we obtain articles that have scores from at least two annotators. We further shortlist the articles only if at least two annotators have agreed whereby we obtain 500 annotated articles. Two annotators are said to have agreed on a given article for a particular dimension if the absolute difference between their scores is less than or equal to 1. For example, resolving mismatch such as high sincerity may mean a score of 4 to one annotator and 5 to another annotator. This normalizes the biases between annotators. We provide the inter-annotator agreement for each dimension in Table 3, which averages to 67.25%. We take the average of the score given by the annotators at this stage and use a static threshold of 3.0 to convert the score to a binary label, indicating whether a particular brand persona is evoked from the text or not.

4.2 Linguistic Features

We extract the following set of linguistic features from each article. We use the concepts proposed by Delin [6] to formulate a number of linguistic features, which aim to capture the trait of the underlying article in a more compact form.

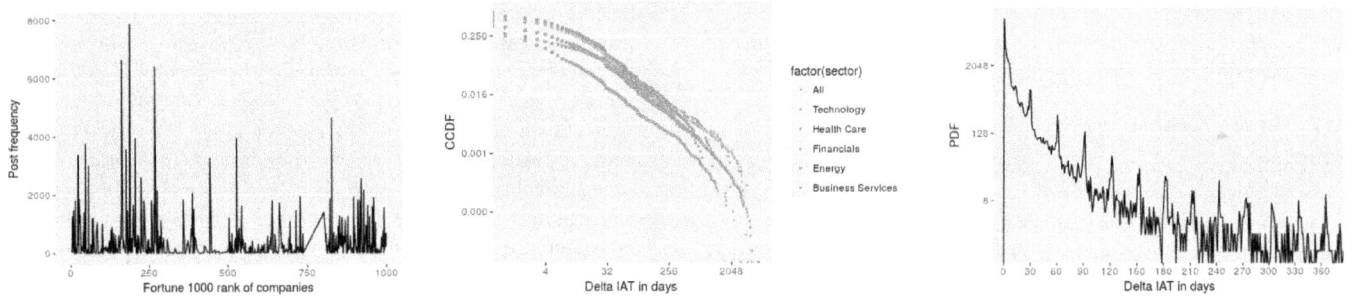

Figure 1: (left) Line plot of total posting volume per company. **(middle)** Heavy-tailed distribution of postings IAT over all companies and also a sector-wise trend. **(right)** Periodic peak pattern: the log-scale histogram of posting's IAT has peaks at 30-33 days interval

Trait	Positive	Negative	Agreement(in %)
sinc	433	67	71.41
exc	339	161	65.02
com	470	30	75.62
rug	190	310	63.50
soph	276	224	60.70

Table 3: Class distribution and inter–annotator agreement per dimension for HT

LIWC: Linguistic Inquiry and Word Count [23] is a dictionary of psycho-linguistics traits. This has been frequently used in social data analysis [26] and psychological trait extraction. We use the values returned by the commercial API version [3] of LIWC for a particular piece of text.

Term Frequency-Inverse Document Frequency (TF-IDF): A TF-IDF vector per document consisting of unigrams, bigrams, and trigrams after removing stop words is considered.

Contractions: These are shortened versions of phrases. Some examples are we are being replaced by we're, is it not being substituted by isn't. Contractions add a degree of informality and a conversational tone to the text.

Collocations: Collocations are word combinations that are known to occur frequently together. Examples include heavy rain, high temperature, etc. We use the Pearson Academic Collocations cite list which consists of 2,469 most frequent lexical collocations in written academic English, to form our dictionary of collocations.

Chains of reference: Chains of reference denote the brand's use of references to itself and closely associated elements. The key elements in this process are the noun phrases in the text, whose content and form can serve either to strongly evoke a brand, reinforce it, or not evoke it at all. Different kinds of relations that can hold between noun phrases and brand concepts as categorized by [6] have been summarized in Table 4. For our model, we use repetition, partial repetition, co-reference, and possessive inferrable as four different features.

Readability: This feature intuitively captures the ease of reading a given piece of text. The feature is based on the Flesch–Kincaid Readability Score [8]. The score considers the word length, sentence

---

[3] www.receptiviti.ai

Link	Definition	Example
Repetition	Repeating the full reference to the brand	Orange...Orange , Target...Target
Partial Repetition	A phrase contains a reference to the brand, but refers to something other than the brand concept	Orange...the Orange Service Promise , Target...Target Stores
Co-reference	Where a concept is reinforced by referring to it again, but not using a full descriptive noun phrase	Orange...We, Target... With us
Possessive inferrables	Where a link is created by referring to something that the brand has, does, or has given to the customer, using a possessive noun phrase	Orange...our network your phone, Target... our stores your cart

Table 4: Categorization of Chains of reference

length, and the number of syllables per word. The higher the value of this score, the easier the content is for reading. It is calculated as follows:

$$Score = 206.835 - 1.015 \frac{TotalWords}{TotalSentences} - 84.6 \frac{TotalSyllables}{TotalWords}$$

4.3 Classification Model

We train separate classifiers for the five traits independently. The classification models, identical for each dimension. The classifier uses only human annotated data. The annotated data act as ground truth while the features discussed in the previous section are fed into a classifier. We consider several classification models which include Naive Bayes, Logistic Regression and Decision Tree, linear support vector machines classification models as well as ensemble algorithms like Random Forest and AdaBoost. During classification, we observe a large class imbalance in the human–annotated data, as summarized in Table 3. We use a data-level approach called SMOTE [5] to address the class-imbalance problem, which works by modifying the training set [24].

Trait	sincerity			excitement			competence			ruggedness			sophistication		
	Prec.	Rec.	F1	Prec.	Rec.	F1	Prec.	Rec.	F1	Prec.	Rec.	F1	Prec.	Rec.	F1
Naive Bayes	0.238	0.851	0.371	0.162	0.791	0.268	0.319	0.941	0.721	0.268	0.622	0.319	0.141	0.854	0.239
Logistic Regres-sion	0.538	0.856	0.659	0.796	0.801	0.798	0.774	0.953	0.853	0.789	0.561	0.654	0.733	0.727	0.725
DecisionTree	0.774	0.871	0.819	0.661	0.742	0.698	0.921	0.954	0.937	0.568	0.536	0.549	0.652	0.671	0.66
RandomForest	0.838	0.865	0.85	0.72	0.795	0.754	0.953	0.939	**0.946**	0.532	0.641	0.575	0.623	0.737	0.673
AdaBoost	0.85	0.868	0.859	0.746	0.761	0.753	0.923	0.95	0.936	0.606	0.585	0.589	0.66	0.69	0.672
SVM (Linear)	0.912	0.861	**0.885**	0.832	0.801	**0.815**	0.919	0.943	0.931	0.773	0.57	**0.655**	0.751	0.707	**0.725**

Table 5: Performance comparison of the different binary classification algorithms for optimal classifer selection

Trait	sincerity			excitement			competence			ruggedness			sophistication			PMax	SpMax
	Prec.	Rec.	F1	Prec.	Rec.	F1	Prec.	Rec.	F1	Prec.	Rec.	F1	Prec.	Rec.	F1		
liwc (base-line)	0.912	0.861	0.885	0.832	0.801	0.815	0.919	0.943	0.931	0.773	0.57	**0.655**	0.751	0.707	**0.725**	0.409	0.372
liwc+ tfidf	0.988	0.867	0.923	0.9	0.787	**0.839**	0.998	0.94	**0.968**	0.527	0.573	0.545	0.726	0.704	0.707	0.407	0.429
tfidf*+ contractions	0.989	0.867	0.923	0.894	0.784	0.834	0.998	0.94	0.968	0.527	0.578	0.548	0.725	0.7	0.708	0.406	0.424
cont*+ collo-cations	0.989	0.867	0.923	0.897	0.787	0.837	0.998	0.94	0.968	0.522	0.579	0.545	0.722	0.708	0.709	0.405	0.428
coll*+ chain-ref	0.991	0.867	**0.925**	0.894	0.787	0.836	0.998	0.94	0.968	0.559	0.587	0.569	0.729	0.693	0.706	0.404	0.407
chainref*+ readability	0.989	0.868	0.924	0.862	0.805	0.837	0.998	0.94	0.968	0.59	0.6	0.592	0.722	0.718	0.72	0.406	0.419
Best features (FLCS)	0.991	0.867	0.925	0.9	0.787	0.839	0.998	0.94	0.968	0.773	0.57	0.655	0.751	0.707	0.725	**0.426**	**0.431**

Table 6: Comparing performance across different feature sets and forming the Final Linear Classifier Set (FLCS)

4.4 Metrics to test the classifier

We observe an uneven ratio of the number of positive and negative class data points across all the traits as evident in Table 3 and thus solely maximizing accuracy will tend to favor the class with more number of data points. We compare the performance of the different classification models by reporting the precision, recall and F1 score. As previously observed, there is a significant class imbalance. Therefore we use F1 score as a single metric for both selecting the optimal classification model and also for choosing the optimal feature set. We thus perform a 7-fold cross-validation strategy and compute our final score as the average of the obtained scores.

4.5 Results

We first perform experiments to select the best classification model. We then identify the set of feature sets which produce the best result, We further validate our methodology by correlating the trait-wise scores, and the ranks provided the annotators (explained in Section 4.1) over the metrics of Pearson coefficient and Spearman's rank correlation coefficient.

4.6 Best classification model

To determine which classifier among the alternatives performs best, we first need to choose a feature set that is already established in terms of the brand personality detection task. Xu et al. [27] use LIWC to characterize the factors contributing to shaping brand personality on social media. We, therefore, decide to use LIWC comprising of 64 categories as our feature set for determining FLC. We, therefore, train all the candidate supervised classification models. We observe that linear SVM reports the highest F1-score for all the brand personality traits except competence as shown in Table 5. We, therefore, choose linear SVM as our final classifier since it has the **highest average F1-score of 0.802**, combining all traits.

4.7 Feature addition

After the selection of linear SVM, we add different linguistic features as described in Section 4.2, on top of the established feature set of LIWC. We incrementally expand the feature sets and choose the optimal set of features which give the highest accuracy. We are able to achieve a very high F1-score for our brand personality consistency task for sincerity, excitement, and competence. For the remaining two traits, ruggedness and sophistication, we observe a good precision score of 0.773 and 0.751 respectively. If we consider the best set of features for each class, we are able to achieve an **a F1-score of 0.822**, which is an improvement over the (limited-feature-set) linear SVM by 2.49%.

We further validate our model by utilizing the ground-truth in which the annotators have provide the ranks of the five brand personality traits in order of their presence in the provided text as well as individual trait-wise score. For each text, we obtain individual trait-wise confidence score from their respective classifiers and create a ranking among the five traits. We then compute the Pearson correlation coefficient between the individual trait-wise scores provided by the annotators with the confidence score provided by the classifiers. We also compute the Spearman rank correlation coefficient between the ranks provided by the annotators and the rank that we obtain based on the confidence scores. We observe from Table 6 that the improvement (deterioration) due to feature addition highly correlate with both the Pearson and Spearman score. More importantly, we observe that the classifier set formed using the best feature set (which is different for different traits), also performs the best in both these two metrics (Pearson - 0.426, Spearman - 0.431). This provides an extra validation to our proposed methodology.

We call the set of five classifiers with the best performing features (different for each trait) model as FLCS (Final Linear Classifier Set), and we use it for annotating MT_{large} required for the brand consistency study, covered in the next section.

4.8 High Fidelity Points

We now use FLCS to classify the MT_{large} data and only select those data points which are classified with high confidence (≥ 0.095), to carry out our brand consistency study. We manually cross-check whether the selected dataset indeed confirms to the class to which it is annotated. A random checking of 50 data points yields just two errors. We name this dataset as MT_{high} which comprises of 93321 data points covering 536 companies. Here, we determine the points have high confidence based on the distance value from the decision boundary, which we obtain for each of the five traits for each text article. We now empirically determine a threshold value for each trait, above which we will tag the text with that particular trait to be present, else tag it to be absent. This acts as a sanity check for our high fidelity dataset. We finally construct the MT_{high} dataset, as having points which have at least one trait present. We now describe the different data collection steps that we perform until now in Table 7.

Dataset name	Number of posts	Number of companies	Collection strategy
MT_{large}	298112	643	Web scraping from official websites based on accept and deny keywords
HT	500	-	Randomly selected 600 points from MT_{large}, which satisfy strict annotation criteria
MT_{high}	93321	536	Subset of MT_{large}, which is annotated with high confidence by FLCS
MT_{time}	49833	242	Subset of MT_{high} having timestamp data
MT_{noTime}	43488	512	Subset of MT_{high} without having timestamp data

Table 7: Summary of the different data collection steps

5 BRAND CONSISTENCY ANALYSIS

We now perform a characterization study where we investigate how well a company exhibits and maintains its brand personality across the web content both across time and also over different content categories. As per our knowledge, this is the first study which investigates the notion of brand consistency computationally. To conduct the study, we first define the consistency between the two texts.

5.1 Brand Consistency - Definition

Consumers tend to interact with companies in a manner similar to humans, where they closely try to follow their inter-personal and social relationships. Therefore, when a company's action violates the relationship norms, consumers develop a more negative perception of the brand as compared to when the brand actions are consistent with those relationship norms [2]. InterBrand [4] - a global brand agency, considered consistency to be among the ten strengths of companies, responsible for sustainable growth of brands among other properties like clarity, commitment, governance, responsiveness, authenticity, relevance, differentiation, presence and engagement.

Formulation: As discussed each post can be represented by two 5-dimensional vectors - *label vector* and *rank vector*. Label vector stores the binary label of whether a trait is present or absent in the text article. Rank vector stores an order of precedence of the brand personality traits from the textual content computed based on its confidence score (higher is the distance from the decision boundary, higher is its confidence score). We first scale this distance value by subtracting the trait-specific threshold value (as mentioned in Section 4.8, before computing the order. We calculate the similarity between a post and the representative vectors (static post) of the respective company using two measures - *binLabelSim* and *rankLabelSim*. Based on their values, we categorize the consistency level into four categories as shown in Table 8. We only choose the most frequently occurring label and rank vector among all the static posts as the respective representative vectors (stands for the company's brand personality). Here, we observe that the static posts are highly consistent among themselves with the average pair-wise binLabelSim being 0.935 (std. deviation of 0.129) and rankVectorSim being 0.861 (std. deviation of 0.285). On the other hand, dynamic posts show an overall average value of binLabelSim as 0.65 and rankVectorSim as -0.03.

Similarity Measure: We now explain how we compute the similarity distance value between two texts, each of which is represented by the above-mentioned label vector and a rank vector.

binLabelSim: To compute the distance between two posts (static and dynamic), we consider their label vectors and use standard distance measures of hamming and Levenshtein distance and compute a composite score termed as *binLabelDist*, which is the simple average of their hamming and Levenshtein distance measures. *binLabelSim* is 1 - *binLabelDist*.

rankVectorSim: We use Pearson, Kendall tau and Spearman's rank correlation coefficient to compute the similarity between two such rank vectors. We calculate a composite score (*rankVectorSim*) which is simply the average of Pearson, Spearman and Kendall

---

[4]https://www.interbrand.com/best-brands/

tauś rank correlation scores. An important point to mention here is that Spearman and Kendall's tau compute correlation using the respective rank vectors, whereas, for computing Pearson correlation, we directly use the scaled confidence score from each of the trait-specific classifiers.

Consistency Levels: We empirically determine the conditions for the different brand consistency levels (see Table 8). The conditions are somewhat arbitrarily determined. From manual inspection, we have noticed that binLabelSim has a higher importance in reflecting the level of brand consistency. Accordingly, a strict ordering of bin-LabelSim is maintained while rankVectorSim is used as a secondary measure to ensure consistency.

Consistency Score: Given a set of posts whose *binLabelSim* and *rankVectorSim* is calculated, consistency score (ConsScr) is defined as the ratio of the number of consistent post(label 1-3) and the total number of posts within that time-frame. For example, say for Microsoft Corporation in temporal bin index 1, which is for first 3 months, we have 10 such dynamic web posts, with the following brand consistency level breakup - strongly consistent (0 out of 10), partially consistent (1), somewhat consistent (3) and not consistent (6 out of 10). We will then say that ConsScr is equal to 0.4 in this case. A ConsScr closer to 1.0 indicates a higher degree of consistency. We consider a given temporal bin for a company to be consistent if $ConsScr \geq 0.5$.

Brand consistency level	binLabelSim	rankVectorSim
Strongly consistent	≥ 0.8	≥ 0.6
Partially consistent	≥ 0.8	≥ 0.2
Somewhat consistent	≥ 0.5	≥ 0.6
Not consistent	Otherwise	Otherwise

Table 8: Conditions associated with different degrees of brand consistency

5.2 Experimental Setup

Since brand consistency is an attribute of the company, we only consider the companies which satisfy a strict data requirement criteria. We only consider companies which have at least one static post with at least one trait present in it. This reduces the number of companies covered to 204. We also mention here that we have times-tamp information for only 49833 points of MT_{high} (53.4%), which we call as MT_{time} and those not having time-stamp information as MT_{noTime}. We use both MT_{time} and MT_{noTime} for the studies. Figure. 2 shows consistency score vis-a-vis fraction of companies maintaining that consistency. As can be seen, only a very few companies can maintain high consistency highlighting the extent of the problem which we have already mentioned. Table 9 shows the top five companies displaying the maximum number of posts in each of the five categories.

5.3 Product promotion posts

The posts related to event or product promotions formed a significant portion of all posts. This corresponds to the description of *products & services* category, which is one of the seven reputation dimensions of the RepTrak Framework as described in the related

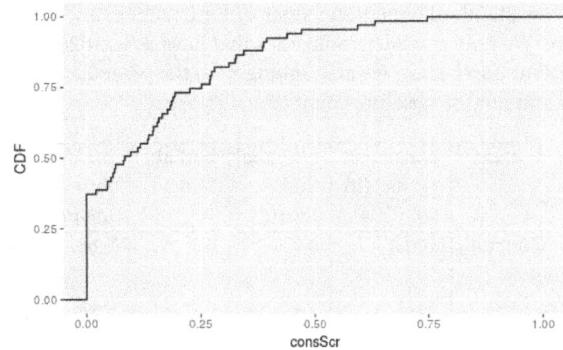

Figure 2: CDF showing consistency score across the companies.

Trait	Top 5 most prominent companies(number of posts)
sinc	Hospitality Properties Trust (159), Discover Financial Services (53), DaVita Inc. (41), Calpine Corporation (29), Darden Restaurants, Inc. (26)
exc	Microsoft Corporation (164), Tribune Media Company (42), Tutor Perini Corporation (29)
com	The Carlyle Group L.P. (67), CSX Corporation (51), Ally Financial Inc. (46), F5 Networks, Inc. (42), Vornado Realty Trust (37)
sop	Oceaneering International, Inc. (69), Tailored Brands, Inc. (62), Hawaiian Holdings, Inc. (45)

Table 9: Top 5 companies in terms of dominant trait in overall event promotions

work (Section 2). This category primarily contains information about the company's products and services, as well as about consumer satisfaction. We first construct a data subset by performing a lexicon based search to automate the identification of such posts. We check whether the following keywords - *event, promotions, promot, products, product-launch, announce, launch*, are present in web page URL. We thus obtain 3255 such data points which satisfy all the above criteria. We observe competence is the primary trait with product promotion followed by sincerity. Individual count where a trait major : sincerity - 839 (out of 3255), excitement - 462, competence - 1334, ruggedness - 0, sophistication - 620.

5.4 Top companies maintaining brand consistency

Here, we identify the Fortune 1000 companies that are best able to maintain brand consistency across their company postings. We measure this property in terms of the percentage of its company postings being strongly consistent and is outlined in Table 10. We also observe that all of these companies have a very high mean and very low standard deviation values of binLabelSim and rankVectorSim. We only consider companies that have at least 20 strongly consistent posts, since we are ranking with the percentage of such posts and not the absolute count of such posts.

spec domain	consistent posts (in %)	binLabelSim mean	binLabelSim sd	rankVectorSim mean	rankVectorSim sd
FTI Consulting, Inc.	100.0	0.9	0.1	0.68	0.08
Regis Corporation	54.0	0.88	0.1	0.67	0.06
Engility Holdings, Inc.	84.0	0.08	0.42	0.66	0.05
Caesars Entertainment Corporation	41.0	0.8	0.0	0.81	0.1
Prudential Financial, Inc.	23.0	0.91	0.1	0.68	0.08

Table 10: Top 5 companies with highest percentage of consistent dynamic posts

5.5 Top Companies maintaining temporal brand consistency

We now study the notion of brand consistency as a company attribute, rather than as a post attribute. Here, we quantify brand consistency score for a company in terms of the different brand consistency categories as mentioned in Table 8. Here we follow a temporal binning strategy where posts of 12 weeks are binned together. We mention the top 5 companies ranked in terms of the total number of such consistent temporal bins in Table 11. We see that only two of the top five companies overlap in the two sets shown by Tables 10 and 11.

spec domain	ConsScr mean	ConsScr sd	Total number of bins
Engility Holdings, Inc.	0.747	0.154	11
Regis Corporation	0.633	0.174	4
Principal Financial Group, Inc.	0.595	0.152	4
Westlake Chemical Corporation	0.47	0.316	11
Capital One Financial Corporation	0.438	0.241	45

Table 11: Top 5 companies with with temporal consistency score across bins

5.6 Top-ranked company vis-a-vis brand consistency

We consider the companies ranked within 150 among the Fortune 1000 companies as the top-ranked companies and those companies

between the rank of 850 and 1000 as our lower ranked companies. We only consider companies that have at least 25 dynamic web pages, thus having a strict minimum data requirement. We are thus left with 18 top-ranked companies and 20 bottom-ranked companies for studying this research question. Here, we consider temporal bins of a duration of 6 months instead of the previous 12 weeks, since the number of data points per bin was observed to be very sparse. The first 5 top companies in terms of dynamic posts count - Microsoft Corporation (5365), Bank of America Corporation (467), Intel Corporation (294), Capital One Financial Corporation (282), Starbucks Corporation (143); similarly the first 5 bottom-ranked companies are - Red Hat, Inc. (732), Autodesk, Inc. (270), Engility Holdings, Inc. (225), Akamai Technologies, Inc. (180), Overstock.com, Inc. (128).

We observe that the top-ranked Fortune 1000 companies can maintain a higher average consistency score as compared to the bottom-ranked companies for the first 12 months, after which its consistency score drops to a score which is equal to the bottom-ranked companies (see Figure 3). On the other hand, bottom-ranked companies maintain a low, consistent score throughout the observed period of 2 years.

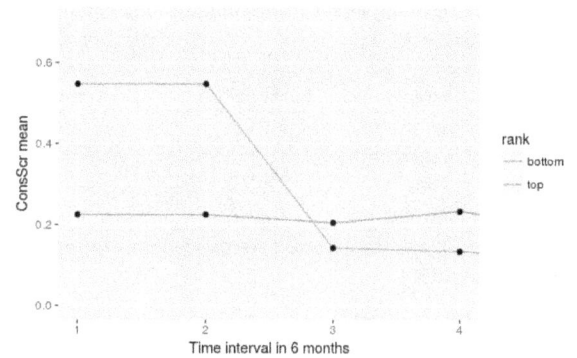

Figure 3: Consistency mean over temporal bins of duration 6 months comparing top and bottom ranked companies

6 CONCLUSION

To the best of our knowledge, this is one of the first attempts towards quantifying brand personality from the text content of an organization's official website. We launch a major crawling activity and are able to collect 298112 web page content covering 643 Fortune 1000 companies. We classify the dataset of each company into static content and dynamic posts and undertake a rigorous approach to find the timestamp of the dynamic posts. Further to it, we annotate a random sample of the data (around 600 data points); we undertake double checking measure whereby the same data points are annotated through labeling as well as ranking. We build five independent classifiers (linear SVM) one for each trait and finally optimize the feature set for each of them; the final classifier set is called FLCS. FLCS provides branding information to each of the text - the classification of the high confidence points is almost 100% correct. With the dataset thus annotated, we study the brand characteristics of companies. For that, we define several metrics and determine four levels of consistency. We discover companies which post consistently and find that more wealthy companies are better at maintaining consistency.

Limitations: We only consider textual content of web articles posted by the companies themselves and do not cover any form of user-generated content regarding the companies. Another important limitation is that we do not cover the visual or content-independent aspects of a brand style guide like color, typography and positioning of different sections and headers of a brand website.

Future Work: In the current work, we develop independent classifiers for each trait. However, it might be possible that one trait (weakly) implies one or more of the others; thus jointly learning all the traits together would be an important future work. We will use the insights derived from this work dealing with document-level text classification and move onto finer granularity like sentence level and identify the most contributing sentences towards the expression of a brand. We will further extend our work to develop a helper tool for the content writers and brand managers, which sentences should be modified for making the text articles more consistent with the targeted brand personality. These would be our next future endeavors.

ACKNOWLEDGMENTS

The first author is currently supported by the Junior Research fellowship from the project titled "IoTDiff: Service Differentiation for Personal Hubs", which is sponsored by Science & Engineering Research Board, New Delhi. A part of the work was carried out during the summer internship at Big Data Experience Lab, Adobe Research, Bangalore, India.

REFERENCES

[1] Jennifer L Aaker. 1997. Dimensions of brand personality. *Journal of marketing research* (1997), 347–356.
[2] Pankaj Aggarwal. 2004. The effects of brand relationship norms on consumer attitudes and behavior. *Journal of consumer research* 31, 1 (2004), 87–101.
[3] Enrique Amigó, Jorge Carrillo-de Albornoz, Irina Chugur, Adolfo Corujo, Julio Gonzalo, Edgar Meij, Maarten de Rijke, and Damiano Spina. 2014. Overview of RepLab 2014: Author Profiling and Reputation Dimensions for Online Reputation Management. In *Information Access Evaluation. Multilinguality, Multimodality, and Interaction*, Evangelos Kanoulas, Mihai Lupu, Paul Clough, Mark Sanderson, Mark Hall, Allan Hanbury, and Elaine Toms (Eds.). Springer International Publishing, Cham, 307–322.
[4] Enrique Amigó, Jorge Carrillo-de Albornoz, Irina Chugur, Adolfo Corujo, Julio Gonzalo, Edgar Meij, Maarten de Rijke, and Damiano Spina. 2014. Overview of RepLab 2014: Author Profiling and Reputation Dimensions for Online Reputation Management. In *Information Access Evaluation. Multilinguality, Multimodality, and Interaction*, Evangelos Kanoulas, Mihai Lupu, Paul Clough, Mark Sanderson, Mark Hall, Allan Hanbury, and Elaine Toms (Eds.). Springer International Publishing, Cham, 307–322.
[5] Nitesh V. Chawla, Kevin W. Bowyer, Lawrence O. Hall, and W. Philip Kegelmeyer. 2002. SMOTE: Synthetic Minority Over-sampling Technique. *J. Artif. Int. Res.* 16, 1 (June 2002), 321–357. http://dl.acm.org/citation.cfm?id=1622407.1622416
[6] Judy Delin. 2007. Brand Tone of Voice. *Journal of Applied Linguistics* 2, 1 (2007). https://journals.equinoxpub.com/index.php/JAL/article/view/1471
[7] Alecia Douglas, Juline Mills, and Raphael Kavanaugh. 2007. Exploring the use of emotional features at romantic destination websites. *Information and Communication Technologies in Tourism 2007* (2007), 331–340.
[8] J Peter Kincaid, Robert P Fishburne Jr, Richard L Rogers, and Brad S Chissom. 1975. *Derivation of new readability formulas (automated readability index, fog count and flesch reading ease formula) for navy enlisted personnel.* Technical Report. DTIC Document.
[9] Shibamouli Lahiri. 2015. SQUINKY! A Corpus of Sentence-level Formality, Informativeness, and Implicature. *arXiv preprint arXiv:1506.02306* (2015).
[10] Wang Ling, Tiago Luís, Luís Marujo, Ramón Fernandez Astudillo, Silvio Amir, Chris Dyer, Alan W Black, and Isabel Trancoso. 2015. Finding function in form: Compositional character models for open vocabulary word representation. *arXiv preprint arXiv:1508.02096* (2015).
[11] Fei Liu, Julien Perez, and Scott Nowson. 2017. A Language-independent and Compositional Model for Personality Trait Recognition from Short Texts. In *Proceedings of the 15th Conference of the European Chapter of the Association for Computational Linguistics: Volume 1, Long Papers*, Vol. 1. 754–764.
[12] Liu Liu, Daria Dzyabura, and Natalie Mizik. 2018. Visual listening in: Extracting brand image portrayed on social media. In *Workshops at the Thirty-Second AAAI Conference on Artificial Intelligence*.
[13] X. Liu, A. Xu, L. Gou, H. Liu, R. Akkiraju, and H. Shen. 2016. SocialBrands: Visual analysis of public perceptions of brands on social media. In *2016 IEEE Conference on Visual Analytics Science and Technology (VAST)*. 71–80. https://doi.org/10.1109/VAST.2016.7883513
[14] Zhe Liu, Anbang Xu, Yi Wang, Jerald Schoudt, Jalal Mahmud, and Rama Akkiraju. 2017. Does Personality Matter?: A Study of Personality and Situational Effects on Consumer Behavior. In *Proceedings of the 28th ACM Conference on Hypertext and Social Media (HT '17)*. ACM, New York, NY, USA, 185–193. https://doi.org/10.1145/3078714.3078733
[15] Natalia Maehle, Cele Otnes, and Magne Supphellen. 2011. Consumers' perceptions of the dimensions of brand personality. *Journal of Consumer Behaviour* 10, 5 (2011), 290–303.
[16] François Mairesse, Marilyn A Walker, Matthias R Mehl, and Roger K Moore. 2007. Using linguistic cues for the automatic recognition of personality in conversation and text. *Journal of artificial intelligence research* 30 (2007), 457–500.
[17] Brigitte Müller and Jean-Louis Chandon. 2003. The impact of visiting a brand website on brand personality. *Electronic Markets* 13, 3 (2003), 210–221.
[18] Ellie Pavlick and Joel Tetreault. 2016. An empirical analysis of formality in online communication. *Transactions of the Association of Computational Linguistics* 4, 1 (2016), 61–74.
[19] Joseph T. Plummer. 2000. How Personality Makes a Difference. *Journal of Advertising Research* 40, 6 (2000), 79–83. https://doi.org/10.2501/JAR-40-6-79-83 arXiv:http://www.journalofadvertisingresearch.com/content/40/6/79.full.pdf
[20] Damiano Spina, Julio Gonzalo, and Enrique Amigó. 2014. Learning Similarity Functions for Topic Detection in Online Reputation Monitoring. In *Proceedings of the 37th International ACM SIGIR Conference on Research & Development in Information Retrieval (SIGIR '14)*. ACM, New York, NY, USA, 527–536. https://doi.org/10.1145/2600428.2609621
[21] Ming-Hsiang Su, Chung-Hsien Wu, and Yu-Ting Zheng. 2016. Exploiting turn-taking temporal evolution for personality trait perception in dyadic conversations. *IEEE/ACM Transactions on Audio, Speech, and Language Processing* 24, 4 (2016), 733–744.
[22] X. Sun, B. Liu, J. Cao, J. Luo, and X. Shen. 2018. Who Am I? Personality Detection Based on Deep Learning for Texts. In *2018 IEEE International Conference on Communications (ICC)*. 1–6. https://doi.org/10.1109/ICC.2018.8422105
[23] Yla R. Tausczik and James W. Pennebaker. 2010. The Psychological Meaning of Words: LIWC and Computerized Text Analysis Methods. (2010). http://homepage.psy.utexas.edu/homepage/students/Tausczik/Yla/index.html
[24] Jing Wang and Min-Ling Zhang. 2018. Towards Mitigating the Class-Imbalance Problem for Partial Label Learning. In *Proceedings of the 24th ACM SIGKDD International Conference on Knowledge Discovery & Data Mining, KDD 2018, London, UK, August 19-23, 2018.* 2427–2436. https://doi.org/10.1145/3219819.3220008
[25] Honghao Wei, Fuzheng Zhang, Nicholas Jing Yuan, Chuan Cao, Hao Fu, Xing Xie, Yong Rui, and Wei-Ying Ma. 2017. Beyond the Words: Predicting User Personality from Heterogeneous Information. In *Proceedings of the Tenth ACM International Conference on Web Search and Data Mining (WSDM '17)*. ACM, New York, NY, USA, 305–314. https://doi.org/10.1145/3018661.3018717
[26] Anbang Xu and Brian Bailey. 2012. What do you think?: a case study of benefit, expectation, and interaction in a large online critique community. In *Proceedings of the ACM 2012 conference on Computer Supported Cooperative Work*. ACM, 295–304.
[27] Anbang Xu, Haibin Liu, Liang Gou, Rama Akkiraju, Jalal Mahmud, Vibha Sinha, Yuheng Hu, and Mu Qiao. 2016. Predicting Perceived Brand Personality with Social Media. In *Proceedings of the Tenth International Conference on Web and Social Media, Cologne, Germany, May 17-20, 2016.* 436–445. http://www.aaai.org/ocs/index.php/ICWSM/ICWSM16/paper/view/13078
[28] Zichao Yang, Diyi Yang, Chris Dyer, Xiaodong He, Alex Smola, and Eduard Hovy. 2016. Hierarchical attention networks for document classification. In *Proceedings of the 2016 Conference of the North American Chapter of the Association for Computational Linguistics: Human Language Technologies*. 1480–1489.

Prevalence and Psychological Effects of Hateful Speech in Online College Communities

Koustuv Saha
Georgia Tech
koustuv.saha@gatech.edu

Eshwar Chandrasekharan
Georgia Tech
eshwar3@gatech.edu

Munmun De Choudhury
Georgia Tech
munmund@gatech.edu

ABSTRACT

Background. Hateful speech bears negative repercussions and is particularly damaging in college communities. The efforts to regulate hateful speech on college campuses pose vexing socio-political problems, and the interventions to mitigate the effects require evaluating the pervasiveness of the phenomenon on campuses as well the impacts on students' psychological state.

Data and Methods. Given the growing use of social media among college students, we target the above issues by studying the online aspect of hateful speech in a dataset of 6 million Reddit comments shared in 174 college communities. To quantify the prevelence of hateful speech in an online college community, we devise College Hate Index (CHX). Next, we examine its distribution across the categories of hateful speech, *behavior, class, disability, ethnicity, gender, physical appearance, race, religion,* and *sexual orientation*. We then employ a causal-inference framework to study the psychological effects of hateful speech, particularly in the form of individuals' online stress expression. Finally, we characterize their psychological endurance to hateful speech by analyzing their language– their discriminatory keyword use, and their personality traits.

Results. We find that hateful speech is prevalent in college subreddits, and 25% of them show greater hateful speech than non-college subreddits. We also find that the exposure to hate leads to greater stress expression. However, everybody exposed is not equally affected; some show lower psychological endurance than others. Low endurance individuals are more vulnerable to emotional outbursts, and are more neurotic than those with higher endurance.

Discussion. Our work bears implications for policy-making and intervention efforts to tackle the damaging effects of online hateful speech in colleges. From technological perspective, our work caters to mental health support provisions on college campuses, and to moderation efforts in online college communities. In addition, given the charged aspect of speech dilemma, we highlight the ethical implications of our work. Our work lays the foundation for studying the psychological impacts of hateful speech in online communities in general, and situated communities in particular (the ones that have both an offline and an online analog).

CCS CONCEPTS

• **Human-centered computing** → *Empirical studies in collaborative and social computing*; *Social media*.

KEYWORDS

social media; Reddit; hateful speech; mental health; stress; natural language analysis; college subreddits; psychological endurance

ACM Reference Format:
Koustuv Saha, Eshwar Chandrasekharan, and Munmun De Choudhury. 2019. Prevalence and Psychological Effects of Hateful Speech in Online College Communities. In *11th ACM Conference on Web Science (WebSci '19), June 30-July 3, 2019, Boston, MA, USA*. ACM, New York, NY, USA, 10 pages. https://doi.org/10.1145/3292522.3326032

1 INTRODUCTION

Colleges are places where intellectual debate is considered as a key aspect of the educational pursuit, and where viewpoint diversity is venerated. Many colleges in the U.S. have been homes of the free speech movement of the 1960s, that catalyzed positive outcomes, ranging from women's suffrage movement to civil rights protests [64]. However, the last few decades has also witnessed several instances where minority groups in colleges have been targeted with verbal altercations, slander, defamation, and hateful speech [37]. In fact, between 2015 and 2016, there has been a 25% rise in the number of reported hate crimes on college campuses [9].

Because colleges are close-knit, diverse, and geographically situated communities of students, the harmful effects of hateful speech are manifold. In addition to being a precursor to potential hate crimes and violence, hateful speech and its exposure can have profound psychological impacts on a campus's reputation, climate, and morale, such as heightened stress, anxiety, depression, and desensitization [49, 78]. Victimization, direct or indirect, has also been associated with increased rates of alcohol and drug use [71]—behaviors often considered risky in the formative college years. Further, hateful speech exposure has negative effects on students' academic lives and performance, with lowered self-esteem, and poorer task quality and goal clarity—disrupting the very educational and vocational foundations that underscore college experience [14, 56].

Given the pervasive adoption of social media technologies in the college student population [62], and as hateful speech has begun to manifest online [16], adds a new dimension to the existing issues surrounding college speech. It is an exacerbating factor behind harassment, bullying, and other violent incidents targeting vulnerable students, often making people feel unwelcome in both digital and physical spaces [44, 71], and even causing psychological upheavals, akin to its offline counterpart [58, 77]. Campus administrators and other stakeholders have therefore struggled with mitigating the negative effects of online hateful speech on campuses, while at the same time valuing students' First Amendment rights [7, 45]. An important step towards addressing existing challenges is to first assess the pervasiveness of online hateful speech and the vulnerability in terms of psychological wellbeing presented to marginalized communities on college campuses. However, present methods of assessments are heavily limited. Most existing reports are anecdotal that are covered in popular media outlets [47], and are based on discrete events. Again, there is no empirical way to comprehensively and proactively quantify and characterize hateful speech that surface online in student communities. In addition, social confounds such as the stigma of being exposed to, and the psychological ramifications of hate often lead to underestimates of the effects of online hate, further tempering the mitigation efforts that aim to help these very marginalized groups.

To bridge these gaps, this paper leverages an extensive dataset of over 6 million comments from the online communities of 174 U.S. colleges on Reddit to examine the online dimension of hateful speech in college communities, addressing two research questions:

RQ1: *How prevalent is hateful speech in online college communities, across the demographic categories such as gender, religion, race?*
RQ2: *How does exposure to online hate affect an individual's expression of their psychological state on social media, particularly stress?*

We operationalize hateful speech in online college communities on the hateful content posted in them. We devise College Hate Index (CHX) to quantify the manifestation of hateful speech across various target categories of hate in an online college community. Our findings suggest that, despite existing moderation policies on college subreddits [41], hateful speech remains prevalent. Adopting a causal inference framework, we find that an individual's exposure to online hateful speech impacts their online stress expression. In fact, when exposed to hate, these individuals show a wide range of stress levels, which we characterize using a grounded construct of psychological endurance to hate. Individuals with lower endurance tend to show greater emotional vulnerability and neuroticism.

Although this work does not capture offline hateful speech on college campuses, it advances the body of research in *online* hateful speech by examining it in a hitherto under-explored community – college campuses, and by surfacing its psychological effects – a hitherto under-explored research direction. We discuss the implications of our work in providing an important empirical dimension to the college speech debate, and for supporting policy-making and well-being support and intervention efforts to tackle the psychological effects of *online* hateful speech in college communities.

Privacy, Ethics, and Disclosure. Given the sensitive nature of our study, despite working with public de-identified data from Reddit, we do not report any information that associates hateful speech and its psychological effects with specific individuals or college campuses. To describe our approach and to ground our research better, this paper includes paraphrased and partially masked excerpts of hateful comments, for which we suggest caution to readers.

2   RELATED WORK

Hateful Speech on College Campuses. Despite being attributed as a form of "words that wound" [53], hate speech lacks a universally accepted definition. In the specific setting of college campuses, we adopt Kaplin's definition as a way to operationalize hateful speech in the online college communities [45]:

> ..verbal and written words, and symbolic acts, that convey a grossly negative assessment of particular persons or groups based on their race, gender, ethnicity, religion, sexual orientation, or disability, which is not limited to a face-to-face confrontation or shouts from a crowd, but may also appear on T-shirts, on posters, on classroom blackboards, on student bulletin boards, in flyers and leaflets, in phone calls, etc.

College campuses harbor many diverse communities of race, religion, ethnicity, and sexual orientation. Although argued to be "safe spaces" [74], colleges suffer from many problems related to hate speech, some of which have also escalated to hate crime and violence over the years [7]. The situation is not only alarming, but also

controversial, because U.S. colleges have been unable to successfully regulate hateful speech on campuses based on the long ongoing debate over the freedom of expression per the First Amendment [45], and hate speech legislation, or the "speech debate" [52]. Therefore, examining hateful speech in colleges remains a subject of interest from the standpoint of legal, political, and social sciences [38].

To measure the pervasiveness of hateful speech in colleges, stakeholders have adopted a handful of methodologies. Most of these are based on discrete and subjective reports of personal experiences [25, 35], whose recollection can be unpleasant and traumatizing to the victims. A significant limitation of this approach, is that they generate 'optimisitic' estimates—many targets of hateful speech refrain from reporting their experiences for the fear of being victimized, and due to social stigma [12, 49].

Researchers have studied hateful speech through crisis reaction model to find that it shows similar three-phase consequences of feelings (affect), thoughts (cognition), and actions (behavior) as other traumatic events [49]. Further, the victims of hateful speech experience psychological symptoms, similar to post-traumatic stress disorder, such as pain, fear, anxiety, nightmares, and intrusive thoughts of intimidation and denigration [53, 78]. Some early work also outlined that prejudice, discrimination, intolerance, hatred, and factors hindering a student's integration into their social and academic environments can lead to stress and lowered self-esteem among minorities in college campuses, even if they are not the direct victims of specific events [14, 56, 71]. However, assessing the psychological impacts of exposure to hateful speech on college campuses is challenging and has so far been unexplored at scale.

As many of students' discussions have moved online and many social media platforms provide open forum of conversation to students [62, 67], these tools have also paved the way for speech that is usually reserved for the edges of society. In fact, many incidents of hateful speech on campuses, that are targeted at marginalized groups, have recently been reported to have been initiated online [71]. Assessing the repercussions of online hateful speech has been challenging, for the same reasons as its offline counterpart. Our work addresses the above noted gaps by utilizing unobtrusively gathered social media data from online college communities to estimate the pervasiveness of online hateful speech, and how it psychologically impacts the exposed individuals.

Online Hateful Speech and Its Effects. Online hateful speech differs from its offline counterpart in various ways, as a consequence of affordances of online platforms, such as anonymity, mobility, ephemerality, size of audience, and the ease of access [13]. Under the veil of (semi)-anonymity, and the ability to exploit limited accountability that comes with anonymous online activity, perpetrators receive reinforcement from like-minded haters, making hatred seem normal and acceptable [10, 72].

However, both online and offline hateful speech are sometimes inter-related with regards to their causes and effects. For instance, Timofeeva studied online hate speech and additional complexities that it brings to the constitutional right to free speech, and Olteanu et al. demonstrated that offline events (e.g., extremist violence) causally stimulate online hateful speech on social media platforms like Twitter and Reddit [59, 79].

Over the past few years, a number of studies have focused on detecting and characterizing hateful speech [42, 73], such as distinguishing hateful speech from other offensive language [27], annotating hateful posts on Twitter based on the critical race theory [81], and conducting a measurement study of hateful speech on Twitter and Whisper [54]. Recently, ElSherief et al. studied the distinctive characteristics of hate instigators and targets on social media in terms of their profile self-presentation, activities, and online visibility, and Cheng et al. explored the relationship between one's mood and antisocial behavior on online communities [20, 34]. Other research has also studied moderation of online antisocial behaviors like undesirable posting [15, 21] and online abuse [11, 18, 43].

Apart from understanding online hateful language, some, although limited studies have also examined its *effects* on the online activities of individuals [3]. [44] showed that victims of online abuse leave the platforms, [77] found that the victims feel increased prejudice, and [16] found that the ban of Reddit communities which incited hateful content was effective towards reducing the manifestation of hateful content on the platform. Similarly, other work found that exposure to online hate among young social media users is associated with psychological and emotional upheavals and heightened distancing from family members [58].Our study advances this critical, yet relatively under-explored line of research by examining how the exposure to online hateful speech can psychologically affect the exposed users, or students in our particular setting of online college communities.

Social Media and Psychological Wellbeing. Psychology literature established that analyzing language helps us understand the psychological states [61]. Several studies have showed that social media data can help us infer the psychological and mental health states of individuals and communities [24, 28, 66]. ,Prior work has also used social media to analyze personality traits and their relationship to wellbeing [75]. Social media data has also facilitated psychological assessments in settings where survey-based assessments are difficult, due to the sensitivities of the situations [30, 67].

Pertaining to college students, Manago et al. found that social media helped college students to satisfy enduring psychosocial needs [51]. Given the ubiquity of social media use among youth [62], and because social media platforms enable them to share and disclose mental health issues [31], researchers have also leveraged social media as an unobtrusive source of data to understand mental health of college students [50]. Of particular relevance are two recent pieces of work using college social media (Reddit) datasets: Bagroy et al., who built a collective mental health index of colleges [5], and Saha and De Choudhury, who studied the evolution of stress following gun violence on college campuses [67].

Although these studies provide us with a foundational background, it remains largely understudied how online community dynamics, such as the exposure to hateful speech affects psychological climate of college campuses. Drawing on the recent success of causal analyses in social media research related to both online hateful speech [16, 59], and mental health [29, 68, 70], we focus on a specific online community behavior (hateful speech in online college communities), and examine its psychological impacts on the online expression of stress of community members.

3 DATA

Online College Community Dataset. Reddit, the source of data in this paper, is one of the most popular social media platforms which caters to the age group between 18-29 years: 65% of Reddit users are young adults [62]. We note that this age demography aligns with the typical college student population, making Reddit a suitable choice for our study. Further, Reddit is a social discussion website which consists of diverse communities known as "subreddits" that offer demographic, topical, or interest-specific discussion boards. Many colleges have a dedicated subreddit community,

which provides a common forum for the students to share and discuss about a variety of issues related to their personal, social, and academic life (see e.g., [5, 67, 70]). In fact, the college subreddits name themselves after the college communities that they represent and they often customize their pages with college logos and campus images to signal their identity.

These observations, taken together, indicate that college communities on Reddit can be a source of data to study the research questions posed in this paper. Moreover, such a subreddit dataset has been leveraged in a number of prior work surrounding the study of online college communities [5, 67, 70]. Notably, Bagroy et al. showed that this Reddit data adequately represents the rough demographic distribution of the campus population of over 100 U.S. colleges, is sufficiently widely adopted in these college campuses, and can be employed as a reliable data source to infer the broader college communities' mental wellbeing [5]. While college students likely use other social media platforms as well, such as Facebook, Twitter, Instagram, and Snapchat, obtaining college-specific data from these sources is challenging because many of these platforms restrict public access of data, and they lack defined community structures, precluding gathering sufficiently representative data for specific college campuses. Moreover, these other platforms introduce difficulties in identifying college students users and their college-related discussions on the respective platforms, unless they self-identify themselves, which can limit both scalability and generalizability. In the following subsection we describe how we identify and collect data from college subreddits.

Data Collection. We began by compiling a list of 200 major ranked colleges in the U.S. by crawling the U.S. News (*usnews.com*) website. Next, we crawled the SnoopSnoo (*snoopsnoo.com*) website, which groups subreddits into categories, one of which is "Universities and Colleges". For 174 of these 200 colleges, we found a corresponding subreddit. As of December 2017, these subreddits had 3010 members on an average, and the largest ones were r/UIUC, r/berkeley, r/aggies, r/gatech, r/UTAustin, r/OSU, and r/ucf with 13K to 19K members.

Next, we built our dataset by running nested SQL-like queries on the public archives of Reddit dataset hosted on Google BigQuery. Our final dataset for 174 college subreddits included 5,884,905 comments, posted by 453,781 unique users between August 2008 and November 2017. Within this dataset, 4,144,161 comments were posted by 425,410 unique users who never cross-posted across subreddit communities. Students seek and share information and opinion on a variety of topics spanning across academics, partying, leisure, relationship, emotional support, and other miscellaneous aspects of college life in particular, and youth life in general.

4 RQ1: PREVALENCE OF HATEFUL SPEECH

4.1 Operationalizing Hateful Speech

A first step in our work revolves around identifying hateful speech in the comments posted on the college subreddits. We adopt a pattern (keyword) matching approach by using a high-precision lexicon from two research studies on hateful speech and social media [27, 54]. This lexicon was curated after multiple iterations of filtering through automated classification, followed by crowd-sourced and expert inspection. It consists of 157 phrases that are categorized into: *behavior, class, disability, ethnicity, gender, physical, race, religion, sexual orientation*, and *other*.

Motivation and Validity. Using this lexicon suits our work because we require aggregative assessment of the prevalence of hateful speech— we do not exclusively focus on detecting individual instances of hateful commentary or the specific victims of hate. A

Table 1: Excerpts of paraphrased snippets per hate category in the college subreddit dataset.

Category	Example Snippet
Behavior	*Jesus f*cking Christ, hide that and move the f*ck on. Stop whining like a bunch of b*tchy snowflakes.*
Class	*When some hick says some questionable stuff pre 2016 it's just some hick.*
Disability	*I don't want to be called out as a Retarded, dont assume your retarded worldview is correct and try to force such on others.*
Ethnicity	*you are a hispanic? hispanics came from native american p*ssies. this is your land, but you live under shit built by whites!*
Gender	*If you disagree with us, then you are an anti-consumerist c*nt. I told you I'd call you a c*nt twice.*
Physical	*That guy is fat and ugly so I didn't read it*
Racial	*Damn n*ggah youze is just a little dude with a litte ole baby dick.*
Religious	*It is just like the post about religious fanatics that yell shit on the quad.*
Sexual Ort.	*BIG SHOT, U WANNA FIGHT? U WANNA BOX F*GGOT?*
Other	*U f*cking uneducated kid. Ill ruin ur chances of admission in over 700 ways.*

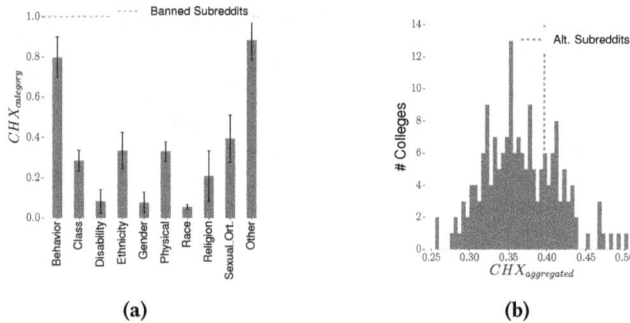

(a)

(b)

Figure 1: (a) Distribution of category-specific CHX; (b) Histogram of category-aggregated CHX over college subreddits

lexicon matching approach casts a wider net on all possible manifestations of online hateful speech, compared to supervised learning based detection techniques which are more tuned to keep false positives at a minimum when incorporated in automatic moderation.

Additionally, we frame our reasoning behind the choice of this approach with *validity theory* [26]. First, since we operationalize hate speech by using this validated, crowdsourced, and expert-annotated lexicon, developed and used in prior work, it offers strong *face* and *construct validity*. This lexicon was compiled on hateful words reported by users on the web; thus it offers a better mechanism to capture the subjective interpretation of hate speech, than bag of words based machine learning approaches. From a *convergent validity* perspective, lexicon approaches have performed as good as sophisticated approaches in hate speech detection [27, 54].

This approach is inclusive, using a rich set of cues covering several forms of online hate, it offers rigor in *content validity*, like in prior work [16, 59], [16] used lexicon of as few as 23 phrases to measure hate speech on Reddit. *Content validity* is valuable here because, unlike most work, our goal is not to detect if a post is hateful for moderation, but to get a collective sense of hatefulness in an online community and to support cross-college community comparisons. Finally, we also manually annotated a random sample of 200 college subreddit comments to check *concurrent validity* of the approach. Two researchers familiar with the literature on online hateful speech, independently rated if using the lexicon-based approach, these comments were correctly identified to have hateful content. We found a Cohen's κ of 0.8, suggesting a strong agreement on the comments identified to have evidence of hateful speech and those manually rated.

Approach. Using the above hate lexicon, for every subreddit in our dataset, we obtain a normalized occurrence of hateful speech,

given as the fraction of keywords that matched the lexicon, to the total number of words in the subreddit's comments. We obtain both category-specific and category-aggregated measures of hateful speech given in the lexicon.

4.2 College Hate Index (CHX)

Next, we discuss the computation of CHX using the above normalized measure of hate in comments. We first identify five subreddits, which were banned by Reddit primarily due to severe hateful speech usage: *r/CoonTown, r/fatpeoplehate, r/KikeTown, r/nazi, r/transf*gs* [16, 57]. These subreddits glorified hateful speech against certain groups. For example, *r/CoonTown* which grew over 15,000 subscribers self-described itself as "a noxious, racist corner of Reddit" [55]. Our motivation to collect this data stems from the conjecture that hateful speech in these banned subreddits would serve as an upper bound to the amount of hateful speech in any other subreddit (such as the 174 college subreddits, none of which were banned at the time of writing this paper). Accordingly, CHX is a measure to calibrate and standardize the prevalence of hateful speech in a college subreddit, allowing aggregative analysis as well as cross subreddit comparison.

Using the same data collection strategy as explained in the *Data* section, we collect 1,436,766 comments from the five banned subreddits mentioned above. Then, per hate category in our hate lexicon, we compute category-specific and category-aggregated normalized occurrences of hate keywords in the comments of banned subreddits using the method described above. Together with the normalized measures of hate in college subreddits, *we define CHX of an online college community to be the ratio of the normalized hate measure (category-specific or category-aggregated) in the college subreddit to the same measure in banned subreddits:*

$$CHX_T(S) = P_T(S)/P_T(B), \qquad (1)$$

S is a college subreddit, B denotes banned subreddits, T indicates type of hate speech assessment: category-specific or category-aggregated, $P_T(S)$ and $P_T(B)$ respectively denote the normalized occurrence of hate keywords for T in S and B. For category-aggregated CHX, T includes *all* hate keywords, and for category-specific CHX, it includes *category-specific* ones.

Based on the above equation 1, a college subreddit with no hate shows CHX of 0, whereas if its hateful speech prevalence matches that in banned subreddits, it shows a CHX of 1. Note that, practically speaking, in a college subreddit the normalized occurrence of hate words can exceed that in the banned subreddits. However, it is less likely based on our reasoning above; thus, we cap the maximum value of CHX at 1, allowing us to bound it in the [0, 1] range.

4.3 Measuring the Prevalence

We find that hateful speech in college subreddits is non-uniformly distributed across the different categories of hate (Figure 1a). A Kruskal-Wallis one-way analysis of variance reveals significant differences in the category-specific occurrences of hate ($H = 1507, p < 0.05$). Among the hate categories, *Other* (mean CHX=0.9) and *behavior* (mean CHX=0.8) show the highest occurrence in college subreddits. While hateful speech targeted at ethnicity, race, and religion have been a major concern for many college campuses [45], we observe varied distribution of online hate for these categories. E.g., CHX for *race* ranges between 0.01 and 0.10, for *ethnicity* it ranges between 0 and 0.70, and for *religion* it ranges between 0.01 and 1.00. Hateful speech towards *disability* ranges between 0 and 0.57, and it shows lower average prevalence (mean CHX = 0.08) than all other categories except *race* (mean CHX = 0.05).

Table 1 reports paraphrased comment excerpts that occur per hate category in the college subreddits. The *Other* category, that demonstrated the highest prevalence, includes keywords like "indecisive", "drunk", and "uneducated". When we examined a random sample of comments, we found that these words are frequently used by the authors to target other members of the community or even the college community in general, e.g., *"They admit gifted students with bright futures but produce uneducated hobos who can't get a job and rely on State alumni for welfare.".* At an aggregate level, hateful speech in college subreddits ranges between 0.26 and 0.51 (mean=0.37; stdev.=0.05) (see Figure 1b). We find that there are no college subreddits with CHX above 0.51; this reveals reasonable civility in these communities, unlike the banned ones. However, the fact that there are no college subreddits at all with CHX below 0.26 indicates the pervasiveness of the phenomenon.

We next ask, how does the prevalence of hateful speech in online college communities compare against elsewhere on Reddit? To answer this, we identify 20 subreddits (alt. subreddits hereon) from the landing page of Reddit, which harbor a diversity of interests and are subscribed by a large number of Reddit users (e.g., *r/AskReddit, r/aww, r/movies*). From these, we collect a random sample of 2M comments (100K comments per subreddit), and using the same strategy to measure the prevalence of hateful speech (as CHX), we calculate the hate index in these subreddits at an aggregate level, and find it to be 0.40. This shows that although a majority of the online college communities reveal lower CHX (Figure 1b), over 25% of them have *greater* hateful speech than the average prevalence in non-college subreddits.

5 RQ2: PSYCHOLOGICAL EFFECTS OF HATE

Recall that our RQ2 asks whether and how the hatefulness in college subreddits affects the psychological state of the community members. To first operationalize psychological state of these online communities, we refer to prior literature that shows that hateful speech is associated with emotional upheavals and distress [53, 78], with stress being one of the most prominent responses in those exposed to hate both directly and indirectly.

5.1 Defining and Quantifying Hate Exposure

Without the loss of generality, we define hate exposure for an individual to be the volume of hateful words shared by others that they are exposed to as a result of participation via commentary in a college subreddit. We calculate this exposure per user as an aggregated percentage of hateful words used by others on all the threads the user has participated in. We use the same lexicon of hate keywords as described in the previous section.

We note that this is a *conservative definition* of online hate exposure, because individuals can be exposed without commenting on a thread with hateful speech; for instance, by simply browsing such a thread. Exposure may also have offline or spill over effects, such as offline hateful expressions whose effects can get amplified when an individual engages with similar content online. However our definition yields a high precision dataset of exposed users, as commentary explicitly signals that individuals have almost certainly consumed some of the hateful content shared by others in a thread.

Further, through this definition of exposure, we choose to not restrict our analysis only to the intended individual targets of hateful speech, but to examine the effects of hateful speech more broadly, at a community-level. Since college subreddits have an offline analog—the offline community on campus, our choice for this broader definition of "exposure" is also inspired by prior psychology literature

which revealed that a toxic (or negative) environment can affect individuals in various forms of presence or relatedness [60].

5.2 Stress Expressed in College Subreddits

Our next objective is to quantify that user's online stress expression, with the psychologically grounded assumption that stress is a manifestation of their psychological state. For this, we appropriate prior work that demonstrated that online stress expression can be measured from content shared in the college subreddits [67, 69].

Specifically, we reproduce a supervised learning based stress detector (classifier) from [67]. This classifier (a SVM model with a linear kernel) employs a supervised learning methodology on a Reddit dataset comprising 2000 posts shared on a stress disclosure and help seeking subreddit, *r/stress* (positive ground truth examples or High Stress), and another 2000 posts obtained from Reddit's landing page that were not shared in any mental health related subreddit (negative examples or Low Stress). Using n-grams and sentiment of the posts as features and based on k-fold ($k = 5$) cross-validation, the classifier predicts a binary stress label (High or Low Stress) for each post with a mean accuracy and mean F1-score of 0.82. This classifier was expert-validated using the Perceived Stress Scale [23] (expert validation accuracy = 81%) on college subreddit data like ours [67]. Similar supervised learning approaches have also been recently used in other work to circumvent the challenges of limited ground-truth [5, 70].

In our case, first, applying this stress classifier, we machine label the 4,144,161 comments in our dataset as high and low stress. Then we aggregate the labeled posts per user for the 425,410 users, to assess their online stress expression. Example comments labeled high stress in our dataset include, *"That sounds very challenging for me. I am a CS major"*, *"College can be very tough at times like this."*, *"Got denied, but I had to act, I'm very disappointed"*.

5.3 Matching For Causal Inference

Next, we aim to quantify the effects of exposure to hateful speech with regard to the stress expressed by users in the college subreddits. This examination necessitates testing for causality in order to eliminate (or minimize) the confounding factors that may be associated with an individual's expression of stress. Ideally such a problem is best tackled using Randomized Controlled Trials (RCTs). However, given that our data is observational and an RCT is impractical and unethical in our specific context involving hateful speech exposure and an individual's psychological state, we adopt a causal inference framework based on statistical matching. This approach aims to simulate a randomized control setting by controlling for observed covariates [39]. For our problem setting, we "match" pairs of users using the propensity score matching technique [39], considering covariates that account for online and offline behaviors of users.

5.3.1 Treatment and Control Groups, and Matching Covariates. We define two comparable cohorts of users who are otherwise similar, but one that was exposed to hateful speech (*Treatment* group) whereas the other was not (*Control* group). To obtain statistically matched pairs of *Treatment* and *Control* users, we control for a variety of covariates such that the effect (online stress) is examined between comparable groups of users showing similar offline and online behaviors: 1) First, we control for users within the *same college subreddits*, which accounts for *offline behavioral changes* attributable to seasonal, academic calendar, or local factors [67]. 2) Next, we account for the *user activity* on Reddit with covariates, per prior work [16, 70], which includes the *number of posts and comments, karma* (aggregated score on the user's posts and comments), *tenure* (duration of participation) in the community. 3) Finally, to minimize the confounding effects of latent factors of those associated with an individual's stress, we limit our analysis in the period after 2016, and among those 217,109 users who participated in discussion threads *both* before and after 2016. Note that our choice of 2016 hinges on the notion that it enables us roughly 2 years of data for our causal analysis, which is half of the typical period of undergraduate education (4 years). This enables us to obtain a *baseline stress* and a *baseline hate exposure* of every user, which are obtained from the comments posted (shared and encountered) before 2016. This baseline stress measures allows us to account for the fact that the psychological wellbeing of an individual can be impacted by both intrinsic and extrinsic historical factors.

5.3.2 Matching Approach. We use the propensity score matching technique [39] to match 143,075 *Treatment* users with a pool of 74,034 users who were not exposed to any hate on the college subreddits in the period from January 2016 to November 2017. First, we train a logistic regression classifier that predicts the propensity score (p) of each user using the above described covariates as features. Next, for every *Treatment* (T_i) user, we find the most similar *Control* user, conditioning to a maximum caliper distance (c) (with $\alpha = 0.2$), i.e., $| T_i(p) - \neg T_i(p) | \le c$, where $c = \alpha * \sigma_{pooled}$ (σ_{pooled} is the pooled standard deviation, and $\alpha \le 0.2$ is recommended for "tight matching" [4]). Thereby, we find a matched *Control* user for each of the 143,045 *Treatment* users.

5.3.3 Quality of Matching. To ensure that our matching technique effectively eliminated any imbalance of the covariates, we use the effect size (Cohen's d) metric to quantify the standardized differences in the matched *Treatment* and the *Control* groups across each of the covariates. Lower values of Cohen's d imply better similarity between the groups, and magnitudes lower than 0.2 indicates "small" differences between the groups [22]. We find that the Cohen's d values for our covariates range between 0.001 and 0.197, with a mean magnitude of 0.07 suggesting a good balance in our matching approach (see Figure 2a). Finally, to eliminate any biases in our findings due to the differences in the degree of participation, we also validate whether the matched pairs of users were exposed to similar quantity of keywords in our period of analysis (post 2016). For the number of keywords they were exposed to, the two cohorts of matched users (*Treatment* and *Control*) show a Cohen's d of 0.02, suggesting minimal differences in their exposure to comment threads or their degree of participation in college subreddits.

We further assess the similarity in topical interests between the commenting behavior of *Treatment* and *Control* pairs of users. Here a high value of topical similarity would ascertain minimal confounds introduced due to topical differences (such as high stressed users being more interested in hateful threads). We adopt a word-embedding based similarity approach [6, 67], where for every user, we obtain a word-embedding representation in 300-dimensional vector space of all the subject titles of the discussion threads that they commented on. We choose subject titles because of their prominence on the homepage of a subreddit, and they likely influence users to consume and subsequently comment on the thread. Next, we compute the vector similarity of the subject titles' word-vectors for every pair of *Treatment* and *Control* users, which essentially quantifies their topical interests. Across all the pairs of *Treatment* and *Control* users, we find an average cosine similarity of 0.67 (stdev. = 0.17), indicating that our matched users share similar interests in the posts on which they commented on.

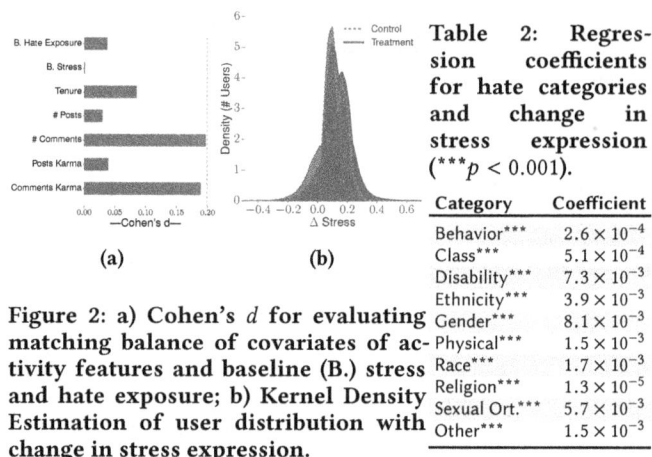

Figure 2: a) Cohen's *d* for evaluating matching balance of covariates of activity features and baseline (B.) stress and hate exposure; b) Kernel Density Estimation of user distribution with change in stress expression.

Table 2: Regression coefficients for hate categories and change in stress expression (***$p < 0.001$).

Category	Coefficient
Behavior***	2.6×10^{-4}
Class***	5.1×10^{-4}
Disability***	7.3×10^{-3}
Ethnicity***	3.9×10^{-3}
Gender***	8.1×10^{-3}
Physical***	1.5×10^{-3}
Race***	1.7×10^{-3}
Religion***	1.3×10^{-5}
Sexual Ort.***	5.7×10^{-3}
Other***	1.5×10^{-3}

5.4 Does Hate Exposure Impact Stress Level?

Following statistical matching, we examine the relationship between the exposure to hate and the expression of stress in college subreddits. Drawing on the widely adopt "Difference in Differences" technique in causal inference research, we evaluate the effects of hate exposure on stress by measuring the shifts in online stress for the *Treatment* group and comparing that with the same in the *Control* group. According to Rubin's causal framework, such an evaluation averages the *effect* (online stress expression) caused by the *treatment* (online hate exposure) on the treated individuals by comparing that with what the same individuals would have shown had they not been treated (the individual's matched pair) [39].

We find that compared to their baseline stress, the stress level of the *Treatment* users (mean=139%) is higher than the *Control* users (mean=106%). Both effect size (Cohen's d=0.40) and paired t-test indicate statistically significance (t=93.3, $p < 0.05$). Figure 2b shows the changes in stress level for the *Treatment* and *Control* users subject to hate speech exposure in the college subreddits. Given that these two groups are matched on offline and online factors, such revealing differences in stress between them following online hate exposure suggest that this exposure likely has a causal relationship with the online stress expression of the users.

We next study how various categories of hate lead to shifts in online stress expression among the *Treatment* users. For this, we fit a linear regression model with the hate categories as independent variables and the change in stress expression as the dependent variable. Table 2 reports the coefficients in the regression model where all of them showed statistical significance. These coefficients could be interpreted as—every unit change in online hate exposure from a category leads to an approximate change in online stress expression by the magnitude of the coefficient. We find that each of the hate categories shows a positive coefficient, indicating that an increase in exposure to any category of hate increases the stress expression of members of the college subreddits. Among these categories, we find that *gender* (0.81%) and *disability* (0.73%) show the greatest coefficients, and therefore affect most towards the online stress expression of the community members.

5.5 Psychological Endurance to Hate Exposure

Within our *Treatment* group, we observe that users are not *equally* affected in their stress levels. In fact, they show a wide range of online stress (median = 0.05, stdev. = 0.80) at varying magnitudes of online hate exposure (median = 0.68, stdev. = 3.61) (see Figure 3). So, besides observing that hate exposure in these communities bears

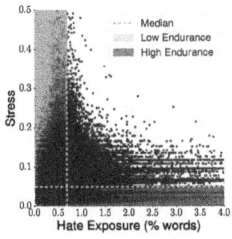

Figure 3: Dist. *Tr.* users.

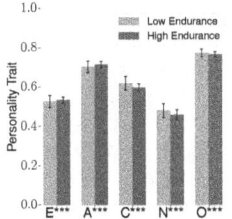

Figure 4: Personality traits in *Tr.* users. Stat. significance reported after Bonferroni correction on independent sample *t*-tests ($***p < 0.001$).

Table 3: Top 25 discriminating *n*-grams ($n = 1, 2$) used by Low and High Endurance users (SAGE [32]).

Low Endurance		High Endurance	
n-gram	SAGE	*n*-gram	SAGE
education code	1.99	guitar	-1.19
prerequisite course	1.68	discord	-1.15
general education	1.64	baylor	-1.15
classes mentioned	1.26	esports	-1.09
mathematics	1.07	smash	-1.00
credit course	1.03	bath	-0.98
upper division	0.95	bands	-0.97
prerequisite	0.95	tournament	-0.93
preassessment	0.89	phi	-0.92
therapy	0.88	garden	-0.90
senate	0.85	shots	-0.89
task	0.84	pokemon	-0.89
cse	0.83	delicious	-0.86
immigrants	0.82	temple	-0.85
prereq	0.81	wings	-0.84
cs1	0.79	used work	-0.84
mathematical	0.78	players	-0.83
irrelevant	0.78	song	-0.83
mentor	0.78	jazz	-0.80
tasks	0.76	anime	-0.80
division	0.75	basement	-0.79
comptia	0.75	rock	-0.79
assessment	0.73	student section	-0.78
anxiety	0.73	yo	-0.78
sql	0.73	sublease	-0.77

a causal relationship with online stress expressions, we also find that online hate does not affect everybody's stress expression uniformly. This aligns with the notion that individuals differ in their resilience to the vicissitudes of life [49]. We call this phenomenon of varied tolerance among users as the *psychological endurance* to online hateful speech. Our motivation to examine this endurance construct comes from the psychology literature, which posits that different people have different abilities to deal with specific uncontrollable events, and stress results from the perception that the demands of these situations exceed their capacity to cope [40].

To understand psychological endurance to online hate, we look at two groups of users who express the extremes of online stress at the opposing extremes of online hate exposure. One group comprises those *Treatment* users with low endurance who have lower tolerance to online hate than most other users and show high (higher than median) stress changes when exposed to low (lower than median) online hate (quadrant 4 in Figure 3). The other group consists of those users who have much higher tolerance, and show low (lower than median) stress changes when exposed to high (higher than median) hate (quadrant 2 in Figure 3). We refer to these two groups as *low endurance* and *high endurance* users—we find 38,503 low and 38,478 high endurance users in our data.

Our analyze the attributes of high and low endurance users as manifested in the college subreddits. We focus on two kinds of attributes— users' online linguistic expression, and their personality traits as inferred from their language. Given that we distinguish the psychological behaviors of two cohorts (individuals with low and high endurance to hateful speech), the choice of these attributes stem from prior work that studied psychological *traits* and *states* of individuals as gleaned from their social media activity [19].

Linguistic Expression. To understand in what ways the low and high endurance users differ in language use, we employ an unsupervised language modeling technique, Sparse Additive Generative Model (SAGE) [32], that has been widely applied in computational linguistic problems on social media data [18, 69, 76]. Given any

two documents, SAGE selects discriminating keywords by comparing the parameters of two logistically parameterized multinomial models, using a self-tuned regularization parameter to control the tradeoff between frequent and rare terms. We use the SAGE model to identify discriminating *n*-grams (n=1,2) between the comments of low and high endurance users. The magnitude of SAGE value of a linguistic token signals the degree of its "uniqueness", and in our case a positive SAGE more than 0 indicates that the *n*-gram is more representative for the low endurance users, whereas a negative SAGE denotes greater representativeness for high endurance users.

Table 3 reports the top 25 *n*-grams ($n = 1, 2$) for low and high endurance users. One pattern evident in these *n*-grams is that low endurance users tend to use more classroom-oriented and academic-related topics, such as "education", "prerequisite", "assessment", "mathematical", etc.. Whereas, the high endurance group demonstrates greater usage of words that relate to a more relaxed and leisure-like context, as well as to diverse non-academic topics/interests, such as "pokemon", "guitar", "delicious", "anime", and "garden". We also find mental health related terms such as "therapy" and "anxiety" for low endurance users, which can be associated with these users self-disclosing their condition or with their help-seeking behaviors around these concerns.

Personality Traits. Our final analysis focuses on understanding the personality differences between individuals showing varied levels of psychological endurance to online stress. Personality refers to the traits and characteristics that uniquely define an individual [75]. Psychology literature posits personality traits as an important aspect to understand the drivers of people's underlying emotional states, trust, emotional stability, and locus of control [1]. For instance, certain personality traits, such as extraversion and neuroticism, represent enduring dispositions that directly lead to subjective wellbeing in individuals, including the dimensions of happiness and negative affect [1]. We study relationship of psychological endurance with personality traits, which can be inferred from social media data of the users [63, 75].

To characterize the personality traits of the users who show low and high psychological endurance, we run their comments' dataset through the Watson Personality Insights API [2], to infer personality in five dimensions of traits: *openness, agreeableness, extraversion, neuroticism,* and *conscientiousness*. Prior research has used this method to extract and characterize several linguistic and psychological constructs from text [19, 34]. Figure 4 shows the distribution of personality traits for low and high endurance users. Paired *t*-tests revealed statistically significant differences between the two groups. Drawing from seminal work on the big-five factor structure of personality [36], we situate our observations as follows:

We observe that the high endurance group reveals 2% greater *agreeableness* (*t*=-66.31) and *extraversion* (*t*=-42.62). Agreeableness characterizes an attribute of being well-mannered, and those who show higher values are generally considered to be less reactive to challenges or an attack (here online hateful speech). *Extraversion* indicates greater sociability, energy, and positive emotions, and lower values signal a reflective personality, which suggests that even lower exposure to online hate can negatively impact users with low endurance. The low endurance users also show 4% greater *neuroticism* (*t*=89.42) and *conscientiousness* (*t*=109.31). *Neuroticism* indicates the degree of emotional stability and higher values signal increased tendency to experience unpleasant emotions easily. Despite these posthoc conjectures, we do acknowledge that understanding these relationships between endurance and personality would require deeper investigation beyond the scope of this paper.

Based on these observations and what we already found in SAGE analysis of the low and high endurance users (Table 3), we infer that even with comparable hate exposure in the college subreddits, different individuals may respond psychologically differently, and these differences may be observed via attributes such as their language of expression on social media and their underlying personality traits.

6 DISCUSSION

6.1 Socio-Political and Policy Implications

The speech debate has been a part of the American socio-political discussions for many years now [52]. In particular, on college campuses, it presents many complexities in decision or policy making that seeks to combat hateful speech within campuses [45]. While this paper does not provide any resolution to this debate, it makes empirical, objective, and data-driven contributions and draws valuable insights towards an informed discussion on this topic.

First, while the speech debate so far has largely focused in the *offline* context, as our study shows, hateful speech in the *online* domain also bears negative impacts on the exposed population, especially in situated communities like college campuses. Our findings align with prior work on the psychological impacts on hateful speech in the offline context [53, 78]. At the same time, they extend the literature by showing that there are not only pronounced differences in the prevalence of various hate speech types, but also the exposure to hate affects individuals' online stress expression. Here we note that antisocial behaviors like hateful speech continue to be a pressing issue for online communities [16, 20], but the effects of online hateful speech remains the subject of little empirical research. Thus, these findings help to account for a previously under-explored, but a critical facet of the speech debate, especially in the context of college campuses.

Second, our findings add new dimensions to the college speech debate centering around legal, ownership, and governance issues. These issues involve not only those who trigger and those who are exposed to online hateful speech, but also the owners, the moderators, the users, and the creators of social media platforms, who may not necessarily be part of the college community.

Third, our work highlights a new policy challenge: how to decipher when online and offline hateful speech reinforce each other, and to delineate their psychological effects, particularly in a situated community where there is likely overlap between the online and offline social worlds. Our work indicates that the affordances of social media, such as anonymity and low effort information sharing amplify the complexities of the speech debate on college campuses. Typically, colleges can choose to restrict the time, place, and manner of someone's speech. However, when speech is not physically located on campus, these affordances can be exploited to quickly reach large segments of the campus population, posing new threats. Consequently, how should college stakeholders respond, when, based on our approach, a student is found to use online hate, observably outside of the physical setting of the campus, targeting a person of marginalized identity?

Finally, our work opens up discussions about the place of "counter-speech" in these communities to undermine the psychological effects of hate, alongside accounting for the legal concerns and governance challenges that enforcing certain community norms may pose [65]. We do note that any such discussions promoting counter speech would need to factor in the general etiquette of conduct expected from the members of the college community to avoid misethnic or chauvinistic phrasing, and to maintain a vibrant and inclusive environment which is respectful of other members [46].

6.2 Technological Implications

6.2.1 Mental Health Support Provisions on College Campuses. The ease of interpretation and the ability to track language changes over time allows our empirical measure of online hateful speech in college campuses to be robust and generalizable across different online college communities, and also accessible to various stakeholders, unlike what is supported by existing hate speech detection techniques [73]. Our methods can thus be leveraged by college authorities to make informed decisions surrounding the speech dilemma on campuses, promote civil online discourse among students, and employ timely interventions when deemed appropriate. While our approach to assess the prevalence of hateful speech is likely to be not perfectly accurate, alongside human involvement in validating these outcomes, timely interventions to reduce the harmful effects of online hateful language can be deployed. As Olteanu et al. [59] recently pointed out that exogenous events can lead to online hatefulness, our framework can assist to proactively detect the psychological ramifications of online hate at their nascent stage to prevent negative outcomes.

Additionally, our work helps us draw insights about the attributes of individuals with higher vulnerability and lower psychological endurance to online hateful speech. This can assist in instrumenting tailored and timely support efforts, and evidence-based decision strategies on campuses. We further note that, any form of hateful speech, whether online or offline, elicits both problem- and emotion- focused coping strategies, and the victims of hateful speech seek support [49]. Many colleges already provide various self, peer, and expert-help resources to cater to vulnerable students. These efforts may be aligned to also consider the effects of *online* hateful speech exposure as revealed in our work.

6.2.2 Moderation Efforts in Online College Communities. Our findings suggest that hateful speech *does* prevail in college subreddits. However, unlike most other online communities, banning or extensively censoring content on college subreddits—a strategy widely adopted today [16, 57] as a measure to counter online antisocial behavior can have counter-effects. Such practices would potentially preclude students from accessing an open discussion board with their peers where not only many helpful information is shared, but also which enables them to socialize and seek support around academic and personal life related topics. Rather, our work can be considered to be a "call-to-action" for the moderators to adopt measures that go beyond blanket banning or censorship. For instance, our approach to assess the stress and hate exposure of users can assist moderators to tune community environment and adapt norms in a way that discourages hateful speech. This could be subreddit guidelines that outline moderation strategies not only discouraging offensive and unwelcoming content, but also around content that *affects* community members. For example, the subreddit r/lifeprotips explicitly calls out against *"tips or comments that encourage behavior that can cause injury or harm to others can cause for a (user) ban"*. Other moderation strategies can also be adopted: such as using labels in specific posts which are perturbing, along the lines of r/AskReddit which uses "[Serious]" to particularly label very important and relevant discussion threads.

Moderators can also provide assistance and support via peer-matching, and include pointers to external online help resources, especially to members who are vulnerable to the negative psychological impacts of online hateful content. Complementarily, as argued in recent research [10], making the harmful effects of hateful language transparent to the community members in carefully planned and strategic manner, could curb the prevalence of antisocial practices including hateful speech. Specifically in online college communities, where the members are geographically situated and embedded in their offline social ties [8, 33], knowledge of the negative psychological repercussion of certain online practices could influence them to refrain from or not engage with such behaviors.

In the offline context, the college speech debate has also aroused discussions surrounding *safe spaces*: particular sites of campuses where students join peers, and *trigger warnings*: explicit statements that certain material discussed in an academic environment might upset sensitive students [46, 80]. These measures are advocated to help in minimize hateful speech and its effects. We argue that analogous measures are possible in online communities as well, using the design affordances of the social media platforms (e.g., creating separate subreddits for minority communities in a college, or providing pop-up warnings on certain posts). However, both safe spaces and trigger warnings are critiqued as they are exclusionary and are harmful for open discourse in colleges. So, any such possible consequences should also be carefully evaluated before such measures are adopted in online communities of college students.

6.3 Ethical Implications

Amid the controversy surrounding the freedom of expression, defining (online) hateful speech remains a complex subject of ethical, legal, and administrative interest, especially on college campuses that are known to value inclusiveness in communities, and to facilitate progressive social exchange. While our definition of hateful speech in online college communities may not be universal, our measurement approach provides an objective understanding of the dynamics and impacts of hateful environment within online college communities. Nevertheless, any decision and policy making based on our findings requires careful and in-depth supplemental ethical analysis, beyond the empirical analysis we present in this paper. For instance, to what extent online hateful speech infringes on the speech provisions on specific campuses remains a topic that needs careful evaluation. Importantly, supported by our analysis, campus stakeholders must navigate a two-prong ethical dilemma: one around engaging with those who use online hateful speech, and two, around treating its extreme manifestations, like hate related threats and altercations directed at campus community members, or its interference with the institution's educational goals.

We finally caution against our work being perceived as a means to facilitate surveillance of student speech on college campuses, or as a guideline to censor speech on campus. Our work is not intended to be used to intentionally or inadvertently marginalize or influence prejudice against those groups who are already marginalized (by gender, race, religion, sexual orientation etc.), or vulnerable, and are often the targets of hateful speech on campuses.

6.4 Limitations and Future Work

Our study has limitations, and some of these suggest promising directions for future work. Although our work is grounded in prior work [5] that college subreddits are representative of their student bodies, we cannot claim that the results extrapolate directly to offline hateful speech on college campuses [13]. Similarly, we cannot claim if these results generalize to other online communities on Reddit or beyond. Importantly, we did not assess the clinical nature of stress in our data, and focused only on inferred stress expression from social media language [67]; future work can validate the extent to which online hate speech impacts the mental health of students. Like many observational studies, we also cannot establish a *true causality* between an individual's exposure to online hate and their

stress expressions. To address these limitations, future work can gather ground truth data about individual stress experiences and clinically validate them with social media derived observations.

We note that our work is sensitive to the uniqueness of the Reddit platform, where the content is already moderated [17, 43, 57]. It is possible that the definition of hateful content qualifying for content removal could vary across the college subreddits, and our work is restricted to only the non-removed comments. Importantly, the norms and strategies to moderate content can vary across different college subreddits. Therefore, our study likely provides a "lower bound estimate" of hateful content on these communities. Additionally, users also use multiple accounts and throwaway accounts on Reddit [48], and we do not identify individual users' experiences of online hate or stress in our dataset. Our findings about the psychological endurance to hate is interesting and inspires further theoretical and empirical investigations—e.g., how can we generalize the relationship between online hate and psychological wellbeing both on campuses and elsewhere, what factors influence the endurance of an individual, and how can we characterize endurance in terms of direct victimization or indirect influence of the ripple effects of online hateful speech on campuses.

7 CONCLUSION

In this paper, we first modeled College Hate Index (CHX) to measure the degree of hateful speech in college subreddits. We found that hateful speech does prevail in college subreddits. Then, we employed a causal inference framework to find that the exposure to hateful speech in college subreddits impacted greater stress expression of the community members. We also found that the exposed users showed varying psychological endurance to hate exposure, i.e, all users exposed to similar levels of hate reacted differently. We analyzed the language and personality of these low and high endurance users to find that, low endurance users are vulnerable to more emotional outbursts, and are more conscientious and neurotic than those showing higher endurance to hate.

8 ACKNOWLEDGEMENT

We thank Eric Gilbert, Stevie Chancellor, Sindhu Ernala, Shagun Jhaver, and Benjamin Sugar for their feedback. Saha and De Choudhury were partly supported by research grants from Mozilla (RK677) and the NIH (R01GM112697).

REFERENCES

[1] Gordon Willard Allport. 1937. Personality: A psychological interpretation. (1937).
[2] IBM Watson Personality API. 2018. personality-insights-demo.ng.bluemix.net.
[3] Pinar Arslan, Michele Corazza, Elena Cabrio, and Serena Villata. 2019. Overwhelmed by Negative Emotions? Maybe You Are Being Cyber-bullied!. In *The 34th ACM/SIGAPP Symposium On Applied Computing (ACM SAC 2019)*.
[4] Peter C Austin. 2011. Optimal caliper widths for propensity-score matching when estimating differences in means and differences in proportions in observational studies. *Pharmaceutical statistics* 10, 2 (2011), 150–161.
[5] Shrey Bagroy, Ponnurangam Kumaraguru, and Munmun De Choudhury. 2017. A Social Media Based Index of Mental Well-Being in College Campuses. In *Proceedings of the 2017 CHI Conference on Human Factors in Computing Systems*.
[6] Timothy Baldwin, Paul Cook, Marco Lui, Andrew MacKinlay, and Li Wang. 2013. How noisy social media text, how diffrnt social media sources?. In *IJCNLP*.
[7] Katharine T Bartlett and Jean O'Barr. 1990. The Chilly Climate on College Campuses: An Expansion of the" Hate Speech" Debate. *Duke Law J.* (1990).
[8] Victor Battistich and Allen Hom. 1997. The relationship between students' sense of their school as a community and their involvement in problem behaviors. *American journal of public health* 87, 12 (1997), 1997–2001.
[9] Dan Bauman. 2018. chronicle.com/article/After-2016-Election-Campus/242577.
[10] Lindsay Blackwell, Tianying Chen, Sarita Schoenebeck, and Cliff Lampe. 2018. When Online Harassment is Perceived as Justified. In *ICWSM*.
[11] Lindsay Blackwell, Jill Dimond, Sarita Schoenebeck, and Cliff Lampe. 2017. Classification and Its Consequences for Online Harassment: Design Insights from HeartMob. *Proc. ACM Hum.-Comput. Interact.* CSCW (2017), 24:1–24:19.

[12] Robert Boeckmann and Jeffrey Liew. 2002. Hate speech: Asian American students' justice judgments and psychological responses. *J. Soc. Issues* (2002).

[13] Alexander Brown. 2017. What is so special about online (as compared to offline) hate speech? *Ethnicities* (2017).

[14] Alberto F Cabrera, Amaury Nora, Patrick T Terenzini, Ernest Pascarella, and Linda Serra Hagedorn. 1999. Campus racial climate and the adjustment of students to college: A comparison between White students and African-American students. *The Journal of Higher Education* (1999).

[15] Stevie Chancellor, Jessica Annette Pater, Trustin Clear, Eric Gilbert, and Munmun De Choudhury. 2016. #Thyghgapp: Instagram Content Moderation and Lexical Variation in Pro-Eating Disorder Communities. In *Proc. CSCW*. 1201–1213.

[16] Eshwar Chandrasekharan, Umashanthi Pavalanathan, Anirudh Srinivasan, Adam Glynn, Jacob Eisenstein, and Eric Gilbert. 2017. You Can't Stay Here: The Efficacy of Reddit's 2015 Ban Examined Through Hate Speech. *PACM HCI (CSCW)* (2017).

[17] Eshwar Chandrasekharan, Mattia Samory, Shagun Jhaver, Hunter Charvat, Amy Bruckman, Cliff Lampe, Jacob Eisenstein, and Eric Gilbert. 2018. The Internet's Hidden Rules: An Empirical Study of Reddit Norm Violations at Micro, Meso, and Macro Scales. *PACM HCI* CSCW (2018).

[18] Eshwar Chandrasekharan, Mattia Samory, Anirudh Srinivasan, and Eric Gilbert. 2017. The Bag of Communities: Identifying Abusive Behavior Online with Preexisting Internet Data. In *Proc. CHI*.

[19] Jilin Chen, Gary Hsieh, Jalal U Mahmud, and Jeffrey Nichols. 2014. Understanding individuals' personal values from social media word use. In *CSCW*.

[20] Justin Cheng, Michael Bernstein, Cristian Danescu-Niculescu-Mizil, and Jure Leskovec. 2017. Anyone Can Become a Troll: Causes of Trolling Behavior in Online Discussions. In *Proc. CSCW*.

[21] Justin Cheng, Cristian Danescu-Niculescu-Mizil, and Jure Leskovec. 2015. Anti-social Behavior in Online Discussion Communities. In *International AAAI Conference on Web and Social Media*.

[22] Jacob Cohen. 1992. Statistical power analysis. *Curr. Dir. Psychol. Sci.* (1992).

[23] Sheldon Cohen, Tom Kamarck, and Robin Mermelstein. 1983. A global measure of perceived stress. *Journal of health and social behavior* (1983), 385–396.

[24] Glen Coppersmith, Craig Harman, and Mark Dredze. 2014. Measuring post traumatic stress disorder in Twitter. In *ICWSM*.

[25] Gloria Cowan and Cyndi Hodge. 1996. Judgments of hate speech: The effects of target group, publicness, and behavioral responses of the target. *Journal of Applied Social Psychology* 26, 4 (1996), 355–374.

[26] Linda Crocker and James Algina. 1986. *Introduction to classical and modern test theory*. ERIC.

[27] Thomas Davidson, Dana Warmsley, Michael Macy, and Ingmar Weber. 2017. Automated Hate Speech Detection and the Problem of Offensive Language.

[28] Munmun De Choudhury, Michael Gamon, Scott Counts, and Eric Horvitz. 2013. Predicting depression via social media. In *ICWSM*.

[29] Munmun De Choudhury, Emre Kiciman, Mark Dredze, Glen Coppersmith, and Mrinal Kumar. 2016. Discovering shifts to suicidal ideation from mental health content in social media. In *Proc. CHI*.

[30] Munmun De Choudhury, Andres Monroy-Hernandez, and Gloria Mark. 2014. Narco emotions: affect and desensitization in social media during the mexican drug war. In *CHI*. ACM, 3563–3572.

[31] Daniel Eisenberg, Justin Hunt, and Nicole Speer. 2012. Help seeking for mental health on college campuses: Review of evidence and next steps for research and practice. *Harvard review of psychiatry* (2012).

[32] Jacob Eisenstein, Amr Ahmed, and Eric P Xing. 2011. Sparse additive generative models of text. (2011).

[33] Nicole B Ellison, Charles Steinfield, and Cliff Lampe. 2007. The benefits of Facebook "friends": Social capital and college studentsúse of online social network sites. *Journal of Computer-Mediated Communication* (2007).

[34] Mai ElSherief, Shirin Nilizadeh, Dana Nguyen, Giovanni Vigna, and Elizabeth Belding. 2018. Peer to Peer Hate: Hate Speech Instigators and Their Targets. *International AAAI Conference on Web and Social Media (ICWSM)* (2018).

[35] Steve France. 1990. Hate goes to college. *ABA Journal* 76 (1990), 44.

[36] Lewis R Goldberg. 1990. An Alternative "Description of Personality": The Big-Five Factor Structure. *J. Pers. Soc. Psychol.* (1990).

[37] Daniel Goleman. 1990. As bias crime seems to rise, scientists study roots of racism. *New York Times* (1990), C1.

[38] Jon B Gould. 2001. The precedent that wasn't: College hate speech codes and the two faces of legal compliance. *Law Soc. Rev.* (2001).

[39] Guido W Imbens and Donald B Rubin. 2015. *Causal inference in statistics, social, and biomedical sciences*. Cambridge.

[40] Rick E Ingram and David D Luxton. 2005. Vulnerability-stress models. *Dev. Psychopathol.: A vulnerability-stress perspective* (2005).

[41] Business Insider. 2018. businessinsider.com/what-is-a-reddit-moderator-2016-1.

[42] Shagun Jhaver, Larry Chan, and Amy Bruckman. 2018. The view from the other side: The border between controversial speech and harassment on Kotaku in Action. *First Monday* 23, 2 (2018).

[43] Shagun Jhaver, Sucheta Ghoshal, Amy Bruckman, and Eric Gilbert. 2018. Online harassment and content moderation: The case of blocklists. *ACM TOCHI* (2018).

[44] Ruogu Kang, Laura Dabbish, and Katherine Sutton. 2016. Strangers on your phone: Why people use anonymous communication applications. In *CSCW*.

[45] William A Kaplin. 1992. A proposed process for managing the First Amendment aspects of campus hate speech. *J. High. Educ.* (1992).

[46] Mae Kuykendall and Charles Adside III. 2013. Unmuting the Volume: Fisher, Affirmative Action Jurisprudence, and the Legacy of Racial Silence. (2013).

[47] L.A.Times. 2017. latimes.com/local/lanow/la-me-berkeley-free-speech-20170605-story.html. Acc: 2018-01-17.

[48] Alex Leavitt. 2015. This is a throwaway account: Temporary technical identities and perceptions of anonymity in a massive online community. In *Proc. CSCW*.

[49] Laura Leets. 2002. Experiencing hate speech: Perceptions and responses to anti-semitism and antigay speech. *Journal of social issues* 58, 2 (2002), 341–361.

[50] Sam Liu, Miaoqi Zhu, and Sean D Young. 2018. Monitoring freshman college experience through content analysis of tweets: observational study. *JMIR public health and surveillance* 4, 1 (2018), e5.

[51] Adriana M Manago, Tamara Taylor, and Patricia M Greenfield. 2012. Me and my 400 friends: the anatomy of college students' Facebook networks, their communication patterns, and well-being. *Developmental psychology* (2012).

[52] Toni M Massaro. 1990. Equality and freedom of expression: The hate speech dilemma. *Wm. & Mary L. Rev.* (1990).

[53] Mari J Matsuda. 1993. *Words that wound: Critical race theory, assaultive speech, and the first amendment*. Westview.

[54] Mainack Mondal, Leandro Araújo Silva, and Fabrício Benevenuto. 2017. A Measurement Study of Hate Speech in Social Media. In *Proc. ACM HT*.

[55] Justin Wm Moyer. 2015. wapo.st/1JmimPm?tid=ss_tw-bottom&utm_term=.75ee6968b36d. Accessed: 2018-07-05.

[56] Daniel G Muñoz. 1986. Identifying areas of stress for Chicano undergraduates. *Latino college students* (1986), 131–156.

[57] Edward Newell, David Jurgens, Haji Mohammad Saleem, Hardik Vala, Jad Sassine, Caitrin Armstrong, and Derek Ruths. 2016. User Migration in Online Social Networks: A Case Study on Reddit During a Period of Community Unrest.

[58] Atte Oksanen, James Hawdon, Emma Holkeri, Matti Näsi, and Pekka Räsänen. 2014. Exposure to online hate among young social media users. *Soul of society: a focus on the lives of children & youth* (2014).

[59] Alexandra Olteanu, Carlos Castillo, Jeremy Boy, and Kush Varshney. 2018. The Effect of Extremist Violence on Hateful Speech Online. In *ICWSM*.

[60] Ellen E Pastorino and Susann M Doyle-Portillo. 2012. *What is psychology? Essentials*. Cengage Learning.

[61] James W Pennebaker and Cindy K Chung. 2007. Expressive writing, emotional upheavals, and health. *Handbook of health psychology* (2007), 263–284.

[62] Pew. 2018. pewinternet.org/fact-sheet/social-media. Accessed: 2018-04-18.

[63] Daniele Quercia, Michal Kosinski, David Stillwell, and Jon Crowcroft. 2011. Our twitter profiles, our selves: Predicting personality with twitter. In *SocialCom*.

[64] Robert A Rhoads. 1998. *Freedom's web: Student activism in an age of cultural diversity*. Hopkins.

[65] Robert D Richards and Clay Calvert. 2000. Counterspeech 2000: A New Look at the Old Remedy for Bad Speech. *BYU L. Rev.* (2000), 553.

[66] Koustuv Saha, Larry Chan, Kaya De Barbaro, Gregory D Abowd, and Munmun De Choudhury. 2017. Inferring Mood Instability on Social Media by Leveraging Ecological Momentary Assessments. *Proc. ACM IMWUT* (2017).

[67] Koustuv Saha and Munmun De Choudhury. 2017. Modeling Stress with Social Media Around Incidents of Gun Violence on College Campuses. (2017).

[68] Koustuv Saha, Benjamin Sugar, John Torous, Bruno Abrahao, Emre Kiciman, and Munmun De Choudhury. 2019. A Social Media Study on The Effects of Psychiatric Medication Use. In *ICWSM*.

[69] Koustuv Saha, John Torous, Sindhu Kiranmai Ernala, Conor Rizuto, Amanda Stafford, and Munmun De Choudhury. 2019. A computational study of mental health awareness campaigns on social media. *TBM* (2019).

[70] Koustuv Saha, Ingmar Weber, and Munmun De Choudhury. 2018. A Social Media Based Examination of the Effects of Counseling Recommendations After Student Deaths on College Campuses. In *ICWSM*.

[71] Allison M Schenk and William J Fremouw. 2012. Prevalence, psychological impact, and coping of cyberbully victims among college students. *Journal of School Violence* 11, 1 (2012), 21–37.

[72] Ari Schlesinger, Eshwar Chandrasekharan, Christina A Masden, Amy S Bruckman, W Keith Edwards, and Rebecca E Grinter. 2017. Situated anonymity: Impacts of anonymity, ephemerality, and hyper-locality on social media. In *Proc. CHI*.

[73] Anna Schmidt and Michael Wiegand. 2017. A survey on hate speech detection using natural language processing. In *SocialNLP*.

[74] Nicholas A Schroeder. 2017. Avoiding Deliberation: Why the Safe Space Campus Cannot Comport with Deliberative Democracy. *BYU Educ. & LJ* (2017), 325.

[75] H Andrew Schwartz, Johannes C Eichstaedt, Margaret L Kern, Lukasz Dziurzynski, Stephanie M Ramones, Megha Agrawal, Achal Shah, Michal Kosinski, David Stillwell, Martin EP Seligman, et al. 2013. Personality, gender, and age in the language of social media: The open-vocabulary approach. *PloS one* (2013).

[76] Eva Sharma, Koustuv Saha, Sindhu Kiranmai Ernala, Sucheta Ghoshal, and Munmun De Choudhury. 2017. Analyzing ideological discourse on social media: A case study of the abortion debate. In *Proc. CSS*. ACM.

[77] Wiktor Soral, Michał Bilewicz, and Mikołaj Winiewski. 2017. Exposure to hate speech increases prejudice through desensitization. *Aggress. Behav.* (2017).

[78] Megan Sullaway. 2004. Psychological perspectives on hate crime laws. *Psychology, Public Policy, and Law* 10 (2004).

[79] Yulia A Timofeeva. 2002. Hate Speech Online: Restricted or Protected-Comparison of Regulations in the United States and Germany. *J. Transnat'l L. & Pol'y* 12 (2002), 253.

[80] Alexander Tsesis. 2016. Campus speech and harassment. *Minn. L. Rev.* (2016).

[81] Zeerak Waseem and Dirk Hovy. 2016. Hateful symbols or hateful people? predictive features for hate speech detection on twitter. In *NAACL-HLT*.

Trust It or Not: Effects of Machine-Learning Warnings in Helping Individuals Mitigate Misinformation

Haeseung Seo
hxs378@psu.edu
The Pennsylvania State University
University Park, PA, USA

Aiping Xiong
axx29@psu.edu
The Pennsylvania State University
University Park, PA, USA

Dongwon Lee
dongwon@psu.edu
The Pennsylvania State University
University Park, PA, USA

ABSTRACT

Despite increased interests in the study of fake news, how to aid users' decision in handling suspicious or false information has not been well understood. To obtain a better understanding on the impact of warnings on individuals' fake news decisions, we conducted two online experiments, evaluating the effect of three warnings (i.e., one Fact-Checking and two Machine-Learning based) against a control condition, respectively. Each experiment consisted of three phases examining participants' recognition, detection, and sharing of fake news, respectively. In Experiment 1, relative to the control condition, participants' detection of both fake and real news was better when the Fact-Checking warning but not the two Machine-Learning warnings were presented with fake news. Post-session questionnaire results revealed that participants showed more trust for the Fact-Checking warning. In Experiment 2, we proposed a Machine-Learning-Graph warning that contains the detailed results of machine-learning based detection and removed the source within each news headline to test its impact on individuals' fake news detection with warnings. We did not replicate the effect of the Fact-Checking warning obtained in Experiment 1, but the Machine-Learning-Graph warning increased participants' sensitivity in differentiating fake news from real ones. Although the best performance was obtained with the Machine-Learning-Graph warning, participants trusted it less than the Fact-Checking warning. Therefore, our study results indicate that a transparent machine learning warning is critical to improving individuals' fake news detection but not necessarily increase their trust on the model.

CCS CONCEPTS

• **Human-centered computing** → **Empirical studies in HCI**;

KEYWORDS

Misinformation; warnings; trust; algorithm transparency

ACM Reference format:
Haeseung Seo, Aiping Xiong, and Dongwon Lee. 2019. Trust It or Not: Effects of Machine-Learning Warnings in Helping Individuals Mitigate

Misinformation. In *Proceedings of Websci '19: 11th ACM Conference on Web Science, Boston, MA, June 30–July 03, 2019 (Websci '19)*, 10 pages.
https://doi.org/10.1145/1122445.1122456

1 INTRODUCTION

We currently live in a historical era called the "information age". The advent of modern information technology fundamentally changes the ways how people access, communicate and share information. Specifically, the rise of the Internet and more recently social media platforms (e.g., Facebook, Twitter) have made it possible for individuals to produce, consume, and share diverse multi-modal information (e.g., text, picture, video). With the boundary between information source and information receiver becoming blurred and often invisible, then, issues arise with regard to the quantity and quality of the information to which people are exposed [3]. Especially, it must be acknowledged that people are not necessarily good at evaluating the quality of online information. *Fake News* often refers to (intentionally) false stories or fabricated information written and published for various incentives including political agenda or financial gain [8, 13, 34]. In recent years, the spread of fake news has been identified as a major risk for individuals and society [35]. For instance, fake news has fostered people's bias and false belief of climate change [39] and greatly influenced elections and democracies [6].

Two venues of approaches have been investigated to mitigate the negative impacts of fake news: (1) computation-based detection and prevention of fake news; (2) decision-aid methods to warn users when a piece of fake news has been identified. Among the latter venue of approaches (the focus of this study), attaching warnings to the news that was suspicious or fact-checked to be fake news was implemented to discourage users' consumption and belief in fake news. One such example once was used by Facebook. While some studies showed that exposure to a fact-checking warning under Facebook style headlines reduced the perceived accuracy of fake news compared to a control condition [9], other studies did not [27], motivating our study.

Also, with more fact-checking work being done by machine learning algorithms [35], one interesting but rarely investigated question related to both venues is: *After computational methods detect fake news, how to convincingly present the result to users to make informed decisions consequently?* To answer this intriguing question, we investigate the following research questions:

(1) RQ1: Will the presence of a fact-checking warning increase participants' fake news detection relative to a control condition in which there is no warning?

(2) RQ2: Will the presence of automatic fake news detection results using machine learning algorithms increase participants' fake news detection relative to the control condition?

(3) RQ3: What is the best way to communicate the result of machine learning based on fake news detection?

In our study, we proposed new machine-learning warnings in response to an emphasis on "algorithm transparency" [11, 26, 31]. A *Fact-Checking* warning that was used in the study of [9] was also used to see whether we could replicate their results. Using a between-subjects design, we conducted two online experiments on Amazon Mechanical Turk (MTurk), in each of which the immediate, short-term, and long-term effectiveness of three warnings against a control condition was evaluated in three phases, respectively. Across two experiments, 1,176 MTurk workers completed three interrelated decision tasks of *recognition*, *detection*, and *sharing* to different news (half real and half fake) in each phase. In addition to the analysis of decision rates, we used a *signal-detection theory* (SDT) [24, 37] approach assessing individuals' susceptibility and bias at detecting fake news.

Across all phases of Experiment 1, participants showed limited recognition and cautious sharing decisions in general. Compared to the control condition, participants increased their correct detection of both fake and real news in the *Fact-Checking* condition but not the others. In Experiment 2, when the news source, a cue that most participants used to identify news' legitimacy, was removed from each news headline, similar results were obtained for the recognition and sharing tasks. But the effect of the *Fact-Checking* warning obtained in Experiment 1 disappeared. Instead, compared to the control condition, a *Machine-Learning-Graph* warning increased participants' sensitivity in differentiating fake and real news.

Our work makes the following three key contributions:

(1) We proposed and evaluated the use of warnings to communicate the results of machine-learning detected fake news to users. Across three machine-learning warnings, only the *Machine-Learning-Graph* warning that includes the detail results of machine-learning based detection increased individuals' correct detection of fake news, suggesting that a transparent machine learning algorithm is critical to improve people's fake news detection.

(2) Our results showed that the *Fact-Checking* warning increased participants' correct detection of both fake and real news when the source was included in news headlines but not when the source was excluded. Participants showed more trust on the *Fact-Checking* warning even though the best detection performance was obtained with the *Machine-Learning-Graph* warning, suggesting promoting users' fake news detection does not necessarily promoting users' trust on the warning.

(3) We introduced a SDT approach to investigate individuals' fake news detection and obtained that the *Machine-Learning-Graph* warning increased participants' sensitivity to differentiate fake from real news but not the *Fact-Checking* warning.

These contributions bridge the two venues of fake news mitigation and should help researchers and practitioners improve their understanding of people's decision-making in facing fake news and propose usable and transparent algorithms to address fake news problems.

2 RELATED WORK
2.1 Human Fake News Detection

Within experimental settings, a few factors have been investigated to understand their impact on people's belief in and willingness to share fake news on social media. Pennycook et al. [27] conducted online studies examining the influence of warning and repetition. In their Experiments 2 and 3, participants were asked to evaluate different pieces of news in multiple stages. In stage 1, participants were asked to indicate whether they were to share news headlines (half fake and half real) on social media. Also, half of the participants were randomly assigned to a warning condition, in which all fake news stories were flagged with a caution symbol and the text "Disputed by 3rd Party Fact-Checkers". The rest half were assigned to a control condition in which no warning was presented. After a distracting stage, in stage 3, participants were asked to rate familiarity and accuracy of real and fake news headlines (a half from stage 1 and a half from a new set of headlines). Each participant in Experiment 3 was also invited to return for a follow-up session one week later in which the same headlines were seen in stage 3 and a new set of headlines were presented. Results showed that repeated headlines were rated as more "real" than novel headlines regardless of headlines' legitimacy and warning. The increased accuracy perception obtained with a single exposure lasted even after a week regardless of the warning. Although the main effect of warning and its interaction with news legitimacy were significant in Experiment 2, neither terms were significant in Experiment 3.

Clayton et al. [9] conducted an online study to further investigate the effect of warning. To eliminate confounding variables, they removed the source within all news headlines. In one condition, they implemented a "Fact-Checking" warning similar to that in [27] but specified the third parties' names within the warning. 413 participants in the condition indicated their perceived accuracy and likelihood to "Like" or share nine news (six fake, four of which with a warning, and three real). Compared to a control condition, participants' perceived accuracy of fake news with the warning was reduced, indicating the effectiveness of using warning to reduce participants' belief in fake news.

A comparison between the studies of [27] and [9] revealed several critical differences, which may cause the ineffectiveness of the warning in Experiment 3 of [27] but the effect obtained by [9]. First, warnings were presented at the familiarity phase of [27] but the evaluation phase of [9]. Thus, Clayton et al. [9] evaluated the effect of warning but Pennycook et al. [27] evaluated its short-term effect. Second, the source was removed for each news headline used by [9], which may increase participants' reliance on using warning to assess the legitimacy of news headlines. Also, the 3rd party names were specified in [9], which may increase individuals' trust on the warning. Accordingly, in our work, we investigated a warning like [9] during the assessment phase but varied the presence and absence of the source to understand how it impacts individuals' belief in fake news with warnings. Besides, we evaluated the immediate, short-term, and long-term effects of the warning in different phases, and asked participants to indicate their trust level on the warning.

2.2 Computational Fake News Detection

In recent years, much attention has been made to detect fake news using computational means (e.g., [10, 36, 38]), especially using various features such as single-modal [4, 30] and multi-modal features [20, 40]. The single-modal methods mainly focus on analyzing the textual contents of news, for example, counting the number of assertive words which are shown more in trusted sources [30] or evaluating the consistency between topic sentence and main text [4]. Meanwhile, multi-modal methods include features derived from various sources, such as contents of news, users who posted news, publishers of news, or how news has propagated in a network. For instance, those features can be several textual features including news contents and user's comments [33] or different data types including a combination of text, image, or video [20, 25, 40].

In addition, to provide the accountability of algorithmic solutions, researchers have started offering details about the inner mechanisms of machine learning algorithms [5]. With more fact-checks done by machine learning algorithms [35], we study how to present the result *after* the detection of fake news occurs. Specifically, the machine-learning warnings in our study were not generated by machine learning algorithms. Instead, we used hypothetical evaluation metrics (e.g., accuracy) and multi-modal features (e.g., text, picture) of machine learning algorithms within various warning signs (e.g., one with the wording "Machine Learning") to leverage the advancements in computational solutions.

2.3 Signal Detection Theory

Accuracy measure, such as the number of correct identification of fake news, is incomplete to understand individuals' vulnerability to fake news because they ignore factors, such as the influence of real news. Accordingly, in our work, in addition to measures of decision rates, we use SDT [16] to understand individuals' detection in response to fake news. SDT has been implemented for investigating decision-making in the context of perceptual uncertainties and risk [24], such as susceptibility to a phishing email and web pages [7, 42].

In SDT, participants' responses are defined as two normal distributions of pieces of evidence, representing both *signal* and *noise*. The difference between the means of signal and noise distributions reflects participants' sensitivity (d'), e.g., their ability to tell whether a piece of news is fake. Independent from d', SDT also allows a measure of participants' response criterion (c), e.g., their tendency to treat a piece of news as fake. In the context of fake news detection, the signal will be fake news to detect and the noise will be real news. If the news is fake and the decision for the news judgment is suspicious, the trial is a *H*: hit. If there is a piece of real news but is judged suspicious, it is a *FA*: false alarm. If fake news is misjudged as non-suspicious, it is a miss. Finally, if real news is judged as non-suspicious, it is a correct decision. d' and c are derived as follows:

$$d' = z(H) - z(FA) \qquad (1)$$
$$c = -0.5[z(H) + z(FA)] \qquad (2)$$

Therefore, using SDT, the evaluation of how well a participant detects fake news will be not influenced by whether the participant is biased or not.

2.4 Current Work

The question of whether machine learning warning reduces individuals' fake news susceptibility has consequences for a broader perspective on the deployment of transparent machine learning algorithms. In this paper, we conducted two experiments investigating the three *RQs* by examining participants' recognition, detection, and willingness to share fake and real news. The detailed data from all our experiments is available for download at http://pike.psu.edu/download/websci19/.

3 EXPERIMENT 1

We conducted a between-subjects online study investigating the effect of two machine-learning and one fact-checking warning in mitigating fake news. In addition to the three warning conditions, a control group (*CON*) in which no warning was presented, was also included in the study. Participants made recognition, detection, and sharing decisions on fake and real news in three phases. In Phase 1, participants got warnings on fake news trials except for those participants in *CON*. After a distraction task of filling demographic information, Phase 2 started, in which participants did the same task as Phase 1 without warning to evaluate the short-term effect of the warning. One week later, we invited each participant back to Phase 3 to do the same task as Phase 2 to evaluate the long-term effect of the warning. Half of the trials in Phase 3 were news headlines that were already presented in Phases 1 and 2, which were used to investigate participants' decisions of repeated fake news.

3.1 Methodology

The study was conducted on Amazon MTurk, and all participants were (1) at least 18 years old; (2) located at the United States; and (3) with a human intelligence task approval rate above 95%. Participants were allowed to participate in the study once. Our online study was programmed using Qualtrics. This and the following study were approved by the Institutional Research Board of The Pennsylvania State University.

Materials. We created 24 news headlines in the format of Facebook posts, consisting of a picture, source, header, and a short description (see Figure 1). 12 were verified fake news from *snope.com* and *politifact.com*, well-known third-party fact-checking websites. The other 12 news headlines were real news chosen from major news media, such as *huffpost.com* and *reuters.com*. The 24 pieces of news were divided into three groups (half real and half fake in each group). For each condition, a Latin-square design was implemented to balance the order of the groups across three phases. We proposed three warnings: Fact-Checking (*FC*), Machine-Learning (*ML*), and Machine-Learning-Accuracy (*MLA*). Each warning was attached to the bottom of the fake news in the study. Figure 1 gives a depiction of the warning design and the content of each warning. The two machine-learning warnings were the same except a hypothetical value, 97%, was described in the *MLA* warning to indicate the accuracy of the machine learning algorithm.

The selected news was released from April to June in 2018, and the topic of news was limited to politics because 1) political news is one type of the most popular news that most individuals will read every day, so most of the people have a certain sense to judge

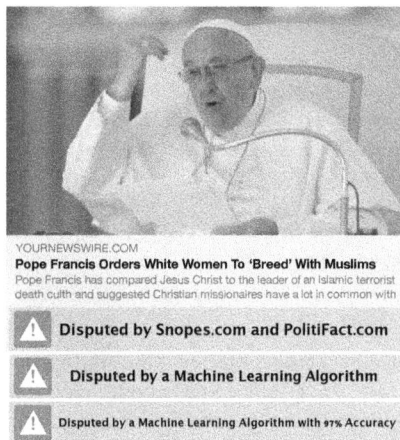

Figure 1: Warnings presented in Experiment 1, top row: A piece of fake news with Fact-Checking (*FC*) warning, center row: Machine-Learning (*ML*) warning, and bottom row: Machine-Learning-Accuracy (*MLA*) warning.

its credibility without professional knowledge; 2) the negative effect caused by the fake political news has become a critical issue in our daily life [6]. For example, in the 2016 American presidential election period, a piece of news titled "Pope Francis Shocks World, Endorses Donald Trump for President" [1] shook the world and commoved voters. Therefore, we believe political news should be treated as one of the top priority news types in solving fake news problems.

Procedure. Figure 2 illustrates the flow chart of Experiment 1. Participants were randomly assigned to one of the four conditions. After participants made an informed consent, Phase 1 started. Eight different news (half fake) were presented one at a time in a randomized order. Participants were instructed to view the headline first and then decide whether they have heard about the news (i.e., *Yes, Unsure, No*). Then, participants were asked to judge the accuracy and decide their willingness to share the news on a 5-point Likert scale, respectively (1 means "Very inaccurate" or "I would never share news like this one", 5 means "Very accurate" or "I would love to share news like this one").

After Phase 1, participants completed a demographic questionnaire that asked for age, gender, and etc., as a distraction. Then Phase 2 started, in which participants completed the same three tasks with another set of eight news as Phase 1, except that the warning labels were *removed*. At the end of Phase 2, participants completed additional questions about their computer skill, social media experience, interest in politics, factors that impact their decisions on three tasks, and their trust on the warning on a 5-point Likert scale (1 means they did not trust the warning at all, 5 means they trust the warning a great deal). Phase 3 was conducted one week after Phases 1 and 2. Each participant received emails inviting him/her to evaluate a set of 16 news (half real and half fake) as in Phase 2. The given news included a new set of eight news, and four from Phase 1, and another four from Phase 2. Each participant was

---

[1]https://www.snopes.com/fact-check/pope-francis-donald-trump-endorsement/

compensated for $0.5 for the completion of Phases 1 and 2, and participants who finished Phase 3 received an extra $0.5.

3.2 Results From Experiment 1

We recruited 800 MTurk workers on July 27, 2018. After removing nine incomplete submissions, 44 responses with both duplicate GPS coordinates (longitude and latitude provided by Quarltrics) and IP addresses, 178 responses with duplicate GPS coordinates but different IP addresses (rationales adopted from [2]), and 17 responses submitted within 3 minutes (median completion time is about 7 minutes), the numbers of participants that we accepted for the three warning conditions were 132, 136, and 138, respectively. The number of participants recruited in the *CON* condition was 146. In total, 552 participants (55.2% female) were included for data analyses. Participants' average age was 39, with 75% between 20 to 40 years. 55% of participants were college students or professionals who had a bachelor or higher degrees. The demographic distributions were similar among the four conditions.

For our analysis, selection rates of "Yes" for the recognition task were calculated for fake news and real news, respectively. For the detection task, choices of "Very inaccurate" and "Inaccurate" for fake news, and choices of "Accurate" and "Very accurate" for real news, were counted and coded as correct. The selection ratio of "Probably yes" and "I would love to share news like this one" of the sharing task were counted for fake and real news, respectively. For each task, we also measured participants' selection rates of "Unsure" option.

For each phase, specified decision rates (range from 0 to 1) of each participant for each task were transferred into arcsine values, and then entered into 2 (news' legitimacy: *fake, real*) × 2 (condition: *CON*, one warning label) mixed analysis of variances (ANOVAs), with a significance level of .05. At Phase 3, we included eight news from Phases 1 and 2, so repetition (*repeated, non-repeated*) was added as another within-subject factor for the tests.

Because the proportion of successful fake news *detection* ignores the influence from real news, we also used the SDT examining participants' sensitivity (d') and response bias (c) based on their correct detection of fake news (H) and incorrect detection of real news (FA). To accommodate H and FA rates of 0 or 1, a log-linear correction added 0.5 to the number of H, 0.5 to the number of FA, 1 to the number of signals (fake news), and 1 to the number of noise (real news) [7, 18]. Although the true d' values were underestimated by the log-linear correction [18], the relatively differences across the conditions should reflect differences apparent in the raw accuracy data. Measures of d' and c of detection decisions from Phases 1 and 2 were submitted to two-sample t-tests. At Phase 3, ANOVAs were conducted with repetition added as a within-subject factor.

Phase 1: Effect of warning. Table 1 lists the specified decision rates of each task for each condition in each phase, as well as the SDT measures for the detection task.

Recognition decisions. Across all phases, participants recognized more real news (34.6%) than fake ones (4.6%), $F_s > 99.29, p_s < .001, \eta_{ps}^2 > .459$, and were more unsure about the recognition of real news (20.4%) than fake news (7.5%), $F_s > 32.64, p_s < .001, \eta_{ps}^2 > .248$. No term involved *condition* was significant except the unsure recognition in *FC* (10.9%) was smaller than in *CON* (14.3%),

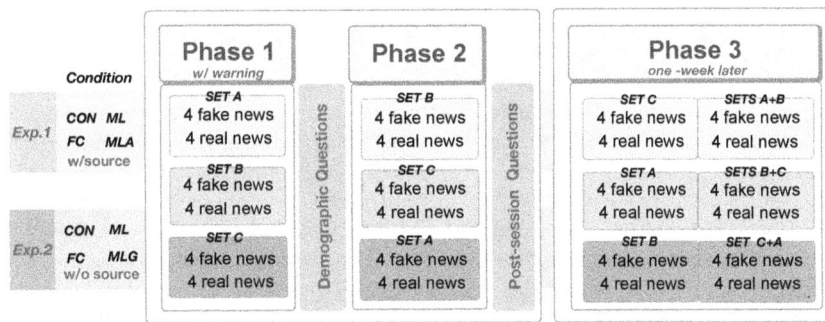

Figure 2: A flow chart showing the experimental design of each phase for both Experiments 1 and 2.

Table 1: Recognition, unsure recognition, correct detection, unsure detection, d', c, sharing, and unsure sharing results of fake and real news of each condition in each phase for Experiments 1 and 2. Sub. means subject, recog. means recognition.

Decision			Exp.1											Exp.2										
	Cond.	Sub. No.	Phase 1		Phase 2		Sub. No.	Phase 3 (New)		Phase 3 (Repeated)		Cond.	Sub. No.	Phase 1		Phase 2		Sub. No.	Phase 3 (New)		Phase 3 (Repeated)	
			Fake	Real	Fake	Real		Fake	Real	Fake	Real			Fake	Real	Fake	Real		Fake	Real	Fake	Real
Recog.	CON	146	4.3%	33.0%	3.9%	31.5%	61	4.9%	31.6%	11.1%	44.7%	CON	153	5.1%	35.8%	5.4%	34.6%	47	2.7%	23.4%	14.9%	39.4%
	FC	132	3.0%	30.3%	3.8%	28.4%	58	2.2%	29.0%	14.7%	45.1%	FC	160	7.5%	33.9%	6.3%	28.4%	60	4.6%	31.3%	16.7%	45.4%
	ML	136	5.9%	38.8%	5.7%	30.3%	58	9.1%	32.3%	17.7%	41.8%	ML	160	4.1%	31.3%	5.2%	29.4%	45	1.1%	25.6%	13.3%	47.2%
	MLA	138	4.0%	28.4%	3.8%	33.2%	50	2.0%	31.0%	9.0%	44.0%	MLG	151	3.6%	37.1%	3.8%	31.5%	54	2.3%	25.0%	13.4%	43.1%
Recog_Unsure	CON	146	8.4%	20.2%	8.7%	24.5%	61	6.6%	21.7%	16.0%	23.4%	CON	153	8.7%	19.6%	9.8%	23.5%	47	9.6%	23.4%	17.0%	27.7%
	FC	132	6.1%	15.7%	9.3%	18.9%	58	5.4%	23.2%	10.3%	19.6%	FC	160	6.1%	21.9%	10.6%	27.8%	60	9.6%	22.9%	15.4%	19.6%
	ML	136	6.4%	19.9%	12.9%	23.5%	58	8.2%	18.1%	18.1%	25.9%	ML	160	8.1%	23.6%	8.9%	25.6%	45	7.2%	20.6%	17.8%	21.7%
	MLA	138	9.1%	25.9%	9.8%	21.7%	50	7.0%	21.0%	15.5%	21.5%	MLG	151	6.8%	19.4%	10.6%	22.5%	54	11.1%	27.8%	19.0%	25.0%
Detection	CON	146	72.6%	39.7%	71.1%	39.7%	61	79.5%	38.9%	60.7%	43.9%	CON	153	70.1%	44.8%	69.0%	41.0%	47	72.3%	38.3%	61.2%	43.6%
	FC	132	79.2%	45.1%	72.0%	40.9%	58	73.7%	42.0%	62.9%	49.1%	FC	160	73.9%	42.5%	68.1%	39.4%	60	70.4%	42.9%	65.0%	51.7%
	ML	136	71.7%	38.4%	65.3%	35.7%	58	67.2%	36.6%	59.1%	42.2%	ML	160	73.8%	39.8%	65.0%	39.5%	45	72.8%	34.4%	63.9%	43.9%
	MLA	138	74.5%	39.7%	72.1%	38.9%	50	72.0%	37.0%	62.5%	47.0%	MLG	151	78.3%	43.0%	67.7%	37.6%	54	76.9%	35.2%	67.1%	43.1%
Detection_Unsure	CON	146	21.6%	35.6%	22.4%	38.7%	61	15.2%	34.8%	27.9%	34.0%	CON	153	21.1%	34.2%	23.4%	40.2%	47	16.5%	39.9%	28.7%	33.0%
	FC	132	13.8%	31.1%	20.3%	34.5%	58	20.5%	36.6%	25.9%	31.3%	FC	160	18.4%	37.2%	22.8%	40.2%	60	21.3%	40.8%	20.4%	29.6%
	ML	136	20.4%	35.8%	27.6%	42.6%	58	23.3%	35.3%	27.2%	35.3%	ML	160	19.4%	37.7%	25.5%	43.3%	45	23.9%	42.8%	28.3%	35.0%
	MLA	138	19.7%	40.4%	22.8%	38.6%	50	21.5%	36.0%	27.0%	33.0%	MLG	151	17.7%	35.8%	27.2%	41.1%	54	18.1%	39.8%	26.4%	30.6%
d'	CON	146	1.17		1.22		61	1.30		0.94		CON	153	1.20		1.22		47	1.20		0.92	
	FC	132	1.37		1.14		58	1.28		1.06		FC	160	1.33		1.19		60	1.34		1.13	
	ML	136	1.12		1.07		58	0.96		0.89		ML	160	1.26		1.17		45	1.21		1.03	
	MLA	138	1.34		1.23		50	1.11		1.05		MLG	151	1.41		1.14		54	1.26		0.97	
c	CON	146	0.04		0.09		61	-0.07		0.22		CON	153	0.11		0.15		47	0.08		0.19	
	FC	132	-0.04		0.04		58	0.06		0.21		FC	160	0.06		0.15		60	0.17		0.21	
	ML	136	0.03		0.16		58	0.06		0.23		ML	160	0.04		0.23		45	0.06		0.18	
	MLA	138	0.07		0.07		50	0.01		0.21		MLG	151	-0.004		0.14		54	-0.03		0.08	
Sharing	CON	146	6.5%	13.7%	6.9%	13.2%	61	9.8%	19.7%	13.1%	20.5%	CON	153	7.8%	15.0%	6.5%	15.0%	47	7.4%	11.2%	7.4%	15.4%
	FC	132	4.5%	15.9%	5.3%	13.6%	58	7.6%	12.1%	9.8%	16.10	FC	160	9.7%	15.2%	10.5%	20.2%	60	11.7%	13.3%	10.8%	15.8%
	ML	136	7.9%	15.4%	7.7%	14.9%	58	11.2%	18.5%	11.2%	13.40	ML	160	5.0%	13.6%	7.0%	12.0%	45	5.6%	8.9%	4.4%	9.4%
	MLA	138	4.7%	14.5%	6.9%	13.2%	50	8.5%	17.0%	5.5%	16.00	MLG	151	5.5%	15.4%	4.5%	12.6%	54	6.5%	12.5%	7.9%	15.3%
Sharing_Unsure	CON	146	6.2%	12.8%	9.1%	14.0%	61	7.4%	16.0%	8.6%	13.9%	CON	153	7.4%	13.1%	8.3%	16.7%	47	5.9%	10.1%	12.2%	11.2%
	FC	132	3.2%	8.0%	6.4%	10.0%	58	4.5%	12.1%	4.9%	15.2%	FC	160	5.6%	14.5%	9.7%	12.2%	60	7.9%	15.4%	6.3%	13.3%
	ML	136	8.8%	16.2%	11.6%	20.2%	58	9.1%	15.1%	10.8%	19.0%	ML	160	7.0%	10.9%	4.8%	12.5%	45	8.3%	9.4%	6.7%	11.1%
	MLA	138	9.2%	16.7%	9.4%	15.6%	50	6.5%	13.5%	13.5%	15.5%	MLG	151	6.8%	12.7%	11.3%	14.1%	54	9.7%	15.3%	7.4%	8.8%

$F_{(1,276)} = 4.31, p = .039, \eta_p^2 = .015$. So we focus on the analyses of detection and sharing decisions in the following parts, but return to recognition decisions in the General Discussion.

Detection decisions. Analyses of correct detection decisions revealed that main effects of news legitimacy were significant across all comparisons, $F_s > 160.56, p_s < .001, \eta_{ps}^2 > .368$. Regardless of conditions, participants correctly detected more fake news (74.4%) than real news (40.7%). Relative to CON (56.2%), the overall correct detection rate was higher for FC (62%), $F_{(1,276)} = 5.99, p = .015, \eta_p^2 = .021$, but not the other conditions (ML: 55%, MLA: 57.1%), $F_s < 1.0$. However, the two-way interaction of news legitimacy and the condition was not significant, $F < 1.0$. Thus, the FC warning not only increased participants' correct detection of fake news but also increased their correct detection of real news, suggesting that participants may rely on the presence and absence of the warning to judge the legitimacy of news headlines.

Across all comparisons, participants were more unsure in detecting real news (35.8%) than fake news (18.9%), $F_s > 56.92, p_s <$

$.001, \eta_{ps}^2 > .169$, which made sense since the warning label was presented with fake news only. Relative to CON (28.6%), only participants in FC (22.4%) showed less unsure about their detection, $F_{(1,276)} = 6.05, p = .015, \eta_p^2 = .014$, but not the other conditions (ML: 28.1%, MLA: 29.9%), $F_s < 1.0$. Also, the reduced unsure detection rate (about 6%) of the FC warning was almost equal to the increased correct detection rate of the FC warning (about 6%), suggesting that participants relied on the FC warning to make decisions mainly when they were uncertain about the news' legitimacy. The main effect of condition did not interact with news legitimacy, $F < 1.0$, indicating the effect of FC was similar between fake and real news.

SDT measures. When warning was present, participants showed minimal bias toward detecting news as fake across all conditions (c = 0.02). Compared to CON ($d' = 1.17$), participants' sensitivity to differentiate fake and real news were similar for all warnings (FC: $d' = 1.37, t_{(276)} = 1.80, p = .073$; ML: $d' = 1.12, t < 1.0$; and MLA: $d' = 1.34, t_{(282)} = 1.50, p = .135$).

Sharing decisions. Participants' overall willingness to sharing the news was low (see Table 1), but their willingness to share real news (14.9%) was higher than that of fake news (5.9%), $F_s >$ 41.78, $p_s < .001$, $\eta^2_{ps} > .130$. Neither the main effect of condition (*CON* vs. *FC* vs. *ML* vs. *MLA*: 10.1% vs. 10.2% vs. 11.7% vs. 9.6%) nor its interaction with news legitimacy were significant, $F_s < 3.51$.

Participants were more unsure about sharing real news (13.5%) than fake news (6.9%), $F_s > 28.89$, $p_s < .001$, $\eta^2_{ps} > .095$. Compared to *CON* (9.5%), participants in *FC* (5.6%) were less unsure about their decisions, $F_{(1, 276)} = 6.46$, $p = .012$, $\eta^2_p = .016$, but not participants in *ML* (12.5%) or *MLA* (12.9%) conditions, $F_s < 1.0$. Consistent with the results of unsure detection decisions, the *FC* warning also reduced participants' uncertainty during sharing decision-making.

Phase 2: Short-term effect of warning. Specified decision rates and SDT measures for Phase 2 are listed in Table 1.

Detection decision. As in Phase 1, the main effect of news legitimacy was significant, $F_s > 149.60$, $p_s < .001$, $\eta^2_{ps} > .352$. When the warning was absent in Phase 2, participants' correct detection of fake news (70.1%) was still better than that of real news (38.8%). For unsure option selection, the main effect of news legitimacy was also significant, $F_s > 67.55$, $p_s < .001$, $\eta^2_{ps} > .197$. Same as in Phase 1, participants showed less unsure of fake news (23.3%) than that of real news (38.6%). Regardless of the warning's presence or absence, more uncertainty at detecting real news than fake news probably was not due to the lack of decision aid for real news trials. No other terms were significant or approached significance.

SDT measures. When the warning was absent in Phase 2, across all conditions, participants showed similar sensitivity ($d' = 1.17$) and minimal bias toward detecting news as real ($c = 0.09$), see Table 1. Neither measures showed difference across conditions, $t_s \leq 1.35$. Taken the results of detection decision and SDT measures together, participants' reasonably accurate detection of fake news but not real news seems mainly due to their uncertainty of real news.

Sharing decision. Without warnings, participants were more willing to share real news (13.7%) than fake news (6.9%), $F_s > 24.25$, $p_s < .001$, $\eta^2_{ps} > .079$, and were more unsure about sharing of real news (15%) than fake news (9.1%), $F_s > 12.56$, $p_s < .001$, $\eta^2_{ps} > .043$. No term involved condition was significant.

Phase 3: Long-term effect of warning. A total of 225 participants returned for Phase 3. Return rates (*CON*: 41.8%, *FC*: 42.4%, *ML*: 42.7%, *MLA*: 36.2%) and demographics were similar across conditions. Decision results and SDT measures for Phase 3 also are shown in Table 1.

Detection decisions. Correct detection of fake news (67.2%) was still better than that of real news (42.1%), $F_s > 50.46$, $p_s < .001$, $\eta^2_{ps} > .305$. And the main effect of news legitimacy interacted with repetition across all comparisons, $F_s > 20.84$, $p_s < .001$, $\eta^2_{ps} > .151$. Participants correctly detect more fake news which was presented in Phase 3 only (73.2%) than those from Phases 1 and 2 (61.2%). But an opposite pattern was obtained for the real news: participants correctly detect less real news which was presented in Phase 3 only (38.7%) than those from prior phases (45.4%).

For unsure option selection, both the main effect of news legitimacy and its interaction with repetition were significant across all comparisons, $F_s > 4.03$, $p_s < .047$, $\eta^2_{ps} > .033$. Same as prior two phases, participants were more unsure at detecting real news (34.5%)

than fake news (23.5%). Besides, participants' uncertainty selection difference between repeated and non-repeated pieces of news was larger for fake news (repeated: 27.0%, non-repeated: 20.0%) than for real news (repeated: 33.4%, non-repeated: 35.7%)

SDT measures. Across conditions, there were no differences for both d' and c for the detection decisions, $F_s < 1.0$. But participants were biased to judge repeated pieces of news as real ($c = 0.22$) and non-repeated news as fake ($c = -0.28$), $F_s > 116.58$, $p_s < .001$, $\eta^2_{ps} > .517$. Also, participants tended to be less sensitive for repeated news ($d' = 0.99$) than non-repeated news ($d' = 1.16$), with the effect of repetition was significant for *FC* and *ML*, $F_s > 3.94$, $p_s > .049$, $\eta^2_{ps} > .033$, but not *MLA*, $F_{(1, 109)} = 2.95$, $p = .088$, $\eta^2_p = .026$.

Sharing decisions. One week later, the willingness to share real news (16.7%) was still higher than that of fake news (9.7%), $F_s > 14.34$, $p_s < .001$, $\eta^2_{ps} = .109$. No other effects were significant, except there was a main effect of repetition for the group of *FC*, $F_{(1, 115)} = 4.14$, $p = .044$, $\eta^2_p = .035$. Participants' willingness to share news was reduced for *FC* (11.4%) than for *CON* (15.8%). For unsure option, only the main effects of news legitimacy were significant, $F_s > 16.47$, $p_s < .001$, $\eta^2_{ps} = .131$. Again, participants showed more unsure to share real news (15%) than fake news (8.1%).

Post-session questions. 72.6% participants did not have a major or work experience in computer-related fields, and 97.5% of participants did not show concern about using computers successfully in diverse situations. 73.2% of participants indicated that they used social media, such as Facebook and Twitter, daily or a few times a week. 82.6% of participants had an interest in politics.

When asked participants to confirm factors that impact their decisions on news' credibility and sharing on social media, Most participants selected source as the most influential factor for their detection (59.2%) and sharing (46.7%) decisions. Overall, participants did not show much trust on warnings, with 31.8% gave "a great deal" or "a lot" trust, 30.8% indicated their trust was moderate, and 37.4% showed a little or no trust. A chi-squared test showed that participants' trust on warning varied across conditions, $\chi^2_{(2)} = 7.27$, $p = .026$, mainly due to more trust obtained for *FC* (40.2%) than *ML* (25%), $p_{adj.} = .023$.

3.3 Discussion

In Experiment 1, we proposed two machine-learning warning and evaluated their effects and one fact-checking warning in help individuals mitigate fake news. In Phase 1, relative to *CON* in which no warning was present, better detection results were obtained for the *FC* warning but not the *ML* and *MLA* warnings. The *FC* warning improved the correct detection of both fake and real news, suggesting that participants may use the presence and absence of warning as the criterion to make their detection decision, which is in agreement with the more trust obtained for the *FC* warning in post-session questions. When no warnings were displayed with fake news in Phases 2 and 3, the effect of *FC* disappeared. The *FC* warning did not show any short-term or long-term effect in helping participants detect fake news, probably because there were no details to inform participants about why the fake news was labeled. Although machine learning is a buzzword, participants showed less trust on the two machine learning warnings than the fact-checking warning, suggesting that they may not necessarily understand what it is and consequently, distrust its use for fake news detection.

4 EXPERIMENT 2

In Experiment 2, to increase the transparency of machine learning algorithms, we proposed a Machine-Learning-Graph (*MLG*) warning in which factors that a machine learning algorithm considers during the fact checking are provided under "Disputed by a Machine Learning Algorithm" label. Because participants identified the news source as the most influential factor in their judgment of the news headlines' legitimacy, we also assessed the robustness of the effect of the *FC* warning from Experiment 1 by removing the source information. We also included *CON* and *ML* without sources to provide baselines for evaluation.

4.1 Participants, Materials, Procedure

We recruited extra 800 MTurk workers on October 16, 2018. The requirements to participate in this study was same as Experiment 1. Furthermore, any participants who already participated in the previous study were excluded.

Materials and procedures of Experiment 2 were identical to Experiment 1 except as noted. First, we removed the source for all the 24 news headlines used in Experiment 1. Second, for the *MLG* condition, we added an extra bar chart below the warning label to represent factors that our hypothetical multi-modal machine learning algorithm considers (e.g., [20, 25, 33, 40]). Three factors, "Source Reliability", "Content Trustfulness", and "Picture/Video Truthfulness", were listed from top to bottom. A filled bar graph was accompanying each factor, and the length of each bar indicates values that the machine learning algorithm derived for the evaluation of the factor. The shorter the filled blue bar, the less reliable or accuracy for the news (see Figure 3)

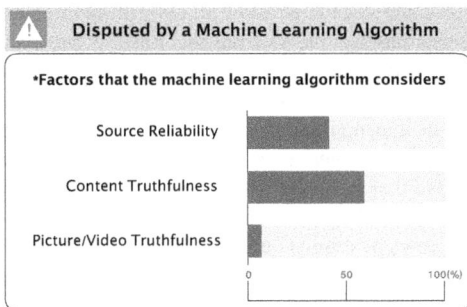

Figure 3: Machine-Learning-Graph (*MLG*) warning of Experiment 2.

4.2 Results From Experiment 2

Using the same criterion as Experiment 1, we got a total of 624 (54.9% female) valid responses, with 153, 160, 160, and 151, for *CON*, *FC*, *ML*, and *MLG*, accordingly. Participants' average age was 39.5 years. 54.2% of participants hold a bachelor or higher degree. For each task in each phase, specified decision rates and SDT measures as a function of the condition were calculated for each participant. Analyses of the decisions rates and SDT measures were conducted in the same way as Experiment 1.

Phase 1: Effect of warning. Table 1 lists the specified decision rates and SDT measures. Same as Experiment 1, participants recognized more real news (34.5%) than fake news (5.1%) regardless of conditions or phases, $F_s > 103.94, ps < .001, \eta_{ps}^2 > .512$, and were more unsure about recognizing real news (21.1%) than fake news (7.4%), $F_s > 19.83, ps < .001, \eta_{ps}^2 > .181$. Again, we focus on the analyses of detecting and sharing decisions in the following parts, but return to recognition decisions in the General Discussion.

Detection decisions. The main effect of news legitimacy was significant across all comparisons, $F_s > 130.56, ps < .001, \eta_{ps}^2 > .296$. Participants correctly detected more fake news (74.0%) than real news (42.5%). Moreover, for *MLG*, compared to *CON*, there was a two-way interaction of news legitimacy and condition, $F_{(1, 302)} = 5.48, p = .020, \eta_p^2 = .018$. Those participants made more correct decisions on fake news with the *MLG* warning (78.3%) than without warning (70.1%), but their correct decision on real news was similar between the two conditions (*CON*: 44.8%, *MLG*: 43.0%), suggesting the effectiveness of *MLG* in reducing participants' fake news susceptibility. Relative to *CON*, neither the main effect of condition nor its interaction with the condition was significant for the correct detection with *FC* or *ML* warnings, $F_s < 3.05$.

For unsure detection, compared to the *CON*, only the main effect of news legitimacy was significant across all comparisons, $F_s > 74.86, ps < .001, \eta_{ps}^2 > .194$, Participants were more uncertain about the accuracy of real news (36.2%) than fake news (19.2%).

SDT measures. When warning was present, compared to *CON* ($d' = 1.20$), participants' sensitivity to differentiate fake and real news was better for *MLG* ($d' = 1.41$), $t_{(302)} = 1.98, p = .048$, but not other conditions (*FC*: $d' = 1.33, t_{(311)} = 1.17, p = .242$, and *ML*: $d' = 1.26$, $t < 1.0$). Relative to *CON* ($c = 0.11$), participants showed similar bias for each warning [*MLG* ($c = -0.004$): $t_{(302)} = -1.84, p = .067$; *FC* ($c = 0.06$): $t < 1.0$; and and *ML* ($c = 0.04$): $t_{(311)} = -1.05, p = .294$].

Sharing decisions. Compared to *CON*, only the main effect of news legitimacy was significant for both sharing and unsure decisions for all warnings, $F_s > 15.31, ps < .001, \eta_{ps}^2 > .047$. In general, participants were more willing to share real news (14.8%) than fake news (7.0%), and they also showed more uncertainty at sharing real news (12.8%) than fake news (6.7%).

Phase 2: Short-term effect of warning. Decision results and SDT measures of each task are shown in Table 1.

Detection decisions. When the warning was absent after a short distraction task, the main effect of news legitimacy was still significant across all comparisons, $F_s > 119.49, ps < .001, \eta_{ps}^2 > .278$. Participants correct detection of fake news (67.4%) was better than that of real news (39.4%). However, the effect of *MLG* obtained in Phase 1 disappeared, $F < 1.0$. For unsure option selection, participants still showed more unsure for real news (41.2%) than fake news (24.7%) across all comparisons, $F_s > 68.11, ps < .001, \eta_{ps}^2 > .184$.

SDT measures. When the warning was absent, neither measures showed difference across conditions, $t_s \leq -1.29, ps \geq .197$.

Sharing decisions. Sharing decisions also showed the same pattern as prior results (see Table 1). Participants were more willing to share real news (15.0%) than fake news (7.2%), $F_s > 36.69, ps < .001, \eta_{ps}^2 > .106$. For unsure option selection, participants also showed more uncertainty about sharing real news (13.8%) than fake news (8.5%), $F_s > 18.69, ps < .001, \eta_{ps}^2 > .058$. Moreover, the effect of warning was revealed in all comparisons. Relative to *CON*, participants who saw the *MLG* warning in Phase 1, increased their uncertainty about sharing fake news but reduced their uncertainty about sharing real news, $F_{(1, 302)} = 4.14, p = .043, \eta_p^2 = .014$. Participants who saw the *FC* warning in Phase 1 showed the similar pattern as participants in *MLG*, $F_{(1, 311)} = 3.87, p = .050, \eta_p^2 = .012$. But their increased susceptibility of fake news was numerically smaller than that of *MLG* and reduced susceptibility of real news was numerically larger than that of *MLG*. And for participants in *ML*, they reduced their uncertainty of sharing both fake and real news, $F_{(1, 311)} = 4.61, p = .033, \eta_p^2 = .015$.

Phase 3: Long-term effect of warning. After one week, 206 participants returned for Phase 3. Return rates (*CON*: 30.7% , *FC*: 37.5%, *ML*: 28.1%, *MLG*: 35.8%) and demographics were similar across conditions. Decision results were also shown in Table 1.

Detection decisions. Same as Experiment 1, participants still correctly detected more fake news (68.8%) than real news (41.9%) one week later, $F_s > 37.17, ps < .001, \eta_{ps}^2 > .261$, and their correct detection pattern varying as a function of repetition, $F_s > 9.76, ps < .002, \eta_{ps}^2 > .098$. Across all conditions, participants' correct detection of repeated fake news (64.4%) was smaller than their correct detection of non-repeated fake news (73.1%). However, participants correctly detected more repeated real news (45.9%) than non-repeated real news (38.0%). Although participants in the *MLG* condition showed numerically better results in detecting fake news, the long-term effects of *MLG* were not significant, $F_s < 1.0$.

Participants were more unsure about the selection of real news (36.4%) than fake news (23.0%), $F_s > 18.80, ps < .001, \eta_{ps}^2 > .173$. Although the main effect of repetition was not significant, it interacted with the news legitimacy, $F_s > 10.41, ps < .002, \eta_{ps}^2 > .104$. Participants were more unsure about detecting fake news from real news which was repeated than those which were non-repeated.

SDT measures. Same as Experiment 1, there were no differences for both d' and c for the detection decisions across conditions, $F_s < 1.0$. Nevertheless, participants showed less sensitivity for the repeated news headlines ($d' = 1.01$) than for the non-repeated news headlines ($d' = 1.26$), $F_s > 4.61, ps < .035, \eta_{ps}^2 > .045$. They also tended to be biased to judge repeated news as real ($c = 0.16$) than non-repeated news ($c = 0.07$), with the effect of repetition was significant for *ML* and *MLG*, $F_s > 5.55, ps < .021, \eta_{ps}^2 > .058$, but not *FC*, $F_{(1, 105)} = 3.51, p = .064, \eta_p^2 = .032$.

Sharing decisions. Same as prior phases, participants showed more willingness to share real news (12.6%) than fake news (8.0%), $F_s > 8.42, ps < .005, \eta_{ps}^2 > .074$. Participants only showed more unsure about sharing real news than fake news for the comparison between *CON* and *FC*, $F_{(1, 105)} = 9.95, p = .002, \eta_p^2 = .087$. The two-way interaction of repetition and condition was significant for the comparison between *CON* and *MLG*, $F_{(1, 99)} = 8.62, p = .004, \eta_p^2 = .080$. Compared to *CON*, participants in *MLG* condition showed more uncertainty at sharing news that was non-repeated but less uncertainty at sharing news that were repeated.

Post-session questions. Overall results of post-session questions in Experiment 2 were similar to those from Experiment 1. 72.4% of participants did not have a major or work experience in computer-related fields, and 98.2% of participants did not concern about using computers successfully in diverse situations. 74.2% of

participants indicated that they used social media, such as Facebook and Twitter more than a few times a week, and 84.8% of participants had an interest in politics. When asked how much their trust on the warning when evaluating the accuracy of news during the study, participants did not show much trust on warnings in general, with 16.8% gave "a great deal" or "a lot" trust, 28.2% indicated their trust was moderate, and 55% showed a little or no trust. Participants' trust level also varied across warnings, $\chi_{(2)}^2 = 34.40, p < .001$. Participants showed more trust for *FC* (30.6%) than *ML* (7.5%), $p_{adj.} < .001$, and *MLG* (11.9%), $p_{adj.} < .001$, respectively.

4.3 Discussion

After removing source within each news headlines at Experiment 2, we did not obtain the effect of the *FC* warning as in Experiment 1. Compared to *CON* in which no warning was presented, the *MLG* warning improved participants' detection of fake news and increased their sensitivity to differentiate fake and real news while the *ML* warning did not. When warnings were absent in Phases 2 and 3, neither the main effect of warning nor its interaction with other factors were significant for detection decisions. However, the effect of *MLG* and *FC* were revealed in participants' increased uncertainty of sharing fake news but reduced uncertainty in sharing real news in Phase 2, suggesting a short-term effect for both warnings. Although participants showed better fake news detection with *MLG* in Phase 1, their trust on the *MLG* warning was less than that of the *FC* warning, suggesting that participants' better detection of fake news with *MLG* in Phase 1 was mostly due to their reliance on the factors that presented within the warning.

5 GENERAL DISCUSSION

Across two experiments, we proposed three machine-learning warnings and evaluated their effects and a fact-checking warning in helping individuals mitigate fake news. Both decision rates and SDT measures showed the effect of *MLG* warning in helping participants differentiate fake news from real ones. When no warnings were displayed in Phase 2, although the *MLG* warning did not impact individuals' detection decisions, participants increased their uncertainty in sharing fake news but reduced their uncertainty in sharing real news, suggesting a short-term effect of the warning.

We obtained that the effect of *FC* warning increased participants' correct detection of both fake and real news when the source was included in news headlines but not when sources were excluded. Although the *FC* warning did not impact individuals' detection decisions when the source was excluded, they increased participants' uncertainty in sharing fake news and reduced their uncertainty in sharing real news when the warning was not displayed in Phase 2, suggesting a short-term effect. Thus, our results did not replicate [9], but are somewhat consistent with [27], showing a small effect of the warning. With the *FC* warning, participants not only increased the correct detection of fake news to which the warning was attached but also the correct detection of real news, suggesting that participants probably relied on the presence and absence of the warning to make the detection decision.

5.1 Limited Effect of Warning Labels

All the warnings that have been implemented in current and prior studies (e.g., [27]) revealed a small effect on mitigating the fake news. One possible reason is that all those proposed warnings are passive, which indicate misinformation to participants without interrupting their primary task. i.e., viewing news headlines and obtaining new information. Prior studies on cybersecurity, e.g., phishing [19, 22], showed that participants ignored passive security indicators and relied instead mainly on the website contents to decide the trustworthiness of a web page. The results of current Experiment 1 showed a similar pattern, in that participants mainly relied on the source of news to make the news' legitimacy decisions even when the warning labels were present. Therefore, one way to improve the effectiveness of warning is to make it active, which will capture users' attention and force users to choose one of the options that were presented by the warning [12, 14, 41].

However, a zero-day exploit of fake news will leave no opportunity for automatic detection and prevention, and people need to make a decision on their own [29]. Therefore, the ability to tell fake news from real ones is an important skill for individuals to acquire. Training is one promising approach to address individuals' inability to differentiate fake and real news. Also, prior studies in cybersecurity provided evidences that knowledge gained from training enhanced the effectiveness of phishing warnings [43]. Therefore, another way to improve the effect of warning is to embed training within the warning and use each warning as an opportunity to train users on how to mitigate fake news.

5.2 Better Recognition of Real News

A point to note about the present study is that overall participants recognized more real news than fake news, and also showed more uncertainty at recognizing real news than fake news. "Recognition" and "unsure" decisions represent two distinct processes for recognition memory, *recollection*, and *familiarity* [21]. The distinction is that people could recognize a piece of news as familiar but not being able to recollect where he or she previously saw it.

Across three phases, participants appeared reasonably accurate at detecting fake news, but their correct detection of real news was less than chance. SDT measures did not show that participants were biased in judging news as fake, thus the poor detection of real news was mainly due to participants' more uncertainty about detecting real news than fake news. A further Pearson correlation analysis revealed that the unsure recognition of real news had a statistically significant positive linear relationship with the unsure detection of real news for both experiments, $p_s < .001$. The strength of the association was approximately moderate for Experiment 1, $r = .294$, and there was a small correlation $r = .245$ for Experiment 2.

Consistent with [17], our results showed that participants' willingness to share news was low in general and was lower for fake news than real news. Moreover, our study revealed that participants were more uncertain about sharing real news than fake news. For both experiments, Pearson correlation analysis showed a significant positive association between unsure recognition and the unsure sharing, $p_s < .003$, but with a small correlation, $r = .268$ for Experiment 1, and $r = .119$ for Experiment 2.

Altogether, the better recognition and more uncertainty of real news suggest that participants may have been exposed to those pieces of real news previously, and their familiarity (uncertainty)

with real news seems to have impaired their evaluation of news' accuracy and their sharing decisions.

5.3 Effect of Repetition

At Phase 3, for those pieces of news that were repeated, participants showed better recognition. Moreover, the increase of recognition was more evident for real news than fake news, suggesting the repetition increased more recollection of real news than fake news. Consistent with the effect of repetition obtained by [27], SDT measures further revealed that participants were less sensitive and more biased to judge news headlines as real for news from prior phases than the news that presented in Phase 3 only. Participants' unsure detection was also increased for the repeated pieces of news, however, the increase was more evident for fake news than real news, suggesting that the repetition mainly increased participants' familiarity (uncertainty) of fake news. Therefore, our study provided evidence that the repetition probably impacts the detection of fake and real news differently.

Human memory has been described an optimization of information retrieval, which uses the statistics derived from past experience to estimate which knowledge will be currently relevant [1]. Besides allowing individuals remembering objects and events that they have actual experience, human memory systems are subject to distortion, bias, and the creation of illusions [23, 32]. Combining the overall better recognition of real news, increased recollection of repeated real news and increased familiarity with repeated fake news, our study further indicates the important role that memory plays in individuals' belief in fake news. Further research should be conducted to explore the extent to which memory affects individuals' belief in fake news.

5.4 Limitations

In our experiments, the effectiveness of warning labels was evaluated with a convenience sample of Amazon MTurk workers, who tended to be young, more educated, and more tech-savvy than the general public. Thus, the generalization of current findings to participants with different demographics needs to be further examined. In addition, the experiment design is limited in its ecological validity. We considered a more ecologically valid method, such as providing social media interface during the study, but we decided to present news headlines to exclude extraneous variables that may have an effect on the outcomes, which increased our confidence of the internal validity of obtained results. Note that such a design was the same as the prior studies [9, 27], which made our results comparable to the prior ones.

Another possible confound was that participants may have experienced the fact-checking warning previously but not the machine learning warnings. Better performance only obtained for the *MLG* warning but not *ML* and *MLA* warnings indicate that novelty may be not critical. Finally, all news headlines in our study are politically related, so generalizing the findings to other types of misinformation needs to be further investigated. Finally, in this study, we did not consider participants' political stance as a factor due to our main interest in warning labels and prior study showed that the partisan bias did not significantly affect participants' susceptibility to fake news [28]. However, recently Gao et al. [15] obtained results indicating that the warning label are more effective for participants in the liberal group than participants in the conservative group. Therefore, to understand whether pre-existing political stance interacts with a machine-learning warning, the future studies can consider political stance of participants as an extra factor and measure how it impacts participants' belief in fake news.

6 CONCLUSION

In this work, we conducted two online experiments to understand the impact of machine-learning warning on reducing individuals' fake news susceptibility. Each experiment consisted of three phases examining participants' recognition, detection, and sharing of fake news, respectively. Across three machine-learning warnings, the Machine-Learning-Graph warning increased participants' sensitivity in differentiating fake from real news, but participants showed limited trusted on it. Our study results imply that a transparent machine learning algorithm (that explains the detail results) may be critical to improving individuals' fake news detection but not necessarily to increase their trust.

7 ACKNOWLEDGEMENT

This work was in part supported by NSF awards #1742702, #1820609, and #1915801, and ORAU-directed R&D program in 2018.

REFERENCES

[1] John R Anderson and Robert Milson. 1989. Human memory: An adaptive perspective. *Psychological Review* 96, 4 (1989), 703–719.
[2] Hui Bai. 2018. Evidence that a large amount of low quality responses on MTurk can be detected with repeated GPS coordinates. (2018). https://goo.gl/19KCHG.
[3] David Bawden and Lyn Robinson. 2009. The dark side of information: Overload, anxiety and other paradoxes and pathologies. *J. of Information Science* 35, 2 (2009), 180–191.
[4] Gaurav Bhatt, Aman Sharma, Shivam Sharma, Ankush Nagpal, Balasubramanian Raman, and Ankush Mittal. 2018. Combining neural, statistical and external features for fake news stance identification. In *The Web Conf. (WWW)*. 1353–1357.
[5] Jenna Burrell. 2016. How the machine 'thinks': Understanding opacity in machine learning algorithms. *Big Data & Society* 3, 1 (2016), 1–12.
[6] Carole Cadwalladr. 2017. The great British Brexit robbery: how our democracy was hijacked. https://tinyurl.com/lkhgkdk. (2017). Accessed: 2019-01-10.
[7] Casey Inez Canfield, Baruch Fischhoff, and Alex Davis. 2016. Quantifying phishing susceptibility for detection and behavior decisions. *Human Factors* 58, 8 (2016), 1158–1172.
[8] Michaela Cavanagh. 2018. Climate change: 'Fake news', real fallout. (2018). https://goo.gl/tCbwYq Accessed: 2019-01-10.
[9] Katherine Clayton, Spencer Blair, Jonathan A Busam, and et al. 2019. Real solutions for fake news? Measuring the effectiveness of general warnings and fact-check tags in reducing belief in false stories on social media. *Political Behavior* (2019), 1–23. https://doi.org/10.1007/s11109-019-09533-0
[10] Niall J Conroy, Victoria L Rubin, and Yimin Chen. 2015. Automatic deception detection: Methods for finding fake news. In *78th ASIS&T Annual Meeting: Information Science with Impact: Research in and for the Community*, Vol. 52. 1–4.
[11] Amit Datta, Michael Carl Tschantz, and Anupam Datta. 2015. Automated experiments on ad privacy settings. In *Privacy Enhancing Technologies*. 92–112.
[12] Serge Egelman, Lorrie Faith Cranor, and Jason Hong. 2008. You've been warned: An empirical study of the effectiveness of web browser phishing warnings. In *ACM CHI*. ACM, 1065–1074.
[13] Craig Silverman et al. 2016. Hyperpartisan Facebook pages are publishing false and misleading information at an alarming rate. (2016). https://goo.gl/6pWtTT
[14] Adrienne Porter Felt, Alex Ainslie, Robert W Reeder, Sunny Consolvo, Somas Thyagaraja, Alan Bettes, Helen Harris, and Jeff Grimes. 2015. Improving SSL warnings: Comprehension and adherence. In *ACM CHI*. ACM, 2893–2902.
[15] Mingkun Gao, Ziang Xiao, Karrie Karahalios, and Wai-Tat Fu. 2018. To label or not to label: The effect of stance and credibility labels on readers' selection and perception of news articles. *ACM CHI* 2, CSCW (2018), 55.
[16] David M Green and John A Swets. 1966. *Signal detection theory and psychophysics*. Wiley, New York, NY.
[17] Andrew Guess, Jonathan Nagler, and Joshua Tucker. 2019. Less than you think: Prevalence and predictors of fake news dissemination on Facebook. *Science Advances* 5, 1 (2019), eaau4586.
[18] Michael J Hautus. 1995. Corrections for extreme proportions and their biasing effects on estimated values of d'. *Behavior Research Methods, Instruments, & Computers* 27, 1 (1995), 46–51.
[19] Amir Herzberg and Ahmad Gbara. 2004. *Trustbar: Protecting (even naive) web users from spoofing and phishing attacks*. Technical Report. Cryptology ePrint Archive, Report 2004/155. http://eprint. iacr. org/2004/155.
[20] Zhiwei Jin, Juan Cao, Han Guo, Yongdong Zhang, and Jiebo Luo. 2017. Multimodal fusion with recurrent neural networks for rumor detection on microblogs. In *ACM Multimedia Conf.* 795–816.
[21] Colleen M Kelley and Larry L Jacoby. 2000. Recollection and familiarity: Process-dissociation. In *The Oxford handbook of memory*, Endel E. Tulving and Fergus I. M. Craik (Eds.). Oxford University Press, New York, 215–228.
[22] Eric Lin, Saul Greenberg, Eileah Trotter, David Ma, and John Aycock. 2011. Does domain highlighting help people identify phishing sites?. In *ACM CHI*. ACM, 2075–2084.
[23] Elizabeth F Loftus. 2005. Planting misinformation in the human mind: A 30-year investigation of the malleability of memory. *Learning & Memory* 12, 4 (2005), 361–366.
[24] Neil A Macmillan and Douglas C Creelman. 2004. *Detection theory: A user's guide*. Lawrence Erlbaum, Mahwah, NJ.
[25] Shivam B Parikh and Pradeep K Atrey. 2018. Media-rich fake news detection: A survey. In *IEEE Conf. on Multimedia Information Processing and Retrieval (MIPR)*. IEEE, 436–441.
[26] Frank Pasquale. 2015. *The black box society: The secret algorithms that control money and information*. Harvard University Press, Cambridge, MA.
[27] Gordon Pennycook, Tyrone Cannon, and David G Rand. 2018. Prior exposure increases perceived accuracy of fake news. *J. of Experimental Psychology: General* 147, 12 (2018), 1865–1880.
[28] Gordon Pennycook and David G Rand. 2018. Lazy, not biased: Susceptibility to partisan fake news is better explained by lack of reasoning than by motivated reasoning. *Cognition* (2018). https://doi.org/10.1016/j.cognition.2018.06.011
[29] Robert W Proctor and Jing Chen. 2015. The role of human factors/ergonomics in the science of security: decision making and action selection in cyberspace. *Human Factors* 57, 5 (2015), 721–727.
[30] Hannah Rashkin, Eunsol Choi, Jin Yea Jang, Svitlana Volkova, and Yejin Choi. 2017. Truth of varying shades: Analyzing language in fake news and political fact-checking. In *Conf. on Empirical Methods in Natural Language Processing (EMNLP)*. 2931–2937.
[31] Marco Tulio Ribeiro, Sameer Singh, and Carlos Guestrin. 2016. Why should i trust you?: Explaining the predictions of any classifier. In *ACM SIGKDD int'l conf. on knowledge discovery and data mining (KDD)*. ACM, 1135–1144.
[32] Henry L Roediger III and Kathleen B McDermott. 2000. Tricks of memory. *Current Directions in Psychological Science* 9, 4 (2000), 123–127.
[33] Natali Ruchansky, Sungyong Seo, and Yan Liu. 2017. Csi: A hybrid deep model for fake news detection. In *ACM Conf. on Information and Knowledge Management (CIKM)*. ACM, 797–806.
[34] Scott Shane. 2017. From headline to photograph, a fake news masterpiece. (2017). https://goo.gl/tmiw7s
[35] Kai Shu, Amy Sliva, Suhang Wang, Jiliang Tang, and Huan Liu. 2017. Fake news detection on social media: A data mining perspective. *ACM SIGKDD Explorations Newsletter* 19, 1 (2017), 22–36.
[36] Kai Shu, Suhang Wang, and Huan Liu. 2018. Understanding user profiles on social media for fake news detection. In *IEEE Conf. on Multimedia Information Processing and Retrieval (MIPR)*. 430–435.
[37] John A Swets. 1964. Signal detection and recognition in human observers: Contemporary readings. Wiley, New York, NY.
[38] Eugenio Tacchini, Gabriele Ballarin, Marco L Della Vedova, Stefano Moret, and Luca de Alfaro. 2017. Some like it hoax: Automated fake news detection in social networks. *arXiv preprint arXiv:1704.07506* (2017).
[39] Sander Van der Linden, Anthony Leiserowitz, Seth Rosenthal, and Edward Maibach. 2017. Inoculating the public against misinformation about climate change. *Global Challenges* 1, 2 (2017).
[40] Yaqing Wang, Fenglong Ma, Zhiwei Jin, Ye Yuan, Guangxu Xun, Kishlay Jha, Lu Su, and Jing Gao. 2018. Eann: Event adversarial neural networks for multimodal fake news detection. In *Proceedings of the 24th ACM SIGKDD International Conference on Knowledge Discovery & Data Mining*. ACM, 849–857.
[41] Min Wu, Robert C Miller, and Simson L Garfinkel. 2006. Do security toolbars actually prevent phishing attacks?. In *ACM CHI*. ACM, 601–610.
[42] Aiping Xiong, Robert W Proctor, Weining Yang, and Ninghui Li. 2017. Is domain highlighting actually helpful in identifying phishing web pages? *Human Factors* 59, 4 (2017), 640–660.
[43] Aiping Xiong, Robert W Proctor, Weining Yang, and Ninghui Li. 2018. Embedding training within warnings improves skills of identifying phishing webpages. *Human Factors* (2018). https://doi.org/10.1177/0018720818810942

A Reverse Turing Test for Detecting Machine-Made Texts

Jialin Shao
Jialin_Shao@outlook.com
Beijing University of Technology
Beijing, China

Adaku Uchendu
azu5030@psu.edu
The Pennsylvania State University
University Park, PA, USA

Dongwon Lee
dongwon@psu.edu
The Pennsylvania State University
University Park, PA, USA

ABSTRACT

As AI technologies rapidly advance, the artifacts created by machines will become prevalent. As recent incidents by the *Deepfake* illustrate, then, being able to differentiate man-made vs. machine-made artifacts, especially in social media space, becomes more important. In this preliminary work, in this regard, we formulate such a classification task as the *Reverse Turing Test* (RTT) and investigate on the contemporary status to be able to classify man-made vs. machine-made texts. Studying real-life machine-made texts in three domains of financial earning reports, research articles, and chatbot dialogues, we found that the classification of man-made vs. machine-made texts can be done at least as accurate as 0.84 in F1 score. We also found some differences between man-made and machine-made in sentiment, readability, and textual features, which can help differentiate them.

CCS CONCEPTS

• **Computing methodologies** → *Supervised learning by classification*; • **Applied computing** → *Document analysis*.

KEYWORDS

Reverse turing test, supervised learning, machine-made text

ACM Reference Format:
Jialin Shao, Adaku Uchendu, and Dongwon Lee. 2019. A Reverse Turing Test for Detecting Machine-Made Texts. In *11th ACM Conference on Web Science (WebSci '19), June 30–July 3, 2019, Boston, MA, USA*. ACM, New York, NY, USA, 5 pages. https://doi.org/10.1145/3292522.3326042

1 INTRODUCTION

Recent advancements in AI technologies have enabled the machine-generation of realistic artifacts that are a little different from genuine artifacts. For instance, BigGAN [2] or Deepfake[1] introduced novel synthesis methods capable of generating realistic (but fake) images or videos, respectively. In the domain of "text" that is the focus of this work, similarly, the advancement of *Natural Language Generation* (NLG) has led to the automation of realistic text generation. It has advanced from heavy rule/template-based approaches to algorithm-based automatic methods using data ontology and

[1] https://github.com/deepfakes/faceswap

Figure 1: Turing Test (left) vs. Reverse Turing Test (right)

user inputs. Currently, for instance, news media such as Associated Press, Forbes, and LA times reportedly use machine learning methods to generate realistic-looking financial earning and weather reports [10]. As such novel technologies become more sophisticated, however, pitfalls and risk of technologies also rapidly increase. Adversaries may use such technologies to generate realistic artifacts to trick naive users in fraudulent activities (e.g., a fake image in a tweet to spread fake news or machine-made chatbot conversation in a phishing scam). To prepare for such a cybersecurity problem better, in this work, we ask if one can accurately distinguish machine-made texts from man-made ones by solely looking at the contents of texts.

This research question that we pose bears a similarity to the *Turing Test*, developed by Alan Turing in 1950, that determines if a human judge (A) is observing a machine (B) or human (C) in some task. If the machine (B) shows the behavior indistinguishable from a human, thus fools the human judge (A), it is said to "passed the Turing Test." In our setting, we aim to develop a machine learning model (A') that determines if the give texts in question were generated by a machine (B) or human (C). To emphasize the fact that the observing judge is a machine (A'), not a human (A), this problem is referred to as the **Reverse Turing Test (RTT)**[2]. Figure 1 illustrates the subtle but important difference.

The underlying hypothesis of this research is to ask if there exists a subtle but fundamental difference (e.g., information loss or patterns of expressions) that can differentiate man-made texts from machine-made ones. As AI technologies rapidly advance, of course, such differences will diminish, making the RTT problem harder. This preliminary work, therefore, aims to investigate on the contemporary status to distinguish machine-made vs. man-made texts. As the work [11] recently showed that the "eye blinking" could be exploited to detect AI-generated videos, we hope to find a similar finding in machine-made texts.

Studying real-life machine-made texts in three domains—e.g., financial earning reports, research articles, and chatbot dialogues, our preliminary results indicate that it is indeed possible to accurately detect machine-made texts *for now* with the classification accuracy in the range of 0.84 – 1 in F1 score. Through the lens such as sentiment analysis, readability analysis, and topic model analysis, we show that man-made texts can be distinguished from machine-made ones.

[2] https://tinyurl.com/yc62z7wk

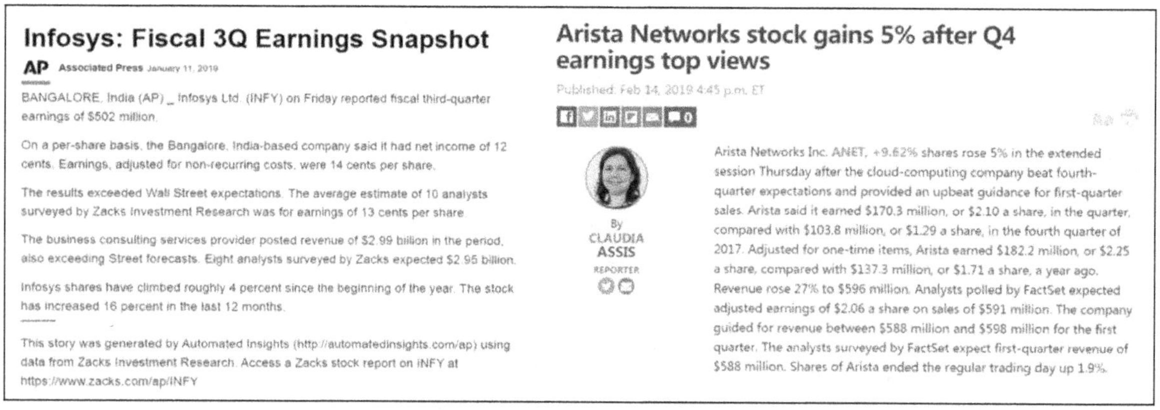

Infosys: Fiscal 3Q Earnings Snapshot

AP Associated Press January 11, 2019

BANGALORE, India (AP) _ Infosys Ltd. (INFY) on Friday reported fiscal third-quarter earnings of $502 million.

On a per-share basis, the Bangalore, India-based company said it had net income of 12 cents. Earnings, adjusted for non-recurring costs, were 14 cents per share.

The results exceeded Wall Street expectations. The average estimate of 10 analysts surveyed by Zacks Investment Research was for earnings of 13 cents per share.

The business consulting services provider posted revenue of $2.99 billion in the period, also exceeding Street forecasts. Eight analysts surveyed by Zacks expected $2.95 billion.

Infosys shares have climbed roughly 4 percent since the beginning of the year. The stock has increased 16 percent in the last 12 months.

This story was generated by Automated Insights (http://automatedinsights.com/ap) using data from Zacks Investment Research. Access a Zacks stock report on INFY at https://www.zacks.com/ap/INFY

Arista Networks stock gains 5% after Q4 earnings top views

Published: Feb 14, 2019 4:45 p.m. ET

By CLAUDIA ASSIS REPORTER

Arista Networks Inc. ANET, +9.62% shares rose 5% in the extended session Thursday after the cloud-computing company beat fourth-quarter expectations and provided an upbeat guidance for first-quarter sales. Arista said it earned $170.3 million, or $2.10 a share, in the quarter, compared with $103.8 million, or $1.29 a share, in the fourth quarter of 2017. Adjusted for one-time items, Arista earned $182.2 million, or $2.25 a share, compared with $137.3 million, or $1.71 a share, a year ago. Revenue rose 27% to $596 million. Analysts polled by FactSet expected adjusted earnings of $2.06 a share on sales of $591 million. The company guided for revenue between $588 million and $598 million for the first quarter. The analysts surveyed by FactSet expect first-quarter revenue of $588 million. Shares of Arista ended the regular trading day up 1.9%.

Figure 2: Examples of machine-made (left) and man-made (right) earning reports.

2 RELATED WORK

Natural Language Generation (NLG) has matured from the most basic template-based methods to coded grammatical and statistical software. It has fostered the generation of tailored reports for specific audiences [1, 6]. Companies, such as the Associated Press, Forbes and the LA Times, have adopted this NLG technology to generate weather forecast, earnings reports, and sports recap news [9].

While NLG evaluation is marked by a great deal of variety, it is hard to compare them due to the diverse inputs and different evaluation purpose and criteria. Currently, the evaluation of NLG outputs is dominated by two methods: (1) one relying on human judgments (i.e., *Turing Test*) which is subjective, and (2) the other using corpora and (i.e., *Reverse Turing Test*) [6]. The *Turing Test* mainly focuses on clarity, fluency, and readability. However, as judged by human evaluators, it may exhibit high variance across domains [3]. For the *Reverse Turing Test*, a variety of corpus-based metrics (e.g., BLEU, CIDEr and ROUGE) are used to evaluate translation, academic summarization, and image description [12, 13, 17]. While the aforementioned methods are concerned with the evaluation of the outputs from NLG, [4] has used TF-IDF and comprehensive profiles as features to build a SVM classifier to identify man-made texts. Related, [16] used meta data in a cluster model to find strong predictors for social bots in twitter.

3 DATASET

We have collected or generated man-made vs. machine-made texts in three domains as follows:

(1) **Academic Papers**: Using *SCIgen*[3], an automatic CS paper generator, developed at MIT, we have generated 908 synthetically-generated Computer Science papers. The collection is named as raw_paper$_M$. For the man-made academic papers, next, we first collected an open-source dataset from Kaggle, which contains papers published in the AAAI Neural Information Processing Systems (NIPS) conferences, and papers from the *Translation Archive* that includes papers from 52 different computer science conferences. Due to the influence from NIPS, note that man-made academic paper dataset has more AI flavour. A total of 7,876 papers in this collection is named as raw_paper$_H$.

(2) **Earnings Reports**: For machine-made news articles, we crawled and scraped data from media websites, such as Yahoo Finance and Forbes. Two leading companies, *Automated Insights* and *Narrative Science*, are in partnership with Yahoo Finance and Forbes, respectively, providing auto-generated financial earning reports. Merging the reports of these two websites together and removing each company's canned copyright message (e.g., "this story is generated by Automated Insights"), we obtained a total of 4,210 earning reports, named as raw_report$_M$. For man-made news articles, next, we chose earnings report of similar lengths and topics, written by human reporters. We collected 2,100 earnings reports from a financial website MarketWatch[4] and named it as raw_report$_H$. Figure 2 provides the examples of man-made vs. machine-made earnings reports in our datasets.

(3) **Chatbot Dialogues**: The chatbot dialogue data comprises of machine-made and man-made texts from a chatbot competition, known as the Society for the Study of Artificial

Table 1: Summary of three datasets.

Dataset Name	# of files	AVG # of words	S.D. # of words
raw_paper$_M$	908	2,087.91	229.56
raw_paper$_H$	7,876	3,835.14	1,846.20
paper$_M$	908	2,090.11	241.99
paper$_H$	1031	2,554.87	602.76
raw_report$_M$	4,210	158.89	47.76
raw_report$_H$	2,100	139.97	57.74
report$_M$	1,450	159.00	33.20
report$_H$	1,516	140.00	27.42
raw_dialog$_M$	993	7.99	5.04
raw_dialog$_H$	993	11.18	10.59
dialog$_M$	979	6.52	2.23
dialog$_H$	955	7.87	4.90

[3]https://pdos.csail.mit.edu/archive/scigen/

[4]https://www.marketwatch.com/

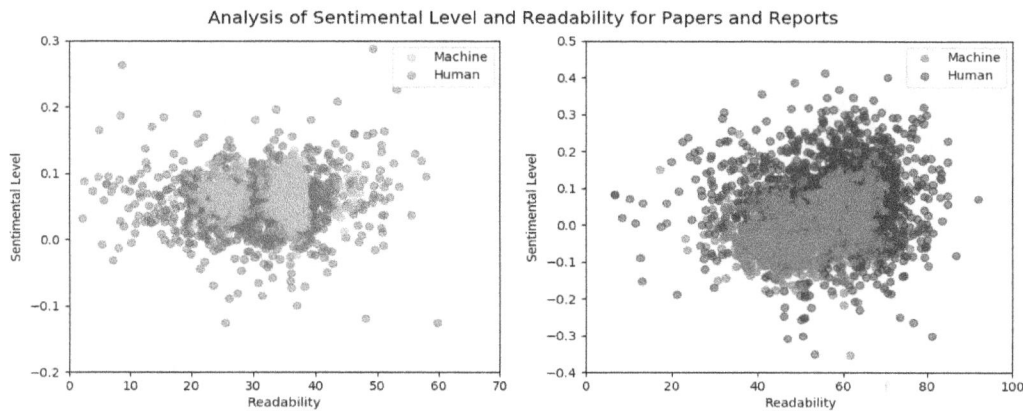

Figure 3: Readability and sentimental level analysis of papers datasets (left) and of reports datasets (right).

Intelligence and Simulation of Behaviour (AISB)[5]. In this competition, a human judge (A) converses with a counterpart who can be either another human (B) or a chatbot (C) (i.e., identity hidden). The response from the counterpart is generated in texts and rated by the human judge (A) for the ability to pass the Turing Test (i.e., how response is likely to be written by a human). The dataset, consisting of 993 dialogues, is named as raw_dialog_M and raw_dialog_H, for the machine-made and man-made texts, respectively.

In pre-processing three datasets, we first eliminate outliers in each dataset according to the 3-sigma principle, which is to say that the length of texts in each dataset is within the three standard deviations of mean length. Capital letters are converted to lowercase and numbers within texts are ignored. Words shorter than 3 characters are also removed. Some stop words, which are provided by Scikit-learn [14], are taken out. To make the dataset of machine-made and man-made texts more comparable, in addition, we delete the machine-made texts whose length deviates too much from the average length of human-made dataset. At the end, we obtain three pairs of human-made vs. machine-made texts with comparable lengths. The pre-processed human-made vs. machine-made data is then named as $paper_H$, $paper_M$, $report_H$, $report_M$, $dialog_H$, and $dialog_M$, respectively. Summary of statistics is shown in Table 1. The final pre-processed datasets are available for download at GitHub[6].

4 CHARACTERIZING MAN-MADE VS. MACHINE-MADE

To understand the characteristics of man-made and machine-made texts better, we investigate the datasets from three angles: (1) sentiment analysis, (2) readability via Flesch Reading Ease [5], and (3) topic model via Latent Dirichlet Allocation (LDA) as follows:

(1) **Sentiment**: By borrowing the definition of "polarity" from *Textblob*[7], we define the sentiment level as a float value within the range $[-1.0, 1.0]$ where 0 indicates neutral, +1.0

[5]https://www.aisb.org.uk/
[6]https://tinyurl.com/y9d4wh3j
[7]https://textblob.readthedocs.io/en/dev/

indicates a very positive sentiment, and -1.0 represents a very negative sentiment. Figure 3, for instance, shows the distributions of sentiment scores in Y-axis from two datasets– i.e., earnings reports ($report_M$ and $report_H$) and academic papers ($paper_M$ and $paper_H$). In both datasets, note that the range of sentiment scores for man-made texts is wider and stronger than that for machine-made ones.

(2) **Readability**: The readability is defined by *the Flesch Reading Ease* as a formula, that generates a score usually between 0 and 100. A higher readability score means that text is more readable. In general, a score between $70 - 80$ is viewed as equivalent to the *7th* grade level. Figure 3 shows the distributions of readability scores in X-axis from the same two datasets. Similar to sentiment, readability of man-made texts varies more widely. However, in general, it is not trivial to differentiate man-made from machine-made by only using readability scores. Additionally, for the chatbot dataset, due to short texts, the differences in both sentiment and readability between man-made and machine-made texts are shown to be negligible.

(3) **Topic Model**: To further explore the differences between man-made and machine-made datasets, we conducted a topic model analysis. Using LDA, we found out that even though each pair of man-made and machine-made datasets are in the same domain (such as earnings reports, computer science academic papers, and chatbot dialogues), there still exist differentiating factors in their textual expressions, attitudes, and concerns. For the academic papers datasets ($paper_M$ and $paper_H$), the most notable top topic words in $paper_H$ include: *datasets*, *model*, *learning*, and *training*. On the other hand, $paper_M$ talks more about *algorithms*, *evaluation*, *methodology*, and *results*. This is expected as $paper_M$, generated by SCIgen, covers broader and older computer science topics, algorithm and methodology, while $paper_H$ covers more recent and AI-ish topics. Second, for the earning report datasets, the top topic words of $report_M$ include *analysts*, *reported*, and *estimate*, that tend to quote analysts' point of view. In addition, $report_M$ prefers to quote numbers. On the other hand,

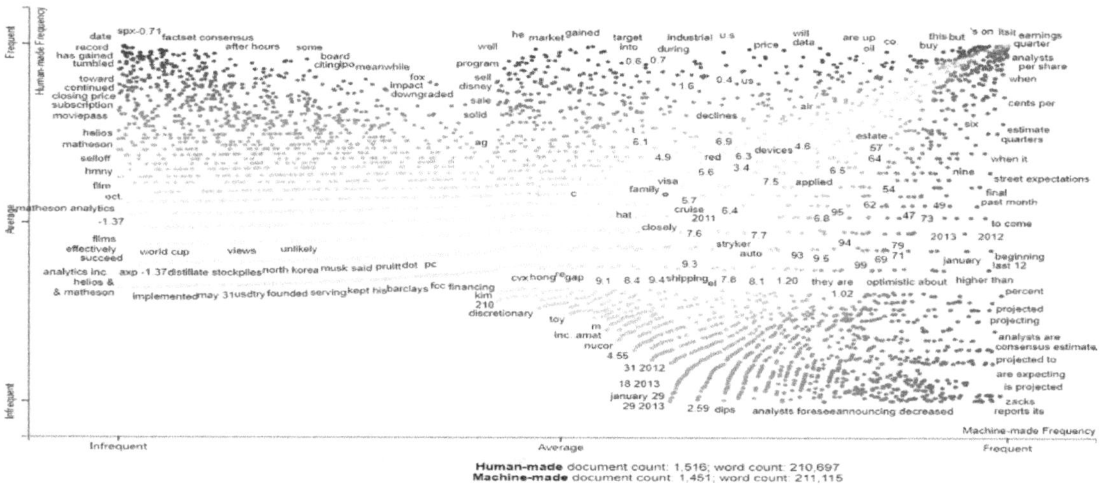

Human-made document count: 1,516; word count: 210,697
Machine-made document count: 1,461; word count: 211,115

Figure 4: Term associations of earnings reports dataset.

report$_H$ has a set of notable topic words, including *gained* and *gains*, that sometimes contribute to the positive sentiment scores. In order to visualize the words and phrases that represent the characteristics of machine-made and human-made texts better, we use *Scattertext* [8] to plot the the words of the earning reports datasets, shown in Figure 4. The X-axis and Y-axis indicate the term frequency in machine-made and human-made texts, respectively. For instance, the upper-left area in Figure 4 shows the terms frequently occurring in man-made texts, while the lower-right area shows the frequent terms in machine-made texts. As to the dialogue datasets, there were no particularly interesting topic words, except that many dialogues in dialog$_H$ contain question-types as the original corpus focused on question-answering scenarios.

5 PREDICTING MAN-MADE VS. MACHINE-MADE

Based on the characterization, in this section, we test if it is possible to build a prediction model to differentiate between man-made and machine-made texts. We studied mainly two types of features in building a machine learning model: (1) syntactic frequency based feature via TF-IDF, and (2) linguistic context based word embedding via word2vec [7].

In order to achieve an accurate classification, we built a classifier using Support Vector Machines (SVM), a machine learning algorithm trained to maximize the margin of separation between positive and negative examples [15]. We tag different class labels for machine-made and man-made texts and split the training and test sets in the 8:2 ratio. Since the number of features is similar to the number of samples in the dataset, we used the Linear Kernel. We tested each model using 10-fold cross validation, with arbitrarily generated seeds to ensure the randomness as much as possible. All classifications are evaluated using F1 score which considers both precision and recall of the test. The model building was performed using Scikit-learn.

Figure 5 shows the F1 scores of classification over all three datasets–i.e., academic papers, earning reports, and chatbot dialogues. X-axis indicates % of text used in learning. For instance, 50% means that we used the half of the contents in the training data in learning. A few findings are notable. First, word2vec based features in general outperform TF-IDF based ones. Linguistic context and subtle differences in semantics captured by word2vec are able to distinguish man-made from machine-made texts much better than a simple frequency-based scheme. Second, after about 50% of training contents are used in learning, the SVM model for papers and reports datasets can differentiate man-made vs. machine-made texts with a near perfect accuracy. However, when less than 50% of contents are used in learning, the accuracy significantly drops, especially using TF-IDF features. On the other hand, it is interesting to see that using as little as 20% of contents in texts, word2vec achieves over 0.95 in F1 score. Finally, for the dialogues dataset that has much less contents than the other two datasets, the classification accuracy is comparatively lower–i.e., 0.84 in F1 score using word2vec and degrades to 0.82 in F1 score using TF-IDF.

6 DISCUSSION

There are several limitations in our study. First, because many commercial NLG technologies are still trade secrets, it was difficult to get sufficient amount of NLG-generated machine-made datasets. In addition, due to the limited amount of texts, classifiers took in length and genre features which could lead to a small degree of overfitting.

Second, as the topics and genres between man-made and machine-made texts in our datasets are not completely aligned, one may not achieve the reported F1 scores for more challenging datasets. Reversely, at the same time, one could improve the prediction accuracy further by using more more powerful learning models (e.g., deep learning) or sophisticated features.

That said, from the prediction experiments, it is clear that using simple features such as TF-IDF or word2vec, it is already possible

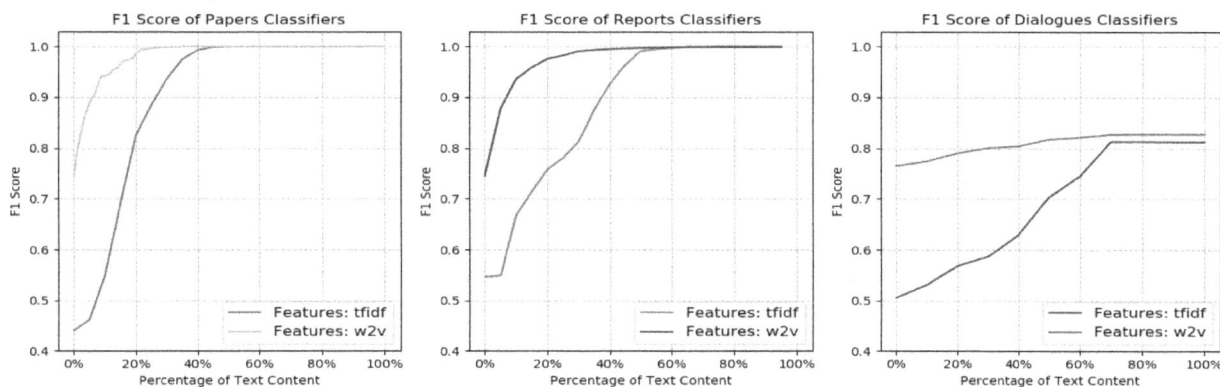

Figure 5: F1 scores of: papers classifiers (left), earning reports classifiers (middle), and chatbot dialogues classifiers (right)

to accurately detect machine-made texts from man-made texts, especially long texts such as academic papers and earning reports. This may be due to the limited datasets but also it is possible that there is subtle but clear difference in the way machine generates texts, different from what humans write or speak. In order to generalize the findings, however, we plan to collect more datasets of man-made and machine-made in different domains.

As NLG technologies are advancing rapidly, in near future, it will become more challenging to detect machine-made texts from man-made ones. One can imagine a scenario where malicious adversaries use an NLG technology to mislead users. For instance, adversaries may use machine-made texts in a chatbot discussion based phishing attack. If a computational solution can tell naive users whether the part of chatbot dialogue is likely to be man-made or machine-made, it can warn a potential victim that she is conversing with a machine, not a human. Therefore, our research is a good starting point toward this important research direction and novel security applications.

7 CONCLUSION

We have formulated the Reverse Turing Test (RTT) problem as the binary classification to differentiate between man-made and machine-made texts. The results of the analysis of the characteristics of machine-made and man-made texts using three real datasets, suggested that machine-made texts tend to be more neutral and relatively more difficult to read than man-made texts. We also demonstrated that there are some special expressions and concerns of machine-made texts in different domains, compared to man-made texts. Further, having the F1 scores of at least 0.84 from binary classifications, we showed that it was possible to differentiate machine-made texts from man-made ones accurately. However, as the relevant technologies rapidly advance, in near future, one may not be able to distinguish machine-made texts from man-made ones effectively.

ACKNOWLEDGMENTS

This work was in part supported by NSF awards #1742702 and #1820609, and ORAU-directed R&D program award in 2018.

REFERENCES

[1] Elizabeth Blankespoor, Christina Zhu, et al. 2018. Capital market effects of media synthesis and dissemination: Evidence from robo-journalism. *Review of Accounting Studies* 23, 1 (2018), 1–36.
[2] Andrew Brock, Jeff Donahue, and Simonyan Karen. 2018. Large Scale GAN Training for High Fidelity Natural Image Synthesis. *arXiv preprint arXiv:1809.11096* (2018).
[3] Matt Carlson. 2015. The robotic reporter: Automated journalism and the redefinition of labor, compositional forms, and journalistic authority. *Digital journalism* 3, 3 (2015), 416–431.
[4] Mehmet M Dalkilic, Wyatt T Clark, James C Costello, and Predrag Radivojac. 2006. Using compression to identify classes of inauthentic texts. In *Proceedings of the 2006 SIAM International Conference on Data Mining*. SIAM, 604–608.
[5] R.F. Flesch. 1979. *How to write plain English: a book for lawyers and consumers*. Harper & Row. https://books.google.com/books?id=-kpZAAAAMAAJ
[6] Albert Gatt and Emiel Krahmer. 2018. Survey of the State of the Art in Natural Language Generation: Core tasks, applications and evaluation. *Journal of Artificial Intelligence Research* 61 (2018), 65–170.
[7] Yoav Goldberg and Omer Levy. 2014. word2vec Explained: deriving Mikolov et al.'s negative-sampling word-embedding method. *arXiv preprint arXiv:1402.3722* (2014).
[8] Jason S Kessler. 2017. Scattertext: a browser-based tool for visualizing how corpora differ. *arXiv preprint arXiv:1703.00565* (2017).
[9] Celeste Lecompte. 2015. Automation in the Newsroom. *Nieman Reports* 69, 3 (2015), 32–45.
[10] Leo Leppänen, Myriam Munezero, Mark Granroth-Wilding, and Hannu Toivonen. 2017. Data-Driven News Generation for Automated Journalism. In *Proceedings of the 10th International Conference on Natural Language Generation*. 188–197.
[11] Yuezun Li Li, Ming-Ching Chang, and Siwei Lyu. 2018. Large Scale GAN Training for High Fidelity Natural Image Synthesis. *arXiv preprint arXiv:1806.02877* (2018).
[12] Chin-Yew Lin. 2004. Rouge: A package for automatic evaluation of summaries. *Text Summarization Branches Out* (2004).
[13] Kishore Papineni, Salim Roukos, Todd Ward, and Wei-Jing Zhu. 2002. BLEU: a method for automatic evaluation of machine translation. In *Proceedings of the 40th annual meeting on association for computational linguistics*. 311–318.
[14] Fabian Pedregosa, Gaël Varoquaux, Alexandre Gramfort, Vincent Michel, Bertrand Thirion, Olivier Grisel, Mathieu Blondel, Peter Prettenhofer, Ron Weiss, Vincent Dubourg, et al. 2011. Scikit-learn: Machine learning in Python. *Journal of machine learning research* 12, Oct (2011), 2825–2830.
[15] Bernhard Scholkopf and Alex Smola. 2002. *Support Vector Machines and Kernel Algorithms*. The Handbook of Brain Theory and Neural Networks, MA Arbib (Eds.), MIT Press.
[16] Onur Varol, Emilio Ferrara, Clayton A Davis, Filippo Menczer, and Alessandro Flammini. 2017. Online human-bot interactions: Detection, estimation, and characterization. *arXiv preprint arXiv:1703.03107* (2017).
[17] Ramakrishna Vedantam, C Lawrence Zitnick, and Devi Parikh. 2015. Cider: Consensus-based image description evaluation. In *Proceedings of the IEEE conference on computer vision and pattern recognition*. 4566–4575.

Algorithmic Privacy and Gender Bias Issues in Google Ad Settings

Nisha Shekhawat*
nisha.shekhawat.y16@lnmiit.ac.in
The LNM Institute of Information Technology
Jaipur, India

Aakanksha Chauhan
aakanksha.chauhan.y16@lnmiit.ac.in
The LNM Institute of Information Technology
Jaipur, India

Sakthi Balan Muthiah
sakthi.balan@lnmiit.ac.in
The LNM Institute of Information Technology
Jaipur, India

ABSTRACT

For more than three years, Google has been facilitating users with four gender options – "Male", "Female", "Rather Not Say" and "Custom". "Rather Not Say" is for users who do not prefer to disclose their gender identity and "Custom" is for users who do not identify themselves among the conventional gender labels (male or female). By this, it is evident that Google provides choice to its users to classify themselves among non-conventional gender groups. This work makes an attempt to assess choice, transparency and privacy in Google Ad Settings when the option "Rather Not Say" is selected as gender. It was observed that even though the gender was set as "Rather Not Say", a conventional gender was displayed as demographic in Ad Personalization page of Google Ad Settings. Therefore, even though it provides choice to the user, it is not an absolute choice as Google still classifies an individual into one of the two traditional categories. Our experiment infers that the websites might be categorized as Male or Female-oriented. Therefore, while trying to create a preference of websites for a particular user, the system often introduces bias towards a gender for a predefined interest demographic in Google Ad Personalization page. This paper focuses on the statistical analysis of the prediction of gender for the different categories of websites and how this effects a user's choice, privacy and transparency.

CCS CONCEPTS

• **Security and privacy** → *Social aspects of security and privacy.*

KEYWORDS

Google ads, gender, bias, preference, transparency, privacy, choice and online browsing behaviour

ACM Reference Format:
Nisha Shekhawat, Aakanksha Chauhan, and Sakthi Balan Muthiah. 2019. Algorithmic Privacy and Gender Bias Issues in Google Ad Settings. In *11th ACM Conference on Web Science (WebSci '19), June 30–July 3, 2019, Boston, MA, USA.* ACM, New York, NY, USA, 5 pages. https://doi.org/10.1145/3292522.3326033

1 INTRODUCTION

Google currently provides its users with four gender options – "Male", "Female", "Rather Not Say" and "Custom", which was first introduced in Dec 2014[2]. "Male" and "Female" options correspond to conventional gender demographics. The option "Rather Not Say" refers to the group of users who do not want to reveal their gender identity, and "Custom" is for the users who are part of the non-conventional gender groups. These policies are formed to provide users with a large domain of non-conventional options to opt from.

For every user, there are two categories of information that is collected by Google to facilitate the users with its services as stated in policies. First one is provided by the user while creating the account and second one is collected as the user employs the services provided by Google like web search, ads, geolocation, history, and many more as listed in Figure 1.

To cater transparency and choice, Google provides the service of Ad Personalization to the users. It displays the demographics which include, first, the information provided by the users, i.e., age group and gender, and second, the interests which are inferred by Google from the user's online browsing behaviour. This online browsing behaviour includes the website visits and web searches (keywords) conducted by a user. Google also provides the facility to disable these interest demographics if a user is not inclined towards them.

As the choice opted by a user is a major consideration by Google, this work attempts to develop an insight about the online browsing behaviour of the simulated users and how it is effecting their choice. This experiment shows that how the analysis of online browsing behaviour of a user, eventually, deprives him or her of the choice while making a selection for the sensitive attribute (gender), i.e., despite of choosing "Rather Not Say", a conventional gender is assigned. Furthermore, it also includes some observations that show how this gender prediction is thereby making the system less transparent for the user. Moreover, it can also be said that a user's privacy is hampered when this predicted information is shared with third party websites[5][7].

This paper is a study on two fronts: one it shows that the gender choice offered by Google is not absolute with respect to Google Ad scenario. And second, when Google assigns a gender in the Google Ad Settings it assigns with respect to the websites a Google user searches, visits or clicks – this shows that the algorithm follows the general societal perception of how male and female interests are stereo-typically differentiated. Both of these present various privacy and bias issues for the user. This work is to indicate that there is a bias and privacy issue associated with Google Ad Settings especially when the user selects "Rather Not Say" category of gender.

Prior work relevant to our study is discussed in Section 2. Method and categorization of outcomes obtained from this experiment are explained in Section 3. Section 4 emphasizes on the statistical analysis of outcomes obtained from this study. The issues detected in Google Ad Settings are discussed in Section 5 while conclusion and future work are explained in Section 6.

2 LITERATURE SURVEY

Several studies have been conducted on Google ads and the relevant works are discussed here. Datta et al.[3] examined Google ads to explore the effect of browsing behaviour on the displayed ads. They developed Adfisher tool to detect differences between the ads shown to the experimental and control groups. These groups had separately defined treatment for various simulated users. While Datta examined transparency for interest demographics in Ad Settings, our work majorly focuses on gender demographic. Craig E. Wills[10] assessed the ads shown to users during controlled browsing as well as examined the inferred demographics and interests shown in the Ad Preference Manager. They also observed profile based ads and found that Google does show non-contextual ads related to sensitive topics like health and finance.

The usage study closest to this work is that of Michael Carl Tschantz[8] who experimented to determine the accuracy of Google ad demographics. They monitored the user's browsing behaviour and recorded interests in Google Ad Settings to conclude whether inferred interests match with user-provided information. On the other hand, this paper studies patterns in user's online browsing behaviour which identifies the user as male or female and also concludes whether the algorithm is leading to a preference or bias. Small-scale anecdotal examinations of the accuracy of Ad Settings have appeared in the popular press, as has a survey looking at the accuracy of Google's geolocation abilities[8].

Other related works differ in both objectives and methodologies. They all focus on how visiting web pages change the ads seen. While our work examines which gender is assigned to a user, when the gender is set as "Rather Not Say", in accordance with the online browsing behaviour of the user and also makes an attempt to develop an insight into Google's algorithm which might be classifying websites as Male or Female-oriented.

3 METHODOLOGY

3.1 Google Ads Policy

As examined on January 2019[4], Google Ads Policy under the subsection of Data Transparency clearly distinguishes between "the information they collect as we use the services" and "the information we create or provide to them" as shown in Figure 1. The former includes the collection of data from browsing, videos, ads, location, website, and apps. This collected data serves as an alley to make the Google services[4] better for the users. An instance of the efficacy that Google provides is making Google Maps faster as the bits of a user's location are collected, which when combined with the location of other users, it is able to recognize a better traffic pattern to aid the users. The latter, whereas, is the information that a user provides while creating a Google account. Google also claims to protect this information as the user utilizes the services. This information includes name, date of birth (age), gender, phone

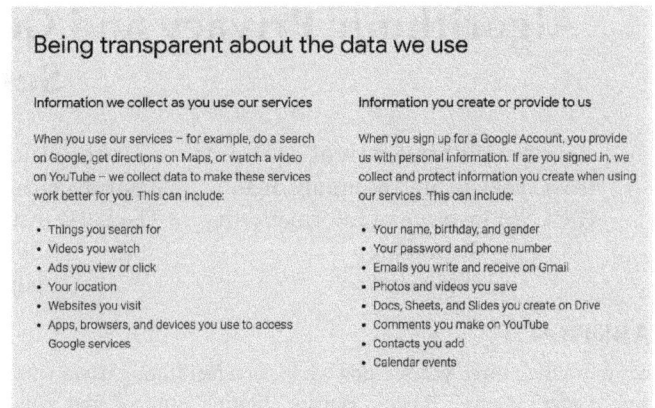

Figure 1: Google Ads Privacy Policy (https://safety.google/privacy/data/).

number, and other sensitive data[4]. Privacy is one of the main concerns as stated in the policy and a comprehensive review process is promised, thereby making it a key consideration at each level of development of any service[4].

3.2 Approach

This experiment aims to assess the choice provided for gender demographic in Google Ad Settings by determining what kind of browsing behaviour pertains to a specific conventional gender according to Google ads algorithm. To conduct this experiment, fifty Gmail accounts were created manually. Gmail account creation includes mobile number verification and the number of accounts that can be validated with a unique mobile number is limited[6]. Therefore, automation of the Gmail account creation is not feasible.

This experiment is implemented using Firefox private browsing. Private browsing was necessary to ensure that no past history or bookmarks were stored that could effect observations of the current browsing behaviour of the simulated users. It was commenced by creating fifty Gmail accounts having same date of birth, no recovery email address or mobile number and gender being set as "Rather Not Say". At the beginning of the experiment, age group (18-24) was the only displayed demographic (inferred from date of birth) in the Ad Personalization page of Google Ad Settings. Each simulated user was then subjected to a different treatment and Ad Personalization page was monitored. The treatment for a simulated user involved searching a keyword, followed by visiting websites for that search. As Google ad profiles are dynamic and may change (e.g., new interests are added) therefore, Ad Personalization page is monitored after visiting each website. Outcomes for the above mentioned procedure are further stated in Section 4.1 and 4.2.

3.3 Categorization of collected information

The results that are collected by applying the approach (described in Section 3.2) to the Google accounts can be divided into two categories – "Label" and "Result". The first category holds record of the websites after each visit and states whether Ad Personalization page has displayed any changes in the interest demographics. This information is kept under the "Label" column which is classified

Table 1: Table for Label categorization

Username (@gmail.com)	Keywords	Treatment	Label
adfisher0002	web dev jobs	linkedin.com	Radical
		glassdoor.com	Radical
adfisher0003	highest paying finance jobs	cnbc.com	Steady
		businessinsider.com	Steady
		emolument.com	Radical

Table 2: Table for Result categorization

Username (@gmail.com)	Keywords	Treatment	Label	Result
adfisher0002	web dev jobs	linkedin.com	Radical	Female
		glassdoor.com	Radical	
adfisher0003	highest paying finance jobs	cnbc.com	Steady	Male
		businessinsider.com	Steady	
		emolument.com	Radical	
adfisher0015	parenting	parenting.com	Steady	No Gender
		psychologytoday.com	Radical	
		apa.org	Steady	
		ted.com	Radical	
		nytimes.com	Steady	

into "Radical" and "Steady". "Radical" is labelled when there is an addition of interest demographics in the Ad Personalization page, which is a consequence of the most recent and the preceding website visits of the simulated user. Whereas "Steady" is labelled when there is no addition or change in the Ad Personalization page after a web search and website visit of a unique user.

This categorization has been shown in Table 1[1] whose first column is Username of the Gmail account on which the treatment is done and second column is Keywords which are searched on web. The third column is Treatment which includes the websites that are visited from that account. The fourth column is Label which is the above mentioned categorization.

The other category is "Result" which is outcome of the complete treatment imparted to a unique account and is obtained from all demographics corresponding to that account. These are analyzed by the algorithm to respond with a gender which was supposed to be absent as "Rather Not Say" option was selected. On the basis of these outcomes, "Result" is classified into three groups i.e, Male, Female and No Gender. No Gender is stated if no result is acknowledged, even after subjecting an account to the complete treatment. For Male and Female classes, the treatment is completed when one of the two genders, either "Male" or "Female" is predicted. For No Gender, the treatment is supposed to be complete when an account visits a significant number (average of 7 to 10 sites) of websites to get a prediction but is still unable to classify one.

The categorization of Result is shown in Table 2[1] in which the first column is Username of the Gmail account, second column is Keywords of the web search, third column is Treatment that is provided to the simulated accounts, fourth column is Label that categorizes changes in interest demographics due to website visits into Radical and Steady. The fifth column is Result that shows the above stated categorization of the outcome of the treatment given to the accounts.
1

4 OBSERVATION

4.1 Observation of Label

"Label" holds the record of each web search and website visit, and whether the Ad Personalization page has responded with any change in the interest demographics or not. In this work, 86 out of 190 visited websites showed Radical behaviour, where 15 sites displayed Radical behaviour in the first visiting only whereas there

Table 3: Table of significant observations

S.No.	Keywords	Treatment	No. of simulated users	Result
1	yoga	yoga+online dating yoga+teaching +shopping	2	Female
	gym	gym gym+art of living	2	Male
2	buying apartments	apartment renting websites	2	Female
3	machine learning conferences	machine learning conferences	2	Male
		machine learning conferences+data science jobs	1	Female
4	data science jobs	data science jobs	4	Male
		machine learning conferences+data science jobs	1	Female
5	high paying finance jobs	finance jobs+chartered accountant	2	Male
6	software development	software development +data science	2	Male
		software developer+full stack developer	2	
		software developer +full stack developer	1	Female
		software developer+jewellery +soccer+home decor+cricket +nail art+bridal dress+pregnancy +pinterest	1	No Gender
7	disability parenting horoscope english literature alcohol support groups	disability+hospital parenting horoscope+demons english literature +political news alcohol support groups +stress management	8	No Gender
8	cooking and cooking jobs	chef jobs	1	Male
		cooking	1	Female
9	medical	doctor jobs	1	Male
		nurse jobs	1	Female

were only 5 sites that showed Steady behaviour even after the treatment was completed. For instance, sites like *indeed.com, pic.nic.in* were labelled Radical because they displayed change in Ad Personalization page in their respective visits. On the other hand, sites

---
[1] https://github.com/nisha987/Google-gender

like *nhs.uk, parenting.com* were labelled Steady which means they did not immediately effect the Ad Personalization page.

4.2 Observation of Result

This experiment classified websites into three classes in accordance with general societal perception – Male-oriented, Female-oriented and Gender Neutral as shown in Table 4[1]. These categories were permuted to create a treatment comprising of websites from one or more of the above three classes. The inferred results of this experiment are stated in Table 3[1] in which the Keywords are being compared, along with the Treatment provided to various accounts, to show the number of simulated users that are showing deviation towards a single gender through their online browsing behaviour.

It was observed that if a user searches for career websites, the user was mostly predicted as "Male". Out of 21 searches for jobs, 13 were high paying professions, where 8 of these were predicted as "Male", 3 as "Female" and 2 accounts were not assigned any gender. For remaining 8 low paying professions, 7 were predicted as "Female" and 1 as "Male"[1]. It was startling to learn that visiting sites for cooking predicted that the user is female while searching for chef jobs predicted that the user is male. Two simulated users visited career websites of tech giants like Adobe, Google, Microsoft, IBM and Amazon searching for data science jobs and were classified as male. This implies that the skewed ratio of male to female employees is also effecting the job opportunities available to the female applicants. Another result demonstrated yoga as an interest for females and gym for males. Four simulated users visited expenditure associated websites and the algorithm concluded that the users were female. Bollywood and machine learning conferences represent male interests whereas flowers, home decor, embroidery, Bacardi, quit smoking, kitchen gardens, motivational talks serve as female interests in Google ad algorithms. For websites and web searches related to parenting, disability, alcohol support groups and horoscope, " No Gender" was concluded for Result column. We also observed that gender field along with other interests in Google Ad Personalization page changes with changing user browsing behaviour like inactivity (mostly vanishes) for a few weeks.

5 DISCUSSION

5.1 Choice

The absolute choice, when given to a user, refers to the fact that every option chosen by the user is respected by Google. In this experiment, for the gender "Rather Not Say", it is found that after a few website visits, a gender field appears in Ad Personalization page, identifying the user as Male, Female or No Gender on the basis of online browsing behaviour of the user (Section 3.3). The prediction of gender deprives the user from the facility of absolute choice.

5.2 Transparency

A user's online browsing behaviour is monitored and recorded to benefit him or her by improving the services as stated in the Google Ads Policy. But here, it can be analyzed that the property of transparency is not delivered entirely because this collected information,

along with improving the services, also leads to prediction of gender (sensitive attribute), which according to the Google Ads Policy, is meant to be provided by the user. The prediction of gender, as observed in Section 4.2, might be a result of the classification of websites into either Male or Female-oriented or as Gender Neutral. This, eventually, might cater for bias while a user goes for any browsing activity. The classification that was observed from this experiment is stated in Table 4[1] .

Table 4: Categorization of websites

S. No.	Classes	Websites
1.	Female-oriented	Web Development Jobs – LinkedIn, Glassdoor
		Fashion designer jobs – LinkedIn, shine, indeed
		Nurse jobs – aetnacareers, glassdoor, indeed
		Online dating
		Yoga – verywellfit.com
		Hairdresser – Naukri, indeed, glassdoor
		Cooking
		Flowers
		Myntra, streetstyle
		Home decor, embroidery, nykaa
		Novels
		Adventure sports like skydiving, canoeing, desert camping, paragliding
		Kitchen gardens
		Teaching jobs and nursery rhymes
		Apartments in New York
		Product trainer and motivational speaker
		Software engineer + full stack developer (indeed, glassdoor)
		Conferences in ml + data science jobs
2.	Male-oriented	Finance job articles – CNBC businessinsider, emolument
		Data scientist – kdnuggets, glassdoor, datajobs, coursera
		Software development and software engineering
		Bollywood and small screen news
		Doctor jobs – naukri.com, Glassdoor, monsterindia, freshersworld
		Chef – catererglobal, indeed
		Gym
		Visiting career websites like IBM, Microsoft, Adobe,Google, Github for data science jobs
		Ml conferences
3.	Overlap between male and female gender	jobs of software engineer
4.	Gender Neutral	Event management – Naukri, indeed, LinkedIn
		When treatment comprises of both male and female interests
		Horoscope and interests pertaining to a culture
		Pinterest
		Alcohol support stress management
		Parenting
		Disability

5.3 Privacy

As the Google Ads Policy states , the privacy of user's information is taken into serious consideration whenever it is being used for improving the services[4]. Gender is one such information that is being pulled. When "Rather Not Say" is chosen, it is meant that the user does not want to reveal the gender. Yet predicting a gender by taking the online browsing behaviour into account contradicts the fact that the user wants to keep the gender private. Also, this predicted gender when shared with the third party websites may hamper the privacy of the user.

5.4 Preferences and bias

Preference can be described as having an inclination for an alternative over other while bias is prejudice for one alternative without any well established fact[9]. For website visits and web searches, all the data is preserved by Google as mentioned in Section 3.1. This data is modeled and analyzed by an algorithm which predicts demographics with reference to the web activity.

When a male user visits cooking, jewellery, makeup related websites, searches such keywords, he is predicted as "Female". This result, though inappropriate and prejudiced, won't effect one's day to day life in a significant manner. Whereas if one searches for career and finance related keywords, visits corresponding websites, and is predicted as "Male", it can be inferred that only males are thought to be eligible for big career opportunities. This also leads to denial of opportunities to many eligible candidates. Out of 21 jobs – for the web searches made, it was startling to discover that Google ads algorithm classifies more than fifty percent of the users searching for high paying jobs as "Male". Even web search for keywords like machine learning conference also predicts that the user is "Male" which can be termed as bias on basis of gender.

6 CONCLUSION

The results of this experiment indicate that there are privacy and bias issues associated with Google Ad Settings. Firstly, even when a Google user does not want to reveal the gender, the Google Ad algorithm predicts a conventional gender and it displays it in the Google Ad Personalization page. This is an indication of choice and privacy issues. Secondly, when it assigns a gender it is based on the websites searched, clicked or visited. This indicates that there is bias towards the websites a user visits – some websites might be male or female oriented while others are gender neutral. This indicates that there is a bias issue. We feel that this work will lead to a more comprehensive research on the algorithms used by Google Ads. An extended statistical analysis over a larger number of accounts may derive more generalized results and distinctions in the classification of websites which are leading to the prediction of gender.

This experiment can be conducted with a larger number of simulated users over a longer span of time to attain a better perception of what websites are more likely to identify the user as Male or Female. It can also be used to capture the difference between Male and Female online browsing behaviour as learned by the Google Ads algorithm.

REFERENCES

[1] 2019. Link to code and appendix,[Last visited on May 1, 2019]. https://github.com/nisha987/Google-gender
[2] Rachael Bennett. 2014. Google-Announcement for addtion of Rather Not Say and Custom gender options. https://plus.google.com/118279113645730324236/posts/FKK2trDERAC
[3] Amit Datta, Michael Carl Tschantz, and Anupam Datta. 2015. Automated experiments on ad privacy settings. *Proceedings on privacy enhancing technologies* 2015, 1 (2015), 92–112.
[4] Google. 2019. Making it easy to understand what data we collect and why, [Last visited on May 1, 2019]. https://safety.google/privacy/data/
[5] Google. 2019. Third-party sites apps with access to your account,[Last visited on May 1, 2019]. https://support.google.com/accounts/answer/3466521?hl=en
[6] Google. 2019. Verify your account,[Last visited on May 1, 2019]. https://support.google.com/accounts/answer/114129?hl=en&visit_id=636849961386601652-3618412408&rd=1
[7] Jonathan R Mayer and John C Mitchell. 2012. Third-party web tracking: Policy and technology. In *2012 IEEE Symposium on Security and Privacy*. IEEE, 413–427.
[8] Michael Carl Tschantz, Serge Egelman, Jaeyoung Choi, Nicholas Weaver, and Gerald Friedland. 2018. The accuracy of the demographic inferences shown on Google's Ad Settings. In *Proceedings of the 2018 Workshop on Privacy in the Electronic Society*. ACM, 33–41.
[9] WikiDiff. 2019. What is the difference between bias and preference?,[Last visited on May 1, 2019]. https://wikidiff.com/bias/preference
[10] Craig E Wills and Can Tatar. 2012. Understanding what they do with what they know. In *Proceedings of the 2012 ACM Workshop on Privacy in the Electronic Society*. ACM, 13–18.

How Gullible Are You? Predicting Susceptibility to Fake News

Tracy Jia Shen
jqs5443@psu.edu
The Pennsylvania State University
University Park, PA, USA

Robert Cowell
rhc5082@psu.edu
The Pennsylvania State University
University Park, PA, USA

Aditi Gupta
ajg6035@psu.edu
The Pennsylvania State University
University Park, PA, USA

Thai Le
tql3@psu.edu
The Pennsylvania State University
University Park, PA, USA

Amulya Yadav
amulya@psu.edu
The Pennsylvania State University
University Park, PA, USA

Dongwon Lee
dongwon@psu.edu
The Pennsylvania State University
University Park, PA, USA

ABSTRACT

In this research, we hypothesize that some social users are more *gullible* to fake news than others, and accordingly investigate on the susceptibility of users to fake news–i.e., how to identify susceptible users, what are their characteristics, and if one can build a prediction model.Building on the crowdsourced annotations of 5 types of susceptible users in Twitter, we found out that: (1) susceptible users are correlated with a combination of user, network, and content features; (2) one can build a reasonably accurate prediction model with 0.82 in AUC-ROC for the multinomial classification task; and (3) there exists a correlation between the dominant susceptibility level of center nodes and that of the entire network.

CCS CONCEPTS

• **Human-centered computing** → **Empirical studies in collaborative and social computing**; • **Machine Learning** → *Social Media*.

KEYWORDS

Fake news, user susceptibility, machine learning

ACM Reference Format:
Tracy Jia Shen, Robert Cowell, Aditi Gupta, Thai Le, Amulya Yadav, and Dongwon Lee. 2019. How Gullible Are You? Predicting Susceptibility to Fake News. In *11th ACM Conference on Web Science (WebSci '19), June 30–July 3, 2019, Boston, MA, USA*. ACM, New York, NY, USA, 2 pages. https://doi.org/10.1145/3292522.3326055

1 INTRODUCTION

Since the 2016 US election, the public interest on fake news has exploded, resulting in many early solutions to computationally detect fake news and understand how it spreads in social media. While they are effective solutions to the problem of fake news, however, we believe that another important problem that has received little attention to date is to study on users' susceptibility to fake news,

Class	Tweets
Strong Agreement	Always knew these kids had ties to #Soros . The parents need to have a Mental background check.
Weak Agreement	Florida is his home base! He found more Useful Idiots!
Neutral	They all look SO saddened by the loss of their classmates....don't they???!!!
Weak Disagreement	Youre a con man too.
Strong Disagreement	Wow. Imagine being a bad enough human to attack teenagers who just survived a mass shooting.

Figure 1: Five levels of susceptibility and their examples.

i.e., why and how some people become susceptible to fake news (while others do not). In this work, therefore, we ask two research questions (RQs): (1) what are the characteristics of Twitter users who are susceptible (or not susceptible) to fake news?, and (2) is it possible to build an accurate model to predict susceptible users in Twitter? To answer these RQs, first, we need to create labeled samples (i.e., Twitter users who are determined to be susceptible to fake news). As there exists no such dataset, however, we instead resort to crowdsourced samples with an assumption that Twitter users who express their agreement or disagreement toward verified fake news are treated as *susceptible* or *not-susceptible* users. Figure 1 shows real Tweet examples of five degrees of agreement to fake news–highly-susceptible (= strong agreement), slightly-susceptible (= weak agreement), neutral, not-quite susceptible (= weak disagreement), and not-at-all susceptible (= strong disagreement).

There exists very few prior work which studies user's susceptibility to fake news. For instance, [1] studied user susceptibility as a behavioral factor to predict viral diffusion of general information rather than fake news. [5] studied user susceptibility to fake news created by bot activities and limit their definition of 'susceptible users' as the ones that interacted at least once with a social bot. [3] studied research questions similar to ours, but used the methodology from cognitive science. Unlike these works, we focus on multiple degrees of susceptibility to fake news by employing machine learning methods.

2 EXPERIMENT AND PREDICTION

Dataset: We first identified 7 verified fake news about the "Parkland Shooting" incident where a gunman killed 17 students and staffs at Marjory Stoneman Douglas High School in Parkland, Florida on Feb. 14, 2018. We then identified 896 users who replied to the 7 fake news from Feb 14 to May 20, 2018, and scraped additional 13,000

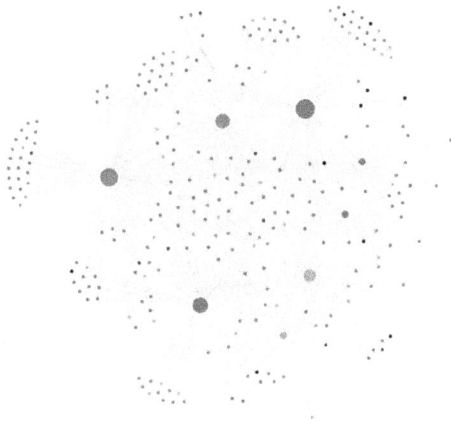

Figure 2: Center nodes network (the biggest 8 nodes), where red=strong-agreement, orange=weak-agreement, grey=neutral, blue=weak-disagreement, and black=strong-disagreement.

Twitter users who were followers or friends of the repliers). Next, for each reply, we assign 5 English-literate Amazon Mechanical Turk (MTurk) workers ($\geq$ 95% approval rate) to label it into one of five classes. We used the majority voting to determine the final class for each reply.

Preliminary Analysis: We checked the spreading network to see if susceptibility is infectious or not. Since we don't have labels for the followers/friends, we only formed the repliers' susceptibility network. The largest component in the network contained 63% of all nodes, including 8 center nodes, 5 of which have more than 100 connections (following relationships). Among 8 center nodes, 4 were labeled as strong agreement (bigger red nodes in Figure 2). Among the nodes connected to these 8 center nodes, about 51% were strong agreement, when strong agreement users accounted for 37% of the entire network. Therefore, it appears that the dominant susceptibility level of center nodes in the largest component of a network is correlated with the dominant susceptibility of the entire network, if majority of center nodes are labeled as strong agreement (in our case, 50%).

Feature Engineering: We considered three types of features: (1) *Content:* linguistic (LIWC) features including usage of punctuation, latent emotions, perception, cognitive thinking in Twitter posts; (2) *User:* # followers, # friends, # lists, # statuses, create_time, circulation_time, and membership_year; and (3) *Network:* clustering features (measuring how users cluster), centrality features (measuring how close users are), influence and special connection features.

Prediction Result: We used four learning models (e.g., KNN, Random Forest, Decision Tree, and XGBoost) to solve the proposed multinomial classification task. Due to the scarcity of training samples, we did not test data-hungry algorithms such as deep learning algorithms. We evaluated the learned models using the Area-Under-the-Curve of the Receiver Operating Characteristics (AUC-ROC) to judge the robustness of the model [2, 4]. Using four learning models, we compared the prediction performance of seven combinations of features–i.e., content-only, user-only, network-only, content + user, content + network, user + network, and all features

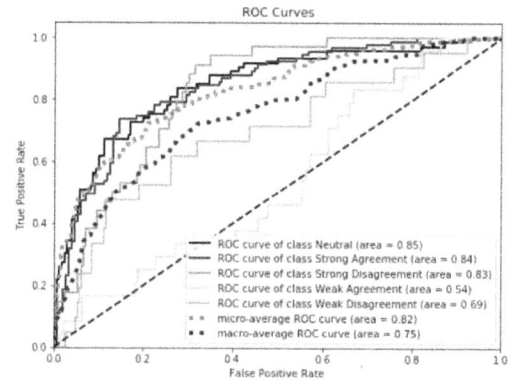

Figure 3: ROC curves of all five classes by XGBoost.

Table 1: Micro-AVG AUC-ROC for all classes

	Content	User	Network	Content + User	Content + Network	User + Network	All Features
KNN	0.60	0.59	0.63	0.65	0.68	0.61	0.62
Decision Tree	0.54	0.62	0.56	0.68	0.57	0.64	0.65
Random Forest	0.66	0.74	0.68	0.71	0.68	0.73	0.77
XGBoost	0.69	0.76	0.68	0.8	0.75	0.77	0.82

combined. The experimental results are summarized in Table 1. In Figure 3, using the best performing XGBoost model to predict both strong-agreement and strong-disagreement data (i.e., highly-susceptible and not-at-all susceptible users), we have over 0.83 AUC performance. The model, however, does not predict the minority classes well, with only 0.54 for weak-agreement and 0.69 for weak-disagreement in AUC. However, the poor performance for minority classes could be due to the scarcity of training data.

3 CONCLUSION

First, we found that the high susceptibility level of center nodes has high correlation with the entire network susceptibility level. Second, we demonstrated that it is possible to differentiate one of five susceptibility levels of users using various features trained in XGBoost model, achieving 0.82 in AUC-ROC.

4 ACKNOWLEDGEMENT

This work was in part supported by NSF awards #1742702 and #1820609, and ORAU-directed R&D program 2018.

REFERENCES

[1] Tuan-anh Hoang and Ee-peng Lim. 2012. Virality and Susceptibility in Information Diffusions. *Proceedings of the Sixth International AAAI Conference on Weblogs and Social Media 2010* (2012), 146–153.
[2] M Hossin and Sulaiman. 2015. A REVIEW ON EVALUATION METRICS FOR DATA CLASSIFICATION EVALUATIONS. *International Journal of Data Mining & Knowledge Management Process (IJDKP)* 5, 2 (2015). https://doi.org/10.5121/ijdkp.2015.5201
[3] Gordon Pennycook and David G. Rand. 2018. Lazy, not biased: Susceptibility to partisan fake news is better explained by lack of reasoning than by motivated reasoning. *Cognition* September 2017 (2018), 1–12. https://doi.org/10.1016/j.cognition.2018.06.011
[4] Sebastian Raschka. [n. d.]. Machine Learning FAQ. https://sebastianraschka.com/faq/docs/multiclass-metric.html
[5] Claudia Wagner, Markus Strohmaier, Silvia Mitter, and Christian Körner. 2012. When social bots attack : Modeling susceptibility of users in online social networks. *#MSM2012 Workshop proceedings* (2012), 41–48. http://ceur-ws.org/Vol-838

Pwned: The Risk of Exposure From Data Breaches*

Gaurav Sood*
gsood07@gmail.com

Ken Cor†
mcor@ualberta.ca
The University of Alberta
Edmonton, Canada

ABSTRACT

News about massive data breaches is increasingly common. But what proportion of Americans are exposed in these breaches is still unknown. We combine data from a large, representative sample of American adults (n = 5,000), recruited by YouGov, with data from *Have I Been Pwned* to estimate the lower bound of the number of times Americans' private information has been exposed. We find that at least 82.84% of Americans have had their private information, such as account credentials, Social Security Number, etc., exposed. On average, Americans' private information has been exposed in at least three breaches. The better educated, the middle-aged, women, and Whites are more likely to have had their accounts breached than the complementary groups.

CCS CONCEPTS

• **Security and privacy** → **Social aspects of security and privacy**.

KEYWORDS

Security risk, Privacy risk, Data breaches, Digital divide

ACM Reference Format:
Gaurav Sood and Ken Cor. 2019. Pwned: The Risk of Exposure From Data Breaches. In *11th ACM Conference on Web Science (WebSci '19), June 30-July 3, 2019, Boston, MA, USA*. ACM, New York, NY, USA, 4 pages. https://doi.org/10.1145/3292522.3326046

1 INTRODUCTION

On the Internet, nobody knows you're a dog. So the adage goes. But increasingly, others know that you like dog food and hate cats. Many of us have made our peace with this new reality. A slew of massive account breaches in recent years, however, threatens to pull the rug from under all illusions of anonymity [9].[1]

---

*Data, scripts, and supporting information can be downloaded from http://github.com/themains/pwned.

[1]On September 22, 2016, for instance, Yahoo! revealed that 500M accounts had been compromised in a breach [4]. Less than three months later, on December 14, 2016, Yahoo! announced that data had been stolen from nearly 1B user accounts in a different breach [11]. In all, Wikipedia lists 272 separate breaches between 2004 and 2018 (see https://en.wikipedia.org/wiki/List_of_data_breaches)

But there is little existing research on how frequently Americans' private information is part of such breaches. Much of the research on data breaches has focused on the downstream impact on corporations, e.g., [5, 14, 16], and people, e.g., [2, 3, 10]. Such research is vital—it informs data breach notification policies, e.g., [6, 8, 12]. But absent from the literature is data that is important for developing effective public policy on corporate liability for data breaches—data on the average American's risk of their private information being exposed in a data breach. In this note, we shed light on this question.

Using a unique dataset, we estimate the lower bound of the average number of breached online accounts per person. We merge data from a large representative sample from YouGov (n = 5,000) with data from Have I Been Pwned (HIBP). We check whether the email associated with the YouGov account is part of the 293 public breaches cataloged by HIBP. We also study how exposure to breaches varies by socio-economic factors including ethnicity, sex, age, and education.

2 DATA AND METHODS

In July 2018, YouGov drew a nationally representative sample of 5,000 adult Americans. YouGov draws the sample as follows: it starts with a random sample of a high-quality sample of American adults, e.g., Current Population Survey, and then finds people on its panel that match the drawn sample most closely [13]. Some research suggests that the quality of samples drawn by YouGov is comparable to those drawn using probability sampling [1]. The sample that YouGov drew here, however, is better than its traditional survey samples. Non-response bias in our sample is zero because YouGov did not have to send out surveys; it used the emails associated with the accounts to collect the data. (YouGov never shared the emails with us.) Table 1 presents the marginals on key socio-demographic variables (see here for the codebook). (Table Supporting Information (SI)[2] 1.1 presents the comparison between the Current Population Survey (CPS) and YouGov on key demographic variables. The upshot is that on key marginals, the difference between YouGov and CPS is less than 5%.)

After drawing the sample, YouGov used the emails associated with the accounts to query the HIBP API. (YouGov did the lookups so that it didn't have to share the email IDs.) HIBP is a non-profit clearinghouse of information about online account breaches. HIBP's stated aim is to provide a way for people to check if they are at risk from online breaches. It currently carries data from 293 breaches covering 278 unique domains and 5,235,843,322 accounts, including data from prominent breaches like the two Yahoo! breaches covering nearly 1.5 billion accounts. The HIPB data are, however, not

---

[2]Supporting information can be downloaded from http://github.com/themains/pwned.

Table 1: YouGov Sample Characteristics

	proportion
race	
white	.67
hispanic/latino	.13
black	.12
asian	.03
middle eastern	.02
mixed race	.01
native american	.01
other	.00
sex	
female	.54
age	
(18, 25]	.09
(25, 35]	.19
(35, 50]	.26
(50, 65]	.28
(65, 100]	.18
education	
no hs	.06
hs grad.	.32
some college	.20
2-year college degree	.11
4-year college degree	.19
postgrad degree	.11

comprehensive. Security researchers believe that there are many breaches that the companies are unaware of and at least a few cases where a company doesn't share information about a breach it knows about. HIBP also refuses to provide data on sensitive breaches—breached accounts where a person's inclusion may adversely affect them—from their public API[3]. So data from HIBP only gives us a lower bound.

HIPB provides an easy way to get all the breached accounts associated with a particular email ID—you just need to make a simple API call passing the email that you want to get data on. This method gives us data on all the breaches logged by HIPB for all the 5,000 profiles. There is one caveat. Our YouGov sample provides data associated with only one email ID, the email people used to register with YouGov. People often have multiple email IDs. And that is another reason why all we get from this data is a lower bound. The actual number of breached accounts per person is likely much higher.

With each request, HIBP returns some metadata on the kind of breaches. (See the codebook for details about all the data that it returns.) Two pieces of information are material here. HIBP classifies each breach as verified or unverified. And it defines unverified

---

[3]HIBP website notes that it does not share whether or not an account has been part of the breach at Adult Friend Finder, Ashley Madison, Beautiful People, Bestialitysextaboo, Brazzers, CrimeAgency vBulletin Hacks, Fling, Florida Virtual School, Freedom Hosting II, Fridae, Fur Affinity, HongFire, Mate1.com, Muslim Match, Naughty America, Non Nude Girls, Rosebutt Board, The Candid Board, The Fappening, xHamster and 1 more.

breaches as breaches whose "legitimacy" it cannot "establish beyond [a] reasonable doubt." HIBP includes these unverified breaches because "they still contain personal information about individuals who want to understand their exposure on the web." The other material column that HIBP returns relates to whether a breach is part of a "spam list." HIBP defines *SpamList* as cases where "large volumes of personal data are found being utilized for the purposes of sending targeted spam." HIBP adds, "This often includes many of the same attributes frequently found in data breaches such as names, addresses, phones numbers and dates of birth. The lists are often aggregated from multiple sources, frequently by eliciting personal information from people with the promise of a monetary reward." And the reason HIBP includes these data is: "whilst the data may not have been sourced from a breached system, the personal nature of the information and the fact that it's redistributed in this fashion unbeknownst to the owners warrants inclusion here."

3 RESULTS

In all, 14,979 breaches are associated with the 5,000 emails on file. Or on average, there are three breaches per person. The median is also three. And at least 82.84% of Americans' accounts have been breached at least once.

The relationship between the number of breaches and socioeconomic is counter to what focusing on traditional concerns around the digital divide would lead us to believe. If anything, the data suggest that people who use online services more are somewhat more likely to have their accounts breached. (See SI 1 Tables and SI 2 Figures for corresponding regressions and figures illustrating group-wise means along with the 95% confidence intervals.)

The number of breaches increases roughly monotonically with education (see Table SI 1.4 and Figure SI 2.3). The average number of breaches among people with no high school degree is 2.35. Compare this to postgraduates, who are part of 3.20 breaches on average (or 1.3 times the average of people with no high school degree).

In contrast to the relationship between education and the number of breaches, the relationship between the number of breaches and age is curvilinear (see Table SI 1.5), with young people's and seniors' accounts least likely to be breached, and middle-aged adults' accounts most likely to be breached. But, as the loess illustrates (see Figure SI 2.4), the relationship is modest.

When we compare the average number of breaches among men and women, we find that women's accounts are 1.12 times more likely to be breached than men's (see Table 2 and Table SI 1.3; $p < .05$). Analyzing breaches by ethnicity, Blacks' and Whites' accounts are most frequently breached. The mean number of breaches associated with the emails for Blacks and Whites is 3.12 and 3.16 respectively. For Hispanics/Latinos, the corresponding number is 2.5 (see Table SI 1.2; $p < .05$). And for Asians, the mean is 2.82.

To assess the source of the exposure, we checked the source of the breaches. The 14,979 breaches stemmed from 156 different sites, but there was a sharp skew with 21 sites with more than 100 breaches accounting for 11,783 of the breaches. Table 3 lists the 21 sites. Prominent websites like linkedin.com, adobe.com, dropbox.com, lastfm.com, among others feature on the list.

In the analysis presented until now, we don't distinguish between different kinds of breaches. But not all breaches are equally grave. So

Table 2: Frequency of Account Breaches By Socio-economic Factors

	mean	se
Ethnicity		
White	3.12	0.05
Black	3.16	0.11
Hispanic/Latino	2.50	0.08
Asian	2.82	0.21
Native American	2.96	0.26
Middle Eastern	2.66	0.24
Mixed Race	2.45	0.22
Other	2.92	1.32
Sex		
Female	3.17	0.05
Male	2.82	0.05
Age		
(18,25]	1.96	0.10
(25,35]	3.12	0.09
(35,50]	3.34	0.08
(50,65]	3.29	0.07
(65,100]	2.95	0.07
Missing	1.19	0.16
Education		
No HS	2.35	0.12
HS Grad.	2.89	0.06
Some College	3.04	0.09
2-year College Degree	3.07	0.10
4-year College Degree	3.22	0.09
Postgrad Degree	3.20	0.11

Table 3: Most Frequently Implicated Domains

domain name	n
rivercitymediaonline.com	2,913
linkedin.com	1,089
modbsolutions.com	1,067
myspace.com	1,059
data4marketers.com	996
cashcrate.com	856
adobe.com	609
disqus.com	570
ticketfly.com	393
tumblr.com	340
dropbox.com	288
dailymotion.com	255
last.fm	248
evony.com	171
clixsense.com	150
cafemom.com	145
imesh.com	144
kickstarter.com	140
edmodo.com	130
zomato.com	112
neopets.com	108

4 CONCLUSION

Nearly 83% of Americans' have had their accounts breached at least once. In total, the 5,000 email accounts on file are associated with 14,979 breaches. Or, on average, people's accounts have been breached thrice. This number, though, is the lower bound for three reasons. First, not all breaches are made public. Second, HIBP doesn't allow access to data on sensitive breaches—breached online accounts on services that may have reputational consequences for people—via its public API. Third, many Americans have multiple email accounts. We only had one email ID per person.

We also find that the kinds of people who are most likely to use online services—the better educated, Whites, etc.—are generally the most exposed. This finding is consistent with Laohaprapanon and Sood, who find that the better educated, people with higher incomes, and racial majorities spend a smaller proportion of time online on problematic sites, but because they are online more often, they end up visiting more such sites [7]. This is contrary to the traditional narrative about the digital divide [15].

next, we shed light on the type of breaches. Of the 15,837 breaches, 14,979 or 94.58% were part of verified breaches. And about a third of the 15,837 breaches are categorized as *SpamList*. In all, we have 10,188 breaches that are verified and not categorized as *SpamList*. We focus our attention on these plausibly graver breaches, checking whether the relationship with socio-economic variables we see above hold in this smaller subset.

When we look at education, the pattern holds up. Once again, the number of breached accounts per person for people with a college degree or more is higher than for people who only got as far as high school (see Table 4). Moving to sex, the pattern is more attenuated with women just nudging ahead of men—the mean for women and men is 2.15 and 2.05 respectively. The general pattern for age remains roughly similar to what we saw above, with the middle-aged more likely to have their accounts breached compared to people younger than 25 and older than 65. Breaking down by race, we see some interesting changes. Asians join Whites near the top of the pile, with means of about 2.2. Accounts of Hispanics or Latinos are less likely to be part of verified non-spam-list breaches (mean = 1.73, $p < .05$). The big relative change is for Blacks; African-Americans are likelier to be part of unverified, *SpamList* breaches.

REFERENCES

[1] Stephen Ansolabehere and Brian F Schaffner. 2014. Does survey mode still matter? Findings from a 2010 multi-mode comparison. *Political Analysis* 22, 3 (2014), 285–303.

[2] Cassandra Cross, Megan Parker, and Daniel Sansom. 2019. Media discourses surrounding "non-ideal" victims: The case of the Ashley Madison data breach. *International Review of Victimology* 25, 1 (2019), 53–69.

[3] Shelby R Curtis, Jessica Rose Carre, and Daniel Nelson Jones. 2018. Consumer security behaviors and trust following a data breach. *Managerial Auditing Journal* 33, 4 (2018), 425–435.

[4] Seth Fiegerman. 2016. Yahoo says 500 million accounts stolen. https://money.cnn.com/2016/09/22/technology/yahoo-data-breach/

[5] Ramkumar Janakiraman, Joon Ho Lim, and Rishika Rishika. 2018. The effect of a data breach announcement on customer behavior: Evidence from a multichannel retailer. *Journal of Marketing* 82, 2 (2018), 85–105.

Table 4: Frequency of Verified, Non-SpamList Account Breaches By Socioeconomic Factors

	mean	se
Ethnicity		
White	2.21	0.04
Black	2.03	0.08
Hispanic/Latino	1.73	0.07
Asian	2.16	0.18
Native American	1.85	0.18
Middle Eastern	2.05	0.21
Mixed Race	1.70	0.19
Other	2.69	1.19
Sex		
Female	2.15	0.04
Male	2.05	0.05
Age		
(18,25]	1.63	0.10
(25,35]	2.44	0.08
(35,50]	2.37	0.07
(50,65]	2.16	0.06
(65,100]	1.78	0.05
Missing	0.91	0.13
Education		
No HS	1.53	0.09
HS Grad.	1.91	0.05
Some College	2.22	0.08
2-year College Degree	2.10	0.08
4-year College Degree	2.37	0.08
Postgrad Degree	2.30	0.08

[6] McKenzie L Kuhn. 2018. 147 Million Social Security Numbers for Sale: Developing Data Protection Legislation After Mass Cybersecurity Breaches. *Iowa L. Rev.* 104 (2018), 417.

[7] Suriyan Laohaprapanon and Gaurav Sood. 2018. Domain Knowledge: Predicting the Kind of Content Hosted by a Domain. http://www.gsood.com/research/papers/domain_knowledge.pdf

[8] Daniel J Marcus. 2018. The Data Breach Dilemma: Proactive Solutions for Protecting Consumers' Personal Information. *Duke LJ* 68 (2018), 555.

[9] David McCandless. 2017. World's Biggest Data Breaches & Hacks. http://www.informationisbeautiful.net/visualizations/worlds-biggest-data-breaches-hacks/

[10] Vyacheslav Mikhed and Michael Vogan. 2018. How data breaches affect consumer credit. *Journal of Banking & Finance* 88 (2018), 192–207.

[11] Lily Hay Newman. 2016. Hack Brief: Hackers Breach A Billion Yahoo Accounts. A Billion. https://www.wired.com/2016/12/yahoo-hack-billion-users/

[12] Bernold Nieuwesteeg and Michael Faure. 2018. An analysis of the effectiveness of the EU data breach notification obligation. *Computer Law & Security Review* 34, 6 (2018), 1232–1246.

[13] Douglas Rivers. 2010. Decennial Census Surname Files (2010, 2000). Sample Matching: Representative Sampling from Internet Panels, https://github.com/themains/pwned/lit/rivers.pdf.

[14] Pierangelo Rosati, Peter Deeney, Mark Cummins, Lisa Van der Werff, and Theo Lynn. 2019. Social media and stock price reaction to data breach announcements: Evidence from US listed companies. *Research in International Business and Finance* 47 (2019), 458–469.

[15] Alexander Van Deursen and Jan Van Dijk. 2011. Internet skills and the digital divide. *New media & society* 13, 6 (2011), 893–911.

[16] Kimberly A Whitler and Paul W Farris. 2017. The impact of cyber attacks on brand image: Why proactive marketing expertise is needed for managing data breaches. *Journal of Advertising Research* 57, 1 (2017), 3–9.

Live It Up: Analyzing Emotions and Language Use in Tweets during the Soccer World Cup Finals

Marisa Vasconcelos
IBM Research
marisaav@br.ibm.com

Jussara Almeida
UFMG
jussara@dcc.ufmg.br

Paulo Cavalin
IBM Research
pcavalin@br.ibm.com

Claudio Pinhanez
IBM Research
csantosp@br.ibm.com

ABSTRACT

In this paper, we present a study to identify similarities and differences in how users express themselves on Twitter during two editions of the most watched sports events in the world, the finals of the FIFA Soccer World Cup of 2014 and 2018. Our findings suggest in 2014 users tended to post more negative content than in 2018, while less hateful and offensive messages were posted in 2018 than in 2014. This study also showcases the challenges of performing analysis of emotional reactions on sports-related posts due to the specificity of the colorful language employed by the fans.

1 INTRODUCTION

Sports are known by their capacity of generating emotional responses which influence both players and spectators. However, it is difficult to measure emotion dynamics of fans during a match, especially during a major worldwide event like the FIFA's Soccer World Cup. With the popularization of mobile phones, sports fans increasingly interact among themselves using social media during the match, displaying their emotions in social posts [5].

We chose to analyze the online behavior of soccer spectators because they are known by their strong emotional reactions which can vary depending on the spectator perspective [2]. Also, the World Cup is the most watched sports competition in the world: an estimated 700 million people followed the final match of the 2014 World Cup.

Our main contribution is a quantitative exploration of the use of emotional language during the 2014 and 2018 final matches of the FIFA's Soccer World Cup. Our findings suggest that the emotional language used in each edition differs in many ways, for instance, tweets posted during 2104 final present a more negative tone on average, compared to the 2018 edition.

In both datasets, we found a low fraction of tweets classified as hate speech or offensive language and we discuss the false positive issues with the hate speech detection approach. Soccer is particularly a game where unfortunately it is common for fans to use offensive vocabulary (for instance, racism, sexism, and homophobia) what makes hate speech and offensive classification important. We discuss some of the challenges of detecting hateful and offensive messages shared during those matches, pointing out limitations on the existing hate-detection tools.

2 THE WORLD CUP TWEET DATASETS

The datasets used in this work are comprised of Twitter posts in English language collected during the final matches of the 2014 and 2018 World Cups: Argentina vs. Germany (July 13th of 2014) and Croatia vs. France (July 14th of 2018). Those sets have been downloaded from different sources. The posts from 2014, to which we refer here as *Firehose 2014* dataset were gathered by means of the use of the Twitter *Firehose*, and contains over 4 million tweets. On the other hand, the posts from 2018, referred to here as the *Streaming 2018* dataset, were collected with the Twitter *Streaming API* (around 771 thousand tweets).

We are aware that a direct comparison of those two datasets has to be done with caution due to the fact that the sampling methodology of the Streaming 2018 dataset is not completely known. However, we argue that, for the goals of this paper, comparing the data in the two sets is fair, following the discussion and arguments of previous work [4]. Wang *et al.* [4] showed that Twitter data samples are able to preserve enough information for analyses focused on the general tweets (e.g., user activity pattern characterization, event detection) or content statistics (e.g., sentiment analysis).

Analyzing the Polarity of the Tweets. We start analyzing the textual content of the tweets by extracting the polarity of the fan's opinions. For this analysis, we utilized *SentiStrength*[1] a state-of-the-art sentiment analysis tool which gives a score that varies from -4 to +4 (negative to positive polarity). Before applying the tool, we filtered out from the tweets URLs, symbols, emojis, and mentions, and we perform lemmatization to the final tweet texts.

Figure 1 shows the mean polarity of the tweets over time in the two datasets. Note that tweets posted in 2014 stays most of the time below the neutral line while the tweets posted in 2018 seem to be more positive than negative. In both datasets, we found that most of the tweets were neutral (45% in 2014 and 53% in 2018). However, 21% and 34% of the tweets were classified as positive and negatives, respectively, in 2014; while in 2018 27% and 20% were classified as positive and negative, respectively.

Analyzing each selected event, we see that users were on average more positive right before the full time completion in both years. In 2014, the weird collision of Argentinian player Higuain with German goalkeeper Neuer had on average a negative view from users while in 2018, the second Croatia goal was also seen as negative, probably because of the failure of the French goalkeeper.

Hate Speech and Offensive Language. We also studied the presence of hate and offensive language. We follow the same hate speech definition proposed by Davidson *et al.* [1]: a "*language that is used to expresses hatred towards a targeted group or is intended to be derogatory, to humiliate, or to insult the members of the group*".

---

[1]http://sentistrength.wlv.ac.uk/

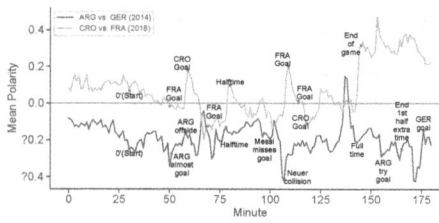

Figure 1: Mean polarity over time.

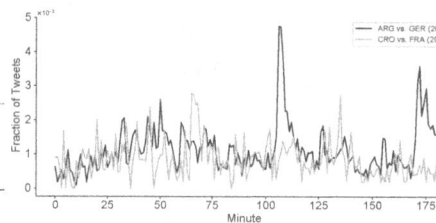

Figure 2: Hate speech tweets over time.

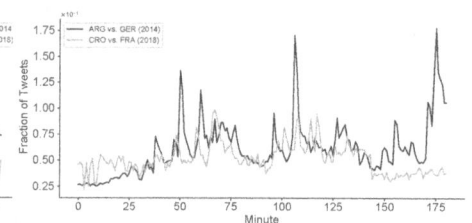

Figure 3: Offensive tweets over time.

For this analysis, we start using a classifier trained with generic tweets composed by posts labeled in three classes (hate speech, offensive language, and regular posts) released as described in [1]. Figures 2 and 3 plot the percentages of hate speech and use of offensive language over time during each match, respectively. Surprisingly, the fraction of tweets classified as hate speech is very low reaching up to only 0.005 in 2014 and 0.003 in 2018. Similarity, offensive language is also considered lower reaching up to 0.18 in 2014 and 0.1 in 2018.

We have also investigated some of the peaks shown in the plots (see Table 1). In 2014, the peak corresponds to the "Neuer collision", in which German goalkeeper Neuer clashed and knocked out Argentinian forward player Higuain. We observed many posts using the word "kill". This type of expression is common in soccer, a kind of hyperbolic language which is not necessarily a real case of hate speech. In 2018, the fourth goal of France team also reached a peak of hate speech due to the use of the word "kill". Offensive words seem to coincide with some major events in matches.

We also use another approach to detect hate speech proposed by Mondal *et al.* [3] which is based on the sentence structure of the text. Using that method, we found posts which match the template with "hate" expression accounted for the majority of matches in both datasets (57% for 2014 and 41% for 2018), while the word "n*igga" and "n*gger" accounted for 51% and 1.52% of the 2014 and 2018 posts. We did not find clear hate speech posts targeting specific nationalities, gender, or ethnicity using this tool.

As we notice, detecting hate speech in soccer (e.g., sports) related posts is not trivial. While analyzing the datasets, we observed many examples of false positives of both hate and offensive language. As mentioned, sports events evoke strong emotions from spectators who often use very expressive and colorful language [2] which tends to "mislead" automatic detection tools. Both state-of-the-art strategies of hate speech detection used here were not efficient to detect hate speech on soccer events [3]. We manually foraged for examples of false positives analyzing some of the posts which were not classified as hate speech and listed some of them in Table 2.

It is important to point out that the frequency of real hate speech may be lower in the Streaming 2018 dataset since Twitter has started restricting hate speech use on its platform in 2017. Their *hateful conduct policy* forbids users from directly attacking individuals on basis of characteristics such as race, sexual orientation or gender.

3 CONCLUSION AND FUTURE WORK

We present a quantitative analysis of the content posted on Twitter during the two FIFA Soccer World Cup final matches of 2014

Example	Class	Event	Dataset
I think Neuer just tried to **kill** Higuain. How the f*ck did Higuain foul him.	hate offensive	Neuer collision	2014
Argentina is so g*y f*cking If you dare f*cking injure Messi	hate offensive	Peak before GER goal	2014
What a stupid decision! F*ck VAR **Bullsh*t** penalty. Joke final.	hate offensive	2nd FRA goal	2018
Mbappe that **n*gga** Holy **sh*t** Mbappe!!	hate offensive	4th FRA goal	2018

Table 1: Tweets found during hate speech peaks.

Examples	Dataset
You'd swear Germany watched Hitler's WWII speech in the locker room at halftime.	2014
Who say "Go Germany" actually mean "Heil Hitler"	2014
100 yrs from now". The last non-colored Frenchm...	2018
Kante is one of the most intelligent players I have ever seen. The pundits will never talk about a black player like that.	2018
Afrikans supporting France coz "they're represented by black players" shows how ignorant we are in this continent	2018

Table 2: Examples of no detected hate speech.

and 2018. The analysis consisted of applying emotional language techniques, such as polarity analysis, and hate speech and offensive language detection to evaluate two large sets of tweets collected during those events. Our work demonstrates the need to improve emotional language analysis tools since we show that current methods seem to suffer from lack of context or biases towards some words which may not be offensive on many occasions.

ACKNOWLEDGMENTS

This work received financial support from CNPq and FAPEMIG.

REFERENCES

[1] T. Davidson, D. Warmsley, M. Macy, and I. Weber. 2017. Automated Hate Speech Detection and the Problem of Offensive Language. In *Proc. of ICWSM'17*.
[2] J. Gratch, G. Lucas, N. Malandrakis, E. Szablowski, E. Fessler, and J. Nichols. 2015. GOAALLL!: Using Sentiment in the World Cup to Explore Theories of Emotion. In *Proc. of the ACII*.
[3] M. Mondal, L. Silva, and F. Benevenuto. 2017. A Measurement Study of Hate Speech in Social Media. In *Proc. of the HT*.
[4] Y. Wang, J. Callan, and B. Zheng. 2015. Should We Use the Sample? Analyzing Datasets Sampled from Twitter's Stream API. *ACM Transactions on the Web* 9, 3, Article 13 (June 2015), 23 pages.
[5] Y. Yu and X. Wang. 2015. World Cup 2014 in the Twitter World: A big data analysis of sentiments in U.S. sports fans' tweets. *Computers in Human Behaviour* 48, C (jul 2015), 392–400.

Characterizing Transport Perception using Social Media: Differences in Mode and Gender

Paula Vasquez-Henriquez
Universidad del Desarrollo
Santiago, Chile
pvasquezh@udd.cl

Eduardo Graells-Garrido
Universidad del Desarrollo
Santiago, Chile
egraells@udd.cl

Diego Caro
Universidad del Desarrollo
Santiago, Chile
dcaro@udd.cl

ABSTRACT

Transport planners face the growing need to understand the behavior of their users, who base their mobility decisions on several factors, including travel time, quality of service, and security. However, transportation is usually designed with an average user in mind, without considering the needs of important groups, such as women. In this context, we analyzed 300K tweets about transportation in Santiago, Chile. We classified users into modes of transportation, and then we estimated the associations between mode of transportation, gender, and the categories of a psycho-linguistic lexicon. Our results include that women express more anger and sadness than expected, and are worried about sexual harassment. Conversely, men focus more on the spatial aspects of transportation, leisure, and work. Thus, our work provides evidence on which aspects of transportation are relevant in the daily experience, enabling the measurement of the travel experience using social media.

CCS CONCEPTS

• **Information systems** → **Web mining**; • **Applied computing** → Transportation;

KEYWORDS

sentiment analysis; twitter; gender differences; transportation

ACM Reference Format:
Paula Vasquez-Henriquez, Eduardo Graells-Garrido, and Diego Caro. 2019. Characterizing Transport Perception using Social Media: Differences in Mode and Gender. In *11th ACM Conference on Web Science (WebSci '19), June 30–July 3, 2019, Boston, MA, USA.* ACM, New York, NY, USA, 5 pages. https://doi.org/10.1145/3292522.3326036

1 INTRODUCTION

Transportation plays a key role in people's development in society, greatly affecting the quality of life [7, 32] of its users, who base their mobility decisions on factors such as cost, comfort, accessibility, punctuality, quality of service, and security [10]. For this reason, transport policy-makers face the growing need to understand their needs and perceptions to better plan and manage transportation networks and public policy. However, there is a gap between the perceptions of transportation administrators and those from users, since information is collected with an "average" user in mind, usually with little consideration of the needs and opinions of other important user groups, such as women [30].

In this paper, we characterized the perception of transportation through Twitter, taking into account differences in mode of transportation and gender. We hypothesized that, if different modes of transportation have their own specific issues, or if women experience any mode of transportation in a different way than men, then this should be reflected in a difference in the linguistic components of the texts they publish. We measured these linguistic components in a two-step process. First, we classified users and their transportation-related tweets into mode(s) of transportation using semi-supervised topic modeling [9, 20]. Then, we measured perception using a psycho-linguistic lexicon and gross-community perception metrics [25].

We applied our proposed method to 300K tweets published in Santiago, Chile. We found that public transport users use Twitter to interact with service providers, while reporting a higher association with sexual and swear words. Motorized transport discussion focuses on taxis and ride-hailing apps, and the state of the driving system, where users show to be sensitive to space usage. Non-motorized transportation discussion is centered around the leisure aspect of this mode [21], where users report more optimism. In terms of gender differences, we confirmed the differences in perception and focus. Women are more associated with sociability, sexual harassment, and positive words, pointing to an ambivalence between concerns and positive experiences. Conversely, men are more associated with the spatial aspect of transportation, work discussion, and swear words.

Our work contributes a methodology to infer mode of transportation usage from social media content, and a case study of measured differences between modes of transportation, with a gender perspective, using Twitter data from a big city. Our results provide evidence on which aspects of transportation are relevant in the travel experience, as measured from social media. Our metrics could be put into operation to allow transportation planners to consider a wider range of needs and dynamics into their work, complementing traditional data sources with fine-grained data.

2 RELATED WORK

Data used to plan and manage transportation is traditionally collected through surveys [1, 8]. Women's travel patterns differ greatly from those of men due to the role they play in society, combining the tasks of workers, home-care givers and those responsible for children and the elderly [2, 19]. However, these differences often do not appear on survey data, where budget constraints of traditional transportation questionnaires may not allow to incorporate gender-specific questions. As result, most of the planning is targeted at average users, with a lack of a gender perspective.

The role of social media in transport analysis has rapidly grown over the last years, allowing to obtain information regarding trips and activities, while highlighting the benefits of using this type of data sources [26]. Social platforms such as Twitter, and other specialized platforms like Waze, allow users to organize in communities, contributing information about transportation, which has been used to infer patterns and dynamics of urban behavior [14, 28]. To the extent of our knowledge, there is not much literature on alternative ways to approach transport perception, except for a descriptive analysis of public transport perception from tweets in the city of Chicago [5], and the monitoring of malfunctions in public transport in Madrid [6].

Our work can be seen as a deeper analysis on the travel experience than those from previous work [5, 6], due to our focus on all modes of transportation and to our structured lexical analysis.

3 METHODOLOGY

The main goal of this study is to characterize the perception of transportation as seen on Twitter, quantifying differences per mode of transport and gender. In this section, we explain the three steps of the pipeline we used to achieve this purpose: user representation and inference of gender, inference of mode of transportation, and measurement of perception.

User Features. A Twitter user profile contains the following attributes used in our study: *id, name, description,* and *tweets.* Tweets are textual micro-posts of 280 characters at most that may contain mentions to other users, hashtags to indicate themes within the post, URLs, emoji, *etc.* To these features, we also added *gender.* We focused on a binary gender separation: {male, female}. Without losing generality, we inferred gender based on self-reported information [12, 17]. The inference was based on two heuristics. The first one matched the first name of each user with a database of known names, built from census data and from manually crafted lists. The second one matched expressions in the self-reported description (*e.g.,* "Mother, Sister, Daughter......", and so on). Then, we propagated gender labels using *SGD Classifier* implemented in *scikit-learn* [23]. We did so by predicting gender based on the description content.

Mode of Transportation Inference. To measure perception per mode of transportation, we needed a way to classify users and tweets into each mode. We used the following high-level categorization of mode(s) of transportation: 1) Public Transportation (*e.g.,* bus, subway); 2) Motorized Transportation (*e.g.,* cars, ride-apps); and 3) Non-Motorized Transportation (*e.g.,* bicycles). These modes can be characterized by vocabulary usage, for instance, public transportation operators have support accounts, and use specific terms like station names. Thus, it is possible to train a model that infers the relationships between users and modes, as well as terms and modes based on the co-occurrences of words. Based on a model to infer modes(s) of transportation from mobile phone data [9], we used a semi-supervised method named Topic-Supervised Non-Negative Matrix Factorization (TS-NMF) [20], which associates users and tweets to latent features interpreted as modes of transportation.

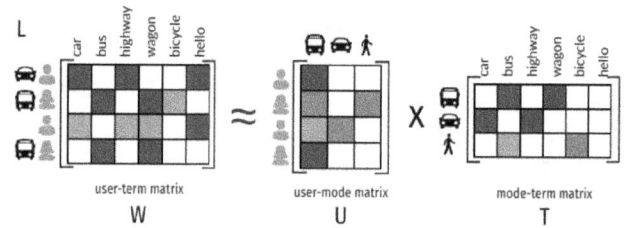

Figure 1: Topic-Supervised Non-Negative Matrix Factorization technique. The document-term matrix W holds the vocabulary used by each user in all their tweets, where each row represents an user, and columns represent the number of times a term is used. As W is positive definite, it can be decomposed in two matrices U and T of lower dimensions. These two matrices represent the latent features associations between terms and modes of transportation.

The TS-NMF method receives as input a document-term matrix W and a supervision matrix L. The matrix W was built from the concatenation of user timelines (*i.e.,* all tweets by the same user), which we treated as documents. A document d_u is defined as a vector: $d_u = [w_1, w_2, ..., w_{|V|}]$, where w_i represents the normalized frequency of term i posted by user u, and $|V|$ is the size of the vocabulary. Terms include words and n-grams (up to three), hashtags, mentions, URL hostnames, and emojis. The matrix L contains a subset of pre-labeled users with modes of transportation. For each mode, we had a list of seed words and phrases that represent it (*e.g., platform* is associated with public transport, *Uber* is associated with motorized transport). Users were pre-labeled based on a calculated score defined as the sum of normalized frequencies of these seed words for each mode. Those with a score higher than a threshold were labeled with the corresponding mode (in our experiments, we defined 0.25 as a compromise between confidence and number of users labeled).

The TS-NMF method decomposes W into the product of two matrices of lower dimensions. This factorization allowed us to arrange the vocabulary into clusters (or latent components) according to the mode of transportation described by users. To do so, we decomposed the matrix into $W \approx U \times T$, where U was a $|u| \times k$ matrix that encodes k latent features of users (i.e their mode of transportation), and T is a $k \times |V|$ matrix, that encodes k latent features over the vocabulary (c.f. Fig. 1). The TS-NMF factorization takes into account the pre-labeled users in L to promote a meaningful semantic structure in the decomposition of the k latent features. For a deep review in topic-supervised factorization see [20].

In this way, the matrix U characterizes users, and the matrix T characterizes the vocabulary, allowing us to classify user tweets into modes of transportation according to their vocabulary usage.

Gross Transport Perception. We quantified transportation perception through the usage of the psycho-linguistic lexicon Linguistic Inquiry and Word Count (LIWC) [24]. This lexicon has been used to characterize perception and emotions on Twitter [11]. Particularly, it defines three high-level categories that we deemed relevant for our study: *Emotionality, Relativity,* and *Personal Concerns.* Emotionality includes both negative emotions such as *anger, sadness,* *fear* and *anxiety*, and positive emotions such as *optimism* and *positive feelings*. Relativity includes notions of *time, motion*, and *space*. Personal Concerns include themes such as *job, leisure, social, swear words*, and *sexual*-related words.

However, just counting words of each LIWC category is not enough, as social media content is subject to factors that may bias analysis. For instance, it can be expected to have more tweets about public transport than motorized modes given that transit riders may use their phones while moving. Previous work on Gross Perception [25] tackles this issue by analyzing the standardized usage of LIWC categories. We built upon these metrics by defining the Gross Transportation Perception *GTP*, which measured the relative use of words per each mode and LIWC category as:

$$GTP_x^{p_{ij}} = \frac{x_{ij}^p - \mu_i^p}{\sigma_i^p},$$

where p is a LIWC category, i is a mode of transportation, j is a day, and x is the normalized frequency of words belonging to the category p in said day for a given group of tweets, μ_i^p and σ_i^p are the mean and sd of the fraction of words belonging to the category p of the mode of transport i. It may be a single user, a group of users, all tweets following specific criteria, *etc*. We carried out this analysis at the transport mode level, in periods of three hours, and at the gender level, at daily periods.

Having into account the previous definition, we defined the *gender gap in perception* as $GAP_i^p = GTP_{f,i}^p - GTP_{m,i}^p$, where p is a LIWC category, i is a mode of transportation, f is the set of tweets by women, and m is the set of tweets by men in a given period. As result, *GAP* tells us if the tendency of using a certain category is associated with females (GAP > 0) or males (GAP < 0).

4 CASE STUDY: SANTIAGO, CHILE

Santiago, Chile, is a densely populated city with almost 7 million people. We collected tweets related to transportation from March to November of 2017, leaving out the summer period in which mobility patterns change. We filtered out tweets that contain URLs of media outlets and unrelated topics, and users with a reported location different from the city of Santiago. We queried the Twitter Streaming API with words related to transportation, such as operator names, station names, and transport-application names. We collected a total of 303,800 tweets from 56,624 users living in the Santiago metropolitan area. We were able to identify 19,012 users as women, and 29,166 as men, which together represent over 85% of the sample. Note that users without inferred gender were later considered to measure differences in modes of transportation.

Figure 2 shows the aggregated hourly frequency distribution of tweets. One can see that the frequency resembles the morning and afternoon peak hours in transportation [33]. The most common terms are the institutional accounts of public transport services (@transantiago and @metrodesantiago). Such frequency hints that a big part of the discussion is held by public transport.
Mode of Transportation Inference. To associate modes of transportation to users and terms we defined seed keywords for each mode, including account names, hashtags, plain words, and emojis. With this schema, we pre-labeled 16,375 users to public transport, 2,449 users to motorized transport, and 2,447 users to non-motorized

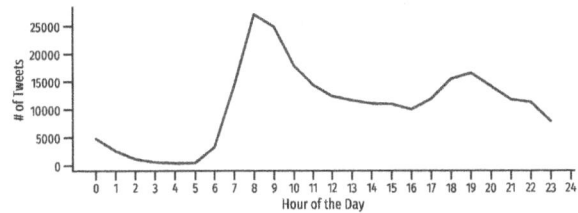

Figure 2: Tweet Frequency per hour of day. The transport-related tweeting frequency resembles the morning and the afternoon peak hours in the Santiago transportation system.

Mode	Seed Word	# Users	# Tweets
Motorized	*driving, highway, @uber_chile*	2,449	41,152
Non-Motorized	*bicycle, walking, @mobikecl*	2,447	29,051
Public	@transantiago, 🚌, @metrodesantiago	16,375	233,597

Table 1: Seed words used to characterize transportation mode. Some users were pre-labeled based according to their usage of the seed words of each mode of transportation.

transport. The TS-NMF model propagated these labels to the rest of the data set (*c.f.* Table 1).

Figure 3 shows one wordcloud per mode of transportation, with their corresponding associated words according to the TS-NMF model. The motorized transport discussion focused on terms related to taxis and ride-hailing apps (*@uber_chile, cabify, taxis, taxi drivers, #uber*), possibly due to conflicts about the legality of these services. Other related terms include the state of the driving system (*highway, driving, accident*), service providers (*@uoct_rm, @autopcentral*), and trip information via Waze, a community-driven GPS navigation software where users (who refer themselves as *wazers*) share travel times and route details. Non-motorized terms relate to riding the bicycle (*bicycle, cyclists, @mfc_stgo*) and their users show more relationship with accounts from municipalities (*@muni_stgo*) andauthorities (*@alessandrifelip*, the mayor of Santiago; or *@orrego*, the former city's intendant). This may be due to two things: people mentioning them to communicate an opinion or a retweet of information published by them. Terms related to public transportation are in respect to the Transantiago system (which integrates the buses and subway), with users mentioning station names (*e.g., Baquedano*, a downtown connection hub), and using hashtags related to the line services and service status (Lines 1 and 6, *#l1, #l6*). Also, they often interact with the Ministry of Transport and Telecommunications (*@mtt_chile*), or bus providers (*@alsaciaexpress*). They mention fewer accounts in comparison to other modes, but use more terms to describe the state and characteristics of the system (*day, minutes, wait, bus stop, wagons*).
Gross Transport Perception per Mode. Figure 4 shows the gross-perception per mode of transportation and LIWC categories. The emotionality associations show that *anger* is a less associated emotion with non-motorized transportation, which is consistent with studies that show that walking and cycling are more related to well-being and higher satisfaction [29, 31]. *Anxiety* is present in public transportation, which could indicate that there is a situation that triggers feelings of fear in users. *Optimism* signals a difference between the non-motorized and motorized transportation, where

Figure 3: Wordclouds of the most associated words per mode of transportation. Motorized transportation discussion focuses on terms related to taxis, ride-hailing apps and the state of the driving system, while non-motorized transportation talk mainly about bicycles and public transportation focuses on interactions with service providers.

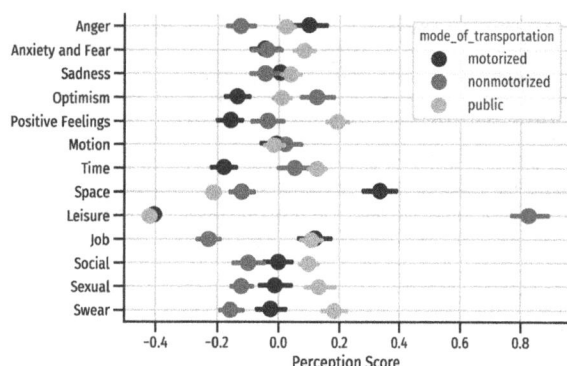

Figure 4: Gross Perception per Mode of Transportation (GTP), a measure of the relative usage of LIWC categories between modes of transportation. For instance, leisure is more associated with non-motorized transportation, in comparison to the other modes.

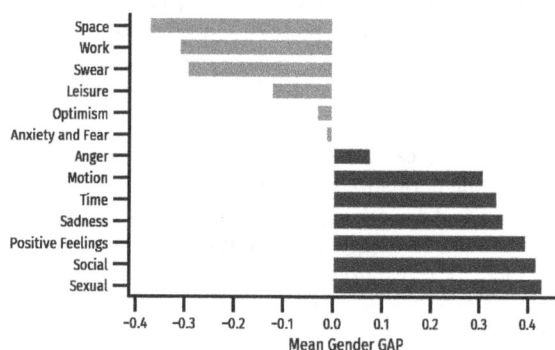

Figure 5: Mean Gender Gaps in Gross-Perception, calculated as the difference between GTPs. LIWC Categories with positive (negative) values present higher association with women (men). For instance, women report higher association to sexual words.

the latter seem to experience fewer feelings of optimism during their travels, which could be related to the stress drivers experience, as studies have shown [15]. *Positive feelings* are more associated to public transportation, contrary to the intuition that Twitter is used only for complains [13].

In terms of relativity, *time* is more associated with non-motorized and public transportation. For example, public transport users may talk about how long they have been waiting for a bus to arrive; non-motorized users may comment on their trip times. Motorized transport users pay more attention to *space*, due to issues such as the state of roads, traffic jams, and accidents. It is important to study these factors since users base their transportation decisions on them [10]. This applies even to single trips, due to the dynamic conditions of transportation, such as crowding at peak hours.

Regarding personal concerns, *leisure* is more associated with non-motorized transport. This may be related to the fact that non-motorized transportation has a strong use for entertainment purposes such as biking or taking a walk for pleasure [21]. In a similar way, public transport association to *work* emerges in the higher use of words from this feature, due to its high use for commuting. In Santiago, commuting represents more than a third of the total trips per day [33]. Public transport users seem to use more *sexual* and *swear* words. In addition to the various studies that have shown that public transport users present negative feelings during the trip [3]; factors such as crowding, delays, and accessibility increase stress, and that this perception differs according to factors such as

gender [4]. It is in this mode of transport where people report high rates of sexual harassment [27].

Gender Differences. Figure 5 shows the mean gender gaps in gross-perception of LIWC categories, after estimating *GTP* for each gender. Men are more associated to the *space* category, which we theorize is because they tend to be the main users of motorized transport [33], where these terms are frequently used. Men are also associated with words related to *work* and *leisure*, consistent with results that show that they talk more about external events, objects, and processes, using more *swear* words [22].

On the other hand, women are more associated with words that talk about the context of transport (*motion, time*). As discussed, this may be due to factors such as time influencing their transportation decisions. It is notable that women also report a high association with *positive* words while also being highly associated with feelings such as *sadness* or *anger*, resulting in an ambivalence.We theorize that this may be caused by the use of sarcasm, or other reasons that should be explored in greater depth. Negative feelings could be related to their higher use of words from the *sexual* sphere, in accordance with studies that point to the violence they suffer in transportation [18], especially in the public type [27]. We explored the words that co-occur with those belonging to the sexual category, finding words such as *harassment, rape, street, man, sexual*, and mentions of public transport (*metro, transantiago, @transantiago, micro*), which is where women report suffering more harassment.

5 DISCUSSION AND CONCLUSIONS

Transportation is fundamental for the development in society, and the way it is perceived has a great impact on the quality of life. Hence, it is important to characterize the perception of people with respect to this activity. In this paper, we have established a method to quantify and compare the perception of modes of transportation, including gender as a factor of analysis. This method captures the subjective travel experience in an inexpensive and dynamic way. Entities such as service providers and transportation system administrators can benefit from the knowledge gained through social network data.

The creation of gender-aware subjective experience metrics could help to identify relevant issues regarding the travel experience that are ignored when transport is designed with the "average user" in mind. For instance, even though sexual harassment is a problem for women, the last travel survey in Santiago only referred to safety, potentially including harassment, but also confounding it with other unsafe situations [33]. This is of special importance in countries with high levels of gender inequality, where women are more often victims of sexual harassment in the public space [18]. Transport riding quality and satisfaction are often measured in terms of the needs of the business [5], which may be oblivious to social problems.

It could be argued that the use of social media data may be biased in terms of representativeness. Although the proportion of men and women may not be representative of the population, patterns within each group could be, particularly in commuter populations [16]. Nevertheless, future work should address this factor, not only by validating gender distribution but also including other demographic factors such as age and income. Finally, a potential line of research is the characterization of context surrounding perception, to answer questions such as: Is the *sexual* category completely related to harassment, or does vernacular language play a relevant role? What is the effect of interventions against harassment? These kinds of insights may be of value for practitioners and policymakers.

Acknowledgements. P.V. and E.G. were partially funded by Fonde-cyt de Iniciación project #11180913. All authors were partially funded by Concurso Interno de Investigación UDD #CI18.

REFERENCES

[1] Reeti Agarwal. 2008. Public transportation and customer satisfaction: the case of Indian railways. *Global Business Review* 9, 2 (2008), 257–272.

[2] Orna Blumen. 1994. Gender differences in the journey to work. *Urban geography* 15, 3 (1994), 223–245.

[3] Mairead Cantwell, Brian Caulfield, and Margaret O'Mahony. 2009. Examining the factors that impact public transport commuting satisfaction. *Journal of Public Transportation* 12, 2 (2009), 1.

[4] Yung-Hsiang Cheng. 2010. Exploring passenger anxiety associated with train travel. *Transportation* 37, 6 (2010), 875–896.

[5] Craig Collins, Samiul Hasan, and Satish V Ukkusuri. 2013. A novel transit rider satisfaction metric: Rider sentiments measured from online social media data. *Journal of Public Transportation* 16, 2 (2013), 2.

[6] Mariluz Congosto, Damaris Fuentes-Lorenzo, and Luis Sánchez. 2015. Microbloggers as sensors for public transport breakdowns. *IEEE Internet Computing* 19, 6 (2015), 18–25.

[7] Giovanni Costal, Laurie Pickup, and Vittorio Di Martino. 1988. Commuting—a further stress factor for working people: evidence from the European Community. *International archives of occupational and environmental health* 60, 5 (1988), 377–385.

[8] JM Del Castillo and FG Benitez. 2013. Determining a public transport satisfaction index from user surveys. *Transportmetrica A: Transport Science* 9, 8 (2013), 713–741.

[9] Eduardo Graells-Garrido, Diego Caro, and Denis Parra. 2018. Inferring modes of transportation using mobile phone data. *EPJ Data Science* 7, 1 (2018), 49.

[10] Joe B Hanna and John T Drea. 1998. Understanding and predicting passenger rail travel: an empirical study. *Transportation Journal* 38, 1 (1998), 38–46.

[11] GACCT Harman and Mark H Dredze. 2014. Measuring post traumatic stress disorder in Twitter. *In ICWSM* (2014).

[12] Brent Hecht, Lichan Hong, Bongwon Suh, and Ed H Chi. 2011. Tweets from Justin Bieber's heart: the dynamics of the location field in user profiles. In *Proceedings of the SIGCHI conference on human factors in computing systems*. ACM, 237–246.

[13] Thorsten Hennig-Thurau, Caroline Wiertz, and Fabian Feldhaus. 2015. Does Twitter matter? The impact of microblogging word of mouth on consumers' adoption of new movies. *Journal of the Academy of Marketing Science* 43, 3 (2015), 375–394.

[14] Daehan Kwak, Daeyoung Kim, Ruilin Liu, Liviu Iftode, and Badri Nath. 2014. Tweeting traffic image reports on the road. In *2014 6th International Conference on Mobile Computing, Applications and Services (MobiCASE)*. IEEE, 40–48.

[15] Alexander Legrain, Naveen Eluru, and Ahmed M El-Geneidy. 2015. Am stressed, must travel: The relationship between mode choice and commuting stress. *Transportation research part F: traffic psychology and behaviour* 34 (2015), 141–151.

[16] Wendy Liu, Faiyaz Al Zamal, and Derek Ruths. 2012. Using social media to infer gender composition of commuter populations. In *Proceedings of the when the city meets the citizen workshop, the international conference on weblogs and social media*.

[17] Wendy Liu and Derek Ruths. 2013. What's in a Name? Using First Names as Features for Gender Inference in Twitter.. In *AAAI spring symposium: Analyzing microtext*, Vol. 13. 10–16.

[18] Anastasia Loukaitou-Sideris and Camille Fink. 2009. Addressing women's fear of victimization in transportation settings: A survey of US transit agencies. *Urban Affairs Review* 44, 4 (2009), 554–587.

[19] Gary Lynch and Susan Atkins. 1988. The influence of personal security fears on women's travel patterns. *Transportation* 15, 3 (1988), 257–277.

[20] Kelsey MacMillan and James D Wilson. 2017. Topic supervised non-negative matrix factorization. *arXiv preprint arXiv:1706.05084* (2017).

[21] Mehdi Menai et al. 2015. Walking and cycling for commuting, leisure and errands: relations with individual characteristics and leisure-time physical activity in a cross-sectional survey. *International Journal of Behavioral Nutrition and Physical Activity* 12, 1 (2015), 150.

[22] Matthew L Newman, Carla J Groom, Lori D Handelman, and James W Pennebaker. 2008. Gender differences in language use: An analysis of 14,000 text samples. *Discourse Processes* 45, 3 (2008), 211–236.

[23] Fabian Pedregosa et al. 2011. Scikit-learn: Machine learning in Python. *Journal of machine learning research* 12, Oct (2011), 2825–2830.

[24] James W Pennebaker, Matthias R Mehl, and Kate G Niederhoffer. 2003. Psychological aspects of natural language use: Our words, our selves. *Annual review of psychology* 54, 1 (2003), 547–577.

[25] Daniele Quercia, Jonathan Ellis, Licia Capra, and Jon Crowcroft. 2012. Tracking gross community happiness from tweets. In *Proceedings of the ACM 2012 conference on computer supported cooperative work*. ACM, 965–968.

[26] Taha H Rashidi, Alireza Abbasi, Mojtaba Maghrebi, Samiul Hasan, and Travis S Waller. 2017. Exploring the capacity of social media data for modelling travel behaviour: Opportunities and challenges. *Transportation Research Part C: Emerging Technologies* 75 (2017), 197–211.

[27] Servicio Nacional de la Mujer. 2012. Estudio Acoso y Abuso Sexual en lugares públicos y medios de transporte colectivos. http://estudios.sernam.cl/documentos/?eMjI0MDIzOA==-Estudio_Acoso_y_Abuso_Sexual_en_lugares_publicos_y_medios_de_transporte_colectivos_. pp. 15.

[28] Thiago H Silva et al. 2013. Traffic condition is more than colored lines on a map: characterization of waze alerts. In *International Conference on Social Informatics*. Springer, 309–318.

[29] Patrick A Singleton. 2018. Walking (and cycling) to well-being: Modal and other determinants of subjective well-being during the commute. *Travel Behaviour and Society* (2018).

[30] Daphne Spain. 2000. Run, don't walk: how transportation complicates women's balancing act. In *Women's Travel Issues Second National ConferenceDrachman Institute of the University of Arizona; Morgan State University; Federal Highway Administration*.

[31] Evelyne St-Louis, Kevin Manaugh, Dea van Lierop, and Ahmed El-Geneidy. 2014. The happy commuter: A comparison of commuter satisfaction across modes. *Transportation research part F: traffic psychology and behaviour* 26 (2014), 160–170.

[32] Alois Stutzer and Bruno S Frey. 2008. Stress that doesn't pay: The commuting paradox. *Scandinavian Journal of Economics* 110, 2 (2008), 339–366.

[33] Universidad Alberto Hurtado, Observatorio Social. 2012. Encuesta Origen Destino Santiago 2012 (Informe Ejecutivo). http://www.sectra.gob.cl/biblioteca/detalle1.asp?mfn=3253. pp. 14, Accessed: 2018-09-24.

Modelling Web Based Socio-Technical Systems Through Formalising Possible Sequences of Human Experience

Rob Walton
Dept. of Engineering Science
Oxford, United Kingdom
rob.walton@eng.ox.ac.uk

David De Roure
Oxford e-Research Centre
Oxford, United Kingdom
david.deroure@oerc.ox.ac.uk

ABSTRACT

When people interact through technical infrastructure such as that of organisations or the World Wide Web, this infrastructure will change and in some cases new identifiable structures or even ecosystems may emerge. Examples of such emergent socio-technical systems on the Web include some social machines and phenomena such as echo chambers. To model these complex social systems we develop a method for formalising the moments, or occasions, of experience of an individual person by contriving a 'chemistry' encoding possible sequences of their external stimuli, internal experience and reactions to this internal experience. We take a process oriented approach and formalise this as a stochastic Petri net. We wire together a number of these to form a fixed social network in which experience is shared. The resulting model unfolds into many possible causal graphs of occasions of experience which we show using an interactive visualisation. We demonstrate the utility of this method by encoding models exhibiting information diffusion and what we call multiple phase diffusion, and then consensus formation, before encoding a mechanism of echo chamber formation. We then demonstrate the conflation of individuals' positions on otherwise separate issues through emotion. The approach results in a single Petri net model which may be analysed using qualitative and quantitative techniques supporting web science research. It provides a way to describe and reason about the internal experience of individuals within multi-scale socio-technical systems.

ACM Reference format:
Rob Walton and David De Roure. 2019. Modelling Web Based Socio-Technical Systems Through Formalising Possible Sequences of Human Experience. In *Proceedings of 11th ACM Conference on Web Science, Boston, MA, USA, June 30–July 3, 2019 (WebSci '19)*, 10 pages.
https://doi.org/10.1145/3292522.3326049

1 INTRODUCTION

When people interact through technical infrastructure such as that of organisations or the World Wide Web, this infrastructure and the social networks that form around it may coexist and adapt together. When this occurs we may identify a socio-technical system,

examples of which, on the Web, include some social machines [21] and phenomena such as echo chambers. In some cases new identifiable structures or ecosystems may emerge [5]. Understanding the mechanisms behind these behaviours and the life-cycle of the resulting structures is important if we are to model the Web and shape its evolution.

The Web exhibits interesting and difficult to model behaviour across multiple scales. We might consider the Web itself a single piece of technical infrastructure and ask how its structure evolves alongside that of a single social network coevolving with it. At this level we see an ecosystem of social machines competing and cooperating for the attention of individuals and for access to their parts of this social network. Within some of these social machines we see the same processes forming local communities with particular interests or goals [5]. Within some of these we see similar behaviours acting to drive individuals to form short-lived communities around topics as fleeting perhaps as a passing joke or a disagreement over spelling. There is no such absolute hierarchy in reality though: topics or ideas spread through these structures in a peer to peer like way, and longer lived structures such as echo chambers form among them, some with influence from outside the Web.

Early work to understand and learn to optimise socio-technical systems focused on organisations at the scale of businesses. The Web and the social structures on it may be considered instances of Large-Scale Socio-Technical Systems identified by Thomas Hughes' system theory [23] and described by Igor Nikolic as "a class of systems that span technical artefacts embedded in a social network, by which a large-scale, complex socio-technical artefact emerges"[17]. At this scale, a lot of research has gone into modelling electricity systems all the way from power generation and distribution up to regulatory frameworks. Modelling these systems is complex in that more than one formalism, possibly described with different languages from different fields of study, is required to capture all relevant aspects of the system. Bringing these together requires simulation in the form of agent based modelling.

John Holland identifies some agent based modelling as *exploratory modelling* which he describes as: "starting with a designated set of of mechanisms, such as the various bonds between amino acids, with the objective of finding out what can happen when these mechanisms interact" [12]. For example, Schelling showed in his study of segregation that for spatially segregated subpopulations to form there is no need for individuals to avoid others: it is sufficient that individuals have a weak preference to be surrounded by those like themselves [19]. More recently and with access to computers Starnini et al. asked which behaviours are sufficient for the metapopulations and echo chambers to emerge in populations of mobile agents [25]. They studied the interplay between mobility,

Schelling's homophily and social influence in models of opinion dynamics.

Such exploratory modelling is powerful but models with analytically derivable or empirically measurable properties have historically had more impact. For example, graph growth algorithms based on properties of generic networks, such as Watts and Strogatz's small-world property [26] or power-law degree distributions, are in common use. Also, Girvan and Newman identified a basic property of community structure in social and biological networks [8]. Such models are powerful, as unlike exploratory models, they provide mathematically solid foundations for further work. For example, algorithms for identifying community structure in networks are often based on properties of classes of randomly growable graphs. In addition to these idealised physical or behavioural based models, statistical models such as those describing the recurrence patterns of words or topics in individual writing or collective discussion[3] are derived from empirical measurement. Holland describes exploratory modelling as a first step toward building such analytical models.

Improved models for understanding the socio-technical systems which form on the Web might help us understand and quantify the changes as they are adopted by users and society. They might help us build social machines which have desirable properties such as encouraging discourse between otherwise polarised social groups or which are not 'owned' centrally [10]. Better theory might help us keep such decentralised social machines answerable to society and prevent capture by external organisations. We might identify echo chambers and determine if they are natural or driven by external agenda and we might further investigate the formation mechanisms of filter bubbles [24]. We might ask in the long term how far into our lives these structures might reach, expanding as they will into Internet of Things (IoT) devices and administered increasingly efficiently by algorithms and artificial intelligence, and what the limits to their influence over our behaviour may be. This helps ensure that the new futures the Web offers are shaped with society's most positive aspirations and not left to selection by chance or short-term thinking.

Our goal is to devise a method for formalising enough of the aspects governing a person's internal and social behaviour on the Web to build generative models of individual and collective human experience. The method should be suitable for modelling the emergence of new structures as social networks co-evolve with technical Web infrastructure. The resulting models should be explorable through simulation but may also, in limiting cases of symmetry or low complexity, have analytically derivable properties. These properties might define for example a rigorous relationship between a model describing operation at the scale of coherent interacting communities and at the level of interactions of individuals within or across these community boundaries.

We propose a model with a formal place for capturing moments, or occasions, of human sense awareness. Given the importance of modelling the behaviours that lead to the emergence of structures on the Web this formalism is based on process rather than material or 'solid' systems. The model has two layers. On the top we propose the use of Alfred Whitehead's *Philosophy of Organism* as a framework and language for modelling our large-scale socio-technical systems. This is a process philosophy reasoned from Whitehead's

observations of the limitations of the way we perceive reality. To produce mathematically tractable models we map this layer down onto Petri nets. The mapping is incomplete which limits the expressiveness of the resulting modelling framework. However it is complete enough to capture a range of behaviours as demonstrated by the simple models developed and verified in Section 3.4. Further background on Whitehead's Philosophy of Organism is given in Section 2.1 and further background on Petri net modelling is given in Section 2.2. The method is developed in Section 3.

Results from simulating the verification models of Section 3.4 are shown in Section 4 in the form of causal graphs of occasions of experience. These models demonstrate, on a fixed social network, diffusion and what we call multiple phase diffusion, percolation and then consensus formation. They also show that an accepted mechanism of echo chamber formation encourages the separation of opinion on networks with pre-existing community structure. We also demonstrated the conflation of individuals' position on otherwise separate issues through emotion. These simple models build toward analysing the development of echo chambers. They can be considered to form an initial collection of primitives that may be combined to produce more realistic models.

2 METHOD BACKGROUND

Our method depends on two components not described above. We introduce Whitehead's *Philosophy of Organism*[27] and Petri nets here.

2.1 Philosophy of Organism

We chose Alfred Whitehead's process metaphysics as the top layer of our modelling framework for two reasons. First, Whitehead describes a system capable of explaining how events of sense awareness form and relate, thus providing a formal way of handling this. Second, although there are other choices that meet this goal, this moves us away from speaking of the boundary of a socio-technical system or of them as material things at all, and instead to speaking about interacting processes.

Whitehead describes the coming and going of acts of sense awareness. Each such act he considers unique. He also considers them ultimately private. For example, we may not quite know what went into building our internal experience of a mug on our desk, but when we look away and that act ends we see that it was clearly unique, and that the subjective experience constituent to it is private, not only to us as an individual, but to that act itself. Whitehead labels these moments of sense awareness *occasions*. An occasion of new experience, Whitehead argues, comes to us at some level preformed like a droplet. Only after we experience this may we analyse it to see what went into its formation. Whitehead describes the mechanisms behind the formation of these occasions, or droplets, of experience.

Whitehead's Philosophy of Organism is a process rather than material metaphysics. We believe it provides a very useful way to understand ecosystems of socio-technical systems in which defining solid material-like boundaries between parts is not possible. In developing his system Whitehead conceived no pre-existing 'screen' onto which these drops of sense-awareness or occasions are projected. Instead these are continually and actively pulled as much as pushed into a model of the present which is always based on prior experience. Whitehead says that 'what we perceive as present is the vivid fringe of memory tinged with anticipation'. As such this model is of a short-lived slice through reality rather than an instant of zero length. Our perception of reality, and Whitehead actually argues, reality itself, being always a duration through time, is necessarily of things going on.

The only physical entities in this system of process metaphysics are occasions. These are the atomic building blocks of Whitehead's view of both physical and perceptual reality. They form through a process Whitehead labels *concrescence*. They are the transient *creatures* of his *Philosophy of Organism*. An occasion is rooted in the branching causal networks of the upstream occasions which was its cause. In the case for mental rather than physical systems, pieces of a-priori knowledge and propositional statements will also have been folded in to these causal roots. As each occasion of awareness exists only in its capacity as an addition to a pre-existing model of the present, they often form part of a process of building some aspect of this model.

Where a procession of similar but evolving occasions form, for example, those formed while watching a leaf drop, or as a family regroups every year to recreate Christmas, Whitehead identifies a longer lived *process*. Once formed and experienced each occasion in this process dies. The leaf falling though still attracts attention and Christmas comes again. Such occasions as these then are destined to form the ancestors to the next generation of 'themselves'. There is a definite causal relationship in which such a subsequent occasion occurs after the former. Whitehead describes across eight categories the rules governing which occasions may form and how they do so. Key to understanding the scenario presented here is that two occasions will not form from exactly the same cause.

In this way, each occasion is what Whitehead calls a *superject*, both subject and object. While living, or forming, an occasion builds a subjective view of the objective data formed by its predecessors. Once it has formed then it becomes just another object to subsequent occasions. The predominantly held material view, that one system forms a subjective view of another, or that one system measures or observes another, is no longer primary. This is a big change from the way are used to understanding our reality.

Now the operation of a process of related occasions coming and going is actually more interesting than this. While an occasion is forming from what Whitehead calls its *actual world* (the collection of dead occasions which are its potential cause) a number of neighbours will be forming contemporaneously (that is with no way of influencing each other but with overlapping actual worlds). These neighbours will be 'picking out' different combinations of occasions from the actual world for inclusion. Each such combination results in not one but a set of occasions, for while forming an occasion not only 'picks' which upstream occasions to include, but from the elements that went into forming those. Whitehead says that each such element is *prehended*. It is to these acts of prehension themselves which a prehension reaches back toward (possible through the *medium* of a series of occasions) bringing their data forward into the occasion of which it is a part.

Whitehead's approach results in structures of such processes of occasions, or more broadly a nest-able partial hierarchy of *societies* of occasions. Whitehead identifies a collection of causally related

occasions as a *duration*. Every duration contains other durations and every pair of durations is part a broader duration[15, chapter 13]. For example, we might pick out processes of causally related occasions associated with work and home life and section these into separate durations. Zooming 'outwards' we might find these contained by the duration of our entire lives and then that of life on Earth. Zooming back 'inwards' from here we find processes such as staying alive as a society, staying alive as an individual or maintaining good hygiene and relationships, which are all prerequisite to at least the duration containing work events. Thus we see that processes of occasions may be situated 'next to each other' and may depend on each other. This interdependency results in what Whitehead considers a society of occasions, or of overlapping societies of occasions. The resulting structure is suitable for modelling processes at the scale of the Web while at the same time is key in Whitehead's understanding of individual and communal perception.

2.2 Petri net modelling

Petri nets, or place/transition nets, are a graphical tool used for the description and analysis of systems with concurrent actions. Invented by Carl Petri in 1939 for describing chemical processes [18] they were used a lot during the development of early computers. There are more general formalisms including process algebras such as Milner's π-calculus but we feel Petri nets provide a good balance between ease of use and modelling power. Their representation in graph form provides an intuitive formalism describing the evolution of distributed systems such as the large-scale socio-technical systems on the Web we seek to develop methods to model. Beneath this they may be represented as an incidence matrix around which have developed a collection of mathematical techniques for qualitative and quantitative analysis. As shown in the remainder of this article they are also capable of encoding sufficient aspects of Whitehead's Philosophy of Organism to model well characterised behaviours of the Web.

2.2.1 Petri net definition. As shown in Figure 1 a Petri net is a bipartite graph comprised of places, shown as circles, and transitions, shown as rectangles, connected with directed edges. The top half of Figure 2 show the standard elements of common Petri net definitions. The state, or *marking*, of a Petri net is represented by tokens inside the places and shown as black disks. A transition *fires* if the places feeding into it through the net's directed arcs all have tokens. This firing is a single atomic event in which a token is removed from each input place and a token is placed in each place connected by outgoing arcs. Tokens need not be conserved. If more than one transition is enabled then the order of firing is random. Basic Petri nets have no encoding of time. If the Petri net of Figure 1 were simulated t_a would first fire causing the tokens in x_{p1} and x_{p2} to disappear as a token appears in x_a. The transition t_b would then fire causing the tokens in x_a and x_{p3} to disappear as a token appears in x_b.

A Petri net PN may be represented more formally as places P, transitions T, input and output arcs A, and an initial marking M:

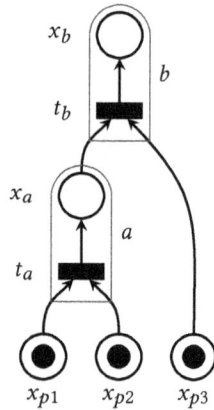

Figure 1: A generative Petri net encoding the potential to experience two occasions *a* and *b* identified by blue surrounds. Each is modelled as a transition *t* with out place *x* indicating that a transition has been experienced. The input places to an occasion's transition represent its prehended occasions.

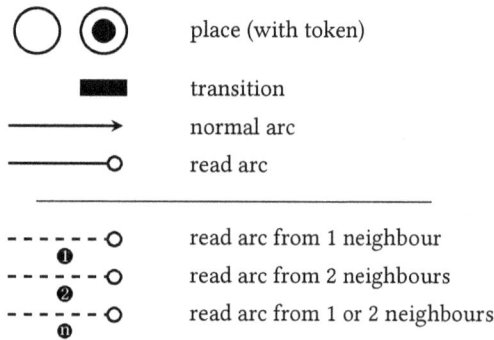

Figure 2: Common Petri net elements above shorthand used in this article

$$
\begin{aligned}
PN &= (P, T, A, M) \\
P &= \{p_1, p_2, ..., p_l\} \\
T &= \{t_1, t_2, ..., t_m\} \\
A &\subset \{P \times T\} \cup \{T \times P\} \\
M &= \{\mu_1, \mu_2, ..., \mu_n\}
\end{aligned}
\tag{1}
$$

where μ_i are the integer number of tokens at a place [2].

A net may be *simulated* resulting in a possible sequence of firings. There are also many analytical techniques for testing if certain markings are reachable for example, or if a net will remain live, or if the number of tokens at any place is bounded [2]. Going in the reverse direction Aalst et al. pioneered the concept of process mining, where a estimates of the net describing the interacting process that result in a given *log* of events may be inferred [1].

2.2.2 Stochastic Petri nets. Petri nets run without time, the result of a simulation being simply a sequence of changing markings or log of firings. Molloy extended the model of Equation (1) to include

a set of transition rates $\Lambda = \{\lambda_1, \lambda_2, ..., \lambda_m\}$ [16]. Where λ_i are, possibly marking dependent, rates for exponentially distributed transition firing times:

$$
f(\tau|\lambda) = \begin{cases} \lambda e^{-\lambda \tau} & \tau \geq 0 \\ 0 & \tau < 0 \end{cases}
\tag{2}
$$

In the resulting continuous-time stochastic Petri net, when a transition becomes enabled an activation time, τ, is chosen randomly and the transition will fire only if the transition remains enabled for this time. The effect is that an enabled transition will fire continuously and independently at a constant average rate while enabled—acting as a *Poisson point process* with average rate λ.

The transition firing rates of the stochastic Petri nets ultimately only affect the ordering of transition firing of the standard Petri net, but in doing so they open up new interpretations of models. Molloy showed that with some limitations a stochastic Petri net with exponentially distributed firing rates is isomorphic to a finite Markov process. These models may also be converted to a set of ordinary differential equations which may be solved numerically, or in simple or symmetric cases, analytically. For example, stable or relatively stable states may be identified using approaches from nonlinear systems analysis.

2.2.3 Coloured Petri nets. Kurt Jensen introduced a generalisation of Petri nets and showed that this can be used to describe and analyse complex systems[14]. In this extension, tokens may have different *colour* or type. This colour may, and will in this article, be associated with an instance of a repeating unit. Places and arcs are given expressions limiting which coloured tokens may enter or traverse them. Transitions may be given optional guard functions which determine if the combination of coloured tokens at their input places meet constraints additional to these.

Coloured Petri nets then can be used to model systems succinctly with repeated structure. In the field of systems biology for example Gao et al. used Coloured Petri Nets as a method for modelling multicellular organisms across multiple scales[7]. They applied this approach to modelling planar cell polarity (PCP) signalling in a Drosophila wing. PCP is the coordinated alignment of cell polarity across a plane of tissue, describing for example the emergence of patterns on the butterfly wing or of our fingerprints.

As an example, Figure 3 shows a coloured Petri net defined in the Snoopy software used for this work and introduced in Section 3.3. The 'Unit' identifier on the places is the set of colours those places may take, in this case the colours $\{1, 2, 3\}$ representing three people. The red text describes, as a multi-set, the colours of the tokens in each place: x_0 has 1 token of colour 2 and one of colour 3, while x_a has one of colour 1. The transition t_a accepts a token of any colour u from the set *Unit* and moves a token of the same colour to place x_a. Without the read arc this coloured Petri net would unfold into three separate units. The read arc presents tokens to the transition via the variable n. The *is_neighbour* function on the transition guards it from firing unless the colours of the tokens in variables u and n meet some criteria.

Looking forward to Section 3 in our work we used a function that enables the transition only if the token in n and the token in u are from neighbouring cells. Figure 4 shows this model unfolded onto the linear graph $n_1 \longleftrightarrow n_2 \longleftrightarrow n_3$. This would be done by

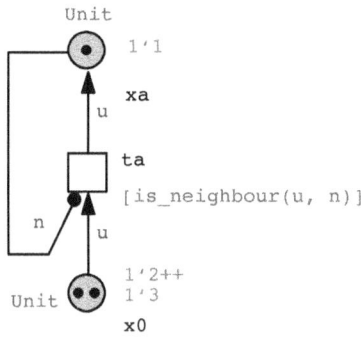

Figure 3: Representation of the diffusion model as displayed in the software package Snoopy. Figure 5a shows the same structure.

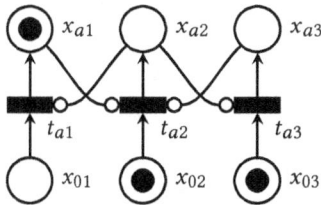

Figure 4: Diffusion model unfolded onto a graph $n_1 \longleftrightarrow n_2 \longleftrightarrow n_3$

specifying is_neighbour(u, n) = (u=1 & n=2) | (u=2 & (n=1|n=3)) | (u=2 & (n=1|n=3)).

3 METHOD DEVELOPMENT AND VERIFICATION

In our goal to model large-scale socio-technical systems on the Web, particularly social machines or echo chambers, we needed to model many interacting individuals. Our approach was to develop generators of possible sequences of human experience, not unlike the n-gram language models introduced by Claude Shannon [22] but for experiences rather than words. We present this 'idea chemistry', based on a simple reading of Whitehead's Philosophy of Organism, in Section 3.1. We then expand this into a 'social idea chemistry' presented in Section 3.2 in which the experience of a neighbour may be followed. Whitehead's Philosophy of Organism is involved, as any attempt to fully describe reality must be, and our goal was just to capture its essence.

3.1 Idea chemistry

In this method, we start building a model by identifying an alphabet O of occasions that may be experienced by an individual. Occasions representing the experience of an idea are labeled with $\{a, b, c...\}$. In this paper we limit these to the experience of statements that might form part of an argumentation map. Where an occasion represents a feeling of emotion, or similar, it is taken from $\{\alpha, \beta, \gamma...\}$. When two occasions represent opposing reactions to a common choice o they are labelled o^+ and o^-.

The experience of an occasion depends on the upstream occasions which are its cause. We capture this in a limited form by formalising which occasions may follow one another. As shown in Figure 1 we represent an occasion o as the combination of i) a transition t_o connected to ii) an output place x_o indicating that the occasion has been experienced and iii) a list of prehensions required for the occasion in the form of input edges to this transition. An occasion's input places are the output places of the occasions it may be caused by. In this example the individual will first experience occasion a before then going on to experience b. This implementation does not capture the way that the formation of an occasion from a given upstream structure could result in differing subjective experience due to the inclusion or exclusion of parts of this structure. With this method we might approximate this by adding each of these possible versions of an occasion to the alphabet O.

3.2 Social idea chemistry

The mapping from Whitehead's model onto Petri nets just proposed affords no social interaction. This mapping was expanded to attribute to each individual person a society of possible occasions which they might experience if both their past experience and now also their environment—formed exclusively by their neighbours in this article—is suitable. We encoded this 'social idea chemistry' as a unit U repeatable on a coloured Petri net, and coloured this with a set of colours, one per individual.

We included just one type of social occasion: the occasion of experiencing an occasion that a neighbour has experienced, or *following* a neighbour. This type of occasion depends on the underlying technical medium M capable of communicating experience—a fixed social network with n nodes throughout this work—and the underlying abilities of each individual to both share an experience and to experience what is shared. To create the final *system model S* we connected together the n coloured 'copies' of U by constructing an is_neighbour guard function on U's transitions in order to represent the social network of the medium M.

For example, and already introduced, Figure 3 shows an example of U on a network of three individuals $n_1 \longleftrightarrow n_2 \longleftrightarrow n_3$ exported from the software package Snoopy introduced in Section 3.3. It represents a single occasion of experience which may be experienced just once, such as that of first experiencing a particular rumour and possibly a reaction to this. Figure 4 shows its expansion onto a non-coloured Petri net with numerical subscripts labelling the three individuals. This model is described in more detail in Section 3.4.1 and encodes an information diffusion process.

Figure 5a shows a shorthand form of this model. The dotted arc indicates a connection from a neighbour's place, and the open circle arrow head that it is a read arc. The one in the black circle indicates that a guard function on the transition will block firing unless one (or more) neighbours has a token in place x_a indicating that they have experienced the occasion a and are in the position to share it.

In summary the resulting mathematical objects were:

(1) A repeatable coloured Petri net unit U encoding the possible sequences of occasions of experience of an individual. This might be 'compiled' from a directed graph of possible occasion orderings, but in this work was hand crafted.

(2) A set of colours, one for each of n individuals with which to colour U.

(3) A medium graph M representing a fixed social network with n nodes.

(4) A complete coloured system Petri net model S obtained by calculating the `is_neighbour` guard function on U from M.

3.3 Simulation software

The Snoopy suite of Petri net modelling software[1] was used in the early development of these methods [11]. We then created a Python based package, occmodeler[2], for more quickly building models, simulating them and analysing and visualising the results. Snoopy's scriptable component, Spike[4], was used for the simulation phase. Python's NetworkX package[3] was used for graph generation and representation [9].

3.4 Experiments

The utility of this method was explored by encoding models exhibiting information diffusion and what we call multiple phase diffusion, and then consensus formation, before then encoding a mechanism of echo chamber formation. We then demonstrated the conflation of individuals' position on otherwise separate issues through emotion. The time step of the simulation run with Spike was 0.02 units, all single neighbour transitions had a firing rate λ of 1 firings per time unit, and all two neighbour transitions (introduced below) a firing rate of 2 firings per time unit. We present these models as illustrative of the potential for these methods, and as possible primitives, rather than as interesting results in their own sense.

The models capture the process nature of Whitehead's model in that occasions depend always on upstream occasions for their cause, and once experienced then go on to form the cause of subsequent downstream occasions. None however draw out the nature of occasions to truly form part of a process—in the way that we earlier described those formed while watching a leaf drop might.

3.4.1 Diffusion. We simulated the model of Figure 5a on a graph created by joining two communities of 7 nodes with small world structure. A marking was chosen such that all nodes started with a token in place x_0 except for one which started in node x_a. We expected all individuals to follow this single individuals' experience of a resulting in a diffusion process. The occasion a may represent an idea or emotion.

3.4.2 Multiphase diffusion. We simulated the model in Figure 5b on the same graph medium as above. This is an extension to the previous model in that the occasion b can only be experienced after the occasion a. A marking was chosen such that all individuals started with a token in place x_0 except for one which started in node x_b and three of its neighbours which started in x_a. A single 14 node small-world network was used. In this model we expect to see the experience of occasion a spreading and then the experience of occasions b spreading on top of this.

[1]http://www-dssz.informatik.tu-cottbus.de/DSSZ/Software/Snoopy
[2]https://github.com/robwalton/occmodeler
[3]https://networkx.github.io

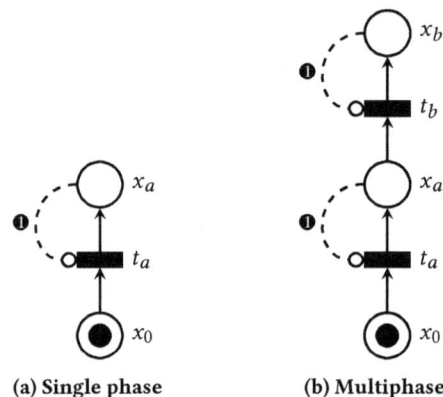

(a) Single phase   (b) Multiphase

Figure 5: Diffusion models

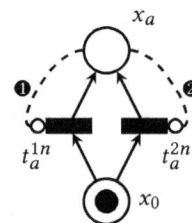

Figure 6: Diffusion with echo model

3.4.3 Diffusion with echo. We built models demonstrating the multi-path effect that Jasny et al. identified as a mechanism occurring in social networks that contributes to echo chamber formation [13]. The authors identified a behaviour in which people are more likely to believe something (or in our case, experience it in the same way as their neighbours) if they hear it from two sources or if they hear it multiple times. We simulated the model in Figure 6 which captures both of these mechanisms. This was the same diffusion model used above but with the addition of a second transition in parallel with the first. The second transition had a guard function requiring two neighbours to have a token in x_a to fire. We set a λ of two firings per time unit for this, rather than the one firing per unit used for the single neighbour transitions elsewhere in this article.

A marking was chosen such that all nodes started with a token in place x_0 except for two which started in place x_a. We ran this simulation once with the rate of t_a^{1n} set to zero and once with it set to one. The rate of t_a^{2n} was set at two firings per time unit for both cases. In the first experiment an occasion is experienced only if two neighbours have experienced it, and in the second experiment an individual may follow either one or two neighbours, but will follow two neighbours at twice the rate.

3.4.4 Single issue consensus. We then ran simulations demonstrating consensus formation of a single issue with two possible opinions a person might choose. We simulated just the left hand issue a of Figure 7 (comprised of the competing occasions a^+ and a^-). We placed this on our two community network and started each person with a randomly chosen opinion. In this model the

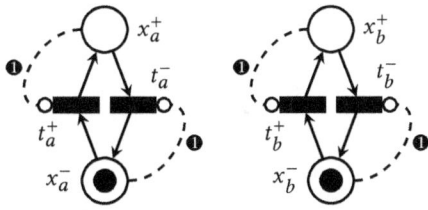

Figure 7: Orthogonal consensus formation model

individual will experience only the occasion of changing ones mind: if they had experience a^- they may subsequently experienced a^+. This model is the same as that introduced by Morris DeGroot in his work "Reaching a consensus" in 1974 [6].

3.4.5 Issue conflation. Above we simulated just issue a of Figure 7. We then created a model containing both issues a and b. As expected, and not shown here, an individual's opinion on each of the two issues was uncorrelated.

We then went on to simulate the model of Figure 8 with the goal of demonstrating how our method might be used to model scenarios in which an individual's opinion on two issues can be conflated via emotion. This model has two issues a and b like that of Figure 7, and as before, an individual may undergo the experience of believing an opinion if a neighbour has experienced it. However in this model the individual must have last experienced a compatible emotion γ. In this model to experience $a^\pm$ or $b^\pm$ requires $\gamma^\pm$ to have been most recently experienced. To illustrate this, a possible interpretation might be: a^+ is to experience a belief in freedom of gun ownership, b^+ is to experience a belief in closed borders, and γ^+ is to experience the feeling of closed-ness or wanting to secure what one has.

In this model, the emotion γ diffuses between individuals and as just stated it must be experienced before an opinion that depends on it may be. In addition the emotion γ will also tend to follow a currently internally held belief: if an individual experiences a^+ before then experiencing the incompatible γ^- then there is tension from the place x_a^+ to cause γ^+ to be re-experienced.

For this experiment, a marking was chosen such that all individuals on one half of the graph started having most recently experienced the emotion γ^+ and the compatible opinions a^+ and b^+ and on the other half γ^-, a^- and b^-.

3.5 Result interpretation and visualisation

The result of simulating these models with Spike was, for each node on the network, a time series of token count in each place and the number of times a transition fired in the prior time interval. With this data it is easy to create a movie showing how the marking of each individual node changes across the network. However we took the approach of showing this temporal data as a causal graph such as that shown in Figure 9.

Figure 9 shows the causal graph resulting from a simulation run. The social network or medium M is shown at the bottom of the plot with initial markings indicated by colour. Time increases upwards from this plane. Following up from each vertex a new occasion is marked as a disk when the individual at that vertex has experienced it. The dashed edges indicate the local cause of

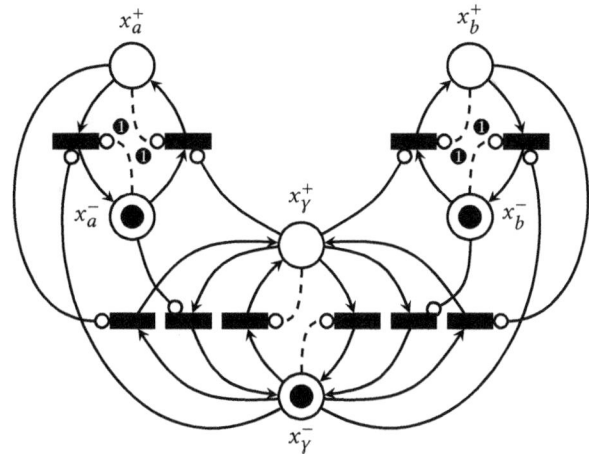

Figure 8: Issue conflation model. Transitions are not labelled and all had a λ of one firing per unit of time.

the occasion, and the solid edges the cause from a neighbour. The curvature of these edges represents nothing and is present only to make the resulting visualisation easier to interpret: these arcs leave a prehended occasion horizontally (through the 'space' of the network) and curve upwards (to become parallel with the time axis) as they enter a new occasion.

4 RESULTS

We present and then discuss the results from the experiments and then from the method as a whole.

4.1 Experiments

The individual experiments described in Section 3.4 are presented and discussed below. Interactive versions of the figures are available online[4], along with results of simulating the same U models on larger networks.

4.1.1 Diffusion. Figure 9 shows a representative causal graph from the diffusion model of Section 3.4.1. As expected the result is a spreading of the experience across the whole network. We observe that, at least on these small networks, there are a countable number of possible graphs. These however expand to an infinite number of particular timings between occasions.

4.1.2 Multiphase diffusion. Figure 10 shows a representative causal graph from the multiphase diffusion model of Section 3.4.2. Here there is a progression of each individual experiencing first a and then b.

4.1.3 Diffusion with echo. Figure 11 shows a representative causal graph from the first run of the diffusion with echo model of Section 3.4.3. The b message can be seen to spread requiring always the prehension of two neighbours having most recently experienced b. In this run the rate of firing of the transition which follows a single neighbour was set to zero. We see, as we would

---

[4]https://robwalton.github.io/posts/2019/websci19/

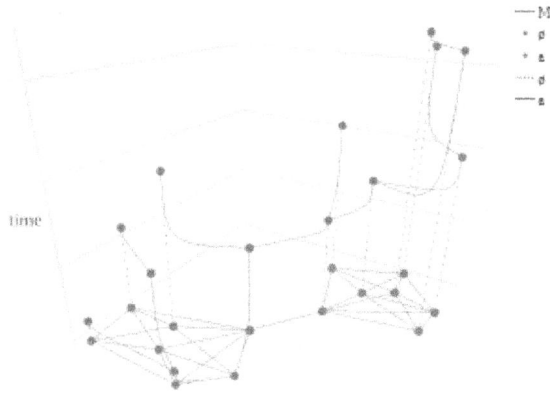

Figure 9: Causal graph for a run of the *diffusion* model

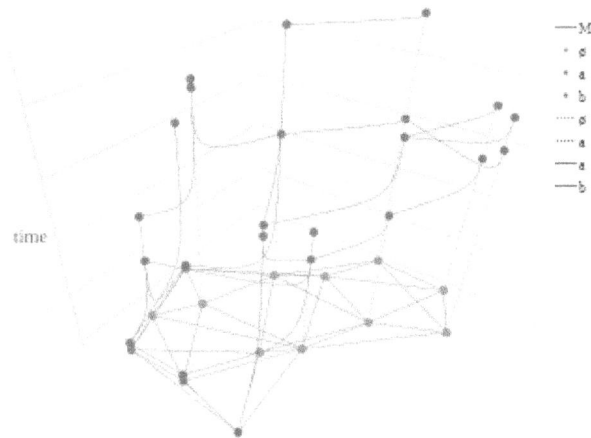

Figure 10: Causal graph for a run of the *multiphase diffusion* model

expect, that the causal path cannot hop from the initial community to its neighbour.

Figure 12 shows the same model extended to also include single neighbour sharing. Two instances of single neighbour sharing are indicated with arrows.

4.1.4 Single issue consensus formation. Figure 13 shows a representative causal graph from the single issue consensus model of Section 3.4.4. This model is the same as that introduced by Morris DeGroot in his work "Reaching a consensus" in 1974 [6]. DeGroot showed that such a model will always converge on a connected graph and modelled the dynamics of opinion across the graph. In about half of the runs the two communities had opposing views. The extreme separation of the two communities reduces the chance of convergence to a single view if the initial random marking results in disagreement. However, all a^+ and all a^- are the only completely stable states and given long enough the system will find itself in one of these. It is interesting that there are two long term stable

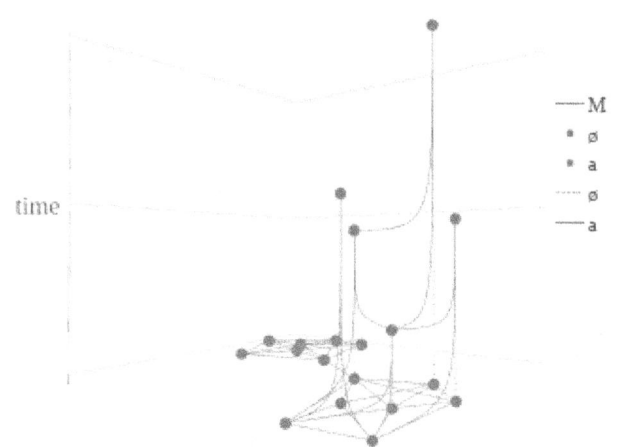

Figure 11: Causal graph for a run of the *diffusion with echo* model with only two neighbour following

Figure 12: Causal graph for a run of the *diffusion with echo* model with both one and two neighbour following. Two instances of single neighbour sharing are indicated with arrows.

states and two short term stable states. We might liken these to attractors from non-linear dynamics. We present the result from this particular simulation run because the a^- opinion made an exciting but brief foray into a^+ territory.

4.1.5 Issue conflation. Fig 14 shows a representative causal graph from the conflation through emotion model of Section 4.1.5. Figure 15 shows, as a function of time, the number of nodes with positive rather than negative opinions for this run. In this run, where both communities converged to the same opinions, the positive opinions were both chosen along with the positive emotion. In all cases the communities tended to either all positively labelled or all negatively labelled choices.

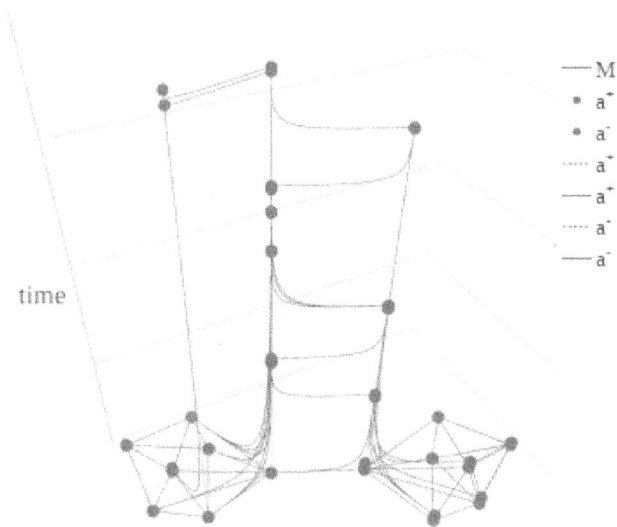

Figure 13: Causal graph for a run of the *single issue consensus* model showing two communities fighting out differing opinions

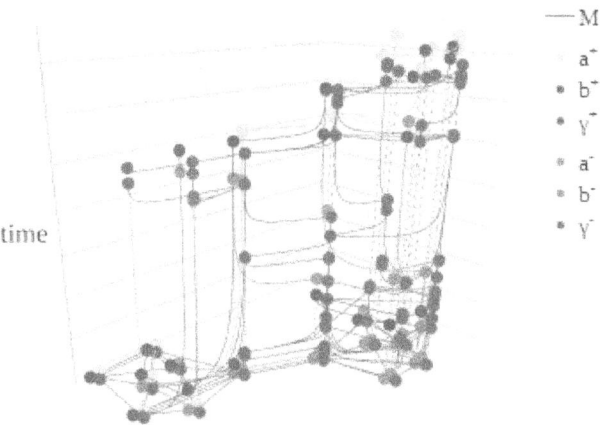

Figure 14: Causal graph for the *conflation through emotion* model

4.2 Method

We developed a two step method of modelling behaviours found in some socio-technical system scenarios on the Web. The mapping from a scenario onto Whitehead's concepts of occasions, with individuals represented as societies of occasions formalised by the possible paths through these occasions was natural. The subsequent mapping from this to Petri nets and from simulated results to causal graphs worked well. The resulting models' basis in Whitehead's metaphysics provides room to attach richly nuanced interpretation—although this may not be evident from looking at the shape of the

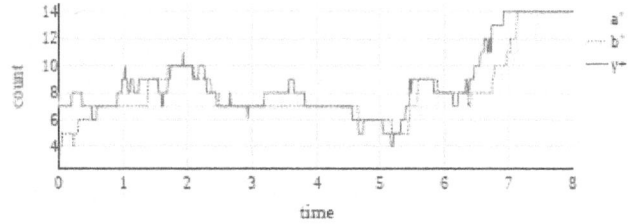

Figure 15: Place count for graph for the *conflation through emotion* model. Traces are shown only for positive opinions (negative counts and positive counts sum to the network's size).

resulting Petri nets themselves or of the unfolded causal graphs of experience. We did not validate the results of experiment against other modelling methods, although the models were simple and the results were as expected. These models should be considered primitives which might be combined together to form more complex sequences of experience.

In some cases, when generating a causal graph from the Spike software's simulation results, multiple firings of the same transition occurred in the same time bin. In these cases there was not enough information to generate a causal graph with all certainty and a heuristic approach was used.

5 DISCUSSION

In this paper we developed and tested a method for the exploratory modelling of emergent socio-technical systems on the Web. We proposed a mapping for describing a fixed social network of interacting people as a partially overlapping collection of Whitehead's societies of occasions. We created a single model for each person which formalised every sequence of occasions they might conceivably experience by contriving a 'chemistry' relating their external stimuli, internal experience and reactions to this internal experience. Interaction between people was limited to one person experiencing what a neighbour had experienced, but only if their own history was compatible. We proposed a mapping from this representation onto a single stochastic coloured Petri net. This was done by creating a unit describing a single 'chemistry' applicable to all, and then encoding the shape of a fixed network into the model in a way that it can be potentially unfolded into a single non-coloured stochastic Petri net in the shape of that network. When simulated the resulting models unfolded into one of many possible causal graphs of occasions of experience which we showed using an interactive visualisation.

We verified the method by developing open source software built on top of the Petri net simulation software Spike. With this we encoded exploratory models exhibiting information diffusion and what we called multiple phase diffusion, and then consensus formation, before then encoding a mechanism of echo chamber formation. We then demonstrated the conflation of individuals' positions on otherwise separate issues through emotion. The results were as expected.

A limitation to the work is that the network individuals interact on is fixed. There is a mechanism for an edge between two people to break in that they may reach markings which prevent future interaction. However there is no way for new edges to form. Although the obvious solution of providing a fully connected network provides a good place to reason from it would result in prohibitively large simulations. Also, at first glance the requirement that every individual be identical appears limiting. However the single 'chemistry' describing the possible sequences of experience might include places with tokens placed during the initial marking which determine permanent characteristics such as character. Although there is no limit to how big models might be in theory the software in its current form will not scale past running on a single machine.

Andrew Selbst et al. identify a number of traps discovered while developing approaches to designing socio-technical systems that behave fairly—for example when performing an automated resume screen or making legal judgements [20]. Among more detailed recommendations they note that system designers must draw abstraction boundaries around social actors rather than just technical ones. The method presented here offers one way of doing this.

6 CONCLUSION

In this paper we developed and tested a method for the exploratory modelling of emergent large-scale socio-technical systems on the Web. Based around modelling possible sequences of human experience with Petri nets the method provides a formalism not seen in other work. It was shown that models exhibiting simple diffusion or consensus formation were simple to build. Highlighting the method's intended use for exploratory modelling we showed that an accepted mechanism for echo chamber formation resulted in relatively stable polarised views on a network with pre-existing community structure. We were also able to demonstrate a plausible model showing how opinion on otherwise unrelated issues may be coupled through an emotion common to both.

This method may be useful to those interested in understanding the mechanisms behind the emergence of complex ecosystems of social machines, echo chambers and other structures on the web. The use of Petri nets at the base of the method blurs the lines between ad-hoc agent based modelling and more analytical modelling. Properties of small or suitably symmetric models might be derived analytically through a mapping onto sets of ordinary differential equations or Markov models. Some properties might help for example build multi-scale models comprised of a perspective formalising operation at the scale of coherent interacting communities and other perspectives formalising interactions of individuals within or across these community boundaries. More generally, this method and the open source occmodeler software which implements it provides a good place from which to explore process based approaches to modelling social systems in general.

REFERENCES

[1] Wil Van Der Aalst, Ton Weijters, and Laura Maruster. 2004. Workflow mining: Discovering process models from event logs. *IEEE Trans. on Knowl. and Data Eng* (2004).

[2] Tilak Agerwala. 1979. Putting Petri nets to work. *Computer* 12, 12 (1979), 85–94.

[3] Eduardo G. Altmann, Janet B. Pierrehumbert, and Adilson E. Motter. 2009. Beyond Word Frequency: Bursts, Lulls, and Scaling in the Temporal Distributions of

Words. *PLOS ONE* 4, 11 (Nov. 2009), e7678. https://doi.org/10.1371/journal.pone.0007678

[4] J Chodak and M Heiner. 2018. Spike - a command line tool for continuous, stochastic & hybrid simulation of (coloured) Petri nets. In *Proc. 21th German Workshop on Algorithms and Tools for Petri Nets (AWPN 2018)*. University of Augsburg, 1–6. https://opus.bibliothek.uni-augsburg.de/opus4/frontdoor/deliver/index/docId/41861/file/awpn18-lorenz-metzger-OPUS.pdf#page=9

[5] David De Roure, Clare Hooper, Megan Meredith-Lobay, Kevin Page, Ségolène Tarte, Don Cruickshank, and Catherine De Roure. 2013. Observing Social Machines Part 1: What to Observe?. In *Proceedings of the 22Nd International Conference on World Wide Web (WWW '13 Companion)*. ACM, New York, NY, USA, 901–904. https://doi.org/10.1145/2487788.2488077

[6] Morris H. DeGroot. 1974. Reaching a Consensus. *J. Amer. Statist. Assoc.* 69, 345 (March 1974), 118. https://doi.org/10.2307/2285509

[7] Qian Gao, Fei Liu, David Gilbert, Monika Heiner, and David Tree. 2011. A multiscale approach to modelling planar cell polarity in Drosophila wing using hierarchically coloured Petri nets. In *Proceedings of the 9th International Conference on Computational Methods in Systems Biology - CMSB '11*. ACM Press, Paris, France, 209. https://doi.org/10.1145/2037509.2037538

[8] M. Girvan and M. E. J. Newman. 2002. Community structure in social and biological networks. *Proceedings of the National Academy of Sciences* 99, 12 (June 2002), 7821–7826. https://doi.org/10.1073/pnas.122653799

[9] Aric A. Hagberg, Daniel A. Schult, and Pieter J. Swart. 2008. Exploring Network Structure, Dynamics, and Function using NetworkX. In *Proceedings of the 7th Python in Science Conference*, Gaël Varoquaux, Travis Vaught, and Jarrod Millman (Eds.). 11–15. event-place: Pasadena, CA USA.

[10] Mark Hartswood and Luc Moreau. 2016. A Social Charter for Smart Platforms. (2016). https://eprints.soton.ac.uk/410307/1/SmartSocietySocialCharterforSmartPlatforms_final.pdf

[11] Monika Heiner, Mostafa Herajy, Fei Liu, Christian Rohr, and Martin Schwarick. 2012. Snoopy – A Unifying Petri Net Tool. In *Application and Theory of Petri Nets (Lecture Notes in Computer Science)*, Serge Haddad and Lucia Pomello (Eds.). Springer Berlin Heidelberg, 398–407.

[12] John H. Holland. 2012. *Signals and Boundaries : Building Blocks for Complex Adaptive Systems*. MIT Press, Cambridge, Mass., UNITED STATES.

[13] Lorien Jasny, Joseph Waggle, and Dana R. Fisher. 2015. An empirical examination of echo chambers in US climate policy networks. *Nature Climate Change* 5, 8 (Aug. 2015), 782–786. https://doi.org/10.1038/nclimate2666

[14] Kurt Jensen. 1981. Coloured petri nets and the invariant-method. *Theoretical Computer Science* 14, 3 (Jan. 1981), 317–336. https://doi.org/10.1016/0304-3975(81)90049-9

[15] G. T. Kneebone. 1963. The application of mathematics to the natural world. In *Mathematical logic and the foundations of mathematics : an introductory survey*.

[16] Michael K. Molloy. 1982. Performance analysis using stochastic Petri nets. *IEEE Transactions on computers* 9 (1982), 913–917.

[17] Nikolic, I. 2009. *Co-Evolutionary Method For Modelling Large Scale Socio-Technical Systems Evolution*. Ph.D. Dissertation. NGInfra / TU Delft. http://resolver.tudelft.nl/uuid:b6855afa-e8ab-442d-ac5a-f645f7639c73

[18] C. Adam Petri and W. Reisig. 2008. Petri net. *Scholarpedia* 3, 4 (2008), 6477. https://doi.org/10.4249/scholarpedia.6477 revision #91647.

[19] Tucmas C. Schelling. 1969. Models of Segregation. *American Economic Review* 59, 2 (May 1969), 488.

[20] Andrew D. Selbst, Danah Boyd, Sorelle Friedler, Suresh Venkatasubramanian, and Janet Vertesi. 2018. *Fairness and Abstraction in Sociotechnical Systems*. SSRN Scholarly Paper ID 3265913. Social Science Research Network, Rochester, NY. https://papers.ssrn.com/abstract=3265913

[21] Nigel Shadbolt, Kieron O'Hara, David De Roure, and Dame Wendy Hall. 2019. *The Theory and Practice of Social Machines*. Springer International Publishing. https://www.springer.com/us/book/9783030100885

[22] C. E. Shannon. 1948. A mathematical theory of communication. *The Bell System Technical Journal* 27, 3 (July 1948), 379–423. https://doi.org/10.1002/j.1538-7305.1948.tb01338.x

[23] John Kenly Smith. 1988. The Social Construction of Technological Systems: New Directions in the Sociology and History of Technology. Edited by Wiebe E. Bijker, Thomas P. Hughes, and Trevor Pinch. Cambridge, Mass.: MIT Press, 1987. 405 pp. Illustrations, charts, notes, bibliography, and index. $35.00. *Business History Review* 62, 2 (1988), 341–342. https://doi.org/10.2307/3116018

[24] Larissa Spinelli and Mark Crovella. 2017. Closed-Loop Opinion Formation. In *the 2017 ACM*. ACM Press, New York, New York, USA, 73–82.

[25] Michele Starnini, Mattia Frasca, and Andrea Baronchelli. 2016. Emergence of metapopulations and echo chambers in mobile agents. *Scientific Reports* 6, 1 (Oct. 2016). https://doi.org/10.1038/srep31834 arXiv: 1603.04789.

[26] Duncan J Watts and Steven H Strogatz. 1998. Collective dynamics of 'small-world' networks. *nature* 393, 6684 (1998), 440. bibtex*[publisher=Nature Publishing Group].

[27] Alfred North Whitehead and Donald W Sherburne. 1957. *Process and reality*. Macmillan New York, NY.

EAN: Event Attention Network for Stock Price Trend Prediction based on Sentimental Embedding

Yaowei Wang
City University of Hong Kong
Department of Computer Science
Hong Kong, China
yaowwang@cityu.edu.hk

Qing Li
The Hong Kong Polytechnic
University
Department of Computing
Hong Kong, China
csqli@comp.polyu.edu.hk

Zhexue Huang, Junjie Li
Shenzhen University
College of Computer Science &
Software Engineering
Shen Zhen, China
{zx.huang,jj.li}@szu.edu.cn

ABSTRACT

It is only natural that events related to a listed company may cause its stock price to move (either up or down), and the trend of the price movement will be very much determined by the public opinions towards such events. With the help of the Internet and advanced natural language processing techniques, it becomes possible to predict the stock trend by analyzing great amount of online textual resources like news from websites and posts on social media. In this paper, we propose an event attention network (EAN) to exploit sentimental event-embedding for stock price trend prediction. Specially, this model combines the merits from both event-driven prediction and sentiment-driven prediction models, in addition to exploiting sentimental event-embedding. Furthermore, we employ attention mechanism to figure out which event contributes the most to the result or, in another word, which event is the main cause of the price fluctuation. In our model, a convolution neural network (CNN) layer is used to extract salient features from transformed event representations, and the latter are originated from a bi-directional long short-term memory (BiLSTM) layer. We conduct extensive experiments on a manually collected real-world dataset. Experimental results show that our model performs significantly better in terms of short-term stock trend prediction.

CCS CONCEPTS

• **Computing methodologies → Natural language processing**; • **Information systems → World Wide Web**; *Web applications*.

KEYWORDS

stock trend prediction; financial text mining; sentimental event embedding; attention-based deep learning

ACM Reference Format:
Yaowei Wang, Qing Li, and Zhexue Huang, Junjie Li. 2019. EAN: Event Attention Network for Stock Price Trend Prediction based on Sentimental Embedding. In *11th ACM Conference on Web Science, June 30–July 3, 2019, Boston, MA, USA*. ACM, New York, NY, USA, 10 pages. https://doi.org/10.1145/3292522.3326014

1 INTRODUCTION

The stock trend prediction aims to predict the future trends of a stock in order to help investors to make good investment decisions. It has become a challenging problem because of highly volatile and non-stationary nature of the market [1]. Nevertheless, the pursuit of maximizing profits has attracted both stock investors and market researchers to make continuous attempts on stock movement prediction.

So far, existing prediction approaches can be divided into technical analysis based vs. peripheral analysis based. The technical analysis based approach is to make predictions on time-series historic market data. It is conducted by analyzing the patterns of historical and current market behavior. Three principles are usually employed: the market behaviors involve all relevant information; the prices move along with the trend; and the history will repeat. Engle [8] was the first to explore this approach. He adapted autoregressive conditional heteroscedasticity, and Taylor [21] applied stochastic volatility to construct time-series data modeling. However, the accuracy and confidence of such these approaches have their limitations, because they omit the interests-driven nature of the market, and neglect the influence on the stock trend from recent social events, new policies on the industry, public opinions and emotions. All of those have the potential to produce large amounts of abnormal transactions and unusual market behaviors, which lead to severe price fluctuations.

On the other hand, peripheral analysis based approaches focus on the impact of social events and real life news on the financial market. With the help of the Internet and the advanced natural language processing, researchers can access abundant instant online resources as references and be capable of processing the information efficiently in order to make more accurate in-time predictions. Two major sources, *i.e.*, news from financial websites and opinions from social media, are widely studied nowadays. Financial news receive more attention because most of the financial articles are written by professional analysts, so that explicit and in-depth views can be delivered from financial news, including interpretations on specific events that could have impacts on some companies' income or the confidence of general public, and new policies that may influence the future macroeconomy indicators or industry development. Many research works have been conducted on Wall Street Journal [2], Bloomberg [6], Yahoo Finance [19], *etc.* For example, Li *et.al* [16] applied a sentence-level summarization model to full-length financial news and built a prediction model on Hong Kong Hang Sang Index. Another popular text mining source is the social media. Though more noisy data (*e.g.*, ungrammatical twitter), the contents generated by public users are representative of the opinions and emotions from the majority of individual investors. Indeed, the public opinions extracted from social media are widely correlate to the stock movement. Gilbert *et.al* [9] showed the degree of public anxiety is a considerable factor of price movement by using Granger Causality Test. Bollen [4] explored seven emotional dimensions and revealed that the prediction results can be enhanced if the scores of Calm and Happiness are evaluated together with historical transaction data. Many researchers [4][25][3][22] made some breakthroughs using twitter texts for market prediction.

From our preliminary empirical studies, we have found that online textual contents from different sources function well in different ways. News contents are more suited than those from social media for event extraction and clustering, because news can tell a relatively complete story about a specific event and we can use the information provided in the news to index the event. However, due to the nature of professionalism (*i.e.*, neutral statements), it is difficult to label the public opinions of such news, especially (expert) financial news. The contents from social media and public forums indicate strong sentiment preference towards a single event, yet the textual descriptions from the social media usually are lexically incomplete, sometimes inconsistent, which makes them unsuitable for event extraction. To utilize the advantages of both sources, we propose a model to detect the events from multi-sourced textual contents and predict the trend of stocks based on related events and public sentiment. In particular, our approach is to conduct event-based sentiment analysis to reveal the causality relationship between the public opinions on social events and unusual market reactions.

The contributions of our work include the following:

(1) We propose a novel sentiment-driven event representation for predicting stock price movement, which is the first piece of work which introducing a sentimental event model into stock trend prediction.
(2) We develop an attention-based hybrid framework to better integrate extracted temporal event information with feature embedding, and exploit the short-term influence of sentimental events.
(3) We adopt Convolutional Neural Networks (CNNs) to handle the prediction task, and the experimental results on real-world datasets indicate the superiority of our model in comparison with several baselines.

The rest of this paper is organized as follows: Section 2 reviews the prior work on technical, event and sentiment analysis for stock prediction. The architecture of the proposed event attention network (EAN) is presented in Section 3. Section 4 provides the details of the datasets we use, and shows the performance of the proposed framework, compared with various baselines on real-world datasets. Finally, in Section 5 we discuss some characteristics of our framework and present the direction of our future research.

2 RELATED WORK

Stock trend prediction is a crucial reference for maximizing profits and avoiding risks. Continuous efforts with implementing various techniques, from machine learning methods to deep learning models, have been applied in stock trend prediction. Meanwhile, peripheral analysis based on online textual resources is also a hot research direction in recent years.

2.1 Technical analysis based prediction

Many machine learning techniques including support vector machine (SVM) [12][11][20] have been exploited to analyze time-series numerical data for stock trend prediction. Tay and Cao [20] modeled multiple features based on a five-day time window, and their experiments show that the SVM can outperform a back-propagate neural network. The limitation of this approach is that it cannot correctly react after significant events happen (for example, the tariff conflicts between China and the US), since it only takes the past numerical data into account. Another typical trend prediction model is the Autoregressive (AR) model [14], which is a time-series-based model. In particular, the AR model uses linear and stationary time-series data to predict the trend of next time step by looking at the current and previous statuses. However, due to the non-linear and non-stationary nature of the stock market, the AR model suffers from the same dilemma as SVM, so it performs terrible after some unprecedented market shocks occur. With the development of deep learning techniques, more attempts have been made on financial prediction. For instance, some recurrent models, especially, Long Short-Term Memory (LSTM) model [18] to better model the time dependency of historic stock data, have been deployed for financial prediction. Nevertheless, the reliability and accuracy of those technical analysis methods suffer from neglecting some outside-market factors, such as events and opinions.

2.2 Event analysis for stock price prediction

To seek the correlation between real life events and stock price turbulence, Yoshihara *et.al* [24] examined temporal effects of past significant events. For example, the prices of many stocks plummeted after the bankruptcy of Lehman Brothers. In their paper, RNN-RBM is adopted to automatically identify useful features from a large amount of texts. Jin *et.al* [13] detected events from Google search trend and

Twitter burst features, and mined the opinion factor from Bloomberg news. The Delta Naïve Bayes model is used to make predictions. Ding [7] used structured events with different time intervals to make stock movement predictions on S&P 500 Index and several individual stocks. Nascimento *et.al* [17] adopted structured-event embedding technique to extract events from news stream, and utilized the event embeddings as input to forecast the stock trend. However, their methods may neglect most of the small enterprises because of few related events to report.

2.3 Sentiment analysis for stock price prediction

Besides event-driven prediction, sentiment analysis prediction is also widely studied because public emotions and opinions about specific events can affect the stock movement more profoundly than events themselves. Li *et.al* [15] implemented a stock price prediction framework analyzing the sentiments from financial news. However, it is difficult to retrieve emotion labels from news articles because of the proficiency nature of the financial news, instead, strong e-motion and opinion expressions can be identified from social media. Vu *et.al* [22] explored the correlation between public emotions and trend of stock movement on Twitter, and utilized sentiment features in financial prediction. Most recently, Hu *et.al* [10] designed an attention-based news-oriented stock trend perdition model based on the sequence of recent related news. Their experiment was conducted on Chinese stock market, and the results show that the confidence of prediction can be elevated considerably after the sentiment of related news is counted. While there have been many efforts in exploiting sentiment from single data source (*e.g.*, news) for stock predication, few of them considered the link between sentiment and events.

3 THE FRAMEWORK OF THE EVENT ATTENTION NETWORK

In this section, we start with characterizing the underlying perspective of events for the task of stock trend prediction, followed by a detailed description of our proposed framework.

3.1 Event Characteristics

To better model the influence of the events on relevant stocks, we address the challenges in the stock trend prediction using events, which can be summarized into following characteristics:

- Imbalanced distribution of events: during the same period of time, there may exist very few news for many small-volumed companies, but more frequent news reports for some big enterprises or companies under some critical and abnormal conditions, which can cause the event dictionary to be either too sparse or too dense for different stocks.

- Inconsistent effect of events: it is important for event processing to distinguish the effect of the same news on different stocks, especially those stocks across industries. For example, the news that "petroleum prices decline due to new energy source emerges" may have a positive effect on auto industry but negative effect on petrochemical industry.
- Distinct importance of events: when multiple events emerge together during a given time window, it is critical for the model to determine which event is the most significant and plays a vital role in stock trend prediction task.
- Different life-time of events: sequential and temporal properties can help reveal the inner relationships between or among the events. It is also vital to determine the life-time of influence, dependency, and causality relationships. However, these are difficult to capture when extracting the events.

Taking into account these characteristics, an ideal learning framework for stock trend prediction should have the ability to distinguish those events holding more intensive and durable influence. In the next subsection, we present our EAN approach as an attempt to address these issues holistically.

3.2 Model Description

We regard the problem of stock trend prediction as a classification problem. For a given date t, a given stock s and the target date (*e.g.*, $t + 5$ days), we can calculate its rise percent by:

$$R(s,t) = \frac{Close\_Price_{t+5} - Close\_Price_t}{Close\_Price_t}, \quad (1)$$

where $Close\_Price_t$ and $Close\_Price_{t+5}$ represents the closing price of the t-th day and t-th+5 day, respectively. Similar to many previous studies, we use the price change to represent the stock movement in order to obtain a binary label (1 for price going up, and -1 for price going down):

$$L(s,t) = \begin{cases} 1 & R(s,t) > 0; \\ -1 & R(s,t) \leq 0. \end{cases} \quad (2)$$

The stock trend prediction task can be formulated as follows: given the length of a time sequence N, the stock s and date t, the goal is to use the news and social media corpora sequence from time $t - N + 1$ to t, denoted as $[C_{t-N+1}, C_{t-N+2}, ..., C_t]$, to predict the class of $R(s,t)$ (*e.g.*, 5 days). Note that each corpus C_i contains a set of documents with the size of D, *i.e.*, $C_i = [n_{i,1}, n_{i,2}..., n_{i,D}]$ denoting D related pieces of news on date i.

The architecture of our proposed Event Attention Network is shown in Fig. 1. It is composed of two parts: the Input Attention Mechanism, and Temporal Hidden Represent. The first part is to encode the event and sentiment information, and generate the contextualized event representation with the attention mechanism. At the beginning, an event embedding layer transforms the news corpus of i-th day into the event and sentiment vector with the size of L, *i.e.*,

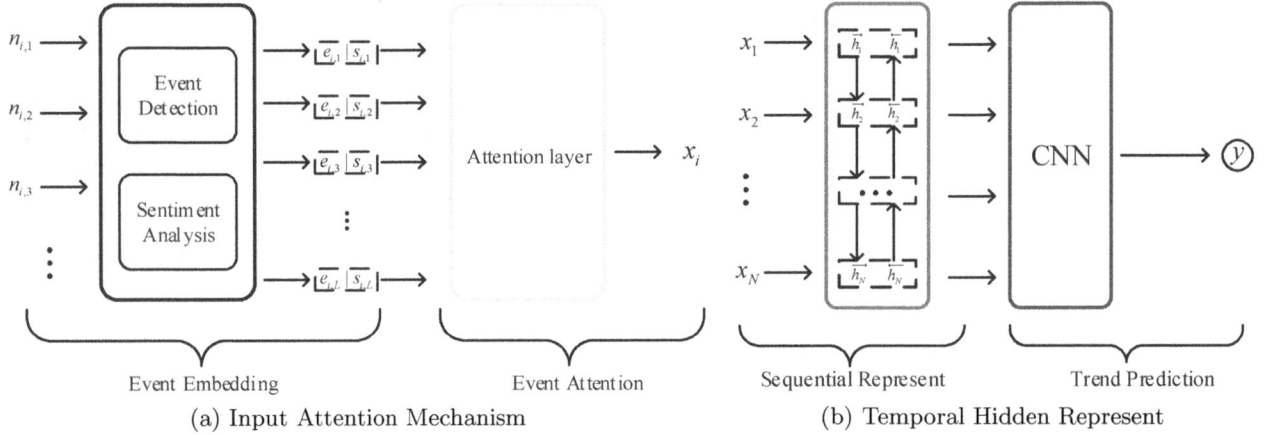

(a) Input Attention Mechanism   (b) Temporal Hidden Represent

Figure 1: The overall framework of the Event Attention Network.

$[(e_{i,1}; s_{i,1}), (e_{i,2}; s_{i,2}), ..., (e_{i,L}; s_{i,L})]$ which denotes L related sentimental events on date i. An event attention layer is next assigned with an attention value for each event vector on date i, and the weighted mean of such event vectors are calculated as a feature vector x_i for this date. The second part is to predict the stock trend using these event vectors within N days, $[x_1, x_2, ..., x_N]$. These feature vectors are encoded by a BiLSTM, which results in the hidden sequential representation $[(\overrightarrow{h_1}; \overleftarrow{h_1}), (\overrightarrow{h_2}; \overleftarrow{h_2}), ..., (\overrightarrow{h_N}; \overleftarrow{h_N})]$. Finally, we adopt the CNN to produce the stock trend prediction result y, based on the sequential representation of the sentimental event information.

3.2.1 Event Embedding Layer.
To tackle the problems of sparsity and uniqueness in the representation space of events, we devise a method for normalized sentimental event embedding representation. In particular, we calculate the sentimental indicators by the sentiment classifier (*e.g.*, Linear Regression). Based on the event tuple vectors and two dimensional emotion values, we then obtain $(e; s)$ called sentimental event representation which is the more effective for stock trend prediction.

Event Detection: Following the previous work [23], we reconstruct the related textual content with features representation by extracting the information like date, location, entities and actions. To handle the information properly, an unsupervised event dictionary (D_e^{Time}, $D_e^{Location}$, D_e^{Name}, D_e^{Action}) is built to retrieve the reconstruction representation (X_d^{Time}, $X_d^{Location}$, X_d^{Name}, X_d^{Action}) from daily related news. The new event dictionary is gifted with significant advantages over complexity and robustness, which makes it more efficient to process large amount of data and noisy data. The objective function with constraints of low rank and local invariance is as follows:

$$\min_{\tilde{E}_i, D_e^m} \sum_{d=1}^{D} \sum_{m=1}^{M} \|X_d^m - D_e^m \tilde{E}_i\|_F^2 + \gamma_1 \|\tilde{E}_i\|_F^2 + \gamma_2 tr(\tilde{E}_i \tilde{E}_i^T),$$

(3)

where M is the number of event components, $\|M\|_F$ is the *Frobenius* norm of matrix M, $\tilde{E}_i$ is the reconstruction of a set of daily events, and the terms γ_1, γ_2 represent the regularization parameters.

Secondly, a batch alignment model is designed to conduct events clustering and obtain the event dictionary. We adopt incremental event detection to automatically filter the content and reconstruct the representation. By introducing a specific optimization algorithm, we can obtain high-quality low-noise event representation from retrieved documents.

Sentiment Analysis: We construct the sentiment model with hierarchical neural networks. Furthermore, we adopt the research findings of Bollen *et.al.* [4], in which user moods are measured in terms of six dimensions (*Calm, Alert, Sure, Vital, Kind,* and *Happy*); the results indicate that the accuracy of stock prediction can be significantly improved by specific dimensions, namely, *Calm* and *Happiness*. When the *Calm* value and *Happiness* value are calculated by feeding relevant documents into the model, these two sentiment values are concatenated together and treated as two dimensional emotion vector of each document.

Sentimental Event Encoding: It is no strange that different stocks may share the same event, which makes the representation space for events very sparse. Thus, a sentimental event encoder is designed to encode the entire event set for tackling the sparsity and uniqueness problems. Specifically, the sentimental event encoding is obtained by aggregating sentiment values of the related documents, as detailed below. For each event $\tilde{e}_{i,l}$, the event-based *Calm* value of related news can be calculated on a daily basis according to the following:

$$\tilde{s}_{i,l}^C = \ln \frac{\zeta + N_{i,l}^p}{\zeta + N_{i,l}^n},$$

(4)

where $N_{i,l}^p$ and $N_{i,l}^n$ represent the numbers of positive and negative documents related the event l on the i-th day, respectively; ζ is a tiny number for smoothing. Similarly, the event-based *Happiness* value has the indicator $\tilde{s}_{i,l}^H$. To enable fair ensemble for $\tilde{e}_{i,l}$ and $(\tilde{s}_{i,l}^C; \tilde{s}_{i,l}^H)$, we use the z-score to normalize the data within a sliding window of length N. The z-scores for $\tilde{e}_{i,l}$ is:

$$e_{i,l} = \frac{\tilde{e}_{i,l} - \mu(\sum_{i,l} \tilde{e}_{i,l})}{\sigma(\sum_{i,l} \tilde{e}_{i,l})}, \quad (5)$$

where μ and σ are the means and standard deviations of all $N \times L$ temporal events related to a stock, respectively. Similarly, we also normalize the sentiment values using z-score. For simplicity, we use the notation $s_{i,l}$ to represent the two dimensions of emotion values $(s_{i,l}^C; s_{i,l}^H)$.

Note that the sentimental event representation $(e_{i,l}; s_{i,l})$ is more significant and robust than the original event tuple represent $\tilde{e}_{i,l}$. Supposing that two different stocks are influenced by the same event, they still may have distinct event representations because of different sets of events and sentiment values. Simultaneously, they also extend the representation space of events, which avoids the learning to stop early in the training process of the stock trend prediction model.

3.2.2 Event Attention Layer.
Since not all events contribute equally to the movement of a stock price, we devise an attention mechanism to aggregate the events by an assigned attention value, i.e., higher weights are assigned to the more significant events automatically. Specifically,

$$u_{i,l} = \delta(W_{e;s}(e_{i,l}; s_{i,l}) + b_{e;s})$$

$$\alpha_{i,l} = \frac{e^{u_{i,l}}}{\sum_l e^{u_{i,l}}} \quad (6)$$

$$x_i = \sum_{l=1}^{L} \alpha_{i,l}(e_{i,l}; s_{i,l}),$$

where $u_{i,l}$ is the latent representation of encoded sentimental event vectors $(e_{i,l}; s_{i,l})$ through one-layer network with parameters $W_{e;s}$ and $b_{e;s}$ plus a sigmoid function δ. By combining them through a *softmax* layer, we can get a normalized attention weight $\alpha_{i,l}$ to distinguish the importance of different events. Finally, we calculate the overall event feature vector x_i by a weighted sum of each sentimental event vector, and use this vector x_i to represent all event expressions on the i-th date.

Consequently, we get a temporal sequence of feature vector $X = \{x_1, x_2, ..., x_N\}$ with N being the size of time sliding window. The attention layer can gradually learn to assign higher attention value to the reliable and important event based on its sentimental event information.

3.2.3 Bi-directional LSTM layer.
To combine the temporal information of events in the convolution-based architecture, we employ a BiLSTM to accumulate the context information for each input event sequence. Belonging to RNN, LSTM is used as an event encoder to obtain a latent distributional representation for two main reasons: (1) The content lengths of events are usually different, and RNN is known to be good at dealing with the variable length problem; (2) LSTM has the ability to handle sequential input and semantics of events.

A common LSTM unit is composed of a cell, an input gate, an output gate and a forget gate. The compact form

of the equations for the LSTM unit can be given as:

$$f_t = \delta(W_f x_t + U_f h_{t-1} + b_f)$$
$$i_t = \delta(W_i x_t + U_i h_{t-1} + b_i)$$
$$o_t = \delta(W_o x_t + U_o h_{t-1} + b_o) \quad (7)$$
$$c_t = f_t \circ c_{t-1} + i_t \circ \delta(W_c x_t + U_c h_{t-1} + b_c)$$
$$h_t = o_t \circ \delta(c_t),$$

where t denotes a given date, f_t denotes the forget gate controlling how much past information should be kept, i_t is the input gate deciding how much new information should be added, and o_t means the output gate expressing how much information should be exhibited. Particularly, c_t represents the state of current time, controlling how mush past state should be used for updating the new state. Finally, the hidden represent h_t is linearly computed by the current state and output.

Therefore, we can get the latent representation for the t-th day through LSTM. In order to capture the information from the past and future of an event, we construct a bi-directional LSTM encoding h_i as follows:

$$\overrightarrow{h_i} = \overrightarrow{LSTM}(x_i), i \in [1, N]$$
$$\overleftarrow{h_i} = \overleftarrow{LSTM}(x_i), i \in [1, N] \quad (8)$$
$$h_i = [\overrightarrow{h_i}; \overleftarrow{h_i}].$$

The result h_i incorporates the information of both its surrounding events and itself. Thus we transfer the sentimental event to temporal sequence representation.

3.2.4 Convolutional Feature Extractor.
We adopt a CNN to extract stock-driven feature representation. We know that big stock price fluctuation is usually determined by key events. The CNN is therefore preferred as the top-level prediction module for its capability of extracting the local features. Note that, the same event might cause different effects on different stocks. Thus, we must take stock company information into consideration to construct event relevance. Specifically, we first calculate the relevance v_i between the collection of events on i-th day and the target stock prices:

$$v_i = \begin{cases} \frac{e^{r_i}}{\sum_i e^{r_i}} & |p_i - p_A| > \epsilon \\ 0 & |p_i - p_A| \le \epsilon, \end{cases} \quad (9)$$

where p_i and p_A are the target stock price of i-th day and average value of N days, respectively, ϵ is a pre-specified constant to avoid flat stock, and $r_i = w_r(h_i; p_i) + b_r$ is a linear transformation between events and target stock price. Then, for a given stock, we use the relevance v to help CNN locate the key event:

$$h_i^{conv} = h_i * v_i, i \in [1, N]. \quad (10)$$

We feed the weighted representation using relevance to the convolutional layer to generate the feature map, as follows:

$$m_i = ReLU(\mathbf{w}_{conv}^T \mathbf{h}_{i:i+s-1}^{conv} + b_{conv}), \quad (11)$$

where $\mathbf{h}_{i:i+s-1}$ is the concatenated vector of $h_i, ..., h_{i+s-1}$ and s is the kernel size, $\mathbf{w}_{conv}$ and $\mathbf{b}_{conv}$ are learnable weights of the convolutional kernel. To capture the most informative features, we apply max pooling and obtain the latent feature z by employing k kernels:

$$z = [max(m_1), max(m_2), ..., max(m_k)]^T. \quad (12)$$

Finally, we pass z to a *softmax* output layer for the final stock trend prediction:

$$p(y|z) = Softmax(W_f z + b_f), \quad (13)$$

where W_f and b_f are learnable parameters.

4 PERFORMANCE EVALUATION

In this section, we firstly describe the collecting process of real-world data. Then, we present the experimental setup, and conduct comprehensive experiments to verify the effectiveness of our proposed Event Attention Network (EAN).

4.1 Datasets

To make the experimental results and conclusions convincing and close to the real market, two groups of datasets from Shenzhen (SZ) and Hong Kong (HK) markets are collected and used to evaluate our framework. These datasets are from the following three data sources:

(1) Stock Price Data: We collect stock price data from Yahoo Finance by employing different strategies for the two markets. For HK market, we select 10 famous companies because their names frequently appeared in the news. Most of these stocks tend to be quite stable when compared with other stocks. To test the effectiveness of our model for different stock market, we randomly select 10 balanced stocks from the SZ market. The balanced stocks have the following conditions: fluctuating market performance, ample amount of related news, and diverse public opinions. Interestingly, these companies are listed as small or medium-sized enterprises. In general, these potential stocks are more difficult to predict[1].

(2) Financial News Data: We obtain relevant news documents from news publishing websites, namely, Hong Kong news from the Finet, and Shenzhen stock news from the Tencent News and Sina News. These financial news documents fall into the period from April 2015 to April 2018. In total, there are 202,156 documents from HZ stocks and 145,714 from HK stocks. News titles and contents are extracted from HTML. The timestamps of the news are also extracted. As our focus is on the 20 stocks from SZ and HK, queries against these 20 stocks can be easily issued and processed based on stock id, name, symbol of company, and so on.

(3) Sentiment Corpus Data: For the sentimental comments on financial news, we obtain the data from an influential social medial platform called the East Money Forum, which is one of the biggest and specialized stock forums. Different from public forums like Facebook or Twitter, each stock has its own sub-forum to ensure that most posts there are published by the investors who hold or sell that particular stock.

We automatically align the 20 stocks of daily trading data with news titles and contents, 2/3 of which are used for training, 1/6 for validating, and 1/6 for testing. The statistics of the datasets are summarized in Table 1. The training, validating and testing datasets are split temporally, with the data from 01/04/2015 to 31/03/2017 for training, the data from 01/04/2017 to 31/09/2017 for validating, and the data from 01/10/2017 to 01/04/2018 for testing.

Table 1: Statistics of the datasets.

		Training	Validation	Testing
#documents	SZ	134,770	33,692	33,694
	HK	97,142	24,285	24,287
#positive labels	SZ	8,652	1,344	1,421
	HK	11,345	2,684	2,533
#words	SZ	83,321,869	27,749,044	27,764,352
	HK	65,732,769	23,744,578	23,766,825
#avg events per day	SZ	13	8	11
	HK	34	31	28
time interval	SZ & HK	01/04/2015-31/03/2017	01/04/2017-31/09/2017	01/10/2015-01/04/2018

4.2 Experimental Setup

In the following experiments, the evaluation metrics are the Accuracy and MacroAveraged F1, the latter is more appropriate for datasets with unbalanced classes. We compare our results with the performance of the following methods on the short-term (5 days) prediction:

- RAND: a naive predictor ignoring all the news, simply adopting random guess for up (+1) or down (-1) at the chance of 50%. We also use this model to check the balance of our datasets.

- ARIMA [14]: Autoregressive Integrated Moving Average, a traditional analysis method using only price information.

- SVM [20] a classical model with extensive feature engineering. To construct the input, a corpus vector for one day is used by averaging all news vectors of a certain date, and the corpus vectors in N days (with the same window size) are concatenated.

- MLP [5]: the multi-layer perceptron (MLP) classifier, which has five layers sized as 500, 400, 300, 200 and 100, respectively. The input of MLP is the same as that in SVM.

- HAN [10]: a state-of-the-art deep neural network with hierarchical attention which predicts stock trend by using a sequence of recent related news through a self-paced learning mechanism.

---

[1]It is more reasonable to assume that people would be more interested in investing such potential stocks, because the famous stocks are usually very expensive and less fluctuations, which lend to less investment opportunities.

In order to make a detailed analysis of all the main components of EAN, we also construct the following three variations:

- EAN-SVM: It uses the SVM as a replacement of the CNN in EAN.
- EAN-MLP: The model changes the final decision layer of EAN to MLP.
- EAN-E: It only uses news event information, the purpose of which is to test the effectiveness of the sentimental event embedding.

We tokenize each news and remove the stop words. For out-of-vocabulary words, we randomly sample their embeddings from the uniform distribution. Then, we tune our model by the validation set to find the best fitted hyper parameters. Table 2 summarizes the final hyper-parameters combinations which strive to balance the speed and prediction accuracy.

Table 2: Setting of hyper-parameters.

Hyper-parameters	EAN-E		EAN	
	SZ	HK	SZ	HK
ζ	0.0001		0.01	
ϵ	0.01	0.3	0.05	0.1
L	3		15	
dim_h^{lstm}	300		300	
dim_h^{cnn}	50		50	
batch size	1024	512	512	256
dropout rates (p_{lstm}, p_{cnn})	(0.3,0.6)		(0.5,0.5)	
kernel size k	40		40	
learning rate	0.001	0.1	0.001	0.01

4.3 Main Results

As shown in Table 3, EAN consistently achieves the best performance on all the datasets, which verifies the efficacy of whole EAN framework. Moreover, EAN can perform well for different kinds of news contents, such as news with relatively formal sentences, and reviews with ungrammatical sentences. The reason is due to its CNN-based predictor which enables EAN to extract more accurate latent features from ungrammatical sentences.

Table 3: Overall experimental results

	Models	SZ		HK	
		ACC	Macro-F1	ACC	Macro-F1
Baselines	RandomGus	51.32	53.27	43.24	45.48
	ARIMA	53.27	52.36	51.93	49.38
	SVM	55.86	58.31	57.23	51.86
	MLP	56.11	56.85	58.35	52.95
	HAN	65.77	63.20	64.29	62.96
EAN variants	EAN-SVM	59.33	57.54	58.33	55.40
	EAN-MLP	61.32	59.35	64.36	63.57
	EAN-E	62.37	60.58	63.52	61.40
	EAN	**66.80**	**70.32**	**65.55**	**67.38**

On the other hand, the performance of the baseline methods varies for the two different markets. For RandomGus, we

can see that its performance on the stocks of SZ is closer to the norm (50%). For the "famous" companies in HK, however, their stocks are mostly stable. Thus, RandomGus cannot perform as effectively as it does for SZ stocks. Note that the Macro-F1 measure is more significant and indicative for such unbalanced data.

We can also make some further observations and conclusions based on the overall experimental results, as follows:

1. LSTM-based models relying on sequential information can perform well for financial news by capturing more useful context features.
2. For ungrammatical text and sentimental reviews, CNN-based approaches have some advantages because CNN aims to extract the most informative features, and is less sensitive to informal texts without strong sequential patterns.
3. The news-based methods (EAN-E and EAN) perform better than those price-based methods.
4. The sentimental information is useful in improving the news-based models (ref. EAN vs. EAN-E).
5. Different from HAN [10], the sentimental event embedding is employed by our EAN to represent the news features, which enables EAN to outperform HAN for the two markets under all measures.

4.4 Effects of window size

A natural and interesting question related to events is how long the life cycles of these events are in terms of influence. In other word, what is the effect of the time window for such events? We investigate two alternatives here: event embedding only (*i.e.*, EAN-E) and event with sentimental information (*i.e.*, EAN). Table 4 shows the experimental results of these two alternatives.

As can be seen, both EAN-E and EAN perform the best when the window size N of SZ market is about $10 \sim 11$. In contrast, the effect of the historical news only lasts, on average, 4 days for HK market. The major reason as we observing is that news from big companies are more frequent than small unknown enterprises. Thus, the "famous" companies have a shorter event life cycle.

The lag window also varies for the individual stocks. We can see that events get updated faster for the more popular domains. For example, the 0700.HK is a famous technological company, whose effective window size is only one day. On the contrary, the financial enterprise 1398.HK needs to feed more historical events in order to achieve good performance. Also note that the lag window is mainly the property of specific stocks, *i.e.*, no matter EAN-E (without sentiment information) or EAN (with sentiments), the average lag window remains similar to each other.

4.5 Performance of Sentimental Event

To investigate the impact of sentimental event features, we look at Table 3 again by comparing EAN and EAN-E. In general, the sentimental information improved the accuracy by 4.43% and 2.03% in SZ market and HK market, respectively.

Table 4: Performance and the best N for different stocks

	Stocks	EAN-E			EAN		
		N	ACC	Macro-F1	N	ACC	Macro-F1
SZ	000573	11	57.33	58.64	10	61.30	64.11
	000886	10	52.40	55.41	8	67.75	68.34
	100017	12	60.50	58.47	12	61.30	60.17
	159938	11	64.55	60.26	11	66.54	60.50
	163819	13	69.82	67.88	12	71.64	70.45
	168301	9	62.32	60.58	9	62.32	60.58
	300031	15	60.29	57.63	13	64.68	65.25
	300488	10	55.43	58.56	12	60.45	64.12
	200056	11	60.17	60.54	8	63.27	64.91
	300622	10	73.44	70.66	10	75.11	74.33
	Avg	**11.5**	**61.63**	**60.86**	**10.5**	**65.44**	**65.28**
HK	0700	1	76.40	74.82	1	80.65	81.51
	0939	1	76.25	72.54	1	78.55	79.71
	0941	3	58.73	60.38	3	59.65	61.33
	0005	4	63.50	63.22	3	65.94	65.88
	1299	5	52.73	55.56	8	61.74	64.17
	2318	3	72.60	67.39	3	73.28	70.66
	1398	9	66.50	64.82	9	66.50	64.85
	0883	4	65.20	61.69	5	66.45	61.55
	2388	2	66.40	63.97	4	68.20	70.53
	3333	11	57.95	58.35	9	63.21	64.88
	Avg	**4.3**	**65.63**	**64.27**	**4.6**	**68.42**	**68.51**

Furthermore, EAN has some distinguished improvements on the Macro-F1 measure: it has 70.32% and 67.34% Macro-F1 value for SZ and HK, respectively. The reason is that many stock prices often maintain a stable state for a certain period of time, i.e., they do not flip up and down everyday. Thus, a crucial task is to predict more accurately the turning point after a stable state. Lacking of the sentimental information, the attention values of events in EAN-E make a little difference. Such an event-only model tends to predict the same label with a stable historical state, resulting in unbalanced labels hence leading to a lower Macro-F1 value. But the sentimental event is more sensitive to new events. Our model assigns a higher attention value for a bursting event with the fluctuation of public sentiments, and this applies to each individual stock. As shown in Table 4, EAN has higher Macro-F1 values than EAN-E does. We can also find that for stocks on which the event-only model (i.e., EAN-E) performs poorly, adding sentiment information can achieve obvious improvement. For example, the 000886 in SZ and 1299 in HK get improved by 15.35% and 9.01% accuracy, respectively, i.e., from 52.40% (by EAN-E) to 67.75% (by EAN), and from 52.73% (by EAN-E) to 61.74% (by EAN).

Fig 2 shows some intuitive examples, from which we can see that sentimental events help achieve better results, especially when N is near the optimal setting. More notably, in Fig 2 (b), the blue curve lags behind the red curve for about 3 days, which shows that the added sentiment information is more helpful in capturing new burst events. In other

word, the events with sentimental information can be captured faster. The approach is also more robust. From Fig 2 (d), we can see that the blue curve improves sharply when N increases towards 9. For a large N, the performance of EAN-E becomes more sensitive, probably due to that more events may involve more noisy and fake information.

4.6 Case Study

Table 5 provides some examples for case study. To show the relationship between events and stocks more clearly, we change the event tuples to natural sentences, and symbolize the sentimental values by using the notations P and N in the table, representing positive and negative, respectively. For each sentiment, we highlight the label with a particular color (red for Happiness and blue for Calm), and the most informative event feature captured by EAN-E is the same as that by EAN, very similar to news title in HAN. To test whether our framework can select significant events and filter out those less informative ones, we also show some detailed results of these (normalized) event attention values. The final prediction uses the binary label pos and neg to indicate whether the price goes up or down.

By capturing news features correctly, all the three methods (HAN, EAN-E, EAN) can predict stock price trend accurately for the first stock 0700.HK which is a famous company with many news articles everyday. It is a relatively simple task to extract key information from the news. For the second stock, its first and second most informative events did

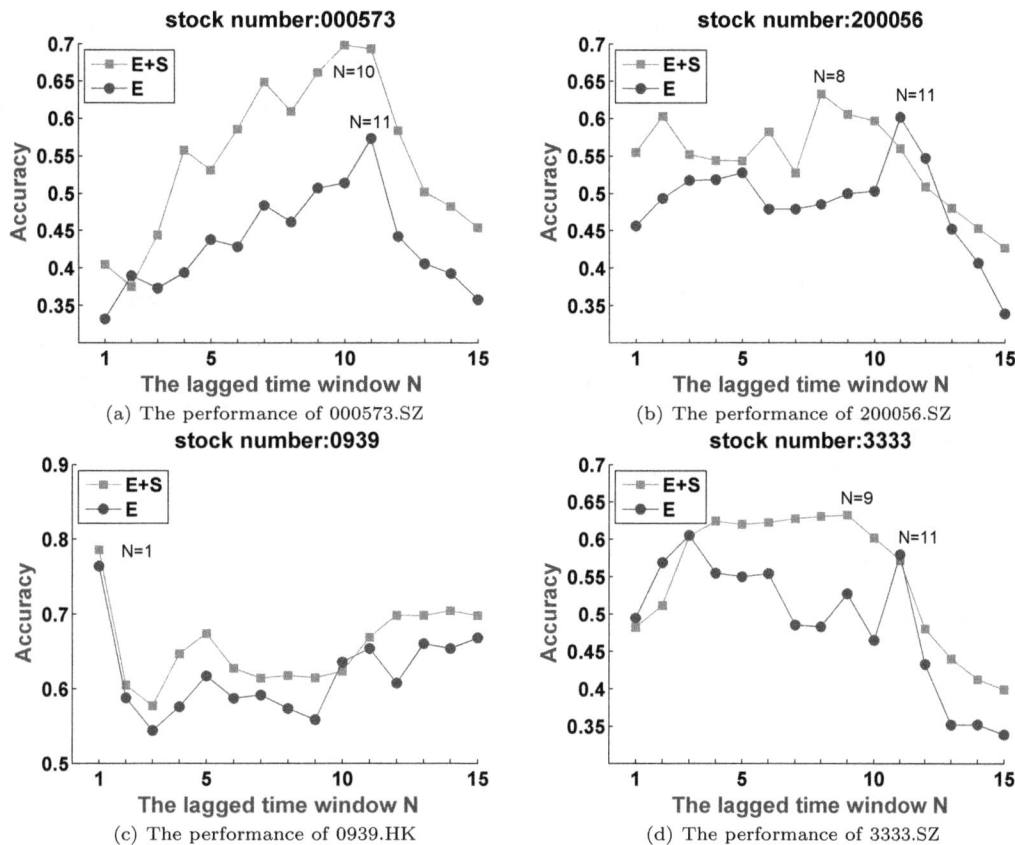

(a) The performance of 000573.SZ

(b) The performance of 200056.SZ

(c) The performance of 0939.HK

(d) The performance of 3333.SZ

Figure 2: The influence of different size of lagged window for events and sentimental events.

Table 5: Example predictions. ✓indicates correct prediction.

Stock	Sentimental Events	Attention	HAN	EAN-E	EAN
0700.HK	Naspers sells out Tencent shares (N,N)	0.54	$neg^{\checkmark}$	$neg^{\checkmark}$	$neg^{\checkmark}$
	Tencent buys out New Classics Media (N,P)	0.14			
	Tencent video reached 62.59 million members (P,P)	0.13			
	Others $(-,-)$	0.19			
000573.SZ	One big transaction occurred (P,N)	0.71	neg	$pos^{\checkmark}$	$pos^{\checkmark}$
	New policy for free trade (P,N)	0.23			
	DongGuan Winnerway Industrial Zone was fined (N,N)	0.03			
	Others $(-,-)$	0.03			
0005.HK	HSBC publish the Annual Report (P,P)	0.36	neg	neg	$pos^{\checkmark}$
	HKMA support the HK\$ (P,P)	0.36			
	HSBC applies blockchain to trade finance (N,P)	0.17			
	Others $(-,-)$	0.11			

not mention the stock and company. Both EAN-E and EAN can still make correct prediction even when the features are hidden. For the third stock which usually does not publish any unusual information except annual report, EAN can still make correct prediction while the other two cannot. As reported in [4], the important event sentiments to stocks are the positive Happiness and positive Calm. The annual report is very beneficial to its stock holders who either feel happy

or at least calm. Our sentimental event embedding, armed with the event-level feature representation with sentimental information, is capable of handling such cases.

Another useful facility of our framework is the temporal event attention mechanism. In general, events happened recently have higher impact on the current stock price movement than those happened earlier. However, there may exist some events which affect a specific stock for a long period of time. For example, the third event in stock 0700.HK is the latest related event, but the attention value of the first event dominates all events, which likely leads to the final prediction correctly. This example also demonstrates a phenomenon that if a company loses some important share holders, the stock price of this company will fall in next several days. Another interesting observation is on financial enterprises. The result indicates that economic policies announced by the government tend to have higher attention values, hence have a great influence on the financial companies, especially on banks.

5 CONCLUSIONS

In this paper, we have proposed a sentimental event embedding approach called EAN for short-term stock price trend prediction, which can generate event representation integrated with not only temporal effect but also sentiment attributes. The attention mechanism is adopted to assign a weighted value to each event according to its significance on stock price movement. A Bi-directional LSTM layer is deployed to figure out the sequential dependency of a series of events. A CNN layer is deployed to extract both event features and sentiment features from the encoded information, and those features are fed to the convolutional layer to make the predictions of stock movement. The experimental results show the superiority of our model, as well as the efficacy of its different modules, thereby verifying the rationality of the EAN architecture.

For our future work, we will investigate on how to address the sparsity of stocks-related news for more accurate stock price trend prediction. And we plan to extract events from multiple data sources. In our current experiment, many significant events are found from the social media and entertainment news rather than finical news. Moreover, the posts from the social media may contain a lot of fake and noisy information that may confuse the general public. These issues will be considered by our subsequent research.

ACKNOWLEDGMENTS

The research presented in this article has been supported by an ITF grant from the Innovation and Technology Commission (Project No. GHP/036/17SZ) and Shenzhen-Hong Kong Technology Cooperation Fund (Project No. SGLH2016 12091011009 26).

REFERENCES

[1] Klaus Adam, Albert Marcet, and Juan Pablo Nicolini. 2016. Stock market volatility and learning. *The Journal of Finance* 71, 1 (2016), 33–82.
[2] Werner Antweiler and Murray Z Frank. 2004. Is all that talk just noise? The information content of internet stock message boards. *The Journal of finance* 59, 3 (2004), 1259–1294.
[3] Johan Bollen and Huina Mao. 2011. Twitter mood as a stock market predictor. *Computer* 44, 10 (2011), 91–94.
[4] Johan Bollen, Huina Mao, and Xiaojun Zeng. 2011. Twitter mood predicts the stock market. *Journal of computational science* 2, 1 (2011), 1–8.

[5] Robert Goodell Brown. 2004. *Smoothing, forecasting and prediction of discrete time series.* Courier Corporation.
[6] Arjun Chatrath, Hong Miao, Sanjay Ramchander, and Sriram Villupuram. 2014. Currency jumps, cojumps and the role of macro news. *Journal of International Money and Finance* 40 (2014), 42–62.
[7] Xiao Ding, Yue Zhang, Ting Liu, and Junwen Duan. 2014. Using structured events to predict stock price movement: An empirical investigation. In *Proceedings of the 2014 Conference on Empirical Methods in Natural Language Processing (EMNLP).* 1415–1425.
[8] Robert F Engle. 1982. Autoregressive conditional heteroscedasticity with estimates of the variance of United Kingdom inflation. *Econometrica: Journal of the Econometric Society* (1982), 987–1007.
[9] Eric Gilbert and Karrie Karahalios. 2010. Widespread Worry and the Stock Market.. In *ICWSM.* 59–65.
[10] Ziniu Hu, Weiqing Liu, Jiang Bian, Xuanzhe Liu, and Tie-Yan Liu. [n. d.]. Listening to chaotic whispers: A deep learning framework for news-oriented stock trend prediction. In *Proceedings of the Eleventh ACM International Conference on Web Search and Data Mining.* ACM, 261–269.
[11] Wei Huang, Yoshiteru Nakamori, and Shou-Yang Wang. 2005. Forecasting stock market movement direction with support vector machine. *Computers & Operations Research* 32, 10 (2005), 2513–2522.
[12] Kyoung jae Kim. 2003. Financial time series forecasting using support vector machines. *Neurocomputing* 55, 1-2 (2003), 307–319.
[13] Fang Jin, Wei Wang, Prithwish Chakraborty, Nathan Self, Feng Chen, and Naren Ramakrishnan. 2017. Tracking multiple social media for stock market event prediction. In *Industrial Conference on Data Mining.* Springer, 16–30.
[14] Lili Li, Shan Leng, Jun Yang, and Mei Yu. 2016. Stock Market Autoregressive Dynamics: A Multinational Comparative Study with Quantile Regression. *Mathematical Problems in Engineering* 2016 (2016).
[15] Xiaodong Li, Haoran Xie, Li Chen, Jianping Wang, and Xiaotie Deng. 2014. News impact on stock price return via sentiment analysis. *Knowledge-Based Systems* 69 (2014), 14–23.
[16] Xiaodong Li, Haoran Xie, Yangqiu Song, Shanfeng Zhu, Qing Li, and Fu Lee Wang. 2015. Does summarization help stock prediction? A news impact analysis. *IEEE intelligent systems* 30, 3 (2015), 26–34.
[17] Janderson B Nascimento and Marco Cristo. 2015. The Impact of Structured Event Embeddings on Scalable Stock Forecasting Models. In *Proceedings of the 21st Brazilian Symposium on Multimedia and the Web.* ACM, 121–124.
[18] Akhter Mohiuddin Rather, Arun Agarwal, and VN Sastry. 2015. Recurrent neural network and a hybrid model for prediction of stock returns. *Expert Systems with Applications* 42, 6 (2015), 3234–3241.
[19] Robert P Schumaker, Yulei Zhang, Chun-Neng Huang, and Hsinchun Chen. 2012. Evaluating sentiment in financial news articles. *Decision Support Systems* 53, 3 (2012), 458–464.
[20] Francis EH Tay and Lijuan Cao. 2001. Application of support vector machines in financial time series forecasting. *omega* 29, 4 (2001), 309–317.
[21] Stephen J Taylor. 2008. *Modelling financial time series.* world scientific.
[22] Tien-Thanh Vu, Shu Chang, Quang Thuy Ha, and Nigel Collier. 2012. An experiment in integrating sentiment features for tech stock prediction in twitter. (2012).
[23] Hang Yang, Yubo Chen, Kang Liu, Yang Xiao, and Jun Zhao. 2018. DCFEE: A Document-level Chinese Financial Event Extraction System based on Automatically Labeled Training Data. In *Proceedings of ACL 2018, System Demonstrations.* 50–55.
[24] Akira Yoshihara, Kazuhiro Seki, and Kuniaki Uehara. 2015. Leveraging temporal properties of news events for stock market prediction. *Artificial Intelligence Research* 5, 1 (2015), 103.
[25] Yang Yu, Wenjing Duan, and Qing Cao. 2013. The impact of social and conventional media on firm equity value: A sentiment analysis approach. *Decision Support Systems* 55, 4 (2013), 919–926.

Building Sociality through Sharing:
Seniors' Perspectives on Misinformation

Mahika Wason*
Sharmistha Swasti Gupta*
mahika16241@iiitd.ac.in
sharmistha16193@iiitd.ac.in
Indraprastha Institute of Information
Technology
New Delhi, India

Shriram Venkatraman
shriramv@iiitd.ac.in
Indraprastha Institute of Information
Technology
New Delhi, India

Ponnurangam Kumaraguru
pk@iiitd.ac.in
Indraprastha Institute of Information
Technology
New Delhi, India

ABSTRACT

This paper attempts to understand the perspectives of the seniors (aged 65 years and above) on misinformation in the Indian context. Interviews with 33 seniors who use social media regularly revealed three themes. The seniors viewed and rationalized sharing news irrespective of its veracity as a process of building sociality. Sharing information was also based on the logic of superimposing information with an epistemic ascription to the networks from where they received it. Finally, a kind of normative dualism becomes apparent from an acknowledgment of the role they may play in the spread of misinformation as agents on the one hand and a resounding need to stop it on the other due to its potential social ramifications.

CCS CONCEPTS

• **Social and professional topics** → **Age**; **Seniors**.

KEYWORDS

Misinformation; Seniors; Sharing; Sociality; Social Media

ACM Reference Format:
Mahika Wason, Sharmistha Swasti Gupta, Shriram Venkatraman, and Ponnurangam Kumaraguru. 2019. Building Sociality through Sharing: Seniors' Perspectives on Misinformation. In *11th ACM Conference on Web Science (WebSci '19), June 30-July 3, 2019, Boston, MA, USA.* ACM, New York, NY, USA, 2 pages. https://doi.org/10.1145/3292522.3326052

1 INTRODUCTION AND RELATED WORK

The surge of fake news online has given rise to several studies on both its macro and micro effects. An often-studied topic has been the millennial consumption of news through social media and their vulnerability in being exposed to hybrid sources of information [1, 4, 5], alongside issues such as echo chambers, network homogeneity, information literacy, ideological alignment and confirmation bias [1, 3, 7]. However, with the rise of the participation of seniors on social media [11, 12], especially in countries such

*Both authors contributed equally to this research.

as India which has the world's second largest online sphere [2], a paucity of studies on the fake news consumption by this demographic acts as the key motivator for this study. In the recent years, India has witnessed the rise of the new middle class, the emergence of cosmopolitan nuclear families, increase in transnational dispersal of families due to global labor markets [9] and the upsurge of smartphones providing digitally connected affordances to families [6]. All of these have contributed to the digitally-savvy middle-class seniors effectively mediating social media to ensure digital connectedness. In this paper, we explore the differential attitudes that the seniors who use social media have on the spread of misinformation. We also explore if information sharing has deeper social roots situated within the paradigm of the Indian ethos.

2 METHODOLOGY

The study adopted a semi-structured ethnographic interview format. Interviews were conducted with 33 seniors (aged 65 years to 82 years) in both the National Capital Region (north of India) and Chennai (south of India). There was a total of 14 men and 19 women participants, recruited through snowball sampling. All were either upper middle class or middle-class Indian citizens and were regular users of Facebook and WhatsApp. The interviews ranged from 12 minutes to 3.5 hours. Pseudonyms have been used to protect the privacy and confidentiality of the participants.

3 RESULTS

We discuss three distinct themes that emerged from our interviews.
i) Sharing to Build Sociality: The loneliness and isolation arising from the changing structure of the new middle-class families in India (due to the rise of transnational and trans-local settlements) impact seniors. Connectedness is ensured through weekly or monthly video calls through social media. For example, though Ravinder, a 70-year-old homemaker interacts with her children overseas a couple of times a week, the rest of the time she feels bored and lonely. To combat this, for over six hours a day she exchanges WhatsApp messages from over 23 groups. Though she does not read these messages in detail, she forwards them as received. This hints at non-consumption of messages that are shared. Sharing became more important than the content of the information. Though normative discourses on functionality and the use of information sharing did surface, the practicality of socializing in everyday lives was key to them. Spreading messages on social

media was perceived as non-agenda driven sharing and pure sociality building process with no functional attributes. Information shared was more often as received and rarely followed by a remarks stating their thoughts on what they shared. Affirmations of testing the reliability of information shared online were frequently brought up with a qualifier that trust on the person who shared the information was a key criterion when information is exchanged as it was impossible to verify everything. Though the usefulness of shared information was an often-heard normative statement, it was apparent that passing information to groups was a an attempt to build sociality.

ii) Epistemic Ascriptions to Networks: The epistemic validity of the information received by these seniors on online groups was mostly accepted at face value. Information is assessed as either falling into personal or non-personal categories and each has its valuation performed on it. It is deciphered based on who passed this information, often ascribing the veracity and the epistemic value of the information to the network or the person who shared it. For example, Rajat, a 70-year-old retired business-man stated "*I once received a piece of information on a change of a health insurance policy for seniors from a group which was a reading group with no seniors in it...I waited for the same message to be passed by the senior friends' group that I am a member of before I took it seriously...you just can't believe anyone...it should come from the right group*". However, on interviewing again, Rajat said that the information was a fake marketing strategy and his network had fallen for it. There were other cases where the ascriptions placed on the network had proved to be false, but that did not deter their faith in the information passed by the right kind of group (which was perceived as possessing the expertise for that kind of information). In case of non-personal information, on the contrary, there were cases where information, irrespective of its authenticity, was passed on just basing it on the ascriptions they associated with specific groups. The best examples pertain to religion. Messages with pictures of a god or goddess which when asked to be passed onto at least 20 people for their wish to be fulfilled, were passed with no questions asked.

iii) Normative Dualism: The seniors rationalized their practice of sharing information as a normative practice embedded deeply in the cultural framework of their native societies. Questions of how to categorize gossip or propaganda abound their interviews. Very often cultural attitudes and the existence of information dispersal processes in their societies even before the proliferation of digital tools and their role as a catalyst in helping spread information and thereby falling prey to misinformation was brought up. The spread of misinformation was often distanced from subjective personal practices and associated with the general nature of human behavior. Misinformation for them would coexist with information, and nothing could be done to stop it. However, they cognized on the ramifications of misinformation given the rate of its spread has increased with the proliferation of social media tools and felt a profound need to curb it's spread.

4 DISCUSSION AND CONCLUSION

Building sociality or having a more natural way to communicate with larger or smaller networks now have a platform-based affordance which these social media platforms offer. With this as a point of inflection, delving deeper into the mechanics of the spread of information by these seniors point to some significant aspects. They typically employ a variegated sharing strategy. For example, impersonal messages generally shared in larger groups are seldom shared with their children over direct channels. Information shared on personal channels rarely makes it to the groups. However, epistemic validations through discussions of certain news could happen over phone calls, WhatsApp calls/messages, Facebook or even face to face communication with a close social circle. This is typical of the theory of scalable sociality [7] where these seniors strategically tend to move between the smaller and the larger groups depending on the nature of information shared. These can be viewed through the lenses of both polymedia [10] where there is a strategic choice of media based on what needs to be communicated and media multiplexity [8], which suggests that stronger ties communicate over multiple media. Non-consumption-based sharing is a significant aspect of these seniors who act as nodes in a larger social network. The more natural the form and the function of the information shared, the higher seems to be the receptivity with the seniors. Deception due to the congruence of form and function of shared information is apparent in the way the seniors describe their vulnerability. Though this study has a regional limitation, we hope that with the paucity of studies on the elderly and their participation on social media in an era of rising misinformation, this paper will act as a call for more such studies in the global south, specifically in countries like India which have a vast and growing digital population.

REFERENCES

[1] [n. d.]. News and America's Kids: How Young People Perceive and Are Impacted by the News | Common Sense Media. https://www.commonsensemedia.org/research/news-and-americas-kids

[2] 2019. List of countries by number of Internet users. https://en.wikipedia.org/w/index.php?title=List_of_countries_by_number_of_Internet_users&oldid=894730851 Page Version ID: 894730851.

[3] Eytan Bakshy, Solomon Messing, and Lada A. Adamic. 2015. Political science. Exposure to ideologically diverse news and opinion on Facebook. *Science (New York, N.Y.)* 348, 6239 (June 2015), 1130–1132. https://doi.org/10.1126/science.aaa1160

[4] Meital Balmas. 2014. When Fake News Becomes Real: Combined Exposure to Multiple News Sources and Political Attitudes of Inefficacy, Alienation, and Cynicism. *Communication Research* 41, 3 (April 2014), 430–454. https://doi.org/10.1177/0093650212453600

[5] Danah Boyd. [n. d.]. *It's Complicated: The Social Lives of Networked Teens.* Yale University Press. http://journals.openedition.org/lectures/17628

[6] Elana D. Buch. 2015. Anthropology of Aging and Care. *Annual Review of Anthropology* 44, 1 (2015), 277–293. https://doi.org/10.1146/annurev-anthro-102214-014254

[7] Martin Flintham, Christian Karner, Khaled Bachour, Helen Creswick, Neha Gupta, and Stuart Moran. 2018. Falling for Fake News: Investigating the Consumption of News via Social Media. In *Proceedings of the 2018 CHI Conference on Human Factors in Computing Systems (CHI '18)*. ACM, New York, NY, USA, 376:1–376:10. https://doi.org/10.1145/3173574.3173950 event-place: Montreal QC, Canada.

[8] Caroline Haythornthwaite. 2002. Strong, Weak, and Latent Ties and the Impact of New Media. *The Information Society* 18, 5 (Oct. 2002), 385–401. https://doi.org/10.1080/01972240290108195

[9] Sarah E. Lamb. 2009. *Aging and the Indian Diaspora: Cosmopolitan Families in India and Abroad.* Indiana University Press. https://muse.jhu.edu/book/3852

[10] Mirca Madianou and Daniel Miller. 2013. Polymedia: Towards a new theory of digital media in interpersonal communication. *International Journal of Cultural Studies* 16, 2 (March 2013), 169–187. https://doi.org/10.1177/1367877912452486

[11] Amy Mitchell, Jocelyn Kiley, Jeffrey Gottfried, and Emily Guskin. 2013. The Role of News on Facebook | Pew Research Center. https://www.journalism.org/2013/10/24/the-role-of-news-on-facebook/

[12] Shriram Venkatraman. 2017. *Social Media in South India.* London: UCL Press. http://discovery.ucl.ac.uk/1558928/1/Social-Media-in-South-India.pdf

Debunking Rumors in Social Networks: A Timely Approach

Liang Wu
School of Computing, Informatics, and Decision Systems
Engineering
Arizona State University
Tempe, AZ
liangwu1@asu.edu

Huan Liu
School of Computing, Informatics, and Decision Systems
Engineering
Arizona State University
Tempe, AZ
huanliu@asu.edu

ABSTRACT

Social networks have been instrumental in spreading rumor such as fake news and false rumors. Research in rumor intervention to date has concentrated on launching an intervening campaign to limit the number of infectees. However, many emerging and important tasks focus more on *early* intervention. Social and psychological studies have revealed that rumors might evolve 70% of its original content after 6 transmissions. Therefore, ignoring earliness of intervention makes the intervening campaign downgrade rapidly due to the evolved content. In real social networks, the number of social actors is usually *large*, while the budget for an intervening campaign is relatively *small*. The limited budget makes early intervention particularly challenging. Nonetheless, we present an efficient containment method that promptly terminates the diffusion with least cost. To our knowledge, this work is the first to study the earliness of rumor intervention in a large real-world social network. Evaluations on a network of 3 million users show that the key social actors who earliest terminate the spread are not necessarily the most influential users or friends of rumor initiators, and the proposed method effectively reduces the life span of rumors.

CCS CONCEPTS

• **Mathematics of computing** → **Graph theory**; • **Networks** → **Online social networks**.

KEYWORDS

Graph Mining; Social Network Analysis; Social Media Mining; Classification

ACM Reference Format:
Liang Wu and Huan Liu. 2019. Debunking Rumors in Social Networks: A Timely Approach. In *11th ACM Conference on Web Science (WebSci'19), June 30–July 3, 2019, Boston, MA, USA*. ACM, New York, NY, USA, 9 pages. https://doi.org/10.1145/3292522.3326025

1 INTRODUCTION

With the blistering expansions in recent years, social media has become an attractive platform for information dissemination. The interconnections between social actors allow for the communication of time-sensitive information. However, social networks

have also cultivated the widespread of rumors. For example, a piece of rumor sent by a compromised Associated Press Twitter account wiped out over $136 billion in equity market value within ten minutes[1].

Despite its importance in maintaining "quality" real-time communications, surprisingly little has been studied about the ***earliness*** of intervention, *i.e.*, how quickly the rumor diffusion can be terminated. Existing intervening systems mainly focus on reducing the ultimate number of infectees [7, 35, 38]. However, according to the traditional social and psychological studies, a rumor evolves so rapidly that most details would be altered after 6 transmissions [2]. Therefore, ignoring the lifespan of rumors leads to more variants being generated that may result in greater influence. An example is the urban legend of Ebola: when potential cases appeared in Newark, false rumors of pandemic outbreaks arose in social media. As a common practice of reducing infectees, authoritative and influential sources broadcast to debunk it. However, the rumor evolved into different variants that circulated for a long time, such as the virus can spread through air and salt water cures Ebola[2].

Existing intervention methods that focus on reducing infectees unnecessarily result in an early termination. They model rumor intervention as a multiparty influence maximization problem, and the main intuition is to find those key influential users, given a particular group of rumor initiators, that minimize (or maximize) the influence of rumors (or factual information). Therefore, influential nodes with a higher centrality measure are usually selected for the campaign of factual information, while users that locate remotely from the *centered* nodes are overlooked. Allocating more budget to the center leads to fewer infectees, but rumors may circulate a longer time among less approachable users.

In this work, we postulate an alternative debunking strategy that rapidly terminates the diffusion of rumors, and we also give the justification behind our choices with theoretical analysis and empirical evaluations. The main contributions of the work are summarized below,

- We propose to study the earliness of rumor intervention and formally formulate the problem in the context of social networks;
- Prove the NP-completeness and provide an approximation approach that efficiently captures the key factual information initiators that terminate rumor diffusion at an early stage.
- Conduct extensive experiments with three real-world social network datasets to understand the working of different aspects for the proposed approach.

---

[1] https://www.washingtonpost.com/news/worldviews/wp/2013/04/23/syrian-hackers-claim-ap-hack-that-tipped-stock-market-by-136-billion-is-it-terrorism/
[2] http://time.com/3479254/ebola-social-media/

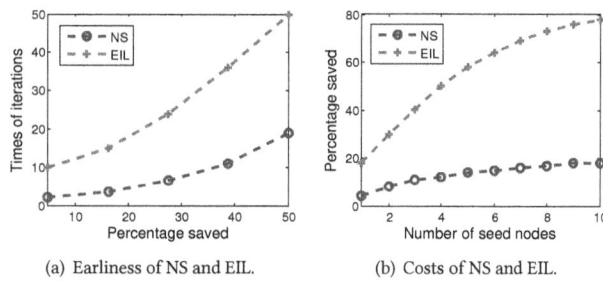

(a) Earliness of NS and EIL.

(b) Costs of NS and EIL.

Figure 1: We compare NS and EIL in terms of costs and earliness. As shown in Figure 1(a), to achieve similar results, NS is much faster and requires fewer iterations. As shown in Figure 1(b), EIL requires a smaller budget to achieve the same result.

Rest of the work is organized as follows: in Section 2, we employ exploratory studies to present the motivation of the work. In Section 3, we formulate the problem of early intervention of rumors. In Section 4, we prove the NP-completeness of the problem and provide an approximation method that is theoretically bounded. Experimental results on real-world social networks are described in Section 5. Section 6 presents related research and Section 7 concludes the work.

2 EXPLORATORY STUDY

The current containment methods can be classified into immunization and real-time intervention approaches. In the first, *before* a rumor starts spreading, the optimal set of nodes and/or links are immunized (*e.g.*, blocking and removing) to make the social network robust to future attacks [9, 39, 48]. In the second, the optimal set of users are found to launch a debunking campaign *after* a rumor starts spreading [7, 17, 20, 27–29, 35, 37, 38]. Although the term "early" has been mentioned in previous work [28], however, all existing approaches only optimize and evaluate the number of infectees. In order to explore the possible way to early intervention, we compare the earliness and influence of two frameworks.

Without loss of generality, we choose generic methods in each category. We choose NetShield (NS) [9, 39] for immunization methods, which is the state-of-the-art approach. It first exploits the spectral property [14] of graphs for large-scale immunization and it is efficient to optimize. The problem of real-time rumor intervention has been first introduced by Budak *et al.*, and they prove that it is an NP-complete problem and they offer a near-optimal solution named EIL [7]. Both EIL and NS have been well studied and extended to various intervention tasks [9, 17, 27]. We conduct experiments with real-world Twitter data, consisting of 19,240 nodes (users) and 3,933,718 edges. The dataset is publicly available through the Social Computing Data Repository[3].

Figure 1(a) shows the earliness of the two methods. Since they both focus on the number of "saved" infectees, we vary the percentage of saved nodes and observe the time needed by each method. A node is *saved* if it would be infected in the absence of the

[3]http://socialcomputing.asu.edu/

intervention [7]. Time is represented by iterations of transmissions which is discrete. We can see that to save the same number of nodes, NS terminates the rumor spread at the earlier stage. Since the required budget (number of seed nodes) is a main concern in real applications, in Figure 1(b), we vary the budget size and observe the percentage of saved nodes. Given the same number of seed nodes, EIL significantly outperforms NS in saving more nodes.

Based on the results, we draw the following observation: though NS seems to be a better tool to achieve the goal of early intervention, the required large budget makes it less practically useful. NS aims to find the optimal set of nodes for decreasing the vulnerability of the global graph in the context of network design, such as computer network intrusion. The size of the optimal set of nodes linearly increases with the number of nodes in a graph. Whereas in digital rumor intervention, the budget for a particular piece of rumor is usually limited; and it is also impractical to permanently block a large number of nodes for immunization purposes. In this work, we will seek to early intervene rumor spread with least cost. Our main intuition is that given the locality of the initial infection, many nodes that lead to a global robustness are redundant to a particular piece of rumor.

3 PROBLEM DEFINITIONS

Traditional information diffusion models study the roles of certain nodes during the process of information being viral. Since they mainly focus on a single-party campaign, information diffusion models cannot be used to model the interaction between multiple campaigns. Though several methods have been proposed to model multi-party information diffusion, the factor of earliness, which is of practical significance in real applications, has been ignored. In this work, we try to model earliness directly.

3.1 Information Diffusion Model

In this subsection, we introduce the diffusion model of rumors in a social network. In the diffusion model, a social network is considered as a directed graph $G = (N, E)$, consisting of nodes (people) N and edges (social relationships) E. Let M and F denote the diffusion of a *rumor* and *factual* information respectively. For each node in a network, it can be infected by either information or be inactive as initialized. The initial set of nodes influenced by M and F are denoted as $P(M)$ and $P(F)$. We assume that people highly rely on social influence in forming their opinions [19], as a result, the infection can be caused by initialization or sequentially by one of the neighbors.

Considering the characteristics of rumors, we introduce three properties of the diffusion model. First, for the brevity of presentation, we let the diffusion of M and F start at the same time. The setting is generalizable to cases where M starts earlier than F since all infected nodes before F starts can be regarded as initialized rumor infectees in another instance of the same problem. Second, we assume people are more likely to believe the factual information than a rumor [21], so when an inactive individual is influenced by M and F at the same time, the individual will be influenced by F. Third, in order to make the problem computationally tractable, we assume the diffusion to be *progressive*, *i.e.*, an inactive individual would be influenced by either information, and once being active, it cannot turn back to inactive or switch to the other status.

The diffusion starts with the network G, and two initial sets of nodes $P(M)$ and $P(F)$. If an individual node u becomes infected by rumor M or immunized by the factual information F at timestamp t, it attempts to influence all its inactive neighbors at timestamp $t+1$. In this work, we assume the time to be discrete as timestamps. Therefore, an early intervention means fewer timestamps and fewer times of rumors to be transmitted. The diffusion happens only once for every edge, and it operates in discrete timestamps. The diffusion keeps running until no more inactive nodes are infected.

3.2 The Computational Problem

Based on the conceptual definitions, we introduce our problem and formally define the computational problem of the real-time early intervention of rumors.

As discussed earlier, immunization methods are faster in containing rumors. Immunization methods like NS exploit the structural and spectral properties of social graphs. In particular, the structural property implies that nodes in a graph are usually scattered into different clusters (communities), and the spectral property indicates that nodes between different clusters have a higher value in the first eigenvector. Therefore, the main idea of NS is to block nodes between communities, and when the infection starts, only the local area will be influenced and the global graph is immunized. To better illustrate the idea, we show the process of a rumor spread under different intervention methods in Figure 2. The x-axis represents the progress of the diffusion, where 30% means 30% of all timestamps have passed. The y-axis represents the inter-group entropy. We first calculate the community membership of social actors with the CESNA method in SNAP toolkit [25], which can efficiently detect communities in big graphs. Given the community membership $C \in \mathbb{R}^{|N| \times K}$, where K is the number of communities, and the probability of a community is $p_i = \frac{\sum_{j=1}^{|N|} C_{i,j}}{|N|}$, and the inter-group entropy can be calculated as,

$$e = -\sum_{i=1}^{K} p_i \log(p_i), \quad (1)$$

which measures how well nodes from different communities are blended. It can be seen that, under EIL, rumors are viral in more clusters of nodes, while NS constrains rumors in fewer communities. Containing rumors in fewer communities not only leads to early intervention, but may also be more practically useful: as investigated in recent work [12], online communities are formed with the coherence of beliefs [1, 5], and they may quickly turn into an *echo chamber* of rumors due to the biased self-confirmation and their selective narrative.

Our main intuition to reduce the budget of NS is that many nodes selected by NS are "covered" by others given a particular (set of) seed node(s). Through empirical studies, we show that intuitive measures such as distance to the seed cannot be used to determine the relationship of being covered, and it is actually an NP-complete problem. Here, we denote the set of nodes that best immunize the graph as the immunization set I [39, 48]. Next, we will formally

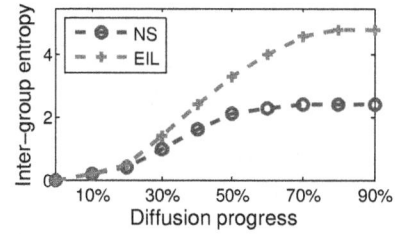

Figure 2: The change of inter-group entropy with the progress of rumor diffusion. A higher entropy value indicates more groups are infected.

define the problem of Early Intervention of rumors with Minimum Cost (EIMMC) as follows.

Definition 3.1. Early Intervention of rumors with Minimum Cost (EIMMC) : Given a social network $G = (N, E)$, and rumor originators $P(M) \in N$ and the immunization set $I \in N$, the target of EIMMC is to find the minimum budget k and the corresponding optimal set of factual information originators $P(F) \in N, |P(F)| = k$, so that all nodes in I are guaranteed to be immunized before being reached by the rumor.

4 EARLY INTERVENTION OF RUMORS

In this section, we introduce how we conduct early intervention of rumors. We first prove the NP-completeness of the proposed approach. In order to provide an efficient solution, we introduce a greedy strategy that is theoretically bounded.

4.1 NP-Completeness of EIMMC

In order to prove the NP-completeness of EIMMC, we introduce the definition of the Set Cover problem below,

Definition 4.1. Set Cover problem(SC): Given a set of elements $U = \{1, 2, \cdots, n\}$ and a set of m subsets of $S = S_1, S_2, \cdots, S_m$, the Set Cover problem is to find the minimum number of sets covering all elements in U such that the union of S is U.

SC is an NP-complete problem and cannot be solved in polynomial time. Later we will use SC to help prove the NP-completeness of EIMMC. As it may be easier to convince a user of the factual information, we assume the high effectiveness property of F, meaning that an individual in $P(F)$ will activate its neighbors in the next timestamp in a deterministic manner. The assumption alleviates the difficulty of solving EIMMC, however, we will show that the simplified problem is also difficult.

THEOREM 4.2. *EIMMC is NP-complete even with the high effectiveness property.*

Proof: Let $S = \{S_1, S_2, \cdots, S_m\}$ be the sets of an SC problem and $S_1 \cup S_2 \cup \cdots S_m = \{a_1, a_2, \cdots, a_n\}$, we construct an EIMMC problem below.

- We create a graph G' with two kinds of nodes u and v, and create a node u_i for a set S_i, and a node v_j for each element a_j. We build an edge from u_i to v_j if $a_j \in S_i$.

- Introduce an infected node set $P'(M)$, and construct an edge from any node in $P(M)$ to $v_1, v_2, \cdots, v_n$.
- Let the immunization set I' include all v, i.e., $I' = \{v_1, v_2, \cdots, v_n\}$.

Therefore, the SC problem is reduced to an EIMMC problem with the graph G', the rumor originators $P'(M)$ and the immunization set I'. Since the problem is NP-complete, we will provide an approximate solution that is theoretically bounded.

4.2 Approximate Solution for EIMMC

THEOREM 4.3. *There is no $o(\ln(n))$-approximation solution for the problem of EIMMC.*

Proof: Since there is no $o\ln(n)$-approximation for the SC problem according to the result of inapproximability [13], following the proof of Theorem 4.2, there is no $o\ln(n)$-approximation for the problem of EIMMC.

THEOREM 4.4. *There exists $O(\ln(n))$-approximation solution for the problem of EIMMC.*

Proof: Given the rumor originators M, using *Breadth First Search* (BFS) method, we can estimate the earliest time of each individual in I that will be infected. Then the problem of EIMMC is to find the minimum set of nodes in the graph that can influence individuals in I before being infected. In particular, we define these nodes as the *roots* of the search trees named $R = r_1, r_2, \cdots, r_l$, and l is the least number of roots that protects I given a particular $P(M)$. Therefore, each node in R immunizes (covers) a certain number of nodes in I. So EIMMC can be transformed to an instance of the SC problem within polynomial time. Since there is an $O(\ln(n))$-approximation for SC, there is also an $O(\ln(n))$-approximation for the problem of EIMMC.

Details of the approximation algorithm can be found in Algorithm 1. In line 1, we use BFS to search nodes that need to be immunized in the immunization set I given a particular M. In line 2, we find nodes that can reach $I'(M)$ before they are infected, and $I'(M)_i$ is the ith element of $I'(M)$. V are the candidates for $P(F)$. From line 3 to line 11, we find the covered nodes H of each candidate seed in V. Therefore, the problem is transformed to finding the least number of sets (H) that cover all units ($I'(M)$). From line 12 to line 15, we search for the optimal sets in a hill-climbing scheme, and the approximation threshold is tightly bounded by $(1 - 1/e)$ [13]. Line 16 returns the optimal set of nodes for the factual information campaign with the least budget. The candidate immunization set $I(M)$ can be obtained beforehand in an offline manner.

4.3 Submodularity of EIMMC

Due to the NP-completeness of the EIMMC problem, we proposed an approximation algorithm to greedily search for a near-optimal solution. However, an approximation method is bounded by a margin of $(1 - \frac{1}{e})$ only if the outcome function is submodular [30, 41]. We define the outcome function as $O(P(F))$, and it denotes the users that are influenced by a certain set of factual information initiators. We need to prove that $O(\cdot)$ is submodular by showing it has a diminishing return. That is, given $P(F)$ and $P'(F)$ where $P(F) \subseteq P'(F)$, the marginal benefit of adding another initiator i to $P(F)$ is always greater or equal to adding it to $P'(F)$: $|O(P(F) \cup \{i\}) - O(P(F))| \geq |O(P'(F) \cup \{i\}) - O(P'(F))|$.

In our work, we aim to cover as many nodes in immunization set as possible. If immunization set can be better covered, the rumor spread can be terminated in an early stage. Since it is extremely difficult to accurately estimate the exact number of infected nodes, for simplicity, we denote $O(P(F))$ by the nodes in the immunization set that can be covered by immunizing $P(F)$. Following conventional practice, we assume the diffusion process is happened in discrete timestamps [18, 35]: active nodes infect their neighbors at each timestamp, and the timestamp will be tagged with the edge between the active node and the infectee. Note that every edge will be assigned at most one timestamp since a node can be activated only once.

Given a graph $G = (V, E)$ with $P(F)$ and $P(M)$ simultaneously starting their campaign, we derive two activation graphs G_F and G_M for the cascade of factual information and rumors, respectively. From the first timestamp, for each node $i \in P(F)$ and node $j \in PM$, we randomly select i, u and (j, v) and activate the corresponding node u and v and assign the timestamp to the edge. The selection is based on the node degree $\frac{1}{d_u}$, where d_u is the degree of node u.

By repeatedly infecting more nodes, some nodes in immunization set will be influenced by the factual information campaign. The expected outcome in terms of coverage of immunization set can be denoted by $O(P(F)) = |E(G_F)(I)|$, which is the number of edges that are linked to immunization set nodes activated by factual information. We prove the diminishing return by presenting the following lemma.

LEMMA 4.5. *In the activation graph G_M, there exists at least one path from a node in $P(M)$ to a node that is both in the immunization set and G_M. In the activation graph G_F, there exists at least one path from a node in $P(F)$ to a node that is both in the immunization set and G_F. For both paths, we denote the timestamp as t_i^M for node $i \in G_M$ and t_j^F for node $j \in G_F$.*

In order to prove $|O(P(F) \cup \{i\}) - O(P(F))| \geq |O(P'(F) \cup \{i\}) - O(P'(F))|$, we need to show that there exists a node $v \in I$, such that $v \in O(P(F))$ and $v \in O(P'(F) \cup \{i\}) \backslash O(P'(F))$. To this end, we present the following two lemmas to prove equivalence:

LEMMA 4.6. *The sufficient conditions for $v \in O_(P(M))$ are*

- $v \in G_F(P(F))$ and $v \in G_M(P(M))$;
- *There exists a timestamp t_v^F for any edge of v in $G_F(P(F))$ that is smaller than or equal to the smallest timestamp of any edge of $v \in G_M(P(M))$.*

LEMMA 4.7. *The sufficient conditions for $v \in O(P'(F) \cup \{i\}) \backslash O(P'(F))$ are as follows*

- $v \in G_M(P(M))$ and $v \in G_F(P(F) \cup \{i\})$;
- *There exists a timestamp t_v^F for any edge of v in $G_F(P(F) \cup \{i\})$ that is smaller than or equal to the smallest timestamp of any edge of $v \in G_M(P(M))$;*
- *For all $j \in P'(F)$, the smallest time stamp among all edges in $G_F(P'(F))$ is larger than the smallest timestamp in $G_M(P(M))$.*

THEOREM 4.8. *The outcome function $O(\cdot)$ is submodular.*

It is easy to prove that $O(\cdot)$ is monotonic. Therefore, the marginal gain of $O(\cdot)$ is diminishing and the greedy approximation is tightly bounded by $(1 - \frac{1}{e})$.

Algorithm 1 Algorithm of Solving EIMMC

Input: $G = N, E, P(M), I(M), D = \emptyset, P(F) = \emptyset$
Output: $P(F)$
1: For $n \in P(M)$, use BFS to construct paths from n to nodes in $I(M)$. Denote the connected nodes (leaves of BFS paths) as $I'(M)$

2: For $n \in I'(M)$, reversely use BFS to find nodes v^i that can reach n, i is the length of the shortest path, *i.e.,* $v^0 = n$, $\forall w \in P(M)$, $w = v^j, j \geq i$; Denote the set of v^i as V_n
3: For $i = 1$ to $|I'(M)|$
4:     For $u \in V_i \cup_{k=1}^{i-1} V_k$
5:         Add edge from u to $I'(M)_i$
6:         For $j = i + 1$ to $|I'(M)|$
7:             If $u \in V_j$, add edge from u to $I'(M)_j$;
8:         End for
9:         Denote nodes that connect by u as H_u
10:    End for
11: End for
12: While $|D| < |I'(M)|$
13:    Select $w = \arg\max_{u \in \cup_{i=1}^{|I'(M)|} V_i} |H_u \setminus D|$
14:    $P(F) = P(F) \cup w, D = D \cup H_u$
15: End while
16: Return $P(F)$

Table 1: Notations and corresponding descriptions

$G = \{N, E\}$	A graph G with nodes N and edges E
$M, P(M)$	rumor and its initiators
$F, P(F)$	Factual information and its initiators
t	Timestamp
I	Immunization set
u, v, w	Nodes in a graph

5 EXPERIMENTS

In this section, we evaluate our approach, compare the results with established baselines, and discuss insights gained. In particular, we aim to evaluate the proposed approach from the following aspects: (1) effectiveness at different networks with different distributions; (2) effectiveness at different rumor originators. Here the effectiveness means the earliness of intervention and the required budget size for intervention.

5.1 Datasets

We use three real-world networks, including the Twitter social network[4], the contact network of Flickr[5], and the collaboration network of DBLP[6]. Twitter and Flickr datasets have been widely used in social network studies. The academic network is a relatively sparse network that captures key features of social networks [34].

- *Twitter Social Network*: This dataset is extracted from the Twitter social network. A node is a Twitter user, and a directed edge from i to j means i is followed by j. The dataset

---

[4]https://www.twitter.com/
[5]https://www.flickr.com/
[6]http://dblp.uni-trier.de/

contains 19,240 nodes and 3,933,718 edges with an average node degree of 204.
- *Flickr Contact Network*: This network covers all the contacts of Flickr users. A directed edge is established from i to j if i contacts j. This dataset consists of 20,809 nodes connected by 390,629 edges with an average node degree of 18.
- *DBLP Collaboration Network*: The DBLP network is extracted from the DBLP computer science bibliography that covers the co-authorship. A connection is established between two nodes (authors) if they publish at least one paper together. The network contains 317,080 nodes connected by 1,049,866 edges with an average degree of 3.

The Twitter and Flickr datasets are obtained through the Social Computing Data Repository[7], and the collaboration network is also publicly available[8].

5.2 Comparison Results

Baselines: In order to compare with competitive methods that tackle the problem of early intervention, we compare with the real-time intervention method EIL. Since the immunization method such as NS requires a budget significantly greater than that of real-time intervention methods, NS is not adopted for the first experiment on real-time intervention. In order to prove the necessity of the proposed framework and test whether simple heuristics can effectively terminate rumor spread and reduce the budget for NS, we construct two baseline methods below.

- PROXIMITY: Given $P(M)$ and a budget k, we select nodes according to the increasing order of the shortest *distance* to $P(M)$. Here, *distance* is the length of the shortest path between two nodes and we adopt the shortest distance between the node and any node of $P(M)$. This method is to test the heuristic that *neighbors of rumor initiators can quickly intervene the spread*.
- NS+PROXIMITY: Given $I(M)$ and a budget k, we select nodes according to the increasing order of the shortest distance to $P(M)$. This method is to test the heuristic that *the immunization set nodes that are closer to the rumor initiators can quickly terminate the spread*.

Earliness of intervention: To the best of our knowledge, this paper is the first work that aims to deal with the earliness issue. To evaluate earliness, we conduct experiments as follows. Intuitively, the number of timestamps can be reduced by increasing the budget (the number of factual information initiators). For example, an extreme case is that all neighbor nodes of the rumor initiators are selected to be immunized, then the diffusion only happens in zero timestamp. Hence, comparing the earliness is equivalent to comparing the needed budget for each method to contain rumors within certain time.

On the three datasets, we set the timestamps for rumor intervention to be 2, 5 and 10. We test each method with a large budget and keep reducing it until the time request cannot be fulfilled. We randomly select nodes to be rumor initiators 10 times, and the average least budget is reported to constrain rumors within

---

[7]http://socialcomputing.asu.edu/
[8]https://snap.stanford.edu/data/com-DBLP.html

T timestamps. As depicted in Figure 3, the proposed approach performs the best among all the methods under different settings, *i.e.*, requiring the least budget for early intervention. For most cases (DBLP $|T| = 2, 5, 10$; Flickr $|T| = 2, 5, 10$ Twitter $|T| = 5$), NS+PROXIMITY is the runner-up method. The result shows that nodes that are both close to the rumor initiators and in the immunization set of NS are relatively more effective for early intervention. PROXIMITY, which is another heuristic-based baseline method, is outperformed by NS on most cases (DBLP $|T| = 2, 10$, Flicker $|T| = 2$; Twitter $|T| = 2, 5$), which shows the redundancy of NS in intervening a specific rumor campaign. Since reducing the number of infectees is an NP-complete problem, and EIL is the approximation method that is bounded by $(1 - \frac{1}{e})$, EIL is theoretically the best tractable method. However, according to the empirical results, directly applying EIL does not necessarily produce an early plan. Our method can well complement with existing quantity-based methods by providing an approach toward reducing the timespan of rumor spread.

A trade-off between earliness and quantity: To meet the target of early intervention, methods other than EIL suffer from a greater number of rumor infectees. Now we are investigating the trade-off between earliness and the quantity of infected nodes of the proposed method.

We denote the number of rumor initiators as $|M|$. By varying the size of M, from (1) the **y-axis** we can observe the quantity of infected nodes; and from (2) the **x-axis** we can observe how early the intervention was. For each setting, we repeat experiments 10 times and report the average results. The M rumor initiators are chosen at random. For each method, the time of intervention may vary in different rounds of experiments, so we also average time length.

As depicted in Figure 4, the proposed approach performs best among all the methods under different settings in terms of earliness. On the other hand, EIL best reduces the ultimate number of rumor infectees. On the Twitter network (from Figure 4(a) to Figure 4(c)), EIMCC reduces over 50% of the rumor's lifespan comparing with the best baseline method, and on the Flickr and DBLP network, the reduction is over 60%. Although we do not focus on the final influence, EIMCC outperforms baselines other than EIL in most experiments (except $|M| = 100$ and $|M| = 500$ of DBLP) while delivering the best of earliness.

We can also see that EIMMC constrains the rumors within the least number of communities and prevents it from further spreading. Through observing the curves in Figure 4, we find that the increase of infectees usually has a big jump, *e.g.*, EIL, Proximity and EIMMC between the second and third timestamp in Figure 4(a). This is because a rumor reaches the "tipping point" and becomes viral in another community. Such "jump" is unfavorable since it shows a community has turned into the "echo chamber" of the rumor, and the rumor may be better trusted, quickly evolved, and more difficult to deal with. Traditional approaches, such as EIL on Flickr dataset with $|M| = 500$, may have more than one "jump", while EIMMC has only one of such jumps in all the experiments.

We see that simple heuristics cannot deal with either the ultimate influence or the earliness of intervention. It would be convenient if nodes that are closer to $P(M)$ or nodes in the immunization set

Table 2: Budget of EIMMC and NS with different datasets and size of M.

$|M|$		10	20	30	40	50	100	500
Twitter	NS	153	172	179	188	201	220	240
	EIMMC	28	33	36	40	55	63	45
Flickr	NS	140	146	155	163	170	182	200
	EIMMC	36	41	48	53	51	58	66
DBLP	NS	130	142	147	153	155	170	201
	EIMMC	31	33	34	47	49	53	61

that are closer to $P(M)$ can lead to an early intervention. However, Proximity, which is based on the shortest distance to $P(M)$, result in the largest number of infectees under most settings as well as the longest lifespan. Proximity+NS performs better comparing with Proximity. However, it still leads to a longer timespan than EIMMC. This is because the nodes in the immunization set that are closer to $P(M)$ may be redundant given a particular rumor.

Another interesting finding is that, comparing results on different networks, the rumor diffusion in a denser graph where the average degree is higher is easier to intervene at an early stage. Intuitively, a denser graph makes it easier for rumors to reach more nodes. However, a denser graph also enables the factual information campaign (F) to easily influence more users. Therefore, with proper selection of nodes, a denser graph may be easier to protect. In this work, we regard the problem of EIMMC as an instance of the vertex cover problem. A denser graph leads to larger sets in SC, which makes it easier to cover vertices with fewer sets.

Budget of intervention: In this work, we postulate the redundancy in the immunization set. Here we will discuss how much EIMMC reduces the budget of intervention given particular rumor campaigns. In order to determine the budget for the proposed method, we first use NS to calculate the immunization set and the budget for NS. Then we apply Algorithm 1 to calculate the budget for EIMMC. The immunization set is greedily expanded until the earliness of the intervention can no longer be improved. Details of NS can be found in [39].

Table 2 illustrates the budget of EIMMC and NS. We vary the size of rumor initiators and observe the corresponding budget. Note that we increase the budget of EIMMC if it leads to a slower intervention. Therefore, the results show how much EIMMC can reduce the budget without any loss of earliness. According to the results, over 70% of the immunization set can be removed, and the required budget of EIMMC linearly increases with $|M|$.

6 RELATED WORK

Since the famous study on the psychology of inaccurate and false information [2], *e.g.*, rumors and urban legends, much work has been done in understanding the mechanism of rumors. There is ample previous work on building mathematical models for the spreading of rumors, *i.e.*, describing the growth and decay of the actual spreading process with simulated population and networks [11]. Such models are typically proposed for characterizing dynamics of rumors with stochastic approaches, in specific network structures such as

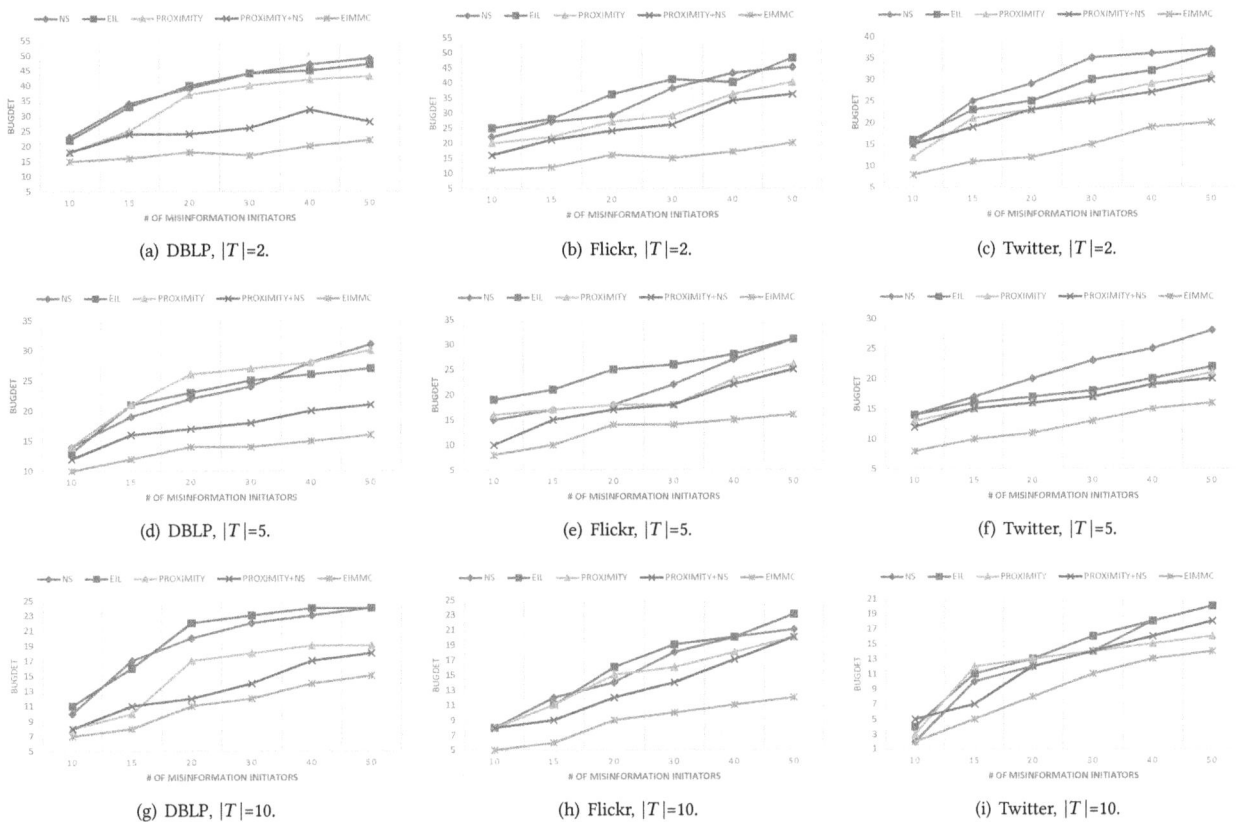

(a) DBLP, $|T|=2$.   (b) Flickr, $|T|=2$.   (c) Twitter, $|T|=2$.

(d) DBLP, $|T|=5$.   (e) Flickr, $|T|=5$.   (f) Twitter, $|T|=5$.

(g) DBLP, $|T|=10$.   (h) Flickr, $|T|=10$.   (i) Twitter, $|T|=10$.

Figure 3: Given a certain social network, we vary the size of rumor initiators $|M|$ and observe the budget of each method needed to terminate rumor diffusion within a target time $|T|$. Methods that require a smaller budget are more effective in early intervening rumors.

scale-free [32]. However, existing information and misinformation diffusion work focuses on estimating the impact of rumors on simulated networks in a small scale [46]. We focus on approaches that directly intervene rumors in real time.

In the context of rumor intervention, Budak *et al.* explore augmenting the traditional influence diffusion techniques to find the optimal nodes to launch an intervening campaign [7], by introducing a competitive party into the traditional *Influence Maximization* (IM) approaches. There are two classical models for IM, *i.e.*, *Linear Threshold* (LT) and *Independent Cascade* (IC). Borodin *et al.* study competitive influence diffusion under the extension of the LT model [6]. Bharathi *et al.* study the IC model and provide an approximation algorithm to maximize the spread of the influence of a single factual information spreader. In addition, Kostka *et al.* regard rumor intervention as a game theoretical problem and analyze the effect of the time lag of a delayed factual information campaign [23]. Since the budget in real-time intervention is usually limited, Nguyen *et al.* aim to limit the spread of rumors to a predefined rate with the least possible set of nodes [35]. However, the existing approaches emphasize on reducing the ultimate number of infected nodes. By contrast, we address the problem of early intervention. As a result, our work first introduces the earliness as

a metric to evaluate intervention approaches, which is important in dealing with rumors due to the quick spread and evolved content [2].

Tong *et al.* first propose to immunize a certain number of nodes to increase the robustness of the network to future attacks [39]. Their idea is to contain the rumors or virus in a small group locally, and they provide a greedy algorithm to efficiently find the optimal set of nodes via leveraging the structural and spectral properties of graphs. The method has been well studied and extended to solve node immunization problems [9] such as group immunization. However, given a particular set of rumor initiators, we postulate the redundancy of the immunization set given a specific rumor campaign, and the proposed approach can be applied to more problems such as the epidemic containment and the group-level immunization that share strong contagion patterns.

Our work is also related to studies on information diffusion. There are various models which are designed to abstract the pattern of information diffusion, such as *SIR Model* [22], *Tipping Model* [8], *Independent Cascade Model* [21] and *Linear Threshold Model* [21]. Traditional information diffusion models ignore the interaction between multiple campaigns, which cannot be directly applied here. In order to accelerate the diffusion models, more scalable methods

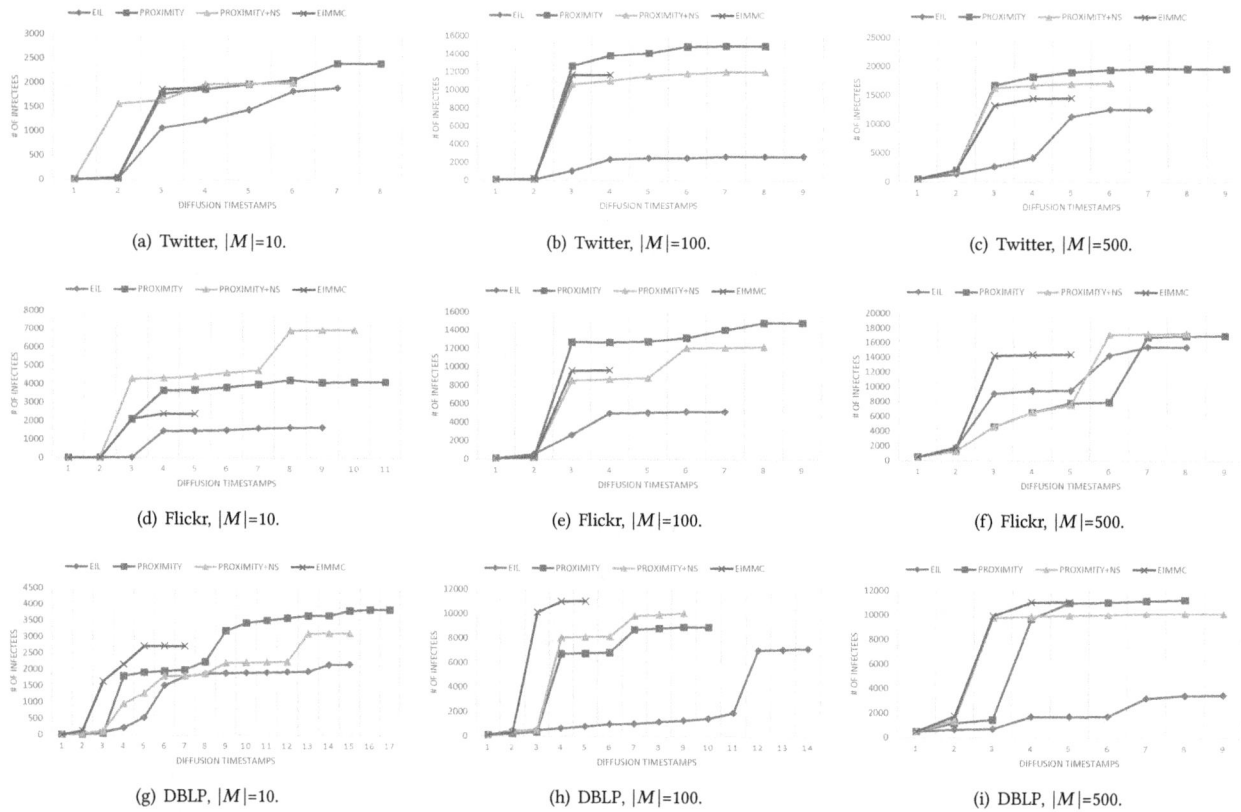

(a) Twitter, $|M|$=10.

(b) Twitter, $|M|$=100.

(c) Twitter, $|M|$=500.

(d) Flickr, $|M|$=10.

(e) Flickr, $|M|$=100.

(f) Flickr, $|M|$=500.

(g) DBLP, $|M|$=10.

(h) DBLP, $|M|$=100.

(i) DBLP, $|M|$=500.

Figure 4: The diffusion progress with different number of rumor initiators and on different datasets. A curve stops progressing to the next timestamp if the rumor is terminated then. We report the lifespan of rumors (horizontally) and the number of infectees (vertically). For the task of early intervention, a shorter lifespan is more favorable.

have been proposed. SIMPATH [15] reduces the computational time through filtering out paths without enough confidence, and Maximum Influence Arborescence (MIA) [10] was also proposed to accelerate the computation of independent cascade model. Various other acceleration algorithms are also available [16, 31]. Our work can also be accelerated by integrating with MIA.

Another stream of research focuses on spreaders of rumors. They aim to find patterns revealing a malicious account, and use these patterns to block potential spreaders. For example, profiles of automatic generated accounts may look similar, duplication of profiles between malicious accounts can be used to detect rumor spreaders [33, 40, 42, 43]. Lee and Kim propose to reveal the patterns hidden behind malicious accounts [24], so as to filtering them in an early stage [44]. Agglomerative hierarchical clustering is adopted in their work, where the likelihood of two names being generated by an identical Markov chain is used for measuring distance, and characters are used as features. After obtaining clusters of similar account names, a supervised method is adopted to classify whether a name cluster is a group of malicious accounts. Account names have also been quantitatively examined [47]. More features including behavioral ones are further incorporated in such algorithms [4]. In contrast to existing work that focuses

on the spreader of rumors [3, 36], network properties of rumor propagation [26, 45] or the content of rumors, we concentrate on finding the key users in a network to early intervene the propagation.

7 CONCLUSION

An early intervention is especially crucial in containing widespread of devastating rumors, such as fake news and false rumors. This work is the first to study the earliness of intervening rumors spread in a real-world social network. We focus on social interactions between people, and we aim to find the key social actors that can terminate the spread of rumors at an early stage. Although the budget is relatively small compared with the nodes in a social network, we can identify the least number of nodes that lead to early intervention. We achieve this by proving the NP-completeness, which is a precondition for finding a near-optimal approximation, and developing a hill-climbing method that is theoretically bounded.

ACKNOWLEDGMENTS

This material is based upon work supported by, or in part by, the National Science Foundation (NSF) grant 1614576, and the Office of Naval Research (ONR) grant N00014-16-1-2257.

REFERENCES

[1] Luca Maria Aiello, Alain Barrat, Rossano Schifanella, Ciro Cattuto, Benjamin Markines, and Filippo Menczer. 2012. Friendship prediction and homophily in social media. *ACM Transactions on the Web (TWEB)* 6, 2 (2012), 9.

[2] Gordon W Allport and Leo Postman. 1947. The psychology of rumor. (1947).

[3] Despoina Antonakaki, Iasonas Polakis, Elias Athanasopoulos, Sotiris Ioannidis, and Paraskevi Fragopoulou. 2016. Exploiting abused trending topics to identify spam campaigns in Twitter. *Social Network Analysis and Mining* 6, 1 (2016), 1–11.

[4] Fabricio Benevenuto, Tiago Rodrigues, Virgilio Almeida, Jussara Almeida, Chao Zhang, and Keith Ross. Identifying video spammers in online social networks. In *International Workshop on Adversarial Information Retrieval on the Web*. ACM, 45–52.

[5] Alessandro Bessi, Fabio Petroni, Michela Del Vicario, Fabiana Zollo, Aris Anagnostopoulos, Antonio Scala, Guido Caldarelli, and Walter Quattrociocchi. 2015. Viral misinformation: The role of homophily and polarization. In *Proceedings of the 24th International Conference on World Wide Web*. ACM, 355–356.

[6] Allan Borodin, Yuval Filmus, and Joel Oren. 2010. Threshold models for competitive influence in social networks. In *International Workshop on Internet and Network Economics*. Springer, 539–550.

[7] Ceren Budak, Divyakant Agrawal, and Amr El Abbadi. 2011. Limiting the spread of misinformation in social networks. In *Proceedings of the 20th international conference on World Wide Web*. ACM, 665–674.

[8] Damon Centola. 2010. The spread of behavior in an online social network experiment. *science* 329, 5996 (2010), 1194–1197.

[9] Chen Chen, Hanghang Tong, B Aditya Prakash, Charalampos E Tsourakakis, Tina Eliassi-Rad, Christos Faloutsos, and Duen Horng Chau. 2016. Node Immunization on Large Graphs: Theory and Algorithms. *IEEE Transactions on Knowledge and Data Engineering* 28, 1 (2016), 113–126.

[10] Wei Chen, Chi Wang, and Yajun Wang. 2010. Scalable influence maximization for prevalent viral marketing in large-scale social networks. In *KDD*. ACM, 1029–1038.

[11] Daryl J Daley and David G Kendall. 1964. Epidemics and rumours. (1964).

[12] Michela Del Vicario, Alessandro Bessi, Fabiana Zollo, Fabio Petroni, Antonio Scala, Guido Caldarelli, H Eugene Stanley, and Walter Quattrociocchi. 2016. The spreading of misinformation online. *Proceedings of the National Academy of Sciences(PNAS)* 113, 3 (2016), 554–559.

[13] Uriel Feige. 1998. A threshold of ln n for approximating set cover. *Journal of the ACM (JACM)* 45, 4 (1998), 634–652.

[14] Miroslav Fiedler. 1973. Algebraic connectivity of graphs. *Czechoslovak mathematical journal* 23, 2 (1973), 298–305.

[15] Amit Goyal, Wei Lu, and Laks VS Lakshmanan. 2011. Simpath: An efficient algorithm for influence maximization under the linear threshold model. In *Data Mining (ICDM), 2011 IEEE 11th International Conference on*. IEEE, 211–220.

[16] Daniel Gruhl, Ramanathan Guha, David Liben-Nowell, and Andrew Tomkins. 2004. Information diffusion through blogspace. In *Proceedings of the 13th international conference on World Wide Web*. ACM, 491–501.

[17] Xinran He, Guojie Song, Wei Chen, and Qingye Jiang. 2012. Influence Blocking Maximization in Social Networks under the Competitive Linear Threshold Model.. In *SDM*. SIAM, 463–474.

[18] Zaobo He, Zhipeng Cai, Jiguo Yu, Xiaoming Wang, Yunchuan Sun, and Yingshu Li. 2017. Cost-efficient strategies for restraining rumor spreading in mobile social networks. *IEEE Transactions on Vehicular Technology* 66, 3 (2017), 2789–2800.

[19] Andrew Hiles, This Chapter Covers, and How Rumors Spread. 2011. How Firms Should Fight Rumors. *Reputation Management: Building and Protecting Your Company'âĂŹs Profile in a Digital World* (2011), 1–44.

[20] Ken-ichi Kawarabayashi. 2014. Optimal budget allocation: Theoretical guarantee and efficient algorithm. (2014).

[21] David Kempe, Jon Kleinberg, and Éva Tardos. 2003. Maximizing the spread of influence through a social network. In *Proceedings of the ninth ACM SIGKDD international conference on Knowledge discovery and data mining*. ACM, 137–146.

[22] William O Kermack and Anderson G McKendrick. 1927. A contribution to the mathematical theory of epidemics. In *Proceedings of the Royal Society of London A: Mathematical, Physical and Engineering Sciences*, Vol. 115. 700–721.

[23] Jan Kostka, Yvonne Anne Oswald, and Roger Wattenhofer. 2008. Rumor dissemination in social networks. In *International Colloquium on Structural Information and Communication Complexity*. Springer, 185–196.

[24] Sangho Lee and Jong Kim. 2014. Early filtering of ephemeral malicious accounts on Twitter. *Computer Communications* 54 (2014), 48–57.

[25] Jure Leskovec and Rok Sosič. 2016. SNAP: A General-Purpose Network Analysis and Graph-Mining Library. *ACM Transactions on Intelligent Systems and Technology (TIST)* 8, 1 (2016), 1.

[26] Chaz Lever, Platon Kotzias, Davide Balzarotti, Juan Caballero, and Manos Antonakakis. 2017. A Lustrum of malware network communication: Evolution and insights. In *Security and Privacy (SP), 2017 IEEE Symposium on*. IEEE, 788–804.

[27] Hui Li, Sourav S Bhowmick, Jiangtao Cui, Yunjun Gao, and Jianfeng Ma. 2015. Getreal: Towards realistic selection of influence maximization strategies in competitive networks. In *ACM SIGMOD International Conference on Management of Data*. ACM, 1525–1537.

[28] Iouliana Litou, Vana Kalogeraki, Ioannis Katakis, and Dimitrios Gunopulos. 2016. Real-Time and Cost-Effective Limitation of Misinformation Propagation. (2016).

[29] Wei Lu, Francesco Bonchi, Amit Goyal, and Laks VS Lakshmanan. 2013. The bang for the buck: fair competitive viral marketing from the host perspective. In *International Conference on Knowledge Discovery and Data Dining (KDD)*. ACM, 928–936.

[30] Carsten Lund and Mihalis Yannakakis. 1994. On the hardness of approximating minimization problems. *Journal of the ACM (JACM)* 41, 5 (1994), 960–981.

[31] Baharan Mirzasoleiman, Ashwinkumar Badanidiyuru, Amin Karbasi, Jan Vondrák, and Andreas Krause. 2014. Lazier Than Lazy Greedy. *arXiv preprint arXiv:1409.7938* (2014).

[32] Yamir Moreno, Maziar Nekovee, and Amalio F Pacheco. 2004. Dynamics of rumor spreading in complex networks. *Physical Review E* 69, 6 (2004), 066130.

[33] Fred Morstatter, Liang Wu, Tahora H Nazer, Kathleen M Carley, and Huan Liu. 2016. A new approach to bot detection: striking the balance between precision and recall. In *2016 IEEE/ACM International Conference on Advances in Social Networks Analysis and Mining (ASONAM)*. IEEE, 533–540.

[34] Mark EJ Newman. 2001. The structure of scientific collaboration networks. *Proceedings of the National Academy of Sciences (PNAS)* 98, 2 (2001), 404–409.

[35] Nam P Nguyen, Guanhua Yan, My T Thai, and Stephan Eidenbenz. 2012. Containment of misinformation spread in online social networks. In *Proceedings of the 4th Annual ACM Web Science Conference*. ACM, 213–222.

[36] Shirin Nilizadeh, François Labrèche, Alireza Sedighian, Ali Zand, José Fernandez, Christopher Kruegel, Gianluca Stringhini, and Giovanni Vigna. 2017. POISED: Spotting Twitter Spam Off the Beaten Paths. *arXiv preprint arXiv:1708.09058* (2017).

[37] Michael Simpson, Venkatesh Srinivasan, and Alex Thomo. 2016. Clearing contamination in large networks. *IEEE Transactions on Knowledge and Data Engineering* 28, 6 (2016), 1435–1448.

[38] Chonggang Song, Wynne Hsu, and Mong Li Lee. 2015. Node Immunization over Infectious Period. In *Proceedings of the 24th ACM International on Conference on Information and Knowledge Management*. ACM, 831–840.

[39] Hanghang Tong, B Aditya Prakash, Charalampos Tsourakakis, Tina Eliassi-Rad, Christos Faloutsos, and Duen Horng Chau. 2010. On the vulnerability of large graphs. In *International Conference on Data Mining*. IEEE, 1091–1096.

[40] Steve Webb, James Caverlee, and Calton Pu. 2008. Social Honeypots: Making Friends With A Spammer Near You.. In *CEAS*.

[41] Laurence A Wolsey. 1982. An analysis of the greedy algorithm for the submodular set covering problem. *Combinatorica* 2, 4 (1982), 385–393.

[42] Liang Wu, Xia Hu, Fred Morstatter, and Huan Liu. 2017. Adaptive spammer detection with sparse group modeling. In *Eleventh International AAAI Conference on Web and Social Media*.

[43] Liang Wu, Xia Hu, Fred Morstatter, and Huan Liu. 2017. Detecting camouflaged content polluters. In *Eleventh International AAAI Conference on Web and Social Media*.

[44] Liang Wu, Jundong Li, Xia Hu, and Huan Liu. 2017. Gleaning wisdom from the past: Early detection of emerging rumors in social media. In *Proceedings of the 2017 SIAM International Conference on Data Mining*. SIAM, 99–107.

[45] Liang Wu and Huan Liu. 2018. Tracing fake-news footprints: Characterizing social media messages by how they propagate. In *Proceedings of the Eleventh ACM International Conference on Web Search and Data Mining*. ACM, 637–645.

[46] Liang Wu, Fred Morstatter, Xia Hu, and Huan Liu. 2016. Mining misinformation in social media. *Big Data in Complex and Social Networks* (2016), 123–152.

[47] Reza Zafarani and Huan Liu. 10 Bits of Surprise: Detecting Malicious Users with Minimum Information *(CIKM'15)*. ACM.

[48] Yao Zhang, Sudip Saha, Anil Vullikanti, B Aditya Prakash, and others. 2015. Near-optimal Algorithms for Controlling Propagation at Group Scale on Networks. *IEEE Transactions on Knowledge and Data Engineering* (2015).

A Broad Evaluation of the Tor English Content Ecosystem

Mahdieh Zabihimayvan
Department of Computer Science and Engineering
Kno.e.sis Research Center, Wright State University
Dayton, OH, USA
zabihimayvan.2@wright.edu

Reza Sadeghi
Department of Computer Science and Engineering
Kno.e.sis Research Center, Wright State University
Dayton, OH, USA
sadeghi.2@wright.edu

Derek Doran
Department of Computer Science and Engineering
Kno.e.sis Research Center, Wright State University
Dayton, OH, USA
derek.doran@wright.edu

Mehdi Allahyari
Department of Computer Science
Georgia Southern University
Statesboro, GA, USA
mallahyari@georgiasouthern.edu

ABSTRACT

Tor is among most well-known dark net in the world. It has noble uses, including as a platform for free speech and information dissemination under the guise of true anonymity, but may be culturally better known as a conduit for criminal activity and as a platform to market illicit goods and data. Past studies on the content of Tor support this notion, but were carried out by targeting popular domains likely to contain illicit content. A survey of past studies may thus not yield a complete evaluation of the content and use of Tor. This work addresses this gap by presenting a broad evaluation of the content of the English Tor ecosystem. We perform a comprehensive crawl of the Tor dark web and, through topic and network analysis, characterize the 'types' of information and services hosted across a broad swath of Tor domains and their hyperlink relational structure. We recover nine domain types defined by the information or service they host and, among other findings, unveil how some types of domains intentionally silo themselves from the rest of Tor. We also present measurements that (regrettably) suggest how marketplaces of illegal drugs and services do emerge as the dominant type of Tor domain. Our study is the product of crawling over 1 million pages from 20,000 Tor seed addresses, yielding a collection of over 150,000 Tor pages. The domain structure is publicly available as a dataset at https://github.com/wsu-wacs/TorEnglishContent.

KEYWORDS

Tor, Content Analysis, Structural Analysis

ACM Reference format:
Mahdieh Zabihimayvan, Reza Sadeghi, Derek Doran, and Mehdi Allahyari. 2019. A Broad Evaluation of the Tor English Content Ecosystem. In *Proceedings of 11th ACM Conference on Web Science, Boston, MA, USA, June 30–July 3, 2019 (WebSci '19)*, 10 pages.
https://doi.org/10.1145/3292522.3326031

1 INTRODUCTION

The deep web defines content on the World Wide Web that cannot or has not yet been indexed by search engines. Services of great interest to parties that want to be anonymous online is a subset of the deep web called *dark nets*: networks running on the Internet that require unique application layer protocols and authorization schemes to access. While many dark nets exist (i.e. I2P [6], Riffle [13], and Freenet [7]), Tor [24] has emerged as the most popular [30]. It is used as a tool for circumventing government censorship [17], for releasing information to the public [24], for sensitive communication between parties [29], and as an (allegedly) private space to buy and sell goods and services [25].

It is an open question whether the fundamental and often necessary protections that Tor provides its users is worth its cost: the same features that protect the privacy of virtuous users also make Tor an effective means to carry out illegal activities and to evade law enforcement. Various positions on this question have been documented [25], but empirical evidence is limited to studies that have crawled, extracted, and analyzed *specific subsets of Tor* based on the type of hosted information, such as drug trafficking [10], homemade explosives [16], terrorist activities [5], or forums [29].

A holistic understanding of how Tor is utilized and its structure as an information ecosystem cannot be gleaned by surveying this body of past work. This is because previous studies focus on a particular subset of this dark web and take measurements that aim to answer unique collections of hypotheses. But such a holistic understanding of Tor's utilization and ecosystem is crucial to answer broader questions about this dark web, such as: *How diverse is the information and the services provided on Tor? Is the argument that the use of Tor to buy and sell illicit goods and services and to enable criminal activities valid? Is the domain structure of Tor 'siloed', in the sense that the Tor domain hyperlink network is highly modular conditioned on content? Does the hyperlink network between domains exhibit scale-free properties?* Answers to such questions can yield an understanding of the kinds of services and information available on Tor, reveal the most popular and important (from a structural perspective) services it provides, and enable a comparison of Tor against the surface web and other co-reference complex systems.

Towards this end, we present a quantitative characterization of the types of information available across a large swath of English language Tor webpages. We conduct a massive crawl of Tor starting from 20,000 different seed addresses and harvest **only** the html page of each visited address[1]. Our crawl encompasses over 1 million addresses, of which 150,473 are hosted on Tor and the remaining 1,085,960 returns to the visible web. We focus on 40,439 Tor pages belonging to 3,347 English language domains and augment LDA with a topic-labeling algorithm that uses DBpedia to assign semantically meaningful labels to the content of crawled pages. We further extract and study a logical network of English Tor domains connected by hyperlinks. We limit our study to the subset of Tor domains with information written in **English** in an attempt to control for any variability in measurements and insights that could be caused by the confluence of information posted in unique languages, structure, and possibly unique subdomains of Tor (for example, VPN services specifically targeting users in countries with government controlled censorship or marketplaces exclusively for users living in a particular country). We summarize our insights to the following research questions:

- RQ1: *Is the information and services of Tor diverse?*
  - We find that Tor services can be described by just nine types. Over 50% of all domains discovered are either directories to other Tor domains, or serve as marketplaces to buy and sell goods and services. Just 24% of all Tor domains are used to publicly post, privately send, or to discover information anonymously. We do find, however, that different types of domains relate to each other in unique ways, including marketplaces that enable payment by forcing gameplay on a gambling site, and that domains involving money transactions have a surprisingly weak reliance to Tor Bitcoin domains.
- RQ2: *What are the 'core' services of Tor? Is there even a core?*
  - An importance analysis from some centrality metrics finds the Dream market to be the most structurally important, "core" service Tor provides by a wide margin. The Dream market is the largest marketplace for illicit goods and services on Tor. Directory sites to find and access Tor domains have dominant betweenness centrality, making them important sources for Tor browsing.
- RQ3: *How siloed are Tor information sources and services?*
  - A connectivity analysis shows how Tor services tend to isolate themselves which makes them difficult to discover by simple browsing and implies the need for a comprehensive seed list of domains for data collection on Tor. We also find patterns suggesting competitive and cooperative behavior between domains depending on their domain type, and that Tor is not particularly introspective: few news domains reference a large number of other domains across this dark web.
- RQ4: *How can the structure of Tor domain hyperlinks be modeled? What are the implications of Tor's domain connectivity?*
  - We find that the hyperlink network of Tor domains does not follow the scale-free structure observed in other sociotechnological systems or the surface web. Also, investigating within content communities denotes a power-tailed

pattern in the in-degree distributions of about half of all Tor domains.

To the best of our knowledge, this study reports on the largest measurements of Tor taken to date, and is the first to study the relationship between Tor domains conditioned on the type of information they hold. We publish the hyperlink structure of this massive dataset to the public at: https://github.com/wsu-wacs/TorEnglishContent. Contrasting our findings for subsets of Tor written in other languages will be an exciting direction for future work.

This paper is organized as follows: Section 2 discusses related work on characterizing and evaluating Tor. Section 3 presents the procedure used for data collection and processing. Section 4 provides an evaluation on Tor content while Section 5 describes the logical network of the domains connected by hyperlinks and presents the analyses results. Finally, Section 6 summarizes the main conclusions and discusses the future work.

2 RELATED WORK

Previous research on Tor have focused on characterizing particular types of hosted content, on traffic-level measurements, and on understanding the security, privacy, and topological properties of Tor relays at the network layer. Towards understanding types of content on Tor, Dolliver *et al.* use geovisualizations and exploratory spatial data analyses to analyze distributions of drugs and substances advertised on the Agora Tor marketplace [10]. Chen *et al.* seek an understanding of terrorist activities by a method incorporating information collection, analysis, and visualization techniques from 39 Jihad Tor sites [5]. Mörch *et al.* analyze 30 Tor domains to investigate the accessibility of information related to suicide [21]. Dolliver *et al.* crawls *Silk Road 2* with the goal of comparing its nature in drug trafficking operations with that of the original site [9]. Other related works propose tools to support the collection of specific information, such as a focused crawler by Iliou *et al.* [16], new crawling frameworks for Tor by Zhang *et al.* [29], and advanced crawling and indexing systems like LIGHTS by Ghosh *et al.* [12].

Tor traffic monitoring is another related area of work. This monitoring is often done to detect security risks and information leakage on Tor that can compromise the anonymity of its users and the paths packets take. Mohaisen *et al.* study the possibility of observing Tor requests at global DNS infrastructure that could threaten the private location of servers hosting Tor sites, such as the name and onion address of Tor domains [20]. McCoy *et al.* study the clients using and routers that are a part of Tor by collecting data from exit routers [18]. Biryukov *et al.* analyze the traffic of Tor hidden services to evaluate their vulnerability against deanonymizing and take down attacks. They demonstrate how to find the popularity of a hidden service, harvest their descriptors in a short time, and find their guard relays. They further propose a large-scale attack to disclose the IP address of a Tor hidden service [2]. We consider such work, operating at the traffic level, as studying Tor payloads that pass through networks, rather than in understanding the content of these payloads or of the inter-connected structure of Tor domains.

The topological properties of Tor, at physical and logical levels, are only beginning to be studied. Xu *et al.* quantitatively evaluated the structure of four terrorist and criminal related networks,

---

[1]For privacy purposes no embedded resources of any kind, including images, scripts, videos, or other multimedia, were downloaded in our crawl.

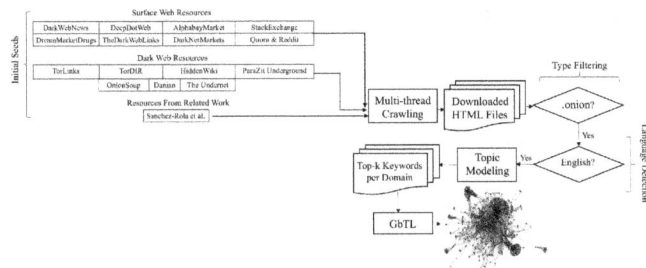

Figure 1: Tor data collection process

one of which is from Tor [25]. They find such networks are efficient in communication and information flow, but are vulnerable to disruption by removing weak ties that connect large connected components. Sanchez-Rola *et al.* conducted a broader structural analysis over 7,257 Tor domains [23]. Their experiments indicate that domains are logically organized in a sparse network, and finds a surprising relation between Tor and the surface web: there are more links from Tor domains to the surface web than to other Tor domains. They also find evidence to suggest a surprising amount of user tracking performed on Tor. Part of this work extends their study by examining the structure between Tor domains *conditioned on the type of information they host.*

3 DATASET COLLECTION AND PROCESSING

We performed a comprehensive crawl of the Tor network to extract data for this study. Figure 1 illustrates this data collection process. We developed a multi-threaded crawler that collects the html of any Tor website reachable by a depth first search (up to depth 4) starting from a seed list of 20,000 Tor addresses. This seed list was constructed by concatenating the list used in a recent study [23] along those identified by the author's manual search of *Reddit, Quora,* and *Ahima,* and other major surface web directories in the days predating the crawl. Although a manual list of seeds runs the inevitable risk of a crawl that can miss portions of Tor, the hidden nature of Tor websites make it unlikely for there to ever be a single authoritative directory of Tor domains. We are confident that our seed list leads to a comprehensive crawl of Tor because: (i) The Reddit, Quora, Ahima, and surface web directories are well-known for providing up to date links to Tor domains and are often used by Tor users to begin their own searches for information. This suggest that these entry points into Tor are at worst practically useful, and at best are ideal starting points to search and find Tor domains associated with the most common uses of the service; (ii) The list adapted from [23] are noted to be sources commonly utilized to discover current Tor addresses. Furthermore, we assign our crawlers to cover all hyperlinks up to depth 4 from every seed page to make our data collection as comprehensive as possible. Out seed list is published online.[2]

Because of the rapidly changing content and structure of Tor [23], including temporary downtime for some domains, we executed two crawls 30 days apart from each other in June and July 2018. To try to control for some variability in the up and down time of domains, the union of the Tor sites captured during the two crawls were stored for subsequent analysis. It is worth noting that we only request html and follow hyperlinks, and do not download the full content

---

[2]https://github.com/wsu-wacs/TorEnglishContent/blob/master/seeds

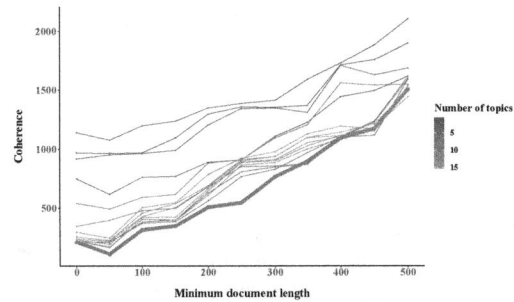

Figure 2: LDA topic coherence score for different number of topic and minimum lengths of document; bold trend representing scores using 9 topics

of a web page. This prevents any access control polices, request rate limiters, and crawler blockers [27] from interrupting our data collection. A total of 1,236,433 distinct pages were captured across both crawls. The collected data was post-processed to identify English pages and to classify the crawled pages as being from the surface or from Tor. Any webpage with suffix *.onion* was classified as a Tor page, while the remainder are considered to be from the surface web. A language identification method proposed by [11] was used to remove non-English onion pages based on their text content regardless of the value set in their HTML language tag. 40,439 English Tor pages remained after this filtering. We chose to only focus on English pages to facilitate our content analysis; an evaluation of non-English pages will be the topic of future work.

3.1 Tor content discovery and labeling

We subjected the corpus of English Tor pages through an unsupervised content discovery and labeling procedure. The process runs the content of every Tor page (where content is defined as any string outside of a markdown tag) through the Latent Dirichlet Allocation (LDA) [3] and Graph-based Topic Labeling (GbTL) [15] algorithms to derive a collection of semantic labels representing broad topics of content on Tor. Each Tor domain is then assigned a label by the dominant topic present across the set of all webpages crawled in the domain.

3.1.1 Topic Modeling. Topic modeling is a method to uncover topics as hidden structures within a collection of documents. By defining a topic as a group of words occurring often together, topic modeling creates semantic links among words within the same context, and differentiates words by their meaning. LDA [3] is a widely used unsupervised learning technique for this purpose. It models a topic t_j $(1 \le j \le T)$ by a probability distribution $p(w_i|t_j)$ over words taken from a corpus $D = \{d_1, d_2, \cdots, d_N\}$ of documents where words are drawn from a vocabulary $W = \{w_1, w_2, \cdots, w_M\}$. The probability of observing word w_i in document d is defined as $p(w_i|d) = \sum_{j=1}^{T} p(w_i|t_j)p(t_j|d)$. Gibbs sampling is used to estimate the word-topic distribution $p(w_i|t_j)$ and the topic-document distribution $p(t_j|d)$ from data.

An important hyperparameter is the number of topics T that should be modeled. We set T by considering the *coherence* [19] of a set of topics inferred for some T, choosing the T with the best coherence C. C is a function of the n words of each t_i having highest probability $P(w_j|t_i)$. Let $W^{(t)} = \{w_1, \cdots, w_n\}$ be the set of top-n

most probable words from $P(w|t)$. Then C is given by:

$$C(t; W^{(t)}) = \sum_{i=2}^{n} \sum_{j=1}^{i-1} \log \frac{F_d(w_i^{(t)}, w_j^{(t)}) + 1}{F_d(w_j^{(t)})}$$

where $w_i^{(t)}, w_j^{(t)} \in W^{(t)}$, $F_d(w)$ indicates the number of documents where w emerges, and $F_d(w_i, w_j)$ gives the number of documents in which both words $w_i^{(t)}$ and $w_j^{(t)}$ exist. Values closer to zero indicate higher coherence for the corresponding topic. T is then chosen as the one that yields the smallest average C over all topics where the summation is ran over a model fitted to T topics.

A final parameter is the minimum length of a document (e.g. Tor page) for it to be considered in the coherence calculation. We determine this length empirically by inspection of Figure 2, which gives topic coherence scores for different values of T and different minimum lengths of the documents where $n = 10$ is considered for each topic. The trend for $T = 9$ yields the closest value to zero for document minimum length of 50 words.

3.1.2 Graph-based Topic Labeling with DBpedia. Word-topic distributions from a fitted topic model are indicative of semantically related words appearing in common contexts. A human may subsequently assign a label to each topic by manually evaluating this distribution However, the manual approach yields a subjective, possibly biased interpretation of the topics present in a corpus. Instead, we incorporate the unsupervised knowledge graph-based labeling algorithm GbTL [15]. It utilizes the DBpedia knowledge graph (KG) which codifies Wikipedia articles and their relationships in the form of an ontology. GbTL finds a concept ζ from DBpedia that would serve as a suitable label to represent t.

To determine ζ, GbTL defines a suitability measure γ. Before defining γ, we note that optimizing any measure over all DBpedia concepts is infeasible due to the massive size of the DBpedia ontology. Instead, GbTL considers a *candidate set* of possible labels for a topic t. The candidate set for topic t are all vertices in the subgraph $G_t = (V_t, E_t)$ of DBpedia where V_t is the set of concepts with labels identical to any word in $W^{(t)}$ along with their directed 1st and 2nd degree neighborhood and E_t is the relations among all concepts in V_t. The choice of 2nd degree neighbors is based on [15] that found this setting to produce a sufficiently large candidate set of labels without adding unrelated ones. Since topic labels can be considered as assigning classes/categories to the topics, we restrict the subgraph relations to those of type **rdfs:type**, **dcterms:subject**, **skos:broader**, **skos:broaderOf**, and **rdfs:sub-ClassOf**. The suitability γ of each concept ζ in V_t is measured by its Focused Random Walk Betweenness Centrality measure [15]. This centrality measures the average amount of time it takes for a random walker to arrive at some node starting from any other node in a network. It is computed as follows:

(1) Let $L = D - A$ be the Laplacian matrix of G_t where A is the adjacency matrix of G_t and D is its diagonal degree matrix.
(2) Arbitrarily remove a row and its corresponding column from L and then invert it. Define T as this inverse with a row and column vector of zeroes inserted at the same index the row and column was removed from L.

(3) Define $\gamma(\zeta, t)$ as follows:

$$\gamma(\zeta, t) = \begin{cases} \dfrac{\sum\limits_{v_x, v_y \in W^{(t)}, x < y} I_i^{xy}}{\binom{n}{2}}, & \text{if } \zeta \notin W^{(t)} \\[3ex] \dfrac{\sum\limits_{v_x, v_y \in W^{(t)}, x < y} I_i^{xy}}{\frac{(n-1)(n-2)}{2}}, & \text{otherwise} \end{cases}$$

where I_i^{xy} is given as:

$$I_i^{(xy)} = \frac{1}{2} \sum_{v_j \in V_t} A_{ij} |T_{ij} - T_{iy} - T_{jx} + T_{jy}|$$

where i is the index of A corresponding to ζ and T_{ab} is the value at row a and column b of T. Since DBpedia is a semantic graph, we assume that vertices playing an important structural role in the graph should be representative of a concept that binds together the concepts in $W^{(t)}$. We use $\arg\max_\zeta \gamma(\zeta, t)$ as the label of topic t.

We built the topic models and derived their subsequent labels using the 7,782 English Tor web pages having more than 50 words. These 7,782 pages come from 1,766 unique onion domains and represents the data we consider in the remainder of our study.[3]

4 CONTENT EVALUATION

We assigned each domain's label by the dominant topic in a concatenation of all of its constituent pages. Application of LDA to this set of documents yielded a set of 9 topics. GbTL labeled these topics Forum, Shopping, Bitcoin, Dream market, Directory, Multimedia, News, Email service, and Gambling. Table 1 lists the 10 most probable words per topic. We supplement this with a manual evaluation of the html code of pages in each domain to better understand the meaning of each topic. For domains where we noticed a number of sub-types identified (e.g. a shopping domain that specialized in particular types of goods or services), we maintained a count of sub-type frequencies and show them in Figure 3. We elaborate on our evaluation of each type of domain below:

Shopping: (359 domains [20.32%]) Shopping domains allow visitors to purchase goods and services, including drugs, medicine, as well as consultancy and investment services. We found the dominant shopping service is to provide money transfer to and from credit cards to buy Visa cards, gift cards, and Bitcoin. Drugs, pornography, hosting Tor services, and forgery services are other types of popular shopping domains. The rest includes pages selling a variety of goods like phone, laptop, movies, and even gold.

Bitcoin: (83 domains [4.7%]) Bitcoin domains provide services for Bitcoin transactions and fund transfers to wallets. Tor Bitcoin services differ in terms of the registration process and personal information needed, registration and transaction fees, the security platforms they use, and fees compared to surface web counterparts.

Dream market: (235 domains [13.3%]) One shopping domain so large that it merited its own topic category is the Dream market. Its pages suggest a wide range of content available for sale, most of which are illicit. This includes drugs, stolen data, and counterfeit consumer goods. Many Dream market pages collected includes login and registration forms (hence words like "Register", "Account",

---

[3]In the remainder of the paper, for sake of brevity we will sometimes refer to the set of English Tor domains as simply 'Tor' or 'Tor domains'.

Table 1: List of 10 most probable words per topic and their label

Label	top-10 words
Directory	Search, Database, Address, Tor, Browse, URL, Directories, Link, Site, Dir
Bitcoin	Btc, Bitcoin, Blockchain, Transaction, Wallet, Deposit, Coin, Buy, Anonymity, Hidden
News	Information, Newspaper, News, Tor, Events, Censorship, Web, Press, Tor, Comment
Email	PM, Privacy, Massage, Mail, GPG, Cypherpunk, AES, Webmail, IRC, Darkmail
Multimedia	Copyright, Book, Video, Music, Free, pdf, Library, TV, FLAC, Paper
Shopping	Supplier, Market, Hidden, Commerce, Product, buy, Order, Price, Marketplace, Money
Forum	NSFW, Invite, Friend, Group, Share, Private, BBS, IM, Chat, Forum
Gambling	Online, Gambling, game, Casino, Lottery, Roulette, Table, Value, Money, Play
Dream market	Marketplace, Online, Buy, Register, Dream, Support, Hidden, Account, User, Tor

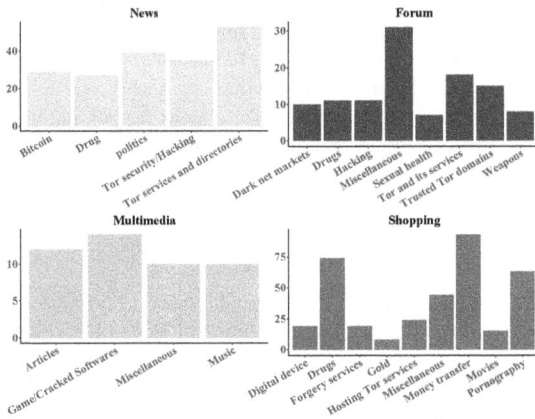

Figure 3: Services provided by news, multimedia, forum, and shopping domains

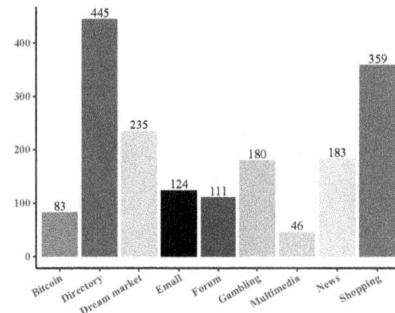

Figure 4: Topic distribution of Tor domains

and "User" emerge in the list of top-10 terms in Table 1) limiting further access for our crawlers.

Directory: (445 domains [25.19%]) Addresses in Tor are made up of meaningless combinations of digits and characters that sometimes change and are hard to memorize. Moreover, most domains may disappear after a short amount of time or move to new addresses [23]. It is thus no surprise to find directory domains emerge in our study. Directories are a convenient way of finding Tor domains without knowing their addresses. Domains labeled as a directory include unnamed pages with lists of .onion domains along with the better known *TorDir* and *The Hidden Wiki* services, as well as search engines like *DeepSearch* and *Ahmia*.

Multimedia: (46 domains [2.6%]) Multimedia domains are sites to download and purchase multimedia products like e-books, movies, musics, games, and academic and press articles even if they are copyright protected. Among all multimedia domains, we measured 28% of them to exclusively offer articles and e-books while 22% offer free download of music or audio files, and to even obtain login information for stolen TV accounts. The remaining provides resources like hacked video game accounts, cracked software, and a mixture of the above.

Forum: (111 domains [6.3%]) Forum domains host bulletin board and social network services for Tor users to discuss ideas and thoughts. Among all forums, 72% have a range of topic discussions including information on Tor and its services, hacking, sexual health, dark net markets, weapons, drugs, and trusted Tor domains. Some forums require payment via Bitcoin to register.

News: (183 domains [10.36%]) Whereas forums facilitate interaction among Tor users, news domains host pages akin to personal weblogs

where an author writes an essay and visitors can post follow-up comments. Links to Tor e-mail services are included to contact post authors. Information on current Tor services and directories is presented by most news domains, along with politics, Bitcoin, drug, and Tor security related posts.

Email service: (124 domains [7.02%]) Email domains offer communication services like email, chat room, and Tor VPNs. Email services vary in the encryption protocol they use, the advertisements they serve for other services, and policies for keeping user log files. Our investigation finds that many email domains use secure protocols like SSL, AES, and PGP to secure user accounts and messages. IRC-based chat rooms are also common. Some email services charge recurring subscription fees.

Gambling: (180 domains [10.19%]) Gambling domains offer services to bet money on games, to purchase gambling advice and consulting, and to read gambling-related news. Gambling domains have a number of links to payment processing options including Ethereum, Monero, DASH, Vertcoin, Visa, and MasterCard.

Figure 4 gives the distribution of topics assigned to each Tor domain. It illustrates how directory and shopping domains, and the Dream market dominate English domains on Tor by accounting for 58.83% of all domain types. This suggests that Tor's main utility for users may be to browse information and shop on marketplaces that require secrecy. In contrast, domains related to the free exchange of ideas and information (a powerful and positive use-case of Tor, particular to users in countries facing Internet censorship [17]), represented by Forum, Email, and News sites, account for just 23.66% of all domains. It should be noted, however that services used in countries that most benefit from the freedom of expression of Tor may not be well-represented in our sample. Gambling domains represent a surprisingly large (10.19%) percentage of domains, suggesting that people may now be turning to Tor to play online gambling games that are otherwise illegal to host in many countries around the

Table 2: Summary statistics of the domain network

Statistic	Value
Domain count ($|V|$)	1,766
Hyperlink count ($|E|$)	5,523
Mean degree ($\bar{k}$)	12
Max degree (max k)	389
Density (ρ)	0.0064
W.C.C. Count ($|C^w|$)	25
S.C.C. Count ($|C^s|$)	756
Max W.C.C. Size (max C_i^w)	955 (54%)
Max S.C.C. Size (max C_i^s)	13 (0.73%)

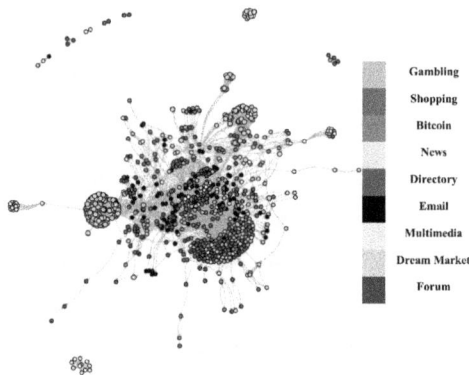

Figure 5: Network of domains with degree > 0

world. Finally, and perhaps surprisingly, Bitcoin and multimedia domains respectively constitute the smallest proportion of English Tor domains. Our initial expectation was that Bitcoin domains would be popular given the prevalence of the Dream market and shopping domains where purchases are made via cryptocurrency. We postulate that sites having a Bitcoin domain may host wallets, search a blockchain, or be markets that covert currency to BTC. Such sites hence may only need to be visited infrequently. Moreover, the mainstream popularity of Bitcoin has led to reputable surface web domains offering similar Bitcoin services.

5 DOMAIN RELATIONSHIPS

We next examine the *structure of relationships* between different sources of information on Tor. Such structural analyses realize the inter and intra-connectivity of domains on Tor conditioned by the type of information or content they host. The structural analysis also seeks to identify the topological properties of the Tor domain network to evaluate similarities and differences between the structure and formation process of Tor domains compared to the surface web and other sociotechnological systems. We build a graph where vertices are domains and a directed relation means a page in a domain has a hyperlink to a page in a different domain.

We measure simple statistics on the connectivity and connected components of the graph in Table 2 to make sense of the structure visualized in Figure 5 (note that all domains with degree 0 are excluded from the figure). The network is sparse, with only 5,523 undirected edges among 1,766 domains and a network density $\rho = 0.006$. The network also has $|C^w| = 25$ weakly connected components (W.C.C.) with the largest one having 955 domains. That only 54% of all vertices fall in the largest W.C.C. is somewhat surprising as many sociotechnological systems including the surface

web hyperlink graph exhibit a single massive connected component that the vast majority of all vertices participate in [4]. This suggests that the underlying process for linking between websites is fundamentally different than in most sociotechnological systems: rather than encouraging connections to make information dissemination easier, the modus operandi of Tor domain owners may be to discourage linking to other domains, so that information on this "hidden" web becomes difficult to arbitrarily discover and disseminate. This hypothesis is further supported by examining the set of strongly connected components C^s. We measure $|C^s| = 756$ and max $C_i^s = 13$, suggesting that an extraordinarily small number of domains collectively co-link with each other. It may be the case that the relatively larger $|C^w|$ and max C_i^w are simply caused by directory websites that offer links to a variety of other domains. These interesting deviations from other types of Web graphs collectively suggest that information on Tor may be intentionally isolated and difficult to discover by simple browsing. The small maximum connected component size speaks to the need of a comprehensive seed list of domains to for any comprehensive crawl of Tor.

5.1 Connectivity analysis

We next examine hyperlink relationships across domains, within domains, and the tendency of domains to link to like domains.

5.1.1 Inter-connectivity. To investigate the relationship between specific domains, we redraw the network with a carpet layout where vertices are spatially grouped in a grid by their domain type in Figure 6. We also list the sum of in- and out-degree from each community to every other community in Figure 7. There are some notable domain relationships observed in the two figures. For example, we find a small number of outgoing edges from shopping to gambling domains (Panel 1 of Figures 6 and 7). Our manual investigation of these relations find that some shopping domains actually provide customers with a method of payment by gambling, where a customer and seller play an online game to determine an amount of payment. We further note that shopping websites are isolated from the Dream market, perhaps to maintain some distinction between their offerings and the largest marketplace on Tor [9]. Another interesting observation is that there are a few number of edges from shopping to Bitcoin domains. Our manual investigation indicates that in addition to some shopping domains providing in-person cash payment (usually local drug vendors), marketplaces that use cryptocurrency for payment tend to link to providers on the surface web, sometimes with instructions for the user to purchase cryptocurrency from a trading house or market, thus explaining the small number of out-going edges from marketplaces to Bitcoin domains. Such links to the surface web, however have been noted as a major Achilles heel to privacy on Tor as a cause of Tor information leakage [23]. Links incoming to Bitcoin domains (Panel 2 of Figures 6 and 7) are dominated by directory ($\approx$ 53%) and email ($\approx$ 32%) domains. This finding defeats our intuition that marketplaces, the Dream market, and gambling sites would have been services most reliant on Bitcoin domains. We also investigated the email domains having edges to Bitcoins and found that many email services on Tor charge customers for anonymous messaging services or suggest a donation be made via Tor Bitcoin services. The sparse relation between multimedia and Bitcoin domains are due to the fact that some

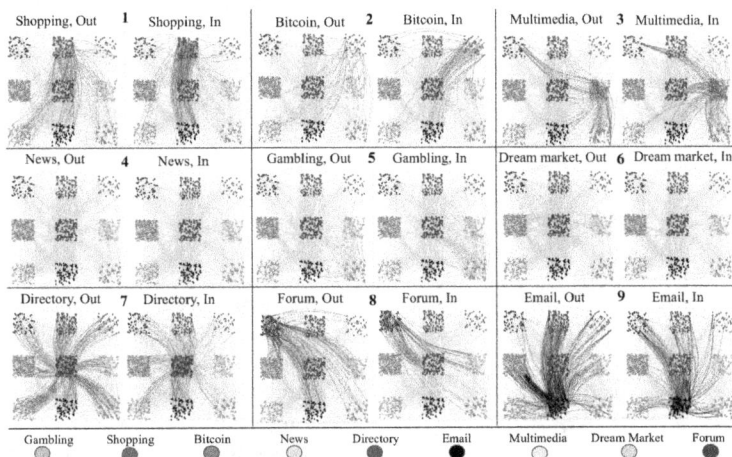

Figure 6: The Tor domain network. Panels 1 through 9 each highlight the incoming and outgoing edges of a particular domain. The figure is best viewed digitally and in color.

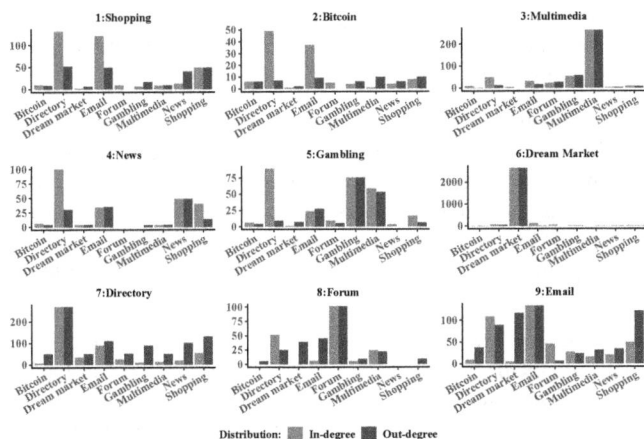

Figure 7: In/out degree distribution of each community

multimedia domains charge users for the services they provide, and of those, many utilize surface web cryptocurrency providers.

Other insights can be gleaned from the carpet and inter-domain degree distributions. For example, the outgoing connections from Dream market websites (Panel 6 of Figures 6 and 7) show that this marketplace has very few incoming or outgoing edges to other domains. Incoming links tend to originate from directory, email, and forum communities, which could be a byproduct of forum threads and email links to this secret marketplace. The Dream market thus appears to be especially siloed on the dark web, despite the fact that it represents 13.3% of all domains. The outgoing edges from directory domains (Panel 7 of Figures 6 and 7) indicate that a large collection of directories on Tor may be sufficient to include sites across all major Tor domains. Email domains exhibit a similar phenomena (Panel 9 of Figures 6 and 7) where they tend to connect to all other types of domains. This suggests that Tor e-mail services are not necessarily exclusive to only marketplace or forum users, but may be a useful service for most Tor visitors. Finally, we see that news and forums have no hyperlinks to each other (Panel 4 of Figures 6 and 7 and Panel 8 of Figures 6 and 7) which implies that although both services are information providers on Tor, they work independently of each other.

5.1.2 Intra-connectivity.
Next, we investigate the connectivity within each domain to evaluate how tightly knit and accessible particular types of Tor domains are among each other. This can reveal how often domains encourage their visitors to visit other domains having similar types of content. Figure 8 separately visualizes all intra-domain connections for each domain type. Perhaps unsurprisingly, Dream market domains are tightly connected compared to others, splitting into only four connected components and the smallest number of isolated domains. Shopping domains are almost entirely disconnected from each other, indicating that marketplaces may intentionally disassociate themselves with others. Gambling, multimedia, and Bitcoin domains are similarly disconnected, likely reflecting a competition for users within domains that tend to charge service fees. On the other hand, email, forum, and directory domains all exhibit a single large connected component. This implies that in email and directory communities, domains have more support from each other and refer their visitors to other similar service providers. News domains have a larger percentage of isolated domains which implies that most of the news websites work independently from each other.

Table 3: R_κ for Tor domain networks

Community	R_b	R_c	R_d
Shopping	.07	.04	.03
Bitcoin	.09	.08	.08
Multimedia	.22	.12	.11
News	.10	.05	.04
Gambling	.11	.06	.06
Dream Market	.10	.35	.03
Directory	.17	.11	.02
Forum	.24	.14	.09
Email	.52	.18	.05

We also quantify the intra-connectivity of topic domains by a Robustness coefficient R_κ proposed by [22]. This coefficient reflects the degree to which a network shatters into multiple connected components as vertices and their incident edges are removed. To compute R_κ, an ordering O_κ is induced on the vertices of the network by a centrality measure κ such that $O_\kappa(k)$ gives the vertex with the kth highest κ centrality. Letting $C_i^{(\kappa)}$ be the size of the largest connected component of the network after removing $\{O_\kappa(1), O_\kappa(2), ..., O_\kappa(i)\}$

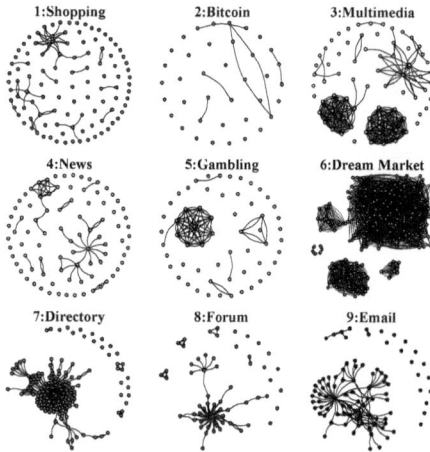

Figure 8: Intra-relations within domains

and their incident edges, R_κ is given by:

$$R_\kappa = \frac{S_1}{S_2} = \frac{\sum_{i=0}^{|V|} i \cdot C_i^{(\kappa)}}{\sum_{i=0}^{|V|} i|V| - \sum_{i=0}^{|V|} i^2} = \frac{6 \sum_{i=0}^{|V|} i \cdot C_i^{(\kappa)}}{|V|(|V|+1)(|V|-1)}$$

R_κ ranges in $[0, 1]$ and smaller values suggest that the network shatters faster as vertices having high κ betweenness are removed. The idea behind R_κ's formulation is to quantify the change in the largest network component size $C_i^{(\kappa)}$ as nodes are removed from the network. The network is 'maximally robust' if a plot of $C_i^{(\kappa)}$ vs the number of nodes removed shows a simple linear decreasing trend. Then the ratio of area under such a plot for a given network, S_1, over the area under the plot for an ideal network, S_2, defines the robustness coefficient for that network. Technical details about the measure are discussed in [22]. Table 3 lists R_κ for each intra-domain network under Betweenness b, closeness c, and degree d centrality. d is defined as the undirected degree of a node, b is defined as the number of shortest paths in the network that a node participates in, and c is defined as the inverse of the average path length from the node to all others in its connected component [28].

Studying Table 3 shows a correlation between R_κ and the competitive or cooperative intra-domain behaviors noted above. There are some networks whose R_d is close to R_c, namely those communities that are sparse networks (shopping, Bitcoin, news, gambling, multimedia), where competition for users and attention is natural. For domains where R_c and R_d are differentiated (directory, email, forum, Dream market), their structure has fewer connected components. This is best illustrated by Dream market where the difference of these coefficients has its maximum value, while exhibiting the fewest connected components. Also, we see that for networks with more supportive interlinking among domains (directory, email, and forum) the difference between R_c and R_d are larger.

In comparing R_b between domains, we observe two groups with similarly small (shopping, Bitcoin, news, Dream market, gambling) and large (multimedia, directory, forum, email) values. This suggests that the intra-connectivity of domains in the first group is dependent on a small percentage of domains, or has a high number of isolated domains which have zero Betweenness centrality. On the other hand, high R_b in the second category implies that their intra-connectivity is more robust to domain failures.

Table 4: Modularity score of each topic community

Community	M
Dream market	0.452
Directory	0.068
Forum	0.034
Email	0.032
Gambling	0.024
News	0.019
Multimedia	0.017
Shopping	0.012
Bitcoin	0.002

It is worth mentioning that for Dream market, R_b and R_c are significantly different due to the separated connected components also seen in Figure 5. Since a high percentage of domains in this community are located in a single connected component, their closeness centralities will be greater than zero. On the other hand, the separated connected components can cause low values for Betweenness centrality since this metric is based on paths between pairs of domains. This finding also indicates that based on the information we have from home pages of Dream markets, there exist separated Dream market communities that link to similar types of goods and services.

5.1.3 Modularity. Finally, we study the modularity of the network as a means to understand the relationship between the inter- and intra-domain connectivity conditioned on the content type of the domain. A domain will have high modularity if it tends to link to pages of the same content type, and low modularity if it tends to link to pages of a different type. The modularity M of a network [28] is given as $M = \frac{1}{2|E|} \sum_{i,j} \left(A_{ij} - \frac{d_i d_j}{2|E|} \right) \Delta_{type_i = type_j}$ where A is a binary network adjacency matrix with $A_{ij} = 1$ if v_i and v_j are adjacent and d_i and d_j are the undirected degree of nodes i and j, and Δ_E is an indicator that returns 1 if statement E is true and 0 otherwise. Table 4 shows that Dream market domains exhibit highest modularity by a wide margin, reinforcing the idea that Dream market domains are largely siloed from all other domains in the Tor ecosystem. Directories have lower but non-negligible modularity, leaving the impression that directory domains weakly cooperate by linking to each other. The remaining domains have substantially lower modularity; thus the majority of Tor domains strongly prefer to link to other types. This suggests that Tor domains prefer to remain isolated within their community of like domains, electing not to link to domains that offer the same type of information or services.

5.2 Importance analysis

We further examine the "importance" of particular domains as defined by various measures of network centrality. The centrality analysis only considers domains having in- or out-degree ≥ 1. We show the CDF [26] of betweenness centralities b_c of domains in Figure 9a. It shows how virtually every Tor domain has a betweenness centrality near or lower than 0.05; in fact there are only 6 domains with betweenness centrality greater than 0.05. These domains are the directory *HiddenWiki* ($b_c = 0.4$) (matching previous reports suggesting this domain is the principle Tor directory [6]), the Email domain *TorBox* ($b_c = 0.17$) and *VFEmail* ($b_c = 0.06$), a Dream market domain ($b_c = 0.07$), and two directories in the *TorWiki* domain ($b_c = 0.19$ and 0.11 respectively). An attack, removal, or failure of such directories may thus directly impact the number of Tor domains reachable by a casual browser exploring this dark web. These domains may further be crucial entry points for probes or crawlers seeking to map the structure of Tor.

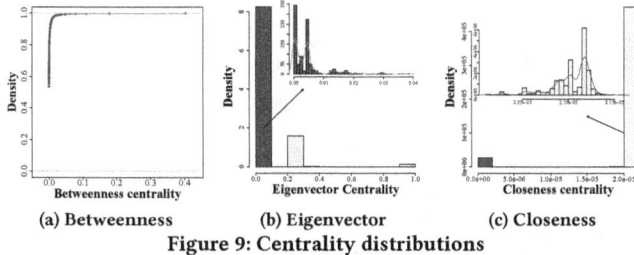

(a) Betweenness   (b) Eigenvector   (c) Closeness

Figure 9: Centrality distributions

Figure 9b shows the distribution of eigenvector centralities across Tor domains. We use a histogram rather than a CDF plot to better illustrate the variability between centrality values. Eigenvector centrality [28] describes the structural importance of a node as a function of the importance of its neighboring nodes. The eigenvector centrailty of vertex v_i is given by the ith component of the eigenvector of A whose corresponding eigenvalue is largest. We find a heavily skewed distribution of eigenvector centralities where a majority are close to zero. Further investigation revealed that all domains with eigenvector centrality ≥ 0.2 are part of the Dream market. Although high eigenvector centrality does not correlate with its relative popularity or frequency of visits from users, the naturally developed organization of Tor's domain structure places the Dream market as the most meaningful Tor domain by a wide margin (note that the highest eigenvector centrality of a non-Dream market domain is only 0.04). This establishes the Dream market as the most structurally important, "core" service Tor provides. The inlet of Figure 9b gives a sense of the distribution for the remaining domains. Here, the distribution exhibits a number of modes corresponding to connected components of the network that is disconnected from the Dream market. The especially low eigenvector centralities of these domains are further indicative of the significance of the Dream market's structural importance in Tor.

Figure 9c shows the distribution of closeness centralities. Like eigenvector centrality, we find a division of domains by those that exhibit extremely low or high scores, but here the majority of domains have very high closeness centrality. It is interesting to find that most domains exhibit a high closeness centrality despite intraconnectivity analysis from Section 5.1.2 suggesting that the intraconnectivity of Tor domains is sparse and has a small largest W.C.C. This outcome is likely the product of the directories *HiddenWiki* and *TorWiki* having high betweenness centrality that enables many pairs of domains to be few hops away from each other via these directories. This underscores the central importance of directory domains to connect Tor pages across domains, and the fact that Tor domains tend to remain undiscoverable without directories.

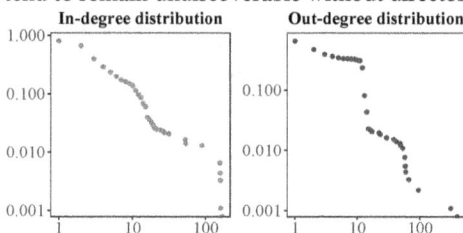

Figure 10: CCDF of network degree distributions

Table 5: Power-tail distribution hypothesis test results

Community	In-degree distribution	Out-degree distribution
Bitcoin	$p = .7623, \alpha = 2.69$	$p = .0114$
Forum	$p = .8996, \alpha = 3.01$	$p = .0001$
Email	$p = .3377, \alpha = 2.08$	$p = .0086$
News	$p = .0344$	$p = .5681, \alpha = 2.73$
Directory	$p = .3407, \alpha = 2.65$	$p = .0002$
Shopping	$p = .2021, \alpha = 2.85$	$p = .0001$
Gambling	$p = .0002$	$p = .0002$
Multimedia	$p = .0003$	$p = .0002$
Dream Market	$p = .0005$	$p = .0007$

5.3 Scale-free structure

We also investigate signs that the hyperlink structure of domains, and structure within domains, take on the same scale-free structure seen in many other sociotechnological systems [1] including the hyperlink structure of the surface web [4]. Figure 10 show the CCDF [26] of the degree distributions on log-log scale. The in-degree distribution does not exhibit a straight line pattern indicative of a power-law, with a rapid drop in the CCDF occurring in the body of the distribution around an in-degree of 10. The out-degree distribution takes on a bimodal pattern, with a set of domains having degree less than 10 and another with degrees between 10 and 100. The distribution's patterns may be explained by the variety of inter- and intra-connectivity patterns observed within each of the domains studied in Sections 5.1.1 and 5.1.2. To quantitatively confirm the distribution is not a power-law we apply Clauset *et al.* hypothesis test presented in [8]. The test checks the null hypothesis H_0: *the network degree distribution is power-tailed* against the alternative that it is **not** power-tailed, and provides an estimate of the power-law exponent α under H_0. The test leaves little doubt that the in- and out-degree distributions of the network (Figure 10) are not power-tailed with $p = 0.0001$, $p = 0.056$, respectively. If we consider the edges to be undirected we still have evidence to reject H_0 with $p = 0.0003$. These measurements confirm the analysis presented in [23] that the hyperlink structure of Tor domains does not have the same scale-free structure as the surface web.

Noting the variety of intra-connectivity patterns discussed in Section 5.1.2, we also check if the degree distribution of sites within each domain are power-tailed. These measurements include intradomain connections as well as those connections incident to a different domain. We list the p-value of the test for the in- and out-degree of each domain in Table 5 and include the estimate of α when H_0 cannot be rejected. Interestingly, we note that it is only for the in-degree distributions of Bitcoin, forum, email, shopping, and directory domains, and the out-degree of the news domain, where there is insufficient evidence to reject H_0. The popularity of about half of all Tor domains (where popularity is defined by an incoming hyperlink) thus has a power-tailed pattern suggesting that a a small number of Bitcoin, forum, email, shopping, and directories are linked to many times more frequently than is typical. That the news domain is the only one with a power law out-degree distribution may suggest the presence of a small number of highly active news sites that offer posts discussing a far wider variety of other Tor domains compared to other news domains. The majority of news domains may thus focus on a specific topic, or are otherwise used to discuss events outside of the Tor network.

6 CONCLUSIONS AND FUTURE WORK

This paper presented a broad overview of the content of English language Tor domains captured in a large crawl of the Tor network. The paper makes revelations about not the physical or logical (hyperlink) structure of Tor, but of the particular domains of information or services hosted on the service and the structure between and within such domains. Such birds-eye insights, and especially those related to the inter-connectivity of domains, cannot be acquired by synthesizing the existing low-level content analysis work that focuses on a single type of Tor domain. Content analysis carried out by LDA and GbTL, using measures of topic coherence and label suitability, identified just nine principal types of domains. Manual analysis of each domain was done to describe the meaning of each topic, and any standout 'sub-types' seen within them. Over half of all domains constitute site directories or marketplaces to purchase and sell goods or services, with money tansfer, drugs, and pornography servicing as the most popular types of marketplaces. Our measurements identified the Dream market as perhaps the 'core' service of Tor, as Dream market domains exhibit especially high closeness and eignevector centralities. The inter-connectivity of the Tor domain network is surprisingly sparse with a small maximum W.C.C. but interesting domain inter-connection patterns discussed in Section 5.1.1. Patterns in the intra-connectivity structure are further indicative of levels of cooperation (where some pages hyperlink to pages in the same domain) and competition (where pages in a domain are more likely to isolate themselves from pages in the same domain) that may be measured by robustness coefficients R_κ for varying centrality scores κ. We further note evidence for rejecting the hypothesis that the global domain structure is scale-free, yet there is insufficient evidence in the in-degree distributions of some domain intra-networks and the out-degree distribution of the news domain intra-network to conclude that these subnetworks are not power law. This is indicative of different underlying processes that form connections in different intra-domain networks.

Future work can expand this work further by studying the evolution of the topics and communities over time using a richer topic extraction analysis based on algorithm discussed in [14]. Another direction of future work is to combine this study with a modern crawl of similar domains on the surface web to be able to directly compare and contrast surface and dark web hyper-link structure. Such a comparative analysis could shed light around the differences in use between the surface and dark web.

ACKNOWLEDGMENTS

This paper is based on work supported by the National Science Foundation (NSF) under Grant No. 1464104. Any opinions, findings, and conclusions or recommendations expressed are those of the author(s) and do not necessarily reflect the views of the NSF.

REFERENCES

[1] Albert-László Barabási and Eric Bonabeau. 2003. Scale-free Networks. *Scientific American* 288, 5 (2003), 60–69.
[2] Alex Biryukov, Ivan Pustogarov, and Ralf-Philipp Weinmann. 2013. Trawling for Tor Hidden Services: Detection, measurement, deanonymization. In *Symposium on Security and Privacy*. 80–94.
[3] David M Blei, Andrew Y Ng, and Michael I Jordan. 2003. Latent Dirichlet Allocation. *Journal of Machine Learning Research* 3, Jan (2003), 993–1022.
[4] Andrei Broder, Ravi Kumar, Farzin Maghoul, Prabhakar Raghavan, Sridhar Rajagopalan, Raymie Stata, Andrew Tomkins, and Janet Wiener. 2000. Graph Structure in the Web. *Computer Networks* 33, 1-6 (2000), 309–320.
[5] Hsinchun Chen, Wingyan Chung, Jialun Qin, Edna Reid, Marc Sageman, and Gabriel Weimann. 2008. Uncovering the Dark Web: A case study of Jihad on the Web. *Journal of the American Society for Information Science and Technology* 59, 8 (2008), 1347–1359.
[6] Michael Chertoff and Tobby Simon. 2015. The Impact of the Dark Web on Internet Governance and Cyber Security. *GCIG Paper Series* 6 (2015).
[7] Ian Clarke, Oskar Sandberg, Matthew Toseland, and Vilhelm Verendel. 2010. Private Communication through a Network of Trusted Connections: The Dark Freenet. *Network* (2010).
[8] Aaron Clauset, Cosma Rohilla Shalizi, and Mark EJ Newman. 2009. Power-law Distributions in Empirical Data. *SIAM review* 51, 4 (2009), 661–703.
[9] Diana S Dolliver. 2015. Evaluating Drug Trafficking on the Tor Network: Silk Road 2, the Sequel. *Int. Journal of Drug Policy* 26, 11 (2015), 1113–1123.
[10] Diana S Dolliver, Steven P Ericson, and Katherine L Love. 2018. A Geographic Analysis of Drug Trafficking Patterns on the Tor Network. *Geographical Review* 108, 1 (2018), 45–68.
[11] Ingo Feinerer, Christian Buchta, Wilhelm Geiger, Johannes Rauch, Patrick Mair, and Kurt Hornik. 2013. The Textcat Package for N-gram based Text Categorization in R. *Journal of statistical software* 52, 6 (2013), 1–17.
[12] Shalini Ghosh, Ariyam Das, Phil Porras, Vinod Yegneswaran, and Ashish Gehani. 2017. Automated Categorization of Onion Sites for Analyzing the Darkweb Ecosystem. In *Proc. of the 23rd ACM SIGKDD Int. Conf. on Knowledge Discovery and Data Mining*. 1793–1802.
[13] Vanessa Henri. 2017. The Dark Web: Some Thoughts for an Educated Debate. *Canadian Journal of Law and Technology* 15, 1 (2017).
[14] Thomas Hofmann. 2017. Probabilistic Latent Semantic Indexing. In *ACM SIGIR Forum*, Vol. 51. 211–218.
[15] Ioana Hulpus, Conor Hayes, Marcel Karnstedt, and Derek Greene. 2013. Unsupervised Graph-based Topic Labelling using DBpedia. In *Proc. of the sixth ACM Int. Conf. on Web Search and Data Mining*. 465–474.
[16] Christos Iliou, George Kalpakis, Theodora Tsikrika, Stefanos Vrochidis, and Ioannis Kompatsiaris. 2016. Hybrid Focused Crawling for Homemade Explosives Discovery on Surface and Dark Web. In *11th Int. Conf. on Availability, Reliability and Security*. 229–234.
[17] Karsten Loesing, Steven J Murdoch, and Roger Dingledine. 2010. A Case Study on Measuring Statistical Data in the Tor Anonymity Network. In *Int. Conf. on Financial Cryptography and Data Security*. 203–215.
[18] Damon McCoy, Kevin Bauer, Dirk Grunwald, Tadayoshi Kohno, and Douglas Sicker. 2008. Shining Light in Dark Places: Understanding the Tor Network. In *Privacy Enhancing Technologies*. 63–76.
[19] David Mimno, Hanna M. Wallach, Edmund Talley, Miriam Leenders, and Andrew McCallum. 2011. Optimizing Semantic Coherence in Topic Models. In *Proc. of the Conf. on Empirical Methods in Natural Language Processing*. 262–272.
[20] Aziz Mohaisen and Kui Ren. 2017. Leakage of. onion at the DNS Root: Measurements, Causes, and Countermeasures. *IEEE/ACM Transactions on Networking* 25, 5 (2017), 3059–3072.
[21] Carl-Maria Mörch, Louis-Philippe Côté, Laurent Corthésy-Blondin, Léa Plourde-Léveillé, Luc Dargis, and Brian L Mishara. 2018. The Darknet and Suicide. *Journal of Affective Disorders* 241 (2018), 127–132.
[22] Mahendra Piraveenan, Shahadat Uddin, and Kon Shing Kenneth Chung. 2012. Measuring Topological Robustness of Networks under Sustained Targeted Attacks. In *Proc. of the Int. Conf. on Advances in Social Networks Analysis and Mining*. 38–45.
[23] Iskander Sanchez-Rola, Davide Balzarotti, and Igor Santos. 2017. The Onions Have Eyes: A Comprehensive Structure and Privacy Analysis of Tor Hidden Services. In *Proc. of the 26th Int. Conf. on World Wide Web*. 1251–1260.
[24] Paul Syverson, R Dingledine, and N Mathewson. 2004. Tor: The Second-generation Onion Router. In *Usenix Security*.
[25] Jennifer Xu and Hsinchun Chen. 2008. The topology of Dark Networks. *Commun. ACM* 51, 10 (2008), 58–65.
[26] Mahdieh Zabihimayvan and Derek Doran. 2018. Some (Non-) Universal Features of Web Robot Traffic. In *Annual Conf. on Information Sciences and Systems*. 1–6.
[27] Mahdieh Zabihimayvan, Reza Sadeghi, H Nathan Rude, and Derek Doran. 2017. A Soft Computing Approach for Benign and Malicious Web Robot Detection. *Expert Systems with Applications* 87 (2017), 129–140.
[28] Reza Zafarani, Mohammad Ali Abbasi, and Huan Liu. 2014. *Social Media Mining: an Introduction*.
[29] Yulei Zhang, Shuo Zeng, Chun-Neng Huang, Li Fan, Ximing Yu, Yan Dang, Catherine A Larson, Dorothy Denning, Nancy Roberts, and Hsinchun Chen. 2010. Developing a Dark Web Collection and Infrastructure for Computational and Social Sciences. In *Int. Conf. on Intelligence and Security Informatics*. 59–64.
[30] Ahmed T. Zulkarnine, Richard Frank, and Bryan Monk. 2016. Surfacing Collaborated Networks in Dark Web to Find Illicit and Criminal Content. In *Int. Conf. on Intelligence and Security Informatics*.

Investor Retention in Equity Crowdfunding

Igor Zakhlebin
Northwestern University
izakhlebin@u.northwestern.edu

Emőke-Ágnes Horvát
Northwestern University
a-horvat@northwestern.edu

ABSTRACT

Crowdfunding platforms promise to disrupt investing as they by-pass traditional financial institutions through peer-to-peer trans-actions. To stay functional, these platforms require a supply of investors who are willing to contribute to campaigns. Yet, little is known about the retention of investors in this setting. Using four years of data from a leading equity crowdfunding platform, we empirically study the length and success of investor activity on the platform. We analyze temporal variations in these outcomes and ex-plain patterns using statistical modeling. Our models are based on information about user's past and current investment decisions, i.e., content-based and structural similarities between the campaigns they invest in. We uncover the role of past successes and diversity of investment decisions for novice vs. serial investors. Our results inform potential strategies for increasing the retention of investors and improving their decisions on crowdfunding platforms.

KEYWORDS

Equity crowdfunding; Investing; User retention; Investment success; Portfolio diversity.

ACM Reference Format:
Igor Zakhlebin and Emőke-Ágnes Horvát. 2019. Investor Retention in Equity Crowdfunding. In *11th ACM Conference on Web Science (WebSci '19), June 30-July 3, 2019, Boston, MA, USA.* ACM, New York, NY, USA, 9 pages. https://doi.org/10.1145/3292522.3326037

1 INTRODUCTION

Online crowdfunding platforms enable their users to contribute to proposed campaigns without the involvement of an institutional mediator between them and the people requesting funds [2, 42]. Since funding is determined by a large group of people instead of a small number of decision makers, campaigns can benefit from the aggregated wisdom of crowds, which promises to recognize valuable projects that would have remained unfunded by traditional financial organizations [9]. In only a couple of years, crowdfunding expanded from funding aspirant creative works and supplying pro-social donations to enabling large citizen-funded urban projects and providing commercial interest-based unsecured loans, as well as angel investments [22]. Due to this growth and diversification, the industry has been increasingly a subject of scholarly interest, mainly in entrepreneurship and management literature [30, 39, 50, 55].

The latest addition to various types of crowdfunding is equity crowdfunding, which allows startups to attract funds from a large group of investors in return for a stake in company ownership [3]. What makes it key among other forms of crowdfunding is that it competes with venture capital by scaling up from the "family and friends" funding model to professional financial markets [42, 50] where investors are motivated by a stake in company ownership and future financial returns instead of an immediate deliverable [13]. Given the quick expansion and current maturity of equity crowd-funding [17], this format promises to truly transform decentralized markets and is thus a crucial subject of study [26, 28].

Regardless of the specific form of crowdfunding, understanding investor participation is crucial. Crowdfunding platforms function as marketplaces that match investments with campaigns. The effi-ciency of such matching determines how well the platform fulfills its purpose, to the extent that all major platforms use the amount of money successfully invested as one of their core key perfor-mance indicators. A lack of investors makes it harder for individual campaigns to receive the requested funding, which decreases the efficiency of the entire platform and, in extreme cases, can lead to the platform becoming defunct [1].

Recent developments demonstrate that crowdfunding platforms cannot rely solely on extensive growth to fund their campaigns. A recent analysis of Kickstarter shows that the platform has reached a plateau in the amount of money pledged to successful cam-paigns [10]. Considering that the growth of this platform was histor-ically fueled by intake of new crowd investors [11], this slowdown may be attributed to the saturation of the market as most of the interested users have either already joined Kickstarter or one of its competitors. Additionally, some existing investors inherently lose interest in crowdfunding over time, a phenomenon that was dubbed "crowdfunding fatigue" by the media [44, 57].

We therefore focus on the following question in the context of equity crowdfunding: *What factors contribute to the retention of investors?* Using comprehensive data about investments made on a popular equity crowdfunding platform over the span of four years, we explore how investment decisions affect investor retention on the platform. Our main contributions can be summarized as follows:

- In light of existing literature (Section 2) and based on our data (Section 3), we introduce variables to describe individual invest-ments and assess the success of crowd investors (Section 4.1–4.2). To better understand the factors associated with investor re-tention, we construct new measures that enable exploring the usefulness of portfolio-based investment rules in the context of equity crowdfunding. Our measures capture the dissimilarity of investments within a "portfolio" with respect to their categories, descriptions, and shared investor bases (Sections 4.3-4.4).

- We show that, as expected, investors who remain on the plat-form have higher success rates than the ones who leave and that over time serial investors become less aligned with the crowds' investment choices (Section 5.1). We also document and explain a counterintuitive uptake of success rate for investors prior to leaving the platform.

- Using survival analysis, we explain the rate of attrition over time based on the proposed variables (Section 5.2). Results show that for novice investors, an exploration of different campaigns is important for retention. Serial investors who stay longer on the platform tend to invest in tandem in the same campaigns and they are more likely to be successful when they choose significantly different campaigns from the same category.

We then discuss our results in the context of broader crowdfunding and crowdwork literature (Section 6) and conclude by outlining directions for future work (Section 7).

2 RELATED WORK

Although there are few papers that focus on the question of investor retention, some closely related questions have been explored in the following bodies of literature.

Contributor retention. Since crowdfunding is enabled by online platforms and relies on contributions from many participants, it can be regarded as a special case of peer production or crowdsourcing, where contributors bring campaign proposals and personal finances instead of ideas, opinions, or effort [22]. This allows us to leverage the rich literature about contributor retention in peer production and crowdwork that covers platforms like Wikipedia [23, 24], Wikia [48], OpenStreetMap [15], Q&A sites [16, 43, 54], forums [37], newsgroups [7, 31], and social media sites [34, 53].

The shared theme of this research is the retention of newcomers, which is strongly affected by their experience during the first contributions on the platform [24, 31, 48]. Current performance, as captured by the frequency, speed, and overall number of contributions, has a positive impact on retention of novice [15, 16, 37, 43] and continuing contributors [53].

While we expect these findings to be general enough to apply to crowdfunding, this is not a given. The types of actors and contributions on such platforms are significantly different [25]. For example, campaigns typically remain fixed once proposed and sourced money are primarily considered as a lump sum. Most importantly, unlike in peer production and crowdsourcing scenarios, there is no explicit coordination in crowdfunding.

Crowdfunding research. Literature systematizing existing research and setting future agenda has focused on classifying crowdfunding platforms and their business models [25] and outlined both similarities with previous funding models, as well as important theoretical and empirical differences from them [22]. Research on user behavior has primarily focused on the project creator's experience on crowdfunding platforms. Several studies have uncovered factors associated with the success of individual campaigns in obtaining the requested funds by assessing the role of creditworthiness [30], effect of social capital [19, 27, 29, 39], and presentation of the idea [4, 18, 28]. The most studied aspects from the investor's point of view have been the motivations for participation [20, 21, 47], the choice of campaigns [6], and the temporal dynamics of contributions towards individual campaigns [12, 36, 55].

The *only* studies related to contributor retention in crowdfunding to date are based on a single education-centric donation platform,

Campaign Name

| | Short campaign description, succinctly explaining what is it about. | INVESTMENT SOUGHT: £10,000 | EQUITY OFFERED: 10.00% |

Location
www.website.com
Category 1   Category 2

INVESTMENT ALREADY FUNDED: £6,000   VALUATION (PRE-MONEY): £100,000

60%

Figure 1: Mock-up of platform's user interface card with information about a single campaign. The detailed description associated with the campaign is not shown here.

DonorsChoose.org [5, 51]. Our paper fills an important gap in the literature by providing a second, significantly different study of investor retention in a novel and high-stakes form of crowdfunding. We also move beyond analysis of first-time investors and develop models explaining the behavior of serial investors. This is essential since only 1% of donors on DC.org had five or more contributions, while the percentage of serial investors in our case is 11.8%.

3 DATA

We received comprehensive data from one of the leading equity crowdfunding platforms operating in the UK and the greater European area. Project creators on this platform are primarily start-ups and later-stage companies that raise capital for their subsequent rounds of funding. The platform thus favors large campaigns, the mean campaign target being £163,800. The investor side is represented both by small private and larger institutional investors. Our data includes information about all crowdfunding campaigns and all individual investments made by platform users between July 2012 and January 2016. We only consider users who have made at least one investment on the platform, and we will heretofore refer to them as "investors." The data comprises 16,907 investors who have collectively made 59,370 investments into 727 campaigns during the considered time period.

On platform's web interface, campaigns are summarised in the form of cards, displaying their requested amount, offered share in equity, current status, and other relevant information (see Fig. 1). Additionally, each campaign features a comprehensive description typically consisting of a few paragraphs of text and is tagged by its creators with one or more predefined categories, such as "Energy," "Consumer products," or "Media and Entertainment." The platform operates by an "all or nothing" principle, meaning that a campaign succeeds only if it reaches its target amount by the campaign expiration date. Otherwise, it is cancelled and all collected money are returned to investors. Campaigns in our sample have an average duration of 83 days, and only 33.6% of them are successful. Finally, each investment is associated with a time stamp and an amount in £ or €, which we convert for consistency into £ according to the exchange rate at the time of investment.

4 MEASURES AND MODELS

To describe investor participation on the platform, we use the pipeline shown in Fig. 2. Investors are presented with a variety of ongoing campaigns to choose from. Based on campaign details and previously made investments, they decide which campaign

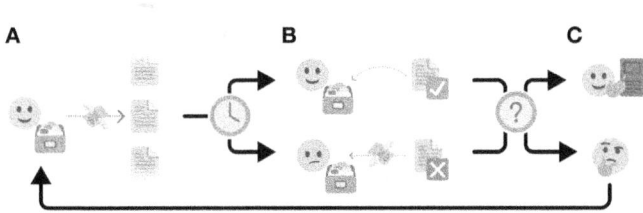

Figure 2: Pipeline of participation in equity crowdfunding. (A) The investor chooses a campaign to invest in. (B) After waiting, they learn whether the funds have been accepted and, given this outcome, (C) they either decide to leave the platform or adjust their strategy and invest again.

they will invest in and how much money they will invest. Upon each campaign's expiration, investors learn whether the requested amount was reached and, therefore, whether their investments have been accepted. Then investors decide whether to repeat this process and make an investment in another campaign or to leave the platform. Our study particularly focuses on this last step: the choice of investors to stay on the platform or to leave.

In order to make further analyses feasible, we add a simplifying assumption to our model. Instead of allowing multiple pending investments, we require investors to decide about new contributions only after they find out whether their previous investment was successful or not. This assumption is supported by research that found previous activity to impact user retention on various platforms [24, 54]. To formalize the intuition that the behavior of individuals changes in response to the outcome of their actions, we thus assume that decisions about ongoing participation on the platform are made successively after learning about the success of the prior investment [8].

In what follows, we examine a number of measures previously shown in the context of peer production and crowd donations to affect the retention of contributors. We additionally introduce measures of campaign dissimilarity to evaluate (1) how diverse the portfolio is thus far and (2) how novel an investment is given the preceding investments. To estimate the effects of the selected variables on the retention of investors, we fit Cox's proportional hazard models [14]. The code for these computations is provided on GitHub[1].

4.1 Quantifying investor success

Just like other platforms involving crowd contributors, crowdfunding platforms benefit from users who participate for long periods of time and make several investments. To capture the longevity of investors through their ongoing interaction with the platform, we look at the *number of investments* they have made throughout the period of study. This variable allows us to track investor attrition from the platform and parallels the number of contributions in other studies [53].

Investors are interested in supporting campaigns that hit their target to avoid locking up funds until a campaign's expiration date. Such investments incur a cost of missed opportunity. To quantify how successful each user is at investing, we measure their *success*

rate, i.e., the fraction of times the user has invested in a successful campaign. It has been shown that crowd investors who invest in successful campaigns are more likely to return to the platform [5]. We are interested in testing this effect based on our data and learning how success rate influences retention of investors in the studied equity crowdfunding platform.

4.2 Characterizing individual investments

Our aim is to capture different aspects of investment behavior that may correlate with sustained contributions on the platform. Relying on existing literature, we use the following variables to describe each individual investment:

Amount. Investment amount in £. Larger investments may indicate investors' higher involvement with the platform and could influence retention similar to effort exerted by contributors in peer production [15].

Time gap. Number of days passed since the previous investment in a given campaign. For the first investment, we define time gap as the time passed since the start of the campaign. Similarly to observations of other online resources [40, 43], we expect that users who take longer to invest again are less likely to return.

Campaign stage. Fraction of the requested capital amassed by a campaign before the user invests in it. Previous studies have used similar measures to separate investors into "early movers" and followers and found important distinctions between them in terms of their rates of return [5] and their contribution to a campaign's success [36, 38].

4.3 Evaluating the dissimilarity of campaigns

To understand how individual campaigns chosen by an investor relate to each other, we quantify their dissimilarity based on salient campaign characteristics as follows:

Category-based dissimilarity. Proposers on our platform tag each campaign with one or more preset category that can be used to define coarse-grained differences between campaigns. Based on these categories, each campaign i can be described by a bit vector $x^{(i)}$ whose elements are equal to 1 if the campaign belongs to the corresponding category and 0 otherwise. We use the *Jaccard distance* to compare two campaign vectors $x^{(i)}$ and $x^{(j)}$:

$$\delta^{\text{categ}}(x^{(i)}, x^{(j)}) = 1 - \frac{x^{(i)} \cdot x^{(j)}}{\sum x^{(i)} + \sum x^{(j)} - x^{(i)} \cdot x^{(j)}}.$$

Here, $x^{(i)} \cdot x^{(j)}$ denotes the element-wise (dot) product of two campaign vectors and $\sum x^{(i)}$ denotes the number of category labels associated with campaign i.

Lexical dissimilarity. It has been shown that linguistic content is important in contexts when one needs to convince others to contribute to a campaign [4, 28]. We use the full-text description of campaigns to make finer-grained distinctions between them based on specific words used. To construct vector representations of these campaign descriptions, we apply a number of common transformations to them. First, we split them into tokens and filter out tokens that represent punctuation and common English words[2]. Then, we stem the remaining tokens, enumerate them, and build vectors with

---

[1]https://github.com/inguar/equity-crowdfunding-code

[2]English language list of stop words was taken from https://www.nltk.org.

the tokens' corresponding *TF-IDF* coefficients [32]. We start with a set of campaign descriptions D and a set of tokens T. Denoting the count of appearances of token t in campaign description d with $f_{t,d}$, we derive a vector $x^{(d)}$ to describe that campaign as follows:

$$x_t^{(d)} = TF(t,d) \cdot IDF(t,D) = \frac{f_{t,d}}{|d|} \cdot \log \frac{|D|}{d \in D: \, t \in d}.$$

Here, $|d|$ denotes the number of tokens in campaign description d and $|D|$ is the total number of campaigns. Then, to compute the dissimilarity of these vectors, we use the standard *cosine distance* as follows:

$$\delta^{\text{lex}}(x^{(i)}, x^{(j)}) = 1 - \cos(x^{(i)}, x^{(j)}) = 1 - \frac{x^{(i)} \cdot x^{(j)}}{||x^{(i)}|| \, ||x^{(j)}||}.$$

Again, $x^{(i)} \cdot x^{(j)}$ denotes the element-wise (dot) product of two vectors and $||x^{(i)}||$ is the Euclidean norm of a vector, i.e., the square root of its elements' sum of squares.

Structural dissimilarity. In equity crowdfunding, it has been shown that initial contributions by investors with public profiles can increase subsequent contributions from both early and late-stage investors [49]. Emerging groups of investors who systematically invest in the same campaigns, i.e., who co-invest, could thus be correlated both with campaign success and investor participation. To quantify this association, we measure the (dis)similarity of campaigns based on investors who participate in them. Specifically, we use the principle of structural equivalence from social network analysis literature [52]. This principle posits that two nodes connected to the same others are structurally equivalent to one another. A corollary to this principle is that the amount of common neighbors in a network reveals how similar two nodes are. Analogously, campaigns that have a large overlap in investors are considered to be more similar to each other than the ones having a small or no overlap at all. To quantify this similarity, we construct an investor-campaign adjacency matrix, where each binary entry indicates whether an investor has contributed to a certain campaign before a given time point. To compare campaigns, we measure the cosine distance between their corresponding adjacency vectors, as defined above.

Viewed jointly, category-based and lexical dissimilarity allow us to evaluate the distance between campaigns based on their topic on a coarse level (*Do they belong to the same categories?*) and on a fine-grained level (*Was the wording in their descriptions similar?*). Structural dissimilarity evaluates campaigns' shared investor base, indicating whether collective behavior and personal influence might be contributing to the decision of staying on the platform or leaving.

4.4 Defining portfolio diversity and investment novelty

Having different notions of campaign dissimilarity, we adapt portfolio-based investment approaches to the crowdfunding scenario. Similarly to traditional investing, it can be assumed that new investments are decided on with existing ones in mind, which together form a *portfolio*. Modern portfolio theory postulates that owning different kinds of financial assets is less risky than owning one type alone [41]. In particular, having a portfolio of assets with uncorrelated returns allows investors to mitigate the risk posed by the potential failure or underperformance of individual assets. Since investors in equity crowdfunding typically don't have historical

data on the previous performance of companies, they try to select a diverse set of campaigns by other means. They can assess dissimilarity based on campaign descriptions and signals from other investors.

We estimate the diversity of a portfolio using the *average pairwise distance* from Ziegler et al. [56]. This measure of diversity can be considered a particular case of the Rao diversity coefficient when elements (here campaigns) are equally probable [45]. Given a set of descriptions of n campaigns $\mathbf{X} = \{x^{(1)}, \ldots, x^{(n)}\}$ that a user has already invested in and a distance or dissimilarity measure δ defined on the elements of $\mathbf{X}$, we have:

$$APD(\mathbf{X}) = \frac{1}{n(n-1)/2} \sum_{i=1}^{n} \sum_{j=i+i}^{n} \delta(x^{(i)}, x^{(j)}).$$

There is a problem with using *APD* as a measure of diversity. Since we utilize it for predicting future events, we re-compute *APD* with every new investment based on information about investments made up to that time point. For the initial investments, thus, the portfolio is comprised of few campaigns, meaning that *APD* is heavily influenced by potential outliers. To mitigate their influence, we add m "fake" distance terms to each computation that are equal to the average pairwise distance $\overline{\delta}$ across all campaigns that were co-invested into in the entire dataset. This way, we incorporate our prior belief that average distances should be close to the mean distance across the population [35], which yields the *Bayesian average pairwise distance* defined as:

$$BAPD(\mathbf{X}) = \frac{1}{m+n(n-1)/2}(m\overline{\delta} + \sum_{i=1}^{n} \sum_{j=i+i}^{n} \delta(x^{(i)}, x^{(j)})).$$

To quantify investment novelty, we can similarly measure the difference between the new campaign x' that the user invests in and all campaigns he or she has previously invested in. For that, we average the pairwise distances between x' and all the prior campaigns $\mathbf{X}$:

$$BAD(\mathbf{X}, x') = \frac{1}{m+n}(m\overline{\delta} + \sum_{i=1}^{n} \delta(x^{(i)}, x')).$$

We find that the median number of n across all computations of diversity and novelty is 4. Based on that, we use $m = 4$ when computing *BAD* and $m = 4(4-1)/2 = 6$ when computing *BAPD*. Given a portfolio of $n = 4$ campaigns, the weights of actual dissimilarities in the average would sum up to $1/2$ and grow for larger values of n.

Having these measures as a general framework, we compute diversity and novelty using the vector representations of campaigns and the introduced dissimilarity measures (see Section 4.3). This gives us three definitions of portfolio diversity ($BAPD^{\text{categ}}$, $BAPD^{\text{lex}}$, and $BAPD^{\text{struct}}$) as well as three definitions of investment novelty (BAD^{categ}, BAD^{lex}, and BAD^{struct}). These measures capture the diversity of the portfolio and the novelty of the current investment given previous investments along three different dimensions. Figures 3 and 4 show the correlation and variance relative to the mean for the category-based, lexical, and structural versions of diversity and novelty, respectively. Accordingly, the correlation between diversity and novelty is typically weak despite the same underlying formulations of dissimilarity. The variance relative to the mean is limited for both measures. The very low variance in *BAPD* in case of the first few investments makes this measure less suited to study novice investors. For this group, *BAD* has an appropriate sensitivity due to its focus on single new investments.

When studying investor retention, we use *BAPD* to measure *portfolio diversity* and *BAD* to quantify a new campaign's dissimilarity to the existing portfolio, i.e., *investment novelty*. We hypothesize

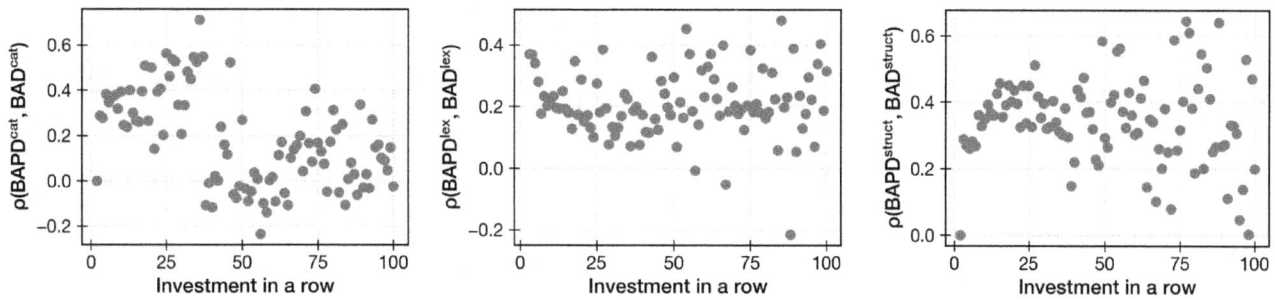

Figure 3: Pearson correlations between *BAPD* and *BAD* measures, by investment number.

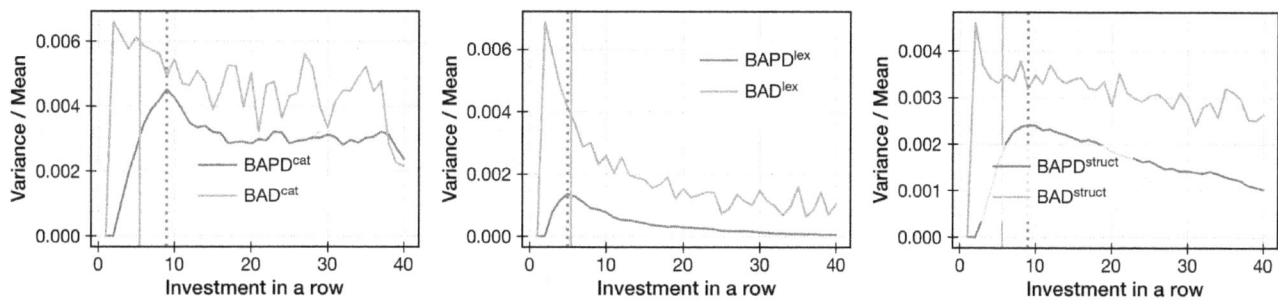

Figure 4: Variance of different *BAPD* and *BAD* measures relative to their means, by investment number. Grey line separates the first five investments from the rest, and blue dotted line shows the maximum of *BAPD*.

that investors with higher portfolio diversity are more likely to make successful investments and to stay on the platform. The expected effect of investment novelty on retention is less clear. On the one hand, it could increase the probability of leaving the platform, because if the chosen campaign is unlike the previous ones, the investor is probably less experienced with the new investment and is making a rather risky decision. On the other hand, it could help with retention, because it shows an interest that makes the investor overcome the cost of including a dissimilar campaign to their portfolio [46].

4.5 Analyses

We consider that users have left the platform if they have not made an investment at least six months prior to the end of our data collection[3]. If a user has made an investment in that period, we presume that they are still active. In statistical terms, the information about the moment when they leave the platform is *right-censored*. We exclude from our analysis users who have joined the platform in the last six months. According to these definitions, 61.5% of users have left the platform; for 9.3% the outcome is right-censored; and 29.3% are excluded as late-joiners. We estimate the user survival function using the Kaplan-Meyer method [33] and find that the median life expectancy of a user is 66.5 days or two investments.

---

[3]We replicated our results with different time windows, including 3 months and 1 year, which yielded similar results.

Data preprocessing. Most platform users invest once in a campaign and occasionally they reinvest in the same campaign. Some investors, however, repeatedly target the same set of campaigns. Since this behavior can point to attempts by campaign creators to generate visibility of traction or can even represent automated investment activity, we exclude users for whom the fraction of re-investments was above 50%. To additionally control for re-investments into the same campaigns, we add a dummy variable *repeated investment* into all models: Its value is 1 if the investor has previously contributed to that campaign and 0 otherwise.

Survival models. We build a number of survival models to estimate the hazard rate of user attrition based on the variables associated with individual's investment events. Since covariates in these models change with time, we use Cox's proportional hazard model with time-varying covariates [14]. As an independent variable, we use the occurrence of an event (leaving the platform) by the end of our time period: 1 if the user has left and 0 if the information about them is right-censored and their outcome is unknown.

We fit two sets of models. The first models are for investments 1 to 5 (novice investors), and the second models are for investment 6 and higher (serial investors). We do this separation for two reasons. If we look at the hazard rate, the probability that an investor would leave the platform after each individual investment (Fig. 5), we see that there is a change around investment 5. Most investors leave the platform after the first few investments (high hazard rate), while investors who placed more than a few investments have a much lower probability of leaving (low hazard rate). This indicates that

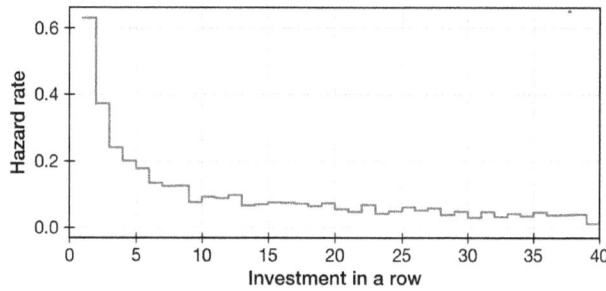

Figure 5: Hazard rates for subsequent investments.

different factors can lead to novices and serial investors leaving the platform. Fitting separate sets of models also allows us to see the changes in effect sizes and significance between these two cases. Our diversity variable naturally supports this separation as well given that the measure reaches its maximum relative variance close to the sixth investment (c.f. Figure 4). We construct multiple models for both novice and serial investors including individual campaign variables along diversity and/or novelty measures.

5 RESULTS

5.1 Success rate and retention

Overall, success rates tend to remain stable over time with a slight downward trend (Fig. 6). Success rates for investors who left the platform after many investments tend to be lower than for the ones who made few investments. Figure 7, left shows how success rate changes over time with each subsequent investment for the entire population of platform users. It similarly has a downward trend showing that over time users tend to make more investments into less successful campaigns. When we split investors with respect to attrition status (Fig. 7, center), we see that investors who leave the platform at later stages are less successful than the ones who remained. This observation hints at the lower success rate as possible reason for user attrition. When we re-scale the plot with investors' final number of investments (Fig. 7, right), we find that the success rate of the last investment for leaving investors is higher than the success rate of their first investment, something we do not observe for remaining users (not shown). This observation points to a tendency of users to leave after a successful investment.

5.2 Survival analyses

The results of fitting Cox's survival models to our data are presented in Tables 1 and 2. In Models 1–4, which describe the first 5 investments (Table 1), almost all single-investment variables are significant. The investment amount and repeated investments are positively associated with attrition. These are most likely users who are trying to leave the platform. They might have been drawn to the platform by a specific campaign and do not explore further opportunities. Additionally, the more time that passes since the previous investment, the more time it takes the investor to return to the platform. Finally, if the current investment is successful and is placed late in the campaign, the investor is more likely to leave.

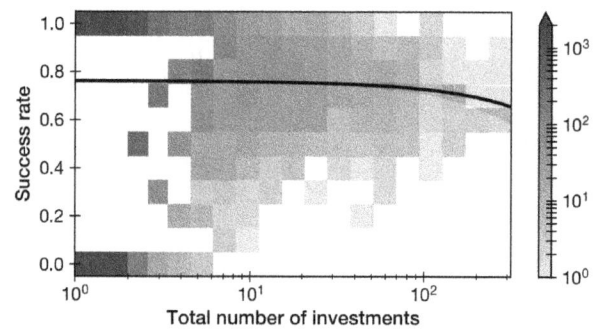

Figure 6: Distribution of success rates with respect to the total number of investments. Color denotes the number of investors in each bin and regression line shows the best linear fit to the data.

Table 1: Coefficients of Cox's proportional hazards model for novice investors, i.e., based on the first 5 investments.

	Model 1	Model 2	Model 3	Model 4
amount	0.03**	0.02*	0.03**	0.02*
	(0.01)	(0.01)	(0.01)	(0.01)
time gap	0.17***	0.16***	0.19***	0.16***
	(0.01)	(0.01)	(0.01)	(0.01)
campaign stage	−0.14***	−0.13***	−0.15***	−0.14***
	(0.01)	(0.01)	(0.01)	(0.01)
repeated inv.	0.10***	0.05**	0.08***	0.04*
	(0.01)	(0.02)	(0.02)	(0.02)
inv. success	0.09***	0.09***	0.09***	0.09***
	(0.01)	(0.01)	(0.01)	(0.01)
categ. novelty	−0.11***			0.04
	(0.02)			(0.02)
lex. novelty		−0.18***		−0.21***
		(0.02)		(0.03)
struct. novelty			−0.12***	−0.01
			(0.02)	(0.03)
observations	24, 451	24, 451	24, 451	24, 451
investors	12, 742	12, 742	12, 742	12, 742
lik. ratio	558.84	637.79	534.45	640.5

Note: $* \, p < 0.05$; $** \, p < 0.01$; $*** \, p < 0.001$.

When included in the model individually, all novelty variables are negatively associated with attrition and are highly significant (Models 1–3). This indicates that novice investors profit from choosing campaigns that are dissimilar to the ones they selected before. Our finding underscores the importance of exploration in the retention of novice investors. When portfolio distance measures are combined (Model 4), only lexical distance remains significant.

For serial investors (Models 5–8), we obtain different results. The effect of time gap on attrition remains positive and highly significant, and repeated investments become occasionally significant with the same sign. Investment amount and campaign stage,

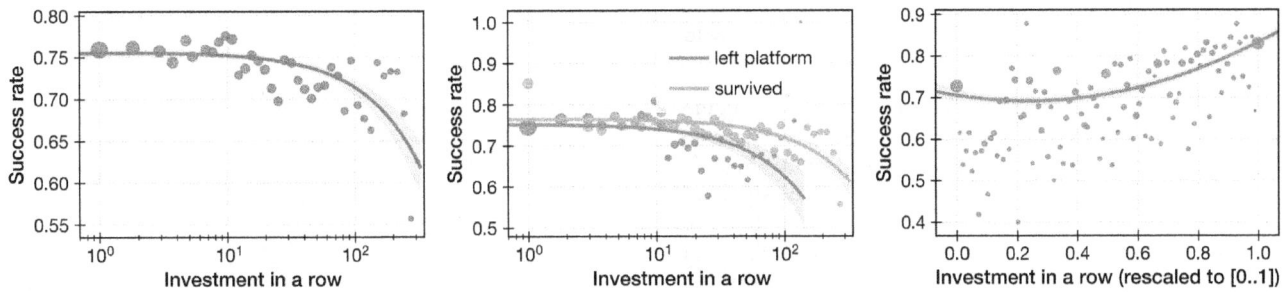

Figure 7: Success rates of subsequent investments overall (left), separated by whether investor has stayed on the platform (center), and for investors who have left (right). Solid lines represent best linear (left and center) or quadratic (right) fit to the data and shaded areas show the 95% confidence intervals. Areas of bubbles reflect the number of aggregated data points.

however, change sign: the less money invested and the later in the campaign, the more likely that this investment would be the last one. This indicates that, in order to stay, serial investors need to invest different amounts, at different campaign stages in comparison with novice investors.

With respect to diversity and novelty measures, category novelty is not significant, but category diversity is significant and positive. Users who have invested in campaigns across different categories are more likely to leave than users who have only participated in one or a few. Lexical novelty and diversity are negative and significant only in the combined Model 8: the more dissimilar campaigns users add to their portfolios, the more likely they are to continue investing. As for structural variables, they are both positive and significant. This indicates that "trail blazers" are at a higher risk of attrition. Naturally, when there is less confirmation and support through other investors who would have also recognized merit, campaigns fail to hit their target and that penalizes investors.

6 DISCUSSION

Our results provide novel explorations into the overlooked parallels between crowdfunding and peer production, suggesting new ways to improve retention of investors on equity crowdfunding platforms.

Retention of contributors. As in peer production, our results demonstrate the existence of a feedback loop in the number of contributions: with more investments, the probability to remain on the platform steadily increases [53]. In other words, users contributing to campaigns less frequently have a significantly higher rate of attrition, mimicking trends found on question answering sites [16]. Similar to the conclusions of Althoff & Leskovec [5], investors with higher success rates are more likely to remain on the platform than investors with lower success rates. However, in our data, investors become less aligned with mainstream investment decisions. We also find that investors continue investing until they make a contribution to at least one funded campaign. In line with previous research about rational herding, preexisting relations between users and campaigns are important for user retention [55]. Based on the introduced measures, we also find that both lexical and structural novelty and diversity are important factors for the retention of

Table 2: Coefficients of Cox's proportional hazards models for serial investors, i.e., based on investment 6 and higher.

	Model 5	Model 6	Model 7	Model 8
amount	−0.10*	−0.12**	−0.09*	−0.11**
	(0.04)	(0.04)	(0.04)	(0.04)
time gap	0.57***	0.55***	0.51***	0.48***
	(0.04)	(0.04)	(0.04)	(0.04)
campaign stage	0.06	0.07	0.11*	0.16**
	(0.05)	(0.05)	(0.06)	(0.06)
repeat inv.	−0.02	−0.06	0.24***	0.15*
	(0.06)	(0.06)	(0.06)	(0.07)
inv. success	0.28***	0.28***	0.32***	0.29***
	(0.06)	(0.06)	(0.06)	(0.06)
categ. novelty	−0.07			−0.00
	(0.05)			(0.06)
categ. diversity	0.10*			0.17**
	(0.04)			(0.05)
lex. novelty		−0.07		−0.13**
		(0.04)		(0.05)
lex. diversity		−0.03		−0.10**
		(0.03)		(0.03)
struct. novelty			0.37***	0.43***
			(0.07)	(0.07)
struct. diversity			0.13*	0.11*
			(0.05)	(0.05)
observations	23,648	23,648	23,648	23,648
investors	1,476	1,476	1,476	1,476
lik. ratio	254.53	255.91	299.48	332.77

Note: $* p < 0.05$; $** p < 0.01$; $*** p < 0.001$.

serial investors. Additionally, we find that all forms of investment novelty are beneficial for retention of novice investors.

Implications for equity crowdfunding. We find that there are two distinctive stages in investor participation. Novice investors should be exposed to a wider variety of campaigns, while serial investors should choose their target categories, settle in them, and monitor the activity of similar investors who might have already tried to add the new combination of campaigns to their portfolios. Our findings could be leveraged in a recommender system, similarly to the proposition of An et al. [6].

Future work. Our research reiterates the role of investors in the crowdfunding process and motivates further research into contributor retention. Specifically, our observational study could be supplemented by controlled experiments that could establish causal effects between the considered variables. Additionally, similarly comprehensive data from several other crowdfunding platforms could test differences in attrition rates as function of platform design and regulations.

7 CONCLUSION

Our research contributes to the existing body of knowledge about crowdfunding by analyzing the retention of investors in an equity crowdfunding platform. In particular, we used empirical data from a market-leading platform to build models that explain investor retention based on information about their individual investments and dissimilarities between the chosen campaigns. Our results demonstrate an exploration-exploitation trade-off in investor retention: in the initial stages, investors are more likely to stay on the platform if they are exposed to a diverse set of campaigns. For serial investors, stability in terms of category and having choices aligned with other serial investors matters. These findings provide new knowledge about how investors can improve the growth prospects of crowdfunding platforms and thereby contribute to the democratization of investment opportunities online.

ACKNOWLEDGMENTS

The authors would like to thank the equity crowdfunding company for providing the data. The authors would also like to thank Eleanor Burgess and the anonymous reviewers for their valuable comments and helpful suggestions. The work is supported by the U.S. National Science Foundation under Grant No. IIS-1755873.

REFERENCES

[1] [n. d.]. Crowdfunding Platforms (Defunct) - Wikipedia. https://en.wiki pedia.org/wiki/Category:Crowdfunding_platforms_(defunct).
[2] Ajay Agrawal, Christian Catalini, and Avi Goldfarb. 2014. Some Simple Economics of Crowdfunding. *Innovation Policy and the Economy* 14, 1 (2014), 63–97. https://doi.org/10.1086/674021
[3] Gerrit K.C. Ahlers, Douglas Cumming, Christina Günther, and Denis Schweizer. 2015. Signaling in Equity Crowdfunding. *Entrepreneurship Theory and Practice* 39, 4 (2015), 955–980. https://doi.org/10.1111/etap.12157
[4] Tim Althoff, Cristian Danescu-Niculescu-Mizil, and Dan Jurafsky. 2014. How to Ask for a Favor: A Case Study on the Success of Altruistic Requests. In *Proceedings of ICWSM'14*. 12–21.
[5] Tim Althoff and Jure Leskovec. 2015. Donor Retention in Online Crowdfunding Communities: A Case Study of DonorsChoose.Org. In *Proceedings of WWW'15*. 34–44. https://doi.org/10.1145/2736277.2741120
[6] Jisun An, Daniele Quercia, and Jon Crowcroft. 2014. Recommending Investors for Crowdfunding Projects. In *Proceedings of WWW'14*. 261–270. https://doi.org/10.1145/2566486.2568005
[7] Jaime Arguello, Brian S. Butler, Lisa Joyce, Robert Kraut, Kimberly S. Ling, and Xiaoqing Wang. 2006. Talk to Me: Foundations for Successful Individual-Group Interactions in Online Communities. In *Proceedings of CHI'06*. 959–968. https://doi.org/10.1145/1124772.1124916
[8] Gerard Beenen, Kimberly Ling, Xiaoqing Wang, Klarissa Chang, Dan Frankowski, Paul Resnick, and Robert E. Kraut. 2004. Using Social Psychology to Motivate Contributions to Online Communities. In *Proceedings of CSCW'04*. 212–221. https://doi.org/10.1145/1031607.1031642
[9] Paul Belleflamme, Thomas Lambert, and Armin Schwienbacher. 2014. Crowdfunding: Tapping the Right Crowd. *Journal of business venturing* 29, 5 (2014), 585–609. https://doi.org/10.1016/j.jbusvent.2013.07.003

[10] Thomas Bidaux. 2018. Kickstarter in 2017 - Year in Review. http://icopartners.com/2018/01/kickstarter-2017-year-review/.
[11] Salvador Briggman. 2015. Is Kickstarter's Growth Slowing Down? http://www.crowdcrux.com/kickstarters-growth-slowing/.
[12] Simla Ceyhan, Xiaolin Shi, and Jure Leskovec. 2011. Dynamics of Bidding in a P2P Lending Service: Effects of Herding and Predicting Loan Success. In *Proceedings of WWW'11*. 547–556. https://doi.org/10.1145/1963405.1963483
[13] Magdalena Cholakova and Bart Clarysse. 2015. Does the Possibility to Make Equity Investments in Crowdfunding Projects Crowd out Reward-Based Investments? *Entrepreneurship Theory and Practice* 39, 1 (2015), 145–172. https://doi.org/10.1111/etap.12139
[14] D. R. Cox. 1972. Regression Models and Life-Tables. *Journal of the Royal Statistical Society. Series B (Methodological)* 34, 2 (1972), 187–220.
[15] Martin Dittus, Giovanni Quattrone, and Licia Capra. 2016. Analysing Volunteer Engagement in Humanitarian Mapping: Building Contributor Communities at Large Scale. In *Proceedings of CSCW'16*. 108–118. https://doi.org/10.1145/2818048.2819939
[16] Gideon Dror, Dan Pelleg, Oleg Rokhlenko, and Idan Szpektor. 2012. Churn Prediction in New Users of Yahoo! Answers. In *Proceedings of WWW'12 Companion*. 829. https://doi.org/10.1145/2187980.2188207
[17] Will Drover, Matthew S. Wood, and Andrew Zacharakis. 2017. Attributes of Angel and Crowdfunded Investments as Determinants of VC Screening Decisions. *Entrepreneurship Theory and Practice* 41, 3 (2017), 323–347. https://doi.org/10.1111/etap.12207
[18] Jefferson Duarte, Stephan Siegel, and Lance Young. 2012. Trust and Credit: The Role of Appearance in Peer-to-Peer Lending. *Review of Financial Studies* 25, 8 (2012), 2455–2484. https://doi.org/10.1093/rfs/hhs071
[19] Seth Freedman and Ginger Zhe Jin. 2008. Do Social Networks Solve Information Problems for Peer-to-Peer Lending? Evidence from Prosper.Com. (2008). https://papers.ssrn.com/sol3/papers.cfm?abstract_id=1936057
[20] Elizabeth M. Gerber and Julie Hui. 2013. Crowdfunding: Motivations and Deterrents for Participation. *ACM Transactions on Computer-Human Interaction* 20, 6 (2013), 1–32. https://doi.org/10.1145/2530540
[21] Elizabeth M Gerber, Julie S Hui, and Pei-Yi Kuo. 2012. Crowdfunding: Why People Are Motivated to Post and Fund Projects on Crowdfunding Platforms. *Proceedings of CSCW'12* (2012), 10.
[22] Rob Gleasure and Joseph Feller. 2016. Emerging Technologies and the Democratisation of Financial Services: A Metatriangulation of Crowdfunding Research. *Information and Organization* 26, 4 (2016), 101–115. https://doi.org/10.1016/j.infoandorg.2016.09.001
[23] Aaron Halfaker, R. Stuart Geiger, Jonathan T. Morgan, and John Riedl. 2013. The Rise and Decline of an Open Collaboration System: How Wikipedia's Reaction to Popularity is Causing its Decline. *American Behavioral Scientist* 57, 5 (2013), 664–688. https://doi.org/10.1177/0002764212469365
[24] Aaron Halfaker, Aniket Kittur, and John Riedl. 2011. Don't Bite the Newbies: How Reverts Affect the Quantity and Quality of Wikipedia Work. In *Proceedings of WikiSym'11*. 163–172. https://doi.org/10.1145/2038558.2038585
[25] Joachim Hemer. 2011. *A Snapshot on Crowdfunding*. Technical Report R2/2011. Fraunhofer ISI, Karlsruhe.
[26] Lars Hornuf and Matthias Schmitt. 2016. Success and Failure in Equity Crowdfunding. *CESifo DICE Report* 14, 2 (2016), 16–22.
[27] Emőke-Ágnes Horvát, Jayaram Uparna, and Brian Uzzi. 2015. Network vs Market Relations: The Effect of Friends in Crowdfunding. In *Proceedings of ASONAM'15*. 226–233. https://doi.org/10.1145/2808797.2808904
[28] Emőke-Ágnes Horvát, Johannes Wachs, Rong Wang, and Anikó Hannák. 2018. The Role of Novelty in Securing Investors for Equity Crowdfunding Campaigns. In *Proceedings of HCOMP'18*. 50–59.
[29] Julie S. Hui, Michael D. Greenberg, and Elizabeth M. Gerber. 2014. Understanding the Role of Community in Crowdfunding Work. In *Proceedings of CSCW'14*. 62–74. https://doi.org/10.1145/2531602.2531715
[30] Rajkamal Iyer, Asim Ijaz Khwaja, Erzo F. P. Luttmer, and Kelly Shue. 2009. Screening in New Credit Markets: Can Individual Lenders Infer Borrower Creditworthiness in Peer-to-Peer Lending? (2009). https://doi.org/10.2139/ssrn.1570115
[31] Elisabeth Joyce and Robert E. Kraut. 2006. Predicting Continued Participation in Newsgroups. *Journal of Computer-Mediated Communication* 11, 3 (2006), 723–747. https://doi.org/10.1111/j.1083-6101.2006.00033.x
[32] Dan Jurafsky and James H Martin. 2009. *Speech and Language Processing: An Introduction to Natural Language Processing, Computational Linguistics, and Speech Recognition*. Prentice Hall, Pearson Education International.
[33] E. L. Kaplan and Paul Meier. 1958. Nonparametric Estimation from Incomplete Observations. *J. Amer. Statist. Assoc.* 53, 282 (1958), 457–481. https://doi.org/10.1080/01621459.1958.10501452
[34] Marcel Karnstedt, Matthew Rowe, Jeffrey Chan, Harith Alani, and Conor Hayes. 2011. The Effect of User Features on Churn in Social Networks. In *Proceedings of WebSci'11*. 1–8. https://doi.org/10.1145/2527031.2527051
[35] Daphne Koller and Nir Friedman. 2009. *Probabilistic Graphical Models: Principles and Techniques*. MIT press.

[36] Venkat Kuppuswamy and Barry L. Bayus. 2013. Crowdfunding Creative Ideas: The Dynamics of Project Backers in Kickstarter. *SSRN Electronic Journal* (2013). https://doi.org/10.2139/ssrn.2234765

[37] Cliff Lampe and Erik Johnston. 2005. Follow the (Slash) Dot: Effects of Feedback on New Members in an Online Community. In *Proceedings of GROUP'05*. ACM Press, 11. https://doi.org/10.1145/1099203.1099206

[38] Yan Li, Vineeth Rakesh, and Chandan K. Reddy. 2016. Project Success Prediction in Crowdfunding Environments. In *Proceedings of WSDM'16*. 247–256. https://doi.org/10.1145/2835776.2835791

[39] Mingfeng Lin, Nagpurnanand R Prabhala, and Siva Viswanathan. 2013. Judging Borrowers by the Company They Keep: Friendship Networks and Information Asymmetry in Online Peer-to-Peer Lending. *Management Science* 59, 1 (2013), 17–35. https://doi.org/10.1287/mnsc.1120.1560

[40] Caroline Lo, Justin Cheng, and Jure Leskovec. 2017. Understanding Online Collection Growth over Time: A Case Study of Pinterest. In *Proceedings of WWW'17*. 545–554. https://doi.org/10.1145/3041021.3054189

[41] Harry Markowitz. 1952. Portfolio Selection. *The Journal of Finance* 7, 1 (1952), 77–91. https://doi.org/10.1111/j.1540-6261.1952.tb01525.x

[42] Ethan Mollick. 2014. The Dynamics of Crowdfunding: An Exploratory Study. *Journal of business venturing* 29, 1 (2014), 1–16. https://doi.org/10.2139/ssrn.2088298

[43] Jagat Sastry Pudipeddi, Leman Akoglu, and Hanghang Tong. 2014. User Churn in Focused Question Answering Sites: Characterizations and Prediction. In *Proceedings of WWW'14 Companion*. 469–474. https://doi.org/10.1145/2567948.2576965

[44] PYMNTS. 2017. Crowded Crowdfunding and the Rise of Social Fundraising Fatigue. https://www.pymnts.com/platform-payments/2017/crowdfunding-social-platforms-fatigue/.

[45] Radhakrishna Rao. 1980. *Diversity and Dissimilarity Coefficients: A Unified Approach*. Technical Report 80-10. Air Force Office of Scientific Research. 38 pages. https://doi.org/10.1016/0040-5809(82)90004-1

[46] Paul Resnick, Joseph Konstan, Yan Chen, and Robert E Kraut. 2011. Starting New Online Communities. In *Building Successful Online Communities: Evidence-Based Social Design*. MIT Press, 231–280.

[47] Jeremy C. Short, David J. Ketchen, Aaron F. McKenny, Thomas H. Allison, and R. Duane Ireland. 2017. Research on Crowdfunding: Reviewing the (Very Recent) Past and Celebrating the Present. *Entrepreneurship Theory and Practice* 41, 2 (2017), 149–160. https://doi.org/10.1111/etap.12270

[48] Nathan TeBlunthuis, Aaron Shaw, and Benjamin Mako Hill. 2018. Revisiting "the Rise and Decline" in a Population of Peer Production Projects. In *Proceedings of CHI'18*. 1–7. https://doi.org/10.1145/3173574.3173929

[49] Silvio Vismara. 2018. Information Cascades among Investors in Equity Crowdfunding. *Entrepreneurship Theory and Practice* 42, 3 (2018), 467–497. https://doi.org/10.1111/etap.12261

[50] Nir Vulkan, Thomas Åstebro, and Manuel Fernandez Sierra. 2016. Equity Crowdfunding: A New Phenomena. *Journal of Business Venturing Insights* 5 (2016), 37–49. https://doi.org/10.1016/j.jbvi.2016.02.001

[51] Rick Wash. 2013. The Value of Completing Crowdfunding Projects. In *Proceedings of ICWSM'13*.

[52] Stanley Wasserman and Katherine Faust. 1994. *Social Network Analysis: Methods and Applications*. Cambridge University Press.

[53] Fang Wu, Dennis M. Wilkinson, and Bernardo A. Huberman. 2009. Feedback Loops of Attention in Peer Production. (2009). arXiv:0905.1740

[54] Jiang Yang, Xiao Wei, Mark S Ackerman, and Lada A Adamic. 2010. Activity Lifespan: An Analysis of User Survival Patterns in Online Knowledge Sharing Communities. In *Proceedings of ICWSM'10*.

[55] Juanjuan Zhang and Peng Liu. 2012. Rational Herding in Microloan Markets. *Management science* 58, 5 (2012), 892–912. https://doi.org/10.1287/mnsc.1110.1459

[56] Cai-Nicolas Ziegler, Sean M. McNee, Joseph A. Konstan, and Georg Lausen. 2005. Improving Recommendation Lists through Topic Diversification. In *Proceedings of WWW'05*. 22. https://doi.org/10.1145/1060745.1060754

[57] Randi Zuckerberg. 2013. On Kickstarter Etiquette and Crowd-Funding Fatigue. https://www.huffingtonpost.com/randi-zuckerberg/kickstarter-etiquette_b_3055863.html.

Who Let The Trolls Out? Towards Understanding State-Sponsored Trolls

Savvas Zannettou
Cyprus University of Technology
sa.zannettou@edu.cut.ac.cy

Tristan Caulfield
University College London
t.caulfield@ucl.ac.uk

William Setzer
University of Alabama at Birmingham
wjsetzer@uab.edu

Michael Sirivianos
Cyprus University of Technology
michael.sirivianos@cut.ac.cy

Gianluca Stringhini
Boston University
gian@bu.edu

Jeremy Blackburn
University of Alabama at Birmingham
blackburn@uab.edu

Abstract

Recent evidence has emerged linking coordinated campaigns by state-sponsored actors to manipulate public opinion on the Web. Campaigns revolving around major political events are enacted via mission-focused "trolls." While trolls are involved in spreading disinformation on social media, there is little understanding of how they operate, what type of content they disseminate, how their strategies evolve over time, and how they influence the Web's information ecosystem. In this paper, we begin to address this gap by analyzing 10M posts by 5.5K Twitter and Reddit users identified as Russian and Iranian state-sponsored trolls. We compare the behavior of each group of state-sponsored trolls with a focus on how their strategies change over time, the different campaigns they embark on, and differences between the trolls operated by Russia and Iran. Among other things, we find: 1) that Russian trolls were pro-Trump while Iranian trolls were anti-Trump; 2) evidence that campaigns undertaken by such actors are influenced by real-world events; and 3) that the behavior of such actors is not consistent over time, hence detection is not straightforward. Using Hawkes Processes, we quantify the influence these accounts have on pushing URLs on four platforms: Twitter, Reddit, 4chan's Politically Incorrect board (/pol/), and Gab. In general, Russian trolls were more influential and efficient in pushing URLs to all the other platforms with the exception of /pol/ where Iranians were more influential. Finally, we release our source code to ensure the reproducibility of our results and to encourage other researchers to work on understanding other emerging kinds of state-sponsored troll accounts on Twitter.

ACM Reference Format:
Savvas Zannettou, Tristan Caulfield, William Setzer, Michael Sirivianos, Gianluca Stringhini, and Jeremy Blackburn. 2019. Who Let The Trolls Out? Towards Understanding State-Sponsored Trolls. In *11th ACM Conference on Web Science (WebSci '19), June 30–July 3, 2019, Boston, MA, USA*. ACM, New York, NY, USA, 10 pages. https://doi.org/10.1145/3292522.3326016

1 Introduction

Recent political events and elections have been increasingly accompanied by reports of disinformation campaigns attributed to state-sponsored actors [14]. In particular, "troll farms," allegedly employed by Russian state agencies, have been actively commenting and posting content on social media to further the Kremlin's political agenda [23].

Despite the growing relevance of state-sponsored disinformation, the activity of accounts linked to such efforts has not been thoroughly studied. Previous work has mostly looked at campaigns run by bots [14, 19, 35]. However, automated content diffusion is only a part of the issue. In fact, recent work has shown that human actors are actually key in spreading false information on Twitter [42]. Overall, many aspects of state-sponsored disinformation remain unclear, e.g., how do state-sponsored trolls operate? What kind of content do they disseminate? How does their behavior change over time? And, more importantly, is it possible to quantify the influence they have on the overall information ecosystem on the Web?

In this paper, we aim to address these questions, by relying on two different sources of ground truth data about state-sponsored actors. First, we use 10M tweets posted by Russian and Iranian trolls between 2012 and 2018 [18]. Second, we use a list of 944 Russian trolls, identified by Reddit, and find all their posts between 2015 and 2018 [36]. We analyze the two datasets across several axes in order to understand their behavior and how it changes over time, their targets, and the content they shared. For the latter, we leverage word embeddings to understand in what context specific words/hashtags are used and shed light to the ideology of the trolls. Also, we use Hawkes Processes [29] to model the influence that the Russian and Iranian trolls had over multiple Web communities; namely, Twitter, Reddit, 4chan's Politically Incorrect board (/pol/) [20], and Gab [52].

Main findings. Our study leads to several key observations:

(1) Our influence estimation results reveal that Russian trolls were extremely influential and efficient in spreading URLs on Twitter. Also, by comparing Russian to Iranian trolls, we find that Russian trolls were more efficient and influential in spreading URLs on Twitter, Reddit, Gab, but not on /pol/.

(2) By leveraging word embeddings, we find ideological differences between Russian and Iranian trolls (e.g., Russian trolls were pro-Trump, while Iranian trolls were anti-Trump).

(3) We find evidence that the Iranian campaigns were motivated by real-world events. Specifically, campaigns against France

and Saudi Arabia coincided with real-world events that affect the relations between these countries and Iran.

(4) We observe that the behavior of trolls varies over time. We find substantial changes in the use of language and Twitter clients over time for both Russian and Iranian trolls.These insights allow us to understand the targets of the orchestrated campaigns for each type of trolls over time.

(5) Wefind that the topics of discussion vary across Web communities. For example, wefind that Russian trolls on Reddit were discussing about cryptocurrencies, while this does not apply in great extent for the Russian trolls on Twitter.

Finally, we make our source code publicly available [41] for reproducibility purposes and to encourage researchers to further work on understanding other types of state-sponsored trolls on Twitter (i.e., on January 31, 2019, Twitter released data related to trolls originating from Venezuela and Bangladesh [38]).

2 Related Work

Opinion manipulation. The practice of swaying opinion in Web communities has become a hot-button issue as malicious actors are intensifying their efforts to push their subversive agenda. Kumar et al. [27] study how users create multiple accounts, called *sockpuppets*, that actively participate in some communities with the goal to manipulate users' opinions. Mihaylov et al. [31] show that trolls can indeed manipulate users' opinions in online forums. In follow-up work, Mihaylov and Nakov [32] highlight two types of trolls: those paid to operate and those that are called out as such by other users. Then, Volkova and Bell [47] aim to predict the deletion of Twitter accounts because they are trolls, focusing on those that shared content related to the Russia-Ukraine crisis . Elyashar et al. [13] distinguish authentic discussions from campaigns to manipulate the public's opinion. Also, Steward et al. [43] focus on discussions related to the Black Lives Matter movement and how content from Russian trolls was retweeted by other users. Using community detection techniques, they unveil that Russian trolls infiltrated both left and right leaning communities, setting out to push specific narratives. Finally, Varol et al. [46] aim to identify memes (ideas) that become popular due to *coordinated* efforts.

False information on the political stage. Conover et al. [7] focus on Twitter activity during the 2010 US midterm elections and the interactions between right and left leaning communities. Ratkiewicz et al. [35] study political campaigns using controlled accounts to disseminate support for an individual or opinion.They use machine learning to detect the early stages of false political information spreading on Twitter. Wong et al. [50] aim to quantify the political leanings of users and news outlets during the 2012 US election on Twitter by considering tweeting and retweeting behavior of articles. Yang et al. [51] investigate the topics of discussions on Twitter for 51 US political persons showing that Democrats and Republicans are active in a similar way on Twitter. Le et al. [28] study 50M tweets related to the 2016 US election primaries and note the importance of three factors in political discussions on social media, namely the *party*, *policy considerations*, and *personality* of the candidates. Howard and Kollanyi [21] study the role of bots in Twitter conversations during the 2016 Brexit referendum.They find that most tweets are in favor of Brexit and that there are bots

Platform	Origin of trolls	# trolls	# trolls with tweets/posts	# of tweets/posts
Twitter	Russia	3,836	3,667	9,041,308
	Iran	770	660	1,122,936
Reddit	Russia	944	335	21,321

Table 1: Overview of Russian and Iranian trolls on Twitter and Reddit. We report the overall number of identified trolls, the trolls that had at least one tweet/post, and the overall number of tweets/posts.

with various levels of automation.Also, Hegelich and Janetzko [19] study whether bots on Twitter are used as political actors. By analyzing 1.7K bots on Twitter during the Russia-Ukraine conflict, they uncover their political agenda and show that bots exhibit various behaviors like trying to hide their identity and promoting topics through the use of hashtags.Badawy et al. [1] predict users that are likely to spread information from state-sponsored actors, while Dutt et al. [11] focus on the Facebook platform and analyze ads shared by Russian trolls in order tofind the cues that make them effective. Finally, a large body of work focuses on social bots [3, 8, 14, 15, 45] and their role in spreading political disinformation, highlighting that they can manipulate the public's opinion at a large scale.

Remarks. In contrast, our study focuses on a set of Russian and Iranian trolls that were independently identified and suspended by Twitter and Reddit. To the best of our knowledge, this constitutes thefirst effort not only to characterize a ground truth of troll accounts, but also to quantify their influence on the greater Web.

3 Troll Datasets

Twitter. On October 17, 2018, Twitter released a large dataset of Russian and Iranian troll accounts [18]. Although the exact methodology used to determine that these accounts were state-sponsored trolls is unknown, based on the most recent Department of Justice indictment [9], the dataset appears to have been constructed in a manner that we can assume essentially no false positives, while we cannot make any postulation about false negatives. Table 1 summarizes the troll dataset.

Reddit. On April 10, 2018, Reddit released a list of 944 accounts which they determined were Russian state-sponsored trolls [36]. We recover the submissions, comments, and account details for these accounts using two mechanisms: 1) Reddit dumps provided by Pushshift[33]; and 2) crawling the user pages of those accounts. Although omitted for lack of space, we note that the union of these two datasets reveals some gaps in both, likely due to a combination of subreddit moderators removing posts or the troll users themselves deleting them, which would affect the two datasets in different ways. In any case, we merge the two datasets, with Table 1 describing thefinal dataset. Note that only 335 of the accounts released by Reddit had at least one submission or comment in our dataset. We suspect the rest were simply used as dedicated voting accounts used in an effort to push (or bury) specific content.

Ethics. We only work with anonymized public data and we follow standard ethical guidelines [37].

4 Analysis

4.1 Accounts Characteristics

Account Creation. Fig. 1 plots the Russian and Iranian troll accounts creation dates on Twitter and Reddit. We observe that the majority of Russian troll accounts were created around the time of

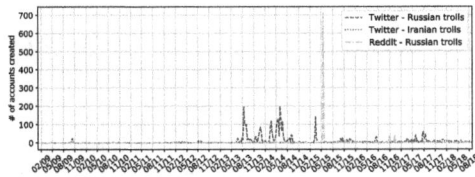

Figure 1: Number of Russian and Iranian troll accounts created per week.

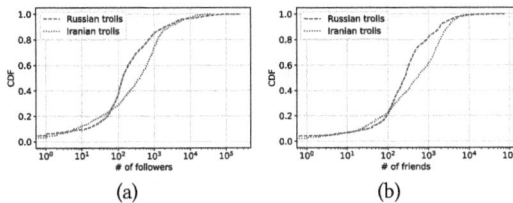

(a)   (b)

Figure 2: CDF of the number of a) followers and b) friends for the Russian and Iranian trolls on Twitter.

the Ukrainian conflict: 80% of them have an account creation date earlier than 2016. Th at said, there are some meaningful peaks in account creation during 2016 and 2017. 57 accounts were created between July 3-17, 2016, which was right before the Republican National Convention (July 18-21) where Donald Trump was named the Republican nominee for President [48] . Later, 190 accounts were created between July and August, 2017, during the run up to the infamous Unite the Right rally in Charlottesville [49]. Taken together, this might be evidence of coordinated activities aimed at manipulating users' opinions on Twitter with respect to specific events. Th is is further evidenced when examining the Russian trolls on Reddit: 75% of the accounts on Reddit were created in a single massive burst in the fi rst half of 2015. Also, there are a few smaller spikes occurring just prior to the 2016 US election. For the Iranian trolls on Twitter we observe that they are much "younger," with the larger bursts of account creation *after* the 2016 US election.

Followers/Friends. Fig. 2 plots the CDF of the number of followers and friends for both Russian and Iranian trolls. 25% of Iranian trolls had more than 1k followers, while the same applies for only 15% of the Russian trolls. In general, Iranian trolls tend to have more followers than Russian trolls (median of 392 and 132, respectively). Both Russian and Iranian trolls tend to follow a large number of users, probably in an attempt to increase their follower count via reciprocal follows. Iranian trolls have a median followers to friends ratio of 0.51, while Russian trolls have a ratio of 0.74. Th is might indicate that Iranian trolls were more effective in acquiring followers without resorting in massive followings of other users, or perhaps that they used services that offer followers for sale [44].

4.2 Temporal Analysis

We next explore troll activity over time, looking for behavioral patterns. Fig. 3(a) plots the (normalized) volume of tweets/posts shared per week in our dataset. We observe that both Russian and Iranian trolls on Twitter became active during the Ukrainian conflict. Although lower in overall volume, there an increasing trend starts around August 2016 and continues through summer of 2017. We also see three major spikes in activity by Russian trolls on Reddit. Th e fi rst is during the latter half of 2015, approximately around the time that Donald Trump announced his candidacy for

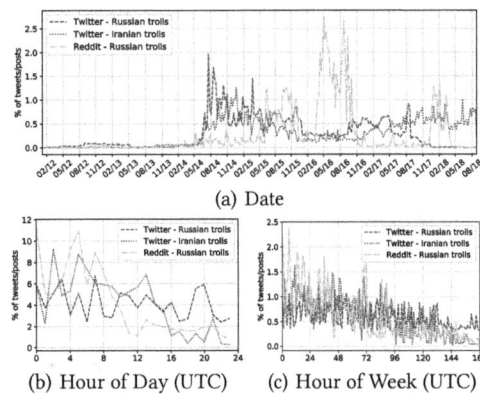

(a) Date

(b) Hour of Day (UTC)   (c) Hour of Week (UTC)

Figure 3: Temporal characteristics of tweets from Russian and Iranian trolls.

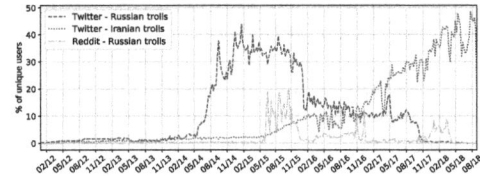

Figure 4: Percentage of unique trolls that were active per week.

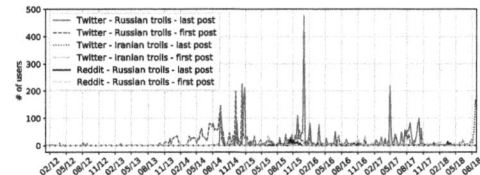

Figure 5: Number of trolls that posted their fi rst/last tweet/post for each week in our dataset.

President. Next, we see solid activity through the middle of 2016, trailing off shortly before the election. Finally, we see another burst of activity in late 2017 through early 2018, at which point the trolls were detected and had their accounts locked by Reddit.

Furthermore, we examine the hour of day and week that the trolls post. Fig. 3(b) shows that Russian trolls on Twitter are active throughout the day, while on Reddit they are particularly active during the fi rst hours of the day. Similarly, Iranian trolls on Twitter tend to be active from early morning until 13:00 UTC. When looking at the activity based on hour of the week (Fig. 3(c)), we fi nd that Russian trolls on Twitter follow a diurnal pattern with slightly less activity during Sunday. In contrast, Russian trolls on Reddit and Iranian trolls on Twitter are particularly active during the fi rst days of the week, while their activity decreases during the weekend. For Iranians this is likely due to the Iranian work week being from Sunday to Wednesday with a half day on Th ursday.

But are *all* trolls in our dataset active throughout the span of our datasets? To answer this question, we plot the percentage of unique troll accounts that are active per week in Fig. 4 from which we draw the following observations. First, the Russian troll campaign on Twitter targeting Ukraine was much more diverse in terms of accounts when compared to later campaigns. Th ere are several possible explanations for this. One explanation is that trolls learned from their Ukrainian campaign and became more efficient in later campaigns, perhaps relying on large networks of bots in their earlier

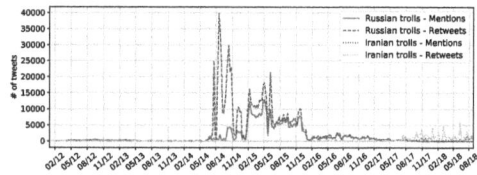

Figure 6: Number of tweets that contain mentions among Russian trolls and among Iranian trolls on Twitter.

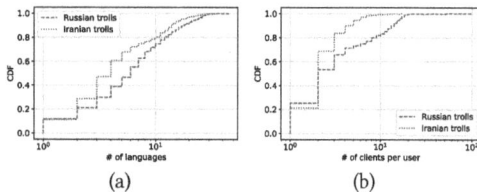

(a)   (b)

Figure 7: CDF of number of (a) languages used (b) clients used for Russian and Iranian trolls on Twitter.

campaigns which were later abandoned in favor of more focused campaigns like project Lakhta [10]. Another explanation could be that attacks on the US election might have required "better trained" trolls, perhaps those that could speak English more convincingly. The Iranians, on the other hand, seem to be slowly building their troll army over time. There is a steadily increasing number of active trolls posting per week over time. We speculate that this is due to their troll program coming online in a slow-but-steady manner, perhaps due to more effective training. Finally, on Reddit we see most Russian trolls posted irregularly, possibly performing other operations on the platform like manipulating votes on other posts.

Next, we investigate the point in time when each troll in our dataset made his first and last tweet. Fig. 5 shows the number of users that made their first/last post for each week in our dataset, which highlights when trolls became active as well as when they "retired." We see that Russian trolls on Twitter made their first posts during early 2014, almost certainly in response to the Ukrainian conflict. When looking at the last tweets of Russian trolls on Twitter we see that a substantial portion of the trolls "retired" by the end of 2015. This is likely because the Ukrainian conflict was over and Russia turned their attention to other targets (e.g., the USA, this is also aligned with the increase in the use of English language, see Section 4.3). When looking at Russian trolls on Reddit, we do not see a spike in first posts close to the time that the majority of the accounts were created (see Fig. 1). This indicates that the newly created Russian trolls on Reddit started posting gradually.

Finally, we assess whether Russian and Iranian trolls mention or retweet each other, and how this behavior occurs over time. Fig. 6 shows the number of tweets that were mentioning/retweeting other trolls' tweets. Russian trolls were particularly fond of this strategy during 2014 and 2015, while Iranian trolls started using this strategy after August, 2017. This again highlights how the strategies employed by trolls adapts and evolves to new campaigns.

4.3 Languages and Clients

Languages. First we study the languages used by trolls as it provides an indication of their targets. The language information is included in the datasets released by Twitter. Fig. 7(a) plots the CDF of the number of languages used by troll accounts. We find that

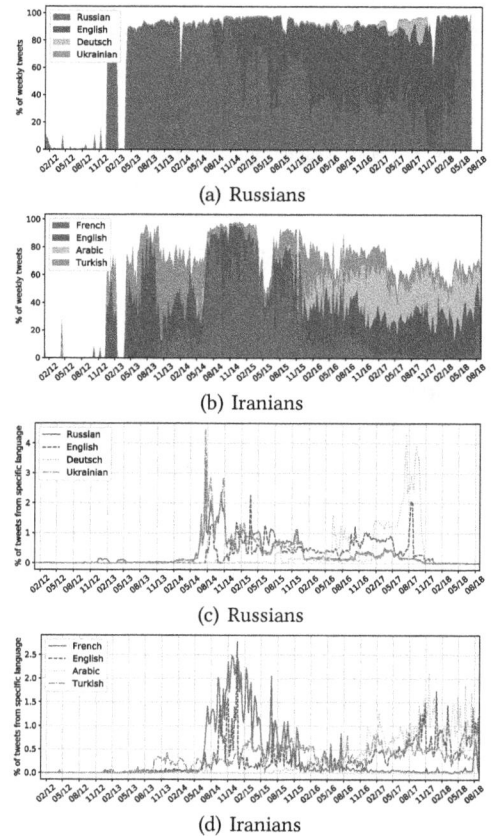

(a) Russians

(b) Iranians

(c) Russians

(d) Iranians

Figure 8: Use of the four most popular languages by Russian and Iranian trolls over time on Twitter. (a) and (b) show the percentage of weekly tweets in each language. (c) and (d) show the percentage of total tweets per language that occurred in a given week.

80% and 75% of the Russian and Iranian trolls, respectively, use more than 2 languages. Next, we note that in general, Iranian trolls tend to use fewer languages than Russian trolls. The most popular language for Russian trolls is Russian (53% of all tweets), followed by English (36%), German (1%), and Ukrainian (0.9%). For Iranian trolls we find that French is the most popular language (28% of tweets), followed by English (24%), Arabic (13%), and Turkish (8%).

Fig. 8 plots the use of different languages over time. Fig. 8(a) and Fig. 8(b) plot the percentage of tweets that were in a given language on a given week for Russian and Iranian trolls, respectively, in a stacked fashion, which lets us see how the usage of different languages changed over time relative to each other. Fig. 8(c) and Fig. 8(d) plot the language use from a different perspective: normalized to the overall number of tweets in a given language. This view gives us a better idea of how the use of each particular language changed over time. We make the following observations. First, there is a clear shift in targets based on the campaign. For example, Fig. 8(a) shows that the majority of early tweets by Russian trolls were in Russian, with English only reaching the volume of Russian language tweets in 2016. This coincides with the "retirement" of several Russian trolls on Twitter (see Fig 5). Next, we see evidence of other campaigns, for example German language tweets begin showing up in early to mid 2016, and reach their highest volume in the latter half of 2017, close to the 2017 German Federal

(a) Russians

(b) Iranians

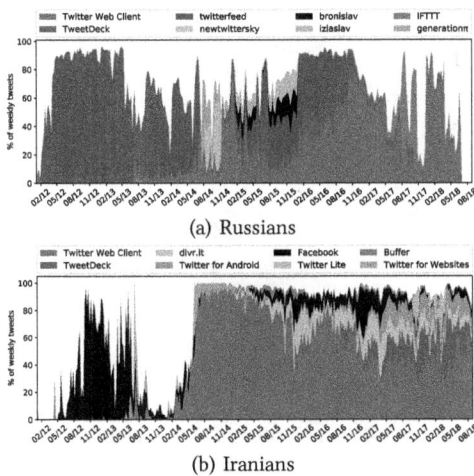

Figure 9: Use of the eight most popular clients by Russian and Iranian trolls over time on Twitter.

elections. Additionally, we note that Russian language tweets have a huge drop off in activity the last two months of 2017.

For the Iranians, we see more obvious evidence of multiple campaigns. For example, although Turkish and English are present for most of the timeline, French quickly becomes a commonly used language in the latter half of 2013, becoming the dominant language used from around May 2014 until the end of 2015. This is likely due to political events that happened during this time period. E.g., in November, 2013 France blocked a stopgap deal related to Iran's uranium enrichment program [26], leading to some fiery rhetoric from Iran's government. As tweets in French fall off, we also observe a dramatic increase in the use of Arabic in early 2016. This coincides with an attack on the Saudi embassy in Tehran [22], the primary reason the two countries ended diplomatic relations.

When looking at the language usage normalized by the total number of tweets in that language, we can get a more focused perspective. In particular, from Fig. 8(c) it becomes strikingly clear that the initial burst of Russian troll activity was targeted at Ukraine, with the majority of Ukrainian language tweets coinciding directly with the Crimean conflict [2]. From Fig. 8(d) we observe that English language tweets from Iranian trolls, while consistently present over time, have a relative peak corresponding with French language tweets, likely indicating an attempt to influence non-French speakers with respect to the campaign against French speakers.

Client usage. Finally, we analyze the clients used to post tweets. When looking at the most popular clients, we find that Russian and Iranian trolls use the main Twitter Web Client (28.5% for Russian trolls, and 62.2% for Iranian trolls). This is in contrast with what normal users use: using a random set of Twitter users, we find that mobile clients make up a large chunk of tweets (48%), followed by the TweetDeck dashboard (32%). We next look at how many different clients trolls use throughout our dataset: in Fig. 7(b), we plot the CDF of the number of clients used per user. 25% and 21% of the Russian and Iranian trolls, respectively, use only one client, while in general Russian trolls tend to use more clients than Iranians.

Fig. 9 plots the usage of clients over time in terms of weekly tweets by Russian and Iranian trolls. We observe that the Russians (Fig. 9(a)) started off with almost exclusive use of the "twitterfeed"

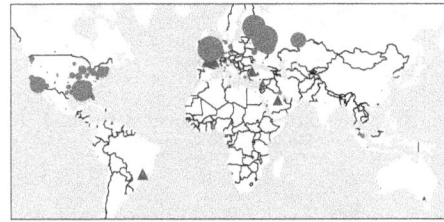

Figure 10: Distribution of reported locations for tweets by Russian (red circles) and Iranian trolls (green triangles) on Twitter.

client. Usage of this client drops off when it was shutdown in October, 2016. During the Ukrainian crisis, however, we see several new clients come into the mix. Iranians (Fig. 9(b)) started off almost exclusively using the "facebook" Twitter client, which automatically Tweets any posts you make on Facebook, indicating that Iranians likely started with a campaign on Facebook. At the beginning of 2014, we see a shift to using the Twitter Web Client, which only begins to decrease towards the end of 2015. Of particular note in Fig. 9(b) is the appearance of "dlvr.it," an automated social media manager, in the beginning of 2015. This corresponds with the creation of IUVM [24], which is a fabricated ecosystem of (fake) news outlets and social media accounts created by the Iranians, and might indicate that Iranian trolls stepped up their game around that time, starting using services that allowed them for better account orchestration to run their campaigns more effectively.

4.4 Geographical Analysis

We then study users' location, relying on the self-reported location field in their profiles, since only very few tweets have actual GPS coordinates. Note that the self-reported field is not required, and users are also able to change it whenever they like, so we look at locations for each tweet. We find that 16.8% and 20.9% of the tweets from Russian and Iranians trolls, respectively, do not include a self-reported location. To infer the geographical location from the self-reported text, we use pigeo [34], which provides geographical information (e.g., latitude, longitude, country, etc.) given the text that corresponds to a location. Specifically, we extract 626 self-reported locations for the Russian trolls and 201 locations for the Iranian trolls. Then, we use pigeo to obtain a geographical location (and its coordinates) for each text that corresponds to a location. Fig. 10 shows the locations inferred for Russian trolls (red circles) and Iranian trolls (green triangles). The size of the shapes on the map indicates the number of tweets that appear on each location. We observe that most of the tweets from Russian trolls come from Russia (34%), the USA (29%), and some from European countries, like United Kingdom (16%), Germany (0.8%), and Ukraine (0.6%). This suggests that Russian trolls may be pretending to be from certain countries, e.g., USA or United Kingdom, aiming to pose as locals and manipulate opinions. A similar pattern exists with Iranian trolls, which were active in France (26%), Brazil (9%), the USA (8%), Turkey (7%), and Saudi Arabia (7%). Also, Iranians trolls, unlike Russian trolls, did not report locations from their country, indicating that these trolls were primarily used for campaigns targeting foreign countries. Finally, we note that the location-based findings are in-line with the findings on the languages analysis (see Section 4.3), further evidencing that both Russian and Iranian trolls were specifically targeting different countries over time.

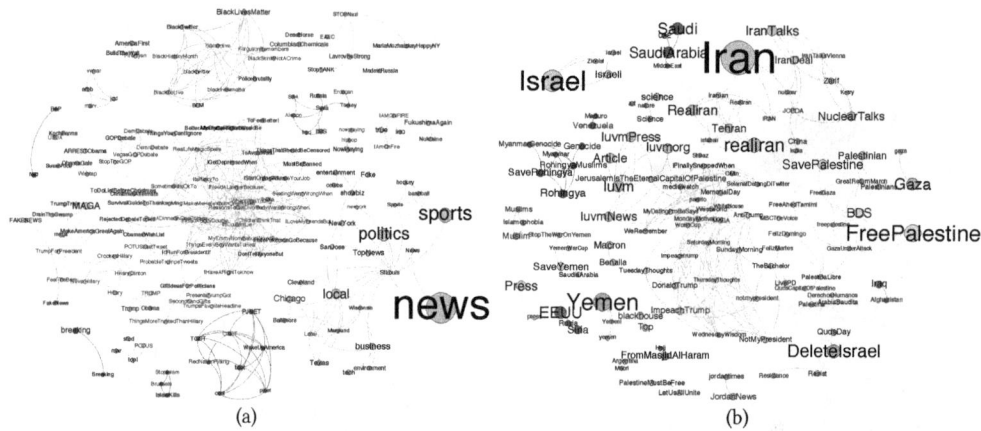

(a)   (b)

Figure 11: Visualization of the top hashtags used by a) Russian trolls and b) Iranian trolls on Twitter (see [40] and [39] for interactive versions).

Russian trolls on Twitter		Iranian trolls on Twitter	
Word	Cosine Similarity	Word	Cosine Similarity
trumparmi	0.68	impeachtrump	0.81
trumptrain	0.67	stoptrump	0.80
votetrump	0.65	fucktrump	0.79
makeamericagreatagain	0.65	trumpisamoron	0.79
draintheswamp	0.62	dumptrump	0.79
trumppenc	0.61	ivankatrump	0.77
@realdonaldtrump	0.59	theresist	0.76
wakeupamerica	0.58	trumpresign	0.76
thursdaythought	0.57	notmypresid	0.76
realdonaldtrump	0.57	worstpresidentev	0.75

Table 2: Top 10 similar words to "maga" and their respective cosine similarities (obtained from the word2vec models).

Russian trolls on Twitter				Iranian trolls on Twitter			
Hashtag	(%)	Hashtag	(%)	Hashtag	(%)	Hashtag	(%)
news	9.5%	USA	0.7%	Iran	1.8%	Palestine	0.6%
sports	3.8%	breaking	0.7%	Trump	1.4%	Syria	0.5%
politics	3.0%	TopNews	0.6%	Israel	1.1%	Saudi	0.5%
local	2.1%	BlackLivesMatter	0.6%	Yemen	0.9%	EEUU	0.5%
world	1.1%	true	0.5%	FreePalestine	0.8%	Gaza	0.5%
MAGA	1.1%	Texas	0.5%	QudsDay4Return	0.8%	SaudiArabia	0.4%
business	1.0%	NewYork	0.4%	US	0.7%	Iuvm	0.4%
Chicago	0.9%	Fukushima2015	0.4%	realiran	0.6%	InternationalQudsDay2018	0.4%
health	0.8%	quote	0.4%	ISIS	0.6%	Realiran	0.4%
love	0.7%	Foke	0.4%	DeleteIsrael	0.6%	News	0.4%

Table 3: Top 20 (English) hashtags in tweets from Russian and Iranian trolls on Twitter.

4.5   Content Analysis

Word Embeddings. Recent indictments by the US Department of Justice have indicated that troll messaging was crafted, with certain phrases and terminology designated for use in certain contexts. To get a better handle on how this was expressed, we build two word2vec models on the tweets: one for the Russian trolls and one for the Iranian trolls. To train the models, we first extract the tweets posted in English, according to the data provided by Twitter. Then, we remove stop words, perform stemming, tokenize the tweets, and keep only words that appear at least 500 and 100 times for the Russian and Iranian trolls, respectively. Table 2 shows the top 10 most similar terms to "maga" for each model. "Maga" refers to Donald Trump's slogan and means "Make America Great Again". We see a marked difference between its usage by Russian and Iranian trolls. Russian trolls are clearly pushing heavily in favor of Donald Trump, while it is the exact opposite with Iranians.

Hashtags. Next, we study the use of hashtags with a focus on the ones written in English. In Table 3, we report the top 20 English hashtags for both Russian and Iranian trolls. Trolls appear to use hashtags to disseminate news (9.5%) and politics (3.0%) related

content, but also use several that might be indicators of propaganda or controversial topics, e.g., #BlackLivesMatter. For instance, one notable example is: "WATCH: Here is a typical #BlackLivesMatter protester: 'I hope I kill all white babes!' #BatonRouge".

Fig. 11 shows a visualization of hashtag usage built from the two word2vec models. Here, we show hashgtags used in a similar context, by constructing a graph where nodes are words that correspond to hashtags from the word2vec models, and edges are weighted by the cosine distances (as produced by the word2vec models) between the hashtags. After trimming out all edges between nodes with weight less than a threshold, based on methodology from [16], we run the community detection heuristic presented in [5], and mark each community with a different color. Finally, the graph is layed out with the ForceAtlas2 algorithm [25], which considers the weight of the edges when laying out the nodes. Note that the size of the nodes is proportional to the number of times the hashtag appeared in each dataset. We first observe that, in Fig. 11(a) there is a central mass of what we consider "general audience" hashtags (see green community on the center of the graph): hashtags related to a holiday or a specific trending topic (but non-political) hashtag. In the bottom right portion of the plot we observe "general news" related categories; in particular American sports related hashtags (e.g., "baseball"). Next, we see a community of hashtags (light blue, towards the bottom left of the graph) clearly related to Trump's attacks on Hillary Clinton. The Iranian trolls again show different behavior. There is a community of hashtags related to nuclear talks (orange), a community related to Palestine (light blue), and a community that is clearly anti-Trump (pink). The central green community exposes some of the ways they pushed the IUVM fake news network by using innocuous hashtags like "#MyDatingProfileSays" as well as politically motivated ones like "#JerusalemIsTheEternalCapitalOfPalestine."

We also study *when* these hashtags are used by the trolls, finding that most of them are well distributed over time. However we find some interesting exceptions. We highlight a few of these in Fig. 12, which plots the top ten hashtags that Russian and Iranian trolls posted with substantially different rates before and after the 2016 US election. The set of hashtags was determined by examining the relative change in posting volume before and after the election (a hashtag is selected when it has a ratio of appearance of before/after or after/before election of 0.5 or less, this is the reason that we can

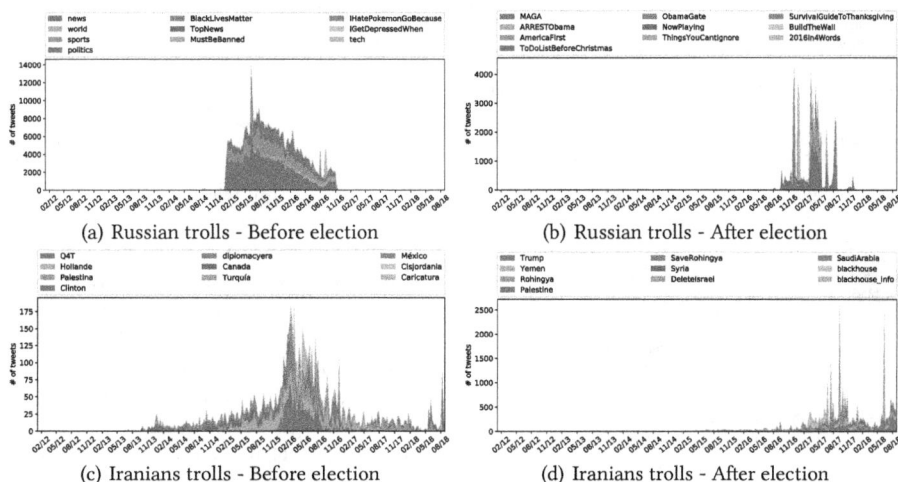

(a) Russian trolls - Before election

(b) Russian trolls - After election

(c) Iranians trolls - Before election

(d) Iranians trolls - After election

Figure 12: Top ten hashtags that appear a) c) substantially more times before the US elections rather than after the elections; and b) d) substantially more times after the elections rather than before.

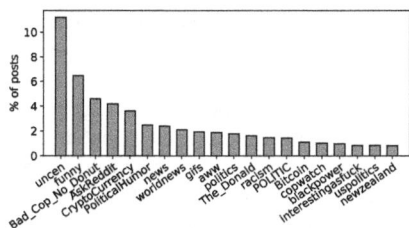

Figure 13: Top 20 subreddits that Russian trolls were active.

see hashtag usage both before and after election in Fig. 12(c)). We make several observations. First, we note that more general audience hashtags remain a staple of Russian trolls before the election (the relative decrease corresponds to the overall relative decrease in troll activity following the Crimea conflict).They also use relatively innocuous/ephemeral hashtags like #IHatePokemonGoBeacause, likely in an attempt to hide the true nature of their accounts.That said, we also see them attaching to politically divisive hashtags like #BlackLivesMatters around the time that Donald Trump won the Republican Presidential primaries in June 2016. In the ramp up to the 2016 election, we see a variety of clearly political related hashtags, with #MAGA seeing peaks starting in early 2017 (higher than any peak during the 2016 Presidential campaigns). We also see a large number of politically ephemeral hashtags attacking Obama and a campaign to push the border wall between Mexico. In addition to these politically oriented hashtags, we again see the usage of ephemeral hashtags related to holidays. #SurvivalGuideToThanksgiving in late November 2016 is interesting as it was heavily used for discussing how to deal with interacting with family members with wildly different view points on the recent election results.This hashtag was exclusively used to give trolls a vector to sow discord. When it comes to Iranian trolls, we note that, prior to the 2016 election, they share many posts with hashtags related to Hillary Clinton (see Fig. 12(c)). After the election they shift to posting negatively about Donald Trump (see Fig. 12(d)).

LDA analysis. We also use the Latent Dirichlet Allocation (LDA) model [4] to analyze tweets' semantics. We train an LDA model for each of the datasets and extract ten distinct topics with ten words,

as reported in Table 4. While both Russian and Iranian trolls tweet about politics, for Iranian trolls, this seems to be focused more on regional, and possibly even internal issues. For example, "iran" itself is a common term in several of the topics, as is "israel," "saudi," "yemen," and "isis." While both sets of trolls discuss the proxy war in Syria, the Iranian trolls have topics pertaining to Russia and Putin, while the Russian trolls do not make any mention of Iran, instead focusing on more vague political topics like gun control and racism. For Russian trolls on Reddit (see Table 5) we againfind topics related to politics and cryptocurrencies (e.g., topic 4).

Subreddits. Fig. 13 shows the top 20 subreddits that Russian trolls on Reddit exploited and their respective percentage of posts over our dataset.Th e most popular subreddit is /r/uncen (11% of posts), which is a subreddit created by a specific Russian troll and, via manual examination, appears to be mainly used to share news articles of questionable credibility. Other popular subreddits include general audience subreddits like /r/funny (6%) and /r/AskReddit (4%), likely in an attempt to hide the fact that they are state-sponsored trolls in the same way that innocuous hashtags were used on Twitter. Finally, it is worth noting that the Russian trolls were particularly active on communities related to cryptocurrencies like /r/CryptoCurrency (3.6%) and /r/Bitcoin (1%) possibly attempting to influence the prices of specific cryptocurrencies.Th is is particularly noteworthy considering cryptocurrencies have been reportedly used to launder money, evade capital controls, and perhaps used to evade sanctions [6].

URLs. We next analyze the URLs included in the tweets/posts. In Table 6, we report the top 20 domains for both Russian and Iranian trolls. Livejournal (5.4%) is the most popular domain in the Russian trolls dataset on Twitter, likely due the Ukrainian campaign. Overall, we can observe the impact of the Crimean conflict, with essentially all domains posted by the Russian trolls being Russian language or Russian oriented. One exception to Russian language sites is RT, the Russian-controlled propaganda outlet.Th e Iranian trolls similarly post more "localized" domains, for example, jordan-times, but we also see them pushing the IUVM fake news network. When it comes to Russian trolls on Reddit, wefi nd that they were posting random images through Imgur (27.6% of the URLs), likely in an attempt to

Topic	Terms (Russian trolls on Twitter)	Topic	Terms (Iranian trolls on Twitter)
1	news, showbiz, photos, baltimore, local, weekend, stocks, friday, small, fatal	1	isis,fi rst, american, young, siege, open, jihad, success, sydney, turkey
2	like, just, love, white, black, people, look, got, one, didn	2	can, people, just, don, will, know, president, putin, like, obama
3	day, will, life, today, good, best, one, usa, god, happy	3	trump, states, united, donald, racist, society, structurally, new, toonsonline, president
4	can, don, people, get, know, make, will, never, want, love	4	saudi, yemen, arabia, israel, war, isis, syria, oil, air, prince
5	trump, obama, president, politics, will, america, media, breaking, gop, video	5	iran, front, press, liberty, will, iranian, irantalks, realiran, tehran, nuclear
6	news, man, police, local, woman, year, old, killed, shooting, death	6	attack, usa, days, terrorist, cia, third, pakistan, predict, cfb, cfede
7	sports, news, game, win, words, nfl, chicago, star, new, beat	7	israeli, israel, palestinian, palestine, gaza, killed, palestinians, children, women, year
8	hillary, clinton, now, new,fb i, video, playing, russia, breaking, comey	8	state,fi re, nation, muslim, muslims, rohingya, syrian, sets, ferguson, inferno
9	news, new, politics, state, business, health, world, says, bill, court	9	syria, isis, turkish, turkey, iraq, russian, president, video, girl, erdo
10	nyc, everything, tcot, miss, break, super, via, workout, hot, soon	10	iran, saudi, isis, new, russia, war, chief, israel, arabia, peace

Table 4: Terms extracted from LDA topics of tweets from Russian and Iranian trolls on Twitter.

Topic	Terms (Russian trolls on Reddit)
1	like, also, just, sure, korea, new, crypto, tokens, north, show
2	police, cops, man, officer, video, cop, cute, shooting, year, btc
3	old, news, matter, black, lives, days, year, girl, iota, post
4	tie, great, bitcoin, ties, now, just, hodl, buy, good, like
5	media, hahaha, thank, obama, mass, rights, use, know, war, case
6	man, black, cop, white, eth, cops, american, quite, recommend, years
7	clinton, hillary, one, will, can, definitely, another, job, two, state
8	trump, will, donald, even, well, can, yeah, true, poor, country
9	like, people, don, can, just, think, time, get, want, love
10	will, can, best, right, really, one, hope, now, something, good

Table 5: LDA topics of posts from Russian trolls on Reddit.

Domain (Russian trolls on Twitter)	(%)	Domain (Iranian trolls on Twitter)	(%)	Domain (Russian trolls on Reddit)	(%)
livejournal.com	5.4%	awdnews.com	29.3%	imgur.com	27.6%
riafan.ru	5.0%	dlvr.it	7.1%	blackmattersus.com	8.3%
twitter.com	2.5%	fb.me	4.8%	donotshoot.us	3.6%
ift.tt	1.8%	whatsupic.com	4.2%	reddit.com	1.9%
ria.ru	1.8%	googl.gl	3.9%	nytimes.com	1.5%
googl.gl	1.7%	realnienovosti.com	2.1%	theguardian.com	1.4%
dlvr.it	1.5%	twitter.com	1.7%	cnn.com	1.3%
gazeta.ru	1.4%	libertyfrontpress.com	1.6%	foxnews.com	1.2%
yandex.ru	1.2%	iuvmpress.com	1.5%	youtube.com	1.2%
j.mp	1.1%	buff.ly	1.4%	washingtonpost.com	1.2%
rt.com	0.8%	7sabah.com	1.3%	huffingtonpost.com	1.1%
nevnov.ru	0.7%	bit.ly	1.2%	photographyisnotacrime.com	1.0%
youtu.be	0.6%	documentinterdit.com	1.0%	butthis.com	1.0%
vesti.ru	0.5%	facebook.com	0.8%	thefreethoughtproject.com	0.9%
kievsmi.net	0.5%	al-hadath24.com	0.7%	dailymail.co.uk	0.7%
youtube.com	0.5%	jordan-times.com	0.7%	rt.com	0.7%
kiev-news.com	0.5%	iuvmonline.com	0.6%	politico.com	0.6%
inforector.ru	0.4%	youtu.be	0.6%	reuters.com	0.6%
lenta.ru	0.4%	alwaght.com	0.6%	youtu.be	0.6%
emaidan.com.ua	0.3%	ift.tt	0.5%	nbcnews.com	0.6 %

Table 6: Top 20 domains included in tweets/posts from Russian and Iranian trolls on Twitter and Reddit.

URLs shared by	Events per community							Total	
	/pol/	Reddit	Twitter	Gab	The_Donald	Iran	Russia	Events	URLs
Russians	76,155	366,319	1,225,550	254,016	61,968	0	151,222	2,135,230	48,497
Iranians	3,274	28,812	232,898	5,763	971	19,629	0	291,347	4,692
Both	331	2,060	85,467	962	283	334	565	90,002	153

Table 7: Number of events for URLs shared by a) Russian trolls; b) Iranian trolls; and c) Both Russian and Iranian trolls.

accumulate karma score. We also note a substantial portion URLs to (fake) news sites linked with the Internet Research Agency like blackmattersus.com (8.3%) and donotshootus.us (3.6%).

5 Influence Estimation

Thus far, we have analyzed the behavior of Russian and Iranian trolls on Twitter and Reddit, with a focus on how they evolved over time. Allegedly, one of their main goals is to manipulate the opinion of other users and extend the cascade of information that they share (e.g., lure other users into posting similar content) [12]. Therefore, we now set out to determine their impact in terms of the dissemination of information on Twitter, and on the greater Web.

To assess their influence, we look at three different groups of URLs: 1) URLs shared by Russian trolls on Twitter, 2) URLs shared by Iranian trolls on Twitter, and 3) URLs shared by both Russian *and* Iranian trolls on Twitter. We thenfi nd all posts that include any of these URLs in Reddit, Twitter (from the 1% Streaming API, with posts from confirmed Russian and Iranian trolls removed), Gab, and 4chan's Politically Incorrect board (/pol/). For Reddit and Twitter our dataset spans January 2016 to October 2018, for /pol/ it spans July 2016 to October 2018, and for Gab it spans August 2016 to October 2018. We select these communities as previous work shows they play an important and influential role on the dissemination of news [54] and memes [53]. Table 7 summarizes the

number of events (i.e., URL occurrences) for each community/group of users that we consider (Russia refers to Russian trolls on Twitter, while Iran refers to Iranian trolls on Twitter). Note that we decouple The_Donald from the rest of Reddit as previous work showed that it is quite efficient in pushing information in other communities [53]. From the table we observe: 1) Twitter has the largest number of events in all groups of URLs mainly because it is the largest community and 2) Gab has a considerably large number of events; more than /pol/ andThe _Donald, which are bigger communities.

For each unique URL, wefi t a Hawkes Processes model [29, 30], which allows us to estimate the strength of connections between each of these communities in terms of how likely an event – the URL being posted by either trolls or normal users to a particular platform – is to cause subsequent events in each of the groups. We fit each Hawkes model using the methodology presented by [53]. In a nutshell, byfitt ing a Hawkes model we obtain all the necessary parameters that allow us to assess the root cause of each event (i.e., the community that is "responsible" for the creation of the event). By aggregating the root causes for all events we are able to measure the influence and efficiency of each Web community we considered. We show our results with two different metrics: 1) the absolute influence, or percentage of events on the destination community caused by events on the source community and 2) the influence relative to size, which shows the number of events caused on the destination platform as a percent of the number of events on the *source* platform.Th e latter can also be interpreted as a measure of how *efficient* a community is in pushing URLs to other communities.

Fig. 14 reports our results for the absolute influence for each group of URLs. When looking at the influence for the URLs from Russian trolls on Twitter (Fig. 14(a)), wefi nd that Russian trolls were particularly influential to Gab (1.9%), the rest of Twitter (1.29%), and /pol/ (1.08%). When looking at the communities that influenced the Russian trolls wefi nd the rest of Twitter (7%) and Reddit (4%). By looking at URLs shared by Iranian trolls on Twitter (Fig. 14(b)), wefi nd that Iranian trolls were most successful in pushing URLs toThe _Donald (1.52%), the rest of Reddit (1.39%), and Gab (1.05%). This is ironic consideringThe _Donald and Gab's zealous pro-Trump leanings and the Iranian trolls' clear anti-Trump leanings [17, 52]. Similarly to Russian trolls, the Iranian trolls were most influenced by Reddit (5.6%) and the rest of Twitter (4.6%). When looking at the URLs posted by both Russian and Iranian trolls wefi nd that, overall, the Russian trolls were more influential in spreading URLs to the other Web communities with the exception of /pol/.

But how do these results change when we normalize the influence with respect to the number of events that each community creates (i.e., efficiency)? Fig. 15 shows the efficiency for each pair of communities/groups of users. For URLs shared by Russian trolls (Fig. 15(a)) wefi nd that Russian trolls were particularly efficient in spreading the URLs to Twitter (10.4%)—which is not a surprise,

Figure 14 (a) Russian trolls

Source \ Destination	/pol/	Reddit	Twitter	Gab	T_D	Russia
/pol/	60.99%	1.45%	0.33%	1.47%	4.85%	0.28%
Reddit	14.84%	85.32%	4.30%	13.76%	18.74%	4.00%
Twitter	5.48%	5.19%	91.33%	9.57%	6.65%	7.08%
Gab	5.72%	2.51%	1.29%	63.45%	7.09%	2.01%
T_D	11.89%	4.55%	1.46%	9.85%	61.61%	1.14%
Russia	1.08%	0.97%	1.29%	1.90%	1.06%	85.49%

Figure 14 (b) Iranian trolls

Source \ Destination	/pol/	Reddit	Twitter	Gab	T_D	Iran
/pol/	77.38%	0.48%	0.18%	2.23%	2.06%	0.11%
Reddit	13.64%	91.07%	2.00%	21.62%	25.12%	5.66%
Twitter	4.15%	5.39%	97.24%	13.72%	10.94%	4.61%
Gab	2.70%	1.05%	0.16%	57.41%	7.68%	0.32%
T_D	1.14%	0.62%	0.12%	3.97%	52.68%	0.05%
Iran	0.98%	1.39%	0.31%	1.05%	1.52%	89.25%

Figure 14 (c) Both

Source \ Destination	/pol/	Reddit	Twitter	Gab	T_D	Iran	Russia
/pol/	57.97%	1.21%	0.15%	0.45%	1.91%	1.39%	0.09%
Reddit	27.35%	90.06%	1.83%	24.69%	27.85%	4.99%	6.12%
Twitter	3.87%	3.81%	97.67%	6.18%	8.13%	53.31%	13.59%
Gab	6.61%	1.96%	0.15%	65.23%	15.01%	0.84%	1.46%
T_D	3.90%	2.34%	0.09%	2.76%	46.75%	0.34%	0.61%
Iran	0.27%	0.13%	0.03%	0.15%	0.00%	37.35%	0.88%
Russia	0.03%	0.50%	0.07%	0.53%	0.35%	1.78%	77.26%

(a) Russian trolls   (b) Iranian trolls   (c) Both

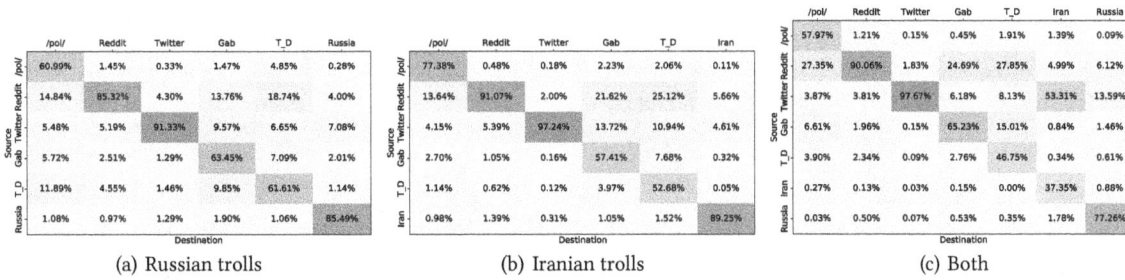

Figure 14: Percent of *destination* events caused by the source community to the destination community for URLs shared by a) Russian trolls; b) Iranian trolls; and c) both Russian and Iranian trolls.

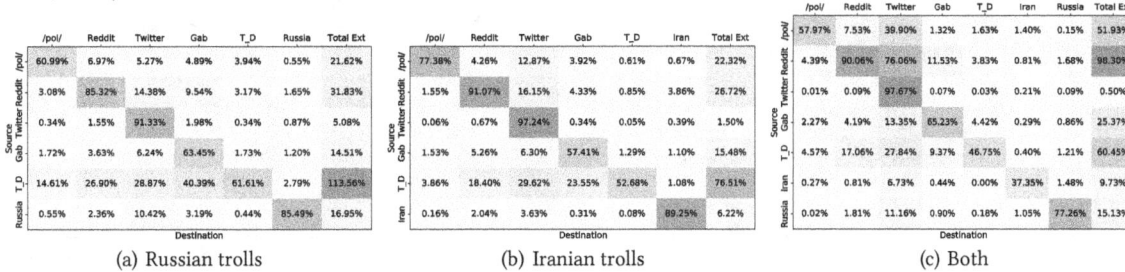

Figure 15 (a) Russian trolls

Source \ Destination	/pol/	Reddit	Twitter	Gab	T_D	Russia	Total Ext
/pol/	60.99%	6.97%	5.27%	4.89%	3.94%	0.55%	21.62%
Reddit	3.08%	85.32%	14.38%	9.54%	3.17%	1.65%	31.83%
Twitter	0.34%	1.55%	91.33%	1.98%	0.34%	0.87%	5.08%
Gab	1.72%	3.63%	6.24%	63.45%	1.73%	1.20%	14.51%
T_D	14.61%	26.90%	28.87%	40.39%	61.61%	2.79%	113.56%
Russia	0.55%	2.36%	10.42%	3.19%	0.44%	85.49%	16.95%

Figure 15 (b) Iranian trolls

Source \ Destination	/pol/	Reddit	Twitter	Gab	T_D	Iran	Total Ext
/pol/	77.38%	4.26%	12.87%	3.92%	0.61%	0.67%	22.32%
Reddit	1.55%	91.07%	16.15%	4.33%	0.85%	3.86%	26.72%
Twitter	0.06%	0.67%	97.24%	0.34%	0.05%	0.39%	1.50%
Gab	1.53%	5.26%	6.30%	57.41%	1.29%	1.10%	15.48%
T_D	3.86%	18.40%	29.62%	23.55%	52.68%	1.08%	76.51%
Iran	0.16%	2.04%	3.63%	0.31%	0.08%	89.25%	6.22%

Figure 15 (c) Both

Source \ Destination	/pol/	Reddit	Twitter	Gab	T_D	Iran	Russia	Total Ext
/pol/	57.97%	7.53%	39.90%	1.32%	1.63%	1.40%	0.15%	51.93%
Reddit	4.39%	90.06%	76.06%	11.53%	3.83%	0.81%	1.68%	98.30%
Twitter	0.01%	0.09%	97.67%	0.07%	0.03%	0.21%	0.09%	0.50%
Gab	2.27%	4.19%	13.35%	65.23%	4.42%	0.29%	0.86%	25.37%
T_D	4.57%	17.06%	27.84%	9.37%	46.75%	0.40%	1.21%	60.45%
Iran	0.27%	0.81%	6.73%	0.44%	0.00%	37.35%	1.48%	9.73%
Russia	0.02%	1.81%	11.16%	0.90%	0.18%	1.05%	77.26%	15.13%

(a) Russian trolls   (b) Iranian trolls   (c) Both

Figure 15: Influence from source to destination community, normalized by the number of events in the *source* community for URLs shared by a) Russian trolls; b) Iranian trolls; and c) Both Russian and Iranian trolls. We also include the total external influence of each community.

given that the accounts operate directly on this platform—and Gab (3.19%). For the URLs shared by Iranian trolls, we again observe that they were most efficient in pushing the URLs to Twitter (3.6%), and the rest of Reddit (2.04%). Also, it is worth noting that in both groups of URLs The _Donald had the highest external influence to the other platforms. This highlights that The _Donald is an impactful actor in the information ecosystem and is quite possibly exploited by trolls as a vector to push specific information to other communities. Finally, when looking at the URLs shared by both groups of trolls, we find that Russian trolls were more efficient (greater impact relative to the number of URLs posted) at spreading URLs in all the communities except /pol/, where Iranians were more efficient.

6 Discussion & Conclusion

In this paper, we analyzed the behavior and evolution of Russian and Iranian trolls on Twitter and Reddit during several years. We shed light to the campaigns of each group of trolls, we examined how their behavior evolved over time, and what content they disseminated. Furthermore, we find some interesting differences between the trolls depending on their origin and the platform from which they operate. For instance, for the latter, we find discussions related to cryptocurrencies only on Reddit by Russian trolls, while for the former we find that Russian trolls were pro-Trump and Iranian trolls anti-Trump. Also, we quantify the influence that these state-sponsored trolls had on several Web communities (Twitter, Reddit, /pol/, and Gab), showing that Russian trolls were more efficient and influential in spreading URLs on other Web communities than Iranian trolls, with the exception of /pol/. In addition, we make our source code publicly available [41], which helps in reproducing our results and it is a leap towards understanding other types of trolls.

Our findings have serious implications for society at large. First, our analysis shows that while troll accounts use peculiar tactics and talking points to further their agendas, these are not completely disjoint from regular users, and therefore developing automated systems to identify and block such accounts remains an open challenge. Second, our results also indicate that automated systems to detect trolls are likely to be difficult to realize: trolls change their behavior over time, and thus even a classifier that works perfectly on one campaign might not catch future campaigns. Third, and perhaps most worrying, we find that state-sponsored trolls have a meaningful amount of influence on fringe communities like The_Donald, 4chan's /pol/, and Gab, and that the topics pushed by the trolls resonate strongly with these communities. This might be due to users on these communities that sympathize with the views the trolls aim to share (i.e., "useful idiots" [55]) or to unidentified state-sponsored actors. In either case, considering recent tragic events like the Tree of Life Synagogue shootings, perpetrated by a Gab user seemingly influenced by content posted there, the potential for mass societal upheaval cannot be overstated. Due to this, we implore the research community, as well as governments and non-government organizations to expend whatever resources are at their disposal to develop technology and policy to address this new, and effective, form of digital warfare.

Acknowledgments. This project has received funding from the EU's Horizon 2020 Research and Innovation program under the Marie Skłodowska Curie ENCASE project (GA No. 691025) and under the CYBERSECURITY CONCORDIA project (GA No. 830927).

References

[1] A. Badawy, K. Lerman, and E. Ferrara. Who Falls for Online Political Manipulation? *ArXiv 1808.03281*, 2018.

[2] BBC. Ukraine crisis: Timeline. https://www.bbc.com/news/world-middle-east-26248275, 2014.

[3] A. Bessi and E. Ferrara. Social bots distort the 2016 US Presidential election online discussion. *First Monday*, 2016.

[4] D. M. Blei, A. Y. Ng, and M. I. Jordan. Latent dirichlet allocation. *JMLR*, 2003.

[5] V. D. Blondel, J.-L. Guillaume, R. Lambiotte, and E. Lefebvre. Fast unfolding of communities in large networks. *Journal of statistical*

mechanics: theory and experiment, 2008.

[6] Bloomberg. IRS Cops Are Scouring Crypto Accounts to Build Tax Evasion Cases. https://www.bloomberg.com/news/articles/2018-02-08/irs-cops-scouring-crypto-accounts-to-build-tax-evasion-cases, 2018.

[7] M. Conover, J. Ratkiewicz, M. R. Francisco, B. Gonalves, F. Menczer, and A. Flammini. Political Polarization on Twitter. In *ICWSM*, 2011.

[8] C. A. Davis, O. Varol, E. Ferrara, A. Flammini, and F. Menczer. BotOrNot: A System to Evaluate Social Bots. In *WWW*, 2016.

[9] Department of Justice. Grand Jury Indicts 12 Russian Intelligence Officers for Hacking Offenses Related to the 2016 Election. https://goo.gl/SCyrm6, 2018.

[10] Department of Justice. Russian National Charged with Interfering in U.S. Political System. https://goo.gl/HAUehB, 2018.

[11] R. Dutt, A. Deb, and E. Ferrara. 'Senator, We Sell Ads': Analysis of the 2016 Russian Facebook Ads Campaign. *ArXiv 1809.10158*, 2018.

[12] S. Earle. TROLLS, BOTS AND FAKE NEWS. https://goo.gl/nz7E8r, 2017.

[13] A. Elyashar, J. Bendahan, and R. Puzis. Is the Online Discussion Manipulated?Qu antifying the Online Discussion Authenticity within Online Social Media. *CoRR*, abs/1708.02763, 2017.

[14] E. Ferrara. Disinformation and social bot operations in the run up to the 2017 French presidential election. *ArXiv 1707.00086*, 2017.

[15] E. Ferrara, O. Varol, C. A. Davis, F. Menczer, and A. Flammini.Th e rise of social bots. *Commun. ACM*, 2016.

[16] J. Finkelstein, S. Zannettou, B. Bradlyn, and J. Blackburn. AQuantitative Approach to Understanding Online Antisemitism. *ArXiv 1809.01644*, 2018.

[17] C. Flores-Saviaga, B. C. Keegan, and S. Savage. Mobilizing the trump train: Understanding collective action in a political trolling community. In *ICWSM '18*, 2018.

[18] V. Gadde and Y. Roth. Enabling further research of information operations on Twitter. https://blog.twitter.com/official/en_us/topics/company/2018/enabling-further-research-of-information-operations-on-twitter.html, 2018.

[19] S. Hegelich and D. Janetzko. Are Social Bots on Twitter Political Actors? Empirical Evidence from a Ukrainian Social Botnet. In *ICWSM*, 2016.

[20] G. E. Hine, J. Onaolapo, E. De Cristofaro, N. Kourtellis, I. Leontiadis, R. Samaras, G. Stringhini, and J. Blackburn. Kek, Cucks, and God Emperor Trump: A Measurement Study of 4chan's Politically Incorrect Forum and Its Effects on the Web. In *ICWSM '17*, 2017.

[21] P. N. Howard and B. Kollanyi. Bots, #StrongerIn, and #Brexit: Computational Propaganda during the UK-EU Referendum. *CoRR*, abs/1606.06356, 2016.

[22] B. Hubbard. Iranian Protesters Ransack Saudi Embassy After Execution of Shiite Cleric. https://nyti.ms/1P7RKUZ, 2016.

[23] Independent. St Petersburg 'troll farm' had 90 dedicated staff working to influence US election campaign. https://ind.pn/2yuCQdy, 2017.

[24] IUVM. IUVM's About page. https://iuvm.org/en/about/, 2015.

[25] M. Jacomy, T. Venturini, S. Heymann, and M. Bastian. ForceAtlas2, a continuous graph layout algorithm for handy network visualization designed for the Gephi software. *PloS one*, 2014.

[26] Julian Borger and Saeed Dehghan. Geneva talks end without deal on Iran's nuclear programme. https://www.theguardian.com/world/2013/nov/10/iran-nuclear-deal-stalls-reactor-plutonium-france, 2013.

[27] S. Kumar, J. Cheng, J. Leskovec, and V. S. Subrahmanian. An Army of Me: Sockpuppets in Online Discussion Communities. In *WWW*, 2017.

[28] H. T. Le, G. R. Boynton, Y. Mejova, Z. Shafiq, and P. Srinivasan. RevisitingTh e American Voter on Twitter. In *CHI*, 2017.

[29] S. W. Linderman and R. P. Adams. Discovering Latent Network Structure in Point Process Data. In *ICML*, 2014.

[30] S. W. Linderman and R. P. Adams. Scalable Bayesian Inference for Excitatory Point Process Networks. *ArXiv 1507.03228*, 2015.

[31] T. Mihaylov, G. Georgiev, and P. Nakov. Finding Opinion Manipulation Trolls in News Community Forums. In *CoNLL*, 2015.

[32] T. Mihaylov and P. Nakov. Hunting for Troll Comments in News Community Forums. In *ACL*, 2016.

[33] Pushshift. Reddit Dumps. https://files.pushshift.io/reddit/, 2018.

[34] A. Rahimi, T. Cohn, and T. Baldwin. pigeo: A python geotagging tool. *ACL*, 2016.

[35] J. Ratkiewicz, M. Conover, M. R. Meiss, B. Gonalves, A. Flammini, and F. Menczer. Detecting and Tracking Political Abuse in Social Media. In *ICWSM*, 2011.

[36] Reddit. Reddit's 2017 transparency report and suspect accountfindings. https://www.reddit.com/r/announcements/comments/8bb85p/reddits_2017_transparency_report_and_suspect/, 2018.

[37] C. M. Rivers and B. L. Lewis. Ethical research standards in a world of big data. *F1000Research*, 3, 2014.

[38] Y. Roth. Empowering further research of potential information operations. https://blog.twitter.com/en_us/topics/company/2019/further_research_information_operations.html, 2019.

[39] S. Zannettou et al. Interactive Graph of Hashtags - Iranian trolls on Twitter. https://trollspaper2018.github.io/trollspaper.github.io/index.html#iranians_graph.gexf, 2018.

[40] S. Zannettou et al. Interactive Graph of Hashtags - Russian trolls on Twitter. https://trollspaper2018.github.io/trollspaper.github.io/index.html#russians_graph.gexf, 2018.

[41] S. Zannettou et al. Source code. https://github.com/zsavvas/trolls_analysis, 2019.

[42] K. Starbird. Examining the Alternative Media EcosystemTh rough the Production of Alternative Narratives of Mass Shooting Events on Twitter. In *ICWSM*, 2017.

[43] L. Steward, A. Arif, and K. Starbird. Examining Trolls and Polarization with a Retweet Network. In *MIS2*, 2018.

[44] G. Stringhini, G. Wang, M. Egele, C. Kruegel, G. Vigna, H. Zheng, and B. Y. Zhao. Follow the green: growth and dynamics in twitter follower markets. In *IMC*, 2013.

[45] O. Varol, E. Ferrara, C. A. Davis, F. Menczer, and A. Flammini. Online Human-Bot Interactions: Detection, Estimation, and Characterization. In *ICWSM*, 2017.

[46] O. Varol, E. Ferrara, F. Menczer, and A. Flammini. Early detection of promoted campaigns on social media. *EPJ Data Science*, 2017.

[47] S. Volkova and E. Bell. Account Deletion Prediction on RuNet: A Case Study of Suspicious Twitter Accounts Active During the Russian-Ukrainian Crisis. In *NAACL-HLT*, 2016.

[48] Wikipedia. Republican National Convention. https://en.wikipedia.org/wiki/2016_Republican_National_Convention, 2016.

[49] Wikipedia. Unite the Right rally. https://en.wikipedia.org/wiki/Unite_the_Right_rally, 2017.

[50] F. M. F. Wong, C.-W. Tan, S. Sen, and M. Chiang.Qu antifying Political Leaning from Tweets and Retweets. In *ICWSM*, 2013.

[51] X. Yang, B.-C. Chen, M. Maity, and E. Ferrara. Social Politics: Agenda Setting and Political Communication on Social Media. In *SocInfo*, 2016.

[52] S. Zannettou, B. Bradlyn, E. De Cristofaro, M. Sirivianos, G. Stringhini, H. Kwak, and J. Blackburn. What is Gab? A Bastion of Free Speech or an Alt-Right Echo Chamber? In *WWW Companion*, 2018.

[53] S. Zannettou, T. Caulfield, J. Blackburn, E. De Cristofaro, M. Sirivianos, G. Stringhini, and G. Suarez-Tangil. On the Origins of Memes by Means of Fringe Web Communities. In *IMC*, 2018.

[54] S. Zannettou, T. Caulfield, E. De Cristofaro, N. Kourtellis, I. Leontiadis, M. Sirivianos, G. Stringhini, and J. Blackburn.Th e Web Centipede: Understanding How Web Communities Influence Each OtherTh rough the Lens of Mainstream and Alternative News Sources. In *IMC*, 2017.

[55] S. Zannettou, M. Sirivianos, J. Blackburn, and N. Kourtellis.Th e web of false information: Rumors, fake news, hoaxes, clickbait, and various other shenanigans. *arXiv preprint arXiv:1804.03461*, 2018.

The Six Relative Advantages in Multichannel Retail for Three-Dimensional Virtual Worlds and Two-Dimensional Websites

Alex Zarifis

Business School, University of Mannheim

Mannheim

azarifis@mail.uni-mannheim.de

ABSTRACT

Multichannel retail is now prevalent with retailers and consumers utilizing a number of channels in parallel or in some instances in an interconnected way. There is a degree of understanding on what each channel can offer but the Relative Advantage of each channel in relation to the others is less understood. This research evaluates the Relative Advantage between the three channels of three-dimensional Virtual Worlds, two-dimensional websites and offline retail stores. The consumer's preferences across the three channels were distinguished across six Relative Advantages. The three channels were then compared across the six Relative Advantages identified. Participants showed a preference for offline and 2D in most situations apart from enjoyment, entertainment, sociable shopping, the ability to reinvent yourself, convenience and institutional trust where the Virtual Worlds were preferred.

CCS CONCEPTS

• Applied computing → Electronic commerce → Online shopping

KEYWORDS: Virtual Worlds; Virtual reality; e-Commerce; Multichannel; Trust.

ACM Reference format:

Alex Zarifis. 2019. The Six Relative Advantages in Multichannel Retail for Three-Dimensional Virtual Worlds and Two-Dimensional Websites. In 11th ACM Conference on Web Science (WebSci '19), June 30-July 3, 2019, Boston, MA, USA. ACM, New York, NY, USA, 10 pages. https://doi.org/10.1145/3292522.3326038

WebSci '19, June 30–July 3, 2019, Boston, MA, USA
© 2019 Association for Computing Machinery.
ACM ISBN 978-1-4503-6202-3/19/06…$15.00
https://doi.org/10.1145/3292522.3326038

1 Introduction

Three retail channels are compared to evaluate their respective Relative Advantage (RA). The first channel is the physical 'brick and mortar' retail stores, the second channel is websites that are navigated and display information in two dimensions (2D websites) and the third channel is three dimensional online environments known as Virtual Worlds (VW) [2]. The foundation of this research is Choudhury and Karahanna [5] that compared two channels. Six RAs were identified that capture the consumer's preferences across the three channels. These six RAs serve as categories of the many specific issues that influence the consumer's behavior across multiple channels. Purchases in 2D websites are increasing, potentially surpassing physical 'brick and mortar' shops in a few years. Physical, offline, shops still play a significant role and have advantages that 2D websites find difficult to replicate.

VWs have been with us for over a decade but their potential to replicate features of the physical world has not been fully realized. Their adoption is at low levels and it has not yet reached a majority in the diffusion of innovation curve [27]. There is however renewed interest in this area [6] with major technology companies starting to drive adoption [33, 36], in a number of ways including augmented reality and virtual reality headsets. It is therefore useful to explore their advantages in relation to each other, as perceived by the consumer. A better understanding of the relationship between the three channels will support organizations in developing their multichannel or omni-channel approach by integrating the channels in a way that fully utilizes their RAs. It will also support the optimization of the many information systems that enable these processes.

The first objective to explore was whether a RA of VWs compared to the 2D navigation Internet, was the aspects of offline retail that it includes, that do not exist in the 2D websites. The second objective explores the same topic between the other pair: Could a RA of VWs over offline be aspects of 2D navigation websites that it includes that are not included in the offline retail environment? The third objective was to explore whether the consumer changes the way a VW is used across the different stages of the purchase. Furthermore, if the consumer changed the way a VW is used across the steps of purchasing process, it would be useful to evaluate whether the significance of the dimensions identified in Choudhury and Karahanna [5] also changed. The fourth objective was to evaluate whether the consumer's usage of VW is different for simple and complex products. The consumer approaches a purchase of a simple and a complex product differently and it is therefore possible that some characteristics of VWs are valued differently in these different processes. The fifth objective was to explore whether VWs may have the RA of a higher degree of institutional trust compared to the 2D websites. The sixth objective was to explore whether a RA of VWs compared to 2D websites for e-commerce is that they offer a higher level of enjoyment. The next section offers an overview of the literature on multichannel retail followed by the methodology applied in this research. The fourth section covers the qualitative findings and identifies the issues to be further evaluated. The fifth section presents the quantitative findings followed by the discussion and finally the conclusion.

2 Multichannel Retail

Evaluating multichannel retail presents a formidable challenge as it requires an understanding of a number different channels, each with their particular characteristics. These channels can be utilized independently or in an interrelated way. Identifying the aspects that are important to the consumer and the aspects that give each channel unique characteristics and a RA is far from simple.

Most research in this area compares traditional brick and mortar shops and 2D websites. The third channel that should be incorporated into the discussion on multichannel retail is VWs. VWs are online three dimensional physically persistent environments where people inhabit and interact with other people, software agents and objects through the use of avatars [18]. Social virtual worlds are VWs where there are no specific goals, sometimes referred to as 'free-form' [13]. There are VWs that focus on gaming but may have a social element such as massively multiplayer online role-playing games (MMORPG) and others that focus on the social element but may include games such as Twinity, There.com, Second Life and Active Worlds. People use VWs for several reasons, some of which are different to why they use 2D websites. Five themes that motivate people to use VWs are self-therapy, instant pleasures, avoiding social norms, self-expression and the appeal of exploration and novelty [25]. Shen and Eder [32] identified perceived usefulness and perceived enjoyment as strong reasons for VW adoption. In addition to these issues that seem to be more significant in VWs there is also the importance of virtual communities [18]. Gammoh et al.[9] found evidence that avatars as sales agents can enhance the consumer's satisfaction with the retailer, make the consumer perceive the product more positively and be more willing to make a purchase. Products can be physical such as shoes [8], virtual products such as virtual shoes, services that are utilized within the VWs such as hosting a conference and services utilized outside of them such as financial services. The sale of virtual products can be referred to as v-commerce [16]. Cagnina and Poian [3] identified the use and limitations of the previous models and attempted to capture the value drivers of

each VW and how this impacted the value chain of the business models within them. Therefore, Cagnina and Poian [3] can be used to bring the literature of business models and that of VW together.

An important consideration for the consumer online, whether in two or three-dimensional environments is trust. Trust is central to collaborating online [4] and particularly business to consumer (B2C) e-commerce where a financial transaction is made [31]. It can be separated into two constituent parts, 'trusting beliefs' and 'trusting intention' [22]. Institutional trust is the consumer's trust in the structures in place that aid a positive outcome for the consumer [22]. For B2C, Pavlou and Gefen [26] consider it to be the buyers perception that effective third-party institutional mechanisms are in place to support a successful transaction. These third-party mechanisms vary from 'weak' ones like transaction facilitation offered by PayPal, certification such as Verisign and enabling feedback to 'strong' ones such as the legal framework [26]. The mechanisms that form an institution can also be formal or informal. An example of a formal institution is the legal framework already mentioned, and examples of informal institutions are communities or group ties [35]. Some constituent parts of institutional trust may be common across all channels such as paying with a specific bank card while others are specific to a channel such as the consumer protection in the specific country where a brick and mortar shop is situated.

One of the behaviors identified in multichannel research is seeking information on one channel and purchasing on another [14]. This has been referred to as cross channel free-riding and is clearly not to the benefit of the organization not rewarded [14]. There is evidence that the consumer prefers different channels for different actions [30]. Searching for information about a purchase such as price, and making a purchase have a distinct nature and different channels may be preferred for each stage [28]. Each channel is found to have different utility [28]. Additional distinctions are examining and picking up the product that is being considered for purchase [12].

Discussion of multiple channels inevitably leads to strategy and business models [21]. Synergies are often sought out when making strategic decisions but in multichannel research they are a priority [20] and must be based on the customer's perspective [29]. With all strategic decisions resource allocation is important and this is also the case in multichannel strategies [28]. Once each channel's advantages and disadvantages are understood to a high granularity an organization can move on to assessing which ones to use and how to use them together. For example, would an organization want to offer the same functionality and products through different channels or would the organization adapt their presence to each channel to utilize that channel's characteristics? Making these choices correctly can lead to an increase in customers and market share [12].

The multitude of strategies can be perceived on a spectrum from entirely homogenized channels to entirely separate offerings. Some examples of multi-channel strategies with less homogenized offerings are: Offering more products on the online shop than the bricks and mortar shop because a company may have one warehouse that serves the online orders and that makes stock management easier and cheaper than in the case of the bricks and mortar shops. A second strategy is to offer more specialized products that sell in smaller numbers online [12]. If the strategy would involve having a different approach to each channel, then it may also incorporate an attempt to migrate from one channel to the other [7].

A more homogenous strategy would attempt to achieve a more coherent user experience, brand, product and service offering across channels regardless of their particularities [37]. This coherence also reduces the risk of causing confusion and dissatisfaction with different prices, products, services [19] and return policies including returns to different channels. It is clear that choosing the right point on the spectrum between homogenization and an entirely different offering is important and far from straight forward [38]. This process has been referred to as harmonization of the channel and has been considered to be a craft [39]. The word craft was chosen to suggest this is not a problem for which one solution can be offered. A number of decisions, supported with a greater understanding of the nuances involved is necessary. Choudhury and Karahanna [5] explored the RA of two electronic channels as illustrated in figure 1. Based on the theory of diffusion of innovation [27] it assumes that a new channel, as with any innovation, must offer a RA in order for consumers to adopt it. Adding VWs and exploring the RA of three retail channels would be useful.

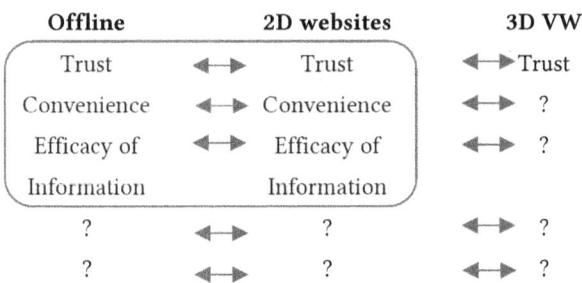

Figure 1. Current literature and research gap

3 Method

3.1 Data Collection

The epistemological approach was critical realist using mixed methods. The qualitative stage involved four focus groups with three to five participants and twelve interviews. This was followed by a quantitative survey that was used to evaluate the consumer's beliefs on the six objectives identified in the qualitative stage. The survey allowed the participant to rank the three channels according to preference on a number of questions related to the six objectives. The questions emerged from the initial qualitative focus groups and interviews. Each question evaluated an important aspect of each RA and together with other related questions they evaluated the RA itself. The survey applied random sampling with a target of 550 participants. A message was sent from within the VW including a link to the

survey to potential participants that met the requirements set. The first requirement was for a minimum of six months of experience in a VW. This could be verified by checking when an avatar was created. The second requirement was for the participants to have made a purchase of a product in the VW. This was checked in question 10 and 97% stated that they had made a purchase in a VW. The participants were also paid and vetted so they were considered responsible and knowledgeable.

Fifty-nine questions were compulsory closed ended questions where the participant answered by selecting a point on a scale that represented their views. This was done mostly by using a slider enabling the data to fit a Gaussian scale better than if they had to choose from a limited set of options such as a five-point Likert scale. The first 12 questions enquired about the participant and their use of VWs. The next eight covered how long, how intensely and for what purpose the participant used VWs. After those demographic questions the first section of the main survey had ten questions covering different aspects related to purchasing products from VWs. The feedback was given on a scale from 'strongly disagree', minus fifty, to 'strongly agree', fifty, using a slider. The second section of the main part of the survey focused on the RA of the three channels by directly comparing them. There were fourteen questions about different aspects of purchasing a product. Under each question there were three sliders one for each retail channel, offline, online 2D website and VWs. The participant chose the degree to which they agreed with the statement in the context of each channel. The scale was the same as in section one. Surveys that were not completed were taken out of the data set. Therefore 616 participants can be considered to have taken the survey.

3.2 Data Analysis

The qualitative data was analyzed using open coding to clarify the issues that would be further evaluated in the quantitative part. The quantitative analysis was on the responses to the survey. The analysis would compare the participants' preferences between three retail channels across several issues identified in the extensive exploratory phase that involved focus groups and interviews. The mean, the standard of deviation and ANOVA were used to explore the data. For the second and third sections the analysis compared between pairs of channels using the t-test to evaluate whether the channels are perceived differently or not, in relation to the given issue.

The second section had three scales for each question. Each scale allowed the participant to show how much they valued one of the three channels for the given issue. The three scales were divided into three pairs to carry out the two-group t-test. This is both statistically and logically sound. The purpose is to identify an RA of one channel compared to another. The pairs were the first scale with the second, the first with the third and the second with the third. The two means that resulted from the responses to the two scales were compared using the t-test to determine whether those means represented different populations. The third section had two scales for each question only comparing two channels. An example of a possible insight from this analysis could be that customers find buying offline more convenient than buying from a VW.

To limit the risk of type one errors the p-value for this research was set at 0.025. When multiple t-tests are used together the risk of type one errors increases. The analysis in this research implements the t-tests separately comparing two channels. If the t-tests in this section were combined to create an order of preference for all three channels the risk of type one errors would increase. The two-sample paired t-test was applied to questions 24 to 37. The one sample t-test was applied to questions 38 to 59. The analysis provides several findings beyond the t-test value. The key results of the t-test are presented and discussed in the next two sections.

4 Findings

4.1 The Relative Advantages of Multichannel Retail to be Evaluated

The RAs identified from the literature were explored and clarified by initial qualitative analysis before they were verified with quantitative analysis. VWs incorporate some characteristics from the two other channels, but they offer a unique combination of these characteristics. The first two RAs of VWs for retail are based on the characteristics they draw from the 2D websites and the 'bricks and mortar' environment.

The first objective explored in the qualitative stage was the RA of VWs compared to 2D websites. Many participants' responses were on this objective and subcategories were identified. These were primarily enjoyment, which will be discussed in more detail in the sixth RA to be explored; social shopping, a richer and more emotive 3D environment, 'face to face', the shopping assistant and to a lesser extent location. In relation to which channel was most emotive, all participants considered the offline environment to be first, which is understandable, and most considered VWs to be more emotive than 2D websites. Therefore, based on the exploratory qualitative stage:

RA1: A relative advantage of VWs to 2D websites for e-commerce, are aspects of the offline environment that VWs include, that do not exist in the 2D websites.

The second objective in the qualitative stage, explored what the RA of VWs is, compared to offline. The nature of the information systems of VWs operating on the Internet guarantees that they will contain some of the Internet's benefits compared to offline. It is therefore not controversial since it is based directly on the functionality of the information systems and not its implementation by a specific organization. When the issue in question results from a specific implementation of a technology the user's perceptions can have greater variety. The data collected on this issue is nevertheless useful as it illustrates this point with empirical evidence and more detail. There was extensive interest from the participants on this issue and four related subcategories of this RA were identified as convenience, speed, 24-7 availability and global reach. Therefore, based on the qualitative stage:

RA2: A relative advantage of VWs for the consumer compared to offline, are 2D website features that VWs include, that are not included in the offline environment.

Choudhury and Karahanna [5] suggested that a consumer would adopt a new channel only if it was perceived to offer an advantage over existing channels. This argument is built on the theory of diffusion of innovation [27]. The third objective states that the 'variable' dimension of RA, will vary across the 'variable' of the stages of the purchasing process. If a consumer prefers a different channel for each stage, this would be a strong indication of the benefit of organizations utilizing a multichannel approach. There was evidence that participants had specific beliefs on each channel's advantages and disadvantages and chose the one they would use for a given task accordingly. They often did not have an outright favorite for all the stages. What could be considered surprising is that no participant chose the same channel for all the stages. Therefore, based on the qualitative stage:

RA3: The consumer may vary their intended usage of VWs across the different stages of the purchase process because the significance of the dimensions may vary across those stages.

The nature of gathering information and making a purchase for a complex product in comparison to a simple product is different [5]. Because of this, the nature of how the technology and the other aspects of a channel are used, is different. Therefore, the variables to compare are consumer usage, product complexity and purchase stages. Most participants considered the 2D websites and offline as best for simple products. For complex products, overall, most participants considered the offline environment as the best. Some considered two dimensional websites better because you can get more information in a shorter space of time. The other reason given for preferring 2D was that they preferred to absorb information in text form. There is of course information in two-dimensional text in VWs but there is usually some navigation involved before it can be viewed. Those that considered VWs to be better than 2D websites, believed this primarily because of the shopping assistant. Therefore, based on the qualitative stage:

RA4: The consumer's usage of VWs may be different for simple and complex products.

Based on the literature on trust as it has been defined and modelled by McKnight et al. [23], institutional trust has been identified as the most relevant aspect of trust. This is in agreement with Choudhury and Karahanna [5]. When considering institutional trust for VWs it is important to clarify what the institution being considered is. For this study the institution is a specific VW, as opposed to VWs in general. There were four types of responses from the participants. The most common was to group the two dimensional and three dimensional together because the underlying technology was the same. There were some that trusted two dimensional websites, the most common reason being that it was more established, and you can read feedback.

Channel	RA 1 Aspects of offline	RA 2 Aspects of 2D websites	RA 3 Vary usage as RA of issues varies	RA 4 Usage different for simple and complex products	RA 5 Level of institutional trust	RA 6 Level of enjoyment
Offline	High or low?	High or low?	High or low?	High or low?	High or low?	High or low?
2D website	High or low?	High or low?	High or low?	High or low?	High or low?	High or low?
VW	High or low?	High or low?	High or low?	High or low?	High or low?	High or low?

(Consumer → table → Product or Service)

Figure 2. Three channels and the six Relative Advantages

There were some that preferred the VWs sighting the payment system. Some highlighted how a VW as an 'institution' influenced 'institutional trust' positively. Some participants noted that the owner of the VW informs users about retailers that are not trustworthy. This illustrates how the fact that a VW is owned by a specific organization has the potential to cultivate greater

institutional trust. That logic was the reason why this issue was identified as an area to investigate. Therefore, based on the qualitative stage:

RA5: VWs may have the RA of more institutional trust for the consumer compared to the 2D websites.

One additional RA of VWs for retail is that of enjoyment and entertainment. Some participants linked the higher level of enjoyment directly to the 3D environment. Therefore, based on the qualitative stage the sixth RA was put forward. Figure 2 illustrates how insight into the six RAs can support the multi-channel strategy.

RA6: A RA for the consumer of VWs to 2D websites, is that they offer a higher level of enjoyment.

Based on the qualitative findings it is also suggested that the model put forward by Choudhury and Karahanna [5] could be extended. The model by Choudhury and Karahanna [5], stated that for the purpose of assessing the RA of a channel for retail: Relative Advantage (RA) = Convenience + Trust + Efficacy of Information. The initial qualitative stage supported the importance of Convenience and Efficacy of Information. There was evidence supporting that institutional trust (RA5) was the type of trust most relevant and that enjoyment (RA6) was important in the choice of channel, particularly when the consumer considered VWs along with 2D websites and offline stores. The findings of RA1, 2, 3 and 4 are also relevant to the model. Therefore, the model can be extended as follows: RA of a

retail channel = Convenience + Institutional Trust + Efficacy of Information + Enjoyment + RA of unique channel functionalities + RA in specific purchasing stage + RA for specific type of product.

4.2 Channel Comparison on Key Variables

4.2.1 Analysis of Questions Comparing Three Channels. A summary of the results of this section is provided in table 1. The first question for which the two-sample dependent t-test was applied was question 24. For question 24 the vignette stated: 'I would learn all I need to know about a product from this channel', when comparing offline (M=66.46, SE=0.97) to online 2D (M=71.18, SE=0.85), t(607)=-4.49, p<0.025, r=0.18, participants on average considered the latter to be preferable out of the two to

a significant degree. When comparing offline to VWs, (M=70.84, SE=0.93), t(607)=-3.52, p<0.025, r=0.14, participants on average considered the latter to be significantly preferable. When comparing online 2D to VWs, t(607)=0.34, p>0.025, r=0.01, participants on average considered the former to

be preferable. All three however had a very small effect size accounting for less than 1% of total variance. The questions from 24 to 37 had this format and were evaluated in this way.

4.2.2 Analysis of Questions Comparing Two Channels. Questions 38 to 59 also discussed RA like the ones above. However, each question only covered two channels. The 38th question will be used as an example to illustrate this: '... I can do it with my friends, so it is more sociable'. If the average response was at 'neither' this would indicate that there was no difference in the perception of the two channels. A positive average would indicate a preference to VWs. The results are summarized in table 2 and discussed in the following section.

Question	Comparing offline to online 2D							Comparing offline to VWs					Comparing online 2D to VW		
	Offline		Online 2D					VW							
	M	SE	M	SE	t(607)	p	r	M	SE	t(607)	p	r	t(607)	p	r
24. I would learn all I need to know about a product from this channel	66.46	0.97	71.18	0.85	-4.49	<0.025	0.18	70.84	0.93	-3.52	<0.025	0.14	0.34	>0.025	0.01
25. I would find it convenient to purchase car insurance from this channel	65.76	1.14	58.87	1.17	4.89	<0.025	0.19	40.30	1.23	15.17	<0.025	0.52	14.90	<0.025	0.52
26. I would find it convenient to purchase a book from this channel	73.87	1.04	74.70	0.98	-0.96	>0.025	0.04	57.82	1.18	11.84	<0.025	0.43	13.72	<0.025	0.49
27. I would feel confident purchasing the car insurance policy through this channel	71.42	1.15	57.18	1.20	11.04	<0.025	0.41	37.36	1.21	20.57	<0.025	0.64	15.99	<0.025	0.54
28. I would feel confident purchasing a book through this channel	78.80	1.04	75.13	1.01	4.62	<0.025	0.18	57.35	1.24	15.39	<0.025	0.53	14.42	<0.025	0.51
29. To determine what I want to buy I like using this channel	72.17	0.98	78.43	0.90	-6.92	<0.025	0.27	60.11	1.13	8.53	<0.025	0.33	14.03	<0.025	0.49
30. To purchase a product I like using this channel	76.63	0.95	75.81	0.92	0.91	>0.025	0.04	59.27	1.11	12.23	<0.025	0.44	13.14	<0.025	0.47
31. For after sales service I like using this channel	72.74	1.01	68.87	0.98	3.25	<0.025	0.13	57.25	1.11	10.14	<0.025	0.38	9.06	<0.025	0.35
32. For a simple product that is always the same and does not involve contracts and negotiation such as a book I would use this channel	75.93	0.99	77.21	0.96	-1.44	>0.025	0.06	63.09	1.11	9.41	<0.025	0.36	12.47	<0.025	0.45
33. For a complex product that is not always the same and may need negotiation such as car insurance, I would prefer this channel	77.10	1.07	57.57	1.15	13.72	<0.025	0.49	41.71	1.19	20.68	<0.025	0.64	12.90	<0.025	0.46
34. I enjoy shopping on this channel for its own sake, not just for the items I may have purchased	70.25	1.01	69.85	0.96	0.41	>0.025	0.02	69.85	1.05	0.75	>0.025	0.03	0.52	>0.025	0.02
35. This channel doesn't just sell products-it entertains me	62.17	1.02	64.88	0.96	-2.85	<0.025	0.11	76.61	0.97	-11.87	<0.025	0.43	-11.05	<0.025	0.41
36. Shopping from this channel "gets me away from it all"	58.10	1.00	61.00	0.93	-2.71	<0.025	0.11	69.50	1.05	-9.35	<0.025	0.35	-8.49	<0.025	0.33
37. I find this channel is not as good as other channels at informing me about the product	50.80	1.06	48.79	1.01	1.80	>0.025	0.07	56.82	0.99	-4.21	<0.025	0.17	-6.67	<0.025	0.26

Table 1. Comparing the channels in section 2 of the survey

4.3 The Six Relative Advantages of Multichannel Retail

4.3.1 Findings Related to the First Relative Advantage. The first objective stated 'a RA of VWs compared to the 2D websites is aspects of offline retail VWs include that do not exist in the 2D websites'. The issues relevant to this were primarily enjoyment, social shopping, a richer and more emotive 3D environment, 'face to face' and the shopping assistant, and to a lesser extent location. There was no preference for the shopping assistant in comparison to offline on average. There was however significant support that the salesperson was a RA compared to 2D websites. The findings therefore suggest that, on average, the aspect from offline of having a shopping assistant, is a RA of VWs compared to the 2D internet. For navigation, in the quantitative section, VWs were considered to have an advantage over both offline and 2D websites. It was considered a greater RA when compared to 2D

websites. Therefore, the findings suggest that on average the aspect that offline and VWs share, compared to navigation in 2D is a RA of VWs compared to 2D websites. For sociability, the quantitative analysis indicated a significant preference for VWs over 2D websites with a medium effect. Therefore, it can be concluded that sociable shopping is a RA of shopping in VWs in comparison to 2D navigation websites. In terms of location VWs were preferred significantly but with a medium effect to 2D websites. In the context of B2C e-commerce in VWs location refers to how the virtual shops are located in the virtual environment. This could be considered the virtual geography. The last relevant issue was the ability to reinvent yourself and be

someone you are not. The results showed that the ability to reinvent oneself was a RA of shopping in VWs compared to 2D websites. Overall, the findings related to this RA support the increased sense of involvement VWs can offer in comparison to 2D websites [1].

4.3.2 Findings Related to the Second Relative Advantage. The second objective stated, 'a relative advantage of VWs for the consumer compared to offline, are 2D website features that VWs include, that are not included in the offline environment'. These were found to be convenience, speed, twenty-four-seven availability, global reach and additional information such as reviews and profiles. The participants were asked to compare the channels based on which one would enable them to learn all they wanted to know about the product. 2D navigation websites were preferred to both other channels. VWs were preferred to offline by some margin. This was an indication that features that VWs and 2D websites included, but were missing from offline, were considered a RA. In terms of convenience, VWs were at a disadvantage to both other channels.

Issues that arose in the qualitative section such as twenty-four-hour availability, access from the convenience of your home, on average were outweighed by the other conveniences of offline and inconveniences of VWs.

4.3.3 Findings Related to the Third Relative Advantage. The third objective stated 'consumers vary their intended usage of VWs across the different stages of the purchase process because the significance of the dimensions of RA may vary across those stages'. The foundation that this research builds on [5], concluded that there was evidence of three stages in the purchasing process.

Question	Compared to VW	M	Stand. error mean	t-statistic	P (sign.)	R (e.s.)
38. A relative advantage of shopping in a VW compared to offline shopping is that I can do it with my friends, so it is more sociable	offline	61.19	1.08	9.44	<0.025	0.36
39. A relative advantage of shopping in a VW compared to a 2D navigation website is that I can do it with my friends, so it is more sociable	2D web	66.80	1.01	15.55	<0.025	0.53
40. A relative advantage of shopping in a VW compared to offline shopping is that there is a shop assistant and you can talk to them 'face to face''	offline	50.67	1.08	-0.31	>0.025	0.01
41. A relative advantage of shopping in a VW compared to a 2D navigation website is that there is a shop assistant and you can talk to them 'face to face''	2D web	60.38	1.02	9.21	<0.025	0.35
42. A relative advantage of shopping in a VW compared to offline shopping is the convenience and speed	offline	69.03	0.95	19.10	<0.025	0.61
43. A relative advantage of shopping in a VW compared to a 2D navigation website is the convenience and speed	2D web	59.02	1.02	7.85	<0.025	0.30
44. A relative advantage of shopping in a VW is the payment method which is easy to use compared to offline shopping	offline	58.68	1.15	6.68	<0.025	0.26
45. A relative advantage of shopping in a VW is the payment method which is easy to use compared to a 2D navigation website	2D web	59.97	1.09	8.20	<0.025	0.32
46. A relative advantage of shopping in a VW is the payment method which is safe compared to offline shopping	offline	50.17	1.13	-7.31	>0.025	0.03
47. A relative advantage of shopping in a VW is the payment method which is safe compared to a 2D navigation website	2D web	56.06	1.05	4.81	<0.025	0.19
48. A relative advantage of shopping in a VW is the after sales service which is good compared to offline shopping	offline	52.91	1.01	1.90	>0.025	0.08
49. A relative advantage of shopping in a VW is the after sales service which is good compared to a 2D navigation website	2D web	56.79	0.94	6.16	<0.025	0.24
50. A relative advantage of shopping in a VW compared to offline shopping is the way you navigate the world as it enhances the browsing experience	offline	66.08	1.00	15.15	<0.025	0.52
51. A relative advantage of shopping in a VW compared to a 2D navigation website is the way you navigate the world as it enhances the browsing experience	2D web	70.10	0.91	21.00	<0.025	0.65
52. A relative advantage of shopping in a VW compared to offline shopping is that good stores are located near each other	offline	59.16	1.02	8.00	<0.025	0.31
53. A relative advantage of shopping in a VW compared to a 2D navigation website is that good stores are located near each other	2D web	57.58	1.01	6.53	<0.025	0.26
54. A relative advantage of shopping in a VW compared to offline shopping is that I can become something I am not in real life, reinvent myself	offline	74.00	0.99	23.29	<0.025	0.69
55. A relative advantage of shopping in a VW compared to a 2D navigation website is that I can become something I am not in real life, reinvent myself	2D web	69.21	1.05	17.35	<0.025	0.58
56. A relative advantage of shopping in a VW compared to offline shopping is that I can purchase virtual versions of real-life products at a much lower price	offline	68.13	1.01	17.05	<0.025	0.57
57. A relative advantage of shopping in a VW compared to a 2D navigation website is that I can purchase virtual versions of real-life products at a much lower price	2D web	66.55	1.00	15.59	<0.025	0.54
58. A relative advantage of shopping in a VW compared to offline shopping is that I can purchase virtual product that are instantly delivered	offline	75.68	0.95	26.00	<0.025	0.73
59. A relative advantage of shopping in a VW compared to a 2D navigation website is that I can purchase virtual product that are instantly delivered	2D web	75.55	0.92	26.60	<0.025	0.73

Table 2. Comparing VWs to the other channels in the survey

For requirements determination, the quantitative analysis found that 2D was more popular than both the other channels. Offline was preferred to VWs. 2D navigation websites are ideal for searching and viewing information on products, while offline products can be physically handled, so this result can be considered logical. For the purchasing stage, offline and 2D websites had no significant difference between them with VWs having a significant difference and effect. Therefore, VWs were at a disadvantage for both stages. The change in the preference, for offline and 2D websites, between this stage and the one preceding it, illustrates the distinct perceptions of the value of each channel. For the last stage, after sales service, offline was more popular than both other channels and 2D websites were more popular than VWs. The margin however between VWs and the other channels was much smaller for this stage. This is an indication that VWs are more useful for after sales service than the other two stages.

4.3.4 Findings Related to the Fourth Relative Advantage. The fourth issue stated that a consumer's purchasing behavior in VWs is different for simple and complex products. The quantitative analysis for complex products found that offline was by far preferable to the other two channels. 2D websites were preferred to VWs. These were the most typical results. All the differences were significant with a large effect. From the participants that considered VWs to be better than 2D websites, most valued the ability to negotiate with a real person such as the shop assistant. They found this to be especially beneficial for complex products.

When comparing complex products, specifically in terms of which they would feel more confident with, offline was preferred to the other two channels and 2D websites were preferred to VWs. The differences were very large and the average for VWs was negative, meaning on average participants would not use it to purchase such products. This is particularly insightful. The theory this research uses posits that a channel needs a RA to be chosen. If the consumer's perception of a VW for complex products is negative, then the channel is inherently ill-suited for this regardless of the alternative channels.

For simple products, offline and 2D websites were close together and both were preferred to VWs by some margin. For the similar question focusing on confidence, the results were similar with a small but significant preference for offline over both other channels. VWs were not preferred in either comparison, as in complex products, but for simple products however the average was positive. This means on average the consumer would use it, but other channels are preferred. These nuances in the perceived value of a channel are the type of findings this research was designed to identify. If an organization was not pursuing standardization/homogenization strategy and pursuing either a differentiation or harmonization strategy, avoiding or de-emphasizing simple products in VWs may help optimize the multichannel retail results.

4.3.5 Findings Related to the Fifth Relative Advantage. The fifth objective stated that VWs may have the RA of more institutional trust compared to 2D websites. In the responses to the question asking whether the payment method was safer offline or in VWs there was no significant difference. The response showed no preference between the two channels; they were almost perfectly matched. When making the comparison with 2D websites, VWs were preferred significantly, with small to medium effect. This is an indication that VWs have the RA of higher institutional trust compared to 2D websites. There were indications from the qualitative analysis that consumers valued the role of VWs as an institution in relation to trust but it was not expected to be as trustworthy as offline. A feature that was especially appreciated was the buyer not receiving your banking details. Other participants valued the role of the VWs administration in identifying and warning about specific threats. These were indications that a VW as an institution influenced institutional trust positively.

As posited by Choudhury and Karahanna [5] trust can be used to compare retail channels. Therefore, a better understanding of trust improves the ability to make those comparisons. Secondly a better understanding of trust can be used to improve the value a retailer offers to the consumer. This can be achieved by adapting the business model to optimize value [10] or in some other way. Lastly the institution, in this case the VW can take measures to improve the level of institutional trust the consumer perceives

[26]. The findings also support the role of institutional trust in relation to the RA of retail channels model: RA of retail channel = Convenience + Institutional Trust + Efficacy of Information + Enjoyment + RA of unique channel functionalities + RA in specific purchasing stage + RA for specific type of product.

4.3.6 Findings Related to the Sixth Relative Advantage. For some of the questions comparing the channels in relation to enjoyment, there was no significant preference between the three. The average of the results was very high, indicating that participants considered all channels to offer significant enjoyment. For the related questions focusing on the entertainment value, VWs were valued far more than the other two channels. 2D websites were preferred to offline. This was one of the few issues where VWs were preferred to both channels and this indicates that entertainment is a RA of VWs. This is in agreement with other research into VWs that found entertainment to be one of the main strengths [15]. In a second related question about escapism, it was also valued as a RA of VWs over both the other channels. This is also in agreement with other research [17]. While enjoyment was not considered a RA, the support showed this was a strength of VWs.

This is also in agreement with other research that identify enjoyment as a strength of VWs [11]. The findings also support the role of enjoyment, including entertainment, in relation to the RA of retail channels model: RA of retail channel = Convenience + Institutional Trust + Efficacy of Information + Enjoyment + RA of unique channel functionalities + RA in specific purchasing stage + RA for specific type of product.

4.3.7 The Six Relative Advantages of Multichannel Retail Matrix. The findings related to the six RAs are summarized in figure 3. The figure illustrates how the consumer's preference varies across the three channels and six RAs. An organization pursuing a multichannel strategy can adapt their offerings in each channel to fully utilize these different preferences as outlined in this figure. While the initial exploratory qualitative stages showed that VWs were the last preference of the three channels on most issues discussed, framing the comparison with the six RAs shows how they can have a useful and complementary role to play in multichannel retail.

5   Discussion

The terms multichannel and omni-channel are widely used for e-commerce by retail practitioners, the financial sector and the business media. While they are often used inconsistently and without an agreed definition they are sometimes presented as a 'silver bullet' that can optimize and futureproof an organization. Knowing the general principle behind multi or omni-channel retail however is of limited benefit. The reality is that understanding the consumer, who is at the same time a technology user [34], is an ongoing challenge that necessitates further exploration.

In parallel, the consumer is exploring the new options constantly being made available to them across all the stages of the purchasing process. The results of this mixed methods research are useful in several ways.

Channel		RA 1 Aspects of offline	RA 2 Aspects of 2D websites	RA 3 Vary usage as RA of issues varies	RA 4 Usage different for simple and complex products	RA 5 Level of institutional trust	RA 6 Level of enjoyment
Consu-mer	Offline	High	Low	Medium	High (complex) High (simple)	High	High (Enjoy) Low (Entert.)
	2D website	Low	High	Medium	Low (complex) Medium (simple)	Low	High (Enjoy) Medium (Entert.)
	VW	Medium	Medium	Low	Medium (complex) Medium (simple)	Medium	High (Enjoy) High (Entert.)

(Product or Service)

Figure 3. The six Relative Advantages and three channels

Overall, the combination of several qualitative and quantitative methods gave a deeper understanding of multichannel retail. Applying a methodology similar to comparative case study analysis, the channels were compared between each other on the issues identified in the qualitative analysis that preceded.

For most comparisons, there was a significant difference, that indicated that the sample and the population it represented, had a distinct view about each channel in relation to the question being asked. The most common result for the section comparing three channels, was to consider offline to be preferable to both 2D websites and VWs. 2D was usually preferred to VWs but not always. The differences in preference were usually consistent without great fluctuations. While VWs were usually the least preferable of the pair of channels, the difference was not very big.

This is an indication that VWs could in the future compete with the other two established channels. A notable exception was question 35 where VWs were preferred to both offline and 2D websites. This question asked which retail channel was the most entertaining. A second question was 36 that asked which channel made the participant feel they 'got away from it all', resulted in VWs on average having a RA over both other channels in terms of escapism. These results are in line with the findings of the qualitative research that lay the foundations for this work. VWs were also preferred to the other two channels for question 37 that enquired about which channel was more informative about the product. This was not in line with the qualitative analysis where the 2D websites seemed to be preferred.

For the second section, that compared VWs to the two other channels one at a time, VWs were preferred significantly in most cases. The reason for VWs being more popular in this section to the previous one, was because while the previous section focused on important issues in retail from the consumer's perspective in general, the latter section focused on potential RAs of VWs that arose from the qualitative research. The issue with the most substantial preference was in question 51, the benefit of navigation over online 2D, 54 and 55, being able to be someone you are not, 58 and 59, instantly delivered virtual products.

6 Conclusion

This research explored the RAs of three retail channels. The three channels were evaluated by a survey of 616 participants across 59 issues that had been identified in the qualitative stage of the research. The quantitative analysis revealed the consumer's preferences across these issues.

The first contribution was identifying six RAs summarized in the matrix of three retail channels. The six RAs support a multichannel strategy by enabling a more informed utilization of each channel. Each channel not only has its strengths and weaknesses but also its RA in relation to the other channels. The second contribution was the insight gained on all three channels. The insight gained for VWs was the most significant as they are the newest and least mature. While participants showed a preference for offline and 2D websites in most situations, there was evidence that the emotional reaction, enjoyment, entertainment, sociable shopping, the ability to reinvent yourself, convenience and institutional trust are RAs of VWs in relation to the other two channels. A third contribution was extending Choudhury and Karahanna [5] to include VWs. Originally the model was only used to compare bricks and mortar and 2D websites. A fourth related contribution is the extension of that model by incorporating the RAs identified in order to be effective when considering VWs. Enjoyment has been used in many similar models in the past in relation to technology adoption but not for the RA of retail channels. Previous research had identified enjoyment, including entertainment, as a factor in purchasing virtual products [9] and using VWs for business activities [32]. The model proposed is: RA of retail channel = Convenience + Institutional Trust + Efficacy of Information + Enjoyment + RA of unique channel functionalities + RA in specific purchasing stage + RA for specific type of product.

A fifth and final contribution, was that by allowing the many and varied beliefs of the participants to emerge, the advantage of a value/customer-orientated business model over an activity-role orientated one [24] were supported. The value/customer-orientated business model is considered more useful in a multichannel environment. To satisfy the customer, business models should start from the multichannel customer's needs and develop the activities to satisfy those needs rather than implementing typical structures and models regardless of the channel. This is in agreement with Cagnina and Poian [3].

REFERENCES

[1]   Ahn, S.J.G. et al. 2016. Experiencing Nature: Embodying Animals in Immersive Virtual Environments Increases Inclusion of Nature in Self and Involvement With Nature. *Journal of Computer-Mediated Communication.* 21, 6 (2016), 399–419. DOI:https://doi.org/10.1111/jcc4.12173.

[2]   Benford, S. et al. 2001. Collaborative virtual environments. *Communications of the ACM.* 44, 7 (Jul. 2001), 79–85. DOI:https://doi.org/10.1145/379300.379322.

[3]   Cagnina, M.R. and Poian, M. 2009. Beyond e-business models: the road to virtual worlds. *Electronic Commerce Research.* 9, 1–2 (Jun. 2009), 49–75. DOI:https://doi.org/10.1007/s10660-009-9027-3.

[4]   Cheng, X. et al. 2013. Modeling individual trust development in computer mediated collaboration: A comparison of approaches. *Computers in Human Behavior.* 29, 4 (2013), 1733–1741.

[5]   Choudhury, V. and Karahanna, E. 2008. The Relative Advantage of Electronic Channels: A Multidimensional View. *Management Information Systems Quarterly.* 32, 1 (2008), 179–200.

[6]   Chui, M. et al. 2013. Ten IT-enabled business trends for the decade ahead. *McKinsey Global Institute White Paper.* (2013).

[7]   Dholakia, U.M. et al. 2010. Consumer Behavior in a Multichannel, Multimedia Retailing Environment. *Journal of Interactive Marketing.* 24, 2 (2010), 86–95.

[8]   Eisenbeiss, M. et al. 2012. The (Real) World Is Not Enough: Motivational Drivers and User Behavior in Virtual Worlds. *Journal of Interactive Marketing.* 26, 2 (2012), 4–20.

[9]   Gammoh, B.S. et al. 2018. Consumer Attitudes Toward Human-Like Avatars in Advertisements: The Effect of Category Knowledge and Imagery and Imagery. *International Journal of Electronic Commerce.* 22, 3 (2018), 325–348. DOI:https://doi.org/10.1080/10864415.2018.1462939.

[10]   Goel, L. and Prokopec, S. 2009. If you build it will they come?-An empirical investigation of consumer perceptions and strategy in virtual worlds. *Electronic Commerce Research.* 9, 1 (2009), 115–134.

[11]   Hamari, J. and Keronen, L. 2017. Why do people buy virtual goods: A meta-analysis. *Computers in Human Behavior.* 71, (2017), 59–69. DOI:https://doi.org/10.1016/j.chb.2017.01.042.

[12]   Harris, P. et al. 2018. Understanding multichannel shopper journey configuration: An application of goal theory. *Journal of Retailing and Consumer Services.* 44, May (2018), 108–117. DOI:https://doi.org/10.1016/j.jretconser.2018.06.005.

[13]   Hassouneh, D. and Brengman, M. 2013. A motivation-based typology of

[14]   Heitz-Spahn, S. 2013. Cross-channel free-riding consumer behavior in a multichannel environment: An investigation of shopping motives, sociodemographics and product categories. *Journal of Retailing and Consumer Services.* 20, 6 (2013), 570–578.

[15]   Huvila, I. et al. 2010. Social capital in Second Life. *Online Information Review.* 34, 2 (2010), 295–316.

[16]   Kaplan, A.M. and Hanlein, M. 2009. The fairyland of Second Life: Virtual social worlds and how to use them. *Business Horizons.* 52, 6 (2009), 563–572.

[17]   Keng, C.J. et al. 2011. Effects of virtual-experience combinations on consumer-related 'sense of virtual community.' *Internet Research.* 21, 4 (2011), 408–434.

[18]   Kim, H.W. et al. 2012. What Motivates People to Purchase Digital Items on Virtual Community Websites? The Desire for Online Self-Presentation. *Information Systems Research.* 23, 4 (2012), 1232–1245.

[19]   Konus, U. et al. 2008. Multichannel Shopper Segments and Their Covariates. *Journal of Retailing.* 84, 4 (2008), 398–413.

[20]   Kumar, V. and Venkatesan, R. 2005. Who are the multichannel shoppers and how do they perform?: Correlates of the multichannel shopping behaviour. *Journal of Interactive Marketing.* 19, 2 (2005), 44–62.

[21]   Levy, M. and Weitz, B. 2009. *Retailing Management.* McGraw Hill.

[22]   McKnight, H. et al. 1998. Initial Trust Formation in New Organizational elationships. *Academy of Management Review.* 23, 3 (1998), 473–490.

[23]   McKnight, H. et al. 2002. The impact of initial consumer trust on intentions to transact with a web site: a trust building model. *Journal of Strategic Information Systems.* 11, 3–4 (2002), 297–323.

[24]   Osterwalder, A. et al. 2005. Communications of the Association for Information Systems Clarifying Business Models: Origins, Present, and Future of the Concept. *Communications of the Association for Information Systems.* 16, 16 (2005), 1–25. DOI:https://doi.org/10.1.1.83.7452.

[25]   Partala, T. 2011. Psychological needs and virtual worlds: Case Second Life. *International Journal of Human Computer Studies.* 69, 12 (2011), 787–800.

[26]   Pavlou, P. A., Gefen, D. 2004. Building effective online marketplaces with institution-based trust. *Information Systems Research.* 15, 1 (2004), 667–675. DOI:https://doi.org/10.1287/isre.1040.0015.

[27]   Rogers, E.M. 1995. *Diffusion of Innovations.* Free Press.

[28]   Saghiri, S. et al. 2017. Toward a Three-dimensional Framework for Omni-channel. *Journal of Business Research.* (2017), 53–67. DOI:https://doi.org/10.1016/j.jbusres.2017.03.025.

[29]   Schoenbachler, D.D. and Gordon, G.L. 2002. Multi-channel shopping: Understanding what drives channel choice. *Journal of Consumer Marketing.* 19, 1 (2002), 42–53.

[30]   Schroder, H. and Zaharia, S. 2012. Linking multi-channel customer behavior with shopping motives: An empirical investigation of a German retailer. *Journal of Retailing and Consumer Services.* 15, 6 (2012), 452–468.

[31]   Sfenrianto, S. et al. 2018. Assessing the Buyer Trust and Satisfaction Factors in the 2 Research Design. *Journal of Theoretical and Applied Electronic Commerce Research.* 13, 2 (2018), 43–57. DOI:https://doi.org/10.4067/S0718-18762018000200105.

[32]   Shen, J. and Eder, L.B. 2009. Exploring Intentions to Use Virtual Worlds for Business. *Journal of Electronic Commerce Research.* 10, 2 (2009), 94–103.

[33]   Steed, A. et al. 2016. An 'In the Wild' Experiment on Presence and Embodiment using Consumer Virtual Reality Equipment. *IEEE Transactions on Visualization and Computer Graphics.* (2016).

[34]   Venkatesh, V. et al. 2016. Unified Theory of Acceptance and Use of Technology: A Synthesis and the Road Ahead. *Journal of the Association for Information Systems.* 17, 5 (2016), 328–376.

[35]   Wang, L. and Gordon, P. 2011. Trust and institutions: A multilevel analysis. *The Journal of Socio-Economics.* 40, 5 (2011), 583–593.

[36]   Williams, A. 2015. Reality check [Consumer Electronics Virtual Reality 3D]. *Engineering & Technology.* 10, 2 (2015), 52–55.

[37]   Yan, R. et al. 2011. Product distribution and coordination strategies in a multi-channel context. *Journal of Retailing and Consumer Services.* 18, 1 (2011), 19–26.

[38]   Zhang, J. et al. 2010. Crafting integrated multichannel retailing strategies. *Journal of Interactive Marketing.* 24, 2 (2010), 168–180. DOI:https://doi.org/10.1016/j.intmar.2010.02.002.

[39]   Zhang, Z. and Gu, C. 2015. Effects of Consumer Social Interaction on Trust in Online Group-Buying Contexts: an Empirical Study in China. *Journal of Electronic Commerce Research.* 16, 1 (2015), 1–21.

In What Mood Are You Today? An Analysis of Crowd Workers' Mood, Performance and Engagement

Mengdie Zhuang
University of Sheffield
Sheffield, United Kingdom
mzhuang1@sheffield.ac.uk

Ujwal Gadiraju
L3S Research Center
Leibniz Universität Hannover
Hannover, Germany
gadiraju@L3S.de

ABSTRACT

The mood of individuals in the workplace has been well-studied due to its influence on task performance, and work engagement. However, the effect of mood has not been studied in detail in the context of microtask crowdsourcing. In this paper, we investigate the influence of one's mood, a fundamental psychosomatic dimension of a worker's behaviour, on their interaction with tasks, task performance and perceived engagement. To this end, we conducted two comprehensive studies; (i) a survey exploring the perception of crowd workers regarding the role of mood in shaping their work, and (ii) an experimental study to measure and analyze the actual impact of workers' moods in information findings microtasks. We found evidence of the impact of mood on a worker's perceived engagement through the feeling of reward or accomplishment, and we argue as to why the same impact is not perceived in the evaluation of task performance. Our findings have broad implications on the design and workflow of crowdsourcing systems.

CCS CONCEPTS

• **Human-centered computing**; • **Information systems**;

ACM Reference Format:
Mengdie Zhuang and Ujwal Gadiraju. 2019. In What Mood Are You Today? An Analysis of Crowd Workers' Mood, Performance and Engagement. In *11th ACM Conference on Web Science (WebSci '19), June 30-July 3, 2019, Boston, MA, USA.* ACM, New York, NY, USA, 10 pages. https://doi.org/10.1145/3292522.3326010

1 INTRODUCTION

Crowdsourcing has been flourishing as a type of gig economy, and has found wide use in both industry and academia, fostering particular interest for conducting *Web Science* research [19]. The motivation for using crowdsourcing has mostly focused on the ease and cost-effective nature of acquiring human input; and a considerable number of prior works have addressed challenges to improve the effectiveness of this paradigm [8, 31].

Theoretical and empirical research suggests that people's moods have an effect on lexical decision making [5], learning and training in the workplace [59], the perception, encoding, storage, and retrieval of information [3, 56], and workplace outcomes, such as productivity [57], behavior and engagement [1]. The popular notion is that people with a positive mood perform better in their work assignments and are more likely to have increased intrinsic motivation. However, there have been diverging opinions among researchers.

Early studies suggest the existence of an indirect causality link between mood and work/task performance intermediated by a spectrum of psychosomatic states. Seibert and Ellis found that students in non-neutral moods displayed greater propensity towards ineffectual thinking, which in turn produced a negative impact on the outcome of tasks such as memory recall [54]. More recent work has been focused on sociability [58] as the mediator between mood and performance, in which they found that workers in positive moods may perform better through interpersonal processes such as helping and seeking help among co-workers. Apart from sociability, non-neutral mood is found to increase vulnerability to distractions [48], which might lead to unwanted behavior at work (e.g., long response time). On the other hand, unpleasant mood states also facilitate work withdrawal behavior due to the individual's need for mood repair [40].

An aspect that resonates throughout the aforementioned studies is the importance of establishing clear links with actionable implications between an individual's mood and its impact and efficacy in the workplace. However, these links and their implications have not previously been established within the context of microtask crowdsourcing, a branch of online labor which is gaining increased traction among the exponents of the current generation, and having an outreaching impact upon human data driven research.

The key difference in the context of microtask crowdsourcing stems from the nature of the work setting. It is both a form of gig work – hence temporary, and on demand – but also remote, which allows the workers to cater their workspace to their own needs [18]. Moreover, the overarching rules and laws that govern traditional workplace interactions fade in the online crowdsourcing context where there is a flexibility in time, space and with respect to organizational boundaries [15, 31]. To the best of our knowledge, prior work has not comprehensively studied the role of worker moods in shaping crowd work in microtask marketplaces.

In this paper, we aim to address this knowledge gap by presenting two studies that aim to understand the role of crowd worker moods in shaping their work outcomes. First, we explore how workers think their moods affect the task outcomes such as worker performance and engagement by using a survey addressing 100 workers. Our findings from the survey further inform and direct the second study, in which we collected data from 300 crowd workers completing information finding microtasks and analyzed how their moods affect their interaction, performance and behavior. We build upon the previously mentioned studies in order to inform and direct discussion together with work design theory on task design, workflows and interventions in crowdsourcing marketplaces, thereby improving the overall effectiveness of the paradigm and at the same time serving the interest of the growing crowd workers community.

Original Contributions. We make the following contributions:

- We enhance and enrich the existing understanding of workers' mental states within the context of microtask crowdsourcing, by quantifying task outcomes and identifying work characteristics in this novel setting in relation to worker moods.
- We find support for the hypothesis that there is an impact of mood on a worker's perceived reward, and shed light on contrary evidence of its impact on performance.
- This work challenges the status quo, by pitting quantitative evidence against the biased understanding of workers themselves in how mood is perceived and how it impacts their engagement and performance.

2 BACKGROUND AND RELATED LITERATURE

2.1 Mood and Emotion

Although both *mood* and *emotion* are valenced affective responses, prior work has elaborately discussed the difference between the two [9]. Firstly, moods last longer than emotions [2, 60]. Secondly, emotions are always targeted towards an event, person or object, while moods are globally diffused [17]. Emotions are triggered by explicit causes and monitor our environment, while moods have combined causes and monitor our internal state [33, 44]. Further, emotions are elicited by threats or opportunities [17], while moods are responses to one's overall position in general [49]. However, note that moods and emotions are not entirely independent; they interact with each other dynamically. Accumulated emotions can lead to specific moods, and moods can lower the degree of emotional arousal [7].

The concept of workplace mood has been traditionally associated with workplace quality (e.g., productivity [57], engagement [1]). We build on the substantial prior works that have established an understanding of *moods* to unearth the background role that mood plays on workers within a microtask crowdsourcing environment. We investigate (a) the *moods* that crowd workers are typically in, while contributing to piecework, and (b) how particular mood dispositions affect task outcomes.

2.2 Exploiting '*Mood*' in Microtask Crowdsourcing

Recently, [55] proposed to leverage the relationship between people's mood and their productivity to operationalize a concept from workforce management research known as 'productive

laziness'[47]. The authors argue that crowd workers need to efficiently schedule when to work and rest, to maximize their overall productivity and sustain the long-term function of the crowdsourcing system. The dynamic scheduling method introduced by the authors jointly minimizes the effort exerted by crowd workers while maximizing the overall throughput. In closely related work, [43] explored the relationship between the mood of crowd workers and their capacity for creative outcomes. The authors proposed two approaches for enhancing worker performance in creative tasks; affective priming, and affective pre-screening. Their findings suggest that workers in a positive mood exhibit enhanced creativity. Other empirical works have established that happiness makes individuals more productive [34, 41].

In contrast to these prior works, we use a robust tool called '*Pick-A-Mood*' (described later in Section 3), which only requires a single click from the participants, to explicitly gather self-reports of worker moods, and test their effect on task outcomes such as worker performance and engagement.

2.3 Worker Engagement and Performance in Crowdsourcing

Previous works have addressed the issue of boredom and fatigue in crowdsourcing marketplaces resulting due to the repetitive nature of long batches of tasks that workers often encounter. Thus, a variety of means to retain and engage workers have been proposed. [52] suggested introducing micro-breaks into workflows to refresh workers, and showed that under certain conditions micro-breaks aid in worker retention and improve their accuracy marginally. Similarly, [6] proposed to intersperse diversions (small periods of entertainment) to improve worker experience in lengthy, monotonous microtasks and found that such micro-diversions can significantly improve worker retention rate while maintaining worker performance. Other works proposed the use of gamification to increase worker retention and throughput [16, 50]. [36] studied worker engagement, characterized how workers perceive tasks and proposed to predict when workers would stop performing tasks. [12] introduced pricing schemes to improve worker retention, and showed that paying periodic bonuses according to pre-defined milestones has the biggest impact on retention rate of workers. More recently, [20] proposed the use of achievement priming to increase worker retention in crowdsourcing microtasks.

In contrast to these prior works in microtask crowdsourcing that measure worker engagement using the proxy of prolonged retention, we measure worker engagement using a standardized questionnaire [45], obtaining direct feedback from the workers. The concept of work engagement has been discussed in the field of work psychology [28], showing long term benefits on workers' development and well being [4]. However, crowd workers are gig economy workers who are fundamentally different from the workers discussed in previous work engagemnt studies; they do not have contracts or regular hours of work, and can pick and choose what jobs they complete and when. To the best of our knowledge, there is no engagement measurement developed specifically for piecework and gig economy workers. Since engaged employees experience a sense of reward and the presence of the necessary supporting resources for the job [28], we propose to measure work engagement of crowd workers using the concepts of *usability* and *reward* [45].

3 STUDY I: PRELIMINARY SURVEY

In this first study, we survey 100 distinct crowd workers on FigureEight[1] (a primary microtask crowdsourcing platform) to understand the following:

(1) How do crowd workers feel during task completion?
(2) What is the perception of crowd workers regarding the influence of their moods on their task performance and engagement?
(3) To what extent do crowd workers perceive their moods to effect their task performance and engagement?

We aim to reveal the distribution of worker moods, and juxtapose the *perceived impact* of moods on engagement and performance.

3.1 Study Design

3.1.1 Measuring the Mood of Workers. To measure the *mood* of crowd workers in an intuitive and easy manner, we use *Pick-A-Mood* (PAM), a character-based pictorial scale for reporting moods [9]. Compared to other measures, this is ideal for the microtask crowdsourcing context where time is of the essence, since it was specifically made to be suitable for design research applications in which people have little time or motivation to report their moods. The PAM is designed on two principal dimensions: arousal and valence. In this study, we focus on the valence dimension. The eight non-neutral moods measured by PAM, can be grouped into two main mood groups [9]: **pleasant** (*excited, cheerful, relaxed, calm*), and **unpleasant** (*tense, irritated, bored, sad*) [62]. The *neutral* mood group stands on its own. The scale has been tested with a general population (with people from 31 different nationalities in the validation study)[9], revealing that the expressions presented by the visual characters are correctly interpreted (see Figure 1). This scale has also been used in other works [61]. In our study, workers were asked to select the pictorial representation of the mood that most closely resembled their current moods.

3.1.2 Survey Design. To achieve a comprehensive understanding of workers perspective on the effect of mood, the survey questions were developed to cover two broad areas (see examples of questions in Figure 2): 1) general perception and reasons for the perceived effect of mood on task performance, 2), perception and reasons for perceived effect of mood on detailed aspects of performance and engagement.

To begin with, the current mood of the workers was collected using the *Pick-A-Mood* scale. Next, the survey presented workers with questions regarding the demographics, educational and general background of the workers. Then, questions related to worker opinions on whether they believe their (current self-reported) mood would influence their work performance and engagement, are presented. The rationale behind using the mood that workers just self-reported is to enable the workers to associate the question to their own feelings. After collecting the general opinion, a set of statements related to their answer to the previous question (but diving into further details) was presented, and a binary response (agree/

[1]http://www.figure-eight.com/

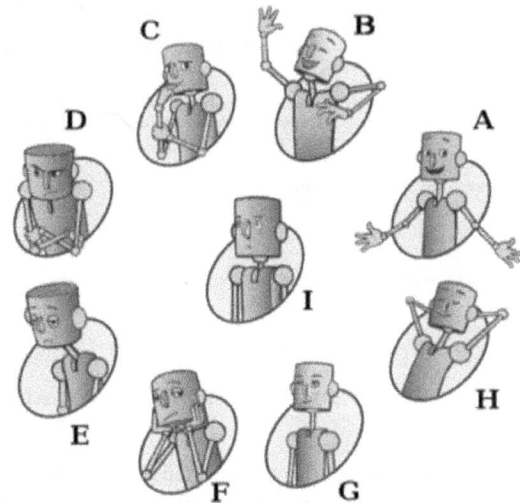

Figure 1: *Pick-A-Mood* scale to measure the self-reported mood of crowd workers in different conditions.

disagree) was required for each statement. For the statements pertaining to engagement, we adapted the three items belonging to *Perceived Usability* (PU) and *Reward* (RW) from the User Engagement Scale [45]. A detailed description of these two concepts is presented in the section 4.1.1. We finally added statements corresponding to each of task accuracy and completion speed which are the two main performance related attributes. In total the survey spanned a mixture of open-ended, multiple-choice, and Likert-type questions designed to filter out malicious workers and motivate workers to provide high quality responses; we collected the responses from 100 workers. In order to collect more specific answers, participants were asked to provide reasons for each of their response.

3.1.3 Study Procedure. We deployed the survey on FigureEight. To ensure high quality responses, we restricted the participation to *Level-3 workers*[2] on the platform. We presented workers with an overview at the beginning of the survey including the purpose of this study and the research impact, to motivate participants into providing genuine and detailed responses. We explicitly encouraged workers to report moods genuinely, assuring that it would have no bearings on their payment. We also used attention check questions to filter out untrustworthy workers [37]. In total, we collected responses from 100 workers and 95 workers passed the attention check. On average workers took ~10 mins to complete the survey and were compensated at a fixed hourly rate of 7.5 USD.

3.2 Results

Of the 95 workers after filtering, 34 were female and 61 were male. This is typical of crowdsourcing platforms, given the demographics of workers [11]. Most of the workers were found to be under 45 years old (N=83), of which 16 were between 18-25 years old. 61 of the workers reported to have at least a Bachelor's degree. Finally,

[2]*Level-3 contributors* on FigureEight comprise workers who completed over 100 test questions across hundreds of different types of tasks, and have a near perfect overall accuracy. They are workers of the highest quality.

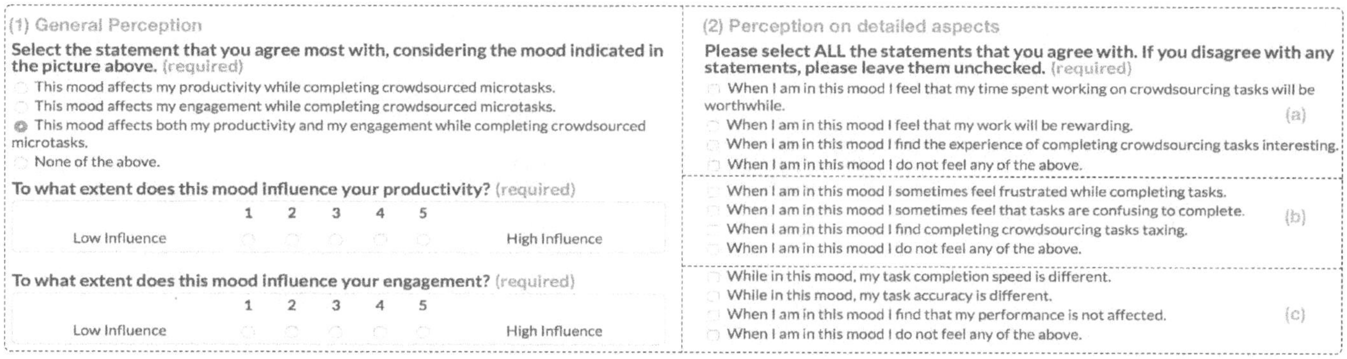

Figure 2: Main survey questions used. (a) Reward, (b) Preceived usability, and (c) Performance.

nearly half of the workers (N=45) reported crowdsourcing to be their primary source of income. The distribution of worker moods as collected using the PAM scale is presented in Figure 3. 63 workers reported pleasant moods, while 28 reported unpleasant moods.

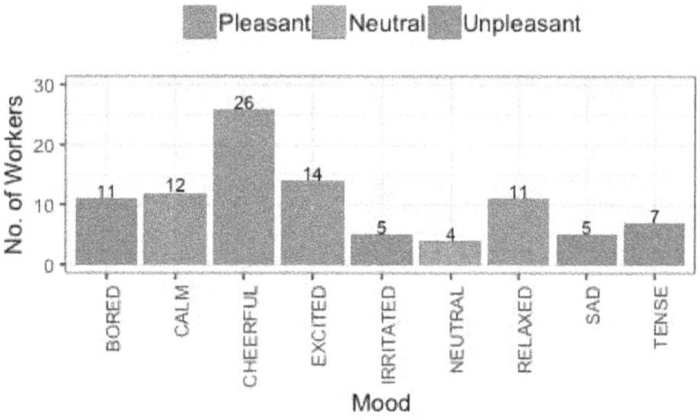

Figure 3: Mood distribution of workers who completed the survey in Study I.

Several important observations emerged from the responses collected using the survey. First, the distribution of moods reported by crowd workers is skewed towards pleasant, and very few people reported to have a neutral mood (N=4, 4.2%). This may be caused by the general conditions under which workers choose to complete crowdsourcing tasks, i.e., on their own terms. As three workers reported in their open-ended remarks, they typically do not feel like working on crowdsourcing tasks when they are in unpleasant moods. This stands in stark contrast to the typically rigid work hours that employees are expected to comply with in traditional workplaces.

Secondly, regarding the general perception of the effect of workers' moods, we found that workers' opinions diverge. As shown in Table 1, 33.68% workers (Pleasant: N= 22, Unpleasant: N= 7, Neutral: N= 3) believed that their mood would not affect either their task performance or work engagement, and 4 of them mentioned that regardless of their mood, they always wanted to perform well in their tasks. This zeal to constantly perform well is arguably due to the existence of the reputation system on FigureEight, where

Table 1: No. of worker agreed on the effect option of mood on their engagement and performance.

	None	Eng.	Perf.	Eng.&Perf.
Pleasant (N=63)	22	6	22	13
Neutral (N=4)	3	0	0	1
Unpleasant (N=28)	7	2	9	10
Total (N=95)	32	8	31	24

workers are awarded level badges based on their accuracy across several tasks, and their level goes on to dictate their general access to available tasks. Thus, workers often aim to maintain a high accuracy and good reputation [18, 39]. 63 workers expressed that their mood affects their engagement or performance. We found that 42 workers provided detailed reasons explaining their choice, or suggested the particular aspects of engagement and performance which are affected.

Table 2: The extent to which workers perceive their moods to effect their engagement and performance on a 5-point scale (Mean (SD), N= No. of responses).

	Pleasant	Unpleasant	Ple.& Un.
Eng.	4.21 (0.63), N=19	4.08 (0.99), N=12	4.18 (0.78)
Perf.	4.17 (0.78), N=35	3.84 (1.01), N=19	4.07 (0.88)

Those workers who believe that their moods do have an effect described attention as the mediator between mood and performance (N=8, keywords in the feedback: "attention", "concentrate", "focus" etc.). In line with our intuition, they mentioned that failing to concentrate on the task instructions in the past, resulted in a decrease in their performance. This is similar to the observation of ineffectual thinking in memory recall tasks [54] in which students with non-neutral mood exhibit more ineffectual thinking, which in turn decreases their performance. Lasecki et al. recognized this link as an upper bound on the memory capacity of an individual in crowdsourcing, and suggested to distribute the cognitive load required by the task among crowd workers [32]. Table 2 presents the 63 workers who rated the extent to which their mood affects their engagement and performance. Although fewer workers (no. of responses =32) indicate that mood has an effect on their engagement, the average value is larger than the average value of the effect of mood on performance (no. of responses =55) in all three groups (pleasant, unpleasant, and the combined non-neutral mood) with a smaller standard deviation.

Regarding the statements, within the 32 workers (Pleasant: N= 19, Unpleasant: N= 12, Neutral: N= 1) who agreed that mood has effect on engagement, 21 of them agreed on RW and 17 on PU. Only one worker didn't pick any of them and leave no more suggestions on the aspects of engagement. Within the 55 workers (Pleasant: N= 35, Unpleasant: N= 1, Neutral: N= 19) who agreed that mood has effect on performance, 36 agreed on the statements we provided and the rest of them did not provide details on the aspects of performance which are influenced.

Overall, we note that a predominant prior belief exists among crowdworkers as to how their mood influences their engagement and performance. However, crowdsourcing is fundamentally different from other types of work as the workers are self-motivated. These observations motivate our subsequent study, in which we collect and analyze data which tests this belief as a null hypothesis.

4 STUDY II: ANALYZING THE IMPACT OF MOOD

Given our findings in Study I, we hypothesize that the mood of crowd workers has an effect on their work engagement and performance. Thus, in Study II we aim to measure and analyze the *actual impact* of worker moods and whether it is consistent with worker beliefs. To this end, we designed a crowdsourcing task and collected data from 300 crowd workers on FigureEight.

Since several workers (N=8) cited attention as a mediator in the preliminary study, in Study II we gather and analyze workers' low-level behavioral traces (keypresses and mouse events) which have been shown to serve as indicators of attention while interacting with an interface [10, 53].

4.1 Study Design

4.1.1 Measuring Engagement. Psychometric scales were used to capture the crowd workers engagement; the User Engagement Scale Short Form (UES-SF) [45], which contains four sub-scales with 12 items. Each item is presented as a statement using a 5 point scale from "*1: Strongly Disagree*" to "*5: Strongly Agree*". The reason we chose the UES-SF is that it has been validated in other HCI contexts, and to date, it is the most tested questionnaire that measures user engagement. Each of the four dimensions only has three items, which is practical in the microtask crowdsourcing context; in that it is easy to motivate workers to respond. Note that it is valid to sample sub-scales to fit the application [45].

To better measure engagement within the crowdsourcing context, we extracted two sub-scales which align with the concept of work engagement [28]: *Perceived Usability* (PU) and *Reward* (RW). Perceived usability measures the challenges workers face when performing the task, and whether the workers could conduct the task using the system the way they wanted to. Reward measures how well the experience with systems can satisfy worker needs,

measures whether workers perceived the interaction as being 'successful', 'rewarding', and 'worthwhile'.

4.1.2 Task Design – Information Finding. We consider *information finding* tasks since prior work has shown a thriving market for information finding tasks on the popular microtask crowdsourcing platform, Amazon's Mechanical Turk (AMT) [13, 22]. We adopt the task of finding the middle-names of famous people, orchestrating the workflow of typical information finding microtasks where workers are asked to find contact details, addresses, or names of particular people, organizations or companies. Depending on the information that is to be searched for, these tasks possess various difficulties [63]. To account for varying levels of the inherent task difficulty in our tasks , we model task difficulty objectively into 3 levels, wherein workers need to consider an additional aspect in each progressively difficult level as shown in Figure 4. In *level-I*, workers are presented with unique names of famous persons, such that the middle-names can be found using a simple search on Google[3] or Wikipedia[4]. In *level-II* workers are additionally provided with the profession of the given person. We manually selected the names such that there are at least two different individuals with the given names in *level-II*, and the distinguishing factor that the workers need to rely upon is their profession. In *level-III* workers are presented names of persons, their profession, and a year during which the persons were active in the given profession. There are multiple distinct individuals with the given names, associated with the same profession in *level-III*. The workers are required to identify the accurate middle-name by relying on the year in which the person was active in the given profession.

4.1.3 Study Procedure. In this study, we deployed 3 crowdsourcing jobs on FigureEight corresponding to each of the 3 difficulty levels of the information finding tasks. In each case, we first administered the PAM scale, which was also used in our preliminary survey, to gather self-reports of worker moods. Following this, we asked participating workers to respond to a few general background questions regarding their age, gender, education, ethnicity, marital status and income. Next, workers received a batch of 20 information finding tasks at random corresponding to a difficulty level. The first 10 tasks in the batch were made mandatory, while the remaining 10 tasks were made optional. We offered workers a bonus of 5 USD cents for completing each of the optional tasks accurately. On completion of the information finding tasks, we administered the engagement questionnaire as described earlier. To ensure high quality responses, we also restricted the participation to *level 3 workers* on FigureEight. Enforcing reputation restrictions is a typically method adapted by requesters to ensure reliability [31]. We followed the guidelines laid down by prior work [24] and used attention check questions to label untrustworthy workers [23]. We examined the responses of workers to further flag those with an overall accuracy of 0% as being untrustworthy. We found 10, 18 and 27 untrustworthy workers in the difficulty levels I, II and III respectively. All workers were paid at an hourly rate of 7.5 USD.

---
[3]http://www.google.com/
[4]http://www.wikipedia.org/

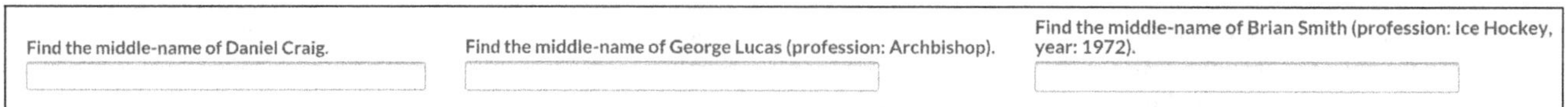

Find the middle-name of Daniel Craig.	Find the middle-name of George Lucas (profession: Archbishop).	Find the middle-name of Brian Smith (profession: Ice Hockey, year: 1972).
(a) Difficulty Level-I	(b) Difficulty Level-II	(c) Difficulty Level-III

Figure 4: Progressive difficulty-levels in the *information finding* task of finding the middle-names of famous persons.

We implemented mousetracking using Javascript and the JQuery library, and logged user activity data ranging from mouse movements to keypresses. We took measures to distinguish between workers who use a mouse and those who use a touchpad. Apart from this data, we use a Javascript implementation[5] of *browser fingerprinting* [14] in order to prevent workers from participating in tasks multiple times (*'repeaters'*) by virtue of using different worker-ids. We take measures to avoid privacy intrusion of workers, by storing only the final hashed fingerprints. Workers were also given an opportunity to opt-out of the Javascript tracking. In this way, we gathered worker activity data from each of the jobs corresponding to the 3 difficulty levels deployed on FigureEight.

We recruited 300 workers in total; 100 distinct workers for each of the three difficulty levels. From the 300 workers, 55 workers (18.3%) did not pass the attention check questions or had 0% accuracy. In addition, some workers opted-out of our Javascript tracking and we could not track their mouse and keypress events thereby. After filtering out these workers, we were left with 216 reliable workers whose behavior we were able to track across the three levels of difficulty.

5 STUDY II RESULTS AND ANALYSIS

5.1 Demographics

Among the 216 workers after filtering, we observe a slightly unbalanced gender distribution (N=142, 65.7% male), which is typical of large crowdsourcing platforms depending on the country of origin of workers [11]. Most of the participants (N=191, 88.4%) are under 46 years old (18-24 years old: N=67 ;26-35 years old: N=72, ; 36-45 years old: N=52,). 119 of them have at least a Bachelor's degree. More than half (N=120, 55.5%) of the workers reported that crowdsourcing is their secondary source of income, and 40.3% of the workers (N=87) reported it is their primary source of income.

5.2 In What Mood Are You Today? Mood of Workers

Previous work has established that moods act as an affective background canvas of our actions and behaviour [7]. By using Pick-A-Mood (PAM) as described earlier, we obtained self-reported assessments of mood from workers before they began the actual tasks. We analyzed the responses of the 216 trustworthy workers and their mood distribution. Our findings are presented in the Figure 5. We found that on average across all conditions, most trustworthy workers claimed to be either *cheerful* (28.38%), *relaxed* (17.25%), *calm* (15.88%), or *bored* (12.5%). Relatively fewer workers were found to be *excited* (7.88%), *sad* (6.41%), *irritated* (3.56%), or *tense* (2.85%). Just

over 5% of the trustworthy workers reported to be in *neutral* moods (see Figure 5).

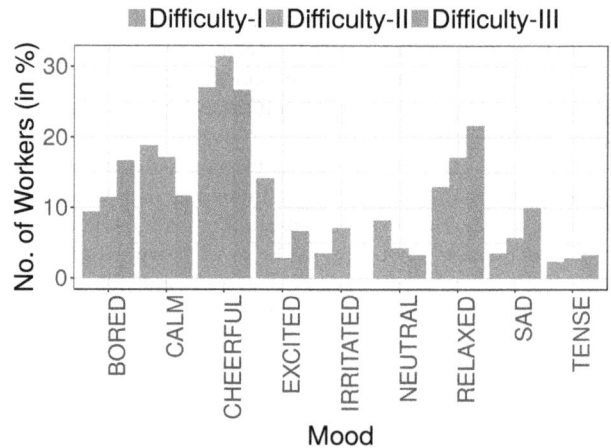

Figure 5: Mood distribution of workers who completed information findings tasks across the three different difficulty conditions (level-I, level-II and level-III).

Of the 216 trustworthy workers, 150 reported **pleasant** moods, 13 reported a **neutral** mood and 53 workers reported **unpleasant** moods.

5.3 Overview of Measures of Task Performance, Work Engagement and workers' behavior

In order to assess the task outcomes of workers in a comprehensive manner, we analyze our results through the distinct lens of *task performance*, *work engagement*, and *worker behavior*. We measured the task performance of workers using their accuracy in the first 10 mandatory information finding tasks ($Acc@10$), overall task accuracy in all the information finding tasks that they completed (Acc), and also time spent on completing the tasks (TCT). On average, we found that the workers achieved 75.6% $Acc@10$, 76.3% Acc, and spent 19.58 minutes to complete the entire crowdsourcing job.

Apart from the task performance, work engagement was measured through a subset of the UES-SF questionnaire [45] that covered two dimensions, Perceived Usability (PU) and Reward (RW), and number of tasks completed (*No. Tasks*). Workers completed 19.22 tasks by average, and 83.7% of them (N=181) completed all 20 tasks. PU measures whether workers think they complete the task the way they want, and RW measures whether the workers perceive the task as being successful and worthwhile. The Reliability Analysis (Cronbach's $\alpha = 0.83$ (PU), and 0.81 (RW)) indicates good internal consistency for both measures. To assign scores for

---

[5]http://github.com/Valve/fingerprintjs

the two sub-scales, we summed all the items within one sub-scale and divided the sum by the number of items for this sub-scale as recommended in [45]. The mean values of the two sub-scales were above 3 ($M = 3.8$ (PU), and 3.7 (RW)), signifying that on average crowd workers had a positive impression of the information finding microtasks. The correlation between these two dimensions (Spearman's $\rho = 0.324$, $p < .001$) is low, suggesting that these two dimensions do cover different aspects of engagement.

Previous works have shown that worker activity logs can be used to profile and model workers based on their behavior [51, 53], and their behavior is an indicator of attention [10]. We logged mouse events such as mouse movements[6], clicks, and the mouse entering or leaving the screen in which the job is open. We analyzed worker behavior, measured by *Mouse Events, Scroll Events, Window Events* and *Keypress Events*, based on their activity logs (mousetracking and keypresses). Mouse and Scroll events are the number of times that a mouse event or scroll event is detected. Mouse events include moving the mouse, and any clicks (right, left, middle). The scroll events we logged include scrolling up or down. We also logged window events such as the window blurring out of focus, or the window coming back into focus based on the worker activity. Every keypress executed by the workers was also logged.

To summarize, we have three measures for task performance (*Acc@10, Accuracy*, and *TCT* (in mins)); three measures for work engagement (*PU, RW*, and *No.Tasks*); and four measures for workers' behavior (*Mouse Events, Scroll Events, Window Events* and *Keypress Events*).

5.4 Effect of Mood on Task Performance and Work Engagement

We analyzed the mean values of crowd workers' task performance and user engagement with different moods, and compare the *Pleasant* mood group against the *Unpleasant* mood group using a corrected t-test. The rationale behind comparing only the two non-neutral groups is based on the small sample size ($N = 13$) of the *Neutral* mood group. Our analysis of statistical significance in this paper is comprised of multiple t-tests. To control for Type-I error inflation in our multiple comparisons, we used the Holm-Bonferroni correction for family-wise error rate (FWER) [26], at the significance level of $\alpha < .05$.

Table 3 summarizes the mean value for the 6 measures, namely *Acc@10, Accuracy, TCT, PU, RW*, and *No.Tasks*, for three types of mood (Pleasant, Neutral, and Unpleasant). With the unbalanced sample size, crowd workers with neutral mood performed the best with a mean *Acc@10* of 80.7% ± 17.1% , and over all accuracy of 81.8% ± 18.6%. Crowd workers in pleasant moods performed better (*Acc@10*: 75.7% ± 20.3%, *Accuracy*: 76.5% ± 20.7%) than those in unpleasant ones (*Acc@10*: 74% ± 22.3%, *Accuracy*: 74.3% ± 23.6%), without significant differences on the two accuracy measures. Although workers in the neutral mood performed the best among the three groups, this result may be a reflection of the small sample size ($N = 13$). The mean value of *Accuracy* is higher than *Acc@10* across all three groups, suggesting a well-known learning effect in crowd work [12, 20]. Crowd workers in an unpleasant mood spent less time on the task, completed fewer tasks and reported a

[6]Mouse movement events were logged at an interval of 500ms.

lower usability score than workers in a pleasant mood or those who reported neutral moods, but all those differences are not significant. Significant differences were observed between the *Pleasant* and *Unpleasant* groups on *RW* (t=3.061, $p < 0.01$), in which pleasant workers ((M=3.86)) felt that the tasks were more rewarding than unpleasant workers ((M=3.45)). This aligns with previous findings [28, 57] in traditional workplace settings, wherein workers in a positive mood perceived their work to be rewarding and tended to invest more in their role.

Table 3: Average values for the 10 task performance, work engagement, and task behavior measures for each of the three mood conditions (corrected t-test to compare the Pleasant group against the Unpleasant group, significance level (2-tailed): ** = $\alpha < 0.01$.

		Pleasant N=150	Neutral N=13	Unpleasant N=53
Perf.	Acc.@10	75.7%	80.7%	74%
	Acc.	76.5%	81.8%	74.3%
	TCT	19.68	19.61	19.28
Eng.	PU	3.81	3.82	3.67
	RW	3.86**	3.59	3.45**
	No. Tasks	19.26	19.46	19.03
Beh.	Mouse Eve.	666.53	616.85	637.87
	Scroll Eve.	928.18	811.77	765.1
	Window Eve.	87	75.92	89.23
	Keypress Eve.	50.23	25.08	57.56

To analyze the effect of mood on the behavior of workers, we conducted t-tests for each type of the events between two non-neutral mood groups. For all four types of events, no significant differences were observed between workers in pleasant moods when compared to those in unpleasant moods. The workers in a pleasant mood performed more mouse events (M=666.53, SD= 352.70) and scroll events (M= 928.18, SD= 749.97) than the workers in unpleasant moods (*mouse events* : M=637.86, SD= 312.03; *scroll events* : M= 765.1, SD= 535.55). This trend was reversed on the frequency with which workers left and re-entered the active window where the crowdsourcing job was open; here workers in pleasant moods (M=87, SD=52.07) corresponded to fewer events than those in unpleasant moods (M=89.23, SD=59.01). Similarly, workers in pleasant moods (M=50.23, SD=48.61) performed fewer key presses than those in unpleasant moods (M=57.56, SD= 60.26). The large standard deviation values of all behavior measures indicate that the data are spread out over a wide range of values. With a close look at the log files, we noticed that it is caused by workers' different interaction habits. For example, in order to check materials in the lower position of the web page, some workers scrolled down, which count as scroll events in the log, while others moved their mouse and clicked a lower position on the scroll bar, which count as mouse events. Similar in performing searching, instead of typing in the search box, some workers copy-pasted the names to the box.

6 DISCUSSION, CAVEATS AND LIMITATIONS

Our analysis provides several complex insights into the role that the mood of workers plays in relation to their performance, engagement and outcomes in the microtask crowdsourcing context. We shape our main arguments around the following job characteristics model for crowdsourcing work. The Job Characteristics Model (JCM) [25], a dominant and widely tested model from work psychology (see detailed tests of JCM in [27]), identifies five core job characteristics: skill variety, task identity, task significance, autonomy, and feedback. The first three characteristics are related to the skills required for completing the task, task difficulty and task impact; thus, they are intrinsically task-centered. Autonomy is the degree to which the job provides substantial freedom, independence, and discretion to the individual in scheduling the work and in determining the procedures to be used in its performance, and is the only characteristic positively linked to objectively measured work performance. Feedback is the degree to which the individual obtains direct and clear information about the effectiveness of his or her performance. The five characteristics promote individual motivation, job satisfaction, and performance through critical psychological states such as experienced responsibility for the outcomes of the work.

6.1 Effects on Performance

No significant differences are observed between workers in a pleasant mood and those in an unpleasant mood with respect to their task performance, namely *Acc@10*, *Accuracy*, and *TCT*, although 55 out of 95 workers (57.9%) participating in the preliminary study reported they believe otherwise. This lack of impact can potentially be explained by the inherent characteristics of crowdsourcing. Contrary to traditional types of labour, gig work, including microtask crowdsourcing, represents an on-demand work activity that benefits from the worker's self-directed decision to work. This is in turn a multi-faceted act, comprising of several micro-choices on the aspect of time, environment and content. Such a latitude of options reflects the high autonomy of the subject in performing their tasks. Furthermore, the choice of whether to work or not represents a primer on the subject's behaviour, which could potentially dampen the effects of mood on the subject's interaction with the system and their task. Based on the tests performed on the JCM [27], we know that autonomy is principally related to the objective task outcome, and, in light of the previous discussion, it is likely that this component accounts for the relative insensitivity of performance metrics to the worker's mood. Moreover, the differences between these findings and prior work in affective computing, where authors found people in happier moods tend to be more creative [34] might be due to the fact that creativity is measured subjectively [34], and subjective performance is often influenced by a spectrum of psychological factors. Another explanation can draw from the drive for compensation among workers. It is well understood that crowd workers on paid microtask crowdsourcing platforms primarily seek monetary rewards, and platforms and requesters introduce various forms of quality control and may subsequently refuse payment if the work produced is suboptimal. Thus a worker's desire to be compensated will drive them to perform at least as well as necessary to achieve this goal. It is also worth noting that our selection of workers (all *level 3 workers*), motivated primarily by the need for high-quality data renders the underlying performance distribution rather sharp. Investigating unleveled crowdworkers from this perspective could be the subject of future work.

6.2 Effects on Engagement

As reported, we found a significant difference between workers in a pleasant mood in comparison to those in an unpleasant mood with respect to their perceived reward (*RW*). The perceived reward, i.e. the inherent gratification obtained through the task completion, irrespective of other material compensation interacts on a primal level with the subject's motivation for tasking (maximizing both the personal and monetary gain). Experiencing meaningfulness is a critical psychological state derived from the five job characteristics and it is thus unsurprising that workers in a pleasant mood are influenced more heavily (cf. [27]). This is furthermore inline with our intuition, due to the reported results of the preliminary survey.

Apart from perceived reward, no significant difference is found with respect to perceived usability (*PU*) and *No.Tasks*. PU is fundamentally a characteristic of the system and task design. Although surprising, it becomes apparent as an outcome of this study that mood has very little influence on this dimension, a fact which could be due to multiple factors. As the batch of tasks in Study II correspond to information finding, an ordinary crowdsourcing task [13], this may result in workers falling out of a *meta-critical* state of mind. This in turn can explain the very low variance in this dimension. The lack of variance in the *No. Tasks* can be accounted for by the fact that most workers completed the entire batch of tasks immaterial of the corresponding task difficulty (fewer than 17% failed to complete the entire batch). It is plausible that a larger batch would result in more variance in *No. Tasks*, but considering that workers spent almost 20 mins to complete 20 tasks on average, it is a large enough batch for microtasks. Prior works have revealed that paying workers well could help in worker retention [12], which is also the likely explanation for our observation.

6.3 Effects on Behavior

The lack of significant difference between the worker's low-level behaviour (comprising of *Mouse Events*, *Scroll Events*, *Window Events* and *Keypress Events*) carries perhaps a more trivial explanation, namely that multiple combinations of different actions can lead to the same outcome within the interaction (two *Keypress Events* can substitute for two *Mouse Events* and vice-versa). Analyzing behaviour at either higher or lower level (e.g., aggregating behaviour patterns based on intent or goal achieved) could prove far more fruitful. We defer this analysis to future studies.

6.4 Implications for Crowsdsourcing Systems

Our paper reflects on how different crowdsouring is from more traditional work settings. The effects of mood have been studied in order to capture this difference through its impact on performance and engagement. But how different is crowdsourcing really, and what are the commonalities it shares with all types of work? For one, the psychological factors present in workers seem to coincide at least at a macro-scale. Considering human factors in improving the effectiveness of the crowdsourcing results is the object of many studies such as [29–31]. But worker-centric studies of this nature could highlight how these goals could be better achieved while developing a system which is sensitive to the principles of work psychology we have been relying on for decades. Several studies have focused on improving the effectiveness of crowdsourcing results through matching eligible workers to the most appropriate task [38, 46]. The main orientation of these tools is derived as an extension of the task-setters' goals and perspective, and constitute a brute-force approach for harnessing more accurate results. Self-assessment has also been proposed as an effective ingredient in crowd work [21], however, none of these artifacts focus on the worker's well-being. Understanding the nature of the crowd worker's environment, interactions, incentives and gratification can serve to achieve the same goals but with a less heavy-handed, more *bottom-up* philosophy.

Stimulating crowd workers to improve engagement, more than accuracy, which we have already scoped as relatively constant across worker experience levels, could be far more beneficial and could be as easily achievable as providing new task designs focused on enhancing perceived reward, or introducing a function which serves as a source of constant positive reinforcement such as a continuously updating performance dashboard.

To summarize, the results of such studies potentially carry keys to providing major improvements to the lives, well-being and mental health of crowdworkers, by recognizing their particular type of work economy as fundamentally innovative and disjoint from its more traditional counterparts. Worker-centric studies shift the focus from the task requester's goals by recognizing and identifying the virtues behind the particular types of interactions of the worker with their task. We show how maximizing task performance measures needn't be a concern when it comes to crowdsourcing in as much as it interacts with a worker's mood, and we remark how improving a worker's feeling of reward can be far more beneficial with an impact on the worker's long term career development. Tailoring tasks to this goal will also help create more quality crowdsouring jobs in the future.

7 CONCLUSIONS AND FUTURE WORK

We have presented a study in which the effects of crowdworkers' moods have been explored through the contrast between prior beliefs of workers, with actual quantitative evidence stemming from behavioral analysis of data gathered from exponents of the very same marketplace. In summary, we take away how mood provides a high impact on perceived reward or task gratification and far less so on performance or perceived usability.

We emphasize how our findings are central to better understanding this work sector, and encourage a shift in focus to worker-centric studies that would take these findings into account to improve the crowdsourcing system in a manner aligned with the worker's own interests, namely enhancing worker engagement without the need for negative reinforcement. We identify task design and system design (e.g., using positively valenced music can enhance the creative performance of workers on AMT [42]) as prime opportunities in achieving this goal.

In the imminent future, we aim to carry out additional studies across different types of crowdsourced tasks (for example, content creation tasks, verification and validation tasks, interpretation and analysis, etc.) to analyze how sensitive a type of task is to crowd worker moods based on the task type. Additionally, we will consider more worker types (e.g., unleveled workers, or workers with

different culture background [35]) while collecting mood for the generalizability of the results. We will also explore methods that can robustly induce positive moods to improve task related outcomes in crowdsourced microtasks.

ACKNOWLEDGEMENTS

We would like to thank all the anonymous crowd workers who participated in our experiments. This research has been supported in part by the Erasmus+ project DISKOW (grant no. 60171990), and the EU Horizon 2020 transnational access program under SoBigData (grant agreement no. 654024).

REFERENCES

[1] Arnold B Bakker, Wilmar B Schaufeli, Michael P Leiter, and Toon W Taris. 2008. Work engagement: An emerging concept in occupational health psychology. *Work & Stress* 22, 3 (2008), 187–200.

[2] Christopher Beedie, Peter Terry, and Andrew Lane. 2005. Distinctions between emotion and mood. *Cognition & Emotion* 19, 6 (2005), 847–878.

[3] Borong Chen, Weiping Hu, and Jonathan A Plucker. 2016. The effect of mood on problem finding in scientific creativity. *The Journal of Creative Behavior* 50, 4 (2016), 308–320.

[4] Michael S. Christian, Adela S. Garza, and Jerel E. Slaughter. 2011. Work engagement: A quantitative review and test of its relations with task and contextual performance. *Personnel Psychology* 64, 1 (2011), 89–136.

[5] David M Clark, John D Teasdale, Donald E Broadbent, and Maryanne Martin. 1983. Effect of mood on lexical decisions. *Bulletin of the Psychonomic Society* 21, 3 (1983), 175–178.

[6] Peng Dai, Jeffrey M Rzeszotarski, Praveen Paritosh, and Ed H Chi. 2015. And now for something completely different: Improving crowdsourcing workflows with micro-diversions. In *Proceeding of The 18th ACM Conference on Computer-Supported Cooperative Work and Social Computing*. ACM, 628–638.

[7] Richard J Davidson. 1994. On emotion, mood, and related affective constructs. *The nature of emotion: Fundamental questions* (1994), 51–55.

[8] Gianluca Demartini, Djellel Eddine Difallah, Ujwal Gadiraju, Michele Catasta, et al. 2017. An introduction to hybrid human-machine information systems. *Foundations and Trends® in Web Science* 7, 1 (2017), 1–87.

[9] Pieter MA Desmet, Martijn H Vastenburg, and Natalia Romero. 2016. Mood measurement with Pick-A-Mood: review of current methods and design of a pictorial self-report scale. *Journal of Design Research* 14, 3 (2016), 241–279.

[10] Fernando Diaz, Ryen White, Georg Buscher, and Dan Liebling. 2013. Robust models of mouse movement on dynamic web search results pages. In *Proceedings of the 22nd ACM international conference on Conference on information & knowledge management*. ACM, 1451–1460.

[11] Djellel Difallah, Elena Filatova, and Panos Ipeirotis. 2018. Demographics and Dynamics of Mechanical Turk Workers. In *Proceedings of the Eleventh ACM International Conference on Web Search and Data Mining*. ACM, New York, NY, USA, 135–143.

[12] Djellel Eddine Difallah, Michele Catasta, Gianluca Demartini, and Philippe Cudré-Mauroux. 2014. Scaling-up the crowd: Micro-task pricing schemes for worker retention and latency improvement. In *Second AAAI Conference on Human Computation and Crowdsourcing*.

[13] Djellel Eddine Difallah, Michele Catasta, Gianluca Demartini, Panagiotis G Ipeirotis, and Philippe Cudré-Mauroux. 2015. The dynamics of micro-task crowdsourcing: The case of amazon mturk. In *Proceedings of the 24th International Conference on World Wide Web*. 238–247.

[14] Peter Eckersley. 2010. How unique is your web browser?. In *Privacy Enhancing Technologies*. Springer, 1–18.

[15] Alek Felstiner. 2011. Working the crowd: employment and labor law in the crowdsourcing industry. *Berkeley J. Emp. & Lab. L.* 32 (2011), 143.

[16] Oluwaseyi Feyisetan, Elena Simperl, Max Van Kleek, and Nigel Shadbolt. 2015. Improving paid microtasks through gamification and adaptive furtherance incentives. In *Proc. WWW'15*. 333–343.

[17] Nico H Frijda et al. 1994. Varieties of affect: Emotions and episodes, moods, and sentiments. (1994).

[18] Ujwal Gadiraju, Alessandro Checco, Neha Gupta, and Gianluca Demartini. 2017. Modus operandi of crowd workers: The invisible role of microtask work environments. *Proceedings of the ACM on Interactive, Mobile, Wearable and Ubiquitous Technologies* 1, 3, 49.

[19] Ujwal Gadiraju, Gianluca Demartini, Djellel Eddine Difallah, and Michele Catasta. 2016. It's getting crowded!: how to use crowdsourcing effectively for web science research. In *Proceedings of the 8th ACM Conference on Web Science*. ACM, 11–11.

[20] Ujwal Gadiraju and Stefan Dietze. 2017. Improving learning through achievement priming in crowdsourced information finding microtasks. In *proceedings of the*

Seventh International Learning Analytics & Knowledge Conference. ACM, 105–114.

[21] Ujwal Gadiraju, Besnik Fetahu, Ricardo Kawase, Patrick Siehndel, and Stefan Dietze. 2017. Using Worker Self-Assessments for Competence-Based Pre-Selection in Crowdsourcing Microtasks. *ACM Transactions on Computer-Human Interaction* 24, 4, Article 30 (Aug. 2017), 26 pages.

[22] Ujwal Gadiraju, Ricardo Kawase, and Stefan Dietze. 2014. A taxonomy of microtasks on the web. In *Proceedings of the 25th ACM conference on Hypertext and social media*. ACM, 218–223.

[23] Ujwal Gadiraju, Ricardo Kawase, Stefan Dietze, and Gianluca Demartini. 2015. Understanding malicious behavior in crowdsourcing platforms: The case of online surveys. In *Proceedings of the 33rd Annual ACM Conference on Human Factors in Computing Systems*. ACM, 1631–1640.

[24] Ujwal Gadiraju, Jie Yang, and Alessandro Bozzon. 2017. Clarity is a worthwhile quality: On the role of task clarity in microtask crowdsourcing. In *Proceedings of the 28th ACM Conference on Hypertext and Social Media*. ACM, 5–14.

[25] J Richard Hackman and Greg R Oldham. 1976. Motivation through the design of work: Test of a theory. *Organizational behavior and human performance* 16, 2 (1976), 250–279.

[26] Sture Holm. 1979. A simple sequentially rejective multiple test procedure. *Scandinavian journal of statistics* (1979), 65–70.

[27] Stephen E Humphrey, Jennifer D Nahrgang, and Frederick P Morgeson. 2007. Integrating motivational, social, and contextual work design features: a meta-analytic summary and theoretical extension of the work design literature. *Journal of applied psychology* 92, 5 (2007), 1332.

[28] William A Kahn. 1990. Psychological conditions of personal engagement and disengagement at work. *Academy of management journal* 33, 4 (1990), 692–724.

[29] Nicolas Kaufmann, Thimo Schulze, and Daniel Veit. 2011. More than fun and money. Worker Motivation in Crowdsourcing-A Study on Mechanical Turk.. In *AMCIS*, Vol. 11. 1–11.

[30] Gabriella Kazai, Jaap Kamps, and Natasa Milic-Frayling. 2013. An analysis of human factors and label accuracy in crowdsourcing relevance judgments. *Information retrieval* 16, 2 (2013), 138–178.

[31] Aniket Kittur, Jeffrey V Nickerson, Michael Bernstein, Elizabeth Gerber, Aaron Shaw, John Zimmerman, Matt Lease, and John Horton. 2013. The future of crowd work. In *Proceedings of the 19th ACM Conference on Computer Supported Cooperative Work*. ACM, 1301–1318.

[32] Walter S Lasecki, Samuel C White, Kyle I Murray, and Jeffrey P Bigham. 2012. Crowd memory: Learning in the collective. In *Proceedings of the Collective Intelligence*.

[33] Richard Lazarus. 1994. The stable and the unstable in emotion. *The nature of emotion: Fundamental questions* (1994), 79–85.

[34] Sheena Lewis, Mira Dontcheva, and Elizabeth Gerber. 2011. Affective computational priming and creativity. In *Proceedings of the SIGCHI Conference on Human Factors in Computing Systems*. ACM, 735–744.

[35] Nangyeon Lim. 2016. Cultural differences in emotion: differences in emotional arousal level between the East and the West. *Integrative Medicine Research* 5, 2 (2016), 105–109.

[36] Andrew Mao, Ece Kamar, and Eric Horvitz. 2013. Why stop now? predicting worker engagement in online crowdsourcing. In *First AAAI Conference on Human Computation and Crowdsourcing*.

[37] Catherine C Marshall and Frank M Shipman. 2013. Experiences surveying the crowd: Reflections on methods, participation, and reliability. In *Proceedings of the 5th Annual ACM Web Science Conference*. ACM, 234–243.

[38] Panagiotis Mavridis, David Gross-Amblard, and Zoltán Miklós. 2016. Using hierarchical skills for optimized task assignment in knowledge-intensive crowdsourcing. In *Proceedings of the 25th International Conference on World Wide Web*. International World Wide Web Conferences Steering Committee, 843–853.

[39] Brian McInnis, Dan Cosley, Chaebong Nam, and Gilly Leshed. 2016. Taking a HIT: Designing around rejection, mistrust, risk, and workers' experiences in Amazon Mechanical Turk. In *Proceedings of the 2016 CHI conference on human factors in computing systems*. ACM, 2271–2282.

[40] Andrew G. Miner and Theresa M. Glomb. 2010. State mood, task performance, and behavior at work: A within-persons approach. *Organizational Behavior and Human Decision Processes* 112, 1 (2010), 43 – 57.

[41] Robert R Morris, Mira Dontcheva, Adam Finkelstein, and Elizabeth Gerber. 2013. Affect and creative performance on crowdsourcing platforms. In *Proceedings of the 2013 Humaine Association Conference on Affective Computing and Intelligent Interaction*. 67–72.

[42] Robert R Morris, Mira Dontcheva, Adam Finkelstein, and Elizabeth Gerber. 2013. Affect and creative performance on crowdsourcing platforms. In *2013 Humaine Association Conference on Affective Computing and Intelligent Interaction*. IEEE, 67–72.

[43] Robert R Morris, Mira Dontcheva, and Elizabeth M Gerber. 2012. Priming for better performance in microtask crowdsourcing environments. *IEEE Internet Computing* 16, 5 (2012), 13–19.

[44] William N Morris. 2012. *Mood: The frame of mind*. Springer Sci. & Business Media.

[45] Heather L. O'Brien, Paul Cairns, and Mark Hall. 2018. A practical approach to measuring user engagement with the refined user engagement scale (UES) and new UES short form. *Intl. J. Human-Computer Studies* 112 (2018), 28 – 39.

[46] Peter Organisciak, Jaime Teevan, Susan Dumais, Robert C Miller, and Adam Tauman Kalai. 2014. A crowd of your own: Crowdsourcing for on-demand personalization. In *Second AAAI Conference on Human Computation and Crowdsourcing*.

[47] Andrew J Oswald, Eugenio Proto, and Daniel Sgroi. 2015. Happiness and productivity. *Journal of Labor Economics* 33, 4 (2015), 789–822.

[48] Antonia Pilar Pacheco-Unguetti and Fabrice B. R. Parmentier. 2016. Happiness increases distraction by auditory deviant stimuli. *British Journal of Psychology* 107, 3 (2016), 419–433.

[49] Jesse J Prinz. 2004. *Gut reactions: A perceptual theory of emotion*. Oxford UP.

[50] Markus Rokicki, Sergiu Chelaru, Sergej Zerr, and Stefan Siersdorfer. 2014. Competitive game designs for improving the cost effectiveness of crowdsourcing. In *Proceedings of the 23rd ACM International Conference on Conference on Information and Knowledge Management*. ACM, 1469–1478.

[51] Jeffrey Rzeszotarski and Aniket Kittur. 2012. CrowdScape: interactively visualizing user behavior and output. In *Proceedings of the 25th annual ACM symposium on User interface software and technology*. ACM, 55–62.

[52] Jeffrey M Rzeszotarski, Ed Chi, Praveen Paritosh, and Peng Dai. 2013. Inserting micro-breaks into crowdsourcing workflows. In *First AAAI Conference on Human Computation and Crowdsourcing*.

[53] Jeffrey M Rzeszotarski and Aniket Kittur. 2011. Instrumenting the crowd: using implicit behavioral measures to predict task performance. In *Proceedings of the 24th Annual ACM Symposium on User Interface Software & Technology*. ACM, 13–22.

[54] Pennie S Seibert and Henry C Ellis. 1991. Irrelevant thoughts, emotional mood states, and cognitive task performance. *Memory & Cognition* 19, 5 (1991), 507–513.

[55] Han Yu Zhiqi Shen, Simon Fauvel, and Lizhen Cui. 2017. Efficient scheduling in crowdsourcing based on workers' mood. In *Agents (ICA), 2017 IEEE International Conference on*. IEEE, 121–126.

[56] Melanie J Taylor and Peter J Cooper. 1992. An experimental study of the effect of mood on body size perception. *Behaviour research and therapy* 30, 1 (1992), 53–58.

[57] Elizabeth R Tenney, Jared M Poole, and Ed Diener. 2016. Does positivity enhance work performance?: Why, when, and what we donâĂŹt know. *Research in Organizational Behavior* 36 (2016), 27–46.

[58] Wei-Chi Tsai, Chien-Cheng Chen, and Hui-Lu Liu. 2007. Test of a model linking employee positive moods and task performance. *Journal of Applied Psychology* 92, 6 (2007), 1570.

[59] Viswanath Venkatesh and Cheri Speier. 1999. Computer technology training in the workplace: A longitudinal investigation of the effect of mood. *Organizational behavior and human decision processes* 79, 1 (1999), 1–28.

[60] Philippe Verduyn, Iven Van Mechelen, and Francis Tuerlinckx. 2011. The relation between event processing and the duration of emotional experience. *Emotion* 11, 1 (2011), 20.

[61] Bjørn Villa, Katrien De Moor, Poul Heegaard, and Anders Instefjord. 2013. Investigating quality of experience in the context of adaptive video streaming: findings from an experimental user study. In *Norsk informatikkonferanse NIK 2013, Universitetet i Stavanger, 18.-20. november 2013*. Akademika forlag, 122–133.

[62] David Watson and Auke Tellegen. 1985. Toward a consensual structure of mood. *Psychological bulletin* 98, 2 (1985), 219.

[63] Jie Yang, Judith Redi, Gianluca Demartini, and Alessandro Bozzon. 2016. Modeling task complexity in crowdsourcing. In *Fourth AAAI Conference on Human Computation and Crowdsourcing*.

Author Index

www.ingramcontent.com/pod-product-compliance
Lightning Source LLC
Chambersburg PA
CBHW080703220326
41598CB00033B/5289